PRENTICE HALL
LITERATURE
GRADE 7

COMMON CORE EDITION ©

Upper Saddle River, New Jersey

Boston, Massachusetts

Chandler, Arizona

Glenview, Illinois

PEARSON

ISBN-13: 978-0-13-319553-8
ISBN-10:   0-13-319553-8
8 9 10 V063 15 14 13 12

Master Teacher Board

Contributing Authors

The contributing authors guided the direction and philosophy of Pearson Prentice Hall Literature. *Working with the development team, they helped to build the pedagogical integrity of the program and to ensure its relevance for today's teachers and students.*

Grant Wiggins, Ed.D., is the President of Authentic Education in Hopewell, New Jersey. He earned his Ed.D. from Harvard University and his B.A. from St. John's College in Annapolis. Grant consults with schools, districts, and state education departments on a variety of reform matters; organizes conferences and workshops; and develops print materials and Web resources on curricular change. He is the coauthor, with Jay McTighe, of *Understanding by Design* and *The Understanding by Design Handbook,* the award-winning and highly successful materials on curriculum published by ASCD. His work has been supported by the Pew Charitable Trusts, the Geraldine R. Dodge Foundation, and the National Science Foundation. *The Association for Supervision of Curriculum Development (ASCD), publisher of the "Understanding by Design Handbook" co-authored by Grant Wiggins and registered owner of the trademark "Understanding by Design," has not authorized, approved, or sponsored this work and is in no way affiliated with Pearson or its products.*

Jeff Anderson has worked with

struggling writers and readers for almost 20 years. Anderson's specialty is the integration of grammar and editing instruction into the processes of reading and writing. He has published two books, *Mechanically Inclined: Building Grammar, Usage, and Style into Writer's Workshop* and *Everyday Editing: Inviting Students to Develop Skill and Craft in Writer's Workshop,* as well as a DVD, *The Craft of Grammar.* Anderson's work has appeared in *English Journal.* Anderson won the NCTE Paul and Kate Farmer Award for his *English Journal* article on teaching grammar in context.

Arnetha F. Ball, Ph.D., is a

Professor at Stanford University. Her areas of expertise include language and literacy studies of diverse student populations, research on writing instruction, and teacher preparation for working with diverse populations. Dr. Ball has also served as an academic specialist for the United States Information Services Program in South Africa. She is the author of *African American Literacies Unleashed* with Dr. Ted Lardner, and *Multicultural Strategies for Education and Social Change.*

Sheridan Blau is Professor of

Education and English at the University of California, Santa Barbara, where he directs the South Coast Writing Project and the Literature Institute for Teachers. He has served in senior advisory roles for such groups as the National Board for Professional Teaching Standards, the College Board, and the American Board for Teacher Education. Blau served for twenty years on the National Writing Project Advisory Board and Task Force, and is a former president of NCTE. Blau is the author of *The Literature Workshop: Teaching Texts and Their Readers,* which was named by the Conference on English Education as the 2004 Richard Meade Award winner for outstanding research in English education.

William G.

Brozo, Ph.D., is a Professor of Literacy at George Mason University in Fairfax, Virginia. He has taught reading and language arts in junior and senior high school and is the author of numerous texts on literacy development. Dr. Brozo's work focuses on building capacity among teacher leaders, enriching the literate culture of schools, enhancing the literate lives of boys, and making teaching more responsive to the needs of all students. His recent publications include *Bright Beginnings for Boys: Engaging Young Boys in Active Literacy* and the *Adolescent Literacy Inventory.*

Doug Buehl is a teacher, author, and

national literacy consultant. He is the author of *Classroom Strategies for Interactive Learning* and coauthor of *Reading and the High School Student: Strategies to Enhance Literacy;* and *Strategies to Enhance Literacy and Learning in Middle School Content Area Classrooms.*

Jim Cummins, Ph.D, is a profes-

sor in the Modern Language Centre at the University of Toronto. He is the author of numerous publications, including *Negotiating Identities: Education for Empowerment in a Diverse Society.* Cummins coined the acronyms BICS and CAPT to help differentiate the type of language ability students need for success.

Harvey Daniels, Ph.D., has been

a classroom teacher, writing project director, author, and university professor. "Smokey" serves as an international consultant to schools, districts, and educational agencies. He is known for his work on student-led book clubs, as recounted in *Literature Circles: Voice and Choice in Book Clubs & Reading Groups* and *Mini Lessons for Literature Circles.* Recent works include *Subjects Matter: Every Teacher's Guide to Content-Area Reading* and *Content Area Writing: Every Teacher's Guide.*

Jane Feber taught language arts in  Jacksonville, Florida, for 36 years. Her innovative approach to instruction has earned her several awards, including the NMSA Distinguished Educator Award, the NCTE Edwin A. Hoey Award, the Gladys Prior Award for Teaching Excellence, and the Florida Council of Teachers of English Teacher of the Year Award. She is a National Board Certified Teacher, past president of the Florida Council of Teachers of English and is the author of *Creative Book Reports* and *Active Word Play*.

Danling Fu, Ph.D., is Professor of Language and Culture in the College of Education at the University of Florida. She researches and provides inservice to public schools nationally, focusing on literacy instruction for new immigrant students. Fu's books include *My Trouble is My English* and *An Island of English* addressing English language learners in the secondary schools. She has authored chapters in the *Handbook of Adolescent Literacy Research* and in *Adolescent Literacy: Turning Promise to Practice*.

Kelly Gallagher is a full-time English  teacher at Magnolia High School in Anaheim, California. He is the former co-director of the South Basin Writing Project at California State University, Long Beach. Gallagher wrote *Reading Reasons: Motivational Mini-Lessons for the Middle and High School, Deeper Reading: Comprehending Challenging Texts 4-12,* and *Teaching Adolescent Writers.* Gallagher won the Secondary Award of Classroom Excellence from the California Association of Teachers of English—the state's top English teacher honor.

Sharroky Hollie, Ph.D., is an  assistant professor at California State University, Dominguez Hills, and an urban literacy visiting professor at Webster University, St. Louis. Hollie's work focuses on professional development, African American education, and second language methodology. He is a contributing author in two texts on culturally and linguistically responsive teaching. He is the Executive Director of the Center for Culturally Responsive Teaching and Learning and the co-founding director of the Culture and Language Academy of Success, an independent charter school in Los Angeles.

Dr. Donald J. Leu, Ph.D., teaches  at the University of Connecticut and holds a joint appointment in Curriculum and Instruction and in Educational Psychology. He directs the New Literacies Research Lab and is a member of the Board of Directors of the International Reading Association. Leu studies the skills required to read, write, and learn with Internet technologies. His research has been funded by groups including the U.S. Department of Education, the National Science Foundation, and the Bill & Melinda Gates Foundation.

Jon Scieszka founded GUYS READ,  a nonprofit literacy initiative for boys, to call attention to the problem of getting boys connected with reading. In 2008, he was named the first U.S. National Ambassador for Young People's Literature by the Library of Congress. Scieszka taught from first grade to eighth grade for ten years in New York City, drawing inspiration from his students to write *The True Story of the 3 Little Pigs!, The Stinky Cheese Man*, the *Time Warp Trio* series of chapter books, and the *Trucktown* series of books for beginning readers.

Sharon Vaughn, Ph.D., teaches at the University of Texas at Austin. She is the previous Editor-in-Chief of the *Journal of Learning Disabilities* and the co-editor of *Learning Disabilities Research and Practice.* She is the recipient of the American Education Research Association SIG Award for Outstanding Researcher. Vaughn's work focuses on effective practices for enhancing reading outcomes for students with reading difficulties. She is the author of more than 100 articles and numerous books designed to improve research-based practices in the classroom.

Karen K. Wixson is Dean of the School of Education at the University of North Carolina, Greensboro. She has published widely in the areas of literacy curriculum, instruction, and assessment. Wixson has been an advisor to the National Research Council and helped develop the National Assessment of Educational Progress (NAEP) reading tests. She is a past member of the IRA Board of Directors and co-chair of the IRA Commission on RTI. Recently, Wixson served on the English Language Arts Work Team that was part of the Common Core State Standards Initiative.

Each unit addresses a BIG Question to enrich exploration of literary concepts and reading strategies.

What is the best way to find the *truth*?

INFORMATIONAL TEXT HIGHLIGHTED

PHLit Online!
www.PHLitOnline.com
Interactive resources provide personalized instruction and activities online.

Skills at a Glance

This page provides a quick look at the skills you will learn and practice in Unit 1.

Reading Skills

Context Clues

  Unlock Meaning

  Reread or Read Ahead to
  Confirm Meaning

Author's Purpose

  Recognize Details

  Use Background Information

Reading for Information

Locate Types of Information

Analyze Structure and Purpose

Literary Analysis

Theme

Central Idea

Narrative Writing

Point of View

Comparing Fiction and Nonfiction

Setting

Historical Context

Comparing Characters

Vocabulary

Big Question Vocabulary

Prefixes: *re-, in-, trans-, ac-*

Roots: *-vita-, -man-, -dict-, -sper-*

Using a Dictionary and Thesaurus

Conventions

Common and Proper Nouns

Possessive Nouns

Revising Incorrect Forms of Plural Nouns

Personal Pronouns

Possessive Pronouns

Checking Pronoun-Antecedent Agreement

Writing

Writing About the Big Question

Essay

Description

News Report

Letter

Timed Writing

Writing Workshop: Informative Text:
  Descriptive Essay

Writing Workshop: Narrative Text:
  Autobiographical Narrative

Speaking and Listening

Dramatic Reading

Discussion

Interview

Delivering a Narrative Presentation

Research and Technology

Biographical Report

 **Common Core State Standards
Addressed in This Unit**

Reading Literature RL.7.1, RL.7.2, RL.7.3, RL.7.6, RL.7.10
Reading Informational Text RI.7.1, RI.7.2, RI.7.3,
RI.7.5, RI.7.6, RI.7.10
Writing W.7.2, W.7.2.a–e, W.7.3, W.7.3.a–e, W.7.5, W.7.7,
W.7.9.a, W.7.9.b, W.7.10
Speaking and Listening SL.7.1.a–c, SL.7.3, SL.7.4,
SL.7.6
Language L.7.1, L.7.2, L.7.2.b, L.7.3, L.7.3.a, L.7.4,
L.7.4.a–d, L.7.5, L.7.5.b, L.7.6
[For the full wording of the standards, see the standards
chart in the front of your textbook.]

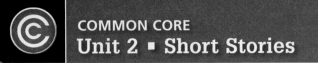

Does every *conflict* have a winner?

Point of View

Theme

Make Predictions
Plot

Make Predictions
Character

Understand Text
Structure and
Purpose

INFORMATIONAL TEXT HIGHLIGHTED

PHLit Online!
www.PHLitOnline.com
Interactive resources provide
personalized instruction and
activities online.

Skills at a Glance

This page provides a quick look at the skills you will learn and practice in Unit 2.

Reading Skills

Make Predictions

  Use Prior Knowledge to Make Predictions

  Read Ahead to Verify Predictions

Make Inferences

  Recognize Details

  Read Between the Lines
  by Asking Questions

Reading for Information

Understand Text Structure and Purpose

Connecting Ideas to Make Inferences
and Generalizations

Literary Analysis

Plot and Plot Devices

Point of View

Character

Comparing Idioms

Conflict and Resolution

Theme

Comparing Irony

Vocabulary

Big Question Vocabulary

Prefixes: *mal-, per-*

Suffixes: *-ance, -tion, -ment, -ious*

Roots: *-tract-, -spir-*

Word Origins

Conventions

Verbs

The Principal Parts of Verbs

Word Choice

Adjectives

Adverbs

Revising for Correct Verb Tense

Writing

Writing About the Big Question

Informative Article

Journal Entry

Anecdote

Letter to the Editor

Timed Writing

Writing Workshop: Argumentative Text:
  Response to Literature

Writing Workshop: Narrative Text: Short Story

Speaking and Listening

Informal Debate

News Story

Delivering an Oral Summary

Research and Technology

Outline

 **Common Core State Standards
Addressed in This Unit**

Reading Literature RL.7.1, RL.7.2, RL.7.3, RL.7.4,
RL.7.6, RL.7.10

Reading Informational Text RI.7.1, RI.7.4, RI.7.5,
RI.7.9, RI.7.10

Writing W.7.1, W.7.1.a–e, W.7.2, W.7.2.a, W.7.2.d–f,
W.7.3, W.7.3.a–e, W.7.5, W.7.7, W.7.9, W.7.9.a

Speaking and Listening SL.7.1, SL.7.1.a, SL.7.3,
SL.7.5, SL.7.6

Language L.7.1, L.7.2.a, L.7.2.b, L.7.3, L.7.4.b, L.7.4.c,
L.7.5.a, L.7.5.c, L.7.6

[For the full wording of the standards, see the standards
chart in the front of your textbook.]

What should we *learn*?

INFORMATIONAL TEXT HIGHLIGHTED

PHLit Online!
www.PHLitOnline.com
Interactive resources provide personalized instruction and activities online.

Skills at a Glance

This page provides a quick look at the skills you will learn and practice in Unit 3.

Reading Skills

Main Idea

Adjust Your Reading Rate to Recognize Main Ideas and Key Points

Make Connections Between Key Points and Supporting Details

Classifying Fact and Opinion

Recognize Clues That Indicate an Opinion

Use Resources to Check Facts

Reading for Information

Analyze Author's Argument

Understand Structure and Purpose

Literary Analysis

Point of View and Purpose

Development of Ideas

Word Choice and Tone

Expository Essay

Reflective Essay

Comparing Biography and Autobiography

Persuasive Essay

Word Choice and Diction

Comparing Humor

Vocabulary

Big Question Vocabulary

Suffixes: *-ness, -able*

Roots: *-rupt-, -leg-, -peti-, -vers-, -sol-*

Words With Multiple Meanings

Conventions

Conjunctions

Prepositions and Prepositional Phrases

Revising to Combine Sentences Using Conjunctions

Subjects and Predicates

Compound Subjects and Predicates

Revising Errors in Adjective and Adverb Usage

Writing

Writing About the Big Question

Analogy

Outline

Persuasive Letter

Adaptation

Timed Writing

Writing Workshop: Explanatory Text: How-to Essay

Writing Workshop: Informative Text: Comparison-and-Contrast Essay

Speaking and Listening

Response

Public Service Announcement

Oral Summary

Evaluating a Persuasive Presentation

Research and Technology

Help-Wanted Ad

 Common Core State Standards Addressed in This Unit

Reading Literature RL.7.3, RL.7.10

Reading Informational Text RI.7.1, RI.7.2, RI.7.3, RI.7.4, RI.7.5, RI.7.6, RI.7.7, RI.7.8, RI.7.9, RI.7.10

Writing W.7.1.a, W.7.1.b, W.7.2, W.7.2.a–e, W.7.3.d, W.7.4, W.7.5, W.7.8, W.7.9, W.7.9.b

Speaking and Listening SL.7.1, SL.7.1.b, SL.7.2, SL.7.3, SL.7.4

Language L.7.1, L.7.1.a, L.7.1.c, L.7.2.b, L.7.3, L.7.3.a, L.7.4, L.7.4.b–d, L.7.5.b, L.7.6

[For the full wording of the standards, see the standards chart in the front of your textbook.]

What is the best way to *communicate?*

Figurative Language

Poetic Form and Structure

Drawing Conclusions
Forms of Poetry

Draw Conclusions
Figurative Language

INFORMATIONAL TEXT HIGHLIGHTED

Skills at a Glance

This page provides a quick look at the skills you will learn and practice in Unit 4.

Reading Skills

Drawing Conclusions

  Asking Questions

  Connecting the Details

Paraphrase

  Read Poetry Aloud, According to Punctuation

  Restate Passages

Reading for Information

Follow Technical Directions

Determine the Main Idea

Literary Analysis

Poetic Form and Structure

Forms of Poetry

Figurative Language

Comparing Narrative Poems

Sound Devices

Rhythm and Rhyme

Comparing Imagery

Vocabulary

Big Question Vocabulary

Prefixes: *un-, im-*

Suffixes: *-ly, -y, -ancy or -ency, -less*

Roots: *-gram-, -leg-, -peti-, -vers-, -sol-*

Connotation and Denotation

Conventions

Infinitives and Infinitive Phrases

Appositives and Appositive Phrases

Revising Sentences Using Participles

Independent and Subordinate Clauses

Sentence Structures

Revising Fragments and Run-on Sentences

Writing

Writing About the Big Question

Lyric Poem, Concrete Poem, or Haiku

Metaphor

Paraphrase

Poem

Timed Writing

Writing Workshop: Argumentative Text:
  Problem-and-Solution Essay

Writing Workshop: Argumentative Text:
  Persuasive Essay

Speaking and Listening

Presentation

Poetry Reading

Evaluating Media Messages and Advertisements

Research and Technology

Scientific Explanation

Survey

 **Common Core State Standards
Addressed in This Unit**

Reading Literature RL.7.1, RL.7.4, RL.7.5, RL.7.6, RL.7.7, RL.7.10

Reading Informational Text RI.7.1, RI.7.4, RI.7.5, RI.7.10

Writing W.7.1, W.7.1.a, W.7.1.b–e, W.7.2, W.7.2.a, W.7.2.b, W.7.2.d–f, W.7.4, W.7.5, W.7.7, W.7.9, W.7.9.a, W.7.10

Speaking and Listening SL.7.1, SL.7.1.c, SL.7.2, SL.7.3, SL.7.4, SL.7.5, SL.7.6

Language L.7.1, L.7.1.a–c, L.7.2, L.7.2.b, L.7.4.b, L.7.4.c, L.7.5.b, L.7.5.c, L.7.6

[For the full wording of the standards, see the standards chart in the front of your textbook.]

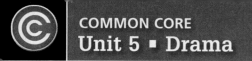
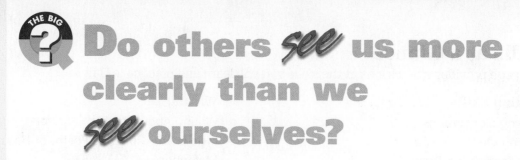

Do others *see* us more clearly than we *see* ourselves?

INFORMATIONAL TEXT HIGHLIGHTED

PHLit Online!
www.PHLitOnline.com
Interactive resources provide personalized instruction and activities online.

Skills at a Glance

This page provides a quick look at the skills you will learn and practice in Unit 5.

Reading Skills

Purpose for Reading

Adjust Your Reading Rate

Preview a Text Before Reading

Summarize

Distinguish Between Important and Unimportant Details

Reading for Information

Identify Author's Perspective

Identify Bias and Stereotyping

Literary Analysis

Conflict

Character

Elements of Drama

Stage Directions

Dialogue

Comparing Characters

Characters' Motives

Comparing Dramatic Speeches

Vocabulary

Big Question Vocabulary

Prefixes: *inter-*

Roots: *-grat-, -sist-*

Borrowed and Foreign Words

Conventions

Interjections

Double Negatives

Revising to Avoid Common Usage Problems

Sentence Functions and Endmarks

Correcting Subject-Verb Agreement With Compound Subjects

Writing

Writing About the Big Question

Letter

Tribute

Summary

Timed Writing

Writing Workshop: Informative Text: Multimedia Report

Writing Workshop: Explanatory Text: Cause-and-Effect Essay

Speaking and Listening

Dramatic Monologue

Conducting an Interview

Research and Technology

Costume Plans

Film Version

 Common Core State Standards Addressed in This Unit

Reading Literature RL.7.1, RL.7.2, RL.7.3, RL.7.5, RL.7.6, RL.7.7, RL.7.10

Reading Informational Text RI.7.1, RI.7.6, RI.7.9, RI.7.10

Writing W.7.1, W.7.1.a–c, W.7.2, W.7.2.a–c, W.7.4, W.7.7, W.7.8, W.7.9, W.7.9.a

Speaking and Listening SL.7.1, SL.7.1.a–c, SL.7.5, SL.7.6

Language L.7.1, L.7.2, L.7.2.b, L.7.3, L.7.4.b–d, L.7.6

[For the full wording of the standards, see the standards chart in the front of your textbook.]

INFORMATIONAL TEXT HIGHLIGHTED

Skills at a Glance

This page provides a quick look at the skills you will learn and practice in Unit 6.

Reading Skills

Cause and Effect

Ask Questions to Analyze
Cause-and-Effect Relationships

Reread to Look for Connections

Compare and Contrast

Using Your Prior Knowledge
to Compare and Contrast

Using a Venn Diagram

Reading for Information

Analyze Cause-and-Effect Organization

Analyze Point of View

Literary Analysis

Theme

Structure and Theme

Myth

Legend and Fact

Comparing Universal Themes

Cultural Context

Folk Tale

Comparing Tone and Themes

Vocabulary

Big Question Vocabulary

Prefixes: *out-, uni-*

Suffixes: *-ity*

Roots: *-vac-, -dom-, -myst-, -know-*

Figurative Language

Conventions

Punctuation Marks

Commas

Revising Incorrect Use of Commas

Capitalization

Abbreviations

Revising to Correct Use of Pronoun Case

Writing

Writing About the Big Question

Myth

Description and Comparison

Plot Summary

Review

Timed Writing

Writing Workshop: Informative Text:
Business Letter

Writing Workshop: Informative Text:
Research Report

Speaking and Listening

Debate

Persuasive Speech

Story

Television News Report

Research Presentation

 **Common Core State Standards
Addressed in This Unit**

Reading Literature RL.7.1, RL.7.2, RL.7.3, RL.7.5,
RL.7.9, RL.7.10

Reading Informational Text RI.7.1, RI.7.5, RI.7.6,
RI.7.9, RI.7.10

Writing W.7.1, W.7.1.a, W.7.1.b, W.7.1.e, W.7.2,
W.7.2.a–c, W.7.2.e, W.7.2.f, W.7.3, W.7.3.a, W.7.3.b,
W.7.4, W.7.5, W.7.7, W.7.8, W.7.9, W.7.9.a

Speaking and Listening SL.7.1, SL.7.1.a–c, SL.7.4,
SL.7.5, SL.7.6

Language L.7.1, L.7.2, L.7.2.a, L.7.2.b, L.7.3.a, L.7.4.b,
L.7.5, L.7.5.a, L.7.5.b, L.7.6

[For the full wording of the standards, see the standards
chart in the front of your textbook.]

Literature

Informational Text—Literary Nonfiction

▶ **Functional Text**

▶ **Literature in Context—Reading in the Content Areas**

▶ Writing Workshops

▶ Vocabulary Workshops

▶ Communications Workshop

The Common Core State Standards will prepare you to succeed in college and your future career. They are separated into four sections—Reading (Literature and Informational Text), Writing, Speaking and Listening, and Language. Beginning each section, the College and Career Readiness Anchor Standards define what you need to achieve by the end of high school. The grade-specific standards that follow define what you need to know by the end of your current grade level.

©Common Core Reading Standards

College and Career Readiness Anchor Standards

Key Ideas and Details

1. Read closely to determine what the text says explicitly and to make logical inferences from it; cite specific textual evidence when writing or speaking to support conclusions drawn from the text.

2. Determine central ideas or themes of a text and analyze their development; summarize the key supporting details and ideas.

3. Analyze how and why individuals, events, and ideas develop and interact over the course of a text.

Craft and Structure

4. Interpret words and phrases as they are used in a text, including determining technical, connotative, and figurative meanings, and analyze how specific word choices shape meaning or tone.

5. Analyze the structure of texts, including how specific sentences, paragraphs, and larger portions of the text (e.g., a section, chapter, scene, or stanza) relate to each other and the whole.

6. Assess how point of view or purpose shapes the content and style of a text.

Integration of Knowledge and Ideas

7. Integrate and evaluate content presented in diverse formats and media, including visually and quantitatively, as well as in words.

8. Delineate and evaluate the argument and specific claims in a text, including the validity of the reasoning as well as the relevance and sufficiency of the evidence.

9. Analyze how two or more texts address similar themes or topics in order to build knowledge or to compare the approaches the authors take.

Range of Reading and Level of Text Complexity

10. Read and comprehend complex literary and informational texts independently and proficiently.

Grade 7 Reading Standards for Literature

Key Ideas and Details

1. Cite textual evidence to support analysis of what the text says explicitly as well as inferences drawn from the text.

2. Determine a theme or central idea of a text and analyze its development over the course of the text; provide an objective summary of the text.

3. Analyze how particular elements of a story or drama interact (e.g., how setting shapes the characters or plot).

Craft and Structure

4. Determine the meaning of words and phrases as they are used in a text, including figurative and connotative meanings; analyze the impact of rhymes and other repetitions of sounds (e.g., alliteration) on a specific verse or stanza of a poem or section of a story or drama.

5. Analyze how a drama's or poem's form or structure (e.g., soliloquy, sonnet) contributes to its meaning.

6. Analyze how an author develops and contrasts the points of view of different characters or narrators in a text.

Integration of Knowledge and Ideas

7. Compare and contrast a written story, drama, or poem to its audio, filmed, staged, or multimedia version, analyzing the effects of techniques unique to each medium (e.g., lighting, sound, color, or camera focus and angles in a film).

8. (Not applicable to literature)

9. Compare and contrast a fictional portrayal of a time, place, or character and a historical account of the same period as a means of understanding how authors of fiction use or alter history.

Range of Reading and Level of Text Complexity

10. By the end of the year, read and comprehend literature, including stories, dramas, and poems, in the grades 6–8 text complexity band proficiently, with scaffolding as needed at the high end of the range.

Grade 7 Reading Standards for Informational Text

Key Ideas and Details

1. Cite several pieces of textual evidence to support analysis of what the text says explicitly as well as inferences drawn from the text.

2. Determine two or more central ideas in a text and analyze their development over the course of the text; provide an objective summary of the text.

3. Analyze the interactions between individuals, events, and ideas in a text (e.g., how ideas influence individuals or events, or how individuals influence ideas or events).

Craft and Structure

4. Determine the meaning of words and phrases as they are used in a text, including figurative, connotative, and technical meanings; analyze the impact of a specific word choice on meaning and tone.

5. Analyze the structure an author uses to organize a text, including how the major sections contribute to the whole and to the development of the ideas.

6. Determine an author's point of view or purpose in a text and analyze how the author distinguishes his or her position from that of others.

Integration of Knowledge and Ideas

7. Compare and contrast a text to an audio, video, or multimedia version of the text, analyzing each medium's portrayal of the subject (e.g., how the delivery of a speech affects the impact of the words).

8. Trace and evaluate the argument and specific claims in a text, assessing whether the reasoning is sound and the evidence is relevant and sufficient to support the claims.

9. Analyze how two or more authors writing about the same topic shape their presentations of key information by emphasizing different evidence or advancing different interpretations of facts.

Range of Reading and Level of Text Complexity

10. By the end of the year, read and comprehend literary nonfiction in the grades 6–8 text complexity band proficiently, with scaffolding as needed at the high end of the range.

© Common Core Writing Standards

College and Career Readiness Anchor Standards

Text Types and Purposes

1. Write arguments to support claims in an analysis of substantive topics or texts, using valid reasoning and relevant and sufficient evidence.

2. Write informative/explanatory texts to examine and convey complex ideas and information clearly and accurately through the effective selection, organization, and analysis of content.

3. Write narratives to develop real or imagined experiences or events using effective technique, well-chosen details, and well-structured event sequences.

Production and Distribution of Writing

4. Produce clear and coherent writing in which the development, organization, and style are appropriate to task, purpose, and audience.

5. Develop and strengthen writing as needed by planning, revising, editing, rewriting, or trying a new approach.

6. Use technology, including the Internet, to produce and publish writing and to interact and collaborate with others.

Research to Build and Present Knowledge

7. Conduct short as well as more sustained research projects based on focused questions, demonstrating understanding of the subject under investigation.

8. Gather relevant information from multiple print and digital sources, assess the credibility and accuracy of each source, and integrate the information while avoiding plagiarism.

9. Draw evidence from literary or informational texts to support analysis, reflection, and research.

Range of Writing

10. Write routinely over extended time frames (time for research, reflection, and revision) and shorter time frames (a single sitting or a day or two) for a range of tasks, purposes, and audiences.

Grade 7 Writing Standards

Text Types and Purposes

1. Write arguments to support claims with clear reasons and relevant evidence.
   a. Introduce claim(s), acknowledge alternate or opposing claims, and organize the reasons and evidence logically.
   b. Support claim(s) with logical reasoning and relevant evidence, using accurate, credible sources and demonstrating an understanding of the topic or text.
   c. Use words, phrases, and clauses to create cohesion and clarify the relationships among claim(s), reasons, and evidence.
   d. Establish and maintain a formal style.
   e. Provide a concluding statement or section that follows from and supports the argument presented.

2. Write informative/explanatory texts to examine a topic and convey ideas, concepts, and information through the selection, organization, and analysis of relevant content.
   a. Introduce a topic clearly, previewing what is to follow; organize ideas, concepts, and information, using strategies such as definition, classification, comparison/contrast, and cause/effect; include formatting (e.g., headings), graphics (e.g., charts, tables), and multimedia when useful to aiding comprehension.
   b. Develop the topic with relevant facts, definitions, concrete details, quotations, or other information and examples.
   c. Use appropriate transitions to create cohesion and clarify the relationships among ideas and concepts.
   d. Use precise language and domain-specific vocabulary to inform about or explain the topic.
   e. Establish and maintain a formal style.
   f. Provide a concluding statement or section that follows from and supports the information or explanation presented.

3. Write narratives to develop real or imagined experiences or events using effective technique, relevant descriptive details, and well-structured event sequences.
   a. Engage and orient the reader by establishing a context and point of view and introducing a narrator and/or characters; organize an event sequence that unfolds naturally and logically.
   b. Use narrative techniques, such as dialogue, pacing, and description, to develop experiences, events, and/or characters.
   c. Use a variety of transition words, phrases, and clauses to convey sequence and signal shifts from one time frame or setting to another.
   d. Use precise words and phrases, relevant descriptive details, and sensory language to capture the action and convey experiences and events.
   e. Provide a conclusion that follows from and reflects on the narrated experiences or events.

Production and Distribution of Writing

4. Produce clear and coherent writing in which the development, organization, and style are appropriate to task, purpose, and audience.

5. With some guidance and support from peers and adults, develop and strengthen writing as needed by planning, revising, editing, rewriting, or trying a new approach, focusing on how well purpose and audience have been addressed.

6. Use technology, including the Internet, to produce and publish writing and link to and cite sources as well as to interact and collaborate with others, including linking to and citing sources.

Research to Build and Present Knowledge

7. Conduct short research projects to answer a question, drawing on several sources and generating additional related, focused questions for further research and investigation.

8. Gather relevant information from multiple print and digital sources, using search terms effectively; assess the credibility and accuracy of each source; and quote or paraphrase the data and conclusions of others while avoiding plagiarism and following a standard format for citation.

9. Draw evidence from literary or informational texts to support analysis, reflection, and research.

  a. Apply *grade 7 Reading standards* to literature (e.g., "Compare and contrast a fictional portrayal of a time, place, or character and a historical account of the same period as a means of understanding how authors of fiction use or alter history").

  b. Apply *grade 7 Reading standards* to literary nonfiction (e.g., "Trace and evaluate the argument and specific claims in a text, assessing whether the reasoning is sound and the evidence is relevant and sufficient to support the claims").

Range of Writing

10. Write routinely over extended time frames (time for research, reflection, and revision) and shorter time frames (a single sitting or a day or two) for a range of discipline-specific tasks, purposes, and audiences.

© Common Core
Speaking and Listening Standards

College and Career Readiness Anchor Standards

Comprehension and Collaboration

1. Prepare for and participate effectively in a range of conversations and collaborations with diverse partners, building on others' ideas and expressing their own clearly and persuasively.

2. Integrate and evaluate information presented in diverse media and formats, including visually, quantitatively, and orally.

3. Evaluate a speaker's point of view, reasoning, and use of evidence and rhetoric.

Presentation of Knowledge and Ideas

4. Present information, findings, and supporting evidence such that listeners can follow the line of reasoning and the organization, development, and style are appropriate to task, purpose, and audience.

5. Make strategic use of digital media and visual displays of data to express information and enhance understanding of presentations.

6. Adapt speech to a variety of contexts and communicative tasks, demonstrating command of formal English when indicated or appropriate.

Grade 7 Speaking and Listening Standards

Comprehension and Collaboration

1. Engage effectively in a range of collaborative discussions (one-on-one, in groups, and teacher-led) with diverse partners on *grade 7 topics, texts, and issues,* building on others' ideas and expressing their own clearly.

   a. Come to discussions prepared, having read or researched material under study; explicitly draw on that preparation by referring to evidence on the topic, text, or issue to probe and reflect on ideas under discussion.

   b. Follow rules for collegial discussions, track progress toward specific goals and deadlines, and define individual roles as needed.

   c. Pose questions that elicit elaboration and respond to others' questions and comments with relevant observations and ideas that bring the discussion back on topic as needed.

   d. Acknowledge new information expressed by others and, when warranted, modify their own views.

2. Analyze the main ideas and supporting details presented in diverse media and formats (e.g., visually, quantitatively, orally) and explain how the ideas clarify a topic, text, or issue under study.

3. Delineate a speaker's argument and specific claims, evaluating the soundness of the reasoning and the relevance and sufficiency of the evidence.

Presentation of Knowledge and Ideas

4. Present claims and findings, emphasizing salient points in a focused, coherent manner with pertinent descriptions, facts, details, and examples; use appropriate eye contact, adequate volume, and clear pronunciation.

5. Include multimedia components and visual displays in presentations to clarify claims and findings and emphasize salient points.

6. Adapt speech to a variety of contexts and tasks, demonstrating command of formal English when indicated or appropriate. (See grade 7 Language standards 1 and 3 for specific expectations.)

© Common Core Language Standards

College and Career Readiness Anchor Standards

Conventions of Standard English

1. Demonstrate command of the conventions of standard English grammar and usage when writing or speaking.

2. Demonstrate command of the conventions of standard English capitalization, punctuation, and spelling when writing.

Knowledge of Language

3. Apply knowledge of language to understand how language functions in different contexts, to make effective choices for meaning or style, and to comprehend more fully when reading or listening.

Vocabulary Acquisition and Use

4. Determine or clarify the meaning of unknown and multiple-meaning words and phrases by using context clues, analyzing meaningful word parts, and consulting general and specialized reference materials, as appropriate.

5. Demonstrate understanding of figurative language, word relationships, and nuances in word meanings.

6. Acquire and use accurately a range of general academic and domain-specific words and phrases sufficient for reading, writing, speaking, and listening at the college and career readiness level; demonstrate independence in gathering vocabulary knowledge when considering a word or phrase important to comprehension or expression.

Grade 7 Language Standards

Conventions of Standard English

1. Demonstrate command of the conventions of standard English grammar and usage when writing or speaking.

   a. Explain the function of phrases and clauses in general and their function in specific sentences.

   b. Choose among simple, compound, complex, and compound-complex sentences to signal differing relationships among ideas.

   c. Place phrases and clauses within a sentence, recognizing and correcting misplaced and dangling modifiers.

2. Demonstrate command of the conventions of standard English capitalization, punctuation, and spelling when writing.

   a. Use a comma to separate coordinate adjectives (e.g., *It was a fascinating, enjoyable movie* but not *He wore an old[,] green shirt*).

   b. Spell correctly.

Knowledge of Language

3. Use knowledge of language and its conventions when writing, speaking, reading, or listening.

   a. Choose language that expresses ideas precisely and concisely, recognizing and eliminating wordiness and redundancy.

Vocabulary Acquisition and Use

4. Determine or clarify the meaning of unknown and multiple-meaning words and phrases based on *grade 7 reading and content*, choosing flexibly from a range of strategies.

   a. Use context (e.g., the overall meaning of a sentence or paragraph; a word's position or function in a sentence) as a clue to the meaning of a word or phrase.

   b. Use common, grade-appropriate Greek or Latin affixes and roots as clues to the meaning of a word (e.g., *belligerent, bellicose, rebel*).

   c. Consult general and specialized reference materials (e.g., dictionaries, glossaries, thesauruses), both print and digital, to find the pronunciation of a word or determine or clarify its precise meaning or its part of speech.

   d. Verify the preliminary determination of the meaning of a word or phrase (e.g., by checking the inferred meaning in context or in a dictionary).

5. Demonstrate understanding of figurative language, word relationships, and nuances in word meanings.

   a. Interpret figures of speech (e.g., literary, biblical, and mythological allusions) in context.

   b. Use the relationship between particular words (e.g., synonym/antonym, analogy) to better understand each of the words.

   c. Distinguish among the connotations (associations) of words with similar denotations (definitions) (e.g., *refined, respectful, polite, diplomatic, condescending*).

6. Acquire and use accurately grade-appropriate general academic and domain-specific words and phrases; gather vocabulary knowledge when considering a word or phrase important to comprehension or expression.

Introductory Unit

Building Academic Vocabulary

Academic vocabulary is the language you encounter in textbooks and on standardized tests and other assessments. Understanding these words and using them in your classroom discussions and writing will help you communicate your ideas clearly and effectively.

There are two basic types of academic vocabulary: general and domain-specific. **General academic vocabulary** includes words that are not specific to any single course of study. For example, the general academic vocabulary word *analyze* is used in language arts, math, social studies, art, and so on. **Domain-specific academic vocabulary** includes words that are usually encountered in the study of a specific discipline. For example, the words *factor* and *remainder* are most often used in mathematics classrooms and texts.

**Common Core
State Standards**

Language 6. Acquire and use accurately grade-appropriate general academic and domain-specific words and phrases; gather vocabulary knowledge when considering a word or phrase important to comprehension or expression.

General Academic Vocabulary

Word	Definition	Related Words	Word in Context
analyze (AN uh lyz) *v.*	break down into parts and examine carefully	analytical	Our assignment is to analyze the story's ending.
appreciate (uh PREE shee ayt) *v.*	be thankful for	appreciative appreciating	Once I read Frost's poem, I learned to appreciate his use of symbols.
assumption (uh SUHMP shuhn) *n.*	belief or acceptance that something is true	assume assuming	The assumption in the essay is well supported by facts.
attitude (AT uh tood) *n.*	mental state involving beliefs, feelings, and values	attitudes	The writer's attitude toward his subject was respectful and full of admiration.
awareness (uh WAIR nehs) *n.*	knowledge gained from one's own perceptions or from information	aware	It is important to develop an awareness of the writer's message.
bias (BY uhs) *n.*	tendency to see things from a slanted or prejudiced viewpoint	biased	You must consider if an advertisement contains bias or tries to mislead the reader.
culture (KUHL chuhr) *n.*	collected customs of a group or community	cultural	Folk tales reveal the values of a culture and teach a lesson.
challenge (CHAL uhnj) *v.*	dare; a calling into question	challenging challenged	Ted invited me to challenge him to a debate.

Ordinary Language:
I **like** poems with strong rhymes and rhythms.

Academic Language:
I **appreciate** poems with strong rhymes and rhythms.

Word	Definition	Related Words	Word in Context
characteristic (kar ihk tuh RIHS tihk) *n.*	trait; feature	character characteristically	One characteristic of poetry is figurative language.
common (KOM uhn) *adj.*	ordinary; expected	commonality	It is common for an essay to contain humor.
communicate (kuh MYOO nuh kayt) *v.*	share thoughts or feelings, usually in words	communication communicating	It is important to be able to communicate thoughts and feelings in writing.
communication (kuh myoo nuh KAY shuhn) *n.*	activity of sharing information or speaking	communicate	There seemed to be a lack of communication between the mother and daughter.
community (kuh MYOO nuh tee) *n.*	group of people who share an interest or who live near each other	communities	Local newspapers serve the community where the paper is published.
conclude (kuhn KLOOD) *v.*	bring to a close; end	concluding conclusion	The writer was able to conclude the essay with a positive memory.
contribute (kuhn TRIHB yut) *v.*	add to; enrich	contribution	Editorials contribute to a public discussion about an issue.
convince (kuhn VIHNS) *v.*	persuade; cause to accept a point of view	convincing	It is important to convince readers of the character's dream.
debate (dih BAYT) *v.*	argue in an attempt to convince	debated debating	The two students tried to debate whether or not the new website was helpful.
define (dih FYN) *v.*	determine the nature of or give the meaning of	defined definition	I was able to define the story's plot quickly.
discover (dihs KUHV uhr) *v.*	find or explore	discovering discovery	The reader tries to discover the reasons for the character's behavior.
diversity (duh VUR suh tee) *n.*	variety, as of groups or cultures	diverse	Reading works from different writers provides diversity.

Ordinary Language: In this essay, I will **tell the meaning** of key terms.

Academic Language: In this essay, I will **define** key terms.

Word	Definition	Related Words	Word in Context
environment (ehn VY ruhn muhnt) *n.*	surroundings; the natural world	environs environmentally	The essay described the beautiful environment where the writer lived.
evaluate (ih VAL yoo ayt) *v.*	judge; determine the value or quality of	evaluated evaluation	The girl was unable to evaluate her friend's work without bias.
examine (ehg ZAM uhn) *v.*	study in depth; look at closely	examining examination	In order to examine the evidence, it was necessary to research the subject.
explain (ehk SPLAYN) *v.*	make plain or clear	explaining explanation	I will explain three key factors in the story's success.
explore (ehk SPLAWR) *v.*	investigate; look into	explored exploration	I wrote a research report to explore my ideas.
facts (fakts) *n.*	accepted truths or reality	factual	I supported my statement with facts and details.
focus (FOH kuhs) *n.*	central point or topic of investigation	focused focusing	The focus of the essay was to provide information about water safety.
generate (JEN uhr ayt) *v.*	create	generated generating	Before researching, I tried to generate a list of topics to explore.
identify (ahy- DEHN tuh fy) *v.*	recognize as being	identification	How do you identify the meaning of this poem?
ignore (ihg NAWR) *v.*	refuse to notice; disregard	ignored ignoring	If we ignore the message, we miss the purpose of the writing.
image (IHM ihj) *n.*	picture; representation	images imaging	The image in the book helped me to visualize the story.
individual (ihn duh VIHJ oo uhl) *n.*	single person or thing	individuals	The story is told from the perspective of one individual.
inform (ihn FORM) *v.*	tell; give information about	information	The purpose of the research paper was to inform the reader about whales.
inquire (ihn KWYR) *v.*	ask in order to learn about	inquiring inquired	We were assigned to inquire about weather patterns and present our findings.
insight (IHN syt) *n.*	ability to see the truth; an understanding	insightful	My teacher shared her insight about the characters with us.
investigate (ihn VEHS tuh gayt) *v.*	examine thoroughly	investigated investigation	As a team, we were able to investigate each aspect of the problem.

Word	Definition	Related Words	Word in Context
media (MEE dee uh) *n.*	collected sources of information, including newspapers, television, and the Internet		The media are an everyday source of information and entertainment for the public.
opposition (op uh ZIHSH uhn) *n.*	state of being against	oppose opposing	The villain in the story presented the opposition to the hero's happiness.
outcome (OWT kuhm) *n.*	way something turns out		We found the outcome of the problem to be a favorable solution.
perceive (puhr SEEV) *v.*	be aware of; see	perceived perception	I was able to perceive Jenny's character through her actions and words.
perception (puhr SEHP shuhn) *n.*	the act of becoming aware of through one or more of the senses	perceive perceptive	My perception of the character changed over the course of the story.
perspective (puhr SPEHK tihv) *n.*	point of view		I did not agree with the writer's perspective.
produce (pruh DOOS) *v.*	make; create	produced producing	In order to produce a new show, the writing team must provide a script.
reaction (ree AK shuhn) *n.*	response to an influence, action, or statement	react	I had a strong reaction to the claims made in the commercial.
reflect (rih FLEHKT) *v.*	think about; consider	reflected reflection	In order to reflect on what had been said, I took some quiet time.
resolution (rehz uh LOO shuhn) *n.*	end of a conflict in which one or both parties is satisfied	resolved resolving	The resolution of the story helped me to see how a compromise can help many people.
team (teem) *n.*	group united in a common goal		Our team prepared a report, and each member presented a part of it.

Word	Definition	Related Words	Word in Context
technology (tehk NOL uh jee) *n.*	practical application of science to business or industry	technologies	At one time, the computer was considered a new technology.
tradition (truh DIHSH uhn) *n.*	custom, as of a social group or culture	traditional	A tradition is often handed down to a new generation though storytelling.
transmit (trans MIHT) *v.*	send or give out	transmitted transmission	We were able to transmit our message over the school's radio station.
understanding (uhn duhr STAN dihng) *n.*	agreement; end of conflict	understand	The students came to an understanding of how best to organize the club.
unify (YOO nuh fy) *v.*	bring together as one	unified unifying	It is important to unify details so that they support the central idea.
unique (yoo NEEK) *adj.*	one of a kind	uniqueness uniquely	Each writer has a unique way of telling a story.

Practice

Examples of various kinds of domain-specific academic vocabulary appear in the charts below. Some chart rows are not filled in. In your notebook, look up the definitions of the remaining words, provide one or two related words, and use each word in context.

Social Studies: Domain-Specific Academic Vocabulary

Word	Definition	Related Words	Word in Context
communism (KOM yuh niz uhm) *n.*	an economic and social system where the land and all products of industry belong to the government as a whole	commune communist	Communism failed in Eastern Europe.
dissent (dih SENT) *n.*	difference of feeling or opinion	dissention dissenter	There was much dissent and disagreement in the government.
neutrality (noo TRAL i tee) *n.*	the state of being neutral; not taking sides in a conflict	neutral	Switzerland kept its neutrality during World War II.
segregation (seg ri GEY shuhn) *n.*	the separation of people because of race, color, or gender	segregate segregated	The Civil Rights Movement helped to end segregation in the South.
socialism (SOH shuh liz uhm) *n.*	a theory or system of organization in which major sources of production are owned or controlled by the community or government	social socialist	Socialism stresses the community rather than the individual.
adaptation (ad uhp TEY shuhn) *n.*			
emigration (em I GREY shuhn) *n.*			
colonization (KOL uh nih ZAY shuhn) *n.*			
nobility (noh BIL i tee) *n.*			
urbanization (UR buh nuh ZAY shuhn) *n.*			

Mathematics: Domain-Specific Academic Vocabulary

Word	Definition	Related Words	Word in Context
negative number (NEG ah tiv NUHM ber) *n.*	a number below zero on a number line; indicated by a minus sign	positive number	The number −4 is a negative number, while 4 is a positive number.
odds (oddz) *n.*	the probability that something will happen	odd oddity	What are the odds that I will win the lottery?
proportion (pruh PAWR shuhn) *n.*	a statement of the equality of two ratios, or the mathematical relationship of a part to the whole	proportionate	The teacher said that the proportion should be written as 4/2 = 10/5.
range (reynj) *n.*	the difference between the largest and smallest values in a group of numbers	ranging	Find the range in the following number set: 2, 3, 4, 5, and 6.
ratio (REY shee oh) *n.*	proportionate relationship between two numbers	ratios	The ratio of 5 to 2 is written as 5:2.
minimum (MIN uh muhm) *n.*			
property (PROP er tee) *n.*			
rate (reyt) *n.*			
reliability (ri LY uh bil i tee) *n.*			
sequence (SEE kwuhns) *n.*			

Science: Domain-Specific Academic Vocabulary

Word	Definition	Related Words	Word in Context
hypothesis (hy POTH uh sis) *n.*	something not proved but assumed to be true for the purpose of further study or argument	hypothesize	The hypothesis that the earth was flat was later proven to be false.
erosion (ih ROH zhuhn) *n.*	the process by which the surface of the earth is worn away by the action of water and other natural events	erode	The hurricane caused beach erosion.
metamorphic (met uh MAWR fik) *adj.*	changing in form or structure	metamorphosis	Metamorphic rock is formed by heat and pressure within the earth.
solubility (sol yuh BIL i tee) *n.*	the ability of a substance to dissolve	soluble	We tested the solubility of salt in a science lab.
synthesize (SIN thuh syz) *v.*	form by combining parts or elements	synthetic	Scientists synthesize compounds by combining two or more substances.

Science: Domain-Specific Academic Vocabulary (*continued*)

Word	Definition	Related Words	Word in Context
energy (EN er jee) *n.*			
evidence (EV i iduhns) *n.*			
gene (jeen) *n.*			
heredity (huh RED i tee) *n.*			
substance (SUHB stuhns) *n.*			

Art: Domain-Specific Academic Vocabulary

Word	Definition	Related Words	Word in Context
intensity (in TEN si tee) *n.*	the quality of a color's brightness and purity	intense	The intensity of the red paint was stronger than the artist wanted.
linear (LIN ee er) *adj.*	having to do with a line	line	The sculpture of the building was linear and rigid.
saturation (sach uh REY shuhn) *n.*	the degree of purity of a color	saturate	The saturation of the pink paint gave the room a lively feel.
texture (TEKS cher) *n.*	the way things feel, or look as if they might feel, when touched	textured	The carpet had a thick and fluffy texture.
unity (YOO ni tee) *n.*	the look and feel of wholeness in a work of art	unite, unified	The mural had good balance and unity.
definition (def uh NISH uhn) *n.*			
form (fawrm) *n.*			
motion (MOH shuhn) *n.*			
space (speys) *n.*			
value (VAL yoo) *n.*			

Technology: Domain-Specific Academic Vocabulary

Word	Definition	Related Words	Word in Context
database (DEY tuh beys) *n.*	a collection of related information stored in a computerized format	databases	The library has a database of all its books.
digital (DIJ i tl) *adj.*	available in an electronic format	digit, digitize	I have a digital version of that book on my computer.
login (LOG in) *n.*	information related to an electronic account name and its password	logging in	I use my login to access my account on a secure Web site.
network (NET work) *n.*	a group of computers connected together to share information	networking, networked	The Internet is the largest network in the world.
platform (PLAT fawrm) *n.*	a group of compatible computers that can share software	platforms	PC is the computer platform used in our school.
bookmark (BOOK mahrk) *n.*			
copy (KOP ee) *n., v.*			
download (DOUN lohd) *v.*			
input (IN poot) *n., v.*			
output (OUT poot) *n., v.*			

Increasing Your Word Knowledge

Increase your word knowledge and chances of success by taking an active role in developing your vocabulary. Here are some tips for you.

To own a word, follow these steps:

Steps to Follow	Model
1. Learn to identify the word and its basic meaning.	The word *examine* means "to look at closely."
2. Take note of the word's spelling.	*Examine* begins and ends with an *e*.
3. Practice pronouncing the word so that you can use it in conversation.	The *e* on the end of the word is silent. Its second syllable gets the most stress.
4. Visualize the word and illustrate its key meaning.	When I think of the word *examine*, I visualize a doctor checking a patient's health.
5. Learn the various forms of the word and its related words.	*Examination* and *exam* are forms of the word *examine*.
6. Compare the word with similar words.	*Examine*, *peruse*, and *study* are synonyms.
7. Contrast the word with similar words.	*Examine* suggests a more detailed study than *read* or *look at*.
8. Use the word in various contexts.	"I'd like to *examine* the footprints more closely." "I will *examine* the use of imagery in this poem."

Building Your Speaking Vocabulary

Language gives us the ability to express ourselves. The more words you know, the better able you will be to get your points across. There are two main aspects of language: reading and speaking. Using the steps above will help you to acquire a rich vocabulary. Follow these steps to help you learn to use this rich vocabulary in discussions, speeches, and conversations.

Steps to Follow	Tip
1. Practice pronouncing the word.	Become familiar with pronunciation guides, which will help you to sound out unfamiliar words. Listening to audio books as you read the text will help you learn pronunciations of words.
2. Learn word forms.	Dictionaries often list forms of words following the main word entry. Practice saying word families aloud: "generate," "generated," "generation," "regenerate," "generator."
3. Translate your thoughts.	Restate your own thoughts and ideas in a variety of ways, to inject formality or to change your tone, for example.
4. Hold discussions.	With a classmate, practice using academic vocabulary words in discussions about the text. Choose one term to practice at a time, and see how many statements you can create using that term.
5. Tape-record yourself.	Analyze your word choices by listening to yourself objectively. Note where your word choice could be strengthened or changed.

Writing an Objective Summary

The ability to write objective summaries is key to success in college and in many careers. Writing an effective objective summary involves recording the key ideas of a text while demonstrating your understanding.

Common Core State Standards

Literature 2. Determine a theme or central idea of a text and analyze its development over the course of the text; provide an objective summary of the text.
Informational Text 2. Determine two or more central ideas in a text and analyze their development over the course of the text; provide an objective summary of the text.

What Is an Objective Summary?

An effective objective summary is a concise, complete, accurate, and objective overview of a text. The following are key characteristics of an objective summary:

- A good summary focuses on the main theme, or central idea, of a text and specific, relevant details that support that theme, or central idea. Unnecessary supporting details are left out.

- An effective summary is usually brief. However, the writer must be careful not to misrepresent the text by leaving out key elements.

- A successful summary accurately captures the essence of the longer text it is describing.

- An effective summary remains objective—the writer refrains from inserting his or her own opinions, reactions, or personal connections into the summary.

What to Avoid in an Objective Summary

- An objective summary is not a collection of sentences or paragraphs copied from the original source.

- It is not a long recounting of every event, detail, or point in the original text.

- A good summary does not include evaluative words or comments, such as the reader's overall opinion of or reaction to the piece. An objective summary is not the reader's interpretation or critical analysis of the work.

Model Objective Summary

Review the elements of an effective objective summary, which are pointed out in the sidenotes that appear next to the summary. Then, write an objective summary of a selection you recently read. Review your summary, and delete any unnecessary details, personal opinions, or evaluations of the text.

Summary of "Mowgli's Brothers"

"Mowgli's Brothers" is one of the stories in *The Jungle Book,* written by Rudyard Kipling. The setting of the story is a jungle in India, and the ~~enchanting~~ story tells the tale of Mowgli, a young boy who is raised by wolves.

One night Mother and Father Wolf woke from their rest to find Tabaqui, a jackal, at the mouth of their cave, begging for food. No one in the jungle liked Tabaqui. However, the wolves gave him a bone to eat in spite of the fact that he upset Mother Wolf ~~by complimenting her on her four young cubs. The wolves thought it was unlucky to compliment children to their faces.~~ Tabaqui further upset the wolves by bringing the news that Shere Khan, a tiger, was moving into their hunting grounds.

After Tabaqui left, Father Wolf set out on his hunt. He heard Shere Khan's roar and then saw him rolling around on the ground. The tiger had landed in a woodcutter's fire while trying to catch his prey.

Soon after that, something approached the wolves' cave. Father Wolf was ready to pounce until he saw what it was—a smiling, happy baby boy. Father Wolf gently picked up the man's cub and brought him to Mother Wolf. The man's cub was not at all afraid, and he snuggled right up with the wolf cubs.

Before long, Shere Khan stuck his big head into the cave. He wanted the man's cub, which had been his prey. The wolves wouldn't give him up, which angered the tiger. But Mother Wolf was even angrier. She said, "The man's cub is mine…He shall not be killed. He shall live to run with the Pack and to hunt with the Pack; and in the end. . .he shall hunt thee."

Mother Wolf named the man's cub Mowgli, and he was brought before the Wolf Pack for approval. With the help of Baloo the bear and Bagheera the black panther, Mowgli was accepted into the Pack. Shere Khan slinked away into the night, roaring his disapproval.

A one-sentence synopsis, or brief overview, highlighting the theme, or central idea, of the story can be an effective start to a summary.

The adjective *enchanting* indicates an opinion and should not be included in an objective summary.

Unnecessary details should be eliminated.

Transition words and phrases show chronological order and enable readers to easily follow the order of events.

If actual sentences from the story are used to show the essence of a text, they must be placed within quotation marks.

Comprehending Complex Texts

**Common Core
State Standards**

Literature 10. By the end of the year, read and comprehend literature, including stories, dramas, and poems, in the grades 6–8 text complexity band proficiently, with scaffolding as needed at the high end of the range.

Over the course of your school years, you will be required to read increasingly complex texts as preparation for college and a career. A complex text is a text that contains challenging vocabulary; long, complex sentences; figurative language; multiple levels of meaning; or unfamiliar settings and situations.

The selections in this textbook provide you with a range of readings, from short stories to autobiographies, poetry, drama, myths, and even science and social studies texts. Some of these texts will fall within your comfort zone; others will most likely be more challenging.

Strategy 1: Multidraft Reading

Most successful readers know that to fully understand a text, you must reread it several times. Get in the habit of reading a text or portions of a text two to three times in order to ensure that you get the most out of your reading experience. To fully understand a text, try this multidraft reading strategy:

1st Reading

On your first reading, look for the basics. If, for example, you are reading a story, look for who does what to whom, what conflicts arise, and how conflicts are resolved. If the text is nonfiction, look for the main ideas and the ways they are presented. If you are reading a lyric poem, read first to get a sense of who the speaker is. Also take note of the poem's setting and main focus.

2nd Reading

During your second reading of a text, focus on the artistry or the effectiveness of the writing. Look for text structures and think about why the author chose those organizational patterns. Then, examine the author's creative uses of language and the effects of that language. For example, has the author used metaphor, simile, or hyperbole? If so, what effect did that use of figurative language create?

3rd Reading

After your third reading, compare and contrast the text with other similar selections you have read. For example, if you read a haiku, think of other haiku you have read and ways the poems are alike or different. Evaluate the text's overall effectiveness and its central idea, or theme.

Independent Practice

As you read this poem, practice the multidraft reading strategy by completing a chart like the one below. Use a separate piece of paper.

"Prayers of Steel" by Carl Sandburg

Lay me on an anvil, O God.

Beat me and hammer me into a crowbar.

Let me pry loose old walls;

Let me lift and loosen old foundations.

Lay me on an anvil, O God.

Beat me and hammer me into a steel spike.

Drive me into the girders that hold a skyscraper together.

Take red-hot rivets and fasten me into the central girders.

Let me be the great nail holding a skyscraper through blue
nights into white stars.

Multidraft Reading Chart

	My Understanding
1st Reading Look for key ideas and details that unlock basic meaning.	
2nd Reading Read for deeper meanings. Look for ways in which the author used text structures and language to create effects.	
3rd Reading Read to integrate your knowledge and ideas. Connect the text to others of its kind and to your own experience.	

Strategy 2: Close Read the Text

To comprehend a complex text, perform a close reading—a careful analysis of the words, phrases, and sentences within the text. As you close read, use the following tips to comprehend the text:

Tips for Close Reading
1. Break down long sentences into parts. Look for the subject of the sentence and its verb. Then, identify which parts of the sentence modify, or give more information about, the subject.
2. Reread difficult passages to confirm that you understand their meaning.
3. Look for context clues, such as **a.** restatement of an idea. For example, in this sentence, "defeated" restates the verb *vanquished*. The army **vanquished,** or <u>defeated</u>, its enemy. **b.** definition of sophisticated words. In this sentence, the underlined information defines the word *girder*. A **girder's** <u>long beam provides support for the floor above.</u> **c.** examples of concepts and topics. In the following passage, the underlined text provides an example of the adjective *voracious*. <u>Eating his entire dinner, two apples, and a banana</u> finally satisfied Rob's **voracious** appetite. **d.** contrasts of ideas and topics. The following sentence points out a difference between Lori and Ellen. Lori was **vivacious,** <u>unlike her shy, quiet</u> sister Ellen.
4. Identify pronoun antecedents. If long sentences or passages contain pronouns, reread the text to make sure you know to whom or what the pronouns refer. In the following passage, the underlined pronouns all have the antecedent *freedom*. **Freedom** is precious. Through <u>it</u> we prosper. In <u>its</u> absence we doubt, quake, rage, and suffer; <u>it</u> is just as necessary to life as is the air we breathe. For, without <u>it</u>, we surely perish.
5. Look for conjunctions, such as *and, or,* and *yet,* to help understand relationships between ideas.
6. Paraphrase, or restate in your own words, passages of difficult text in order to check your understanding. Remember that a paraphrase is a word-for-word restatement of an original text; it is not a summary.

Close-Read Model

As you read this document, take note of the sidenotes that model ways to unlock meaning in the text.

---

from "Speech to the Constitutional Convention" by Benjamin Franklin

I confess that I do not entirely approve of this Constitution at present; but, sir, I am not sure I shall never approve of it, for, having lived long, I have experienced many instances of being obliged, by better information or fuller consideration, to change opinions even on important subjects, which I once thought right, but found to be otherwise. It is therefore that, the older I grow, the more apt I am to doubt my own judgment of others. Most men, indeed, as well as most sects in religion think themselves in possession of all truth, and that wherever others differ with them, it is so far error. . . . .

In these sentiments, sir, I agree to this Constitution with all its faults—if they are such—because I think a general government necessary for us, and there is no form of government but what may be a blessing to the people if well administered; and I believe, further, that this is likely to be well administered for a course of years, and can only end in despotism, as other forms have done before it, when the people shall become so corrupted as to need a despotic government, being incapable of any other. I doubt, too, whether any other convention we can obtain may be able to make a better Constitution; for, when you assemble a number of men, to have the advantage of their joint wisdom, you inevitably assemble with those men all their prejudices, their passions, their errors of opinion, their local interests, and their selfish views. From such an assembly can a perfect production be expected?

It therefore astonishes me, sir, to find this system approaching so near to perfection as it does. . . .

Break down this long sentence into parts. The text highlighted in yellow conveys the basic meaning of the sentence. The text highlighted in blue provides additional information.

Look for antecedents. In this sentence, the noun *faults* is replaced by the pronoun *they.* The conjunction *because,* highlighted in blue, indicates a cause-and-effect relationship.

Search for context clues. The words in blue are context clues that help you figure out the meaning of the word that appears in yellow.

Strategy 3: Ask Questions

Be an attentive reader by asking questions as you read. Throughout this textbook, we have provided questions for you following each selection. These questions are sorted into three basic categories that build in sophistication and lead you to a deeper understanding of the texts you read.

Here is an example from this text:

Some questions are about Key Ideas and Details in the text. To answer these questions, you will need to locate and cite explicit information in the text or draw inferences from what you have read.

Some questions are about Craft and Structure in the text. To answer these questions, you will need to analyze how the author developed and structured the text. You will also look for ways in which the author artfully used language and how those word choices impacted the meaning and tone of the work.

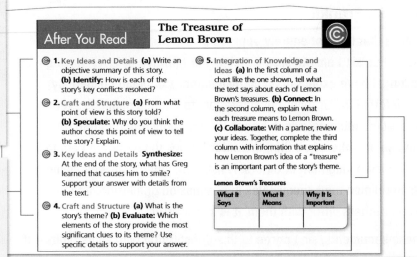

Some questions are about the Integration of Knowledge and Ideas in the text. These questions ask you to evaluate a text in many different ways, such as comparing texts, looking at arguments in the text, and many other methods of analyzing a text's ideas.

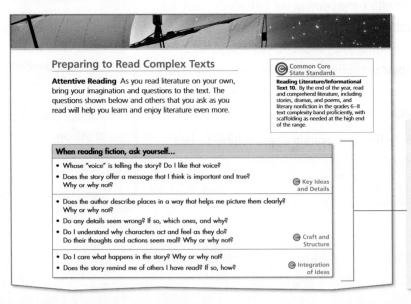

As you read independently, ask similar types of questions to ensure that you fully enjoy and comprehend texts you read for school and for pleasure. We have provided sets of questions for you on the Independent Reading pages at the end of each unit.

INFORMATIONAL TEXT

Model

Following is an example of a complex text. The sidenotes show sample questions that an attentive reader might ask while reading.

Sample questions:

from "Owning Books" by William Lyon Phelps

in a radio broadcast on April 6, 1933:

The habit of reading is one of the greatest resources of mankind; and we enjoy reading books that belong to us much more than if they are borrowed. . . your own books belong to you; you treat them with that affectionate intimacy that annihilates formality. Books are for use, not for show; you should own no book that you are afraid to mark up, or afraid to place on the table wide open and face down. A good reason for marking favorite passages in books is that this practice enables you to remember more easily the significant sayings, to refer to them quickly, and then in later years, it is like visiting a forest where you once blazed a trail. You have the pleasure of going over the old ground, and recalling both the intellectual scenery and your own earlier self.

Key Ideas and Details
Does the first sentence state facts or express an opinion? Who is meant by *we* and *us*?

Craft and Structure
What parallel structures does the writer use in this passage? What effect does that use have on readers?

Integration of Knowledge and Ideas
To what extent do you agree with the author's viewpoint? Explain.

INFORMATIONAL TEXT

Independent Practice

Write three to five questions you might ask yourself as you read this passage from a speech delivered by Theodore Roosevelt at the Grand Canyon in 1903.

from "Speech at the Grand Canyon" by Theodore Roosevelt

. . . In the Grand Canyon, Arizona has a natural wonder which, so far as I know, is, in kind, absolutely unparalleled throughout the rest of the world. I want to ask you to do one thing in connection with it, in your own interest and in the interest of the country—to keep this great wonder of nature as it now is. I was delighted to learn of the wisdom of the Santa Fe railroad people in deciding not to build their hotel on the brink of the canyon. I hope you will not have a building of any kind, not a summer cottage, a hotel, or anything else, to mar the wonderful grandeur, the sublimity, the great loneliness and beauty of the canyon. Leave it as it is. You cannot improve on it. The ages have been at work on it, and man can only mar it. What you can do is to keep it for your children, your children's children and for all who come after you, as one of the great sights which every American, if he can travel at all, should see. . . .

Analyzing Arguments

Common Core State Standards

Informational Text 8. Trace and evaluate the argument and specific claims in a text, assessing whether the reasoning is sound and the evidence is relevant and sufficient to support the claims.

Language 6. Acquire and use accurately general academic and domain-specific words and phrases.

The ability to evaluate an argument, as well as to make one, is an important skill for success in college and in the workplace.

What Is an Argument?

Chances are, you have used the word *argument* to refer to a disagreement between people. This type of argument involves trading opinions and evidence in a conversational way, with both sides contributing to the discussion. A formal argument, however, presents one side of a controversial or debatable issue. Through this type of argument, the writer logically supports a particular belief, conclusion, or point of view. A good argument is supported with reasoning and evidence.

Purposes of Argument

There are three main purposes for writing a formal argument:

- to change the reader's mind about an issue
- to convince the reader to accept what is written
- to motivate the reader to take action, based on what is written

---

Elements of an Argument

Claim (assertion)—what the writer is trying to prove

Example: *Sports programs should be funded by private individuals, not schools.*

Grounds (evidence)—the support used to convince the reader

Example: *Because students who participate in sports get the benefits of that activity, the students should do fund-raising to pay for the use of equipment and training.*

Justification—the link between the grounds and the claim; why the grounds are credible

Example: *For example, participants in sports often get college scholarships—money that is paid to them. Since those students benefit personally from the sports experience, they should help fund the cost of the sports activities.*

Evaluating Claims

When reading or listening to an argument, critically assess the claims that are made. Analyze the argument to identify claims that are based on fact or that can be proved true. Also evaluate evidence that supports the claims. If there is little or no reasoning or evidence provided to support the claims, the argument may not be sound or valid.

Model Argument

from "Speech Supporting Women's Suffrage"
by Robert L. Owen

Women compose one-half of the human race. . . A full half of the work of the world is done by women. A careful study of the matter has demonstrated the vital fact that these working women receive a smaller wage for equal work than men do, and that the smaller wage and harder conditions imposed on the woman worker are due to the lack of the ballot. . . . Equal pay for equal work is the first great reason justifying this change of governmental policy.

There are other reasons which are persuasive: First, women, take it all in all, are the equals of men in intelligence, and no man has the hardihood to assert the contrary. . . .

Every evil prophecy against granting the suffrage has failed. The public men of Colorado, Wyoming, Utah, and Idaho give it a cordial support.

The testimony is universal:

First, it has not made women mannish; they. . .are better able to protect themselves and their children because of the ballot.

Second, they have not become office-seekers. . . It [suffrage] has made women broader and greatly increased the understanding of the community at large of the problems of good government. . . .

It has not absolutely regenerated society, but it has improved it. It has raised the . . .moral standard of the suffrage, because there are more criminal men than criminal women. . . .

The great doctrine of the American Republic that "all governments derive their just powers from the consent of the governed" justifies the plea on one-half of the people, the women, to exercise the suffrage. The doctrine of the American Revolutionary War that taxation without representation is unendurable justifies women in exercising the suffrage.

Claim: Smaller wages and poor working conditions for women are caused by the fact that women cannot vote.

Grounds: Equal pay should be given for equal work.

Grounds: Women are just as intelligent as men.

An opposing argument is acknowledged and refuted.

Justification: Women should have the right to vote because government derives its powers from the consent of the governed, and women are half of the governed population. Also, taxation without representation is against U.S. principles. If women are to be taxed, they should have a vote.

A strong conclusion does more than simply restate the claim.

The Art of Argument: Rhetorical Devices and Persuasive Techniques

Rhetorical Devices

Rhetoric is the art of using language in order to make a point or to persuade listeners. Rhetorical devices such as the ones listed below are accepted elements of argument. Their use does not weaken an argument. Rather, the use of rhetorical devices is regarded as a key part of an effective argument.

Rhetorical Devices	Examples
Repetition The repeated use of words, phrases, or sentences	It is not **fair** to expect this treatment. Nor is it **fair** to pay for this decision.
Parallelism The repeated use of similar grammatical structures	Good students learn <u>to read, to question, and to respond</u>.
Rhetorical Question Calls attention to the issue by implying an obvious answer	Shouldn't consumers get what they pay for?
Sound Device The use of alliteration, assonance, rhyme, or rhythm	The invention is both **p**ractical and **p**rofitable.
Simile and Metaphor Compares two seemingly unlike things or asserts that one thing *is* another	**Teachers** are <u>like sparks</u> igniting the curiosity of their students.

Persuasive Techniques

Persuasive techniques are often found in advertisements and in other forms of informal persuasion. Although techniques like the ones below are sometimes found in informal arguments, they should be avoided in formal arguments.

Persuasive Techniques	Examples
Bandwagon Approach/Anti-Bandwagon Approach Appeals to a person's desire to belong; encourages or celebrates individuality	Anyone with any sense will vote for Richard Rock. Vote your conscience; an election is not a popularity contest.
Emotional Appeal Evokes people's fear, anger, or desire	Without working smoke detectors, your family is in danger.
Endorsement/Testimony Employs a well-known person to promote a product or idea	"I use this toothpaste, and it brightens my movie-star smile."
Loaded Language The use of words that are charged with emotion	The heroic firefighters bravely battled the raging inferno.
Hyperbole Exaggeration to make a point	Our candidate does the work of ten people.

INFORMATIONAL TEXT

Model Speech

The excerpted speech below includes examples of rhetorical devices and persuasive techniques.

from "Inaugural Address" by Dwight D. Eisenhower

My fellow citizens:

... Since this century's beginning, a time of tempest has seemed to come upon the continents of the earth. Masses of Asia have awakened to strike off shackles of the past. Great nations of Europe have fought their bloodiest wars. Thrones have toppled and their vast empires have disappeared. New nations have been born.

> The use of alliteration makes these phrases memorable.

For our own country, it has been a time of recurring trial. We have grown in power and in responsibility. We have passed through the anxieties of depression and of war to a summit unmatched in man's history. Seeking to secure peace in the world, we have had to fight through the forests of the Argonne, to the shores of Iwo Jima, and to the cold mountains of Korea...

> Eisenhower uses parallelism and repetition to emphasize his main points.

How far have we come in man's long pilgrimage from darkness toward light? Are we nearing the light—a day of freedom and of peace for all mankind? Or are the shadows of another night closing in upon us?...

> Rhetorical questions call attention to the speaker's point.

. . . we know that the virtues most cherished by free people—love of truth, pride of work, devotion to country—all are treasures equally precious in the lives of the most humble and of the most exalted. The men who mine coal and fire furnaces and balance ledgers and turn lathes and pick cotton and heal the sick and plant corn—all serve as proudly, and as profitably, for America as the statesmen who draft treaties and the legislators who enact laws.

> Additional examples of parallel structure enable the audience to follow Eisenhower's ideas and to be moved by his words.

...We must be willing, individually and as a Nation, to accept whatever sacrifices may be required of us. A people that values its privileges above its principles soon loses both.

> Sound devices, such as alliteration, are a way to emphasize a phrase.

These basic precepts are not lofty abstractions, far removed from matters of daily living... Patriotism means equipped forces and a prepared citizenry. Moral stamina means more energy and more productivity...Love of liberty means the guarding of every resource that makes freedom possible...

No person, no home, no community can be beyond the reach of this call. We are summoned to act in wisdom and in conscience, to work with industry, to teach with persuasion, to preach with conviction, to weigh our every deed with care and with compassion. For this truth must be clear before us: whatever America hopes to bring to pass in the world must first come to pass in the heart of America.

> The parallelism created by repeated grammatical structures gives the speech rhythm.

Composing an Argument

 Common Core
State Standards

Writing 1.a. Introduce claim(s), acknowledge alternate or opposing claims, and organize the reasons and evidence logically.

Writing 1.b. Support claim(s) with logical reasoning and relevant evidence, using accurate, credible sources and demonstrating an understanding of the topic or text.

Writing 1.e. Provide a concluding statement or section that follows from and supports the argument presented.

Choosing a Topic

You should choose a topic that matters to people—and to you. Brainstorm topics you would like to write about, and then choose the topic that most interests you.

Once you have chosen a topic, check to be sure you can make an arguable claim. Ask yourself:

1. What am I trying to prove? What ideas do I need to get across?

2. Are there people that would disagree with my claim? What alternate, or opposing, opinions might they have?

3. Do I have evidence to support my claim? Is my evidence sufficient or relevant?

If you are able to put into words what you want to prove and answered "yes" to numbers 2 and 3, you have an arguable claim.

Introducing the Claim and Establishing Its Significance

Before you begin writing, think about your audience and what they probably know about the topic. Then, provide only as much background information as necessary. Remember that you are not writing a summary of the issue—you are crafting an argument. Once you have provided context for your argument, clearly state your claim, or thesis. A written argument's claim often, but not always, appears in the first paragraph.

Developing Your Claim with Reasoning and Evidence

Now that you have made your claim, you must support it with evidence, or grounds. A good argument should have at least three solid pieces of evidence to support the claim. Evidence can range from personal experience to researched data or expert opinion. Knowing your audience's knowledge level, concerns, values, and possible biases can help you decide what kind of evidence will have the strongest impact. Make sure your evidence is up to date and comes from a credible source. Don't forget to credit your sources and address the opposing counterclaim.

Writing a Concluding Statement or Section

Restate your claim in the conclusion of your argument, and synthesize, or pull together, the evidence you have provided. Make your conclusion strong enough to be memorable to the reader; leave him or her with something to think about.

Practice

Complete an outline like the one below to help you plan your own argument.

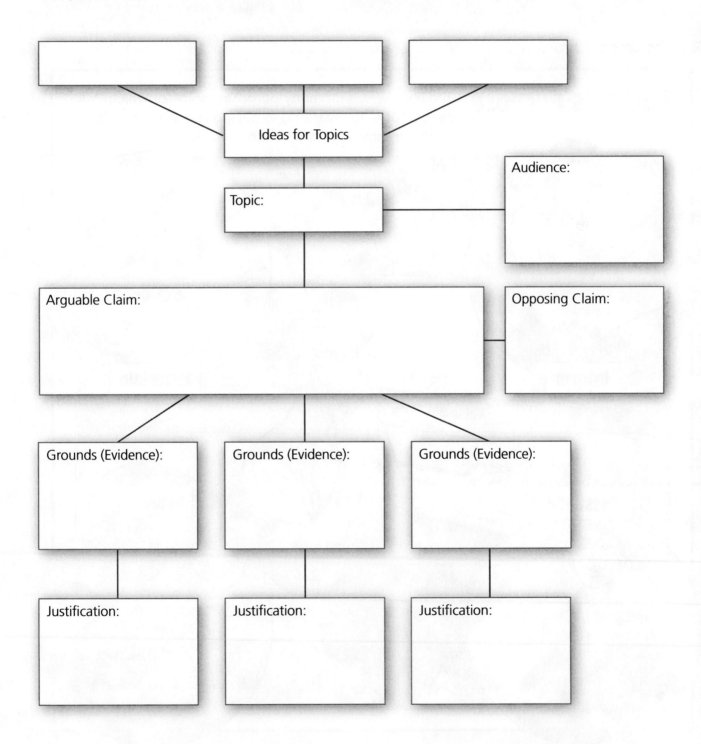

PICTURE IT!
A Comprehension Handbook

Author's Purpose An author writes for many purposes, some of which are to inform, to entertain, to persuade, or to express. An author may have more than one purpose for writing.

Inform

Entertain

Persuade

Express

Cause and Effect

An effect is something that happens. A cause is why that thing happens. An effect sometimes has more than one cause. A cause sometimes has more than one effect. Clue words such as *because*, *as a result*, *therefore*, and *so that* can signal causes and effects.

Cause

Effect

Compare and Contrast

To compare and contrast is to look for similarities and differences in things. Clue words such as *like* or *as* show similarities. Clue words such as *but* or *unlike* show differences.

Context Clues

You can use context clues—the words and phrases around an unfamiliar word—to determine the meaning of an unfamiliar word.

Draw Conclusions

When we draw conclusions, we make sensible decisions or form reasonable opinions after thinking about the facts and details in what we are reading.

Fact and Opinion

A fact is something that can be proved. Facts are based on evidence. Opinions express ideas and are based on interpretation of evidence.

Main Idea and Details

Main idea is the most important idea about a topic.

Details are smaller pieces of information that support the main idea.

Making Predictions

To make predictions, use text, graphics, and prior knowledge to predict what might happen in a story or what you might learn from a text. As you read, new information can lead to new or revised predictions.

Making Inferences

When we make inferences, or infer something, we come to a conclusion based on a detail an author provides in the text.

Paraphrasing

Paraphrasing is restating a sentence or an idea in your own words. Paraphrasing can lead to a better understanding of what we read.

Setting a Purpose for Reading

When we set a purpose for reading, we approach a text with a specific goal or question that we would like answered. Setting a purpose for reading guides comprehension by focusing our attention on specific information.

Summarizing

To summarize, we restate the main ideas of a text or the main events of a plot. In a summary, we leave out the supporting details.

Media Literacy Handbook

INTRODUCTION: Today, messages are transmitted across a variety of media modes, such as film, television, radio, and the Internet. As you interact with these messages each day—in images, advertisements, movies, and an array of different contexts—it is important to consider the potential influence of the medium.

- What is the intention of the message?
- How is it communicated?
- How do specific elements of the medium—such as color, image, or font—help convey the message?
- Why might the creator of the message have selected this medium?

These are the key issues of media literacy, the study of messages in the media and their impact.

Camera Shots and Angles
Filmmakers create camera shots and sequences to help them tell stories. Some shots capture an entire scene; others zoom in on specific characters.

Special Effects

Filmmakers use special effects to create on-screen illusions that bring the imagination to life.

Questions About Film Techniques

- What effect is created by the choice of camera angle shown in the image at left? Choose another camera angle and explain how that shot might convey a different message than the one shown here.

- Study the images above. In what way does the use of special effects make the film better for viewers?

Focus and Framing
A sharp focus captures all details in a photographic image. A softer focus lessens the amount of detail that can be seen. The framing of elements within a photograph directs the eye toward a portion of the image.

Lighting and Shadow
Lighting techniques are used in photography to enhance mood and direct the viewer's focus.

Special Techniques

Most images you see today have been manipulated or changed in some way. Even a small change—such as an added graphic element or a difference in shading—can alter the mood of an image.

Questions About Graphics and Photos

- What would be the effect if the image above left used a sharp focus instead of a combination of a sharp and soft focus?

- In what way does the use of color and light create mood in the photo below left?

- What special techniques were applied to the original photograph shown above? What effect does the use of special techniques create?

Persuasive Techniques

Advertisements use carefully selected visual elements and specific language to appeal to the viewer's emotions.

BRING THIS AD FOR **$1 OFF** ONE ADULT ADMISSION*

Fall is Fabulous
at the Lady Bird Johnson Wildflower Center

Fall Plant Sale and Gardening Festival

9 a.m. to 5 p.m. • Saturday and Sunday, October 18 and 19

Lady Bird Johnson
Wildflowercenter
THE UNIVERSITY OF TEXAS AT AUSTIN

Text and Graphics

Newspaper and magazine layouts are constructed to capture the eye and quickly convey the important ideas of a story. The use of type fonts, imagery, and page space direct the eye to portions of the printed page.

Questions About Print Media

- What image or graphic dominates the advertisement at left? In what way does the use of language in the ad enhance its message?

- Which of the above grabs your attention: the image or the graphic on the magazine cover? Explain.

- What do you notice first on the newspaper's front page? What overall effect does the use of type size and fonts create?

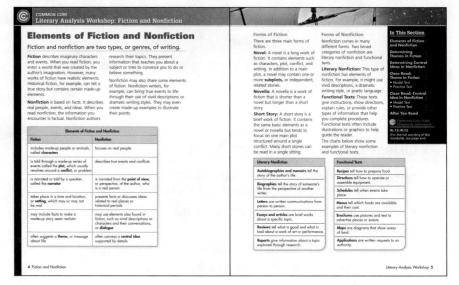
How is this book organized?

- There are six units, each focusing on a specific genre.
- Each unit has a Big Question to get you thinking about important ideas and to guide your reading.
- A Literary Analysis Workshop begins each unit, providing instruction and practice for essential skills.

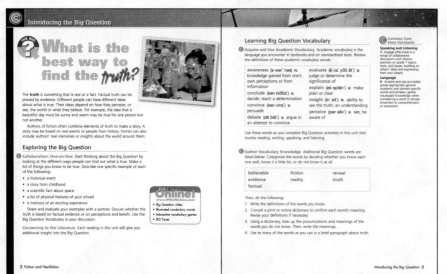

◄ At the beginning of the unit, **Introducing the Big Question** provides a reading focus for the entire unit. Use **academic vocabulary** to think, talk, and write about this question.

A **Literary Analysis Workshop** provides an overview of the unit genre, an in-depth exploration of Common Core State Standards, as well as models and practice opportunities. ▶

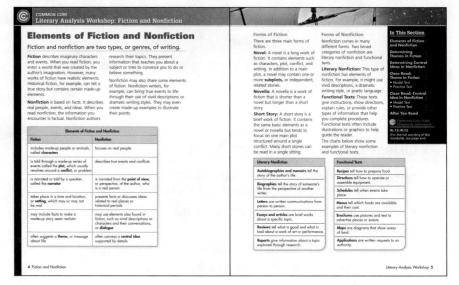

How are the literary selections organized?

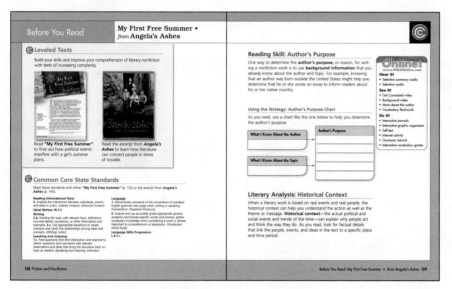

◀ **Before You Read** introduces two selection choices that both teach the same skills. Your teacher will help you choose the selection that is right for you.

Writing About the Big Question is a quick-writing activity that helps you connect the Big Question to the selection you are about to read.

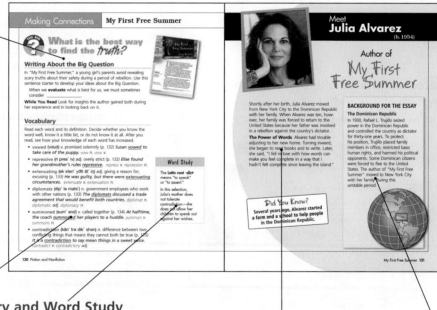

Vocabulary and Word Study introduce important selection vocabulary words and teach you about prefixes, suffixes, and roots.

Meet the Author and Background teach you about the author's life and provide information that will help you understand the selection.

How are the literary selections organized? *(continued)*

After You Read helps you practice the skills you have learned. ▼

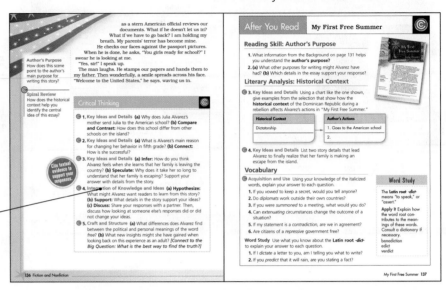

Critical Thinking questions help you reflect on what you have read and apply the Big Question to the selection.

Projects and activities help you deepen your understanding of the selection while strengthening your **writing, listening, speaking, and research skills.**

Integrated Language Skills provides instruction and practice for important grammar skills.

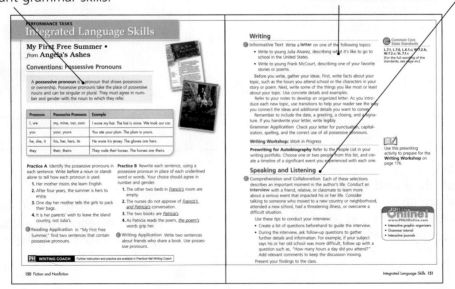

What special features will I find in this book?

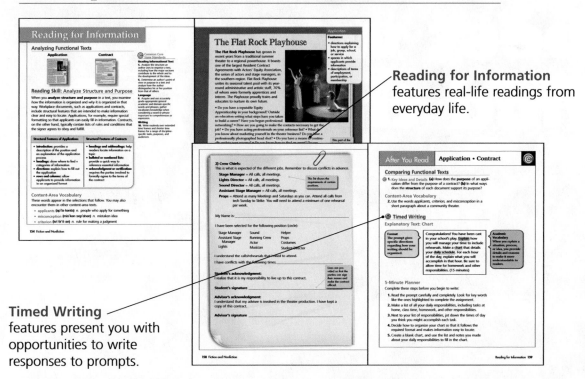

Reading for Information features real-life readings from everyday life.

Timed Writing features present you with opportunities to write responses to prompts.

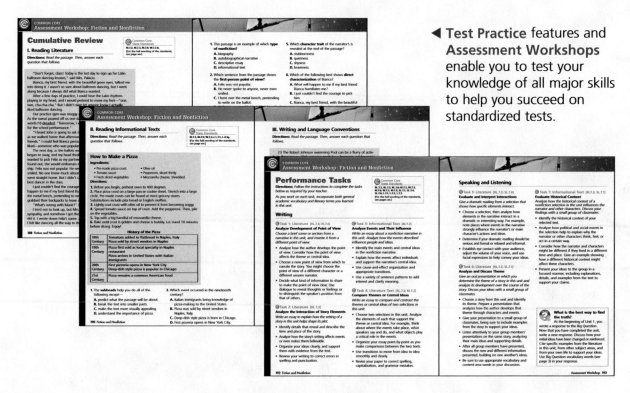

◀ **Test Practice** features and **Assessment Workshops** enable you to test your knowledge of all major skills to help you succeed on standardized tests.

What is the best way to find the *truth*?

Fiction and Nonfiction

PHLit Online!
www.PHLitOnline.com

Hear It!
- Selection summary audio
- Selection audio
- BQ Tunes

See It!
- Author videos
- Big Question video
- Get Connected videos
- Background videos
- More about the authors
- Illustrated vocabulary words
- Vocabulary flashcards

Do It!
- Interactive journals
- Interactive graphic organizers
- Grammar tutorials
- Interactive vocabulary games
- Test practice

THE BIG ? What is the best way to find the *truth?*

The **truth** is something that is real or a fact. Factual truth can be proved by evidence. Different people can have different ideas about what is true. Their ideas depend on how they perceive, or see, the world or what they believe. For example, the idea that a beautiful day must be sunny and warm may be true for one person but not another.

Authors of fiction often combine elements of truth to make a story. A story may be based on real events or people from history. Stories can also include authors' real memories or insights about the world around them.

Exploring the Big Question

Collaboration: One-on-One Discussion Start thinking about the Big Question by looking at the different ways people can find out what is true. Make a list of things you know to be true. Describe one specific example of each of the following:

- a historical event
- a story from childhood
- a scientific fact about space
- a list of physical features of your school
- a memory of an exciting experience

Share and evaluate your examples with a partner. Discuss whether the truth is based on factual evidence or on perceptions and beliefs. Use the Big Question Vocabulary in your discussion.

Connecting to the Literature Each reading in this unit will give you

PHLit Online!
www.PHLitOnline.com

- Big Question video
- Illustrated vocabulary words
- Interactive vocabulary games
- BQ Tunes

Learning Big Question Vocabulary

**Common Core
State Standards**

**Speaking and Listening
1.** Engage effectively in a range of collaborative discussions with diverse partners on grade 7 topics, texts, and issues, building on others' ideas and expressing their own clearly.

**Language
6.** Acquire and use accurately grade-appropriate general academic and domain-specific words and phrases; gather vocabulary knowledge when considering a word or phrase important to comprehension or expression.

Acquire and Use Academic Vocabulary Academic vocabulary is the language you encounter in textbooks and on standardized tests. Review the definitions of these academic vocabulary words.

awareness (ə wer´ nəs) **n.** knowledge gained from one's own perceptions or from information

conclude (kən klood´) **v.** decide; reach a determination

convince (kən vins´) **v.** persuade

debate (dē bāt´) **v.** argue in an attempt to convince

evaluate (ē val´ yoo āt´) **v.** judge or determine the significance of

explain (ek splān´) **v.** make plain or clear

insight (in´ sīt´) **n.** ability to see the truth; an understanding

perceive (pər sēv´) **v.** see; be aware of

Use these words as you complete Big Question activities in this unit that involve reading, writing, speaking, and listening.

Gather Vocabulary Knowledge Additional Big Question words are listed below. Categorize the words by deciding whether you know each one well, know it a little bit, or do not know it at all.

believable	**fiction**	**reveal**
evidence	**reality**	**truth**
factual		

Then, do the following:

1. Write the definitions of the words you know.

2. Consult a print or online dictionary to confirm each word's meaning. Revise your definitions if necessary.

3. Using a dictionary, look up the pronunciations and meanings of the words you do not know. Then, write the meanings.

4. Use as many of the words as you can in a brief paragraph about truth.

Elements of Fiction and Nonfiction

Fiction and nonfiction are two types, or genres, of writing.

Fiction describes imaginary characters and events. When you read fiction, you enter a world that was created by the author's imagination. However, many works of fiction have realistic elements. Historical fiction, for example, can tell a true story but contains certain made-up elements.

Nonfiction is based on facts. It describes real people, events, and ideas. When you read nonfiction, the information you encounter is factual. Nonfiction authors research their topics. They present information that teaches you about a subject or tries to convince you to do or believe something.

Nonfiction may also share some elements of fiction. Nonfiction writers, for example, can bring true events to life through their use of vivid descriptions or dramatic writing styles. They may even create made-up examples to illustrate their points.

Elements of Fiction and Nonfiction	
Fiction	**Nonfiction**
includes made-up people or animals, called **characters**	focuses on real people
is told through a made-up series of events called the **plot,** which usually revolves around a **conflict,** or problem	describes true events and conflicts
is narrated or told by a speaker, called the **narrator**	is narrated from the **point of view,** or perspective, of the author, who is a real person
takes place in a time and location, or **setting,** which may or may not be real	presents facts or discusses ideas related to real places or historical periods
may include facts to make a made-up story seem realistic	may use elements also found in fiction, such as vivid descriptions or characters and their conversations, or **dialogue**
often suggests a **theme,** or message about life	often conveys a **central idea** supported by details

Forms of Fiction

There are three main forms of fiction.

Novel: A novel is a long work of fiction. It contains elements such as characters, plot, conflict, and setting. In addition to a main plot, a novel may contain one or more **subplots,** or independent, related stories.

Novella: A novella is a work of fiction that is shorter than a novel but longer than a short story.

Short Story: A short story is a brief work of fiction. It contains the same basic elements as a novel or novella but tends to focus on one main plot structured around a single conflict. Many short stories can be read in a single sitting.

Forms of Nonfiction

Nonfiction comes in many different forms. Two broad categories of nonfiction are literary nonfiction and functional texts.

Literary Nonfiction: This type of nonfiction has elements of fiction. For example, it might use vivid descriptions, a dramatic writing style, or poetic language.

Functional Texts: These texts give instructions, show directions, explain rules, or provide other types of information that help you complete procedures. Functional texts often include illustrations or graphics to help guide the reader.

The charts below show some examples of literary nonfiction and functional texts.

In This Section

Elements of Fiction and Nonfiction

Determining Theme in Fiction

Determining Central Ideas in Nonfiction

Close Read: Theme in Fiction
- Model Text
- Practice Text

Close Read: Central Idea in Nonfiction
- Model Text
- Practice Text

After You Read

 Common Core State Standards addressed:

RL.7.2; RI.7.2
[For the full wording of the standards, see the standards chart in the front of your textbook.]

Literary Nonfiction
Autobiographies and memoirs tell the story of the author's life.
Biographies tell the story of someone's life from the perspective of another writer.
Letters are written communications from person to person.
Essays and articles are brief works about a specific topic.
Reviews tell what is good and what is bad about a work of art or performance.
Reports give information about a topic explored through research.

Functional Texts
Recipes tell how to prepare food.
Directions tell how to operate or assemble equipment.
Schedules tell when events take place.
Menus tell which foods are available and their cost.
Brochures use pictures and text to advertise places or events.
Maps are diagrams that show areas of land.
Applications are written requests to an authority.

Determining Theme in Fiction

Works of fiction express themes— messages or insights about life.

 **Common Core State Standards**

Reading Literature 2. Determine a theme or central idea of a text and analyze its development over the course of the text; provide an objective summary of the text.

The **theme** is a central message in a literary work. When you read a work of fiction, remember that theme and subject are not the same. The subject is what the story is about. The theme is the writer's message about a particular subject.

Subject	Theme
Competition	Winning isn't everything.
Forces of Nature	Humans can't control the forces of nature.
Failure	Failure may teach more than success teaches.

In some works of fiction, the writer will state the theme directly. More often, however, a fiction writer *implies,* or suggests, a theme through the words and experiences of characters or through events in the story.

Universal Themes A **universal theme** is a message about life that is expressed in many different cultures and time periods. The value of friendship and the power of love are two examples of universal themes. Ideas like these address experiences that are common to many people. Such universal themes can be found in a variety of works, such as tales from ancient Greece or modern novels.

Multiple Themes Some works of fiction express more than one theme. Novels, full-length plays, and some long poems may have multiple themes, while a short story usually expresses a single theme.

Interpreting Themes Different people may interpret the theme of a story in different ways. Consider, for example, the classic myth of Daedalus and Icarus.

Example:
Daedalus constructs wings with feathers held together by wax to help his son Icarus and himself escape an island prison. Daedalus warns Icarus not to fly too close to the sun because the sun's heat could melt the wax. Thrilled by the adventure of flying, Icarus ignores his father's warning. The wax melts, causing Icarus's wings to fall apart, and Icarus falls to his death.

Possible Interpretations of Theme:
• Know your limitations.
• Defying nature leads to disaster.
• Ambition can be costly.

These themes are all different, but each reflects the events of the story.

Determining Central Ideas in Nonfiction

Works of literary nonfiction express central, or main, ideas.

Common Core State Standards

Reading Information 2. Determine two or more central ideas in a text and analyze their development over the course of the text; provide an objective summary of the text.

The **central,** or **main, idea** is the key point in a work of literary nonfiction. All nonfiction works express one or more central ideas. Sometimes the author directly states the central idea, then supports it with key details. In many cases, however, the author *implies*, or suggests, the central idea. Readers can determine the central idea by analyzing the key details and supporting evidence the author provides.

Topic Sentences and Supporting Details In many works of nonfiction, the author conveys one central idea for the entire work, which is supported by central ideas in individual paragraphs. The central idea of a paragraph can often be found in the **topic sentence,** which is usually the first sentence.

The example below shows three paragraphs with topic sentences that support the central idea of the entire work.

> **Example: Topic Sentences**
>
> **Central Idea:** Breakfast is the most important meal of the day.
>
> **Paragraph 1:** Children who eat breakfast do better in school.
>
> **Paragraph 2:** People who skip breakfast may make unhealthy snack choices.
>
> **Paragraph 3:** People who eat breakfast are likely to maintain a healthy weight.

In the same way that each paragraph supports the central idea of the entire work, supporting details support the topic sentence of each paragraph. The following example shows a supporting detail for Paragraph 1.

> **Example: Supporting Detail**
>
> In a recent study, children who ate breakfast made fewer mistakes and worked faster on math tests than children who skipped breakfast.

Author's Purpose and Central Idea An **author's purpose** is his or her main reason for writing. The three most common purposes are to **entertain,** to **inform,** or to **persuade** the reader. An author may have more than one purpose in a single work. The author will also have a *specific* purpose that relates to his or her topic. The central idea is what the author wants readers to believe about that topic.

Author's Purpose	To persuade
Specific Purpose	To persuade citizens to vote to build a wind farm in their town
Central Idea	A wind farm will benefit people in the community.

Close Read: Theme in Fiction

All the elements of a story, from the title to the characters to individual words, work together to support the theme.

Authors of fiction seldom directly state the theme, or central message about life. Instead, they often present the theme indirectly. To discover a theme that is implied, or presented indirectly, pay attention to details in the selection by asking yourself the questions in the chart below. They may provide clues that will help you discover what the work reveals about people or life.

Clues to Theme		
Title The **title** is the name of the story. • Do the words in the title prompt ideas or stir emotions? • Do the words include any "universal theme" words (*love, friendship, nature, time*)?	**Conflict** A **conflict** is a struggle between opposing forces. • What is the main conflict in the story? • How does the conflict affect the characters? • What message about life might the conflict suggest?	**Setting** The **setting** is the time and place of the action. • How does the setting affect the characters? • Could this story take place in a different setting?
Characters A **character** is a person or an animal that takes part in the action of the story. • What is each character's main problem or conflict? • Do the characters change or learn anything about life?	**Statements and Observations** A **statement** or **observation** expresses an idea. • What do the characters say about themselves and each other? • Which of the narrator's statements pertain to life or human nature? • What sentences stand out in your mind? Why?	**Symbols** A **symbol** is something that stands for or represents something else. • What objects are important in the story? • How do characters react to particular objects, people, or words?

Model

About the Text This story is set in Japan in the Middle Ages, when powerful lords lived in palaces and ruled the people who lived on their estates. The lords could do what they wanted, and the people had to obey them.

from *The Tale of the Mandarin Ducks* by Katherine Paterson

Long ago and far away in the Land of the Rising Sun, there lived together a pair of mandarin ducks. Now, the drake was a magnificent bird with plumage of colors so rich that the emperor himself would have envied it. But his mate, the duck, wore the quiet tones of the wood, blending exactly with the hole in the tree where the two had made their nest.

One day while the duck was sitting on her eggs, the drake flew down to a nearby pond to search for food. While he was there, a hunting party entered the woods. The hunters were led by the lord of the district, a proud and cruel man who believed that everything in the district belonged to him to do with as he chose. The lord was always looking for beautiful things to adorn his manor house and garden. And when he saw the drake swimming gracefully on the surface of the pond, he determined to capture him.

The lord's chief steward, a man named Shozo, tried to discourage his master. "The drake is a wild spirit, my lord," he said. "Surely he will die in captivity." But the lord pretended not to hear Shozo. Secretly he despised Shozo, because although Shozo had once been his mightiest samurai, the warrior had lost an eye in battle and was no longer handsome to look upon.

The lord ordered his servants to clear a narrow way through the undergrowth and place acorns along the path. When the drake came out of the water he saw the acorns. How pleased he was! He forgot to be cautious, thinking only of what a feast they would be to take home to his mate.

Just as he was bending to pick up an acorn in his scarlet beak, a net fell over him, and the frightened bird was carried back to the lord's manor and placed in a small bamboo cage.

Characters The narrator describes the lord's cruelty and selfishness. Often, details about a main character can provide a clue to the theme of a work.

Symbols In folk tales, animals or magical creatures often represent people. The lord's attitude toward the drake represents how little he cares for the people he rules.

Statements This statement further illustrates the lord's shallowness and cruelty.

Conflict The wild bird does not want to be caged. Its capture creates a conflict.

© EXEMPLAR TEXT

Model continued

Setting In the society in which the story takes place, the lord has a high position. He likes to show off in front of others.

Conflict The conflict builds as grief causes the captured drake to become ill.

The lord was delighted with his new pet. He ordered a feast to be prepared and invited all the wealthy landowners from miles around, so that he could show off the drake and brag about his wonderful plumage, which was indeed more beautiful than the finest brocade.

But the drake could think only of his mate sitting alone on her eggs, not knowing what had happened to her husband.

As the days wore on, his crested head began to droop. His lovely feathers lost their luster. His proud, wild cry became first a weary *cronk* and then he fell silent. No matter what delicacies the kitchen maid brought him, he refused to eat. He is grieving for his mate, the girl thought, for she was wise in the customs of wild creatures.

The lord, who liked things only so long as they were beautiful and brought him honor, grew angry when he saw that the drake was ailing. "Perhaps we should let him go," Shozo suggested, "since he no longer pleases you, my lord." But the lord did not like anyone to tell him what to do, much less a one-eyed servant. He refused to release the drake, ordering instead that the cage be put out of sight so that he would no longer be annoyed by the bird's sad appearance.

Theme The story continues, but based on details you have learned so far, you can determine one or more possible themes. For example, based on the lord's cruelty, one theme might be that selfish people can do terrible harm to others. Based on the drake's grief, another theme might be that separation from a loved one can cause great pain.

Independent Practice

About the Selection During a visit to a nursing home, a young girl sees a whole new side of her 102-year-old great-grandmother.

"The Three-Century Woman" by Richard Peck

"I guess if you live long enough," my mom said to Aunt Gloria, "you get your fifteen minutes of fame."

Mom was on the car phone to Aunt Gloria. The minute Mom rolls out of the garage, she's on her car phone. It's state-of-the-art and better than her car.

We were heading for Whispering Oaks to see my great-grandmother Breckenridge, who's lived there since I was a little girl. They call it an Elder Care Facility. Needless to say, I hated going.

The reason for Great-grandmother's fame is that she was born in 1899. Now it's January 2001. If you're one of those people who claim the new century begins in 2001, not 2000, even you have to agree that Great-grandmother Breckenridge has lived in three centuries. This is her claim to fame.

We waited for a light to change along by Northbrook Mall, and I gazed fondly over at it. Except for the Multiplex, it was closed because of New Year's Day. I have a severe mall habit. But I'm fourteen, and the mall is the place without homework. Aunt Gloria's voice filled the car.

"If you take my advice," she told Mom, "you'll keep those Whispering Oaks people from letting the media in to interview Grandma. Interview her my foot! Honestly. She doesn't know where she is, let alone how many centuries she's lived in. The poor old soul. Leave her in peace. She's already got one foot in the—"

"Gloria, your trouble is you have no sense of history." Mom gunned across the intersection. "You got a C in history."

"I was sick a lot that year," Aunt Gloria said.

"Sick of history," Mom mumbled.

"I heard that," Aunt Gloria said.

They bickered on, but I tuned them out. Then when we turned in at Whispering Pines, a sound truck from IBC-TV was blocking the drive.

"Good grief," Mom murmured. "TV."

Conflict Why might the narrator hate visiting Whispering Oaks?

Character What do Aunt Gloria's words tell you about her attitude toward her grandmother?

Practice continued

"I told you," Aunt Gloria said, but Mom switched her off. She parked in a frozen rut.

"I'll wait in the car," I said. "I have homework."

"Get out of the car," Mom said.

If you get so old you have to be put away, Whispering Oaks isn't that bad. It smells all right, and a Christmas tree glittered in the lobby. A real tree. On the other hand, you have to push a red button to unlock the front door. I guess it's to keep the inmates from escaping, though Great-grandmother Breckenridge wasn't going anywhere and hadn't for twenty years.

When we got to her wing, the hall was full of camera crews and a woman from the suburban newspaper with a notepad.

Mom sighed. It was like that first day of school when you think you'll be okay until the teachers learn your name. Stepping over a cable, we stopped at Great-grandma's door, and they were on to us.

"Who are you people to Mrs. Breckenridge?" the newspaperwoman said. "I want names."

These people were seriously pushy. And the TV guy was wearing more makeup than Mom. It dawned on me that they couldn't get into Great-grandma's room without her permission. Mom turned on them.

"Listen, you're not going to be interviewing my grandmother," she said in a quiet bark. "I'll be glad to tell you anything you want to know about her, but you're not going in there. She's got nothing to say, and . . . she needs a lot of rest."

"Is it Alzheimer's?"[1] the newswoman asked. "Because we're thinking Alzheimer's."

"Think what you want," Mom said. "But this is as far as you get. And you people with the camera and the light, you're not going in there either. You'd scare her to death, and then I'd sue the pants off you."

They pulled back.

But a voice came wavering out of Great-grandma's room. Quite an eerie, echoing voice.

Setting How might the narrator's description of Whispering Oaks help develop a theme?

Character Based on these comments, what is your impression of Great-grandma?

---

1. **Alzheimer's** (älts′ hī′ mərz) *n.* a progressive disease in which brain cells degenerate, leading to severe dementia.

"Let them in!" the voice said.

It had to be Great-grandma Breckenridge. Her roommate had died. "Good grief," Mom muttered, and the press surged forward.

Mom and I went in first, and our eyes popped. Great-grandma was usually flat out in the bed, dozing, with her teeth in a glass and a book in her hand. Today she was bright-eyed and propped up. She wore a fuzzy pink bed jacket. A matching bow was stuck in what remained of her hair.

"Oh, for pity's sake," Mom said. "They've got her done up like a Barbie doll."

Great-grandma peered from the bed at Mom. "And who are you?" she asked.

"I'm Ann," Mom said carefully. "This is Megan," she said, meaning me.

"That's right," Great-grandma said. "At least you know who you are. Plenty around this place don't."

The guy with the camera on his shoulder barged in. The other guy turned on a blinding light.

Great-grandma blinked. In the glare we noticed she wore a trace of lipstick. The TV anchor elbowed the woman reporter aside and stuck a mike in Great-grandma's face. Her claw hand came out from under the covers and tapped it.

"Is this thing on?" she inquired.

"Yes, ma'am," the TV anchor said in his broadcasting voice. "Don't you worry about all this modern technology. We don't understand half of it ourselves." He gave her his big, fivethirty news smile and settled on the edge of the bed. There was room for him. She was tiny.

"We're here to congratulate you for having lived in three centuries—for being a Three-Century Woman! A great achievement!"

Great-grandma waved a casual claw. "Nothing to it," she said. "You sure this mike's on? Let's do this in one take."

The cameraman snorted and moved in for a closer shot. Mom stood still as a statue, wondering what was going to come out of Great-grandma's mouth next.

Statements What does Megan's use of the word "claw" say about her feelings toward aging?

Character Does Great-grandma appear to have a good understanding of what is going on? Explain.

Practice continued

Character Based on her remarks, has your impression of Great-grandma changed since you began reading this story? Why or why not?

"Mrs. Breckenridge," the anchor said, "to what do you attribute[2] your long life?"

"I was only married once," Great-grandma said. "And he died young."

The anchor stared. "Ah. And anything else?"

"Yes. I don't look back. I live in the present."

The camera panned around the room. This was all the present she had, and it didn't look like much.

"You live for the present," the anchor said, looking for an angle, "even now?" Great-grandma nodded. "Something's always happening. Last night I fell off the bed pan."

Mom groaned.

The cameraman pulled in for a tighter shot. The anchor seemed to search his mind. You could tell he thought he was a great interviewer, though he had no sense of humor. A tiny smile played around Great-grandma's wrinkled lips.

"But you've lived through amazing times, Mrs. Breckenridge. And you never think back about them?"

Great-grandma stroked her chin and considered. "You mean you want to hear something interesting? Like how I lived through the San Francisco earthquake—the big one of oh-six?"

Beside me, Mom stirred. We were crowded over by the dead lady's bed. "You survived the 1906 San Francisco earthquake?" the anchor said.

Great-grandma gazed at the ceiling, lost in thought.

"I'd have been about seven years old. My folks and I were staying at that big hotel. You know the one. I slept in a cot at the foot of their bed. In the middle of the night, that room gave a shake, and the chiffonier walked right across the floor. You know what a chiffonier is?"

"A chest of drawers?" the anchor said.

"Close enough," Great-grandma said. "And the pictures flapped on the walls. We had to walk down twelve flights because the elevators didn't

---

2. **attribute** (ə trib´ yōōt) *v.* think of as caused by.

work. When we got outside, the streets were ankle-deep in broken glass. You never saw such a mess in your life."

Mom nudged me and hissed: "She's never been to San Francisco. She's never been west of Denver. I've heard her say so."

"Incredible!" the anchor said.

"Truth's stranger than fiction," Great-grandma said, smoothing her sheet.

"And you never think back about it?"

Great-grandma shrugged her little fuzzy pink shoulders. "I've been through too much. I don't have time to remember it all. I was on the *Hindenburg* when it blew up, you know."

Mom moaned, and the cameraman was practically standing on his head for a close-up.

"The *Hindenburg*!"

"That big gas thing the Germans built to fly over the Atlantic Ocean. It was called a zeppelin.[3] Biggest thing you ever saw—five city blocks long. It was in May of 1937, before your time. You wouldn't remember. My husband and I were coming back from Europe. No, wait a minute."

Great-grandma cocked her head and pondered for the camera.

"My husband was dead by then. It was some other man. Anyway, the two of us were coming back on the *Hindenburg*. It was smooth as silk. You didn't know you were moving. When we flew in over New York, they stopped the ball game at Yankee Stadium to see us passing overhead."

Great-grandma paused, caught up in the memories.

"And then the *Hindenburg* exploded," the anchor said, prompting her.

She nodded. "We had no complaints about the trip till then. The luggage was all stacked, and we were coming in at Lakehurst, New Jersey. I was wearing my beige coat—beige or off-white, I forget. Then whoosh! The gondola[4] heated up like an oven, and people peeled out of the windows. We hit the ground and bounced. When we hit again, the door fell off, and I walked out and kept going. When they caught up to me in the parking

Statements How might Great-grandma know so much about the San Francisco earthquake if she has never been to San Francisco?

---

3. **zeppelin** (zep´ ə lin) *n.* a large, cigar-shaped airship with separate compartments filled with gas; used from 1900 to 1937.
4. **gondola** (gän´ dō lə) *n.* a cabin attached to the underside of an airship to hold the motors, instruments, passengers, etc.

Practice continued

lot, they wanted to put me in the hospital. I looked down and thought I was wearing a lace dress. The fire had about burned up my coat. And I lost a shoe."

"Fantastic!" the anchor breathed. "What detail!" Behind him the woman reporter was scribbling away on her pad.

"Never," Mom muttered. "Never in her life."

"Ma'am, you are living history!" the anchor said. "In your sensational span of years you've survived two great disasters!"

"Three." Great-grandma patted the bow on her head. "I told you I'd been married."

"And before we leave this venerable lady," the anchor said, flashing a smile for the camera, "we'll ask Mrs. Breckenridge if she has any predictions for this new twenty-first century ahead of us here in the Dawn of the Millennium."

Statements How might this statement relate to a possible theme?

"Three or four predictions," Great-grandma said, and paused again, stretching out her airtime. "Number one, taxes will be higher. Number two, it's going to be harder to find a place to park. And number three, a whole lot of people are going to live as long as I have, so get ready for us."

"And with those wise words," the anchor said, easing off the bed, "we leave Mrs. B—"

Statements Why does Great-grandma say this to the reporter?

"And one more prediction," she said. "TV's on the way out. Your network ratings are already in the basement. It's all web-sites now. Son, I predict you'll be looking for work."

And that was it. The light went dead. The anchor, looking shaken, followed his crew out the door. When TV's done with you, they're done with you. "Is that a wrap?" Great-grandma asked.

But now the woman from the suburban paper was moving in on her. "Just a few more questions, Mrs. Breckenridge."

"Where you from?" Great-grandma blinked pink-eyed at her.

"The Glenview Weekly Shopper."

"You bring a still photographer with you?" Great-grandma asked.

"Well, no."

"And you never learned shorthand[5] either, did you?"

"Well, no."

"Honey, I only deal with professionals. There's the door."

So then it was just Mom and Great-grandma and I in the room. Mom planted a hand on her hip. "Grandma. Number one, you've never been to San Francisco. And number two, you never saw one of those zeppelin things."

Great-grandma shrugged. "No, but I can read." She nodded to the pile of books on her nightstand with her spectacles folded on top. "You can pick up all that stuff in books."

"And number three," Mom said, "Your husband didn't die young. I can remember Grandpa Breckenridge."

"It was that TV dude in the five-hundred-dollar suit who set me off," Great-grandma said. "He dyes his hair, did you notice? He made me mad, and it put my nose out of joint. He didn't notice I'm still here. He thought I was nothing but my memories. So I gave him some."

Now Mom and I stood beside her bed.

"I'll tell you something else," Great-grandma said. "And it's no lie."

We waited, holding our breath to hear. Great-grandma Breckenridge was pointing her little old bent finger right at me. "You, Megan," she said. "Once upon a time, I was your age. How scary is that?"

Then she hunched up her little pink shoulders and winked at me. She grinned and I grinned. She was just this little withered-up leaf of a lady in the bed. But I felt like giving her a kiss on her little wrinkled cheek, so I did.

"I'll come and see you more often," I told her.

"Call first," she said. "I might be busy." Then she dozed.

Statements What has Great-grandma proved to everyone?

Character How has Megan's attitude toward her great-grandmother changed?

Theme What is one possible theme of this story?

---

5. **shorthand** (shôrt´ hand´) *n.* a system of speed writing using symbols to represent letters, words, and phrases.

Close Read: Central Idea in Nonfiction

The central idea is often stated early in the work. Supporting details develop that idea.

A nonfiction work has an overall central idea, but each paragraph in the work also has its key point. The details in each paragraph support its key point, and the paragraphs support the central idea of the whole work.

Stated Central Idea In some cases, an author tells the reader the central idea. The idea can often be found in a topic sentence in the opening paragraph.

Example:

Movie versions of popular novels are almost always disappointments. They can never match the pictures in readers' imaginations and often leave out popular moments from the story.

Implied Central Idea Sometimes authors do not directly state the central idea. Instead, they imply, or suggest, it through a series of related details.

Example:

Restaurant kitchens require a great deal of expensive equipment. They constantly need to maintain a supply of fresh food. A bad location can doom even the best restaurant.

Each sentence points out a difficulty in running a restaurant. The central idea might be stated as follows: It is difficult to run a successful restaurant.

Types of Supporting Details

Authors use different kinds of details to develop their central ideas. As you read, notice the types of details authors choose, and think about why they were selected.

Facts are statements that can be proved. *Example: Polar bears can swim as fast as 6.2 miles per hour.*	**Observations** are reports from eyewitnesses. *Example: During a one-hour period, sixteen cars did not even pause at the stop sign.*
Statistics are facts in the form of numbers. *Example: Only 40% of those polled could remember last year's Best Picture winner.*	**Personal experiences** come from life. *Example: I learned that shoes really matter when I finished the hike with blistered feet.*
Expert statements come from authoritative sources. *Example: Dr. Flynn said the virus could not affect humans.*	**Anecdotes** are stories that make a point. *Example: To encourage me to keep trying, my coach said, "I made many mistakes myself in my first year of playing soccer."*
Examples are concrete illustrations of a concept. *Example: Shoppers have choices. Supermarkets devote entire aisles to ethnic foods.*	**Analogies** use comparisons to make a point. *Example: Baking a cake is like building a house. You need the right tools and materials.*

Model

About the Text This is an excerpt from a book about the Great Chicago Fire of 1871. The fire started in Patrick O'Leary's barn on the night of October 8 and lasted until the 10th, when rain helped put it out. It caused property damage that totaled almost 200 million dollars.

from *The Great Fire* by Jim Murphy

Chicago in 1871 was a city ready to burn. The city boasted having 59,500 buildings, many of them—such as the Courthouse and the Tribune Building—large and ornately decorated. The trouble was that about two-thirds of all these structures were made entirely of wood. Many of the remaining buildings (even the ones proclaimed to be "fireproof") looked solid, but were actually jerry-built affairs; the stone or brick exteriors hid wooden frames and floors, all topped with highly flammable tar or shingle roofs. It was also a common practice to disguise wood as another kind of building material. The fancy exterior decorations on just about every building were carved from wood, then painted to look like stone or marble. Most churches had steeples that appeared to be solid from the street, but a closer inspection would reveal a wooden framework covered with cleverly painted copper or tin.

The situation was worst in the middle-class and poorer districts. Lot sizes were small, and owners usually filled them up with cottages, barns, sheds, and outhouses—all made of fast-burning wood, naturally. Because both Patrick and Catherine O'Leary worked, they were able to put a large addition on their cottage despite a lot size of just 25 by 100 feet. Interspersed in these residential areas were a variety of businesses—paint factories, lumberyards, distilleries, gasworks, mills, furniture manufacturers, warehouses, and coal distributors.

Wealthier districts were by no means free of fire hazards. Stately stone and brick homes had wood interiors, and stood side by side with smaller wood-frame houses. Wooden stables and other storage buildings were common, and trees lined the streets and filled the yards.

Statistics The number of flammable structures supports the statement that the city was ready to burn.

Facts This fact explains how even more buildings had flammable parts.

Examples This example shows how tightly packed the small lots were.

Central Idea The author states the central idea in the opening sentence, then uses facts to support the idea that Chicago was ready to burn.

Independent Practice

About the Selection Michael Morrison's article tells the story of the *Hindenburg* disaster described in "The Three-Century Woman."

Facts Why might the author have opened the article with these facts?

Statistics What idea do these statistics convey?

Observations What emotion does this quotation express? How does it support a central idea?

Expert Statements How does this detail relate to the entire article?

Central Idea What is the central idea of this article?

"The Fall of the Hindenburg" by Michael Morrison

On May 6, 1937, the German airship *Hindenburg* burst into flames 200 feet over its intended landing spot at New Jersey's Lakehurst Naval Air Station. Thirty-five people on board were killed (13 passengers and 22 crewmen), along with one crewman on the ground.

803 Feet Long and 242 Tons The giant flying vessel measured 803.8 feet in length and weighed approximately 242 tons. Its mostly metal frame was filled with hydrogen. It came complete with sleeping quarters, a library, dining room, and a magnificent lounge, but still managed a top speed of just over 80 miles per hour. The zeppelin had just crossed the Atlantic Ocean after taking off from Frankfurt, Germany, $2\frac{1}{2}$ days prior on its first transatlantic voyage of the season. Thirty-six passengers and a crew of 61 were on board.

Disaster Strikes As it reached its final destination in New Jersey, it hovered over its landing spot and was beginning to be pulled down to the ground by landing lines by over 200 crewmen when disaster struck. A burst of flame started just forward of the upper fin, then blossomed into an inferno that engulfed the *Hindenburg*'s tail.

"Oh, the Humanity!" Many jumped from the burning craft, landed on the soft sand of the naval base below, and lived to tell about it; others weren't so lucky. Herb Morrison, a reporter for WLS Radio in Chicago, happened to be covering the event and cried out the now famous words, "Oh, the Humanity!" The majestic ship turned into a ball of flames on the ground in only 34 seconds.

Unknown Cause The cause of the disaster is still uncertain. At the time, many thought the ship had been hit by lightning. Many still believe that the highly flammable hydrogen was the cause. Some Germans even cried foul play, suspecting sabotage intended to sully the reputation of the Nazi regime. NASA research, however, has shown that the highly combustible varnish treating the fabric on the outside of the vessel most likely caused the tragedy.

**Common Core State Standards**

Reading Literature 9. Compare and contrast a fictional portrayal of a time, place, or character and a historical account of the same period as a means of understanding how authors of fiction use or alter history.

After You Read

The Three-Century Woman • The Fall of the Hindenburg

1. Key Ideas and Details (a) In "The Three-Century Woman," find two statements that show details about Megan's character. **(b) Speculate:** Why do you think the author chose to tell the story in Megan's voice?

2. Key Ideas and Details (a) Speculate: Why do you think the reporter believes Great-grandma's version of the truth? **(b) Infer:** What are clues that Great-grandma is not telling the truth?

3. Key Ideas and Details (a) Infer: Why does Great-grandma make up these stories? **(b) Analyze:** What does Great-grandma's storytelling reveal about her character?

4. Key Ideas and Details Analyze: What is Michael Morrison's main **purpose** for writing "The Fall of the Hindenburg"? Explain.

5. Key Ideas and Details (a) Compare: How does the fictional account of the *Hindenburg* disaster differ from the historical account? **(b) Connect:** How does the purpose of each text help determine what key information is presented? Support your answers with details from the texts.

6. Integration of Knowledge and Ideas (a) In the first column of a chart like the one below, write three of Great-grandma's reactions to the reporters. **(b) Infer:** In the second column, explain what Great-grandma's reactions reveal about her character. **(c) Interpret:** In the third column, explain a possible theme or message these reactions might convey.

Her Reaction	Her Character	Message/Theme

(d) Collaborate: Discuss your chart with a classmate to identify the **theme** that best fits the story.

7. Key Ideas and Details (a) Write an objective summary of "The Three-Century Woman." Remember that an objective summary should contain only the most important events or ideas. It should not include your personal opinions. **(b)** Write an objective summary of "The Fall of the Hindenburg."

Leveled Texts

Build your skills and improve your comprehension of fiction and nonfiction with texts of increasing complexity.

Read "**Papa's Parrot**" to find out how a parrot helps a boy understand his father's feelings.

Read "**mk**" to learn how a young girl raised in China tries to find her identity as an American.

Common Core State Standards

Meet these standards with either **"Papa's Parrot"** (p. 26) or **"mk"** (p. 34).

Reading Literature
2. Determine a theme or central idea of a text and analyze its development over the course of the text; provide an objective summary of the text. (*Literary Analysis: Spiral Review*)

Writing
2. Write informative/explanatory texts to examine a topic and convey ideas, concepts, and information through the selection, organization, and analysis of relevant content.
2.b. Develop the topic with relevant facts, definitions, concrete details, quotations, or other information and examples. (*Writing: Compare-and-Contrast Essay*)

Speaking and Listening
6. Adapt speech to a variety of contexts and tasks, demonstrating command of formal English when indicated or appropriate. (*Speaking and Listening: Dramatic Reading*)

Language
2. Demonstrate command of the conventions of standard English capitalization, punctuation, and spelling when

writing. (*Conventions: Common and Proper Nouns*)

4. Determine or clarify the meaning of unknown and multiple-meaning words and phrases based on grade 7 reading and content, choosing flexibly from a range of strategies. **4.a.** Use context as a clue to the meaning of a word or phrase. (*Reading Skill: Context Clues*)

5. Demonstrate understanding of figurative language, word relationships, and nuances in word meanings.
5.b. Use the relationship between particular words to better understand each of the words. (*Vocabulary: Synonyms*)

6. Acquire and use accurately grade-appropriate general academic and domain-specific words and phrases; gather vocabulary knowledge when considering a word or phrase important to comprehension or expression. (*Vocabulary: Word Study*)

Reading Skill: Context Clues

Context, the words and phrases surrounding a word, can help you understand a word you do not know. When you come across an unfamiliar word, **use context clues** to unlock the meaning.

- **Restatement:** The population, or number of people in the country, is stable.
- **Opposite, or contrast:** Average rainfall has not declined, it has increased.
- **Example:** Modes of transportation, such as car, train, and airplane, are available.

You can also use syntactic clues—the word's position or function in the sentence—to determine an unfamiliar word. As you read, use context clues to find possible meanings for unfamiliar words. Verify your understanding by consulting a dictionary.

Literary Analysis: Narrative Text

Narrative text is writing that tells a story. The act or process of telling a story is also called **narration.**

- A narrative is usually told in *chronological order*—the order in which events occurred in time.
- A narrative may be presented in fiction, nonfiction, or poetry.

As you read, think about how the sequence of events is important to the story.

Using the Strategy: Narration Chart

As you read, record the sequence of story events in a chart like this:

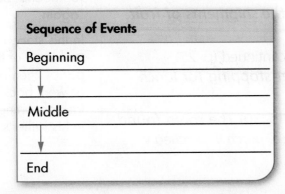

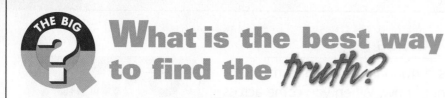

Writing About the Big Question

In "Papa's Parrot," the truth about a father's feelings toward his son are revealed through an unlikely source—his parrot. Use this sentence starter to develop your ideas about the Big Question.

Sometimes we can discover the **truth** by _____.

When we **reveal** our feelings, others _____.

While You Read Look for details that show how Harry's relationship with his father changes as he learns the truth.

Vocabulary

Read each word and its definition. Decide whether you know the word well, know it a little bit, or do not know it at all. After you read, see how your knowledge of each word has increased.

- **merely** (mir´ lē) *adv.* no more than; simply (p. 26) *The child who fell down was __merely__ scared, not injured.* *mere adj.*

- **clusters** (klus´ tərz) *n.* numbers of things of the same sort that are grouped together; bunches (p. 27) *Grapes grow in __clusters__ on vines.* *cluster n. clustering v.*

- **ignored** (ig nôrd´) *v.* paid no attention to (p. 27) *I __ignored__ his rude comment and went on talking.* *ignore v. ignorance n.*

- **shipments** (ship´ mənts) *n.* deliveries or acts of sending goods (p. 27) *A freak snowstorm delayed the __shipments__ of fruit.* *ship v. shipping adj.*

- **resumed** (ri zo͞omd´) *v.* began again; continued (p. 29) *The campers __resumed__ the hike after stopping for lunch.* *resume v. resuming v. resumption n.*

- **perch** (purch) *n.* roost for a bird; seat (p. 30) *The robin found a __perch__ on a high branch of the tree.* *perch v. perched v.*

Word Study

The **Latin prefix** *re-* means "back" or "again."

In this story, Harry took care of the parrot, then **resumed**, or went back to, his task of sorting candy in his father's store.

Meet
Cynthia Rylant
(b. 1954)

Author of
PAPA'S
Parrot

Growing up in a small mountain town in West Virginia, Cynthia Rylant never thought about becoming a writer. Aside from comic books, she did not do much reading, and the only writing she did was for school assignments. A future career as an author was the farthest thing from her mind.

A Change of Plans When Rylant entered college, her plan was to become a nurse. Then, in a required English course, she read a story by Langston Hughes. The story "just knocked me off my feet," Rylant has said. She decided to change her major to English. It was a good choice, as she has found great success as a writer.

BACKGROUND FOR THE STORY

Parrots

Parrots can learn to say words that are repeated over and over to them. Most of a parrot's "vocabulary" is taught on purpose, but a parrot may learn words accidentally. In "Papa's Parrot," the bird's accidental vocabulary plays a key part in the story.

DID YOU KNOW?
Rylant, an animal lover with many pet dogs, often includes animals in her stories.

PAPA'S Parrot

Cynthia Rylant

Though his father was fat and merely owned a candy and nut shop, Harry Tillian liked his papa. Harry stopped liking candy and nuts when he was around seven, but, in spite of this, he and Mr. Tillian had remained friends and were still friends the year Harry turned twelve.

For years, after school, Harry had always stopped in to see his father at work. Many of Harry's friends stopped there, too, to spend a few cents choosing penny candy from the giant bins or to sample Mr. Tillian's latest batch of roasted peanuts. Mr. Tillian looked forward to seeing his son and his son's friends every day. He liked the company.

When Harry entered junior high school, though, he didn't come by the candy and nut shop as often. Nor did his friends. They were older and they had more spending money. They went to a burger place. They played video games. They shopped for records.[1] None of them were much interested in candy and nuts anymore.

A new group of children came to Mr. Tillian's shop now. But not Harry Tillian and his friends.

The year Harry turned twelve was also the year Mr. Tillian got a parrot. He went to a pet store one day and bought one for more money than he could really afford. He brought the parrot to his shop, set its cage near the sign for maple clusters, and named it Rocky.

Harry thought this was the strangest thing his father had ever done, and he told him so, but Mr. Tillian just ignored him.

Rocky was good company for Mr. Tillian. When business was slow, Mr. Tillian would turn on a small color television he had sitting in a corner, and he and Rocky would watch the soap operas. Rocky liked to scream when the romantic music came on, and Mr. Tillian would yell at him to shut up, but they seemed to enjoy themselves.

The more Mr. Tillian grew to like his parrot, and the more he talked to it instead of to people, the more embarrassed Harry became. Harry would stroll past the shop, on his way somewhere else, and he'd take a quick look inside to see what his dad was doing. Mr. Tillian was always talking to the bird. So Harry kept walking.

At home things were different. Harry and his father joked with each other at the dinner table as they always had—Mr. Tillian teasing Harry about his smelly socks; Harry teasing Mr. Tillian about his blubbery stomach. At home things seemed all right. ●

But one day, Mr. Tillian became ill. He had been at work, unpacking boxes of caramels, when he had grabbed his chest and fallen over on top of the candy. A customer had found him, and he was taken to the hospital in an ambulance.

Mr. Tillian couldn't leave the hospital. He lay in bed, tubes in his arms, and he worried about his shop. New shipments of candy and nuts would be arriving. Rocky would be hungry.

---

1. records (rek´ ərdz) *n.* thin grooved discs on which music is recorded and played on a phonograph, or record player.

Narration
What details make this fictional narrative seem realistic?

Vocabulary
clusters (klus´ tərz) *n.* numbers of things of the same sort that are grouped together; bunches

ignored (ig nôrd´) *v.* paid no attention to

shipments (ship´ mənts) *n.* deliveries or acts of sending goods

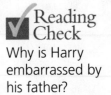

Reading Check
Why is Harry embarrassed by his father?

Who would take care of things?

Harry said he would. Harry told his father that he would go to the store every day after school and unpack boxes. He would sort out all the candy and nuts. He would even feed Rocky.

So, the next morning, while Mr. Tillian lay in his hospital bed, Harry took the shop key to school with him. After school he left his friends and walked to the empty shop alone. In all the days of his life, Harry had never seen the shop closed after school. Harry didn't even remember what the CLOSED sign looked like. The key stuck in the lock three times, and inside he had to search all the walls for the light switch.

The shop was as his father had left it. Even the caramels were still spilled on the floor. Harry bent down and picked them up one by one, dropping them back in the boxes. The bird in its cage watched him silently.

Harry opened the new boxes his father hadn't gotten to. Peppermints. Jawbreakers. Toffee creams. Strawberry kisses. Harry traveled from bin to bin, putting the candies where they belonged.

"Hello!"

Harry jumped, spilling a box of jawbreakers.

"Hello, Rocky!"

Harry stared at the parrot. He had forgotten it was there. The bird had been so quiet, and Harry had been thinking only of the candy.

"Hello," Harry said.

Narration
What does Harry do after school to help his father?

Context Clues
What clues point to the meaning of the word *bin*?

"Hello, Rocky!" answered the parrot.

Harry walked slowly over to the cage. The parrot's food cup was empty. Its water was dirty. The bottom of the cage was a mess.

Harry carried the cage into the back room.

"Hello, Rocky!"

"Is that all you can say, you dumb bird?" Harry mumbled. The bird said nothing else.

Harry cleaned the bottom of the cage, refilled the food and water cups, and then put the cage back in its place and resumed sorting the candy.

"Where's Harry?"

Harry looked up.

"Where's Harry?"

Harry stared at the parrot.

"Where's Harry?"

Chills ran down Harry's back. What could the bird mean? It was something from "The Twilight Zone."[2]

"Where's Harry?"

Harry swallowed and said, "I'm here. I'm here, you stupid bird."

"You stupid bird!" said the parrot.

Well, at least he's got one thing straight, thought Harry.

"Miss him! Miss him! Where's Harry? You stupid bird!"

Harry stood with a handful of peppermints.

---

2. **"The Twilight Zone"** science-fiction television series from the 1960s.

"What?" he asked.

"Where's Harry?" said the parrot.

"I'm here, you stupid bird! I'm here!" Harry yelled. He threw the peppermints at the cage, and the bird screamed and clung to its **perch.**

Harry sobbed, "I'm here." The tears were coming.

Harry leaned over the glass counter.

"Papa." Harry buried his face in his arms.

"Where's Harry?" repeated the bird.

Harry sighed and wiped his face on his sleeve. He watched the parrot. He understood now: someone had been saying, for a long time, "Where's Harry? Miss him."

Harry finished his unpacking and then swept the floor of the shop. He checked the furnace so the bird wouldn't get cold. Then he left to go visit his papa.

Vocabulary
perch (purch) *n.*
roost for a bird; seat

© **Spiral Review**
Theme What has Harry learned? How does this information point to a possible theme?

Critical Thinking ©

© 1. **Key Ideas and Details (a)** In the past, why did Harry and his friends visit Mr. Tillian after school? **(b) Infer:** Why have Harry and his friends stopped visiting Harry's father?

© 2. **Key Ideas and Details (a)** Who is Rocky? **(b) Analyze Cause and Effect:** Why does Mr. Tillian buy Rocky?

© 3. **Key Ideas and Details (a)** Explain how Harry reacts when Rocky says "Where's Harry?" and "Miss him!" **(b) Analyze:** Why does Harry react as he does?

© 4. **Integration of Knowledge and Ideas (a) Analyze:** What does each main character need to understand about the other? **(b) Make a Judgment:** Which character has a greater responsibility to be understanding? Why? **(c) Discuss:** Share your response with a partner. Then, explain how understanding someone else's response did or did not change your opinion.

© 5. **Integration of Knowledge and Ideas (a)** What truth does Rocky reveal about Mr. Tillian's feelings toward Harry? **(b)** Would it have been better for Harry to learn the truth from his father? Explain. *[Connect to the Big Question: What is the best way to find the truth?]*

Cite textual evidence to support your responses.

Reading Skill: Context Clues

1. In a chart like this, write the italicized word in the left column. Then, write the **context clues** and what the word means. Check your response in a dictionary. **(a)** Harry would *stroll* past the pet shop on his way to somewhere else . . . Mr. Tillian was always talking to the bird. So Harry kept on walking. **(b)** He checked the *furnace* so the bird wouldn't get cold.

Unfamiliar Word	Context Clues	Possible Meaning

Literary Analysis: Narrative Text

Ⓒ **2. Craft and Structure** Identify a reason that the story is called a **narrative.**

Ⓒ **3. Craft and Structure** The order of events is important in narration. **(a)** Did Mr. Tillian buy his parrot before or after Harry stopped coming to the store? **(b)** Why is this detail important?

Vocabulary

Ⓒ **Acquisition and Use** Explain your answer to each question.

1. Would you *resume* a meeting before taking a break?
2. If children play in a *cluster,* are they playing together?
3. If *shipments* are ready for delivery, have they already arrived?
4. What part of a bird holds onto a *perch*?
5. If something is *merely* a chance, is it likely to happen?
6. If you *ignored* your friend, would you respond to him?

Word Study Use the context of the sentences and what you know about the **Latin prefix re-** to explain your answers.

1. If a person *rejoins* a group, has he or she been there before?
2. Can you *recall* something you have not learned yet?

Word Study

The **Latin prefix re-** means "back" or "again."

Apply It Explain how the prefix *re-* contributes to the meanings of these words. Consult a dictionary if necessary.

relocate

recede

remove

What is the best way to find the *truth?*

Writing About the Big Question

In "mk," a real historical figure becomes a fictional friend to a young girl. Use these sentence starters to develop your ideas about the Big Question.

Sometimes we **believe** in things that are not true because it helps us _____.

We find what is **real** by _____.

While You Read Look for ways that Jean discovers who she is through her experiences as an American who lives overseas.

Vocabulary

Read each word and its definition. Decide whether you know the word well, know it a little bit, or do not know it at all. After you read, see how your knowledge of each word has increased.

- **relation** (ri lā´ shən) *n.* connection between two or more things (p. 34) *Kim chose a seat based on its relation to her friends.* relationship *n.* relative *adj.* relate *v.* related *adj.*

- **quest** (kwest) *n.* long search for something (p. 35) *The pirates set out on a quest for treasure.* request *n.* question *n.*

- **adequate** (ad´ i kwət) *adj.* enough (p. 36) *The small sandwich was not an adequate lunch for a growing girl.* adequately *adv.* adequacy *n.* inadequate *n.*

- **deceive** (dē sēv´) *v.* make someone believe something that is not true (p. 39) *Sadly, Annie tried to deceive her friend by making up a story.* deceived *v.* deceiving *v.* deception *n.*

- **transformation** (trans´ fər mā´ shən) *n.* change (p. 39) *Lily's transformation from soccer star to prom queen was amazing.* transform *v.* transformative *adj.*

- **ignorant** (ig´ nə rənt) *adj.* not knowing facts or information (p. 43) *The traveler was ignorant of the country's customs and had to ask a lot of questions.* ignorance *n.* ignore *v.* ignored *v.*

Word Study

The **Latin prefix** *in-* means "not."

In this story, Jean thought her greeting to Mrs. Barrett was **adequate**, or enough. However, Mrs. Barrett was displeased because she found it *inadequate.*

Meet
Jean Fritz
(b. 1915)

Author of

mk

Missionary Kid An only child of missionary parents, Jean Fritz grew up in China. Although she had not yet been in the United States, she read and heard from her father about American heroes, such as George Washington and Teddy Roosevelt. Her fascination with these heroes inspired her career as a writer of American history.

Fritz fills her biographies with unusual but true details about her subjects, which she researches thoroughly. "History is full of gossip; it's real people and emotion," she says. The details make her books about historical figures such as Pocahontas or Sam Adams spring to life.

DID YOU KNOW?
As a child, Fritz kept a journal to help her feel less lonely.

BACKGROUND FOR THE SELECTION
Overseas Schools

When American parents live and work outside the United States, their children often attend American schools overseas. At most of these schools, students are taught in English and study many of the things that students study in the United States. International schools, like the one described in this selection, are located all over the world.

mk

Jean Fritz

Vocabulary
relation (ri lā´ shən) *n.* connection between two or more things

I suspect for most of us MKs[1] China not only sharpened our sense of time but our sense of place. We always knew where we were in relation to the rest of the world. And we noticed. Perhaps because we knew we would be leaving China sometime (we wouldn't be MKs or even Ks forever), we developed the habit of observing our surroundings with care. We have strong memories, which explains why as an adult, walking along a beach in Maine, I suddenly found myself on the verge of tears. In front of me, pushing up from the crevice of a rock, was a wild bluebell[2] like the wild bluebells I had known in my summers at Kuling.[3] Suddenly I was a child again. I was back in China, welcoming bluebells back in my life.

---

1. **MKs** (em´ kāz´) *n.* Missionary Kids; the children of missionaries.
2. **bluebell** (blōō´ bel´) *n.* plant with blue, bell-shaped flowers.
3. **Kuling** (kōōl´ iŋ) *n.* now called Lushan, a hill resort south of the Yangtze River in China.

For a long time it was hard for me to unscramble the strings that made up my quest. I have noticed, however, that those MKs who were born in China and stayed there through their high school years were more likely to commit their lives in some way to China. After finishing their higher education in the States, they would return to China as consuls, as teachers, as businessmen and women, as writers, as historians.

I wouldn't be staying through high school. My family planned to return to America when I had finished seventh grade, whether I was finished with China or not. Of course I knew I had to become an American, the sooner the better. So far away from America, I didn't feel like a real American. Nor would I, I thought, until I had put my feet down on American soil.

I had just finished sixth grade at the British School in Wuhan,[4] so I would have one more year to go. Nothing would change that. I knew that there was fighting up and down the Yangtze River, but the Chinese were always fighting—warlord against warlord.[5] That had nothing to do with me. But as soon as I saw the servant from next door racing toward our house with a message for my mother, I knew something was happening. Since we had no phone, we depended on our German neighbors for emergency messages. My father had called, the servant explained. All American women and children had to catch the afternoon boat to Shanghai.[6] The army, which had done so much damage to Nanjing (just down the river), was on its way here. ●

As I helped my mother pack, my knees were shaking. I had only felt this once before. My mother and I had been in a ricksha on the way to the racecourse when farmers ran to the road, calling hateful words at us and throwing stones.

4. **Wuhan** (wōō´ hän´) *n.* city in the central part of China, near the Yangtze River.
5. **warlord** (wôr´ lôrd´) *n.* local leader.
6. **Shanghai** (shaŋ´ hī´) *n.* seaport in eastern China.

Context Clues
Identify examples in this paragraph that help you define *commit*.

Vocabulary
quest (kwest) *n.* long search for something

▼ **Critical Viewing**
Does a ricksha offer much protection to the riders? Explain. **[Speculate]**

Reading Check
As a child, where did the narrator live?

The ricksha-pullers were fast runners, so we weren't hurt, but I told myself this was like Stephen in the Bible who was stoned to death. He just didn't have a ricksha handy. By the time we reached the boat that afternoon, my knees were normal. So was I. And I knew what our plans were. My father and other American men would work in the daytime, but for safety at night they would board one of the gunboats anchored in the river. The women and children going to Shanghai would be protected from bullets by steel barriers erected around the deck. And when we reached Shanghai, then what? I asked my mother.

We would be staying with the Barretts, another missionary family, who had one son, Fletcher, who was two years younger than I and generally unlikable. Mr. Barrett met us in Shanghai and drove us to their home, where his wife was on the front porch. My mother greeted her warmly but I just held out my hand and said, "Hello, Mrs. Barrett," which I thought was adequate. She raised her eyebrows. "Have you become so grown up, Jean," she said, "that I'm no longer your 'Auntie Barrett'?"

I didn't say that I'd always been too grown up for the "auntie" business. I just smiled. In China all MKs called their parents' friends "auntie" or "uncle." Not me. Mrs. B. pushed Fletcher forward.

Vocabulary
adequate
(ad´ i kwət) *adj.* enough

▼ **Critical Viewing**
Jean probably saw boats like this on the Yangtze River. What purpose do you think these boats served?
[Hypothesize]

"Fletcher has been so excited about your visit, Jean," she said. "He has lots of games to show you. Now, run along, children."

Fletcher did have a lot of games. He decided what we'd play—rummy, then patience, while he talked a blue streak. I didn't pay much attention until, in the middle of an Uncle Wiggley game, he asked me a question.

"Have you ever been in love, Jean?" he asked.

What did he think I was? I was twelve years old, for heaven's sakes!

Ever since first grade I'd been in love with someone. The boys never knew it, of course.

Fletcher hadn't finished with love. "I'm in love now," he said. "I'll give you a hint. She's an MK."

"Naturally."

"And she's pretty." Then he suddenly shrieked out the answer as if he couldn't contain it a second longer. "It's you," he cried. "Y-O-U."

Well, Fletcher Barrett was even dumber than I'd thought. No one had ever called me "pretty" before. Not even my parents. Besides, this conversation was making me sick. "I'm tired," I said. "I think I'll get my book and lie down."

At the last minute I had slipped my favorite book in my suitcase. It was one my father and I had read last year—*The Courtship of Miles Standish*[7]—all about the first settlers in America. I knew them pretty well now and often visited with Priscilla Alden.

Settled on the bed in the room I'd been told was mine, I opened the book and let the Pilgrims step off the Mayflower into Shanghai. Priscilla was one of the first.

"You're still a long way from Plymouth," I told her, "but you'll get there. Think you'll like it?"

"I know I will," she answered promptly. "Everything will be better there."

"How do you know?"

"It's a new country. It will be whatever we make it."

"It may be hard," I warned her.

"Maybe," she admitted. "But I'll never give up. Neither will John," she added.

---

7. ***The Courtship of Miles Standish*** *n.* narrative poem by Henry Wadsworth Longfellow, written in 1858. One character in the poem is Priscilla Alden.

Context Clues
Which word restates the meaning of *shrieked* here?

Narration
What problems does reading help Jean solve?

Reading
Check
Why is it necessary for Jean and her mother to travel to Shanghai?

▶ **Critical Viewing**
In what ways do the children in this picture look similar to and different from children of today? **[Compare and Contrast]**

Narration
What world events affect the author of this nonfiction narrative?

I was being called for supper. I waited for the Pilgrims to get back on the Mayflower. Then I closed the book and went downstairs.

The days that followed, I spent mostly with Fletcher, whether I liked it or not. Fletcher was fussing now that the summer was almost over and he'd have to go back to school soon.

"I thought you'd like it," I said. "After all, it's an American school and you're an American."

"So what?"

"Don't you feel like an American when you're in school?"

"What's there to feel?"

He was impossible. If he had gone to a British school, the way I had all my life, he might realize how lucky he was. The Shanghai American School was famous. Children from all over China were sent there to be boarders. Living in Shanghai, Fletcher was just a day student. But even so!

Then one day my mother got a letter from my father. The danger was mostly over, he thought, but some foreign businesses were not reopening. The British School had closed down. (Good news!)

The Yangtze River boats went back in service the next week, so my mother went downtown to buy our tickets back to Wuhan. Fletcher was back in school now, and as soon as he came home, he rushed to see me, his face full of news.

"Your mother is only buying one ticket," he informed me. "You're not going. You're going to the Shanghai American School as a boarder."

"My mother would never do that. You're crazy," I replied. "Where did you get such an idea?"

"I overheard our mothers talking. It's true, Jean."

"Yeah, like cows fly."

When my mother came back, I could see that she was upset. Fletcher did a disappearing act; I figured he didn't want to be caught in a lie.

"Oh, I'm sorry, Jean," my mother said, her eyes filling with tears. She put her arms around me. "Since the British School is closed," she said, "I've arranged

for you to be a boarder at the American School. It won't be for long. We may even go back to America early. At least I'll know you're safe."

I knew my mother was worried that I'd be homesick, so I couldn't let on how I really felt. (Just think, I told myself, I'd have almost a year to practice being an American.) I buried my head on her shoulder. "I'll be okay," I said, sniffing back fake tears. Sometimes it's necessary to deceive your parents if you love them, and I did love mine.

After my mother left on the boat, Mr. Barrett took me to the Shanghai American School (SAS for short). I guess I expected some kind of immediate transformation. I always felt a tingling when I saw the American flag flying over the American consulate. Surely it would be more than a tingling now; surely it would overwhelm me. But when we went through the iron gates of the school grounds, I didn't feel a thing. On the football field a group of high school girls were practicing cheerleading. They were jumping, standing on their hands, yelling rah, rah, rah. It just seemed like a lot of fuss about football. What was the matter with me?

Vocabulary

deceive (dē sēv´) v. make someone believe something that is not true

transformation (trans´ fər mā´ shən) n. change

✓ Reading Check

Why is Jean excited about going to the American school?

Narration
What is the first thing Jean's roommate decides to do for her?

Spiral Review
Central Idea How does Jean's agreement to get a haircut support a central idea of this narrative?

The dormitory where I'd be living was divided in half by a swinging door. The high school girls were on one side of the door; the junior high (which included me) were on the other. On my side there were two Russian girls and two American MKs, the Johnson sisters, who had long hair braided and wound around their heads like Sunday school teachers. And there was Paula, my American roommate, who looked as though she belonged on the other side of the door. Hanging in our shared closet I noticed a black velvet dress. And a pair of high heeled shoes. She wore them to tea dances, she explained, when one of her brother's friends came to town. She was squinting her eyes as she looked at me, sizing up my straight hair and bangs.

"I happen to know you're an MK," she said, "but you don't have to look like one." The latest style in the States, she told me, was a boyish bob.[8] She'd give me one, she decided.

So that night she put a towel around my shoulders and newspaper on the floor, and she began cutting. This might make all the difference, I thought, as I watched my hair travel to the floor.

It didn't. My ears might have felt more American, but not me. After being in hiding all their lives, my ears were suddenly outdoors, looking like jug handles on each side of my face. I'd get used to them, I told myself. Meanwhile I had to admit that SAS was a big improvement over the British School. Even without an American flag feeling, I enjoyed the months I was there.

What I enjoyed most were the dances, except they weren't dances. There were too many MKs in the school, and the Ms didn't approve of dancing. Instead, we had "talk parties." The girls were given what looked like dance cards and the boys were supposed to sign up for the talk sessions they wanted. Of course a girl could feel like a wallflower[9] if her card wasn't filled up, but mine usually was. These parties gave me a chance to look over the boys in case I wanted to fall in love, and actually I was almost ready to make a choice when my parents suddenly appeared. It was early spring. Just as my mother had suspected, we were going to America early.

I knew that three weeks crossing the Pacific would be different from five days on the Yangtze but I didn't know how

---

8. **bob** (bäb) *n.* woman's or child's short haircut.
9. **wallflower** (wôl′ flou′ ər) *n.* person who stands against the wall and watches at a dance due to shyness or lack of popularity.

different. My father had given me a gray-and-green plaid steamer rug that I would put over me when I was lying on my long folding deck chair. At eleven o'clock every morning a waiter would come around with a cup of "beef tea." I loved the idea of drinking beef tea under my steamer rug but it didn't happen often. The captain said this was the roughest crossing he'd ever made, and passengers spent most of their time in their cabins. If they came out for a meal, they were lucky if they could get it down before it came back up again. I had my share of seasickness, so of course I was glad to reach San Francisco.

I couldn't wait to take my first steps on American soil, but I expected the American soil to hold still for me. Instead, it swayed as if we were all still at sea, and I lurched about as I had been doing for the last three weeks. I noticed my parents were having difficulty, too. "Our heads and our legs aren't ready for land," my father explained. "It takes a little while." We spent the night in a hotel and took a train the next day for Pittsburgh where our relatives were meeting us.

It was a three-day trip across most of the continent, but

▲ **Critical Viewing**
How do you think Jean might have felt as she appoached the Golden Gate Bridge in San Francisco by ship? **[Speculate]**

Narration
Why is Jean excited about the end of the crossing?

✓ Reading Check
How long does it take Jean and her family to cross the Pacific?

it didn't seem long. Every minute America was under us and rushing past our windows—the Rocky Mountains, the Mississippi river, flat ranch land, small towns, forests, boys dragging school bags over dusty roads. It was all of America at once splashed across where we were, where we'd been, where we were going. How could you not feel American? How could you not feel that you belonged? By the time we were settled at my grandmother's house, I felt as if I'd always been a part of this family. And wasn't it wonderful to have real aunts and uncles, a real grandmother, and yes, even a real bathroom, for heaven's sakes?

I wanted to talk to Priscilla, so I took my book outside, and when I opened it, out tumbled the Pilgrims, Priscilla first. I smiled. Here we were, all of us in America together, and it didn't matter that we came from different times. We all knew that America was still an experiment and perhaps always

▼ **Critical Viewing**
How does this landscape of the United States compare with Jean's description of where she lived in China? **[Compare and Contrast]**

would be. I was one of the ones who had to try to make the experiment work. ●

"You'll have disappointments," Priscilla said. "But it will help if you get to know Americans who have spent their lives working on the experiment."

I wasn't sure just what she meant, but I knew it was important. "I'll try," I said.

"Try!" Priscilla scoffed. "If you want to be a real American, you'll have to do more than that." Her voice was fading. Indeed, the Pilgrims themselves were growing faint. Soon they had all slipped away.

I learned about disappointment as soon as I went to school. Of course I was no longer an MK, but I was certainly a curiosity. I was the Kid from China. "Did you live in a mud hut?" one boy asked me. "Did you eat rats and dogs? Did you eat with sticks?"

I decided that American children were ignorant. Didn't their teachers teach them anything? After a while, as soon as anyone even mentioned China, I shut up. "What was the name of your hometown?" I was asked, but I never told. I couldn't bear to have my hometown laughed at.

"Not all American children are ignorant," my mother pointed out. "Just a few who ask dumb questions."

Even in high school, however, I often got the same questions. But now we were studying about the American Revolution and George Washington. Of course I'd always known who Washington was, but knowing history and understanding it are two different things. I had never realized how much he had done to make America into America. No matter how much he was asked to do for his country, he did it, even though he could hardly wait to go back home and be a farmer again. Of course there were disappointments on the way; of course he became discouraged. "If I'd known what I was getting into," he said at the beginning of the Revolution, "I would have chosen to live in an Indian teepee all my life." He never took the easiest way. When he thought his work was over at the end of the Revolution, he agreed to work on the Constitution. When the country needed a president, he took the oath of office. When his term was over, he was persuaded to run once again. Everyone had confidence that as long as he was there, the new government would work.

Context Clues
Which clues in this paragraph help you to understand the meaning of *fading*?

Vocabulary
ignorant (ig´ nə rənt) *adj.* not knowing facts or information

Narration
What does Jean learn in high school that she did not understand before?

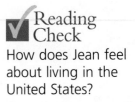
Reading Check

How does Jean feel about living in the United States?

Although Washington was the first, there were many more like him who were, as Priscilla would say, "real" Americans. As I went through college and read about them, I knew I wanted to write about them someday. I might not talk to them in the same way I talked to Priscilla, but I would try to make them as real as they were when they were alive.

I had the feeling that I was coming to the end of my quest. But not quite. One day when someone asked me where I was born, I found myself smiling. I was for the moment standing beside the Yangtze River. "My hometown," I said, "was Wuhan, China." I discovered that I had to take China with me wherever I went.

Critical Thinking

Cite textual evidence to support your responses.

1. **Key Ideas and Details** How does the setting affect the events in this narrative?

2. **Key Ideas and Details** **(a)** Why do Jean and her mother travel to Shanghai? **(b) Infer:** Does the American School in Shanghai live up to Jean's expectations? Why or why not?

3. **Key Ideas and Details** **Take a Position:** What are the pros and cons of living outside the United States? Choose a position and support your answer.

4. **Integration of Knowledge and Ideas** **(a)** How does Jean's connection with Priscilla Alden help her find the truth? **(b)** What does Jean conclude about what makes a person a real American? *[Connect to the Big Question: What is the best way to find the truth?]*

Reading Skill: Context Clues

1. In a chart like this, write the italicized word in the left column. Then, write the **context clues** and what the word means. Check your response in a dictionary. **(a)** I was no longer an MK, but I was certainly a *curiosity*. I was the Kid from China. **(b)** I expected the American soil to hold still for me. Instead, it *swayed* as if we were all still at sea.

Unfamiliar Word	Context Clues	Possible Meaning

Literary Analysis: Narrative Text

2. Craft and Structure Identify the main reason that "mk" is classified as a **narrative.**

3. Craft and Structure The order of events is important in **narration. (a)** What is the first thing Jean sees as she goes through the iron gates of the Shanghai American School? **(b)** Why is this information important to the story?

Vocabulary

Acquisition and Use Rewrite each sentence, replacing each underlined word with a **synonym,** or word with a similar meaning.

1. The travelers were on a *quest* for adventure.

2. They brought *adequate* supplies for a week of camping.

3. When you smile, your face undergoes a *transformation*.

4. The *relation* between extreme sports and injuries is high.

5. Do not try to *deceive* me with that silly mask and fake voice!

6. The players were *ignorant* of the new rules of the game.

Word Study Use the context of the sentences and what you know about the **Latin prefix in-** to explain each answer.

1. If something is *inaccurate,* is it correct or incorrect?

2. Would an *insensitive* person cry during a sad part of a movie?

Word Study

The **Latin prefix *in-*** means "not."

Apply It Explain how the prefix *in-* contributes to the meanings of these words. Consult a print dictionary if necessary.

invisible
inactive
incomplete

Integrated Language Skills

Papa's Parrot • mk

Conventions: Common and Proper Nouns

All nouns can be classified as either **common nouns** or **proper nouns.**

- A common noun names a person, place, or thing.
- A proper noun names a specific person, place, or thing.

Common nouns are not capitalized unless they begin a sentence or a title. Proper nouns are always capitalized.

Common Nouns	Proper Nouns
singer	Jennifer Johnson
city	Phoenix
dog	Prince

Practice A Identify the nouns in each sentence. Then, label each as a common or proper noun.

1. The parrot was good for Mr. Tillian.
2. Harry and his father had fun together.
3. Mr. Tillian fell onto the candy boxes.
4. Harry helped in the store.
5. That parrot talked to Harry.
6. Harry learned a lesson from Rocky.

© **Reading Application** In "Papa's Parrot," find two sentences with common nouns and two sentences with proper nouns.

Practice B Revise each sentence to replace common nouns with proper nouns.

1. The missionary kids knew they would leave the country someday.
2. Jean's favorite book was about the first settlers.
3. Children from around the world attended that school.
4. Many students in her new country asked her silly questions.

© **Writing Application** Write two sentences describing what it might be like to go to school in another country. Use at least one common noun and one proper noun in your description. Capitalize the proper nouns.

PH **WRITING COACH** Further instruction and practice are available in *Prentice Hall Writing Coach.*

Writing

Informative Text Write a brief **compare-and-contrast essay.** If you write about "Papa's Parrot," compare and contrast Harry's behavior before and after he entered junior high school. Before you write, gather details from the story in a two-column chart.

- In the first column, list details that show what Harry was like before junior high school.
- In the second column, list details that show his behavior and thoughts once he entered junior high school.

If you write about "mk," compare and contrast Jean's feelings about America before and after she arrives in the United States. Before you write, gather story details in a two-column chart.

- In the first column, list details that show her thoughts and feelings about America when she was living in China.
- In the second column, list details that show her thoughts and feelings when she lived and went to school in the United States.

Grammar Application Capitalize all the proper nouns in your essay.

Writing Workshop: *Work in Progress*

Prewriting for Descriptive Essay Think of a memorable place. List five qualities or features that make it special for you. Pick one or two items from this list, and jot down sensory details that you associate with each one. Describe the sight, sound, and smell of the places. Save this Place List in your writing portfolio.

Speaking and Listening

Comprehension and Collaboration With a partner, perform a **dramatic reading** of either "Papa's Parrot" or "mk." Read the story and choose a section that is especially moving, emotional, or funny. Divide the text so that each partner can present a portion. As you rehearse, focus on these points:

- Speak clearly so that each word can be heard.
- Raise and lower your voice to express emotion.
- Slow down and stress certain words for effect.
- Make eye contact with your listeners as you read.

Common Core State Standards

L.7.2, L.7.5.b, L.7.6; W.7.2.b; SL.7.6
[For the full wording of the standards, see page 22.]

Use this prewriting activity to prepare for the **Writing Workshop** on page 92.

PHLit Online!
www.PHLitOnline.com

- Interactive graphic organizers
- Grammar tutorial
- Interactive journals

Leveled Texts

Build your skills and improve your comprehension of nonfiction and fiction with texts of increasing complexity.

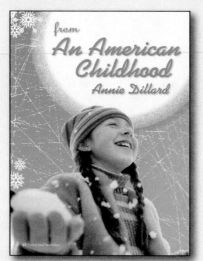

Read the excerpt from ***An American Childhood*** to see the unexpected results that follow when neighborhood children toss snowballs at a car.

Read **"The Luckiest Time of All"** to meet a great-grandmother who believes the time she almost got bitten by a dog was the luckiest time of all.

 Common Core State Standards

Meet these standards with either the excerpt from ***An American Childhood*** (p. 52) or **"The Luckiest Time of All"** (p. 62).

Reading Literature
6. Analyze how an author develops and contrasts the points of view of different characters or narrators in a text. *(Literary Analysis: Point of View)*

Reading Informational Text
6. Determine an author's point of view or purpose in a text and analyze how the author distinguishes his or her position from that of others. *(Literary Analysis: Point of View)*

Spiral Review: RL.7.2; RI.7.2

Writing
2. Write informative/explanatory texts to examine a topic and convey ideas, concepts, and information through the selection, organization, and analysis of relevant content. **d.** Use precise language and domain-specific vocabulary to inform about or explain the topic. *(Writing: Description)*

7. Conduct short research projects to answer a question, drawing on several sources and generating additional related, focused questions for further research and investigation. *(Research and Technology: Biographical Report)*

Language
4. Determine or clarify the meaning of unknown and multiple-meaning words and phrases based on grade 7 reading and content, choosing flexibly from a range of strategies. **4.a.** Use context as a clue to the meaning of a word or phrase. *(Reading Skill: Context Clues)*

5. Demonstrate understanding of figurative language, word relationships, and nuances in word meanings. **b.** Use the relationship between particular words to better understand each of the words. *(Vocabulary: Analogies)*

Reading Skill: Context Clues

Context clues are restatements, examples, definitions, and contrasting details in a text that help you unlock meanings of unfamiliar words and expressions. When you come across an unfamiliar word, use context clues to figure out the word's meaning. Then, **reread and read ahead to confirm the meaning.**

Using the Strategy: Context Clues Chart

Use a chart like the one shown to find out the meanings of words.

Context	Function in Sentence	Meaning
The doll's small feet wore *miniscule* shoes.	It is an adjective that describes a doll's shoes.	*Miniscule* probably means "tiny."

Literary Analysis: Point of View

Point of view is the perspective from which a narrative is told. It affects the kinds of details that are revealed to the reader. Different points of view can affect the *theme* or message of a story because of the information the author shares.

- **First-person point of view:** The narrator is a character who participates in the story and uses the first-person pronoun *I.* The narrator can reveal only his or her own thoughts and feelings.

- **Third-person point of view:** The narrator is not a character in the story. He or she uses third-person pronouns such as *he* and *she* to refer to the characters.

- Third-person narrators can be **omniscient** or **limited.** An omniscient narrator tells what each character thinks and feels. A narrator with a limited point of view reveals the thoughts and feelings of only one character.

Finally, a narrator can be either **objective** or **subjective.** An objective narrator is a neutral observer, much like a reporter. A subjective narrator participates in the story and relates things from a specific point of view.

PHLit
Online!
www.PHLitOnline.com

Hear It!
- Selection summary audio
- Selection audio

See It!
- Get Connected video
- Background video
- More about the author
- Vocabulary flashcards

Do It!
- Interactive journals
- Interactive graphic organizers
- Self-test
- Internet activity
- Grammar tutorial
- Interactive vocabulary games

 **What is the best way to find the** *truth?*

Writing About the Big Question

In the excerpt from *An American Childhood,* a young man energetically chases the narrator and her friends after they throw a snowball at his car. Use this sentence starter to develop your ideas about the Big Question.

Being challenged when we don't expect it gives us **insight** about _____ because _____.

While You Read Look for details that reveal an insight or truth that the narrator has learned.

Vocabulary

Read each word and its definition. Decide whether you know the word well, know it a little bit, or do not know it at all. After you read, see how your knowledge of each word has increased.

- **strategy** (strat´ ə jē) *n.* set of plans used to gain success or achieve a goal (p. 53) *The general presented his strategy for the attack. strategize v. strategic adj.*

- **translucent** (trans lo͞o´ sənt) *adj.* allowing light through (p. 54) *The sun's rays shine through the translucent stained glass. translucence n.*

- **compelled** (kəm peld´) *v.* forced (p. 56) *Honesty compelled him to tell the truth. compel v. compelling adj.*

- **improvising** (im´ prə vīz´ iŋ) *v.* making up or inventing on the spur of the moment (p. 56) *Jazz musicians are good at improvising in performances. improvise v. improvisation n.*

- **perfunctorily** (pər fuŋk´ tə rə lē) *adv.* done without care merely as a routine; superficially (p. 57) *Ella washed her hands perfunctorily even though they were clean. perfunctory adj.*

- **righteous** (rī´ chəs) *adj.* morally good and fair (p. 58) *The principal felt the punishment was righteous. right adj. righteously adv. righteousness n.*

Word Study

The **Latin prefix** *trans-* means "over," "across," or "through."

In this story, the narrator forms a mound of snow into a **translucent** iceball, which, while not quite see-through, allows light to pass through.

Annie Dillard
(b. 1945)

Photograph by Rollie McKenna

Author of
from An American Childhood

Growing up in Pittsburgh, Pennsylvania, Annie Dillard loved reading, drawing, and observing the natural world. During high school, she began reading and writing poetry.

Pulitzer Prize–Winning Book While attending college in Virginia, Dillard lived near a creek in a valley of the Blue Ridge Mountains. In 1974, she published *Pilgrim at Tinker Creek*, which describes her explorations of that environment. While writing the book, Dillard would sit for hours observing sights in the natural world around her, such as a praying mantis laying its eggs. Then she would return home and think about her observations, mixing them with her readings from science and philosophy.

Dillard gives this advice to aspiring writers: "You have enough experience by the time you're five years old. What you need is the library. What you have to learn is the best of what is being thought and said."

DID YOU KNOW?

Dillard's favorite book—which she still reads once a year—is *The Field Book of Ponds and Streams*.

BACKGROUND FOR THE AUTOBIOGRAPHY

The American Suburbs

The events in this narrative take place in a suburban neighborhood. The word *suburban* refers to a residential area on or near the outskirts of a city, or "urban" area. After World War II, many people had cars and were able to leave crowded cities. Suburban living has some of the conveniences of a city—such as shopping and entertainment—in a quieter environment.

from
An American Childhood
Annie Dillard

Some boys taught me to play football. This was fine sport. You thought up a new **strategy** for every play and whispered it to the others. You went out for a pass, fooling everyone. Best, you got to throw yourself mightily at someone's running legs. Either you brought him down or you hit the ground flat out on your chin, with your arms empty before you. It was all or nothing. If you hesitated in fear, you would miss and get hurt: you would take a hard fall while the kid got away, or you would get kicked in the face while the kid got away. But if you flung yourself wholeheartedly at the back of his knees—if you gathered and joined body and soul and pointed them diving fearlessly—then you likely wouldn't get hurt, and you'd stop the ball. Your fate, and your team's score, depended on your concentration and courage. Nothing girls did could compare with it.

Boys welcomed me at baseball, too, for I had, through enthusiastic practice, what was weirdly known as a boy's arm. In winter, in the snow, there was neither baseball nor football, so the boys and I threw snowballs at passing cars. I got in trouble throwing snowballs, and have seldom been happier since.

Vocabulary
strategy (strat´ ə jē)
n. set of plans used to gain success or achieve a goal

◄ **Critical Viewing**
Do you think that children and adults would have the same reaction to this snow scene? Explain. **[Compare and Contrast]**

Point of View
Which words and details in the first two paragraphs indicate that this narrative is told from the first-person point of view?

Reading Check
What sports did the author learn to play?

On one weekday morning after Christmas, six inches of new snow had just fallen. We were standing up to our boot tops in snow on a front yard on trafficked Reynolds Street, waiting for cars. The cars traveled Reynolds Street slowly and evenly; they were targets all but wrapped in red ribbons, cream puffs. We couldn't miss. ●

I was seven; the boys were eight, nine, and ten. The oldest two Fahey boys were there—Mikey and Peter—polite blond boys who lived near me on Lloyd Street, and who already had four brothers and sisters. My parents approved Mikey and Peter Fahey. Chickie McBride was there, a tough kid, and Billy Paul and Mackie Kean too, from across Reynolds, where the boys grew up dark and furious, grew up skinny, knowing, and skilled. We had all drifted from our houses that morning looking for action, and had found it here on Reynolds Street.

It was cloudy but cold. The cars' tires laid behind them on the snowy street a complex trail of beige chunks like crenellated castle walls.[1] I had stepped on some earlier; they squeaked. We could have wished for more traffic. When a car came, we all popped it one. In the intervals between cars we reverted to the natural solitude of children.

I started making an iceball—a perfect iceball, from perfectly white snow, perfectly spherical, and squeezed perfectly translucent so no snow remained all the way through. (The Fahey boys and I considered it unfair actually to throw an iceball at somebody, but it had been known to happen.)

I had just embarked on the iceball project when we heard tire chains come clanking from afar. A black Buick was moving toward us down the street. We all spread out, banged together some regular snowballs, took aim, and, when the Buick drew nigh, fired.

A soft snowball hit the driver's windshield right before the driver's face. It made a smashed star with a hump in the middle.

Often, of course, we hit our target, but this time, the only time in all of life, the car pulled over and stopped. Its wide black door opened; a man got out of it, running. He didn't even close the car door.

---

1. **like crenellated** (kren′ əl āt′ əd) **castle walls** in rows of squares like the notches along the top of castle walls.

He ran after us, and we ran away from him, up the snowy Reynolds sidewalk. At the corner, I looked back; incredibly, he was still after us. He was in city clothes: a suit and tie, street shoes. Any normal adult would have quit, having sprung us into flight and made his point. This man was gaining on us. He was a thin man, all action. All of a sudden, we were running for our lives.

Wordless, we split up. We were on our turf; we could lose ourselves in the neighborhood backyards, everyone for himself. I paused and considered. Everyone had vanished except Mikey Fahey, who was just rounding the corner of a yellow brick house. Poor Mikey, I trailed him. The driver of the Buick sensibly picked the two of us to follow. The man apparently had all day.

Context Clues
What clues clarify the meaning of the expression "gaining on us" in this paragraph?

◄ **Critical Viewing**
In what two ways is this photograph of a snow-covered bicycle a good image for this narrative? **[Support]**

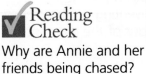

Reading Check
Why are Annie and her friends being chased?

from An American Childhood **55**

He chased Mikey and me around the yellow house and up a backyard path we knew by heart: under a low tree, up a bank, through a hedge, down some snowy steps, and across the grocery store's delivery driveway. We smashed through a gap in another hedge, entered a scruffy backyard and ran around its back porch and tight between houses to Edgerton Avenue; we ran across Edgerton to an alley and up our own sliding woodpile to the Halls' front yard; he kept coming. We ran up Lloyd Street and wound through mazy backyards toward the steep hilltop at Willard and Lang.

He chased us silently, block after block. He chased us silently over picket fences, through thorny hedges, between houses, around garbage cans, and across streets. Every time I glanced back, choking for breath, I expected he would have quit. He must have been as breathless as we were. His jacket strained over his body. It was an immense discovery, pounding into my hot head with every sliding, joyous step, that this ordinary adult evidently knew what I thought only children who trained at football knew: that you have to fling yourself at what you're doing, you have to point yourself, forget yourself, aim, dive. ●

Mikey and I had nowhere to go, in our own neighborhood or out of it, but away from this man who was chasing us. He impelled us forward; we compelled him to follow our route. The air was cold; every breath tore my throat. We kept running, block after block; we kept improvising, backyard after backyard, running a frantic course and choosing it simultaneously, failing always to find small places or hard places to slow him down, and discovering always, exhilarated, dismayed, that only bare speed could save us—for he would never give up, this man— and we were losing speed.

He chased us through the backyard labyrinths of ten

Vocabulary
compelled (kəm peld´)
v. forced

improvising
(im´ prə vīz´ iŋ) *v.*
making up or
inventing on the
spur of the moment

blocks before he caught us by our jackets. He caught us and we all stopped.

We three stood staggering, half blinded, coughing, in an obscure hilltop backyard: a man in his twenties, a boy, a girl. He had released our jackets, our pursuer, our captor, our hero: he knew we weren't going anywhere. We all played by the rules. Mikey and I unzipped our jackets. I pulled off my sopping mittens. Our tracks multiplied in the backyard's new snow. We had been breaking new snow all morning. We didn't look at each other. I was cherishing my excitement. The man's lower pants legs were wet; his cuffs were full of snow, and there was a prow of snow beneath them on his shoes and socks. Some trees bordered the little flat backyard, some messy winter trees. There was no one around: a clearing in a grove, and we the only players.

It was a long time before he could speak. I had some difficulty at first recalling why we were there. My lips felt swollen; I couldn't see out of the sides of my eyes; I kept coughing.

"You stupid kids," he began perfunctorily.

We listened perfunctorily indeed, if we listened at all, for the chewing out was redundant, a mere formality, and beside the point. The point was that he had chased us passionately without giving up, and so he had caught us. Now he came down to earth. I wanted the glory to last forever.

But how could the glory have lasted forever? We could have run through every backyard in North America until we got to Panama. But when he trapped us at the lip of the Panama Canal, what precisely could he have done to prolong the drama of the chase and cap its glory? I brooded about this for the next few years. He could only have fried Mikey Fahey and me in boiling oil, say, or dismembered us piecemeal, or staked us to anthills. None of which I really wanted, and

He impelled us forward; we compelled him to follow our route. The air was cold; every breath tore my throat.

Spiral Review
Central Idea How does the narrator describe the man? How might this description relate to the central idea?

Vocabulary
perfunctorily (pər fuŋk′tə rə lē) *adv.* done without care merely as a routine; superficially

Context Clues
Which words in this paragraph verify the meaning of *redundant* by restating it?

Reading Check
What happens when the man catches the children?

none of which any adult was likely to do, even in the spirit of fun. He could only chew us out there in the Panamanian jungle, after months or years of exalting pursuit. He could only begin, "You stupid kids," and continue in his ordinary Pittsburgh accent with his normal righteous anger and the usual common sense.

If in that snowy backyard the driver of the black Buick had cut off our heads, Mikey's and mine, I would have died happy, for nothing has required so much of me since as being chased all over Pittsburgh in the middle of winter—running terrified, exhausted—by this sainted, skinny, furious red-headed man who wished to have a word with us. I don't know how he found his way back to his car.

Critical Thinking

Cite textual evidence to support your responses.

© 1. **Key Ideas and Details** **(a)** What are Dillard and her friends doing "On one weekday morning after Christmas"? **(b) Describe:** What words would you use to describe the way the man chases Dillard and her friend?

© 2. **Key Ideas and Details** **(a)** What does the man do when he catches Dillard and her friend? **(b) Infer:** How do his actions cause this "hero" to come "down to earth"?

© 3. **Key Ideas and Details** **(a) Analyze:** In general, what does the young Dillard value and not value in people? **(b) Evaluate:** Do you think this episode from Dillard's early life has a larger meaning, or is it just an entertaining story? Explain.

© 4. **Integration of Knowledge and Ideas** **(a)** How do our memories of an event give us greater insight? **(b)** Can we find the truth about something by reflecting on it? Why or why not? *[Connect to the Big Question: What is the best way to find the truth?]*

Reading Skill: Context Clues

Read these lines from the narrative: *In the <u>intervals</u> between cars we reverted to the natural solitude of children.*

1. What is a possible meaning for <u>intervals</u>?

2. What **context clues** suggest this meaning?

Literary Analysis: Point of View

Ⓒ **3. Craft and Structure** In a chart like this, give two examples in which the narrator shares her thoughts or feelings.

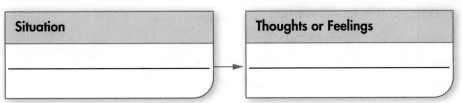

Situation		Thoughts or Feelings
	→	

Ⓒ **4. Craft and Structure (a)** What are three details that could have been included if the **first-person narrator** had been the man? **(b)** How might this different point of view affect the **theme**?

Ⓒ **5. Craft and Structure** Is the narrator's point of view objective or subjective? Use text evidence to explain.

Vocabulary

Ⓒ **Acquisition and Use** Explain why each is either true or false.

1. Few doctors feel *compelled* to help others.

2. We are *improvising* by using garbage bags for rain ponchos.

3. A granite rock is *translucent* when held to the light.

4. A friend who has been wronged feels *righteous* anger.

5. Studying hard is a good *strategy* for passing a test.

6. You are happy if you do something *perfunctorily*.

Word Study Use what you know about the **Latin prefix trans-** to explain your answer to each question.

1. Does a *transatlantic* flight bring you across an ocean?

2. If you want to *transplant* a tree, must you dig it up first?

Word Study

The **Latin prefix trans-** means "over," "across," or "through."

Apply It Explain how the prefix *trans-* contributes to the meanings of these words. Consult a dictionary if necessary.
transferral
transportation
transcontinental

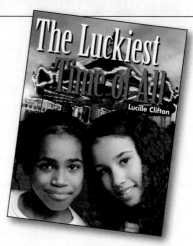

What is the best way to find the *truth?*

Writing About the Big Question

In "The Luckiest Time of All," a woman shares with her great-granddaughter the story of how she met her husband. She describes the way something most people would call bad luck turned out to be good luck. Use these sentence starters to develop your ideas about the Big Question.

When we **believe** something is lucky, we feel _____.

We **reveal** our experiences to others so that _____.

While You Read Think about what the great-grandmother gives to her great-granddaughter by sharing her memories.

Vocabulary

Read each word and its definition. Decide whether you know the word well, know it a little bit, or do not know it at all. After you read, see how your knowledge of each word has increased.

- **plaited** (plāt′ əd) *v.* braided (p. 63) *Annie looked cute as she plaited her hair.* plait *n.* plaited *adj.*

- **wonders** (wun′dərz) *n.* things that cause astonishment; marvels (p. 63) *A rainbow is one of the wonders of nature.* wonder *n.* wonderful *adj.*

- **twine** (twīn) *n.* strong string or cord of strands twisted together (p. 65) *The twine held the kite in the wind.* twined *v.* twining *v.* intertwined *adj.*

- **hind** (hīnd) *adj.* rear (p. 65) *The dog injured his hind legs.* behind *adj.*

- **spied** (spīd) *v.* watched secretly (p. 65) *The detective spied on his suspect.* spy *v.* spies *n.* spying *v.*

- **acquainted** (ə kwānt′ əd) *adj.* familiar (p. 66) *Before the party, I was not acquainted with her brother.* acquaint *v.* acquaintance *n.*

Word Study

The **Latin prefix** *ac-* means "motion toward," "addition to," or "nearness to."

In this story, Mrs. Pickens becomes **acquainted**, or familiar, with her future husband.

Meet
Lucille Clifton
(1936–2010)

Author of
The Luckiest Time of All

Lucille Sayles Clifton was born into a large, working-class family in Depew, New York. Although her parents were not formally educated, they taught their children to appreciate books and poetry. During her childhood, Clifton also developed a deep respect for her African American culture and its storytelling tradition.

A Life of Achievement After she became the first member of her family to graduate from high school, Clifton entered college. Two years later, she left school and began her writing career. Her first collection of poems was published in 1969, and *The New York Times* called it one of the best books of the year.

DID YOU KNOW?
From 1979 to 1982, Clifton served as Poet Laureate of Maryland.

BACKGROUND FOR THE STORY
Dialect

Dialect is a form of language spoken by people in a specific region or group. Dialects differ from standard formal language in pronunciation, grammar, and word choice. In "The Luckiest Time of All," Lucille Clifton uses a dialect of the rural South. The informal language contributes to the feeling that readers are listening to a story told aloud.

The Luckiest

Time of All

Lucille Clifton

Mrs. Elzie F. Pickens was rocking slowly on the porch one afternoon when her Great-granddaughter, Tee, brought her a big bunch of dogwood blooms, and that was the beginning of a story.

"Ahhh, now that dogwood reminds me of the day I met your Great-granddaddy, Mr. Pickens, Sweet Tee.

"It was just this time, spring of the year, and me and my best friend Ovella Wilson, who is now gone, was goin to join the Silas Greene. Usta be a kinda show went all through the South, called it the Silas Greene show. Somethin like the circus. Me and Ovella wanted to join that thing and see the world. Nothin wrong at home or nothin, we just wanted to travel and see new things and have high times. Didn't say nothin to nobody but one another. Just up and decided to do it.

"Well, this day we plaited our hair and put a dress and some things in a crokasack[1] and started out to the show. Spring day like this.

"We got there after a good little walk and it was the world, Baby, such music and wonders as we never had seen! They had everything there, or seemed like it.

"Me and Ovella thought we'd walk around for a while and see the show before goin to the office to sign up and join.

"While we was viewin it all we come up on this dancin dog. Cutest one thing in the world next to you, Sweet Tee, dippin

---

1. **crokasack** (krō´ kər sak) *n.* usually spelled *croker sack,* a bag made of burlap or similar material.

Context Clues
Read ahead to identify clues that show you that Silas Greene is not the name of a person in this context.

Vocabulary
plaited (plāt´ əd)
v. braided

wonders (wun´dərz)
n. things that cause astonishment; marvels

✓ Reading Check
Where did Ovella and Tee's great-grandmother go?

Culture Connection

A Matter of Luck

Most people believe that hard work contributes more than luck to a person's success. However, there is scientific evidence that a positive attitude increases a person's chances for success. In this sense, any action or object that contributes to a person's positive attitude could be considered lucky. Here is how some accomplished Americans approach the issue:

- Basketball superstar Michael Jordan always wore his blue University of North Carolina shorts under his Chicago Bulls uniform when he played.

- When she is on the ice, skating star Michelle Kwan wears a Chinese good luck charm around her neck. It was a gift from her grandmother.

Connect to the Literature

Why do you think Elzie considers the stone to be lucky?

and movin and head bowin to that music. Had a little ruffly skirt on itself and up on two back legs twistin and movin to the music. Dancin dancin dancin till people started throwin pennies out of they pockets.

"Me and Ovella was caught up too and laughin so. She took a penny out of her pocket and threw it to the ground where that dog was dancin, and I took two pennies and threw 'em both.

"The music was faster and faster and that dog was turnin and turnin. Ovella reached in her sack and threw out a little pin she had won from never being late at Sunday school. And me, laughin and all excited, reached in my bag and threw out my lucky stone!

"Well, I knew right off what I had done. Soon as it left my hand it seemed like I reached back out for it to take it back. But the stone was gone from my hand and Lord, it hit that dancin dog right on his nose!

"Well, he lit out after me, poor thing. He lit out after me and I flew! Round and round the Silas Greene we run, through every place me and Ovella had walked before, but now that dancin dog was a runnin dog and all the people was laughin at the new show, which was us!

"I felt myself slowin down after a while and I thought I would turn around a little bit to see how much gain that cute little dog was makin on me. When I did I got such a surprise! Right behind me was the dancin

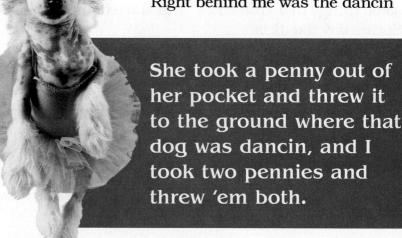

She took a penny out of her pocket and threw it to the ground where that dog was dancin, and I took two pennies and threw 'em both.

dog and right behind him was the finest fast runnin hero in the bottoms of Virginia.

"And that was Mr. Pickens when he was still a boy! He had a length of twine in his hand and he was twirlin it around in the air just like the cowboy at the Silas Greene and grinnin fit to bust.

"While I was watchin how the sun shined on him and made him look like an angel come to help a poor sinner girl, why, he twirled that twine one extra fancy twirl and looped it right around one hind leg of that dancin dog and brought him low.

"I stopped then and walked slow and shy to where he had picked up that poor dog to see if he was hurt, cradlin him and talkin to him soft and sweet. That showed me how kind and gentle he was, and when we walked back to the dancin dog's place in the show he let the dog loose and helped me to find my stone. I told him how shiny black it was and how it had the letter A scratched on one side. We searched and searched and at last he spied it! ●

"Ovella and me lost heart for shows then and we walked on home. And a good little way, the one who was gonna be your Great-granddaddy was walkin on behind. Seein us safe. Us walkin kind of slow. Him seein us safe. Yes." Mrs. Pickens'

Vocabulary

twine (twīn) *n.* strong string or cord of strands twisted together

hind (hīnd) *adj.* rear

spied (spīd) *v.* watched secretly

Point of View

In Elzie's narrative, why are Mr. Pickens's thoughts not revealed?

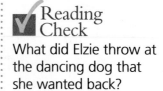

Reading Check

What did Elzie throw at the dancing dog that she wanted back?

Vocabulary
acquainted (ə kwānt´
əd) *adj.* familiar

Point of View
How does the writer
indicate that the point
of view changes from a
first-person narrative by
Elzie to a third-person
narrative about Elzie
and Tee?

Spiral Review
Theme What message
about luck does this
story convey?

voice trailed off softly and Tee noticed she had a little smile on
her face.

"Grandmama, that stone almost got you bit by a dog that
time. It wasn't so lucky that time, was it?"

Tee's Great-grandmother shook her head and laughed out
loud.

"That was the luckiest time of all, Tee Baby. It got me
acquainted with Mr. Amos Pickens, and if that ain't luck,
what could it be! Yes, it was luckier for me than for anybody, I
think. Least mostly I think it."

Tee laughed with her Great-grandmother though she didn't
exactly know why.

"I hope I have that kind of good stone luck one day," she
said.

"Maybe you will someday,"
her Great-grandmother said.

And they rocked a little
longer and smiled together.

Critical Thinking

Cite textual
evidence to
support your
responses.

1. **Key Ideas and Details (a)** Why do Ovella and Elzie go to
   the Silas Greene show? **(b) Infer:** What does this tell you
   about Elzie as a young woman? **(c) Connect:** In what ways
   is Elzie similar or different as an older woman?

2. **Key Ideas and Details (a)** When does Elzie first see Mr.
   Pickens? **(b) Infer:** Why does he save Elzie from the dog?
   (c) Analyze: How does Elzie know that Mr. Pickens is a
   good man?

3. **Key Ideas and Details (a) Speculate:** Would you say that
   Elzie has been happy with her life? Support your opinion
   with examples. **(b) Synthesize:** What might Tee learn from
   her great-grandmother's story?

4. **Craft and Structure (a)** What does the great-grandmother
   believe about her lucky stone? **(b)** How can what we
   believe help us discover the truth? *[Connect to the Big
   Question: What is the best way to find the truth?]*

Reading Skill: Context Clues

Read the following lines from the story: *Well, he <u>lit out</u> after me, poor thing. He lit out after me and I flew! Round and round the Silas Greene we run . . . but now that dancing dog was a runnin dog. . . .*

1. What is a possible meaning for *lit out*?

2. What **context clues** suggest this meaning?

Literary Analysis: Point of View

3. Craft and Structure Using a chart like the one shown, give two examples from Elzie's story in which she shares her thoughts or feelings about a situation.

Situation	Thoughts or Feelings

4. Craft and Structure **(a)** How might Elzie's story be different if it were told from a limited third-person **point of view?** **(b)** How might this different point of view affect the theme?

Vocabulary

Acquisition and Use An **analogy** shows a relationship between a pair of words. Use a word from the vocabulary list on page 60 to complete each analogy. Your choice should make a word pair that matches the relationship between the first two words.

1. *Harmed* is to *hurt* as _____ is to *known*.

2. *Thread* is to *sewing* as _____ is to *tying*.

3. *Shy* is to *bashful* as *saw* is to _____.

4. *Front* is to *fore* as *rear* is to _____.

5. *Comedians* are to *funny* as _____ are to *exciting*.

6. *Trousers* are to *pleated* as *hair* is to _____.

Word Study Use what you know about the **Latin prefix ac-** to explain your answer to each question.

1. Would a car collector want to *acquire* a convertible?

2. Would you *accelerate* to go faster?

Word Study

The **Latin prefix ac-** means "motion toward," "addition to," or "nearness to."

Apply It Explain how the prefix *ac-* contributes to the meanings of these words. Consult a dictionary if necessary.
accept
accessible
accumulate

Integrated Language Skills

An American Childhood •
The Luckiest Time of All

Conventions: Possessive Nouns

Possessive nouns show ownership. Possessives are formed in different ways for plural and singular nouns.

Singular noun: add an apostrophe and *-s*
Plural noun that ends in *-s*: add an apostrophe
Plural noun not ending in *-s*: add an apostrophe and *-s*

Type of Noun	Rule	Example
Singular: player	Add apostrophe and *-s*.	The player's bat.
Singular ending in *-s*: Jones	Add apostrophe and *-s*.	The Jones's farm.
Plural that ends in *-s*: bees	Add apostrophe.	The bees' buzzing.
Plural that does not end in *-s*: children	Add apostrophe and *-s*.	The children's toys.

Practice A Identify the correct possessive form in each sentence.

1. The (narrators'/narrator's) friends joined her outside one snowy morning.
2. They made snowballs and threw them at a young (mans'/man's) windshield.
3. The (snowballs'/snowballs's) impact startled the driver.
4. The man chased the children through their (neighbors'/neighbor's) yards.

ⓒ **Reading Application** Find two sentences containing possessive nouns in the excerpt from *An American Childhood*.

Practice B Rewrite each of the following using the possessive form.

1. the story of Elzie Pickens
2. the great-grandmother of Sweet Tee
3. the decision of the girls to join the circus
4. the Sunday school pin of Ovella
5. the stone that Great-grandmother carried
6. the performance of the dancing dog
7. the laughter of the people

ⓒ **Writing Application** Write a sentence about each photograph on pages 62–66. Use at least one possessive noun in each sentence.

PH WRITING COACH | Further instruction and practice are available in *Prentice Hall Writing Coach*.

Writing

Explanatory Text In the excerpt from *An American Childhood,* Annie Dillard uses **hyperbole,** an exaggeration for effect. Describing a chase, she says: "We could have run through every backyard in North America until we got to Panama." Lucille Clifton also uses hyperbole in "The Luckiest Time of All," when Elzie Pickens describes Mr. Pickens as "the finest fast runnin hero in the bottoms of Virginia."

Choose one of the following options to write a **description** that contains hyperbole. Use precise language to create a strong impression.

- Think of an extreme circumstance or situation. For example, to describe being very cold, you might write, "I felt as if my blood was frozen solid in my veins. If I had cut myself, I would have bled icicles."

- Think of a strong quality or skill a person could have. For example, to describe someone very smart, you might write, "She knew more than all the professors at the university. She had answers to questions that had not even been thought of yet."

Grammar Application Check your writing to be sure you have correctly punctuated all possessive nouns.

Writing Workshop: *Work in Progress*

Prewriting for Description Revise the details of your Place List from your writing portfolio. Look at the words you used to describe sensory images. If you wrote "the place smells bad," revise to use a more descriptive word or phrase, such as *sickening*, *musty*, or *sour*. Save this Descriptive Word List in your writing portfolio.

Research and Technology

Build and Present Knowledge Use the Internet and library resources to research the life of Annie Dillard or Lucille Clifton. Consult multiple sources to answer the questions below, as well as other questions you may have.

- What was the author's childhood like?

- What were major events in her life?

- What are the highlights of her writing career?

Use note cards as you research to jot down your findings. Then, present a **biographical report** to the class that includes visuals. Using a word processing program will allow you to use special fonts for headings and subheadings.

Common Core State Standards

L.7.5.b; W.7.2.d; W.7.7
[For the full wording of the standards, see page 48.]

Use this prewriting activity to prepare for the **Writing Workshop** on page 92.

PHLit Online!
www.PHLitOnline.com

- Interactive graphic organizers
- Grammar tutorial
- Interactive journals

Test Practice: Reading

Context Clues

Fiction Selection

Directions: *Read the selection. Then, answer the questions.*

After we toured the Egyptian wing at the museum, my Aunt Margaret and I <u>browsed</u> in the gift shop. I had only planned to look, but I found the perfect birthday gift for my mother. It was a <u>replica</u> of a piece of jewelry that was found when King Tut's tomb was discovered. My mother is very interested in archaeology and the Egyptian <u>antiquities</u> found in King Tut's tomb. I really wanted to buy the necklace for her, but then I remembered that my aunt was with me. I did not know if I could trust her to keep my gift a secret. But I overcame my <u>hesitation</u> after my aunt promised to keep quiet. "My lips are <u>sealed</u>, Megan," she said. "I will not tell a soul."

1. What does the word *browsed* mean in this passage?
   A. opened things
   B. looked over things
   C. bought things
   D. tested things

2. What context clue helps you clarify the meaning of *browsed*?
   A. we toured the Egyptian wing
   B. my Aunt Margaret and I
   C. I had only planned to look
   D. the perfect birthday gift

3. What does the word *antiquities* mean?
   A. ancient objects
   B. the act of digging up
   C. newly-made jewelry
   D. the rooms inside a tomb

4. What is the meaning of the word *hesitation*?
   A. excitement
   B. uncertainty
   C. fear
   D. anger

5. In the passage, which words do *not* help you understand the expression *my lips are sealed*?
   A. keep my gift a secret
   B. overcame my hesitation
   C. promised to keep quiet
   D. will not tell a soul

Writing for Assessment

Write a paragraph of your own in which you correctly use two of the words from this selection. As you write, build in context clues to help readers figure out the meanings of those words.

Nonfiction Selection

Directions: *Read the selection. Then, answer the questions.*

In 1922, an Egyptologist named Howard Carter discovered a buried staircase that led to a <u>sealed</u> tomb. When the tomb was opened, Carter found fantastic treasures—items made of gold, <u>alabaster</u>, ebony, and precious stones. It was the greatest collection of Egyptian artifacts ever discovered. The mummified body of King Tutankhamen, the 18-year-old Egyptian boy king, had been buried with jewelry and other items that indicated his importance. He had clearly been of <u>noble</u> birth. Many people had tried to find the tomb of King Tutankhamen, also known as King Tut, but Carter was the first to discover the tomb. It was no easy task. Carter searched for almost eight years before he and his crew discovered the boy king's final resting place.

1. What does the word *sealed* mean in the context of this selection?
- **A.** open
- **B.** missing
- **C.** tightly closed
- **D.** damp

2. What context clue helps you clarify the meaning of *sealed*?
- **A.** a buried staircase
- **B.** when the tomb was opened
- **C.** Howard Carter discovered a buried staircase
- **D.** Carter found fantastic treasures

3. Which phrase helps you clarify the meaning of the word *noble*?
- **A.** mummified body
- **B.** Egyptian boy king
- **C.** buried staircase
- **D.** fantastic treasures

4. In the selection, which word does *not* hint at the meaning of *alabaster*?
- **A.** gold
- **B.** treasures
- **C.** precious
- **D.** opened

Writing for Assessment

Connecting Across Texts
Explain how the meaning of the word *sealed* differs in each passage. Write a brief paragraph, using details from both passages to support your answer.

• Online practice
• Instant feedback

Reading for Information

Analyzing Functional and Expository Texts

Atlas Entry

Public Document

Common Core State Standards

Reading Informational Text
5. Analyze the structure an author uses to organize a text, including how the major sections contribute to the whole and to the development of the ideas.

Language
4.a. Use context as a clue to the meaning of a word or phrase.

Writing
10. Write routinely over extended time frames and shorter time frames for a range of discipline-specific tasks, purposes, and audiences.

Reading Skill: Locate Types of Information

When you read informational texts, such as consumer, workplace, and public documents, use structural features to **locate specific types of information**. Features such as headings can help you to quickly find information about a particular subject. Captions for photographs and other graphic elements can help you to find information that is provided visually. As you read, remember that you can locate useful information both in the body of the text and in supporting visuals. This chart shows some features that will help you locate information in atlases and public documents.

Features in Atlases	Features in Public Documents
• headings • bold print • map keys or legends • captions for graphs	• headings • images and captions • direct quotations

Content-Area Vocabulary

These words appear in the selections that follow. You may also encounter them in other content-area texts.

- **industrial** (in dus´ trē əl) *adj.* having highly developed forms of business, trade, or manufacture

- **decipher** (di sī´ fər) *v.* make out the meaning of

- **interrogations** (in ter´ə gā´ shənz) *n.* formal examinations that involve questioning the subject

EAST ASIA

China, Mongolia, Taiwan

China is the world's third-largest country and its most populous—over one billion people live there. Under its communist government, which came to power in 1949, China has became a major **industrial** nation, but most of its people still live and work on the land as they have for thousands of years. Taiwan also has a booming economy and exports its products around the world. Mongolia is a vast, remote country with a small population, many of whom are nomads.

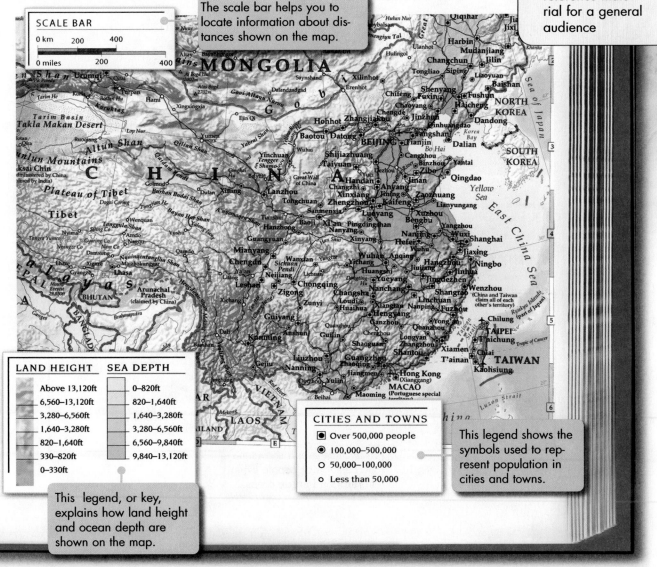

The scale bar helps you to locate information about distances shown on the map.

SCALE BAR

| 0 km | 200 | 400 |

| 0 miles | 200 | 400 |

LAND HEIGHT

	Above 13,120ft
	6,560–13,120ft
	3,280–6,560ft
	1,640–3,280ft
	820–1,640ft
	330–820ft
	0–330ft

SEA DEPTH

	0–820ft
	820–1,640ft
	1,640–3,280ft
	3,280–6,560ft
	6,560–9,840ft
	9,840–13,120ft

This legend, or key, explains how land height and ocean depth are shown on the map.

CITIES AND TOWNS

◉	Over 500,000 people
◉	100,000–500,000
○	50,000–100,000
∘	Less than 50,000

This legend shows the symbols used to represent population in cities and towns.

Population

Most of China's people live in the eastern part of the country, where climate, landscape, and soils are most favorable. Urban areas there house more than 250 million people, but almost 75% of the population lives in villages and farms the land. Taiwan's lowlands are very densely populated. In Mongolia, about 50% of the people live in the countryside.

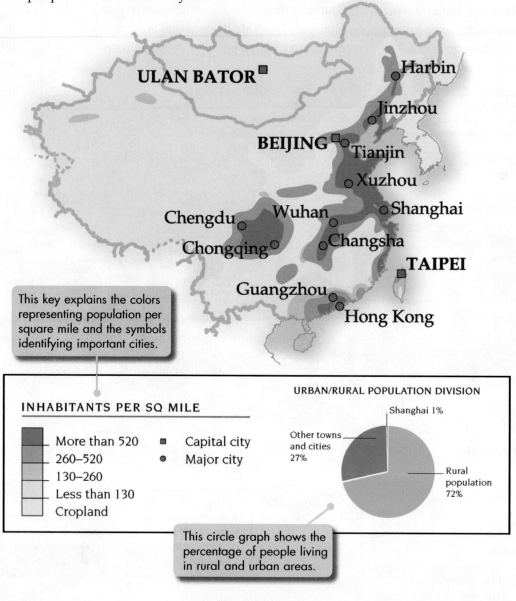

ULAN BATOR

Harbin

Jinzhou

BEIJING
Tianjin

Xuzhou

Chengdu
Wuhan
Shanghai

Chongqing
Changsha

TAIPEI

Guangzhou

Hong Kong

This key explains the colors representing population per square mile and the symbols identifying important cities.

INHABITANTS PER SQ MILE

- More than 520
- 260–520
- 130–260
- Less than 130
- Cropland

- ■ Capital city
- ● Major city

URBAN/RURAL POPULATION DIVISION

Shanghai 1%

Other towns and cities 27%

Rural population 72%

This circle graph shows the percentage of people living in rural and urban areas.

The Statue of Liberty - Ellis Island Foundation, Inc.

Byron Yee: Discovering a Paper Son

For actor Byron Yee, family history provides the inspiration for his one-man show. "My name is Byron Yee. I am the second son of Bing Quai Yee. I am the son of a paper son.

"My father was an immigrant. He came to America to escape the Japanese invasion of China in 1938. He was 15 years old and he didn't know a word of English. He didn't have a penny in his pocket and he was living in a crowded apartment in New York City with relatives he had never met. I know nothing about my father's history, about his past."

Most Chinese immigrants came through Angel Island in San Francisco Bay.

This photo shows where Byron Yee first searched for his father's immigration records.

With little to go on, Byron set out to **decipher** his father's story. He started at Angel Island, located in the middle of San Francisco Bay. "Angel Island has been called the Ellis Island of the West and for the most part, all the Chinese who came to the United States came through here, from a period of 1910 to 1940. But the rules were a little bit different. European settlers, Russian settlers were processed within an hour. The Japanese were kept for one day. But the Chinese were detained anywhere from three weeks to two years for their **interrogations**. So this was not so much the Ellis Island of the West for the Chinese; it was more like Alcatraz."

In 1882, Congress passed a law prohibiting Chinese laborers from immigrating to the United States. The Chinese Exclusion Act was the only immigration law ever based on race alone. But people found ways around the act: US law states that children of American citizens are automatically granted citizenship themselves, no matter where they were born. Taking advantage of that opening, some immigrants claimed to be legitimate offspring of U.S. citizens when in fact they were not. These individuals, mostly male, were called paper sons.

Byron's next step was to find his father's immigration file. The National Archives regional office in San Bruno, California contains thousands of files related to Angel Island. While Byron did not find his father's records there, he did find those of his grandfather, Yee Wee Thing. In one of the documents in his grandfather's file, Byron found a cross reference to his father, Yee Bing Quai. To avoid the scrutiny of Angel Island, Byron's father had sailed through Boston. Byron found his file at the National Archives in Massachusetts.

The Chinese Exclusion Act prohibited the immigration of Chinese laborers.

This caption highlights a key fact provided in the text.

"My father at 15. He is asked 197 questions: 'When did your alleged father first come to the United States?' 'Have you ever seen a photograph of your alleged father?' 'How many trips to China has your alleged father made since first coming to the United States?'" The lengthy interrogation made Byron suspect that his father was in fact a paper son. Maybe this was why he never knew his father's story.

Though Byron's mother knew very little about her husband's past, she did have an old photo, which she sent to Byron—a portrait of his father's family back in China. Byron learned that the baby on the left was his father. The boy in the middle was Yee Wee Thing, not Byron's grandfather at all, but his uncle.

"It kind of floored me because all of a sudden it made a lot of sense—why he was the way he was, why he never really talked about his past, why he was very secretive. It explained a lot about him and about his history.

"You see my story is no different from anyone else's. . . In all of our collective past, we've all had that one ancestor that had the strength to break from what was familiar to venture into the unknown. I can never thank my father and uncle enough for what they had to do so that I could be here today. One wrong answer between them and I would not be here."

Comparing Functional and Expository Texts

Ⓒ **1. Key Ideas and Details (a)** Which text presents more information in the form of visual elements? **(b)** Which text presents more information through quotations? **(c)** How do visuals and quotations each help you to understand a topic? Explain.

Content-Area Vocabulary

2. (a) Explain how context clues in the selections suggest the meanings of *industrial, decipher,* and *interrogations.* **(b)** Use each word in a sentence that shows its meaning.

⏱ Timed Writing

Informative Text: Letter

> **Format and Audience**
> The prompt gives instructions to write a letter. Because the letter will be addressed to family members, it can be informal.

Write a letter from the perspective of a "paper son," like Byron Yee's father, arriving in America for the first time. Write to your family and describe your experiences. Use the public document you have read to add details to your letter. (15 minutes)

> **Academic Vocabulary**
> When you *describe* something, you use words that appeal to the senses to create a vivid picture in your reader's mind.

5-Minute Planner

Complete these steps before you begin to write:

1. Read the prompt carefully and completely. Notice key words like the ones highlighted.

2. Reread the public document to locate information related to the assignment. Look for details that help you understand the experience of Chinese immigrants arriving in America during the early twentieth century. **TIP:** Quotations in public documents often include detailed information about people's experiences.

3. Make a list of the people, places, events, and experiences that you want to describe in your letter. Next to each, jot down a few details you can provide in your description, based on text information and on your own imagination.

4. Refer to your list as you draft your letter.

Comparing Fiction and Nonfiction

Fiction is prose writing that tells about imaginary characters and events. Novels, novellas, and short stories are types of fiction. **Literary nonfiction** is prose writing that tells about real people, places, objects, or events. Biographies, memoirs, and historical accounts are types of nonfiction.

While one is fiction and the other nonfiction, the selections here are both examples of **narrative writing** that include the following elements:

- a *narrator* who tells the story
- *characters,* or people living the story
- *dialogue,* or the conversations that the characters have
- story *events* that make up the action
- a *theme* or *central idea*

These elements work together to develop the narratives. For example, both writers use dialogue to convey the impact that a specific event or situation has upon the characters.

Narrators are another important element of fiction and literary nonfiction. The narrator in the excerpt from *Barrio Boy* tells about an important real event in the writer's life. In contrast, the narrator in "A Day's Wait" tells the story of an imagined boy on a single day. As you read, use a chart like the one shown to note ways in which the elements and features of the works are similar and different.

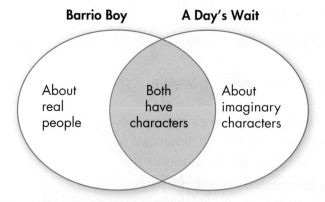

Barrio Boy   **A Day's Wait**

About real people

Both have characters

About imaginary characters

Common Core
State Standards

Reading Literature
3. Analyze how particular elements of a story or drama interact.

Reading Informational Texts
3. Analyze the interactions between individuals, events, and ideas in a text.

Writing
2.a. Introduce a topic clearly, previewing what is to follow; organize ideas, concepts, and information, using strategies such as definition, classification, comparison/contrast, and cause/ effect; include formatting, graphics, and multimedia when useful to aiding comprehension.

PHLit Online!
www.PHLitOnline.com

- Vocabulary flashcards
- Interactive journals
- More about the authors
- Selection audio
- Interactive graphic organizers

What is the best way to find the *truth?*

Writing About the Big Question

In each of these narratives, a boy faces a situation—real or imagined—that he perceives as frightening. Use this sentence starter to develop your ideas.

When something is **explained** to us, it makes us less afraid because _____.

Meet the Authors

Ernesto Galarza (1905–1984)

Author of "Barrio Boy"

When he was seven years old, Ernesto Galarza moved from Mexico to California. There, his family harvested crops in the fields of Sacramento and struggled to make ends meet. Galarza learned English quickly and won a scholarship for college.

Helping Farm Workers From 1936 to 1947, Galarza served as chief of the Division of Labor and Social Information for the Pan-American Union, dealing with education and labor in Latin America. When he returned to California, he worked to gain rights for farm workers.

Ernest Hemingway (1899–1961)

Author of "A Day's Wait"

A true adventurer, Ernest Hemingway based much of his writing on his own experiences. He served as an ambulance driver in World War I, worked as a journalist, traveled the world, and enjoyed outdoor sports.

Writing About the Familiar Hemingway's fiction celebrates his spirit of adventure. The story "A Day's Wait" captures the quiet bravery of many of his characters.

from Barrio Boy

Ernesto Galarza

My mother and I walked south on Fifth Street one morning to the corner of Q Street and turned right. Half of the block was occupied by the Lincoln School. It was a three-story wooden building, with two wings that gave it the shape of a double-T connected by a central hall. It was a new building, painted yellow, with a shingled roof that was not like the red tile of the school in Mazatlán. I noticed other differences, none of them very reassuring. We walked up the wide staircase hand in hand and through the door, which closed by itself. A mechanical contraption screwed to the top shut it behind us quietly.

Up to this point the adventure of enrolling me in the school had been carefully rehearsed. Mrs. Dodson had told us how to find it and we had circled it several times on our walks. Friends in the barrio[1] explained that the director was called a principal, and that it was a lady and not a man. They assured us that there was always a person at the school who could speak Spanish.

Exactly as we had been told, there was a sign on the door in both Spanish and English: "Principal." We crossed the hall and entered the office of Miss Nettie Hopley.

Miss Hopley was at a roll-top desk to one side, sitting in a swivel chair that moved on wheels. There was a sofa against the opposite wall, flanked by two windows and a door that opened on a small balcony. Chairs were set around a table and framed pictures hung on the walls of a man with long white hair and another with a sad face and a black beard.

The principal half turned in the swivel chair to look at us

---

1. barrio (bär´ ē ō) *n.* part of a town or city where most of the people are Hispanic.

over the pinch glasses crossed on the ridge of her nose. To do this she had to duck her head slightly as if she were about to step through a low doorway.

What Miss Hopley said to us we did not know but we saw in her eyes a warm welcome and when she took off her glasses and straightened up she smiled wholeheartedly, like Mrs. Dodson. We were, of course, saying nothing, only catching the friendliness of her voice and the sparkle in her eyes while she said words we did not understand. She signaled us to the table. Almost tiptoeing across the office, I maneuvered myself to keep my mother between me and the gringo lady. In a matter of seconds I had to decide whether she was a possible friend or a menace.[2] We sat down.

Then Miss Hopley did a formidable thing. She stood up. Had she been standing when we entered she would have seemed tall. But rising from her chair she soared. And what she carried up and up with her was a buxom superstructure,[3] firm shoulders, a straight sharp nose, full cheeks slightly molded by a curved line along the nostrils, thin lips that moved like steel springs, and a high forehead topped by hair gathered in a bun. Miss Hopley was not a giant in body but when she mobilized[4] it to a standing position she seemed

---

2. **menace** (men′ əs) *n.* danger; threat.
3. **buxom superstructure** full figure.
4. **mobilized** (mō′ bə līzd′) *v.* put into motion.

a match for giants. I decided I liked her.

She strode to a door in the far corner of the office, opened it and called a name. A boy of about ten years appeared in the doorway. He sat down at one end of the table. He was brown like us, a plump kid with shiny black hair combed straight back, neat, cool, and faintly obnoxious.

Miss Hopley joined us with a large book and some papers in her hand. She, too, sat down and the questions and answers began by way of our interpreter. My name was Ernesto. My mother's name was Henriqueta. My birth certificate was in San Blas. Here was my last report card from the Escuela Municipal Numero 3 para Varones of Mazatlán,[5] and so forth. Miss Hopley put things down in the book and my mother signed a card.

As long as the questions continued, Doña[6] Henriqueta could stay and I was secure. Now that they were over, Miss Hopley saw her to the door, dismissed our interpreter and without further ado took me by the hand and strode down the hall to Miss Ryan's first grade. Miss Ryan took me to a seat at the front of the room, into which I shrank—the better to survey her. She was, to skinny, somewhat runty me, of a withering height when she patrolled the class. And when I least expected it, there she was, crouching by my desk, her blond radiant face level with mine, her voice patiently maneuvering me over the awful idiocies of the English language.

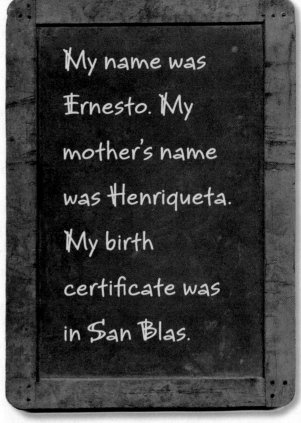

During the next few weeks Miss Ryan overcame my fears of tall, energetic teachers as she bent over my desk to help me with a word in the pre-primer. Step by step, she loosened me and my classmates from the safe anchorage of the desks for recitations at the blackboard and consultations at her desk. Frequently she burst into happy announcements to the whole class. "Ito can read a sentence," and small Japanese Ito, squint-eyed and shy, slowly read aloud while the class listened in wonder: "Come, Skipper, come. Come and run." The Korean, Portuguese, Italian, and

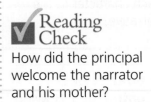

Reading Check

How did the principal welcome the narrator and his mother?

---

5. **Escuela Municipal Numero 3 para Varones of Mazatlán** (es kwä lä mōō nē sē päl′ nōō′ me rō träs pä′ rä bä rō′ nes mä sät län′) Municipal School Number 3 for Boys of Mazatlán.

6. **Doña** (dō′ nyä) Spanish title of respect meaning "lady" or "madam."

from Barrio Boy **83**

Polish first graders had similar moments of glory, no less shining than mine the day I conquered "butterfly," which I had been persistently pronouncing in standard Spanish as boo-ter-flee. "Children," Miss Ryan called for attention. "Ernesto has learned how to pronounce *butterfly*!" And I proved it with a perfect imitation of Miss Ryan. From that celebrated success, I was soon able to match Ito's progress as a sentence reader with "Come, butterfly, come fly with me."

Like Ito and several other first graders who did not know English, I received private lessons from Miss Ryan in the closet, a narrow hall off the classroom with a door at each end. Next to one of these doors Miss Ryan placed a large chair for herself and a small one for me. Keeping an eye on the class through the open door she read with me about sheep in the meadow and a frightened chicken going to see the king, coaching me out of my phonetic ruts in words like *pasture, bow-wow-wow, hay,* and *pretty,* which to my Mexican ear and eye had so many unnecessary sounds and letters. She made me watch her lips and then close my eyes as she repeated words I found hard to read. When we came to know each other better, I tried interrupting to tell Miss Ryan how we said it in Spanish. It didn't work. She only said "oh" and went on with *pasture, bow-wow-wow,* and *pretty.* It was as if in that closet we were both discovering together the secrets of the English language and grieving together over the tragedies of Bo-Peep. The main reason I was graduated with honors from the first grade was that I had fallen in love with Miss Ryan. Her radiant, no-nonsense character made us either afraid not to love her or love her so we would not be afraid, I am not sure which. It was not only that we sensed she was with it, but also that she was with us. Like the first grade, the rest of the Lincoln School was a sampling of the lower part of town where many races made their home. My pals in the second grade were Kazushi, whose parents spoke only Japanese; Matti, a skinny Italian boy; and Manuel, a fat Portuguese who would never get into a fight but wrestled you to the ground and just sat on you. Our assortment of nationalities included Koreans, Yugoslavs, Poles, Irish, and home-grown Americans.

At Lincoln, making us into Americans did not mean scrubbing away what made us originally foreign. The teachers called us as our parents did, or as close as they could pronounce our names in Spanish or Japanese. No one was ever scolded or punished for speaking in his native tongue on

Nonfiction
What details in this section help you appreciate the importance of the author's actual experience?

Nonfiction
What details in this passage tell about each character in the narrative?

Ⓒ
Spiral Review
Central Idea How do Galarza's memories of Lincoln School relate to a central idea?

the playground. Matti told the class about his mother's down quilt, which she had made in Italy with the fine feathers of a thousand geese. Encarnación acted out how boys learned to fish in the Philippines. I astounded the third grade with the story of my travels on a stagecoach, which nobody else in the class had seen except in the museum at Sutter's Fort. After a visit to the Crocker Art Gallery and its collection of heroic paintings of the golden age of California, someone showed a silk scroll with a Chinese painting. Miss Hopley herself had a way of expressing wonder over these matters before a class, her eyes wide open until they popped slightly. It was easy for me to feel that becoming a proud American, as she said we should, did not mean feeling ashamed of being a Mexican.

▲ **Critical Viewing**
What do you think it would be like to travel in a stagecoach like the one in this picture? **[Speculate]**

Critical Thinking

1. **Key Ideas and Details Summarize:** Describe Galarza's experiences as a newcomer in school.

2. **Key Ideas and Details (a)** Why is Galarza afraid of Miss Ryan at first? **(b) Interpret:** What does Galarza mean when he says Miss Ryan "was with it" and "with us"?

3. **Integration of Knowledge and Ideas Analyze:** What experiences in Lincoln School help Galarza realize his dream of "becoming a proud American"?

4. **Integration of Knowledge and Ideas (a)** What is the unknown that frightens Galarza in this story? **(b)** How does Galarza use his experience at school to discover the truth about those around him? *[Connect to the Big Question: What is the best way to find the truth?]*

Cite textual evidence to support your responses.

▲ **Critical Viewing**
Describe how you think
the boy in this picture
might feel. **[Connect]**

He came into the room to shut the windows while we were still in bed and I saw he looked ill. He was shivering, his face was white, and he walked slowly as though it ached to move.

"What's the matter, Schatz[1]?"

"I've got a headache."

"You better go back to bed."

"No. I'm all right."

"You go to bed. I'll see you when I'm dressed."

But when I came downstairs he was dressed, sitting by the fire, looking a very sick and miserable boy of nine years. When I put my hand on his forehead I knew he had a fever.

"You go up to bed," I said, "you're sick."

"I'm all right," he said.

When the doctor came he took the boy's temperature.

"What is it?" I asked him.

"One hundred and two."

Downstairs, the doctor left three different medicines in different colored capsules with instructions for giving them. One was to bring down the fever, another a purgative, the

---

1. Schatz (shäts) German term of affection, used here as a loving nickname.

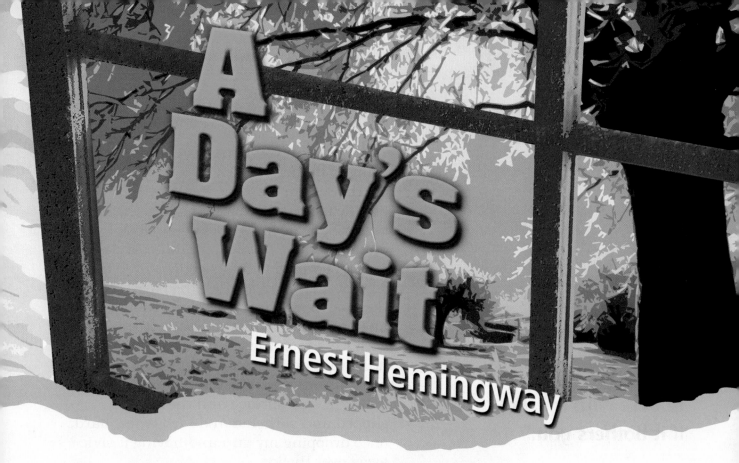

A Day's Wait
Ernest Hemingway

third to overcome an acid condition. The germs of influenza can only exist in an acid condition, he explained. He seemed to know all about influenza and said there was nothing to worry about if the fever did not go above one hundred and four degrees. This was a light epidemic of flu and there was no danger if you avoided pneumonia.

Back in the room I wrote the boy's temperature down and made a note of the time to give the various capsules.

"Do you want me to read to you?"

"All right. If you want to," said the boy. His face was very white and there were dark areas under his eyes. He lay still in the bed and seemed very detached from what was going on.

I read aloud from Howard Pyle's *Book of Pirates*; but I could see he was not following what I was reading.

"How do you feel, Schatz?" I asked him.

"Just the same, so far," he said.

I sat at the foot of the bed and read to myself while I waited for it to be time to give another capsule. It would have been natural for him to go to sleep, but when I looked up he was looking at the foot of the bed, looking very strangely.

"Why don't you try to go to sleep? I'll wake you up for the medicine."

Vocabulary
epidemic (ep´ ə dem´ ik)
n. outbreak of a contagious disease

"You don't have to stay in here with me, Papa, if it bothers you."

Vocabulary
flushed (flusht) *v.*
drove from hiding

Fiction
Who is the narrator of this work? How do you know?

"I'd rather stay awake."

After a while he said to me, "You don't have to stay in here with me, Papa, if it bothers you."

"It doesn't bother me."

"No. I mean you don't have to stay if it's going to bother you."

I thought perhaps he was a little lightheaded and after giving him the prescribed capsules at eleven o'clock I went out for a while. It was a bright, cold day, the ground covered with a sleet that had frozen so that it seemed as if all the bare trees, the bushes, the cut brush and all the grass and the bare ground had been varnished with ice. I took the young Irish setter for a little walk up the road and along a frozen creek, but it was difficult to stand or walk on the glassy surface and the red dog slipped and slithered and I fell twice, hard, once dropping my gun and having it slide away over the ice.

We flushed a covey of quail under a high clay bank with overhanging brush and I killed two as they went out of sight over the top of the bank. Some of the covey lit in trees but most of them scattered into brush piles and it was necessary to jump on the ice-coated mounds of brush several times before they would flush. Coming out while you were poised unsteadily on the icy, springy brush they made difficult shooting, and I killed two, missed five, and started back pleased to have found a covey close to the house and happy there were so many left to find on another day.

At the house they said the boy had refused to let anyone come into the room.

"You can't come in," he said. "You mustn't get what I have."

I went up to him and found him in exactly the position I had left him, white-faced, but with the tops of his cheeks flushed by the fever, staring still, as he had stared at the foot of the bed.

I took his temperature.

"What is it?"

"Something like a hundred," I said. It was one hundred and two and four tenths.

"It was a hundred and two," he said.

"Who said so?"

"The doctor."

"Your temperature is all right," I said. "It's nothing to worry about."

"I don't worry," he said, "but I can't keep from thinking."

"Don't think," I said. "Just take it easy."

"I'm taking it easy," he said and looked straight ahead. He was evidently holding tight on to himself about something.

"Take this with water."

"Do you think it will do any good?"

"Of course it will."

I sat down and opened the *Pirate* book and commenced to read, but I could see he was not following, so I stopped.

"About what time do you think I'm going to die?" he asked.

"What?"

"About how long will it be before I die?"

"You aren't going to die. What's the matter with you?"

"Oh, yes, I am. I heard him say a hundred and two."

LITERATURE IN CONTEXT

Science Connection

Temperature Scales
You might have been taught that ice and snow melt when the temperature is 32°F, or Fahrenheit. Another commonly known temperature is 98.6°F—normal body temperature. Using the Celsius scale is another matter. Water freezes at 0° Celsius, or C, and boils at 100°C.

When temperature is expressed one way and must be converted to the other, there are formulas or conversion charts to help. Today, only the United States and Jamaica still use Fahrenheit as the standard for most measurements.

Connect to the Literature

Why is the boy's temperature important to him and his father?

Vocabulary
evidently (ev´ ə dent´ lē) *adv.* clearly; obviously

Reading
Check

How does the boy know his temperature?

"People don't die with a fever of one hundred and two. That's a silly way to talk."

"I know they do. At school in France the boys told me you can't live with forty-four degrees. I've got a hundred and two."

He had been waiting to die all day, ever since nine o'clock in the morning.

"You poor Schatz," I said. "Poor old Schatz. It's like miles and kilometers. You aren't going to die. That's a different thermometer. On that thermometer thirty-seven is normal. On this kind it's ninety-eight."

"Are you sure?"

"Absolutely," I said. "It's like miles and kilometers. You know, like how many kilometers we make when we do seventy miles in the car?"

"Oh," he said.

But his gaze at the foot of the bed relaxed slowly. The hold over himself relaxed too, finally, and the next day it was very slack and he cried very easily at little things that were of no importance.

> "At school in France the boys told me you can't live with forty-four degrees. I've got a hundred and two."

Spiral Review
Theme What critical information has the boy learned from this conversation with his father? How does his reaction relate to a possible theme?

Critical Thinking

Cite textual evidence to support your responses.

1. **Key Ideas and Details (a)** Why does the boy tell his father to leave the sickroom? **(b) Infer:** What does this reveal about the boy?

2. **Key Ideas and Details (a)** Why does the boy think he will die? Use details from the story to support your response. **(b) Interpret:** What is the meaning of the story's title?

3. **Key Ideas and Details (a) Analyze:** Which of the boy's words and actions give clues that he believes something terrible is wrong? **(b) Evaluate:** Do you think the story is about the boy's bravery or about the boy's fear? Explain. **(c) Speculate:** What might have happened if the boy had shared his fears?

4. **Integration of Knowledge and Ideas** When the truth of the boy's illness is explained to him, what truth has he learned about his character? *[Connect to the Big Question: What is the best way to find the truth?]*

Comparing Fiction and Nonfiction

1. Craft and Structure (a) For each selection, tell whether the narrator and events are real or imagined. **(b)** Based on your answer, what rules about truth and accuracy did each writer follow for writing these selections?

2. Key Ideas and Details Complete a chart like the one shown to help you analyze one character in each story.

Character	Detail	Fiction or Nonfiction?
The boy in "A Day's Wait"		
Miss Ryan in *Barrio Boy*		

3. Integration of Knowledge and Ideas (a) How might "A Day's Wait" be different if it were nonfiction? **(b)** How might *Barrio Boy* change if it were fiction?

⏱ Timed Writing

Explanatory Text: Essay

In a brief essay, compare and contrast the narrators of *Barrio Boy* and "A Day's Wait." State your topic in the introduction and discuss how the narrator presents the events in each work. Consider adding a chart to show what is the same and different. **(40 minutes)**

5-Minute Planner

1. Gather your ideas by jotting down answers to these questions:

   • Which work includes more personal details about the narrator?

   • How is dialogue used in each work?

   • Do the narrator's thoughts and actions build toward a specific theme or insight? Why or why not?

   • Which narrator is central to the narrative's action?

2. Choose an organizational strategy. If you use the block method, present all the details about one narrator, then all the details about the other narrator. If you use the point-by-point method, discuss one aspect of both narrators, then another aspect of both narrators, and so on.

3. Reread the prompt and then draft your essay.

Writing Workshop

Common Core State Standards

Writing

2.a. Introduce a topic clearly, previewing what is to follow; organize ideas, concepts, and information, using strategies such as definition, classification, comparison/contrast, and cause/effect.

2.d. Use precise language and domain-specific vocabulary to inform about or explain the topic.

2.e. Establish and maintain a formal style.

5. With some guidance and support from peers and adults, develop and strengthen writing as needed by planning, revising, editing, rewriting, or trying a new approach, focusing on how well purpose and audience have been addressed.

Write an Informative Text

Description: Descriptive Essay

Defining the Form A **descriptive essay** creates a picture of a person, place, thing, or event. Descriptive language engages your attention by creating vivid images that help you "see" the action. You might use descriptive language in short stories, poems, and journals.

Assignment Write a descriptive essay about a place or an event that is meaningful to you. Your essay should feature these elements:

✔ vivid *sensory details* to appeal to the five senses

✔ a *main impression* supported by each detail

✔ clear, *consistent organization*

✔ links between details and the feelings or thoughts they inspire

✔ effective *transitions*

✔ error-free writing, including *correct spelling of plural nouns*

To preview the criteria on which your descriptive essay may be judged, see the rubric on page 97.

 Writing Workshop: *Work in Progress*

Review the work you did on pages 47 and 69.

Prewriting/Planning Strategy

Use cubing to gather details. Follow these steps to "cube" your subject and uncover information that will bring your description to life for readers.

1. Describe it. Explain how it looks, sounds, feels, tastes, or smells.

2. Associate it. List feelings or stories it calls to mind.

3. Apply it. Show how your topic can be used.

4. Analyze it. Divide it into parts.

5. Compare and contrast it. Compare it with a related subject.

6. Argue for or against it. Show its good and bad points.

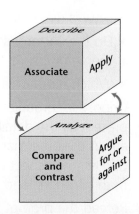

Find Your Voice

Voice describes a writer's distinctive style and can be influenced by word choice, sentence structure, and tone—the writer's attitude toward his or her subject. A professional writer usually has a distinct voice that makes his or her writing instantly recognizable. For example, think of how a jazz musician and a hip-hop artist might play "The Star-Spangled Banner" completely differently. Developing a unique voice can take time. These tips and activities will help get you started.

Learning from the Professionals Next time you are reading a descriptive passage that you enjoy, think about the writer's voice. Filling in a chart like the one shown will help you analyze voice. This chart refers to Ernest Hemingway's "A Day's Wait," which appears on pages 86–90, but you can use it for any text that you enjoy.

Word Choice	*Varnished with ice; glassy surface; covey of quail*
Sentence Structure	Long sentences; many short phrases joined together
Tone	Sentence structure makes narrator sound breathless, rushed.

Checking Your Voice As you write your descriptive essay, review your draft for word choice, sentence structure, and tone. Remember to consider your purpose and audience. Decide if your style of writing should be formal or informal. Are you happy with the voice you are using? If not, try changing some of these elements to change your voice. Ask yourself these questions:

- *Word Choice*: What kinds of words have I chosen? Have I used precise language to create a strong impression?
- *Sentence Structure*: How did I arrange the words in my sentences? What type of sentences do I typically create?
- *Tone*: How do I feel about my subject?

Then, ask a partner to read your draft and give feedback. By adjusting the elements above, you can adjust your voice. Many writers refer to this process as "finding their voice."

PH WRITING COACH

Further instruction and practice are available in *Prentice Hall Writing Coach*.

Drafting Strategies

Organize your ideas. Present your details in a pattern that will make sense to readers. Use a chart like the one shown to select a general organizational plan for your essay. Keep in mind that you may use elements of more than one plan as you write. For example, you may use chronological order as your *overall* organization to describe an event. You may also use elements of spatial order to describe the setting.

Spatial Order	Chronological Order	Order of Importance
If you are writing about a place or object, use a form of spatial order, such as near to far, left to right, front to back, or bottom to top.	If you are describing an event, present details in the order they happen.	If you are describing to show the significance of your subject, begin with your least important details and build up to the most important.

Elaborate to create a main impression. Set a mood or use an idea to unify your essay. For example, you might create a feeling of suspense, a calm atmosphere, or a flurry of activity. Include sensory details that support and strengthen this overall impression.

Revising Strategies

Revise for organization and transition. Review your draft with a partner to find places you can improve the organization of your composition in order to fit your purpose and audience. Add transition words and phrases to show the connections between details and ideas.

Revise word choice. Highlight vague or empty adjectives like *nice* and *good*, which do not add information to your description. Then, use a print or digital **thesaurus** to help you find words that have the same basic meaning but are more precise.

Vague Adjective: A *bad* wind blew.
Precise Adjective: A *ferocious* wind blew.

Vague Adverb: He sang *well*.
Precise Adverb: He sang *angelically*.

Revising Incorrect Forms of Plural Nouns

The plural form of a noun indicates that more than one person, place, or thing is named. Plural forms are either regular or irregular.

Identifying Incorrect Forms of Plural Nouns To identify and fix incorrect forms of plural nouns, you must first know how to create plural nouns. Regular nouns form their plurals by adding -s or -es.

Regular Plural Nouns

Singular:	bus	monkey	radio
Plural:	bus**es**	monkey**s**	radio**s**

Sometimes the singular and plural forms of a noun are the same.

Irregular Plural Nouns

Singular:	ox	goose	woman	mouse	deer	clothes
Plural:	oxen	geese	women	mice	deer	clothes

Forming Regular Plural Nouns	
Word Ending	**Rule**
-o or -y preceded by a vowel -ff	Add -s
-s, -ss, -x, -z, -zz, -sh, -ch -o preceded by a consonant	Add -es (exceptions: solo and other musical terms)
-y preceded by a consonant	Change y to i and add -es
-fe	Change f to v and add -es
-f	Add -s OR change f to v and add -es

PH WRITING COACH

Further instruction and practice are available in *Prentice Hall Writing Coach*.

Fixing Incorrect Forms of Plural Nouns To fix an incorrect form of a plural noun, verify the spelling using one of these methods:

1. **Review the rules for forming regular plural nouns.** First, write the singular form of the noun and circle the last two letters. Then, find the corresponding rule in the chart.

2. **Use a dictionary to look up the correct spelling.**

Grammar in Your Writing

Choose two paragraphs in your draft and circle each plural noun. If the spelling is faulty, correct it using one of the methods described.

Common Core
State Standards

Language
2.b. Spell correctly.

Spring Into Spring

Spring is the perfect time to get outdoors and get active. The spring season brings the freshness of a new beginning. If you've been cooped up all winter, the perfect start to spring is a brisk walk. If you walk during the day, you will feel the sunshine warming up the pavement; a breeze may ruffle your hair; you'll hear the songs of birds that you'd almost forgotten about over the winter. If you walk in the early evening, in the purple-gray dusk, you may even hear the "spring peepers," little frogs that become suddenly vocal around April. You might mistake them for crickets, because they have that same high-pitched monotonous chirping sound, but peepers are more shrill and persistent. Any one of these sensations by itself is enough to raise a little hope that winter is over. If you're lucky enough to experience them all at once on your first spring walk, you'll feel uplifted and energized by the knowledge that soon that stuffy old winter coat can be put in storage for many months.

During the rest of the season, if you continue to walk, you will experience new additions to the spring line-up. Not long after you've heard the peepers, you'll start to smell the earth. As the ground warms up, it gives off a soft, distinct "spring-like" smell. The scent of warm earth says "spring" the way the scent of pine says "winter." Because the ground is warming up, the smell of flowers can't be far behind! The first flowers of spring, though, are more a treat for the eyes than the nose. The brilliant yellow forsythia don't have much of an aroma, but they're so bright, they don't really need one to announce their arrival! The shy hyacinth, which blooms shortly after, is not as easily spotted, but your nose will tell you that the strong perfume in the air means a hyacinth is hiding somewhere nearby. Neighbors working their gardens—some of whom you may not have seen all winter—will call a friendly hello. Everyone seems friendlier at the beginning of spring.

Later in the season, when you begin to hear the growl and grumble of lawnmowers around the neighborhood, you'll know that spring has done its work. When the grass grows tall enough to need mowing, it's time to start thinking about those summer sensations!

Sensory details about sunshine, breezes, birdsongs, and the colors of dusk appeal to the senses of touch, hearing, and sight.

Charity reinforces the overall impression of lightness and energy to contrast with the stuffy winter coat.

The description is organized in time order—new details are introduced in the order in which they appear as spring progresses.

Here, and at various points in the essay, Charity includes her feelings and reactions to what she is describing.

Transitions that indicate time help readers follow the chronological organization of the description.

Editing and Proofreading

Proofread your essay to fix errors in grammar and punctuation.

Focus on Spelling: Troublesome Words Use a dictionary to confirm the spelling of troublesome words in your essay. If you used a word-processor to draft, use the spell-check function to search for errors. Then, review each word because spell-check will not catch **homophones** such as *there* and *their*—words that are spelled correctly but have several correct spellings and meanings. Use **mnemonic devices**, or memory aids, to help you remember which spelling to use. For example, to distinguish between *there* and *their,* notice that the word that is the opposite of *here* also contains the word *here.*

Publishing and Presenting

Consider one of the following ways to share your writing.

Tape-record your essay. Read your description aloud on tape. Add sound effects or background music that reinforces the main impression of your description. Play the tape for your classmates.

Post your composition. Put your description on a class bulletin board or post it on a school Web site. Add photos or art if possible.

Reflecting on Your Writing

Writer's Journal Jot down your answer to this question:

Which strategy was most useful for creating vivid details?

Rubric for Self-Assessment

Find evidence in your writing to address each category. Then, use the rating scale to grade your work.

Spiral Review

Earlier in the unit, you learned about **common and proper nouns** (p. 46) and **possessive nouns** (p. 68). Check the capitalization of the common and proper nouns in your narrative. Review your descriptive essay to be sure you have placed apostrophes correctly in possessive nouns.

PH   WRITING COACH

Further instruction and practice are available in *Prentice Hall Writing Coach.*

Criteria	Rating Scale				
	not very				*very*
Focus: How clear is the main impression?	1	2	3	4	5
Organization: How clear and consistent is the organization?	1	2	3	4	5
Support/Elaboration: How effectively do you use sensory details in your description?	1	2	3	4	5
Style: How effective are your transitions?	1	2	3	4	5
Conventions: How correct is your grammar, especially your use of plural nouns?	1	2	3	4	5
Voice: How consistent is the style of your writing?	1	2	3	4	5

© Leveled Texts

Build your skills and improve your comprehension of fiction with texts of increasing complexity.

Read **"All Summer in a Day"** to learn about a day when the sun shines briefly on the wet, dark planet Venus.

Read **"Suzy and Leah"** to find out what happens when two girls from very different backgrounds struggle to be friends.

© Common Core State Standards

Meet these standards with either **"All Summer in a Day"** (p. 102) or **"Suzy and Leah"** (p. 114).

Reading Literature
3. Analyze how particular elements of a story or drama interact. *(Literary Analysis: Setting)*
Spiral Review: RL.7.2

Writing
2. Write informative/explanatory texts to examine a topic and convey ideas, concepts, and information through the selection, organization, and analysis of relevant content. *(Writing: News Report)*

Speaking and Listening
1.a. Come to discussions prepared, having read or researched material under study; explicitly draw on that preparation by referring to evidence on the topic, text, or issue to probe and reflect on ideas under discussion.
1.b. Follow rules for collegial discussions, track progress toward specific goals and deadlines, and define individual roles as needed. **1.c.** Pose questions that elicit elaboration and respond to others' questions and comments with relevant observations and ideas that bring the discussion back on topic as needed. **1.d.** Acknowledge new information expressed by others and, when warranted, modify their own views. *(Speaking and Listening: Discussion)*

Language
4.b. Use common, grade-appropriate Greek or Latin affixes and roots as clues to the meaning of a word. *(Vocabulary: Word Study)*

6. Acquire and use accurately grade-appropriate general academic and domain-specific words and phrases; gather vocabulary knowledge when considering a word or phrase important to comprehension or expression. *(Vocabulary: Word Study)*

Reading Skill: Author's Purpose

Fiction writers may write for a variety of **purposes.** To achieve their purpose, writers use details that entertain, teach, call readers to action, or reflect on experiences. **Recognizing details that indicate the author's purpose** can give you a rich understanding of a literary work.

Using the Strategy: Details Chart

As you read, use a **details chart** like the one below. Record details in the story that help you identify the author's purpose for writing.

Entertain	Teach	Reflect
Funny details or details that create interest	Explanations	Details that create a mood

Literary Analysis: Setting

The **setting** of a story is the time and place of the action. In this example, the details in italics help establish the story's setting:

As *night fell,* the hungry raccoons roamed the *forest* for food.

- In some stories, setting is just a backdrop. The same story events could take place in a completely different setting.

- In other stories, setting is very important. It develops a specific atmosphere or mood in the story. The setting may even relate directly to the story's central **conflict,** or problem.

As you read, notice the details and information that build the setting. Then, decide whether the time and place of the story shapes the story's characters or events.

What is the best way to find the *truth?*

RAY BRADBURY

ALL SUMMER IN A DAY

Writing About the Big Question

In "All Summer in a Day," a group of students live on a planet where it rains all the time. Only one girl remembers seeing the sun because she once lived on Earth. Use this sentence starter to develop your ideas about the Big Question.

When we have **evidence** that something exists, but others don't believe us, we can _____.

While You Read Look for ways the author shows that Margot is treated differently by the others because of what she knows.

Vocabulary

Read each word and its definition. Decide whether you know the word well, know it a little bit, or do not know it at all. After you read, see how your knowledge of each word has increased.

- **intermixed** (in´ tər mikst´) *adj.* mixed together (p. 103) *All of the puzzle pieces were intermixed. intermix v. intermixing v.*

- **slackening** (slak´ ən iŋ) *adj.* easing; becoming less active (p. 104) *The dying man's strength was slackening. slacken v. slacker n. slack adj.*

- **vital** (vīt´ 'l) *adj.* extremely important or necessary (p. 106) *Food and water are vital for survival. vitally adv. vitality n. vitamin n.*

- **tumultuously** (tōō mul´ chōō əs lē) *adv.* noisily and violently (p. 108) *The angry crows protested tumultuously. tumult n. tumultuous adj.*

- **resilient** (ri zil´ yənt) *adj.* able to spring back into shape (p. 108) *Rubber is a resilient material. resilience n. resiliency n.*

- **savored** (sā´ vərd) *v.* tasted or experienced with delight (p. 109) *Eric savored his hot fudge sundae. savor v. savory adj.*

> ### Word Study
>
> The **Latin root -vit-** or **-viv-** means "life."
>
> In this story, Margot's parents believe it is **vital,** or extremely important for her life, for Margot to return to Earth.

Author of
ALL SUMMER IN A DAY

As a boy, Ray Bradbury loved magicians, circuses, and science-fiction stories. He began writing his own imaginative tales and by age seventeen had his first story published in a magazine called *Imagination!*

A Science-Fiction Wonder In 1950, Bradbury won fame for his book of science-fiction stories called *The Martian Chronicles*. One story describes how a group of Earthlings struggle on the rainy world of Venus. Bradbury began to wonder how a child might react to the sun's brief appearance on Venus. Four years later, he answered his own question by writing "All Summer in a Day."

BACKGROUND FOR THE STORY

Venus

"All Summer in a Day" is set on Venus, the second planet from the sun. Today, we know that Venus has a surface temperature of almost 900° Fahrenheit. In 1950, when Ray Bradbury wrote this story, some scientists believed that the clouds of Venus concealed a watery world. That information may have led Bradbury to create a setting of soggy jungles and constant rain.

DID YOU KNOW?
Many of Bradbury's stories were adopted for the television series **The Twilight Zone.**

RAY BRADBURY

All Summer in a Day

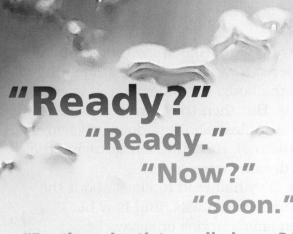

◄ **Critical Viewing**
Based on the emotion this image conveys to you, do you expect this story to be happy or sad? **[Predict]**

"Ready?"
"Ready."
"Now?"
"Soon."

"Do the scientists really know? Will it happen today, will it?"

"Look, look; see for yourself!"

The children pressed to each other like so many roses, so many weeds, intermixed, peering out for a look at the hidden sun.

It rained.

It had been raining for seven years; thousands upon thousands of days compounded and filled from one end to the other with rain, with the drum and gush of water, with the sweet crystal fall of showers and the concussion of storms so heavy they were tidal waves come over the islands. A thousand forests had been crushed under the rain and grown up a thousand times to be crushed again. And this was the way life was forever on the planet Venus and this was the schoolroom of the children of the rocket men and women who had come to a raining world to set up civilization and live out their lives.

"It's stopping, it's stopping!"

"Yes, yes!"

Margot stood apart from them, from these children who could never remember a time when there wasn't rain and rain and rain. They were all nine years old, and if there had been a day, seven years ago, when the sun came out for an hour and showed its face to the stunned world, they could not recall. Sometimes, at night, she heard them stir, in remembrance, and she knew they were dreaming and remembering gold or a yellow crayon or a coin large enough

Vocabulary
intermixed
(in´ tər mikst´) *adj.*
mixed together

Author's Purpose
List three details Bradbury provides to describe conditions on the Venus that he imagines.

Setting
How have seven years of constant rain affected the children?

✓ Reading Check
What do the children hope will happen today?

to buy the world with. She knew they thought they remembered a warmness, like a blushing in the face, in the body, in the arms and legs and trembling hands. But then they always awoke to the tatting drum, the endless shaking down of clear bead necklaces upon the roof, the walk, the gardens, the forests, and their dreams were gone.

All day yesterday they had read in class about the sun. About how like a lemon it was, and how hot. And they had written small stories or essays or poems about it:

I think the sun is a flower,
That blooms for just one hour.

That was Margot's poem, read in a quiet voice in the still classroom while the rain was falling outside.

"Aw, you didn't write that!" protested one of the boys.

"I did," said Margot. "I did."

"William!" said the teacher.

But that was yesterday. Now the rain was slackening, and the children were crushed in the great thick windows.

"Where's teacher?"

"She'll be back."

"She'd better hurry, we'll miss it!"

They turned on themselves, like a feverish wheel, all fumbling spokes.

Margot stood alone. She was a very frail girl who looked as if she had been lost in the rain for years and the rain had washed out the blue from her eyes and the red from her mouth and the yellow from her hair. She was an old photograph dusted from an album, whitened away, and if she spoke at all her voice would be a ghost. Now she stood, separate, staring at the rain and the loud wet world beyond the huge glass.

"What're you looking at?" said William.

Margot said nothing.

"Speak when you're spoken to." He gave her a shove. But she did not move; rather she let herself be moved only by him and nothing else.

They edged away from her, they would not look at her. She felt them go away. And this

Vocabulary
slackening (slak´ ən iŋ) *adj.* easing; becoming less active

◀ **Critical Viewing**
What aspects of
the story's setting
do you see in this
picture? **[Connect]**

was because she would play no games with them in the
echoing tunnels of the underground city. If they tagged her
and ran, she stood blinking after them and did not follow.
When the class sang songs about happiness and life and
games her lips barely moved. Only when they sang about the
sun and the summer did her lips move as she watched the
drenched windows. ●

And then, of course, the biggest crime of all was that
she had come here only five years ago from Earth, and she
remembered the sun and the way the sun was and the sky
was when she was four in Ohio. And they, they had been on
Venus all their lives, and they had been only two years old
when last the sun came out and had long since forgotten
the color and heat of it and the way it really was. But
Margot remembered.

"It's like a penny," she said once, eyes closed.

"No, it's not!" the children cried.

"It's like a fire," she said, "in the stove."

"You're lying, you don't remember!" cried the
children.

But she remembered and stood quietly apart from
all of them and watched the patterning windows.

Setting
How was Margot's
former home on
Earth different from
her home on Venus?
What effect does
this difference have
on Margot?

✔ Reading
Check
What is the difference
between Margot and
the other children?

THAT BLOOMS FOR JUST ONE HOUR.

Vocabulary
vital (vīt´ 'l) *adj.*
extremely important or necessary

And once, a month ago, she had refused to shower in the school shower rooms, had clutched her hands to her ears and over her head, screaming the water mustn't touch her head. So after that, dimly, dimly, she sensed it, she was different and they knew her difference and kept away. •

There was talk that her father and mother were taking her back to Earth next year; it seemed vital to her that they do so, though it would mean the loss of thousands of dollars to her family. And so, the children hated her for all these reasons of big and little consequence. They hated her pale snow face, her waiting silence, her thinness, and her possible future.

"Get away!" The boy gave her another push. "What're you waiting for?"

Then, for the first time, she turned and looked at him. And what she was waiting for was in her eyes.

"Well, don't wait around here!" cried the boy savagely. "You won't see nothing!"

Her lips moved.

"Nothing!" he cried. "It was all a joke, wasn't it?" He turned to the other children. "Nothing's happening today. Is it?"

They all blinked at him and then, understanding, laughed and shook their heads. "Nothing, nothing!"

"Oh, but," Margot whispered, her eyes helpless. "But this is the day, the scientists predict, they say, they know, the sun . . ."

"All a joke!" said the boy, and seized her roughly. "Hey, everyone, let's put her in a closet before teacher comes!"

"No," said Margot, falling back.

They surged[1] about her, caught her up and bore her, protesting, and then pleading, and then crying, back into a tunnel, a room, a closet, where they slammed and locked the door. They stood looking at the door and saw it tremble from her beating and throwing herself against it. They heard her muffled cries. Then, smiling, they turned and went out and back down the tunnel, just as the teacher arrived.

"Ready, children?" She glanced at her watch.

---

1. surged (surjd) *v.* moved in a violent swelling motion.

"Yes!" said everyone.

"Are we all here?"

"Yes!"

The rain slackened still more.

They crowded to the huge door.

The rain stopped.

It was as if, in the midst of a film concerning an avalanche, a tornado, a hurricane, a volcanic eruption, something had, first, gone wrong with the sound apparatus, thus muffling and finally cutting off all noise, all of the blasts and repercussions and thunders, and then, second, ripped the film from the projector and inserted in its place a peaceful tropical slide which did not move or tremor. The world ground to a standstill. The silence was so immense and unbelievable that you felt your ears had been stuffed or you had lost your hearing altogether. The children put their hands to their ears. They stood apart. The door slid back and the smell of the silent, waiting world came in to them.

The sun came out.

It was the color of flaming bronze and it was very large. And the sky around it was a blazing blue tile color. And the jungle burned with sunlight as the children, released from their spell, rushed out, yelling, into the springtime.

"Now, don't go too far," called the teacher after them. "You've only two hours, you know. You wouldn't want to get caught out!"

But they were running and turning their faces up to the sky and feeling the sun on their cheeks like a warm iron; they were taking off their jackets and letting the sun burn their arms.

"Oh, it's better than the sun lamps, isn't it?"

"Much, much better!"

Author's Purpose
How do the details in this paragraph affect your response to the story?

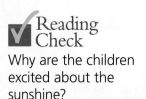

Reading Check

Why are the children excited about the sunshine?

Vocabulary
tumultuously
(to͞o mul´ cho͞o əs
lē) *adv.* noisily
and violently

resilient
(ri zil´ yənt) *adj.* able
to spring back
into shape

▼ **Critical Viewing**
Do you think this pic-
ture illustrates emo-
tions that the children
feel while playing
outside? Why or why
not? **[Connect]**

They stopped running and stood in the great jungle
that covered Venus, that grew and never stopped growing,
tumultuously, even as you watched it. It was a nest of
octopi, clustering up great arms of fleshlike weed, wavering,
flowering in this brief spring. It was the color of rubber and
ash, this jungle, from the many years without sun. It was
the color of stones and white cheeses and ink, and it was the
color of the moon.

The children lay out, laughing, on the jungle mattress, and
heard it sigh and squeak under them, resilient and alive.
They ran among the trees, they slipped and fell, they pushed
each other, they played hide-and-seek and tag, but most of
all they squinted at the sun until tears ran down their faces,
they put their hands up to that yellowness and that amazing
blueness and they breathed of the fresh, fresh air and
listened and listened to the silence which suspended them
in a blessed sea of no sound and no motion. They looked

at everything and savored everything. Then, wildly, like animals escaped from their caves, they ran and ran in shouting circles. They ran for an hour and did not stop running.

And then—

In the midst of their running one of the girls wailed.

Everyone stopped.

The girl, standing in the open, held out her hand.

"Oh, look, look," she said, trembling.

They came slowly to look at her opened palm.

In the center of it, cupped and huge, was a single raindrop.

She began to cry, looking at it.

They glanced quietly at the sky.

"Oh, Oh."

A few cold drops fell on their noses and their cheeks and their mouths. The sun faded behind a stir of mist. A wind blew cool around them. They turned and started to walk back toward the underground house, their hands at their sides, their smiles vanishing away.

A boom of thunder startled them and like leaves before a new hurricane, they tumbled upon each other and ran. Lightning struck ten miles away, five miles away, a mile, a half mile. The sky darkened into midnight in a flash.

They stood in the doorway of the underground for a moment until it was raining hard. Then they closed the door and heard the gigantic sound of the rain falling in tons and avalanches, everywhere and forever. ●

"Will it be seven more years?"

"Yes. Seven."

Then one of them gave a little cry.

"Margot!"

"What?"

"She's still in the closet where we locked her."

"Margot."

They stood as if someone had driven them, like so many stakes, into the floor. They looked at each other and then looked away. They glanced out at the world that was raining now and raining and raining steadily. They could not meet each other's glances. Their faces were solemn and pale. They looked at their hands and feet, their faces down.

Vocabulary
savored (sā´ vərd)
v. tasted or experienced with delight

Setting
How does the change in the weather affect the children's mood?

Spiral Review
Theme What details hint at the importance of the setting to the story? How does the setting relate to a possible theme?

Reading Check
What do the children do when the sun comes out?

"Margot."

One of the girls said, "Well . . .?"

No one moved.

"Go on," whispered the girl.

They walked slowly down the hall in the sound of cold rain. They turned through the doorway to the room in the sound of the storm and thunder, lightning on their faces, blue and terrible. They walked over to the closet door slowly and stood by it.

Behind the closet door was only silence.

They unlocked the door, even more slowly, and let Margot out.

Author's Purpose
What details here help to reveal the author's purpose? Explain.

Critical Thinking

Cite textual evidence to support your responses.

1. **Key Ideas and Details** **(a)** What details in the story indicate how Margot knows what the sun is like? **(b) Infer:** Why do the children reject her description of the sun?

2. **Key Ideas and Details** **(a)** Why do the children want the teacher to hurry back to the classroom at the beginning of the story? **(b) Infer:** Who is the "leader" of the class when the teacher is out of the room? **(c) Draw Conclusions:** Why do the children go along with the prank that is played on Margot?

3. **Key Ideas and Details** **(a)** How do the children react when they realize that Margot missed the sun because of their prank? **(b) Draw Conclusions:** Why do you think they react as they do? **(c) Generalize:** What might the children have learned from their experiences?

4. **Integration of Knowledge and Ideas** **(a) Speculate:** How do you think Margot will respond to the children after the incident? **(b) Support:** Why do you think so? **(c) Discuss:** In a small group, discuss your responses. As a group, choose one answer to share with the class.

5. **Integration of Knowledge and Ideas** How would the story be different if the children had believed Margot when she told them about the sun? *[Connect to the Big Question: What is the best way to find the truth?]*

Reading Skill: Author's Purpose

1. What are two things the author might have wished to teach his audience through this story?

2. (a) In your own words, what was the author's main **purpose** in writing this story? **(b)** Which details support your answer?

Literary Analysis: Setting

3. Key Ideas and Details How does the **setting** of this story affect the characters and events?

4. Key Ideas and Details Using a chart like the one shown, give two examples from the story to show how setting affects the story's mood.

Setting	Story's Mood

Vocabulary

Acquisition and Use An **analogy** shows a relationship between a pair of words or phrases. Use a word from the vocabulary list on page 100 to complete each analogy. Your choice should create a word pair whose relationship matches the relationship between the first two words or phrases.

1. *More* is to *increasing* as *less* is to _____.

2. *Beautiful day* is to *enjoyed* as *good meal* is to _____.

3. *Singing* is to *optional* as *breathing* is to _____.

4. *Quickly* is to *rapidly* as *noisily* is to _____.

5. *One person* is to *separate* as *crowd* is to _____.

6. *Steel* is to *unbreakable* as *rubber* is to _____.

Word Study Use the context of the sentences and what you know about the **Latin root -vit-** or **-viv-** to explain your answer to each question.

1. If a doctor *revitalizes* a patient, does the patient live or die?

2. Would a *vivacious* dog lie down when you enter the room?

Word Study

The **Latin root -vit-** or **-viv-** means "life."

Apply It Explain how the root contributes to the meanings of these words. Consult a dictionary if necessary.
survive
vitamin
revive

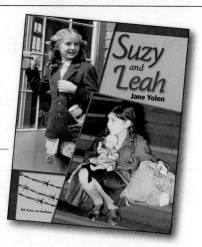

What is the best way to find the *truth?*

Writing About the Big Question

In "Suzy and Leah," two girls struggle to understand each other until the truth is revealed about one of their lives. Use this sentence starter to develop your ideas about the Big Question.

When we have **insight** about someone's life, we can _____.

While You Read Look for ways that Yolen reveals the truth about each of these characters—and the way she weaves true historical details into the story.

Vocabulary

Read each word and its definition. Decide whether you know the word well, know it a little bit, or do not know it at all. After you read, see how your knowledge of each word has increased.

- **refugee** (ref´ yōō jē´) *n.* person who flees home or country to seek shelter from war or cruelty (p. 115) *The refugee crossed the border into safety.* *refugees n. refuge n.*

- **penned** (pend) *v.* locked up in a small enclosure (p. 115) *The horses were penned in a corral.* *pen v. pen n.*

- **porridge** (pôr´ ij) *n.* soft food made of cereal boiled in water or milk (p. 116) *Oatmeal is a type of porridge.*

- **cupboard** (kub´ ərd) *n.* cabinet with shelves for cups, plates, and food (p. 117) *Her grandmother built a special cupboard for her collection of teacups.* *cupboards n.*

- **falsely** (fôls´ lē) *adv.* incorrectly; untruthfully (p. 118) *Vicky insisted she had been falsely accused.* *false adj. falsehood n.*

- **permanent** (pʉr´ mə nənt) *adj.* lasting for all time (p. 120) *His accident left a permanent scar.* *permanently adj. permanence n.*

Word Study

The **Latin root word** *manere* means to "remain" or "dwell."

In this story, Suzy describes Leah as having a **permanent** frown, or a frown that remains on her face always.

Author of

Suzy and Leah

Jane Yolen has written more than two hundred books. "I am a person in love with story and with words," says Yolen. "I wake up, and I have to write."

Finding Inspiration Yolen is never at a loss for ideas. Whenever an idea strikes her, she jots it down and places it in an "idea file" that she keeps. Then, when searching for a new story to write, she simply consults the file. "I don't care whether the story is real or fantastical," she explains. "I tell the story that needs to be told."

A Personal Interest Although Yolen is known primarily for her fantasy stories, her Jewish heritage inspired her to write "Suzy and Leah," the story of a Holocaust survivor. Yolen wrote about the Holocaust so that her own children could understand and remember what happened to Jews in Europe during World War II.

Did You Know?
Jane Yolen's storytelling career began in first grade, when she wrote a class musical about vegetables.

BACKGROUND FOR THE STORY
War Refugee Board
"Suzy and Leah" is based on actual events. The United States established the War Refugee Board in January 1944. The goal of the Board was to rescue victims of Nazi persecution from death in German-occupied Europe. In one rescue effort, 982 people from eighteen countries were brought to a refugee camp in Oswego, New York.

Suzy
and
Leah

Jane Yolen

Dear Diary,

Today I walked past that place, the one that was in the newspaper, the one all the kids have been talking about. Gosh, is it ugly! A line of rickety wooden buildings just like in the army. And a fence lots higher than my head. With barbed wire[1] on top. How can anyone—even a refugee—live there?

I took two candy bars along, just like everyone said I should. When I held them up, all those kids just swarmed over to the fence, grabbing. Like in a zoo. Except for this one girl, with two dark braids and bangs nearly covering her eyes. She was just standing to one side, staring at me. It was so creepy. After a minute I looked away. When I looked back, she was gone. I mean gone. Disappeared as if she'd never been.

Suzy

August 5, 1944

My dear Mutti,[2]

I have but a single piece of paper to write on. And a broken pencil. But I will write small so I can tell all. I address it to you, Mutti, though you are gone from me forever. I write in English, to learn better, because I want to make myself be understood.

Today another girl came. With more sweets. A girl with yellow hair and a false smile. Yonni and Zipporah and Ruth, my friends, all grabbed for the sweets. Like wild animals. Like . . . like prisoners. But we are not wild animals. And we are no longer prisoners. Even though we are still penned in.

I stared at the yellow-haired girl until she was forced to look down. Then I walked away. When I turned to look back, she was gone. Disappeared. As if she had never been.

Leah

September 2, 1944

Dear Diary,

I brought the refugee kids oranges today. Can you believe it—they didn't know you're supposed to peel oranges first. One boy tried to eat one like an apple. He made an awful face,

---

Vocabulary
refugee (ref yoō jē′) *n.* person who flees home or country to seek shelter from war or cruelty

penned (pend) *v.* locked up in a small enclosure

◄ **Critical Viewing**
How do these girls look both similar and different? **[Compare and Contrast]**

✓ Reading Check
What did Suzy offer to the children through the fence?

1. **barbed wire** twisted wire with sharp points all along it, used for fences and barriers.
2. **Mutti** (moo′ tē) German equivalent of "Mommy."

but then he ate it anyway. I showed them how to peel oranges with the second one. After I stopped laughing.

Mom says they are going to be coming to school. Of course they'll have to be cleaned up first. Ugh. My hand still feels itchy from where one little boy grabbed it in his. I wonder if he had bugs.

Suzy

Vocabulary
porridge (pôr´ ij) *n.*
soft food made of cereal boiled in water or milk

Author's Purpose
What purpose might the author have for including details about Leah's life before the war?

September 2, 1944

My dear Mutti,

Today we got cereal in a box. At first I did not know what it was. Before the war we ate such lovely porridge with milk straight from our cows. And eggs fresh from the hen's nest, though you know how I hated that nasty old chicken. How often she pecked me! In the German camp, it was potato soup—with onions when we were lucky, without either onion or potato when we were not. And after, when I was running from the Nazis, it was stale brown bread, if we could find any. But cereal in a box—that is something.

I will not take a sweet from that yellow-haired girl, though. She laughed at Yonni. I will not take another orange fruit.

Leah

September 5, 1944

Dear Diary,

So how are those refugee kids going to learn? Our teachers teach in English. This is America, after all.

I wouldn't want to be one of them. Imagine going to school and not being able to speak English or understand anything that's going on. I can't imagine anything worse.

Suzy

September 5, 1944

My dear Mutti,

The adults of the Americans say we are safe now. And so we must go to their school. But I say no place is safe for us. Did not the Germans say that we were safe in their camps? And there you and baby Natan were killed.

And how could we learn in this American school anyway? I have a little English. But Ruth and Zipporah and the others, though they speak Yiddish[3] and Russian and German, they have no English at all. None beyond *thank you* and *please* and *more sweets.* And then there is little Avi. How could he go to this school? He will speak nothing at all. He stopped speaking, they say, when he was hidden away in a cupboard by his grandmother who was taken by the Nazis after she swore there was no child in the house. And he was almost three days in that cupboard without food, without water, without words to comfort him. Is English a safer language than German?

There is barbed wire still between us and the world.

Leah

The adults of the Americans say we are safe now.

Vocabulary
cupboard (kub´ ərd) *n.* a cabinet with shelves for cups, plates, and food

September 14, 1944

Dear Diary,

At least the refugee kids are wearing better clothes now. And they all have shoes. Some of them still had those stripy pajamas on when they arrived in America.

The girls all wore dresses to their first day at school, though. They even had hair bows, gifts from the teachers. Of course I recognized my old blue pinafore.[4] The girl with the dark braids had it on, and Mom hadn't even told me she was giving it away. I wouldn't have minded so much if she had only asked. It doesn't fit me anymore, anyway.

The girl in my old pinafore was the only one without a name tag, so all day long no one knew her name.

Suzy

◄ **Critical Viewing**
Does this girl look like one of the children Suzy describes? Explain. **[Compare]**

Reading Check
What happened to Leah's mother?

---

3. **Yiddish** (yid ´ish) *n.* language spoken by Eastern European Jews and their descendants. It is written with Hebrew letters and contains words from Hebrew, German, Russian, and Polish.
4. **pinafore** (pin´ ə fôr´) *n.* a sleeveless garment worn over a dress, often over a blouse.

Setting
How did Leah's former home on the farm change during the war?

Vocabulary
falsely (fôls' lē) *adv.* incorrectly; untruthfully

Author's Purpose
What purpose might the author have for describing Leah from Suzy's point of view?

September 14, 1944

My dear Mutti,

   I put on the blue dress for our first day. It fit me well. The color reminded me of your eyes and the blue skies over our farm before the smoke from the burning darkened it. Zipporah braided my hair, but I had no mirror until we got to the school and they showed us the toilets. They call it a bathroom, but there is no bath in it at all, which is strange. I have never been in a school with boys before.

   They have placed us all in low grades. Because of our English. I do not care. This way I do not have to see the girl with the yellow hair who smiles so falsely at me.

   But they made us wear tags with our names printed on them. That made me afraid. What next? Yellow stars?[5] I tore mine off and threw it behind a bush before we went in.

Leah

September 16, 1944

Dear Diary,

   Mr. Forest has assigned each of us to a refugee to help them with their English. He gave me the girl with the dark braids, the one without the name tag, the one in my pinafore. Gee, she's as prickly as a porcupine. I asked if I could have a different kid. He said I was the best English student and she already spoke the best English. He wants her to learn as fast as possible so she can help the others. As if she would, Miss Porcupine.

   Her name is Leah. I wish she would wear another dress.

Suzy

September 16, 1944

My dear Mutti,

   Now I have a real notebook and a pen. I am writing to you at school now. I cannot take the notebook back to the shelter. Someone there will surely borrow it. I will instead keep it here. In the little cupboard each one of us has been given.

   I wish I had another dress. I wish I had a different student helping me and not the yellow-haired girl.

Leah

---

5. yellow stars Jews were forced to wear fabric stars during the Holocaust to distinguish them from others.

September 20, 1944

Dear Diary,

Can't she ever smile, that Leah?
I've brought her candy bars and
apples from home. I tried to give
her a handkerchief with a yellow
flower on it. She wouldn't take any
of them.

Her whole name is Leah
Shoshana Hershkowitz. At least,
that's the way she writes it. When
she says it, it sounds all different,
low and growly. I laughed when
I tried to say it, but she wouldn't
laugh with me. What a grouch.

And yesterday, when I took her
English paper to correct it, she
shrank back against her chair
as if I was going to hit her or
something. Honestly!

Mom says I should invite her home
for dinner soon. We'll have to get her a special pass for that.
But I don't know if I want her to come. It's not like she's any
fun at all. I wish Mr. Forest would let me trade.

Suzy

September 20, 1944

My dear Mutti,

The girl with the yellow hair is called Suzy Ann McCarthy. It is a
silly name. It means nothing. I asked her who she was named for,
and she said, "For a book my mom liked." A book! I am named after
my great-grandmother on my mother's side, who was an important
woman in our village. I am proud to carry on her name.

This Suzy brings many sweets. But I must call them candies now.
And a handkerchief. She expects me to be grateful. But how can I
be grateful? She treats me like a pet, a pet she does not really like or
trust. She wants to feed me like an animal behind bars.

If I write all this down, I will not hold so much anger. I have much
anger. And terror besides. *Terror.* It is a new word for me, but an old
feeling. One day soon this Suzy and her people will stop being nice

▲ **Critical Viewing**
Part of this story is set
in a refugee camp,
like the one shown
here. What details in
the photograph are
confirmed in Suzy's
letters? **[Support]**

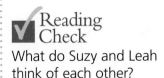

Reading Check

What do Suzy and Leah
think of each other?

to us. They will remember we are not just refugees but Jews, and they will turn on us. Just as the Germans did. Of this I am sure.

Leah

Dear Diary,

Leah's English is very good now. But she still never smiles. Especially she never smiles at me. It's like she has a permanent frown and permanent frown lines between her eyes. It makes her look much older than anyone in our class. Like a little old lady.

I wonder if she eats enough. She won't take the candy bars. And she saves the school lunch in her napkin, hiding it away in her pocket. She thinks no one sees her do it, but I do. Does she eat it later? I'm sure they get dinner at the shelter. Mom says they do. Mom also says we have to eat everything on our plates. Sometimes when we're having dinner I think of Leah Shoshana Hershkowitz.

Suzy

September 30, 1944

My dear Mutti,

Avi loves the food I bring home from school. What does he know? It is not even kosher.[6] Sometimes they serve ham. But I do not tell Avi. He needs all the food he can get. He is a growing boy.

I, too, am growing fast. Soon I will not fit into the blue dress. I have no other.

Leah

October 9, 1944

Dear Diary,

They skipped Leah up to our grade, her English has gotten so good. Except for some words, like victory, which she pronounces "wick-toe-ree." I try not to laugh, but sometimes I just can't help it!

Leah knows a lot about the world and nothing about America. She thinks New York is right next to Chicago, for

---

6. kosher (kō'shər) *adj.* fit to eat according to the Jewish laws of diet.

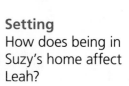

> *Leah knows a lot about the world and nothing about America.*

goodness sakes! She can't dance at all. She doesn't know the words to any of the top songs. And she's so stuck up, she only talks in class to answer questions. The other refugees aren't like that at all. Why is it only my refugee who's so mean?

Suzy

October 9, 1944

My dear Mutti,

   I think of you all the time. I went to Suzy's house because Mr. Forest said they had gone to a great deal of trouble to get a pass for me. I did not want to go so much, my stomach hurt the whole time I was there.

   Suzy's *Mutti* was nice, all pink and gold. She wore a dress with pink roses all over it and it reminded me of your dress, the blue one with the asters. You were wearing it when we were put on the train. And the last time I saw you at the camp with Natan. Oh, *Mutti.* I had to steel my heart against Suzy's mother. If I love her, I will forget you. And that I must never do.

   I brought back food from her house, though, for Avi. I could not eat it myself. You would like the way Avi grows bigger and stronger. And he talks now, but only to me. He says, "More, Leah, please." And he says "light" for the sun. Sometimes when I am really lonely I call him Natan, but only at night after he has fallen asleep.

Leah

Setting
How does being in Suzy's home affect Leah?

Reading Check

What does Leah do with her food at lunchtime?

October 10, 1944

Dear Diary,

Leah was not in school today. When I asked her friend Zipporah, she shrugged. "She is ill in her stomach," she said. "What did she eat at your house?"

I didn't answer "Nothing," though that would have been true. She hid it all in a handkerchief Mom gave her. Mom said, "She eats like a bird. How does she stay alive?"

Suzy

October 11, 1944

Dear Diary,

They've asked me to gather Leah's things from school and bring them to the hospital. She had to have her appendix out and nearly died. She almost didn't tell them she was sick until too late. Why did she do that? I would have been screaming my head off with the pain.

Mom says we have to visit, that I'm Leah's American best friend. Hah! We're going to bring several of my old dresses, but not my green one with the white trim. I don't want her to have it. Even if it doesn't fit me anymore.

Suzy

October 12, 1944

Dear Diary,

I did a terrible thing. I read Leah's diary. I'd kill anyone who did that to me!

At first it made no sense. Who were *Mutti* and Natan, and why were they killed? What were the yellow stars? What does kosher mean? And the way she talked about me made me furious. Who did she think she was, little Miss Porcupine? All I did was bring candy and fruit and try to make those poor refugee kids feel at home.

Then, when I asked Mom some questions, carefully, so she wouldn't guess I had read Leah's diary, she explained. She said the Nazis killed people, mothers and children as well as men. In places called concentration camps. And that all the Jews—people who weren't Christians like us—had to wear yellow stars on their clothes so they could be spotted blocks

▼ **Critical Viewing**
What do the details in this photograph tell you about the lives and backgrounds of these children? **[Infer]**

Author's Purpose
What facts about World War II does the author teach in this entry?

and blocks away. It was so awful I could hardly believe it, but Mom said it was true.

How was I supposed to know all that? How can Leah stand any of us? How could she live with all that pain?

Suzy

October 12, 1944

▼ **Critical Viewing**
The girls pictured here are looking out of a ship's porthole as they prepare to go to America. Which girl has an expression you would expect to see on Leah's face? Explain. **[Connect]**

My dear Mutti,

Suzy and her mother came to see me in the hospital. They brought me my notebook so now I can write again.

I was so frightened about being sick. I did not tell anyone for a long time, even though it hurt so much. In the German camp, if you were sick and could not do your work, they did not let you live.

But in the middle of the night, I had so much fever, a doctor was sent for. Little Avi found me. He ran to one of the guards. He spoke out loud for the first time. He said, "Please, for Leah. Do not let her go into the dark."

The doctor tells me I nearly died, but they saved me. They have given me much medicines and soon I will eat the food and they will be sure it is kosher, too. And I am alive. This I can hardly believe. *Alive!*

Then Suzy came with her *Mutti*, saying, "I am sorry. I am so sorry. I did not know. I did not understand." Suzy did a bad thing. She read my notebook. But it helped her understand. And then, instead of making an apology, she

FEDE
דב הוי

Author's Purpose
What purpose does the author archieve by telling a story through young characters?

did a strange thing. She took a red book with a lock out of her pocket and gave it to me. "Read this," she said. "And when you are out of the hospital, I have a green dress with white trim I want you to have. It will be just perfect with your eyes."

I do not know what this trim may be. But I like the idea of a green dress. And I have a new word now, as well. It is this: *diary.*

A new word. A new land. And—it is just possible—a new friend.

Leah

Critical Thinking

Cite textual evidence to support your responses.

1. **Key Ideas and Details** **(a)** What kind of camp was Leah in before coming to the refugee camp? **(b) Interpret:** What does Leah mean by, "There is barbed wire still between us and the world"?

2. **Key Ideas and Details** **(a)** How are Suzy and Leah forced to get to know each other? **(b) Analyze:** What do Suzy's early reactions to Leah tell you about Suzy? **(c) Analyze:** What do Leah's early reactions to Suzy tell you about Leah?

3. **Key Ideas and Details** **(a)** What does Suzy learn about Leah when she reads her diary? **(b) Infer:** What is the "red book with a lock" that Suzy gives Leah to read? **(c) Draw Conclusions:** How have both girls changed by the end of the story? Use details from the story to support your answer.

4. **Integration of Knowledge and Ideas** **(a) Predict:** Do you think Suzy and Leah will become close friends in the future? **(b) Support:** What evidence from the story makes you feel this way? **(c) Discuss:** In a small group, share and discuss your responses.

5. **Key Ideas and Details** **(a)** What does Suzy's mother say that reveals the truth about the Jewish children's situation? **(b)** How does that explanation change how Suzy perceives Leah? *[Connect to the Big Question: What is the best way to find the truth?]*

Reading Skill: Author's Purpose

1. What are two things the author might have wished to teach her audience through this story?

2. (a) Did the author intend to entertain her audience?
   (b) Which details support your answer? Explain.

3. In your own words, what was the author's main **purpose** in writing this story? Explain.

Literary Analysis: Setting

4. Key Ideas and Details How does the **setting** of this story affect the events that occur between Suzy and Leah?

5. Key Ideas and Details Using a chart like the one shown, give two examples from the story to show how setting affects the story's mood.

Setting	Story's Mood

Vocabulary

Acquisition and Use Using your knowledge of the italicized words, explain your answer to each question.

1. Would a *permanent* stain on a carpet be easy to remove?

2. In what room of a house might you find a *cupboard*?

3. Would a diet of only *porridge* be a healthy choice?

4. Would a wild horse enjoy being *penned* in?

5. Would a *falsely* accused person be guilty?

6. Would a *refugee* be able to go back home safely?

Word Study Use the context of the sentences and what you know about the **Latin root word *manere*** to explain your answer to each question.

1. Would a wealthy person live in a *manor*?

2. If something has *permanence,* is it likely to last a long time?

Word Study

The **Latin root word *manere*** means to "remain" or "dwell."

Apply It Explain how the root contributes to the meanings of these words. Verify your understanding by consulting a dictionary if neccesary.
remain
mansion

Integrated Language Skills

All Summer in a Day • Suzy and Leah

Conventions: Personal Pronouns

A **personal pronoun** takes the place of a noun that names a person. Some personal pronouns take the place of the **subject**—the person doing the action. Other personal pronouns take the place of the **object**—the one receiving the action.

Pronouns, such as those listed in the chart below, are used every day in conversation. Writers use pronouns to avoid the awkwardness of repeating the same noun over and over.

Subject Pronouns	Object Pronouns
I, we, you, he, she, it, they	me, us, you, him, her, it, them

Practice A Identify the personal pronoun in each sentence. Then, identify the noun it replaces.

1. When Margot talked about the sun, she came to life.
2. The children waited for the sun to shine on them.
3. The students locked Margot in the closet and forgot about her.
4. When the sun came out, it made the children happy.

© **Speaking Application** Read "All Summer in a Day" to find two sentences with personal pronouns. Recite these sentences to a partner and identify the personal pronouns.

Practice B Identify the personal pronoun in each sentence. Then, tell whether it is a subject or object pronoun. Use each personal pronoun in a sentence of your own.

1. Suzy gave them oranges as a gift.
2. Leah did not like her at first.
3. They were in the same class.
4. Eventually, she began to understand Leah.

© **Writing Application** Write a dialogue in which two characters from the story you read discuss their experiences. Use at least two subject pronouns and two object pronouns.

PH **WRITING COACH**   Further instruction and practice are available in *Prentice Hall Writing Coach*.

Writing

Informative Text Write a **news report** based on the story you read. Your report should describe either **(a)** the day the sun appeared on Venus, or **(b)** conditions at the refugee camp where Leah is living.

- First, list questions that your news report will answer. Write questions that ask *who, what, where, when, why,* and *how.*
- Before you write your report, answer each question. Use story details to help you gather information.
- Present the most important information in your opening paragraph. Then, write the rest of your report, based on the information you have collected.

Grammar Application Review your news report, looking for places where you can replace repeated nouns with personal pronouns.

Writing Workshop: *Work in Progress*

Prewriting for Narration Jot down a list of five people whom you know. Keep this People List in your portfolio. Refer to this list when you write your autobiographical narrative.

Speaking and Listening

Comprehension and Collaboration With a partner, hold a **discussion** about the underlying message of the story you read. If you read "All Summer in a Day," discuss a lesson the selection taught you about treating others. If you read "Suzy and Leah," discuss how reading the story affected your understanding of the Holocaust.

Follow these steps to complete the assignment:

- Prepare by rereading the selection, keeping in mind the topic of your discussion. Jot down points that support your position.
- Listen carefully to your partner's points.
- Ask your partner questions to clarify his or her position. Look for evidence to support these ideas.
- Write down key points that you and your partner make.
- Identify the strongest points, and share them with the class.
- As a group, identify two lessons readers might learn from the story you read.

Common Core State Standards

W.7.2; SL.7.1.a-d; L.7.4.b, L.7.6
[For the full wording of the standards, see page 98.]

Use this prewriting activity to prepare for the **Writing Workshop** on page 176.

PHLit Online!
www.PHLitOnline.com
- Interactive graphic organizers
- Grammar tutorial
- Interactive journals

© Leveled Texts

Build your skills and improve your comprehension of literary nonfiction with texts of increasing complexity.

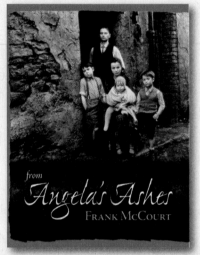

Read **"My First Free Summer"** to find out how political events interfere with a girl's summer plans.

Read the excerpt from ***Angela's Ashes*** to learn how literature can connect people in times of trouble.

© Common Core State Standards

Meet these standards with either **"My First Free Summer"** (p. 132) or the excerpt from ***Angela's Ashes*** (p. 140).

Reading Informational Texts
1. Cite several pieces of textual evidence to support analysis of what the text says explicitly as well as inferences drawn from the text. *(Reading Skill: Author's Purpose)*

3. Analyze the interactions between individuals, events, and ideas in a text. *(Literary Analysis: Historical Context)*

Spiral Review: RI.7.2

Writing
2.b. Develop the topic with relevant facts, definitions, concrete details, quotations, or other information and examples. **2.c.** Use appropriate transitions to create cohesion and clarify the relationships among ideas and concepts. *(Writing: Letter)*

Speaking and Listening
1.c. Pose questions that elicit elaboration and respond to others' questions and comments with relevant observations and ideas that bring the discussion back on topic as needed. *(Speaking and Listening: Interview)*

Language
1. Demonstrate command of the conventions of standard English grammar and usage when writing or speaking. *(Conventions: Possessive Pronouns)*

6. Acquire and use accurately grade-appropriate general academic and domain-specific words and phrases; gather vocabulary knowledge when considering a word or phrase important to comprehension or expression. *(Vocabulary: Word Study)*

Reading Skill: Author's Purpose

One way to determine the **author's purpose,** or reason, for writing a nonfiction work is to use **background information** that you already know about the author and topic. For example, knowing that an author was born outside the United States might help you determine that he or she wrote an essay to inform readers about his or her native country.

Another way to determine author's purpose is to look for details in the text that help you make inferences about author's purpose. For example, if an author provides detailed descriptions about a historical setting, you might infer that the author's purpose is to educate the reader.

Using the Strategy: Author's Purpose Chart

As you read, use a chart like the one below to help you determine the author's purpose.

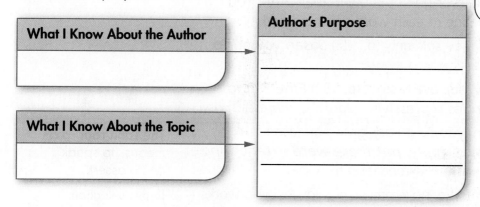

PHLit Online!
www.PHLitOnline.com

Hear It!
• Selection summary audio
• Selection audio

See It!
• Get Connected video
• Background video
• More about the author
• Vocabulary flashcards

Do It!
• Interactive journals
• Interactive graphic organizers
• Self-test
• Internet activity
• Grammar tutorial
• Interactive vocabulary games

Literary Analysis: Historical Context

When a literary work is based on real events and real people, the historical context can help you understand the action as well as the theme or message. **Historical context**—the actual political and social events and trends of the time—can explain why people act and think the way they do. As you read, look for factual details that link the people, events, and ideas in the text to a specific place and time period.

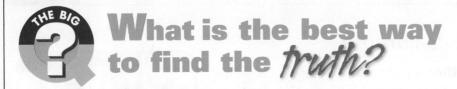

What is the best way to find the *truth?*

Writing About the Big Question

In "My First Free Summer," a young girl's parents avoid revealing scary truths about their safety during a period of rebellion. Use this sentence starter to develop your ideas about the Big Question.

When we **evaluate** what is best for us, we must sometimes consider _____.

While You Read Look for insights the author gained both during her experience and in looking back on it.

Vocabulary

Read each word and its definition. Decide whether you know the word well, know it a little bit, or do not know it at all. After you read, see how your knowledge of each word has increased.

- **vowed** (voud) *v.* promised solemnly (p. 132) *Susan vowed to take care of the puppy.* *vow n. vow v.*

- **repressive** (ri pres´ iv) *adj.* overly strict (p. 132) *Elise found her grandmother's rules repressive.* *repress v. repression n.*

- **extenuating** (ek sten´ yoo āt´ iŋ) *adj.* giving a reason for; excusing (p. 133) *He was guilty, but there were extenuating circumstances.* *extenuate v. extenuation n.*

- **diplomats** (dip´ lə mats´) *n.* government employees who work with other nations (p. 133) *The diplomats discussed a trade agreement that would benefit both countries.* *diplomat n. diplomatic adj. diplomacy n.*

- **summoned** (sum´ ənd) *v.* called together (p. 134) *At halftime, the coach summoned her players to a huddle.* *summon v. summons n.*

- **contradiction** (kän´ trə dik´ shən) *n.* difference between two conflicting things that means they cannot both be true (p. 135) *It is a contradiction to say mean things in a sweet voice.* *contradict v. contradictory adj.*

Word Study

The **Latin root -dict-** means "to speak" or "to assert."

In this selection, Julia's mother does not tolerate **contradiction**—she does not allow her children to speak out against her wishes.

Author of

My First Free Summer

Shortly after her birth, Julia Alvarez moved from New York City to the Dominican Republic with her family. When Alvarez was ten, however, her family was forced to return to the United States because her father was involved in a rebellion against the country's dictator.

The Power of Words Alvarez had trouble adjusting to her new home. Turning inward, she began to read books and to write. Later, she said, "I fell in love with how words can make you feel complete in a way that I hadn't felt complete since leaving the island."

BACKGROUND FOR THE ESSAY

The Dominican Republic

In 1930, Rafael L. Trujillo seized power in the Dominican Republic and controlled the country as dictator for thirty-one years. To protect his position, Trujillo placed family members in office, restricted basic human rights, and harmed his political opponents. Some Dominican citizens were forced to flee to the United States. The author of "My First Free Summer" moved to New York City with her family during this unstable period.

Did You Know?
Several years ago, Alvarez started a farm and a school to help people in the Dominican Republic.

My First Free Summer
Julia Alvarez

I never had summer—I had summer school. First grade, summer school. Second grade, summer school. Thirdgrade-summerschoolfourthgradesummerschool. In fifth grade, I **vowed** I would get interested in fractions, the presidents of the United States, Mesopotamia; I would learn my English.

That was the problem. English. My mother had decided to send her children to the American school so we could learn the language of the nation that would soon be liberating us. For thirty years, the Dominican Republic had endured a bloody and **repressive** dictatorship. From my father, who was involved in an underground plot, my mother knew that los américanos[1] had promised to help bring democracy to the island.

"You have to learn your English!" Mami kept scolding me.

"But why?" I'd ask. I didn't know about my father's activities. I didn't know the dictator was bad. All I knew was that my friends who were attending Dominican schools were often on holiday to honor the dictator's birthday, the dictator's saint day, the day the dictator became the dictator, the day the dictator's oldest son was born, and so on. They marched in parades and visited the palace and had their picture in the paper.

---

1. los américanos (lōs ä me′ rī kä′ nōs) *n.* Spanish for "the Americans."

Meanwhile, I had to learn about the pilgrims with their funny witch hats, about the 50 states and where they were on the map, about Dick and Jane[2] and their tame little pets, Puff and Spot, about freedom and liberty and justice for all—while being imprisoned in a hot classroom with a picture of a man wearing a silly wig hanging above the blackboard. And all of this learning I had to do in that impossibly difficult, rocks-in-your-mouth language of English!

Somehow, I managed to scrape by. Every June, when my prospects looked iffy, Mami and I met with the principal. I squirmed in my seat while they arranged for my special summer lessons.

"She is going to work extra hard. Aren't you, young lady?" the principal would quiz me at the end of our session.

My mother's eye on me, I'd murmur, "Yeah."

"Yes, what?" Mami coached.

"Yes." I sighed. "Sir."

It's a wonder that I just wasn't thrown out, which was what I secretly hoped for. But there were extenuating circumstances, the grounds on which the American school stood had been donated by my grandfather. In fact, it had been my grandmother who had encouraged Carol Morgan to start her school. The bulk of the student body was made up of the sons and daughters of American diplomats and business people, but a few Dominicans—most of them friends or members of my family—were allowed to attend.

"You should be grateful!" Mami scolded on the way home from our meeting. "Not every girl is lucky enough to go to the Carol Morgan School!"

In fifth grade, I straightened out. "Yes, ma'am!" I learned to say brightly. "Yes, sir!" To wave my hand in sword-wielding swoops so I could get called on with the right answer. What had changed me? Gratitude? A realization of my luckiness? No, sir! The thought of a fun summer? Yes, ma'am! I wanted to run with the pack of cousins and friends in the common yard that connected all our properties. To play on the

---

2. Dick and Jane characters in a reading book commonly used by students in the 1950s.

trampoline and go off to la playa[3] and get brown as a berry. I wanted to be free. Maybe American principles had finally sunk in!

The summer of 1960 began in bliss: I did not have to go to summer school! *Attitude much improved. Her English progressing nicely. Attentive and cooperative in classroom.* I grinned as Mami read off the note that accompanied my report card of Bs.

But the yard replete with cousins and friends that I had dreamed about all year was deserted. Family members were leaving for the United States, using whatever connections they could drum up. The plot had unraveled. Every day there were massive arrests. The United States had closed its embassy and was advising Americans to return home.

My own parents were terrified. Every night black Volkswagens blocked our driveway and stayed there until morning. "Secret police," my older sister whispered.

"Why are they secret if they're the police?" I asked.

"Shut up!" my sister hissed. "Do you want to get us all killed?"

Day after day, I kicked a deflated beach ball around the empty yard, feeling as if I'd been tricked into good behavior by whomever God put in charge of the lives of 10-year-olds. I was bored. Even summer school would have been better than this!

One day toward the end of the summer, my mother summoned my sisters and me. She wore that

Historical Context
What daily events cause the U.S. government to advise Americans to return home?

▶ **Critical Viewing**
Rafael Trujillo was dictator of the Dominican Republic from 1930 to 1961. What details in the photograph make him look important? **[Analyze]**

Vocabulary
summoned (sum´ ənd) *v.* called together

---

3. la playa (lä plä´ yä) *n.* Spanish for "the beach."

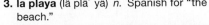

too-bright smile she sometimes pasted on her terrified face.

"Good news, girls! Our papers and tickets came! We're leaving for the United States!"

Our mouths dropped. We hadn't been told we were going on a trip anywhere, no less to some place so far away.

I was the first to speak up, "But why?"

My mother flashed me the same look she used to give me when I'd ask why I had to learn English.

I was about to tell her that I didn't want to go to the United States, where summer school had been invented and everyone spoke English. But my mother lifted a hand for silence. "We're leaving in a few hours. I want you all to go get ready! I'll be in to pack soon." The desperate look in her eyes did not allow for contradiction. We raced off, wondering how to fit the contents of our Dominican lives into four small suitcases.

Our flight was scheduled for that afternoon, but the airplane did not appear. The terminal lined with soldiers wielding machine guns, checking papers, escorting passengers into a small interrogation room. Not everyone returned.

"It's a trap," I heard my mother whisper to my father.

This had happened before, a cat-and-mouse game the dictator liked to play. Pretend that he was letting someone go, and then at the last minute, their family and friends conveniently gathered together—wham! The secret police would haul the whole clan away.

Of course, I didn't know that this was what my parents were dreading. But as the hours ticked away, and afternoon turned into evening and evening into night and night into midnight with no plane in sight, a light came on in my head. If the light could be translated into words, instead, they would say: Freedom and liberty and justice for all . . . I knew that ours was not a trip, but an escape. We had to get to the United States.

The rest of that night is a blur. It is one, then two the next morning. A plane lands, lights flashing. We are walking on the runway, climbing up the stairs into the cabin. An American lady wearing a cap welcomes us. We sit down, ready to depart. But suddenly, soldiers come on board. They go seat by seat, looking at our faces. Finally, they leave, the door closes, and with a powerful roar we lift off and I fall asleep. ●

Next morning, we are standing inside a large, echoing hall

Author's Purpose
How does your background knowledge of Julia and her mother help you understand the look described here?

Vocabulary
contradiction
(kän´ trə dik´ shən) *n.* difference between two conflicting things that means they cannot both be true

▼ **Critical Viewing**
Describe Julia based on this passport photo and what you have read. **[Infer]**

✓ Reading Check
Where did many of Julia's relatives go during the summer of 1960?

as a stern American official reviews our documents. What if he doesn't let us in? What if we have to go back? I am holding my breath. My parents' terror has become mine.

He checks our faces against the passport pictures. When he is done, he asks, "You girls ready for school?" I swear he is looking at me.

"Yes, sir!" I speak up.

The man laughs. He stamps our papers and hands them to my father. Then wonderfully, a smile spreads across his face. "Welcome to the United States," he says, waving us in.

Author's Purpose
How does this scene point to the author's main purpose for writing this story?

Spiral Review
Central Idea
How does the historical context help you identify the central idea of this essay?

Critical Thinking

1. **Key Ideas and Details** **(a)** Why does Julia Alvarez's mother send Julia to the American school? **(b) Compare and Contrast:** How does this school differ from other schools on the island?

2. **Key Ideas and Details** **(a)** What is Alvarez's main reason for changing her behavior in fifth grade? **(b) Connect:** How is she successful?

3. **Key Ideas and Details** **(a) Infer:** How do you think Alvarez feels when she learns that her family is leaving the country? **(b) Speculate:** Why does it take her so long to understand that her family is escaping? Support your answer with details from the story.

4. **Integration of Knowledge and Ideas** **(a) Hypothesize:** What might Alvarez want readers to learn from this story? **(b) Support:** What details in the story support your ideas? **(c) Discuss:** Share your responses with a partner. Then, discuss how looking at someone else's responses did or did not change your ideas.

5. **Craft and Structure** **(a)** What differences does Alvarez find between the political and personal meanings of the word *free*? **(b)** What new insights might she have gained when looking back on this experience as an adult? *[Connect to the Big Question: What is the best way to find the truth?]*

Cite textual evidence to support your responses.

Reading Skill: Author's Purpose

1. What information from the Background on page 131 helps you understand the **author's purpose?**

2. (a) What other purposes for writing might Alvarez have had? **(b)** Which details in the essay support your response?

Literary Analysis: Historical Context

3. Key Ideas and Details Using a chart like the one shown, give examples from the selection that show how the **historical context** of the Dominican Republic during a rebellion affects Alvarez's actions in "My First Free Summer."

Historical Context		Author's Actions
Dictatorship	→	1. Goes to the American school
		2.

4. Key Ideas and Details List two story details that lead Alvarez to finally realize that her family is making an escape from the island.

Vocabulary

Acquisition and Use Using your knowledge of the italicized words, explain your answer to each question.

1. If you *vowed* to keep a secret, would you tell anyone?

2. Do *diplomats* work outside their own countries?

3. If you were *summoned* to a meeting, what would you do?

4. Can *extenuating* circumstances change the outcome of a situation?

5. If my statement is a *contradiction*, are we in agreement?

6. Are citizens of a *repressive* government free?

Word Study Use what you know about the **Latin root** *-dict-* to explain your answer to each question.

1. If I *dictate* a letter to you, am I telling you what to write?

2. If you *predict* that it will rain, are you stating a fact?

Word Study

The **Latin root** *-dict-* means "to speak," or "assert."

Apply It Explain how the word root contributes to the meanings of these words. Consult a dictionary if necessary.

benediction
edict
verdict

What is the best way to find the *truth?*

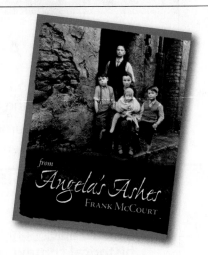

Writing About the Big Question

In this excerpt from *Angela's Ashes,* a young boy discovers the joy of language while recovering from a serious illness. Use this sentence starter to develop your ideas about the Big Question.

A difficult experience can increase our **awareness** of _____ _____ because _____.

While You Read Look for places where the author uses humor and truth to describe his childhood stay in the hospital.

Vocabulary

Read each word and its definition. Decide whether you know the word well, know it a little bit, or do not know it at all. After you read, see how your knowledge of each word has increased.

- **miracle** (mir´ ə kəl) *n.* remarkable event or thing; marvel (p. 141) *It was a miracle that he survived the fall.* *miraculous adj.*

- **saluting** (sə loot´ iŋ) *v.* honoring by performing an act or gesture (p. 142) *The soldiers were saluting as they passed the general.* *salute v. salutation n.*

- **desperate** (des´ pər it) *adj.* without hope; having a great desire or need (p. 143) *John was desperate for a new pair of shoes.* *desperation n. desperately adv.*

- **patriotic** (pā trē ät´ ik) *adj.* showing love and support for one's own country (p. 143) *The crowds waved the American flag in a patriotic show.* *patriot n. patriotism n.*

- **ban** (ban) *n.* order forbidding something (p. 146) *The theater has a ban on cell phone use while a film is playing.* *ban v. banned v. banish v.*

- **guzzled** (guz´ əld) *v.* drank greedily (p. 147) *Ted guzzled water while hiking in the desert.* *guzzle v. guzzler n.*

Word Study

The **Latin root *-sper-*** or ***-spes-*** means "hope."

In this story, Frank has recovered from a **desperate,** or nearly hopeless, illness.

Meet
Frank McCourt
(1930–2009)

Author of
Angela's Ashes

Frank McCourt was born in Brooklyn, New York, but he was raised in Ireland. His father struggled to keep a job, and the family often went hungry. Because of the family's squalid living conditions, McCourt nearly died of typhoid fever when he was ten years old. At age thirteen, McCourt left school and worked at a series of odd jobs in an effort to help feed his family. At age nineteen, he sailed for America, where he eventually enrolled at New York University and became an English teacher. *Angela's Ashes*, McCourt's Pulitzer Prize-winning memoir, describes the author's youth in Ireland.

BACKGROUND FOR THE SELECTION

Infectious Diseases in Ireland

In Ireland during the 1940s, infectious diseases such as typhoid and diphtheria claimed the lives of many children. This was especially true in poor and working-class districts where conditions could be very unsanitary. In some neighborhoods, entire blocks of houses shared a single outhouse, or outdoor toilet, which often overflowed and attracted rats and flies. These pests would then make their way into surrounding homes, and spread disease by tainting food and water.

Did You Know?

McCourt taught English for twenty-seven years in New York City high schools before becoming a writer.

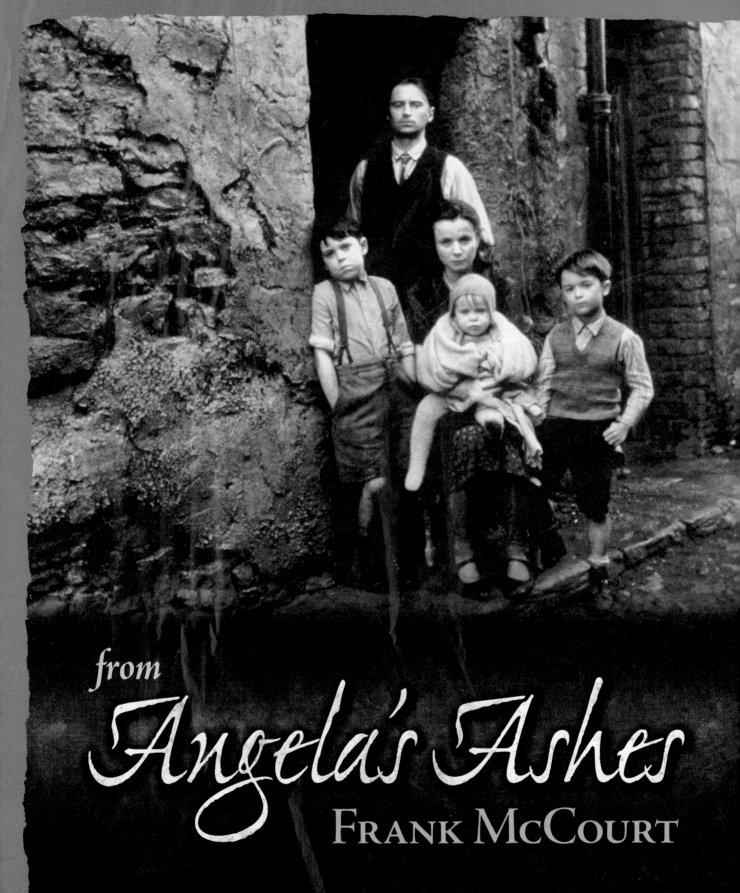

from

Angela's Ashes

FRANK McCOURT

$\mathcal{T}$he other two beds in my room are empty. The nurse says I'm the only typhoid[1] patient and I'm a miracle for getting over the crisis.

The room next to me is empty till one morning a girl's voice says, Yoo hoo, who's there?

I'm not sure if she's talking to me or someone in the room beyond.

Yoo hoo, boy with the typhoid, are you awake?

I am.

Are you better?

I am.

Well, why are you here?

I don't know. I'm still in the bed. They stick needles in me and give me medicine.

What do you look like?

I wonder, What kind of a question is that? I don't know what to tell her.

Yoo hoo, are you there, typhoid boy?

I am.

What's your name?

Frank.

That's a good name. My name is Patricia Madigan. How old are you?

Ten.

Oh. She sounds disappointed.

But I'll be eleven in August, next month.

Well, that's better than ten. I'll be fourteen in September. Do you want to know why I'm in the Fever Hospital?

I do.

I have diphtheria[2] and something else.

What's something else?

They don't know. They think I have a disease from foreign parts because my father used to be in Africa. I nearly died. Are you going to tell me what you look like?

I have black hair.

You and millions.

I have brown eyes with bits of green that's called hazel.

---

1. **typhoid** (tī´ foid´) *n.* severe infectious disease causing fever and intestinal disorders.
2. **diphtheria** (dif thir´ ē ə) *n.* severe infectious disease causing high fever and leading to the blockage of breathing passages.

Vocabulary
miracle (mir´ ə kəl) *n.* remarkable event or thing; marvel

Author's Purpose
How can you tell that the author is describing a personal experience?

Reading Check
Why is Frank in the hospital?

from Angela's Ashes **141**

You and thousands.

I have stitches on the back of my right hand and my two feet where they put in the soldier's blood.

Oh, . . . did they?

They did.

You won't be able to stop marching and saluting.

There's a swish of habit[3] and click of beads and then Sister Rita's voice. Now, now, what's this? There's to be no talking between two rooms especially when it's a boy and a girl. Do you hear me, Patricia?

I do, Sister.

Do you hear me, Francis?

I do, Sister.

You could be giving thanks for your two remarkable recoveries. You could be saying the rosary. You could be reading *The Little Messenger of the Sacred Heart* that's beside your beds. Don't let me come back and find you talking.

She comes into my room and wags her finger at me. Especially you, Francis, after thousands of boys prayed for you at the Confraternity. Give thanks, Francis, give thanks.

She leaves and there's silence for a while. Then Patricia whispers, Give thanks, Francis, give thanks, and say your rosary, Francis, and I laugh so hard a nurse runs in to see if I'm all right. She's a very stern nurse from the County Kerry[4]

Vocabulary
saluting (sə lo͞ot´ iŋ) v. honoring by performing an act or gesture

Author's Purpose
What humorous details here help you understand the situation better?

---

3. **habit** (hab´ it) n. the costume traditionally worn by nuns.
4. **County Kerry** (ker´ ē) southwestern county of Ireland.

and she frightens me. What's this, Francis? Laughing? What is there to laugh about? Are you and that Madigan girl talking? I'll report you to Sister Rita. There's to be no laughing for you could be doing serious damage to your internal apparatus.

She plods out and Patricia whispers again in a heavy Kerry accent, No laughing, Francis, you could be doin' serious damage to your internal apparatus. Say your rosary, Francis, and pray for your internal apparatus.

Mam visits me on Thursdays. I'd like to see my father, too, but I'm out of danger, crisis time is over, and I'm allowed only one visitor. Besides, she says, he's back at work at Rank's Flour Mills and please God this job will last a while with the war on and the English desperate for flour.[5] She brings me a chocolate bar and that proves Dad is working. She could never afford it on the dole.[6] He sends me notes. He tells me my brothers are all praying for me, that I should be a good boy, obey the doctors, the nuns, the nurses, and don't forget to say my prayers. He's sure St. Jude pulled me through the crisis because he's the patron saint of desperate cases and I was indeed a desperate case. ●

Patricia says she has two books by her bed. One is a poetry book and that's the one she loves. The other is a short history of England and do I want it? She gives it to Seamus, the man who mops the floors every day, and he brings it to me. He says, I'm not supposed to be bringing anything from a dipteria room to a typhoid room with all the germs flying around and hiding between the pages and if you ever catch dipteria on top of the typhoid they'll know and I'll lose my good job and be out on the street singing patriotic songs with a tin cup in my hand, which I could easily do because there isn't a song ever written about Ireland's sufferings I don't know. . . .

Oh, yes, he knows Roddy McCorley. He'll sing it for me right

✓ **Reading Check**

Why does the nurse run into Frank's room?

---

5. **with the war on and the English desperate for flour** (1939–1945) The Second World War caused shortages of food and other basic supplies in England.
6. **on the dole** unemployed and receiving money from the government in compensation.

Author's Purpose
What is the effect of the author's choice to omit quotation marks to show when people are speaking?

Historical Context
What historical information about Ireland do you learn from Seamus's comments about the book he gives Frank?

enough but he's barely into the first verse when the Kerry nurse rushes in. What's this, Seamus? Singing? Of all the people in this hospital you should know the rules against singing. I have a good mind to report you to Sister Rita.

Ah, . . . don't do that, nurse.

Very well, Seamus. I'll let it go this one time. You know the singing could lead to a relapse in these patients.

When she leaves he whispers he'll teach me a few songs because singing is good for passing the time when you're by yourself in a typhoid room. He says Patricia is a lovely girl the way she often gives him sweets from the parcel her mother sends every fortnight. He stops mopping the floor and calls to Patricia in the next room, I was telling Frankie you're a lovely girl, Patricia, and she says, You're a lovely man, Seamus. He smiles because he's an old man of forty and he never had children but the ones he can talk to here in the Fever Hospital. He says, Here's the book, Frankie. Isn't is a great pity you have to be reading all about England after all they did to us, that there isn't a history of Ireland to be had in this hospital.

The book tells me all about King Alfred and William the Conqueror and all the kings and queens down to Edward, who had to wait forever for his mother, Victoria, to die before he could be king. The book has the first bit of Shakespeare I ever read.

I do believe, induced by potent circumstances
That thou art mine enemy.

The history writer says this is what Catherine, who is a wife of Henry the Eighth, says to Cardinal Wolsey, who is trying to have her head cut off. I don't know what it means and I don't care because it's Shakespeare and it's like having jewels in my mouth when I say the words. If I had a whole book of Shakespeare they could keep me in the hospital for a year. • Patricia says she doesn't know what induced means or potent circumstances and she doesn't care about Shakespeare, she has her poetry book and she reads to me from beyond the wall a poem about an owl and a pussycat that went to sea in a green boat with honey and money and it makes no sense and when I say that Patricia gets huffy and says that's the last poem she'll ever read to me. She says I'm always reciting the lines from Shakespeare and they make no sense either. Seamus stops mopping again

Reading Skill: Author's Purpose

1. What information from the Background on page 139 helps you understand the **author's purpose**?

2. (a) What other purposes for writing might McCourt have had? **(b)** Which details in the passage support your response?

Literary Analysis: Historical Context

© **3. Key Ideas and Details** Use a chart like the one shown to record factual details that give clues about the work's historical context.

Historical Context	Details
Widespread disease	1. Many children die from typhoid and diphtheria.
	2.

© **4. Key Ideas and Details** How does the historical context help you understand Seamus's actions in the selection?

Vocabulary

© **Acquisition and Use** Use your understanding of the italicized words to explain your answer to each question.

1. If you *guzzled* your lemonade, did you drink it slowly?

2. In what professions is *saluting* most common?

3. Is a *miracle* an everyday occurrence?

4. If you feel *desperate,* are you happy?

5. Does a *patriotic* person care about his or her country?

6. If your parents *ban* television, are you allowed to watch it?

Word Study Use the context of the sentences and what you know about the **Latin root *-spes-*** to explain your answer to each question.

1. Does a *prosperous* person have trouble paying bills?

2. If you feel *despair,* have you lost all hope?

Word Study

The **Latin root *-sper-*** or *-spes-* means "hope."

Apply It Explain how the root contributes to the meanings of these words. Consult a print or digital dictionary if necessary.
despair
prosper
prosperous

Integrated Language Skills

My First Free Summer •
from Angela's Ashes

Conventions: Possessive Pronouns

A **possessive pronoun** is a pronoun that shows possession or ownership. Possessive pronouns take the place of possessive nouns and can be singular or plural. They must agree in number and gender with the noun to which they refer.

Pronouns	Possessive Pronouns	Examples
I, we	my, mine, our, ours	I wore *my* hat. The hat is *mine*. We took *our* car.
you	your, yours	You ate *your* plum. The plum is *yours*.
he, she, it	his, her, hers, its	He wore *his* jersey. The gloves are *hers*.
they	their, theirs	They rode *their* horses. The horses are *theirs*.

Practice A Identify the possessive pronouns in each sentence. Write *before a noun* or *stands alone* to tell how each pronoun is used.

1. Her mother insists that she learn English.
2. After four years, the summer is hers to enjoy.
3. One day her mother tells the girls to pack their bags.
4. It is her parents' wish to leave the island country, not Julia's.

ⓒ Reading Application In "My First Free Summer," find two sentences that contain possessive pronouns.

Practice B Rewrite each sentence, using a possessive pronoun in place of each underlined word or words. Your choice should agree in number and gender.

1. The other two beds in *Francis's* room are empty.
2. The nurses do not approve of *Francis's and Patricia's* conversation.
3. The two books are *Patricia's*.
4. As Patricia reads the poem, *the poem's* words grip her.

ⓒ Writing Application Write two sentences about friends who share a book. Use possessive pronouns.

PH WRITING COACH	Further instruction and practice are available in *Prentice Hall Writing Coach*.

Writing

Common Core State Standards

L.7.1, L.7.6; W.7.2.b, W.7.2.c; SL.7.1.c
[For the full wording of the standards, see page 128.]

Informative Text Write a **letter** on one of the following topics:

- Write to young Julia Alvarez, describing what it's like to go to school in the United States.
- Write to young Frank McCourt, describing one of your favorite stories or poems.

Before you write, gather your ideas. First, write facts about your topic, such as the hours you attend school or the characters in your story or poem. Next, write some of the things you like most or least about your topic. Use concrete details and examples.

Refer to your notes to develop an organized letter. As you introduce each new topic, use transitions to help your reader see the way you connect the ideas and additional details you want to convey.

Remember to include the date, a greeting, a closing, and a signature. If you handwrite your letter, write legibly.

Grammar Application Check your letter for punctuation, capitalization, spelling, and the correct use of all possessive pronouns.

Writing Workshop: *Work in Progress*

Prewriting for Autobiography Refer to the People List in your writing portfolio. Choose one or two people from this list, and create a timeline of a significant event you experienced with each one.

Use this prewriting activity to prepare for the **Writing Workshop** on page 176.

Speaking and Listening

Comprehension and Collaboration Each of these selections describes an important moment in the author's life. Conduct an **interview** with a friend, relative, or classmate to learn more about a serious event that impacted his or her life. Consider talking to someone who moved to a new country or neighborhood, attended a new school, had a threatening illness, or overcame a difficult situation.

Use these tips to conduct your interview:

- Create a list of questions beforehand to guide the interview.
- During the interview, ask follow-up questions to gather further details and information. For example, if your subject says his or her old school was more difficult, follow up with a question such as, "How many hours a day did you attend?" Add relevant comments to keep the discussion moving.

Present your findings to the class.

- Interactive graphic organizers
- Grammar tutorial
- Interactive journals

Test Practice: Reading

Author's Purpose

Fiction Selection

Directions: *Read the selection. Then, answer the questions.*

My dad loves to play pranks on April Fools' Day. He started many years ago by shaking our hands with a hidden buzzer that tickled us. My sisters and I loved that joke. Each year, he would think of creative ways to make us laugh for weeks before April 1st. Over time, the pranks got funnier and more creative. One April 1st, we awoke to find the furniture in our house rearranged! He liked to think of ways to surprise each of us with a special prank. Mom's favorite joke was when Dad wrote her a big check and told her to cash it the next day. That's when she discovered it had been written in disappearing ink!

1. What is the author's purpose for writing this passage?
   A. to inform
   B. to persuade
   C. to entertain
   D. to teach

2. Which of the following details does *not* support the author's purpose?
   A. Dad shakes hands with a tickling buzzer.
   B. The narrator has sisters.
   C. Dad rearranges the furniture.
   D. Mom gets a check written with disappearing ink.

3. Which word *best* describes the narrator's father?
   A. serious
   B. nervous
   C. thoughtful
   D. playful

4. Which of these words *best* describes the author's tone—her feelings about her father and his April Fools' Day tradition?
   A. wistful
   B. sarcastic
   C. loving
   D. alarmed

Writing for Assessment

Reread the passage, and write a paragraph in which you describe the author's purpose. Cite specific details from the passage that help the author achieve her purpose for writing.

Nonfiction Selection

Directions: *Read the selection. Then, answer the questions.*

Ready to laugh and make others laugh? The annual International Clown Convention will take place November 3rd through 5th at the Civic Center in downtown Portland. Register now for side-splitting classes taught by clowning professionals from around the world. It is never too late to try something new! Learn how to juggle, ride a unicycle, apply clown makeup like a pro, and more! While you're here, be sure to visit our huge costume and gift shop on the second floor of the Civic Center, where you'll find hilarious gag gifts as well as Portland's widest selection of wacky costumes and accessories. The convention runs every day from 10 a.m. to 10 p.m. Space is limited, so register now before this circus leaves town!

1. What is the author's purpose for writing this passage?
   A. The author wants to stress the importance of humor.
   B. The author wants to inform readers that the Civic Center is crowded.
   C. The author wants to persuade readers to register for the clown convention.
   D. The author wants to entertain readers with facts about clowning.

2. Which possible title would *best* support the author's purpose?
   A. The Clowns Are Coming
   B. Register Now for Clown Classes
   C. Learn Something New
   D. Clowns Are No Joke

3. Why does the author include information about the costume and gift shop?
   A. to encourage readers to visit the shop
   B. to mention the store hours
   C. to appeal to people who do not like classes
   D. to convince people to be funny

4. What words from the article *best* support the author's purpose?
   A. side-splitting; clowning professionals; Portland's widest selection
   B. International Clown Convention; juggle; gift shop
   C. November 3rd through 5th; Civic Center; downtown Portland
   D. around the world; try something new; circus leaves town

Writing for Assessment

Connecting Across Texts
If the father in the first passage read the second passage in his local newspaper, do you think the author of the second passage would partly achieve his purpose for writing? Write a brief response, using details from the two passages to support your answer.

www.PHLitOnline.com
- Online practice
- Instant feedback

Reading for Information

Analyzing Functional Texts

Application	Contract

© Common Core State Standards

Reading Informational Text
5. Analyze the structure an author uses to organize a text, including how the major sections contribute to the whole and to the development of the ideas.
6. Determine an author's point of view or purpose in a text and analyze how the author distinguishes his or her position from that of others.

Language
6. Acquire and use accurately grade-appropriate general academic and domain-specific words and phrases; gather vocabulary knowledge when considering a word or phrase important to comprehension or expression.

Writing
10. Write routinely over extended time frames and shorter time frames for a range of discipline-specific tasks, purposes, and audiences.

Reading Skill: Analyze Structure and Purpose

When you **analyze structure and purpose** in a text, you examine *how* the information is organized and *why* it is organized in that way. Workplace documents, such as applications and contracts, include structural features that are intended to make information clear and easy to locate. Applications, for example, require special formatting so that applicants can easily fill in information. Contracts, on the other hand, typically contain lists of rules and conditions that the signer agrees to obey and fulfill.

Structural Features of Applications	Structural Features of Contracts
• **introduction:** provides a description of the position and an explanation of the application process • **headings:** show where to find categories of information • **directions:** explain how to fill out the application • **rows and columns:** allow applicants to provide information in an organized format	• **headings and subheadings:** help readers locate information on a topic • **bulleted or numbered lists:** provide a quick way to reference essential information • **acknowledgment or certification:** requires the parties involved to formally agree to the terms of the contract

Content-Area Vocabulary

These words appear in the selections that follow. You may also encounter them in other content-area texts.

- **applicants** (ap´lə kənts) *n.* people who apply for something
- **misconception** (mis´kən sep´shən) *n.* mistaken idea
- **criterion** (krī tir´ē ən) *n.* rule for making a judgment

The Flat Rock Playhouse

Application

Features:
- directions explaining how to apply for a job, group, school, or service
- spaces in which applicants provide information
- descriptions of terms of employment, participation, or membership

The Flat Rock Playhouse has grown in recent years from a traditional summer theater to a regional powerhouse. It boasts one of the largest Resident Contract Agreements with Actors' Equity Association, the union of actors and stage managers, in the southern region. Flat Rock Playhouse unites its seasonal talent pool with its year-round administrative and artistic staff, 70% of whom were formerly apprentices and interns. The Playhouse proudly trains and educates to nurture its own future.

• Do you have a reputable Equity Apprenticeship in your background? Outside an education setting what steps have you taken to build a career? Have you begun professional networking? • How are you going to make the contacts necessary to get the job? • Do you have acting professionals on your reference list? • What do you know about marketing yourself in the theater business? Do you have a professionally photographed head shot? • Do you have a means to continually update your resume? • Do you know how to find an agent? Do you know how to get call backs at a cattle-call audition? • Would you feel comfortable in a professional environment? • Are you ready to join a union? Are you a triple-threat talent?

This part of the introduction describes the application process.

We will be attending SETC (Southeastern Theatre Conference) in March and will be happy to contact all serious applicants who have already initiated contact regarding their audition numbers. Applicants can, of course, call and set up personal auditions at the Playhouse if they are not attending SETC. However, if one's schedule or geographic distance from the Playhouse makes a personal audition impossible, one may send a videotaped audition consisting of two monologues and if applicable examples of singing and dance work. Also to expedite our selection and registration process, be sure to include two reference letters with the return correspondence. An application form and descriptive material about the program are subject to change due to variations in the talents and needs of each student class. Please complete and return the application at your earliest convenience if you wish to be considered among this year's candidates.

Apprentice Application Form for the Vagabond School of Drama

TO ENROLL: PLEASE **PRINT** THIS FORM, COMPLETE IT, AND RETURN IT WITH A HEADSHOT OR SNAP SHOT, as well as any other information you deem necessary. Videotapes are welcome. Auditions and/or interviews by the Executive Director or his appointee are required.

Student Name		Social Security
Address		
City	State	Zip
Home Phone	Work Phone	E-mail
Age Date of Birth / /	Weight Height	Hair Color

Instruction

Song	Dance	Instruments

Theater Training		
Parent/Guardian Name		
Address		
City	State	Zip
Home Phone	Work Phone	E-mail

Please provide a character reference

Name		
Address		
City	State	Zip
Home Phone	Work Phone	E-mail

The Vagabond School of the Drama, Inc. is a not-for-profit educational institution that admits students of any race, creed, sex, national, or ethnic origin.

> The directions at the top of the page explain what applicants are required to do.

> The application provides spaces for applicants to give information about themselves.

Contract

Features:

- explanation of terms of agreement
- lists of responsibilities of each party
- lines on which parties sign their names

"Theater Show Contract"

Crew and Cast Contract for the completion of school work.

Dear Faculty and Students,
This is the play contract. With the current show, the crew and cast will be working very hard at rehearsals and performances. This work often requires late hours and leaves minimal time to complete homework assignments.

- This contract was designed to help the student and teacher reach a mutual agreement for completion of the work.

- If the class work is not completed under the terms of this agreement, the student will be held responsible for missing assignments.

- In most cases, this contract is used as a tool to *extend* assignment due dates and not as an excuse to get out of the work.

> The bulleted list calls out some important terms of the contract.

- If students and teachers have difficulty reaching a workable solution, it is advised that the student contact his/her advisor to help with this process.

- It is a common **misconception** that the play is over on Saturday night. Actually, all members of the cast and crew are required to participate in the "Strike" clean-up on Sunday. Please consider this fact when arranging new deadlines. Strike will often consume the better part of the day.

Thank you very much for your understanding. Hope to see you at the show!

Crew Commitments

> This subheading introduces the section dealing with crew responsibilities.

Saturday Set Crew

Anyone can come and help on Saturdays. You can come as often as you like and stay for any amount of time you can spare. {The Crew members, who come to the most Saturdays, have the best chance of being on Running Crew.} Lunch is usually at 1 pm and typically costs $5.

Running Crew, Crew Chiefs, and Props

Crew members who are crew chiefs or on Running Crew will need to be available at specific times. When you accept a job on Crew you are accepting the calls that go with that job. Any problems or conflicts you have with these times need to be discussed and confirmed in advance.

1) Running Crew:

Come to as many Saturdays as you can. Our first **criterion** for selecting Running Crew is how many Saturdays you attended to help build the set. You need to come to all calls from tech Sunday through Strike.

2) Crew Chiefs:

This is what is expected of the different jobs. Remember to discuss conflicts in advance.

Stage Manager = All calls, all meetings.

Lights Director = All calls, all meetings.

Sound Director = All calls, all meetings.

Assistant Stage Manager = All calls, all meetings.

Props = Attend as many Meetings and Saturdays as you can. Attend all calls from tech Sunday to Strike. You will need to attend a minimum of one rehearsal per week.

> This list shows the requirements of certain positions.

My Name is: _____

I have been selected for the following position (circle):

Stage Manager	Sound	Helper
Assistant Stage	Running Crew	Props
Manager	Actor	Costumes
Lights	Musician	Student Director

I understand the calls/rehearsals that I need to attend.

I have conflicts with the following times. _____

> Lines are provided so that the parties can sign their names and make the contract official.

Student's acknowledgment:

I realize that it is my responsibility to live up to this contract.

Student's signature _____

Advisor's acknowledgment:

I understand that my advisee is involved in the theater production. I have kept a copy of this contract.

Advisor's signature _____

Comparing Functional Texts

1. Key Ideas and Details (a) How does the **purpose** of an application differ from the purpose of a contract? **(b)** In what ways does the **structure** of each document support its purpose?

Content-Area Vocabulary

2. Use the words *applicants, criterion,* and *misconception* in a short paragraph about a community theater.

Timed Writing

Explanatory Text: Chart

> **Format**
> The prompt gives specific directions regarding how your writing should be organized.

Congratulations! You have been cast in your school's play. Explain how you will manage your time to include rehearsals. Make a chart that details your daily schedule. For each hour of the day, explain what you will accomplish in that hour. Be sure to allow time for homework and other responsibilities. (15 minutes)

> **Academic Vocabulary**
> When you *explain* a situation, process, or idea, you provide details and reasons to make it more understandable to readers.

5-Minute Planner

Complete these steps before you begin to write:

1. Read the prompt carefully and completely. Look for key words like the ones highlighted to complete the assignment.
2. Make a list of all your daily responsibilities, including tasks at home, class time, homework, and other responsibilities.
3. Next to your list of responsibilities, jot down the times of day you think you might accomplish each task.
4. Decide how to organize your chart so that it follows the required format and makes information easy to locate.
5. Create a blank chart, and use the list and notes you made about your daily responsibilities to fill in the chart.

Comparing Characters

A **character** is a person, animal, or being that takes part in the action of a literary work. In literature, you will find characters with a range of personalities and attitudes. For example, a character might be dependable and smart but also stubborn. The qualities that make each character unique are called **character traits.** Writers use the process of **characterization** to create and develop characters. There are two types of characterization:

- **Direct characterization:** The writer directly states or describes the character's traits.

- **Indirect characterization:** The writer reveals a character's personality through his or her words and actions, and through the thoughts, words, and actions of others.

A character's responses may be internal or external. An **internal response** reveals a character's thoughts, while an **external response** consists of a character's actions or deeds. Writers use the internal and external responses of characters to **develop the plot** of a literary work. For example, the characters' responses can strongly influence the conflict—the problem or struggle that increases the tension in a story.

As you read, look for character traits that show each narrator's qualities, attitudes, and values. Use a chart like the one below to analyze how the writer develops the narrator's character.

**Common Core
State Standards**

**Reading Literature
3.** Analyze how particular elements of a story or drama interact.

**Reading Informational Texts
3.** Analyze the interactions between individuals, events, and ideas in a text.

**Writing
2.a.** Introduce a topic clearly, previewing what is to follow; organize ideas, concepts, and information, using strategies such as definition, classification, comparison/contrast, and cause/effect.

	"The Night the Bed Fell"	"Stolen Day"
Main character		
Direct descriptions		
Character's words and actions		
What others say about character		

www.PHLitOnline.com

- Vocabulary flashcards
- Interactive journals
- More about the authors
- Selection audio
- Interactive graphic organizers

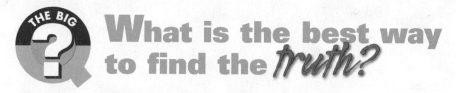

What is the best way to find the *truth?*

Writing About the Big Question

Each of these stories describes a misunderstanding that happened when people's own beliefs got in the way of what is true. Use this sentence starter to develop your ideas.

When people **misunderstand** a situation, it creates confusion because _____.

Meet the Authors

James Thurber (1894–1961)
Author of "The Night the Bed Fell"

According to James Thurber, if you had lived in his Ohio home, you would have observed absurd events. He wrote of such events—but always showed affection for his quirky relatives.

Understanding Humor To Thurber, humor results from the contrast between the confusion of a moment and the insight gained later. In "The Night the Bed Fell," Thurber calmly recounts and makes sense of an instance of total confusion—and the result is laughter. Thurber's literary home was *The New Yorker* magazine, where he wrote essays that gently poked fun at the world. He often did line drawings for his essays, even when his sight began to fail him.

Sherwood Anderson (1876–1941)
Author of "Stolen Day"

As a teenager, Sherwood Anderson worked as a newsboy, housepainter, and stable groom. Later, he fought in Cuba in the Spanish-American War. Even though Anderson did not begin to write professionally until he was forty years old, he is considered an important writer of the twentieth century.

A Powerful Influence Anderson's novel *Winesburg, Ohio* was published in 1919. In it, Anderson used simple, everyday language to capture the sense of loneliness and lost hope of characters living in a small town.

The Night the Bed Fell

James Thurber

I suppose that the high-water mark of my youth in Columbus, Ohio, was the night the bed fell on my father. It makes a better recitation (unless, as some friends of mine have said, one has heard it five or six times) than it does a piece of writing, for it is almost necessary to throw furniture around, shake doors, and bark like a dog, to lend the proper atmosphere and verisimilitude[1] to what is admittedly a somewhat incredible tale. Still, it did take place.

It happened, then, that my father had decided to sleep in the attic one night, to be away where he could think. My mother opposed the notion strongly because, she said, the old wooden bed up there was unsafe: it was wobbly and the heavy headboard would crash down on father's head in case the bed fell, and kill him. There was no dissuading him, however, and at a quarter past ten he closed the attic door behind him and went up the narrow twisting stairs. We later heard ominous creakings as he crawled into bed. Grandfather, who usually slept in the attic bed when he was with us, had disappeared some days before. On these occasions he was usually gone six or eight days and returned growling and out of temper, with the news that the

Vocabulary
ominous (äm´ ə nəs) *adj.* threatening

---

1. verisimilitude (ver´ ə si mil´ ə tōōd) *n.* appearance of truth or reality.

Federal Union[2] was run by a passel of blockheads and that the Army of the Potomac[3] didn't have a chance.

We had visiting us at this time a nervous first cousin of mine named Briggs Beall, who believed that he was likely to cease breathing when he was asleep. It was his feeling that if he were not awakened every hour during the night, he might die of suffocation. He had been accustomed to setting an alarm clock to ring at intervals until morning, but I persuaded him to abandon this. He slept in my room and I told him that I was such a light sleeper that if anybody quit breathing in the same room with me, I would wake instantly. He tested me the first night—which I had suspected he would—by holding his breath after my regular breathing had convinced him I was asleep. I was not asleep, however, and called to him. This seemed to allay his fears a little, but he took the precaution of putting a glass of spirits of camphor[4] on a little table at the head of his bed. In case I didn't arouse him until he was almost gone, he said, he would sniff the camphor, a powerful reviver. Briggs was not the only member of his family who had his crotchets.[5] Old Aunt Melissa Beall (who could whistle like a man, with two fingers in her mouth) suffered under the premonition that she was destined to die on South High Street, because she had been born on South High Street and married on South High Street. Then there was Aunt Sarah Shoaf, who never went to bed at night without the fear that a burglar was going to get in and blow chloroform[6] under her door through a tube. To avert this calamity—for she was in greater dread of anesthetics than of losing her household goods—she always piled her money, silverware, and other valuables in a neat stack just outside her bedroom, with a note reading: "This is all I have. Please take it and do not use your chloroform, as this is all I have." Aunt Gracie Shoaf also had a burglar phobia, but she met it with more fortitude. She was confident that burglars had been getting into her house every night for forty years. The fact that she never missed anything was to her no proof to the contrary. She always claimed that she scared them off before they could take anything, by throwing shoes down the hallway. When she went to bed she piled, where she could get at them handily, all the shoes

Character
What details about this character are probably exaggerated?

Character
What are the contrasts between the aunts' beliefs and reality?

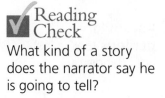
Reading Check
What kind of a story does the narrator say he is going to tell?

---

2. **Federal Union** northern side during the Civil War of the 1860s. He is under the illusion that the Civil War has not yet ended.
3. **Army of the Potomac** one of the northern armies during the Civil War.
4. **spirits of camphor** liquid with a powerful odor.
5. **crotchets** (kräch′ its) *n.* peculiar ideas.
6. **chloroform** (klôr′ ə fôrm′) *n.* substance used at one time as an anesthetic.

Vocabulary
perilous (per´ ə ləs) *adj.* dangerous

there were about her house. Five minutes after she had turned off the light, she would sit up in bed and say "Hark!" Her husband, who had learned to ignore the whole situation as long ago as 1903, would either be sound asleep or pretend to be sound asleep. In either case he would not respond to her tugging and pulling, so that presently she would arise, tiptoe to the door, open it slightly and heave a shoe down the hall in one direction, and its mate down the hall in the other direction. Some nights she threw them all, some nights only a couple of pair.

But I am straying from the remarkable incidents that took place during the night that the bed fell on father. By midnight we were all in bed. The layout of the rooms and the disposition[7] of their occupants is important to an understanding of what later occurred. In the front room upstairs (just under father's attic bedroom) were my mother and my brother Herman, who sometimes sang in his sleep, usually "Marching Through Georgia" or "Onward, Christian Soldiers." Briggs Beall and myself were in a room adjoining this one. My brother Roy was in a room across the hall from ours. Our bull terrier, Rex, slept in the hall.

My bed was an army cot, one of those affairs which are made wide enough to sleep on comfortably only by putting up, flat with the middle section, the two sides which ordinarily hang down like the sideboards of a drop-leaf table. When these sides are up, it is perilous to roll too far toward the edge, for then the cot is likely to tip completely over, bringing the whole bed down on top of one, with a tremendous banging crash. This, in fact, is precisely what happened about two o'clock in the morning. (It was my mother who, in recalling the scene later, first referred to it as "the night the bed fell on your father.")

---

7. **disposition** (dis´ pə zish´ ən) *n.* arrangement.

Always a deep sleeper, slow to arouse (I had lied to Briggs), I was at first unconscious of what had happened when the iron cot rolled me onto the floor and toppled over on me. It left me still warmly bundled up and unhurt, for the bed rested above me like a canopy. Hence I did not wake up, only reached the edge of consciousness and went back. The racket, however, instantly awakened my mother, in the next room, who came to the immediate conclusion that her worst dread was realized: the big wooden bed upstairs had fallen on father. She therefore screamed, "Let's go to your poor father!" It was this shout, rather than the noise of my cot falling, that awakened Herman, in the same room with her. He thought that mother had become, for no apparent reason, hysterical. "You're all right, Mamma!" he shouted, trying to calm her. They exchanged shout for shout for perhaps ten seconds: "Let's go to your poor father!" and "You're all right!" That woke up Briggs. By this time I was conscious of what was going on, in a vague way, but did not yet realize that I was under my bed instead of on it. Briggs, awakening in the midst of loud shouts of fear and apprehension, came to the

▼ **Critical Viewing**
What part of the story does this picture show? **[Connect]**

Character
How does the mother's reaction make this situation humorous?

Reading Check
What type of bed does the narrator sleep on this night?

He came to the conclusion that he was suffocating. by James Thurber

quick conclusion that he was suffocating and that we were all trying to "bring him out." With a low moan, he grasped the glass of camphor at the head of his bed and instead of sniffing it poured it over himself. The room reeked of camphor. "Ugf, ahfg," choked Briggs, like a drowning man, for he had almost succeeded in stopping his breath under the deluge of pungent spirits. He leaped out of bed and groped toward the open window, but he came up against one that was closed. With his hand, he beat out the glass, and I could hear it crash and tinkle on the alleyway below. It was at this juncture that I, in trying to get up, had the uncanny sensation of feeling my bed above me! Foggy with sleep, I now suspected, in my turn, that the whole uproar was being made in a frantic endeavor to extricate me from what must be an unheard-of and perilous situation. "Get me out of this!" I bawled. "Get me out!" I think I had the nightmarish belief that I was entombed in a mine. "Gugh," gasped Briggs, floundering in his camphor.

By this time my mother, still shouting, pursued by Herman, still shouting, was trying to open the door to the attic, in order to go up and get my father's body out of the wreckage. The door was stuck, however, and wouldn't yield. Her frantic pulls on it only added to the general banging and confusion. Roy and the dog were now up, the one shouting questions, the other barking.

Father, farthest away and soundest sleeper of all, had by this time been awakened by the battering on the attic door. He decided that the house was on fire. "I'm coming, I'm coming!" he wailed in a slow, sleepy voice—it took him many minutes to regain full consciousness. My mother,

Character
What action does Briggs perform that helps to reveal his nervous personality?

▶ **Critical Viewing**
How does the action in this drawing capture the mood of the story? **[Analyze]**

Roy had to throw Rex. by James Thurber

still believing he was caught under the bed, detected in his "I'm coming!" the mournful, resigned note of one who is preparing to meet his Maker. "He's dying!" she shouted.

"I'm all right!" Briggs yelled to reassure her. "I'm all right!" He still believed that it was his own closeness to death that was worrying mother. I found at last the light switch in my room, unlocked the door, and Briggs and I joined the others at the attic door. The dog, who never did like Briggs, jumped for him—assuming that he was the culprit in whatever was going on—and Roy had to throw Rex and hold him. We could hear father crawling out of bed upstairs. Roy pulled the attic door open, with a mighty jerk, and father came down the stairs, sleepy and irritable but safe and sound. My mother began to weep when she saw him. Rex began to howl. "What in the name of heaven is going on here?" asked father.

The situation was finally put together like a gigantic jigsaw puzzle. Father caught a cold from prowling around in his bare feet but there were no other bad results. "I'm glad," said mother, who always looked on the bright side of things, "that your grandfather wasn't here."

Character
What characteristics make the mother amusing?

Vocabulary
culprit (kul´ prit)
n. guilty person

Spiral Review
Central Idea What are two central ideas in this humorous essay?

Critical Thinking

Cite textual evidence to support your responses.

1. **Key Ideas and Details** **(a)** Who is in the house on the night Thurber describes? **(b) Compare:** What quality or qualities do these characters share? **(c) Support:** What examples illustrate the shared qualities?

2. **Key Ideas and Details** **(a)** Describe the layout of the rooms. **(b) Analyze:** Why is the placement of the rooms in the house important to the events?

3. **Key Ideas and Details** **(a)** What do Briggs, Aunt Sarah Shoaf, and Aunt Gracie Shoaf do before going to bed? **(b) Infer:** What do you suppose the author, looking back, thinks of this behavior? **(c) Make a Judgment:** Do you think the author treats his relatives fairly in the essay? Why or why not?

4. **Integration of Knowledge and Ideas** **(a)** How do the misunderstandings in this essay help reveal each character's beliefs? **(b)** How can we use a misunderstanding to bring us closer to the truth? *[Connect to the Big Question: What is the best way to find the truth?]*

It must be that **all children** are actors.

Stolen Day

Sherwood Anderson

It must be that all children are actors. The whole thing started with a boy on our street named Walter, who had inflammatory rheumatism.[1] That's what they called it. He didn't have to go to school.

Still he could walk about. He could go fishing in the creek or the waterworks pond. There was a place up at the pond where in the spring the water came tumbling over the dam and formed a deep pool. It was a good place. Sometimes you could get some big ones there.

I went down that way on my way to school one spring morning. It was out of my way but I wanted to see if Walter was there.

He was, inflammatory rheumatism and all. There he was, sitting with a fish pole in his hand. He had been able to walk down there all right.

It was then that my own legs began to hurt. My back too. I went on to school but, at the recess time, I began to cry. I did it when the teacher, Sarah Suggett, had come out into the schoolhouse yard.

She came right over to me.

"I ache all over," I said. I did, too.

---

1. **inflammatory rheumatism** (in flam´ ə tôr´ ē rōō´ mə tiz´ əm) *n.* a disease which causes the joints to swell painfully and gradually break down.

Character
What can you tell about the narrator based on the pain he experiences?

I kept on crying and it worked all right.

"You'd better go on home," she said.

So I went. I limped painfully away. I kept on limping until I got out of the schoolhouse street.

Then I felt better. I still had inflammatory rheumatism pretty bad but I could get along better.

I must have done some thinking on the way home.

"I'd better not say I have inflammatory rheumatism," I decided. "Maybe if you've got that you swell up."

I thought I'd better go around to where Walter was and ask him about that, so I did—but he wasn't there.

"They must not be biting today," I thought.

I had a feeling that, if I said I had inflammatory rheumatism, Mother or my brothers and my sister Stella might laugh. They did laugh at me pretty often and I didn't like it at all.

"Just the same," I said to myself, "I have got it." I began to hurt and ache again.

I went home and sat on the front steps of our house. I sat there a long time. There wasn't anyone at home but Mother and the two little ones. Ray would have been four or five then and Earl might have been three.

It was Earl who saw me there. I had got tired sitting and was lying on the porch. Earl was always a quiet, solemn little fellow.

He must have said something to Mother for presently she came.

"What's the matter with you? Why aren't you in school?" she asked.

I came pretty near telling her right out that I had inflammatory rheumatism but I thought I'd better not. Mother and Father had been speaking of Walter's case at the table just the day before. "It affects the heart," Father had said. That frightened me when I thought of it. "I might die," I thought. "I might just suddenly die right here; my heart might stop beating."

Character
Why does the narrator's pain suddenly disappear?

Spiral Review
Theme How might the narrator's so-called pain relate to a possible theme?

Vocabulary
solemn (säl´ əm) *adj.* serious; somber

I kept on crying and it worked all right.

On the day before I had been running a race with my brother Irve. We were up at the fairgrounds after school and there was a half-mile track.

"I'll bet you can't run a half-mile," he said. "I bet you I could beat you running clear around the track."

And so we did it and I beat him, but afterwards my heart did seem to beat pretty hard. I remembered that lying there on the porch. "It's a wonder, with my inflammatory rheumatism and all, I didn't just drop down dead," I thought. The thought frightened me a lot. I ached worse than ever.

"I ache, Ma," I said. "I just ache."

She made me go in the house and upstairs and get into bed.

It wasn't so good. It was spring. I was up there for perhaps an hour, maybe two, and then I felt better.

I got up and went downstairs. "I feel better, Ma," I said.

Mother said she was glad. She was pretty busy that day and hadn't paid much attention to me. She had made me get into bed upstairs and then hadn't even come up to see how I was.

I didn't think much of that when I was up there but when I got downstairs where she was, and when, after I had said I felt better and she only said she was glad and went right on with her work, I began to ache again.

I thought, "I'll bet I die of it. I bet I do."

I went out to the front porch and sat down. I was pretty sore at Mother.

"If she really knew the truth, that I have the inflammatory rheumatism and I may just drop down dead any time, I'll bet

▲ **Critical Viewing**
Does this boy look genuinely upset, or do you think he is making himself cry, as the story's narrator does? Explain. **[Evaluate]**

Character
What character trait do the narrator's thoughts suggest?

Reading Check
What does the narrator believe is wrong with him?

she wouldn't care about that either," I thought.

I was getting more and more angry the more thinking I did.

"I know what I'm going to do," I thought; "I'm going to go fishing."

I thought that, feeling the way I did, I might be sitting on the high bank just above the deep pool where the water went over the dam, and suddenly my heart would stop beating.

And then, of course, I'd pitch forward, over the bank into the pool and, if I wasn't dead when I hit the water, I'd drown sure.

They would all come home to supper and they'd miss me.

"But where is he?"

Then Mother would remember that I'd come home from school aching.

She'd go upstairs and I wouldn't be there. One day during the year before, there was a child got drowned in a spring. It was one of the Wyatt children.

Right down at the end of the street there was a spring under a birch tree and there had been a barrel sunk in the ground.

Everyone had always been saying the spring ought to be kept covered, but it wasn't.

So the Wyatt child went down there, played around alone, and fell in and got drowned.

Mother was the one who had found the drowned child. She had gone to get a pail of water and there the child was, drowned and dead.

This had been in the evening when we were all at home, and Mother had come running up the street with the dead, dripping child in her arms. She was making for the Wyatt house as hard as she could run, and she was pale.

She had a terrible look on her face, I remembered then.

"So," I thought, "they'll miss me and there'll be a search made. Very likely there'll be someone who has seen me sitting by the pond fishing, and there'll be a big alarm and all the town will turn out and they'll drag the pond."

I was having a grand time, having died. Maybe, after they found me and had got me out of the deep pool, Mother would grab me up in her arms and run home with me as she had run with the Wyatt child.

Character
Based on this imaginary scene, what words would you use to describe the narrator?

I got up from the porch and went around the house. I got my fishing pole and lit out for the pool below the dam. Mother was busy—she always was—and didn't see me go. When I got there I thought I'd better not sit too near the edge of the high bank.

By this time I didn't ache hardly at all, but I thought.

"With inflammatory rheumatism you can't tell," I thought.

"It probably comes and goes," I thought.

"Walter has it and he goes fishing," I thought.

I had got my line into the pool and suddenly I got a bite. It was a regular whopper. I knew that. I'd never had a bite like that.

I knew what it was. It was one of Mr. Fenn's big carp.

Mr. Fenn was a man who had a big pond of his own. He sold ice in the summer and the pond was to make the ice. He had bought some big carp and put them into his pond and then, earlier in the spring when there was a freshet,[2] his dam had gone out.

So the carp had got into our creek and one or two big ones had been caught—but none of them by a boy like me.

The carp was pulling and I was pulling and I was afraid he'd break my line, so I just tumbled down the high bank holding onto the line and got right into the pool. We had it out, there in the pool. We struggled. We wrestled. Then I got a hand under his gills and got him out.

He was a big one all right. He was nearly half as big as I was myself. I had him on the bank and I kept one hand under his gills and I ran.

I never ran so hard in my life. He was slippery, and now and then he wriggled out of my arms; once I stumbled and fell on him, but I got him home.

So there it was. I was a big hero that day. Mother got a washtub and filled it with water. She put the fish in it and all the neighbors came to look. I got into dry clothes and went

"I know what I'm going to do," I thought; "I'm going to go fishing."

Character
What do the narrator's actions with the carp reveal about his physical condition?

Reading Check
What happened to the Wyatt child?

---

2. freshet (fresh′ it) a great rise or overflowing of a stream caused by heavy rains or melted snow.

I was a **BIG** *hero that day.*

down to supper—and then I made a break that spoiled my day.

There we were, all of us, at the table, and suddenly Father asked what had been the matter with me at school. He had met the teacher, Sarah Suggett, on the street and she had told him how I had become ill.

"What was the matter with you?" Father asked, and before I thought what I was saying I let it out.

"I had the inflammatory rheumatism," I said—and a shout went up. It made me sick to hear them, the way they all laughed.

It brought back all the aching again, and like a fool I began to cry.

"Well, I *have* got it—I *have*, I *have*," I cried, and I got up from the table and ran upstairs.

I stayed there until Mother came up. I knew it would be a long time before I heard the last of the inflammatory rheumatism. I was sick all right, but the aching I now had wasn't in my legs or in my back.

Critical Thinking

Cite textual evidence to support your responses.

1. **Key Ideas and Details** **(a)** What inspires the narrator to think he has inflammatory rheumatism? **(b) Infer:** Why does the narrator think this would be an appealing disease to have? **(c) Respond:** What do you think of his idea? Explain.

2. **Key Ideas and Details** **(a)** What does the narrator do after he gets home? **(b) Infer:** Why does his mother pay him little attention?

3. **Integration of Knowledge and Ideas** **(a)** How does his family respond when the narrator says he has inflammatory rheumatism? **(b) Defend:** Do you think the narrator's family should have been more understanding? Why or why not?

4. **Integration of Knowledge and Ideas** How does discovering what is *not* real help us determine what is real? Explain. *[Connect to the Big Question: What is the best way to find the truth?]*

Comparing Characters

© **1. Key Ideas and Details** Identify one example of **direct characterization** and one example of **indirect characterization** in each selection.

© **2. Key Ideas and Details (a)** What happens to the narrator's army cot in "The Night the Bed Fell"? **(b)** What does his mother think happened?

© **3. Key Ideas and Details (a)** What does the narrator of "Stolen Day" do that causes his teacher to send him home? **(b)** Why does he do this?

© **4. Integration of Knowledge and Ideas** Use the chart below to compare how the narrators of both stories are alike and how they are different.

	How similar?	How different?
Narrator: "Stolen Day"	A boy	Believes he is sick
Narrator: "The Night the Bed Fell"		

⏱ Timed Writing

Explanatory Text: Essay

In an essay, compare and contrast the narrators in these selections. Describe ways in which the narrators' internal and external responses to conflict affect the development of the plot. Cite evidence from the texts to support your analysis. **(30 minutes)**

5-Minute Planner

1. Read the prompt carefully and completely.

2. Answer these questions to help you gather your ideas.

   • What are a few traits of each narrator? How does each respond to conflict?

   • To what extent do the narrators' responses affect the plot of each selection?

   • Which narrator do you think will learn the most from his experiences? Why?

3. Create an outline in which you organize the details of your essay.

4. Reread the prompt, and then use your outline to draft your essay.

Writing Workshop

Write a Narrative

Narration: Autobiographical Narrative

Defining the Form Stories that tell of real events in a writer's life are called **autobiographical narratives.**

Assignment Write an autobiographical narrative about an event in your life that helped you grow or changed your outlook. Include

- ✔ a clear *sequence of events* involving you, the writer
- ✔ a problem or *conflict,* or a clear contrast between past and present viewpoints
- ✔ a *plot* line that includes a beginning, rising action, climax, and resolution, or *denouement*
- ✔ *pacing* that effectively builds the action
- ✔ *specific details and quotations*
- ✔ well-developed *major and minor characters*
- ✔ error-free writing, including *correct use of pronouns*

To preview the criteria on which your autobiographical narrative may be judged, see the rubric on page 183.

 Writing Workshop: *Work in Progress*

Review the work you did on pages 127 and 151.

WRITE GUY
Jeff Anderson, M.Ed.

What Do You Notice?

Structure and Style

These sentences are from Richard Peck's "The Three-Century Woman." Read them several times.

"I was wearing my beige coat—beige or off-white, I forget. Then whoosh! The gondola heated up like an oven, and people peeled out of the windows. We hit the ground and bounced."

Discuss these questions with a partner:

- What do you notice about the structure of these sentences?
- How does the sentence style add interest or increase action?

Think about ways to use structure to add interest to your writing.

 **Common Core State Standards**

Writing
3. Write narratives to develop real or imagined experiences or events using effective technique, relevant descriptive details, and well-structured event sequences.
3.a. Engage and orient the reader by establishing a context and point of view and introducing a narrator and/or characters; organize an event sequence that unfolds naturally and logically.

Reading-Writing Connection
To get the feel for narrative nonfiction, read *An American Childhood* by Annie Dillard (p. 52) and *Angela's Ashes* by Frank McCourt (p. 140)

Prewriting/Planning Strategies

Choose a topic. To choose the right event from your life to narrate, use one of the following strategies:

- **Freewriting** Write for five minutes about whatever comes to mind on these general topics: *funny times*, *sad times*, and *lessons I have learned*. When you are finished, review what you have written and circle any ideas that could make a good topic for your purpose and audience.

- **Listing** Fill in a chart like the one below. In each column, list names or descriptions of memorable people and things that you know or have a particular viewpoint about from home, school, or travel. Review your chart to find connections between the items. For each connection you find, circle the two items and draw an arrow between them. Finally, review the connections you have found, and jot down ideas for engaging stories that they suggest.

PHLit Online!
www.PHLitOnline.com
- Illustrated vocabulary words
- Interactive vocabulary games
- Vocabulary flashcards

People	Places	Things	Events

Make a timeline. Once you have decided on a topic, begin to gather the details that you will use in your narrative. Fill out a timeline like the one shown to organize your details in time order.

Timeline

Event 1: I meet Mark.

Event 2: We decide to join the swim team.

Event 3: Mark and I compete in the freestyle.

Detail 1: Mark has red hair, carries his knapsack everywhere.

Detail 2: Cold day—everybody lines up nervously by the pool waiting for the coach.

Detail 3: I feel funny about trying to beat Mark. He is probably my best friend.

Drafting Strategies

Common Core
State Standards

Writing
3. Write narratives to develop real or imagined experiences or events using effective technique, relevant descriptive details, and well-structured event sequences.
3.a. Engage and orient the reader by establishing a context and point of view and introducing a narrator and/or characters; organize an event sequence that unfolds naturally and logically.
3.d. Use precise words and phrases, relevant descriptive details, and sensory language to capture the action and convey experiences and events.
3.e. Provide a conclusion that follows from and reflects on the narrated experiences or events.

Map out your story. Make a conflict chart like the one below. In the center, write a brief description of the conflict. Fill in linked circles with specific narrative action related to the conflict. Number the circles to help put the events of your story in order. As you draft, refer to your chart to help connect details to your central conflict.

Develop the plot line. Once you have mapped out the plot, make sure that you arrange the pace in the story so that the conflict intensifies during the **rising action.** The climax should be the highest point of interest in your story. The **resolution,** or **denouement,** should be the conclusion in which your conflict is resolved.

Develop a setting. A vivid setting can bring your story to life and help readers understand your characters. When describing a setting, try to appeal to several of your readers' senses. Draw a word picture of the place with precise and colorful nouns, adjectives, verbs, and adverbs.

> **Vague Description:** We lived in a small town.
>
> **Vivid Description:** Main Street smelled like pine trees because the woods were only steps away.

Develop characters through dialogue. Bring people to life by using dialogue—quoting what people said as they said it. Do not report everything a character says. Instead, create conversations that vividly show the character's feelings, gestures, and expressions as he or she reacts to events.

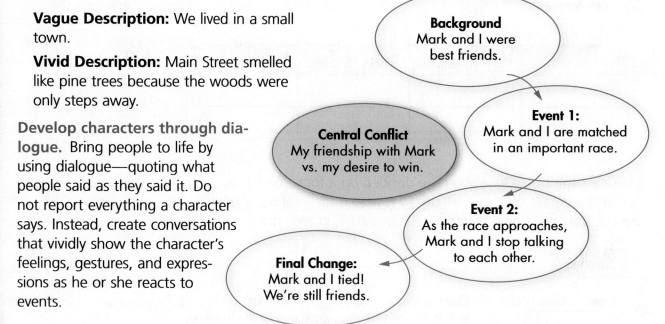

Background
Mark and I were best friends.

Central Conflict
My friendship with Mark vs. my desire to win.

Event 1:
Mark and I are matched in an important race.

Event 2:
As the race approaches, Mark and I stop talking to each other.

Final Change:
Mark and I tied! We're still friends.

Writers on Writing

Richard Peck On Conflict in Fiction

Richard Peck is the author of "The Three-Century Woman" (p. 11).

My novel *Fair Weather* is about a farm girl named Rosie Beckett who's never been anywhere until she and her family have the adventure of their lives. They visit the World's Columbian Exposition, the great Chicago World's Fair of 1893. It's in the Women's Building at the fair where Rosie finds her future. But the story begins down on the farm because all fiction is based on contrast: young, old; male, female; country, city. . . .

"I wrote 'The Three-Century Woman' twelve times. . . ."
— Richard Peck

Professional Model:

from *Fair Weather*

It was the last day of our old lives and we didn't even know it.

I didn't. It looked like any old day to me, a sultry, summer morning hot enough to ruffle the roofline. But then, any little thing could come as a surprise to us. We were just plain country people. I suppose we were poor, but we didn't know it. Poor, but proud. There wasn't a ~~scrap~~ **blister** of paint in the house, but there were no hogs under the porch, ~~and no rust on the implements~~.

I was sitting out in the old rope swing at the back of our place because the house was too full of Mama and my sister Lottie. I wasn't swinging. I thought I was pretty nearly too old to ~~be swinging~~ **swing**. In the fall I'd be fourteen, with only one more year of school to go.

Strangely, this book was published on September 10, 2001.

I decided to leave it with hogs. The detail about the rust wasn't necessary, as further evidence of the family's pride.

I wanted to suggest a conflict here between sister and mother, but to let the reader wonder what the problem is.

Revising Strategies

Common Core
State Standards

Writing
3.a. Engage and orient the reader by establishing a context and point of view and introducing a narrator and/or characters; organize an event sequence that unfolds naturally and logically.

3.b. Use narrative techniques, such as dialogue, pacing, and description, to develop experiences, events, and/or characters.

3.c. Use a variety of transition words, phrases, and clauses to convey sequence and signal shifts from one time frame or setting to another.

3.d. Use precise words and phrases, relevant descriptive details, and sensory language to capture the action and convey experiences and events.

5. With some guidance and support from peers and adults, develop and strengthen writing as needed by planning, revising, editing, rewriting, or trying a new approach, focusing on how well purpose and audience have been addressed.

Review sequence of events. Read through your narrative to make sure that the events you describe are in chronological order. Add transition words, such as *first, next, later,* and *finally,* to clarify the sequence of events.

Check your pacing. A good story builds to a single most exciting moment, called the **climax.** The secret of building to a climax is **pacing**—the speed at which your story moves along. Pace your story to build suspense. To improve the pacing of your story, use the following strategies:

- Cut details and events that do not build suspense or heighten readers' interest.
- Revise or delete any paragraph that is not clearly connected to the central conflict.
- Make clear connections between other events to show readers how events relate to each other.

Use specific, precise nouns. Look for nouns that are vague or general and might leave the reader wondering *what kind.* Replace general and vague nouns with specific and precise ones. Review your draft, circling any nouns that do not answer the questions *What exactly?* and *What kind?* Replace these nouns with specific, precise nouns that convey a lively picture. Use a dictionary to confirm the precise meaning of the words you are using.

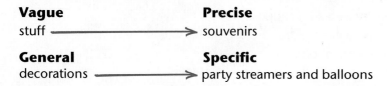

| **Vague** | **Precise** |
| stuff | ⟶ souvenirs |

| **General** | **Specific** |
| decorations | ⟶ party streamers and balloons |

Peer Review
Give your draft to one or two classmates to read. Ask them to highlight details that slow the story down or ideas that are unconnected to the central conflict. Use the feedback to eliminate any unnecessary details from your draft. As you review comments and revise your draft, adjust your writing to your purpose and audience as needed.

Checking Pronoun-Antecedent Agreement

Incorrect pronoun-antecedent agreement occurs when a personal pronoun disagrees with its antecedent in person, number, or gender.

Identifying Incorrect Pronoun-Antecedent Agreement An **antecedent** is the word or words for which a pronoun stands. A pronoun's antecedent may be a noun, a group of words acting as a noun, or another pronoun.

Antecedent   **Pronoun**

Example: I told <u>Alexis</u> to bring a bathing suit with <u>her</u>.

In this example, the pronoun *her* is third person and singular. It agrees with its feminine antecedent, *Alexis*, which is also third person (the person spoken about) and singular.

Fixing Agreement Errors To fix an incorrect pronoun-antecedent agreement, identify both the pronoun and the antecedent for which it stands. Then use one of the following methods.

1. **Identify the person of the antecedent** as first, second, or third. Choose a pronoun that matches the antecedent in person.

2. **Identify the number of the antecedent** as singular or plural. Choose a pronoun that matches the antecedent in number.

3. **Identify the gender of the antecedent** as masculine or feminine. Choose a pronoun that matches the antecedent in gender.

> **PH** **WRITING COACH**
>
> Further instruction and practice are available in *Prentice Hall Writing Coach*.

Personal Pronouns		
	Singular	**Plural**
First Person	I, me, my, mine	we, us, our, ours
Second Person	you, your, yours	you, your, yours
Third Person	**Feminine:** she, her, hers **Masculine:** he, him, his **Neutral:** it, its	they, them, their, theirs

Grammar in Your Writing
Read your draft. Draw an arrow from each personal pronoun to its antecedent. If the agreement is incorrect, fix it using one of the methods above.

Bicycle Braking Blues

Crash! Once again, I found myself flying off my bike and toward the grass. At age eight, crashes were an everyday occurrence, and I reminded myself that it was better to practice braking here by the lawn than to risk another episode like "The Club Hill Clobbering."

It all started when I arrived at my grandparents' house in Galesburg to spend the summer. I made many friends in their neighborhood, but they spent most of their time riding bikes, and I didn't have one. Then, my step-grandmother gave me the almost new, metallic green bike that her grandson had outgrown. I was over-joyed to have a bike. . . . I learned to ride it well enough—what I didn't learn was how to use the brakes. On the flat ground near my grandparents' house, I just let the bike slow down until I could put my feet down.

One day my babysitter took me for lunch at the club grill. She rode my grand-father's golf cart while I rode my bike. When we had to climb the big hill leading up to the club, I walked my bike alongside the cart. After lunch, I mounted my bike while Erika drove Grandpa's golf cart. As we headed toward home, neither of us gave a thought to . . . the HILL.

As we came around the corner of the bike path, I started picking up speed. By the time I realized what was happening, it was too late. "The hill!" I yelled to Erika. "Your brakes! Use your brakes!" she shouted. With the wind rushing in my ears, I could hardly hear her. Looking down the hill, I saw a golf cart was block-ing the path. It seemed to be getting bigger and closer by the second. "Well," I thought to myself, "it's now or never." I steered my speeding bike toward the grass alongside the path and jumped off sideways. I leapt off and BAM! The world turned upside down and inside out. The next sound I heard was the grumbling of a golf cart engine. It sounded annoyed about the jumble of parts in its path. The next thing I saw was Erika's face. She was so scared that her face was stiff and pale. I stood up to show Erika that I was fine. The only damage I sustained was some dirt on my jeans, and the bike survived without too many scratches too. Also, my pride was hurt. How can you ride a bike if you can never go down hill? So every day, Erika took me to the hill and we'd go a little further up. That way, I learned to brake on a hill, little by little, rather than getting clob-bered again!

With this hint, Alexander clearly con-nects his introduction to the central conflict of his story.

Adding this detail helps move the story along—it shows why a bike is so important to Alexander.

Alexander narrates events in clear sequence.

Using this precise noun helps vividly convey the scene to readers.

Details such as *stiff* and *pale* help readers vividly imagine Erika's expression.

Editing and Proofreading

Review your draft to correct errors in spelling, grammar, and punctuation.

Focus on the Dialogue: As you proofread your story, pay close attention to the correct punctuation of **dialogue**—the actual words spoken by a character. Use the examples as a guide. All dialogue should be enclosed in quotation marks. A **split dialogue** is when a quotation is split up with additional information in the middle, such as identifying the speaker.

"She went home," I said.

"Wow!" I yelled. "I love it."

Publishing and Presenting

Consider one of the following ways to share your writing:

Present an oral narrative. Practice telling your story, using notes rather than reading from your draft, until you can deliver it smoothly and naturally. Practice using gestures to emphasize key points. Tell your story to the class.

Make a poster. Arrange photos, artwork, or small souvenirs, along with a neat copy of your narrative, on posterboard to display in class.

Reflecting on Your Writing

Writer's Journal Jot down your answer to this question:

As you wrote, what new insights into your story did you have?

Rubric for Self-Assessment

Find evidence in your writing to address each category. Then, use the rating scale to grade your work.

Spiral Review
Earlier in the unit, you learned about **personal pronouns** (p. 126) and **possessive pronouns** (p. 150). Check the use of possessive pronouns in your narrative. Review your autobiographical narrative to be sure you have avoided inappropriate shifts in pronoun number (singular or plural) and person.

PH **WRITING COACH**
Further instruction and practice are available in *Prentice Hall Writing Coach.*

Criteria	Rating Scale				
	not very				*very*
Focus: How clearly does the narrative present the problem or conflict?	1	2	3	4	5
Organization: How clearly is the sequence of events presented?	1	2	3	4	5
Support/Elaboration: How vivid are details and quotations?	1	2	3	4	5
Style: How effectively is the action of the story paced?	1	2	3	4	5
Conventions: How correct is your grammar, especially your use of pronouns and antecedents?	1	2	3	4	5

Vocabulary Workshop

Using a Dictionary and Thesaurus

If you need to know the meaning, the pronunciation, or the part of speech of a word, you can find that information in a **dictionary.** In addition, a dictionary can show you a word's **etymology,** or origin. Etymologies explain how words come into the English language and how they change over time. Check the front or back of a dictionary for a guide to the symbols and abbreviations used in etymologies.

Here is an example of a dictionary entry. Notice what it tells you about the word *anthology*.

Dictionary

> **anthology** (an ·äl´ ß jè) *n.*, *pl.* **-gies** [Gr. *anthologia*, a garland, collection of short poems < *anthologos*, gathering flowers < *anthos*, flower + *legein*, to gather] a collection of poems, stories, songs, excerpts, etc., chosen by the compiler

In a **thesaurus,** you will find a list of a word's synonyms, or words with similar meanings. You can use a thesaurus when you are looking for alternate word choices in your writing. Look at this example of a thesaurus entry.

Thesaurus

> **clarify** *v.* interpret, define, elucidate, see EXPLAIN.

Note that a thesaurus does not provide definitions of words. Before you use a word you find in a thesaurus, check a dictionary to be sure you understand the word's meaning.

Where to Find a Dictionary and Thesaurus

You can find these resources in book form at your school or library. You can also use *digital tools,* such as *online dictionaries* and *thesauruses,* to find the most precise words to express your ideas. Ask your teacher to recommend the best online word study resources.

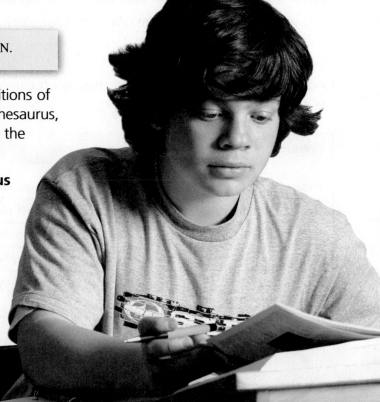

Common Core State Standards

Language
4.c. Consult general and specialized reference materials, both print and digital, to find the pronunciation of a word or determine or clarify its precise meaning or its part of speech.
4.d. Verify the preliminary determination of the meaning of a word or phrase.

Practice A Find each of the following words in a print or online dictionary. Write down the first pronunciation, part of speech, and definition of each word. Then, use each word in a sentence that shows its meaning.

1. voyage   **2.** robust   **3.** engulf   **4.** intricate

Practice B Use a print or online thesaurus to find an alternate word for the italicized word in each sentence. Choose a more expressive word that means the same thing as the original. Verify the meaning of the word you choose in a dictionary.

1. I had to *run* down the street to catch the school bus on time.

2. After soccer practice, all we wanted to do was *sit* on the couch.

3. On our class trip to the nature trail, our assignment was to *find* as many bugs as possible.

4. After the storm, Damian had to *make* his storage shed again.

5. We had to *push* the trash down to make it fit in the can.

Activity Create a quick-reference thesaurus of some commonly used words. Make notecards like the one shown for the words *big*, *nice*, and *interesting*. Share your notecards with classmates and collect more synonyms. Then, with a partner, distinguish the shades of meaning that each word conveys. Use cards like these to help you find precise words when you write.

Word:
Part of Speech:
Definition:
Synonym 1:
Synonym 1 Definition:
Shades of Meaning:
Synonym 2:
Synonym 2 Definition:
Shades of Meaning:

Comprehension and Collaboration

With a partner, look up the meanings of the words *bolt* and *preserve*. Note that each word can be used as both a noun and a verb. For each word, write one sentence using the word as a noun and another sentence using the word as a verb.

Communications Workshop

Delivering a Narrative Presentation

A **narrative presentation** is similar to a written narrative. In a presentation, however, you can add interest by using your voice, gestures, and facial expressions. These techniques and strategies will help make your presentation effective and interesting.

Learn the Skills

Use these strategies to complete the activity on page 187.

Develop a plot line. A narrative presentation tells events in order. Begin by introducing a conflict. Then, develop rising action leading to a climax. Consider adding suspense to keep your audience engaged. Finally, provide a clear resolution. Determine the point of view from which the story will be told and write your narrative from that perspective.

Establish setting and characters. Think about how you will describe the setting—the time and place of your narrative. Describe major and minor characters and bring them to life through dialogue and descriptions of their actions.

Consider your audience. As you write, think about your audience. Choose words and a tone, such as serious or playful, that will appeal to that audience.

Deliver Your Narrative

Rehearse your delivery. Read through your narrative to become familiar with it. If you plan to use a script, remember to look up frequently, use clear pronunciation, and make eye contact with your audience.

- **Vary the volume.** For example, you might speak loudly to express how a coach peps up her team or softly to describe how a baby falls asleep.
- **Switch the pitch.** For example, you might use a high voice to show panic and a low voice to show sternness or tiredness.
- **Use clear pronunciation.** For example, be careful to pronounce each sound that a letter makes in a word and make sure not to drop sounds that appear at the ends of words.

Common Core State Standards

Speaking and Listening

4. Present claims and findings, emphasizing salient points in a focused, coherent manner with pertinent descriptions, facts, details, and examples; use appropriate eye contact, adequate volume, and clear pronunciation.

Presentation Tips for Specific Audiences

Younger Audience	Older Audience
• Exaggerate reactions with dramatic facial expressions.	• Use more realistic voices and facial expressions.
• Use short sentences and simple vocabulary.	• Use varied sentences and sophisticated vocabulary level.
• Insert questions that invite audience participation. Make frequent eye contact.	• Maintain audience attention by changing your position and moving about as you speak. Make frequent eye contact.

Practice the Skills

© **Presentation of Knowledge and Ideas** Use what you have learned in this workshop to perform the following task.

ACTIVITY: Prepare and Deliver a Narrative

Choose a fictional story to present to your class. It may be either a story you write yourself or a story written by another author. Use the strategies in this workshop to organize and practice your presentation. Finally, deliver your presentation. Answer the following questions as you prepare:

• Who is my audience?
• From whose point of view will I tell the story?
• What descriptions and details can I include to add interest to my story?
• How can I build drama or suspense to engage my audience?
• What is the tone of the story, and how can I convey that tone during my presentation?
• How will I use my voice effectively?

Practice your presentation, using the checklist below to help you prepare. Try using different tones of voice and different speaking rates until you find the most effective delivery. When you feel you are ready, present your story to your classmates.

Presentation Checklist

Presentation Delivery
❏ Is the overall presentation suitable for the audience?
❏ Does the speaker's style of speaking fit the characters and plot?
❏ Is the tone of the story clearly communicated through the speaker's volume, pitch, facial expressions, and gestures?
❏ Does the pace of the presentation fit the story's action?
❏ Does the speaker pronounce words clearly and precisely?
❏ Does the speaker make frequent eye contact with the audience?
❏ What could the speaker do to improve the presentation?

© **Comprehension and Collaboration** After your presentation, ask your classmates to give you feedback by completing the Presentation Checklist. Then use the checklist to provide feedback on your classmates' presentations.

Cumulative Review

I. Reading Literature

Common Core
State Standards

RI.7.2, RI.7.3, RI.7.6; W.7.2.b.
[For the full wording of the standards, see the standards chart in the front of your textbook.]

Directions: *Read the passage. Then, answer each question that follows.*

"Don't forget, class! Today is the last day to sign up for Latin ballroom dancing lessons," said Mrs. Palacio.

Bianca, my best friend, with the beautiful green eyes, talked me into doing it. I wasn't so sure about ballroom dancing, but I went along because I always did what Bianca wanted.

After a few days of practice, I could hear the Latin rhythms playing in my head, and I would pretend to move my feet—"one, two, cha-cha-cha." But I didn't dare let anyone know I actually liked ballroom dancing.

Our practice gym was muggy and lit only by faint sunlight. As the sweat poured off us one day, Mrs. Palacio said the terrible words I'd <u>dreaded</u>. "Tomorrow, I want you to select your partner for the school performance."

"I heard John is going to ask me," Bianca said with excitement as we walked home that afternoon. "You should choose one of his friends." I could feel Bianca pressuring me to choose someone she liked—someone who was popular.

The next day, as the ballots were passed out, the gym walls began to sway, and my head throbbed. I had a huge secret. I wanted to pick Felix as my partner. But I figured that if Bianca found out, she would embarrass me, maybe even end our friendship. Felix was not popular. He never spoke to anyone, never even smiled. No one knew much about him except that after practice, he went straight home. But I didn't care. Felix was handsome and the best dancer in the class.

I just couldn't find the courage to pick him. I froze. What will happen to me if my best friend Bianca humiliates me? I bent over the metal bench, pretending to write on the ballot. The other kids grabbed their backpacks to leave as I sat there with tears welling up.

"What's wrong with Marie?" John asked on his way out.

I tried not to look up, but Mrs. Palacio caught my eye. I felt her sympathy, and somehow I got the courage to make my decision. I did it. I wrote down Felix's name. A weight was suddenly lifted, and I felt like dancing all the way to the moon—on my own two feet.

1. This passage is an example of which **type of nonfiction?**
   A. biography
   B. autobiographical narrative
   C. descriptive essay
   D. informational text

2. Which sentence from the passage shows the **first-person point of view?**
   A. Felix was not popular.
   B. He never spoke to anyone, never even smiled.
   C. I bent over the metal bench, pretending to write on the ballot.
   D. "What's wrong with Marie?" John asked on his way out.

3. Which sentence from the passage describes the **setting?**
   A. But I didn't dare let anyone know I actually liked ballroom dancing.
   B. Felix was not popular.
   C. I tried not to look up, but Mrs. Palacio caught my eye.
   D. Our practice gym was muggy and lit only by faint sunlight.

4. Which of the following statements *best* describes the **central idea** of the passage?
   A. Do what you feel is right, no matter what others may think.
   B. If you practice hard, you will improve.
   C. If you like something, practice after school.
   D. It is important to do what your friends think is right in order to fit in.

5. Which **character trait** of the narrator's is revealed at the end of the passage?
   A. stubbornness
   B. quietness
   C. shyness
   D. braveness

6. Which of the following *best* shows **direct characterization** of Bianca?
   A. What will happen to me if my best friend Bianca humiliates me?
   B. I just couldn't find the courage to pick him.
   C. Bianca, my best friend, with the beautiful green eyes, talked me into doing it.
   D. But I figured that if Bianca found out, she would embarrass me, maybe even end our friendship.

7. **Vocabulary** Which word or phrase is closest in meaning to the underlined word dreaded?
   A. feared
   B. hoped for
   C. practiced
   D. forgotten

Timed Writing

8. In a paragraph, explain how the writer uses **indirect characterization** to describe the narrator. **Support** your ideas with at least three specific examples from the passage.

II. Reading Informational Texts

Directions: *Read the passage. Then, answer each question that follows.*

Common Core
State Standards

RI.7.3, RI.7.5; W.7.2.c; L.7.1, L.4.1.g
[For the full wording of the standards, see the standards chart in the front of your textbook.]

How to Make a Pizza

Ingredients:

- Pre-made pizza crust
- Tomato sauce
- Fresh sliced vegetables
- Olive oil
- Pepperoni, sliced thinly
- Mozzarella cheese, shredded

Directions:

1. Before you begin, preheat oven to 400 degrees.
2. Place pizza crust on a large pan or cookie sheet. Stretch into a large circle. Pre-made crusts can be found at most grocery stores. Substitutions include pita bread or English muffins.
3. Lightly coat crust with olive oil to prevent it from becoming soggy.
4. Spread tomato sauce on top of crust. Add the pepperoni. Then, pile on the vegetables.
5. Top with a big handful of mozzarella cheese.
6. Bake until crust is golden and cheese is bubbly. Let stand 10 minutes before slicing. Enjoy!

History of the Pizza

18th Century	Tomatoes added to flatbread in Naples, Italy Pizza sold by street vendors in Naples
19th Century	Pizza first sold as local specialty in Naples restaurant Pizza arrives in United States with Italian immigrants
20th Century	First pizzeria opens in New York City Deep-dish style pizza is popular in Chicago
21st Century	Pizza remains a common American food

1. The **subheads** help you do all of the following *except*—

A. predict what the passage will be about.
B. break the text into smaller parts.
C. make the text more visually appealing.
D. understand the importance of pizza.

2. Which event occurred in the nineteenth century?

A. Italian immigrants bring knowledge of pizza-making to the United States.
B. Pizza was sold by street vendors in Naples, Italy.
C. Deep-dish style pizza is born in Chicago.
D. First pizzeria opens in New York City.

III. Writing and Language Conventions

Directions: *Read the passage. Then, answer each question that follows.*

(1) The Robert Johnson swimming Pool can be a flurry of activity in the summer. (2) Swimming pools have been around for centuries. (3) The squealing children jump repeatedly into the turquoise water. (4) Across the pool you can hear faint voices engaged in a "Marco Polo" game. (5) Childrens beach balls fly across the pool. (6) When the swimmers finally get out, the scorching pavement burns there feet. (7) Labor Day comes. (8) That unique feeling of summer ends when the lifeguard locks the gate, closing the pool until next year.

1. How could the writer revise sentence 3 to appeal to the **sense** of touch?
- **A.** The squealing children smell the chlorine in the pool water.
- **B.** The squealing children jump repeatedly into the water, making loud splashes.
- **C.** The squealing children eat candy and chips by the turquoise water.
- **D.** The squealing children jump into the chilly water to escape the summer heat.

2. How could the writer *best* revise sentence 7 to include a **transition?**
- **A.** Labor Day comes.
- **B.** By the way, Labor Day comes.
- **C.** Finally, Labor Day comes.
- **D.** After all, Labor Day comes.

3. Which sentence should the writer remove from the passage because it does not add to the **main impression?**
- **A.** sentence 1
- **B.** sentence 2
- **C.** sentence 7
- **D.** sentence 8

4. What is the correct way to capitalize the **proper nouns** in sentence 1?
- **A.** The Robert Johnson swimming pool can be a flurry of activity in the summer.
- **B.** The Robert Johnson Swimming Pool can be a flurry of activity in the summer.
- **C.** The Robert Johnson Swimming pool can be a flurry of activity in the summer.
- **D.** The Robert johnson swimming pool can be a flurry of activity in the summer.

5. What is the correct way to punctuate the **possessive noun** in sentence 5?
- **A.** Childrens beach ball's fly across the pool.
- **B.** Childrens' beach ball fly across the pool.
- **C.** Children's beach balls' fly across the pool.
- **D.** Children's beach balls fly across the pool.

6. How can the writer revise sentence 6 to correctly spell a **troublesome word?**
- **A.** Change *there* to *their*.
- **B.** Change *there* to *they're*.
- **C.** Change *there* to *they*.
- **D.** The sentence is correct.

Performance Tasks

Directions: *Follow the instructions to complete the tasks below as required by your teacher.*

As you work on each task, incorporate both general academic vocabulary and literary terms you learned in this unit.

Common Core State Standards

RL.7.2, RL.7.3, RL.7.6; RI.7.2, RI.7.3; W.7.2, W.9.a, W.9.b; SL.7.1, SL.7.4, SL.7.6; L.7.1, L.7.2, L.7.3
[For the full wording of the standards, see the standards chart in the front of your textbook.]

Writing

Task 1: Literature [RL.7.6]
Analyze Point of View

Analyze how the author develops the points of view of two different characters in a story from this unit.

- Choose a story in which two characters clearly display their points of view.

- Write an analysis that tells how the author develops these distinct points of view through the characters' words and actions.

- Include examples from the story that show how the author makes each character's point of view clear to readers. Explain how one character's perspective is similar to or different from the perspective of the other character.

Task 2: Literature [RL.7.3]
Analyze the Interaction of Story Elements

Write an essay to explain how the setting of a story in this unit helps shape its plot.

- Identify details that reveal and describe the time and place of the story you chose.

- Analyze how the story's setting affects events or even makes them believable.

- Organize your ideas clearly, and support them with evidence from the text.

- Review your writing to correct errors in spelling and punctuation.

Task 3: Informational Text [RI.7.3]
Analyze Events and Their Influence

Write an essay about a nonfiction narrative in this unit. Analyze how the events described influence people and ideas.

- Identify the main events and central ideas in the nonfiction narrative.

- Explain how the events affect individuals and support the narrative's central idea.

- Use cause-and-effect organization and appropriate transitions.

- Use a variety of sentence patterns to add interest and clarify meaning.

Task 4: Literature [RL.7.2; RI.7.2]
Compare Themes or Central Ideas

Write an essay to compare and contrast the themes or central ideas of two selections in this unit.

- Choose two selections in this unit. Analyze the elements of each that support the theme or central idea. For example, think about where the events take place, what speakers say and do, and what objects play a critical role in the events.

- Organize your essay point-by-point to clearly show comparisons between the two texts.

- Use transitions to move smoothly from one idea to the next.

- Revise your essay to correct spelling, capitalization, and grammar mistakes.

Speaking and Listening

ⓒ Task 5: Literature [RL.7.3; SL.7.6]

Evaluate and Interpret Interactions

Give a dramatic reading from a selection in this unit that shows how specific elements interact.

- Choose a selection, then analyze how elements in the narrative interact in a dramatic or interesting way. For example, note places where events in the narrative strongly influence the narrator's or main character's actions and ideas.

- Determine if your dramatic reading should be serious and formal or relaxed and informal.

- Begin by explaining to your audience how the elements interact. Then, read one or two passages of the text that clearly illustrate this interaction.

- Establish eye contact with your audience, adjust the volume of your voice, and use facial expressions to help convey your ideas.

ⓒ Task 6: Literature [RL.7.2; SL.7.1]

Analyze and Discuss Theme

Give an oral presentation in which you determine the theme of a story in this unit and analyze its development over the course of the story.

- Choose a story from this unit and identify its theme. Prepare a presentation that analyzes how the author develops that theme through characters and events.

- Give your presentation to a small group of classmates, being sure to include examples from the story to support your ideas.

- Listen attentively to your group members' presentations, analyzing their main ideas and supporting details.

- Be sure to use appropriate vocabulary and content-area words in your discussion.

ⓒ Task 7: Informational Text [RI.7.3; SL.7.1]

Evaluate Historical Context

Analyze how the historical context of a nonfiction selection in this unit influences the narrator and other characters. Discuss your findings with a small group of classmates.

- Identify the historical context of your selected text.

- Analyze how political and social events in the selection help to explain why the narrator or other characters think, feel, or act in a certain way.

- Consider how the narrator and characters might be different if they lived in a different time and place. Give an example showing how a different historical context might affect these characters.

- Present your ideas to the group in a focused manner, including explanations, details, and examples from the text to support your claims.

What is the best way to find the truth?

At the beginning of Unit 1, you wrote a response to the Big Question. Now that you have completed the unit, write a new response. Discuss how your initial ideas have been changed or reinforced. Cite specific examples from the literature in this unit, from other subject areas, and from your own life to support your ideas. Use Big Question vocabulary words (see page 3) in your response.

Featured Titles

In this unit, you have read a variety of fiction and literary nonfiction. Continue to read on your own. Select books that you enjoy, but challenge yourself to explore new topics, new authors, and works of increasing depth and complexity. The titles suggested below will help you get started.

Literature

Amanda/Miranda
by Richard Peck

In this long, fictional story, or **novel,** a servant girl trades identities with her look-alike mistress during the real-life sinking of the ship *Titanic*.

Letters from Rifka
by Karen Hesse

This work of **fiction** is set in Russia after World War II, an era in which Jews were brutally treated. Many, like 12-year-old Rifka and her family, fled the country. Rifka's story unfolds in a series of **letters** that describe her separation from her family and her ultimate reunion with them in America.

Little Women
by Louisa May Alcott   EXEMPLAR TEXT

Based on the author's life, this classic **novel** tells the story of the four March sisters—Meg, Joe, Beth, and Amy— who are growing up during the Civil War. The sisters face great challenges but never lose their determination.

A Fire in My Hands
by Gary Soto   EXEMPLAR TEXT

This collection of free-verse **poems,** including "Oranges" and "That Girl," reflects on Soto's experiences as a young Mexican American. The book also includes **essays** by Soto about his writing process.

Blessing the Boats:
New and Selected Poems
by Lucille Clifton

In this collection, celebrated poet Lucille Clifton describes both ordinary life and extraordinary experiences. Her **poems** use few words to achieve great beauty and power.

Informational Texts

The Emperor's Silent Army
by Jane O'Connor
Viking, 2002

In 1974, farmers digging in China uncovered an army of life-sized clay soldiers buried for over 2,000 years. This work of **historical nonfiction** tells that story.

Discoveries: Truth Is Stranger Than Fiction

Find out new information in this book, which contains **essays** about different subject areas. You will read "The Wonders of the World," "Snakes in the Sky!," "Reel Time," and "Math Tricks."

A Night to Remember
by Walter Lord   EXEMPLAR TEXT

This work of **historical nonfiction,** based on true accounts by survivors of the *Titanic*, details the sinking of the famous ship.

Preparing to Read Complex Texts

Attentive Reading As you read literature on your own, bring your imagination and questions to the text. The questions shown below and others that you ask as you read will help you learn and enjoy literature even more.

 **Common Core State Standards**

Reading Literature/Informational Text 10. By the end of the year, read and comprehend literature, including stories, dramas, and poems, and literary nonfiction in the grades 6–8 text complexity band proficiently, with scaffolding as needed at the high end of the range.

When reading fiction, ask yourself...

- Whose "voice" is telling the story? Do I like that voice?
- Does the story offer a message that I think is important and true? Why or why not?

© Key Ideas and Details

- Does the author describe places in a way that helps me picture them clearly? Why or why not?
- Do any details seem wrong? If so, which ones, and why?
- Do I understand why characters act and feel as they do? Do their thoughts and actions seem real? Why or why not?

© Craft and Structure

- Do I care what happens in the story? Why or why not?
- Does the story remind me of others I have read? If so, how?

© Integration of Ideas

When reading nonfiction, ask yourself...

- Who is the author? Why did he or she write the work?
- Has the author made me care about the subject? Why or why not?

© Key Ideas and Details

- Does the author organize ideas well, or is the text hard to follow?
- Does the author use evidence that helps me understand the ideas?
- Does the author support his or her claims with solid evidence?

© Craft and Structure

- Does the author leave out ideas I think are important?
- Do I agree with some of the author's ideas, but not with others? If so, why?
- What else have I read about this topic? How is this work similar to or different from those other works?
- What have I learned from this text?

© Integration of Ideas

THE BIG ?

Does every *conflict* have a winner?

Short Stories

www.PHLitOnline.com

Hear It!
- Selection summary audio
- Selection audio
- BQ Tunes

See It!
- Author videos
- Big Question video
- Get Connected videos
- Background videos
- More about the authors
- Illustrated vocabulary words
- Vocabulary flashcards

Do It!
- Interactive journals
- Interactive graphic organizers
- Grammar tutorials
- Interactive vocabulary games
- Test practice

Does every *conflict* have a winner?

A **conflict** is a struggle between opposing forces. A conflict can be as small as a disagreement between friends about what movie to see. On the other hand, it can be as large as a civil war. When you struggle with a decision, you have a conflict within yourself. There are many kinds of conflict. Some can be dangerous. Others, like a sports competition, can be exciting. When a conflict is worked out, it is resolved. Different kinds of conflicts are resolved in different ways.

Exploring the Big Question

Ⓒ Collaboration: One-on-One Discussion Start thinking about the Big Question by making a list of different conflicts you have experienced or heard about. Describe one specific example of each of the following types of conflict.

- An argument or disagreement between friends
- A misunderstanding between two people
- A competition between teams or in a contest
- A struggle to make a decision
- A struggle to overcome a challenge or an obstacle

   Share your examples with a partner. Talk about the cause of each conflict and the way the conflict worked out. Use the Big Question vocabulary in your discussion.

Connecting to the Literature Each reading in this unit will give you additional insight into the Big Question.

PHLit Online!
www.PHLitOnline.com

- Big Question video
- Illustrated vocabulary words
- Interactive vocabulary games
- BQ Tunes

Learning Big Question Vocabulary

Ⓒ Acquire and Use Academic Vocabulary Academic vocabulary is the language you encounter in textbooks and on standardized tests. Review the definitions of these academic vocabulary words.

attitude (at´ ə tōōd´) *n.* a person's opinions and feelings about someone or something

challenge (chal´ ənj) *n.* a demanding task that tests your skills and abilities

communication (kə myōō´ ni kā´ shən) *n.* the giving and receiving of information

conflict (kän´ flikt´) *n.* a struggle between opposing forces

opposition (äp´ ə zish´ ən) *n.* a person, group, or force that tries to prevent you from accomplishing something

outcome (out´ kum´) *n.* the way a situation turns out

resolution (rez´ə lōō´ shən) *n.* the working out of a problem or conflict

understanding (un´dər stan´ diŋ) *n.* an agreement

Use these words as you complete Big Question activities in this unit that involve reading, writing, speaking, and listening.

Speaking and Listening
1. Engage effectively in a range of collaborative discussions with diverse partners on grade 7 topics, texts, and issues, building on others' ideas and expressing their own clearly.

Language
6. Acquire and use accurately grade-appropriate general academic and domain-specific words and phrases; gather vocabulary knowledge when considering a word or phrase important to comprehension or expression.

Ⓒ Gather Vocabulary Knowledge Additional Big Question words are listed below. Categorize the words by deciding whether you know each one well, know it a little bit, or do not know it at all.

competition	desire	obstacle
compromise	disagreement	struggle
danger	misunderstanding	

Then, do the following:

1. Work with a partner to say each word and explain what you think each word means.

2. Consult a print or online dictionary to confirm each word's pronunciation and meaning.

3. Then, use at least four of the words in a brief paragraph about a conflict you experienced or heard about.

4. Take turns reading your paragraphs aloud.

Elements of Short Stories

A short story is a brief work of fiction. No two stories are identical, but they all share some common elements.

A **short story** takes readers on a quick, focused journey. Authors use the following elements of fiction to make the trip interesting.

Characters are the people or animals that take part in a story's action. They are driven by **motivation,** their reasons for acting as they do.

Conflict is the central problem or struggle that the characters face. A short story typically has one central conflict.

Plot is the sequence of events in a story. Events are often presented in chronological order, though they may be told out of sequence.

Setting is the time and place of a story. The setting can create a **mood,** or atmosphere.

Point of view is the perspective from which a story is told.

Theme is the central message expressed in a story. A theme is a general truth or observation about life or human nature.

Characters: the people or animals in a story
- In **direct characterization,** the author describes a character.
- In **indirect characterization,** the author reveals a character through speech and actions.

Conflict: a problem the characters face
- An **external conflict** is a struggle between a character and an outside force.
- An **internal conflict** takes place within a character's mind.

Plot: the sequence of events in a story
- **Exposition** introduces the situation.
- **Rising action** introduces the **conflict.**
- **Climax** is the turning point.
- **Falling action** is when the conflict eases.
- **Resolution** is the conclusion.

Short Story Elements

Setting: the time and place of the action, including
- historical period;
- physical location;
- season of year and time of day;
- climate and weather;
- culture and social systems or traditions.

Theme: a central message or insight
- **Stated themes** are expressed directly.
- **Implied themes** are suggested by the author.
- **Universal themes** recur in different cultures and time periods.

Point of View

The perspective from which a short story is told, or narrated, affects the kinds of information readers receive. When a story is told from the **first-person** point of view, the narrator is a character in the story. Readers learn only what that character knows, thinks, or feels.

When a story is told from the **third-person** point of view, the narrator is not a character, but a voice outside the story. A third-person narrator may be either **omniscient** or **limited.** An omniscient narrator is able to relate the inner thoughts and feelings of all the characters. A narrator with a limited point of view reveals the thoughts and feelings of only one character.

Example: Points of View

First Person
I could hear the footsteps, but I couldn't see a thing. Where was the light switch?

Third-Person Omniscient
Ted heard someone approaching, but in the darkness, he had no idea it was a burglar.

Another difference among types of narrators is that some narrators are objective, while others are subjective. An **objective narrator** is a neutral observer who reports on story events without adding personal comments. A **subjective narrator,** however, participates in the story and offers opinions about what takes place. This type of narrator can influence the way readers understand events and characters.

Some subjective narrators are unreliable, which means that readers cannot trust everything they say. For example, a story might be narrated from the perspective of a small child who is too young to understand certain story events. In this case, readers may have to piece together clues to fully grasp what is happening in the story.

Comparing Narrators

Objective	Subjective
At the news conference, Max responded to each question in a careful, measured tone. It was over in less than ten minutes.	Like every good politician, Max knew how to hide his feelings. In front of the camera, he became a slick advertisement for himself.

A narrator is a filter through which readers get information. However, the narrator does not reflect the only point of view in a story. Each character has his or her perspective as well. Two characters in a story may have very different perspectives on the same event. Readers can make inferences about a character's point of view based on the information and details the narrator provides.

In This Section

Elements of Short Stories

Analyzing How Elements Interact

Close Read: Analyzing Story Elements
• Model Text
• Practice Text

After You Read

 Common Core State Standards

RL.7.3, RL.7.6
[For the full wording of the standards, see the standards chart in the front of your textbook.]

Analyzing How Elements Interact

The interaction of key story elements reveals the **theme** of a story.

Common Core State Standards

Reading Literature 3. Analyze how particular elements of a story or drama interact.

Reading Literature 6. Analyze how an author develops and contrasts the points of view of different characters or narrators in a text.

In the best short stories, story elements interact to convey a meaningful **theme,** or message about life or human nature.

Inferring a Theme Most authors do not simply state a story's theme. Instead, they develop it over the course of the story through elements such as character, conflict, and plot. Readers must infer, or figure out, the theme by analyzing story clues and thinking about how they add up to a central message or insight.

Characters and Theme To determine the theme of a story, notice the words, thoughts, and actions of the characters. Characters' **motivations,** or reasons for doing what they do, may also contribute to the theme. Note the **dialogue,** or what the characters say, as well as the narrator's observations and descriptions.

Narrator's Observations	Theme
Dee grinned at me as she left the stage. My shy, timid friend was standing tall and proud.	A friend can help you overcome fears and develop your potential.
Dialogue	
"I made it!" Dee shouted to Carla in the hall. "Thanks for talking me into trying out for the play!"	

Conflict and Theme Most stories focus on a **conflict,** or struggle between opposing forces. When the conflict is **external,** a character struggles with an outside force. When the conflict is **internal,** a character struggles with himself or herself. A story's central conflict often ties directly to its theme. Look at these examples:

External Conflict	Possible Theme
Character versus a force of nature	Humans should not underestimate the power of nature.
Character versus society	Individuals must carve out their own paths in life.

Internal Conflict	Possible Theme
Character versus his or her fears	People may be stronger than they realize.
Character facing a difficult decision	People should trust their instincts.

The ways that characters respond to a story's conflict can provide clues to theme. In particular, pay attention to how the main character changes during the story and what he or she may have learned by the end.

Plot and Theme Events in the plot help develop a story's theme. The **exposition** and **rising action** develop the focus of the story. The **climax,** or turning point, often reveals a shift that points to an underlying message. As the story winds down to its **resolution,** that message becomes clearer.

Remember that story events may not flow in chronological order. An author may interrupt the sequence of events with a **flashback**—a scene from the past—or by **foreshadowing,** giving clues that hint at events to come. Such devices can move the story along while conveying the author's message.

Point of View and Theme A story may be told from the point of view of a character in the story or of an outside narrator. The narrator's point of view is crucial to the message of the story because readers know only what the narrator knows or chooses to tell. Use point of view to help you determine theme by determining who is telling the story and considering what message the narrator seems to think is important.

Setting and Theme The place and time in which a story occurs can affect everything from the characters' motivations to the central conflict. Therefore, setting may have a strong influence on a story's message. In some cases, the setting is so important that the events of the story could not take place in any other time or location.

Symbols and Theme A **symbol** is a person, a place, or an object that represents something else. A dove, for example, is often a symbol for peace. Authors may use symbols to highlight or emphasize key concepts. As you read, pay attention to objects that seem to represent important ideas. Understanding the deeper meaning of a symbol can help you determine a story's theme.

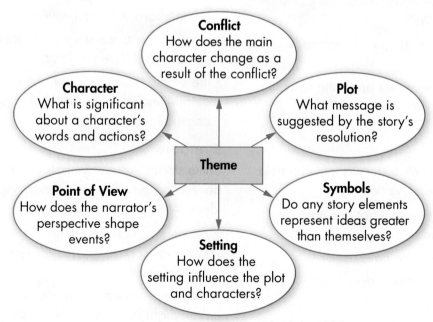

Conflict
How does the main character change as a result of the conflict?

Character
What is significant about a character's words and actions?

Plot
What message is suggested by the story's resolution?

Theme

Point of View
How does the narrator's perspective shape events?

Symbols
Do any story elements represent ideas greater than themselves?

Setting
How does the setting influence the plot and characters?

Close Read: Analyzing Story Elements

Authors use all the elements of a short story to develop a theme.

A good story does more than capture a reader's interest and stir deep feelings—it also develops a **theme,** or insight about life. Readers can analyze a variety of clues to determine how the theme is revealed through a story's key elements.

Clues That Show How Story Elements Interact to Develop Theme	
Characters Characters' actions, decisions, and dialogue can highlight a story's theme. As you read, consider • characters' words, actions, and interactions with other characters; • the motivations, or reasons, for characters' actions; • changes that characters undergo.	**Conflict** A story's central conflict fuels the plot and often ties directly to the theme. Identify • external or internal conflicts in the story; • what each side in the conflict has at stake and is willing to fight for; • whether the main character changes or learns something as a result of the conflict.
Plot Consider the sequence of events in a story to infer a story's theme. As you read, note • key background information in the exposition; • what happens to the characters at the plot's climax, or turning point; • the use of plot devices, such as foreshadowing or flashback; • the way events are wrapped up in the resolution, or conclusion, of the story.	**Setting** The time and place of a story can influence the theme directly or indirectly. As you read, think about • the role setting plays in the conflicts and in the characters' motivations; • whether the same story could take place in a different setting; • the emotional associations of setting details, including the cultural and social context in which events occur.
Point of View The perspective from which a story is told can help reveal theme. As you read, notice • who is telling the story and what this narrator knows or does not know; • observations made by the narrator; • how the narrator's point of view affects what readers know; • how the author develops and contrasts different characters' points of view.	**Symbols** Some stories include symbols that may point to a theme by representing important ideas. As you read, look for • people, objects, or events that may stand for something greater than themselves; • ideas mentioned in the title of the story that might have symbolic meanings.

Model

About the Text This story is set during India's colonial period, when the country was ruled by England.

"The Dinner Party" by Mona Gardner

The country is India. A colonial official and his wife are giving a large dinner party. They are seated with their guests—army officers, and government attachés with their wives, and a visiting American naturalist—in their spacious dining room. It has a bare marble floor, open rafters, and wide glass doors opening onto a veranda.

A spirited discussion springs up between a young girl who insists that women have outgrown the jumping-on-a-chair-at-the-sight-of-a-mouse era and a colonel who says that they haven't.

"A woman's unfailing reaction in any crisis," the colonel says, "is to scream. And while a man may feel like it, he has that ounce more of nerve control than a woman has. And that last ounce more is what counts."

The American does not join in the argument but watches the other guests. As he looks, he sees a strange expression come over the face of the hostess. She is staring straight ahead, her muscles contracting slightly. With a slight gesture, she summons the native boy standing behind her chair and whispers to him. The boy's eyes widen, and he quickly leaves the room.

Of the guests, none except the American notices this or sees the boy place a bowl of milk on the veranda just outside the open doors.

The American comes to with a start. In India, milk in a bowl means only one thing—bait for a snake. He realizes there must be a cobra in the room. He looks up at the rafters—the likeliest place—but they are bare. Three corners of the room are empty, and in the fourth the servants are waiting to serve the next course. There is only one place left—under the table.

His first impulse is to jump back and warn the others, but he knows the commotion would frighten the cobra into striking. He speaks quickly, the tone of his voice so arresting that it sobers everyone.

Characters The colonel believes that women lack self-control. Characters' opinions and beliefs may be clues to theme.

Point of View The narrator's point of view is limited to what the American notices. This heightens suspense by leaving the cause of the hostess's expression unknown.

Plot The author uses foreshadowing. Readers sense there is something significant about the bowl of milk but do not yet know what it is.

Setting The setting of this story is crucial to the plot. In India, the bowl of milk has a special significance.

Conflict The American faces an internal conflict. He wants to warn the others, but does not want to endanger them. He must exercise *self-control*, which begins to emerge as a central idea in the story.

Model continued

Characters The host's statement recalls the argument at the beginning of the story. A repeated idea may point to the theme of a story.

Plot In the resolution, we discover that Mrs. Wynnes has shown more self-control than any other character. The final sentence suggests the theme: *Courage and self-control are not specific to a gender.*

"I want to know just what control everyone at this table has. I will count to three hundred—that's five minutes—and not one of you is to move a muscle. Those who move will forfeit fifty rupees[1]. Ready!"

The twenty people sit like stone images while he counts. He is saying "two hundred and eighty" when, out of the corner of his eye, he sees the cobra emerge and make for the bowl of milk. Screams ring out as he jumps to slam the veranda doors safely shut.

"You were right, Colonel!" the host exclaims. "A man has just shown us an example of perfect control."

"Just a minute," the American says, turning to his hostess. "Mrs. Wynnes, how did you know the cobra was in the room?"

A faint smile lights up the woman's face as she replies, "Because it was crawling across my foot."

---

1. **rupee** (roo pē') *n.* the unit of money of several Asian countries such as India, Pakistan, and Sri Lanka.

Independent Practice

About the Text Walter Dean Myers bases much of his work on his childhood experiences growing up in New York City's Harlem.

"The Treasure of Lemon Brown" by Walter Dean Myers

The dark sky, filled with angry, swirling clouds, reflected Greg Ridley's mood as he sat on the stoop of his building. His father's voice came to him again, first reading the letter the principal had sent to the house, then lecturing endlessly about his poor efforts in math.

"I had to leave school when I was thirteen," his father had said, "that's a year younger than you are now. If I'd had half the chances that you have, I'd . . ."

Greg had sat in the small, pale green kitchen listening, knowing the lecture would end with his father saying he couldn't play ball with the Scorpions. He had asked his father the week before, and his father had said it depended on his next report card. It wasn't often the Scorpions took on new players, especially fourteen-year-olds, and this was a chance of a lifetime for Greg. He hadn't been allowed to play high school ball, which he had really wanted to do, but playing for the Community Center team was the next best thing. Report cards were due in a week, and Greg had been hoping for the best. But the principal had ended the suspense early when she sent that letter saying Greg would probably fail math if he didn't spend more time studying.

"And you want to play *basketball*?" His father's brows knitted over deep brown eyes. "That must be some kind of a joke. Now you just get into your room and hit those books."

That had been two nights before. His father's words, like the distant thunder that now echoed through the streets of Harlem, still rumbled softly in his ears.

It was beginning to cool. Gusts of wind made bits of paper dance between the parked cars. There was a flash of nearby lightning, and soon large drops of rain splashed onto his jeans. He stood to go upstairs, thought of the lecture that probably awaited him if he did anything except shut himself in his room with his math book, and started walking down the street instead. Down the block there was an old tenement[1] that had been abandoned for some months. Some of the guys had held an impromptu checker tournament there the week before, and Greg had noticed that the door, once boarded over, had been slightly ajar.

---

1. tenement (ten´ ə mənt) *n.* old, run-down apartment house.

Plot What conflict does this flashback reveal?

Characters What is Greg's motivation for staying out in the bad weather rather than going home?

Practice continued

Setting How does the weather echo Greg's state of mind?

Conflict How do Greg's feelings about his father reflect a conflict?

Pulling his collar up as high as he could, he checked for traffic and made a dash across the street. He reached the house just as another flash of lightning changed the night to day for an instant, then returned the graffiti-scarred building to the grim shadows. He vaulted over the outer stairs and pushed tentatively on the door. It was open, and he let himself in.

The inside of the building was dark except for the dim light that filtered through the dirty windows from the streetlamps. There was a room a few feet from the door, and from where he stood at the entrance, Greg could see a squarish patch of light on the floor. He entered the room, frowning at the musty smell. It was a large room that might have been someone's parlor at one time. Squinting, Greg could see an old table on its side against one wall, what looked like a pile of rags or a torn mattress in the corner, and a couch, with one side broken, in front of the window.

He went to the couch. The side that wasn't broken was comfortable enough, though a little creaky. From the spot he could see the blinking neon sign over the bodega[2] on the corner. He sat awhile, watching the sign blink first green then red, allowing his mind to drift to the Scorpions, then to his father. His father had been a postal worker for all Greg's life, and was proud of it, often telling Greg how hard he had worked to pass the test. Greg had heard the story too many times to be interested now.

For a moment Greg thought he heard something that sounded like a scraping against the wall. He listened carefully, but it was gone.

Outside the wind had picked up, sending the rain against the window with a force that shook the glass in its frame. A car passed, its tires hissing over the wet street and its red taillights glowing in the darkness.

Greg thought he heard the noise again. His stomach tightened as he held himself still and listened intently. There weren't any more scraping noises, but he was sure he had heard something in the darkness—something breathing!

He tried to figure out just where the breathing was coming from; he knew it was in the room with him. Slowly he stood, tensing. As he turned, a flash of lightning lit up the room, frightening him with its sudden brilliance. He saw nothing, just the overturned table, the pile of rags and an old newspaper on the floor. Could he have been imagining the sounds? He continued listening, but heard nothing and thought that it might have just been rats. Still, he thought, as soon as the rain let up he would leave. He went to the window and was about to look when he heard a voice behind him.

---

2. bodega (bō dä´ gə) *n.* small grocery store serving a Latino neighborhood.

"Don't try nothin' 'cause I got a razor here sharp enough to cut a week into nine days!"

Greg, except for an involuntary tremor[3] in his knees, stood stock still. The voice was high and brittle, like dry twigs being broken, surely not one he had ever heard before. There was a shuffling sound as the person who had been speaking moved a step closer. Greg turned, holding his breath, his eyes straining to see in the dark room.

The upper part of the figure before him was still in darkness. The lower half was in the dim rectangle of light that fell unevenly from the window. There were two feet, in cracked, dirty shoes from which rose legs that were wrapped in rags.

"Who are you?" Greg hardly recognized his own voice.

"I'm Lemon Brown," came the answer. "Who're you?"

"Greg Ridley."

"What you doing here?" The figure shuffled forward again, and Greg took a small step backward.

"It's raining," Greg said.

"I can see that," the figure said.

The person who called himself Lemon Brown peered forward, and Greg could see him clearly. He was an old man.

His black, heavily wrinkled face was surrounded by a halo of crinkly white hair and whiskers that seemed to separate his head from the layers of dirty coats piled on his smallish frame. His pants were bagged to the knee, where they were met with rags that went down to the old shoes. The rags were held on with strings, and there was a rope around his middle. Greg relaxed. He had seen the man before, picking through the trash on the corner and pulling clothes out of a Salvation Army box. There was no sign of the razor that could "cut a week into nine days."

"What are you doing here?" Greg asked.

"This is where I'm staying," Lemon Brown said. "What you here for?"

"Told you it was raining out," Greg said, leaning against the back of the couch until he felt it give slightly.

"Ain't you got no home?"

"I got a home," Greg answered.

3. **involuntary** (in väl′ ən ter′ ē) **tremor** (trem′ ər) *n.* automatic trembling or shaking.

Characters What do you learn about Lemon Brown based on his own words? What do you learn based on the narrator's description?

Point of View What character's perspective does the narrator share?

Plot How does the tension of the story lessen when Greg sees Lemon Brown?

Practice continued

Symbols Lemon Brown mentions the treasure of the story's title. What ideas and associations are conveyed by the word *treasure*?

Characters What do you learn about Lemon Brown through this dialogue?

Characters What does this dialogue reveal about Brown's feelings toward both his son and Greg? How might these feelings connect to a possible theme?

"You ain't one of them bad boys looking for my treasure, is you?" Lemon Brown cocked his head to one side and squinted one eye. "Because I told you I got me a razor."

"I'm not looking for your treasure," Greg answered, smiling. "If you have one."

"What you mean, if I have one," Lemon Brown said. "Every man got a treasure. You don't know that, you must be a fool!"

"Sure," Greg said as he sat on the sofa and put one leg over the back. "What do you have, gold coins?"

"Don't worry none about what I got," Lemon Brown said.

"You know who I am?"

"You told me your name was orange or lemon or something like that."

"Lemon Brown," the old man said, pulling back his shoulders as he did so, "they used to call me Sweet Lemon Brown."

"Sweet Lemon?" Greg asked.

"Yes sir. Sweet Lemon Brown. They used to say I sung the blues so sweet that if I sang at a funeral, the dead would commence to rocking with the beat. Used to travel all over Mississippi and as far as Monroe, Louisiana, and east on over to Macon, Georgia. You mean you ain't never heard of Sweet Lemon Brown?"

"Afraid not," Greg said. "What . . . what happened to you?"

"Hard times, boy. Hard times always after a poor man. One day I got tired, sat down to rest a spell and felt a tap on my shoulder. Hard times caught up with me."

"Sorry about that."

"What you doing here? How come you didn't go on home when the rain come? Rain don't bother you young folks none."

"Just didn't." Greg looked away.

"I used to have a knotty-headed boy just like you." Lemon Brown had half walked, half shuffled back to the corner and sat down against the wall. "Had them big eyes like you got, I used to call them moon eyes. Look into them moon eyes and see anything you want."

"How come you gave up singing the blues?" Greg asked.

"Didn't give it up," Lemon Brown said. "You don't give up the blues; they give you up. After a while you do good for yourself, and it ain't nothing but foolishness singing about how hard you got it. Ain't that right?"

"I guess so."

"What's that noise?" Lemon Brown asked, suddenly sitting upright.

Greg listened, and he heard a noise outside. He looked at Lemon Brown and saw the old man pointing toward the window.

Greg went to the window and saw three men, neighborhood thugs, on the stoop. One was carrying a length of pipe. Greg looked back toward Lemon Brown, who moved quietly across the room to the window. The old man looked out, then beckoned frantically for Greg to follow him. For a moment Greg couldn't move. Then he found himself following Lemon Brown into the hallway and up darkened stairs. Greg followed as closely as he could. They reached the top of the stairs, and Greg felt Lemon Brown's hand first lying on his shoulder, then probing down his arm until he finally took Greg's hand into his own as they crouched in the darkness.

"They's bad men," Lemon Brown whispered. His breath was warm against Greg's skin.

"Hey! Rag man!" A voice called. "We know you in here. What you got up under them rags? You got any money?"

Silence.

"We don't want to have to come in and hurt you, old man, but we don't mind if we have to."

Lemon Brown squeezed Greg's hand in his own hard, gnarled fist.

There was a banging downstairs and a light as the men entered. They banged around noisily, calling for the rag man.

"We heard you talking about your treasure." The voice was slurred. "We just want to see it, that's all."

"You sure he's here?" One voice seemed to come from the room with the sofa.

"Yeah, he stays here every night."

"There's another room over there; I'm going to take a look. You got that flashlight?"

"Yeah, here, take the pipe too."

Greg opened his mouth to quiet the sound of his breath as he sucked it in uneasily. A beam of light hit the wall a few feet opposite him, then went out.

"Ain't nobody in that room," a voice said. "You think he gone or something?"

"I don't know," came the answer. "All I know is that I heard him talking about some kind of treasure. You know they found that shopping bag lady with that money in her bags."

Plot During this rising action, how does the relationship between Greg and Lemon Brown change?

Point of View How does the narrator's point of view affect what you know at this point in the story?

Practice continued

"Yeah. You think he's upstairs?"

"Hey, old man, are you up there?"

Silence.

"Watch my back, I'm going up."

There was a footstep on the stairs, and the beam from the flashlight danced crazily along the peeling wallpaper. Greg held his breath. There was another step and a loud crashing noise as the man banged the pipe against the wooden banister[4]. Greg could feel his temples throb as the man slowly neared them. Greg thought about the pipe, wondering what he would do when the man reached them—what he *could* do.

Then Lemon Brown released his hand and moved toward the top of the stairs. Greg looked around and saw stairs going up to the next floor. He tried waving to Lemon Brown, hoping the old man would see him in the dim light and follow him to the next floor. Maybe, Greg thought, the man wouldn't follow them up there. Suddenly, though, Lemon Brown stood at the top of the stairs, both arms raised high above his head.

"There he is!" A voice cried from below.

"Throw down your money, old man, so I won't have to bash your head in!"

Lemon Brown didn't move. Greg felt himself near panic. The steps came closer, and still Lemon Brown didn't move. He was an eerie sight, a bundle of rags standing at the top of the stairs, his shadow on the wall looming over him. Maybe, the thought came to Greg, the scene could be even eerier.

Greg wet his lips, put his hands to his mouth and tried to make a sound. Nothing came out. He swallowed hard, wet his lips once more and howled as evenly as he could.

"What's that?"

As Greg howled, the light moved away from Lemon Brown, but not before Greg saw him hurl his body down the stairs at the men who had come to take his treasure. There was a crashing noise, and then footsteps. A rush of warm air came in as the downstairs door opened, then there was only an ominous silence.

Greg stood on the landing. He listened, and after a while there was another sound on the staircase.

"Mr. Brown?" he called.

"Yeah, it's me," came the answer. "I got their flashlight."

Plot How does the narrator's point of view increase tension and suspense as the story nears its climax?

---

4. **banister** (ban´ is tər) *n.* railing along a staircase.

Greg exhaled in relief as Lemon Brown made his way slowly back up the stairs.

"You OK?"

"Few bumps and bruises," Lemon Brown said.

"I think I'd better be going," Greg said, his breath returning to normal. "You'd better leave, too, before they come back."

"They may hang around outside for a while," Lemon Brown said, "but they ain't getting their nerve up to come in here again. Not with crazy old rag men and howling spooks. Best you stay a while till the coast is clear. I'm heading out west tomorrow, out to East St. Louis."

"They were talking about treasures," Greg said. "You *really* have a treasure?"

"What I tell you? Didn't I tell you every man got a treasure?" Lemon Brown said. "You want to see mine?"

"If you want to show it to me," Greg shrugged.

"Let's look out the window first, see what them scoundrels be doing," Lemon Brown said.

They followed the oval beam of the flashlight into one of the rooms and looked out the window. They saw the men who had tried to take the treasure sitting on the curb near the corner. One of them had his pants leg up, looking at his knee.

"You sure you're not hurt?" Greg asked Lemon Brown.

"Nothing that ain't been hurt before," Lemon Brown said. "When you get as old as me all you say when something hurts is, 'Howdy, Mr. Pain, sees you back again.' Then when Mr. Pain see he can't worry you none, he go on mess with somebody else."

Greg smiled.

"Here, you hold this." Lemon Brown gave Greg the flashlight.

He sat on the floor near Greg and carefully untied the strings that held the rags on his right leg. When he took the rags away, Greg saw a piece of plastic. The old man carefully took off the plastic and unfolded it. He revealed some yellowed newspaper clippings and a battered harmonica.

"There it be," he said, nodding his head. "There it be."

Greg looked at the old man, saw the distant look in his eye, then turned to the clippings. They told of Sweet Lemon Brown, a blues singer and harmonica player who was appearing at different theaters in the South.

Plot What happens at the climax of the story? What clues suggest that the story has now entered the falling action?

Symbols Lemon Brown once again says that "every man got a treasure." What possible theme might this idea support?

Characters How have Greg's feelings toward Lemon Brown changed since the two first met?

Practice continued

One of the clippings said he had been the hit of the show, although not the headliner. All of the clippings were reviews of shows Lemon Brown had been in more than 50 years ago. Greg looked at the harmonica. It was dented badly on one side, with the reed holes on one end nearly closed.

"I used to travel around and make money for to feed my wife and Jesse— that's my boy's name. Used to feed them good, too. Then his mama died, and he stayed with his mama's sister. He growed up to be a man, and when the war come he saw fit to go off and fight in it. I didn't have nothing to give him except these things that told him who I was, and what he come from. If you know your pappy did something, you know you can do something too.

"Anyway, he went off to war, and I went off still playing and singing. 'Course by then I wasn't as much as I used to be, not without somebody to make it worth the while. You know what I mean?"

"Yeah," Greg nodded, not quite really knowing.

"I traveled around, and one time I come home, and there was this letter saying Jesse got killed in the war. Broke my heart, it truly did.

"They sent back what he had with him over there, and what it was is this old mouth fiddle and these clippings. Him carrying it around with him like that told me it meant something to him. That was my treasure, and when I give it to him he treated it just like that, a treasure. Ain't that something?"

"Yeah, I guess so," Greg said.

"You *guess* so?" Lemon Brown's voice rose an octave as he started to put his treasure back into the plastic. "Well, you got to guess 'cause you sure don't know nothing. Don't know enough to get home when it's raining."

"I guess . . . I mean, you're right."

"You OK for a youngster," the old man said as he tied the strings around his leg, "better than those scalawags[5] what come here looking for my treasure. That's for sure."

"You really think that treasure of yours was worth fighting for?" Greg asked. "Against a pipe?"

"What else a man got 'cepting what he can pass on to his son, or his daughter, if she be his oldest?" Lemon Brown said. "For a big-headed boy you sure do ask the foolishest questions."

Lemon Brown got up after patting his rags in place and looked out the window again.

Plot What do these past events reveal about Lemon Brown's treasure? What theme does the author develop here?

Conflict Why does Greg ask if the treasure was worth fighting for? How does Lemon Brown's response reinforce the developing theme?

---

5. **scalawags** (skal´ ə wagz´) *n.* people who cause trouble; scoundrels.

"Looks like they're gone. You get on out of here and get yourself home. I'll be watching from the window so you'll be all right."

Lemon Brown went down the stairs behind Greg. When they reached the front door the old man looked out first, saw the street was clear and told Greg to scoot on home.

"You sure you'll be OK?" Greg asked.

"Now didn't I tell you I was going to East St. Louis in the morning?" Lemon Brown asked. "Don't that sound OK to you?"

"Sure it does," Greg said. "Sure it does. And you take care of that treasure of yours."

"That I'll do," Lemon said, the wrinkles about his eyes suggesting a smile. "That I'll do."

The night had warmed and the rain had stopped, leaving puddles at the curbs. Greg didn't even want to think how late it was. He thought ahead of what his father would say and wondered if he should tell him about Lemon Brown. He thought about it until he reached his stoop, and decided against it. Lemon Brown would be OK, Greg thought, with his memories and his treasure.

Greg pushed the button over the bell marked Ridley, thought of the lecture he knew his father would give him, and smiled.

Setting How does a change in the setting echo a change that has taken place in Greg?

Conflict How might Greg's experience with Lemon Brown have changed his attitude toward his father?

After You Read

The Treasure of Lemon Brown

1. Key Ideas and Details (a) Write an objective summary of this story. **(b) Identify:** How is each of the story's key conflicts resolved?

2. Craft and Structure (a) From what point of view is this story told? **(b) Speculate:** Why do you think the author chose this point of view to tell the story? Explain.

3. Key Ideas and Details Synthesize: At the end of the story, what has Greg learned that causes him to smile? Support your answer.

4. Craft and Structure (a) What is the story's theme? **(b) Evaluate:** Which elements of the story provide the most significant clues to its theme? Explain.

5. Integration of Knowledge and Ideas (a) In the first column of a chart like the one shown, tell what the text says about each of Lemon Brown's treasures. **(b) Connect:** In the second column, explain what each treasure means to Lemon Brown. **(c) Collaborate:** With a partner, review your ideas. Together, complete the third column with information that explains how Lemon Brown's idea of a "treasure" is an important part of the story's theme.

Lemon Brown's Treasures

What It Says	What It Means	Why It Is Important

The Bear Boy • Rikki-tikki-tavi

Ⓒ Leveled Texts

Build your skills and improve your comprehension of short stories with texts of increasing complexity.

Read **"The Bear Boy"** to discover how a father and son learn an important lesson from bears.

Read **"Rikki-tikki-tavi"** to meet a brave mongoose who battles a deadly family of cobras.

Ⓒ Common Core State Standards

Meet these standards with either **"The Bear Boy"** (p. 220) or **"Rikki-tikki-tavi"** (p. 228).

Reading Literature
3. Analyze how particular elements of a story or drama interact. *(Literary Analysis: Plot)*

Writing
2.d. Use precise language and domain-specific vocabulary to inform about or explain the topic. *(Writing: Informative Article)*
2.e. Establish and maintain a formal style. *(Writing: Informative Article)*

Speaking and Listening
1.a. Come to discussions prepared, having read or researched material under study; explicitly draw on that preparation by referring to evidence on the topic, text, or issue to probe and reflect on ideas under discussion. *(Speaking and Listening: Informal Debate)*

3. Delineate a speaker's argument and specific claims, evaluating the soundness of the reasoning and the relevance and sufficiency of the evidence. *(Speaking and Listening: Informal Debate)*

Language
4.b. Use common, grade-appropriate Greek or Latin affixes and roots as clues to the meaning of a word. *(Vocabulary: Word Study)*

6. Acquire and use accurately grade-appropriate general academic and domain-specific words and phrases; gather vocabulary knowledge when considering a word or phrase important to comprehension or expression. *(Vocabulary: Word Study)*

Reading Skill: Make Predictions

Predicting means making an intelligent judgment about what will happen next in a story based on details in the text. You can also **use prior knowledge to make predictions.** For example, if a character in a story sees dark clouds, you can predict that there will be a storm. That is because your prior knowledge tells you that dark clouds often mean stormy weather.

As you read, use details from the story and your prior knowledge to make predictions about what characters will do.

Literary Analysis: Plot

Plot is the related sequence of events in a short story and other works of fiction. Each event serves to move the story forward. Some plot events drop hints about what might happen next. Such events create **foreshadowing.** A plot has the following elements:

- **Exposition:** introduction of the setting, the characters, and the basic situation

- **Rising Action:** events that introduce a **conflict,** or struggle, and increase the tension; events that explain character's past actions

- **Climax:** the story's high point, at which the eventual outcome becomes clear

- **Falling Action:** events that follow the climax

- **Resolution:** the final outcome and tying up of loose ends

Using the Strategy: Plot Diagram

Record story details on a **plot diagram** like this one.

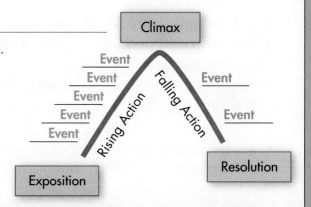

Does every *conflict* have a winner?

Writing About the Big Question

In "The Bear Boy," a family of bears help resolve a conflict by teaching a father how to care for his son. Use this sentence starter to develop your ideas about the Big Question.

When a person does not **understand** how to care for others, _____ can be lost.

While You Read Think about who benefits from the boy's encounter with the bears.

Vocabulary

Read each word and its definition. Decide whether you know the word well, know it a little bit, or do not know it at all. After you read, see how your knowledge of each word has increased.

- **timid** (tim´ id) *adj.* shy; fearful (p. 220) *The timid child was afraid of me.* timidity *n.* timidly *adv.*

- **initiation** (i nish´ ē ā´ shən) *n.* process that makes a person a member of a group (p. 220) *Jo looked forward to her initiation into the Honor Society.* initiate *v.* initiated *v.* initiating *v.*

- **canyon** (kan´ yən) *n.* long narrow valley between high cliffs (p. 221) *Many tourists hike from the rim to the valley of the Grand Canyon.*

- **approvingly** (ə prōōv´ iŋ lē) *adv.* with acceptance (p. 221) *The coach clapped approvingly at the pitcher's strikeout.* approve *v.* approved *v.* approval *n.*

- **neglected** (ni glekt´ əd) *v.* failed to take care of (p. 221) *The cat neglected her kittens, so we raised them.* neglect *v.* neglectful *adj.*

- **guidance** (gīd´ 'ns) *n.* advice or assistance (p. 222) *Students need guidance when choosing their classes.* guide *n.* guide *v.* guided *v.*

Word Study

The **Latin suffix -ance** means "the act of" and indicates a noun form.

In this story, Kuo-Haya's father asks for **guidance,** or the act of providing direction, in dealing with the mother bear.

Author of
THE BEAR BOY

Joseph Bruchac was raised by his grandparents in the foothills of the Adirondack Mountains in New York State. There, his grandfather, who was of Abenaki Indian descent, taught Bruchac to appreciate the forest. From his grandmother, a law school graduate, Bruchac inherited a love of books and writing. Bruchac has written more than seventy books for children and has performed worldwide as a teller of Native American folk tales.

Respect for Tradition Bruchac respects the role that storytelling plays in Native American cultures. Like "The Bear Boy," many of his stories are based on traditional folk tales and on his ancestors' way of life. He has said, "I always go back to what I have heard, what I have seen, what I have experienced. And whatever I imagine or create new always comes out of that life experience."

DID YOU KNOW?
Bruchac's younger sister and his two sons, James and Jesse, work for the preservation of Abenaki culture.

BACKGROUND FOR THE STORY
Animals in Native American Folk Tales

In early times, Native Americans depended on animals for food, clothing, and shelter. As a result, Native Americans felt gratitude toward animals and included them as important characters in their oral stories. "The Bear Boy" is a Native American story that focuses on a mother bear and her cubs.

THE Bear Boy

Joseph Bruchac

Long ago, in a Pueblo village, a boy named Kuo-Haya lived with his father. But his father did not treat him well. In his heart he still mourned the death of his wife, Kuo-Haya's mother, and did not enjoy doing things with his son. He did not teach his boy how to run. He did not show him how to wrestle. He was always too busy.

As a result, Kuo-Haya was a timid boy and walked about stooped over all of the time. When the other boys raced or wrestled, Kuo-Haya slipped away. He spent much of his time alone.

Time passed, and the boy reached the age when his father should have been helping him get ready for his initiation into manhood. Still Kuo-Haya's father paid no attention at all to his son.

One day Kuo-Haya was out walking far from the village, toward the cliffs where the bears lived. Now the people of the village always knew they must stay away from these cliffs, for the bear was a very powerful animal. It was said that if someone saw a bear's tracks and followed them, he might never come

Vocabulary
timid (tim′ id) *adj.* shy; fearful

initiation (i nish′ ē ā′ shən) *n.* process that makes a person a member of a group

back. But Kuo-Haya had never been told about this. When he came upon the tracks of a bear, Kuo-Haya followed them along an arroyo, a small canyon cut by a winding stream, up into the mesas.[1] The tracks led into a little box canyon below some caves. There, he came upon some bear cubs.

When they saw Kuo-Haya, the little bears ran away. But Kuo-Haya sat down and called to them in a friendly voice.

"I will not hurt you," he said to the bear cubs. "Come and play with me." The bears walked back out of the bushes. Soon the boy and the bears were playing together. As they played, however, a shadow came over them. Kuo-Haya looked up and saw the mother bear standing above him.

"Where is Kuo-Haya?" the people asked his father.

"I do not know," the father said.

"Then you must find him!"

So the father and other people of the pueblo began to search for the missing boy. They went through the canyons calling his name. But they found no sign of the boy there. Finally, when they reached the cliffs, the best trackers found his footsteps and the path of the bears. They followed the tracks along the arroyo and up into the mesas to the box canyon. In front of a cave, they saw the boy playing with the bear cubs as the mother bear watched them approvingly, nudging Kuo-Haya now and then to encourage him.

The trackers crept close, hoping to grab the boy and run. But as soon as the mother bear caught their scent, she growled and pushed her cubs and the boy back into the cave.

"The boy is with the bears," the trackers said when they returned to the village.

"What shall we do?" the people asked.

"It is the responsibility of the boy's father," said the medicine man. Then he called Kuo-Haya's father to him.

"You have not done well," said the medicine man. "You are the one who must guide your boy to manhood, but you have neglected him. Now the mother bear is caring for your boy as you should have done all along. She is teaching him to be strong as a young man must be strong. If you love your son, only you can get him back."

Every one of the medicine man's words went into the

---

1. **mesas** (mā´ səz) *n.* plateaus (or flat-topped hills) with steep sides.

Vocabulary
canyon (kan´ yən) *n.* long narrow valley between high cliffs

Make Predictions
Based on your knowledge of bears, what do you think will happen to Kuo-Haya?

▲ **Critical Viewing**
What does this artifact show about the relationship between Pueblo people and bears? **[Connect]**

Vocabulary
approvingly
(ə prōōv´ iŋ lē) *adv.* with acceptance.
neglected
(ni gleckt´ əd) *v.* failed to take care of

Reading Check
How does Kuo-Haya end up living with the bears?

▲ **Critical Viewing**
How does this bear figurine compare with the description of the mother bear in the story? **[Compare and Contrast]**

Vocabulary
guidance (gīd´ ′ns) *n.* advice or assistance

Plot
What is the climax of the story? How do you know?

father's heart like an arrow. He began to realize that he had been blind to his son's needs because of his own sorrow.

"You are right," he said. "I will go and bring back my son."

Kuo-Haya's father went along the arroyo and climbed the cliffs. When he came to the bears' cave, he found Kuo-Haya wrestling with the little bears. As the father watched, he saw that his son seemed more sure of himself than ever before.

"Kuo-Haya," he shouted. "Come to me."

The boy looked at him and then just walked into the cave. Although the father tried to follow, the big mother bear stood up on her hind legs and growled. She would not allow the father to come any closer.

So Kuo-Haya's father went back to his home. He was angry now. He began to gather together his weapons, and brought out his bow and his arrows and his lance.[2] But the medicine man came to his lodge and showed him the bear claw that he wore around his neck.

"Those bears are my relatives!" the medicine man said. "You must not harm them. They are teaching your boy how we should care for each other, so you must not be cruel to them. You must get your son back with love, not violence."

Kuo-Haya's father prayed for guidance. He went outside and sat on the ground. As he sat there, a bee flew up to him, right by his face. Then it flew away. The father stood up. Now he knew what to do!

"Thank you, Little Brother," he said. He began to make his preparations. The medicine man watched what he was doing and smiled.

Kuo-Haya's father went to the place where the bees had their hives. He made a fire and put green branches on it so that it made smoke. Then he blew the smoke into the tree where the bees were. The bees soon went to sleep.

Carefully Kuo-Haya's father took out some honey from their hive. When he was done, he placed pollen and some small pieces of turquoise[3] at the foot of the tree to thank the bees for their gift. The medicine man, who was watching all this, smiled again. Truly the father was beginning to learn.

Kuo-Haya's father traveled again to the cliffs where the bears

---

2. **lance** (lans) *n.* long spear.
3. **turquoise** (tʉr´ koiz´) *n.* greenish-blue gemstone.

lived. He hid behind a tree and saw how the mother bear treated Kuo-Haya and the cubs with love. He saw that Kuo-Haya was able to hold his own as he wrestled with the bears.

He came out from his hiding place, put the honey on the ground, and stepped back. "My friends," he said, "I have brought you something sweet."

The mother bear and her cubs came over and began to eat the honey. While they ate, Kuo-Haya's father went to the boy. He saw that his little boy was now a young man.

"Kuo-Haya," he said, putting his hands on his son's shoulders, "I have come to take you home. The bears have taught me a lesson. I shall treat you as a father should treat his son."

"I will go with you, Father," said the boy. "But I, too, have learned things from the bears. They have shown me how we must care for one another. I will come with you only if you promise you will always be friends with the bears." The father promised, and that promise was kept. Not only was he friends with the bears, but he showed his boy the love a son deserves.

Plot
Is this scene part of the rising action? Explain your answer.

✓ **Reading Check**
Why did Kuo-Haya's father gather the honey?

LITERATURE IN CONTEXT

Social Studies Connection

The Pueblo
The word pueblo refers to the village-dwelling Native Americans of the southwestern United States. Pueblo villages, like this one, are made of adobe and contain hundreds of rooms.

▶ *Pueblo pottery is known for the beauty of its shape and decoration.*

▶ *This is the entrance to a kiva, or sacred ceremonial room.*

Connect to the Literature

How was living in a village like the one shown an advantage to Kuo-Haya's father?

And he taught him all the things a son should be taught.

Everyone in the village soon saw that Kuo-Haya, the bear boy, was no longer the timid little boy he had been. Because of what the bears had taught him, he was the best wrestler among the boys. With his father's help, Kuo-Haya quickly became the greatest runner of all. To this day, his story is told to remind all parents that they must always show as much love for their children as there is in the heart of a bear.

Cite textual evidence to support your responses.

Critical Thinking

1. **Key Ideas and Details** **(a)** What kind of relationship does Kuo-Haya have with his father at the beginning of the story? **(b) Analyze Cause and Effect:** Describe the effect this relationship has on Kuo-Haya. **(c) Interpret:** Why does Kuo-Haya choose to spend so much time alone?
(d) Discuss: Share your responses with a partner. Then, discuss how your partner's responses did or did not change your interpretation.

2. **Key Ideas and Details** **(a)** What does Kuo-Haya do when he first sees the bear cubs? **(b) Compare and Contrast:** How is Kuo-Haya's life with the bears different from his life in the village? Support your answer with details from the story.

3. **Key Ideas and Details** **(a)** What advice does the medicine man offer the father? **(b) Connect:** How does seeing a bee help the father decide how to get his son back?

4. **Integration of Knowledge and Ideas** **(a) Analyze:** Native American folk tales often teach a lesson. What lesson does this folk tale teach? **(b) Evaluate:** Do you think the lesson applies to people of all cultures? Explain.

5. **Integration of Knowledge and Ideas** How do Kuo-Haya, his father, and the bears all benefit from conflict? *[Connect to the Big Question: Does every conflict have a winner?]*

Reading Skill: Make Predictions

1. What **prior knowledge** did you have from reading the Background note on page 219 that helped you **predict** that Kuo-Haya would be accepted by the bears?

2. Choose another prediction based on prior knowledge that you made as you read this story. Use a graphic organizer like the one here to show how you made your prediction.

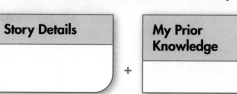

Story Details   +   **My Prior Knowledge**   = 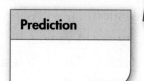 **Prediction**

Literary Analysis: Plot

3. **Key Ideas and Details** Identify two **plot** events that increase the tension of the story.

4. **Key Ideas and Details** Identify two or three events that move the plot toward the **climax,** when Kuo-Haya's father asks his son to come home.

Vocabulary

Acquisition and Use Answer each question. Then, explain your answer.

1. Would a *timid* child enjoy performing for a crowd?

2. Does an *initiation* mark a new beginning?

3. Is a *canyon* considered a wide open space?

4. If someone looks at you *approvingly*, does he or she dislike what you are doing?

5. If you *neglected* a houseplant, what would happen to it?

6. Do you ask for *guidance* if you know what to do?

Word Study Use the context of the sentences and what you know about the **Latin suffix -ance** to explain your answer.

1. If someone is asking for *assistance,* does she need help?

2. If you have no *tolerance* for your noisy neighbors, do you put up with them?

Word Study

The **Latin suffix -ance** means "the act of."

Apply It Explain how the suffix **-ance** contributes to the meanings of these words. Consult a dictionary if necessary.

utterance
disturbance
reliance

Does every *conflict* have a winner?

Writing About the Big Question

"Rikki-tikki-tavi" tells the story of a fierce battle between a mongoose and two cobras. Use this sentence starter to develop your ideas about the Big Question.

Sometimes in a **conflict,** innocent victims _____.

While You Read Consider who suffers as a result of the conflict between Rikki-tikki-tavi and the cobras.

Vocabulary

Read each word and its definition. Decide whether you know the word well, know it a little bit, or do not know it at all. After you read, see how your knowledge of each word has increased.

- **revived** (ri vīvd´) *v.* came back to life or consciousness (p. 229) *A brave bystander revived the man who almost drowned.* *revive v. reviving v. revival n.*

- **immensely** (i mens´ lē) *adv.* a great deal; very much (p. 230) *We enjoyed ourselves immensely at the circus.* *immense adj. immensity n.*

- **veranda** (və ran´də) *n.* an open porch, usually with a roof (p. 230) *In the summer, we like to eat dinner on the veranda.*

- **mourning** (môr´ niŋ) *adj.* expressing grief, especially after someone dies (p. 239) *The young widow was in mourning.* *mourning n. mourn v. mourner n. mournful adj.*

- **consolation** (kän´ sə lā´ shən) *n.* something that comforts a disappointed person (p. 240) *The sick boy got a toy as consolation for missing the party.* *console v. consolable adj. consolingly adv.*

- **cunningly** (kun´ iŋ lē) *adv.* cleverly (p. 240) *He cunningly took the plate with the largest slice of pizza.* *cunning adj.*

Word Study

The **Latin suffix -*tion*** is an ending that turns a verb into a noun, meaning "the thing that is."

In this story, Nagaina suggests that Teddy's death will be a **consolation**, or something that is consoling or comforting, for Darzee's wife.

Author of
RIKKI-TIKKI-TAVI

Rudyard Kipling was born in Bombay, India, to English parents. Although he moved to England when he was five, Kipling remained attached to the land of his birth. In 1882, he returned there as a journalist and began writing the stories that would make him famous.

International Popularity Kipling's stories became an immediate success when they were published in England because they brought the details of Indian life to an eager audience. Soon after, the stories became popular in the U.S., too. Kipling traveled a great deal and wrote several books of stories and poems, including *The Jungle Book* and *Captains Courageous*. In 1907, Kipling became the first English writer to win the Nobel Prize in Literature.

BACKGROUND FOR THE STORY
Mongoose *vs.* Cobra

In this story, a brave mongoose takes on a family of snakes known as Indian cobras. Cobras feed on small animals. The mongoose is a brown, furry animal about fifteen inches long—the perfect size for a cobra's meal. However, the fast, fierce mongoose usually wins a battle with a cobra.

Did You Know?
Organizations such as the Boy Scouts and Girl Scouts grew out of ideas found in Kipling's Jungle Book.

RIKKI-TIKKI

Rudyard Kipling

This is the story of the great war that Rikki-tikki-tavi fought, single-handed, through the bathrooms of the big bungalow in Segowlee cantonment.[1] Darzee, the tailorbird bird, helped him, and Chuchundra (chōō chun´ drə) the muskrat, who never comes out into the middle of the floor, but always creeps round by the wall, gave him advice; but Rikki-tikki did the real fighting.

He was a mongoose, rather like a little cat in his fur and his tail, but quite like a weasel in his head and his habits. His eyes and the end of his restless nose were pink; he could scratch himself anywhere he pleased, with any leg, front or back, that he chose to use; he could fluff up his tail till it looked like a bottle brush, and his war cry as he scuttled through the long grass, was: "*Rikk-tikk-tikki-tikki-tchk!*"

One day, a high summer flood washed him out of the burrow where he lived with his father and mother, and carried him, kicking and clucking,

---

1. **Segowlee cantonment** (sē gou´ lē kan tän´ mənt) *n.* living quarters for British troops in Segowlee, India.

down a roadside ditch. He found a little wisp of grass floating there, and clung to it till he lost his senses. When he **revived**, he was lying in the hot sun on the middle of a garden path, very draggled[2] indeed, and a small boy was saying: "Here's a dead mongoose. Let's have a funeral."

"No," said his mother; "let's take him in and dry him. Perhaps he isn't really dead."

They took him into the house, and a big man picked him up between his finger and thumb and said he was not dead but half choked; so they wrapped him in cotton wool, and warmed him, and he opened his eyes and sneezed.

"Now," said the big man (he was an Englishman who had just moved into the bungalow); "don't frighten him, and we'll see what he'll do."

It is the hardest thing in the world to frighten a mongoose, because he is eaten up from nose to tail with curiosity. The motto of all the mongoose family is, "Run and find out"; and Rikki-tikki was a true mongoose. He looked at the cotton wool, decided that it was not good to eat, ran all round the table, sat up and put his fur in order, scratched himself, and jumped on the small boy's shoulder.

"Don't be frightened, Teddy," said his father. "That's his way of making friends."

"Ouch! He's tickling under my chin," said Teddy.

Rikki-tikki looked down between the boy's collar and neck, snuffed at his ear, and climbed down to the floor, where he sat rubbing his nose.

"Good gracious," said Teddy's mother, "and that's a wild creature! I suppose he's so tame because we've been kind to him."

"All mongooses are like that," said her husband. "If Teddy

---

2. **draggled** (drag´ əld) *adj.* wet and dirty.

Vocabulary
revived (ri vīvd´)
v. came back to life or consciousness

Plot
What important details about the mongoose are revealed in the exposition on the previous page?

Reading
Check

Who is Rikki-tikki-tavi, and how does he meet Teddy?

Vocabulary
immensely
(i mens′ lē) *adv.* a
great deal; very much

veranda (və ran′də) *n.*
an open porch, usually
with a roof

doesn't pick him up by the tail, or try to put him in a cage, he'll run in and out of the house all day long. Let's give him something to eat."

They gave him a little piece of raw meat. Rikki-tikki liked it immensely, and when it was finished he went out into the veranda and sat in the sunshine and fluffed up his fur to make it dry to the roots. Then he felt better.

"There are more things to find out about in this house," he said to himself, "than all my family could find out in all their lives. I shall certainly stay and find out."

He spent all that day roaming over the house. He nearly drowned himself in the bathtubs, put his nose into the ink on a writing table, and burned it on the end of the big man's cigar, for he climbed up in the big man's lap to see how writing was done. At nightfall he ran into Teddy's nursery to watch how kerosene lamps were lighted, and when Teddy went to bed Rikki-tikki climbed up too; but he was a restless companion, because he had to get up and attend to every noise all through the night, and find out what made it. Teddy's mother and father came in, the last thing, to look at their boy, and Rikki-tikki was awake on the pillow. "I don't like that," said Teddy's mother; "he may bite the child." "He'll do no such thing," said the father. "Teddy's safer with that little beast than if he had a bloodhound to watch him. If a snake came into the nursery now—"

But Teddy's mother wouldn't think of anything so awful.

Early in the morning Rikki-tikki came to early breakfast in the veranda riding on Teddy's shoulder, and they gave him banana and some boiled egg; and he sat on all their laps one after the other, because every well-brought-up mongoose always hopes to be a house mongoose some day and have rooms to run about in, and Rikki-tikki's mother (she used to live in the General's house at Segowlee) had carefully told Rikki what to do if ever he came across Englishmen.

Then Rikki-tikki went out into the garden to see what was to be seen. It was a large garden, only half cultivated, with bushes as big as summer houses of Marshal Niel roses, lime and orange trees, clumps of bamboos, and thickets of high grass. Rikki-tikki licked his lips. "This is a splendid hunting ground," he said, and his tail grew bottlebrushy at the thought of it, and he scuttled up and down the garden,

Make Predictions
Based on the parents' thoughts about Rikki, what do you predict will happen in the story?

snuffing here and there till he heard very sorrowful voices in a thornbush.

It was Darzee, the tailorbird, and his wife. They had made a beautiful nest by pulling two big leaves together and stitching them up the edges with fibers, and had filled the hollow with cotton and downy fluff. The nest swayed to and fro, as they sat on the rim and cried.

"What is the matter?" asked Rikki-tikki.

"We are very miserable," said Darzee.

"One of our babies fell out of the nest yesterday and Nag ate him."

"H'm!" said Rikki-tikki, "that is very sad—but I am a stranger here. Who is Nag?"

Darzee and his wife only cowered down in the nest without answering, for from the thick grass at the foot of the bush there came a low hiss—a horrid cold sound that made Rikki-tikki jump back two clear feet. Then inch by inch out of the grass rose up the head and spread hood of Nag, the big black cobra, and he was five feet long from tongue to tail. When he had lifted one third of himself clear of the ground, he stayed balancing to and fro exactly as a dandelion tuft balances in the wind, and he looked at Rikki-tikki with the wicked snake's eyes that never change their expression, whatever the snake may be thinking of. •

"Who is Nag?" he said. "*I* am Nag. The great god Brahm[3] put his mark upon all our people when the first cobra spread his hood to keep the sun off Brahm . . . as he slept. Look, and be afraid!"

He spread out his hood more than ever, and Rikki-tikki saw the spectacle mark on the back of it that looks exactly like the eye part of a hook-and-eye fastening. He was afraid for the minute; but it is impossible for a mongoose to stay frightened for any length of time, and though Rikki-tikki had never met a live cobra

Rikki-tikki licked his lips.

"This is a splendid hunting ground," he said ...

✓ Reading Check

How do Teddy's parent's feel about Rikki-tikki-tavi staying at their house?

---

3. Brahm (bräm) short for Brahma, the name of the chief god in the Hindu religion.

before, his mother had fed him on dead ones, and he knew that all a grown mongoose's business in life was to fight and eat snakes. Nag knew that too, and at the bottom of his cold heart he was afraid.

"Well," said Rikki-tikki, and his tail began to fluff up again, "marks or no marks, do you think it is right for you to eat fledglings out of a nest?"

Nag was thinking to himself, and watching the least little movement in the grass behind Rikki-tikki. He knew that mongooses in the garden meant death sooner or later for him and his family; but he wanted to get Rikki-tikki off his guard. So he dropped his head a little, and put it on one side.

"Let us talk," he said. "You eat eggs. Why should not I eat birds?"

"Behind you! Look behind you!" sang Darzee.

Rikki-tikki knew better than to waste time in staring. He jumped up in the air as high as he could go, and just under him whizzed by the head of Nagaina (nə gī′nə), Nag's wicked wife. She had crept up behind him as he was talking, to make an end of him; and he heard her savage hiss as the stroke missed. He came down almost across her back, and if he had been an old mongoose he would have known that then was the time to break her back with one bite; but he was afraid of the terrible lashing return stroke of the cobra. He bit, indeed, but did not bite long enough, and he jumped clear of the whisking tail, leaving Nagaina torn and angry.

"Wicked, wicked Darzee!" said Nag, lashing up high as he could reach toward the nest in the thornbush; but Darzee had built it out of reach of snakes; and it only swayed to and fro.

Plot
What details intensify the conflict here?

▼ **Critical Viewing**
Based on this photograph, which animal would you expect to win a match to the death—the cobra or the mongoose? Why? **[Speculate]**

Rikki-tikki felt his eyes growing red and hot (when a mongoose's eyes grow red, he is angry), and he sat back on his tail and hind legs like a little kangaroo, and looked all around him, and chattered with rage. But Nag and Nagaina had disappeared into the grass. When a snake misses its stroke, it never says anything or gives any sign of what it means to do next. Rikki-tikki did not care to follow them, for he did not feel sure that he could manage two snakes at once. So he trotted off to the gravel path near the house, and sat down to think. It was a serious matter for him. ●

If you read the old books of natural history, you will find they say that when the mongoose fights the snake and happens to get bitten, he runs off and eats some herb that cures him. That is not true. The victory is only a matter of quickness of eye and quickness of foot—snake's blow against mongoose's jump—and as no eye can follow the motion of a snake's head when it strikes, that makes things much more wonderful than any magic herb. Rikki-tikki knew he was a young mongoose, and it made him all the more pleased to think that he had managed to escape a blow from behind. It gave him confidence in himself, and when Teddy came running down the path, Rikki-tikki was ready to be petted.

Make Predictions
What do you predict will be the outcome of the conflict? What prior knowledge helps you make that prediction?

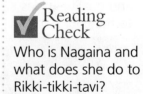

Reading Check
Who is Nagaina and what does she do to Rikki-tikki-tavi?

Science Connection

Cobra Fact and Fiction

Although the snakes in this story have fictional abilities and characteristics, many of their qualities are accurately based on those of real animals.

- Cobras do have spectacle-shaped markings on their hood, as shown in the picture below.

- Cobras are known to enter houses, just as Nag and Nagaina do in the story.

- A female cobra is extremely dangerous and vicious after laying eggs.

- Unlike the snakes in the story, however, real cobras do not travel in pairs or work together to hatch their eggs.

Connect to the Literature

What fictional characteristics and qualities does Kipling give to the cobras in this story?

But just as Teddy was stooping, something flinched a little in the dust, and a tiny voice said: "Be careful. I am death!" It was Karait (kə rīt´), the dusty brown snakeling that lies for choice on the dusty earth; and his bite is as dangerous as the cobra's. But he is so small that nobody thinks of him, and so he does the more harm to people. •

Rikki-tikki's eyes grew red again, and he danced up to Karait with the peculiar rocking, swaying motion that he had inherited from his family. It looks very funny, but it is so perfectly balanced a gait that you can fly off from it at any angle you please; and in dealing with snakes this is an advantage. If Rikki-tikki had only known, he was doing a much more dangerous thing than fighting Nag, for Karait is so small, and can turn so quickly, that unless Rikki bit him close to the back of the head, he would get the return stroke in his eye or lip. But Rikki did not know: his eyes were all red, and he rocked back and forth, looking for a good place to hold. Karait struck out. Rikki jumped sideways and tried to run in, but the wicked little dusty gray head lashed within a fraction of his shoulder, and he had to jump over the body, and the head followed his heels close.

Teddy shouted to the house: "Oh, look here! Our mongoose is killing a snake"; and Rikki-tikki heard a scream from Teddy's mother. His father ran out with a stick, but by the time he came up, Karait had lunged out once too far, and Rikki-tikki had sprung, jumped on the snake's back, dropped his head far between his fore legs, bitten as high up the back as he could get hold, and rolled away. That bite paralyzed Karait, and Rikki-tikki was just going to eat him up from the tail, after the custom of his family at dinner, when he remembered that a full meal makes a slow mongoose, and if he wanted all his strength and quickness ready, he must keep himself thin.

He went away for a dust bath under the castor-oil bushes, while Teddy's father beat the dead Karait. "What is the use of that?" thought Rikki-tikki. "I have settled it all"; and then Teddy's mother picked him up from the dust and hugged him, crying that he had saved Teddy from death, and Teddy's father said that he was a providence,[4] and Teddy looked on with big scared eyes. Rikki-tikki was rather amused at all the fuss, which, of course, he did not understand. Teddy's mother might just as well have petted Teddy for playing in the dust. Rikki was thoroughly enjoying himself.

That night, at dinner, walking to and fro among the wineglasses on the table, he could have stuffed himself three times over with nice things; but he remembered Nag and Nagaina, and though it was very pleasant to be patted and petted by Teddy's mother, and to sit on Teddy's shoulder, his eyes would get red from time to time, and he would go off into his long war cry of "*Rikk-tikk-tikki-tikki-tchk!*"

Teddy carried him off to bed, and insisted on Rikki-tikki sleeping under his chin. Rikki-tikki was too well bred to bite or scratch, but as soon as Teddy was asleep he went off for his nightly walk round the house, and in the dark he ran up against Chuchundra the muskrat, creeping round by the wall. Chuchundra is a brokenhearted little beast. He whimpers and cheeps all the night, trying to make up his mind to run into the middle of the room, but he never gets there.

"Don't kill me," said Chuchundra, almost weeping. "Rikki-tikki don't kill me."

"Do you think a snake-killer kills muskrats?" said Rikki-tikki scornfully.

"Those who kill snakes get killed by snakes," said Chuchundra, more sorrowfully than ever. "And how am I to be sure that Nag won't mistake me for you some dark night?"

"There's not the least danger," said Rikki-tikki; "but Nag is in the garden, and I know you don't go there."

4. **a providence** (präv´ ə dəns) *n.* a godsend; a valuable gift.

Plot
What details in this paragraph show that the tension is over?

Chuchundra is a brokenhearted little beast.

Reading Check
What happens when Rikki meets Karait?

"My cousin Chua, the rat, told me—" said Chuchundra, and then he stopped.

"Told you what?"

"H'sh! Nag is everywhere, Rikki-tikki. You should have talked to Chua in the garden."

"I didn't—so you must tell me. Quick, Chuchundra, or I'll bite you!"

Chuchundra sat down and cried till the tears rolled off his whiskers. "I am a very poor man," he sobbed. "I never had spirit enough to run out into the middle of the room. H'sh! I mustn't tell you anything. Can't you *hear*, Rikki-tikki?"

Rikki-tikki listened. The house was as still as still, but he thought he could just catch the faintest scratch-scratch in the world—a noise as faint as that of a wasp walking on a windowpane—the dry scratch of a snake's scales on brickwork.

"That's Nag or Nagaina," he said to himself; "and he is crawling into the bathroom sluice.[5] You're right, Chuchundra; I should have talked to Chua."

He stole off to Teddy's bathroom, but there was nothing there, and then to Teddy's mother's bathroom. At the bottom of the smooth plaster wall there was a brick pulled out to make a sluice for the bath water, and as Rikki-tikki stole in by the masonry curb where the bath is put, he heard Nag and Nagaina whispering together outside in the moonlight.

"When the house is emptied of people," said Nagaina to her husband, "*he* will have to go away, and then the garden will be our own again. Go in quietly, and remember that the big man who killed Karait is the first one to bite. Then come out and tell me, and we will hunt for Rikki-tikki together."

"But are you sure that there is anything to be gained by killing the people?" said Nag.

"Everything. When there were no people in the bungalow, did we have any mongoose in the garden? So long as the bungalow is empty, we are king and queen of the garden; and remember that as soon as our eggs in the melon bed hatch (as they may tomorrow), our children will need room and quiet."

---

5. **sluice** (slo͞os) *n.* drain.

Plot
What details add to the conflict as Rikki overhears this conversation?

"I had not thought of that," said Nag. "I will go, but there is no need that we should hunt for Rikki-tikki afterward. I will kill the big man and his wife, and the child if I can, and come away quietly. Then the bungalow will be empty, and Rikki-tikki will go."

Rikki-tikki tingled all over with rage and hatred at this, and then Nag's head came through the sluice, and his five feet of cold body followed it. Angry as he was, Rikki-tikki was very frightened as he saw the size of the big cobra. Nag coiled himself up, raised his head, and looked into the bathroom in the dark, and Rikki could see his eyes glitter.

"Now, if I kill him here, Nagaina will know;—and if I fight him on the open floor, the odds are in his favor. What am I to do?" said Rikki-tikki-tavi.

Nag waved to and fro, and then Rikki-tikki heard him drinking from the biggest water jar that was used to fill the bath. "That is good," said the snake. "Now, when Karait was killed, the big man had a stick. He may have that stick still, but when he comes in to bathe in the morning he will not have a stick. I shall wait here till he comes. Nagaina—do you hear me?—I shall wait here in the cool till daytime."

There was no answer from outside, so Rikki-tikki knew Nagaina had gone away. Nag coiled himself down, coil by coil, round the bulge at the bottom of the water jar, and Rikki-tikki stayed still as death. After an hour he began to move, muscle by muscle, toward the jar. Nag was asleep, and Rikki-tikki looked at his big back, wondering which would be the best place for a good hold. "If I don't break his back at the first jump," said Rikki, "he can still fight; and if he fights—O Rikki!" He looked at the thickness of the neck below the hood, but that was too much for him; and a bite near the tail would only make Nag savage.

"It must be the head," he said at last; "the head above the hood; and, when I am once there, I must not let go."

Then he jumped. The head was lying a little clear of the water jar, under the curve of it; and, as his teeth met, Rikki braced his back against the bulge of the red earthenware to hold down the head. This gave him just one second's purchase,[6] and he made the most of it. Then he was battered

---

Reading Check

Where are Nag and Nagaina and what are they planning?

to and fro as a rat is shaken by a dog—to and fro on the floor, up and down, and round in great circles: but his eyes were red, and he held on as the body cart-whipped over the floor, upsetting the tin dipper and the soap dish and the fleshbrush, and banged against the tin side of the bath. As he held he closed his jaws tighter and tighter, for he made sure he would be banged to death, and, for the honor of his family, he preferred to be found with his teeth locked. He was dizzy, aching, and felt shaken to pieces when something went off like a thunderclap just behind him; a hot wind knocked him senseless and red fire singed his fur. The big man had been wakened by the noise, and had fired both barrels of a shotgun into Nag just behind the hood.

Rikki-tikki held on with his eyes shut, for now he was quite sure he was dead; but the head did not move, and the big man picked him up and said: "It's the mongoose again, Alice; the little chap has saved our lives now." Then Teddy's mother came in with a very white face, and saw what was left of Nag, and Rikki-tikki dragged himself to Teddy's bedroom and spent half the rest of the night shaking himself tenderly to find out whether he really was broken into forty pieces, as he fancied. ●

When morning came he was very stiff, but well pleased with his doings. "Now I have Nagaina to settle with, and she will be worse than five Nags, and there's no knowing when the eggs she spoke of will hatch. Goodness! I must go and see Darzee," he said.

Without waiting for breakfast, Rikki-tikki ran to the thornbush where Darzee was singing a song of triumph at the top of his voice. The news of Nag's death was all over the garden, for the sweeper had thrown the body on the rubbish heap.

"Oh, you stupid tuft of feathers!" said Rikki-tikki, angrily. "Is this the time to sing?"

"Nag is dead—is dead—is dead!" sang Darzee. "The valiant Rikki-tikki caught him by the head and held fast. The big man brought the bang-stick and Nag fell in two pieces! He will never eat my babies again."

"All that's true enough; but where's Nagaina?" said Rikki-tikki, looking carefully round him.

▲ **Critical Viewing**
What role does Darzee, the tailor-bird, play in the conflict between Rikki-tikki-tavi and the cobras? **[Analyze]**

Plot
Why is the death of Nag part of the rising action rather than the resolution?

"Nagaina came to the bathroom sluice and called for Nag," Darzee went on; "and Nag came out on the end of a stick—the sweeper picked him up on the end of a stick and threw him upon the rubbish heap. Let us sing about the great, the red-eyed Rikki-tikki!" and Darzee filled his throat and sang.

"If I could get up to your nest, I'd roll all your babies out!" said Rikki-tikki. "You don't know when to do the right thing at the right time. You're safe enough in your nest there, but it's war for me down here. Stop singing a minute, Darzee."

"For the great, the beautiful Rikki-tikki's sake, I will stop," said Darzee. "What is it, O Killer of the terrible Nag!"

"Where is Nagaina, for the third time?"

"On the rubbish heap by the stables, mourning for Nag. Great is Rikki-tikki with the white teeth."

"Bother my white teeth! Have you ever heard where she keeps her eggs?"

"In the melon bed, on the end nearest the wall, where the sun strikes nearly all day. She had them there weeks ago."

"And you never thought it worthwhile to tell me? The end nearest the wall, you said?"

"Rikki-tikki, you are not going to eat her eggs?"

"Not eat exactly; no. Darzee, if you have a grain of sense you will fly off to the stables and pretend that your wing is broken, and let Nagaina chase you away to this bush! I must get to the melon bed, and if I went there now she'd see me."

Darzee was a featherbrained little fellow who could never hold more than one idea at a time in his head; and just because he knew that Nagaina's children were born in eggs like his own, he didn't think at first that it was fair to kill them. But his wife was a sensible bird, and she knew that cobra's eggs meant young cobras later on; so she flew off from the nest, and left Darzee to keep the babies warm, and continue his song about the death of Nag. Darzee was very like a man in some ways.

She fluttered in front of Nagaina by the rubbish heap, and cried out, "Oh, my wing is broken! The boy in the house threw a stone at me and broke it." Then she fluttered more desperately than ever.

Nagaina lifted up her head and hissed, "You warned Rikki-tikki when I would have killed him. Indeed and truly, you've chosen a bad place to be lame in." And she moved toward

consolation
(kän´ sə lā´ shən) *n.*
something that com-
forts a disappointed
person

cunningly (kun´ iŋ
lē) *adv.* cleverly

Plot
Do you think this scene
is the climax or part
of the rising action?
Why?

Darzee's wife, slipping along over the dust.

"The boy broke it with a stone!" shrieked Darzee's wife.

"Well! It may be some consolation to you when you're dead to know that I shall settle accounts with the boy. My husband lies on the rubbish heap this morning, but before night the boy in the house will lie very still. What is the use of running away? I am sure to catch you. Little fool, look at me!"

Darzee's wife knew better than to do *that*, for a bird who looks at a snake's eyes gets so frightened that she cannot move. Darzee's wife fluttered on, piping sorrowfully, and never leaving the ground, and Nagaina quickened her pace.

Rikki-tikki heard them going up the path from the stables, and he raced for the end of the melon patch near the wall. There, in the warm litter about the melons, very cunningly hidden, he found twenty-five eggs, about the size of a bantam's eggs,[7] but with whitish skin instead of shell.

"I was not a day too soon," he said; for he could see the baby cobras curled up inside the skin, and he knew that the minute they were hatched they could each kill a man or a mongoose. He bit off the tops of the eggs as fast as he could, taking care to crush the young cobras, and turned over the litter from time to time to see whether he had missed any. At last there were only three eggs left, and Rikki-tikki began to chuckle to himself, when he heard Darzee's wife screaming:

"Rikki-tikki, I led Nagaina toward the house, and she has gone into the veranda, and—oh, come quickly—she means killing!"

Rikki-tikki smashed two eggs, and tumbled backward down the melon bed with the third egg in his mouth, and scuttled to the veranda as hard as he could put foot to the ground. Teddy and his mother and father were there at early breakfast; but Rikki-tikki saw that they were not eating anything. They sat stone-still, and their faces were white. Nagaina was coiled up on the matting by Teddy's chair, within easy striking distance of Teddy's bare leg, and she was swaying to and fro singing a song of triumph.

"Son of the big man that killed Nag," she hissed, "stay still. I am not ready yet. Wait a little. Keep very still, all you three. If you move I strike, and if you do not move I strike, Oh, foolish

---

7. bantam's (ban´ təmz) **eggs** *n.* eggs of a small chicken.

people, who killed my Nag!"

Teddy's eyes were fixed on his father, and all his father could do was to whisper, "Sit still, Teddy. You mustn't move. Teddy, keep still."

Then Rikki-tikki came up and cried: "Turn round, Nagaina; turn and fight!"

"All in good time," said she, without moving her eyes. "I will settle my account with *you* presently. Look at your friends, Rikki-tikki. They are still and white; they are afraid. They dare not move, and if you come a step nearer I strike."

"Look at your eggs," said Rikki-tikki, "in the melon bed near the wall. Go and look, Nagaina."

The big snake turned half round, and saw the egg on the veranda. "Ah-h! Give it to me," she said.

Rikki-tikki put his paws one on each side of the egg, and his eyes were blood-red. "What price for a snake's egg? For a young cobra? For a young king cobra? For the last—the very last of the brood? The ants are eating all the others down by the melon bed."

Nagaina spun clear round, forgetting everything for the sake of the one egg; and Rikki-tikki saw Teddy's father shoot out a big hand, catch Teddy by the shoulder, and drag him across the little table with the teacups, safe and out of reach of Nagaina.

"Tricked! Tricked! Tricked! *Rikk-tck-tck!*" chuckled Rikki-tikki."The boy is safe, and it was I—I—I that caught Nag by the hood last night in the bathroom." Then he began to jump up and down, all four feet together, his head close to the floor. "He threw me to and fro, but he could not shake me off. He was dead before the big man blew him in two. I did it. *Rikki-tikki-tck-tck!* Come then, Nagaina. Come and fight with me. You shall not be a widow long."

Nagaina saw that she had lost her chance of killing Teddy, and the egg lay between Rikki-tikki's paws. "Give me the egg, Rikki-tikki. Give me the last of my eggs, and I will go away and never come back," she said, lowering her hood.

"Yes, you will go away, and you will never come back; for you will go to the rubbish heap with Nag. Fight, widow! The big man has gone for his gun! Fight!"

Rikki-tikki was bounding all round Nagaina, keeping just out of reach of her stroke, his little eyes like hot coals.

Spiral Review
Setting How would a fight with Nagaina in an open space like the veranda be different from Rikki-tikki's fight with Nag?

Plot
What details increase the tension in the story at this point?

Reading Check
What does Rikki bring with him to the veranda?

Nagaina gathered herself together, and flung out at him. Rikki-tikki jumped up and backward. Again and again and again she struck, and each time her head came with a whack on the matting of the veranda and she gathered herself together like a watchspring. Then Rikki-tikki danced in a circle to get behind her, and Nagaina spun round to keep her head to his head, so that the rustle of her tail on the matting sounded like dry leaves blown along by the wind.

He had forgotten the egg. It still lay on the veranda, and Nagaina came nearer and nearer to it, till at last, while Rikki-tikki was drawing breath, she caught it in her mouth, turned to the veranda steps, and flew like an arrow down the path, with Rikki-tikki behind her. When the cobra runs for her life, she goes like a whiplash flicked across a horse's neck.

Rikki-tikki knew that he must catch her, or all the trouble would begin again. She headed straight for the long grass by the thornbush, and as he was running Rikki-tikki heard Darzee still singing his foolish little song of triumph. But Darzee's wife was wiser. She flew off her nest as Nagaina came along, and flapped her wings about Nagaina's head. If Darzee had helped they might have turned her; but Nagaina only lowered her hood and went on. Still, the instant's delay brought Rikki-tikki up to her, and as she plunged into the rat hole where she and Nag used to live, his little white teeth were clenched on her tail, and he went down with her—and very few mongooses, however wise and old they may be, care to follow a cobra into its hole. It was dark in the hole; and Rikki-tikki never knew when it might open out and give Nagaina room to turn and strike at him. He held on savagely, and struck out his feet to act as brakes on the dark slope of the hot, moist earth.

Then the grass by the mouth of the hole stopped waving, and Darzee said: "It is all over with Rikki-tikki! We must sing his death song. Valiant Rikki-tikki is dead! For Nagaina will surely kill him underground."

So he sang a very mournful song that he made up all on the spur of the

Spiral Review
Setting How does the setting of the cobra's hole introduce uncertainty into the plot?

Plot
How does Darzee's comment here add to the tension?

minute, and just as he got to the most touching part the grass quivered again, and Rikki-tikki, covered with dirt, dragged himself out of the hole leg by leg, licking his whiskers. Darzee stopped with a little shout. Rikki-tikki shook some of the dust out of his fur and sneezed. "It is all over," he said. "The widow will never come out again." And the red ants that live between the grass stems heard him, and began to troop down one after another to see if he had spoken the truth.

Rikki-tikki curled himself up in the grass and slept where he was—slept and slept till it was late in the afternoon, for he had done a hard day's work.

"Now," he said, when he awoke, "I will go back to the house. Tell the Coppersmith, Darzee, and he will tell the garden that Nagaina is dead."

The Coppersmith is a bird who makes a noise exactly like the beating of a little hammer on a copper pot; and the reason he is always making it is because he is the town crier to every Indian garden, and tells all the news to everybody who cares to listen. As Rikki-tikki went up the path, he heard his "attention" notes like a tiny dinner gong; and then the steady "*Ding-dong-tock!* Nag is dead—*dong!* Nagaina is dead! *Ding-dong-tock!*" That set all the birds in the garden singing, and the frogs croaking; for Nag and Nagaina used to eat frogs as well as little birds.

When Rikki got to the house, Teddy and Teddy's mother and Teddy's father came out and almost cried over him; and that night he ate all that was given him till he could eat no more, and went

Plot
What part of the plot does Rikki's comment illustrate?

Reading Check
What happens when Nagaina goes down the snake hole?

to bed on Teddy's shoulder, where Teddy's mother saw him when she came to look late at night.

"He saved our lives and Teddy's life," she said to her husband. "Just think, he saved all our lives."

Rikki-tikki woke up with a jump, for all the mongooses are light sleepers.

"Oh, it's you," said he. "What are you bothering for? All the cobras are dead; and if they weren't, I'm here."

Rikki-tikki had a right to be proud of himself; but he did not grow too proud, and he kept that garden as a mongoose should keep it, with tooth and jump and spring and bite, till never a cobra dared show its head inside the walls.

Critical Thinking

Cite textual evidence to support your responses.

1. **Key Ideas and Details (a)** How does Rikki feel about the cobras? How do they feel about Rikki? **(b) Compare:** Using details from the story, compare Rikki's and the cobras' personalities.

2. **Key Ideas and Details (a)** What is the relationship between Nag and Nagaina? **(b) Analyze:** What does Nagaina do to make matters worse for Nag and herself? **(c) Draw Conclusions:** Why does this plan make her a villain?

3. **Key Ideas and Details (a) Analyze:** What role does Darzee play in the story? **(b) Compare and Contrast:** Whose approach to life, Darzee's or Rikki's, do you think is more effective? Why?

4. **Integration of Knowledge and Ideas (a) Analyze:** "Rikki-tikki-tavi" is among the most widely read short stories ever written. Why do you think it is so popular? **(b) Evaluate:** Do you think the story deserves this standing? Explain. **(c) Discuss:** Share your responses with a partner. Then, discuss how looking at someone else's responses did or did not change your evaluation.

5. **Integration of Knowledge and Ideas (a)** In what way are Nagaina's eggs innocent victims of the conflict? **(b)** How do Teddy and his family suffer? *[Connect to the Big Question: Does every conflict have a winner?]*

Reading Skill: Make Predictions

1. What **prior knowledge** did you have from reading the Background note on page 227 that helped you **predict** that Rikki-tikki-tavi would be able to defeat the cobras?

2. Choose another prediction based on prior knowledge that you made as you read this story. Use a graphic organizer like the one here to show how you made your prediction.

Rudyard Kipling

Story Details

+

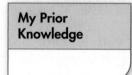

My Prior Knowledge

=

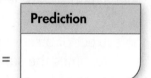

Prediction

Literary Analysis: Plot

3. Key Ideas and Details Identify two **plot** events that increase the tension between Rikki and Nag.

4. Key Ideas and Details Identify two or three events that move the plot toward the **climax,** when Rikki and Nagaina battle.

Vocabulary

Acquisition and Use Answer each question. Then, explain your response.

1. Is someone who has just been *revived* ready to run a race?

2. If you like a man *immensely,* how do you feel about him?

3. When you sit on a *veranda,* are you inside the house?

4. If you are *mourning* someone, are you smiling?

5. Is missing dinner *consolation* for getting home late?

6. If you are *cunningly* disguised, can you be recognized?

Word Study Use the context of the sentences and what you know about the **Latin suffix -*tion*** to explain your answer.

1. If a painting is an *imitation,* is it the original?

2. If someone offers a *suggestion,* is he being helpful?

Integrated Language Skills

The Bear Boy • Rikki-tikki-tavi

Conventions: Verbs

A **verb** is a word that expresses an action or a state of being.
Every complete sentence must have at least one verb.

- An **action verb** tells what action someone or something is doing.
- A **linking verb** joins the subject of a sentence with a word or phrase that describes or renames the subject. The most common linking verbs are forms of *be*, such as *am, is, was, were, has been,* and *will be*. Other linking verbs include *seem, become, stay, feel, taste,* and *look.*

Action Verbs	Linking Verbs
John *rode* his bike. Let's *skate* in the park.	Jessica *seems* happy. James *is* a member of the club. The theater *will be* crowded.

Practice A Identify the verb or verbs in each sentence, and indicate whether they are action verbs or linking verbs.

1. Kuo-Haya felt shy in front of the other boys.
2. Kuo-Haya followed bear tracks into a canyon.
3. Kuo-Haya's father searched for Kuo-Haya among the cliffs.
4. Kuo-Haya's father was angry at the mother bear.

© **Reading Application** In "The Bear Boy," find one sentence with a linking verb and one with an action verb.

Practice B Identify the action verb in each sentence. Then, write a new sentence for each, using the verb as a linking verb.

1. Rikki-tikki-tavi looked all around the bungalow.
2. Rikki-tikki-tavi felt the soft pillow on Teddy's bed.
3. Karait, the dusty brown snakeling, appeared in the dust.
4. Nagaina turned to see her only remaining egg.

© **Writing Application** Choose a photo from pages 228–244 and write two sentences: one using a linking verb, and one using an action verb.

PH WRITING COACH | Further instruction and practice are available in *Prentice Hall Writing Coach.*

Writing

Common Core State Standards

W.7.2.d, W.7.2.e, SL.1.a, SL.3
[For the full wording of the standards, see page 216.]

Informative Text Write an **informative article** based on the story you read.

- If you read "Bear Boy," write about how a mother bear raises cubs.
- If you read "Rikki-tikki-tavi," write about cobras or mongooses.

An informative article teaches readers about a topic and contains these elements:

- an introduction, a body, and a conclusion
- details that tell *when, how much, how often,* or *to what extent*
- a formal style that avoids slang and incomplete sentences
- terms specific to your topic, such as *den, venom, predator*

Grammar Application Check your writing to make sure your use of action and linking verbs is correct.

Writing Workshop: *Work in Progress*

Preview for Response to Literature Answer the following: *What stories have I read that I enjoyed or did not enjoy? What characters stand out?* Save this Story List in your writing portfolio.

Use this prewriting activity to prepare for the **Writing Workshop** on page 302.

Speaking and Listening

Comprehension and Collaboration With a partner, engage in an **informal debate** based on the story you read. Each of you should pick an opposing viewpoint to present.

- If you read "The Bear Boy," debate whether it is ethical to train wild animals for entertainment purposes, such as circuses or shows.
- If you read "Rikki-tikki-tavi," defend the actions of either the mongoose or the cobras in the story. Explain your position.

Follow these steps to complete the assignment.

- Convince your partner of your viewpoint by supporting your ideas with valid arguments based on credible research.
- Respect your partner's time to talk. Do not interrupt.
- As you listen to your partner, take note of his or her argument. When it is your turn to talk, do one of three things:

  (1) Explain why there is not enough evidence to support your partner's argument. (2) Explain why the evidence contradicts your partner's argument. (3) Find an inconsistency with one of your partner's earlier arguments.

www.PHLitOnline.com
- Interactive graphic organizers
- Grammar tutorial
- Interactive journals

from **Letters from Rifka** • **Two Kinds**

Leveled Texts

Build your skills and improve your comprehension of short stories with texts of increasing complexity.

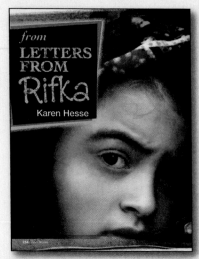

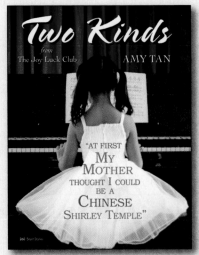

Read ***Letters from Rifka*** to find out what happens when a Russian family attempts a daring escape.

Read **"Two Kinds"** to learn how a daughter struggles to fulfill her mother's wishes.

Common Core State Standards

Meet these standards with either the excerpt from ***Letters from Rifka*** (p. 252) or **"Two Kinds"** (p. 260).

Reading Literature
6. Analyze how an author develops and contrasts the points of view of different characters or narrators in a text. *(Literary Analysis: Character)*

Writing
3.a. Engage and orient the reader by establishing a context and point of view and introducing a narrator and/or characters; organize an event sequence that unfolds naturally and logically. **3.b.** Use narrative techniques, such as dialogue, pacing, and description, to develop experiences, events, and/or characters. *(Writing: Journal Entry)*

7. Conduct short research projects to answer a question, drawing on several sources and generating additional related, focused questions for further research and investigation. *(Research and Technology: Outline)*

Language
1. Demonstrate command of the conventions of standard English grammar and usage when writing or speaking. *(Conventions: The Principal Parts of Verbs)*

4.b. Use common, grade-appropriate Greek or Latin affixes and roots as clues to the meaning of a word. *(Vocabulary: Word Study)*

6. Acquire and use accurately grade-appropriate general academic and domain-specific words and phrases; gather vocabulary knowledge when considering a word or phrase important to comprehension or expression. *(Vocabulary: Word Study)*

Reading Skill: Make Predictions

A **prediction** is an informed judgment about what will happen. Use details in the text to make predictions as you read. Then, **read ahead to verify predictions**—to check whether your predictions are correct.

- As you read, ask yourself whether new details support your predictions. If they do not, revise your predictions based on the new information.

- If the predictions you make turn out to be wrong, **reread to look for details** you might have missed.

Using the Strategy: Prediction Chart

Record details in a **prediction chart** like this one.

Prediction	Revised or Confirmed Prediction	Actual Outcome
Details	New details	Details from rereading (if necessary)

Literary Analysis: Character

A **character** is a person or animal in a literary work.

- A **character's motives** are the emotions or goals that drive him or her to act one way or another.

- **Character traits** are the individual qualities that make each character unique. Identify character traits by noticing how characters think, act, and speak throughout a story.

- A character's **point of view** is his or her unique perspective.

Characters' motives, traits, and point of view influence what characters do and how they interact with others. As you read, think about how the author shows what the characters are like and why they do what they do.

PHLit
Online!
www.PHLitOnline.com

Hear It!
- Selection summary audio
- Selection audio

See It!
- Get Connected video
- Background video
- More about the author
- Vocabulary flashcards

Do It!
- Interactive journals
- Interactive graphic organizers
- Self-test
- Internet activity
- Grammar tutorial
- Interactive vocabulary games

Writing About the Big Question

In *Letters from Rifka*, a family must escape from their country after a war. Use these sentence starters to develop your ideas about the Big Question.

The **struggles** of war sometimes cause people to _____.

People often face the **danger** of losing _____.

While You Read Look for things Rifka and her family lose as they make their escape.

Vocabulary

Read each word and its definition. Decide whether you know the word well, know it a little bit, or do not know it at all. After you read, see how your knowledge of each word has increased.

- **distract** (di strakt´) *v.* draw attention away (p. 253) *A toy will* <u>*distract*</u> *a crying child.* distract *v.* distracted *adj.* distraction *n.*

- **emerged** (ē murjd) *v.* came into view; became visible (p. 254) *The sun finally* <u>*emerged*</u> *from behind the heavy clouds.* emerge *v.* emerging *v.* emergent *adj.*

- **deserts** (di zurts´) *v.* leaves, especially a military post (p. 254) *A soldier who* <u>*deserts*</u> *is committing a crime.* desert *v.* deserter *n.* desertion *n.*

- **peasants** (pez´ ənts) *n.* owners of small farms, or farm laborers (p. 256) *The* <u>*peasants*</u> *bought and sold vegetables at the village market.*

- **huddled** (hud´ 'ld) *v.* crowded or nestled close together (p. 256) *The newborn kittens* <u>*huddled*</u> *together for warmth.* huddle *v.* huddle *n.* huddling *v.*

- **precaution** (pri kô´ shən) *n.* something you do to prevent something bad or dangerous from happening (p. 256) *Wearing a bike helmet is a good* <u>*precaution*</u> *against head injuries.* precautionary *adj.* caution *n.* cautioned *v.*

Word Study

The **Latin root -*tract*-** means "pull" or "drag."

In this story, a character is asked to **distract** some guards, or pull their attention away from someone who does not want to be noticed.

Meet
Karen Hesse

Author of

LETTERS FROM
Rifka

Growing up in Baltimore, Maryland, Karen Hesse dreamed of many different careers—archaeologist, actress, and author. Hesse discovered that she was "good with words" in the fifth grade. She began her writing career sitting in her closet after school and writing poetry. Thirty years later, she published her first book, *Wish on a Unicorn*.

Discovering Vermont Hesse and her husband, Randy, took a six-month tent-camping trip across the United States in 1976. At the end of that trip, they discovered Brattleboro, Vermont, which is where they live today.

BACKGROUND FOR THE STORY

Jews in Russia

For most of the nineteenth and early twentieth centuries, the Jews of Russia faced prejudice and unfair treatment. This caused thousands of Jews to leave the country, many fleeing to the United States. In this excerpt from *Letters from Rifka*, a Jewish family begins their escape from Russia after the turmoil of World War I.

DID YOU KNOW?

Hesse started writing *Letters from Rifka* about twenty times, until she was happy with the "voice" of the main character.

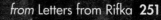

from Letters from Rifka **251**

from

LETTERS FROM Rifka

Karen Hesse

My Dear Cousin Tovah,

We made it! If it had not been for your father, though, I think my family would all be dead now: Mama, Papa, Nathan, Saul, and me. At the very best we would be in that filthy prison in Berdichev,[1] not rolling west through Ukraine on a freight train bound for Poland.

I am sure you and Cousin Hannah were glad to see Uncle Avrum come home today. How worried his daughters must have been after the locked doors and whisperings of last night.

Soon Bubbe Ruth, my dear little grandmother, will hear of our escape. I hope she gives a big pot of Frusileh's cream to Uncle Avrum. How better could she thank him?

When the sun rose above the trees at the train station in Berdichev this morning, I stood alone outside a boxcar, my heart knocking against my ribs.

I stood there, trying to look older than my twelve years. Wrapped in the new shawl Cousin Hannah gave to me, still I trembled.

"Wear this in health," Hannah had whispered in my ear as she draped the shawl over my shoulders early this morning, before we slipped from your house into the dark.

"Come," Papa said, leading us through the woods to the train station.

I looked back to the flickering lights of your house, Tovah.

"Quickly, Rifka," Papa whispered. "The boys, and Mama, and I must hide before light."

"You can distract the guards, can't you, little sister?" Nathan said, putting an arm around me. In the darkness, I could not see his eyes, but I felt them studying me.

"Yes," I answered, not wanting to disappoint him.

At the train station, Papa and Mama hid behind bales of hay in boxcars to my right. My two giant brothers, Nathan and Saul, crouched in separate cars to my left. Papa said that we should hide in different cars. If the guards discovered only one of us, perhaps the others might still escape.

---

1. **Berdichev** (byir d ē′ chif) *n.* a city in Russia, now Ukraine.

Predict
Based on the first paragraph, what do you think this story will be about?

Character
What do Rifka's remarks about her grandmother and Uncle Avrum reveal about her character?

Vocabulary
distract (di strakt′) *v.* draw attention away

✓ Reading Check
Where is Rifka as she writes this letter?

Behind me, in the dusty corner of a boxcar, sat my own rucksack. It waited for me, holding what little I own in this world. I had packed Mama's candlesticks, wrapped in my two heavy dresses, at the bottom of the sack.

Your gift to me, the book of Pushkin, I did not pack. I kept it out, holding it in my hands.

I would have liked to fly away, to race back up the road, stopping at every door to say good-bye, to say that we were going to America.

But I could not. Papa said we must tell no one we were leaving, not even Bubbe Ruth. Only you and Hannah and Uncle Avrum knew. I'm so glad at least you knew, Tovah.

As Papa expected, not long after he and Mama and the boys had hidden themselves, two guards **emerged** from a wooden shelter. They thundered down the platform in their heavy boots climbing in and out of the cars, making their search.

They did not notice me at first. Saul says I am too little for anyone to notice, but you know Saul. He never has a nice word to say to me. And I am small for a girl of twelve. Still, my size did not keep the guards from noticing me. I think the guards missed seeing me at first because they were so busy in their search of the train. They were searching for Nathan.

You know as well as I, Tovah, that when a Jewish boy **deserts** the Russian Army, the army tries hard to find him. They bring him back and kill him in front of his regiment[2] as a warning to the others. Those who have helped him, they also die. •

---

2. regiment (rej´ ə mənt) *n.* a military unit consisting of a large number of persons.

Late last night, when Nathan slipped away from his regiment and appeared at our door, joy filled my heart at seeing my favorite brother again. Yet a troubled look worried Nathan's face. He hugged me only for a moment. His dimpled smile vanished as quickly as it came.

"I've come," he said, "to warn Saul. The soldiers will soon follow. They will take him into the army."

I am ashamed, Tovah, to admit that at first hearing Nathan's news made me glad. I wanted Saul gone. He drives me crazy. From his big ears to his big feet, I cannot stand the sight of him. Good riddance, I thought.

How foolish I was not to understand what Nathan's news really meant to our family.

"You should not have come," Mama said to Nathan. "They will shoot you when you return."

Papa said, "Nathan isn't going to return. Hurry! We must pack!"

We all stared at him.

"Quickly," Papa said, clapping his hands. "Rifka, run and fill your rucksack[3] with all of your belongings." I do not know what Papa thought I owned.

Mama said, "Rifka, do you have room in your bag for my candlesticks?"

"The candlesticks, Mama?" I asked.

"We either take them, Rifka, or leave them to the greedy

---

3. **rucksack** (ruk´ sak´) *n.* a kind of knapsack or backpack worn over the shoulders.

▲ **Critical Viewing**
In what ways do these Russian military officers look different from American military officers today? **[Compare and Contrast]**

© **Spiral Review**
Plot Why is Nathan's escape from the army an important plot event?

✓ Reading Check
What does Rifka carry in her sack?

Vocabulary

peasants (pez´ ənts) *n.* owners of small farms, or farm laborers

huddled (hud´ 'ld) *v.* crowded or nestled close together

precaution (pri kô´ shən) *n.* something you do to prevent something bad or dangerous from happening

peasants. Soon enough they will swoop down like vultures to pick our house bare," Mama said.

Papa said, "Your brothers in America have sent for us, Rifka. It is time to leave Russia and we are not coming back. Ever."

"Don't we need papers?" I asked.

Papa looked from Nathan to Saul. "There is no time for papers," he said.

Then I began to understand.

We huddled in your cellar through the black night, planning our escape. Uncle Avrum only shut you out to protect you, Tovah.

Hearing the guards speak this morning, I understand his precaution. It was dangerous enough for you to know we were leaving. We could not risk telling you the details of our escape in case the soldiers came to question you.

The guards were talking about Nathan. They were saying what they would do to him once they found him, and what they would do to anyone who had helped him.

Nathan hid under a stack of burlap bags, one boxcar away from me. I knew, no matter how frightened I was, I must not let them find Nathan.

Cite textual evidence to support your responses.

Critical Thinking

1. **Key Ideas and Details** **(a) Support:** What details in the story reveal Rifka's age? **(b) Analyze:** How do you think Rifka's age affects the way she feels about the story's events?

2. **Key Ideas and Details** **(a)** What risks did Nathan take by escaping from the Russian Army? **(b) Speculate:** How do you think he felt as he appeared at his family's door? Explain.

3. **Key Ideas and Details** **(a) Analyze:** Why was Rifka not allowed to say goodbye to her friends and neighbors? **(b) Make a Judgment:** Do you think she was wise to have left silently? Why?

4. **Craft and Structure** How might the story be different if it were told from Papa's or Nathan's point of view?

5. **Integration of Knowledge and Ideas** **(a)** What do Rifka and her family lose by leaving their home? **(b)** What do they gain? *[Connect to the Big Question: Does every conflict have a winner?]*

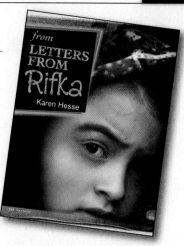

Reading Skill: Make Predictions

1. (a) Did you **predict** that the guards would find Rifka? **(b)** Did reading ahead make you change your prediction? Explain.

2. (a) At what point in the story were you able to predict the family's reason for leaving Russia? **(b)** Did your prediction change as you read? Explain.

Literary Analysis: Character

3. Key Ideas and Details Using a diagram like this one, identify Rifka's **character traits.** Support your answers with story details.

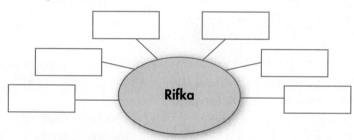

Rifka

4. Key Ideas and Details What are Nathan's **motives** for leaving the Russian Army?

Vocabulary

Acquisition and Use Make up an answer to each question. Use a complete sentence that includes the italicized vocabulary word.

1. How can they *distract* the children?

2. What *emerged* from the egg?

3. What animals *huddled* under the bushes?

4. What *precaution* can you take to prevent sunburn?

5. What happens when a soldier *deserts* the army?

6. Why did the *peasants* gather in the town square?

Word Study Use the context of the sentences and what you know about the **Latin root -*tract*-** to explain each answer.

1. Does a shy person usually want to *attract* attention?

2. Can a *tractor* be useful if you want to pull a heavy object?

Word Study

The **Latin root -*tract*-** means "pull" or "drag."

Apply It Explain how the root -*tract*- contributes to the meanings of these words. Consult a print or online dictionary if necessary.

extract
detract
tractable

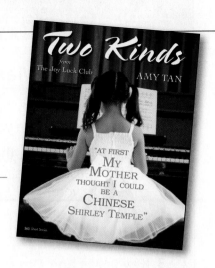

Does every *conflict* have a winner?

Writing About the Big Question

In "Two Kinds," the narrator's mother has dreams of greatness for her daughter. Use these sentence starters to develop your ideas about the Big Question.

Parents and children have **disagreements** about _____.

They can overcome these **obstacles** by _____.

While You Read Look for conflicts between the daughter and her mother in this story.

Vocabulary

Read each word and its definition. Decide whether you know the word well, know it a little bit, or do not know it at all. After you read, see how your knowledge of each word has increased.

- **reproach** (ri prōch´) *n.* disapproval; criticism (p. 262) *Jack's dedicated work in the community was beyond reproach.*
  reproach v. reproachful adj. reproachfully adv.

- **conspired** (kən spīrd) *v.* planned together secretly (p. 269) *The girls conspired to surprise their mother. conspire v. conspiracy n.*

- **devastated** (dev´ ə stat´ əd) *v.* destroyed; completely upset (p. 272) *The uncontrolled fire devastated the city.*
  devastate v. devastation n. devastating v.

- **nonchalantly** (nän´ shə länt´ lē) *adv.* seemingly uninterested (p. 272) *He looked away nonchalantly as the girls talked about the dance. nonchalant adj. nonchalance n.*

- **expectations** (ek´ spek tā´ shənz) *n.* things looked forward to (p. 274) *Ellen had high expectations that the play would be wonderful. expectation n. expect v.*

- **sentimental** (sen tə ment´ əl) *adj.* emotional; showing tender feeling (p. 275) *The sentimental music made her grandmother cry. sentiment n. sentimentally adv.*

Word Study

The **Latin root -*spir*-** means "breath."

If you say something "under your breath," you say it in secret. In this story, two characters **conspire**, or secretly plan, to have the narrator play piano in a talent show.

Meet
Amy Tan
(b. 1952)

Author of
Two Kinds

If Amy Tan's mother had gotten her way, Amy would have two professions—doctor and concert pianist. Although Tan showed early promise in music, at thirty-seven she became a successful fiction writer instead. Tan's first novel, *The Joy Luck Club*, drew on her troubled relationship with her mother, who was born in China.

The Writing Life Tan has written many books—most for adults, some for children. Writing is sometimes tough, says Tan, but she keeps this in mind: "A story should be a gift." That thought propels Tan to keep creating memorable characters and events.

BACKGROUND FOR THE STORY
China

In 1949, the Communist party seized control of China, following years of civil war. Like the mother in "Two Kinds," a number of Chinese who feared Communists fled to the United States. Many of them lost everything except their hopes for a better future. They placed these hopes on the shoulders of the children born in the new land. As you read, note how the daughter in "Two Kinds" deals with her mother's expectations.

Did You Know?
Tan sometimes performs in a rock group with fellow writer Stephen King to raise money for charity.

Two Kinds

from
The Joy Luck Club AMY TAN

"AT FIRST MY MOTHER THOUGHT I COULD BE A CHINESE SHIRLEY TEMPLE"

My mother believed you could be anything you wanted to be in America. You could open a restaurant. You could work for the government and get good retirement. You could buy a house with almost no money down. You could become rich. You could become instantly famous.

"Of course you can be prodigy,[1] too," my mother told me when I was nine. "You can be best anything. What does Auntie Lindo know? Her daughter, she is only best tricky."

America was where all my mother's hopes lay. She had come here in 1949 after losing everything in China: her mother and father, her family home, her first husband, and two daughters, twin baby girls. But she never looked back with regret. There were so many ways for things to get better.

老師

We didn't immediately pick the right kind of prodigy. At first my mother thought I could be a Chinese Shirley Temple.[2] We'd watch Shirley's old movies on TV as though they were training films. My mother would poke my arm and say, "Ni kan" [nè kän]—You watch. And I would see Shirley tapping her feet, or singing a sailor song, or pursing her lips into a very round O while saying, "Oh my goodness."

"*Ni kan*," said my mother as Shirley's eyes flooded with tears. "You already know how. Don't need talent for crying!"

Soon after my mother got this idea about Shirley Temple, she took me to a beauty training school in the Mission district and put me in the hands of a student who could barely hold the scissors without shaking. Instead of getting big fat curls, I emerged with an uneven mass of crinkly black fuzz. My mother dragged me off to the bathroom and tried to wet down my hair.

"You look like Negro Chinese," she lamented, as if I had done this on purpose.

---

1. **prodigy** (präd´ ə jē) *n.* child of unusually high talent.
2. **Shirley Temple** American child star of the 1930s. She starred in her first movie at age three and won an Academy Award at age six.

Character
In what ways might the details in this paragraph contribute to the mother's motives?

Character
What are the mother's motives for taking her daughter to beauty training school?

✓ Reading Check
Whom does the narrator's mother want her to be like?

The instructor of the beauty training school had to lop off these soggy clumps to make my hair even again. "Peter Pan is very popular these days," the instructor assured my mother. I now had hair the length of a boy's, with straight-across bangs that hung at a slant two inches above my eyebrows. I liked the haircut and it made me actually look forward to my future fame.

In fact, in the beginning, I was just as excited as my mother, maybe even more so. I pictured this prodigy part of me as many different images, trying each one on for size. I was a dainty ballerina girl standing by the curtains, waiting to hear the right music that would send me floating on my tiptoes. I was like the Christ child lifted out of the straw manger, crying with holy indignity. I was Cinderella stepping from her pumpkin carriage with sparkly cartoon music filling the air.

In all of my imaginings, I was filled with a sense that I would soon become *perfect*. My mother and father would adore me. I would be beyond reproach. I would never feel the need to sulk for anything.

But sometimes the prodigy in me became impatient. "If you don't hurry up and get me out of here, I'm disappearing for good," it warned. "And then you'll always be nothing." •

老師

Every night after dinner, my mother and I would sit at the Formica kitchen table. She would present new tests, taking her examples from stories of amazing children she had read in *Ripley's Believe It or Not*, or *Good Housekeeping*, *Reader's Digest*, and a dozen other magazines she kept in a pile in our bathroom. My mother got these magazines from people whose houses she cleaned. And since she cleaned many houses each week, we had a great assortment. She would look through them all, searching for stories about remarkable children.

The first night she brought out a story about a three-year-old boy who knew the capitals of all the states and even most of the European countries. A teacher was quoted as

Vocabulary
reproach (ri prōch´)
n. disapproval; criticism

Character
Why is the mother interested in stories about remarkable children?

saying the little boy could also pronounce the names of the foreign cities correctly.

"What's the capital of Finland?" my mother asked me, looking at the magazine story.

All I knew was the capital of California, because Sacramento was the name of the street we lived on in Chinatown. "Nairobi!"[3] I guessed, saying the most foreign word I could think of. She checked to see if that was possibly one way to pronounce "Helsinki" [hel siṅ′ kē] before showing me the answer.

The tests got harder—multiplying numbers in my head, finding the queen of hearts in a deck of cards, trying to stand on my head without using my hands, predicting the daily temperatures in Los Angeles, New York, and London.

One night I had to look at a page from the Bible for three minutes and then report everything I could remember. "Now Jehoshaphat had riches and honor in abundance and . . . that's all I remember, Ma," I said.

And after seeing my mother's disappointed face once again, something inside of me began to die. I hated the tests, the raised hopes and failed expectations. Before going to bed that night, I looked in the mirror above the bathroom sink and when I saw only my face staring back—and that it would always be this ordinary face—I began to cry. Such a sad, ugly girl! I made high-pitched noises like a crazed animal, trying to scratch out the face in the mirror.

And then I saw what seemed to be the prodigy side of me—because I had never seen that face before. I looked at my reflection, blinking so I could see more clearly. The girl staring back at me was angry, powerful. This girl and I were the same. I had new thoughts, willful thoughts, or rather thoughts filled with lots of won'ts. I won't let her change me, I promised myself. I won't be what I'm not.

So now on nights when my mother presented her tests, I performed listlessly, my head propped on one arm. I pretended to be bored. And I was. I got so bored I started counting the bellows of the foghorns out on the bay while my mother drilled me in other areas. The sound was comforting and reminded me of the cow jumping over the

---

3. Nairobi (nī rō′ bē) *n.* capital of Kenya, a country in east central Africa.

Predict
How do you think the narrator will do on the harder tests? Read on to verify your prediction.

Predict
What is your prediction about the mother's reaction when the girl performs poorly on the tests? Why?

Reading Check
What would the narrator and her mother do every night after dinner?

moon. And the next day, I played a game with myself, seeing if my mother would give up on me before eight bellows. After a while I usually counted only one, maybe two bellows at most. At last she was beginning to give up hope.

Two or three months had gone by without any mention of my being a prodigy again. And then one day my mother was watching *The Ed Sullivan Show*[4] on TV. The TV was old and the sound kept shorting out. Every time my mother got halfway up from the sofa to adjust the set, the sound would go back on and Ed would be talking. As soon as she sat down, Ed would go silent again. She got up, the TV broke into loud piano music. She sat down. Silence. Up and down, back and forth, quiet and loud. It was like a stiff embraceless dance between her and the TV set. Finally she stood by the set with her hand on the sound dial.

She seemed entranced by the music, a little frenzied piano piece with this mesmerizing[5] quality, sort of quick passages and then teasing lilting ones before it returned to the quick playful parts.

"*Ni kan*," my mother said, calling me over with hurried hand gestures. "Look here."

I could see why my mother was fascinated by the music. It was being pounded out by a little Chinese girl, about nine years old, with a Peter Pan haircut. The girl had the sauciness[6] of a Shirley Temple. She was proudly modest like a

▼ **Critical Viewing**
How does this photo-graph of the author compare with your own image of the story's narrator? **[Compare and Contrast]**

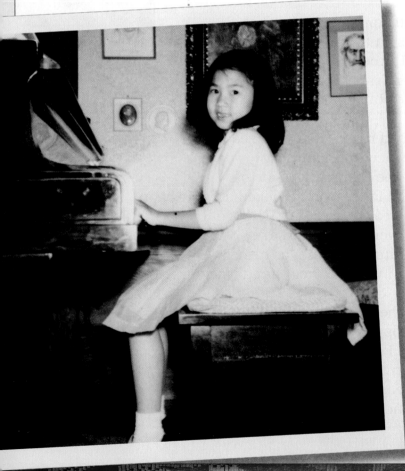

---

4. ***The Ed Sullivan Show*** popular variety show, hosted by Ed Sullivan, that ran from 1948 to 1971.
5. **mesmerizing** (mez´ mər īz iŋ) *adj.* hypnotizing.
6. **sauciness** (sô´ sē nəs) *n.* liveliness; boldness; spirit.

proper Chinese child. And she also did this fancy sweep of a curtsy, so that the fluffy skirt of her white dress cascaded slowly to the floor like the petals of a large carnation.

In spite of these warning signs, I wasn't worried. Our family had no piano and we couldn't afford to buy one, let alone reams of sheet music and piano lessons. So I could be generous in my comments when my mother bad-mouthed the little girl on TV.

"Play note right, but doesn't sound good! No singing sound," complained my mother.

"What are you picking on her for?" I said carelessly. "She's pretty good. Maybe she's not the best, but she's trying hard." I knew almost immediately I would be sorry I said that.

"Just like you," she said. "Not the best. Because you not trying." She gave a little huff as she let go of the sound dial and sat down on the sofa.

The little Chinese girl sat down also to play an encore of "Anitra's Dance" by Grieg.[7] I remember the song, because later on I had to learn how to play it.

Three days after watching *The Ed Sullivan Show*, my mother told me what my schedule would be for piano lessons and piano practice. She had talked to Mr. Chong, who lived on the first floor of our apartment building. Mr. Chong was a retired piano teacher and my mother had traded house cleaning services for weekly lessons and a piano for me to practice on every day, two hours a day, from four until six.

When my mother told me this, I felt as though I had been sent to hell. I whined and then kicked my foot a little when I couldn't stand it anymore.

"Why don't you like me the way I am? I'm not a genius! I can't play the piano. And even if I could, I wouldn't go on TV if you paid me a million dollars!" I cried.

My mother slapped me. "Who ask you be genius?" she shouted. "Only ask you be your best. For you sake. You think I want you be genius? Hnnh! What for! Who ask you!"

"So ungrateful," I heard her mutter in Chinese. "If she

Character
What does this conversation indicate about the difference between the mother's and daughter's traits and motives?

▲ **Critical Viewing**
This television stood four feet tall. How have television and technology changed over the years? **[Connect]**

Reading Check
Why does the mother decide that the narrator should play the piano?

---

7. **Grieg** (grēg) *n.* Edvard Grieg (1843–1907), Norwegian composer.

had as much talent as she has temper, she would be famous now."

Mr. Chong, whom I secretly nicknamed Old Chong, was very strange, always tapping his fingers to the silent music of an invisible orchestra. He looked ancient in my eyes. He had lost most of the hair on top of his head and he wore thick glasses and had eyes that always looked tired and sleepy. But he must have been younger than I thought, since he lived with his mother and was not yet married.

I met Old Lady Chong once and that was enough. She had this peculiar smell like a baby that had done something in its pants. And her fingers felt like a dead person's, like an old peach I once found in the back of the refrigerator; the skin just slid off the meat when I picked it up.

I soon found out why Old Chong had retired from teaching piano. He was deaf. "Like Beethoven!"[8] he shouted to me. "We're both listening only in our head!" And he would start to conduct his frantic silent sonatas.

Our lessons went like this. He would open the book and point to different things, explaining their purpose: "Key! Treble! Bass! No sharps or flats! So this is C major! Listen now and play after me!"

And then he would play the C scale a few times, a simple chord, and then, as if inspired by an old, unreachable itch, he gradually added more notes and running trills and a pounding bass until the music was really something quite grand.

I would play after him, the simple scale, the simple chord, and then I just played some nonsense that sounded like a cat running up and down on top of garbage cans. Old Chong smiled and applauded and then said, "Very good! But now you must learn to keep time!"

So that's how I discovered that Old Chong's eyes were too

> He looked ancient...and had eyes that always looked tired and sleepy.

Predict
How do you think the narrator will react to Old Chong's piano lessons? Read on to verify your prediction.

---

8. **Beethoven** (bā′ tō′ vən) *n.* Ludwig van Beethoven (1770–1827), German composer who began to lose his hearing in 1801. Some of his greatest pieces were written when he was completely deaf.

slow to keep up with the wrong notes I was playing. He went through the motions in half-time. To help me keep rhythm, he stood behind me, pushing down on my right shoulder for every beat. He balanced pennies on top of my wrists so I would keep them still as I slowly played scales and arpeggios.[9] He had me curve my hand around an apple and keep that shape when playing chords. He marched stiffly to show me how to make each finger dance up and down, staccato[10] like an obedient little soldier.

He taught me all these things, and that was how I also learned I could be lazy and get away with mistakes, lots of mistakes. If I hit the wrong notes because I hadn't practiced enough, I never corrected myself. I just kept playing in rhythm. And Old Chong kept conducting his own private reverie.

So maybe I never really gave myself a fair chance. I did pick up the basics pretty quickly, and I might have become a good pianist at that young age. But I was so determined not to try, not to be anybody different that I learned to play only the most ear-splitting preludes, the most discordant hymns.

Over the next year, I practiced like this, dutifully in my own way. And then one day I heard my mother and her friend Lindo Jong both talking in a loud bragging tone of voice so others could hear. It was after church, and I was leaning against the brick wall wearing a dress with stiff white petticoats. Auntie Lindo's daughter, Waverly, who was about my age, was standing farther down the wall about five feet away. We had grown up together and shared all the closeness of two sisters squabbling over crayons and dolls. In other words, for the most part, we hated each other. I thought she was snotty. Waverly Jong had gained a certain amount of fame as "Chinatown's Littlest Chinese Chess Champion."

Character
What motivates the daughter to play piano badly?

Reading Check
What useful information does the narrator learn about her piano teacher?

---

9. arpeggios (är pej´ ē ōz) *n.* notes in a chord played separately in quick succession.
10. staccato (stə kät´ ō) *adv.* played crisply, with clear breaks between notes.

▲ **Critical Viewing**
This photo shows the type of community and time period of the author's child-hood. How may these surroundings have affected the story?
[Connect]

"She bring home too many trophy," lamented Auntie Lindo that Sunday. "All day she play chess. All day I have no time do nothing but dust off her winnings." She threw a scolding look at Waverly, who pretended not to see her.

"You lucky you don't have this problem," said Auntie Lindo with a sigh to my mother.

And my mother squared her shoulders and bragged: "Our problem worser than yours. If we ask Jing-mei wash dish, she hear nothing but music. It's like you can't stop this natural talent."

And right then, I was determined to put a stop to her foolish pride.

老師

A few weeks later, Old Chong and my mother conspired to have me play in a talent show which would be held in the church hall. By then, my parents had saved up enough to buy me a secondhand piano, a black Wurlitzer spinet with a scarred bench. It was the showpiece of our living room.

For the talent show, I was to play a piece called "Pleading Child" from Schumann's[11] *Scenes from Childhood*. It was a simple, moody piece that sounded more difficult than it was. I was supposed to memorize the whole thing, playing the repeat parts twice to make the piece sound longer. But I dawdled over it, playing a few bars and then cheating, looking up to see what notes followed. I never really listened to what I was playing. I daydreamed about being somewhere else, about being someone else.

The part I liked to practice best was the fancy curtsy: right foot out, touch the rose on the carpet with a pointed foot, sweep to the side, left leg bends, look up and smile.

My parents invited all the couples from the Joy Luck Club[12] to witness my debut. Auntie Lindo and Uncle Tin were there. Waverly and her two older brothers had also come. The first two rows were filled with children both younger and older than I was. The littlest ones got to go first. They recited simple nursery rhymes, squawked out tunes on miniature violins, twirled Hula Hoops, pranced in pink ballet tutus, and when they bowed or curtsied, the audience would sigh in unison, "Awww," and then clap enthusiastically.

When my turn came, I was very confident. I remember

Vocabulary
conspired
(kən spīrd´) *v.* planned together secretly

And right then, I was determined to put a stop to her foolish pride.

Reading Check
What do the narrator's mother and Auntie Lindo discuss?

---

11. Schumann (shōō´ män) Robert Alexander Schumann (1810–1856), German composer.
12. Joy Luck Club four Chinese women who have been meeting for years to socialize.

my childish excitement. It was as if I knew, without a doubt, that the prodigy side of me really did exist. I had no fear whatsoever, no nervousness. I remember thinking to myself, This is it! This is it! I looked out over the audience, at my mother's blank face, my father's yawn, Auntie Lindo's stiff-lipped smile, Waverly's sulky expression. I had on a white dress layered with sheets of lace, and a pink bow in my Peter Pan haircut. As I sat down I envisioned people jumping to their feet and Ed Sullivan rushing up to introduce me to everyone on TV.

And I started to play. It was so beautiful. I was so caught up in how lovely I looked that at first I didn't worry how I would sound. So it was a surprise to me when I hit the first wrong note and I realized something didn't sound quite right. And then I hit another and another followed that. A chill started at the top of my head and began to trickle down. Yet I couldn't stop playing, as though my hands were bewitched. I kept thinking my fingers would adjust themselves back, like a train switching to the right track. I played this strange jumble through two repeats, the sour notes staying with me all the way to the end.

When I stood up, I discovered my legs were shaking. Maybe I had just been nervous and the audience, like Old Chong, had seen me go through the right motions and had not heard anything wrong at all. I swept my right foot out, went down on my knee, looked up and smiled. The room was quiet, except for Old Chong, who was beaming and shouting, "Bravo! Bravo! Well done!" But then I saw my mother's face, her stricken face. The audience clapped weakly, and as I walked back to my chair, with my whole face quivering as I tried not to cry, I heard a little boy whisper loudly to his mother, "That was awful," and the mother whispered back, "Well, she certainly tried."

And now I realized how many people were in the audience, the whole world it seemed. I was aware of eyes burning into my back. I felt the shame of my mother and father as they sat stiffly throughout the rest of the show.

We could have escaped during intermission. Pride and some strange sense of honor must have anchored my parents to their chairs. And so we watched it all: the

Predict
How do you predict the mother will react to her daughter's poor piano playing?

Spiral Review
Plot Do you think the narrator's poor performance will inspire a change in her actions and attitude as the story progresses? Why or why not?

eighteen-year-old boy with a fake mustache who did a magic show and juggled flaming hoops while riding a unicycle. The breasted girl with white makeup who sang from *Madama Butterfly* and got honorable mention. And the eleven-year-old boy who won first prize playing a tricky violin song that sounded like a busy bee.

After the show, the Hsus, the Jongs, and the St. Clairs from the Joy Luck Club came up to my mother and father.

"Lots of talented kids," Auntie Lindo said vaguely, smiling broadly.

"That was somethin' else," said my father, and I wondered if he was referring to me in a humorous way, or whether he even remembered what I had done.

Waverly looked at me and shrugged her shoulders. "You aren't a genius like me," she said matter-of-factly. And if I hadn't felt so bad, I would have pulled her braids and punched her stomach.

> *I felt the shame of my mother and father as they sat stiffly throughout the rest of the show.*

✓ **Reading Check**
What happens at the talent show?

◄ **Critical Viewing**
How do you think the narrator felt watching the other children perform? **[Connect]**

Vocabulary
devastated (dev´ ə
stāt´ əd) *v.* destroyed;
completely upset
nonchalantly (nän´
shə länt´ lē) *adv.* seemingly uninterested

Predict
What do you predict
the mother will say to
her daughter now that
the piano recital is over?

But my mother's expression was what devastated me: a quiet, blank look that said she had lost everything. I felt the same way, and it seemed as if everybody were now coming up, like gawkers at the scene of an accident, to see what parts were actually missing. When we got on the bus to go home, my father was humming the busy-bee tune and my mother was silent. I kept thinking she wanted to wait until we got home before shouting at me. But when my father unlocked the door to our apartment, my mother walked in and then went to the back, into the bedroom. No accusations. No blame. And in a way, I felt disappointed. I had been waiting for her to start shouting, so I could shout back and cry and blame her for all my misery. ●

老師

I assumed my talent-show fiasco meant I never had to play the piano again. But two days later, after school, my mother came out of the kitchen and saw me watching TV.

"Four clock," she reminded me as if it were any other day. I was stunned, as though she were asking me to go through the talent-show torture again. I wedged myself more tightly in front of the TV.

"Turn off TV," she called from the kitchen five minutes later.

I didn't budge. And then I decided. I didn't have to do what my mother said anymore. I wasn't her slave. This wasn't China. I had listened to her before and look what happened. She was the stupid one.

She came out from the kitchen and stood in the arched entryway of the living room. "Four clock," she said once again, louder.

"I'm not going to play anymore," I said nonchalantly. "Why should I? I'm not a genius."

She walked over and stood in front of the TV. I saw her chest was heaving up and down in an angry way.

"No!" I said, and I now felt stronger, as if my true self had finally emerged. So this was what had been inside me all along.

"No! I won't!" I screamed.

She yanked me by the arm, pulled me off the floor, snapped off the TV. She was frighteningly strong, half pulling, half carrying me toward the piano as I kicked the throw rugs under my feet. She lifted me up and onto the hard bench. I was sobbing by now, looking at her bitterly. Her chest was heaving even more and her mouth was open, smiling crazily as if she were pleased I was crying.

"You want me to be someone that I'm not!" I sobbed. "I'll never be the kind of daughter you want me to be!"

"Only two kinds of daughters," she shouted in Chinese. "Those who are obedient and those who follow their own mind! Only one kind of daughter can live in this house. Obedient daughter!"

"Then I wish I wasn't your daughter. I wish you weren't my mother," I shouted. As I said these things I got scared. It felt like worms and toads and slimy things crawling out of my chest, but it also felt good, as if this awful side of me had surfaced, at last.

"Too late change this," said my mother shrilly.

And I could sense her anger rising to its breaking point. I wanted to see it spill over. And that's when I remembered the babies she had lost in China, the ones we never talked about. "Then I wish I'd never been born!" I shouted. "I wish I were dead! Like them."

It was as if I had said the magic words. Alakazam!—and her face went blank, her mouth closed, her arms went slack, and she backed out of the room, stunned, as if she were blowing away like a small brown leaf, thin, brittle, lifeless.

It was not the only disappointment my mother felt in me. In the years that followed, I failed her so many times,

> *"You want me to be someone that I'm not!" I sobbed. "I'll never be the kind of daughter you want me to be!"*

Reading Check

How does the narrator feel about her performance at the talent show?

each time asserting my own will, my right to fall short of
expectations. I didn't get straight A's. I didn't become class
president. I didn't get into Stanford. I dropped out of college.

For unlike my mother, I did not believe I could be
anything I wanted to be. I could only be me.

And for all those years, we never talked about the disaster
at the recital or my terrible accusations afterward at the
piano bench. All that remained unchecked, like a betrayal
that was now unspeakable. So I never
found a way to ask her why she had hoped
for something so large that failure was
inevitable.

> *For unlike my mother,
> I did not believe I could
> be anything I wanted to
> be. I could only be me.*

And even worse, I never asked her what
frightened me the most: Why had she given
up hope?

For after our struggle at the piano, she
never mentioned my playing again. The
lessons stopped. The lid to the piano was
closed, shutting out the dust, my misery,
and her dreams.

So she surprised me. A few years ago,
she offered to give me the piano, for my thirtieth birthday. I
had not played in all those years. I saw the offer as a sign of
forgiveness, a tremendous burden removed.

Predict
How do you predict the
narrator will respond to
the gift of the piano?

"Are you sure?" I asked shyly. "I mean, won't you and Dad
miss it?"

"No, this your piano," she said firmly. "Always your piano.
You only one can play."

"Well, I probably can't play anymore," I said. "It's been
years."

"You pick up fast," said my mother, as if she knew this
was certain. "You have natural talent. You could been
genius if you want to."

"No I couldn't."

"You just not trying," said my mother. And she was
neither angry nor sad. She said it as if to announce a fact
that could never be disproved. "Take it," she said.

But I didn't at first. It was enough that she had offered
it to me. And after that, every time I saw it in my parents'

living room, standing in front of the bay windows, it made me feel proud, as if it were a shiny trophy I had won back. •

Last week I sent a tuner over to my parents' apartment and had the piano reconditioned, for purely sentimental reasons. My mother had died a few months before and I had been getting things in order for my father, a little bit at a time. I put the jewelry in special silk pouches. The sweaters she had knitted in yellow, pink, bright orange—all the colors I hated—I put those in moth-proof boxes. I found some old Chinese silk dresses, the kind with little slits up the sides. I rubbed the old silk against my skin, then wrapped them in tissue and decided to take them home with me.

After I had the piano tuned, I opened the lid and touched the keys. It sounded even richer than I remembered. Really, it was a very good piano. Inside the bench were the same exercise notes with handwritten scales, the same secondhand music books with their covers held together with yellow tape.

I opened up the Schumann book to the dark little piece I had played at the recital. It was on the left-hand side of

Vocabulary
sentimental (sen´ tə ment´ əl) *adj.* emotional; showing tender feeling

Predict
What do you think the narrator will do now that the piano has been tuned after so many years?

☑ Reading Check
What gift does the narrator receive for her 30th birthday? Why?

the page, "Pleading Child." It looked more difficult than I remembered. I played a few bars, surprised at how easily the notes came back to me.

And for the first time, or so it seemed, I noticed the piece on the right-hand side. It was called "Perfectly Contented." I tried to play this one as well. It had a lighter melody but the same flowing rhythm and turned out to be quite easy. "Pleading Child" was shorter but slower; "Perfectly Contented" was longer, but faster. And after I played them both a few times, I realized they were two halves of the same song.

老師

Critical Thinking

Cite textual evidence to support your responses.

© 1. **Key Ideas and Details** **(a)** In what ways does the mother pressure her daughter for change? **(b) Draw Conclusions:** How does the difference in their attitudes create problems? Support your answer with details from the text.

© 2. **Key Ideas and Details** **(a)** What are the titles of the two pieces in the Schumann book that the daughter plays at the end of the story? **(b) Connect:** In what ways do the titles and pieces reflect the daughter's feelings about herself?

© 3. **Integration of Knowledge and Ideas** **(a) Evaluate:** Do you agree that people can be anything they want to be? Why or why not? **(b) Make a Judgment:** Should the narrator's mother have pushed the daughter as she did? Explain.

© 4. **Craft and Structure** How might the story be different if it were told from the mother's point of view?

© 5. **Integration of Knowledge and Ideas** In this story, conflict results when a mother pushes her daughter to become a success. Is there a winner in this conflict? Explain. *[Connect to the Big Question: Does every conflict have a winner?]*

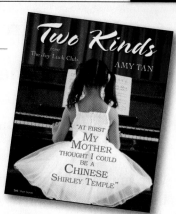

Reading Skills: Make Predictions

1. (a) What **predictions** did you make about how well the narrator would play at the recital? **(b)** Did reading ahead cause you to change your prediction?

2. (a) At what point in the story were you able to **predict** that the daughter would eventually refuse to play the piano? **(b)** Did your prediction change as you read? Explain.

Literary Analysis: Character

3. Key Ideas and Details Using a diagram like this one, list the daughter's **character traits,** supporting your answers with story details.

The Daughter

4. Key Ideas and Details What **motives** does this daughter have to rebel against her mother finally?

Vocabulary

Acquisition and Use Make up an answer to each question. Use a complete sentence that includes the italicized vocabulary word.

1. Who *conspired* to make the party a surprise?

2. Why did the *reproach* bother him?

3. What kind of weather *devastated* the crops?

4. What instruments does the musical *prodigy* play?

5. How did the audience respond to the singer's *debut?*

6. How did the *obedient* child behave at the lecture?

Word Study Use the context of the sentences and what you know about the **Latin root -spir-** to explain each answer.

1. Is a *spirited* person lively or dull?

2. If something *inspires* you, does it make you feel excitement?

Word Study

The **Latin root -*spir*-** means "breath."

Apply It Explain how the root **-*spir*-** contributes to the meanings of these words. Consult a dictionary if necessary.

perspire
transpire
respiration

Integrated Language Skills

from **Letters from Rifka • Two Kinds**

Conventions: The Principal Parts of Verbs

A verb has four **principal parts**: *present, present participle, past,* and *past participle.*

Verb tenses indicate when something occurred. Tenses are formed using the principal parts of verbs. In the chart below, you will find the four principal parts of the verb *talk*. Notice that when you use both the present and past participle, you also include helping verbs. Common helping verbs include *has, have, had, am, is, are, was,* and *were.* A verb and its helping verb is called a "verb phrase."

	Present	Present Participle	Past	Past Participle
Regular	Today I **talk**.	I am **talking** now.	Yesterday we **talked**.	We have **talked** often.
Irregular	He **sits** down.	He is **sitting** down.	Yesterday he **sat** down.	He has often **sat** there.

Practice A Locate the verb or verb phrase in the following sentences and indicate which of the four main tenses they are.
1. The Army searched for Nathan.
2. The family had boarded the train quickly and quietly.
3. Rifka writes a letter to Tovah describing her escape.
4. Rifka was hiding from the guards.

Ⓒ **Reading Application** In "Letters from Rifka," locate at least three of the principal parts of verbs.

Practice B Rewrite each sentence, using a different principal part. Explain how your choice changes the meaning of the sentence.
1. The narrator's mother had hoped her daughter would become a prodigy.
2. The mother bought her daughter, Jing-mei, a piano for her lessons.
3. Jing-mei is performing in the recital.
4. She had trouble pleasing her mother.

Ⓒ **Writing Application** Choose a photograph featured in "Two Kinds" and write four sentences about it. Use at least two of the four principal parts of verbs.

PH | WRITING COACH | Further instruction and practice are available in *Prentice Hall Writing Coach.*

Writing

Narrative Text Write a **journal entry** as a character from either *Letters from Rifka* or "Two Kinds."

- Choose a character and a specific situation from your story.
- Write from the character's point of view, using the word *I*.
- Describe the situation by presenting a clear sequence of events.
- Use dialogue and descriptive details to relay the character's thoughts and feelings.

Grammar Application Check your writing to be sure you have used verb tenses correctly.

Writing Workshop: *Work in Progress*

Prewriting for Response to Literature Review the Story List in your portfolio. For each story you describe, create a two-column chart with the labels "What I Liked" and "What I Disliked." Then, note specific scenes, characters, images, or actions that fit in each column. Keep this Response Chart in your portfolio.

Research and Technology

Build and Present Knowledge Write an **outline** that provides background.

- If you read *Letters from Rifka*, find out more about the unfair treatment of Jews in twentieth-century Russia.
- If you read "Two Kinds," research traditional Chinese beliefs and customs about the relationship between parents and children.

Follow these steps to complete the assignment:

- Generate a list of questions on your topic to guide your research.
- Consult a variety of library or Internet resources to answer your questions.
- Organize your thoughts by jotting down notes.
- In outline form, state briefly and in your own words the main points and key details of what you learned.
- Group your notes by category. Use Roman numerals (I, II, III) to number your most important points. Under each Roman numeral, use capital letters for each supporting detail.
  TIP: Look at the Outline Format model on page 1042.
- Share your findings with other students.

Common Core State Standards

L.7.1, L.7.4.b, L.7.6; W.7.3.a, W.7.3.b, W.7.7
[For the full wording of the standards, see page 248.]

Use this prewriting activity to prepare for the **Writing Workshop** on page 302.

PHLit Online!
www.PHLitOnline.com
- Interactive graphic organizers
- Grammar tutorial
- Interactive journals

Test Practice: Reading

Make Predictions

Fiction Selection

Directions: *Read the selection. Then, answer the questions.*

Outdoors, Jenna and her little brother Tim noticed dark clouds building on the horizon. They decided to go indoors. Jenna had taken a weather safety course, and she knew that there was danger from lightning, even if a storm seemed far away.

Earlier, Mom had called to say she would be a little late getting home. Tim suggested to Jenna that they get dinner started. The two were cutting up vegetables when a loud crack of thunder shook the house. Startled, Jenna went to see the news on television. Just then, there was a flash of lightning and the house lost power. Jenna grabbed Tim by the hand and led him to a hall in the center of the house. Then, the lights came on, and Jenna heard the sound of a car pulling into the driveway.

1. What information in the first paragraph helps you predict that a storm is brewing?
   A. Jenna and Tim are playing soccer.
   B. There are dark clouds on the horizon.
   C. Jenna and Tim go indoors.
   D. Jenna had taken a weather safety course.

2. What detail helps you predict that Jenna will know what to do when the lights go out?
   A. She is Tim's older sister.
   B. She has taken a weather safety course.
   C. She wants to check the news.
   D. She sees dark clouds on the horizon.

3. Which prediction might you make when you learn that the lights have come on?
   A. The storm will become stronger.
   B. The storm will continue.
   C. The storm will soon end.
   D. Lightning will strike their house.

4. Based on details in the story, who do you predict is in the car?
   A. Jenna and Tim's mother is in the car.
   B. A neighbor is in the car.
   C. The town soccer coach is in the car.
   D. A television reporter is in the car.

Writing for Assessment

Based on your prior knowledge and details in the story, write two or three sentences predicting what Jenna will say when her mother gets home. Use details from the story to support your answer.

Nonfiction Selection

Directions: *Read the selection. Then, answer the questions.*

Several severe thunderstorms raced through Connecticut last Wednesday, producing damaging winds and cloud-to-ground lightning. Winds reached as high as 60 miles per hour in some areas, knocking down trees and power lines.

One Connecticut man saw a tree crash through the roof of his home. Another family escaped unharmed through their back door after a power surge caused a fire to erupt in their basement. Approximately 61,000 homes lost power.

As soon as weather conditions allowed, utility crews began removing downed trees and restoring electricity. By the next day, the utility company had restored power to more than half of the homes.

1. What detail in the first paragraph helps you predict that people lost electricity during the storm?
   A. There were several different storms.
   B. The storm took place in the summer.
   C. There was cloud-to-ground lightning.
   D. Winds knocked down power lines.

2. Based on details in the passage, what might you predict would happen two days after the storm?
   A. Another severe storm would sweep through the state.
   B. Power would have been restored for most residents.
   C. Most power lines would remain down.
   D. Many families would order pizza.

3. What do you predict happened after the tree crashed through the man's home?
   A. Rain poured in through the roof.
   B. The wind stopped.
   C. Lightning caused a power outage.
   D. Trees fell on all the neighbors' homes.

4. Based on details in the passage, what do you predict will happen as a result of the storm?
   A. Many branches will need to be cleaned up.
   B. People will move to a safer area.
   C. People will be without power for weeks.
   D. Many houses will be repainted.

Writing for Assessment

Connecting Across Texts
If Jenna and Tim experienced a storm like the one in Connecticut, how might that change your prediction about what Jenna would say when her mother got home? Write a brief response, using details from the two passages to support your answer.

PHLit
Online!
www.PHLitOnline.com
- Online practice
- Instant feedback

Reading for Information

Analyzing Expository and Functional Texts

Magazine Article

Encyclopedia Entry

**Common Core
State Standards**

Reading Informational Text
5. Analyze the structure an author uses to organize a text, including how the major sections contribute to the whole and to the development of the ideas.

9. Analyze how two or more authors writing about the same topic shape their presentations of key information by emphasizing different evidence or advancing different interpretations of facts.

Language
6. Acquire and use accurately grade-appropriate general academic and domain-specific words and phrases; gather vocabulary knowledge when considering a word or phrase important to comprehension or expression.

Reading Skill:
Understand Text Structure and Purpose

Your **purpose,** or reason, for reading affects the way you approach informational texts. When you read to learn about a specific topic, you may consult a variety of texts. Although they share a common topic, each text may present different facts on the topic, or the texts may present evidence in different ways.

   Understanding the text structure will help you decide if a specific text suits your purpose for reading. Text structure includes the special features of each type of writing, as shown in the chart below.

Text Features	Description
Title	The name of the article, which often gives clues about the topic
Subheadings	Boldface words that identify the main idea of each section
Photographs, illustrations, captions	Images and their labels that give additional information about the topic
Charts, graphs, diagrams	Information that is presented visually
Maps, legends	Art that shows geographic information

Content-Area Vocabulary

These words appear in the selections that follow. You may also encounter them in other content-area texts.

- **predators** (pred´ ə tərz) *n.* people or animals that exist by eating other animals
- **burrows** (bʉr´ōz) *n.* tunnels or holes dug into the ground by animals, for shelter

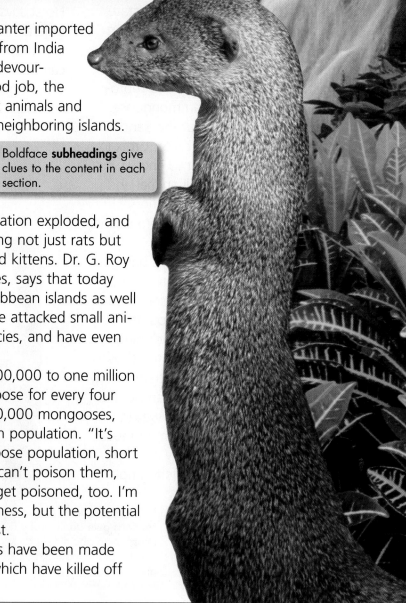

Mongoose on the Loose

Larry Luxner

Magazine Article

Features:

- text meant for leisure reading
- products published at regular intervals
- text published along with photos, ads, and articles by different writers

The **title** and **photo** help you predict what the article will be about.

The **introduction** to the magazine article sets up the topic.

In 1872 a Jamaican sugar planter imported nine furry little mongooses from India to eat the rats which were devouring his crops. They did such a good job, the planter started breeding his exotic animals and selling them to eager farmers on neighboring islands.

Population Explodes

Boldface **subheadings** give clues to the content in each section.

With no natural **predators**—like wolves, coyotes, or poisonous snakes—the mongoose population exploded, and within a few years, they were killing not just rats but pigs, lambs, chickens, puppies, and kittens. Dr. G. Roy Horst, a U.S. expert on mongooses, says that today mongooses live on seventeen Caribbean islands as well as Hawaii and Fiji, where they have attacked small animals, threatened endangered species, and have even spread minor rabies epidemics.

In Puerto Rico there are from 800,000 to one million of them. That is about one mongoose for every four humans. In St. Croix, there are 100,000 mongooses, about twice as many as the human population. "It's impossible to eliminate the mongoose population, short of nuclear war," says Horst. "You can't poison them, because cats, dogs, and chickens get poisoned, too. I'm not a prophet crying in the wilderness, but the potential for real trouble is there," says Horst.

According to Horst, great efforts have been made to rid the islands of mongooses, which have killed off a number of species including the Amevia lizard on St. Croix, presumed extinct for several decades. On Hawaii, the combination of mongooses and sports hunting has reduced the Hawaiian goose, or nene, to less than two dozen individuals.

> A **conclusion** gives a final summary and brings closure to the text.

Scientist Studies Problem

The fifty-nine-year-old biology professor, who teaches at Potsdam College in upstate New York, recently finished his third season at the 500-acre Cabo Rojo National Wildlife Refuge in southwestern Puerto Rico, using microchips to study the life cycle and reproductive habits of the Caribbean mongoose. (He is also doing similar work at the Sandy Point Fish and Wildlife Refuge on St. Croix in the U.S. Virgin Islands.) "I want to know what happens when you take a small animal and put him in an area with no competition. This is a model that doesn't exist anywhere else in the world."

Horst's five-year, $60,000 study is being sponsored by Earthwatch Incorporated, a non-profit group that has funded some 1,300 research projects in eighty-seven countries. Volunteers pay $1,500 each (not including airfare) to come to Puerto Rico for ten days and help Horst set out mongoose traps, study the animals, and keep records. Often he and his volunteers spend a sweaty day walking about ten miles while setting out mongoose traps in the wilderness. Later, they perform surgery on their unwilling subjects to implant the electronic devices that will allow them to track the animal's habits.

Horst has tagged more than 400 mongooses with PITs (permanently implanted transponders), a new microchip technology, which he says has changed his work dramatically. "You couldn't do this with ear tags. It was very hard to permanently mark these animals until this technology came along," he said.

Horst has caught thousands of mongooses and has reached some interesting conclusions. Among them: mongooses have a life expectancy of six to ten years, much longer than the previously accepted figure of three years. Horst says his research will provide local and federal health officials with extremely valuable information if they ever decide to launch a campaign against rabies in Puerto Rico or the U.S. Virgin Islands.

> **Photographs and captions** give additional information about the content of the magazine article.

A mongoose gets tagged.

Indian Grey Mongoose

from WildInfo

Encyclopedia Entry

Features:

- text meant for reference
- information published in print, on CD-ROM, or online
- articles usually organized alphabetically by topic

The **title** tells you what the encyclopedia entry is about.

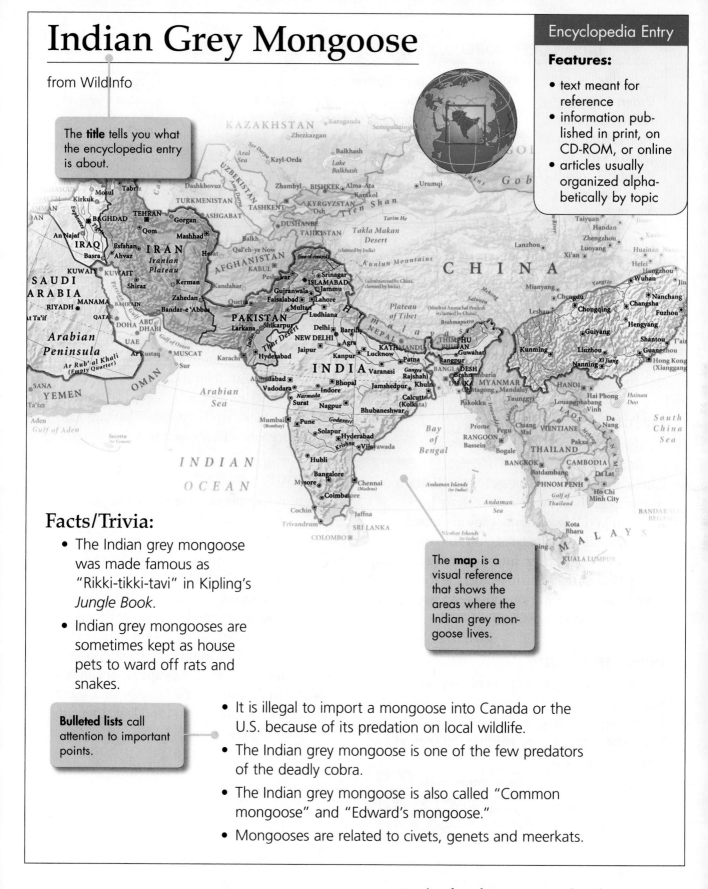

The **map** is a visual reference that shows the areas where the Indian grey mongoose lives.

Facts/Trivia:

- The Indian grey mongoose was made famous as "Rikki-tikki-tavi" in Kipling's *Jungle Book*.

- Indian grey mongooses are sometimes kept as house pets to ward off rats and snakes.

Bulleted lists call attention to important points.

- It is illegal to import a mongoose into Canada or the U.S. because of its predation on local wildlife.

- The Indian grey mongoose is one of the few predators of the deadly cobra.

- The Indian grey mongoose is also called "Common mongoose" and "Edward's mongoose."

- Mongooses are related to civets, genets and meerkats.

INDIAN GREY MONGOOSE (*HERPESTES EDWARDSI*)	
Class: Mammalia **Order:** Carnivora **Family:** Herpestidae **Size:** Length: 9 to 26 inches (23 to 65 cm) **Weight:** 3 pounds (1.4 kg) **Diet:** Rats, insects, lizards, eggs and snakes	**Distribution:** Asia **Young:** 2 to 4, up to 3 times a year **Animal Predators:** None (cobras kill young mongooses) **Terms:** No special terms **Lifespan:** 7 to 12 years in the wild and 20 or more years in captivity

Charts visually call out important information for quick reference.

Description

Indian grey mongooses resemble weasels, with grey-brown fur; a long, slender body; a pointed face and a long, bushy tail. Their fur is dense, providing protection from cobras' fangs. Indian grey mongooses have amazing stamina, and are able to overpower cobras.

Habitat

Indian grey mongooses are found in India, Sri Lanka and Nepal as well as Middle Eastern countries such as Saudi Arabia, Iraq, Iran, Pakistan and Kazakhstan. They are also found on the island of Madagascar, off the coast of Africa. They have been introduced to Italy, the Malay Peninsula, Mauritius and the Ryukyu Islands. Indian grey mongooses can usually be found in wooded areas.

Paragraphs help break up the article into smaller sections of information.

Feeding Habits

Indian grey mongooses tend to prey on small mammals such as rats, but will also eat insects, lizards, eggs, fruit and the occasional snake. They search for prey by sniffing the ground and turning over rocks and stones.

Encyclopedia entries present factual information about many aspects of the mongoose.

Reproduction

Females undergo a two-month pregnancy before giving birth to two to four young. The young are born with some hair but are unable to see for the first few days. Young mongooses are early developers and after several weeks begin hunting with their mother. Once they become skillful hunters, they leave their mother to establish their own territories. They are able to reproduce when they reach two years of age.

Behavior

Indian grey mongooses live alone, but pair up during mating season. They sleep in **burrows** at night and come out during the day to hunt and bask in the sun. They are active, quick hunters. Because of their ability to capture and kill cobras, it was once believed that mongooses were immune to venom, but actually they are so quick when attacking a snake that they manage not to get bitten. Indian grey mongooses are extremely agile animals, capable of climbing walls and trees, running backwards for a short distance, and by using their hind legs, they are able to leap high in the air.

Comparing Expository and Functional Texts

 1. Key Ideas and Details **(a)** What are two differences between the **structure** of a magazine article and the structure of an encyclopedia entry? **(b)** What type of information did you find in the encyclopedia article that was not in the magazine article?

Content-Area Vocabulary

2. (a) Add the suffix *-y* to the base word *predator*. Explain how the suffix alters the meaning of the base word. **(b)** Use two of these words in a sentence that shows you understand the meaning of each word: *predator, predatory, burrows.*

Timed Writing

Informative Text: Description

> **Format**
> The prompt gives specific directions about what to focus on in your description. Narrow your descriptive details to these two items.

> Describe a mongoose. Include specific details from the magazine article and encyclopedia entry that describe its appearance and behavior. Include vivid words and phrases that create strong images for readers.
> (20 minutes)

> **Academic Vocabulary**
> When you *describe* something, you give information and details about it.

5-Minute Planner

Complete these steps before you begin to write:

1. Read the prompt carefully, noting key highlighted words.

2. To prepare your response, fold a piece of paper in half lengthwise, making two columns. Write "Appearance" on one side and "Behavior" on the other.

3. Review the different information about mongooses in the magazine article and the encyclopedia entry. In each column, jot down facts, quotations, or other relevant information from the texts.

4. For each fact you record, write a descriptive word or phrase that will make your writing more vivid.

5. Use your notes to write your description.

Comparing Idioms

Figurative language is writing or speech that is not meant to be understood literally. An **idiom** is one type of figurative language. It is an expression with a meaning that is different from the meanings of the actual words. For example, if your friend asks if you "need a hand," he is not asking if you need an actual hand. Instead, he wants to know if you need help. The meaning of an idiom comes from common use of the expression, which is often unique to a language, region, or community. We are so used to hearing idioms that we forget that they do not make sense if we take them literally.

Writers use idioms to make their writing more interesting and colorful, and to reflect the ways that people actually talk. Both "Seventh Grade" and "Melting Pot" contain idioms. Use a chart like the one shown to record the idioms you find in each story. Then, explain how the use of idioms enables the writers to achieve specific effects.

Common Core State Standards

Reading Literature
4. Determine the meaning of words and phrases as they are used in at text, including figurative and connotative meanings.

Writing
2.a. Introduce a topic clearly, previewing what is to follow; organize ideas, concepts, and information, using strategies such as definition, classification, comparison/contrast, and cause/effect. *(Timed Writing)*
2.f. Provide a concluding statement or section that follows from and supports the information or explanation presented.

Story	Idiom	Literal Meaning	Actual Meaning
"Seventh Grade"			
"Melting Pot"			

www.PHLitOnline.com

- Vocabulary flashcards
- Interactive journals
- More about the authors
- Selection audio
- Interactive graphic organizers

Does every *conflict* have a winner?

Writing About the Big Question

In both of these selections, characters face a conflict when they try to figure out how to fit in with people that seem different from them. Use this sentence starter to develop your ideas about the Big Question.

Sometimes it is a **struggle** to fit in because _____.

Meet the Authors

Gary Soto (b. 1952)
Author of "Seventh Grade"

Like the characters in many of his works, Gary Soto grew up in Fresno and once harvested crops in the fields of California.

A Sense of Belonging Soto began writing while in college. In the fiction and poetry he has written since, he reaches back to the sense of belonging he felt in Fresno. He often writes for young adults, who he knows are also searching for their own community and their own place. When he is not writing, Soto enjoys basketball, karate, and Aztec dance.

Anna Quindlen (b. 1953)

Author of "Melting Pot"

Anna Quindlen spent five years reporting for *The New York Times*, covering issues relating to her family and her neighborhood. "Melting Pot" originally appeared in "Life in the 30's," a popular column that Quindlen wrote for the *Times* from 1986 to 1988.

Building on Success In 1992 Quindlen's regular columns earned her a Pulitzer Prize. Later, she left the newspaper to write novels. She has published several bestsellers, including *One True Thing, Black and Blue,* and *Blessings.*

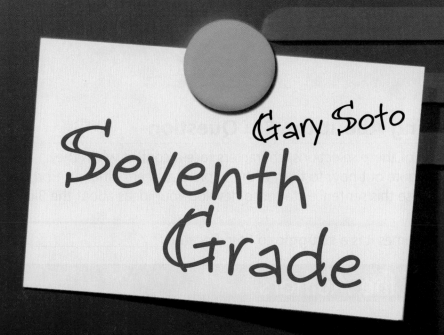

Seventh Grade

Gary Soto

Vocabulary
elective (ē lek´ tiv)
n. optional course

On the first day of school, Victor stood in line half an hour before he came to a wobbly card table. He was handed a packet of papers and a computer card on which he listed his one **elective**, French. He already spoke Spanish and English, but he thought some day he might travel to France, where it was cool; not like Fresno, where summer days reached 110 degrees in the shade. There were rivers in France and huge churches, and fair-skinned people everywhere, the way there were brown people all around Victor.

Besides, Teresa, a girl he had liked since they were in catechism classes at Saint Theresa's, was taking French, too. With any luck they would be in the same class. Teresa is going to be my girl this year, he promised himself as he left the gym full of students in their new fall clothes. She was cute. And good in math, too, Victor thought as he walked down the hall to his homeroom. He ran into his friend, Michael Torres, by the water fountain that never turned off.

They shook hands, *raza*-style, and jerked their heads at one another in a *saludo de vato.*[1] "How come you're making a face?" asked Victor.

"I ain't making a face, *ese.*[2] This is my face." Michael said his face had changed during the summer. He had read a *GQ*

---

1. **raza-style . . . saludo de vato** (sä lōō´ dō dā bä´ tō) Spanish gestures of greeting between friends.
2. **ese** (es´ ā) *n.* Spanish word for "man."

magazine that his older brother had borrowed from the Book Mobile and noticed that the male models all had the same look on their faces. They would stand, one arm around a beautiful woman, and scowl. They would sit at a pool, their rippled stomachs dark with shadow, and *scowl.* They would sit at dinner tables, cool drinks in their hands, and *scowl.*

"I think it works," Michael said. He scowled and let his upper lip quiver. His teeth showed along with the ferocity of his soul. "Belinda Reyes walked by a while ago and looked at me," he said.

Victor didn't say anything, though he thought his friend looked pretty strange. They talked about recent movies, baseball, their parents, and the horrors of picking grapes in order to buy their fall clothes. Picking grapes was like living in Siberia,[3] except hot and more boring.

"What classes are you taking?" Michael said, scowling.

"French. How 'bout you?"

"Spanish. I ain't so good at it, even if I'm Mexican."

"I'm not either, but I'm better at it than math, that's for sure."

A tinny, three-beat bell propelled students to their homerooms. The two friends socked each other in the arm and went their ways, Victor thinking, man, that's weird. Michael thinks making a face makes him handsome.

On the way to his homeroom, Victor tried a scowl. He felt foolish, until out of the corner of his eye he saw a girl looking at him. Umm, he thought, maybe it does work. He scowled with greater conviction.

In homeroom, roll was taken, emergency cards were passed out, and they were given a bulletin to take home to their parents. The principal, Mr. Belton, spoke over the crackling loudspeaker, welcoming the students to a new year, new experiences, and new friendships. The students squirmed in their chairs and ignored him. They were anxious to go to first period. Victor sat calmly, thinking of Teresa, who sat two rows away, reading a paperback novel. This would be his lucky year. She was in his homeroom, and would probably be in his English and math classes. And, of course, French.

The bell rang for first period, and the students herded noisily through the door. Only Teresa lingered, talking with the homeroom teacher.

---

3. Siberia (sī bir´ ē ə) *n.* region in northern Asia known for its harsh winters.

Vocabulary

scowl (skoul) *v.* look at someone or something in an angry or disapproving way

Vocabulary

conviction
(kən vik´ shən) *n.* belief

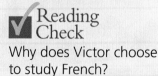

Reading Check

Why does Victor choose to study French?

Idiom
(a) Explain what the teacher means by the phrase "a good bet."
(b) What does it mean when Victor tries to "bump into" Teresa?

▼ **Critical Viewing**
What details suggest that this might be the beginning of a school year? **[Hypothesize]**

"So you think I should talk to Mrs. Gaines?" she asked the teacher. "She would know about ballet?"

"She would be a good bet," the teacher said. Then added, "Or the gym teacher, Mrs. Garza."

Victor lingered, keeping his head down and staring at his desk. He wanted to leave when she did so he could bump into her and say something clever.

He watched her on the sly. As she turned to leave, he stood up and hurried to the door, where he managed to catch her eye. She smiled and said, "Hi, Victor."

He smiled back and said, "Yeah, that's me." His brown face blushed. Why hadn't he said, "Hi, Teresa," or "How was your summer?" or something nice?

As Teresa walked down the hall, Victor walked the other way, looking back, admiring how gracefully she walked, one foot in front of the other. So much for being in the same class, he thought. As he trudged to English, he practiced scowling.

In English they reviewed the parts of speech. Mr. Lucas, a portly man, waddled down the aisle, asking, "What is a noun?"

"A person, place, or thing," said the class in unison.

"Yes, now somebody give me an example of a person—you, Victor Rodriguez."

"Teresa," Victor said automatically. Some of the girls giggled. They knew he had a crush on Teresa. He felt himself blushing again.

"Correct," Mr. Lucas said. "Now provide me with a place."

Mr. Lucas called on a freckled kid who answered, "Teresa's house with a kitchen full of big brothers."

After English, Victor had math, his weakest subject. He sat in the back by the window, hoping that he would not be called on. Victor understood most of the problems, but some of the stuff looked like the teacher made it up as she went along. It was confusing, like the inside of a watch.

After math he had a fifteen-minute break, then social studies, and, finally, lunch. He bought a tuna casserole with buttered rolls, some fruit cocktail, and milk. He sat with Michael, who practiced scowling between bites.

Girls walked by and looked at him.

"See what I mean, Vic?" Michael scowled. "They love it."

"Yeah, I guess so."

They ate slowly, Victor scanning the horizon for a glimpse of Teresa. He didn't see her. She must have brought lunch, he thought, and is eating outside. Victor scraped his plate and left Michael, who was busy scowling at a girl two tables away.

The small, triangle-shaped campus bustled with students talking about their new classes. Everyone was in a sunny mood. Victor hurried to the bag lunch area, where he sat down and opened his math book. He moved his lips as if he were reading, but his mind was somewhere else. He raised his eyes slowly and looked around. No Teresa.

He lowered his eyes, pretending to study, then looked slowly to the left. No Teresa. He turned a page in the book and stared at some math problems that scared him because he knew he would have to do them eventually. He looked to the right. Still no sign of her. He stretched out lazily in an attempt to disguise his snooping.

Then he saw her. She was sitting with a girlfriend under a plum tree. Victor moved to a table near her and daydreamed about taking her to a movie. When the bell sounded, Teresa looked up, and their eyes met. She smiled sweetly and gathered her books. Her next class was French, same as Victor's.

They were among the last students to arrive in class, so all the good desks in the back had already been taken. Victor was forced to sit near the front, a few desks away from Teresa, while Mr. Bueller wrote French words on the chalkboard. The bell rang, and Mr. Bueller wiped his hands, turned to the class, and said, "*Bonjour.*"[4]

"*Bonjour,*" braved a few students.

"*Bonjour,*" Victor whispered. He wondered if Teresa heard him. Mr. Bueller said that if the students studied hard, at the end of the year they could go to France and be understood by the populace.

One kid raised his hand and asked, "What's 'populace'?"

"The people, the people of France."

Mr. Bueller asked if anyone knew French. Victor raised his hand, wanting to impress Teresa. The teacher beamed and said, "*Très bien. Parlez-vous français?*"[5]

> He sat in the back by the window, hoping that he would not be called on.

Reading Check

Who or what is Victor thinking of during lunch?

---

4. **Bonjour** (bōn zhōōr´) French for "hello;" "good day."
5. **Très bien. Parlez-vous français?** (trā byan pär lā vōō´ frän sā´) French for "Very well. Do you speak French?"

Victor didn't know what to say. The teacher wet his lips and asked something else in French. The room grew silent. Victor felt all eyes staring at him. He tried to bluff his way out by making noises that sounded French.

"La me vave me con le grandma," he said uncertainly.

Mr. Bueller, wrinkling his face in curiosity, asked him to speak up.

Great rosebushes of red bloomed on Victor's cheeks. A river of nervous sweat ran down his palms. He felt awful. Teresa sat a few desks away, no doubt thinking he was a fool. Without looking at Mr. Bueller, Victor mumbled, "Frenchie oh wewe gee in September."

Mr. Bueller asked Victor to repeat what he had said.

"Frenchie oh wewe gee in September," Victor repeated.

Mr. Bueller understood that the boy didn't know French and turned away. He walked to the blackboard and pointed to the words on the board with his steel-edged ruler.

"*Le bateau*," he sang.

"*Le bateau*," the students repeated.

"*Le bateau est sur l'eau*,"[6] he sang.

"*Le bateau est sur l'eau.*"

Victor was too weak from failure to join the class. He stared at the board and wished he had taken Spanish, not French. Better yet, he wished he could start his life over. He had never been so embarrassed. He bit his thumb until he tore off a sliver of skin.

The bell sounded for fifth period, and Victor shot out of the room, avoiding the stares of the other kids, but had to return for his math book. He looked sheepishly at the teacher, who was erasing the board, then widened his eyes in terror at Teresa who stood in front of him. "I didn't know you knew French," she said. "That was good."

Mr. Bueller looked at Victor, and Victor looked back. Oh please, don't say anything, Victor pleaded with his eyes. I'll wash your car, mow your lawn, walk your dog—anything! I'll be your best student and I'll clean your erasers after school.

---

6. *Le bateau est sur l'eau* (lə bä tō′ ā soor lō) French for "The boat is on the water."

Mr. Bueller shuffled through the papers on his desk. He smiled and hummed as he sat down to work. He remembered his college years when he dated a girlfriend in borrowed cars. She thought he was rich because each time he picked her up he had a different car. It was fun until he had spent all his money on her and had to write home to his parents because he was broke.

Victor couldn't stand to look at Teresa. He was sweaty with shame. "Yeah, well, I picked up a few things from movies and books and stuff like that." They left the class together. Teresa asked him if he would help her with her French.

"Sure, anytime," Victor said.

"I won't be bothering you, will I?"

"Oh no, I like being bothered."

"*Bonjour,*" Teresa said, leaving him outside her next class. She smiled and pushed wisps of hair from her face.

"Yeah, right, *bonjour,*" Victor said. He turned and headed to his class. The rosebushes of shame on his face became bouquets of love. Teresa is a great girl, he thought. And Mr. Bueller is a good guy.

He raced to metal shop. After metal shop there was biology, and after biology a long sprint to the public library, where he checked out three French textbooks.

He was going to like seventh grade.

Idiom
What does the expression "he was broke" mean?

Spiral Review
Setting Does the setting help make this story appealing to readers? Explain.

Critical Thinking

1. **Key Ideas and Details (a)** Why do you think Michael scowls? **(b) Compare and Contrast:** What is similar about Michael's scowling and Victor's pretending to speak French?

2. **Key Ideas and Details (a) Infer:** How does Victor view Teresa? **(b) Support:** What examples from the story indicate his feelings?

3. **Integration of Knowledge and Ideas (a) Analyze:** What does Victor probably learn from his experiences in seventh grade? **(b) Apply:** How can you apply this lesson to your own life?

4. **Integration of Knowledge and Ideas (a)** How does Mr. Bueller help Victor avoid a conflict when he does not correct Victor's French skills? **(b)** How does this action help Victor be accepted by Teresa? *[Connect to the Big Question: Does every conflict have a winner?]*

Cite textual evidence to support your responses.

MELTING POT

Anna Quindlen

My children are upstairs in the house next door, having dinner with the Ecuadorian family that lives on the top floor. The father speaks some English, the mother less than that. The two daughters are fluent in both their native and their adopted languages, but the youngest child, a son, a close friend of my two boys, speaks almost no Spanish. His parents thought it would be better that way. This doesn't surprise me; it was the way my mother was raised, American among Italians. I always suspected, hearing my grandfather talk about the "No Irish Need Apply" signs outside factories, hearing my mother talk about the

neighborhood kids, who called her greaseball, that the American fable of the melting pot was a myth. Here in our neighborhood it exists, but like so many other things, it exists only person-to-person.

The letters in the local weekly tabloid[1] suggest that everybody hates everybody else here, and on a macro level they do. The old-timers are angry because they think the new moneyed professionals are taking over their town. The professionals are tired of being blamed for the neighborhood's rising rents, particularly since they are the ones paying them. The old immigrants are suspicious of the new ones. The new ones think the old ones are bigots. Nevertheless, on a micro level most of us get along. We are friendly with the Ecuadorian family, with the Yugoslavs across the street, and with the Italians next door, mainly by virtue of our children's sidewalk friendships. It took awhile. Eight years ago we were the new people on the block, filling dumpsters with old plaster and lath, . . . (sitting) on the stoop with our demolition masks hanging around our necks like goiters.[2] We thought we could feel people staring at us from behind the sheer curtains on their windows. We were right.

---

1. **tabloid** (tab´ loid´) *n.* small newspaper.
2. **goiters** (goit´ ərz) *n.* swellings in the lower front of the neck caused by an enlarged thyroid gland.

Spiral Review
Setting What type of neighborhood does Quindlen live in? What details helped you answer?

Vocabulary
bigots (big´ əts) *n.* narrow-minded, prejudiced people

Reading Check
What attitude does Quindlen say most people have toward others who are new or different?

My first apartment in New York was in a gritty warehouse district, the kind of place that makes your parents wince. A lot of old Italians lived around me, which suited me just fine because I was the granddaughter of old Italians. Their own children and grandchildren had moved to Long Island and New Jersey. All they had was me. All I had was them.

I remember sitting on a corner with a group of half a dozen elderly men, men who had known one another since they were boys sitting together on this same corner, watching a glazier install a great spread of tiny glass panes to make one wall of a restaurant in the ground floor of an old building across the street. The men laid bets on how long the panes, and the restaurant, would last. Two years later two of the men were dead, one had moved in with his married daughter in the suburbs, and the three remaining sat and watched dolefully as people waited each night for a table in the restaurant. "Twenty-two dollars for a piece of veal!" one of them would say, apropos of nothing.[3] But when I ate in the restaurant they never blamed me. "You're not one of them," one of the men explained. "You're one of me." It's an argument familiar to members of almost any embattled race or class: I like you, therefore you aren't like the rest of your kind, whom I hate.

Change comes hard in America, but it comes constantly. The butcher whose old shop is now an antiques store sits day after day outside the pizzeria here like a lost child. The old people across the street cluster together and discuss what kind of money they might be offered if the person who bought their building

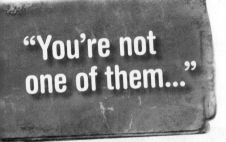

"You're not one of them..."

---

3. **apropos** (ap´ rə pō´) **of nothing** without connection.

wants to turn it into condominiums. The greengrocer stocks yellow peppers and fresh rosemary for the gourmands, plum tomatoes and broad-leaf parsley for the older Italians, mangoes for the Indians. He doesn't carry plantains, he says, because you can buy them in the bodega.[4]

Sometimes the baby slips out with the bath water. I wanted to throw confetti the day that a family of rough types who propped their speakers on their station wagon and played heavy metal music at 3:00 A.M. moved out. I stood and smiled as the seedy bar at the corner was transformed into a slick Mexican restaurant. But I liked some of the people who moved out at the same time the rough types did. And I'm not sure I have that much in common with the singles who have made the restaurant their second home.

Yet somehow now we seem to have reached a nice mix. About a third of the people in the neighborhood think of squid as calamari, about a third think of it as sushi, and about a third think of it as bait. Lots of the single people who have moved in during the last year or two are easygoing and good-tempered about all the kids. The old Italians have become philosophical about the new Hispanics, although they still think more of them should know English. The firebrand community organizer with the storefront on the block, the one who is always talking about people like us as though we stole our houses out of the open purse of a ninety-year-old blind widow, is pleasant to my boys.

---

4. **bodega** (bō dä´ gə) *n.* small, Hispanic grocery store.

Idiom
What do you think the expression "baby slips out with the bath water" really means?

Drawn in broad strokes, we live in a pressure cooker: oil and water, us and them. But if you come around at exactly the right time, you'll find members of all these groups gathered around complaining about the condition of the streets, on which everyone can agree. We melt together, then draw apart. I am the granddaughter of immigrants, a young professional—either an interloper[5] or a longtime resident, depending on your concept of time. I am one of them, and one of us.

---

5. **interloper** (in´ tər lō´ pər) *n.* one who intrudes on another.

We MELT together, then draw apart.

Critical Thinking

Cite textual evidence to support your responses.

1. **Key Ideas and Details (a)** Identify the different groups in Quindlen's neighborhood. **(b) Connect:** What experiences do most of the residents share? **(c) Interpret:** How do these shared experiences both unite and divide the residents?

2. **Key Ideas and Details Draw Conclusions:** What advice would Quindlen give about how people of different cultures can get along?

3. **Integration of Knowledge and Ideas (a) Analyze:** How is Quindlen both "one of them" and "one of us"? **(b) Make a Judgment:** Do you think it is possible to belong to both groups? **(c) Apply:** What does this essay suggest about the way people live in city neighborhoods in the United States?

4. **Integration of Knowledge and Ideas (a)** How were the people in this neighborhood in conflict with one another? **(b)** How did the author find a way to be successful within the different cultural environments? *[Connect to the Big Question: Does every conflict have a winner?]*

Comparing Idioms

© **1. Key Ideas and Details** **(a)** Identify two **idioms** in "Seventh Grade." **(b)** Explain the difference between the literal and intended meaning of each idiom.

© **2. Key Ideas and Details** Identify and explain at least one idiom in "Melting Pot."

© **3. Integration of Knowledge and Ideas** Choose an idiom from each selection. Then, think about how each idiom helps you either understand or enjoy the selection. Record your ideas in a chart like the one below.

	"Seventh Grade"	"Melting Pot"
Idiom		
How it helps my understanding or enjoyment		

⏱ Timed Writing

Explanatory Text: Essay

In an essay, compare and contrast to explain how idioms added to your interest as you read "Seventh Grade" and "Melting Pot." **(25 minutes)**

5-Minute Planner

1. Read the prompt carefully and completely.

2. Choose at least one idiom from each selection to support your response. Discuss both the literal and actual meaning of each idiom.

3. Explain how the writer's use of each idiom adds interest to the description of a character or situation. For example, think about how the idioms help you get to know the narrator in each selection.

4. Reread the prompt, and then draft your essay. Provide a concluding statement in which you make a judgment about which writer uses idioms more effectively.

Writing Workshop

Write an Argument

Response to Literature: Review of a Short Story

Defining the Form In a **response to literature,** the writer develops an argument that addresses one or more aspects of a literary work. You might use elements of a literary response in a letter to an author, or in a book or movie review.

Assignment Choose a short story you feel strongly about and analyze what it means to you. Include these elements:

✔ a strong, *interesting focus* on an aspect of the short story

✔ a logical and consistent *organization*

✔ a *judgment* about the value of the work

✔ sufficient *support* for your ideas and claims

✔ a concluding statement that summarizes your argument

✔ error-free writing, including *correct verb tenses*

To preview the criteria on which your review may be judged, see the rubric on page 307.

 Writing Workshop: *Work in Progress*

Review the work you did on pages 247 and 279.

Prewriting/Planning Strategy

Find connections. After you have decided on a story, read or review the selection carefully to find a topic for your essay. Complete a chart like the one shown. Fill in each column by answering the corresponding question. Look over what you have written and highlight details that connect in ways that interest you. To create a focused topic, sum up the highlighted details in a sentence.

Characters	Settings	Actions	Motivations
Who did the action?	When or where was it done?	What was done?	Why was it done?

Writing
1. Write arguments to support claims with clear reasons and relevant evidence.
1.b. Support claim(s) with logical reasoning and relevant evidence, using credible sources and demonstrating an understanding of the topic or text.
1.c. Use words, phrases, and clauses to clarify the relationship among claim(s) and reasons.
1.d. Establish and maintain a formal style.
9. Draw evidence from literary or informational texts to support analysis, reflection, and research.
Language
5.c. Distinguish among the connotations of words with similar denotations.

Finding the Perfect Word

Word choice is the specific language a writer selects in order to create a strong impression. Critics choose memorable words and phrases to emphasize their arguments and to grab readers' attention. Follow these tips as you write your review.

Developing Tone The tone of your writing reveals your attitude toward your audience or subject. Ask yourself:

- How did the plot of this short story make me feel?
- Did I like the characters or dislike them? Why?
- Would I recommend this story to others?

Write your answers to these questions in complete sentences. Then use your responses as you draft your review, using a formal style that is appropriate for a review.

Choosing Language As you write, use language that helps you develop your arguments and that accurately captures your feelings about an aspect of the story. Include colorful words, phrases, and comparisons. Consider the **connotations** of words, or the feelings and associations they convey, as well as their **denotations,** or meanings. For example, if you liked the climax of a story, you might describe it as *dramatic*. If you did not like it, you might describe it as *exaggerated*. Add examples and quotations to support your descriptions. The chart shows descriptive words that you might use.

> **PH WRITING COACH**
>
> Further instruction and practice are available in *Prentice Hall Writing Coach*.

Plot	Characters	Dialogue	Description
suspenseful predictable confusing	hideous flat intriguing	unrealistic engaging humorous	unique extensive uninteresting

Supporting Claims With Reasons Choose words that support your claims. For example, if you claim that a character is overly dramatic, you might use words that emphasize the character's hysterical reactions to an ordinary event.

Checking Language With a partner, review your word choices for fairness, accuracy, and consistency.

Drafting Strategies

Define and develop your focus. Review your prewriting notes to find a main idea or focus for your response. The focus statement sums up your reaction to one aspect of the story. Answer questions like the ones shown. Then, write one good sentence that states the focus and references a literary element. Include this sentence in your introduction, and elaborate on it in the body of your review.

Common Core State Standards

Writing

1.a. Introduce claim(s) and organize the reasons and evidence clearly.

1.b. Support claim(s) with logical reasoning and relevant evidence, using credible sources and demonstrating an understanding of the topic or text.

1.e. Provide a concluding statement or section that follows from the argument presented.

9. Draw evidence from literary or informational texts to support analysis, reflection, and research.

9.a. Apply grade 7 Reading standards to literature.

1. My Response	**2. What Causes It**	**3. My Focus**
What is my main response to my topic? I thoroughly enjoyed the story.	What features of the story cause my reaction? • the suspense • the believability of the characters	What conclusion can I draw about the story's features? The author creates suspense and believable characters, producing a realistic story.

Use examples to provide support. Rely on examples from the story to help you support your main arguments and claims. Refer to specific scenes, characters, images, and action. Justify your interpretations with direct quotations from the text. However, avoid just retelling the story. It is important to share your responses to the text.

Revising Strategy

Revise to organize around your strongest idea. Review your draft with a partner to find places to support your main point. Follow these steps:

1. Circle your strongest point—your most profound insight or the quotation that pulls your response together. Consider moving this point to the end, just before your concluding statement.

2. If you move your strongest point to the end, revise your last paragraph to add a transition sentence that clearly explains the connection between this point and your other ideas.

3. Go back to other paragraphs to link each paragraph to your concluding point. For example, use connecting language like this: *Another example that shows the story's humor is . . .*

Revising for Correct Verb Tense

A verb indicates an action or a state of being. Verbs have tenses, or different forms, that tell when something happens or exists.

Identifying Verb Tense In standard English, verbs have six tenses: present, past, future, present perfect, past perfect, and future perfect.

Present indicates an action that happens regularly or states a general truth: *I walk my dog Squeegee every morning.*

Past indicates an action that has already happened: *We walked earlier than usual yesterday.*

Future indicates an action that will happen: *We will walk on the beach this summer.*

Present perfect indicates an action that happened sometime in the past or an action that happened in the past and is still happening now: *We have walked here every day for two years.*

Past perfect indicates an action that was completed before another action in the past: *We had walked around the corner when Squeegee started to bark.*

Future perfect indicates an action that will have been completed before another: *We will have walked two hundred miles before I need new shoes.*

> **PH WRITING COACH**
>
> Further instruction and practice are available in *Prentice Hall Writing Coach.*

Fixing Incorrect Verb Tense To fix an incorrect form of a verb, first identify any questionable verbs in your review. Then, verify the correct form using one of the following methods.

1. **Review the basic forms of the six tenses.** First, identify the time—present, past, or future—in which the action occurs. Then, review the examples above to determine which form corresponds with that time. Avoid shifting tenses needlessly.

2. **Rewrite the sentence.** Consider which verb tense will make your idea as precise as possible. Revise using that tense.

Grammar in Your Writing

Choose a paragraph in your draft. Underline the verbs in each sentence of the paragraph. If the tense for any verb is faulty or shifts needlessly, fix it using one of the methods described above.

Language
2.b. Spell correctly.

The Lesson of "Rikki-tikki-tavi"

The short story "Rikki-tikki-tavi" is a well-known short story written by Rudyard Kipling, who also wrote many novels, such as *Kim* and *Captains Courageous*. "Rikki-tikki-tavi" is a story about two natural enemies: a mongoose and a cobra. The message of the story is that although you may be small, you can still overcome major enemies. This story is enjoyable because it can teach you helpful morals while keeping you entertained at the same time.

The beginning of this story is heavyhearted and dramatic. A small boy named Teddy thinks that the mongoose is dead following a bout with its first enemy—a flood that swept him away from his burrow. The mood of the story changes when the boy realizes that the mongoose is still alive, but weak. He decides to keep it, and takes care of it much like a pet, feeding it and naming it Rikki-tikki-tavi.

When Rikki-tikki goes outside into the little boy's garden to explore his surroundings, he comes upon a bird, which he confronts. The story switches back to a gloomy mood when the mongoose discovers that Nag, a cobra, ate one of the bird's eggs. When Rikki-tikki hears this, Nag comes out of the tall grass behind him.

This is when the story gets scary because Rikki faces another enemy. Nag quickly spreads his hood to intimidate the small mongoose. Then, Nagaina, Nag's wife, pulls a surprise attack on Rikki-tikki and nearly eats him. Because Rikki-tikki is young and dodges the cobra's blow from behind, he gains plenty of confidence. Readers wonder whether the mongoose will stay safe.

As the story progresses, Rikki meets Karait, another snake, and this builds excitement and tension. This snake isn't after the mongoose, although he is after the family. When Teddy runs out to pet Rikki-tikki, the snake strikes at the boy, but Rikki-tikki lunges at the snake and paralyzes it by biting it before it can bite Teddy.

Later, after Rikki-tikki discovers that the cobras are going to go after his owners, he is filled with rage and he takes on the challenge. The moment the reader is waiting for arrives. The mongoose and the cobra fight to kill. At one point Rikki-tikki has his teeth in Nag as Nag flings himself about. Readers may think that Rikki-tikki will surely die from the beating that he is taking, but he holds on and, thankfully, Teddy's dad hears the fighting and shoots Nag behind the hood with a shotgun, easily ending the brutal battle, which leaves Nag dead and Rikki-tikki dizzy, but alive.

This story is exciting and thought provoking. It ends, leaving me and other readers to think about its real meaning. Most people can relate to a time when they have faced a challenge in their life but have felt that they were unable to overcome it. However, when they kept trying and put their minds to it, they eventually ended with success, as Rikki-tikki did.

Tyler focuses on the message, or theme, of the story.

Here, Tyler summarizes the most important plot events in the story in the order in which they occur.

Tyler supports his ideas about the story by giving examples of how Rikki-tikki fights several enemies even though he is small.

Tyler explains what message readers can take away from the story.

Editing and Proofreading

Spell tricky syllables correctly. The syllables in some words are barely heard. Because of this, letters are often left out in spelling. Double-check the spellings of words such as *different, average,* and *restaurant* in a dictionary. Notice how each word is broken into syllables. Say the word aloud while you look at it, and exaggerate your pronunciation of the sounds and syllables.

Focus on quotations. A response to a literary work should include a number of quotations from the work. Pay careful attention to the punctuation, indentation, and capitalization of quotations. Use quotation marks to set off short quotations. Longer quotations of four or more lines should be indented, without quotation marks.

Spiral Review

Earlier in the unit, you learned about **verbs** (p. 246) and the **principal parts of verbs** (p. 278). Check your essay to be sure that you have used verbs correctly.

Publishing and Presenting

Consider these ideas to share your writing with a larger audience:

Share your review. Discuss your response with a group of classmates. Invite classmates to respond with their opinions and reactions.

Build a collection. Work with your classmates to assemble a book of responses to literature for your school or local library. Include a rating system and rate each work to which you have responded.

PH WRITING COACH

Further instruction and practice are available in *Prentice Hall Writing Coach.*

Reflecting on Your Writing

Writer's Journal Jot down your answer to this question:

How did writing about the work help you to understand it?

Rubric for Self-Assessment

Find evidence in your writing to address each category. Then, use the rating scale to grade your work.

Criteria	Rating Scale				
	not very				*very*
Focus: How well does your response present a strong, interesting aspect of the work?	1	2	3	4	5
Organization: How logical and consistent is your organization?	1	2	3	4	5
Support/Elaboration: How convincing are your supporting examples?	1	2	3	4	5
Style: How clearly do you express your judgment about the work?	1	2	3	4	5
Conventions: How correct is your grammar, especially your use of verb tense?	1	2	3	4	5
Word Choice: Was the language in your review descriptive enough to create a strong impression?	1	2	3	4	5

© Leveled Texts

Build your skills and improve your comprehension of short stories with texts of increasing complexity.

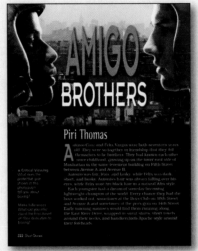

Read "**The Third Wish**" to find out what conflicts arise when a lonely man is granted three wishes.

Read "**Amigo Brothers**" to learn the outcome of a boxing match between two best friends.

© Common Core State Standards

Meet these standards with either **"The Third Wish"** (p. 312) or **"Amigo Brothers"** (p. 322).

Reading Literature

1. Cite several pieces of textual evidence to support analysis of what the text says explicitly as well as inferences drawn from the text. *(Reading Skill: Make Inferences)*

Writing

2.a. Introduce a topic clearly, previewing what is to follow; organize ideas, concepts, and information, using strategies such as definition, classification, comparison/contrast, and cause/effect; include formatting, graphics, and multimedia when useful to aiding comprehension.

2.e. Establish and maintain a formal style. *(Speaking and Listening: News Story)*

3. Write narratives to develop real or imagined experiences or events using effective technique, relevant descriptive details, and well-structured event sequences.

3.e. Provide a conclusion that follows from and reflects on the narrated experiences or events. *(Writing: Anecdote)*

Speaking and Listening

6. Adapt speech to a variety of contexts and tasks, demonstrating command of formal English when indicated or appropriate. *(Speaking and Listening: News Story)*

Language

2.a. Use a comma to separate coordinate adjectives. *(Conventions: Adjectives)*

4.b. Use common, grade-appropriate Greek or Latin affixes and roots as clues to the meaning of a word. *(Vocabulary: Word Study)*

6. Acquire and use accurately grade-appropriate general academic and domain-specific words and phrases; gather vocabulary knowledge when considering a word or phrase important to comprehension or expression. *(Vocabulary: Acquisition and Use)*

Reading Skill: Make Inferences

Authors usually do not directly tell you everything about a story's characters, setting, and events. Instead, readers must **make inferences,** or develop logical ideas about unstated information.

- To form inferences, you must **recognize details** that the author states explicitly, or directly, in the story. Next, connect those details with what you know about life.

- Then, develop an informed idea, or inference, about the story's characters, setting, and events, based on that information.

Using the Strategy: Details Chart

As you read, record details and make inferences using a chart like this one.

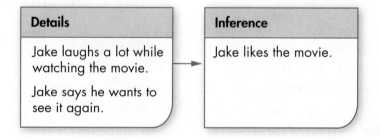

Details	Inference
Jake laughs a lot while watching the movie. Jake says he wants to see it again.	Jake likes the movie.

Literary Analysis: Conflict and Resolution

The plot of most fictional stories centers on a **conflict**—a struggle between opposing forces. There are two kinds of conflict:

- When there is an **external conflict,** a character struggles with an outside force, such as another character or nature.

- When there is an **internal conflict,** a character struggles with himself or herself to overcome opposing feelings, beliefs, needs, or desires.

A story can have a series of small conflicts that contribute to the main conflict. The **resolution,** or outcome, often comes toward the end of the story, when the problem is settled in some way.

Does every *conflict* have a winner?

Writing About the Big Question

In this story, wishes granted do not necessarily bring happiness to everyone involved. Use these sentence starters to develop your ideas about the Big Question:

When we **desire** something for another's happiness, we should consider _____.

Compromise requires that both sides in a conflict _____.

While You Read Look for ways that Mr. Peters and his wife Leita struggle with internal conflicts about their situation.

Vocabulary

Read each word and its definition. Decide whether you know the word well, know it a little bit, or do not know it at all. After you read, see how your knowledge of each word has increased.

- **verge** (vʉrj) *n.* edge; brink (p. 314) *After she lost her favorite bracelet, Sophie was on the verge of tears.* *verged v. verging v.*

- **dabbling** (dab´ ling) *v.* wetting by dipping, splashing, or paddling in the water (p. 314) *The ducks were dabbling their feathers in the pond.* *dabble v.*

- **presumptuous** (prē zump´ chōō əs) *adj.* overconfident; lacking respect (p. 314) *Only a presumptuous person brags a lot.* *presume v. presumptive adj. presumption n.*

- **rash** (rash) *adj.* too hasty (p. 315) *It is rash to marry someone after the first date.* *rashly adv.*

- **remote** (ri mōt´) *adj.* far away from anything else (p. 315) *Living on a remote farm can be lonely.* *remotely, adv. remoter adj. remotest adj.*

- **malicious** (mə lish´ əs) *adj.* hateful; spiteful (p. 317) *Her malicious expression showed she disliked him.* *maliciously adv. malice n.*

Word Study

The **Latin prefix** *mal-* means "bad."

In this story, the old King looks at Mr. Peters with a **malicious**, or hateful, look that shows a desire to cause him harm.

Meet
Joan Aiken
(b. 1924–2004)

Author of
The Third Wish

As a child, Joan Aiken often walked in the fields near her home in England and created stories to amuse herself. She was inspired by her father, stepfather, and mother, who were all writers. She was also inspired by the classic novels her mother read to her when Aiken was young. By five, Aiken was writing her own tales. "Writing is just a family trade," she once said.

An Imaginative Mind Aiken wrote for both children and adults. A typical Aiken tale combines traditional elements of a short story with elements of horror, fantasy, and mystery. "The Third Wish" comes from a collection with a title that sums up much of Aiken's writing—*Not What You Expected.*

BACKGROUND FOR THE STORY

Traditional Tales
Joan Aiken's story is a story about three wishes. Almost every culture in the world has a traditional fairy tale or folk tale about a character who is granted three wishes, uses two unwisely, and then needs the third to undo one or both of the first two wishes.

Did You Know?
Five-year-old Aiken began taking notes and composing on a pad that she bought with her birthday money.

The Third Wish

Joan Aiken

ONCE THERE WAS A MAN WHO WAS DRIVING IN HIS CAR AT DUSK ON A SPRING EVENING THROUGH PART OF THE FOREST OF SAVERNAKE. HIS NAME WAS MR. PETERS. THE PRIMROSES WERE JUST BEGINNING BUT THE TREES WERE STILL BARE, AND IT WAS COLD; THE BIRDS HAD STOPPED SINGING AN HOUR AGO.

As Mr. Peters entered a straight, empty stretch of road he seemed to hear a faint crying, and a struggling and thrashing, as if somebody was in trouble far away in the trees. He left his car and climbed the mossy bank beside the road. Beyond the bank was an open slope of beech trees leading down to thorn bushes through which he saw the gleam of water. He stood a moment waiting to try and discover where the noise was coming from, and presently heard a rustling and some strange cries in a voice which was almost human—and yet there was something too hoarse about it at one time and too clear and sweet at another. Mr. Peters ran down the hill and as he neared the bushes he saw something white among them which was trying to extricate[1] itself; coming closer he found that it was a swan that had become entangled in the thorns growing on the bank of the canal.

The bird struggled all the more frantically as he approached, looking at him with hate in its yellow eyes, and when he took hold of it to free it, it hissed at him, pecked him, and thrashed dangerously with its wings which were powerful enough to break his arm. Nevertheless he managed to release it from the thorns, and carrying it tightly with one arm, holding the snaky head well away with

---

1. **extricate** (eks´ tri kāt´) v. set free.

▶ **Critical Viewing**
What details of this picture could help you predict that this story has elements of fantasy? **[Connect]**

Conflict and Resolution
What external conflict does Mr. Peters face after he finds the swan?

the other hand (for he did not wish his eyes pecked out), he took it to the verge of the canal and dropped it in.

The swan instantly assumed great dignity and sailed out to the middle of the water, where it put itself to rights with much dabbling and preening, smoothing its feathers with little showers of drops. Mr. Peters waited, to make sure that it was all right and had suffered no damage in its struggles. Presently the swan, when it was satisfied with its appearance, floated in to the bank once more, and in a moment, instead of the great white bird, there was a little man all in green with a golden crown and long beard, standing by the water. He had fierce glittering eyes and looked by no means friendly.

"Well, Sir," he said threateningly, "I see you are presumptuous enough to know some of the laws of magic. You think that because you have rescued—by pure good fortune— the King of the Forest from a difficulty, you should have some fabulous reward."

"I expect three wishes, no more and no less," answered Mr. Peters, looking at him steadily and with composure.[2]

"Three wishes, he wants, the clever man! Well, I have yet to hear of the human being who made any good use of his three wishes—they mostly end up worse off than they started. Take your three wishes then"—he flung three dead leaves in the air—"don't blame me if you spend the last wish in undoing the work of the other two."

Mr. Peters caught the leaves and put two of them carefully in his briefcase. When he looked up, the swan was sailing about in the middle of the water again, flicking the drops angrily down its long neck.

Mr. Peters stood for some minutes reflecting on how he should use his reward. He knew very well that the gift of three magic wishes was one which brought trouble more often than not, and he had no intention of being like the forester who first wished by mistake for a sausage, and then in a rage wished it on the end of his wife's nose, and then had to use his last wish in getting it off again. Mr. Peters had most of the things which he wanted and was very content with his life. The only thing that troubled him was that he was a little lonely, and had no companion for his old age. He decided to use his first wish and to keep the other two in case of an emergency. Taking a thorn he pricked his tongue with

---

2. **composure** (kəm pō′ zhər) *n.* calmness of mind.

Vocabulary
verge (vʉrj)
n. edge; brink

dabbling (dab′ ling)
v. wetting by dipping, splashing, or pad-dling in the water

presumptuous
(prē zump′ choo əs)
adj. overconfident; lacking respect

Spiral Review
Plot The King of the Forest grants Mr. Peters three wishes, but not without a warning. How does granting the wishes advance the plot? How does the warning hint at how the plot might develop?

it, to remind himself not to utter rash wishes aloud. Then holding the third leaf and gazing round him at the dusky undergrowth, the primroses, great beeches and the blue-green water of the canal, he said:

"I wish I had a wife as beautiful as the forest."

A tremendous quacking and splashing broke out on the surface of the water. He thought that it was the swan laughing at him. Taking no notice he made his way through the darkening woods to his car, wrapped himself up in the rug and went to sleep.

When he awoke it was morning and the birds were beginning to call. Coming along the track towards him was the most beautiful creature he had ever seen, with eyes as blue-green as the canal, hair as dusky as the bushes, and skin as white as the feathers of swans.

"Are you the wife that I wished for?" asked Mr. Peters.

"Yes, I am," she replied. "My name is Leita."

She stepped into the car beside him and they drove off to the church on the outskirts of the forest, where they were married. Then he took her to his house in a remote and lovely valley and showed her all his treasures—the bees in their white hives, the Jersey cows, the hyacinths, the silver candlesticks, the blue cups and the luster bowl for putting primroses in. She admired everything, but what pleased her most was the river which ran by the foot of his garden.

"Do swans come up there?" she asked.

"Yes, I have often seen swans there on the river," he told her, and she smiled.

Leita made him a good wife. But as time went by Mr. Peters began to feel that she was not happy. She seemed restless, wandered much in the garden, and sometimes when he came back from the fields he would find the house empty and she would return after half an hour or so with no explanation of where she had been. On these occasions she was always especially tender and would put out his slippers to warm and cook his favorite dish—Welsh rarebit[3] with wild strawberries—for supper.

One evening he was returning home along the river path when he saw Leita in front of him, down by the water. A swan had sailed up to the verge and she had her arms round its neck and the swan's head rested against her cheek. She was

---

3. **Welsh rarebit** a dish of melted cheese served on crackers or toast.

Vocabulary
rash (rash) *adj.* too hasty

remote (ri mōt´) *adj.* far away from anything else

Conflict and Resolution
What inner conflict is resolved for Mr. Peters when he gets a wife?

Make Inferences On what details does Mr. Peters base his inference that Leita is not happy?

Reading Check
What happens after Mr. Peters makes his first wish?

The Third Wish **315**

Mythology Connection

A Star Is Born The graceful, noble swan has been celebrated in the myths and literature of many cultures. It is also visible in the skies as a constellation, Cygnus the Swan.

In one version of how the constellation came to be, Phaethon, a human son of Apollo the sun god, borrowed his father's chariot. Phaethon drove dangerously, and to stop him, Zeus hurled a thunderbolt at him. It killed him instantly, and he fell from the sky.

Phaethon's friend Cygnus searched the river for him. As Apollo watched him dive in, he thought Cygnus resembled a swan. When Cygnus died of grief, Apollo took pity and changed him into a swan, placing him forever among the stars.

Connect to the Literature

What similarities can you find between the story of Cygnus and "The Third Wish"?

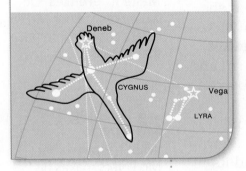

weeping, and as he came nearer he saw that tears were rolling, too, from the swan's eyes.

"Leita, what is it?" he asked, very troubled.

"This is my sister," she answered. "I can't bear being separated from her."

Now he understood that Leita was really a swan from the forest, and this made him very sad because when a human being marries a bird it always leads to sorrow.

"I could use my second wish to give your sister human shape, so that she could be a companion to you," he suggested.

"No, no," she cried, "I couldn't ask that of her."

"Is it so very hard to be a human being?" asked Mr. Peters sadly.

"Very, very hard," she answered.

"Don't you love me at all, Leita?"

"Yes, I do, I do love you," she said, and there were tears in her eyes again. "But I missed the old life in the forest, the cool grass and the mist rising off the river at sunrise and the feel of the water sliding over my feathers as my sister and I drifted along the stream."

"Then shall I use my second wish to turn you back into a swan again?" he asked, and his tongue pricked to remind him of the old King's words, and his heart swelled with grief inside him.

"Who will take care of you?"

"I'd do it myself as I did before I married you," he said, trying to sound cheerful.

She shook her head. "No, I could not be as unkind to you as that. I am partly a swan, but I am also partly a human being now. I will stay with you."

Poor Mr. Peters was very distressed on his wife's account and did his best to make her life happier, taking her for drives in the car, finding beautiful music for her to listen to on the radio, buying clothes for her and even suggesting a trip round the world. But she said no to that; she would prefer to stay in their own house near the river.

He noticed that she spent more and more time baking wonderful cakes—jam puffs, petits fours, eclairs and meringues. One day he saw her take a basketful down to the river and he guessed that she was giving them to her sister.

He built a seat for her by the river, and the two sisters spent hours together there, communicating in some wordless manner. For a time he thought that all would be well, but then he saw how thin and pale she was growing.

One night when he had been late doing the account he came up to bed and found her weeping in her sleep and calling:

"Rhea! Rhea! I can't understand what you say! Oh, wait for me, take me with you!"

Then he knew that it was hopeless and she would never be happy as a human. He stooped down and kissed her goodbye, then took another leaf from his notecase, blew it out of the window, and used up his second wish.

Next moment instead of Leita there was a sleeping swan lying across the bed with its head under its wing. He carried it out of the house and down to the brink of the river, and then he said, "Leita! Leita!" to waken her, and gently put her into the water. She gazed round her in astonishment for a moment, and then came up to him and rested her head lightly against his hand; next instant she was flying away over the trees towards the heart of the forest.

He heard a harsh laugh behind him, and turning round saw the old King looking at him with a malicious expression.

"Well, my friend! You don't seem to have managed so wonderfully with your first two wishes, do you? What will you do with the last? Turn yourself into a swan? Or turn Leita back into a girl?"

"I shall do neither," said Mr. Peters calmly. "Human beings and swans are better in their own shapes."

But for all that he looked sadly over towards the forest where Leita had flown, and walked slowly back to his house.

Next day he saw two swans swimming at the bottom of the garden, and one of them wore the gold chain he had given Leita after their marriage; she came up and rubbed her head against his hand.

Mr. Peters and his two swans came to be well known in that part of the country; people used to say that he talked to swans and they understood him as well as his neighbors. Many people were a little frightened of him. There was a story that once when thieves tried to break into his house they were set upon by two huge white birds which carried them off bodily and dropped them into the river.

Conflict and Resolution
Beyond what he has already done to resolve his wife's conflict, what else do you suggest Mr. Peters could do?

Vocabulary
malicious (mə lishʹ əs) *adj.* hateful; spiteful

Reading Check
Why does Leita want to be a swan again?

As Mr. Peters grew old everyone wondered at his contentment. Even when he was bent with rheumatism[4] he would not think of moving to a drier spot, but went slowly about his work, with the two swans always somewhere close at hand.

Sometimes people who knew his story would say to him: "Mr. Peters, why don't you wish for another wife?"

"Not likely," he would answer serenely. "Two wishes were enough for me, I reckon. I've learned that even if your wishes are granted they don't always better you. I'll stay faithful to Leita."

One autumn night, passers-by along the road heard the mournful sound of two swans singing. All night the song went on, sweet and harsh, sharp and clear. In the morning Mr. Peters was found peacefully dead in his bed with a smile of great happiness on his face. In his hands, which lay clasped on his breast, were a withered leaf and a white feather.

Make Inferences
What inferences can you make from knowing what Mr. Peters held in his hands when he died?

---

4. **rheumatism** (roo′ mə tiz′ əm) *n.* pain and stiffness of the joints and muscles.

Critical Thinking

Cite textual evidence to support your responses.

1. **Key Ideas and Details (a)** How does Mr. Peters get the opportunity to ask for three wishes? **(b) Reflect:** How did you think Mr. Peters's wishing would turn out? Was your prediction correct?

2. **Key Ideas and Details (a)** How does Mr. Peters use his first wish? **(b) Speculate:** Why do you think he does not wish for riches?

3. **Key Ideas and Details (a) Make a Judgment:** Do you think Mr. Peters used his wishes wisely? **(b) Support:** What evidence from the story makes you feel that way?

4. **Integration of Knowledge and Ideas Apply:** Many cultures have traditional tales about wishes that do not work out. Why do you think this kind of story is so common?

5. **Integration of Knowledge and Ideas (a)** Do you think Mr. Peters made the right decision to help him resolve his internal conflict? **(b)** What story details support your response? *[Connect to the Big Question: Does every conflict have a winner?]*

Reading Skill: Make Inferences

1. List details that support the **inference** that Mr. Peters loves Leita more than he loves himself.

2. List details that support the inference that Leita still loves Mr. Peters even after changing back to a swan.

3. List details that suggest that Mr. Peters is not afraid to die.

Literary Analysis: Conflict and Resolution

© **4. Key Ideas and Details (a)** What **conflict** does Mr. Peters's first wish introduce? **(b)** What **resolution** does Mr. Peters find for the conflict?

© **5. Key Ideas and Details** On a chart like the one shown, identify two smaller conflicts that build toward Mr. Peters's main conflict, and tell how each is resolved.

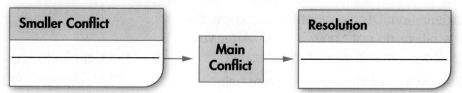

Vocabulary

© **Acquisition and Use** Answer each question, and explain your response.

1. To people in your school, does Australia seem *remote*?

2. Does it take a long time to make a *rash* decision?

3. What would you do if you faced a *malicious* person?

4. Is it safe to stand on the *verge* of a steep cliff?

5. Is it *presumptuous* of a host to invite guests to a party?

6. If you see someone *dabbling* in a pool, is he in danger?

Word Study Use what you know about the **Latin prefix mal-** to explain your answer to each question.

1. If something is *malodorous,* does it smell good?

2. What kind of physical *malady* might a player have after a football game?

Does every *conflict* have a winner?

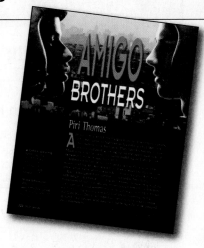

Writing About the Big Question

In "Amigo Brothers," two good friends compete against each other in a boxing match. Use these sentence starters to develop your ideas about the Big Question.

When close friends **compete**, _____.

Conflicts between friends can create feelings of _____.

While You Read Look for internal conflicts in each character as the story builds up to the big fight.

Vocabulary

Read each word and its definition. Decide whether you know the word well, know it a little bit, or do not know it at all. After you read, see how your knowledge of each word has increased.

- **devastating** (dev´ ə stāt iŋ) *adj.* destructive; overwhelming (p. 323) *A devastating storm destroyed the town.*
  devastate v. devastation n. devastating v.

- **perpetual** (pər pəch´ oo əl) *adj.* constant; unending (p. 326) *Toddlers are in perpetual motion, never standing still.*
  perpetually adv. perpetuate v. perpetuity n.

- **dignitaries** (dig´ nə tər´ ēz) *n.* people holding high positions or offices (p. 327) *The people honored the dignitaries by giving them the best seats. dignitary n. dignify v. dignified adj.*

- **improvised** (im´ prə vīzd) *v.* composed or performed on the spur of the moment (p. 327) *Working without a script, they improvised the entire play. improvisation n. improvising v.*

- **dispelled** (di speld´) *v.* driven away; made to disappear (p. 329) *Luckily, my worries were dispelled by the good news. dispel v. dispelling v.*

- **evading** (ē vād´ iŋ) *v.* avoiding (p. 330) *We hid behind the fence, evading the bullies. evade v. evasive adj. evasively adv.*

Word Study

The **Latin prefix** *per-* means "through" or "completely."

In this story, Antonio imagines **perpetual** boxing motions, motions that are unending throughout the night.

Meet
Piri Thomas
(b. 1928)

Author of
AMIGO BROTHERS

Growing up on the streets of New York City's Spanish Harlem, Piri Thomas faced tough challenges like poverty, gangs, and racism. He later related those struggles in his best-selling autobiographical novel, *Down These Mean Streets.* The book introduced many non-Hispanics to the world of *el barrio*—"the neighborhood."

An Avid Reader When he was young, Thomas tried to avoid the difficult world around him by surrounding himself with books. "My one island of refuge in *el barrio* was the public library," Thomas has recalled. "I gorged myself on books. . . . Reading helped me to realize that there was a world out there far vaster than the narrow confines of *el barrio.*"

BACKGROUND FOR THE STORY

Amateur Boxing

In "Amigo Brothers," two teenage boys want to compete in the annual Golden Gloves tournament. This competition is probably the most famous amateur boxing event in the United States. Each year, local and regional elimination bouts lead to final championship matches.

DID YOU KNOW?
Thomas has written many magazine articles reflecting on ways for people everywhere to achieve peace and justice.

AMIGO BROTHERS

Piri Thomas

Antonio Cruz and Felix Vargas were both seventeen years old. They were so together in friendship that they felt themselves to be brothers. They had known each other since childhood, growing up on the lower east side of Manhattan in the same tenement building on Fifth Street between Avenue A and Avenue B.

Antonio was fair, lean, and lanky, while Felix was dark, short, and husky. Antonio's hair was always falling over his eyes, while Felix wore his black hair in a natural Afro style.

Each youngster had a dream of someday becoming lightweight champion of the world. Every chance they had the boys worked out, sometimes at the Boys Club on 10th Street and Avenue A and sometimes at the pro's gym on 14th Street. Early morning sunrises would find them running along the East River Drive, wrapped in sweat shirts, short towels around their necks, and handkerchiefs Apache style around their foreheads.

▲ **Critical Viewing**
What does the protective gear shown in this photograph tell you about boxing?

Make Inferences
What can you infer about the boys based on their dedication to boxing?

While some youngsters were into street negatives, Antonio and Felix slept, ate, rapped, and dreamt positive. Between them, they had a collection of *Fight* magazines second to none, plus a scrapbook filled with torn tickets to every boxing match they had ever attended, and some clippings of their own. If asked a question about any given fighter, they would immediately zip out from their memory banks divisions, weights, records of fights, knock-outs, technical knock-outs, and draws or losses.

Each had fought many bouts representing their community and had won two gold-plated medals plus a silver and bronze medallion. The difference was in their style. Antonio's lean form and long reach made him the better boxer, while Felix's short and muscular frame made him the better slugger. Whenever they had met in the ring for sparring sessions, it had always been hot and heavy.

Now, after a series of elimination bouts, they had been informed that they were to meet each other in the division finals that were scheduled for the seventh of August, two weeks away—the winner to represent the Boys Club in the Golden Gloves Championship Tournament.

The two boys continued to run together along the East River Drive. But even when joking with each other, they both sensed a wall rising between them.

One morning less than a week before their bout, they met as usual for their daily work-out. They fooled around with a few jabs at the air, slapped skin, and then took off, running lightly along the dirty East River's edge.

Antonio glanced at Felix who kept his eyes purposely straight ahead, pausing from time to time to do some fancy leg work while throwing one-twos followed by upper cuts to an imaginary jaw. Antonio then beat the air with a barrage of body blows and short **devastating** lefts with an overhand jaw-breaking right. After a mile or so, Felix puffed and said, "Let's stop a while, bro. I think we both got something to say to each other." Antonio nodded. It was not natural to be acting as though nothing unusual was happening when two ace-boon buddies were going to be blasting each other within a few short days.

They rested their elbows on the railing separating them from the river. Antonio wiped his face with his short towel. The sunrise was now creating day.

Felix leaned heavily on the river's railing and stared across to the shores of Brooklyn. Finally, he broke the silence.

Conflict and Resolution
What external conflict is introduced in this part of the story?

Vocabulary
devastating (dev´ ə stāt´ iŋ) *adj.* destructive; overwhelming

Reading Check
What dream do Antonio and Felix share?

"Man, I don't know how to come out with it."

Antonio helped. "It's about our fight, right?"

"Yeah, right." Felix's eyes squinted at the rising orange sun.

"I've been thinking about it too, *panín*. In fact, since we found out it was going to be me and you, I've been awake at night, pulling punches on you, trying not to hurt you."

"Same here. It ain't natural not to think about the fight. I mean, we both are *cheverote* fighters and we both want to win. But only one of us can win. There ain't no draws in the eliminations."

Make Inferences
What do the details in this conversation suggest about the boys' relationship?

Felix tapped Antonio gently on the shoulder. "I don't mean to sound like I'm bragging, bro. But I wanna win, fair and square."

Antonio nodded quietly. "Yeah. We both know that in the ring the better man wins. Friend or no friend, brother or no . . ."

Felix finished it for him. "Brother. Tony, let's promise something right here. Okay?"

"If it's fair, *hermano*, I'm for it." Antonio admired the courage of a tugboat pulling a barge five times its welterweight size.

"It's fair, Tony. When we get into the ring, it's gotta be like we never met. We gotta be like two heavy strangers that want the same thing and only one can have it. You understand, don'tcha?"

"*Sí*, I know." Tony smiled. "No pulling punches. We go all the way."

"Yeah, that's right. Listen, Tony. Don't you think it's a good idea if we don't see each other until the day of the fight? I'm going to stay with my Aunt Lucy in the Bronx. I can use Gleason's Gym for working out. My manager says he got some sparring partners with more or less your style."

Tony scratched his nose pensively. "Yeah, it would be better for our heads." He held out his hand, palm upward. "Deal?"

"Deal." Felix lightly slapped open skin.

"Ready for some more running?" Tony asked lamely.

"Naw, bro. Let's cut it here. You go on. I kinda like to get things together in my head."

"You ain't worried, are you?" Tony asked.

"No way, man." Felix laughed out loud. "I got too much

smarts for that. I just think it's cooler if we split right here. After the fight, we can get it together again like nothing ever happened."

The amigo brothers were not ashamed to hug each other tightly.

"Guess you're right. Watch yourself, Felix. I hear there's some pretty heavy dudes up in the Bronx. *Suavecito*, okay?"

"Okay. You watch yourself too, *sabe?*"

Tony jogged away. Felix watched his friend disappear from view, throwing rights and lefts. Both fighters had a lot of psyching up to do before the big fight.

The days in training passed much too slowly. Although they kept out of each other's way, they were aware of each other's progress via the ghetto grapevine.

The evening before the big fight, Tony made his way to the roof of his tenement. In the quiet early dark, he peered over the ledge. Six stories below the lights of the city blinked and the sounds of cars mingled with the curses and the laughter of children in the street. He tried not to think of Felix, feeling he had succeeded in psyching his mind. But only in the ring would he really know. To spare Felix hurt, he would have to knock him out, early and quick.

Up in the South Bronx, Felix decided to take in a movie in an effort to keep Antonio's face away from his fists. The flick was *The Champion* with Kirk Douglas, the third time Felix was seeing it.

The champion was getting hit hard. He was saved only by the sound of the bell.

Felix became the champ and Tony the challenger.

The movie audience was going out of its head. The challenger, confident that he had the championship in the bag, threw a left. The champ countered with a dynamite right.

Felix's right arm felt the shock. Antonio's face, superimposed[1] on the screen, was hit by the awesome blow. Felix saw himself in the ring, blasting Antonio against the ropes. The champ had to be forcibly restrained. The challenger was allowed to crumble slowly to the canvas.

When Felix finally left the theatre, he had figured out how

---

1. **superimposed** (soo´ pər im pōzd´) *adj.* put or stacked on top of something else.

Conflict and Resolution
What internal conflict do Tony and Felix each face before the fight?

▲ **Critical Viewing**
Which details in the story would you include in a caption for this photograph? **[Apply]**

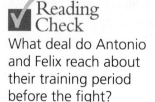

Reading Check
What deal do Antonio and Felix reach about their training period before the fight?

Language Connection

Spanish Terms

amigo (ə mē′ gō) *n.* Spanish for "friend"

panín (pä nēn′) *n.* Spanish for "pal"

cheverote (che bē rō′ tā) Spanish for "the greatest"

hermano (er mä′ nō) *n.* Spanish for "brother"

suavecito (swä vä sē′ tō) Spanish for "take it easy"

sabe (sä′ bā) *v.* Spanish for "understand?"

salsa (säl′ sä) *n.* a style of Latin American music

señores y señoras (se nyō′ res ē se nyō′ räs) Spanish for "Gentlemen and Ladies"

mucho corazón (moo̅′ chō kô rä sôn′) Spanish for "much courage"

Connect to the Literature

Why do you think the author uses Spanish words in this story?

to psyche himself for tomorrow's fight. It was Felix the Champion vs. Antonio the Challenger.

He walked up some dark streets, deserted except for small pockets of wary-looking kids wearing gang colors. Despite the fact that he was Puerto Rican like them, they eyed him as a stranger to their turf. Felix did a fast shuffle, bobbing and weaving, while letting loose a torrent of blows that would demolish whatever got in its way. It seemed to impress the brothers, who went about their own business.

Finding no takers, Felix decided to split to his aunt's. Walking the streets had not relaxed him, neither had the fight flick. All it had done was to stir him up. He let himself quietly into his Aunt Lucy's apartment and went straight to bed, falling into a fitful sleep with sounds of the gong for Round One.

Antonio was passing some heavy time on his rooftop. How would the fight tomorrow affect his relationship with Felix? After all, fighting was like any other profession. Friendship had nothing to do with it. A gnawing doubt crept in. He cut negative thinking real quick by doing some speedy fancy dance steps, bobbing and weaving like mercury.[2] The night air was blurred with perpetual motions of left hooks and right crosses. Felix, his *amigo* brother, was not going to be Felix at all in the ring. Just an opponent with another face. Antonio went to sleep, hearing the opening bell for the first round. Like his friend in the South Bronx, he prayed for victory, via a quick clean knock-out in the first round.

Large posters plastered all over the walls of local shops announced the fight between Antonio Cruz and Felix Vargas as the main bout.

The fight had created great interest in the neighborhood. Antonio and Felix were well liked and respected. Each had his own loyal following. Antonio's fans counted on his boxing skills. On the other side, Felix's admirers trusted in his dynamite-packed fists.

Felix had returned to his apartment early in the morning of August 7th and stayed there, hoping to avoid seeing Antonio.

---

2. **mercury** (mur′ kyoor ē) *n.* the element mercury, also known as quicksilver because it is so quick and fluid.

He turned the radio on to *salsa* music sounds and then tried to read while waiting for word from his manager.

The fight was scheduled to take place in Tompkins Square Park. It had been decided that the gymnasium of the Boys Club was not large enough to hold all the people who were sure to attend. In Tompkins Square Park, everyone who wanted could view the fight, whether from ringside or window fire escapes or tenement rooftops.

The morning of the fight Tompkins Square was a beehive of activity with numerous workers setting up the ring, the seats, and the guest speakers' stand. The scheduled bouts began shortly after noon and the park had begun filling up even earlier.

The local junior high school across from Tompkins Square Park served as the dressing room for all the fighters. Each was given a separate classroom with desk tops, covered with mats, serving as resting tables. Antonio thought he caught a glimpse of Felix waving to him from a room at the far end of the corridor. He waved back just in case it had been him.

The fighters changed from their street clothes into fighting gear. Antonio wore white trunks, black socks, and black shoes. Felix wore sky blue trunks, red socks, and white boxing shoes. Each had dressing gowns to match their fighting trunks with their names neatly stitched on the back.

The loudspeakers blared into the open windows of the school. There were speeches by dignitaries, community leaders, and great boxers of yesteryear. Some were well prepared, some improvised on the spot. They all carried the same message of great pleasure and honor at being part of such a historic event. This great day was in the tradition of champions emerging from the streets of the lower east side.

Make Inferences
What does Antonio's wave from the dressing room suggest about his feelings for Felix?

Reading
Check
Why are so many people in the neighborhood interested in watching the fight?

▼ **Critical Viewing**
How do you think the boxers feel as they wait for the bell to start the match? **[Connect]**

Spiral Review

Plot How does the sequence of events that begins with the boxers entering the ring and builds to the bell ringing increase the tension of the plot? Why are these events part of the rising action of the plot?

Interwoven with the speeches were the sounds of the other boxing events. After the sixth bout, Felix was much relieved when his trainer Charlie said, "Time change. Quick knock-out. This is it. We're on."

Waiting time was over. Felix was escorted from the classroom by a dozen fans in white T-shirts with the word FELIX across their fronts.

Antonio was escorted down a different stairwell and guided through a roped-off path.

As the two climbed into the ring, the crowd exploded with a roar. Antonio and Felix both bowed gracefully and then raised their arms in acknowledgment.

Antonio tried to be cool, but even as the roar was in its first birth, he turned slowly to meet Felix's eyes looking directly into his. Felix nodded his head and Antonio responded. And both as one, just as quickly, turned away to face his own corner.

Bong—bong—bong. The roar turned to stillness.

"Ladies and Gentlemen. *Señores y Señoras.*"

The announcer spoke slowly, pleased at his bilingual efforts.

"Now the moment we have all been waiting for— the main event between two fine young Puerto Rican fighters, products of our lower east side. In this corner, weighing 134 pounds, Felix Vargas. And in this corner, weighing 133 pounds, Antonio Cruz. The winner will represent the Boys Club in the tournament of champions, the Golden Gloves. There will be no draw. May the best man win."

The cheering of the crowd shook the window panes of the old buildings surrounding Tompkins Square Park. At the center of the ring, the referee was giving instructions to the youngsters.

"Keep your punches up. No low blows. No punching on the back of the head. Keep your heads up. Understand. Let's have a clean fight. Now shake hands and come out fighting."

Both youngsters touched gloves and nodded. They turned and danced quickly to their corners. Their head towels and dressing gowns were lifted neatly from their shoulders by their trainers' nimble fingers. Antonio crossed himself. Felix did the same.

BONG! BONG! ROUND ONE. Felix and Antonio turned and faced each other squarely in a fighting pose. Felix wasted no time. He came in fast, head low, half hunched toward his right shoulder, and lashed out with a straight left. He missed a right cross as Antonio slipped the punch and countered with one-two-three lefts that snapped Felix's head back, sending a mild shock coursing through him. If Felix had any small doubt about their friendship affecting their fight, it was being neatly dispelled.

Antonio danced, a joy to behold. His left hand was like a piston pumping jabs one right after another with seeming ease. Felix bobbed and weaved and never stopped boring in. He knew that at long range he was at a disadvantage. Antonio had too much reach on him. Only by coming in close could Felix hope to achieve the dreamed-of knockout.

Antonio knew the dynamite that was stored in his *amigo* brother's fist. He ducked a short right and missed a left hook. Felix trapped him against the ropes just long enough to pour some punishing rights and lefts to Antonio's hard midsection. Antonio slipped away from Felix, crashing two lefts to his head, which set Felix's right ear to ringing.

Bong! Both *amigos* froze a punch well on its way, sending up a roar of approval for good sportsmanship.

Felix walked briskly back to his corner. His right ear had not stopped ringing. Antonio gracefully danced his way toward his stool none the worse, except for glowing glove burns, showing angry red against the whiteness of his midribs.

"Watch that right, Tony." His trainer talked into his ear. "Remember Felix always goes to the body. He'll want you to drop your hands for his overhand left or right. Got it?"

Antonio nodded, spraying water out between his teeth. He felt better as his sore midsection was being firmly rubbed.

Felix's corner was also busy.

"You gotta get in there, fella." Felix's trainer poured water over his curly Afro locks. "Get in there or he's gonna chop you up from way back."

Bong! Bong! Round two. Felix was off his stool and rushed Antonio like a bull, sending a hard right to his head. Beads of water exploded from Antonio's long hair.

Antonio, hurt, sent back a blurring barrage of lefts and rights that only meant pain to Felix, who returned with a short left to the head followed by a looping right to the body. Antonio countered with his own flurry, forcing Felix to give ground. But not for long.

Felix bobbed and weaved, bobbed and weaved, occasionally

Vocabulary
dispelled (di speld´)
v. driven away; made to disappear

Make Inferences
What do their actions here tell you about Felix and Antonio as boxers?

✓ Reading Check
Why can't the fight be a tie?

Amigo Brothers **329**

punching his two gloves together.

Antonio waited for the rush that was sure to come. Felix closed in and feinted[3] with his left shoulder and threw his right instead. Lights suddenly exploded inside Felix's head as Antonio slipped the blow and hit him with a pistonlike left catching him flush on the point of his chin.

Bedlam[4] broke loose as Felix's legs momentarily buckled. He fought off a series of rights and lefts and came back with a strong right that taught Antonio respect.

Antonio danced in carefully. He knew Felix had the habit of playing possum when hurt, to sucker an opponent within reach of the powerful bombs he carried in each fist.

A right to the head slowed Antonio's pretty dancing. He answered with his own left at Felix's right eye that began puffing up within three seconds.

Antonio, a bit too eager, moved in too close and Felix had him entangled into a rip-roaring, punching toe-to-toe slugfest that brought the whole Tompkins Square Park screaming to its feet.

Rights to the body. Lefts to the head. Neither fighter was giving an inch. Suddenly a short right caught Antonio squarely on the chin. His long legs turned to jelly and his arms flailed out desperately. Felix, grunting like a bull, threw wild punches from every direction. Antonio, groggy, bobbed and weaved, evading most of the blows. Suddenly his head cleared. His left flashed out hard and straight catching Felix on the bridge of his nose.

Felix lashed back with a haymaker,[5] right off the ghetto streets. At the same instant, his eye caught another left hook from Antonio. Felix swung out trying to clear the pain. Only the frenzied screaming of those along ringside let him know that he had dropped Antonio. Fighting off the growing haze, Antonio struggled to his feet, got up, ducked, and threw a smashing right that dropped Felix flat on his back.

Felix got up as fast as he could in his own corner, groggy but still game. He didn't even hear the count. In a fog, he heard the roaring of the crowd, who seemed to have gone insane. His head cleared to hear the bell sound at the end of the round. He was very glad. His trainer sat him down on the stool.

In his corner, Antonio was doing what all fighters do when they are hurt. They sit and smile at everyone.

Conflict and Resolution
How does the author increase the external conflict here?

Vocabulary
evading (ē vād′ iŋ) *v.* avoiding

Make Inferences
What can you infer from the fact that Felix is groggy and glad to sit down?

3. **feinted** (fānt′ əd) *v.* pretended to make a blow.
4. **Bedlam** (bed′ ləm) *n.* condition of noise and confusion.
5. **haymaker** punch thrown with full force.

Neither Fighter **WAS GIVING AN INCH.**

The referee signaled the ring doctor to check the fighters out. He did so and then gave his okay. The cold water sponges brought clarity to both *amigo* brothers. They were rubbed until their circulation ran free.

Bong! Round three—the final round. Up to now it had been tic-tac-toe, pretty much even. But everyone knew there could be no draw and this round would decide the winner.

This time, to Felix's surprise, it was Antonio who came out fast, charging across the ring. Felix braced himself but couldn't ward off the barrage of punches. Antonio drove Felix hard against the ropes.

The crowd ate it up. Thus far the two had fought with *mucho corazón.* Felix tapped his gloves and commenced his attack anew. Antonio, throwing boxer's caution to the winds, jumped in to meet him.

Both pounded away. Neither gave an inch and neither fell to the canvas. Felix's left eye was tightly closed. Claret red blood poured from Antonio's nose. They fought toe-to-toe.

The sounds of their blows were loud in contrast to the silence of a crowd gone completely mute. The referee was stunned by their savagery.

Bong! Bong! Bong! The bell sounded over and over again. Felix and Antonio were past hearing. Their blows continued to pound on each other like hailstones.

Finally the referee and the two trainers pried Felix and Antonio apart. Cold water was poured over them to bring

▲ **Critical Viewing**
Why do you think that competitors in boxing matches wear contrasting colors such as the blue and red shown here? **[Hypothesize]**

Reading Check
Does Felix or Antonio fall to the mat first?

them back to their senses.

They looked around and then rushed toward each other. A cry of alarm surged through Tompkins Square Park. Was this a fight to the death instead of a boxing match?

The fear soon gave way to wave upon wave of cheering as the two *amigos* embraced.

No matter what the decision, they knew they would always be champions to each other.

BONG! BONG! BONG! "Ladies and Gentlemen. *Señores* and *Señoras*. The winner and representative to the Golden Gloves Tournament of Champions is . . ."

The announcer turned to point to the winner and found himself alone. Arm in arm the champions had already left the ring.

Critical Thinking

> Cite textual evidence to support your responses.

1. **Key Ideas and Details (a)** What is the boys' plan for training before they face each other in the ring?
   (b) Evaluate: What are the advantages and disadvantages of their plan? **(c) Discuss:** Do you think the plan is mostly good or mostly bad? In a small group, share your responses. As a group, choose one response to share with the class.

2. **Integration of Knowledge and Ideas (a) Analyze:** In what ways does the boys' friendship both help them and hurt them during the fight? **(b) Apply:** Why is it harder for each of them to compete against a friend than a stranger?

3. **Integration of Knowledge and Ideas Speculate:** Do you think the boys will be willing to box against each other in the future? Explain your response.

4. **Integration of Knowledge and Ideas (a)** Why do you think the author chose not to tell you which of the two boys won the fight? **(b)** What do you think the author is saying in this story about winners and losers? *[Connect to the Big Question: Does every conflict have a winner?]*

Reading Skill: Make Inferences

1. List details that support the **inference** that the boys care for each other more than they care for themselves.

2. List details that support the inference that the boys have few other friends besides each other.

3. List two details that show that neither boy gives up easily.

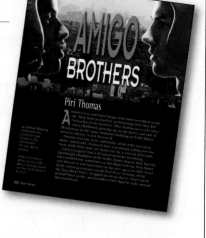

Literary Analysis: Conflict and Resolution

Ⓒ 4. **Key Ideas and Details** **(a)** What **conflict** does the boys' dream introduce? **(b)** What **resolution** do the boys find for their conflict?

Ⓒ 5. **Key Ideas and Details** On a chart like the one shown, identify two smaller conflicts that build toward the main conflict, and tell how each is resolved.

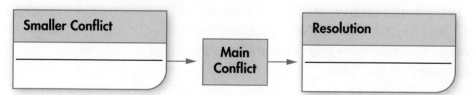

Smaller Conflict		Main Conflict		Resolution

Vocabulary

Ⓒ **Acquisition and Use** Answer each question. Then, explain your response.

1. How do most people respond to *devastating* news?

2. What would you do if a friend's lateness were *perpetual*?

3. How would you *improvise* if you forgot a line in a play?

4. If someone had *dispelled* a rumor, would you believe it?

5. Would you chase a person you were *evading*?

6. If you were to meet a *dignitary*, how would you greet her?

Word Study Use what you know about the **Latin prefix *per-*** to explain your answer to each question.

1. If a teenager has a *permit,* can he or she drive a car?

2. Would the smell of dinner cooking *permeate* the kitchen?

Word Study

The **Latin prefix *per-*** means "through" or "complete."

Apply It Explain how the prefix ***per-*** contributes to the meanings of these words. Consult a dictionary if necessary.

persevere
percolate
persuade

Integrated Language Skills

The Third Wish • Amigo Brothers

Conventions: Adjectives

An **adjective** modifies or describes a noun or pronoun.
An adjective may answer the questions *What kind? How many? Which one?* or *Whose?*

Adjective Questions	
What kind?	Dan bought a <u>sports</u> jacket.
How many?	We sold <u>fifty</u> tickets.
Which one?	Please hand me the <u>green</u> one.
Whose?	We saw <u>Kathy's</u> play.

Compound adjectives are made up of more than one word, such as "one-sided opinion," and most are written as hyphenated words.
Coordinate adjectives are two or more adjectives that modify the same noun and are separated by a comma. You can tell if adjectives are coordinate if the word *and* could be used in place of the comma without altering the meaning.

Practice A Identify the adjective in each sentence and the word it modifies.

1. Mr. Peters rescued the tangled swan.
2. The king warned Mr. Peters against making foolish wishes.
3. Leita made delicious sweets for her sister.
4. Leita's sister often came to the edge of the water to visit.
5. Mr. Peters used his second wish to please Leita.

ⓒ **Reading Application** In "The Third Wish," find a sentence with several adjectives.

Practice B Add one or two adjectives to each sentence based on the question in parenthesis.

1. Antonio and Felix have been friends since childhood. (What kind?)
2. Felix decided to stay at a house before the fight. (Whose?)
3. Felix threw a blow to the side of Antonio's face. (Which side?)
4. The boys were champions in and out of the ring. (What kind?)

ⓒ **Writing Application** Write sentences in which you use coordinate adjectives to describe a competition between friends.

PH **WRITING COACH** | Further instruction and practice are available in *Prentice Hall Writing Coach*.

Writing

 **Common Core State Standards**

L.7.2.a, L.7.4.b, L.7.6; W.7.2.a, W.7.2.e, W.7.3, W.7.3.e; SL.7.6
[For the full wording of the standards, see page 308.]

ⓒ Narrative Text Write an **anecdote,** or brief story, that tells what might have happened if the ending of the story you read were different. If you read "The Third Wish," write an anecdote about what might have happened if Mr. Peters had not turned Leita back into a swan. If you read "Amigo Brothers," write an anecdote about what might have happened if Antonio or Felix had been knocked out during the fight. Follow these steps:

- First, think of how the story would unfold with the new ending.
- Then, make notes on a conflict that could have arisen.
- Next, decide on one resolution to the conflict.
- Finally, conclude by stating a lesson that the characters would learn.

Grammar Application Check your writing to be sure you have used adjectives correctly.

Writing Workshop: *Work in Progress*

Prewriting for Narration Briefly describe four conflicts that you have experienced yourself, witnessed, seen on televised news, or read about in newspapers. These conflicts may have occurred in school, at home, in your community, or in a distant location. Jot down notes about what made each one memorable to you. Put this Conflict List in your writing portfolio.

Use this prewriting activity to prepare for the **Writing Workshop** on page 384.

Speaking and Listening

ⓒ Presentation of Ideas Write a **news story** based on the story you read.

- If you write about "The Third Wish," announce the death of Mr. Peters and hail him as a local hero.
- If you write about "Amigo Brothers," describe the fight between Antonio and Felix from the perspective of a reporter in the audience.

Follow these steps to complete the assignment:

- Organize your story to present your details in the most effective order. For instance, you might present events in the order in which they occurred or in order of importance.
- Practice reading your news story aloud, using proper grammar and a formal style, before presenting it to the class.

Zoo • Ribbons

© Leveled Texts

Build your skills and improve your comprehension of short stories with texts of increasing complexity.

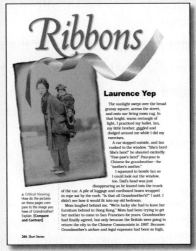

Read **"Zoo"** to see what conflict develops when a spaceship full of creatures makes a visit to Earth.

Read **"Ribbons"** to learn how cultures collide when a Chinese grandmother moves in with her American family.

© Common Core State Standards

Meet these standards with either **"Zoo"** (p. 340) or **"Ribbons"** (p. 346).

Reading Literature

1. Cite several pieces of textual evidence to support analysis of what the text says explicitly as well as inferences drawn from the text. *(Reading Skill: Make Inferences)*

2. Determine a theme or central idea of a text and analyze its development over the course of the text; provide an objective summary of the text. *(Literary Analysis: Theme)*

Writing

1.a. Introduce claim(s), acknowledge alternate or opposing claims, and organize the reasons and evidence logically.

1.b. Support claim(s) with logical reasoning and relevant evidence, using accurate, credible sources and demonstrating an understanding of the topic or text. *(Writing: Letter to the Editor)*

7. Conduct short research projects to answer a question, drawing on several sources and generating additional related, focused questions for further research and investigation. *(Research and Technology: Poster)*

Speaking and Listening

5. Include multimedia components and visual displays in presentations to clarify claims and findings and emphasize salient points. *(Research and Technology: Poster)*

Language

1. Demonstrate command of the conventions of standard English grammar and usage when writing or speaking. *(Conventions: Adverbs)*

4.b. Use common, grade-appropriate Greek or Latin affixes and roots as clues to the meaning of a word. *(Vocabulary: Word Study)*

6. Acquire and use accurately grade-appropriate general academic and domain-specific words and phrases; gather vocabulary knowledge when considering a word or phrase important to comprehension or expression. *(Vocabulary: Word Study)*

Reading Skill: Make Inferences

An **inference** is a conclusion you draw about something that is not directly stated. Use details in the text to make inferences about a story. For example, if a story opens with a man running down a dark alley while looking over his shoulder, you might infer that the man is trying to get away from someone or something.

- One way to make inferences is to **read between the lines by asking questions.** Such questions include "Why is this charcer so upset?" and "Why is this character planning to take this action?"

Using the Strategy: Question and Answer Chart

Jot down questions on a chart like this one to help you make inferences as you read.

Why Does the Writer...	Answer (Inference)
Show the man looking over his shoulder?	To tell readers someone or something is chasing the man
Place the man in a dark alley?	To create an atmosphere of fear
Not start by naming the chaser?	To emphasize the man who looks back

Literary Analysis: Theme

A story's **theme** is its central idea, message, or insight into life. Occasionally, the author states the theme directly. More often, however, the theme is implied.

As you read, look at what the characters say and do, where the story takes place, and what objects in the story seem important. These details will help you determine the theme—what the author wants to teach you about life.

Does every *conflict* have a winner?

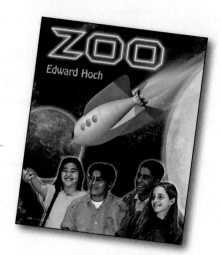

Writing About the Big Question

In "Zoo," human and alien cultures have conflicting ideas about each other. Use these sentence starters to develop your ideas about the Big Question.

When two groups that are very different come together, **misunderstandings** can result because _____.

These groups might get along better if _____.

While You Read Think about ways that the human onlookers see the creatures as different from themselves.

Vocabulary

Read each word and its definition. Decide whether you know the word well, know it a little bit, or do not know it at all. After you read, see how your knowledge of each word has increased.

- **interplanetary** (in´ tər plan´ ə ter´ ē) *adj.* between planets (p. 341) *The interplanetary tour went from Venus to Mars.*

- **wonderment** (wun´ dər mənt) *n.* feeling of surprise or astonishment (p. 341) *The fans stared at the television in wonderment and joy as the goal was scored. wonder n. wonder v. wonderful adj.*

- **awe** (ô) *n.* mixed feelings of fear and wonder (p. 341) *His eyes grew wide in awe at his first sight of a large elephant. awed v. awesome adj.*

- **expense** (ek spens´) *n.* financial cost (p. 341) *Paying for college is a huge expense. expensive adj.*

- **babbled** (bab´ əld) *v.* murmured; talked foolishly or too much (p. 342) *The two friends babbled on the phone for hours. babble v. babbler n. babbling adj.*

- **garments** (gär´ mənts) *n.* clothes (p. 342) *Her suitcase was packed with garments for the trip. garment n.*

Word Study

The **Latin suffix -ment** means "the act of" or "the state of."

In this story, the people waited to see the strange creatures in a state of wonder, or **wonderment.**

Meet
Edward Hoch
(1930–2008)

Author of

When he wrote mystery stories, Edward Hoch did not attempt to create fast-paced scenes with lots of suspense and action. Instead, he preferred to create tension by making his readers guess what would happen next. Hoch created stories that have unusual plots and carefully selected clues for readers to follow.

Magazine Writer Hoch's first mystery story appeared in 1955 in the magazine *Famous Detective Stories*. A few years later, he began writing for *Ellery Queen's Mystery Magazine,* the longest-running magazine in existence for mystery fiction. In his lifetime, Hoch published more than 450 stories for the magazine.

Did You Know?

Many of Hoch's stories feature the same characters. A character named Captain Leopold appears in more than one hundred Hoch stories.

BACKGROUND FOR THE STORY

Zoos

People have studied wild animals since early times. In fact, experts believe that the first zoos were developed as far back as 4500 B.C. Until modern times, animals in zoos lived mostly in cages. However, many of today's zoos house animals in natural habitats, filled with native plants and other animals. In this story, you will read about a zoo that is unlike any other.

ZOO

Edward Hoch

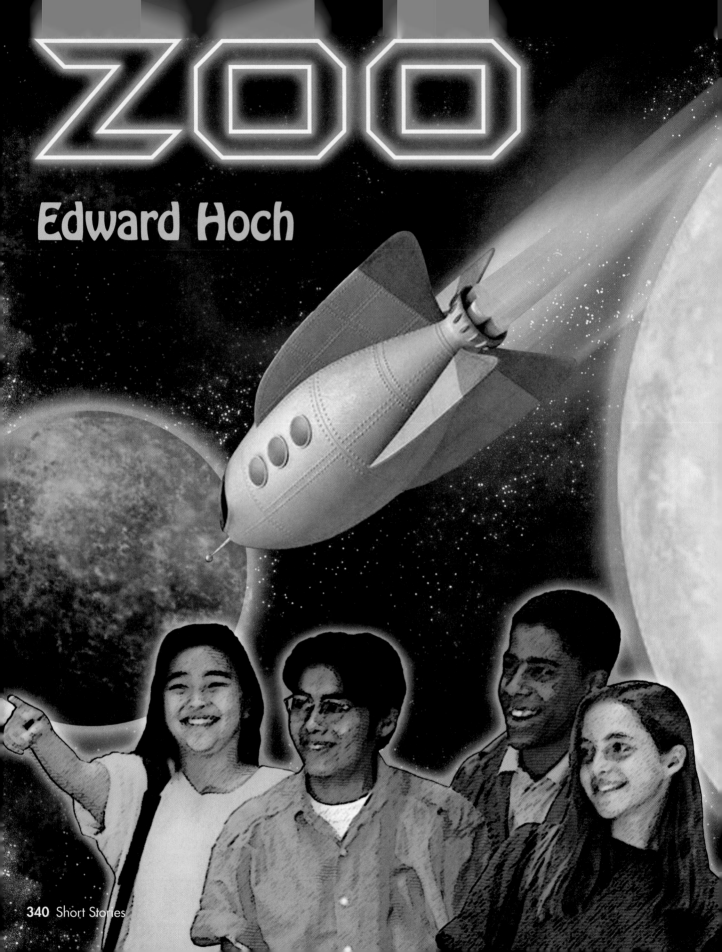

The children were always good during the month of August, especially when it began to get near the twenty-third. It was on this day that the great silver spaceship carrying Professor Hugo's Interplanetary Zoo settled down for its annual six-hour visit to the Chicago area.

Before daybreak the crowds would form, long lines of children and adults both, each one clutching his or her dollar and waiting with wonderment to see what race of strange creatures the Professor had brought this year.

In the past they had sometimes been treated to three-legged creatures from Venus, or tall, thin men from Mars, or even snakelike horrors from somewhere more distant. This year, as the great round ship settled slowly to earth in the huge tri-city parking area just outside of Chicago, they watched with awe as the sides slowly slid up to reveal the familiar barred cages. In them were some wild breed of nightmare—small, horse-like animals that moved with quick, jerking motions and constantly chattered in a high-pitched tongue. The citizens of Earth clustered around as Professor Hugo's crew quickly collected the waiting dollars, and soon the good Professor himself made an appearance, wearing his many-colored rainbow cape and top hat. "Peoples of Earth," he called into his microphone. The crowd's noise died down and he continued. "Peoples of Earth, this year you see a real treat for your single dollar—the little-known horse-spider people of Kaan—brought to you across a million miles of space at great expense. Gather around, see them, study them, listen to them, tell your friends about them. But hurry! My ship can remain here only six hours!"

And the crowds slowly filed by, at once horrified and fascinated by these strange creatures that looked like horses but ran up the walls of their cages like spiders. "This is certainly worth a dollar," one man remarked, hurrying away. "I'm going home to get the wife."

All day long it went like that, until ten thousand people had filed by the barred cages set into the side of the spaceship. Then, as the six-hour limit ran out, Professor Hugo once more took the microphone in hand. "We must go now, but we will return next year on this date. And if you enjoyed our zoo this year, telephone your friends in other cities about it. We will land in New York tomorrow, and next week on to London, Paris, Rome, Hong Kong, and Tokyo. Then on to other worlds!"

Make Inferences
Based on details here, what can you infer about Professor Hugo?

Theme
Why might the people be so eager to see the horse-like animals?

Vocabulary
interplanetary (in´ tər plan´ ə ter´ ē) *adj.* between planets
wonderment (wun´dər mənt) *n.* feeling of surprise or astonishment
awe (ô) *n.* mixed feelings of fear and wonder
expense (ek spens´) *n.* financial cost

◄ **Critical Viewing**
Describe the children's reactions to the space exhibit. **[Analyze]**

Reading Check
What arrives on Professor Hugo's spaceship this year?

He waved farewell to them, and as the ship rose from the ground, the Earth peoples agreed that this had been the very best Zoo yet. . . .

Some two months and three planets later, the silver ship of Professor Hugo settled at last onto the familiar jagged rocks of Kaan, and the odd horse-spider creatures filed quickly out of their cages. Professor Hugo was there to say a few parting words, and then they scurried away in a hundred different directions, seeking their homes among the rocks. •

In one house, the she-creature was happy to see the return of her mate and offspring. She babbled a greeting in the strange tongue and hurried to embrace them. "It was a long time you were gone. Was it good?"

And the he-creature nodded. "The little one enjoyed it especially. We visited eight worlds and saw many things."

The little one ran up the wall of the cave. "On the place called Earth it was the best. The creatures there wear garments over their skins, and they walk on two legs."

"But isn't it dangerous?" asked the she-creature.

"No," her mate answered. "There are bars to protect us from them. We remain right in the ship. Next time you must come with us. It is well worth the nineteen commocs it costs."

And the little one nodded. "It was the very best Zoo ever. . . ."

Vocabulary
babbled (bab´ əld)
v. murmured; talked foolishly or too much

garments (gär´mənts)
n. clothes

Spiral Review
Character What is surprising about the creatures of Kaan? Explain.

Critical Thinking

Cite textual evidence to support your responses.

1. Key Ideas and Details What do the people of Earth see and do at the Interplanetary Zoo?

2. Key Ideas and Details **(a)** How do humans on Earth react to people from Kaan? **(b)** How do Kaan people react to people from Earth? **(c) Compare and Contrast:** In a small group, discuss your answers. Identify details from the story that support your ideas. Together, decide what the similarities and differences tell you.

3. Integration of Knowledge and Ideas **(a)** Why did the horse spiders feel safe on their trip? **(b) Analyze:** How do you think Hoch wants readers to react to the end of the story? **(c) Evaluate:** Is the ending successful? Explain your answer.

4. Integration of Knowledge and Ideas **(a)** Why do the people of Earth and the creatures of Kaan fear each other? **(b)** In what ways are the two worlds similar? *[Connect to the Big Question: Does every conflict have a winner?]*

Reading Skill: Make Inferences

1. What **inference** can you make from the first two sentences of the story?

2. **(a)** What details does the author include about Professor Hugo's clothing? **(b)** What inference can you make about Professor Hugo from these details?

3. What inference did you make when you read that the professor charges one dollar to view the creatures? Explain.

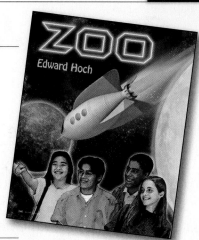

Literary Analysis: Theme

© 4. **Key Ideas and Details** What **theme** does the story convey about people and their differences? In a graphic organizer like this one, list details about the setting and characters that support the theme.

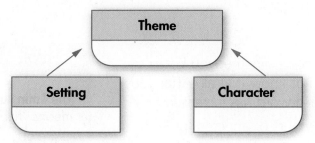

Vocabulary

© **Acquisition and Use** Use your knowledge of the italicized words to answer each question. Explain your responses.

1. What kind of item would be a big *expense*?
2. Do most people use *interplanetary* travel?
3. If a student *babbled* in class, would the teacher be happy?
4. What person, event, or achievement do you look at in *awe*?
5. If you feel a sense of *wonderment*, are you bored?
6. What would a person buy to replace old *garments*?

Word Study Use the context of the sentences and what you know about the **Latin suffix -ment** to explain your answers.

1. What type of performance might you watch in *amazement*?
2. What are you expected to do with an *assignment*?

Word Study

The **Latin suffix -ment** means "the act of" or "the state of."

Apply It Explain how the suffix contributes to the meanings of these words. Consult a print or online dictionary if necessary.

movement
government
development

Does every *conflict* have a winner?

Writing About the Big Question

In "Ribbons," a granddaughter and a grandmother struggle to overcome their differences. Use these sentence starters to develop your ideas about the Big Question.

Family members from different generations often **struggle** to

_____.

They can come to an **understanding** if they _____.

While You Read Look for ways that the characters work to understand each other better.

Vocabulary

Read each word and its definition. Decide whether you know the word well, know it a little bit, or do not know it at all. After you read, see how your knowledge of each word has increased.

- **sensitive** (sen´ sə tiv) *adj.* easily hurt or affected (p. 348) *Sunburned skin is very sensitive.* sensitivity *n.* sensation *n.* sensory *adj.*

- **meek** (mēk) *adj.* timid; not willing to argue (p. 348) *The meek man allowed two people to cut in front of him in line.* meekly, *adv.* meekness *n.*

- **coax** (kōks) *v.* use gentle persuasion (p. 348) *Jack offered the frightened puppy a biscuit to coax him into the water.* coaxingly *adv.* coaxer *n.* coaxed *v.*

- **laborious** (lə bôr´ ē əs) *adj.* taking much work or effort (p. 348) *Ian made cake from scratch, even though it was laborious.* laboriously *adv.* labor *n.*

- **exertion** (eg zʉr´shən) *n.* physical work (p. 349) *The exertion of rowing the boat exhausted Tim.* exert *v.* exerted *v.*

- **furrowed** (fʉr´ ōd) *v.* wrinkled (p. 355) *Her brow was furrowed in concentration during the test.* furrow *n.*

Word Study

The **Latin suffix -ious** means "full of."

In this story, the grandmother's walking is **laborious**, requiring much labor or work, as she climbs the stairs.

Author of

Ribbons

Laurence Yep was born in San Francisco. He grew up in an apartment above his family's grocery store in an African American neighborhood. During his elementary and middle school years, Yep rode a bus to a bilingual school in Chinatown. He feels that these experiences with different cultures led him to write science fiction and fantasy stories in which characters face new worlds and learn new languages and customs.

Adult's Influence Yep decided to become a professional writer when a high school teacher encouraged him to send out his stories for publication. He is the author of more than forty books, including the Newbery Honor Book *Dragonwings*.

Did You Know?

When Yep was 18, he sold his first story to a science-fiction magazine for a penny a word.

BACKGROUND FOR THE STORY

Cultural Differences

The way people show respect for one another often depends on their cultural background. For example, many people in the United States shake hands upon meeting and look directly into other peoples' eyes. In some cultures, however, this behavior is considered rude. In "Ribbons," a young American girl faces the problem of reaching across cultures to get to know her Chinese grandmother.

Ribbons

Laurence Yep

The sunlight swept over the broad grassy square, across the street, and onto our living room rug. In that bright, warm rectangle of light, I practiced my ballet. Ian, my little brother, giggled and dodged around me while I did my exercises.

A car stopped outside, and Ian rushed to the window. "She's here! She's here!" he shouted excitedly. "Paw-paw's here!" *Paw-paw* is Chinese for grandmother—for "mother's mother."

I squeezed in beside Ian so I could look out the window, too. Dad's head was just disappearing as he leaned into the trunk of the car. A pile of luggage and cardboard boxes wrapped in rope sat by the curb. "Is that all Grandmother's?" I said. I didn't see how it would fit into my old bedroom.

Mom laughed behind me. "We're lucky she had to leave her furniture behind in Hong Kong." Mom had been trying to get her mother to come to San Francisco for years. Grandmother had finally agreed, but only because the British were going to return the city to the Chinese Communists in 1997. Because Grandmother's airfare and legal expenses had been so high,

▲ **Critical Viewing**
How do the pictures on these pages compare to the image you have of Grandmother? Explain. **[Compare and Contrast]**

there wasn't room in the family budget for Madame Oblomov's ballet school. I'd had to stop my daily lessons.

The rear car door opened, and a pair of carved black canes poked out like six-shooters. "Wait, Paw-paw," Dad said, and slammed the trunk shut. He looked sweaty and harassed.

Grandmother, however, was already using her canes to get to her feet. "I'm not helpless," she insisted to Dad.

Ian was relieved. "She speaks English," he said.

"She worked for a British family for years," Mom explained.

Turning, Ian ran toward the stairs. "I've got the door," he cried. Mom and I caught up with him at the front door and made him wait on the porch. "You don't want to knock her over," I said. For weeks, Mom had been rehearsing us for just this moment. Ian was supposed to wait, but in his excitement he began bowing to Grandmother as she struggled up the outside staircase.

Grandmother was a small woman in a padded silk jacket and black slacks. Her hair was pulled back into a bun behind her head. On her small feet she wore a pair of quilted cotton slippers

Paw-paw is Chinese for grandmother — for "mother's mother."

 Reading Check

Why does the narrator have to stop her daily ballet lessons?

shaped like boots, with furred tops that hid her ankles.

"What's wrong with her feet?" I whispered to Mom.

"They've always been that way. And don't mention it," she said. "She's sensitive about them."

I was instantly curious. "But what happened to them?"

"Wise grandchildren wouldn't ask," Mom warned. •

Mom bowed formally as Grandmother reached the porch. "I'm so glad you're here," she said.

Grandmother gazed past us to the stairway leading up to our second-floor apartment. "Why do you have to have so many steps?" she said.

Mom sounded as meek as a child. "I'm sorry, Mother," she said.

Dad tried to change the subject. "That's Stacy, and this little monster is Ian."

"*Joe sun, Paw-paw*," I said. "Good morning, Grandmother." It was afternoon, but that was the only Chinese I knew, and I had been practicing it.

Mother had coached us on a proper Chinese greeting for the last two months, but I thought Grandmother also deserved an American-style bear hug. However, when I tried to put my arms around her and kiss her, she stiffened in surprise. "Nice children don't drool on people," she snapped at me.

To Ian, anything worth doing was worth repeating, so he bowed again. "*Joe sun, Paw-paw.*"

Grandmother brightened in an instant. "He has your eyes," she said to Mom.

Mom bent and hefted Ian into her arms. "Let me show you our apartment. You'll be in Stacy's room."

Grandmother didn't even thank me. Instead, she stumped up the stairs after Mom, trying to coax a smile from Ian, who was staring at her over Mom's shoulder.

Grandmother's climb was long, slow, laborious. *Thump, thump, thump.* Her canes struck the boards as she slowly mounted the steps. It sounded like the slow, steady beat of a mechanical heart.

Mom had told us her mother's story often enough. When Mom's father died, Grandmother had strapped my mother to

Make Inferences
Why might Grandmother have complained about "so many steps"?

Vocabulary
sensitive (sen´ sə tiv) *adj.* easily hurt or affected

meek (mēk) *adj.* timid; not willing to argue

coax (kōks) *v.* use gentle persuasion

laborious (lə bôr´ ē əs) *adj.* taking much work or effort

her back and walked across China to Hong Kong to escape the Communists who had taken over her country. I had always thought her trek was heroic, but it seemed even braver when I realized how wobbly she was on her feet.

I was going to follow Grandmother, but Dad waved me down to the sidewalk. "I need you to watch your grandmother's things until I finish bringing them up," he said. He took a suitcase in either hand and set off, catching up with Grandmother at the foot of the first staircase.

While I waited for him to come back, I inspected Grandmother's pile of belongings. The boxes, webbed with tight cords, were covered with words in Chinese and English. I could almost smell their exotic scent, and in my imagination I pictured sunlit waters lapping at picturesque docks. Hong Kong was probably as exotic to me as America was to Grandmother. Almost without thinking, I began to dance.

Dad came back out, his face red from exertion. "I wish I had half your energy," he said. Crouching, he used the cords to lift a box in each hand.

I pirouetted,[1] and the world spun round and round. "Madame Oblomov said I should still practice every day." I had waited for this day not only for Grandmother's sake but for my own. "Now that Grandmother's here, can I begin my ballet lessons again?" I asked.

Dad turned toward the house. "We'll see, hon."

Disappointment made me protest. "But you said I had to give up the lessons so we could bring her from Hong Kong," I said. "Well, she's here."

Dad hesitated and then set the boxes down. "Try to understand, hon. We've got to set your grandmother up in her own apartment. That's going to take even more money. Don't you want your room back?"

Poor Dad. He looked tired and worried. I should have shut up, but I loved ballet almost as much as I loved him. "Madame put me in the fifth division even though I'm only eleven. If I'm absent much longer, she might make me start over again with the beginners."

"It'll be soon. I promise." He looked guilty as he picked up the boxes and struggled toward the stairs.

---

1. pirouetted (pir´ oo et´ əd) v. whirled around on one foot.

▲ **Critical Viewing**
The shoes on the left
are similar to the ones
that Grandmother
wore in China. How
old do you think
Grandmother was
when she wore these
shoes? **[Speculate]**

Dad had taken away the one hope that had kept me going during my exile[2] from Madame. Suddenly I felt lost, and the following weeks only made me more confused. Mom started laying down all sorts of new rules. First, we couldn't run around or make noise because Grandmother had to rest. Then we couldn't watch our favorite TV shows because Grandmother couldn't understand them. Instead, we had to watch Westerns on one of the cable stations because it was easier for her to figure out who was the good guy and who was the bad one.

Worst of all, Ian got all of her attention—and her candy and anything else she could bribe him with. It finally got to me on

---

2. exile (eg´ zīl) *n.* a forced absence.

a warm Sunday afternoon a month after she had arrived. I'd just returned home from a long walk in the park with some friends. I was looking forward to something cool and sweet, when I found her giving Ian an ice cream bar I'd bought for myself. "But that was my ice cream bar," I complained as he gulped it down.

"Big sisters need to share with little brothers," Grandmother said, and she patted him on the head to encourage him to go on eating.

When I complained to Mom about how Grandmother was spoiling Ian, she only sighed. "He's a boy, Stacy. Back in China, boys are everything."

It wasn't until I saw Grandmother and Ian together the next day that I thought I really understood why she treated him so much better. She was sitting on a kitchen chair with her head bent over next to his. She had taught Ian enough Chinese so that they could hold short, simple conversations. With their faces so close, I could see how much alike they were.

Ian and I both have the same brown eyes, but his hair is black, while mine is brown, like Dad's. In fact, everything about Ian looks more Chinese. Except for the shape of my eyes, I look as Caucasian as Dad. And yet people sometimes stare at me as if I were a freak. I've always told myself that it's because they're ignorant and never learned manners, but it was really hard to have my own grandmother make me feel that way.

Even so, I kept telling myself: Grandmother is a hero. She saved my mother. She'll like me just as much as she likes Ian once she gets to know me. And, I thought in a flash, the best way to know a person is to know what she loves. For me, that was the ballet.

Ever since Grandmother had arrived, I'd been practicing my ballet privately in the room I now shared with Ian. Now I got out the special box that held my satin toe shoes. I had been so proud when Madame said I was ready to use them. I was the youngest girl on pointe[3] at Madame's school. As I lifted them out, the satin ribbons fluttered down around my wrists as if in a welcoming caress. I slipped one of the shoes onto my foot, but when I tried to tie the ribbons around my ankles, the ribbons came off in my hands.

---

3. **on pointe** (pwant) dancing on the tip of the toe (of the ballet shoe).

Theme
What does Mom's comment tell you about the treatment of boys in China? What message about life do these details suggest?

Reading Check
How do things change when Grandmother moves into the house?

I could have asked Mom to help me reattach them, but then I remembered that at one time Grandmother had supported her family by being a seamstress. •

Grandmother was sitting in the big recliner in the living room. She stared uneasily out the window as if she were gazing not upon the broad, green lawn of the square but upon a Martian desert.

"Paw-paw," I said, "can you help me?"

Grandmother gave a start when she turned around and saw the ribbons dangling from my hand. Then she looked down at my bare feet, which were callused from three years of daily lessons. When she looked back at the satin ribbons, it was with a hate and disgust that I had never seen before. "Give those to me." She held out her hand.

I clutched the ribbons tightly against my stomach. "Why?"

"They'll ruin your feet." She lunged toward me and tried to snatch them away.

Angry and bewildered, I retreated a few steps and showed her the shoe. "No, they're for dancing!"

All Grandmother could see, though, was the ribbons. She managed to totter to her feet without the canes and almost fell forward on her face. Somehow, she regained her balance. Arms reaching out, she stumbled clumsily after me. "Lies!" she said.

"It's the truth!" I backed up so fast that I bumped into Mom as she came running from the kitchen.

Mom immediately assumed it was my fault. "Stop yelling at your grandmother!" she said.

By this point, I was in tears. "She's taken everything else. Now she wants my toe-shoe ribbons."

Grandmother panted as she leaned on Mom. "How could you do that to your own daughter?"

"It's not like you think," Mom tried to explain.

However, Grandmother was too upset to listen. "Take them away!"

Make Inferences
What can you infer about Grandmother based on her reaction to the ribbons?

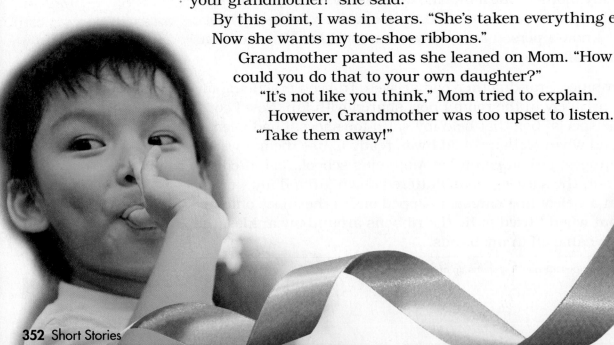

Grandmother gave a start when she turned around and saw the ribbons dangling from my hand.

Mom helped Grandmother back to her easy chair. "You don't understand," Mom said.

All Grandmother did was stare at the ribbons as she sat back down in the chair. "Take them away. Burn them. Bury them."

Mom sighed. "Yes, Mother."

As Mom came over to me, I stared at her in amazement. "Aren't you going to stand up for me?"

But she acted as if she wanted to break any ties between us. "Can't you see how worked up Paw-paw is?" she whispered. "She won't listen to reason. Give her some time. Let her cool off." She worked the ribbons away from my stunned fingers. Then she also took the shoe.

For the rest of the day, Grandmother just turned away every time Mom and I tried to raise the subject. It was as if she didn't want to even think about satin ribbons.

That evening, after the dozenth attempt, I finally said to Mom, "She's so weird. What's so bad about satin ribbons?"

"She associates them with something awful that happened to her," Mom said.

That puzzled me even more. "What was that?"

She shook her head. "I'm sorry. She made me promise never to talk about it to anyone." ●

The next morning, I decided that if Grandmother was

Spiral Review
Character Based on the scene with the ribbons, list one detail you learn about each of these characters: Grandmother, Mom, and Stacy.

Reading Check

How does Grandmother react when she sees the ribbons from the ballet shoes?

going to be mean to me, then I would be mean to her. I began to ignore her. When she entered a room I was in, I would deliberately turn around and leave.

For the rest of the day, things got more and more tense. Then I happened to go into the bathroom early that evening. The door wasn't locked, so I thought it was unoccupied, but Grandmother was sitting fully clothed on the edge of the bathtub. Her slacks were rolled up to her knees and she had her feet soaking in a pan of water.

"Don't you know how to knock?" she snapped, and dropped a towel over her feet.

However, she wasn't quick enough, because I saw her bare feet for the first time. Her feet were like taffy that someone had stretched out and twisted. Each foot bent downward in a way that feet were not meant to, and her toes stuck out at odd angles, more like lumps than toes. I didn't think she had all ten of them, either.

"What happened to your feet?" I whispered in shock.

Looking ashamed, Grandmother flapped a hand in the air for me to go. "None of your business. Now get out."

"Don't you know how to knock?" she snapped, and dropped a towel over her feet.

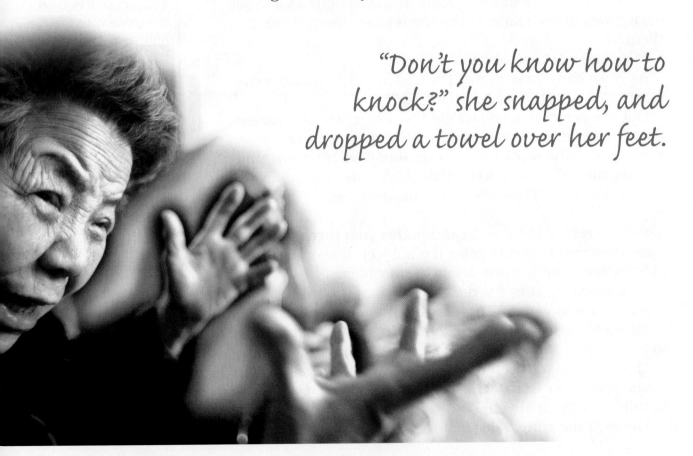

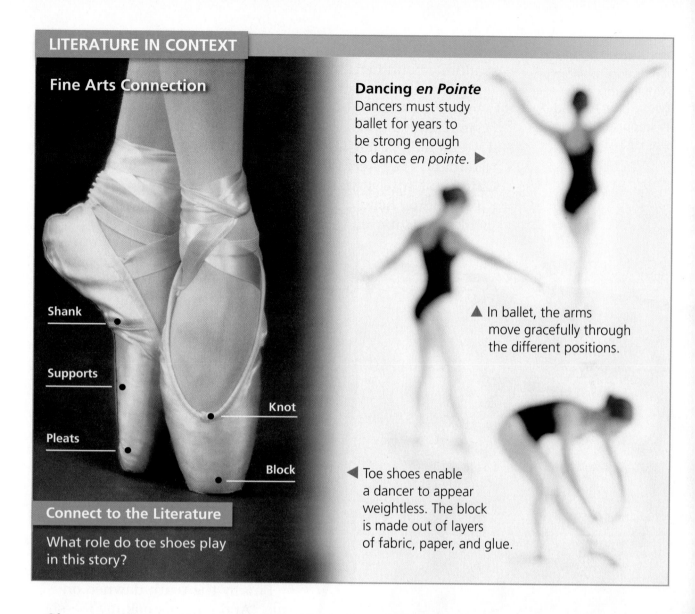

Fine Arts Connection

Shank

Supports

Pleats

Knot

Block

Connect to the Literature

What role do toe shoes play in this story?

Dancing *en Pointe*
Dancers must study ballet for years to be strong enough to dance *en pointe*. ▶

▲ In ballet, the arms move gracefully through the different positions.

◀ Toe shoes enable a dancer to appear weightless. The block is made out of layers of fabric, paper, and glue.

She must have said something to Mom, though, because that night Mom came in and sat on my bed. Ian was outside playing with Grandmother. "Your grandmother's very upset, Stacy," Mom said.

"I didn't mean to look," I said. "It was horrible." Even when I closed my eyes, I could see her mangled feet.

I opened my eyes when I felt Mom's hand on my shoulder. "She was so ashamed of them that she didn't like even me to see them," she said.

"What happened to them?" I wondered.

Mom's forehead furrowed as if she wasn't sure how to explain things. "There was a time back in China when people thought women's feet had to be shaped a certain way to look

Vocabulary
furrowed (fur´ōd) *v.* wrinkled

Reading Check
What did Stacy see that made Grandmother upset?

beautiful. When a girl was about five, her mother would gradually bend her toes under the sole of her foot."

"Ugh." Just thinking about it made my own feet ache. "Her own mother did that to her?"

Mom smiled apologetically. "Her mother and father thought it would make their little girl attractive so she could marry a rich man. They were still doing it in some of the back areas of China long after it was outlawed in the rest of the country."

I shook my head. "There's nothing lovely about those feet."

"I know. But they were usually bound up in silk ribbons."

Mom brushed some of the hair from my eyes. "Because they were a symbol of the old days, Paw-paw undid the ribbons as soon as we were free in Hong Kong—even though they kept back the pain."

I was even more puzzled now. "How did the ribbons do that?"

Mom began to brush my hair with quick, light strokes. "The ribbons kept the blood from circulating freely and bringing more feeling to her feet. Once the ribbons were gone, her feet ached. They probably still do."

I rubbed my own foot in sympathy. "But she doesn't complain."

"That's how tough she is," Mom said.

Finally the truth dawned on me. "And she mistook my toe-shoe ribbons for her old ones."

Mom lowered the brush and nodded solemnly. "And she didn't want you to go through the same pain she had."

I guess Grandmother loved me in her own way. When she came into the bedroom with Ian later that evening, I didn't leave. However, she tried to ignore me—as if I had become tainted by her secret.

When Ian demanded a story, I sighed. "All right. But only one."

Naturally, Ian chose the fattest story he could, which was my old collection of fairy tales by Hans Christian Andersen. Years of reading had cracked the spine so that the book fell open automatically in his hands to the story that had been my favorite when I was small. It was the original story of "The Little Mermaid"—not the cartoon. The picture illustrating the tale showed the mermaid posed like a ballerina in the middle of the throne room.

"This one," Ian said, and pointed to the picture of the Little Mermaid.

When Grandmother and Ian sat down on my bed, I began to read. However, when I got to the part where the Little Mermaid could walk on land, I stopped.

Ian was impatient. "Come on, read," he ordered, patting the page.

"After that," I went on, "each step hurt her as if she were walking on a knife." I couldn't help looking up at Grandmother.

This time she was the one to pat the page. "Go on. Tell me more about the mermaid."

So I went on reading to the very end, where the Little Mermaid changes into sea foam. "That's a dumb ending," Ian said. "Who wants to be pollution?"

"Sea foam isn't pollution. It's just bubbles," I explained. "The important thing was that she wanted to walk even though it hurt."

"I would rather have gone on swimming," Ian insisted.

"But maybe she wanted to see new places and people by going on the land," Grandmother said softly. "If she had kept her tail, the land people would have thought she was odd. They might even have made fun of her."

When she glanced at her own feet, I thought she might be talking about herself—so I seized my chance. "My satin ribbons aren't like your old silk ones. I use them to tie my toe shoes on when I dance." Setting the book down, I got out my other shoe. "Look."

Grandmother fingered the dangling ribbons and then pointed at my bare feet. "But you already have calluses there."

I began to dance before Grandmother could stop me. After a minute, I struck a pose on half-toe. "See? I can move fine."

She took my hand and patted it clumsily. I think it was the first time she had showed me any sign of affection. "When I

Theme
What details in this paragraph support a theme of understanding cultural differences?

Reading Check
What happened to Grandmother's feet when she was a child?

saw those ribbons, I didn't want you feeling pain like I do."

I covered her hands with mine. "I just wanted to show you what I love best—dancing."

"And I love my children," she said. I could hear the ache in her voice. "And my grandchildren. I don't want anything bad to happen to you."

Suddenly I felt as if there were an invisible ribbon binding us, tougher than silk and satin, stronger even than steel; and it joined her to Mom and Mom to me.

I wanted to hug her so badly that I just did. Though she was stiff at first, she gradually softened in my arms.

"'Let me have my ribbons and my shoes," I said in a low voice. "Let me dance."

"Yes, yes," she whispered fiercely.

I felt something on my cheek and realized she was crying, and then I began crying, too.

"So much to learn," she said, and began hugging me back. "So much to learn."

Make Inferences
Why do you think the narrator and her grandmother are crying?

Critical Thinking

© **1. Key Ideas and Details** How are differences in generation and culture revealed in this story? Support your answer.

© **2. Key Ideas and Details** **(a)** Identify two examples from the story that show how Stacy's life changes when Grandmother arrives. **(b) Analyze Cause and Effect:** For each, tell how you would expect Stacy to feel about these changes. **(c) Evaluate:** Discuss with a partner whether or not you sympathize with Stacy. Then discuss how hearing your partner's responses did or did not change your view.

© **3. Key Ideas and Details** **(a)** How does Stacy learn the secret of Grandmother's feet? **(b) Connect:** How does Stacy's attitude change after her mother explains older Chinese customs?

© **4. Integration of Knowledge and Ideas** **(a)** How do Grandmother and Stacy finally overcome their conflict and begin to understand and appreciate one another? **(b)** What lessons does each character learn? *[Connect to the Big Question: Does every conflict have a winner?]*

Cite textual evidence to support your responses.

Reading Skill: Make Inferences

1. The author describes Grandmother's arrival by saying, "The rear car door opened, and a pair of carved black canes poked out like six-shooters." Why do you think he includes those details instead of simply introducing the character by name?

2. Grandmother carried her daughter on her back to Hong Kong to escape her enemy. What questions might you ask to help you make an **inference** about Grandmother's life?

Literary Analysis: Theme

Ⓒ **3. Key Ideas and Details** What **theme** does the story convey about understanding between grandparents and grandchildren? In a graphic organizer like this one, list details about the setting and characters that support the theme.

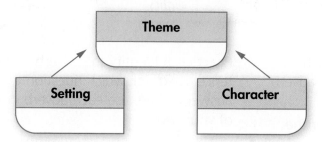

Vocabulary

Ⓒ **Acquisition and Use** Use your knowledge of the italicized words to answer each question. Explain your responses.

1. If a girl is *meek*, how might she answer questions in class?

2. How would you *coax* someone to go somewhere with you?

3. What subject in school is the most *laborious* for you?

4. What is your least favorite type of *exertion*?

5. If your forehead is *furrowed*, how might you feel?

6. If someone is *sensitive*, is it a good idea to tease him?

Word Study Use the context of the sentences and what you know about the **Latin suffix -ious** to explain your answer to each question.

1. If a meal is *nutritious*, what kinds of foods does it include?

2. Who do you know who has *ambitious* goals?

Word Study

The **Latin suffix -ious** means "full of."

Apply It Explain how the suffix **-ious** contributes to the meanings of these words. Consult a dictionary if necessary.

glorious
gracious
hilarious

Integrated Language Skills

Zoo • Ribbons

Conventions: Adverbs

An **adverb** is a word that modifies or describes a verb, an adjective, or another adverb.

Adverbs provide information by answering the question *how? when? where? how often?* or *to what extent?* Many adverbs end in the suffix *-ly*. The chart shows examples:

How?	When?	Where?	How Often?	To What Extent?
She paced *nervously*.	I will finish it *later*.	The robins flew *away*.	Linda *always* laughs.	Luke moved *slightly*.

Practice A Identify the adverb in each sentence. Then, tell which word the adverb modifies.

1. The people waited anxiously for the Professor to lift the sides of the spaceship.

2. The crowds slowly walked by the creatures' cages.

3. Professor Hugo brought the creatures to Chicago annually.

4. When returning home, the little creature thoroughly explained the adventure to his mother.

5. She had never been on an interplanetary trip.

© **Reading Application** In "Zoo," find two sentences with adverbs.

Practice B Identify the adverb in each sentence. Next, tell which question the adverb answers. Then, use each adverb in a sentence of your own.

1. Ian greeted his grandmother courteously when she arrived.

2. Grandmother usually chose to play with Ian instead of showing interest in Stacy.

3. Stacy's mother finally explained Grandmother's strong reaction to the ribbons.

4. I wanted to hug her so badly that I just did.

© **Writing Application** List at least five adverbs that can be used to revise this sentence: *They sometimes talked to each other.* Discuss the effect of each change.

PH **WRITING COACH** | Further instruction and practice are available in *Prentice Hall Writing Coach*.

Writing

Argument Write a **letter to the editor** of a local newspaper as a response to either "Zoo" or "Ribbons." If you write in response to "Zoo," take a position about whether zoo animals should live in natural habitats instead of cages. If you write in response to "Ribbons," take a position about whether young people should participate in extra schooling by taking art classes or participating in sports.

- First, consider both sides of the issue and list at least one reason in support of each one. Then, choose which position to support.
- As you draft, state and support your position. Consult credible sources to find logical reasons and evidence that will convince readers to take your side.
- E-mail your letter to the editor of a newspaper.

Grammar Application Use adverbs correctly in your writing.

Writing Workshop: *Work in Progress*

Prewriting for Narration Choose two ideas from the Conflict List in your writing portfolio and jot down ideas about how each might be resolved. Save the Resolution Ideas List for later development.

Research and Technology

Build and Present Knowledge Create a **poster** based on the story you read.

- If you read "Zoo," your poster should focus on a zoo in your town, city, or state. Provide zoo hours, admission fees, special exhibits, and the animals you would recommend others visit.
- If you read "Ribbons," your poster should give information about the basic arm and foot positions used in ballet and the benefits of learning to dance.

Follow these steps to complete the assignment:

- Identify the topic of your poster. Then, jot down questions to guide your research.
- Develop a search plan. Then, use the Internet and library resources to conduct your research. Use photos, drawings, and diagrams to illustrate your poster.
- Present your poster and research to the class. Add music or sound effects to emphasize key points.

Common Core State Standards

L.7.1, L.7.4.b, L.7.6; W.7.1.a, W.7.1.b, W.7; SL.7.5
[For the full wording of the standards, see page 336.]

Use this prewriting activity to prepare for the **Writing Workshop** on page 384.

PHLit Online!
www.PHLitOnline.com
- Interactive graphic organizers
- Grammar tutorial
- Interactive journals

Test Practice: Reading

Make Inferences

Fiction Selection

Directions: *Read the selection. Then, answer the questions.*

Tina skipped down the boardwalk and onto the sand. The morning sun glistened on the waves, and a warm breeze stirred the dune grass. Humming quietly to herself, Tina walked along, picking up interesting shells as she went. She was assembling a collection for her grandmother, who liked to use them in craft projects. Later, Tina would wrap the shells carefully to prevent them from breaking. Then, she would put them in a box and mail them off to her grandmother. In the meantime, she would enjoy her beautiful surroundings, because tomorrow her family would head back home. She would be glad to see her friends after a two-week absence, but Tina really hated to think of leaving.

1. From details in the first two sentences, what can you infer about the story's setting?
- **A.** The story is set in a park.
- **B.** The story is set at the beach.
- **C.** The story is set near the mountains.
- **D.** The story is set on an island.

2. Which two details *best* help you infer that Tina is on vacation?
- **A.** She is in a place with warm breezes, and she hums to herself.
- **B.** She skips down the boardwalk, and she picks up shells.
- **C.** She is on the sand, and she mails a package to her grandmother.
- **D.** She will go home tomorrow, and she has been away for two weeks.

3. What can you infer about shells from the way Tina packs them to send to her grandmother?
- **A.** Shells are delicate.
- **B.** Shells are hard to find.
- **C.** Shells come in many colors.
- **D.** Shells are popular keepsakes.

4. Based on details in the passage, which word *best* describes how Tina feels at the beginning of the story?
- **A.** contented
- **B.** nervous
- **C.** overjoyed
- **D.** bored

Writing for Assessment

Write a paragraph explaining whether you think that Tina enjoyed her vacation. Use details from the story to support your inference.

Nonfiction Selection

Directions: *Read the selection. Then, answer the questions.*

People collect seashells for many reasons—to decorate their homes, to make crafts, or to impress their friends. Some people find shells while walking along the seashore. Others buy shells at souvenir shops, which are often located in seaside communities.

These souvenir shops offer a variety of small, medium, and large seashells for sale. The shops also sell coral, starfish, sea horses, and sand dollars. Craftspeople can often find mini craft shells as small as a quarter-inch long. The stores usually sell these shells by the pound.

Prices for seashells can vary greatly. A half-inch starfish might cost as little as thirty cents, while a 400-pound Tridacna Gigas clam shell might cost over six hundred dollars.

1. Which of the following details helps you infer that customers can buy large quantities of shells from souvenir shops?
   A. The shops sell large shells.
   B. The shops sell shells by the pound.
   C. The shops sell very expensive shells.
   D. The shops sell starfish.

2. Based on details in the passage, what is a souvenir shop's main reason for collecting and selling shells?
   A. to clean up the seashore
   B. to create an attractive display
   C. to help craftspeople
   D. to make money

3. What inferences can you make based on details in the passage?
   A. People like to collect one type of shell.
   B. It is easy to find shells on the sand.
   C. People buy many types of shells.
   D. Shells are only bought by tourists.

4. Which of the following inferences is *not* supported by details in the passage?
   A. Seashells come in many shapes and sizes.
   B. Some people enjoy making crafts with seashells.
   C. Some people think seashells are beautiful.
   D. People who collect seashells like to swim in the ocean.

Writing for Assessment

Connecting Across Texts
Write a description of how Tina's grandmother might react if she were to visit a souvenir shop like the one in the passage. Use details from both passages to support your ideas.

www.PHLitOnline.com
- Online practice
- Instant feedback

Reading for Information

Analyzing Expository Texts

Government Publication

Web Site

**Common Core
State Standards**

Reading Informational Text
1. Cite several pieces of textual evidence to support analysis of what the text says explicitly as well as inferences drawn from the text.

Language
4.c. Consult general and specialized reference materials, both print and digital, to find the pronunciation of a word or determine or clarify its precise meaning or its part of speech.

6. Acquire and use accurately grade-appropriate general academic and domain-specific words and phrases; gather vocabulary knowledge when considering a word or phrase important to comprehension or expression.

Reading Skill: Connecting Ideas to Make Inferences and Generalizations

An **inference** is a logical conclusion about information that is not directly stated. It is based on details in the text that are stated explicitly, or directly, and your own knowledge and experience. When you apply an inference in a general or nonspecific way, you are making a generalization. A **generalization** is a broad statement that applies to many examples and is supported by evidence. For example, a person who has successfully trained many dogs might make the generalization that all dogs are trainable. Use a chart like the one shown to record evidence that supports a generalization.

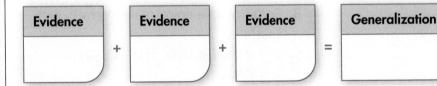

Content-Area Vocabulary

These words appear in the selections that follow. You may also encounter them in other content-area texts.

- **exertion** (eg zur´ shən) *n.* physical or mental effort
- **calories** (kal´ ə rēz) *n.* units used for measuring the energy produced by food
- **infrastructure** (in´ frə struk´ chər) *n.* systems, such as roads, schools, power plants, and so on, that allow a community to continue to exist and grow

Walking for Exercise and Pleasure

Government Publication

Features:

- information provided by a government office or agency free of charge
- content published in print or online
- material available to all people

The President's Council on Physical Fitness and Sports

Walking: An Exercise for All Ages

Walking is easily the most popular form of exercise. Other activities generate more conversation and media coverage, but none of them approaches walking in number of participants. Approximately half of the 165 million American adults (18 years of age and older) claim they exercise regularly, and the number who walk for exercise is increasing every year.

Walking is the only exercise in which the rate of participation does not decline in the middle and later years. In a national survey, the highest percentage of regular walkers (39.4%) for any group was found among men 65 years of age and older.

Unlike tennis, running, skiing, and other activities that have gained great popularity fairly recently, walking has been widely practiced as a recreational and fitness activity throughout recorded history.

Classical and early English literature seems to have been written largely by men who were prodigious walkers, and Emerson and Thoreau helped carry on the tradition in America. Among American presidents, the most famous walkers included Jefferson, Lincoln, and Truman.

Walking: The Slower, Surer Way to Fitness

People walk for many reasons: for pleasure . . . to rid themselves of tensions . . . to find solitude . . . or to get from one place to another. Nearly everyone who walks regularly does so at least in part because of a conviction that it is good exercise.

Often dismissed in the past as being "too easy" to be taken seriously, walking recently has gained new respect as a means of improving

> This subheading contains a **generalization** about exercise.

> The information in this passage supports an **inference** that walking is popular among older men.

> This line tells you which office of the government published the document.

> Topic sentences such as this one can often serve as evidence to support an **inference** or **generalization**.

physical fitness. Studies show that, when done briskly on a regular schedule, it can improve the body's ability to consume oxygen during **exertion**, lower the resting heart rate, reduce blood pressure, and increase the efficiency of the heart and lungs. It also helps burn excess **calories**.

Walking burns approximately the same amount of calories per mile as does running, a fact particularly appealing to those who find it difficult to sustain the jarring effects of long distance jogging. Briskly walking one mile in 15 minutes burns just about the same number of calories as jogging an equal distance in 8½ minutes. In weight-bearing activities like walking, heavier individuals will burn more calories than lighter persons. For example, studies show that a 110-pound person burns about half as many calories as a 216-pound person walking at the same pace for the same distance.

In addition to the qualities it has in common with other activities, walking has several unique advantages. Some of these are:

Almost everyone can do it.
You don't have to take lessons to learn how to walk. Probably all you need to do to become a serious walker is step up your pace and distance and walk more often.

> Given the details listed here, you might **infer** that the writer enjoys walking.

You can do it almost anywhere.
All you have to do to find a place to walk is step outside your door. Almost any sidewalk, street, road, trail, park, field, or shopping mall will do. The variety of settings available is one of the things that makes walking such a practical and pleasurable activity.

You can do it almost anytime.
You don't have to find a partner or get a team together to walk, so you can set your own schedule. Weather doesn't pose the same problems and uncertainties that it does in many sports. Walking is not a seasonal activity, and you can do it in extreme temperatures that would rule out other activities.

It doesn't cost anything.
You don't have to pay fees or join a private club to become a walker. The only equipment required is a sturdy, comfortable pair of shoes.

Listen to Your Body

Listen to your body when you walk. If you develop dizziness, pain, nausea, or any other unusual symptom, slow down or stop. If the problem persists, see your physician before walking again.

> The information in the final paragraph presents a **generalization**.

The most important thing is simply to set aside part of each day and walk. No matter what your age or condition, it's a practice that can make you healthier and happier.

Web site

Features:
- full color, interactive presentation of information
- a home page links to other documents
- content available to all with Internet access

Safe Routes to School
It's Happening in Metro Atlanta

This photo allows you to infer that many students in Atlanta are walking to school.

Many of us over 30 remember walking or biking to school as an important part of childhood—a time to stretch our legs, explore our neighborhoods, make friends, feel the wind.... Many children today no longer have those opportunities. Safe Routes to School programs are developing in many parts of the world to bring that experience back to kids.

The Metro Atlanta Safe Routes to School Demonstration Project is the first comprehensive program to promote walking and biking to school in the state of Georgia. Our pilot project is making environments around schools safer so that more and more kids— and adults!—can walk and bike on their journeys to and from school. Our research will be compiled into a guidebook that will help other communities establish Safe Routes to School programs across Georgia.

The Atlanta Bicycle Campaign is now in its third year of this 4-year project. Many thanks to our partners of the Metro Atlanta Safe Routes to School Coalition and to our funders, the Georgia Department of Transportation/Federal Highway Administration!

This sentence supports the inference that the bicycle campaign has been successful.

Click here to learn more about the Safe Routes to School program.

Click here to learn about some of the tools we have used to implement our program.

The word *Demonstration* supports the inference that other communities will use Atlanta as a model.

The Metro Atlanta Safe Routes to School Demonstration Project

What are the goals of the Metro Atlanta Demonstration Project?

The project has 3 specific goals:

1. To improve the safety of children who walk and bicycle to and from school;

2. To increase the numbers of school community members who walk and/or bicycle safely to and from school;

3. To prepare a guidebook for Safe Routes to School in Georgia.

How is the project carried out?

The project uses the "4 E's" approach:

Engineering—focusing on **infrastructure** improvements around the school that support walking and bicycling;

Enforcement—focusing on legal enforcement of traffic laws as well as school policies that support walking and bicycling;

Education—focusing on bicycle and pedestrian safety training of children and adults in the school community;

Encouragement—focusing on fun, educational, and motivational activities and events that promote safe walking and bicycling.

Where and when is the project taking place?

This project is working at four school sites, two in DeKalb County, representing an urban environment, and two in Gwinnett County, representing a suburban environment.

What will the demonstration project accomplish?

This is a demonstration project for the state of Georgia. At the conclusion of our work with the schools, we will produce a guidebook for use by others interested in establishing a Safe Routes to School program in their communities in Georgia.

Do you want to start a Safe Routes to School program in your neighborhood?

Click here to find out how.

Comparing Expository Texts

1. Key Ideas and Details (a) Make one **inference** and one **generalization** about walking based on each text. Use the graphic organizer on page 364 to support your generalizations with evidence. **(b)** How are the generalizations you made about walking from each text similar to and different from each other?

Content-Area Vocabulary

2. (a) Remove the suffix *-ion* from the word *exertion*. Using a print or online dictionary, explain how removing the suffix alters the meaning of the word and its part of speech. **(b)** Use the word *exert* in a sentence that shows its meaning.

⏱ Timed Writing

Explanatory Text: Directions

Format
To draw a map, first consider the scale by estimating distances between points. Provide a legend, or key, to explain your color coding.

Suppose that you are organizing a Walk to School Week for the students in your neighborhood. Decide on a meeting place, and write clear directions from that spot to the front door of your school. Identify the streets, landmarks, and distances between points in your directions. In addition, draw a detailed map with important information clearly labeled. (30 minutes)

Academic Vocabulary
When you *identify* something, you recognize and bring attention to it.

5-Minute Planner

Complete these steps before you begin to write:

1. Read the prompt carefully, noting that there are two assignments that you must complete—a set of directions and a map.

2. In a rough sketch, map out the location of the school, the meeting place, and streets and landmarks between them.

3. Determine the walking path. Note where you turn left or right and where you cross streets. Estimate the distances between key points. **TIP** If possible, use a map of your town or city to help identify street names and estimate distances.

4. Use your notes and rough map as you draft your directions.

Comparing Irony

Irony is a literary element that involves a contradiction or contrast of some kind. In literature, writers often use irony to entertain and to convey a theme, or message.

- In **situational irony**, something takes place that is the opposite of what we expect to happen. For example, people note the irony when a fire station burns down.

- In **verbal irony,** a speaker or character says something that contradicts what he or she actually means. A jealous runner-up who says to a rival, "You deserved the medal" is speaking ironically if she really means, "You deserved the *second-place* medal."

As you read these stories, ask yourself questions like these to help you understand the author's use of situational irony:

- What details lead me to expect a certain outcome?

- What happened instead of the outcome I expected?

- Does irony in the story help convey a message or insight about life?

Use a chart like this to record your observations.

**Common Core
State Standards**

**Reading Literature
3.** Analyze how particular elements of a story or drama interact.

**Writing
2.a.** Introduce a topic clearly, previewing what is to follow; organize ideas, concepts, and information, using strategies such as definition, classification, comparison/contrast, and cause/effect; include formatting, graphics, and multimedia when useful to aiding comprehension. *(Timed Writing)*

Story		
Expected Outcome		
Actual Ending		
Clues in Story		

- Vocabulary flashcards
- Interactive journals
- More about the authors
- Selection audio
- Interactive graphic organizers

www.PHLitOnline.com

Writing About the Big Question

Both of these stories have events that take characters—and readers—by surprise. Use this sentence starter to develop your ideas.

Unexpected events can **challenge** people by _____.

Meet the Authors

O. Henry (1862–1910)

Author of "After Twenty Years"

O. Henry is the pen name of William Sydney Porter. He is known for his warm, witty short stories featuring ordinary people. Porter held many jobs, including working on a sheep ranch, in a bank, in a newspaper office, and as the publisher of a humor magazine. Later, Porter was sentenced to prison for stealing bank funds, a crime he may not have committed.

Finding a New Identity While serving time, Porter wrote short stories. On his release, he moved to New York City and started a career as a writer. He used the name O. Henry to shield his identity. Many of his 300 stories are inspired by his time in prison, where he gained an understanding of people on both sides of the law.

Shinichi Hoshi (1926–1997)

Author of "He—y, Come On Ou—t!"

Shinichi Hoshi, a Japanese writer, is best known for his "short-short stories," in which he makes observations about human nature and society. Hoshi wrote more than a thousand short-short stories as well as longer fantasy stories, detective stories, biographies, and travel articles. In addition, he was one of the first Japanese science-fiction writers. Hoshi's stories have been translated into many languages, and devoted readers enjoy their unexpected plot turns.

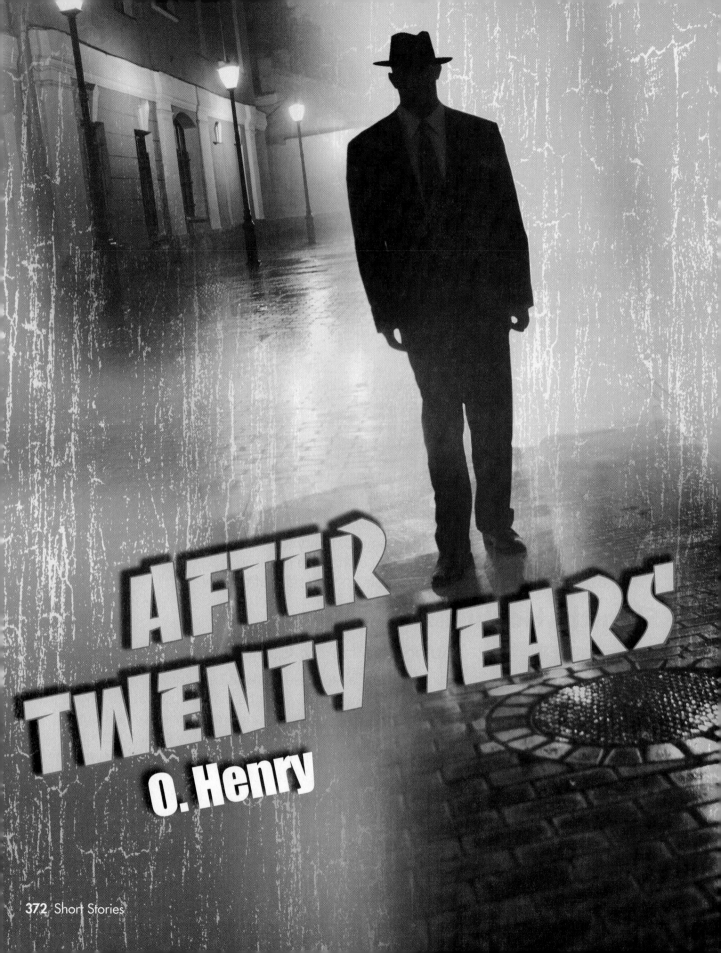

AFTER TWENTY YEARS

O. Henry

The policeman on the beat moved up the avenue impressively. The impressiveness was habitual and not for show, for spectators were few. The time was barely 10 o'clock at night, but chilly gusts of wind with a taste of rain in them had well nigh[1] depeopled the streets.

Trying doors as he went, twirling his club with many intricate and artful movements, turning now and then to cast his watchful eye down the pacific thoroughfare,[2] the officer, with his stalwart form and slight swagger, made a fine picture of a guardian of the peace. The vicinity was one that kept early hours. Now and then you might see the lights of a cigar store or of an all-night lunch counter; but the majority of the doors belonged to business places that had long since been closed.

When about midway of a certain block the policeman suddenly slowed his walk. In the doorway of a darkened hardware store a man leaned, with an unlighted cigar in his mouth. As the policeman walked up to him the man spoke up quickly.

"It's all right, officer," he said, reassuringly. "I'm just waiting for a friend. It's an appointment made twenty years ago. Sounds a little funny to you, doesn't it? Well, I'll explain if you'd like to make certain it's all straight. About that long ago there used to be a restaurant where this store stands—'Big Joe' Brady's restaurant."

"Until five years ago," said the policeman. "It was torn down then."

The man in the doorway struck a match and lit his cigar. The light showed a pale, square-jawed face with keen eyes, and a little white scar near his right eyebrow. His scarfpin was a large diamond, oddly set.

"Twenty years ago tonight," said the man, "I dined here at 'Big Joe' Brady's with Jimmy Wells, my best chum, and the finest chap in the world. He and I were raised here in New York, just like two brothers, together. I was eighteen and Jimmy was twenty. The next morning I was to start for the

---

1. **well nigh** *adv.* very nearly.
2. **pacific thoroughfare** calm street.

Vocabulary

spectators
(spek´ tāt´ erz) *n.*
people who watch

intricate (in´ tri kit) *adj.*
complex; detailed

◀ **Critical Viewing**
Based on this picture, what are three words that might describe the story you are about to read? **[Predict]**

✓ Reading
Check
What is the officer doing?

West to make my fortune. You couldn't have dragged Jimmy out of New York; he thought it was the only place on earth. Well, we agreed that night that we would meet here again exactly twenty years from that date and time, no matter what our conditions might be or from what distance we might have to come. We figured that in twenty years each of us ought to have our destiny worked out and our fortunes made, whatever they were going to be."

"It sounds pretty interesting," said the policeman. "Rather a long time between meets, though, it seems to me. Haven't you heard from your friend since you left?"

"Well, yes, for a time we corresponded," said the other. "But after a year or two we lost track of each other. You see, the West is a pretty big proposition, and I kept hustling around over it pretty lively. But I know Jimmy will meet me here if he's alive, for he always was the truest, stanchest old chap in the world. He'll never forget. I came a thousand miles to stand in this door tonight, and it's worth it if my old partner turns up."

The waiting man pulled out a handsome watch, the lids of it set with small diamonds.

"Three minutes to ten," he announced. "It was exactly ten o'clock when we parted here at the restaurant door."

"Did pretty well out West, didn't you?" asked the policeman.

"You bet! I hope Jimmy has done half as well. He was a kind of plodder, though, good fellow as he was. I've had to compete with some of the sharpest wits going to get my pile. A man gets in a groove in New York. It takes the West to put a razor-edge on him."

The policeman twirled his club and took a step or two.

"I'll be on my way. Hope your friend comes around all right. Going to call time on him sharp?"

"I should say not!" said the other. "I'll give him half an hour at least. If Jimmy is alive on earth he'll be here by that time. So long, officer."

"Good-night, sir," said the policeman, passing on along his beat, trying doors as he went.

There was now a fine, cold drizzle falling, and the wind

Vocabulary
destiny (des′ tə nē) *n.* preplanned course of events

Irony
Based on the story so far, do you expect the old friends to reunite? Explain your answer.

had risen from its uncertain puffs into a steady blow. The few foot passengers astir in that quarter hurried dismally and silently along with coat collars turned high and pocketed hands. And in the door of the hardware store the man who had come a thousand miles to fill an appointment, uncertain almost to absurdity,[3] with the friend of his youth, smoked his cigar and waited.

About twenty minutes he waited, and then a tall man in a long overcoat, with collar turned up to his ears, hurried across from the opposite side of the street. He went directly to the waiting man.

"Is that you, Bob?" he asked, doubtfully.

"Is that you, Jimmy Wells?" cried the man in the door.

"Bless my heart!" exclaimed the new arrival, grasping both the other's hands with his own. "It's Bob, sure as fate. I was certain I'd find you here if you were still in existence. Well, well, well!—twenty years is a long time. The old restaurant's gone, Bob; I wish it had lasted, so we could have had another dinner there. How has the West treated you, old man?"

"Bully;[4] it has given me everything I asked it for. You've changed lots, Jimmy. I never thought you were so tall by two or three inches."

"Oh, I grew a bit after I was twenty."

"Doing well in New York, Jimmy?"

"Moderately. I have a position in one of the city departments. Come on, Bob; we'll go around to a place I know of, and have a good long talk about old times."

The two men started up the street, arm in arm. The man from the West, his egotism enlarged by success, was

▲ **Critical Viewing**
Would it be hard to identify an old friend in a setting like this one? Why? **[Explain]**

Irony
Did you expect Jimmy to show up for the meeting? Why or why not?

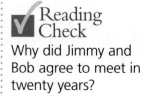

Reading Check
Why did Jimmy and Bob agree to meet in twenty years?

---

3. **absurdity** (ab sur´də tē) *n.* nonsense.
4. **bully** *interj.* very good.

Nighthawks, Edward Hopper, The Art Institute of Chicago

▲ **Critical Viewing**
What details in this painting match the setting of the story? **[Connect]**

Vocabulary
simultaneously
(sī´ məl tā´ nē əs lē) *adv.* at the same time

beginning to outline the history of his career. The other, submerged in his overcoat, listened with interest.

At the corner stood a drug store, brilliant with electric lights. When they came into this glare each of them turned simultaneously to gaze upon the other's face.

The man from the West stopped suddenly and released his arm.

"You're not Jimmy Wells," he snapped. "Twenty years is a long time, but not long enough to change a man's nose from a Roman to a pug."[5]

"It sometimes changes a good man into a bad one," said the tall man. "You've been under arrest for ten minutes, 'Silky' Bob. Chicago thinks you may have dropped over our way and wires us she wants to have a chat with you. Going quietly are you? That's sensible. Now, before we go to the station here's a

---

5. change a man's nose from a Roman to a pug A Roman nose has a high, prominent bridge, but a pug nose is short, thick, and turned up at the end.

note I was asked to hand to you. You may read it here at the window. It's from Patrolman Wells."

The man from the West unfolded the little piece of paper handed him. His hand was steady when he began to read, but it trembled a little by the time he had finished. The note was rather short.

Bob,
I was at the appointed place on time. When you struck the match to light your cigar I saw it was the face of the man wanted in Chicago. Somehow I couldn't do it myself, so I went around and got a plain clothes man to do the job.
Jimmy.

Irony
How does the patrolman's name indicate the irony of the conversation with the policeman at the beginning of this story?

Spiral Review
Conflict What conflict do you think each man felt when Bob was taken to jail?

Critical Thinking

1. **Key Ideas and Details (a)** Where is the story set? **(b) Analyze:** Describe the atmosphere, or mood, using two details from the story.

2. **Key Ideas and Details (a)** How does Bob describe Jimmy's strengths and weaknesses? **(b) Infer:** How did Bob spend his time away from his hometown after he left?

3. **Key Ideas and Details (a)** What evidence shows that both Bob and Jimmy are proud of their accomplishments? **(b) Make a Judgment:** Who has been more successful? Explain your answer.

4. **Integration of Knowledge and Ideas (a)** Do you think Bob's expectations of Jimmy were fulfilled? **(b)** Was there a "winner" in this story? Support your answer with details from the story. *[Connect to the Big Question: Does every conflict have a winner?]*

Cite textual evidence to support your responses.

He-y, Come On Ou-t!

Shinichi Hoshi
Translated by Stanleigh Jones

▲ **Critical Viewing**
In what ways do people who live in towns like the one shown have to depend on their environment? **[Analyze]**

The typhoon had passed and the sky was a gorgeous blue. Even a certain village not far from the city had suffered damage. A little distance from the village and near the mountains, a small shrine had been swept away by a landslide.

"I wonder how long that shrine's been here."

"Well, in any case, it must have been here since an awfully long time ago."

"We've got to rebuild it right away."

While the villagers exchanged views, several more of their number came over.

"It sure was wrecked."

"I think it used to be right here."

"No, looks like it was a little more over there."

Just then one of them raised his voice. "Hey what in the world is this hole?"

Where they had all gathered there was a hole about a meter in diameter. They peered in, but it was so dark nothing could be seen. However, it gave one the feeling that it was so deep it went clear through to the center of the earth.

There was even one person who said, "I wonder if it's a fox's hole."

"He—y, come on ou—t!" shouted a young man into the hole. There was no echo from the bottom. Next he picked up a pebble and was about to throw it in.

"You might bring down a curse on us. Lay off," warned an old man, but the younger one energetically threw the pebble in. As before, however, there was no answering response from the bottom. The villagers cut down some trees, tied them with rope and made a fence which they put around the hole. Then they repaired to the village.

"What do you suppose we ought to do?"

"Shouldn't we build the shrine up just as it was over the hole?"

A day passed with no agreement. The news traveled fast, and a car from the newspaper company rushed over. In no time a scientist came out, and with an all-knowing expression on his face he went over to the hole. Next, a bunch of gawking curiosity seekers showed up; one could also pick out here and there men of shifty glances who appeared to be concessionaires.[1] Concerned that someone might fall into the hole, a policeman from the local substation kept a careful watch.

One newspaper reporter tied a weight to the end of a long cord and lowered it into the hole. A long way down it went. The cord ran out, however, and he tried to pull it out, but it would not come back up. Two or three people helped out, but when they all pulled too hard, the cord parted at the edge of the hole. Another reporter, a camera in hand, who had been watching all of this, quietly untied a stout rope that had been wound around his waist.

The scientist contacted people at his laboratory and had them bring out a high-powered bull horn, with which he was going to check out the echo from the hole's bottom. He tried switching through various sounds, but there was no echo. The scientist was puzzled, but he could not very well give up with everyone watching him so intently. He put the bull horn right up to the hole, turned it to its highest volume, and let it sound continuously for a long time. It was a noise that would

Irony
What expectations does the author create in the reader's mind about the hole?

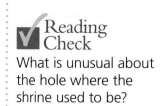

✓ Reading Check
What is unusual about the hole where the shrine used to be?

---

1. **concessionaires** (kən sesh′ ə nerz′) *n.* business people.

have carried several dozen kilometers above ground. But the hole just calmly swallowed up the sound.

In his own mind the scientist was at a loss, but with a look of apparent composure he cut off the sound and, in a manner suggesting that the whole thing had a perfectly plausible explanation, said simply, "Fill it in."

Safer to get rid of something one didn't understand.

The onlookers, disappointed that this was all that was going to happen, prepared to disperse. Just then one of the concessionaires, having broken through the throng and come forward, made a proposal.

"Let me have that hole. I'll fill it in for you."

"We'd be grateful to you for filling it in," replied the mayor of the village, "but we can't very well give you the hole. We have to build a shrine there."

"If it's a shrine you want, I'll build you a fine one later. Shall I make it with an attached meeting hall?"

Before the mayor could answer, the people of the village all shouted out.

"Really? Well, in that case, we ought to have it closer to the village."

"It's just an old hole. We'll give it to you!"

So it was settled. And the mayor, of course, had no objection.

The concessionaire was true to his promise. It was small, but closer to the village he did build for them a shrine with an attached meeting hall.

About the time the autumn festival was held at the new shrine, the hole-filling company established by the concessionaire hung out its small shingle at a shack near the hole.

The concessionaire had his cohorts mount a loud campaign in the city. "We've got a fabulously deep hole! Scientists say it's at least five thousand meters deep! Perfect for the disposal of such things as waste from nuclear reactors."

Government authorities granted permission. Nuclear power plants fought for contracts. The people of the village were a bit worried about this, but they consented when it was explained that there would be absolutely no above-ground contamination² for several thousand years and that they would share in the profits. Into the bargain, very shortly a

Vocabulary
apparent (ə par´ ənt)
adj. seeming
plausible (plô´ zə bəl)
adj. believable
proposal (prə pōz´ əl)
n. plan; offer

Irony
Is this how you would expect the former site of a shrine to be treated? Explain.

---

2. **contamination** (kən tam´ ə nā´ shən) *n.* pollution by poison or other dangerous substances.

magnificent road was built from the city to the village.

Trucks rolled in over the road, transporting lead boxes. Above the hole the lids were opened, and the wastes from nuclear reactors tumbled away into the hole.

From the Foreign Ministry and the Defense Agency boxes of unnecessary classified documents were brought for disposal. Officials who came to supervise the disposal held discussions on golf. The lesser functionaries, as they threw in the papers, chatted about pinball.

The hole showed no signs of filling up. It was awfully deep, thought some; or else it might be very spacious at the bottom. Little by little the hole-filling company expanded its business.

Bodies of animals used in contagious disease experiments at the universities were brought out, and to these were added the unclaimed corpses of vagrants. Better than dumping all of its garbage in the ocean, went the thinking in the city, and plans were made for a long pipe to carry it to the hole.

The hole gave peace of mind to the dwellers of the city. They concentrated solely on producing one thing after another. Everyone disliked thinking about the eventual consequences. People wanted only to work for production companies and sales corporations; they had no interest in becoming junk dealers. But, it was thought, these problems too would gradually be resolved by the hole.

Young girls whose betrothals[3] had been arranged discarded old diaries in the hole. There were also those who were inaugurating new love affairs and threw into the hole old photographs of themselves taken with former sweethearts. The police felt comforted as they used the hole to get rid of accumulations of expertly done counterfeit bills. Criminals breathed easier after throwing material evidence into the hole.

Whatever one wished to discard, the hole accepted it all.

---

3. **betrothals** (bē trōth′ əlz) *n.* promises of marriage.

▲ **Critical Viewing**
What feelings do you think people would have after visiting a shrine like the one shown? **[Connect]**

Irony
Does this use of the hole seem like a good idea? Why or why not?

Reading Check
In what ways has the concessionaire used the hole to his advantage?

The hole cleansed the city of its filth; the sea and sky seemed to have become a bit clearer than before.

Aiming at the heavens, new buildings went on being constructed one after the other.

One day, atop the high steel frame of a new building under construction, a workman was taking a break. Above his head he heard a voice shout:

"He—y, come on ou—t!"

But, in the sky to which he lifted his gaze there was nothing at all. A clear blue sky merely spread over all. He thought it must be his imagination. Then, as he resumed his former position, from the direction where the voice had come, a small pebble skimmed by him and fell on past.

The man, however, was gazing in idle reverie[4] at the city's skyline growing ever more beautiful, and he failed to notice.

---

4. **idle reverie** (rev´ ə rē) *n.* daydreaming.

▲ **Critical Viewing**
Based on the story, why might the man in this picture be looking up? **[Hypothesize]**

Cite textual evidence to support your responses.

Critical Thinking

1. **Key Ideas and Details (a)** What had stood before the hole appeared, and for how long? **(b) Infer:** What is the author suggesting about the site?

2. **Key Ideas and Details (a)** What does the concessionaire offer to do with the hole? **(b) Analyze Causes and Effects:** What is the result of his action?

3. **Integration of Knowledge and Ideas (a) Synthesize:** What comment do you think the author may be making about people and the environment? **(b) Generalize:** What message does the author suggest when a voice and a pebble apparently come out of the hole?

4. **Integration of Knowledge and Ideas (a)** Do you think the author believes that the hole provides a good solution for the community? **(b)** What conflicts do you think the author wants you to see in the ending of the story? **(c)** Do these conflicts have winners and losers? Explain, using details from the story. *[Connect to the Big Question: Does every conflict have a winner?]*

Comparing Irony

1. Craft and Structure Did the end of O. Henry's story entertain or shock you? Explain.

2. Craft and Structure Did the ending of "He—y, Come on Ou—t!" change your mind or confirm your thinking about a social issue? Explain.

3. Integration of Knowledge and Ideas Create a chart to compare irony. **(a)** In the first column, identify the irony you found. **(b)** In the second column, explain what the irony tells you about the characters. **(c)** In the third column, explain what message the author delivers through the use of irony.

	What It Says	What It Means	Why It Is Important
After Twenty Years			
He—y, Come on Ou—t!			

⏱ Timed Writing

Explanatory Text: Essay

In an essay, compare and contrast your responses to the two stories based on the authors' use of irony. Support your ideas with details from the texts. **(40 minutes)**

5-Minute Planner

1. Read the prompt carefully and completely.

2. Gather your ideas in a Venn diagram or by jotting down answers to these questions:

- Is believability important to you when you respond to ironic stories? Why or why not?

- Which story's ironic message did you understand more easily?

3. Use a compare-and-contrast organizational strategy. For example, compare and contrast your reactions to a surprising aspect in each story.

4. Reread the prompt, and then draft your essay.

Writing Workshop

 Common Core State Standards

Writing
3. Write narratives to develop real or imagined experiences or events using effective technique, relevant descriptive details, and well-structured event sequences.
3.a. Engage and orient the reader by establishing a context and point of view and introducing a narrator and/or characters; organize an event sequence that unfolds naturally and logically.

Write a Narrative

Narration: Short Story

Defining the Form A **short story** is a brief, creative fictional narrative. You might use elements of this type of writing in an autobiographical essay, a drama, a feature article, or a biography.

Assignment Write a short story about an interesting or original situation that will capture readers' attention. Include these elements:

✔ well-developed *major and minor characters*

✔ a *conflict* that keeps the reader asking, "What will happen next?"

✔ a clear story line or sequence told from a *consistent point of view*

✔ effective *pacing*

✔ narrative that develops *dialogue, suspense, descriptive details,* and other literary elements and devices

✔ a *title* that catches the reader's attention

✔ precise vocabulary and *effective word choice*

✔ error-free writing, including *correct use of comparatives*

To preview the criteria on which your short story may be judged, see the rubric on page 391.

 Writing Workshop: *Work in Progress*

Review the work you did on pages 335 and 361.

WRITE GUY
Jeff Anderson, M.Ed.

What Do You Notice?

Tone

The following sentences are from Joan Aiken's "The Third Wish."

In the morning, Mr. Peters was found peacefully dead in his bed with a smile of great happiness on his face. In his hands, which lay clasped on his breast, were a withered leaf and a white feather.

Discuss these questions with a partner:
- What do you notice about this passage?
- How does the word choice contribute to the tone?

Think about ways you might use word choice to contribute to the tone of your work.

Reading-Writing Connection

To get the feel for short story, review "Zoo" by Edward Hoch on page 340 or "Ribbons" by Laurence Yep on page 346.

Prewriting/Planning Strategies

Use a "what if" strategy. To help you choose the characters and situation for your story, fill in the blanks of a sentence such as the one shown here. Try a number of situations and choose the one that interests you the most.

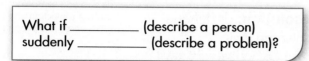

What if _____ (describe a person)
suddenly _____ (describe a problem)?

Identify the conflict. A **conflict** is a struggle between opposing forces. A character's conflict may be *external,* as when a sheriff has a conflict with an outlaw, or *internal,* as when that outlaw struggles with his conscience. Identify the conflict to focus your topic and get your story moving. Ask yourself these questions:

- Who is the main character of my story?
- What does the main character want?
- What is preventing him or her from getting it?

Use listing and itemizing. Your next step is to gather details to include in your story. Review the model shown here and follow these steps to try this strategy:

1. Quickly jot down a list of everything that comes to mind about a general idea.
2. Circle the most interesting item on the list.
3. Itemize that detail—create another list of everything that comes to mind about it.
4. After you have generated several lists, look for connections among all the circled items. These connections will help you decide which details to include in your story.

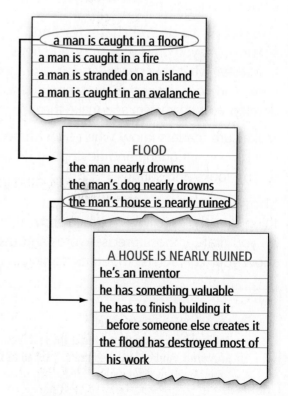

a man is caught in a flood
a man is caught in a fire
a man is stranded on an island
a man is caught in an avalanche

FLOOD
the man nearly drowns
the man's dog nearly drowns
the man's house is nearly ruined

A HOUSE IS NEARLY RUINED
he's an inventor
he has something valuable
he has to finish building it
  before someone else creates it
the flood has destroyed most of
  his work

Drafting Strategies

Create a plot. Begin by mapping out a **plot,** the arrangement of actions in the story. In most stories, the plot follows this pattern:

- The **exposition** introduces the main characters and their basic situation, including the central conflict or problem.
- The **conflict** intensifies during the rising action.
- The **climax** is the high point of interest.
- The story's falling action leads to the **resolution,** or denouement, in which the conflict is resolved in some way.

As you write, use transitional words and phrases, such as *next, then,* and *later* to show how one event in your plot leads to the next.

Use literary elements and devices. A good story builds to a single exciting moment. To achieve this, writers rely on literary elements and devices. For example, **foreshadowing** is the use of clues hinting at future plot events. This creates **suspense,** a technique that makes the reader wonder what will happen next.

Use details to define character and setting. As you draft your story, add details that reveal what your characters look like, how they act, what they think, and how others react to them. By adding these details, you develop your characters and make them more interesting.

Make sure readers know when and where the action is taking place. Use sensory language and descriptive details to describe how your setting looks and sounds.

Show; do not tell. Although it can be useful to tell readers something directly, usually you should show them rather than tell them. As you draft, choose precise words and use narrative techniques to show your characters' thoughts, feelings, actions, and reactions.

Common Core State Standards

Writing
3.c. Use a variety of transition words, phrases, and clauses to convey sequence and signal shifts from one time frame or setting to another.
3.d. Use precise words and phrases, relevant descriptive details, and sensory language to capture the action and convey experiences and events.

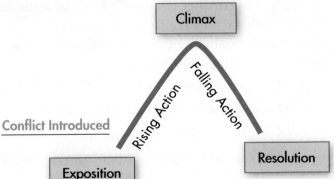

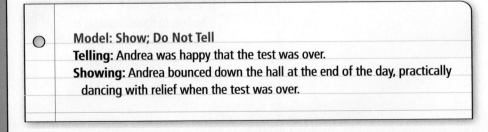

Model: Show; Do Not Tell
Telling: Andrea was happy that the test was over.
Showing: Andrea bounced down the hall at the end of the day, practically dancing with relief when the test was over.

Writers on Writing

Walter Dean Myers On Revising to Heighten Tension

> Walter Dean Myers is the author of "The Treasure of Lemon Brown" (p. 207).

As a child listening to the stories from the Old Testament, I formed images in my mind of what exactly was going on. At first I only sympathized with the character Joseph, but as I grew older I wondered how his eldest brother, Reuben, must have felt. So, I explored Reuben's feelings in a short story entitled "Reuben and Joseph." This section from my draft of the story shows how I revise to heighten tension.

"Often the minor characters interest me the most."
—Walter Dean Myers

Professional Model:

from "Reuben and Joseph"

~~Joseph lives~~. My brother lives. Like a man risen from the dead, he has appeared from the ashes of memory. ~~We are bid~~ He tells us that we are to go home tomorrow and tell our father the good news. But ~~those glad tidings~~ that good news, the joyous celebration he envisions, ~~will also speak of my disgrace~~ is filled with danger and disgrace for the messengers. Grief and fear sit in the pit of my stomach like two huge rocks. If I could scream silently, I would do so. If my tears could speak, I would let them.

~~Tonight I spent hours waiting for sleep and then, when sleep finally came, I awoke with a start, my heart pounding~~. I have been tossing and turning all night. Sleep comes now and again, but then I quickly wake, my heart pounding. The room is too warm, and I hear the breathing of my brothers who lie on mats around me. . . .

It was more important to establish that he is talking about his brother than to give his brother's name. I want the reader to wonder, Why does he worry that his brother lives?

Okay, so I'm into what I imagine to be the jargon of the day, but I need to get on with my story.

Saying that there is danger here immediately heightens the tension. "Also speak of my disgrace" is too stiff.

"I have been tossing and turning all night" is more direct than the sentence I crossed out and creates more drama.

Revising Strategies

Improve your characterization. Cut a five-pointed star out of construction paper and label the points *Dialogue, Movement, Gestures, Feelings,* and *Expressions.* Slide the star down your draft as you look for places where you can add details that reveal more about your characters. When you find a place to include more precise information, make notes in the margin and start over.

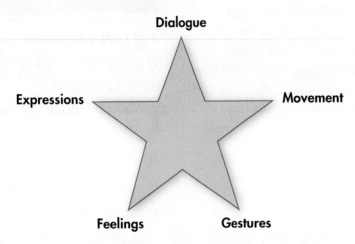

Follow these suggestions as you add information to develop character:

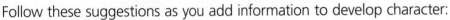

Dialogue: Write conversations that show how the character speaks, using the words and phrasing he or she might use.

Movement: Describe a character's movements using precise words like *rushed, timid,* or *excited.*

Gestures: Tell how the characters stand, move, and act.

Feelings: Consider the way events will make your characters feel, and include relevant descriptive details to reveal these emotions.

Expressions: Describe the facial expressions your characters make to convey their ideas and feelings without words.

Use active voice. A verb in active voice shows that the subject is performing the action: *Ana bought the computer.* A verb in passive voice shows that the subject receives the action: *The computer was bought by Ana.* Sentences written in active voice are less wordy and are usually stronger and more effective.

Peer Review
Give your draft to a few classmates to read. Ask them to highlight places where you can include details to develop stronger characters. Then, revise your draft, focusing on your purpose and audience.

Conventions	Sentence Fluency	Voice	Organization	Word Choice	Ideas

Comparison of Adjectives and Adverbs

Most adjectives and adverbs have three degrees of comparison: the *positive*, the *comparative*, and the *superlative*.

Identifying Degrees of Adjectives and Adverbs The positive is used when no comparison is made. The comparative is used when two things are being compared. The superlative is used when three or more things are being compared.

Positive: Hannah is a *fast* runner.

Comparative: Eva is a *faster* runner than Hannah.

Superlative: Emmy is the *fastest* runner on the team.

Forming Comparative and Superlative Degrees	
Use *-er* or *more* to form the comparative degree.	faster, taller, narrower, sunnier, more intelligent, more expressive
Use *-est* or *most* to form the superlative degree.	fastest, tallest, sunniest, most nutritious, most sorrowful
Use *more* and *most* with modifiers of three or more syllables.	more popular, more intelligently, most popular, most intelligently

PH WRITING COACH

Further instruction and practice are available in *Prentice Hall Writing Coach*.

Fixing Incorrect Use of Comparative and Superlative Degrees
To fix the incorrect use of comparative and superlative degrees of adjectives and adverbs, use one or more of the following methods:

1. **Identify the number of things being compared.** Review the rules for comparison and use the correct word or word ending.

2. **Identify the number of syllables in the modifier.** Review the rules for modifiers with a specific number of syllables and use the correct word or word ending.

3. **Read the words aloud.** If the words sound awkward, combine the modifier with a different word or word ending.

Grammar in Your Writing
Choose two paragraphs in your draft. Underline every sentence that compares two or more things. If the use of a comparative or superlative degree of any adjective or adverb is faulty, fix it.

The Leaky Boat

It was a cold September evening. My linen cuffs flapped uncontrollably in a biting wind baring its white teeth of snow. The sun had long since set, and all was quiet on the sea. A cool mist had settled around the bay, sending a sharp chill down my spine. I continued to row; I had seen worse. I could still hear the voice ringing through my head:

"This is it, son. Either you're ready or you're not."

I was ready. The fire in my lantern flickered as another wind blew across the bay, carrying more frightening sounds from the distance. I gripped my father's pendant for reassurance, clenching the jade cross and willing myself to be strong. I was ready.

No one dared go out on such a night. Tonight was Friday—the 13th. I was the only one traveling the waters, or so I thought. Ever since the coast guard had shown us out, no one dared go fishin' even if it was for a big fish; I mean a big fish, a legend, and a monster! But it wasn't a fish anyone in my family could bring themselves to kill. It was ancient, and it had, in a distant time, saved one of my ancestors from being swallowed by the sea.

Now, I had survived many a boating trip before, but what happened next would become a remarkable memory for the rest of my life.

As I shifted in my seat I could feel it. Something was wrong. I shifted once more and that's when I heard it. The wind blew hard against my face, the cold stinging my eyes. Rushing water all around me—a storm! It had come slowly at first. I had not thought much of it, but now it was at its nastiest, and I was in the middle of it! The waves crashed against my boat like hail pounding on a window. I was violently thrown back and forth in my boat! I turned to the side. How close was I to the rocky shore?

Another wave hit, revealing a large rock off the starboard side. A wave came from the opposite side, drenching me with water, but that was not all. The wave sent me hurtling toward the rock! I slammed into the rock with full force! I was swept aside by another, smaller wave as water poured into my boat! What was I to do? Thunder roared overhead.

As I struggled to keep upright, a massive wave came up from behind, plunging me into the water. I swam with all my strength to the surface, taking in a big breath of air and holding tight to my father's pendant.

The water churned around me fiercely, tossing to and fro. The foam swirled around me, and the salt stung my eyes as it hit me. I was plunged under again. I swam up for air with my strength rapidly leaving me. Disaster struck! I felt a wave come. I could not see it. I felt the necklace being ripped from my neck, leaving the sanctuary of my head and spiraling down to the murky depths. I looked down for it, squinting to open my burning eyes; I saw an eye and a long slender body, and then all went dark.

I awoke the next morning on an unfamiliar shore, not knowing where I was. I felt something cold against my neck—the pendant! How had it been retrieved? How had I survived? The fish. The family fish had saved my family again. I still don't know how I obtained the pendant or where I had to go, for that is another story.

K.C. uses descriptive language to set the scene for the story.

The story is told from a first-person point of view. Readers learn about the narrator from what he thinks and experiences.

K.C. develops suspense by foreshadowing something dangerous.

The varied sentence structure and length make the pacing of the story's conflict suspenseful.

Vivid details and tension make the reader want to know what is going to happen next.

Editing and Proofreading

Review your draft to find and eliminate errors in grammar, spelling, and punctuation.

Focus on dialogue. Enclose a character's exact words in quotation marks. If dialogue comes *before* the words announcing speech, use a comma, question mark, or exclamation point at the end of the quotation—not a period. If dialogue comes *after* the words announcing speech, use a comma before the quotation.

"I heard the siren," Benjamin said.
Sally jumped and shouted, "So did I, but it still surprised me!"

© **Spiral Review**
Earlier in the unit, you learned about **adjectives** (p. 334) and **adverbs** (p. 360). Review your short story to be sure you have used adjectives and adverbs correctly to achieve your intended effect.

Publishing and Presenting

Share your writing with a wider audience:

Submit your story. Submit your story to a school literary magazine, a national publication, an online journal, or a contest.

Give a reading. Read your story aloud to your class or to a group of friends. Prepare posters announcing your reading and distribute signed copies of your story at the event.

Reflecting on Your Writing

Writer's Journal Jot down your answer to this question:

How has your writing experience changed the way you read short stories?

Rubric for Self-Assessment

Find evidence in your writing to address each category. Then, use the rating scale to grade your work.

Criteria	Rating Scale
	not very very
Focus: How well-developed are your characters?	1 2 3 4 5
Organization: How clearly organized is the story line or sequence of events?	1 2 3 4 5
Support/Elaboration: How well do the dialogue and suspense support the plot?	1 2 3 4 5
Style: How precise is your word choice?	1 2 3 4 5
Conventions: How correct is your grammar, especially your use of comparative adjectives and adverbs?	1 2 3 4 5

Vocabulary Workshop

Word Origins

A word's **origin,** or **etymology,** tells the history of the word. Knowing the history of a word or word part can help you understand its meaning. This chart gives the meanings of several Latin, Greek, Old English, and Middle English word parts.

Common Core State Standards

Language
4.b. Use common, grade-appropriate Greek or Latin affixes and roots as clues to the meaning of a word.
4.c. Consult general and specialized reference materials, both print and digital, to find the pronunciation of a word or determine or clarify its precise meaning or its part of speech.
5.a. Interpret figures of speech (e.g., literary, biblical, and mythological allusions) in context.

Latin and Greek Word Parts

Roots	Origin	Meaning	Examples
-aud-	Latin	to hear	audio, audience
-struct-	Latin	to build	structure, instruct
-port-	Latin	to carry	portable, transport
Prefixes	**Origin**	**Meaning**	**Examples**
inter-	Latin	among, between	internet, international
mis-	Old English	wrong, not	misbehave, misfortune
tele-	Greek	distant	telephone, telescope
Suffixes	**Origin**	**Meaning**	**Examples**
-ful	Middle English	full of	joyful, fearful
-less	Middle English	without	careless, thoughtless

Practice A For each word in italics, underline the root, prefix, or suffix. Then, explain how the the meaning of the word part contributes to the meaning of the word. If necessary, consult a print or online dictionary.

1. The *construction* of the new bank building is on schedule.
2. When Samuel *interrupts* me, I can't remember what I have been saying.
3. When the roads are slick, signs alert drivers to be *careful.*
4. The *auditorium* was full of people eager to hear the symphony.
5. The losing candidate suspected that the votes were *miscounted.*

Many words and phrases in English come from **Latin, Greek, and Anglo-Saxon mythology.** Study the chart below to learn the origins of some of these words and phrases.

Words and Phrases From Mythology		
Word or Phrase	**Origin**	**Meaning**
January	Janus, a Roman god, had two faces— one looking forward and one looking backward.	The first month of our calendar year
Achilles heel	Achilles, a great Greek warrior, was known to be weak only in his foot.	A weakness or weak point
Herculean effort	The Greek hero Hercules was known for his strength and for completing twelve difficult tasks.	A difficult task requiring great strength
high horse	In medieval England, nobles were given tall horses to show their importance. The phrase "get off your high horse" developed from this practice.	A superior attitude

Practice B Identify the word or phrase from the chart that is associated with each sentence.

1. When Byron bragged about his new car we told him <u>not to be too proud of himself</u>.

2. It is always good to have a fresh start in <u>the new year</u>.

3. I can usually stick to a healthy diet, but my <u>weakness</u> is brownies

4. Beating the other team will require <u>us to be stronger than ever</u>.

Activity An **allusion** is a reference to a well-known person, event, literary work, or work of art. Many works of literature contain allusions. For example, a writer might describe a long or difficult journey as an "odyssey." This is an allusion to *The Odyssey*, a long epic poem that was written sometime between 600 and 800 B.C. In the poem, the ancient Greek hero Odysseus takes a long, difficult voyage to reach his home. Another ancient Greek hero is Hercules, who was famous for completing amazingly difficult tasks. Write a short tale about an odyssey in which the hero must make a Herculean effort. Your story can be set in the past or present.

Comprehension and Collaboration

Trade your odyssey story with a partner. Rewrite your partner's story to include three new words based on word parts from the chart on the previous page. You may use words that appear in this Vocabulary Workshop, other words you know, or new words you find in a dictionary.

Communications Workshop

Delivering an Oral Summary

An **oral summary** shares many of the characteristics of a written summary. The guidelines below will help you plan what you want to say and help you say it with confidence.

Learn the Skills

Use these strategies to complete the activity on page 395.

Summarize. Like its written counterpart, an oral summary should briefly state the main idea of a work, with only as many details as needed to give a complete, but concise, picture of the work.

Organize your points in sequence. To create a summary to use in an oral presentation, organize your ideas and record them on note cards.

Write the "main idea"—the overall statement of the work's content—on your first note card. Include one or two key details that support the main idea. Make additional cards to present points from the beginning, middle, and end of the work. Write your conclusion on a separate card. Refer to your note cards as you deliver your presentation.

Show a comprehensive understanding. As you prepare your presentation, do not just string together fact after fact. Ask yourself, "What does all this mean?" Try to convey a genuine understanding of what you have seen or read, not just the surface details.

Consider your audience. Include enough information so that your audience can follow the summary accurately.

Plan your delivery. Try to project confidence and a positive attitude. Plan and practice your delivery so that you stay focused when presenting.

- **Vary your sentence structure.** To add interest, vary your sentence structure just as you do when you write. Listen to your words and monitor yourself for errors in grammar.

- **Use your voice well.** Be energetic, but speak clearly and precisely. Enunciate every word. Vary the pitch and speed of your voice to keep your listeners engaged. Make sure that you are speaking loudly enough to be heard clearly.

- **Make eye contact.** Memorize as much of your summary as you can to enable you to make eye contact with listeners.

**Common Core
State Standards**

Speaking and Listening
4. Present claims and findings, emphasizing salient points in a focused, coherent manner with pertinent descriptions, facts, details, and examples; use appropriate eye contact, adequate volume, and clear pronunciation.

Main Idea
Giant pandas have become rare because hunters kill them. **Facts:** There are only about 2,500 living in the wild. There are only about 150 in zoos.

Conclusion
If we can support the efforts to save pandas, maybe there will be more pandas in the world of our children and grandchildren.

Practice the Skills

⊚ Presentation of Knowledge and Ideas Use what you have learned in this workshop to complete the following activity.

ACTIVITY: Prepare and Deliver an Oral Summary

Choose an article, at least three pages long, from a magazine or Web site. Present an oral summary of the article to your class. Use the instruction on page 394 and the following steps to guide you:

- Begin with a strong opening statement. You might use a rhetorical question—a question asked for effect: *Does anyone wonder what happened to the plans for the new park?* You might use an impressive fact contained in the article: *It has been two years since the plans were first approved.*
- Use formal English.
- When presenting, project your voice so that everyone can hear. Pronounce words clearly. Do not rush.
- End with a strong closing statement that relates to your opening statement. *So, that is what has happened to the park plans: repeated budget cuts.*

⊚ Comprehension and Collaboration Ask your classmates to give you feedback by saying how they rated you on the Presentation Evaluation Checklist shown here. While your classmates give their presentations, use the checklist to rate their work.

Presentation Evaluation Checklist

Presentation Content
Was the summary clear and easy to follow?
Check all that apply.

- ☐ It had a strong beginning and ending.
- ☐ It included all key points.
- ☐ I understood the main points of the work based on this summary.

Presentation Delivery
Did the speaker deliver the summary effectively?
Check all that apply.

- ☐ The speaker established good eye contact.
- ☐ The speaker enunciated clearly and maintained good volume.
- ☐ The speaker varied rate and pitch of voice.
- ☐ The speaker used formal English.

Cumulative Review

**Common Core
State Standards**

RL.7.2, RL.7.3, RL.7.6; W.7.10
[For the full wording of the standards,
see the standards chart in the front of
your textbook.]

I. Reading Literature

Directions: *Read the story. Then, answer each question that follows.*

"They say that if you are lost in the Everglades, you die. That is, of course, if you have no food, no shelter, and no survival skills," Alicia said as she stared at the sawgrass prairie stretching before her. Her gaze swept along the distant horizon, where the flat grasslands touched the sky. There was not a mini-mart in sight.

"We're not lost," Petra assured her. "I know exactly where we are." Then she whispered, "I just don't know how to get to where we *were*."

Petra was feeling more guilty than scared. The ride into the saw-grass prairie had been her idea, and she had planned well, packing food, water, and a first-aid kit. All the supplies were loaded on the rented horse that carried both girls along the trail. It was not her fault that the horse had wandered off while she and Alicia explored one of the side trails on foot.

"We should stay where we are," Petra said casually, without a trace of care. "The horse will probably return soon. It knows the trail that will take us back."

Alicia shaded her eyes and searched the western region for the missing horse. The bright sun was blinding and hot. That is why they had decided to explore the marsh, where the ground was soggy but the temperature was cooler. Alicia had never ventured into a marsh before. Her boldness had surprised her, but then she had second thoughts. She felt the presence of unknown creatures and wished she had some way to protect herself against those alligators and poisonous snakes that were surely eyeing her soft flesh. All at once her boldness had evaporated. Her skin felt suddenly clammy, and she had run back to the main trail—into a worse nightmare: the horse was gone.

All at once, Alicia's thoughts were interrupted by the sound of Petra's voice. "The horse!" yelled Petra, pointing excitedly. "It's coming back!"

"Ah!" sighed Alicia. "We live for another day."

1. Which event in the story's **plot** happens first?

   A. Alicia and Petra decide to explore the marsh.
   B. The horse comes back to Alicia and Petra.
   C. Petra decides to wait for the horse.
   D. A snake scares the horse.

2. Which event marks the **climax** of the story?

   A. Alicia finds a mini-mart.
   B. Petra yells that the horse is coming back.
   C. Alicia becomes scared in the marsh.
   D. Petra packs up the first-aid kit.

3. What part of the **plot** reveals that Petra had packed food, water, and a first aid kit?

   A. the exposition
   B. the rising action
   C. the falling action
   D. the resolution

4. Which of the following **character traits** does Petra possess?

   A. She is easily scared.
   B. She does not enjoy hiking.
   C. She stays calm in emergencies.
   D. She does not get along with others.

5. Which of the following story details contributes most to the **external conflict?**

   A. The horse wanders off.
   B. There is no mini-mart.
   C. Petra feels guilty.
   D. The girls have food and water.

6. What is Alicia's **motive** for exploring the marsh?

   A. She wants to get out of the hot sun.
   B. She wants to hide from alligators.
   C. She is looking for her first-aid kit.
   D. She wants to capture a snake.

7. What happens in the **resolution** of the story?

   A. Petra begins feeling guilty.
   B. The horse wanders off.
   C. Petra shows bravery.
   D. The horse returns.

8. Which sentence best conveys the **theme** of the story?

   A. Preparation can save your life.
   B. Staying calm can help in a scary situation.
   C. Friendships are invaluable.
   D. Life can be full of hardships.

⏱ Timed Writing

9. Write an essay in which you **explain** whether you think the **main conflict** of this story is internal or external. Cite evidence from the text to support your analysis.

GO ON ⇨

II. Reading Informational Text

Directions: *Read the excerpt from an encyclopedia entry. Then, answer each question that follows.*

Common Core State Standards

RI.7.1, RI.7.5; W.7; L.7.1., L.7.3
[For the full wording of the standards, see the standards chart in the front of your textbook.]

The American Alligator

Appearance

Alligators look like large lizards with thick bodies and tails. They have strong jaws and many sharp teeth. An alligator's eyes stick up above its skull, allowing it to see above the water while its body is beneath the surface. It swims by moving its powerful tail from side to side.

Average Size				
Length when hatched	Length for adult male	Length for adult female	Weight for adult male	Weight for adult female
9 inches	11–12 feet	9 feet or less	450–550 pounds	160 pounds

Diet

Alligators are meat-eating reptiles that eat birds, fish, snakes, turtles, frogs, and mammals. Alligators are good hunters, partly because they are not easily seen by their prey. That is because they swim with only their eyes and tough, scaly backs visible above the surface. To an unsuspecting creature, an alligator can look like a dead log floating in the water.

1. If you wanted to write a physical description of an American alligator, in which sections of the encyclopedia entry would you look for information?

A. The American Alligator *and* Appearance
B. Appearance *and* Average Size
C. Appearance *and* Diet
D. Average Size *and* Diet

2. What are the **subheads** in this encyclopedia entry?

A. The American Alligator *and* Appearance
B. Appearance *and* Average Size
C. Appearance *and* Diet
D. Average Size *and* Diet

3. Which **generalization** is *not* supported by information in the encyclopedia entry?

A. Male alligators are bigger than females.
B. Alligators spend much of their time in the water.
C. Alligators do not live in the ocean.
D. Alligators use their sense of sight for hunting.

4. What can you **infer** from the information about alligators?

A. Alligators are dangerous.
B. Alligators are found in the South.
C. Alligators are easy to train.
D. Alligators live a long time.

III. Writing and Language Conventions

Directions: *Read the passage below. Then, answer each question that follows.*

> (1) "Seventh Grade" is a funny and believable story. (2) In it, a boy named Victor likes a girl named Teresa. (3) To impress her, Victor pretends to speak French in class. (4) Although he seems smart, he did not really know French. (5) Victor's teacher knows Victor is faking. (6) However, the teacher is very cool. (7) He does not tell the class that Victor's answers are wrong. (8) That is because he remembers what it is like to be a teenager.

1. What sentence states the writer's **claim** about "Seventh Grade"?

A. sentence 1
B. sentence 3
C. sentence 5
D. sentence 7

2. Which additional sentence would *best* **support** the writer's opinion?

A. Victor's secret is safe with his teacher.
B. Gary Soto is the author of "Seventh Grade."
C. You can tell that the story's author, Gary Soto, remembers being young.
D. You should read other stories by the author, Gary Soto.

3. Which word is the **best** replacement for the word **cool** in sentence 6?
A. cold
B. intelligent
C. prepared
D. understanding

4. How would you revise the verb in sentence 6 to use the **future tense?**

A. will be
B. is not
C. was not
D. understand

5. What is the tense of the **principal part** of the verb *tell* in sentence 7?

A. present
B. present participle
C. past
D. past participle

6. How could the writer revise sentence 4 to change the verb to the **present tense?**

A. Although he was smart, he did not really know French.
B. Although he seemed smart, he does not really know French.
C. Although he seems smart, he does not really know French.
D. The sentence is already in the present tense.

Performance Tasks

Directions: *Follow the instructions to complete the tasks below as required by your teacher.*

As you work on each task, incorporate both general academic vocabulary and literary terms you learned in this unit.

Common Core
State Standards

RL.7.1, RL.7.2, RL.7.3, RL.7.6; W.7.9.a; SL.7.5, SL.7.6; L.7.1, L.7.2, L.7.3, L.7.6
[For the full wording of the standards, see the standards chart in the front of your textbook.]

Writing

Task 1: Literature [RL.7.3; W.7.9.a]
Analyze Setting and Character

Write an essay about a story in this unit in which you discuss how the setting shapes the characters.

- Choose a story with a distinct setting. Remember that time, place, climate, and common beliefs of the time are all part of the setting.

- Analyze how the setting shapes the characters. Describe how it affects their beliefs, thoughts, feelings, actions, and reactions.

- Use appropriate transitions to clarify the relationships between ideas in your essay.

- Use a dictionary to check your spelling of commonly confused words, such as *there, their,* and *they're.*

Task 2: Literature [RL.7.6; W.7.9.a]
Analyze Characters' Points of View

Write an essay in which you identify at least two characters' points of view from a story in this unit. Analyze how the author develops and contrasts the points of view of these characters.

- Identify the points of view of at least two characters from a story. Describe what the characters believe and how they feel. Discuss their motives.

- Analyze how the author develops each character's point of view through narration, dialogue, and action. Include concrete details from the text to develop and support your analysis.

- Then, discuss how the author *contrasts* the points of view of your chosen characters through their dialogue, actions, and reactions.

- As you revise, check your writing for correct spelling and punctuation.

Task 3: Literature [RL.7.1; W.7.9.a]
Evaluate Plot

Write an essay in which you evaluate the plot in one of the stories in this unit.

- Choose a story with a plot that you feel is developed in a particularly effective way. Then, write an opening sentence that expresses your view.

- Analyze how well the parts of the plot work together to move the story forward. Focus on the exposition, rising action and conflict, climax, falling action, and resolution.

- Use details from the text to support your evaluation. For example, point out examples of effective narrative techniques such as the use of foreshadowing, descriptive language, or specific details that build tension or suspense.

- Use transitional words or phrases, such as *furthermore, likewise, however, and in addition to,* to create unity between the ideas in sentences or paragraphs.

- Add a conclusion that sums up your main points and ties your essay together.

Speaking and Listening

Task 4: Literature [RL.7.2; SL.7.6]
Analyze and Develop Theme

Write a brief narrative in which you develop the theme of a story from this unit in a different way. Read your story aloud to a group of classmates.

- Determine the theme of a story in this unit and analyze its development over the course of the story.
- Decide on a different way to develop the same theme. Then, write a brief narrative to develop imagined experiences that express the theme.
- As you write, choose language that expresses your ideas clearly and effectively.
- Read your story aloud to a group of classmates.

Task 5: Literature [RL.7.3; SL.7.6]
Analyze Story Elements

Give an oral presentation in which you analyze the ways that literary elements interact in a story in this unit.

- Determine the ways that literary elements work together in your chosen story. For example, consider how the characters and setting affect the plot.
- Explain the impact of these elements on the story as a whole. Determine how the story would be different if it took place in a different setting or if a character had been developed in a different way.
- In your oral presentation, capture your audience's attention by beginning with a powerful opening statement. Vary your volume, pitch, and pacing and establish eye contact as you speak.

Task 6: Literature [RL.7.3; SL.7.5]
Analyze Conflict Development

Give a presentation in which you use multimedia or visual displays to clarify your analysis of how particular story elements interact to develop the conflict of a story in this unit.

- Prepare a presentation that identifies the internal or external conflict faced by the main character in a story of your choice. Analyze how particular story elements, such as setting, plot, and other characters, interact to develop the conflict.
- Create a story map, a cause-and-effect chart, or another graphic to visually display the conflict and the progress of its development.
- Accurately use appropriate vocabulary and content-area words in your presentation.

Does every conflict have a winner?

At the beginning of Unit 2, you wrote a response to the Big Question. Now that you have completed the unit, write a new response. Discuss how your initial ideas have either been changed or reinforced. Cite specific examples from the literature in this unit, from other subject areas, and from your own life to support your ideas. Use Big Question vocabulary words (see p. 199) in your response.

Featured Titles

In this unit, you have read a variety of short stories. Continue to read on your own. Select works that you enjoy, but challenge yourself to explore new authors and works of increasing depth and complexity. The titles suggested below will help you get started.

Literature

The Dark Is Rising

by Susan Cooper

Aladdin, 1973   **EXEMPLAR TEXT** ©

On his eleventh birthday, Will Stanton learns that he is the Sign-Seeker, an immortal who must fight the Dark to keep the world safe from evil. This **novel** is the first in a series of five books that draw inspiration from ominous Welsh and Celtic myths, as well as the action-packed legends of King Arthur.

The Collected Poems of Langston Hughes

by Langston Hughes

Vintage, 1994   **EXEMPLAR TEXT** ©

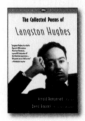

Langston Hughes was just nineteen when his first poem, "The Negro Speaks of Rivers," was published. Critics were soon raving about his original voice, which combined the rhythms of jazz and blues with the words and speech patterns of his African American heritage. This collection of **poetry** spans Hughes's long and brilliant career.

White Fang and The Call of the Wild

by Jack London

White Fang tells the first-person story of a wolf whom a man adopts after enduring a series of hardships. *The Call of the Wild* is about a pampered dog stolen from his home and forced to endure harsh Yukon winters and cruel masters as a sled dog. In both **novels,** the animals rely on instinct to survive in a brutal environment.

Heat

by Mike Lupica

Philomel, 2006

Michael Arroyo is such a skilled pitcher that coaches of rival baseball teams demand proof of his age. In this **novel,** Michael must struggle to find a way to play the game that he loves and to cope with his difficult home life.

The Devil's Arithmetic

by Jane Yolen

In this **historical novel,** a girl finds herself whisked back in time to a Polish village to experience firsthand the horrors her relatives experienced. She learns the history of the Holocaust in a way that no history lesson could teach.

Informational Texts

Geeks: How Two Lost Boys Rode the Internet out of Idaho

by Jon Katz

Villard Books, 2000   **EXEMPLAR TEXT** ©

In this **nonfiction** book, Jesse and Eric, two computer "geeks" with few social skills or future prospects, meet the reporter Jon Katz, who convinces them that they can use their computer savvy to create a better life.

Discoveries: Working It Out

What role does conflict play in social studies, science, music, and mathematics? The **essays** and **stories** in this book explore different types of conflicts and how they are worked out.

Preparing to Read Complex Texts

Attentive Reading As you read on your own, ask yourself questions about the text. The questions below, along with others that you ask as you read, will enrich your reading experience.

 **Common Core State Standards**

Reading Literature/Informational Text 10. By the end of the year, read and comprehend literature, including stories, dramas, and poems, and literary nonfiction in the grades 6–8 text complexity band proficiently, with scaffolding as needed at the high end of the range.

When reading short stories, ask yourself...

- Can I clearly picture the setting of the story? Which details help me do so?
- Can I picture the characters clearly in my mind? Why or why not?
- Do the characters speak and act like real people? Why or why not?
- Which characters do I like? Why? Which characters do I dislike? Why?
- Do I understand why the characters act as they do? Why or why not?
- What does the story mean to me? Does it express a meaning or an insight I find important and true?

© **Key Ideas and Details**

- Does the story grab my attention right from the beginning? Why or why not?
- Do I want to keep reading? Why or why not?
- Can I follow the sequence of events in the story? Am I confused at any point? If so, what information would make the sequence clearer?
- Do the characters change as the story progresses? If so, do their changes seem believable?
- Are there any passages that I find especially moving, interesting, or well written? If so, why?

© **Craft and Structure**

- How is this story similar to and different from other stories I have read?
- Do I care what happens to the characters? Do I sympathize with them? Why or why not?
- How do my feelings toward the characters affect my experience of reading the story?
- Did the story teach me something new or cause me to look at something in a new way? If so, what did I learn?
- Would I recommend this story to others? Why or why not?
- Would I like to read other works by this author? Why or why not?

© **Integration of Ideas**

What should we *learn*?

404

Types of Nonfiction

www.PHLitOnline.com

Hear It!
- Selection summary audio
- Selection audio
- BQ Tunes

See It!
- Author video
- Big Question video
- Get Connected videos
- Background videos
- More about the authors
- Illustrated vocabulary words
- Vocabulary flashcards

Do It!
- Interactive journals
- Interactive graphic organizers
- Grammar tutorials
- Interactive vocabulary games
- Test practice

What should we *learn?*

Everyone has their own ideas about what is important to learn. Some people believe we should learn information that helps us develop practical skills. Others believe we should explore topics driven by our curiosity and talents.

When you think about what we should learn, remember that knowledge includes skills you learn in school and lessons you learn from others. It also includes information that helps you understand other cultures, and ideas that inspire you to investigate the world around you. No matter what is most important to you, the drive to discover new things is something we all have in common.

Exploring the Big Question

Collaboration: Group Discussion Start thinking about the Big Question by making a list of things you believe are important to learn. Describe an example for each of the following:

- A skill that could save someone's life
- A subject you would like to study in school
- A job that requires specific knowledge
- An idea that might make the world a better place
- A personal interest of yours

   With a small group, discuss why you think some of these items are more important to learn than others. During your discussion, speak when it is your turn and listen to others without interrupting. Assign a discussion leader to keep ideas moving forward and a group recorder to list the items in the order of importance the group agrees to support. Ask a timekeeper to monitor your discussion and limit it to fifteen minutes. Finally, choose a speaker to present your group's ideas to the class.

Connecting to the Literature Each reading in this unit will give you additional insight into the Big Question.

PHLit Online!
www.PHLitOnline.com
- Big Question video
- Illustrated vocabulary words
- Interactive vocabulary games
- BQ Tunes

Learning Big Question Vocabulary

Acquire and Use Academic Vocabulary Academic vocabulary is the language you encounter in textbooks and on standardized tests. Review the definitions of these academic vocabulary words.

Common Core State Standards

Speaking and Listening
1.b. Follow rules for collegial discussions, track progress toward specific goals and deadlines, and define individual roles as needed.

Language
4.d. Verify the preliminary determination of the meaning of a word or phrase.
6. Acquire and use accurately grade-appropriate general academic and domain-specific words and phrases; gather vocabulary knowledge when considering a word or phrase important to comprehension or expression.

analyze (an′ə līz′) *v.* break into parts in order to study closely

discover (di skuv′ər) *v.* find something hidden or previously unknown

evaluate (ē val′yoo̅ āt′) *v.* judge or rate

examine (eg zam′ ən) *v.* study in depth in order to find or check something

explore (ek splôr′) *v.* travel through an unfamiliar area to find out what it is like; thoroughly discuss a topic

facts (fakts) *n.* true information about a topic

inquire (in kwīr′) *v.* ask someone for information

investigate (in ves′ tə gāt′) *v.* work to find out the truth

Use these words as you complete Big Question activities in this unit that involve reading, writing, speaking, and listening.

Gather Vocabulary Knowledge Additional Big Question words are listed below. Categorize the words by deciding whether you know each one well, know it a little bit, or do not know it at all.

curiosity	interview	question
experiment	knowledge	understand
information		

Then, do the following:

1. Write the definitions of the words you know.
2. Verify the definitions by looking up each word in a print or online dictionary. Revise your definitions as needed.
3. Continue to use the dictionary to look up the meanings and pronunciations of the unknown words.
4. Then, write a paragraph, using all the vocabulary words, about the types of things you think are important to learn.

Elements of Nonfiction

Nonfiction is writing about actual people, ideas, and events.

Nonfiction writing presents information that is true or thought to be true. Two broad categories of nonfiction are **functional texts,** which are practical documents that help readers perform everyday tasks, and **literary nonfiction,** which features some of the same literary elements and techniques as fiction.

Authors of nonfiction write with one or more **purposes,** or goals, in mind. Usually, these are to inform, describe, or persuade. To fulfill his or her purpose, the writer organizes information in a logical **structure,** or arrangement of parts, using patterns of organization such as these:

- **Chronological,** which presents events in the order in which they happened
- **Spatial,** which describes items as they appear in space—for example, left to right

- **Comparison-and-contrast,** which groups ideas based on their similarities and differences
- **Cause-and-effect,** which explains how one event causes, or leads to, another
- **Problem-and-solution,** which examines a problem and proposes ways to solve it

Literary Nonfiction In addition to informing, describing, or persuading, literary nonfiction may have an additional purpose: to entertain. When a work of literary nonfiction tells a story, it is called **narrative nonfiction.** It may include the elements listed in the right-hand column of the chart below.

Comparison of Storytelling Elements

In Fiction	In Narrative Nonfiction
Characters are developed through • **direct characterization,** or statements about what the characters are like; • **indirect characterization,** or descriptions of what the characters do, say, and think.	**Direct** and **indirect characterization** reveal the personalities of **real people.**
Setting is revealed through • **vivid descriptions** of **time, place,** and **customs;** • **figurative language,** or unusual comparisons, such as similes.	**Vivid descriptions** and **figurative language** describe **real places, real historical eras,** and **real customs.**
Plot, or the sequence of fictional events in a story, is **artfully paced and organized** to sustain readers' interest.	**Artful pacing and organization** describe **actual events.**

Forms of Literary Nonfiction

In addition to narrative nonfiction, three common forms of literary nonfiction are articles, essays, and speeches.

Articles are short prose works that present facts about a subject. They may appear in print sources, such as newspapers, or in online sources, such as Web sites.

Essays are also short prose works that focus on a particular subject. They may be more personal than articles, however. The author of an essay often has a deep emotional connection to the subject.

Speeches are written texts that are delivered orally to an audience. Like an essay, a speech expresses the speaker's point of view, or perspective, on a topic.

Types of Nonfiction

Just as there are different *forms* of nonfiction, there are also different *types*—each with its own general purpose. The chart below shows the most common types of nonfiction and gives examples of ways that a work of each type might address the same general subject: pets.

In This Section

Elements of Nonfiction

Analyzing Structure in Literary Nonfiction

Analyzing Relationships in Literary Nonfiction

Close Read: Determining Author's Purpose
• Model Text
• Practice Text

After You Read

 Common Core State Standards

RI.7.3, RI.7.4, RI.7.5, RI.7.6
[For the full wording of the standards, see the standards chart in the front of your textbook.]

Types and Purposes of Nonfiction

Type	Purpose	Examples
Expository	to present facts and ideas or to explain a process	an online article that explores ways to keep your dog healthy
Persuasive	to convince readers to take an action or to adopt a point of view	a speech urging the audience to adopt a pet
Narrative	to tell the story of a real-life experience	an essay about a dog who saved a person's life
Descriptive	to provide a vivid picture of something	an essay about the writer's favorite pet
Reflective	to explain the writer's insights about an event or experience	an essay describing lessons about life the writer learned from owning a pet
Humorous	to entertain and amuse	an article about the challenges of training a very frisky puppy
Analytical	to break a large idea into parts to show how the parts work as a whole	an article that discusses the criteria used for judging champion show dogs

Analyzing Structure in Literary Nonfiction

The structure of a nonfiction work provides clues to the author's purpose.

Common Core State Standards

Reading Informational Text 5. Analyze the structure an author uses to organize a text, including how the major sections contribute to the whole and to the development of the ideas.

Reading Informational Text 6. Determine an author's point of view or purpose in a text and analyze how the author distinguishes his or her position from that of others.

Writers of nonfiction deliberately arrange their words, sentences, paragraphs, and sections in ways that clearly develop their key ideas.

Text Features You can often tell how a nonfiction work is organized by looking at its arrangement on the page. Text features, such as subheads and charts, can provide clues about the author's purpose.

If a text has . . .	It is probably organized . . .	Its purpose may be . . .
steps or dates	in time order	• to tell a story • to explain a process
section headings	by topic	• to inform • to describe

Key Ideas All nonfiction works communicate one or more key ideas. The opening sentences of a work usually state or suggest the key idea and hint at the author's purpose:

> I was only three when I first smelled the fresh, damp soil of Grandma's garden. Somewhere inside me, a seed of love sprouted and began to grow.

These sentences convey the key idea that the writer began gardening at a very young age. The author's purpose might be to reflect on a personal experience.

Point of View The author's point of view is his or her basic beliefs about a subject. The opening sentences in the previous example tell you that the author has a passion for gardening. Her point of view is that gardening is a worthwhile pursuit.

Major Sections Nonfiction may be organized into sections arranged under headings. Each section supports a key idea and helps fulfill the author's purpose. Consider the section headings in an article about New York City:

Example: Section Headings
How to Get Around
What to See and Do
Where to Eat

↓

Unstated Key Idea
New York City is a good place to visit.

↓

Author's Purpose
To inform tourists

The structure, key idea, and purpose of a text are interrelated. The headings suggest that there are a lot of things to do in New York City. The information presented indicates that the article is meant for visitors. These elements combine to express the author's purpose to offer guidance to tourists.

Analyzing Relationships in Literary Nonfiction

Works of **literary nonfiction** show relationships between people, events, and ideas.

 **Common Core State Standards**

Reading Informational Text 3. Analyze the interactions between individuals, events, and ideas in a text.

Reading Informational Text 4. Determine the meaning of words and phrases as they are used in a text, including figurative, connotative, and technical meanings; analyze the impact of a specific word choice on meaning and tone.

Logical Relationships Nonfiction works show their subjects in relationship to the larger world. For instance, they may show cause-and-effect relationships, such as ways in which people are affected by events and ideas—and vice versa. Here are some specific examples.

If a text is about . . .	It might show . . .
the Civil War	• what events and ideas caused the war • who suffered during the war
the author's life as a spy	• what caused her career choice • how her actions affected others
social networks	• how they have impacted users' lives • why they have become so popular

People do not always agree about the causes or effects of an event. Two writers, given the same facts, may express different opinions. Each writer's point of view affects his or her interpretation of information. In some nonfiction works, the writer may be *biased,* expressing a one-sided opinion. However, a writer is not necessarily biased just because he or she has a particular point of view.

Word Choice Looking closely at an author's choice of words can help you detect his or her point of view. Word choice can also help reveal an author's **tone,** or attitude toward his or her subject and audience. In particular, notice words with positive or negative **connotations,** or emotional associations. For example, the words *curious* and *nosy* have the same basic meaning. However, calling someone "curious" conveys positive connotations, while calling that same person "nosy" conveys negative connotations.

Figurative Language In literary nonfiction, writers often use figurative language, or unusual comparisons, to bring an idea to life and to create a certain tone. Look at the example, in which a girl is described in three very different ways.

Example	Lily is compared to . . .	Tone
"Cyclone Lily" strikes again.	a cyclone	sarcastic
Lily sheds her things like a tree sheds leaves.	a tree	matter-of-fact
Lily is bursting with life. She can't help but drop petals along the way.	a flower	adoring

Close Read: Determining Author's Purpose

To discover the purpose or purposes of a work of literary nonfiction, look closely at key elements of the text.

Literary nonfiction contains elements of nonfiction writing *and* elements of "literary," or creative, writing. Literary nonfiction may please the reader with its graceful use of language. However, it may also persuade, inform, explain, describe, tell a story, or amuse. You can discover an author's purpose by looking closely at the following key elements of a text.

Clues to Author's Purpose

Key Ideas are main points that the author wants readers to understand and remember. To find key ideas and use them as clues, ask yourself:

- Does the beginning of the work directly state a key idea? If so, what is it?
- Do details in the text suggest key ideas? If so, what are those ideas?
- Why does the author include these key ideas?

Relationships are the logical connections between ideas, such as cause-and-effect relationships. To find relationships and use them as clues, ask yourself:

- How does one detail connect to other details?
- How do these connections point to a key idea?
- What do the relationships between ideas suggest about the author's purpose?

Point of View is the author's position and beliefs about a subject. To identify point of view and use it as a clue, ask yourself:

- What are the author's beliefs about his or her subject?
- Which details reveal those beliefs?
- What is the author's reason for expressing this point of view?

Connotation and Tone Connotations are the positive or negative feelings associated with a word. Tone is the author's attitude toward his or her subject and audience. To identify connotations and tone and use them as clues, ask yourself:

- Which words, if any, convey a strongly positive or negative attitude?
- What larger purpose do the words or attitude support?

Text Structure refers to the various parts of the text and their organization. To identify text structure and use it as a clue, ask yourself:

- What overall pattern of organization does the author use?
- Why does the author use that pattern?

Literary Elements are storytelling elements such as characters, setting, and plot, and the techniques associated with them. To use these elements as clues, ask yourself:

- What is the literary element?
- What is the writer's aim in using this element?

Model

About the Text This excerpt is from a nonfiction book about a famous boycott. A boycott is a form of protest in which people refuse to buy a particular product or use a particular service. The first part of the excerpt is the book's introduction. The second part tells the story of a woman who decided to participate in the boycott.

---

from *Freedom Walkers: The Story of the Montgomery Bus Boycott* by Russell Freedman

Not so long ago in Montgomery, Alabama, the color of your skin determined where you could sit on a public bus. If you happened to be an African American, you had to sit in the back of the bus, even if there were empty seats up front.

Back then, racial segregation was the rule throughout the American South. Strict laws—called "Jim Crow" laws—enforced a system of white supremacy that discriminated against blacks and kept them in their place as second-class citizens.

People were separated by race from the moment they were born in segregated hospitals until the day they were buried in segregated cemeteries. Blacks and whites did not attend the same schools, worship in the same churches, eat in the same restaurants, sleep in the same hotels, drink from the same water fountains, or sit together in the same movie theaters.

In Montgomery, it was against the law for a white person and a Negro to play checkers on public property or ride together in a taxi.

Most southern blacks were denied their right to vote. The biggest obstacle was the poll tax, a special tax that was required of all voters but was too costly for many blacks and for poor whites as well. Voters also had to pass a literacy test to prove that they could read, write, and understand the U.S. Constitution. These tests were often rigged to disqualify even highly educated blacks. Those who overcame the obstacles and insisted on registering as voters faced threats, harassment, and even physical violence. As a result, African Americans in the South could not express their grievances in the voting booth, which, for the most part, was closed to them. But there were other ways to protest, and one day a half century ago, the black citizens in Montgomery rose up in protest and united to demand their rights—by walking peacefully.

It all started on a bus.

Point of View This sentence announces that the author will view his subject through the eyes of African Americans.

Relationships These sentences show how the "Jim Crow" laws affected people's daily lives.

Text Structure This paragraph builds up to the key idea of the entire book: black citizens finally refused to stay "in their place."

Literary Elements This sentence sums up, in an intriguing and provocative way, how the protest started.

© EXEMPLAR TEXT

Model continued

Key Ideas This section begins with a key idea: Jo Ann Robinson suffered a very upsetting experience.

Text Structure Transitions signal that the story is being told in chronological order.

Point of View This quotation reveals the bus driver's biased point of view.

Literary Elements The description and quotation build tension.

Relationships The quotation connects this section to the introduction by explaining why this incident caused Robinson to later join the bus boycott.

Author's Purpose Details suggest that the author's purpose is to inform readers about the Montgomery bus boycott while also giving the human side of the story.

Jo Ann Robinson

Looking back, she remembered it as the most humiliating experience of her life, "a deep hurt that would not heal." It had happened just before Christmas in 1949. She was about to visit relatives in Cleveland, Ohio, where she would spend the holidays.

Earlier that day she had driven out to Dannelly Field, the Montgomery, Alabama, airport, and checked her luggage for the flight to Cleveland. Then she drove back to the campus of Alabama State, an all-black college where she had been hired that fall as a professor of English. After parking her car in the campus garage, she took her armful of Christmas gifts, walked to the nearest bus stop, and waited for a ride back to the airport.

Soon a Montgomery City Lines bus rolled into view and pulled up at the stop. Balancing her packages, Jo Ann Robinson stepped aboard and dropped her dime into the fare box. She saw that the bus was nearly empty. Only two other passengers were aboard—a black man in a seat near the back and a white woman in the third seat from the front. Without thinking, Robinson took a seat two rows behind the white woman.

"I took the fifth-row seat from the front and sat down," she recalled, "immediately closing my eyes and envisioning, in my mind's eye, the wonderful two-week vacation I would have with my family and friends in Ohio."

Jolted out of her reverie by an angry voice, she opened her eyes and sat upright. The bus driver had come to a full stop and turned in his seat. He was speaking to her. "If you can sit in the fifth row from the front seat of the other buses in Montgomery," he said, "suppose you get off and ride in one of them."

The driver's message didn't register at first. Robinson was still thinking about her holiday trip. Suddenly the driver rose from his seat, went over to her, and stood with his arm drawn back, as if to strike her. "Get up from there!" he yelled. "Get up from there!"

Shaken and alarmed, Robinson bolted to her feet and stumbled off the bus in tears, packages falling from her arms. She had made the mistake of sitting in one of the front ten seats, which were reserved for white riders only.

"I felt like a dog," she wrote later. "And I got mad, after this was over, and I realized I was a human being, and just as intelligent and far more [educationally] trained than that bus driver was. But I think he wanted to hurt me, and he did. . . . I cried all the way to Cleveland."

Independent Practice

About the Selection In this article, author and educator Richard Mühlberger discusses a famous painting by Rembrandt, a Dutch painter who lived and worked during the 1600s. Rembrandt is generally considered one of the greatest painters of all time.

from *What Makes a Rembrandt a Rembrandt?*
by Richard Mühlberger

Citizen Soldiers

A Dutch poet of Rembrandt's day wrote, "When the country is in danger, every citizen is a soldier." That was the idea behind the militia, or civic guard companies, which trained citizens how to fight and shoot in case their city was attacked. Each company drilled in archery, the crossbow, or the musket. By Rembrandt's time, militia companies were as much social clubs as military organizations.

Captain Frans Banning Cocq, out to impress everyone, chose Rembrandt to paint his militia company, with members of the company paying the artist to have their portraits included in the painting. The huge canvas was to be hung in the new hall of the militia headquarters, where it would be seen at receptions and celebrations along with other militia paintings.

By the mid-seventeenth century, there were more than one hundred big militia paintings hanging in public halls in the important cities of the Netherlands. In all of these group portraits, the men were evenly lined up so that each face got equal attention, just as they had been in traditional anatomy lesson paintings. Rembrandt did not like this way of presenting the scene. He had seen militia companies in action, and there were always people milling about who were not militiamen but who took part in their exercises and parades. To add realism to the piece, he decided to include some of these people, as well as a dog. There was room on the wall for a canvas about sixteen feet wide, large enough for Rembrandt to do what no other painter had ever done before. His idea was to show the exciting commotion before a parade began.

Key Ideas What does the title suggest the text will be about? How might the subhead support that key idea?

Literary Elements Who is the central character of the painting? Do you think he will also be the central "character" of the article? Explain.

Relationships How will Rembrandt's painting differ from earlier militia paintings by other artists?

Practice continued

Text Structure How is this section organized? What words or phrases tell you this?

Key Ideas How does this sentence—and the entire section—help answer the title question?

Two Handsome Officers

Everywhere in the painting, Rembrandt used sharp contrasts of dark and light. Everything that honors the citizen soldiers and their work is illuminated; everything else is in shadow. Captain Frans Banning Cocq is the man dressed in black with a red sash under his arm, striding forward in the center. Standing next to him is the most brightly lighted man in the painting, Lieutenant Willem van Ruytenburgh, attired in a glorious gold and yellow uniform, silk sash, soft leather cavalry boots, and a high hat with white ostrich plumes. His lancelike weapon, called a partisan, and the steel gorget[1] around his neck—a leftover from the days when soldiers wore full suits of armor—are the only hints that he is a military man. Rembrandt links him to Banning Cocq by contrasting the colors of their clothing and by painting the shadow of Banning Cocq's hand on the front of van Ruytenburgh's coat. The captain is giving orders to his lieutenant for the militia company to march off.

Banning Cocq is dressed in a black suit against a dark background, yet he does not disappear. Rembrandt made him the most important person in the composition. Van Ruytenburgh turns to listen to him, which shows his respect for his commander. Banning Cocq's face stands out above his bright red sash and white collar. How well Rembrandt knew that darkness makes faces shine! The captain's self-assured pace, the movement of the tassels at his knees, and the angle of his walking staff are proof of the energy and dignity of his stride.

---

1. gorget (gôr′ jit) *n.* a piece of armor for the throat.

Muskets and Mascots

On either side of these two handsome officers, broad paths lead back into the painting

Rembrandt knew that when the huge group scene was placed above eye level on the wall of the militia headquarters, these empty areas would be the first to be seen. He wanted them to lead the eyes of viewers to figures in the painting who did not have the advantage of being placed in the foreground. In the middle of one of these paths is a man in red pouring gunpowder into the barrel of his musket. Behind the captain, only partially seen, another man shoots his gun into the air, and a third militiaman, to the right of van Ruytenburgh, blows on his weapon to clean it. Loading, shooting, and cleaning were part of the standard drill for musketeers, and so they were included in the painting to demonstrate the men's mastery of their weapons.

Walking in a stream of bright light down the path on the left is a blond girl dressed in yellow with a dead chicken tied to her waist. She has a friend in blue behind her. In their public shows, the militia would choose two young girls to carry the emblems[2] of their company, here the claws of a bird. The yellow and blue of the girls' costumes are the militia's colors. In the parade that is being organized, these mascots will take a prominent place, the fair-haired girl holding aloft the chicken's claws.

Many of the background figures stand on stairs so that their faces can be seen. The man above the girl in yellow is Jan Corneliszoon Visscher, after Banning Cocq and van Ruytenburgh the highest-ranking person in the militia company. He waves a flag that combines the colors of the militia company with the three black crosses of Amsterdam. While Rembrandt did not pose him in bright light, he made him important by placing him high up on the stairs, by showing the sheen in his costume, and by giving him the large flag to unfurl.

Connotation and Tone Does the word *mastery* have positive or negative connotations? How does this word relate to the essay's key idea about Rembrandt?

Connotation and Tone Why do you think the author chose the word *unfurl* instead of *hold* or *wave*?

---

2. emblems *n.* objects that stand for something else; symbols.

Practice continued

Literary Elements
How does this detail create suspense?

Key Ideas What does this fact tell you about the details of Rembrandt's paintings?

Point of View Do you think the author shares this opinion? Explain.

A Red Ribbon and Fine Old Clothes

In spite of his partial appearance, the drummer on the right seems ready to come forward to lead a march with his staccato beat. The sound seems to bother the dusty dog below. Behind the drummer, two men appear to be figuring out their places in the formation. The one in the white collar and black hat outranks many of the others in the scene. His prestige is signaled in an unusual way: A red ribbon dangles over his head, tied to the lance of the man in armor behind van Ruytenburgh. Additional lances can be counted in the darkness, some leaning against the wall, others carried by militiamen. Their crisscross patterns add to the feeling of commotion that Rembrandt has captured everywhere on the huge canvas.

The costumes worn in this group portrait are much more ornate and colorful than what Dutchmen ordinarily wore every day. Some, like the breeches and helmet of the man shooting his musket behind Banning Cocq, go back a hundred years to the beginnings of the militia company. In the eyes of many Dutchmen, clothing associated with a glorious past brought special dignity to the company. What an opportunity for Rembrandt, perhaps the greatest lover of old clothes in Amsterdam!

Not a Night Watch

Night Watch is a mistaken title that was given to the painting over a hundred years after Rembrandt died, but it has stuck, and is what the painting is almost universally called. Although the exaggerated chiaroscuro[3] does give an impression of night time, there is daylight in the scene. It comes from the left, as the shadows under Banning Cocq's feet prove. And it is clear that no one in the painting is on watch, alert to the approach of an enemy. The official title of the painting is *Officers and Men of the Company of Captain Frans Banning Cocq and Lieutenant Willem van Ruytenburgh.*

Rembrandt completed the painting in 1642, when he was thirty-six years old. He probably had no idea that it would be the most famous Dutch painting of all time. In 1678, one of his former students wrote that it would "outlive all its rivals," and within another century the painting was considered one of the wonders of the world.

---

3. **chiaroscuro** (kē är′ ə skoor′ ō) *n.* a dramatic style of light and shade in a painting or drawing.

from What Makes a Rembrandt a Rembrandt?

© 1. **Key Ideas and Details (a)** Why was Rembrandt hired to paint Captain Banning Cocq's militia company? **(b) Analyze:** How did Rembrandt change the way military group portraits were painted?

© 2. **Key Ideas and Details (a) Interpret:** According to the article, what techniques does Rembrandt use to emphasize higher-ranking figures? **(b) Support:** How does the painter make the background figures visible? **(c) Summarize:** What details reveal that a parade is being organized?

© 3. **Integration of Knowledge and Ideas** Based on your reading of the essay, what title would you give Rembrandt's painting? Why?

© 4. **Craft and Structure (a) Describe:** How is this essay organized? **(b) Infer:** Why do you think the author chose to organize it this way?

© 5. **Key Ideas and Details (a)** What might Rembrandt be trying to teach through his artwork? **(b)** How does reading about art help you learn more about it?

© 6. **Integration of Knowledge and Ideas (a)** Use a chart like the one shown to analyze the types of writing Mühlberger uses in the essay.

Examples of Description	Examples of Exposition

(b) Collaborate: With a partner, review your charts. Together, discuss the **author's purpose(s)** for writing the essay. Share your ideas with the class.

Leveled Texts

Build your skills and improve your comprehension of literary nonfiction with texts of increasing complexity.

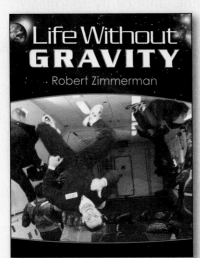

Read **"Life Without Gravity"** to find out about the weightlessness that astronauts experience in space.

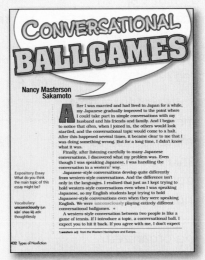

Read **"Conversational Ballgames"** to learn how cultural differences can affect the way people talk to one another.

Common Core State Standards

Meet these standards with either **"Life Without Gravity"** (p. 424) or **"Conversational Ballgames"** (p. 432).

Reading Informational Text

2. Determine two or more central ideas in a text and analyze their development over the course of the text; provide an objective summary of the text. (*Reading Skill: Main Idea*)

5. Analyze the structure an author uses to organize a text, including how the major sections contribute to the whole and to the development of the ideas. (*Literary Analysis: Expository Essay*)

7. Compare and contrast a text to an audio, video, or multimedia version of the text, analyzing each medium's portrayal of the subject. (*Speaking and Listening: Oral Summary*)

Writing

9. Draw evidence from literary or informational texts to support analysis, reflection, and research. **9.b.** Apply *grade 7 Reading standards* to literary nonfiction. (*Writing: Analogy*)

Speaking and Listening

2. Analyze the main ideas and supporting details presented in diverse media and formats and explain how the ideas clarify a topic, text, or issue under study. (*Speaking and Listening: Oral Summary*)

4. Present claims and findings, emphasizing salient points in a focused, coherent manner with pertinent descriptions, facts, details, and examples; use appropriate eye contact, adequate volume, and clear pronunciation. (*Speaking and Listening: Oral Summary*)

Language

1. Demonstrate command of the conventions of standard English grammar and usage when writing or speaking. (*Conventions: Conjunctions*)

4.b. Use common, grade-appropriate Greek or Latin affixes and roots as clues to the meaning of a word. (*Vocabulary: Word Study*)

Reading Skill: Main Idea

The **main idea** is the central point of a nonfiction text. While most texts focus on one main idea, some may address two or more closely related central ideas. The main idea of a paragraph is often stated in a topic sentence. The rest of the paragraph presents **supporting details** that give examples, explanations, or reasons.

When reading nonfiction, **adjust your reading rate to recognize main ideas.**

- **Skim,** or look over the text quickly, to get a sense of the main ideas before you begin reading.
- **Read closely** to learn what the central ideas are.
- **Scan,** or run your eyes over the text, to find answers to questions, to clarify, or to find supporting details.

Using the Strategy: Main Idea Chart

Refer to the chart below as you look for central ideas.

Reading Rate	What to Look For
Skimming before reading	Organization, topic sentences, repeated words
Close reading	Key points, supporting details
Scanning	Particular word or idea

Literary Analysis: Expository Essay

An **expository essay** is a short piece of nonfiction in which an author explains, defines, or interprets ideas, events, or processes. The organization, or structure, of the information depends on the topic and on the author's purpose, or reason for writing. Ideas may be developed in sections or in related paragraphs. Transitional words, such as *finally* and *since,* may clarify the development of ideas.

As you read, analyze the structure the author uses to present ideas.

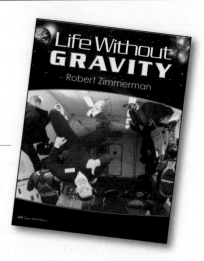

What should we *learn?*

Writing About the Big Question

In "Life Without Gravity," the author describes the ways that astronauts adjust to being weightless in space. Use these sentence starters to develop your ideas about the Big Question.

Reading about other people's experiences can help us **explore** our ideas about _____.

When we are **curious** about unfamiliar experiences, we can find out more by _____.

While You Read Look for information that helps you learn about the astronauts' experiences. For example, identify details that show how a lack of gravity can affect the human body.

Vocabulary

Read each word and its definition. Decide whether you know the word well, know it a little bit, or do not know it at all. After you read, see how your knowledge of each word has increased.

- **manned** (mand) *adj.* having human operators on board (p. 425) *Robotic spacecraft are often cheaper to build than manned ships. man v.*

- **spines** (spīnz) *n.* backbones (p. 425) *Sitting up straight is good for our spines. spiny adj. spinal adj.*

- **feeble** (fē´ bəl) *adj.* weak (p. 426) *The injured bird made a feeble attempt to fly. feebleness n. feebly adv.*

- **blander** (bland´ ər) *adj.* more tasteless (p. 426) *The lack of spices made the chili blander than the cornbread. bland adj. blandest adj.*

- **globules** (gläb´ yo͞olz) *n.* drops of liquid (p. 427) *Globules of water made her hair wet. globule n.*

- **readapted** (rē ə däpt´ əd) *v.* gradually adjusted again (p. 428) *After returning from camp, he readapted to life at home. readapt v. adapt v. adapted v. adaptor n. adaptive adj.*

Word Study

The **Old English suffix -ness** means "the condition or quality of being." It usually indicates the word is a noun.

In this essay, the author explains that **feebleness**, a weakened condition, can be brought on by a lack of gravity.

Meet
Robert Zimmerman
(b. 1953)

Author of
Life Without
GRAVITY

As a boy, Robert Zimmerman became fascinated with science-fiction books. They appealed to him because "the time was the early 1960s, when the first humans were going into space, and these books had an optimistic and hopeful view of that endeavor, as well as the future."

Influence of TV Today, Zimmerman watches little television, but as a child, he remembers viewing the blastoff of *Mercury*, NASA's first manned spacecraft. He recalls thinking, "This is the United States. We can do anything if we put our minds to it!"

DID YOU KNOW? Zimmerman spent twenty years in the movie business as a screenwriter and producer.

BACKGROUND FOR THE ESSAY
Gravity and Weightlessness

Here on Earth, gravity is the force that holds people and objects down and gives them weight. Beyond Earth's atmosphere, however, gravity is weaker. This causes people and things to weigh less. For astronauts in space, the weak gravity environment affects how they eat, drink, and move. It can even affect their bones and muscles, as "Life Without Gravity" points out.

Life without
GRAVITY

Robert Zimmerman

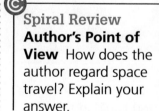

Being weightless in space seems so exciting. Astronauts bounce about from wall to wall, flying! They float, they weave, they do somersaults and acrobatics without effort. Heavy objects can be lifted like feathers, and no one ever gets tired because nothing weighs anything. In fact, everything is fun, nothing is hard.

NOT! Since the first manned space missions in the 1960s, scientists have discovered that being weightless in space isn't just flying around like Superman. Zero gravity is alien stuff. As space tourist Dennis Tito said when he visited the international space station, "Living in space is like having a different life, living in a different world."

Worse, weightlessness can sometimes be downright unpleasant. Your body gets upset and confused. Your face puffs up, your nose gets stuffy, your back hurts, your stomach gets upset, and you throw up. If astronauts are to survive a one-year journey to Mars—the shortest possible trip to the Red Planet—they will have to learn how to deal with this weird environment. ●

Our bodies are adapted to Earth's gravity. Our muscles are strong in order to overcome gravity as we walk and run. Our inner ears[1] use gravity to keep us upright. And because gravity wants to pull all our blood down into our legs, our hearts are designed to pump hard to get blood up to our brains.

In space, the much weaker gravity makes the human body change in many unexpected ways. In microgravity,[2] your blood is rerouted, flowing from the legs, which become thin and sticklike, to the head, which swells up. The extra liquid in your head also makes you feel like you're hanging upside down or have a stuffed-up nose.

The lack of gravity causes astronauts to routinely "grow" between one and three inches taller. Their spines straighten

---

1. **inner ears** (in′ ər irz) *n.* internal parts of the ears that give people a sense of balance.
2. **microgravity** (mī′ krō grav′ i tē) *n.* state of near-weightlessness that astronauts experience as their spacecraft orbits Earth.

Vocabulary
manned (mand) *adj.* having human operators on board

spines (spīnz) *n.* backbones

Expository Essay
What information do you learn about the human body in these paragraphs?

© **Spiral Review**
Author's Point of View How does the author regard space travel? Explain your answer.

Reading Check
What are some disadvantages of weightlessness?

Life Without Gravity **425**

Vocabulary
feeble (fē´ bəl)
adj. weak
blander (bland´ ər)
adj. more tasteless
globules (gläb´ yo̅o̅lz)
n. drops of liquid

out. The bones in the spine and the disks between them spread apart and relax.

But their bones also get thin and spongy. The body decides that if the muscles aren't going to push and pull on the bones, it doesn't need to lay down as much bone as it normally does. Astronauts who have been in space for several months can lose 10 percent or more of their bone tissue. If their bones got much weaker, they would snap once the astronauts returned to Earth.

And their muscles get weak and flabby. Floating about in space is too easy. If astronauts don't force themselves to exercise, their muscles become so feeble that when they return to Earth they can't even walk.

Worst of all is how their stomachs feel. During the first few days in space, the inner ear—which gives people their sense of balance—gets confused. Many astronauts become nauseous. They lose their appetites. Many throw up. Many throw up a lot!

Weightlessness isn't all bad, however. After about a week people usually get used to it. Their stomachs settle down. Appetites return (though

▲ Critical Viewing
Why do you think the red liquid in this picture is floating around? Explain. **[Analyze]**

astronauts always say that food tastes blander in space). The heart and spine adjust.

Then, flying around like a bird becomes fun! Rooms suddenly seem much bigger. Look around you: The space above your head is pretty useless on Earth. You can't get up there to work, and anything you attach to the ceiling is simply something you'll bump your head on.

Main Idea
What is the main idea in this paragraph?

In space, however, that area is useful. In fact, equipment can be installed on every inch of every wall. In weightlessness you choose to move up or down and left or right simply by pointing your head. If you turn yourself upside down, the ceiling becomes the floor.

And you can't drop anything! As you work you can let your tools float around you. But you'd better be organized and neat. If you don't put things back where they belong when you are finished, tying them down securely, they will float away. Air currents will then blow them into nooks and crannies, and it might take you days to find them again.

In microgravity, you have to learn new ways to eat. Don't try pouring a bowl of cornflakes. Not only will the flakes float all over the place, the milk won't pour. Instead, big balls of milk will form. You can drink these by taking big bites out of them, but you'd better finish them before they slam into a wall, splattering apart and covering everything with little tiny milk globules.

Some meals on the space station are eaten with forks and knives, but scooping food with a spoon doesn't work. If the food isn't gooey enough to stick to the spoon, it will float away.

Everyone in space drinks through a straw, since liquid simply refuses to stay in a glass. The straw has to have a clamp at one end, or else when you stop drinking, the liquid will continue to flow out, spilling everywhere.

To prevent their muscles and bones from becoming too weak for life on Earth, astronauts have to follow a boring two-hour exercise routine every single day. Imagine having to run on a treadmill for one hour in the morning and then ride an exercise bicycle another hour before dinner. As Russian astronaut Valeri Ryumin once said, "Ye-ech!"

Even after all this exercise, astronauts who spend more than two months in space are usually weak and uncomfortable when they get back to Earth. Jerry Linenger, who spent more than four months on the Russian space station, *Mir*[3] struggled to walk after he returned. "My

---

3. *Mir* (mēr) *n.* Russian space station.

LITERATURE IN CONTEXT

Science Connection

Weighted Down Your weight in pounds is actually the measure of the downward force of gravity upon your body. How much force gravity puts on you depends on the size and mass of the planet on which you are standing.

Imagine that on Earth you weigh 100 pounds. Because the surface gravity of Jupiter is 2.64 times that of Earth, you would weigh 264 pounds on Jupiter without eating a forkful more. On the other hand, surface gravity on the moon is one-sixth of Earth's gravity. That means your moon weight would be just under 17 pounds, though you would look exactly the same.

Of course, when you are not on a planet or moon, you are out of gravity's pull, so you weigh nothing at all.

Connect to the Literature

Is weightlessness as described in "Life Without Gravity" something you would like to experience? Why or why not?

body felt like a 500 pound barbell," he said. He even had trouble lifting and holding his fifteen-month-old son, John.

When Linenger went to bed that first night, his body felt like it was being smashed into the mattress. He was constantly afraid that if he moved too much, he would float away and out of control.

And yet, Linenger recovered quickly. In fact, almost two dozen astronauts have lived in space for more than six months, and four have stayed in orbit for more than a year. These men and women faced the discomforts of weightlessness and overcame them. And they all **readapted** to Earth gravity without problems, proving that voyages to Mars are possible . . . Even if it feels like you are hanging upside down the whole time!

Vocabulary
readapted (rē ə dapt´ əd) *v.* gradually adjusted again

Critical Thinking

1. **Key Ideas and Details** What is difficult about living in a weightless environment? Support your answer.

2. **Craft and Structure** **(a)** List three unpleasant effects of weightlessness that are explained in the essay. **(b) Cause and Effect:** Describe the cause of each unpleasant effect.

3. **Key Ideas and Details** **(a)** What are some of the fun aspects of weightlessness? **(b) Connect:** What new choices does living in a weightless environment give an astronaut?

Cite textual evidence to support your responses.

4. **Integration of Knowledge and Ideas** **(a) Synthesize:** If the astronauts quoted in the article were offered another trip in space, what advice would you give them about the wisdom of taking the trip again? **(b) Discuss:** Talk about your advice in a small group. As a group, choose three important pieces of advice to share with the class.

5. **Integration of Knowledge and Ideas** **(a)** How do the experiences of other people—such as those of the astronauts in this essay—help us to discover the world? Explain. **(b)** What can we learn from people who experiment with something new? *[Connect to the Big Question: What should we learn?]*

Reading Skill: Main Idea

1. What ideas did you identify from **skimming** the article before you read it?

2. (a) What are three **main ideas** in the article? **(b)** What **supporting details** does the author provide for each idea?

3. Is one main idea more important than the others? Explain.

Literary Analysis: Expository Essay

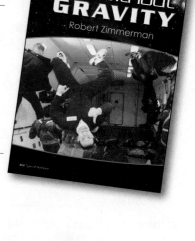

© **4. Craft and Structure** Explain why "Life Without Gravity" is an **expository essay.** Give examples from the text to support your answer.

© **5. Craft and Structure** Fill out a chart like the one shown to organize the information provided in the essay.

What Is Weightlessness?	What Are Its Advantages?	What Are Its Disadvantages?	Author's Conclusion

Vocabulary

© **Acquisition and Use** Rewrite each sentence so that it includes a word from the vocabulary list on page 422 that conveys the same basic meaning as the italicized word or phrase.

1. I could barely hear her *weak* voice over the noise of the radio.

2. My cold makes this food seem *less tasty.*

3. Space flights *with humans aboard* took place in the 1960s.

4. When the thermometer broke, *tiny drops* of mercury spilled onto the table.

5. With no *bones in our backs*, we would not be able to stand.

6. After vacation, we *have gotten used to* being home again.

Word Study Use what you know about the **Old English suffix -*ness*** to explain your answer to each question.

1. If Sara is known for her *nastiness,* does she treat people well?

2. Could *laziness* prevent someone from being productive?

Word Study

The **Old English suffix -*ness*** means "the condition or quality of being."

Apply It Explain how the suffix **-*ness*** contributes to the meanings of these words. Consult a dictionary if necessary.

dreariness
togetherness
greatness

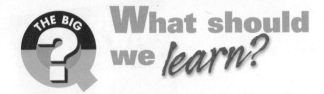

What should we *learn?*

Writing About the Big Question

In "Conversational Ballgames," we learn that Japanese and western cultures have different "rules" for conversation. Use this sentence starter to develop your ideas about the Big Question.

Understanding conversational "rules" can be helpful because _____.

While You Read Look for insights about how communication between people may be affected by cultural beliefs and practices.

Vocabulary

Read each word and its definition. Decide whether you know the word well, know it a little bit, or do not know it at all. After you read, see how your knowledge of each word has increased.

- **unconsciously** (un kän´ shəs lē) *adv.* thoughtlessly (p. 432) *The dog unconsciously scratched his ear.* unconscious *adj.* conscious *adj.*

- **elaboration** (ē lab´ ə rā´ shən) *n.* addition of more details (p. 433) *His elaboration of the main idea helped me grasp his point.* elaborate *v.* elaborately *adv.* elaborateness *n.*

- **murmuring** (mur´ mər iŋ) *v.* making low sounds that cannot be heard clearly (p. 433) *My parents were murmuring in the hallway to each other.* murmur *v.* murmur *n.*

- **parallel** (par´ ə lel´) *adj.* extending in the same direction and at the same distance apart (p. 434) *The train tracks ran parallel to the highway.* parallelism *n.* parallelogram *n.*

- **suitable** (soot´ ə bəl) *adj.* appropriate (p. 434) *The movie was suitable for children.* suitability *n.* suitably *adv.* suit *v.*

- **indispensable** (in´ di spen´ sə bəl) *adj.* absolutely necessary (p. 435) *Sunscreen is indispensable in the strong summer sun.* indispensably *adv.* dispensable *adj.*

Word Study

The **Latin suffix -able** means "capable" or "worthy of being."

In Japanese culture, there is always a **suitable**, or appropriate, pause between speakers.

Meet
Nancy Masterson Sakamoto (b. 1931)

Author of
CONVERSATIONAL BALLGAMES

Nancy Masterson Sakamoto graduated from UCLA with an English degree. She married a Japanese artist and Buddhist priest, and the couple lived in Japan for twenty-four years. There, Sakamoto was a visiting professor at the University of Osaka, where she trained Japanese teachers who taught English to middle school and high school students.

Cultural Differences While living in Japan, Sakamoto was able to observe conversations from both the Japanese and American perspectives.

DID YOU KNOW?
Sakamoto was a professor of American Studies at Shitennoji Gakuen University in Hawaii.

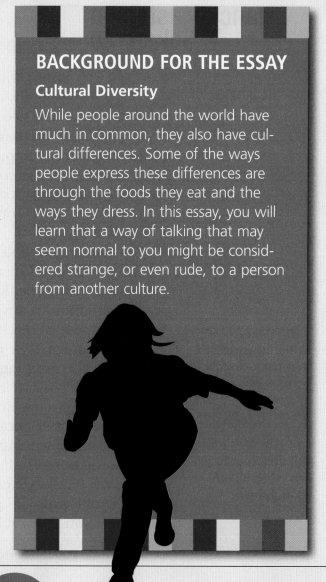

BACKGROUND FOR THE ESSAY
Cultural Diversity
While people around the world have much in common, they also have cultural differences. Some of the ways people express these differences are through the foods they eat and the ways they dress. In this essay, you will learn that a way of talking that may seem normal to you might be considered strange, or even rude, to a person from another culture.

CONVERSATIONAL BALLGAMES

Nancy Masterson Sakamoto

After I was married and had lived in Japan for a while, my Japanese gradually improved to the point where I could take part in simple conversations with my husband and his friends and family. And I began to notice that often, when I joined in, the others would look startled, and the conversational topic would come to a halt. After this happened several times, it became clear to me that I was doing something wrong. But for a long time, I didn't know what it was.

Finally, after listening carefully to many Japanese conversations, I discovered what my problem was. Even though I was speaking Japanese, I was handling the conversation in a western[1] way.

Japanese-style conversations develop quite differently from western-style conversations. And the difference isn't only in the languages. I realized that just as I kept trying to hold western-style conversations even when I was speaking Japanese, so my English students kept trying to hold Japanese-style conversations even when they were speaking English. We were unconsciously playing entirely different conversational ballgames. •

A western-style conversation between two people is like a game of tennis. If I introduce a topic, a conversational ball, I expect you to hit it back. If you agree with me, I don't expect

Expository Essay
What do you think the main topic of this essay might be?

Vocabulary
unconsciously (un kän´ shəs lē) *adv.* thoughtlessly

---

1. **western** *adj.* from the Western Hemisphere and Europe.

you simply to agree and do nothing more. I expect you to add something—a reason for agreeing, another example, or an elaboration to carry the idea further. But I don't expect you always to agree. I am just as happy if you question me, or challenge me, or completely disagree with me. Whether you agree or disagree, your response will return the ball to me.

And then it is my turn again. I don't serve a new ball from my original starting line. I hit your ball back again from where it has bounced. I carry your idea further, or answer your questions or objections, or challenge or question you. And so the ball goes back and forth, with each of us doing our best to give it a new twist, an original spin, or a powerful smash.

And the more vigorous the action, the more interesting and exciting the game. Of course, if one of us gets angry, it spoils the conversation, just as it spoils a tennis game. But getting excited is not at all the same as getting angry. After all, we are not trying to hit each other. We are trying to hit the ball. So long as we attack only each other's opinions, and do not attack each other personally, we don't expect anyone to get hurt. A good conversation is supposed to be interesting and exciting.

If there are more than two people in the conversation, then it is like doubles in tennis, or like volleyball. There's no waiting in line. Whoever is nearest and quickest hits the ball, and if you step back, someone else will hit it. No one stops the game to give you a turn. You're responsible for taking your own turn.

But whether it's two players or a group, everyone does his best to keep the ball going, and no one person has the ball for very long.

A Japanese-style conversation, however, is not at all like tennis or volleyball. It's like bowling. You wait for your turn. And you always know your place in line. It depends on such things as whether you are older or younger, a close friend or a relative stranger to the previous speaker, in a senior or junior position, and so on.

When your turn comes, you step up to the starting line with your bowling ball, and carefully bowl it. Everyone else stands back and watches politely, murmuring encouragement. Everyone waits until the ball has reached the end of the alley, and watches to see if it knocks down all the pins, or only some of them, or none of them. There is a pause, while everyone registers your score.

Main Idea
What details in this paragraph support the idea that conversation is like tennis?

Vocabulary
elaboration (ē lab´ ə rā´ shən) *n.* addition of more details
murmuring (mur´ mər in) *v.* making low sounds that cannot be heard clearly

Spiral Review
Author's Point of View How does the author seem to feel about communication across cultures? Explain your answer.

Reading Check
What happens when the author tries to join Japanese conversations?

Then, after everyone is sure that you have completely finished your turn, the next person in line steps up to the same starting line, with a different ball. He doesn't return your ball, and he does not begin from where your ball stopped. There is no back and forth at all. All the balls run parallel. And there is always a suitable pause between turns. There is no rush, no excitement, no scramble for the ball. No wonder everyone looked startled when I took part in Japanese conversations. I paid no attention to whose turn it was, and kept snatching the ball halfway down the alley and throwing it back at the bowler. Of course the conversation died. I was playing the wrong game.

This explains why it is almost impossible to get a western-style conversation or discussion going with English students in Japan. I used to think that the problem was their lack of English language ability. But I finally came to realize that the biggest problem is that they, too, are playing the wrong game.

Whenever I serve a volleyball, everyone just stands back and watches it fall, with occasional murmurs of encouragement. No one hits it back. Everyone waits until I call on someone to take a turn. And when that person speaks, he doesn't hit my ball back. He serves a new ball. Again, everyone just watches it fall. So I call on someone else. This person does not refer to what the previous speaker has said. He also serves a new ball. Nobody seems to have paid any attention to what anyone

Vocabulary

parallel (par´ ə lel´) *adj.* extending in the same direction and at the same distance apart

suitable (sōōt´ ə bəl) *adj.* appropriate

▼ **Critical Viewing**
How does this image fit the author's description of a conversation between someone from Japan and someone from the west? **[Connect]**

There is no back and forth at all. All the balls run parallel.

else has said. Everyone begins again from the same starting line, and all the balls run parallel. There is never any back and forth. Everyone is trying to bowl with a volleyball.

And if I try a simpler conversation, with only two of us, then the other person tries to bowl with my tennis ball. No wonder foreign English teachers in Japan get discouraged.

Now that you know about the difference in the conversational ballgames, you may think that all your troubles are over. But if you have been trained all your life to play one game, it is no simple matter to switch to another, even if you know the rules. Knowing the rules is not at all the same thing as playing the game.

Even now, during a conversation in Japanese I will notice a startled reaction, and belatedly realize that once again I have rudely interrupted by instinctively trying to hit back the other person's bowling ball. It is no easier for me to "just listen" during a conversation than it is for my Japanese students to "just relax" when speaking with foreigners. Now I can truly sympathize with how hard they must find it to try to carry on a western-style conversation.

If I have not yet learned to do conversational bowling in Japanese, at least I have figured out one thing that puzzled me for a long time. After his first trip to America, my husband complained that Americans asked him so many questions and made him talk so much at the dinner table that he never had a chance to eat. When I asked him why he couldn't talk and eat at the same time, he said that Japanese do not customarily think that dinner, especially on fairly formal occasions, is a suitable time for extended conversation.

Since westerners think that conversation is an indispensable part of dining, and indeed would consider it impolite not to converse with one's dinner partner, I found this Japanese custom rather strange. Still, I could accept it as a cultural difference even though I didn't really understand it. But when my husband added, in explanation, that Japanese consider it extremely rude to talk with one's mouth full, I

▲ **Critical Viewing**
Does this image illustrate the author's ideas about Japanese conversation? Explain. **[Analyze]**

Vocabulary
indispensable (inˊ di spenˊ sə bəl) *adj.* absolutely necessary

 Reading Check
To what two sports does the author compare western-style conversation?

got confused. Talking with one's mouth full is certainly not an American custom. We think it very rude, too. Yet we still manage to talk a lot and eat at the same time. How do we do it?

Main Idea
State the main idea of this paragraph in your own words.

For a long time, I couldn't explain it, and it bothered me. But after I discovered the conversational ballgames, I finally found the answer. Of course! In a western-style conversation, you hit the ball, and while someone else is hitting it back, you take a bite, chew, and swallow. Then you hit the ball again, and then eat some more. The more people there are in the conversation, the more chances you have to eat. But even with only two of you talking, you still have plenty of chances to eat.

Maybe that's why polite conversation at the dinner table has never been a traditional part of Japanese etiquette.[2] Your turn to talk would last so long without interruption that you'd never get a chance to eat.

---

2. **etiquette** (et´ i kit) *n.* formal rules for polite behavior in society or in a particular group.

Critical Thinking

Cite textual evidence to support your responses.

1. **Key Ideas and Details** **(a)** What happened at first when the author joined in during conversations in Japan? **(b) Draw Conclusions:** What misunderstandings took place during those initial conversations? Use examples from the essay to support your response.

2. **Key Ideas and Details** **(a)** To what sports or games does the author compare Japanese-style and western-style conversations? **(b) Apply:** What do the author and her family and friends need to understand about each other?

3. **Key Ideas and Details** **(a)** How do the Japanese feel about conversing during dinner? **(b) Compare and Contrast:** How does their behavior compare with westerners' behavior during a meal?

4. **Integration of Knowledge and Ideas** **(a)** How does awareness of other cultures help us to communicate with people? **(b)** How does it help us to understand the world better? *[Connect to the Big Question: What should we learn?]*

Reading Skill: Main Idea

1. What ideas did you identify from **skimming** the article?

2. **(a)** What are three **main ideas** in the article? **(b)** What **supporting details** does the author provide for each idea?

3. Is one main idea more important than the others? Explain.

Literary Analysis: Expository Essay

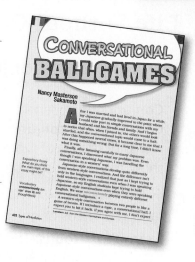

4. **Craft and Structure** Explain why "Conversational Ballgames" is an **expository essay.** Give examples from the text to support your answer.

5. **Craft and Structure** Fill out a chart like the one shown to organize the information provided in the essay.

Describe Polite Conversation in the United States	Describe Polite Conversation in Japan	Author's Conclusion

Vocabulary

Acquisition and Use Rewrite each sentence so that it includes a word from the vocabulary list on page 430 that conveys the same basic meaning as the italicized words or phrases.

1. The lines in the parking lot are *side by side.*

2. I could hear people *talking softly* in the next room.

3. Your descriptive essay should include *many details.*

4. A pencil sharpener is *completely necessary* in a classroom.

5. *Unaware of her actions,* she twirled her hair as she read.

6. Be sure to wear something *appropriate* for the award ceremony at school.

Word Study Use the context of the sentences and what you know about the **Latin suffix -able** to explain your answer to each question.

1. If something is *noticeable,* can you easily see it?

2. Do you reuse a *disposable* camera?

Word Study

The **Latin suffix -able** means "capable" or "worthy of being."

Apply It Explain how the suffix **-able** contributes to the meanings of these words. Consult a dictionary if necessary.

lovable
enjoyable
preferable

Integrated Language Skills

Life Without Gravity • Conversational Ballgames

Conventions: Conjunctions

Conjunctions connect words or groups of words.
Coordinating conjunctions, such as *but* and *so,* connect
words or groups of words that are similar in form. Conjunctions
show the relationship between those two parts.

In the following examples, the coordinating conjunctions are boldface. The words or groups of words they connect are italicized.

Example: **Nouns:** The *pen* **and** *paper* contained fingerprints.
Verbs: Shall we *walk* **or** *ride* our bicycles?
Groups of words: *He ran out the door,* **but** *the bus
had already left.*

Coordinating Conjunctions							
but	or	yet	so	for	and	nor	

Practice A Circle the coordinating conjunction in each sentence. Underline the words or
groups of words connected by the conjunction.

1. Being weightless has both advantages and
disadvantages.
2. You are able to fly, but you also lose your
balance.
3. You have to exercise so your muscles
don't get too weak.
4. I would not like losing my appetite, nor
would I like chasing my food!

© **Reading Application** In "Life Without
Gravity," find two sentences, each with
a different coordinating conjunction, and
identify the words or groups of words the
conjunctions connect.

Practice B Identify the coordinating conjunction in each sentence. Then, use the conjunction in a sentence of your own.

1. Conversations stopped when Sakamoto
joined in, but she did not know why.
2. She wanted to solve the problem, so she
listened carefully to other conversations.
3. She learned that she should not interrupt
or challenge a speaker.
4. She tried not to interrupt, yet sometimes
she could not help herself.

© **Writing Application** Write a paragraph
about how people converse, using three different coordinating conjunctions. Then, circle
the words that the conjunctions connect.

PH WRITING COACH Further instruction and practice are available in *Prentice Hall Writing Coach.*

Writing

Explanatory Text An **analogy** makes a comparison between two or more things that are alike in some ways but otherwise different. For example: A follower without a leader is like a planet without a sun.

- If you read "Life Without Gravity," use this sentence starter to write an analogy: "Life without gravity is like _____."

- If you read "Conversational Ballgames," use this sentence starter to write an analogy: "Communicating with someone from another culture is like _____."

Write several sentences to develop your analogy. Support your statements with details from the selection that you chose. Also use anecdotes (personal stories), examples from real life, and facts or statistics to explain your ideas.

Grammar Application Reread your analogy to make sure you have used conjunctions correctly.

Writing Workshop: *Work in Progress*

Prewriting for Exposition To prepare for a how-to essay that you may write, make a list of five everyday tasks. These tasks can be anything you do, from brushing your teeth to opening your locker. Then, save this Everyday Task List in your writing portfolio.

Speaking and Listening

Presentation of Ideas As your teacher directs, listen to the audio version of either Zimmerman's or Sakamoto's expository essay. Access the audio of the selection by visiting www.PHLitOnline. In a small group, compare and contrast the audio and text versions of your chosen selection. Discuss the ways in which you find each version compelling. Then, prepare and deliver an **oral summary** of the essay.

- Be objective. In your own words, outline the main ideas and supporting details.

- Gather visual aids, such as photographs, illustrations, or charts that support your summary.

- Show each visual aid as you talk about the point it illustrates.

- Provide a clear summarizing concluding statement. Then, as a class, discuss how visual aids clarified each presentation.

Common Core State Standards

L.7.1, L.7.4.b; RI.7.7; W.7.9, W.7.9.b; RI.7.7; SL.7.2, SL.7.4
[For the full wording of the standards, see page 420.]

Use this prewriting activity to prepare for the **Writing Workshop** on page 484.

PHLit Online!
www.PHLitOnline.com

- Interactive graphic organizers
- Grammar tutorial
- Interactive journals

Ⓒ Leveled Texts

Build your skills and improve your comprehension of literary nonfiction with texts of increasing complexity.

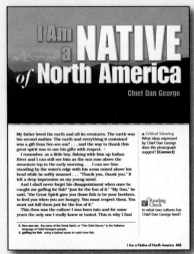

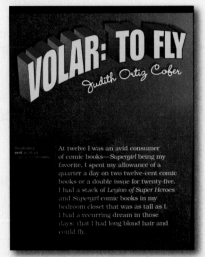

Read **"I Am a Native of North America"** to discover the author's desire to preserve his Native American culture.

Read **"Volar: To Fly"** to learn about the author's childhood wish to escape her life and fly.

Ⓒ Common Core State Standards

Meet these standards with either **"I Am a Native of North America"** (p. 444) or **"Volar: To Fly"** (p. 452).

Reading Informational Text

2. Determine two or more central ideas in a text and analyze their development over the course of the text; provide an objective summary of the text. *(Reading Skill: Main Idea)*

3. Analyze the interactions between individuals, events, and ideas in a text. *(Literary Analysis: Reflective Essay)*

6. Determine an author's point of view or purpose in a text and analyze how the author distinguishes his or her position from that of others. *(Literary Analysis: Spiral Review)*

7. Compare and contrast a text to an audio, video, or multimedia version of the text, analyzing each medium's portrayal of the subject. *(Speaking and Listening: Response)*

Writing

2.a. Introduce a topic clearly, previewing what is to follow; organize ideas, concepts, and information, using strategies such as definition, classification, comparison/contrast, and cause/effect. *(Writing: Outline)*

Language

1.a. Explain the function of phrases and clauses in general and their function in specific sentences. *(Conventions: Prepositions and Prepositional Phrases)*

5.b. Use the relationship between particular words to better understand each of the words. *(Vocabulary: Synonyms and Antonyms)*

6. Acquire and use accurately grade-appropriate general academic and domain-specific words and phrases; gather vocabulary knowledge when considering a word or phrase important to comprehension or expression. *(Vocabulary: Word Study)*

Reading Skill: Main Idea

The **main, or central, idea** is the most important idea in a work or a passage of text. A single main idea may grow out of two or more important ideas that develop throughout the text. Sometimes the author directly states the main idea and then provides the key points that support it. These key points are supported in turn by details such as examples and descriptions.

Other times, the main idea is unstated. The author provides only the key points or supporting details that add up to the main idea. To understand the main idea, **make connections between key points and supporting details.**

- Notice how the writer groups details.
- Look for sentences that pull details together.

Using the Strategy: Main Idea Chart

Use a chart like this one to help you make connections as you read.

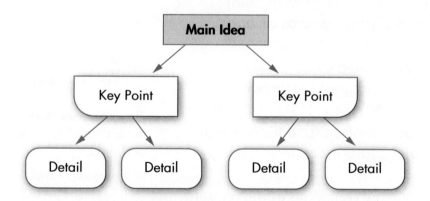

Literary Analysis: Reflective Essay

A **reflective essay** is a brief prose work that presents a writer's thoughts and feelings—or reflections—about an experience or idea. The purpose is to communicate these thoughts and feelings so that readers will respond with thoughts and feelings of their own. As you read a reflective essay, think about the ideas the writer is sharing and analyze the interactions between individuals, events, and ideas in the text.

What should we *learn?*

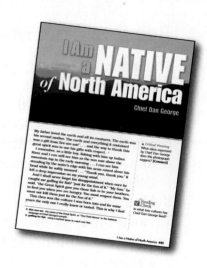

Writing About the Big Question

In "I Am a Native of North America," Chief Dan George recalls the traditions that his Native American culture valued above all. Use this sentence starter to develop your ideas about the Big Question.

It is important to **discover** the traditions and beliefs of people from different cultures because _____.

While You Read Learn how Native Americans' values influenced the way they lived and the choices they made.

Vocabulary

Read each word and its definition. Decide whether you know the word well, know it a little bit, or do not know it at all. After you read, see how your knowledge of each word has increased.

- **distinct** (di stiŋkt´) *adj.* separate and different (p. 444)
  Sparrows and owls are two <u>distinct</u> groups of birds.
  distinctive adj. distinctly adv. distinction n. indistinct adj.

- **communal** (kə myōn´ əl) *adj.* shared by all (p. 444)
  Campers ate together in a <u>communal</u> lunchroom.
  communally adv. commune n. commune v. community n.

- **justifies** (jus´ tə fīz´) *v.* excuses; explains (p. 446) *Her fear <u>justifies</u> her strange behavior. justify v. justifiable adj.*
  justification n.

- **promote** (prə mōt´) *v.* encourage; contribute to the growth of (p. 447) *The teacher tried to <u>promote</u> her students' good habits. promotion n. promotional adj.*

- **hoarding** (hôr´ diŋ) *v.* accumulating and storing a supply as a reserve (p. 447) *After the war, <u>hoarding</u> food made her feel safer. hoard v. hoarder n.*

- **integration** (in´ tə grā´ shən) *n.* the end of separation of cultural or racial groups (p. 448) *<u>Integration</u> allowed students of all races to attend school together. integrate v. integrating v.*

Word Study

The **Latin root -just-** means "law" or "fair and right."

In this essay, Chief Dan George cannot understand a culture that **justifies**, or defends as right, the killing of others in a war.

Meet
Chief Dan George
(1899–1981)

Author of
I Am a Native of North America

Chief Dan George, the son of a tribal chief, was named "Tes-wah-no" but was also known as Dan Slaholt. At age five, he was sent to a mission boarding school, where his last name was changed to George.

At seventeen, Dan George left school and began working. While he was working as a bus driver, he won the role of an aging Indian in a TV series.

Life as an Actor George was called one of the "finest natural actors anywhere." He won acting awards in Canada and earned parts in major motion pictures. With fame, George became a spokesman for Native Americans.

BACKGROUND FOR THE ESSAY

Vancouver-Area Native Americans

Chief Dan George was a member of the Coast Salish Indians in western Canada. His ancestors organized their lives according to a cycle of hunting, food gathering, and cultural activities. During winter, the people stayed in large villages near sheltered bays. In spring, they moved to the beaches, where they fished, hunted, and gathered berries. Then, in the fall, groups met along the rivers to fish. Their cycle of living connected them closely to the natural world.

DID YOU KNOW?

Chief Dan George was more than sixty years old when he became a movie actor.

n the course of my lifetime I have lived in two distinct cultures. I was born into a culture that lived in communal houses. My grandfather's house was eighty feet long. It was called a smoke house, and it stood down by the beach along the inlet.[1] All my grandfather's sons and their families lived in this large dwelling. Their sleeping apartments were separated by blankets made of bull rush reeds, but one open fire in the middle served the cooking needs of all. In houses like these, throughout the tribe, people learned to live with one another; learned to serve one another; learned to respect the rights of one another. And children shared the thoughts of the adult world and found themselves surrounded by aunts and uncles and cousins who loved them and did not threaten them. My father was born in such a house and learned from infancy how to love people and be at home with them.

And beyond this acceptance of one another there was a deep respect for everything in nature that surrounded them.

---

1. inlet (in´ let´) *n.* narrow strip of water jutting into a body of land from a river, a lake, or an ocean.

I Am a NATIVE of North America

Chief Dan George

My father loved the earth and all its creatures. The earth was his second mother. The earth and everything it contained was a gift from See-see-am[2] . . . and the way to thank this great spirit was to use his gifts with respect. ●

I remember, as a little boy, fishing with him up Indian River and I can still see him as the sun rose above the mountain top in the early morning . . . I can see him standing by the water's edge with his arms raised above his head while he softly moaned . . . "Thank you, thank you." It left a deep impression on my young mind.

And I shall never forget his disappointment when once he caught me gaffing for fish[3] "just for the fun of it." "My Son," he said, "the Great Spirit gave you those fish to be your brothers, to feed you when you are hungry. You must respect them. You must not kill them just for the fun of it."

This then was the culture I was born into and for some years the only one I really knew or tasted. This is why I find

▲ **Critical Viewing**
What ideas expressed by Chief Dan George does this photograph suggest? **[Connect]**

✔ Reading Check

What did Chief Dan George's father teach him about the Earth?

---

2. **See-see-am** the name of the Great Spirit, or "The Chief Above," in the Salishan language of Chief George's people.
3. **gaffing for fish** using a barbed spear to catch river fish.

it hard to accept many of the things I see around me.

I see people living in smoke houses hundreds of times bigger than the one I knew. But the people in one apartment do not even know the people in the next and care less about them.

It is also difficult for me to understand the deep hate that exists among people. It is hard to understand a culture that justifies the killing of millions in past wars, and is at this very moment preparing bombs to kill even greater numbers. It is hard for me to understand a culture that spends more on wars and weapons to kill, than it does on education and welfare to help and develop.

It is hard for me to understand a culture that not only hates and fights its brothers but even attacks nature and abuses her. I see my white brother going about blotting out nature from his cities. I see him strip the hills bare, leaving ugly wounds on the face of mountains. I see him tearing things from the bosom of mother earth as though she were a monster, who refused to share her treasures with him. I see him throw poison in the waters, indifferent to the life he kills there; and he chokes the air with deadly fumes.

My white brother does many things well for he is more clever than my people but I wonder if he knows how to love well. I wonder if he has ever really learned to love at all. Perhaps he only loves the things that are his own but never learned to love the things that are outside and beyond him. And this is, of course, not love at all, for man must love all creation or he will love none of it. Man must love fully or he will become the lowest of the animals. It is the power to love that makes him the greatest of them all . . . for he alone of all animals is capable of love.

Love is something you and I must have. We must have it because our spirit feeds upon it. We must have it because without it we become weak and faint. Without love our self-esteem weakens. Without it our courage fails. Without love we can no longer look out confidently at the world. Instead we turn inwardly and begin to feed upon our own personalities and little by little we destroy ourselves.

You and I need the strength and joy that comes from knowing that we are loved. With it we are creative. With it we march tirelessly. With it, and with it alone, we are able to sacrifice for others.

There have been times when we all wanted so desperately to feel a reassuring hand upon us . . . there have been lonely times when we so wanted a strong arm around us . . . I cannot tell you how deeply I miss my wife's presence when I return from a trip. Her love was my greatest joy, my strength, my greatest blessing. ●

I am afraid my culture has little to offer yours. But my culture did prize friendship and companionship. It did not look on privacy as a thing to be clung to, for privacy builds up walls and walls promote distrust. My culture lived in big family communities, and from infancy people learned to live with others.

My culture did not prize the hoarding of private possessions; in fact, to hoard was a shameful thing to do among my people. The Indian looked on all things in nature as belonging to him and he expected to share them with others and to take only what he needed.

Everyone likes to give as well as receive. No one wishes only to receive all the time. We have taken much from your culture . . . I wish you had taken something from our culture . . . for there were some beautiful and good things in it.

Main Idea
What key words or sentences so far have helped you determine the essay's main idea?

Reflective Essay
What experiences does the author reflect on here?

Vocabulary
promote (prə mōt′) v. encourage; contribute to the growth of

hoarding (hôr′ diŋ) v. accumulating and storing a supply as a reserve

Soon it will be too late to know my culture, for integration is upon us and soon we will have no values but yours. Already many of our young people have forgotten the old ways. And many have been shamed of their Indian ways by scorn and ridicule. My culture is like a wounded deer that has crawled away into the forest to bleed and die alone.

The only thing that can truly help us is genuine love. You must truly love us, be patient with us and share with us. And we must love you—with a genuine love that forgives and forgets . . . a love that forgives the terrible sufferings your culture brought ours when it swept over us like a wave crashing along a beach . . . with a love that forgets and lifts up its head and sees in your eyes an answering love of trust and acceptance.

This is brotherhood . . . anything less is not worthy of the name.

I have spoken.

Vocabulary
integration (in´ tə grā´ shən) *n.* the end of separation of cultural or racial groups

Critical Thinking

Cite textual evidence to support your responses.

© 1. **Key Ideas and Details (a)** Name three things that people learn from growing up in communal homes. Use examples from the essay to support your answer. **(b) Compare and Contrast:** Identify several differences between the "two distinct cultures" in which Chief Dan George lived.

© 2. **Craft and Structure (a)** What three things puzzle Chief Dan George about his "white brother"? **(b) Interpret:** When Chief Dan George says, "My white brother . . . is more clever than my people," what does he mean by *clever*?

© 3. **Integration of Knowledge and ideas (a) Analyze:** What is the "brotherhood" that Chief Dan George talks about in the essay? **(b) Evaluate:** Is this brotherhood important? Why or why not?

© 4. **Integration of Knowledge and Ideas Make a Judgment:** Can people maintain a sense of cultural identity while interacting with another group that does not have the same culture? Explain.

© 5. **Integration of Knowledge and Ideas (a)** Why it is important to know the beliefs and traditions of those who came before us? **(b)** What could happen if we ignore the past? *[Connect to the Big Question: What should we learn?]*

Reading Skill: Main Idea

1. (a) What details does Chief Dan George provide about his father's relationship with nature? **(b)** Find a sentence from the work that pulls these details together.

2. What is the **main idea** of the essay?

Literary Analysis: Reflective Essay

3. Craft and Structure Analyze the **reflective essay** in a chart like the one shown. In the first column, write George's reflections on three points. Then, write your response. Trade charts with a partner and discuss your responses. In the third column of your chart, explain whether your responses changed based on your discussion.

George's Reflections	My Responses	After Discussion
Father gives thanks on fishing trip.		

Vocabulary

Acquisition and Use An **antonym** is a word that is opposite in meaning to another word. For the first word in each item, choose the word that is its antonym. Explain your answers.

1. distinct: **(a)** similar **(b)** different **(c)** decided

2. communal: **(a)** busy **(b)** private **(c)** organized

3. justifies: **(a)** supports **(b)** opposes **(c)** excuses

4. promote: **(a)** encourage **(b)** advance **(c)** prevent

5. hoarding: **(a)** storing **(b)** distributing **(c)** saving

6. integration: **(a)** segregation **(b)** assimilation **(c)** mixing

Word Study Use the context of the sentences and what you know about the **Latin root -just-** to explain your answer to each question.

1. If a decision is *unjust,* is it fair?

2. If there is no *justification* for your error, are you to blame?

Word Study

The **Latin root -just-** means "law" or "fair and right."

Apply It Explain how the word root **-just-** contributes to the meanings of these words. Consult a dictionary if necessary.

justice
adjust
injustice

What should we learn?

Writing About the Big Question

In "Volar: To Fly," a daughter learns of her mother's deepest wish. Use this sentence starter to develop your ideas about the Big Question.

Our hopes and dreams help us to **examine** what is important in our lives because they show us _____.

While You Read Look for details that reveal the wishes of the author and her mother. Consider what the author learns from knowing these dreams.

Vocabulary

Read each word and its definition. Decide whether you know the word well, know it a little bit, or do not know it at all. After you read, see how your knowledge of each word has increased.

- **avid** (av´ id) *adj.* eager and enthusiastic (p. 452) *Julia was an avid reader of adventure stories.* *avidly adv.*

- **obsession** (əb sesh´ ən) *n.* extreme interest in something (p. 455) *Her obsession with soccer keeps her from playing other sports.* *obsess v. obsessive adj. obsessed adj.*

- **interrupted** (in´ tə rupt´ əd) *v.* briefly stopped someone from speaking or completing a task (p. 455) *Tim interrupted me as I was speaking.* *interrupt v. interruptive adj. interruption n.*

- **dismal** (diz´ məl) *adj.* dark and gloomy (p. 456) *The grey skies and rainy weather made the day appear dismal.* *dismally adv.*

- **refuse** (ref´ yo͞oz) *n.* trash; waste (p. 456) *The garbage truck collected all the refuse.*

Word Study

The **Latin root -rupt-** means "break" or "burst."

The essay's author knows her parents will be disappointed if their morning talk is **interrupted,** or if their private time is broken.

Meet
Judith Ortiz Cofer
(b. 1952)

Author of
VOLAR: TO FLY

Judith Ortiz Cofer was born in Puerto Rico, but moved to Paterson, New Jersey, with her family when she was very young. Her family made frequent trips between Paterson and Hormigueros, Puerto Rico, where Cofer spent time with her extended family and listened to her grandmother's family stories. In the late 1960s, Cofer's family moved to Augusta, Georgia, where she attended high school and college.

Writing About Cultures Cofer's writing includes fiction, nonfiction, and poetry for both children and adults. Much of Cofer's work addresses differences between the cultures of the United States and Puerto Rico. She is currently a professor of English and creative writing at the University of Georgia.

DID YOU KNOW?
Cofer's first novel, *In The Line of the Sun*, was nominated for the Pulitzer Prize.

BACKGROUND FOR THE ESSAY

Puerto Rico

Puerto Rico is a U.S. territory located between the Caribbean Sea and the North Atlantic Ocean, about 1,000 miles from Miami, Florida. It is approximately three times the size of Rhode Island. Although residents of Puerto Rico were granted U.S. citizenship in 1917, they do not vote in American presidential elections or pay federal taxes. They have their own local government and constitution. Still, as U.S citizens, they can be drafted into military service and must obey federal laws. The dominant language of Puerto Rico is Spanish; however, both English and Spanish are considered official languages.

VOLAR: TO FLY

Judith Ortiz Cofer

At twelve I was an **avid** consumer of comic books—*Supergirl* being my favorite. I spent my allowance of a quarter a day on two twelve-cent comic books or a double issue for twenty-five. I had a stack of *Legion of Super Heroes* and *Supergirl* comic books in my bedroom closet that was as tall as I. I had a recurring dream in those days: that I had long blond hair and could fly.

...and my hair would magically go straight and turn a golden color...

In my dream I climbed the stairs to the top of our apartment building as myself, but as I went up each flight, changes would be taking place. Step by step I would fill out: my legs would grow long, my arms harden into steel, and my hair would magically go straight and turn a golden color. . . Once on the roof, my parents safely asleep in their beds, I would get on tip-toe, arms outstretched in the position for flight and jump out my fifty-story-high window into the black lake of the sky. From up there, over the rooftops, I could see everything, even beyond the few blocks of our barrio; with my X-ray vision I could look inside the homes of people who interested me. Once I saw our landlord, whom I knew my parents feared, sitting in a treasure-room dressed in an ermine coat and a large gold crown. He sat on the floor counting his dollar bills. I played a trick on him. Going up to his building's chimney, I blew a little puff of my super-breath into his fireplace, scattering his stacks of money so that he had to start counting all over again. I could more or less program my Supergirl dreams in those days by focusing on the object

of my current obsession. This way I "saw" into the private lives of my neighbors, my teachers, and in the last days of my childish fantasy and the beginning of adolescence, into the secret room of the boys I liked. In the mornings I'd wake up in my tiny bedroom with the incongruous—at least in our tiny apartment—white "princess" furniture my mother had chosen for me, and find myself back in my body: my tight curls still clinging to my head, skinny arms and legs . . . •

In the kitchen my mother and father would be talking softly over a café con leche. She would come "wake me" exactly forty-five minutes after they had gotten up. It was their time together at the beginning of each day and even at an early age I could feel their disappointment if I interrupted them by getting up too early. So I would stay in my bed recalling my dreams of flight, perhaps planning my next flight. In the kitchen they would be discussing events in the barrio. Actually, he would be carrying that part of the conversation; when it was her turn to speak she would, more often than not, try shifting the topic toward her desire to see her *familia* on the Island: *How about a vacation in Puerto Rico together this year, Querido? We could rent a car, go to the beach. We could . . .* And he would answer patiently, gently, *Mi amor, do*

Vocabulary

dismal (diz´ məl) *adj.*
dark and gloomy

refuse (ref´ yo͞oz)
n. trash; waste

Spiral Review
Author's Point of View In what way do these details about a simple morning routine help convey the author's perspective on the contrast between dreams and reality?

you know how much it would cost for the all of us to fly there? It is not possible for me to take the time off . . . Mi vida, please understand. . . . And I knew that soon she would rise from the table. Not abruptly. She would . . . look out the kitchen window. The view was of a dismal alley that was littered with refuse thrown from windows. The space was too narrow for anyone larger than a skinny child to enter safely, so it was never cleaned. My mother would check the time on the clock over her sink, the one with a prayer for patience and grace written in Spanish. A birthday gift. She would see that it was time to wake me. She'd sigh deeply and say the same thing the view from her kitchen window always inspired her to say: *Ay, si yo pudiera volar.**

---

* Oh, if only I could fly.

Critical Thinking

Cite textual evidence to support your responses.

1. Key Ideas and Details (a) What does the author dream about at night? Use details to support your answer. **(b) Analyze:** What do you think her dreams reveal about her life?

2. Craft and Structure (a) Infer: Why does the author wait in bed in the morning? **(b) Interpret:** Why do you think the mother and father want time to talk?

3. Craft and Structure Connect: Why do both the daughter and mother long to fly? Explain each of their reasons.

4. Craft and Structure (a) What reasons does the author's father give her mother for why they cannot visit Puerto Rico? **(b) Infer:** What does this reveal about their life in the barrio?

5. Integration of Knowledge and Ideas (a) Predict: Do you think that the mother will go to Puerto Rico? Why or why not? **(b) Discuss:** If you were able to fly, where would you go? In a small group, discuss your responses. As a group, choose one idea to share with the class.

6. Integration of Knowledge and Ideas (a) What does the author learn from her dreams? **(b)** How do our imaginations help us to create new possibilities in our lives? *[Connect to the Big Question: What should we learn?]*

Reading Skill: Main Idea

1. (a) What details does Cofer provide about her desire to fly?
(b) Give an example of a sentence from the work that pulls these details together.

2. What is the **main idea** of the essay?

Literary Analysis: Reflective Essay

ⓒ **3. Craft and Structure** Analyze this **reflective essay** in a chart like the one shown. In the first column, write Cofer's reflections on three points, including the one provided. Then, write your responses. Trade charts with a partner and discuss your responses. In the third column, explain whether your responses changed based on your discussion.

Cofer's Reflections	My Responses	After Discussion
Mother longs to visit her family.		

Vocabulary

ⓒ **Acquisition and Use** A **synonym** is a word that is the same or similar in meaning to another word. For the first word in each numbered item, choose the word that is its synonym. Explain your answers.

1. avid: **(a)** apathetic **(b)** eager **(c)** lukewarm

2. interrupted: **(a)** stopped **(b)** appeased **(c)** soothed

3. obsession: **(a)** indifference **(b)** fixation **(c)** coldness

4. refuse: **(a)** treasure **(b)** gift **(c)** rubbish

5. dismal: **(a)** gloomy **(b)** cheerful **(c)** bright

Word Study Use the context of the sentences and what you know about the **Latin root -rupt-** to explain your answer to each question.

1. Would a noisy audience *disrupt* a piano recital?

2. If your appendix *ruptured,* would you need to see a doctor?

Word Study

The **Latin root -rupt-** means "break or burst."

Apply It Explain how the word root **-rupt-** contributes to the meanings of these words. Consult a dictionary if necessary.

corrupt
abrupt
erupt

Integrated Language Skills

I Am a Native of North America • Volar: To Fly

Conventions: Prepositions and Prepositional Phrases

A **preposition** relates a noun or a pronoun that follows the preposition to another noun or pronoun in the sentence. In the sentence *The book is on the table*, the preposition *on* shows the relationship between *table* and *book*.

A **prepositional phrase** begins with a preposition and ends with a noun or pronoun—called the **object of the preposition.** In the prepositional phrase *on the table*, the preposition is *on*, and the object of the preposition is *table*.

Some Commonly Used Prepositions			
above	below	in	over
across	beneath	into	through
after	between	near	to
against	by	of	toward
along	down	on	under
at	during	onto	until
before	for	out	up
behind	from	outside	with

Practice A Identify the prepositional phrase in each sentence. Then, identify the preposition and the object of the preposition.

1. Native Americans lived in big family communities.
2. They learned to live with one another.
3. They had a great respect for nature's gifts.
4. Among their people, hoarding was considered shameful.

© **Reading Application** In "I Am a Native of North America," find three sentences with prepositional phrases.

Practice B Identify the preposition and the object of the preposition in each prepositional phrase. Then, use the prepositional phrase to write a sentence about hopes and dreams.

1. in her bedroom closet
2. during the night
3. through the cloudless sky
4. across the ocean

© **Writing Application** Choose three prepositions from "Volar: To Fly." Then, write a paragraph about a dream you have using the prepositions.

PH WRITING COACH Further instruction and practice are available in *Prentice Hall Writing Coach.*

Writing

Ⓒ **Informative Text** Make an **outline** to show the main idea and supporting details of either "I Am a Native of North America" or "Volar: To Fly." Build your outline using this format:

At the top of your outline, write a sentence stating the main ideas of the essay in your own words. Then, list subtopics for each main idea, and finally, list details.

- Use Roman numerals to identify each key point.
- Use capital letters to identify supporting details.

Grammar Application Check your writing to be sure you have used prepositions and prepositional phrases correctly.

Writing Workshop: *Work in Progress*

Prewriting for Exposition Specific details tell readers exactly how a step should be performed. Review your Everyday Task List for the process you described earlier. Consider what additional details would be useful to readers and include them at the appropriate steps.

Ⓒ **Common Core State Standards**

L.7.1.a, L.7.6; RI.7.7; W.7.2.a
[For the full wording of the standards, see page 440.]

Use this prewriting activity to prepare for the **Writing Workshop** on page 484.

Speaking and Listening

Ⓒ **Presentation of Ideas** In a small group, present a **response** to an audio version of either "I Am a Native of North America" or "Volar: To Fly." Access the audio of the selection by visiting www.PHLitOnline. Once you have listened to the audio version of your chosen selection, follow these steps to complete your response.

- Listen to the audio version of the selection as a group, taking notes on the impact of the selection as it is read aloud. For example, note whether the audio version brings certain words and phrases to life or if the audio version emphasizes a serious or humorous tone that is not evident in the printed version.

- Then, discuss with the group ways in which the audio version enhanced or detracted from the meaning and tone of the printed version. Replay the audio as needed to confirm the group's ideas.

- After your discussion, plan a presentation to the class in which you share your response.

- Assign presenter roles, and rehearse your presentation.

- At the conclusion of your presentation, invite questions and comments from your audience.

PHLit Online!
www.PHLitOnline.com
- Interactive graphic organizers
- Grammar tutorial
- Interactive journals

Test Practice: Reading

Main Idea

Fiction Selection

Directions: *Read the selection. Then, answer the questions.*

When Dad chopped down the pear tree in our back yard, I cried. I loved its short gnarly branches and its pretty white flowers. I was sure I would miss seeing it from my bedroom window. Then Dad transplanted some bushes, and I got upset again. I guess I don't like change very much.

All winter long, I moped about the changes. I especially missed seeing my little tree covered in snow. But a funny thing happened in the spring. When I looked out my window, I realized I could see wetlands in the distance and some rolling hills beyond that. Dad had opened up an amazing view!

Now I spend hours looking through my binoculars. I watch beavers swim in the water. Sometimes I see a large bird with long, slender legs and a long beak fly back and forth. It is amazing how much time my family now spends outside together while bird watching.

1. What is the main idea of this passage?
   A. It is wrong to chop down trees.
   B. Everything looks different in springtime.
   C. Change can be hard, but sometimes it is good.
   D. Spending time together as a family is important.

2. What detail does *not* support the main idea?
   A. The writer's father chopped down a tree.
   B. The writer does not like change.
   C. Without the tree, the writer has an amazing view.
   D. The family now spends hours together outside.

3. Which two words are repeated in the text and hint at the main idea?
   A. chopped and transplanted
   B. change and amazing
   C. upset and missed
   D. spring and family

4. What lesson did the writer learn?
   A. She learned that change can lead to something good.
   B. She learned to enjoy simple things.
   C. She learned to appreciate nature.
   D. She learned to identify different birds.

Writing for Assessment

In a paragraph, identify three details in the passage that show how the writer's attitude changes.

Nonfiction Selection

Directions: *Read the selection. Then, answer the questions.*

You can learn a lot about a bird by looking at its beak, or bill. Birds such as cardinals, sparrows, and finches have strong, thick, cone-shaped beaks. These beaks are perfect for cracking seeds. Bird lovers place feeders filled with seeds in their yards for songbirds. Woodpeckers, on the other hand, have long, chisel-shaped beaks. They use their beaks to peck holes in trees. Tiny hummingbirds have long, tubular bills that they use in much the same way we use a straw.

Herons walk on long, slender legs and often live near wetlands. They have long, straight bills with sharp edges that keep slippery fishes from escaping. Other fish-eaters, like cormorants, have hooks on the end of their beaks for holding fishes. Wading birds with long, narrow bills use their beaks to probe deep in the sand for tasty insects or worms.

1. What is the main idea of this selection?
  A. A bird's beak gives clues about what it eats.
  B. Birds eat a wide variety of foods.
  C. Fish-eaters live near the shore.
  D. It does not really matter what type of beak a bird has.

2. Which detail does *not* directly support the main idea of paragraph 1?
  A. Cone-shaped beaks can crack seeds.
  B. Bird lovers feed songbirds.
  C. Woodpeckers peck holes in trees.
  D. A hummingbird uses its beak like a straw.

3. What is the main idea of paragraph 2?
  A. Herons are fish-eaters.
  B. You can guess a shore bird's diet by looking at its beak.
  C. Most shore birds have long legs.
  D. Shore birds' beaks are different from those of birds that live in the woods.

4. Which detail in paragraph 2 directly supports the main idea of that paragraph?
  A. Herons have long, slender legs.
  B. Fish can be slippery.
  C. A hooked beak can hold a fish.
  D. Birds think insects and worms are tasty.

Writing for Assessment

Connecting Across Texts
Based on information in both passages, write a paragraph describing which birds the writer of the first passage might see through her binoculars.

www.PHLitOnline.com
- Online practice
- Instant feedback

Analyzing Expository Texts

Textbook Article

Magazine Article

Common Core State Standards

Reading Informational Text
8. Trace and evaluate the argument and specific claims in a text, assessing whether the reasoning is sound and the evidence is relevant and sufficient to support the claims.

Writing
1.a. Write arguments to support claims with clear reasons and relevant evidence.

Language
4.b. Use common, grade-appropriate Greek or Latin affixes and roots as clues to the meaning of a word.

6. Acquire and use accurately grade-appropriate general academic and domain-specific words and phrases; gather vocabulary knowledge when considering a word or phrase important to comprehension or expression.

Reading Skill: Analyze Author's Argument

When you read a text that explains a problem and proposes a solution, **analyze the author's argument** to be sure you understand it. Look for a clear statement of the problem and evidence that supports the proposed solution. The evidence that the author presents should come from trustworthy sources and should include facts and statistics. The author's evidence should also be focused, relating directly to his or her claim.

As you read, use a checklist like the one shown to help you trace and analyze an author's argument.

Checklist for Analyzing an Author's Argument

- ❏ Does the author present a clear argument?
- ❏ Is the argument supported by evidence?
- ❏ Is the evidence believable?
- ❏ Does the author use sound reasoning to develop the argument?

Content-Area Vocabulary

These words appear in the selections that follow. You may also encounter them in other content-area texts.

- **decibels** (des´ ə bəlz) *n.* units for measuring the relative loudness of sounds
- **marsh** (märsh) *n.* low land that is permanently or temporarily under water
- **ecology** (ē käl´ə jē) *n.* study of the relationships among plants, animals, and people and their surroundings

Features:
- clear language
- educational purpose
- visual aids such as photos
- text written for a student audience

Keeping It Quiet

from *Prentice Hall Science Explorer*

A construction worker uses a jackhammer; a woman waits in a noisy airport; a spectator watches a car race. All three experience noise pollution. In the United States alone, 40 million people face danger to their health from noise pollution.

> The writer identifies a problem in the opening paragraph.

People start to feel pain at about 120 decibels. But noise that "doesn't hurt" can still damage your hearing. Exposure to 85 decibels (a kitchen blender) can slowly damage the hair cells in your cochlea. As many as 9 million Americans have hearing loss caused by noise. What can be done about noise pollution?

> Supporting facts and statistics explain specific dangers and identify the extent of the problem.

The Issues

What Can Individuals Do?

Some work conditions are noisier than others. Construction workers, airport employees, and truck drivers are all at risk. Workers in noisy environments can help themselves by using ear protectors, which can reduce noise levels by 35 decibels.

Many leisure activities also pose a risk. A listener at a rock concert or someone riding a motorbike can prevent damage by using ear protectors. People can also reduce noise at the source. They can buy quieter machines and avoid using lawnmowers or power tools at quiet times of the day. Simply turning down the volume on headphones for radios and CD players can help prevent hearing loss in young people.

> The writer proposes some solutions to the problem.

What Can Communities Do?

Transportation—planes, trains, trucks, and cars—is the largest source of noise pollution. About 15 million Americans live near airports or under airplane flight paths. Careful planning to locate airports away from dense populations can reduce noise. Cities can also prohibit late-night flights.

This statistic supports the idea that the problem is widespread.

Many communities have laws against noise that exceeds a certain decibel level, but these laws are hard to enforce. In some cities, "noise police" can give fines to people who use noisy equipment.

What Can the Government Do?

A National Office of Noise Abatement and Control was set up in the 1970s. It required labels on power tools to tell how much noise they made. But in 1982, this office lost its funding. In 1997, lawmakers proposed The Quiet Communities Act to bring the office back and set limits to many types of noise. But critics say that national laws have little effect. They want the federal government to encourage—and pay for—research into making quieter vehicles and machines.

The author describes early attempts to solve the problem, as well as more recent solutions.

Marine Extension Service

On the Boardwalk

FOR THE FIRST TIME IN HIS LIFE Savannah native Jay Norris led the way to the water, racing through maritime forest and salt **marsh** toward the Skidaway River, his wheelchair rolling smoothly over the surface of the trail.

"It's the first time he's been on an offroad path and not attached to my back," said his mother, Dawn Norris. "He was out ahead of me, as independent and carefree as you can expect a 9-year-old to be."

Jay Norris can now learn first-hand about salt marsh **ecology** and the Georgia coast thanks to the new Americans with Disabilities Act (ADA)-funded boardwalk and nature trail on Skidaway Island, Ga.

"I saw fiddler crabs, little snails and marsh," said Jay Norris, who cut the ribbon for the trail's grand opening on May 20, 2006. "It was great and awesome. I liked it a bunch."

The University of Georgia's Marine Education Center and Aquarium on Skidaway Island supports year-round educational programs for both youth and adults, and provides an overview of the physical and biological processes that shape the Georgia coast.

"We continually try to expand our offerings to the general public, both locally and regionally," said Bob Williams, interim associate director for marine education. "With the boardwalk and nature trail, we had an opportunity to expand what we have to offer outside the building."

Marine educators imagined building a universally accessible boardwalk that would not only extend over the

The writer takes the position that all people should have access to nature.

space to the laboratories, classrooms and original dirt and gravel pathways already in use.

"Our classes were having some impact on the salt marsh," said marine education specialist John Crawford. "They can't help but trample on the mud. The marsh recovers, but it takes a little while. We were looking for an alternative and thought maybe a boardwalk would be a way to go."

The new Jay Wolf Nature Trail begins at the aquarium and winds through a canopy of live oak and laurel trees dripping with Spanish moss before entering the dense woods of maritime forest. Interpretive signs along the way identify trees, plants, and shrubs and provide information on Georgia's coastal ecology. A few hundred yards into the forest, the trail connects to a new wooden boardwalk that extends over the marsh to the Skidaway River.

A platform at the end of the boardwalk allows marine educators to give presentations to groups overlooking the marsh and the river. Every 100 feet or so, gates in the four-feet-high railing open to allow interactive teaching and interpretive education and better views for children and people with disabilities.

"Now with the gates students using a wheelchair can raise and lower anything from a hula hoop to a meter-square sampling device down to the marsh," Crawford said. That means more interaction with Georgia's coastal environment, especially for people like Jay Norris who live near the water but have been unable to explore their surroundings on their own.

- AMANDA E. SWENNES

The writer quotes an expert to show the impact people can have on the environment.

Savannah native Jay Norris (right) cut the ribbon for the Jay Wolf Nature Trail's grand opening on Skidaway Island, GA, May 20, 2006. The new ADA-approved nature trail and boardwalk (above) make the Georgia coast accessible to all.

Comparing Expository Texts

© 1. Key Ideas and Details (a) What **argument** does the author make in the textbook article? **(b)** What argument does the author make in the magazine article? **(c)** Which argument do you find more convincing? Explain your answer.

Content-Area Vocabulary

2. The word *ecology* is made up of two Greek word parts: the prefix *eco-,* meaning "house" or "environment," and the suffix *-logy,* meaning "the study of." **(a)** List two words with the prefix *eco-* and two words with the suffix *-logy.* Use a dictionary to confirm each word's definition. **(b)** Use each word in a sentence that shows its meaning.

⏱ Timed Writing

Argumentative Text: Propose a Solution

> **Format**
> The prompt calls for a *brief essay.* Therefore, you will need to present and support your ideas in three to five paragraphs.

Noise pollution can be a serious hazard. Write a brief essay in which you propose a solution to this problem in your community. Use information from the text you have read to support your argument. (25 minutes)

> **Academic Vocabulary**
> When you *propose a solution,* you suggest a way to solve a problem. To *support* your idea, use details that show why a solution is needed and why it might work.

5-Minute Planner

Complete these steps before you begin to write:

1. Read the prompt carefully, noting the key highlighted words.

2. Review the textbook article on noise pollution. Note how the author's argument and evidence might apply to your community and be used to support your argument.

3. Think about how noise pollution affects your community, and list a few ideas for possible solutions. **TIP** The evidence you present to support your solutions should include facts, including numerical data, or statistics. Every supporting detail you cite should relate directly to your claim.

4. Use your notes as you begin to draft your essay.

Comparing Biography and Autobiography

In an **autobiography,** a person tells his or her own life story. Authors of autobiographies may write about their own experiences to explain their actions, to provide insight into their choices, or to show the personal side of an event.

In contrast, in a **biography,** an author tells the life story of another person. Authors of biographies often write to analyze a person's experiences and actions. Biographies are often written about famous people, but they can also be written about ordinary people. The subject of a biography may be seen as an example from whom readers can learn a valuable lesson.

Both biography and autobiography focus on actual events and offer insights to explain a person's actions or ideas. However, the two forms have these important differences:

Biography
- More objective
- Based on research
- Should have a balanced viewpoint

Autobiography
- More personal
- Based on memory and emotion
- May present a personal bias, or slant

Text Structures The two forms are often complex because they cover so many parts of a subject's life. To make sense of that complexity, writers may break the information into sections. These sections may have titles or may be woven into a flowing story. As you read, use a chart like the one shown to record details that reveal each subject's personality. Analyze how these details are arranged in sections or episodes that add to your sense of the subject as a whole.

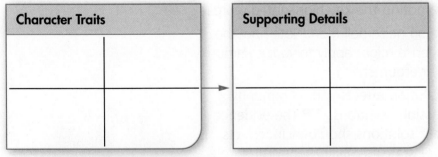

Character Traits		Supporting Details	

Common Core State Standards

Reading Informational Text

5. Analyze the structure an author uses to organize a text, including how the major sections contribute to the whole and to the development of the ideas.

6. Determine an author's point of view or purpose in a text and analyze how the author distinguishes his or her position from that of others.

Writing

2. Write informative/explanatory texts to examine a topic and convey ideas, concepts, and information through the selection, organization, and analysis of relevant content.

4. Produce clear and coherent writing in which the development, organization, and style are appropriate to task, purpose, and audience.

www.PHLitOnline.com

- Vocabulary flashcards
- Interactive journals
- More about the authors
- Selection audio
- Interactive graphic organizers

What should we *learn?*

Writing About the Big Question

In each of these narratives, a boy discovers something that interests him and becomes his lifelong pursuit. Use this sentence starter to develop your ideas about the Big Question.

When you **inquire** about something new, it allows you to _____.

Meet the Authors

Barbara Eaglesham (b. 1957)

Author of "A Special Gift—The Legacy of 'Snowflake' Bentley"

Barbara Eaglesham loves looking through a microscope—especially at snowflakes. When she first read about "Snowflake" Bentley she quickly became a fan, and she wanted to spread the word. "I get very jazzed about science," Eaglesham confesses. "I love to attempt to communicate complicated subjects to young people, and watch them get excited about it, too." Her piece about "Snowflake" Bentley was originally published in *Odyssey: Adventures in Science*.

Russell Baker (b. 1925)

Author of "No Gumption"

Newspaper columnist, author, and humorist Russell Baker grew up during the Great Depression, a period in the 1930s of poor business conditions and major unemployment. Baker's father, a stonemason, died when Baker was five years old. These facts provided the substance for much of Baker's later writing, which mixes humor with sadness.

Winning Honors Baker began his career as a journalist for the *Baltimore Sun* and *The New York Times*. He later won one Pulitzer Prize for his "Observer" column in the *Times* and another for his autobiography *Growing Up*, from which this essay comes.

A Special Gift —
The Legacy of "Snowflake" Bentley

Barbara Eaglesham

Wilson Bentley received a gift on his 15th birthday that was to change his life—an old microscope his mother had once used in teaching. As birthday gifts go, it might not have seemed like much, but to this 1880s Vermont farm boy it was special indeed. "When the other boys of my age were playing with popguns and sling-shots, I was absorbed in studying things under this microscope," he later wrote.

And nothing fascinated him more than snowflakes. It would become a passion that would last a lifetime, earn him the nickname "Snowflake Bentley," and make him known around the world.

Focused on Beauty

If you have ever seen a snowflake design on a mug, or on jewelry, or maybe on a tote bag, chances are it was based on one of Bentley's more than 5,000 photomicrographs[1] of snow crystals (snow crystals are the building blocks of snowflakes).

At first, though, Bentley did not own a camera. He had only his eyes and his microscope, and no way to share his enjoyment of the delicate hexagons other than to draw them. As soon as the snow started to fly (and if his chores were

Vocabulary

hexagons (hek′ sə gänz′) *n.* six-sided figures

---

1. **photomicrographs** photographs made through a microscope.

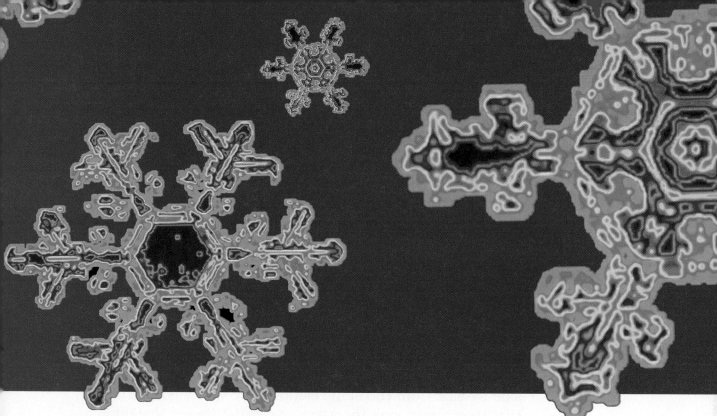

done), he would collect some snow crystals on a board painted black. He'd spend hours inside his woodshed, where he had his microscope, picking up the most perfect ones on the end of a piece of straw from a broom and transferring them to a microscope slide. There, he would flatten them with a bird feather. Then, holding his breath, he would observe the crystal and hurry to draw what he saw before it evaporated into thin air. It was a frustrating business to try to capture all the details in a drawing while simultaneously being in a race against time.

Eventually, a few years later, Bentley noticed an advertisement for a microscope and camera that he knew was the answer to his dreams. The problem was, the equipment cost $100—equal to a whopping $2,000 today. His father, being a serious, hardworking farmer, felt that looking through a microscope was a waste of time. "Somehow my mother got him to spend the money." Bentley wrote, "but he never came to believe it had been worthwhile." That was probably a feeling shared by the locals of Jericho, who nicknamed him "Snowflake" Bentley.

Undeterred, he began his quest to photograph a snow crystal. Once he attached the microscope to the camera and rigged up a way to focus it without running back and forth (he couldn't reach the focus knob from behind the camera),

Spiral Review
Author's Point of View Based on this paragraph, how would you describe the author's perspective on her subject?

Reading Check
Before he had a camera, how did Bentley capture the shapes of snow-flakes?

he began experimenting with photography. In the 1880s, few people owned a camera, so Bentley had no one to ask for help. Time after frustrating time, his negatives appeared blank. Not until the following winter did he figure out that too much light was reaching the camera lens. His solution was to place a metal plate with a pinhole in the center beneath the stage of the microscope, to cut down the stray light and allow only the light waves carrying the image to reach the camera.

This was the key, and on January 15, 1885, at the age of 19, Bentley finally photographed a snowflake! Many hours over the next 45 years were spent in his tiny darkroom beneath the stairs developing negatives that he then carried, often by lantern-light, to the brook for washing. In all that time, he never saw two snow crystals that were exactly alike, although he realized that if he were able to collect two crystals side-by-side from the same cloud, there was a good chance that they might look the same. (Scientist Nancy Knight did just that in 1988, and indeed found two identical snow crystals!)

An artist as well as a scientist, Bentley wanted to find a way to make the shape of the crystal stand out more from the white background of the photo paper. He couldn't bring himself to alter his original glass plate negatives, so he began making copies of them and scraping the photographic emulsion away from the edges of the images with a knife, a time-consuming trick that allowed sunlight through, turning the background black when printed by sunlight.

Bentley's book, *Snow Crystals*, containing 2,453 of his photographs, was finally published and delivered to his house just weeks before his death in 1931. Bentley was pleased. He never made more than a few thousand dollars from his work, but it had been a labor of love and he was satisfied to know that he would finally be able to share the beauty of his snow crystals with the world.

He is remembered primarily for this accomplishment, but to his friends and

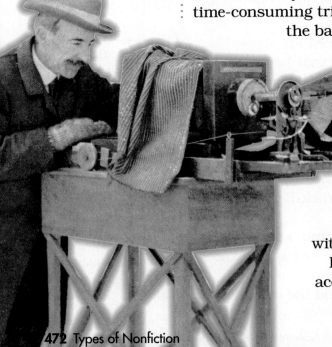

Biography
What details here reveal the author's research into Bentley's life?

family, he was kind, gentle, and funny "Willie." He was the man who would sometimes tie an insect to a blade of grass to photograph it covered with dew the next morning, and who always chewed every bite 36 times. He was a gifted pianist who also played the violin and clarinet. He was the bachelor farmer who lived in the same farmhouse all his life. To scientists, he was the untrained researcher who not only photographed snow crystals, but also kept a detailed daily log of local weather conditions throughout his life and developed a method to measure the size of raindrops. To the people of Jericho, he is remembered as the not-so-flaky-after-all "Snowflake" Bentley.

Critical Thinking

© **1. Key Ideas and Details (a)** What gift did Bentley receive for his fifteenth birthday? **(b) Compare and Contrast:** How was this gift different from the types of gifts that other boys received?

© **2. Key Ideas and Details (a)** What problems did Bentley face when he tried to draw the snowflakes he observed? **(b) Speculate:** Why do you think Bentley's father agreed to buy the expensive equipment?

© **3. Integration of Knowledge and Ideas (a) Analyze:** In what ways was Bentley's work beneficial to science? **(b) Analyze:** What other benefits to society did Bentley's photographs have?

© **4. Integration of Knowledge and Ideas (a)** How did Bentley's curiosity help change the direction of his life? **(b) Determine:** What may have been the author's reason for writing the selection? **(c) Discuss:** With a partner, discuss whether a person has to be accomplished for someone to write about him or her. *[Connect to the Big Question: What should we learn?]*

Cite textual evidence to support your responses.

No Gumption

Russell Baker

I began working in journalism when I was eight years old. It was my mother's idea. She wanted me to "make something" of myself and, after a level-headed appraisal[1] of my strengths, decided I had better start young if I was to have any chance of keeping up with the competition.

The flaw in my character which she had already spotted was lack of "gumption." My idea of a perfect afternoon was lying in front of the radio rereading my favorite Big Little Book,[2] *Dick Tracy Meets Stooge Viller.* My mother despised inactivity. Seeing me having a good time in repose, she was powerless to hide her disgust. "You've got no more gumption than a bump on a log," she said. "Get out in the kitchen and help Doris do those dirty dishes."

My sister Doris, though two years younger than I, had enough gumption for a dozen people. She positively enjoyed washing dishes, making beds, and cleaning the house. When she was only seven she could carry a piece of short-weighted cheese back to the A&P, threaten the manager with legal action, and come back triumphantly with the full quarter-pound we'd paid for and a few ounces extra thrown in for forgiveness. Doris could have made something of herself if she hadn't been a girl. Because of this defect, however, the best she could hope for was a career as a nurse or schoolteacher, the only work that capable females were considered up to in those days.

This must have saddened my mother, this twist of fate that had allocated all the gumption to the daughter and left her with a son who was content with Dick Tracy and Stooge Viller. If disappointed, though, she wasted no energy on self-pity. She would make me make something of myself whether I wanted to or not. "The Lord helps those who help themselves," she said. That was the way her mind worked.

She was realistic about the difficulty. Having sized up

Vocabulary
gumption (gump´ shən) *n.* courage; enterprise

▲ **Critical Viewing**
Judging by the clothing worn in these images, when does the story take place? **[Assess]**

---

1. **appraisal** (ə prāz´ əl) *n.* judgment; evaluation.
2. **Big Little Book** a small, inexpensive picture book that often portrayed the adventures of comic-strip heroes like Dick Tracy.

THE SATURDAY EVENING POST

Fou728klin

5c. the Copy

November 27, 1937

Volume 210, Number 22

WATER BUKIT

Birthday Greetings

Frances Tipton Hunter

THIS PEACE IS A CHEAT—By JOHN GUNTHER

the material the Lord had given her to mold, she didn't overestimate what she could do with it. She didn't insist that I grow up to be President of the United States.

Fifty years ago parents still asked boys if they wanted to grow up to be President, and asked it not jokingly but seriously. Many parents who were hardly more than paupers still believed their sons could do it. Abraham Lincoln had done it. We were only sixty-five years from Lincoln. Many a grandfather who walked among us could remember Lincoln's time. Men of grandfatherly age were the worst for asking if you wanted to grow up to be President. A surprising number of little boys said yes and meant it.

I was asked many times myself. No, I would say, I didn't want to grow up to be President. My mother was present during one of these interrogations.[3] An elderly uncle, having posed the usual question and exposed my lack of interest in the Presidency, asked, "Well, what do you want to be when you grow up?"

I loved to pick through trash piles and collect empty bottles, tin cans with pretty labels, and discarded magazines. The most desirable job on earth sprang instantly to mind. "I want to be a garbage man," I said.

My uncle smiled, but my mother had seen the first distressing evidence of a bump budding on a log. "Have a little gumption, Russell," she said. Her calling me Russell was a signal of unhappiness. When she approved of me I was always "Buddy."

When I turned eight years old she decided that the job of starting me on the road toward making something of myself could no longer be safely delayed. "Buddy," she said one day, "I want you to come home right after school this afternoon. Somebody's coming and I want you to meet him."

When I burst in that afternoon she was in conference in the parlor with an executive of the Curtis Publishing Company. She introduced me. He bent low from the waist and shook my hand. Was it true as my mother had told him, he asked, that I longed for the opportunity to conquer the world of business?

My mother replied that I was blessed with a rare determination to make something of myself.

"That's right," I whispered.

"But have you got the grit, the character, the never-say-quit spirit it takes to succeed in business?"

3. interrogations (in ter ə´ gā´ shənz) *n.* situations in which a person is formally questioned.

Vocabulary
paupers (pô´ pərz)
n. people who
are very poor

Autobiography
What does Baker reveal about himself with these details?

Spiral Review
Author's Point of View What does the author's humorous perspective tell readers about his purpose for writing?

My mother said I certainly did.

"That's right," I said.

He eyed me silently for a long pause, as though weighing whether I could be trusted to keep his confidence, then spoke man-to-man. Before taking a crucial step, he said, he wanted to advise me that working for the Curtis Publishing Company placed enormous responsibility on a young man. It was one of the great companies of America. Perhaps the greatest publishing house in the world. I had heard, no doubt, of the *Saturday Evening Post*?

Heard of it? My mother said that everyone in our house had heard of the *Saturday Post* and that I, in fact, read it with religious devotion.

Then doubtless, he said, we were also familiar with those two monthly pillars of the magazine world, the *Ladies Home Journal* and the *Country Gentleman*.

Indeed we were familiar with them, said my mother.

Representing the *Saturday Evening Post* was one of the weightiest honors that could be bestowed in the world of business, he said. He was personally proud of being a part of that great corporation.

My mother said he had every right to be.

Again he studied me as though debating whether I was worthy of a knighthood. Finally: "Are you trustworthy?"

My mother said I was the soul of honesty.

"That's right," I said.

The caller smiled for the first time. He told me I was a lucky young man. He admired my spunk. Too many young men thought life was all play. Those young men would not go far in this world. Only a young man willing to work and save and keep his face washed and his hair neatly combed could hope to come out on top in a world such as ours. Did I truly and sincerely believe that I was such a young man?

"He certainly does," said my mother.

"That's right," I said.

He said he had been so impressed by what he had seen of me that he was going to make me a representative of the Curtis Publishing Company. On the following Tuesday, he said, thirty freshly printed copies of the *Saturday Evening Post* would be delivered at our door. I would place these magazines,

Vocabulary
crucial (krōō′ shəl) *adj.* important; critical

▼ **Critical Viewing**
How does your image of Russell Baker compare with this photograph of him with his sister? **[Compare and Contrast]**

✔ Reading Check
What job does Russell have?

still damp with the ink of the presses, in a handsome canvas bag, sling it over my shoulder, and set forth through the streets to bring the best in journalism, fiction, and cartoons to the American public.

He had brought the canvas bag with him. He presented it with reverence fit for a chasuble.[4] He showed me how to drape the sling over my left shoulder and across the chest so that the pouch lay easily accessible[5] to my right hand, allowing the best in journalism, fiction, and cartoons to be swiftly extracted and sold to a citizenry whose happiness and security depended upon us soldiers of the free press.

The following Tuesday I raced home from school, put the canvas bag over my shoulder, dumped the magazines in, and, tilting to the left to balance their weight on my right hip, embarked on the highway of journalism.

We lived in Belleville, New Jersey, a commuter town at the northern fringe of Newark. It was 1932, the bleakest year of the Depression. My father had died two years before, leaving us with a few pieces of Sears, Roebuck furniture and not much else, and my mother had taken Doris and me to live with one of her younger brothers. This was my Uncle Allen. Uncle Allen had made something of himself by 1932. As salesman for a soft-drink bottler in Newark, he had an income of $30 a week; wore pearl-gray spats,[6] detachable collars, and a three-piece suit; was happily married; and took in threadbare relatives.

Autobiography
Does Russell have the same goals for himself that his mother has? Explain.

With my load of magazines I headed toward Belleville Avenue. That's where the people were. There were two filling stations at the intersection with Union Avenue, as well as an A&P, a fruit stand, a bakery, a barber shop, Zuccarelli's drugstore, and a diner shaped like a railroad car. For several hours I made myself highly visible, shifting position now and then from corner to corner, from shop window to shop window, to make sure everyone could see the heavy black lettering on the canvas bag that said *The Saturday Evening Post*. When the angle of the light indicated it was suppertime, I walked back to the house.

"How many did you sell, Buddy?" my mother asked.

"None."

"Where did you go?"

---

4. **chasuble** (chaz´ ə bəl) *n.* sleeveless outer garment worn by priests.
5. **accessible** (ak ses´ ə bəl) *adj.* available.
6. **spats** (spats) *n.* cloth or leather material that covers the upper part of shoes or ankles.

"The corner of Belleville and Union Avenues."

"What did you do?"

"Stood on the corner waiting for somebody to buy a *Saturday Evening Post*."

"You just stood there?"

"Didn't sell a single one."

"For God's sake, Russell!"

Uncle Allen intervened. "I've been thinking about it for some time," he said, "and I've about decided to take the *Post* regularly. Put me down as a regular customer." I handed him a magazine and he paid me a nickel. It was the first nickel I earned.

Afterwards my mother instructed me in salesmanship. I would have to ring doorbells, address adults with charming self-confidence, and break down resistance with a sales talk pointing out that no one, no matter how poor, could afford to be without the *Saturday Evening Post* in the home.

I told my mother I'd changed my mind about wanting to succeed in the magazine business.

"If you think I'm going to raise a good-for-nothing," she replied, "you've got another think coming." She told me to hit the streets with the canvas bag and start ringing doorbells the instant school was out next day. When I objected that I didn't feel any aptitude for salesmanship, she asked how I'd like to lend her my leather belt so she could whack some sense into me. I bowed to superior will and entered journalism with a heavy heart.

My mother and I had fought this battle almost as long as I could remember. It probably started even before memory began, when I was a country child in northern Virginia and my mother, dissatisfied with my father's plain workman's life, determined that I would not grow up like him and his people, with calluses on their hands, overalls on their backs, and fourth-grade educations in their heads. She had fancier ideas of life's possibilities. Introducing me to the *Saturday Evening Post*, she was trying to wean me as early as possible from my father's world where men left with lunch pails at sunup, worked with their hands until the grime ate into the pores, and died with a few sticks of mail-order furniture as their legacy. In my mother's vision of the better life there were desks

Autobiography
Why do you think Baker includes this conversation between himself and his mother?

▲ **Critical Viewing**
Does this picture fit your idea of Baker's mother? Explain.
[Connect]

Vocabulary
aptitude (apˊ tə to͞od) *n.* talent; ability

Reading Check
How did Russell do on his first day of selling?

▼ **Critical Viewing**
Based on these covers, do you think *The Saturday Evening Post* would be easy to sell? Why? **[Take a Position]**

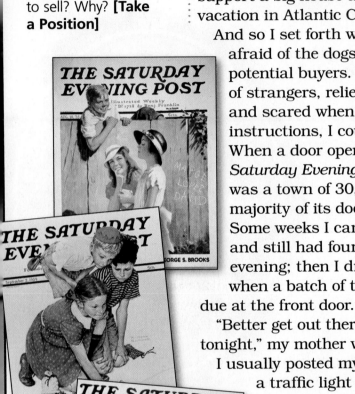

and white collars, well-pressed suits, evenings of reading and lively talk, and perhaps—if a man were very, very lucky and hit the jackpot, really made something important of himself— perhaps there might be a fantastic salary of $5,000 a year to support a big house and a Buick with a rumble seat[7] and a vacation in Atlantic City.

And so I set forth with my sack of magazines. I was afraid of the dogs that snarled behind the doors of potential buyers. I was timid about ringing the doorbells of strangers, relieved when no one came to the door, and scared when someone did. Despite my mother's instructions, I could not deliver an engaging sales pitch. When a door opened I simply asked, "Want to buy a *Saturday Evening Post*?" In Belleville few persons did. It was a town of 30,000 people, and most weeks I rang a fair majority of its doorbells. But I rarely sold my thirty copies. Some weeks I canvassed the entire town for six days and still had four or five unsold magazines on Monday evening; then I dreaded the coming of Tuesday morning, when a batch of thirty fresh *Saturday Evening Posts* was due at the front door.

"Better get out there and sell the rest of those magazines tonight," my mother would say.

I usually posted myself then at a busy intersection where a traffic light controlled commuter flow from Newark. When the light turned red I stood on the curb and shouted my sales pitch at the motorists.

"Want to buy a *Saturday Evening Post*?"

One rainy night when car windows were sealed against me I came back soaked and with not a single sale to report. My mother beckoned to Doris.

"Go back down there with Buddy and show him how to sell these magazines," she said.

Brimming with zest, Doris, who was then seven years old, returned with me to the corner. She took a magazine from the bag, and when the light turned red she strode to the nearest car and banged her small fist against the closed window. The driver, probably startled at what he took to be a midget assaulting his car, lowered the window to stare, and Doris thrust a *Saturday Evening Post* at him.

---

7. rumble seat in the rear of early automobiles, a seat that could be folded shut.

"You need this magazine," she piped, "and it only costs a nickel."

Her salesmanship was irresistible. Before the light changed half a dozen times she disposed of the entire batch. I didn't feel humiliated. To the contrary. I was so happy I decided to give her a treat. Leading her to the vegetable store on Belleville Avenue, I bought three apples, which cost a nickel, and gave her one.

"You shouldn't waste money," she said.

"Eat your apple." I bit into mine.

"You shouldn't eat before supper," she said. "It'll spoil your appetite."

Back at the house that evening, she dutifully reported me for wasting a nickel. Instead of a scolding, I was rewarded with a pat on the back for having the good sense to buy fruit instead of candy. My mother reached into her bottomless supply of maxims[8] and told Doris, "An apple a day keeps the doctor away."

By the time I was ten I had learned all my mother's maxims by heart. Asking to stay up past normal bedtime, I knew that a refusal would be explained with, "Early to bed and early to rise, makes a man healthy, wealthy, and wise." If I whimpered about having to get up early in the morning, I could depend on her to say, "The early bird gets the worm."

The one I most despised was, "If at first you don't succeed, try, try again." This was the battle cry with which she constantly sent me back into the hopeless struggle whenever I moaned that I had rung every doorbell in town and knew there wasn't a single potential buyer left in Belleville that week. After listening to my explanation, she handed me the canvas bag and said, "If at first you don't succeed . . ."

Three years in that job, which I would gladly have quit after the first day except for her insistence, produced at least one valuable result. My mother finally concluded that I would never make something of myself by pursuing a life in business and started considering careers that demanded less competitive zeal.

One evening when I was eleven I brought home a short "composition" on my summer vacation which the teacher had graded with an A. Reading it with her own school-teacher's eye, my mother agreed that it was top-drawer seventh grade

---

8. **maxims** (mak´ simz) *n.* wise sayings.

Autobiography
What do you learn about Russell based on his feelings about his sister's salesmanship?

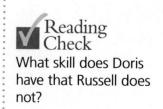
Reading Check
What skill does Doris have that Russell does not?

prose and complimented me. Nothing more was said about it immediately, but a new idea had taken life in her mind. Halfway through supper she suddenly interrupted the conversation.

"Buddy," she said, "maybe you could be a writer."

I clasped the idea to my heart. I had never met a writer, had shown no previous urge to write, and hadn't a notion how to become a writer, but I loved stories and thought that making up stories must surely be almost as much fun as reading them. Best of all, though, and what really gladdened my heart, was the ease of the writer's life. Writers did not have to trudge through the town peddling from canvas bags, defending themselves against angry dogs, being rejected by surly strangers. Writers did not have to ring doorbells. So far as I could make out, what writers did couldn't even be classified as work.

I was enchanted. Writers didn't have to have any gumption at all. I did not dare tell anybody for fear of being laughed at in the schoolyard, but secretly I decided that what I'd like to be when I grew up was a writer.

Autobiography
How would a career in writing have solved a problem that Baker had?

Critical Thinking

Cite textual evidence to support your responses.

1. **Key Ideas and Details (a)** From the passage, find two words or expressions that Baker uses to describe his traits as a young boy. **(b) Analyze:** How did those traits prevent Baker from being a good salesperson?

2. **Key Ideas and Details (a)** Why does Baker's mother get him a job as a newsboy? **(b) Infer:** What goals does Baker's mother set for him as a child? **(c) Compare and Contrast:** Compare Baker's own aims in life as a child with the goals his mother sets for him.

3. **Craft and Structure (a) Analyze:** Identify two examples that show Baker's sense of humor about his poor salesmanship. **(b) Connect:** What does his sense of humor about failure show about his personality?

4. **Integration of Knowledge and Ideas (a)** What does Baker learn about himself through the events he relates here? **(b)** How can learning about someone else's life help us to learn about our own experiences? *[Connect to the Big Question: What should we learn?]*

Comparing Biography and Autobiography

© **1. Key Ideas and Details (a)** In a chart, list three details in the biography that show the writer researched Snowflake Bentley. For each, indicate what source she may have used.

Details	Possible Source

(b) Are there occasions in a biography when readers get opinions directly from the person who is the focus of the biography? Explain.

© **2. Craft and Structure (a)** List two details in "No Gumption" that only Russell Baker could have known. **(b)** How would the narrative be different if Doris were telling the story?

⏱ Timed Writing

Explanatory Text: Essay

Compare and contrast what you learned about Snowflake Bentley with what you learned about Russell Baker. As you write, consider the differences between the genres of biography and autobiography and the sorts of information that each genre delivers. **(40 minutes)**

5-Minute Planner

1. Read the prompt carefully and completely.

2. Gather your ideas by jotting down answers to these questions:

- Which person do you feel you understand better? Why?
- How does the form—autobiography or biography—affect your ability to learn about each person?
- How does the way the story is organized add to your understanding of the subject?

3. Review each selection. Take notes on the types of details, such as facts, descriptions, or plot events, that lead to insights about each subject. Use these notes as you write your comparison-and-contrast essay.

4. Reread the prompt, and then draft your essay.

Writing Workshop

 **Common Core
State Standards**

Writing
2.a. Introduce a topic clearly, previewing what is to follow; organize ideas, concepts, and information, using strategies such as definition, classification, comparison/contrast, and cause/effect; include formatting, graphics, and multimedia when useful to aiding comprehension.
2.d. Use precise language and domain-specific vocabulary to inform about or explain the topic.
4. Produce clear and coherent writing in which the development, organization, and style are appropriate to task, purpose, and audience.
5. With some guidance and support from peers and adults, develop and strengthen writing as needed by planning, revising, editing, rewriting, or trying a new approach, focusing on how well purpose and audience have been addressed.

Write an Explanatory Text

Exposition: How-to Essay

Defining the Form A **how-to essay** is a written, step-by-step explanation of how to do or make something. For example, how-to essays can explain how to repair a bicycle or how to make organic brownies. You may use elements of a how-to essay to write instructions, technical documents, and explanations.

Assignment Write a how-to essay about a process that you know well enough to explain clearly. You should feature these elements:

✔ a *narrow, focused topic* that can be fully explained in the essay

✔ a *list of materials* needed

✔ multi-step directions explained in *sequential order*

✔ *illustrations* that help clarify the directions

✔ appropriate *technical terms* relating to your topic

✔ error-free writing, including *correct use of conjunctions*

To preview the criteria on which your how-to essay may be judged, see the rubric on page 489.

 Writing Workshop: *Work in Progress*

Review the work you did on pages 439 and 459.

Prewriting/Planning Strategies

Choose a topic. List activities you know well in categories such as *sports, assembly and repair,* and *cooking.* Choose one as your topic.

List and itemize. List materials and steps, using the chart as a model. Itemize each part and add specific details.

Making Banana Bread

List

Preheat oven.
Mix dry ingredients.
Mix other ingredients.
Prepare bananas.
Ice the cake.

Itemize

• 2 c. flour	• 1 t. baking soda	• 1/3 c. butter
• 1 c. sugar	• 1 t. cinnamon	• 1 egg
• 1 c. yogurt	• 2 bananas	• 1 t. vanilla

Bananas should be peeled and ripe. Mash them with vanilla and yogurt.

Organization	Word Choice	Ideas	Conventions	Sentence Fluency	Voice

First Things First

Organization is the structure a writer chooses to achieve a desired effect. Use **chronological,** or step-by-step, organization when you write a how-to essay. A reader needs clear, well-organized directions in order to complete a task sucessfully. If the steps are out of order, or if they are unclear, he or she will have a difficult time following your directions.

Creating a List Make a list of all materials or ingredients needed. Organize these items in the order in which they will be used. Doing so will help the reader organize his or her own workspace. Then, list all of the steps in consecutive order—that is, the order in which they should be performed. Use numbers and spacing to make the steps easy to follow.

Clarifying Terms and Steps Once you have your lists, look for any specialized terms or steps that need an explanation. A step or term that is familiar to you may not be familiar to someone else. Make your explanations clear, concise, and easy to follow.

One Simple Plan

To organize your draft, use a chart like the one below. Add lines for materials and instructions as needed.

Title/Introduction _____	
Materials list	**Instructions**
☐ _____ ☐ _____ ☐ _____	1. _____ 2. _____ 3. _____
Conclusion _____	

Checking Your Organization Exchange your completed how-to chart with a classmate for a peer review. As you read your partner's chart, note whether each of the materials and instructions listed are clearly described and appear in a logical and easy-to-follow order. Provide feedback for your partner by suggesting possible edits for clarity or improved organization.

Drafting Strategies

Add details to make your essay more precise. Look for places in your draft that need elaboration or clarification. Add details that show how much, how long, or how to complete a step.

Include helpful illustrations. To help readers follow your directions, include illustrations that clarify one or more steps. Add labels to simple line drawings, photographs, or diagrams to help explain your graphics. Place each illustration in the section of your draft that describes the step it shows.

Revising Strategies

Insert transitions. Time transitions indicate sequential order. They include words such as *first, later, next,* and *finally,* as well as phrases such as *in about an hour* or *when the glue has dried.* Review your draft and add transitions, as necessary, to clarify the order of events.

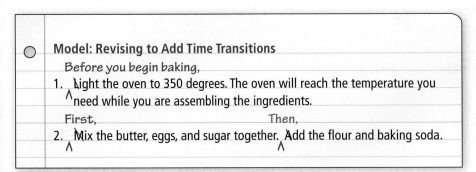

> **Model: Revising to Add Time Transitions**
>
> *Before you begin baking,*
> 1. Light the oven to 350 degrees. The oven will reach the temperature you ^ need while you are assembling the ingredients.
> *First,*   *Then,*
> 2. Mix the butter, eggs, and sugar together. Add the flour and baking soda.
> ^   ^

Upgrade to technical vocabulary. When explaining a process, use appropriate technical terms associated with your topic. Technical words are more precise than general words. Because of this, technical words can make your writing less wordy and can minimize redundancy, or meaningless repetition. For example, in the items shown below, notice how the names of specific kitchen utensils use fewer words and are less repetitive than the general terms. Review your draft, circling all general terms. Replace the general terms with precise words that clarify the process while minimizing wordiness and redundancy.

General	Technical
scraping utensil ——————→	spatula
mixing utensil ——————→	whisk, eggbeater

Common Core State Standards

Writing
2.a. Introduce a topic clearly, previewing what is to follow; organize ideas, concepts, and information, using strategies such as definition, classification, comparison/contrast, and cause/effect; include formatting, graphics, and multimedia when useful to aiding comprehension.
2.b. Develop the topic with relevant facts, definitions, concrete details, quotations, or other information and examples.
2.c. Use appropriate transitions to create cohesion and clarify the relationships among ideas and concepts.
2.d. Use precise language and domain-specific vocabulary to inform about or explain the topic.

Language
3. Use knowledge of language and its conventions when writing, speaking, reading, or listening.
3.a. Choose language that expresses ideas precisely and concisely, recognizing and eliminating wordiness and redundancy.

Revising to Combine Sentences Using Conjunctions

Too many short sentences in a row can make your writing choppy—that is, your writing will seem to have a repetitive stop-start quality. Using conjunctions to combine sentences will help you create a smoother, more varied writing style.

Identifying Sentences to Combine Combine sentences that express similar ideas by using words that clarify the relationship between the ideas. Here are two common ways to combine sentences:

Use a coordinating conjunction, such as *and* or *but*.

CHOPPY: I really wanted to sleep. I had to walk my dogs.

COMBINED: I really wanted to sleep, **but** I had to walk my dogs.

Add a subordinating conjunction, such as *after* or *until*.

CHOPPY: You cannot read the book. I want a chance.

COMBINED: You cannot read the book **until** I get a chance.

Fixing Choppy Sentences To fix choppy sentences, rewrite them using the following method.

1. **Identify relationships between sentences.** Look for a series of related short sentences. Identify whether the ideas in the sentences are of equal importance or unequal importance.

2. **Combine sentences.** Combine sentences showing equal importance by using coordinating conjunctions. Use subordinating conjunctions to combine sentences of unequal importance.

Coordinating Conjunctions	Common Subordinating Conjunctions
and, or, so, for, but, nor, yet	after, although, as, as if, as long as, because, before, even though, if, in order that, since, so that, than, though, unless, until, when, whenever, where, wherever, while

PH **WRITING COACH**

Further instruction and practice are available in *Prentice Hall Writing Coach*.

Grammar in Your Writing

Read your draft aloud, highlighting any passages that sound choppy. Then, revise by combining sentences using the method described.

Student Model: Danielle Spiess, LaPorte, IN

 Common Core
State Standards

Language
2.b. Spell correctly.

How to Serve Overhand in Volleyball

Volleyball is one of the most popular sports around. Knowing how to serve overhand will be useful if you ever decide to try out for a team. If you have ever seen anyone serve, it may look pretty easy, but it is not as easy as it looks. It takes a lot of practice!

To practice, you'll need a volleyball, a practice ball that is heavier than regulation balls, and a net.

1. To start off, use a volleyball that is heavier than normal. It will be more difficult at the beginning, but when you finally get your serve over, it will be a lot stronger. The regular volleyball is lighter, so you won't have to put as much force into your serve during games.

2. Next is the toss, probably the most important part of the serve. Throw the volleyball into the air. Try to get a high, square toss. If your toss is too low or off to one side, the ball will not go over the net the way you want it to. It might also go too far in front of you or behind you. If this happens, catch the volleyball and start over.

    It will take you a while to get the perfect toss. So, you may need extra practice to make sure you can toss the ball well enough to set up a good serve. Work with a partner to get your toss in the right zone—straight up and not too low.

3. The final step is hitting it over. You can use either an open or a closed hand. Using an open hand is easier because when a closed hand is used, you sometimes hit the volleyball off your knuckles. After you toss the ball, wait until your toss reaches its peak, and then hit it. The volleyball may not go over the first time, but soon you will get it.

    In volleyball, serving takes a lot of practice and a lot of effort, but it is a key skill for any serious player. As with any other athletic skill, set a goal for yourself. Then, just keep with it and don't give up!

Danielle focuses her essay on how to serve a volleyball.

This paragraph identifies the items necessary to complete the task.

Danielle explains why using a heavier ball is the best way to get started.

This paragraph clearly identifies the steps for tossing the ball.

Danielle explains all steps in sequential order.

Editing and Proofreading

Review your draft to eliminate errors in grammar, spelling, and punctuation. Use the **spell-check feature on your computer** to help you identify the correct spelling of words.

Focus on sentence fragments. A **sentence fragment** is a group of words that is incorrectly punctuated as a sentence. A fragment is missing a subject, a predicate, or both. Therefore, it does not express a complete thought. Proofread your essay to make sure all of your sentences are complete.

Publishing and Presenting

Consider one of the following ways to share your writing:

Give a demonstration. Use props to give a demonstration of the task you explain in your essay.

Make a class anthology. With classmates, combine your essays into a how-to reference booklet. Display the book in your school or local library, where people can use it.

Reflecting on Your Writing

Writer's Journal Jot down your answer to this question:
Which drafting strategy did you find most useful? Explain.

Spiral Review

Earlier in the unit, you learned about **conjunctions** (p. 438) and **prepositions and prepositional phrases** (p. 458). Check your use of conjunctions, prepositions, and prepositional phrases in your how-to essay.

PH WRITING COACH

Further instruction and practice are available in *Prentice Hall Writing Coach*.

Rubric for Self-Assessment

Find evidence in your writing to address each category. Then, use the rating scale to grade your work.

Criteria	Rating Scale
	not very very
Focus: How well have you focused your topic?	1 2 3 4 5
Organization: How clearly organized are the lists of materials and directions?	1 2 3 4 5
Support/Elaboration: How helpful are the illustrations?	1 2 3 4 5
Style: How appropriate are the technical terms?	1 2 3 4 5
Conventions: How correct is your grammar, especially your use of conjunctions?	1 2 3 4 5

Ⓒ Leveled Texts

Build your skills and improve your comprehension of literary nonfiction with texts of increasing complexity.

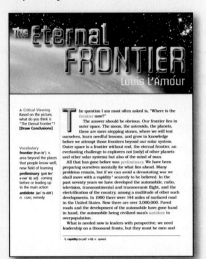

Read **"All Together Now"** to learn how the author encourages people to work together to improve race relations.

Read **"The Eternal Frontier"** to find out why outer space provides endless opportunities to learn about the unknown.

Ⓒ Common Core State Standards

Meet these standards with either **"All Together Now"** (p. 494) or **"The Eternal Frontier"** (p. 500).

Reading Informational Text

8. Trace and evaluate the argument and specific claims in a text, assessing whether the reasoning is sound and the evidence is relevant and sufficient to support the claims. *(Literary Analysis: Persuasive Essay)*

Spiral Review: RI.7.5

Writing

1.a. Introduce claim(s), acknowledge alternate or opposing claims, and organize the reasons and evidence logically.

1.b. Support claim(s) with logical reasoning and relevant evidence, using accurate, credible sources and demonstrating an understanding of the topic or text. *(Writing: Persuasive Letter)*

Speaking and Listening

4. Present claims and findings, emphasizing salient points in a focused, coherent manner with pertinent descriptions, facts, details, and examples. *(Speaking and Listening: Public Service Announcement)*

Language

4.b. Use common, grade-appropriate Greek or Latin affixes and roots as clues to the meaning of a word. *(Vocabulary: Word Study)*

6. Acquire and use accurately grade-appropriate general academic and domain-specific words and phrases; gather vocabulary knowledge when considering a word or phrase important to comprehension or expression. *(Vocabulary: Word Study)*

Reading Skill: Classifying Fact and Opinion

When you read nonfiction, it is important to classify types of information. Distinguishing between fact and opinion is a key skill.

- A **fact** is something that can be proved.
- An **opinion** is a person's judgment or belief. It may be supported by factual evidence, but it cannot be proved.

As you read, **recognize clues that indicate an opinion,** such as the phrases *I believe* or *in my opinion.* Also look for words such as *always, never, must, cannot, best, worst,* and *all,* which may be broad statements that reveal a personal judgment. Emotional statements are very often based on opinion.

Literary Analysis: Persuasive Essay

A **persuasive essay** is a work of nonfiction that presents a series of arguments to convince readers to believe or act in a certain way. When you read persuasive essays, be alert for the use of persuasive techniques. Then decide whether they represent reasonable and relevant support that convinces you to accept or act on the author's ideas.

Using the Strategy: Techniques Chart

This chart shows some techniques that are often used in persuasive essays. As you read, identify and analyze these common persuasive techniques:

Persuasive Techniques	Examples
Appeals to authority using opinions of experts and well-known people	According to the school principal, attendance is at an all-time high.
Appeals to emotion using words that convey strong feelings	Are we going to quietly accept such an insult to our intelligence?
Appeals to reason using logical arguments backed by facts	A healthy breakfast leads to a healthy lifestyle.

What should we *learn?*

Writing About the Big Question

In "All Together Now," Barbara Jordan discusses how people can make a difference in improving race relations. Use this sentence starter to develop your ideas about the Big Question.

When we **examine** the ways that all people are similar, we discover that accepting others is _____.

While You Read Consider how learning about and accepting others can make a difference in race relations.

Vocabulary

Read each word and its definition. Decide whether you know the word well, know it a little bit, or do not know it at all. After you read, see how your knowledge of each word has increased.

- **legislation** (lej´ is lā´ shən) *n.* law (p. 494) *The senators passed legislation to help reduce pollution. legislative adj. legislate v. legislator n.*

- **tolerant** (täl´ ər ənt) *adj.* accepting; free from bigotry or prejudice (p. 494) *A tolerant attitude can help resolve conflicts. tolerate v. tolerance n. intolerant adj.*

- **culminated** (kul´ mə nāt´ əd) *v.* reached its highest point or climax (p. 494) *The movie's plot culminated in a speedy chase scene. culminate v. culminating v. culmination n.*

- **fundamental** (fun´ də ment´ 'l) *adj.* basic; forming a foundation (p. 494) *The ability to read is a fundamental skill. fundamentally adv.*

- **equality** (ē kwôl´ ə tē) *n.* social state in which all people are treated the same (p. 495) *Our after-school club treats all members with equality. equal adj. equaled v. quality n.*

- **optimist** (äp´ tə mist) *n.* someone who takes the most hopeful view of matters (p. 495) *An optimist always sees the positive side of things. optimistic adj. optimism n.*

Word Study

The **Latin root -leg-** means "law."

In this speech, Barbara Jordan argues that we need more than just **legislation**, or laws, to improve race relations.

Author of
All Together Now

Barbara Jordan inherited her skill at public speaking from her father, a Baptist minister. As a high school student in Houston, Texas, Jordan participated in debates and won public speaking competitions.

Keynote Speaker Jordan was elected to the Texas Senate in 1966, and in 1972 she became a member of Congress. During the 1976 Democratic National Convention, she became the first African American to deliver the keynote speech at a major party's political convention. In her dynamic speech she said, ". . . there is something different about tonight. There is something special about tonight. What is different? What is special? I, Barbara Jordan, am a keynote speaker."

DID YOU KNOW?

In 1990, the National Women's Hall of Fame voted Jordan one of the most influential women of the twentieth century.

BACKGROUND FOR THE SPEECH

Rights for All

Before the 1960s, some Americans faced racial discrimination at work, in schools, and on public transportation. Laws such as the Civil Rights Act of 1964 were passed to extend equal rights to all Americans. In "All Together Now," Barbara Jordan expresses support for these important laws, but also emphasizes her belief that people must work together to improve race relations.

All Together Now

Barbara Jordan

▲ **Critical Viewing**
Based on this photo
and the title, what do
you think this essay will
be about? **[Predict]**

▲ **Critical Viewing**
Based on this photo
and the title, what do
you think this essay will
be about? **[Predict]**

Vocabulary
legislation (lej´ is
lā´ shən) *n.* law
tolerant (täl´ ər ənt) *adj.*
accepting; free from
bigotry or prejudice
culminated (kul´ mə
nāt´ əd) *v.* reached its
highest point or climax
fundamental (fun´ də
ment´ ´l) *adj.* basic;
forming a foundation

When I look at race relations today I can see that some
positive changes have come about. But much remains to be
done, and the answer does not lie in more legislation. We
have the legislation we need; we have the laws. Frankly,
I don't believe that the task of bringing us all together can
be accomplished by government. What we need now is soul
force—the efforts of people working on a small scale to build
a truly tolerant, harmonious society. And parents can do a
great deal to create that tolerant society.

We all know that race relations in America have had a
very rocky history. Think about the 1960s when Dr. Martin
Luther King, Jr., was in his heyday and there were marches
and protests against segregation[1] and discrimination. The
movement culminated in 1963 with the March on Washington.

Following that event, race relations reached an all-time
peak. President Lyndon B. Johnson pushed through the Civil
Rights Act of 1964, which remains the fundamental piece of
civil rights legislation in this century. The Voting Rights Act of
1965 ensured that everyone in our country could vote. At last,
black people and white people seemed ready to live together
in peace.

---

1. segregation (seg´ rə gā´ shən) *n.* the practice of forcing racial groups to live apart from
each other.

But that is not what happened. By the 1990's the good feelings had diminished. Today the nation seems to be suffering from compassion fatigue, and issues such as race relations and civil rights have never regained momentum.

Those issues, however, remain crucial. As our society becomes more diverse, people of all races and backgrounds will have to learn to live together. If we don't think this is important, all we have to do is look at the situation in Bosnia[2] today.

How do we create a harmonious society out of so many kinds of people? The key is tolerance—the one value that is indispensable in creating community.

If we are concerned about community, if it is important to us that people not feel excluded, then we have to do something. Each of us can decide to have one friend of a different race or background in our mix of friends. If we do this, we'll be working together to push things forward.

One thing is clear to me: We, as human beings, must be willing to accept people who are different from ourselves. I must be willing to accept people who don't look as I do and don't talk as I do. It is crucial that I am open to their feelings, their inner reality.

What can parents do? We can put our faith in young people as a positive force. I have yet to find a racist baby. Babies come into the world as blank as slates and, with their beautiful innocence, see others not as different but as enjoyable companions. Children learn ideas and attitudes from the adults who nurture them. I absolutely believe that children do not adopt prejudices unless they absorb them from their parents or teachers.

The best way to get this country faithful to the American dream of tolerance and equality is to start small. Parents can actively encourage their children to be in the company of people who are of other racial and ethnic backgrounds. If a child thinks, "Well, that person's color is not the same as mine, but she must be okay because she likes to play with the same things I like to play with," that child will grow up with a broader view of humanity.

I'm an incurable optimist. For the rest of the time that I have left on this planet I want to bring people together. You

---

2. **Bosnia** (bäz´ nē ə) *n.* country, located on the Balkan Peninsula in Europe, that was the site of a bloody civil war between different ethnic and religious groups during the 1990s.

Persuasive Essay
Which persuasive technique does Jordan use with this reference to Bosnia?

Spiral Review
Structure The author organizes her ideas by asking and then answering a question. Do you think this structure is effective? Explain.

Vocabulary
equality (ē kwôl ´ə tē) *n.* a social state in which all people are treated the same

optimist (äp´ tə mist) *n.* someone who takes the most hopeful view of matters

Fact and Opinion
What clue words in this paragraph show that the author is expressing an opinion?

Reading Check
What did the Voting Rights Act of 1965 do?

might think of this as a labor of love. Now, I know that love means different things to different people. But what I mean is this: I care about you because you are a fellow human being and I find it okay in my mind, in my heart, to simply say to you, I love you. And maybe that would encourage you to love me in return.

It is possible for all of us to work on this—at home, in our schools, at our jobs. It is possible to work on human relationships in every area of our lives.

▶ **Critical Viewing**
Does this photograph reflect the attitude Jordan conveys in the essay? Explain. **[Assess]**

Critical Thinking

Cite textual evidence to support your responses.

ⓒ 1. **Key Ideas and Details (a)** How does Jordan summarize the history of race relations from the 1960s to the 1990s? Use examples from the essay to support your answer. **(b) Interpret:** In your own words, describe what Jordan means by "compassion fatigue."

ⓒ 2. **Key Ideas and Details (a)** What "one value" is necessary to create "a harmonious society"? **(b) Analyze:** Why does Jordan suggest Americans "start small" to promote this value? **(c) Apply:** What types of behavior might help reduce the problems Jordan describes?

ⓒ 3. **Key Ideas and Details (a)** According to Jordan, how do children learn ideas and attitudes? **(b) Interpret:** What does Jordan mean when she says "I have yet to find a racist baby"?

ⓒ 4. **Key Ideas and Details (a)** What does Jordan suggest parents do to foster a sense of community? **(b) Evaluate:** Do you think that Jordan's ideas could work to promote tolerance? Explain.

ⓒ 5. **Integration of Knowledge and Ideas (a)** How can learning about the history of race relations help us in the future? **(b)** What can this knowledge teach us? *[Connect to the Big Question: What should we learn?]*

Reading Skill: Classifying Fact and Opinion

1. List two **facts** Jordan uses to support her ideas.

2. In a chart like this, record three **opinions** Jordan expresses, and list the clues that helped you identify each opinion.

Opinion	Clues

Literary Analysis: Persuasive Essay

© 3. Craft and Structure Identify one appeal to authority, one appeal to emotion, and one appeal to reason that Jordan uses in this **persuasive essay.**

© 4. Craft and Structure (a) What is the most convincing argument Jordan makes? **(b)** Why is it convincing?

Vocabulary

© Acquisition and Use Answer each question by writing a complete sentence that includes the italicized vocabulary word. Explain your answer.

1. Is reading a *fundamental* part of education?

2. What does it mean when Congress passes new *legislation*?

3. If Joan is an *optimist*, does she believe things will end well?

4. If people are *tolerant*, are they likely to accept others?

5. If a soccer team's season *culminated* in victory, what happened?

6. If a country is founded on *equality*, are some people treated differently than others?

Word Study Use what you know about the **Latin root -leg-** to explain your answer to each question.

1. Is a thief likely to give a *legitimate* account of his actions?

2. Would you expect an honest person to do something *illegal*?

Word Study

The **Latin root -leg-** means "law."

Apply It Explain how the word root -leg- contributes to the meanings of these words. Consult a dictionary if necessary.

allegation
legacy
privilege

What should we *learn?*

Writing About the Big Question

In "The Eternal Frontier," the author discusses new discoveries that came about because of people's desire to explore outer space. Use these sentence starters to develop your ideas about the Big Question.

Space **exploration** (is / is not) important because _____.

Curiosity can lead to discovery because _____.

While You Read Look for advances that might never have been made if not for space travel.

Vocabulary

Read each word and its definition. Decide whether you know the word well, know it a little bit, or do not know it at all. After you read, see how your knowledge of each word has increased.

- **frontier** (frun tir′) *n.* area beyond the places that people know well; new field of learning (p. 500) *Lewis and Clark mapped the western frontier.* frontiersman *n.* front *n.*

- **preliminary** (prē lim′ ə ner′ ē) *adj.* coming before or leading up to the main action (p. 500) *The doctor will do a preliminary exam before surgery.* preliminaries *n.*

- **antidote** (an′ tə dōt′) *n.* cure; remedy (p. 500) *Laughter can be an antidote for sadness.*

- **atmospheric** (at′ məs fer′ ik) *adj.* having to do with the air surrounding Earth (p. 501) *Air pollution alarms atmospheric scientists.* atmosphere *n.* atmospherically *adv.* sphere *n.*

- **destiny** (des′ tə nē) *n.* things that will happen to someone in the future, or the power that controls this (p. 501) *Laura believed her destiny was in her own hands.* destined *v.* destinies *n.* destination *n.*

- **impetus** (im′ pə təs) *n.* driving force (p. 502) *A strong desire to succeed is her impetus to work hard.* impetuses *n.* impetuous *adj.*

Meet
Louis L'Amour
(1908–1988)

Author of
The Eternal Frontier

It is not surprising that Louis L'Amour became a writer of western novels. He was born in North Dakota and often met cowboys as they traveled by railroad near the farm where he was raised. Two of L'Amour's uncles, who worked on his father's ranch, told the boy fascinating stories of frontier life.

What Makes a Good Story? L'Amour used the rules of all good fiction writing to write his westerns. He has said, "A western starts with a beginning and it goes to an end. It's a story about people, and that's the important thing to remember. Every story is about people—people against the canvas of their time."

BACKGROUND FOR THE ESSAY

Space Exploration

Not everyone agrees that exploring outer space is a good idea. Some people argue that space exploration has led to valuable inventions, such as scratch-resistant lenses and voice-controlled wheelchairs. Others, however, say that space exploration is too expensive. They argue that the money would be better spent dealing with issues here on Earth, such as improving schools and protecting the environment. In "The Eternal Frontier," Louis L'Amour expresses his opinions about the exploration of space.

DID YOU KNOW?
At various times in his life, L'Amour worked as an elephant handler, a fruit picker, and a lumberjack.

FRONTIER

Louis L'Amour

▲ **Critical Viewing**
Based on the picture, what do you think is "The Eternal Frontier"?
[Draw Conclusions]

Vocabulary
frontier (frun tir´) *n.* area beyond the places that people know well; new field of learning

preliminary (prē lim´ ə ner´ ē) *adj.* coming before or leading up to the main action

antidote (an´ tə dōt´) *n.* cure; remedy

The question I am most often asked is, "Where is the frontier now?"

The answer should be obvious. Our frontier lies in outer space. The moon, the asteroids, the planets, these are mere stepping stones, where we will test ourselves, learn needful lessons, and grow in knowledge before we attempt those frontiers beyond our solar system. Outer space is a frontier without end, the eternal frontier, an everlasting challenge to explorers not [only] of other planets and other solar systems but also of the mind of man.

All that has gone before was preliminary. We have been preparing ourselves mentally for what lies ahead. Many problems remain, but if we can avoid a devastating war we shall move with a rapidity[1] scarcely to be believed. In the past seventy years we have developed the automobile, radio, television, transcontinental and transoceanic flight, and the electrification of the country, among a multitude of other such developments. In 1900 there were 144 miles of surfaced road in the United States. Now there are over 3,000,000. Paved roads and the development of the automobile have gone hand in hand, the automobile being civilized man's antidote to overpopulation.

What is needed now is leaders with perspective; we need leadership on a thousand fronts, but they must be men and

---

1. **rapidity** (rə pid´ ə tē) *n.* speed.

women who can take the long view and help to shape the outlines of our future. There will always be the nay-sayers, those who cling to our lovely green planet as a baby clings to its mother, but there will be others like those who have taken us this far along the path to a limitless future.

We are a people born to the frontier. It has been a part of our thinking, waking, and sleeping since men first landed on this continent. The frontier is the line that separates the known from the unknown wherever it may be, and we have a driving need to see what lies beyond . . . ●

A few years ago we moved into outer space. We landed men on the moon; we sent a vehicle beyond the limits of the solar system, a vehicle still moving farther and farther into that limitless distance. If our world were to die tomorrow, that tiny vehicle would go on and on forever, carrying its mighty message to the stars. Out there, someone, sometime, would know that once we existed, that we had the vision and we made the effort. Mankind is not bound by its atmospheric envelope or by its gravitational field, nor is the mind of man bound by any limits at all.

One might ask—why outer space, when so much remains to be done here? If that had been the spirit of man we would still be hunters and food gatherers, growling over the bones of carrion in a cave somewhere. It is our destiny to move out, to accept the challenge, to dare the unknown. It is our destiny to achieve.

Fact and Opinion
Explain whether this paragraph states facts or opinions.

Vocabulary
atmospheric
(at´ məs fer´ ik) *adj.*
having to do with the air surrounding Earth

destiny (des´ tə nē) *n.*
things that will happen to someone in the future, or the power that controls this

Reading Check

Where does the author predict the future will take place?

The Eternal Frontier **501**

Vocabulary
impetus (im´ pə təs) *n.*
driving force

Yet we must not forget that along the way to outer space whole industries are springing into being that did not exist before. The computer age has arisen in part from the space effort, which gave great impetus to the development of computing devices. Transistors, chips, integrated circuits, Teflon, new medicines, new ways of treating diseases, new ways of performing operations, all these and a multitude of other developments that enable man to live and to live better are linked to the space effort. Most of these developments have been so incorporated into our day-to-day life that they are taken for granted, their origin not considered.

If we are content to live in the past, we have no future. And today is the past.

Critical Thinking

Cite textual evidence to support your responses.

1. **Key Ideas and Details (a)** What does L'Amour refer to as "the eternal frontier"? **(b) Compare and Contrast:** How might the "eternal" frontier be similar to and different from the western frontier that L'Amour writes about in his novels?

2. **Key Ideas and Details (a)** What kinds of leaders does L'Amour say we need now? Use examples from the essay to support your answer. **(b) Infer:** In which ways would those leaders support the cause of space travel?

3. **Key Ideas and Details (a)** To what does L'Amour compare the "nay-sayers" who are opposed to funding space exploration? **(b) Make a Judgment:** Do you think that is a fair evaluation? Why or why not?

4. **Integration of Knowledge and Ideas (a) Draw Conclusions:** What message about space does the essay convey? Which reasons best support L'Amour's claim? **(b) Evaluate:** Is the message positive? Explain.

5. **Integration of Knowledge and Ideas (a)** How does our curiosity help us to explore the unknown? **(b)** What can we learn from our desire to explore things that are a mystery? *[Connect to the Big Question: What should we learn?]*

Reading Skill: Classifying Fact and Opinion

1. List two **facts** that L'Amour uses to support his argument about space exploration.

2. In a chart like the one shown, record three **opinions** L'Amour expresses in the essay. Then, list the clues that helped you identify each opinion.

Opinion	Clues

Literary Analysis: Persuasive Essay

© **3. Craft and Structure** Identify one appeal to emotion and one appeal to reason that L'Amour uses in this **persuasive essay.**

© **4. Key Ideas and Details (a)** What is the most convincing argument L'Amour makes? **(b)** Why is it convincing?

Vocabulary

© **Acquisition and Use** Answer each question by writing a complete sentence that includes the italicized vocabulary word. Explain your answer.

1. Was the western United States ever a new *frontier?*

2. Are *preliminary* plans the last plans a person makes?

3. Is eating dessert an *antidote* to feeling full after a heavy meal?

4. Is gravity one of the moon's *atmospheric* qualities?

5. Does your *destiny* lead you to a place you are meant to be?

6. Do some people need an *impetus* to start an assignment?

Word Study Use the context of the sentences and what you know about the **Latin root -peti-** to explain each answer.

1. When you *petition* a teacher, are you hoping for a response?

2. Can *competition* motivate a person to improve her skills?

Word Study

The **Latin root -peti-** means "to ask for, request, or strive after."

Apply It Explain how the word root -peti- contributes to the meanings of these words. Consult a dictionary if necessary.

repetitive
impetuous
appetite

Integrated Language Skills

All Together Now • The Eternal Frontier

Conventions: Subjects and Predicates

Every sentence has two parts—the **subject** and **predicate**—which together express a complete thought. The **subject** describes whom or what the sentence is about. The **predicate** is a verb that tells what the subject does, what is done to the subject, or what the condition of the subject is.

- A **simple subject** is the main noun or pronoun in a complete subject. A **complete subject** is a simple subject and all the words that modify it.
- A **simple predicate** is the main verb or verb phrase in a complete predicate. A **complete predicate** is a simple predicate and all the words that modify it.

Sentence	Simple Subject / Simple Predicate	Complete Subject / Complete Predicate
Lila walked quickly.	Lila / walked	Lila / walked quickly.
Lush green trees provided shade.	trees / provided	Lush green trees / provided shade.
The crashing of the waves soothed me.	crashing / soothed	The crashing of the waves / soothed me.

Practice A Circle the simple subject and underline the simple predicate in each sentence.

1. Civil rights laws caused many positive changes.
2. People in America still have a lot of work to do.
3. Parents must teach children tolerance.
4. They should lead by example.

© **Reading Application** In "All Together Now," identify the simple subject and simple predicate in three different sentences.

Practice B Write sentences, using each simple subject and predicate listed.

1. space, expands
2. explorers, travel
3. shuttles, carry
4. technology, grows
5. scientists, study

© **Writing Application** Write three sentences on any topic. In each sentence, circle the simple subject and the simple predicate. Then, draw a line between the complete subject and the complete predicate.

PH **WRITING COACH** Further instruction and practice are available in *Prentice Hall Writing Coach.*

Writing

Common Core
State Standards

L.7.4.b, L.7.6; W.7.1.a,
W.7.1.b; SL.7.4
[For the full wording of the
standards, see page 490.]

Argument Write a brief **persuasive letter** on one of the following topics from either "All Together Now" or "The Eternal Frontier."

- A letter to community leaders advising them on how people in the community can promote tolerance

- A letter to government leaders advising them about space travel

Demonstrate understanding of your topic as you draft:

- Clearly state your claim, or position. For example, "Promoting tolerance in our community would . . ." or "Space travel is important because . . ."

- Identify your goals, and use the texts or other reliable sources to explain the steps you suggest to meet them.

- Defend your claims with logical reasoning and relevant evidence.

Grammar Application Make sure you have written complete sentences that contain a subject and predicate.

Writing Workshop: *Work in Progress*

Prewriting for Exposition Make a two-column chart of everyday decisions. In the left column, list six recent choices you have made. In the right column, jot down one alternate decision for each item. Keep this Everyday Decisions chart in your writing portfolio.

Use this prewriting activity to prepare for the **Writing Workshop** on page 548.

Speaking and Listening

Comprehension and Collaboration In a small group, write a **public service announcement** (PSA) on one of the following topics:

- Promoting the fair treatment of all people

- Encouraging space travel

Follow these steps to complete the assignment.

- Give all group members a chance to speak, and listen to their ideas.

- Identify your audience, and support your claims with relevant details and descriptions that they will find logical and appealing.

- Use persuasive techniques, such as those shown in the chart on page 491.

- Share your PSA with the class, and request audience feedback.

www.PHLitOnline.com
- Interactive graphic organizers
- Grammar tutorial
- Interactive journals

The Real Story of a Cowboy's Life • Rattlesnake Hunt

ⓒ Leveled Texts

Build your skills and improve your comprehension of literary nonfiction with texts of increasing complexity.

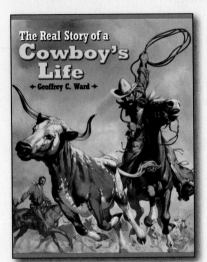

Read **"The Real Story of a Cowboy's Life"** to experience what life was actually like in the early days of the West.

Read **"Rattlesnake Hunt"** to see how the author discovers her courage during an outdoor adventure.

ⓒ Common Core State Standards

Meet these standards with either **"The Real Story of a Cowboy's Life"** (p. 510) or **"Rattlesnake Hunt"** (p. 518).

Reading Informational Text

4. Determine the meaning of words and phrases as they are used in a text, including figurative, connotative, and technical meanings; analyze the impact of a specific word choice on meaning and tone. *(Literary Analysis: Word Choice and Diction)*

Writing

3.d. Use precise words and phrases, relevant descriptive details, and sensory language to capture the action and convey experiences and events. *(Writing: Adaptation)*

4. Produce clear and coherent writing in which the development, organization, and style are appropriate to task, purpose, and audience. *(Writing: Adaptation)*

5. Develop and strengthen writing as needed by planning, revising, editing, and rewriting, focusing on how well purpose and audience have been addressed. *(Writing: Adaptation)*

8. Gather relevant information from multiple print and digital sources, using search terms effectively. *(Research and Technology: Help-wanted Ad)*

Language

4.b. Use common, grade-appropriate Greek or Latin affixes and roots as clues to the meaning of a word. *(Vocabulary: Word Study)*

6. Acquire and use accurately grade-appropriate general academic and domain-specific words and phrases; gather vocabulary knowledge when considering a word or phrase important to comprehension or expression. *(Vocabulary: Word Study)*

Reading Skill: Classifying Fact and Opinion

As you read nonfiction, be alert to the types of details a writer uses to support an idea. You can **classify** these details into two basic categories. A **fact** is information you can prove. An **opinion** is a judgment.

- **Fact:** The room measures ten feet by twelve feet.
- **Opinion:** Green is the best color for the room.

Be aware that some writers present opinions or beliefs as facts. To get to the truth, **use resources to check facts.**

Using the Strategy: Resources Chart

Use a chart like this one to identify information the writer presents. Then, indicate which resource could help you check the facts.

Resources	Statement in Text
almanac	
atlas or map	
biographical dictionary	
dictionary	
encyclopedia	
reliable Web site	

Literary Analysis: Word Choice, or Diction

A writer's word choice, or **diction,** is an important element of his or her writing. The words a writer uses can make writing seem difficult or easy, formal or informal. Diction includes not only individual words but also phrases and expressions the writer uses. The answers to these questions shape a writer's diction:

- *What does the audience already know about the topic?* The writer may have to define terms or use simpler language.

- *What feeling will this work convey?* Word choice can make a work serious or funny, academic or personal. The use of casual or formal language can make a work seem simple or complex.

As you read, notice how the author's word choice and diction affect the way you respond to a text.

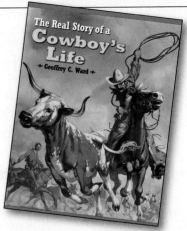

What should we *learn?*

Writing About the Big Question

"The Real Story of a Cowboy's Life" describes the duties and dangers that cowboys experienced in the 1800s. Use this sentence starter to develop your ideas about the Big Question.

The **facts** we can learn from historical accounts are important because _____.

While You Read Look for firsthand details that describe and explain the lives of cowboys. Then, consider which details in the text might be relevant to your life.

Vocabulary

Read each word and its definition. Decide whether you know the word well, know it a little bit, or do not know it at all. After you read, see how your knowledge of each word has increased.

- **discipline** (dis´ ə plin´) *n.* strict control (p. 511) *When the captain slept, there was no discipline on the ship.* disciplined *v.* disciplinary *adj.* disciplinarian *n.*

- **gauge** (gāj) *v.* estimate or judge (p. 511) *She kept a straight face, and it was hard to gauge her reaction.* gauged *v.* gauging *v.* gauge *n.*

- **emphatic** (em fat´ ik) *adj.* expressing strong feeling (p. 511) *She was so emphatic that I believed her.* emphatically *adv.* emphasize *v.* emphasis *n.*

- **ultimate** (ul´ tə mit) *adj.* final (p. 512) *His ultimate goal was to become team captain.* ultimately *adv.* ultimatum *n.*

- **longhorns** (lôn´ hornz´) *n.* breed of cattle with long horns (p. 512) *Longhorns are common on ranches in Texas.* longhorn *n.*

- **diversions** (də vur´ zhənz) *n.* amusements (p. 513) *The park offered diversions for children and adults.* divert *v.* diversion *n.* diversionary *adj.*

Word Study

The **Latin root -vers-** means "to turn."

As this essay describes, cowboys enjoyed few **diversions**, or amusing activities that would turn their attention away from their work.

Meet
Geoffrey C. Ward
(b. 1940)

Author of
The Real Story of a
Cowboy's Life

Historian Geoffrey C. Ward strives to present an accurate portrayal of the past. He has written more than a dozen books about the United States and the people who played key roles in its growth. Ward's book *A First-Class Temperament*, about Franklin D. Roosevelt, won the 1989 National Book Critics Circle Award for biography. Ward has also written biographies of Mark Twain, Susan B. Anthony, Harry Truman, and Billy the Kid.

Screenwriter, Too In addition to his books, Ward has written or co-written more than a dozen screenplays for films, many of which have appeared on public television.

BACKGROUND FOR THE ESSAY

Cowboys

American cowboys were most active from the Civil War through the 1890s. The meat industry was growing, but transportation was lacking. To get cattle to market, cowboys drove them—that is, forced them—to trudge long distances. When people hear the word *cowboy,* they think of a life of daring, romance, and adventure. As this essay shows, that may not be an accurate image.

DID YOU KNOW ?

Ward teamed up with filmmaker Ken Burns to create the Emmy Award-winning PBS documentaries *The Civil War* and *Baseball*.

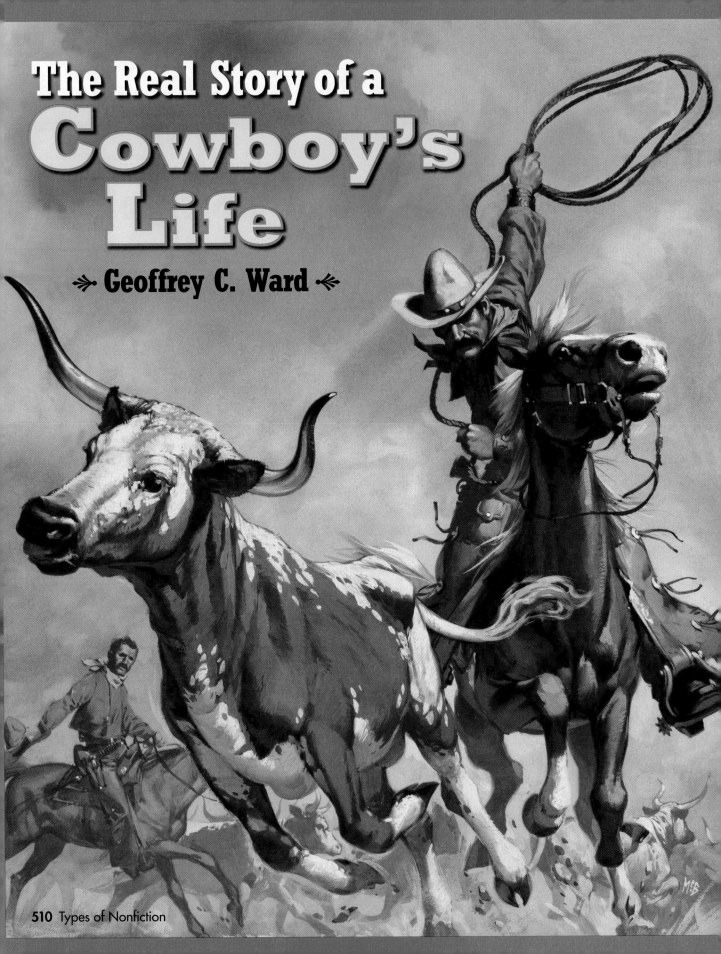

The Real Story of a Cowboy's Life

Geoffrey C. Ward

A drive's success depended on discipline and planning. According to Teddy Blue,[1] most Texas herds numbered about 2,000 head with a trail boss and about a dozen men in charge—though herds as large as 15,000 were also driven north with far larger escorts. The most experienced men rode "point" and "swing," at the head and sides of the long herd; the least experienced brought up the rear, riding "drag" and eating dust. At the end of the day, Teddy Blue remembered, they "would go to the water barrel . . . and rinse their mouths and cough and spit up . . . black stuff. But you couldn't get it up out of your lungs."

They had to learn to work as a team, keeping the herd moving during the day, resting peacefully at night. Twelve to fifteen miles a day was a good pace. But such steady progress could be interrupted at any time. A cowboy had to know how to gauge the temperament of his cattle, how to chase down a stray without alarming the rest of the herd, how to lasso a steer using the horn of his saddle as a tying post. His saddle was his most prized possession; it served as his chair, his workbench, his pillow at night. Being dragged to death was the most common death for a cowboy, and so the most feared occurrence on the trail was the nighttime stampede. As Teddy Blue recalled, a sound, a smell, or simply the sudden movement of a jittery cow could set off a whole herd.

If . . . the cattle started running—you'd hear that low rumbling noise along the ground and the men on herd wouldn't need to come in and tell you, you'd know—then you'd jump for your horse and get out there in the lead, trying to head them and get them into a mill[2] before they scattered. It was riding at a dead run in the dark, with cut banks and prairie dog holes all around you, not knowing if the next jump would land you in a shallow grave.

Most cowboys had guns, but rarely used them on the trail. Some outfits made them keep their weapons in the chuck wagon to eliminate any chance of gunplay. Charles Goodnight[3] was still more emphatic: "Before starting on a trail drive, I made it a rule to draw up an article of agreement,

---

1. **Teddy Blue** Edward C. Abbot, a cowboy who rode in a successful trail drive in the 1880s.
2. **mill** *n.* slow movement in a circle.
3. **Charles Goodnight** cowboy who rode successful trail drives beginning in the 1860s.

Fact and Opinion
What resource could you use to check the size of Texas herds in the nineteenth century?

Vocabulary
discipline (dis´ ə plin´) *n.* strict control

gauge (gāj) *v.* estimate or judge

emphatic (em fat´ ik) *adj.* expressing strong feeling

◀ **Critical Viewing**
How does this painting suggest the "real story" of a cowboy's life? **[Analyze]**

✓ **Reading Check**
What are two dangers cowboys face?

setting forth what each man was to do. The main clause stipulated[4] that if one shot another he was to be tried by the outfit and hanged on the spot, if found guilty. I never had a man shot on the trail." •

Regardless of its ultimate destination, every herd had to ford[5] a series of rivers—the Nueces, the Guadalupe, the Brazos, the Wichita, the Red.

A big herd of longhorns swimming across a river, Goodnight remembered, "looked like a million floating rocking chairs," and crossing those rivers one after another, a cowboy recalled, was like climbing the rungs of a long ladder reaching north.

"After you crossed the Red River and got out on the open plains," Teddy Blue remembered, "it was sure a pretty sight to see them strung out for almost a mile, the sun shining on their horns." Initially, the land immediately north of the Red River was Indian territory, and some tribes charged tolls for herds crossing their land—payable in money or beef. But Teddy Blue remembered that the homesteaders, now pouring onto the Plains by railroad, were far more nettlesome:

> There was no love lost between settlers and cowboys on the trail. Those jay-hawkers would take up a claim right where the herds watered and charge us for water. They would plant a crop alongside the trail and plow a furrow around it for a fence, and then when the cattle got into their wheat or their garden patch, they would come cussing and waving a shotgun and yelling for damages. And the cattle had been coming through there when they were still raising punkins in Illinois.

The settlers' hostility was entirely understandable. The big herds ruined their crops, and they carried with them a disease, spread by ticks and called "Texas fever," that devastated domestic livestock. Kansas and other territories along the route soon established quarantine lines,[6] called "deadlines," at the western fringe of settlement, and insisted that trail drives not cross them. Each year, as settlers continued to move in, those deadlines moved farther west.

Sometimes, farmers tried to enforce their own, as John Rumans, one of Charles Goodnight's hands, recalled:

Vocabulary
ultimate (ul´ tə mit) *adj.* final
longhorns (lôŋ´ hornz´) *n.* breed of cattle with long horns

Word Choice, or Diction
A "jay-hawker" is a slang term for a thief. How does Blue's use of the term contribute to the meaning and feel of this passage?

---

4. stipulated (stip´ yə lāt´ əd) *v.* stated as a rule.
5. ford (fôrd) *v.* cross a river at a shallow point.
6. quarantine (kwôr´ ən tēn) **lines** *n.* boundaries created to prevent the spread of disease.

Some men met us at the trail near Canyon City, and said we couldn't come in. There were fifteen or twenty of them, and they were not going to let us cross the Arkansas River. We didn't even stop. . . . Old man [Goodnight] had a shotgun loaded with buckshot and led the way, saying: "John, get over on that point with your Winchester and point these cattle in behind me." He slid his shotgun across the saddle in front of him and we did the same with our Winchesters. He rode right across, and as he rode up to them, he said: "I've monkeyed as long as I want to with you," and they fell back to the sides, and went home after we had passed.

There were few diversions on the trail. Most trail bosses banned liquor. Goodnight prohibited gambling, too. Even the songs for which cowboys became famous grew directly out of doing a job, remembered Teddy Blue:

The singing was supposed to soothe [the cattle] and it did; I don't know why, unless it was that a sound they was used to would keep them from spooking at other noises. I know that if you wasn't singing, any little sound in the night—it might be just a horse shaking himself—could make them leave the country; but if you were singing, they wouldn't notice it.

The two men on guard would circle around with their horses on a walk, if it was a clear night and the cattle was bedded down and quiet, and one man would sing a

▲ **Critical Viewing**
Why do you think cowboys, like those pictured, wear hats? **[Hypothesize]**

Vocabulary
diversions
(də vʉr´ zhənz) *n.* amusements

✓ Reading Check
Why did the settlers want to stop the cowboys and their herd from coming through the land where they lived?

verse of song, and his partner on the other side of the herd would sing another verse; and you'd go through a whole song that way. . . . "Bury Me Not on the Lone Prairie" was a great song for awhile, but . . . they sung it to death. It was a saying on the range that even the horses nickered it and the coyotes howled it; it got so they'd throw you in the creek if you sang it. •

The number of cattle on the move was sometimes staggering: once, Teddy Blue rode to the top of a rise from which he could see seven herds strung out behind him; eight more up ahead; and the dust from an additional thirteen moving parallel to his. "All the cattle in the world," he remembered, "seemed to be coming up from Texas."

At last, the herds neared their destinations. After months in the saddle—often wearing the same clothes every day, eating nothing but biscuits and beef stew at the chuck wagon, drinking only water and coffee, his sole companions his fellow cowboys, his herd, and his horse—the cowboy was about to be paid for his work, and turned loose in town.

Critical Thinking

1. Key Ideas and Details What qualifies Teddy Blue as a reliable source of information? Support your answer with details.

2. Key Ideas and Details **(a)** Identify two ways violence was kept down on the trail. **(b) Interpret:** Based on this information, what kind of person succeeded as a cowboy?

3. Key Ideas and Details **(a)** Why did settlers object to cattle coming through the land where they lived? **(b) Infer:** Why did cowboys object to going around settled areas? **(c) Make a Judgment:** What solution or compromise would have been most fair? Discuss your response with a classmate.

Cite textual evidence to support your responses.

4. Integration of Knowledge and Ideas **Analyze:** How is the information presented about cowboys the same or different from what you have learned about cowboys or the American West in works of fiction or textbooks? Explain.

5. Integration of Knowledge and Ideas **(a)** What information from this article can you use in your own life? **(b)** Why might it be important to rely on information from others, rather than limiting our knowledge to things we experience ourselves? *[Connect to the Big Question: What should we learn?]*

Reading Skill: Classifying Fact and Opinion

1. Identify one **fact** and one **opinion** in the essay.

2. What resource would you use to check the distance between Canyon City and the Arkansas River?

3. How do both facts and opinions help the writer paint a full picture of his subject?

Literary Analysis: Word Choice, or Diction

4. Craft and Structure Review the author's **word choice,** or **diction,** by completing a chart like the one shown.

Technical Vocabulary	Formal Language	Informal Language

5. Craft and Structure What feeling about cowboys do you think the author wants to convey in this essay? Explain.

Vocabulary

Acquisition and Use For each item, write a sentence correctly using the words indicated.

1. diversions; long train rides

2. gauge; progress

3. ultimate; goal

4. discipline; grades

5. emphatic; message

6. longhorns; stampede

Word Study Use the context of the sentences and what you know about the **Latin root -vers-** to explain your answer to each question.

1. If you *reverse* direction, do you go the opposite way?

2. If you behave in a *subversive* manner, are you being supportive?

Word Study

The **Latin root -vers-** means "to turn."

Apply It Explain how the root **-vers-** contributes to the meanings of these words. Consult a print or online dictionary if necessary.

transverse
versatile
adversary

What should we *learn*?

Writing About the Big Question

In "Rattlesnake Hunt," the author learns to manage her fear of rattlesnakes. Use this sentence starter to develop your ideas about the Big Question.

When we **evaluate** how we feel after trying something that scares us, we sometimes find that our feelings have changed because _____.

While You Read Look for things that Rawlings learns about rattlesnakes that help her to gain courage.

Vocabulary

Read each word and its definition. Decide whether you know the word well, know it a little bit, or do not know it at all. After you read, see how your knowledge of each word has increased.

- **adequate** (ad´ i kwət) *adj.* sufficient (p. 518) *The filling meal was <u>adequate</u> before the hike.* adequacy *n.* adequately *adv.*

- **desolate** (des´ ə lit) *adj.* lonely; solitary (p. 519) *The mountain peak was <u>desolate</u>, but lovely.* desolated *v.* desolation *n.*

- **forage** (fôr´ ij) *n.* food for domestic animals (p. 519) *Hay is good <u>forage</u> for cows.* foraged *v.* foraging *v.* forager *n.*

- **translucent** (trans loo´ sənt) *adj.* allowing some light through (p. 520) *The sun shone through the <u>translucent</u> window panes.* translucency *n.* translucently *adv.*

- **arid** (ar´ id) *adj.* dry and barren (p. 520) *No plants grew in the <u>arid</u> land.* aridity *n.*

- **mortality** (môr tal´ ə tē) *n.* condition of being mortal, or having to die eventually (p. 521) *Every living thing faces <u>mortality</u>.* mortal *adj.* mortally *adv.* immortality *n.* immortal *adj.*

Word Study

The **Latin root -sol-** means "alone."

Rawlings's hunting trip takes her into **desolate**, or lonely, territory.

Meet
Marjorie Kinnan Rawlings (1896–1953)

Author of
Rattlesnake Hunt

After starting out as a journalist, Marjorie Kinnan Rawlings quit and moved to a farm she bought in northern Florida. There, her experiences and close exposure to nature inspired her to write several novels, including the 1939 Pulitzer Prize–winning book, *The Yearling*. Her writing reflects an intimate understanding and appreciation of the outdoors.

A Disciplined Writer Rawlings devoted herself to writing but described it as "agony." She forced herself to type eight hours a day. Her daily goal was to produce at least six pages, although she would settle for three. She remained focused, refusing to let any outsiders interfere with her work. She felt that "living" with her characters was necessary in order to create a successful story.

DID YOU KNOW ?
When she worked on *The Yearling*, Rawlings prepared for key scenes by taking part in several bear hunts.

BACKGROUND FOR THE ESSAY
Snakes
When people hear the word *snake*, they often react with fear, thinking of a dangerous and deadly creature. However, those who study and work with these sometimes poisonous reptiles have strategies for safety. In "Rattlesnake Hunt," you will see how professionals respect the potential danger of snakes while controlling their interactions with these reptiles.

Rattlesnake Hunt

Marjorie Kinnan Rawlings

Ross Allen, a young Florida herpetologist,[1] invited me to join him on a hunt in the upper Everglades[2]—for rattlesnakes. Ross and I drove to Arcadia in his coupé[3] on a warm January day.

I said, "How will you bring back the rattlesnakes?"

"In the back of my car."

My courage was not adequate to inquire whether they were thrown in loose and might be expected to appear between our feet. Actually, a large portable box of heavy close-meshed wire made a safe cage. Ross wanted me to

---

1. **herpetologist** (hʉr´ pə täl´ ə jist) *n.* someone who studies reptiles and amphibians.
2. **Everglades** large region of marshes in southern Florida, about one hundred miles long and averaging fifty miles in width.
3. **coupé** (kōō pā´) *n.* small two-door automobile.

write an article about his work and on our way to the unhappy hunting grounds I took notes on a mass of data that he had accumulated in years of herpetological research. The scientific and dispassionate detachment of the material and the man made a desirable approach to rattlesnake territory. As I had discovered with the insects and varmints,[4] it is difficult to be afraid of anything about which enough is known, and Ross' facts were fresh from the laboratory.

The hunting ground was Big Prairie, south of Arcadia and west of the northern tip of Lake Okeechobee. Big Prairie is a desolate cattle country, half marsh, half pasture, with islands of palm trees and cypress and oaks. At that time of year the cattlemen and Indians were burning the country, on the theory that the young fresh wire grass that springs up from the roots after a fire is the best cattle forage. Ross planned to hunt his rattlers in the forefront of the fires. They lived in winter, he said, in gopher holes, coming out in the midday warmth to forage, and would move ahead of the flames and be easily taken. We joined forces with a big man named Will, his snake-hunting companion of the territory, and set out in early morning, after a long rough drive over deep-rutted roads into the open wilds.

I hope never in my life to be so frightened as I was in those first few hours. I kept on Ross' footsteps, I moved when he moved, sometimes jolting into him when I thought he might leave me behind. He does not use the forked stick of conventional snake hunting, but a steel prong, shaped like an L, at the end of a long stout stick. He hunted casually, calling my attention to the varying vegetation, to hawks overhead, to a pair of the rare whooping cranes that flapped over us. In mid-morning he stopped short, dropped his stick, and brought up a five-foot rattlesnake draped limply over the steel L. It seemed to me that I should drop in my tracks.

"They're not active at this season," he said quietly. "A snake takes on the temperature of its surroundings. They can't stand too much heat for that reason, and when the weather is cool, as now, they're sluggish."

---

4. **varmints** (vär′ mənts) *n.* animals regarded as troublesome.

Spiral Review
Author's Point of View What is the author's attitude toward snakes? Which words in this paragraph show her perspective on the topic?

Vocabulary
desolate (des′ ə lit) *adj.* lonely; solitary
forage (fôr′ ij) *n.* food for domestic animals

Fact and Opinion What reference source could confirm the fact in the last paragraph about a snake's temperature?

Reading Check
Why is the narrator going on a rattlesnake hunt?

Vocabulary
translucent (trans
lσσ´ sənt) *adj.* allowing
some light through

arid (ar´ id) *adj.*
dry and barren

▼ **Critical Viewing**
What makes the snake
in this photograph
appear dangerous?
[Analyze]

The sun was bright overhead, the sky a translucent blue,
and it seemed to me that it was warm enough for any snake
to do as it willed. The sweat poured down my back. Ross
dropped the rattler in a crocus sack and Will carried it. By
noon, he had caught four. I felt faint and ill. We stopped by a
pond and went swimming. The region was flat, the horizon
limitless, and as I came out of the cool blue water I expected
to find myself surrounded by a ring of rattlers. There were
only Ross and Will, opening the lunch basket. I could not eat.
Will went back and drove his truck closer, for Ross expected
the hunting to be better in the afternoon. The hunting was
much better. When we went back to the truck to deposit two
more rattlers in the wire cage, there was a rattlesnake lying
under the truck.

Ross said, "Whenever I leave my car or truck
with snakes already in it, other rattlers
always appear. I don't know whether this is
because they scent or sense the presence
of other snakes, or whether in this arid
area they come to the car for shade in
the heat of the day."

The problem was scientific, but I
had no interest. ●

That night Ross and Will and I
camped out in the vast spaces of

the Everglades prairies. We got water from an abandoned well and cooked supper under buttonwood bushes by a flowing stream. The camp fire blazed cheerfully under the stars and a new moon lifted in the sky. Will told tall tales of the cattlemen and the Indians and we were at peace.

Ross said, "We couldn't have a better night for catching water snakes."

After the rattlers, water snakes seemed innocuous[6] enough. We worked along the edge of the stream and here Ross did not use his L-shaped steel. He reached under rocks and along the edge of the water and brought out harmless reptiles with his hands. I had said nothing to him of my fears, but he understood them. He brought a small dark snake from under a willow root.

"Wouldn't you like to hold it?" he asked. "People think snakes are cold and clammy, but they aren't. Take it in your hands. You'll see that it is warm."

Again, because I was ashamed, I took the snake in my hands. It was not cold, it was not clammy, and it lay trustingly in my hands, a thing that lived and breathed and had mortality like the rest of us. I felt an upsurgence of spirit.

The next day was magnificent. The air was crystal, the sky was aquamarine, and the far horizon of palms and oaks lay against the sky. I felt a new boldness and followed Ross bravely. He was making the rounds of the gopher holes. The rattlers came out in the mid-morning warmth and were never far away. He could tell by their trails whether one had come out or was still in the hole. Sometimes the two men dug the snake out. At times it was down so long and winding a tunnel that the digging was hopeless. Then they blocked the entrance and went on to other holes. In an hour or so they made the original rounds, unblocking the holes. The rattler in every case came out hurriedly, as though anything were preferable to being shut in. All the time Ross talked to me, telling me the scientific facts he had discovered about the habits of the rattlers. ●

"They pay no attention to a man standing perfectly still," he said, and proved it by letting Will unblock a hole while he stood at the entrance as the snake came out. It was exciting to

---

6. **innocuous** (in näk´ yōō əs) *adj.* harmless.

▲ **Critical Viewing**
Snakes are often pictured in art and on artifacts such as this Native American basket. Why do you think that is so? **[Speculate]**

Vocabulary
mortality (môr tal´ ə tē) *n.* the condition of being mortal, or having to die eventually

Reading Check
How are the narrator's feelings changing?

Fact and Opinion
Is Ross stating fact or opinion in this paragraph? How do you know?

Word Choice, or Diction
How would you rephrase "as the sun mounted in the sky and warmed the moist Everglades" in less formal language?

watch the snake crawl slowly beside and past the man's legs. When it was at a safe distance he walked within its range of vision, which he had proved to be no higher than a man's knee, and the snake whirled and drew back in an attitude[7] of fighting defense. The rattler strikes only for paralyzing and killing its food, and for defense.

"It is a slow and heavy snake," Ross said. "It lies in wait on a small game trail and strikes the rat or rabbit passing by. It waits a few minutes, then follows along the trail, coming to the small animal, now dead or dying. It noses it from all sides, making sure that it is its own kill, and that it is dead and ready for swallowing."

A rattler will lie quietly without revealing itself if a man passes by and it thinks it is not seen. It slips away without fighting if given the chance. Only Ross' sharp eyes sometimes picked out the gray and yellow diamond pattern, camouflaged among the grasses. In the cool of the morning, chilled by the January air, the snakes showed no fight. They could be looped up limply over the steel L and dropped in a sack or up into the wire cage on the back of Will's truck. As the sun mounted in the sky and warmed the moist Everglades earth, the snakes were warmed too, and Ross warned that it was time to go more cautiously. Yet having learned that it was we who were the aggressors; that immobility meant complete safety; that the snakes, for all their lightning flash

7. **attitude** (at´ ə tood´) *n.* a position or posture of the body.

in striking, were inaccurate in their aim, with limited vision; having watched again and again the liquid grace of movement, the beauty of pattern, suddenly I understood that I was drinking in freely the magnificent sweep of the horizon, with no fear of what might be at the moment under my feet. I went off hunting by myself, and though I found no snakes, I should have known what to do.

The sun was dropping low in the west. Masses of white cloud hung above the flat marshy plain and seemed to be tangled in the tops of distant palms and cypresses. The sky turned orange, then saffron. I walked leisurely back toward the truck. In the distance I could see Ross and Will making their way in too. The season was more advanced than at the Creek, two hundred miles to the north, and I noticed that spring flowers were blooming among the lumpy hummocks. I leaned over to pick a white violet. There was a rattlesnake under the violet.

If this had happened the week before, if it had happened the day before, I think I should have lain down and died on top of the rattlesnake, with no need of being struck and poisoned. The snake did not coil, but lifted its head and whirred its rattles lightly. I stepped back slowly and put the violet in a buttonhole. I reached forward and laid the steel L across the snake's neck, just back of the blunt head. I called to Ross:

"I've got one."

He strolled toward me.

"Well, pick it up," he said.

I released it and slipped the L under the middle of the thick body.

"Go put it in the box."

He went ahead of me and lifted the top of the wire cage. I made the truck with the rattler, but when I reached up the six feet to drop it in the cage, it slipped off the stick and dropped on Ross' feet. It made no effort to strike.

"Pick it up again," he said. "If you'll pin it down lightly and reach just back of its head with your hand, as you've seen me do, you can drop it in more easily."

I pinned it and leaned over. •

Reading Check

What will a rattler do if it thinks it is not seen?

Cite textual evidence to support your responses.

Word Choice, or Diction

On this page, find an example of an informal expression that is used by the author.

"I'm awfully sorry," I said, "but you're pushing me a little too fast."

He grinned. I lifted it on the stick and again as I had it at head height, it slipped off, down Ross' boots and on top of his feet. He stood as still as a stump. I dropped the snake on his feet for the third time. It seemed to me that the most patient of rattlers might in time resent being hauled up and down, and for all the man's quiet certainty that in standing motionless there was no danger, would strike at whatever was nearest, and that would be Ross.

I said, "I'm just not man enough to keep this up any longer," and he laughed and reached down with his smooth quickness and lifted the snake back of the head and dropped it in the cage. It slid in among its mates and settled in a corner. The hunt was over and we drove back over the uneven trail to Will's village and left him and went on to Arcadia and home. Our catch for the two days was thirty-two rattlers.

I said to Ross, "I believe that tomorrow I could have picked up that snake."

Back at the Creek, I felt a new lightness. I had done battle with a great fear, and the victory was mine.

Critical Thinking

© 1. **Key Ideas and Details** **(a)** Why does Rawlings go on the hunt? **(b) Infer:** Why do Rawlings's feelings about snakes change when she holds one?

© 2. **Craft and Structure** **(a)** Note two ways in which Rawlings shows that she has partly overcome her fears. **(b) Infer:** Why does the author announce at the end of the hunt that she has won a "victory"?

© 3. **Integration of Knowledge and Ideas** **Generalize:** What general truth does this essay suggest?

© 4. **Integration of Knowledge and Ideas** **Analyze:** How is the information presented about snakes the same as or different from information found in works of fiction, popular media, or textbooks? Support your answer with specific examples.

© 5. **Integration of Knowledge and Ideas** **(a)** In what ways does the hunt change how Rawlings thinks about nature and herself? **(b)** How does conquering our fears allow us greater freedom to learn about the world? *[Connect to the Big Question: What should we learn?]*

Reading Skill: Classifying Fact and Opinion

1. Identify one **fact** in the essay and one **opinion.**

2. What resource would you use to check the facts about a rattlesnake's vision?

3. How do both facts and opinions help the writer explain her experience with snakes?

Literary Analysis: Word Choice, or Diction

4. Craft and Structure Review the author's **word choice,** or **diction,** by completing a chart like the one shown.

Technical Vocabulary	Formal Language	Informal Language

5. Craft and Structure Reread the top of page 523. How do phrases like "the liquid grace of movement, the beauty of pattern" reflect the author's new attitude toward snake hunting?

6. Integration of Knowledge and Ideas What feeling about snakes and her own experience do you think the author wanted to convey in this essay? Explain.

Vocabulary

Acquisition and Use For each item, write a single sentence correctly using the words indicated.

1. arid, farmer

2. mortality, medicine

3. desolate, midnight

4. adequate, light

5. forage, horse

6. translucent, marbles

Word Study Use the sentence context and your knowledge of the **Latin root -sol-** to explain your answer to each question.

1. How many people can play a game of *solitaire*?

2. If you seek *solitude*, do you want others around?

Word Study

The **Latin root -sol-** means "alone."

Apply It Explain how the root -sol- contributes to the meanings of these words. Consult a dictionary if necessary.

soliloquy
consolidate
soloist

Integrated Language Skills

The Real Story of a Cowboy's Life • Rattlesnake Hunt

Conventions: Compound Subjects and Predicates

A **compound subject** contains two or more subjects that share the same verb. A **compound predicate** contains two or more verbs that share the same subject.

Both compound subjects and compound predicates are joined by conjunctions such as *and* and *or*.

Compound subject: *Bob* and *I* entertained at the talent show.

Compound predicate: We *clapped* and *laughed*.

Follow these rules for agreement with compound subjects:

Compound Subjects Joined With "and"	Compound Subjects Joined With "or"
Share the same verb and take the plural form	Take the form of the verb that agrees with the subject closest to the verb
Example: Jared and Willa *help* the customers.	**Example:** Jared or Willa *helps* the customers.

Practice A Identify the compound subject or compound predicate in each sentence.

1. Cowboys chased and lassoed steer.
2. A smell or sound could set off a herd.
3. Teddy Blue and Charles Goodnight were cowboys during the 1800s.
4. Homesteaders cussed, threatened, and yelled at the cowboys.

© **Reading Application** In "The Real Story of a Cowboy's Life," find a sentence with a compound subject or a compound predicate.

Practice B Write a sentence using each compound subject or compound predicate listed. Follow the rules for agreement.

1. vegetation, hawks, and whooping cranes
2. picnicked and swam
3. cattlemen and Indians
4. waits and watches
5. Will and Ross

© **Writing Application** Write two sentences using compound subjects and predicates. Review your sentences to ensure subject-verb agreement, and revise them as needed.

PH **WRITING COACH** | Further instruction and practice are available in *Prentice Hall Writing Coach*.

Writing

Common Core State Standards

W.7.3.d, W.7.4, W.7.5, W.7.8
[For the full wording of the standards, see page 506.]

Informative Text Write an **adaptation** of an incident that is described in the essay you read. Retell the incident for a new audience, such as a group of kindergarteners or a class of students learning English. Follow these steps:

- Choose an incident to retell and decide on an audience.
- Draft to reflect the needs and interests of your audience.
- Use precise words and sensory language to add life and immediacy to your description.
- Finally, revise to organize ideas logically, making sure you have met both your purpose and the needs of your audience.

Grammar Application Make sure to follow the rules of agreement for any compound subjects in your essay.

Writing Workshop: *Work in Progress*

Prewriting for Exposition Choose three sets of items from the Everyday Decisions chart in your writing portfolio. For each set, answer the following question: *What do these items have in common?* Save this Comparison Work in your portfolio.

Use this prewriting activity to prepare for the **Writing Workshop** on page 548.

Research and Technology

Build and Present Knowledge Write a **help-wanted ad** for one of the following positions:

- A modern job involving cattle or horses
- A person to work with Ross Allen, the herpetologist

Before you write, use online search terms, such as *veterinarian, experience required,* and *scientist* to find related help-wanted ads to use as models.

- Notice the concise writing style of ads, and review what the ads cover, including job responsibilities, education, experience, skills, and personal traits the employer seeks.
- Use language that is appropriate for a business ad, including correct grammar and tone.
- Type your ad on a computer and use the spell-check feature.
- Add clip art or other visual displays to enhance key ideas, clarify a point, or add interest.
- Experiment with typefaces to emphasize main ideas.

www.PHLitOnline.com
- Interactive graphic organizers
- Grammar tutorial
- Interactive journals

Test Practice: Reading

Classifying Fact and Opinion

Fiction Selection

Directions: *Read the selection. Then, answer the questions.*

On Saturday morning, Rapha woke early. He was meeting his grandfather in Boston. To get there, he would take the Green Line, the oldest line in Boston's subway system. Rapha boarded the train at Woodland station. He thought the seats were incredibly uncomfortable. He was glad the ride would take only thirty minutes. He leaned back and thought about the day ahead.

In Boston, Rapha and his grandfather would have lunch before seeing the Edward Hopper exhibition at the Museum of Fine Arts. Rapha's grandfather believes that Edward Hopper is the greatest American artist. He says Hopper's work is dark and light at the same time and shows everyday America. To Rapha, Hopper's work seems eerie. However, he has seen only a few pieces. The exhibition will include ninety-two of Hopper's most brilliant paintings.

1. Which of these statements should be classified as an opinion?
  A. The Green Line is the oldest line in Boston's subway system.
  B. The train leaves from Woodland station.
  C. The seats on the train are incredibly uncomfortable.
  D. The ride to Boston takes thirty minutes.

2. Which statement can be proved?
  A. The seats on the train are incredibly uncomfortable.
  B. Rapha thought about the day ahead.
  C. Edward Hopper is the greatest American artist.
  D. The Museum of Fine Arts is hosting the exhibition.

3. Which statement should be classified as a fact?
  A. Rapha was glad the ride is short.
  B. Hopper's work seems eerie.
  C. Hopper's work is dark and light.
  D. Ninety-two paintings are on display.

4. Is the final sentence of the selection a fact or an opinion?
  A. It is a fact
  B. It is an opinion
  C. It is both a fact and an opinion
  D. It is neither a fact nor an opinion

Writing for Assessment

In a short paragraph, explain how you would verify the facts in this passage. Name at least two resources you could use to confirm that the facts are accurate.

Nonfiction Selection

Directions: *Read the selection. Then, answer the questions.*

Georgia O'Keeffe is the greatest American artist. She was born in Sun Prairie, Wisconsin, in 1887. O'Keeffe loved experimenting with art as a child. Later, she studied art in college. For a while, she supported herself as a commercial artist. I don't believe this work suited her, though. After a while, she became an art teacher. She taught in schools around the country, winding up in the high plains of Texas.

O'Keeffe's move to the Southwest was wonderful for her. Many think it marked a turning point in her life as an artist. She said that the stark beauty of the land appealed to her. She began painting actively to capture her surroundings on canvas. She painted pictures of flowers, bleached animal bones, rolling hills, and clouds. I believe she did her best work during this period. Many of these paintings are included in museum collections around the world.

1. Which statement cannot be proved?
   A. Georgia O'Keeffe is the greatest American artist.
   B. O'Keeffe loved experimenting with art as a child.
   C. For a while, she supported herself as a commercial artist.
   D. Many think it marked a turning point in her life as an artist.

2. Which statement is an opinion?
   A. She was born in Sun Prairie, Wisconsin, in 1887.
   B. Later, she studied art in college.
   C. For a while, she supported herself as a commercial artist.
   D. I don't believe this work suited her.

3. Which detail can be supported but *not* proved?
   A. Georgia O'Keeffe is the greatest American artist.
   B. She was born in Sun Prairie, Wisconsin, in 1887.
   C. She studied art in college.
   D. She supported herself as a commercial artist.

4. Which statement is an opinion?
   A. She said that the stark beauty of the land appealed to her.
   B. She began painting actively to capture her surroundings on canvas.
   C. She painted pictures of flowers, bleached animal bones, rolling hills, and clouds.
   D. I believe she did her best work during this period.

Writing for Assessment

Connecting Across Texts
If the author of this passage and Rapha's grandfather were to meet, over what opinion might they disagree? Use details from both passages to write a brief response.

PHLit
Online!
www.PHLitOnline.com
- Online practice
- Instant feedback

Reading for Information

Analyzing Functional Texts

Instruction Manual

Signs

Common Core State Standards

Reading Informational Text
5. Analyze the structure an author uses to organize a text, including how the major sections contribute to the whole and to the development of the ideas.
9. Analyze how two or more authors writing about the same topic shape their presentations of key information by emphasizing different evidence or advancing different interpretations of facts.

Language
4.b. Use common, grade-appropriate Latin affixes and roots as clues to the meaning of a word.
4.d. Verify the preliminary definition of the meaning of a word or phrase.
6. Acquire and use accurately grade-appropriate general academic and domain-specific words and phrases; gather vocabulary knowledge when considering a word or phrase important to comprehension or expression.

Reading Skill: Structure and Purpose

When you **analyze the structure** of a text, you examine how the author shapes and organizes information. Doing so can help you to **locate information** and **understand the purpose**—what the text is meant to do. As you read the instruction manual and signs, consider how the structural features of each text relate to its purpose of giving information about snakes. Consider, too, that although the selections are about the same general topic, they emphasize different information based on their specific purposes.

The following chart lists some common structural features and the ways they support the purpose of a text.

Purpose	Category	Structural Features
to warn	sign	• Brief, easy-to-read text in large type • Large graphics
to teach	instruction manual	• Numbered lists that show step-by-step instructions • Labeled graphics that clarify important concepts

Content-Area Vocabulary

These words appear in the selections that follow. You may also encounter them in other content-area texts.

- **immobilize** (i mō′ bə līz′) *v.* prevent from moving
- **tourniquet** (toor′ ni kit) *n.* device that stops bleeding by putting pressure on a blood vessel

How to Recognize Venomous Snakes in North America

Features:
- clearly labeled visual aids
- safety warnings that describe best practices
- lists of steps to follow

Most snakes in North America are not venomous. The two types of poisonous snakes you should be aware of, pit vipers and coral snakes, are described in this chart.

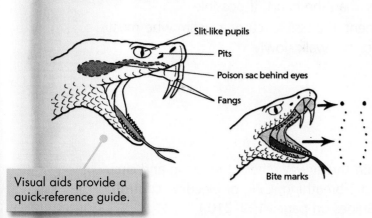

Visual aids provide a quick-reference guide.

Rattlesnakes, copperheads, and cottonmouths are all *pit vipers*. You can recognize a pit viper by its triangular head, fangs, narrow, vertical pupils, and the pits between its nostrils and its eyes. The coral snake has round pupils and is not a pit viper; it does have fangs, but they may not be visible. Nonvenomous snakes have round pupils and no fangs, pits, or rattles.

Rattlers grow up to 8 feet long. There are about 30 species of rattlesnake in the U.S., but any rattler can be recognized by the rattles at the end of its tail.

Copperheads grow up to 4 feet long and have diamond-shaped markings down their backs. They vibrate their tails when angry, but have no rattles.

Color photographs help the reader identify each type of snake.

The cottonmouth, also known as the water moccasin, grows up to 4 feet long. When alarmed, it opens its mouth, revealing the white lining for which it is named.

© Brian Kenney

Coral snakes grow up to 3 feet long and have distinctive red, black, and yellow or white rings and a black nose. Other snakes have similar colors, but only the coral snake has red bands bordered by white or yellow.

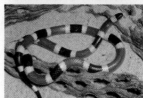

First Aid for a Snake Bite

Follow these guidelines to care for someone bitten by a snake:

- Call 9-1-1 or the local emergency number.
- Wash the wound, if possible.
- **Immobilize** the affected part.
- Keep the affected area lower than the heart, if possible.
- Minimize the victim's movement. If possible, carry a victim who must be transported or have him or her walk slowly.
- Do not apply ice.
- Do not cut the wound.
- Do not apply a **tourniquet**.
- Do not use electric shock.

> This bulleted list describes how to respond to a victim of snake bite.

1. Check the victim's ABCs. Open the airway; check breathing and circulation. If necessary, begin rescue breathing, CPR, or bleeding control. (See the Emergency Action Guides on pages 199–210.)

2. If the victim is having breathing problems, keep his or her airway open. A conscious victim will naturally get into the position in which it is easiest to breathe.

3. Calm and reassure the victim. Anxiety aggravates all reactions.

4. Wash the bite with soap and water.

5. Remove any rings or constricting items, since the bitten area may swell.

6. Take steps to slow the rate at which the venom spreads in the victim's body. Have the victim lie still. Place the injured site below the level of the victim's heart and immobilize it in a comfortable position.

7. Look for signs of shock, such as decreased alertness or increased paleness. If shock develops, lay the victim flat, raise his or her feet 8 to 12 inches, and cover the victim with a coat or blanket. *Do not* elevate the bitten area, and *do not* place the victim in this position if you suspect any head, neck, back, or leg injury or if the position makes the victim uncomfortable. (See **Shock** on page 172.)

8. Stay with the victim until you get medical help.

> Numbered steps help readers follow the instructions for helping a snake-bite victim.

Sign

Features:

- clearly printed text displayed in a public place
- large illustrations or other graphics
- concise language

RATTLESNAKES

Rattlesnakes may be found in this area. They are important members of the natural community, as they help keep rodent and other small animal populations under control. Rattlesnakes are not aggressive, but will strike to defend themselves if disturbed. Please give them distance and respect. Stay on designated trails. Be alert where you place your hands and feet.

A large illustration helps readers to quickly identify a rattlesnake.

The sign uses concise language to convey important information.

LOOK FOR THE DIFFERENCES

NON-VENOMOUS SNAKE

Bold headings show the types of snakes being compared.

RATTLESNAKE

Scales may be smooth or ridged (keeled)

Eyes may have rounded or elliptical pupils

Scales keeled (with a raised ridge in the center of each)

Eyes with vertical, cat-like pupils

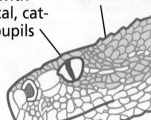

Head, at rest, narrow, barely distinguishable from neck

Head, at rest, broad, "triangular"

Diagrams show key differences between the two snakes.

Body relatively slim or narrow

Body heavy, or relatively "fat" in appearance

Tail tapers to a long, thin point (usually); never with rattles

Tail blunt, ending in a rounded scale (baby snakes) or in a cluster of modified scales (the rattle): never tapers to a thin point

Comparing Functional Texts

 1. Key Ideas and Details (a) What are some of the differences in **structure** and **purpose** between the instructional manual and the warning signs? **(b)** In what ways do structural features support the different purposes of each text?

Content-Area Vocabulary

2. (a) The word *immobilize* is based on the Latin root *-mov-*, which means "to move" and the prefix *im-/in-*, which means "without." Explain how the meaning of the word reflects the meanings of the two word parts. **(b)** Identify two other English words that are based on the root *-mov-*. Write the definition for each word. **(c)** Use a dictionary to verify your definitions.

⏱ Timed Writing

Explanatory Text: Essay

> **Audience**
> Remember that your readers may need to recall this information in an emergency. Your explanation should be clear, brief, and memorable.

In a short essay, explain how to effectively care for a snake-bite victim until help arrives. Include the most important information from the manual to support your response. (25 minutes)

> **Academic Vocabulary**
> When you *explain* a procedure or a process, you tell how to perform a task, using sequence words such as *before, first,* and *next.*

5-Minute Planner

Complete these steps before you begin to write:

1. Read the prompt carefully, noting the highlighted key words.

2. Review the section titled "First Aid for a Snake Bite" in the instruction manual. Jot down the most important and helpful information from both the bulleted list and the numbered list. **TIP** Focus on actions the reader *should* take. Do not focus on what the reader should not do or should do only in certain situations.

3. Review your notes, and identify the essential steps in caring for a snake-bite victim.

4. List the steps you identified in the order in which they should be performed. Then, use that list as the basis for your essay.

Comparing Humor

Humor is a type of writing that is meant to amuse readers. To entertain, authors may use one or more of these comic techniques:

- Present an illogical, inappropriate, improper, or unusual situation
- Contrast reality with the characters' mistaken views
- Exaggerate the truth, or exaggerate the feelings, ideas, and actions of characters
- Play with language by using funny names, nonsense words, humorous ways of speaking, or other forms of wordplay

While most humorists want to entertain the reader, many also write to convey serious messages. Humor usually reflects reality in some way, if only by turning reality upside down. In some humorous works, such as "Alligator," a writer observes a funny situation and captures it in words, managing to communicate the humor to readers. In other humorous works, such as "The Cremation of Sam McGee," the author begins with facts, but exaggerates them for comic effect.

Writers of humorous works often develop humor through the characters they present. In the essay "Alligator" and the narrative poem "The Cremation of Sam McGee," humorous characters are central to the selection. As you read, use a cluster diagram like the one shown to note comic details in the descriptions and actions of Aunt Belle in "Alligator" and Sam McGee in "The Cremation of Sam McGee."

Common Core
State Standards

Reading Literature
3. Analyze how particular elements of a story or drama interact.

Writing
9. Draw evidence from literary or informational texts to support analysis, reflection, and research.

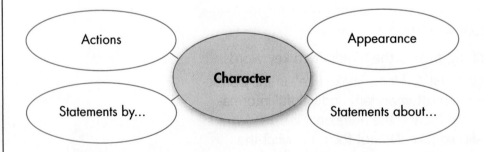

www.PHLitOnline.com

- Vocabulary flashcards
- Interactive journals
- More about the authors
- Selection audio
- Interactive graphic organizers

What should we *learn?*

Writing About the Big Question

In each of these selections, the narrator exaggerates the facts for humorous effect. Use these sentence starters to develop your ideas.

Our **curiosity** sometimes leads us to discover humor because we see _____.

Humor can help us gain insight by _____.

Meet the Authors

Bailey White (b. 1950)
Author of "Alligator"

Bailey White reads her humorous essays on *All Things Considered*, a program on public radio. She describes people and situations she encounters in and around Thomasville, Georgia, where she was born and lives today.

Juggling Two Careers White began writing when she was a teen. On graduation from Florida State University, she returned to Thomasville to teach first grade. During the twenty years she taught, she wrote in her spare time. Today, White pursues her writing career full time.

Robert Service (1874–1958)

Author of "The Cremation of Sam McGee"

Born in England and raised in Scotland, Robert Service went to Canada at age twenty to work for a bank. In the Yukon Territory, he met fur trappers and gold prospectors. Leaving the bank, Service traveled in the Arctic, where he observed the people and recorded his adventures. "The Cremation of Sam McGee" grew out of these experiences.

ALLIGATOR

Bailey White

I remember as a little child watching my Aunt Belle's wide rump disappear into the cattails and marsh grass at the edge of a pond as she crawled on her hands and knees to meet a giant alligator face to face. She was taming him, she said. We children would wait high up on the bank with our eyes and mouths wide open, hoping that the alligator wouldn't eat her up, but not wanting to miss it if he did.

Finally Aunt Belle would get as close to him as she wanted, and they would stare at each other for some minutes. Then my aunt would jump up, wave her arms in the air, and shout, "Whoo!" With a tremendous leap and flop the alligator would

▲ Critical Viewing
Would you want to try to tame an alligator like this one? Why or why not? [Connect]

Vocabulary
cattails (kat´ tālz) *n.* tall reeds with furry spikes found in wetlands

Vocabulary

exultant (eg zult´ 'nt)
adj. expressing great
joy or triumph

bellow (bel´ ō)
v. roar deeply

Spiral Review

Word Choice In this
vivid description of the
alligator, which words
describe his motion?

Humorous Essay
Which details make this
paragraph funny?

▼ Critical Viewing
This alligator appears
to be smiling. Describe
how its smile makes
you feel. **[Connect]**

throw himself into the water. The little drops from that splash would reach all the way to where we were standing, and my aunt would come up the bank drenched and exultant. "I have to show him who's boss," she would tell us.

Later, Aunt Belle taught that alligator to bellow on command. She would drive the truck down to the edge of the pond and gun the engine. We would sit in the back, craning our necks to see him coming. He would come fast across the pond, raising two diagonal waves behind him as he came. He would haul himself into the shallow water and get situated just right. His back was broad and black. His head was as wide as a single bed. His tail would disappear into the dark pond water. He was the biggest alligator anyone had ever seen.

Then my aunt would turn off the engine. We would all stop breathing. The alligator would swell up. He would lift his head, arch his tail, and bellow. The sound would come from deep inside. It was not loud, but it had a carrying quality. It was like a roar, but with more authority than a lion's roar. It was a sound you hear in your bones. If we were lucky, he would bellow ten times. Then Aunt Belle would throw him a dead chicken.

The day came when she could just walk down to the pond and look out across the water. The alligator would come surging up to the bank, crawl out, and bellow.

By this time he was very old. My aunt got old, too. Her children had all grown up. She got to where she was spending a lot of time down at the pond. She'd go down there and just sit on the bank. When the alligator saw her, he'd swim over and climb out. He never bellowed anymore. They would just sit and look at each other. After a while my aunt would walk back to the house. The alligator would swim out to where the water was deep and black, and float for a minute; then he'd just disappear, without even a ripple. That's how he did.

But one day he didn't come when Aunt Belle went to the pond. He didn't come the next day, or the day after. All that summer, Aunt Belle walked around and around the pond looking, listening, and sniffing. "Something as big as that, you'd know if he was dead, this hot weather," she'd say. Finally, she stopped going down to the pond.

But sometimes, on the nights of the full moon in springtime, I can hear an alligator bellow. It comes rolling up through the night. It's not loud, but it makes me sit up in bed and hold my breath. Sometimes I hear it ten times. It's a peaceful sound.

Humorous Essay
Which details in this paragraph are probably exaggerated for effect? Explain.

Critical Thinking

1. **Key Ideas and Details (a)** According to the second paragraph of the essay, what were some early interactions between Aunt Belle and the alligator? **(b) Infer:** What does Aunt Belle mean when she says she has to "show him who's boss"?

2. **Craft and Structure (a)** What words and phrases does White use to describe the bellowing of the alligator? **(b) Speculate:** How would the story have been different if White had used a more realistic style to describe the scene?

3. **Integration of Knowledge and Ideas (a) Compare and Contrast:** How are the alligator and Aunt Belle similar at the end of the essay? **(b) Analyze:** How does the relationship between the alligator and Aunt Belle change over the years?

4. **Integration of Knowledge and Ideas (a)** What does the writer learn from her Aunt Belle? **(b)** Why do you think people sometimes use humor to convey a serious or touching message? *[Connect to the Big Question: What should we learn?]*

Cite textual evidence to support your responses.

The CREMATION of SAM MCGEE

Robert Service

▲ **Critical Viewing**
Why do you think people in the Arctic, like the men in this poem, travel by dog sled as pictured here?
[Hypothesize]

Background In this poem, two men prospect for gold in Canada's Yukon Territory. Located just east of Alaska, where the temperature can reach −60°F, the area long attracted fortune hunters who came for its mineral wealth. Gold was discovered in the Klondike River region in the 1890s, and many people, including poet Robert Service, came to look for it.

There are strange things done in the midnight sun
    By the men who moil[1] for gold;
The Arctic trails have their secret tales
    That would make your blood run cold;
5 The Northern Lights have seen queer sights,
    But the queerest they ever did see
Was that night on the marge[2] of Lake Lebarge
    I cremated Sam McGee.

Now Sam McGee was from Tennessee,
    where the cotton blooms and blows
10 Why he left his home in the South to roam
    'round the Pole, God only knows.

---

1. moil (moil) *v.* toil and slave.
2. marge (märj) *n.* poetic word for the shore of the lake.

He was always cold, but the land of gold
    seemed to hold him like a spell;
Though he'd often say in his homely way
    that "he'd sooner live in hell."

On a Christmas Day we were mushing our way
    over the Dawson trail.
Talk of your cold! through the parka's fold
    it stabbed like a driven nail.
15 If our eyes we'd close, then the lashes froze
    til sometimes we couldn't see;
It wasn't much fun, but the only one
    to whimper was Sam McGee.

And that very night, as we lay packed tight
    in our robes beneath the snow,
And the dogs were fed, and the stars o'erhead
    were dancing heel and toe,
He turned to me, and "Cap," says he,
    "I'll cash in this trip, I guess;
20 And if I do, I'm asking that you
    won't refuse my last request."

▲ **Critical Viewing**
What details of this image make it a good illustration for the poem? Explain. **[Evaluate]**

Vocabulary
whimper (hwim´ pər) *v.* make low, crying sounds

✓ **Reading Check**
Why is Sam McGee in the Arctic?

Humor
Why does McGee
want to be cremated?

Well, he seemed so low that I couldn't say no;
    then he says with a sort of moan:
"It's the cursed cold, and it's got right hold
    till I'm chilled clean through to the bone.
Yet 'tain't being dead—it's my awful dread
    of the icy grave that pains;
So I want you to swear that, foul or fair,
    you'll cremate my last remains."

**Spiral Review Word
Choice** Notice that
there are rhyming
words, such as *need*
and *heed,* in the middle
and end of alternating
lines. How do these
word choices affect the
sound of the poem?

25 A pal's last need is a thing to heed,
    so I swore I would not fail;
And we started on at the streak of dawn;
    but God! he looked ghastly pale.
He crouched on the sleigh, and he raved all day
    of his home in Tennessee;
And before nightfall a corpse was all
    that was left of Sam McGee.

There wasn't a breath in that land of death,
    and I hurried, horror-driven,
30 With a corpse half hid that I couldn't get rid,
    because of a promise given;
It was lashed to the sleigh, and it seemed to say:
    "You may tax your brawn[3] and brains,
But you promised true, and it's up to you
    to cremate those last remains."

Now a promise made is a debt unpaid,
    and the trail has its own stern code.
In the days to come, though my lips were dumb,
    in my heart how I cursed that load.
35 In the long, long night, by the lone firelight,
    while the huskies, round in a ring,

Vocabulary
loathed (lō*th*d) *v.* hated

Howled out their woes to the homeless snows—
    O God! how I loathed the thing.
And every day that quiet clay
    seemed to heavy and heavier grow;
And on I went, though the dogs were spent
    and the grub was getting low;
The trail was bad, and I felt half mad,
    but I swore I would not give in;

---

3. brawn (brôn) *n.* physical strength.

40 And I'd often sing to the hateful thing,
       and it hearkened with a grin.

    Till I came to the marge of Lake Lebarge,
       and a derelict[4] there lay;
    It was jammed in the ice, but I saw in a trice
       it was called the "Alice May."
    And I looked at it, and I thought a bit,
       and I looked at my frozen chum;
    Then "Here," said I, with a sudden cry,
       "is my cre-ma-tor-eum."

45 Some planks I tore from the cabin floor,
       and I lit the boiler fire;
    Some coal I found that was lying around,
       and I heaped the fuel higher;
    The flames just soared, and the furnace roared—
       such a blaze you seldom see;
    And I burrowed a hole in the glowing coal,
       and I stuffed in Sam McGee.

    Then I made a hike, for I didn't like
       to hear him sizzle so;
50 And the heavens scowled, and the huskies howled,
       and the wind began to blow.
    It was icy cold, but the hot sweat rolled
       down my cheeks, and I don't know why;
    And the greasy smoke in an inky cloak
       went streaking down the sky.

    I do not know how long in the snow
       I wrestled with grisly fear;
    But the stars came out and they danced about
       ere again I ventured near;

---

4. **derelict** (der′ ə likt′) *n.* abandoned ship.

Humor
What problem, or conflict, does the speaker face?

Reading Check

What promise does the speaker keep?

55 I was sick with dread, but I bravely said:
        "I'll just take a peep inside.
    I guess he's cooked, and it's time I looked"; . . .
        then the door I opened wide.

    And there sat Sam, looking cool and calm,
        in the heart of the furnace roar;
    And he wore a smile you could see a mile,
        and he said: "Please close that door.
    It's fine in here, but I greatly fear
        you'll let in the cold and storm—
60 Since I left Plumtree, down in Tennessee,
        it's the first time I've been warm."

    There are strange things done in the midnight sun
        By the men who moil for gold;
    The Arctic trails have their secret tales
        That would make your blood run cold;
65 *The Northern Lights have seen queer sights,*
        But the queerest they ever did see
    Was that night on the marge of Lake Lebarge
        I cremated Sam McGee.

Critical Thinking

Cite textual evidence to support your responses.

1. **Key Ideas and Details (a)** What problem does Sam have with his surroundings? **(b) Deduce:** What prevents him from going home?

2. **Key Ideas and Details (a)** Who is the speaker, and what does he promise Sam? **(b) Interpret:** Why is the speaker determined to keep his promise? Use details from the poem to support your answer.

3. **Craft and Structure (a)** What does the speaker find when he opens the furnace door? **(b) Infer:** What reaction does the poet expect you to have to this unexpected occurrence?

4. **Integration of Knowledge and Ideas (a)** What does this selection teach about the Yukon and friendship through its use of humor? **(b)** What can we learn from the things that make us laugh? *[Connect to the Big Question: What should we learn?]*

Comparing Humor

© 1. Craft and Structure Complete a chart like the one shown to analyze the techniques each author uses to create humor.

	Humorous Scene	Details	Humorous Techniques
"Alligator"			
"The Cremation of Sam McGee"			

⏱ Timed Writing

Explanatory Text: Essay

Analyze which selection you think is more humorous: the essay "Alligator" or the poem "The Cremation of Sam McGee." Write a comparison-and-contrast essay, providing details from the selections to support your position. **(25 minutes)**

5-Minute Planner

1. Read the prompt carefully and completely.
2. Gather your ideas by jotting down answers to these questions:
   - What events from each selection amused you most?
   - Whom did you find funnier—Aunt Belle in "Alligator" or Sam McGee in "The Cremation of Sam McGee"?
   - Whom did you find more touching? Why?
   - What purpose might the authors have had beyond amusing you? Explain.
   - Which author would you choose to read again? Why?
3. Choose an organizational strategy. Use either the block method—discussing first one work, then the other—or the point-by-point method—discussing one point per work at a time—to compare elements such as the narrators, characters, and setting.
4. Reread the prompt, and then draft your essay.

Writing Workshop

Write an Explanatory Text

Exposition: Comparison-and-Contrast Essay

Defining the Form A **comparison-and-contrast essay** analyzes the similarities and differences between two or more related subjects. You might use elements of this form in persuasive essays, journals, and reviews.

Assignment Write a comparison-and-contrast essay that helps readers make a decision or see old things in a fresh way. Your essay should feature these elements:

- A *topic involving two or more things* that are neither nearly identical nor extremely different
- *Details illustrating both similarities and differences*
- *Clear organization* that highlights the points of comparison
- An *introduction* that grabs a reader's interest, and a strong, memorable *conclusion*
- Error-free writing, including *correct use of adjectives and adverbs*

To preview the criteria on which your comparison-and-contrast essay may be judged, see the rubric on page 555.

Writing Workshop: *Work in Progress*

Review the work that you did on pages 505 and 527.

WRITE GUY
Jeff Anderson, M.Ed.

What Do You Notice?

Sentence Structure

The following sentences are from Chief Dan George's "I Am a Native of North America." Read them several times.

You and I need the strength and joy that comes from knowing that we are loved. With it we are creative. With it we march tirelessly. With it, and with it alone, we are able to sacrifice for others.

Discuss these questions with a partner:

- What do you notice about these sentences?
- How does the sentence structure and the repetition of certain words help to build ideas?

Think about ways you might use structure to make your writing lively.

Writing
2. Write informative/explanatory texts to examine a topic and convey ideas, concepts, and information through the selection, organization, and analysis of relevant content.
2.a. Introduce a topic clearly, previewing what is to follow; organize ideas, concepts, and information, using strategies such as definition, classification, comparison/contrast, and cause/effect.
2.b. Develop the topic and relevant facts, definitions, concrete details, quotations, or other information and examples.
2.d. Use precise language and domain-specific vocabulary to inform about or explain the topic.
2.e. Establish and maintain a formal style.

Reading-Writing Connection

To get a feel for comparison-and-contrast writing, read "Conversational Ballgames" by Nancy Masterson Sakamoto on page 432.

Prewriting/Planning Strategies

Choose a topic. To choose a topic for your essay, use one of these strategies:

- **Quicklist** Fold a piece of paper in thirds lengthwise. In the first column, list recent choices you have made—for instance, products you have bought or activities you have completed. In the second column, next to each choice, write a precise descriptive phrase. In the third column, give an alternative to your choice.

  Example: polka-dot sweatshirt / playful, silly / team jacket
  Review your list, and choose the most interesting pairing to compare and contrast.

- **BUT Chart** Write the word BUT down the center of a piece of paper. On the left, list items with something in common. List differences among them on the right. Choose your topic from this list.

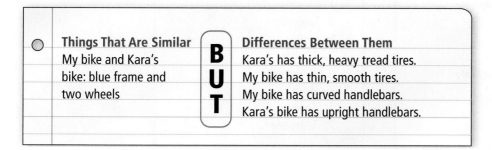

Things That Are Similar	B U T	Differences Between Them
My bike and Kara's bike: blue frame and two wheels		Kara's has thick, heavy tread tires. My bike has thin, smooth tires. My bike has curved handlebars. Kara's bike has upright handlebars.

Get specific. You may find that your topic is too broad to cover in a brief essay. Use these strategies to narrow your topic.

- **Describe it** to someone who is not familiar with it.
- **Apply it,** explaining what you can do with it, on it, or to it.
- **Analyze it** by breaking it into parts.
- **Argue for or against it,** explaining good and bad points, while maintaining a formal style.

Circle details from your notes to create a focused topic.

Show similarities and differences. Focus on gathering details that show similarities and differences between your subjects. Use a Venn diagram to organize your details. Fill in details about one subject on the left side of the diagram and details about the other on the right side. Use the middle section to list common features.

Drafting Strategies

Organize the body of your draft. Your essay should be easy for readers to follow and understand. There are two main ways to organize a comparison-and-contrast essay. Choose the one that is most appropriate to your topic and purpose.

- **Block Method** Present all the details about one of your subjects, then all the details about your next subject. This method works well if you are writing about more than two subjects or if your topic is complex.

- **Point-by-Point Method** Discuss one aspect of both subjects, then another aspect of both subjects, and so on.

Methods of Organization

Block Method
A. Theater
1. Amount of variety
2. Intensity
3. Realism
B. Television
1. Amount of variety
2. Intensity
3. Realism

Point-by-Point Comparison
A. Amount of Variety
1. Theater
2. Television
B. Intensity
1. Theater
2. Television
C. Realism
1. Theater
2. Television

Layer ideas using SEE. Often, the most interesting parts of an essay are the details you offer to support your main ideas. Use the SEE method to develop strong elaboration.

- *State* your main idea in every paragraph to stay on topic.
- *Extend* the idea with an example that proves the main idea.
- *Elaborate* by offering further details to describe your example.

Include formatting, graphics, and multimedia. Use headings to highlight the main sections in your paper. Graphics, such as charts and tables, or multimedia, such as a tape recording or slide show, can strengthen ideas and further comprehension.

Clarify relationships. Use words and phrases to show relationships between ideas. Transitions that show comparisons include *also, just as, like,* and *similarly.* Transitions that show contrasts include *although, but, however, on the other hand, whereas,* and *while.*

Writers on Writing

Richard Mühlberger On Getting Readers Involved

> Richard Mühlberger is the author of "What Makes a Rembrandt a Rembrandt?" (p. 413).

Whether you are writing comparison-and-contrast or another form of exposition, you need to keep the reader's interest and attention. Everyone involved in producing my book about Monet, the French Impressionist painter, knew before it was printed that it would be a success. Monet was the number one artist in popularity among adults. But the book was for middle-school students. My job was to get them involved in exploring Monet's art.

"I write with my audience in mind."
—Richard Mühlberger

Professional Model:

from *"What Makes a Monet a Monet?"*

Oscar-Claude Monet was born in Paris, France, on November 14, 1840. When he was five years old, his family moved to the seaside city of Le Havre. He went to school there, but he was not much of a student. He liked to draw irreverent caricatures of his teachers, who tried in vain to get him to concentrate on other subjects. Monet later confessed that he did not learn much in school except some spelling. "It seemed like a prison, and I could never bear to stay there, even for four hours a day, especially when the sunshine beckoned and the sea was smooth," he said.

Monet's favorite activity was wandering along the beaches, making caricatures of tourists. He usually pictured a person with a very small body and a very large head, exaggerating the nose or some other part of the face. He sold his caricatures for ten to twenty francs, more than what his teachers earned in a day!

I wanted to establish right away that Monet had only one interest in life—making art.

The word *sunshine* summarizes the essence of many of his paintings. Alone, that word may not compel a young person to read on. So I placed it in a context that makes the young artist sound like a maverick who might interest young readers.

My book does not contain a caricature by Monet so I had to come up with a description that would draw a picture in the reader's mind.

Revising Strategies

Heighten interest. Check your essay to make sure it grabs and holds your readers' attention. Use the following strategies:

- Sharpen your introduction to intrigue readers, encouraging them to read further. Consider including a strong image, a surprising comparison, or a thought-provoking question.
- Add details that are surprising, colorful, and important.
- Add headings, relevant graphics, or multimedia.
- Add language to emphasize similarities or differences.
- Rework your conclusion to add impact or leave readers with a lingering question. Be sure your conclusion makes the value of the comparison and contrast clear.

Common Core
State Standards

Writing
2.e. Provide a concluding statement or section that follows from and supports the information or explanation presented.
4. Produce clear and coherent writing in which the development, organization, and style are appropriate to task, purpose, and audience.
5. With some guidance and support from peers and adults, develop and strengthen writing as needed by planning, revising, editing, rewriting, or trying a new approach, focusing on how well purpose and audience have been addressed.

Language
1.c. Place phrases and clauses within a sentence, recognizing and correcting misplaced and dangling modifiers.
3.a. Choose language that expresses ideas precisely and concisely, recognizing and eliminating wordiness and redundancy.

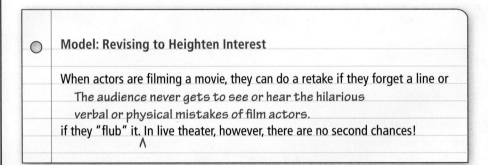

Avoid repetition. Check your writing for unnecessary repetition. Sometimes writers will repeat a point but add something slightly different the second time. Combine the two sentences to preserve your additional material while avoiding repetition and providing interest with sentence variety.

Repetitive: Lastly, the best thing about theater is it's real. What I mean is you see when people make mistakes. You see people being human by making mistakes every so often.

Combined: Lastly, the best thing about theater is it's human and real. What I mean is you see when people make mistakes.

Peer Review

Read your revised draft to a teacher or classmate. Ask whether you repeated information. Together, look for ways to make the writing clearer and less repetitive.

Revising Errors in Adjective and Adverb Usage

The common modifiers *just* and *only* often cause problems in both speaking and writing.

Identifying Errors in Adjective and Adverb Usage Usage problems with adjectives and adverbs typically occur when these words are placed incorrectly in a sentence or are confused because of similar meanings. When used as an adverb, *just* often means "no more than." When *just* has this meaning, place it right before the word it logically modifies.

Incorrect: Do you *just* want one brownie for dessert?

Correct: Do you want *just* one brownie for dessert?

The position of ***only*** can affect the entire meaning of a sentence.

Only he ate the cake. (Nobody else ate it.)

He *only* ate the cake. (He did nothing else with the cake.)

He ate *only* the cake. (He ate nothing else.)

Fixing Errors in Adjective and Adverb Usage To fix a usage problem with adjectives and adverbs, use one of the following methods.

1. **For *only*:** If the word is intended as an adverb meaning "no more than," place it right before the word it logically modifies.

2. **For *just*:** First, identify the intended meaning of the sentence. Then, position *just* in the sentence so that the meaning is clear.

3. **For other common problems:** See the chart or use a dictionary.

> **PH** **WRITING COACH**
>
> Further instruction and practice are available in *Prentice Hall Writing Coach*.

Commonly Confused Modifiers	
bad: (adjective) He was a *bad* skater.	**badly:** (adverb) I played *badly* at the recital.
fewer: answers "How many?" He had *fewer* questions.	**less:** answers "How much?" He drank *less* water today.

Grammar In Your Writing

Choose two paragraphs in your draft. Underline every sentence that contains one of the modifiers discussed or another modifier you think you may have used incorrectly. Fix any usage problems.

Stage vs. Set

Theater or television? If you are under eighteen, you more than likely said "television." Have you ever stopped to consider what the magical world of theater has to offer?

Anyone who has been to the theater can tell you that there is nothing like the feeling of sitting and watching people perform. Actors get something special out of theater, too. Knowing that hundreds of people are watching your every move creates a special kind of excitement.

There's also variety. In live theater, every show is different. When you watch a rerun on television, it's the exact same thing every time. With theater, you get a different experience every night. You can go to see the same show with a different cast or director and the performance will be totally different. Even if you go to a show with the same cast and director, it will be different. An actor might forget a line and improvise or suddenly decide to change the way he or she is playing a character in a scene. The audience never knows exactly what will happen.

Theater is also larger than the drama you see on television. I don't care how big a screen your television has, theater will always be BIGGER—the emotion more passionate, the voices louder, and the effect more profound. In theater, you have to project your voice and movements so that they carry to the back rows of the audience. In television, actors just need to be seen and heard by the cameras and microphones.

Lastly, the best thing about theater is it's human and real. You see when people make mistakes. On television, everything has to be perfect or they do a retake. You never see television actors miss a line or trip over their feet. Since there is no second chance in theater, everything is more spontaneous. When a performance takes an unexpected turn, the audience gets to see the professionalism of the actors as they respond to something new.

Next time you're channel surfing and there's nothing good on, why not take some time to check out what's playing in your community playhouse? Who knows? Maybe you'll discover a rising talent. Even better, maybe you'll decide you want to become an actor or actress after you see how thrilling a live production really is.

In the first paragraph, Mackenzie introduces the comparison in a way that grabs the reader's attention. She compares things that are alike, yet different.

Mackenzie develops her argument by including examples and explanations, using the point-by-point method of organization.

In the final paragraph, Mackenzie offers a strong conclusion that challenges the reader to accept her point of view.

Editing and Proofreading

Review your draft to correct errors in grammar, spelling, and punctuation.

Focus on empty language. Review your work to delete words that do not add value or meaning. Consider cutting words such as *very* and *really* and clauses such as *I think, as I said,* and *you know.*

Publishing and Presenting

Consider one of the following ways to share your writing.

Be a consumer watchdog. If your essay contains information that is useful to consumers, form a Consumer Information Panel. Post your essays to a class blog or school Web site. Include links to reliable, related sites, such as government Web sites that focus on health and safety or consumer issues.

Submit it to a magazine. Submit your essay to a magazine that specializes in the subject you have chosen. You can find publishing information and an address in a recent edition of the magazine.

Reflecting on Your Writing

Writer's Journal Jot down your answer to this question:

What was the most important improvement you made when revising?

Rubric for Self-Assessment

Find evidence in your writing to address each category. Then, use the rating scale to grade your work.

Spiral Review

Earlier in the unit, you learned about **subjects and predicates** (p. 504) and **compound subjects and predicates** (p. 526). Check the use of subjects and predicates in your comparison-and-contrast essay. Review your essay to be sure that each sentence contains at least one subject and predicate and that you have followed rules for agreement with compound subjects.

PH WRITING COACH

Further instruction and practice are available in *Prentice Hall Writing Coach.*

Criteria	Rating Scale
	not very / very
Focus: How clearly does the essay address two or more related subjects?	1 2 3 4 5
Organization: How effectively are points of comparison organized?	1 2 3 4 5
Support/Elaboration: How well do you use details to describe similarities and differences?	1 2 3 4 5
Style: How well have you used language that grabs the reader's interest?	1 2 3 4 5
Conventions: How correct is your grammar, especially your use of adjectives and adverbs?	1 2 3 4 5

Vocabulary Workshop

Words With Multiple Meanings

A **multiple-meaning word** is a word that has more than one definition. Many words in English have multiple meanings; for example, *peach* can be defined as a color or a fruit. To determine the meaning intended in a sentence, you must consider the context, or the words surrounding the word. The following chart shows a multiple-meaning word used in two different sentences.

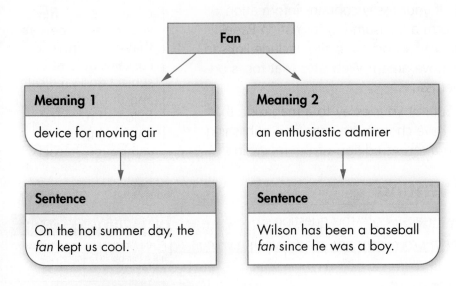

Fan	
Meaning 1	**Meaning 2**
device for moving air	an enthusiastic admirer
Sentence	**Sentence**
On the hot summer day, the *fan* kept us cool.	Wilson has been a baseball *fan* since he was a boy.

 **Common Core State Standards**

Language

4. Determine or clarify the meaning of unknown and multiple-meaning words and phrases based on grade 7 reading and content, choosing flexibly from a range of strategies.

4.a. Use context as a clue to the meaning of a word or phrase.

4.c. Consult general and specialized reference materials, both print and digital, to find the pronunciation of a word or determine or clarify its precise meaning or its part of speech.

4.d. Verify the preliminary determination of the meaning of a word or phrase.

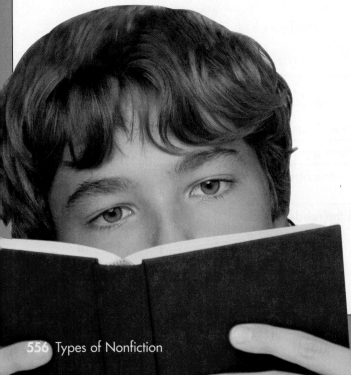

Practice A Write the meaning of each italicized word. Verify the meaning in a dictionary.

1. **a.** When the *bats* swooped down on my head, I let out a scream.

   b. I wish we could get new *bats* for our softball team this year.

2. **a.** Julian was not *present* to collect the prize he won.

   b. I decided to make my sister's birthday *present* this year.

3. **a.** The *second* hand on the clock ticked loudly.

   b. Liliana won *second* prize at the science fair.

4. **a.** We saved the *rest* of the cake for the next class.

   b. After running a mile in track, we all needed a *rest*.

Practice B For each word listed, write two sentences that use different meanings of the word. If necessary, look up the meanings in a dictionary.

1. kind   5. dash

2. object   6. season

3. express   7. desert

4. ring   8. seal

Activity Use a print or digital dictionary to learn about these words with multiple meanings: *power*, *degree*, *dynamite*, *file*, *patient*. Write each word on a separate notecard like the one shown. Fill in the left column of the notecard according to one of the word's meanings. Fill in the right-hand column according to another of the word's meanings. Then, trade note cards with a partner, and discuss the different meanings and uses of the words that each of you found.

www.PHLitOnline.com
- Author video: Writing Process
- Author video: Rewards of Writing

Word: _____	
Part of Speech:	Part of Speech:
Definition:	Definition:
Example Sentence:	Example Sentence:

Comprehension and Collaboration

Work with two or three classmates to write a sentence that uses two different meanings of each of the following words. For example: *While we sat in a traffic jam, I was able to eat my breakfast of toast and* jam.

fair
long
last

Communications Workshop

Evaluating a Persuasive Presentation

Common Core State Standards

Speaking and Listening

2. Analyze the main ideas and supporting details presented in diverse media and formats and explain how the ideas clarify a topic, text, or issue under study.

3. Delineate a speaker's argument and specific claims, evaluating the soundness of the reasoning and the relevance and sufficiency of the evidence.

A **persuasive presentation** is similar to a persuasive composition. Its purpose is to persuade the listener to do, buy, or believe something. Use these strategies to assess persuasive presentations.

Learn the Skills

Use these strategies to complete the activity on page 559.

Evaluate content. Like its written counterpart, an effective persuasive presentation includes a clear statement of the speaker's position and relevant supporting evidence. Listen to every word of a persuasive presentation in order to explain the speaker's purpose. Evaluate whether the speaker is appealing to your emotions or using facts, statistics, and other information that can be proved.

Determine the speaker's attitude. Ask yourself these questions to determine how the speaker feels about his or her subject:

- Does the speaker appeal to emotion or to reason?
- Does he or she use words that convey strong images or associations?
- What do the speaker's body language and facial expressions suggest?
- What is the speaker's tone of voice?

Listen for a logical organization. Follow the argument from point to point. Listen for the connections between ideas. Also, listen for a convincing introduction and conclusion.

Listen for strong evidence. Be aware of the anecdotes, descriptions, facts, statistics, and specific examples that support the speaker's position. Is the support convincing? Why or why not?

Ask questions. Never be afraid to ask questions. You will discover how well the speaker has researched the topic by questioning the evidence.

Challenge bias or faulty logic. If you disagree with something the presenter has said, express your opinion. Respect the speaker's viewpoints if you identify bias or faulty logic. If you suspect a piece of evidence is wrong, challenge it by asking for its source.

Clarify and contribute. Paraphrase a speaker's key points to clarify what you have heard. You might also share a personal anecdote or observation that affirms the speaker's position.

Practice the Skills

© **Presentation of Knowledge and Ideas** Use what you have learned in this workshop to complete the following activity.

ACTIVITY: Evaluating a Persuasive Presentation

Watch a persuasive sales pitch, either live or in a recorded format.
- Identify the speaker's message.
- Evaluate if the speaker's purpose is to inform or influence the audience.
- Explain how you felt listening to the message.
- List questions that the speaker's claims raise for you.
- Jot down notes about the presentation, such as the speaker's tone of voice, body language, and facial expressions.
- Draw conclusions about the speaker's message by considering verbal and nonverbal cues.
- Use the Assessment Guide to evaluate the presentation.

Use the Assessment Guide below to interpret the content and delivery of the persuasive presentation you watched.

Assessment Guide

What is the speaker's purpose behind this message?

Is the speaker's purpose to inform or influence the audience?

What does the speaker hope you will do after hearing the message?

What evidence does the speaker provide to support claims?

How could you research the speaker's claims?

On what points would you challenge the speaker?

How effective was the delivery of the presentation?

What can you conclude about the speaker's nonverbal and verbal communication, including tone of voice, gestures, and facial expressions?

© **Comprehension and Collaboration** Compare your findings with those of your classmates. As a group, discuss how you can use the strategies above to evaluate other messages, such as advertisements, commercials, and additional persuasive presentations. Then, evaluate various ways that media is used to influence and inform audiences.

Cumulative Review

Common Core
State Standards

RI.7.4, RI.7.6, RI.7.8; L.7.4.a; W.7.2.b
[For the full wording of the standards, see the standards chart in the front of your textbook.]

I. Reading Literature/Informational Text

Directions: *Read the passage. Then, answer each question that follows.*

Dear City Council Members,

I am concerned about the dangers of bicycle riding in our city's neighborhoods. I ride my bike to school, and last week, I almost had a very serious accident. Because there are no bike lanes in my neighborhood, I was forced to ride in the street with cars. A car came around a corner fast, honked at me, and almost hit me. I swerved, fell off my bike, and hit my head on the curb. Luckily, I was wearing a helmet. Because I was so close to school, I was able to get help quickly. This incident serves as proof that major improvements to bicycle safety need to be implemented before a worse accident occurs.

The first and most important improvement is providing more bike lanes on neighborhood streets. After some research, I found that there have been many studies on the effectiveness of simply painting bike lanes onto existing streets. In one study, the city of Lakeland, only 100 miles away, spent two percent of their transportation safety budget on bike lanes. The results showed that the bicycle accident rate went down from 45 per year to only 18.

We also need to have driver education. In a questionnaire I sent to 50 of my classmates, they reported that it is common for drivers to honk or yell things like "Get out of the road!" at cyclists. Children are harassed by angry drivers for simply riding their bikes.

If the city could post yellow signs that have a "Bicycle Crossing" symbol, it would alert drivers that this is a bike route. The city currently has these signs posted on major roads. However, the signs are desperately needed in neighborhoods near schools. Young riders would feel safer going across these marked intersections.

Before we have any serious accidents involving children, the city needs to act now. The innocent act of children riding their bicycles is now loaded with angry drivers who take their <u>aggression</u> out at cyclists. This is unacceptable, and the city needs to step to the plate to change it.

Sincerely,
Priya Mandala

1. What is the **author's purpose** in this passage?
   A. to entertain readers
   B. to inform the public
   C. to explain a step-by-step process
   D. to persuade city officials

2. How does the use of **autobiographical details** in the first paragraph contribute to the argument?
   A. It tells the opinion of an expert.
   B. It makes the arguments weaker.
   C. It makes the writer appear more sincere.
   D. It makes the writer seem immature.

3. Which word in this sentence is an example of strong **word choice:** *However, these signs are desperately needed in neighborhoods near schools.*
   A. However
   B. needed
   C. neighborhoods
   D. desperately

4. Which of the following sentences demonstrates an **appeal to reason?**
   A. Because I was close to school, I was able to get help quickly.
   B. The results showed that the bicycle accident rate went down from 45 per year to only 18.
   C. The signs are desperately needed in neighborhoods near schools.
   D. Before we have any serious accidents involving children, the city needs to act now.

5. How does the writer **appeal to emotion?**
   A. She sends her letter directly to the City Council.
   B. She suggests solutions with facts to support her ideas.
   C. She cites a study conducted in Lakeland.
   D. She uses strong language to get her point across.

6. Why does the writer think driver education is necessary?
   A. Drivers get angry with children riding bicycles.
   B. The sidewalks are in poor condition for riding a bicycle.
   C. Streets around schools are used most by bicycle riders.
   D. The existing bicycle lanes are ignored by drivers.

7. **Vocabulary** Which word is closest in meaning to the underlined word <u>aggression</u>?
   A. danger
   B. changes
   C. anger
   D. difficulty

⏱ Timed Writing

8. Make a list of the **author's main arguments.** In an essay, evaluate how well each **argument** is supported with **facts** or **opinions.** Cite evidence from the text to support your analysis.

GO ON

II. Reading Informational Text

Directions: *Read the passage. Then, answer each question that follows.*

Common Core State Standards

RI.7.6; L7.1.c, L7.3.a
[For the full wording of the standards, see the standards chart in the front of your textbook.]

Salamander Population at Risk in Oasis Springs

The Agency for Natural Habitats recently discovered a rare species of salamander living in Oasis Springs, a popular spring-fed pool. We have found that the process used for cleaning the pool is endangering these creatures. To keep the water safe for swimmers, the pool staff currently uses an algae treatment of bleach and brushing. This treatment kills the salamanders. Therefore, we propose three solutions to preserve the salamander population and to keep the pool thriving.

First, we will remove salamanders from the pool for a special breeding program. Ten salamanders will be taken each month to reproduce. They will then be reintroduced into the pool. This program has been proven successful for other endangered species.

Our most important solution involves a new cleaning process. The pool will be cleaned without brushes or bleach. Divers will wipe the rocky bottom with special cloths. No soap products will be used.

Finally, specialists will visit the pool each week to inspect the water quality. An expert committee will then review the results.

These crucial steps will allow both salamanders and people to enjoy Oasis Springs for many years to come.

1. What is the **main purpose** of the passage?
   A. to persuade the public to help to save the salamanders
   B. to explain how to clean the spring-fed pool without harming people
   C. to inform the public about the proposed steps to save the salamander population
   D. to explore the life of the salamander population

2. Which is a **proposed solution?**
   A. Ban swimming in the pool.
   B. Clean the pool without using bleach.
   C. Close the pool to the public.
   D. Bring divers to clean the salamanders.

3. Which of the following sentences *best* shows the **author's purpose?**
   A. Therefore, we propose three solutions to preserve the salamander population and to keep the pool thriving.
   B. The pool will be cleaned without brushes or bleach.
   C. An expert committee will then review the results.
   D. Ten salamanders will be taken each month to reproduce.

III. Writing and Language Conventions

Directions: *Read the passage. Then, answer the questions that follow.*

(1) Have some fun this weekend. (2) Learn how to catch a Frisbee® behind your back! (3) Decide where to catch the disc. (4) Run to that spot. (5) Next, take a step back with the foot that is on the same side as your catching hand. (6) Wrap your catching arm behind your back. (7) Bend your elbow. (8) Face your palm up, and point your thumb up. (9) The last step is to pinch your thumb to your fingers when the disc hits your hand. (10) Now, enjoy all of your friends' applause!

1. Which of these titles *best* supports the **topic** of the passage?

A. How to Catch a Disc at the Park

B. How to Teach Your Dog to Catch a Disc

C. How to Impress Your Friends

D. How to Catch a Disc Behind Your Back

2. Which of the following sentences placed after sentence 2 would *best* clarify the **multi-step directions?**

A. First, watch the disc when it is thrown.

B. Second, throw the disc to your partner.

C. Stand ten feet away from your partner.

D. First, scan the area for obstacles.

3. How should sentence 1 be revised to include a more informative **prepositional phrase?**

A. Have some fun and excitement this weekend.

B. Have some fun at the park this weekend.

C. Have some fun this weekend at school.

D. Have some fun this weekend and learn something new.

4. Which of the following revisions *best* combines sentence 3 and sentence 4 by using a **coordinating conjunction?**

A. Decide where you will catch the disk before you run to that spot.

B. Decide where you will catch the disk, and run to that spot.

C. Decide where you will catch the disk while you run to that spot.

D. Decide where you will catch the disk. In the meantime, run to that spot.

5. Which **transition** could the writer place in sentence 8 to clarify the instruction?

A. first

B. last

C. after

D. then

Performance Tasks

Directions: *Follow the instructions to complete the tasks below as required by your teacher.*

As you work on each task, incorporate both general academic vocabulary and literary terms you learned in this unit.

Common Core State Standards

RI.7.2, RI.7.3, RI.7.4, RI.7.5, RI.7.6, RI.7.8; W.7.9.b; SL.7.3, SL.7.4; L.7.3.a

[For the full wording of the standards, see the standards chart in the front of your textbook.]

Writing

Task 1: Informational Text [RI.7.5; W.7.9.b]
Analyze Text Structure

Write an essay in which you analyze the structure an author uses to organize a work of literary nonfiction in this unit.

- Identify and describe the structure the author uses to organize the text you chose.

- Explain how the major sections contribute to the whole and to the development of the author's ideas.

- Cite evidence from the text to support your analysis, and present your ideas in an organized manner.

- Ensure that each sentence in your essay has a subject and predicate. Use conjunctions to combine choppy sentences that have related ideas.

Task 2: Informational Text [RI.7.5, W.7.9.b]
Analyze Structure and Purpose

Write an essay in which you explain the characteristics of two different types of nonfiction essays in this unit.

- Choose examples of two different types of essays—for example, a persuasive essay and a reflective essay.

- State which essays you chose and briefly explain their topics and purposes.

- Describe how information is organized or presented in each essay.

- Analyze the author's purpose for writing each essay, and evaluate the connection between that purpose and the essay's organization.

- Support the central idea in each paragraph with examples and details from the essays.

- Revise to eliminate unnecessary words. Confirm the spellings and meanings of words by consulting a dictionary.

Task 3: Informational Text [RI.7.6; W.7.9.b; L.7.3.a]
Determine an Author's Point of View

Write an essay in which you identify and analyze the author's point of view in a selection from this unit.

- Choose a selection in which the author presents a clear point of view on a topic. Explain which essay you chose, state the topic, and briefly describe the author's perspective.

- Analyze how the author presents his or her perspective by emphasizing certain evidence or by presenting an interpretation of facts.

- Conclude by telling whether or not you think the author conveys his or her perspective effectively. Support your opinion with examples from the text.

- Use appropriate transitions to create cohesion and to clarify the relationships among ideas.

- Vary your sentences, using coordinating or subordinating conjunctions accurately to combine sentences.

Speaking and Listening

ⓒ Task 4: Informational Text [RI.7.8; SL.7.3]
Evaluate Arguments
Give an oral presentation in which you evaluate the author's argument in a nonfiction text in this unit. Share your presentation with a small group of classmates, then evaluate their assessments of the same text.

- Work as a group to choose the selection you will evaluate.
- As the basis for your presentation, write an essay in which you trace and evaluate the author's argument and specific claims in the text you chose. Include your assessment of the author's reasoning and evidence.
- Take turns presenting your evaluations to the group.
- Evaluate your classmates' arguments by considering their use of clear reasoning and relevant and sufficient evidence.
- Use precise language to express your ideas.

ⓒ Task 5: Informational Text [RI.7.4; SL.7.4]
Analyze the Impact of Word Choice
Give an oral presentation analyzing how word choice and diction impact meaning and tone in a work in this unit.

- Select a text, then choose a specific passage to use as the focus of your analysis. State which work you chose and why you chose it.
- Explain the tone of the selection—formal or informal, serious or funny, and so on.
- Show how the author's word choice affects your response to the text. Consider specific words, sentence length and style, and the feeling the work conveys. Include supporting examples.
- Consider how the author could have achieved a completely different effect by using different words or by putting sentences together in a different way.
- During your presentation, establish eye contact, speak with adequate volume, and pronounce your words clearly.

ⓒ Task 6: Informational Text
[RI.7.2, RI.7.3; SL.7.4]
Deliver a Response to Literature
Give an oral presentation of your response to one of the essays from this unit.

- Choose an essay that provoked a strong response in you—either positive or negative. State which work you chose.
- Explain the central idea or ideas that the author communicates in the essay. Then, describe your response by answering the following questions: *Do I agree with the author? Has the author provided solid support for his or her ideas? Has the author helped me look at something in a different way?*
- In your presentation, include descriptions, facts, and other details from the essay that support your ideas.

THE BIG ❓ What should we learn?
At the beginning of Unit 3, you wrote a response to the Big Question. Now that you have completed the unit, write a new response. Discuss how your initial ideas have been either changed or reinforced. Cite specific examples from the literature in this unit, from other subject areas, and from your own life to support your ideas. Use Big Question vocabulary words (see p. 407) in your response.

Featured Titles

In this unit, you have read a variety of informational texts, including literary nonfiction. Continue to read on your own. Select books that you enjoy, but challenge yourself to explore new topics, new authors, and works of increasing depth and complexity. The titles suggested below will help you get started.

Informational Texts

Barrio Boy

by Ernesto Galarza

As a young boy in the early twentieth century, Galarza moved from a tiny Mexican village to a bustling Latino neighborhood in Sacramento. Follow him on his journey in this **memoir** of his early life.

Astronomy & Space

Edited by Phillis Engelbert   **EXEMPLAR TEXT** ©

Explore outer space in this three-volume **encyclopedia,** which includes a timeline, photographs, biographies, and a glossary of important words to know.

Discoveries: Finding Our Place in the World

This collection of **essays** explores four subject areas. In it, you will find "Stonehenge: Groundbreaking Discoveries," "Where on Earth Are You?" "From Bricks to Mortar to Cyberspace: Art Museums Online," and "Testing the Market."

Nonfiction Readings Across the Curriculum

This collection of **essays** and **stories** features writers such as Beverly Cleary, Gary Paulsen, Joe Namath, and more. Delve into its pages to find interesting observations about sports, literature, science, and social studies.

Vincent van Gogh: Portrait of an Artist

by Jan Greenberg and Sandra Jordan

Yearling, 2003   **EXEMPLAR TEXT** ©

The painter Vincent van Gogh surprised the art world of the late nineteenth century with his broad brushstrokes, vivid colors, and dreamlike landscapes. Meet Van Gogh as a shy boy, an awkward young man, and an ambitious artist in this exciting **biography.**

Green Lantern's Book of Inventions

by Clare Hibbert

With a comic book superhero as your guide, learn about great inventions through the ages—from the wheel to the Internet—in this **nonfiction** book.

Literature

Child of the Owl

by Laurence Yep

When her father is hospitalized, twelve-year-old Casey is sent to live with her grandmother in the strange and unfamiliar world of Chinatown. This **novel** follows Casey as she learns to accept her new situation, drawing strength from family history and Chinese legend.

Slow Dance Heart Break Blues

by Arnold Adoff

In this collection of **poetry,** Adoff uses a hip-hop style and modern imagery to explore issues important to teenagers, such as love, loss, and identity.

Preparing to Read Complex Texts

Attentive Reading As you read on your own, ask yourself questions about the text. The questions below, along with others that you ask as you read, will enrich your reading experience.

 **Common Core State Standards**

Reading Literature/Informational Text 10. By the end of the year, read and comprehend literature, including stories, dramas, and poems, and literary nonfiction in the grades 6–8 text complexity band proficiently, with scaffolding as needed at the high end of the range.

When reading literary nonfiction, ask yourself...

- Who is the author? Why did he or she write the work?
- Is the author writing about a personal experience or a topic he or she has studied? In either case, what are my expectations about the work?
- Are the ideas the author expresses important? Why or why not?
- Did the author live at a different time and place than the present? If so, how does that affect his or her choice of topic and attitude?
- Does the author express beliefs that are very different from mine? If so, how does that affect what I understand and feel about the text?
- Does any one idea seem more important than the others? Why?
- What can I learn from this work?

Ⓒ Key Ideas and Details

- Does the author order ideas so that I can understand them? If not, what is unclear?
- Is the work interesting right from the start? If so, what has the author done to capture my interest? If not, why?
- Does the author give me a new way of looking at a topic? If so, how? If not, why?
- Is the author an expert on the topic? How do I know?
- Does the author use a variety of evidence that makes sense? If not, what is weak?
- Does the author use words in ways that are both interesting and clear? If so, are there any sections that I enjoy more than others? If not, why?

Ⓒ Craft and Structure

- Does the work seem believable? Why or why not?
- Do I agree or disagree with the author's arguments or ideas? Why or why not?
- Does this work remind me of others I have read? If so, in what ways?
- Does this work make me want to read more about this topic? Does it make me want to explore a related topic? Why or why not?

Ⓒ Integration of Ideas

THE BIG ? What is the best way to communicate?

Unit 4

Poetry

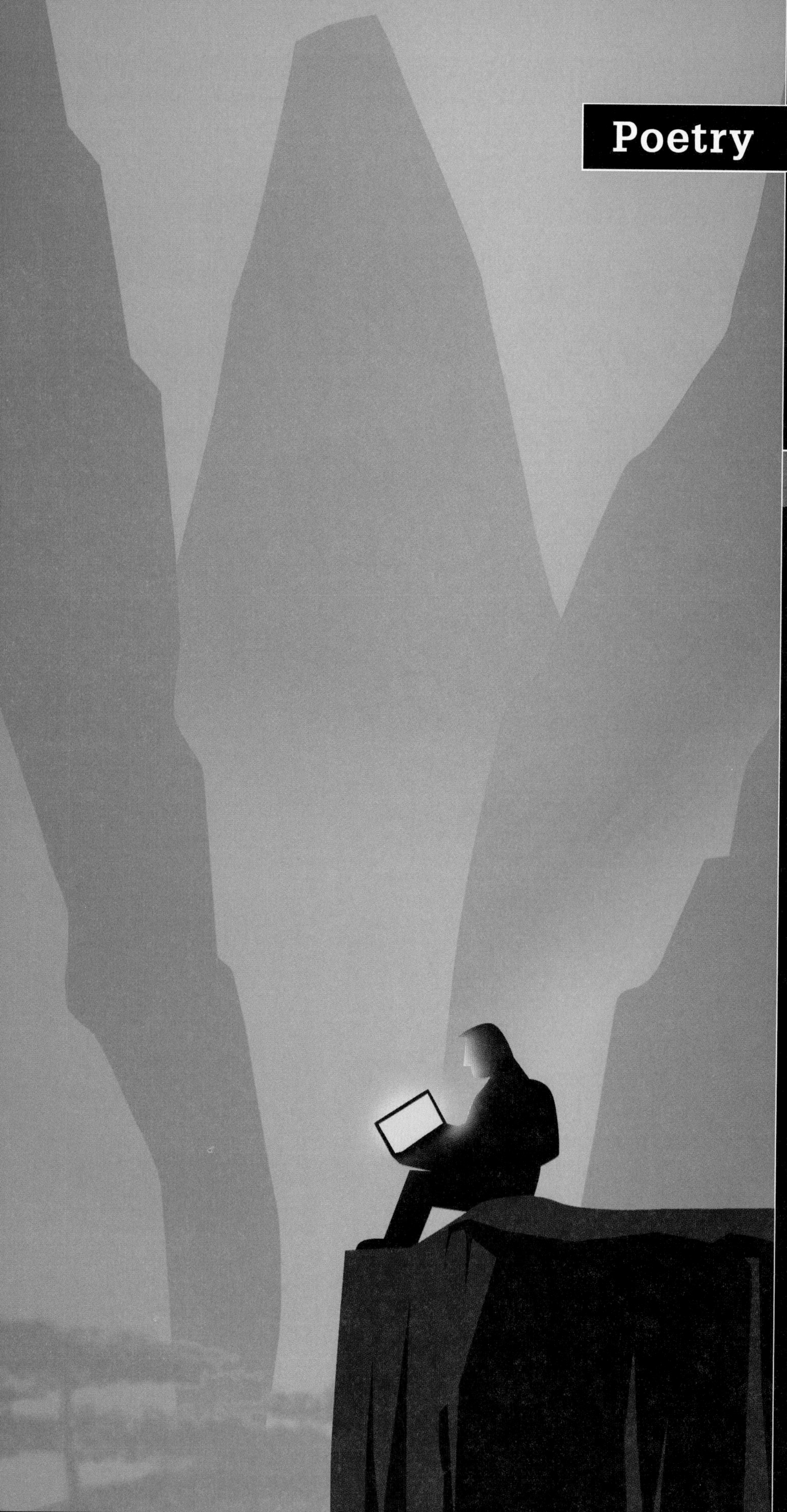

PHLit Online!

www.PHLitOnline.com

Hear It!

- Selection summary audio
- Selection audio
- BQ Tunes

See It!

- Author videos
- Big Question video
- Get Connected videos
- Background videos
- More about the authors
- Illustrated vocabulary words
- Vocabulary flashcards

Do It!

- Interactive journals
- Interactive graphic organizers
- Grammar tutorials
- Interactive vocabulary games
- Test practice

 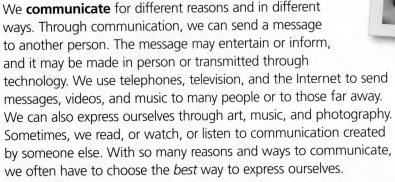

What is the best way to communicate?

We **communicate** for different reasons and in different ways. Through communication, we can send a message to another person. The message may entertain or inform, and it may be made in person or transmitted through technology. We use telephones, television, and the Internet to send messages, videos, and music to many people or to those far away. We can also express ourselves through art, music, and photography. Sometimes, we read, or watch, or listen to communication created by someone else. With so many reasons and ways to communicate, we often have to choose the *best* way to express ourselves.

Exploring the Big Question

© **Collaboration: One-on-One Discussion** Start thinking about the Big Question by making a list of ways that people communicate. Describe one specific example of each of these types of communication:

- telling stories
- transmitting messages through technology
- talking to friends or family members
- filming an event
- speaking in public
- creating music or art

  Share your examples with a partner. With your partner, discuss which items on your lists are the best ways to communicate and why. Build on your partner's ideas, responding to each with related ideas of your own. Ask questions to make sure you have understood each other's points, and clarify your meaning as needed. Use the Big Question vocabulary in your discussion.

Connecting to the Literature Each reading in this unit will give you additional insight into the Big Question.

PHLit Online!
www.PHLitOnline.com

- Big Question video
- Illustrated vocabulary words
- Interactive vocabulary games
- BQ Tunes

Learning Big Question Vocabulary

Acquire and Use Academic Vocabulary Academic vocabulary is the language you encounter in textbooks and on standardized tests. Review the definitions of these academic vocabulary words.

communicate (ke myōō′ ni kāt′) *v.* share thoughts or feelings

contribute (kən′ trib′ yōōt) *v.* add to; enrich

inform (in fôrm′) *v.* tell; give information about

media (mē′ dē ə) *n.* sources of information, such as newspapers, television, and the Internet

produce (prə dōōs′) *v.* make; create

react (rē akt′) *v.* respond to

speak (spēk′) *v.* use oral language

technology (tek näl′ ə jē) *n.* machines, equipment, and ways of doing things that are based on modern knowledge about science

transmit (trans mit′) *v.* send or give out

Use these words as you complete Big Question activities in this unit that involve reading, writing, speaking, and listening.

Gather Vocabulary Knowledge Additional Big Question words are listed below. Categorize the words by deciding whether you know each one well, know it a little bit, or do not know it at all.

enrich	express	listen
entertain	learn	teach

Then, do the following:

1. Work with a partner to write each word on one side of an index card and its definition on the other side.

2. Verify the definitions by looking them up in a print or online dictionary and revising your cards as needed.

3. Place the cards with the words facing up in a pile.

4. Take turns drawing a word card, pronouncing the word and then using it in an original sentence.

Speaking and Listening
1. Engage effectively in a range of collaborative discussions with diverse partners on grade 7 topics, texts, and issues, building on others' ideas and expressing their own clearly.

Language
6. Acquire and use accurately grade-appropriate general academic and domain-specific words and phrases; gather vocabulary knowledge when considering a word or phrase important to comprehension or expression.

Elements of Poetry

Poetry uses the rhythms and sounds of words as well as their meanings to set the imagination in motion.

Poetry is a type of literature that uses the sounds, rhythms, and meanings of words to describe the world in striking and imaginative ways. Poetry comes in many forms, from structured traditional verse to contemporary poems that follow few rules. However varied their forms may be, many poems are made up of the same elements.

Lines and Stanzas Poetry is divided into **lines,** or groups of words. In some poems, the first word of each line is capitalized, even if it is not the beginning of a sentence. A sentence in a poem may stretch over several lines. The first one or two lines may *break,* or end, before the sentence is finished. However, good readers of poetry know that they should read the sentence as a whole, without pausing at the end of every line.

In many poems, lines are organized in units of meaning called **stanzas.** The lines in a stanza work together to express one key idea. A blank line, called a **stanza break,** signals that one stanza has ended and a new stanza is beginning.

As you read the poem below, think about the key idea in each stanza, and identify the relationship between ideas.

Refrains and Repetition Like a catchy song, a poem may repeat lines, either identically or with variations. A line or group of lines that is repeated at regular intervals in a poem is called a **refrain.** In a refrain, a poet reminds readers and listeners of a key idea, image, or event. Often, a refrain is repeated at the end of each stanza. A poet may also repeat lines with **variations**—changing one or more words with each repetition.

As you read the poem at the bottom of the page, notice how the poet uses repetition, including a refrain, to emphasize his key ideas.

"Life"
by Paul Laurence Dunbar

A crust of bread and a corner to sleep in,
A minute to smile and an hour to weep in,
A pint of joy to a peck of trouble,
And never a laugh but the moans come double;
    And that is life!

> This five-line **stanza** compares life's joys to its sorrows. Together, the lines **focus on one key idea:** Life has more sorrow than joy.

A crust and a corner that love makes precious,
With a smile to warm and the tears to refresh us;
And joy seems sweeter when cares come after,
And a moan is the finest of foils for laughter;
    And that is life!

> The **focus changes,** and a **new stanza** starts. Here, the speaker describes life's joys. The **key idea** is that sorrow intensifies joy.

Sound Devices

Rhythm and Meter Most poems have **rhythm,** or a beat, created by the stressed and unstressed syllables in words. To sustain a pattern of rhythm, or **meter,** a poet may arrange words and break lines at certain points.

Meter is measured in **feet,** or units of stressed and unstressed syllables. As you read the following lines, look for the pattern in the arrangement of stressed syllables (′) and unstressed syllables (˘). Feet are divided by slashes (/).

> Whĕn Í/sĕe bírch/ĕš bénd/
> tŏ left/ănd ríght
> Ăcróss/thĕ línes/ŏf stráight/ĕr
> dárk/ĕr treés,
> Ĭ liké/tŏ thínk/sŏme bóy's/
> bĕen swíng/ĭng thém.
> (from "Birches," Robert Frost)

In this example, each foot consists of one unstressed syllable followed by one stressed syllable. This down-up, down-up rhythmic pattern fits the subject of an imagined boy swinging on the branches of trees.

Poets may break a metrical pattern for effect. For example, Frost shifts the accent to the first syllable in this line from "Birches": "Kicking his way down through the air to the ground." The shift emphasizes the boy's movement.

Rhyme Some poems also contain **rhyme,** or the repetition of vowel and consonant sounds at the ends of words, as in _tin_ and _pin_. In many poems, the rhymes follow a particular pattern, or **rhyme scheme.** In the following example, the first line rhymes with the third line, and the second line rhymes with the fourth line. This rhyme scheme is indicated by using a different letter for each rhyme sound: _abab._

> **Rhyme Scheme**
>
> How doth the little crocodile   **a**
>   Improve his shining tail,   **b**
> And pour the waters of the Nile   **a**
>   On every golden scale!   **b**
>
> (from "How Doth the Little Crocodile," Lewis Carroll)

Additional Sound Devices

Poets may also use other sound devices to enhance mood and meaning in their poems.

- **Alliteration** is the repetition of consonant sounds in the beginnings of words, as in _slippery slope._
- **Repetition** is the use of any element of language—a sound, word, or phrase—more than once.
- **Onomatopoeia** is the use of words that imitate sounds. _Splat, hiss,_ and _gurgle_ are all examples of onomatopoeia.

In This Section

Elements of Poetry

Analyzing Poetic Language

Analyzing Poetic Form and Structure

Close Read:
- Model Text
- Practice Text

After You Read

 Common Core State Standards

RL.7.4, RL.7.5
[For the full wording of the standards, see the standards chart in the front of your textbook.]

Analyzing Poetic Language

Poetic language is specific, imaginative, and rich with emotion.

Common Core State Standards

Reading Literature
4. Determine the meaning of words and phrases as they are used in a text, including figurative and connotative meanings; analyze the impact of rhymes and other repetitions of sounds on a specific verse or stanza of a poem or section of a story or drama.

Poetic language begins when a writer weaves together the images and associations called up by words and says something unique that could not be said in different words.

Shade of Meaning The **denotation** of a word is its literal, dictionary definition. The **connotation** consists of the ideas and feelings that the word brings to mind. The chart below lists several words that refer to dogs. Consider the differences in the words' connotations (printed in darker type).

Denotative and Connotative Meanings
canine ⟶ dog
pooch ⟶ **friendly, lovable** dog
mongrel ⟶ **mean, ugly** mixed-breed dog

The technical term *canine* has a neutral connotation, neither positive nor negative. By contrast, the word *pooch* conveys positive feelings, while *mongrel* conveys negative feelings.

Imagery To create vivid word pictures, poets use **imagery,** or descriptions that appeal to the five senses. Imagery helps poets convey what they see, hear, smell, taste, or touch.

The example below appeals to the senses of taste, hearing, and smell.

Example: Imagery
Taste the green in the lettuce,

Hear the crunch of its freshness,

Smell its earth perfume.

Figurative Language To help readers share their perceptions and insights, poets may also use **figurative language,** or language that is not meant to be taken literally. Many types of figurative language are comparisons that show how things are alike in surprising ways. Three common types of figurative language are similes, metaphors, and personification.

A **simile** uses the word *like* or *as* to compare two seemingly unlike things.
- *His hands were as cold as steel.*

A **metaphor** describes one thing as if it were something else.
- *My chores were a mountain waiting to be climbed.*

Personification gives human qualities to a nonhuman subject.
- *The fingertips of the rain tapped a steady beat on the windowpane.*

Analyzing Poetic Form and Structure

Common Core State Standards

Reading Literature 5. Analyze how a drama's or a poem's form or structure contributes to its meaning.

Every **form** of poetry has its own **structure**.

There are many different forms of poetry. A poet chooses the form that best suits his or her intended meaning.

Narrative poetry tells a story in verse. Narrative poems have elements similar to those in short stories, such as plot and characters.

Haiku is a three-line Japanese form that describes something in nature. The first and third lines each have five syllables, and the second line has seven.

Free Verse poetry is defined by its lack of structure. It has no regular meter, rhyme, fixed line length, or specific stanza pattern.

Lyric poetry expresses the thoughts and feelings of a single speaker, often in highly musical verse.

Ballads are songlike poems that tell stories. They often deal with adventure or romance.

Concrete poems are shaped to look like their subjects. The poet arranges the lines to create a picture on the page.

Limericks are humorous, rhyming five-line poems with a specific rhythm pattern and rhyme scheme.

Look at the lyric poem below to see how the structural elements of rhythm, rhyme, and imagery help reinforce the poet's meaning.

Analysis of Lines from "Tiare Tahiti," Rupert Brooke		
Taü here, Mamua!	a	• The poem's meter emphasizes the commands "crown" and "come."
Crown the hair, and come away!	b	
Hear the calling of the moon,	c	• The *c* rhyme sound ties lines 3–5 together, reflecting their focus on the night's beauty. This focus is developed with **imagery**.
And the whispering scents that stray	b	
5 About the idle warm lagoon.	c	
Hasten, hand in human hand,	d	• The new *d* rhyme sound in lines 6–8 introduces a new idea: The speaker urges Mamua to come to the lagoon. The **alliteration** of the *h*, *w*, and *d* sounds reinforces this idea.
Down the dark, the flowered way,	b	
Along the whiteness of the sand,	d	
And in the water's soft caress,	e	• Lines 9–10 rhyme, interrupting the pattern of alternating end rhymes. The interruption shows that these lines express a key idea: Nature can ease the mind.
10 Wash the mind of foolishness,	e	
Mamua, until the day.	b	

Close Read: Analyzing Structure and Meaning

From sound to structure, each element of a poem helps to shape its meaning.

To analyze a poem, follow your ear and your imagination as well as the meanings of words.

- **Read the poem aloud.** Listen for sounds that repeat or that create strong contrasts. Then, reread the poem, thinking about how the sound patterns link ideas and reinforce meaning.

- **Read in complete sentences.** Do not pause at the end of a line unless it ends with a period or other punctuation mark. Instead, read for meaning.
- **Analyze poetic elements.** Follow the tips in the chart below.

Tips for Analyzing Structure and Meaning

Word Choice
- Use context or a dictionary to understand word **denotations** (literal meanings) and **connotations** (associated ideas and feelings).
- Ask yourself what the connotations of key words show about the subject and the speaker (the voice that says the poem).

Imagery
- Identify images—descriptions that appeal to one or more of the five senses.
- Determine your emotional response to each.
- Analyze ways in which images are connected and consider what they show about the poem's subject.

Figurative Language
Identify **similes** (comparisons using *like* or *as*), **metaphors** (comparisons in which one thing is spoken of as if it were another), and **personifications** (comparisons giving human characteristics to a nonhuman subject).

Sound Devices
- Identify any instances of **alliteration** (the repetition of sounds at the beginning of words), **onomatopoeia** (words with sounds that imitate what they name), **repetition** (the reuse of the same word or closely related words), and **rhyme** (the repetition of sounds at the end of words).

Structure
Determine the poem's **form** and notice its patterns of elements such as **rhyme,** line breaks, and **stanzas.**
- If the poem divides into stanzas, determine the main idea in each.

Rhythm
- Identify the pattern of stressed and unstressed syllables in each line.
- Consider how meter reinforces ideas.
- Consider ways in which changes in the rhythm reinforce surprises or shifts in meaning.

Model

About the Selection Emily Dickinson (1830–1886) lived a quiet life in Amherst, Massachusetts, growing increasingly secluded in her later days. Yet the poetry she wrote was daringly original. She is known for her individualistic use of punctuation and capitalization.

Dickinson lived during the Industrial Revolution, a time marked by the rapid expansion of cities, a great increase in the number of factories, and improved methods of transportation, including the growth of the railroad. During her lifetime, the citizens of Amherst debated whether to construct a train line to the town. This poem offers Dickinson's perceptions of a train.

"The Railway Train" by Emily Dickinson

I like to see it lap the miles,
And lick the valleys up,
And stop to feed itself at tanks;
And then, prodigious, step

5 Around a pile of mountains,
And supercilious,[1] peer
In shanties by the sides of roads;
And then a quarry[2] pare

To fit its sides, and crawl between,
10 Complaining all the while
In horrid, hooting stanza;
Then chase itself down hill

And neigh like Boanerges;[3]
Then, punctual as a star,
15 Stop—docile and omnipotent[4]—
At its own stable door.

Sound Devices Alliteration emphasizes words that help to build an image of a speeding train.

Structure Each stanza builds on the comparison of a train to an animal.

Sound Devices The poet uses onomatopoeia to suggest the sound of a train's whistle.

Figurative Language The words *neigh* and *stable* reinforce the comparison of the train to an animal. The train arrives at the station like a horse returning to its stable after a run.

---

1. **supercilious** (sōō´ pər sil´ ē əs) *adj.* full of pride; haughty.
2. **quarry** (kwôr´ ē) *n.* a place where rock for building is mined; a pit or excavation dug in rock.
3. **Boanerges** (bō´ ə nʉr´ jēz´) *n.* a thunderously loud speaker (from the Bible).
4. **docile** (däs´ əl) **and omnipotent** (äm nip´ ə tənt) easy to train or manage and all-powerful.

Independent Practice

About the Text Born in El Paso, Texas, in 1942, Pat Mora enjoys writing about the Mexican American heritage of the Southwest. Bilingual and bicultural, she writes poetry in English and Spanish and often includes Spanish words and phrases in her English-language poems. "Maestro" was inspired by Mora's conversation with a music professor who conducts a local orchestra. In the conversation, he shared the childhood experiences that nourished his interest in music.

Sound Devices What idea is emphasized by the repetition of the words "bows" and "again"?

Structure What shift in topic is marked by the stanza break between lines 6 and 7? Explain.

Word Choice What connotations does the word *snare* have? What do these connotations add to the image of the speaker playing music with his parents?

Imagery What does this final image convey about the speaker's memory of singing and playing music?

"Maestro" by Pat Mora

He hears her
when he bows.
Rows of hands clap
again and again he bows
5 to stage lights and upturned faces
but he hears only his mother's voice

years ago in their small home
singing Mexican songs
one phrase at a time
10 while his father strummed the guitar
or picked the melody with quick fingertips.
Both cast their music in the air
for him to snare with his strings,
songs of lunas[1] and amor[2]
15 learned bit by bit.
She'd nod, smile, as his bow slid
note to note, then the trio
   voz,[3] guitarra,[4] violín[5]
would blend again and again
20 to the last pure note
sweet on the tongue.

1. **lunas** (lo͞o′ näs) *n.* Spanish for "moons."
2. **amor** (ä′ môr′) *n.* Spanish for "love."
3. **voz** (vōs) *n.* Spanish for "voice."
4. **guitarra** (gē tär′ rä) *n.* Spanish for "guitar."
5. **violín** (vē ō lēn′) *n.* Spanish for "violin."

About the Text In describing this poem, Pat Mora has said, "People who don't know the desert may find it bare and frightening. I wanted to show how the desert comforts me."

"The Desert Is My Mother" by Pat Mora

I say feed me.
She serves red prickly pear[1] on a spiked cactus.

I say tease me.
She sprinkles raindrops in my face on a sunny day.

5 I say frighten me.
She shouts thunder, flashes lightning.

I say hold me.
She whispers, "Lie in my arms."

I say heal me.
10 She gives me chamomile, oregano, peppermint.

I say caress me.
She strokes my skin with her warm breath.

I say make me beautiful.
She offers turquoise for my fingers,
15 a pink blossom for my hair.

I say sing to me.
She chants her windy songs.

I say teach me.
She blooms in the sun's glare,
20 the snow's silence,
the driest sand.

The desert is my mother.
El desierto es mi madre.
The desert is my strong mother.

Imagery To what senses does this description appeal?

Structure How does the speaker use repetition and line breaks to structure the poem? What does this structure suggest about the speaker and the desert?

Figurative Language What type of figurative language does the speaker use? In what way does this figure of speech sum up the exchanges between the speaker and the desert in the preceding lines?

---

1. prickly pear *n.* a species of cactus with sharp spines and an edible fruit.

Practice continued   **About the Text** In this poem, Pat Mora describes her aunt. Note how Mora inserts Spanish words into the poem. Think about why she might have chosen to do that.

Structure How does the repetition of words ending in -ing help structure the poem?

Imagery Which words help to create a vivid image of the young girl dancing?

Word Choice What are the connotations of the word *tottering*? What contrast does it establish between the aunt's movements when she was young and her movements now?

"Bailando"[1] by Pat Mora

I will remember you dancing,
spinning round and round
a young girl in Mexico,
your long, black hair free in the wind,
5   spinning round and round
a young woman at village dances
your long, blue dress swaying
to the beat of La Varsoviana,[2]
smiling into the eyes of your partners,
10 years later smiling into my eyes
when I'd reach up to dance with you,
my dear aunt, who years later
danced with my children,
you, white-haired but still young
15 waltzing on your ninetieth birthday,
more beautiful than the orchid
pinned on your shoulder,
tottering now when you walk
but saying to me, "Estoy[3] bailando,"
20 and laughing.

---

1. Bailando (bī län´ dō) *v.* Spanish for "dancing."
2. La Varsoviana (lä bär´ sō byä´ nä) *n.* a lively folk dance.
3. Estoy (es tȯi´) *adj.* Spanish for "I am."

1. Key Ideas and Details (a) Explain what scene is described in lines 1–5 of "Maestro," citing details in support. **(b) Infer:** What does the speaker mean in saying "he hears only his mother's voice" (line 6)? **(c) Infer:** Which is more influential for him—his present audience or his childhood with his family? Explain.

2. Key Ideas and Details Analyze: What effect do the Spanish words contribute to the image of the speaker's childhood in the poem "Maestro"?

3. Craft and Structure (a) Cite: Find one image that appeals to the sense of touch, one that appeals to sight, and one that appeals to hearing in "The Desert Is My Mother." **(b) Analyze:** Do these images help paint an effective picture of the desert? Explain.

4. Key Ideas and Details (a) Infer: In the poem "Bailando," who describes the dancing? **(b) Analyze:** Describe three different times when the aunt dances. How are they connected? How are they different? **(c) Interpret:** What key point does the speaker make using these images of dancing?

5. Craft and Structure Interpret: How does the one-sentence, single-stanza structure of "Bailando" reinforce the ideas in the poem? Support your answer with details from the poem.

6. Craft and Structure (a) Find one example of the use of repetition in each of the three poems. **(b) Analyze:** Choose one of your examples and explain how the repetition conveys an idea or feeling or how it helps to structure the poem.

7. Craft and Structure (a) Analyze: Complete a Venn diagram to analyze **personification** in "The Desert Is My Mother." In one circle, list words that show the desert is like a woman. In the other, list words that describe it as a landscape.

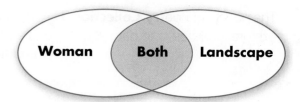

(b) Collaborate: Discuss your Venn diagram with a partner, and use your partner's feedback to guide you in revising your diagram.

8. Integration of Knowledge and Ideas (a) Interpret: Choose one of the poems and identify a lesson it suggests about life. **(b) Evaluate:** Explain how well this lesson applies to life generally, giving examples to support your evaluation.

Leveled Texts

Build your skills and improve your comprehension of poetry with texts of increasing complexity.

The poems in **Poetry Collection 1** explore loneliness and nature.

The poems in **Poetry Collection 2** present ideas about animals, plants, and flowers.

Common Core State Standards

Meet these standards with either **Poetry Collection 1** (p. 586) or **Poetry Collection 2** (p. 594).

Reading Literature

5. Analyze how a drama's or poem's form or structure contributes to its meaning. *(Literary Analysis: Forms of Poetry)*

7. Compare and contrast a written story, drama, or poem to its audio, filmed, staged, or multimedia version, analyzing the effects of techniques unique to each medium. *(Speaking and Listening: Presentation)*

Writing

4. Produce clear and coherent writing in which the development, organization, and style are appropriate to task, purpose, and audience. *(Writing: Lyric Poem, Concrete Poem, or Haiku)*

6. Use technology, including the Internet, to produce and publish writing. *(Writing: Lyric Poem, Concrete Poem, or Haiku)*

Speaking and Listening

1.d. Acknowledge new information expressed by others and, when warranted, modify their own views. *(Speaking and Listening: Presentation)*

Language

1.a. Explain the function of phrases and clauses in general and their function in specific sentences. *(Conventions: Infinitives and Infinitive Phrases)*

6. Acquire and use accurately grade-appropriate general academic and domain-specific words and phrases; gather vocabulary knowledge when considering a word or phrase important to comprehension or expression. *(Vocabulary: Word Study)*

Reading Skill: Drawing Conclusions

The techniques an author uses in poetry may require readers to think critically to determine meaning. **Drawing conclusions** means arriving at an overall meaning or understanding by pulling together several details. Drawing conclusions helps you recognize ideas that are not directly stated.

Asking questions like the ones that follow can help you identify details and make connections that lead to a conclusion.

- What details does the writer include and emphasize?
- How are the details related? Is there a pattern?
- What do the details mean all together?

Using the Strategy: Conclusions Map

Use a **conclusions map** like the one below to record details from the poems and draw conclusions from the details.

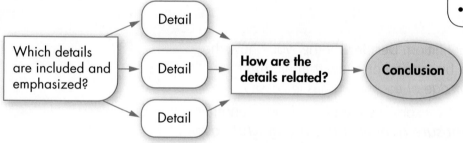

Literary Analysis: Forms of Poetry

There are many different **forms of poetry.** Each form has specific rules that guide the structure of a poem and contribute to its meaning.

- A **lyric poem** expresses the poet's thoughts and feelings about a single image or idea in vivid, musical language.
- In a **concrete poem,** the poet arranges the letters and lines to create a visual image that suggests the poem's subject.
- **Haiku** is a traditional form of Japanese poetry that is often about nature. The first line always has five syllables, the second line has seven syllables, and the third line has five syllables.

What is the best
way to *communicate?*

Writing About the Big Question

In Poetry Collection 1, three poets use patterns of sounds and words to share their thoughts or observations. Use these sentence starters to develop your ideas about the Big Question.

Writers might use poetry as a way to **communicate** because it allows them to _____.

Through poetry, writers can **express** _____.

While You Read Look for ways that each writer arranges words to create a picture or feeling. Later, you can evaluate or judge each author's success in communicating meaning.

Vocabulary

Read each word and its definition. Decide whether you know the word well, know it a little bit, or do not know it at all. After you read, see how your knowledge of each word has increased.

- **translates** (trans´ lāts) *v.* expresses the same thing in another form (p. 586) *I am not sure how well the thoughtful novel translates to the big screen.* translated *v.* translator *n.*

- **luminous** (lōō´ mə nəs) *adj.* giving off light (p. 586) *The luminous moon stood out in the dark sky.* luminosity *n.*

- **minnow** (min´ ō) *n.* small fish (p. 589) *His tank was home to one minnow and three catfish.* minnows *n.*

- **swerve** (swɜrv) *n.* curving motion (p. 589) *With a swerve, the skater avoided hitting me.* swerve *v.* swerving *v.*

- **utter** (ut´ ər) *v.* speak (p. 589) *The shy boy refused to utter a word.* utterance *n.*

- **weasel** (wē´ zəl) *n.* small mammal that eats rats, mice, birds, and eggs (p. 590) *The weasel chased the rabbit but failed to catch it.* weaselly *adj.*

Word Study

The **Latin root -lum-** means "light."

In "The Rider," the speaker sees flowers with **luminous,** or brightly lit, petals.

Naomi Shihab Nye

(b. 1952)

Author of "The Rider" (p. 586)

As a teenager, Naomi Shihab Nye probably felt the loneliness she describes in this poem. When Nye was fourteen, her family moved from Missouri to the Middle East. Though she now values learning about her Arab heritage, the move was not easy. Nye has published volumes of poetry as well as books for children.

William Jay Smith

(b. 1918)

Author of "Seal" (p. 588)

William Jay Smith was born in Winnfield, Louisiana. He has taught college students, written poetry and essays, translated Russian and French poetry, and even served in the Vermont State Legislature for two years. Like "Seal," many of Smith's poems show that poetry can be pure and simple—and fun.

Buson

(1716–1784)

Author of "Haiku" (p. 590)

Japanese poet Buson was not only a skilled writer of haiku, but also a talented painter. His love of color and interest in the visual world are reflected in much of his poetry. At age thirty-six, Buson became the "master" at the haiku school in Kyoto, Japan. When a student asked him to reveal the secret of haiku, Buson responded, "Use the commonplace to escape the commonplace."

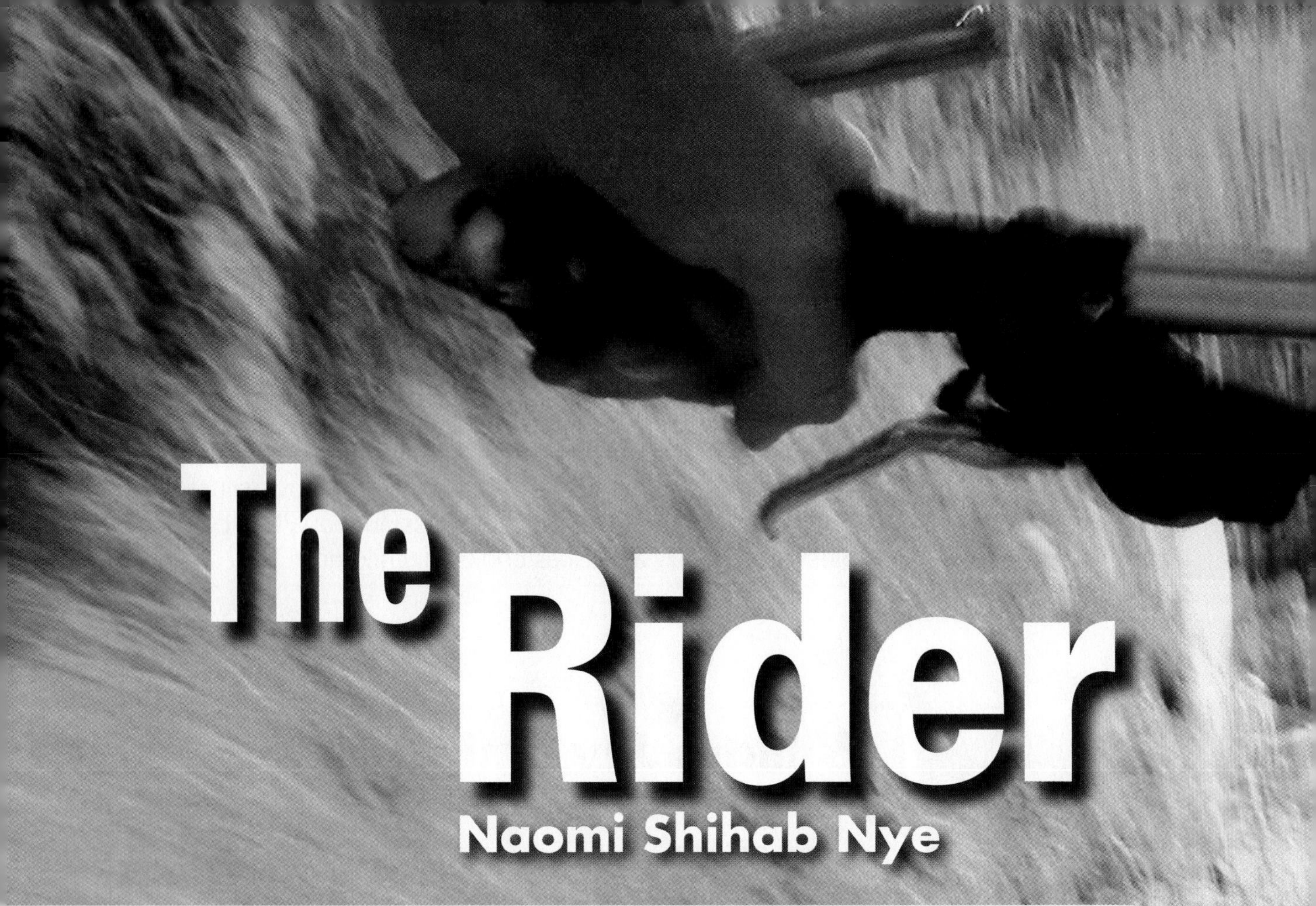

The Rider

Naomi Shihab Nye

A boy told me
if he rollerskated fast enough
his loneliness couldn't catch up to him,

the best reason I ever heard
5   for trying to be a champion.

What I wonder tonight
pedaling hard down King William Street
is if it translates to bicycles.

A victory! To leave your loneliness
10   panting behind you on some street corner
while you float free into a cloud of sudden azaleas,
luminous pink petals that have
    never felt loneliness,
no matter how slowly they fell.

Vocabulary
translates (trans´ lāts)
v. expresses the same
thing in another form
luminous (lōo´ mə nəs)
adj. giving off light

Forms of Poetry
Whose feelings does
the poem express—"a
boy's" or the speaker's?
Explain.

◄ **Critical Viewing** What details of this photograph convey the feelings the poem describes? **[Analyze]**

Seal

WILLIAM JAY SMITH

See how he dives
  From the rocks with a zoom!
    See how he darts
      Through his watery room
5   Past crabs and eels
      And green seaweed,
      Past fluffs of sandy
      Minnow feed!¹
      See how he swims
10   With a swerve and a twist,
      A flip of the flipper,
      A flick of the wrist!
      Quicksilver-quick,
      Softer than spray,
15   Down he plunges
    And sweeps away;
  Before you can think,
Before you can utter
Words like "Dill pickle"
20 Or "Apple butter,"
Back up he swims
Past Sting Ray and Shark,
Out with a zoom,
A whoop, a bark;
25 Before you can say
    Whatever you wish,
      He plops at your side
        With a mouthful of fish!

---

1. **feed** (fēd) *n.* tiny particles that minnows feed on.

Forms of Poetry
Why might the poet have arranged the lines of the poem this way?

Vocabulary
minnow (min ō)
n. small fish
swerve (swɤrv) *n.*
curving motion

Vocabulary
utter (ut´ ər) *v.* speak

◄ **Critical Viewing**
What details in this photograph remind you of the poem? **[Analyze]**

Spiral Review

Words and Phrases
Why is the "windless" detail essential to the central idea of the second haiku?

Vocabulary

weasel (wē′ zəl) *n.* small mammal that eats rats, mice, birds, and eggs

Draw Conclusions

What is the speaker in the first haiku worried about?

HAIKU

BUSON

O foolish ducklings,
you know my old green pond is
watched by a weasel.

Deep in a windless
wood, not one leaf dares to move. . . .
Something is afraid.

After the moon sets,
slow through the forest, shadows
drift and disappear.

Critical Thinking

Cite textual evidence to support your responses.

1. **Key Ideas and Details (a)** What two sports are discussed in "The Rider"? **(b) Compare:** What do the two sports have in common?

2. **Craft and Structure (a)** Identify six words that describe the movement of the seal in "Seal." **(b) Infer:** How would you describe the mood or feeling that these words create?

3. **Key Ideas and Details (a)** In the first haiku, what does the speaker warn the ducklings about? **(b) Analyze:** How would you describe the speaker's attitude toward the ducks?

4. **Craft and Structure (a)** Which techniques or words help to convey ideas, pictures, or feelings most successfully? **(b)** How does form or structure help to communicate a poem's meaning? Explain. *[Connect to the Big Question: What is the best way to communicate?]*

Reading Skill: Draw Conclusions

1. For each poem, ask a question that helps you **draw the conclusion** given. **(a)** The speaker in "The Rider" values speed. **(b)** The seal in "Seal" zooms around quickly. **(c)** The speaker in the haiku values nature.

Literary Analysis: Forms of Poetry

2. Craft and Structure In a chart like this one, check off the characteristics exhibited by each **poetic form.**

Poem	Characteristics of Poem				
	Musical language	Single image or idea	Thoughts of one speaker	Lines shaped like subject	Three lines; 17 syllables
The Rider (lyric)					
Seal (concrete)					
Haiku (haiku)					

3. Craft and Structure How is the form of each poem suited to the ideas each one conveys?

Vocabulary

Acquisition and Use Rewrite each sentence using a vocabulary word from page 584.

1. The small brown mammal ate the eggs.

2. The shining moon was visible in the night sky.

3. The sled made a movement to turn at the bottom of the hill.

4. Frozen by stage fright, the actor could not speak a word.

5. Dan was able to speak the English word in Spanish.

6. John saw hundreds of tiny silver fish in the pond.

Word Study Use what you know about the **Latin root -lum-** to explain your answer to each question.

1. Is a *luminary* someone who is unknown?

2. When you switch on a light, does it *illuminate* the room?

Word Study

The **Latin root -lum-** means "light."

Apply It Explain how the root -lum- contributes to the meanings of these words. Consult a dictionary if necessary.

lumen
luminescence

What is the best way to *communicate?*

Writing About the Big Question

Each poem in Poetry Collection 2 describes an aspect of nature. Use these sentence starters to develop your ideas about the Big Question.

Writers might use poetry to **speak** to readers in a different way because _____.

The descriptive language that poets use can **enrich** their writing because it communicates _____.

While You Read Look for words and phrases in these poems that create pictures in your mind. Later, you can evaluate or judge each author's success in communicating meaning.

Vocabulary

Read each word and its definition. Decide whether you know the word well, know it a little bit, or do not know it at all. After you read, see how your knowledge of each word has increased.

- **burrow** (bur´ ō) *v.* dig a hole for shelter (p. 594) *In the winter, turtles burrow in the mud under ponds.* burrow *n.*

- **forsythia** (fôr sith´ ē ə) *n.* shrub with yellow flowers that blooms in early spring (p. 595) *The forsythia blossoms were a welcome sign of spring.*

- **telegram** (tel´ ə gram) *n.* message transmitted by telegraph (p. 595) *The messenger delivered the telegram that arrived from overseas.*

- **fragrant** (frā´ grənt) *adj.* sweet-smelling (p. 596) *The flowers were colorful, but not very fragrant.* fragrance *n.* fragrantly *adv.*

Word Study

The **Greek root -gram-** means "write," "draw," or "record."

In "Forsythia," a floral **telegram,** or coded message, announces the arrival of spring.

Nikki Giovanni

(b. 1943)

Author of "Winter" (p. 594)

Many of Nikki Giovanni's poems highlight the major events in her life. In "Winter," however, she writes about a universal subject: the changing of the seasons. In addition to being a poet, Giovanni is a college professor who teaches both English literature and African American studies.

Forsythia
MARY ELLEN SOLT

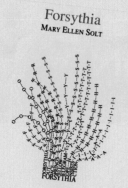

Mary Ellen Solt

(b. 1920)

Author of "Forsythia" (p. 595)

Mary Ellen Solt was born in Iowa. As a writer, she has devoted much of her energy to studying and creating concrete poetry. In the introduction to her book, *Concrete Poetry—A World View*, Solt writes, "[The reader] must now perceive the poem as an object and participate in the poet's act of creating it, for the concrete poem communicates first and foremost its structure."

Matsuo Bashō

(1644–1694)

Author of "Haiku" (p. 596)

Matsuo Bashō was born near Kyoto, Japan. He began studying poetry at an early age and became one of Japan's most famous poets. Along with writing poetry, Bashō taught poetry, served as a noble in the court, and lived in a monastery.

WINTER
Nikki Giovanni

Frogs burrow the mud
snails bury themselves
and I air my quilts
preparing for the cold

5 Dogs grow more hair
mothers make oatmeal
and little boys and girls
take Father John's Medicine[1]

Bears store fat
10 chipmunks gather nuts
and I collect books
For the coming winter

---
1. Father John's Medicine old-fashioned cough syrup.

Forsythia
MARY ELLEN SOLT

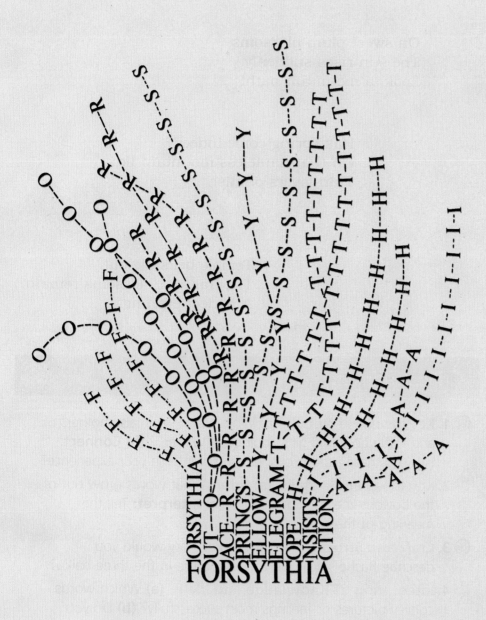

FORSYTHIA

Vocabulary
forsythia (fôr sith´ ē ə) *n.* shrub with yellow flowers that blooms in early spring

telegram (tel´ ə gram) *n.* message transmitted by telegraph

Forms of Poetry
Why might the poet have arranged the words and letters on the page in this way?

HAIKU
BASHŌ

On sweet plum blossoms
The sun rises suddenly.
Look, a mountain path!

Has spring come indeed?
On that nameless mountain lie
Thin layers of mist.

Temple bells die out.
The fragrant blossoms remain.
A perfect evening!

Forms of Poetry
How are these three poems similar?

Vocabulary
fragrant (frā´ grənt)
adj. sweet smelling

Critical Thinking

Cite textual evidence to support your responses.

1. **Key Ideas and Details** **(a)** What are the animals, mothers, and "little boys and girls" doing in "Winter"? **(b) Connect:** How do these actions connect with winter in your experience?

2. **Key Ideas and Details** **(a) Infer:** What words grow out of the bottom line of "Forsythia"? **(b) Interpret:** Tell the meaning of these lines.

3. **Craft and Structure** **(a) Analyze:** How would you describe Bashō's attitude toward nature in the three haiku?

4. **Integration of Knowledge and Ideas** **(a)** Which words convey pictures or feelings most successfully? **(b)** Do you think these poems are meaningful for people your age? Explain. *[Connect to the Big Question: What is the best way to communicate?]*

Reading Skill: Draw Conclusions

1. For each poem, ask a question that helps you **draw the conclusion** given. **(a)** The speaker in "Winter" accepts the changing seasons as part of the natural cycle of life. **(b)** Forsythia grows in a tangled, wild way. **(c)** The speaker in the three haiku values nature.

Literary Analysis: Forms of Poetry

© 2. Craft and Structure On a chart like the one shown, place a checkmark under each characteristic of the **poetic form** that applies.

Poem	Characteristics of Poem				
	Musical language	Single image or idea	Thoughts of one speaker	Lines shaped like subject	Three lines; 17 syllables
Winter (lyric)					
Forsythia (concrete)					
Haiku (haiku)					

© 3. Craft and Structure How is the form of each poem suited to the ideas each one conveys?

Vocabulary

© Acquisition and Use Rewrite each sentence so it includes a vocabulary word from page 592 and conveys that same basic meaning.

1. A woodchuck tried to dig a hole under our tool shed.

2. Tim sent a message to let us know when he would arrive.

3. A row of yellow flowering bushes lines my driveway.

4. The sweet-smelling lilac bushes are my favorite.

Word Study Use what you know about the **Greek root -gram-** to explain your answer to each question.

1. Is a *diagram* useful if you want to show a stadium layout?

2. If you want to personalize your towels, could you get them *monogrammed*?

Word Study

The **Greek root -gram-** means "write," "draw," or "record."

Apply It Explain how the word root *-gram-* contributes to the meanings of these words. Consult a dictionary if necessary.

grammar
gramophone
hologram

Integrated Language Skills

Poetry Collections 1 and 2

Conventions: Infinitives and Infinitive Phrases

An **infinitive** is a verb form that acts as a noun, an adjective, or an adverb. An infinitive usually begins with the word *to*.

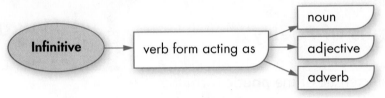

These example sentences show the infinitive in italics.

Examples: *To learn* is her goal. (noun)
She is the one *to see*. (adjective)
Everyone waited *to hear*. (adverb)

An **infinitive phrase** is an infinitive plus its own modifiers or complements. The examples show italicized infinitive phrases acting as different parts of speech.

Examples: <u>*To speak*</u> *Spanish fluently* is my goal. (noun)
She is the one <u>*to see*</u> *for advice*. (adjective)
Everyone waited <u>*to hear*</u> *the news*. (adverb)

Poetry Collection 1

Poetry Collection 2

Practice A Identify the infinitive and infinitive phrase in each sentence.

1. The rider wants to ride away from her loneliness.
2. To swim wild and free like a seal would be thrilling.
3. Weasels like to eat ducklings.
4. To keep perfectly still is difficult.

Ⓒ **Reading Application** In "Poetry Collection 1," find a line of poetry that contains an infinitive. In your own words, explain what an infinitive phrase does.

Practice B Identify the infinitive phrase in each sentence. Determine the function each phrase performs in the sentence. Then, use each infinitive to write a new sentence.

1. In winter, mothers make oatmeal to satisfy hunger.
2. Some people like to read by the fire.
3. I can hardly wait to see the flowers bloom in spring.
4. He wants us to look at the path.

Ⓒ **Writing Application** Choose a line in one of the poems in "Poetry Collection 2," and then rewrite it to include an infinitive.

PH WRITING COACH Further instruction and practice are available in *Prentice Hall Writing Coach*.

Writing

Common Core
State Standards

L.7.1.a, L.7.6; W.7.4, W.7.6;
SL.7.1.d
[For the full wording of the
standards, see page 582.]

Poetry Write a **lyric poem, concrete poem,** or **haiku** to share your thoughts in new, creative ways.

- Pick a subject that interests you. Write the subject in the center of a piece of paper, and create a cluster diagram around it.

- Brainstorm and list vivid descriptions, action words, thoughts, and feelings in a cluster diagram.

- Review the characteristics of each poetic form and decide which form is best suited to your topic. Then, use your notes to draft your poem in the form you have chosen. Add a creative title.

- Use one or more computer programs, such as a word-processing or drawing program, to write and format your poem. Use punctuation, line length, and arrangement to create a desired effect. Publish your poem by posting it on an approved Web site or in your classroom.

Grammar Application Check your writing to be sure you have correctly used all infinitives and infinitive phrases.

Writing Workshop: *Work in Progress*

Prewriting for Exposition For a problem-and-solution essay you may write, list three solutions that might solve a problem caused by cell phone use. Put this Solutions Lists in your writing portfolio.

Use this prewriting activity to prepare for the **Writing Workshop** on page 640.

Speaking and Listening

Presentation of Ideas In the library or online, find a recording of a poet reading his or her own lyric poetry. Listen to one or more of the poems with a small group of classmates. Then, in a brief **presentation** to your group, tell what you like or do not like about the audio version in comparison with the written poem. Follow these steps to complete the assignment.

- Analyze the effects of hearing the words in comparison with reading them. Support your opinion with specific reasons and examples from the recording.

- Listen carefully to each person's opinions and weigh them against your own.

- With your group, acknowledge new information expressed and discuss whether or not your opinion changed after listening to other responses.

PHLit
Online!
www.PHLitOnline.com
- Interactive graphic organizers
- Grammar tutorial
- Interactive journals

Leveled Texts

Build your skills and improve your comprehension of poetry with texts of increasing complexity.

The poems in **Poetry Collection 3** explore the power of life, nature, and courage.

The poems in **Poetry Collection 4** express admiration for both people and nature.

Common Core State Standards

Meet these standards with either **Poetry Collection 3** (p. 604) or **Poetry Collection 4** (p. 613).

Reading Literature
4. Determine the meaning of words and phrases as they are used in a text, including figurative and connotative meanings; analyze the impact of rhymes and other repetitions of sounds on a specific verse or stanza of a poem or section of a story or drama. *(Literary Analysis: Figurative Language)*

Writing
2. Write informative/explanatory texts to examine a topic and convey ideas, concepts, and information through the selection, organization, and analysis of relevant content.
2.d. Use precise language and domain-specific vocabulary to inform about or explain the topic. *(Writing: Metaphor)*
7. Conduct short research projects to answer a question, drawing on several sources. *(Research and Technology: Scientific Explanation)*

Speaking and Listening
5. Include multimedia components and visual displays in presentations to clarify claims and findings and emphasize salient points. *(Research and Technology: Scientific Explanation)*

Language
1.a. Explain the function of phrases and clauses in general and their function in specific sentences. *(Conventions: Appositives and Appositive Phrases)*
6. Acquire and use accurately grade-appropriate general academic and domain-specific words and phrases; gather vocabulary knowledge when considering a word or phrase important to comprehension or expression. *(Vocabulary: Word Study)*

Reading Skill: Draw Conclusions

In poetry, an author's techniques can add musicality and beauty to the work. To interpret meaning, **draw conclusions** after considering the details in a literary work. **Connecting the details** can help. For example, if the speaker in a poem describes beautiful flowers, bright sunshine, and happy children, you might conclude that he or she has a positive outlook. As you read, identify important details. Then, look at the details together to draw a conclusion about the poem's meaning.

Literary Analysis: Figurative Language

Figurative language is language that is not meant to be taken literally. Writers use figures of speech to express ideas in vivid and imaginative ways. Common figures of speech include the following:

- A **simile** compares two unlike things by using the words *like* or *as.*

- A **metaphor** compares two unlike things by saying that one thing *is* another.

- In **personification,** a nonhuman subject is given human characteristics.

- A **symbol** is an object, person, animal, place, or image that represents something other than itself.

Using the Strategy: Figurative Language Chart

As you read, refer to the chart below to identify figurative language.

Simile	Metaphor	Personification	Symbol
My love is like a red, red rose.	Life is a bowl of cherries.	The stars were dancing heel to toe.	dove = peace, harmony heart = love, romance

What is the best way to *communicate?*

Writing About the Big Question

The poets in Poetry Collection 3 make interesting comparisons among objects and ideas. Use this sentence starter to develop your ideas about the Big Question.

Sometimes, a comparison between seemingly unrelated things can **express** the idea that _____.

While You Read Look for comparisons that inspire you to see things in a new way.

Vocabulary

Read each word and its definition. Decide whether you know the word well, know it a little bit, or do not know it at all. After you read, see how your knowledge of each word has increased.

- **fascinated** (fas´ ə nāt´ əd) *adj.* very interested (p. 604) *The fascinated child could not take her eyes off the twinkling lights.* fascinate *v.* fascination *n.* fascinating *v.*

- **prickly** (prik´ lē) *adj.* sharply pointed; thorny (p. 606) *She cried as she fell into the prickly bush.* prickle *n.* prickled *v.* pricklier *adj.*

- **crouches** (krouch´ əz) *v.* stoops or bends low (p. 607) *Rachel crouches to pick a flower.* crouch *v.*

- **unravel** (un rav´ əl) *v.* become untangled or separated (p. 607) *The ball of yarn began to unravel.* unraveled *v.* unraveling *v.*

- **dislodge** (dis läj´) *v.* leave a position or place (p. 607) *The books dislodge and fall off the shelf.* dislodged *v.* dislodging *v.* lodger *n.*

- **granite** (gran´ it) *n.* hard, gray rock (p. 608) *Many of New Hampshire's mountains are made of granite.* granitic *adj.*

Word Study

The **Latin suffix -ly** means "like" or "in the manner of."

In "Loo-Wit," an old woman feels something **prickly**, like sharp points, on her neck.

Naomi Long Madgett

(b. 1923)

Author of "Life" (p. 604)

Naomi Long Madgett first discovered poetry at the age of seven or eight, while reading in her father's study. She was most inspired by the poets Alfred, Lord Tennyson and Langston Hughes, though their styles are quite different. Madgett once said, "I would rather be a good poet than anything else." Her ambition to create good poetry has led her to write more than seven collections of poems.

Wendy Rose

(b. 1948)

Author of "Loo-Wit" (p. 606)

Wendy Rose was born in Oakland, California, to a Hopi father and a Scots-Irish-Miwok mother. In addition to being a poet, Rose is an anthropologist who has worked to protect Native American burial sites from developers. She is also a painter who has illustrated some of her own books. "Loo-Wit" is based on legends of the Cowlitz people of Washington State.

Edna St. Vincent Millay

(1892–1950)

Author of "The Courage That My Mother Had" (p. 608)

Edna St. Vincent Millay's mother was a hard-working nurse who encouraged her daughters to be independent and to love reading. Millay's mother had a powerful influence on young Edna, who grew up to be a widely published writer and political activist. Born in Rockland, Maine, Millay published her first poem at the age of fourteen. In 1923, she became the first woman to win the Pulitzer Prize for poetry.

Life

Naomi Long Madgett

Vocabulary
fascinated (fas´ ə nāt´ əd) *adj.* very interested

Life is but a toy that swings on a bright gold chain
Ticking for a little while
To amuse a fascinated infant,
Until the keeper, a very old man,
5   Becomes tired of the game
And lets the watch run down.

LOO-WIT

Wendy Rose

The way they do
this old woman
no longer cares
what others think
5 but spits her black tobacco
any which way
stretching full length
from her bumpy bed.
Finally up
10 she sprinkles ashes
on the snow,
cold buttes[2]
promise nothing
but the walk
15 of winter.
Centuries of cedar
have bound her
to earth,
huckleberry ropes
20 lay prickly
on her neck.
Around her
machinery growls,
snarls and plows
25 great patches
of her skin.

Vocabulary
prickly (prik´ lē) *adj.*
sharply pointed; thorny

▶ **Critical**
Viewing Which lines
of the poem best cap-
ture the action in this
photograph? **[Assess]**

---

1. **Loo-Wit** name given by the Cowlitz people to Mount St. Helens, an active
   volcano in Washington State. It means "lady of fire."
2. **buttes** (byo͞ots) *n.* steep hills standing alone in flat land.

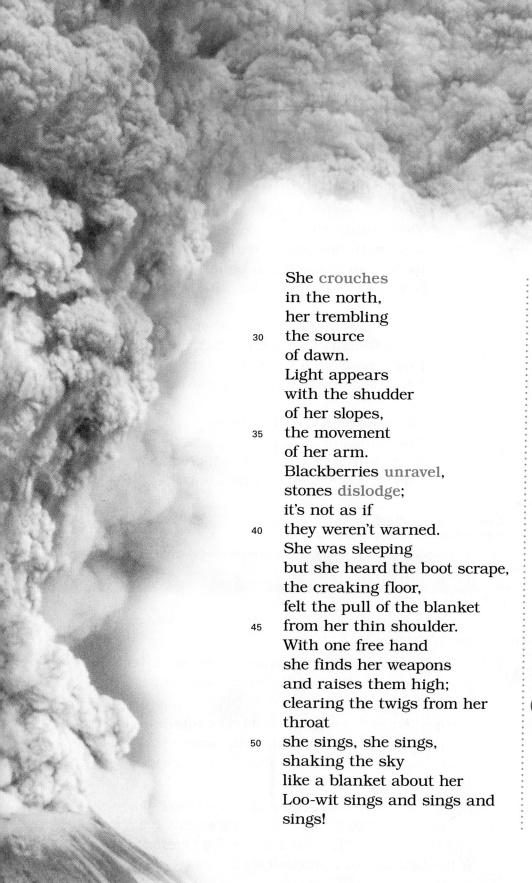

She crouches
in the north,
her trembling
30 the source
of dawn.
Light appears
with the shudder
of her slopes,
35 the movement
of her arm.
Blackberries unravel,
stones dislodge;
it's not as if
40 they weren't warned.
She was sleeping
but she heard the boot scrape,
the creaking floor,
felt the pull of the blanket
45 from her thin shoulder.
With one free hand
she finds her weapons
and raises them high;
clearing the twigs from her
throat
50 she sings, she sings,
shaking the sky
like a blanket about her
Loo-wit sings and sings and
sings!

The Courage That My Mother Had

Edna St. Vincent Millay

Vocabulary
granite (gran´ it) *n.*
hard, gray rock

The courage that my mother had
Went with her, and is with her still:
Rock from New England quarried;[1]
Now granite in a granite hill.

5   The golden brooch[2] my mother wore
She left behind for me to wear;
I have no thing I treasure more:
Yet, it is something I could spare.

    Oh, if instead she'd left to me
10   The thing she took into the grave!—
That courage like a rock, which she
Has no more need of, and I have.

Draw Conclusions
What detail in the third stanza shows how the speaker feels about her mother?

---

1. **quarried** (kwôr´ ēd) *adj.* carved out of the ground.
2. **brooch** (brōch) *n.* large ornamental pin.

Critical Thinking

Cite textual evidence to support your responses.

© **1. Craft and Structure** In "Life," what image does Madgett use to describe life?

© **2. Key Ideas and Details Analyze Causes and Effects:** According to the details in "Loo-Wit," what causes the volcano's eruption?

© **3. Integration of Knowledge and Ideas Interpret:** In "The Courage That My Mother Had," why would the speaker rather have her mother's character than the physical item her mother left her?

© **4. Integration of Knowledge and Ideas** How can a poet use figures of speech to communicate an idea in a new and different way? *[Connect to the Big Question: What is the best way to communicate?]*

Reading Skill: Draw Conclusions

1. Use a graphic organizer like this one to connect details from the poem "Life" to reach the **conclusion** that is given.

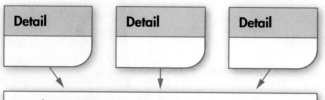

Detail	Detail	Detail

Conclusion: The speaker believes that people lose interest in life as they grow older.

2. Which details from "Loo-Wit" support the conclusion that people are disturbing the mountain?

Literary Analysis: Figurative Language

© 3. Craft and Structure (a) To what is life compared in "Life"? **(b)** Which type of **figurative language** does Madgett use?

© 4. Craft and Structure Give three examples of **personification** in "Loo-Wit."

© 5. Craft and Structure (a) What is a **symbol** for strength in "The Courage That My Mother Had"? **(b)** How do you know?

Vocabulary

© Acquisition and Use Explain your answer to each question.

1. If a tree root is *dislodged*, is it still in the ground?

2. To *unravel* a ball of yarn, do you wind it around?

3. When a dog *crouches*, is he standing on his hind legs?

4. If Michael is *fascinated* by the show, is he bored?

5. If something is made of *granite*, will it break easily?

6. Would a bush that is *prickly* be pleasant to touch?

Word Study Use what you know about the **Latin suffix -ly** to explain your answer to each question.

1. If you speak a language *fluently*, do you speak it poorly?

2. Would it be wise to move *quickly* if you were late for school?

Word Study

The **Latin suffix -ly** means "like" or "in the manner of."

Apply It Explain how the suffix -ly contributes to the meanings of these words. Consult a dictionary if necessary.

haphazardly
proudly
rapidly

What is the best way to *communicate?*

Writing About the Big Question

In Poetry Collection 4, Langston Hughes and Henry Wadsworth Longfellow express admiration for people who have made a difference in their lives. Use this sentence starter to develop your ideas on the Big Question.

> Some writers choose to write poems about people who **enrich** their lives because _____.

While You Read Look for words and images in each poem that communicate the speaker's feelings.

Vocabulary

Read each word and its definition. Decide whether you know the word well, know it a little bit, or do not know it at all. After you read, see how your knowledge of each word has increased.

- **crystal** (kris´ təl) *adj.* made of clear, brilliant glass (p. 613) *Mother was very proud of her crystal glasses.* crystal *n.* crystalize *v.*

- **sinewy** (sin´ yōō wē) *adj.* tough and strong (p. 614) *With sinewy hands, he carved the stone.* sinew *n.*

- **brawny** (brôn´ ē) *adj.* strong and muscular (p. 614) *The piano mover had brawny arms.* brawn *n.* brawnier *adj.*

- **parson** (pär´ sən) *n.* minister (p. 615) *The parson had a deep voice that was easily heard in the rear pews.* parsonage *n.*

- **wrought** (rôt) *adj.* shaped by hammering (p. 615) *The fence was wrought iron.*

- **haunches** (hônch əz) *n.* upper legs and hips of an animal (p. 616) *The dog sat back on his haunches.* haunch *n.*

Word Study

The **Greek suffix -y** means "marked by" or "having."

In his poem, Longfellow describes the village blacksmith's arms as **brawny,** or having strength.

Langston Hughes

(1902–1967)

Author of "Mother to Son" (p. 612)

Langston Hughes published his first work just a year after his high school graduation. Though he wrote in many genres, Hughes is best known for his poetry. He was one of the main figures in the Harlem Renaissance, a creative movement among African Americans that took place in the 1920s in New York City.

Henry Wadsworth Longfellow

(1807–1882)

Author of "The Village Blacksmith" (p. 614)

Although his father wanted him to become a lawyer, Henry Wadsworth Longfellow chose to become a poet and college professor. Longfellow was part of a group of poets called the Fireside Poets, so named because families often gathered around their fireplaces, to read aloud poems such as "The Village Blacksmith."

Carl Sandburg

(1878–1967)

Author of "Fog" (p. 616)

The son of Swedish immigrants, Carl Sandburg was born in Illinois. Although he won the Pulitzer Prize in both poetry and history, he was not a typical scholar. By the time his first book appeared, he had tried many different occupations, including farm worker, stagehand, railroad worker, soldier, and cook.

Mother to Son

Langston Hughes

Well, son, I'll tell you:
Life for me ain't been no crystal stair.
It's had tacks in it,
And splinters,
5   And boards torn up,
And places with no carpet on the floor—
Bare.
But all the time
I'se been a-climbin' on,
10   And reachin' landin's,
And turnin' corners,
And sometimes goin' in the dark
Where there ain't been no light.
So boy, don't you turn back.
15   Don't you set down on the steps
'Cause you finds it's kinder hard.
Don't you fall now—
For I'se still goin', honey,
I'se still climbin',
20   And life for me ain't been no crystal stair.

Vocabulary
crystal (kris´ təl)
adj. made of clear,
brilliant glass

Figurative Language
What does the staircase
symbolize?

Draw Conclusions
What details in the
poem support the
conclusion that life has
not been easy for the
mother?

The Village Blacksmith

Henry Wadsworth Longfellow

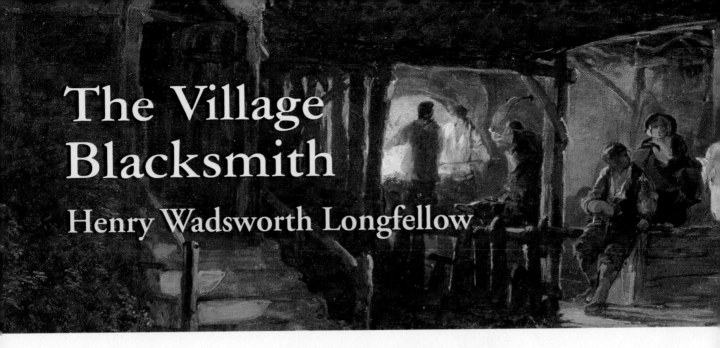

Under a spreading chestnut tree
    The village smithy[1] stands;
The smith, a mighty man is he,
    With large and sinewy hands;
5 And the muscles of his brawny arms
    Are strong as iron bands.

His hair is crisp,[2] and black, and long,
    His face is like the tan;
His brow is wet with honest sweat,
10   He earns whate'er he can,
And looks the whole world in the face,
    For he owes not any man.

Week in, week out, from morn till night,
    You can hear his bellows[3] blow;
15 You can hear him swing his heavy sledge,[4]
    With measured beat and slow,
Like a sexton[5] ringing the village bell,
    When the evening sun is low.

1. **smithy** (smith ē) *n.* workshop of a blacksmith.
2. **crisp** (krisp) *adj.* closely curled and wiry.
3. **bellows** (bel´ ōz) *n.* device for quickening the fire by blowing air in it.
4. **sledge** (slej) *n.* sledgehammer; a long, heavy hammer, usually held with both hands.
5. **sexton** (seks tən) *n.* person who cares for church property and rings church bells.

And children coming home from school
       Look in at the open door;
They love to see the flaming forge,
       And hear the bellows roar,
And catch the burning sparks that fly
       Like chaff from a threshing floor.

He goes on Sunday to the church,
       And sits among his boys;
He hears the parson pray and preach,
       He hears his daughter's voice,
Singing in the village choir,
       And it makes his heart rejoice.
It sounds to him like her mother's voice,
       Singing in Paradise!
He needs must think of her once more,
       How in the grave she lies;
And with his hard, rough hand he wipes
       A tear out of his eyes.

Toiling—rejoicing—sorrowing,
       Onward through life he goes;
Each morning sees some task begin,
       Each evening sees it close;
Something attempted, something done,
       Has earned a night's repose.

Thanks, thanks to thee, my worthy friend,
       For the lesson thou hast taught!
Thus at the flaming forge of life
       Our fortunes must be wrought;
Thus on its sounding anvil shaped
       Each burning deed and thought.

(Line numbers: 20, 25, 30, 35, 40, 45)

Figurative Language
Find an example of a simile in this stanza.

Draw Conclusions
What conclusion can you draw about the blacksmith's wife from the details in lines 25–36?

Vocabulary
parson (pär´ sən) *n.* minister

wrought (rôt) *adj.* shaped by hammering

Reading Check
What kind of hours does the village blacksmith keep?

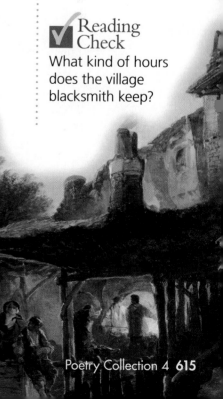

▶ **Critical Viewing**
What is the blacksmith probably doing for these horses?
[Use Prior Knowledge]

FOG
Carl Sandburg

The fog comes
on little cat feet.

It sits looking
over harbor and city
5   on silent haunches
and then moves on.

Vocabulary
haunches (hônch´
əz) *n.* upper legs and
hips of an animal

Critical Thinking

Cite textual evidence to support your responses.

1. **Key Ideas and Details (a) Analyze:** What qualities does the mother in "Mother to Son" demonstrate through her words and actions? **(b) Synthesize:** Why does she need these qualities?

2. **Key Ideas and Details (a)** Identify three details in "The Village Blacksmith" that show how hard the blacksmith works. **(b) Distinguish:** Does the poet present hard work as a positive or a negative thing? Support your answer.

3. **Key Ideas and Details (a)** What three things does the fog do in "Fog"? **(b) Connect:** What qualities of fog make it a good subject for a poem?

4. **Integration of Knowledge and Ideas (a)** How does the speaker in "Mother to Son" communicate her advice and love for her son? **(b)** How can we show admiration for others in our lives? *[Connect to the Big Question: What is the best way to communicate?]*

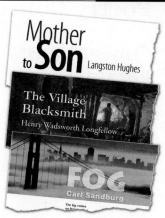

Reading Skill: Draw Conclusions

1. Use a graphic organizer like this one to connect details from "Mother to Son" to reach the **conclusion** that is given.

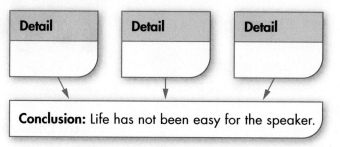

Detail	Detail	Detail

Conclusion: Life has not been easy for the speaker.

2. Which details from "The Village Blacksmith" support the conclusion that the blacksmith sets an example for his family?

Literary Analysis: Figurative Language

© **3. Craft and Structure** Which type of **figurative language** can you identify in lines 15–18 from "The Village Blacksmith"?

© **4. Craft and Structure** What example of **personification** can you identify in lines 20–24 from "The Village Blacksmith"?

© **5. Craft and Structure** In "Mother to Son," identify four **symbols** of hardship.

Vocabulary

© **Acquisition and Use** Explain your answer to each question.

1. Would a dog sit on its *haunches* if it were running?

2. Would you expect a weight lifter to be *brawny*?

3. Who would you expect to have *sinewy* hands?

4. If a glass is made of *crystal*, is it breakable?

5. Would a *parson* likely be found in a church?

6. If something is *wrought*, was it made by hammering?

Word Study Use context and what you know about the **Greek suffix -y** to explain your answer to each question.

1. If a child is *fidgety*, is she sitting still?

2. Is it wise to wear a jacket on a *windy* day?

Word Study

The **Greek suffix -y** means "marked by" or "having."

Apply It Explain how the suffix -y contributes to the meanings of these words. Consult a dictionary if necessary.

sunny
shifty
brainy

Integrated Language Skills

Poetry Collections 3 and 4

Conventions: Appositives and Appositive Phrases

An **appositive** is a noun or pronoun placed after another noun or pronoun to identify, rename, or explain it.

An **appositive phrase** is a noun or pronoun with modifiers. It stands next to a noun or pronoun and adds information that identifies, renames, or explains it.

Poetry Collection 4

Appositives	Appositive Phrases
Michelangelo, the painter, lived in Italy.	Louisa May Alcott, an American author, wrote *Little Women*.
Our cat, Midnight, likes to sleep on my bed.	Karina—a talented violinist—played a solo.

Appositives or appositive phrases are set off with commas or dashes when their meaning is not essential to the sentence.

Practice A Identify the appositive or appositive phrase in each sentence, and indicate which noun it identifies, renames, or explains.

1. My favorite poet, Naomi Madgett, describes life as an amusement.

2. Millay's mother, a powerful influence in her life, was a hard-working nurse.

3. Wendy Rose—an anthropologist, poet, and painter—is also an activist.

4. These poets, all talented women, share their thoughts about the natural world.

© **Reading Application** Find an appositive phrase in "Life."

Practice B Identify the appositive or appositive phrase in each sentence. Then, write a new sentence, using the same appositive or phrase.

1. His mother, a determined woman, continues on despite the obstacles.

2. In the smithy—the blacksmith's workshop—the flames burn yellow and hot.

3. The blacksmith, a worthy friend, has taught us a lesson.

4. Fog, a large curling cat, envelops the city.

© **Writing Application** Write three sentences that contain appositive phrases. Set off nonessential appositives with commas or dashes.

PH **WRITING COACH**   Further instruction and practice are available in *Prentice Hall Writing Coach*.

Writing

Explanatory Text Create a **metaphor** using one of the following topics from the poems in these collections as inspiration:

- life
- a quality, such as loyalty
- an idea, such as love

Use precise language to compare your topic to something else, such as an object, an idea, or an animal. Then, extend the metaphor by making several connected comparisons. Use vivid images and descriptive language to develop your metaphor.

Grammar Application Check your writing to be sure you have correctly used appositives or appositive phrases.

Writing Workshop: *Work-in-Progress*

Prewriting for Exposition Using the Solutions List from your writing portfolio, number your ideas in order from your most to least favorite. Then, write a few sentences to support your number one idea. Save your Main Solution in your writing portfolio.

Research and Technology

Build and Present Knowledge Working with a partner, write a **scientific explanation** of one of the following topics. Then, present your findings to the class in an oral report:

- Research volcanic eruptions, such as how volcanoes form, the warning signs of an eruption, where and why volcanoes typically erupt, or famous eruptions of the past.

- Explain the difference between fog and smog. In your writing, define each term, describe at least one similarity and one difference, and identify two types of fog and smog.

Use library resources to conduct your research. Support your explanation with facts and details.

- If you are using a book, scan the table of contents to see if your topic is addressed. Then, review the index for key words.
- Look up unfamiliar or scientific terms in a glossary.
- Use diagrams, illustrations, photographs, maps, or other visuals to clarify your findings and emphasize key points.
- Put information into your own words.

Common Core State Standards

L.7.1.a; W.7.2, W.7.2.d, W.7.7; SL.7.5
[For the full wording of the standards, see page 600.]

Use this prewriting activity to prepare for the **Writing Workshop** on page 640.

www.PHLitOnline.com
- Interactive graphic organizers
- Grammar tutorial
- Interactive journals

Test Practice: Reading

Drawing Conclusions

Fiction Selection

Directions: *Read the selection. Then, answer the questions.*

On Monday morning, Janelle's alarm rang at 7:00, 7:15, and 7:30. Each time, she reached her arm out from under the warm covers and fumbled around on the nightstand until she found the clock. Then, she hit the snooze button. Finally, at 7:45, she pried one eye open and looked at the clock. She screeched, jumped out of bed, and ran shivering down the hall and into the shower.

By 8:30, Janelle was turning onto the northbound lane of the Golden Gate Bridge. "That's a relief," sighed Janelle. As she drove, she thought about the presentation she would give later that day to the head of her department. As usual, the traffic flowed quickly and smoothly. Janelle checked her watch with a smile. She felt pity for the people caught in the daily bumper-to-bumper traffic on the other side of the bridge.

1. Based on details in this passage, you can conclude that—
   A. Janelle's snooze button is broken.
   B. Janelle meant to get up earlier.
   C. Janelle does not like her boss.
   D. Janelle's presentation will go well.

2. What detail supports the conclusion you drew in question 1?
   A. The alarm rang at 7:00, 7:15, and 7:30.
   B. Janelle screeched, jumped out of bed, and ran down the hall.
   C. Janelle sighed with relief.
   D. Traffic flowed quickly and smoothly.

3. What can you conclude about Janelle based on the second paragraph?
   A. She drives too quickly.
   B. She is on her way to work.
   C. She did not leave her house on time.
   D. She is late every day.

4. What techniques does the author use to convey Janelle's worry about arriving on time?
   A. The author provides a series of facts about the traffic and time.
   B. The author uses humor.
   C. The author uses short, direct sentences.
   D. The author uses direct quotations from Janelle.

Writing for Assessment

Based on details in the second paragraph, what **conclusion** can you draw about morning traffic on the Golden Gate Bridge? Write a few sentences explaining your answer.

Nonfiction Selection

Directions: *Read the selection. Then, answer the questions.*

The Golden Gate Bridge spans the San Francisco Bay, connecting the peninsula of San Francisco to northern California. The Golden Gate is a suspension bridge, with tall towers that hold up thick cables from which the bridge hangs. The floor of the bridge rises 220 feet above the bay. A six-lane road on the bridge is bordered by sidewalks. Movable lane markers control the heavy flow of traffic on the road. There can be more lanes for cars entering the city, or more lanes for cars leaving the city. On weekday mornings, four of the six lanes run southbound into the city and two lanes run northbound out of the city. In the afternoon, the lanes are reversed. Four lanes run northbound and two run southbound. Even with this system, traffic is often heavy.

1. Which of the following conclusions is best supported by the details in this passage?
   A. The bridge connects San Francisco and northern California.
   B. Tourists visit the Golden Gate Bridge.
   C. All suspension bridges have six lanes.
   D. Commuters enjoy driving across the Golden Gate Bridge.

2. Which conclusion can you reach by connecting these details: The bridge is 220 feet above the water; it has tall towers?
   A. The bridge is not very big.
   B. The bridge will not stand for long.
   C. The bridge is visible from far away.
   D. The bridge is very unusual.

3. Which details support the conclusion that many people can move across the bridge?
   A. The bridge hangs from thick cables and is 220 feet above the water.
   B. The bridge spans San Francisco Bay, and San Francisco is on a peninsula.
   C. The towers peek through the fog and are a symbol of San Francisco.
   D. The bridge has six lanes for traffic and sidewalks for pedestrians.

4. What can you conclude based on the last four sentences in the passage?
   A. Tourists enjoy visiting the city.
   B. More people travel to the city in the mornings.
   C. The Golden Gate Bridge is the most popular way to enter San Francisco.
   D. Movable lanes are unsafe for drivers.

Writing for Assessment

Connecting Across Texts

Write a paragraph that describes what Janelle's commute would be like if she were traveling in the opposite direction. Would she have made it to work on time? Use details from both passages to support your **conclusions.**

www.PHLitOnline.com
- Online practice
- Instant feedback

Reading for Information

Analyzing Functional Texts

Technical Directions

Product Warranty

Reading Skill: Follow Technical Directions

Technical directions offer step-by-step instruction on how to assemble, operate, or repair a mechanical device. Technical directions might also include tips or warnings about how *not* to use a device. To be sure that you understand and correctly follow a set of technical directions, use a checklist like the one shown.

Checklist for Following Technical Directions

☐ Read all the directions completely before starting to follow them.

☐ Look for clues such as bold type or capital letters that point out specific sections or important information.

☐ Use diagrams to locate and name the parts of the product.

☐ Follow each step in the exact order given.

☐ Do not skip any steps.

Content-Area Vocabulary

These words appear in the selections that follow. You may also encounter them in other content-area texts.

- **warrants** (wôr′ ənts) *v.* guarantees

- **supersedes** (soo′ pər sēdz′) *v.* takes the place of; causes to be set aside

- **liability** (lī′ ə bil′ ə tē) *n.* condition of being responsible, especially by law

Common Core State Standards

Reading Informational Text

4. Determine the meaning of words and phrases as they are used in a text, including technical meanings.

5. Analyze the structure an author uses to organize a text, including how the major sections contribute to the whole and to the development of the ideas.

Writing

2.d. Use precise language and domain-specific vocabulary to inform about or explain the topic. *(Timed Writing)*

Language

6. Acquire and use accurately grade-appropriate general academic and domain-specific words and phrases; gather vocabulary knowledge when considering a word or phrase important to comprehension or expression.

PHLit Online!
www.PHLitOnline.com
- Online practice
- Instant feedback

How to Download Ringtones for a Cell Phone

Features:

- step-by-step instructions for the use of a mechanical device
- tips or warnings
- some technical language
- text written for a general or a specific audience

The Built-in Method

Instructions

- **STEP 1:** Determine if your wireless carrier provides you with a built-in method for downloading ringtones right from your phone. This is usually the most expensive method, but quite simple.

- **STEP 2:** Press the "Web" or "Internet" button on your phone. Once it loads, go to the "Downloads" section. From there, there should be a section for ringtones.

- **STEP 3:** Preview and download new tones for your phone from the ringtones section.

> Directions are provided in sequential order.

Free Ringtones

> Subheads identify different methods of downloading ringtones.

Instructions

- **STEP 1:** Access a computer with Internet.

- **STEP 2:** Go to your favorite search engine and search for "free ringtones." You will get lots of results.

- **STEP 3:** Choose a site that does not require registration. If you do have to register, make sure that any boxes that would sign you up for emails or additional services are NOT checked.

- **STEP 4:** Find ringtones you like and have them sent to your phone. This will require entering your carrier and phone number if you haven't already. The new ringtones will be sent to your phone.

Tips & Warnings

- You may need to be in your home service area to receive these tones.

Setting Your New Ringtones

Instructions

Bold type and capital letters help to call out the steps of the process.

- **STEP 1:** Decide if you want to set one ringtone as a universal ring, which will play every time you receive a call, or whether you want to set specific ringtones to correspond to specific entries in your phonebook. That way different ringtones will play when different people call you.

- **STEP 2:** Set a universal ringtone in the settings section of your phone. If you cannot find how to do this, consult the manual for your phone. If you do not have the manual, you can probably find it online at either the manufacturer's site or your carrier's site.

- **STEP 3:** Set a ring that is specific to a caller by first finding that person in your phonebook. Select the person for which you want the special ring. Select "Edit." Scroll down in the phonebook entry and select "Ring." Choose the ringtone you want to play when that person calls.

Overall Tips & Warnings

- If at any point you are having trouble, consult the documentation that came with your phone.

Limited Warranty for Cellular Telephones Purchased in the United States

Our Warranty

The company warrants this phone to be free from defects in material and workmanship. During the limited warranty period, the company will repair or replace, at its option, without charge, a defective phone.

How long is the limited warranty period?

The limited warranty period for the phone extends for one (1) year, beginning on the date of its original purchase.

What is not covered by this warranty?

This warranty does not cover cosmetic damage resulting from normal wear and tear. It also does not cover any failure of a phone that has been subjected to misuse, neglect, accident, shipping or other physical damage, exposure to water or moisture, unauthorized repair, or unauthorized connections.

How do you get warranty service?

To make a warranty claim, please follow these step-by-step instructions:

Step 1: Determine if your phone is eligible for warranty service, according to the conditions stated above. Be sure that you have proof of purchase.

Step 2: Contact Customer Service using the company's toll-free phone number. Business hours are Monday through Friday, 9:00AM–5:00PM Eastern Standard Time. Before calling, please have the following ready:

- your receipt or other proof of purchase
- the phone number
- the model number
- the serial number (found on the label under the phone's battery)

Once it has been determined that the phone is eligible for warranty service, the customer service representative will provide you with a return authorization number. You will also receive an address and instructions for shipping the phone to the company's repair facility.

This section of the warranty provides directions for getting repairs made.

Step 3: Ship the phone to the company's repair facility. Phones should be shipped in a well-padded cardboard box. In addition to the phone, the following must be included:

- your return shipping address
- your daytime phone number and/or fax number
- a complete description of the problem
- a copy of your proof of purchase
- your return authorization number

A bulleted list gives important information about how to complete this step in the process.

You will be responsible for the cost of shipping the phone to the repair facility. The company will cover the cost of return shipment.

Step 4: When you receive your new or repaired phone, you must reactivate your cellular service. You can do so by calling the company's toll-free number and following the instructions given.

What are the limits on the company's responsibility?

This warranty is the complete and exclusive agreement between you and the company. It supersedes all other written or oral communications related to this phone. The company provides no other express warranties for this product. The warranty exclusively describes all of the company's responsibilities regarding this phone.

The company shall have no liability for any indirect, special, incidental, consequential, or similar damages (including, but not limited to lost profits or revenue, loss of data, inability to use the phone or other associated equipment, the cost of substitute equipment, and claims by third parties) resulting from the use of this phone.

Comparing Functional Texts

1. Key Ideas and Details (a) What is the most useful structural feature of each document? Explain. **(b)** In what ways do both the technical directions and the warranty help readers make better use of their telephones?

Content-Area Vocabulary

2. Write a brief paragraph summarizing the protections the warranty offers consumers. In your paragraph, accurately use the words *warrants, supersedes,* and *liability*.

⏱ Timed Writing

Explanatory Text: Directions

> **Format**
> The prompt instructs you to explain the use of a mechanical device. Therefore, you will need to write a set of directions.

Show that you understand the technical directions by creating an explanation of how to download and play a new ringtone. Refer to the source document for the steps, but use your own words in your explanation. (30 minutes)

> **Academic Vocabulary**
> A *source* document is a text from which you received information.

5-Minute Planner

Complete these steps before you begin to write:

1. Read the prompt closely, noting highlighted key words.

2. Closely reread each section of the technical document. Jot down ideas about how you can restate the main ideas in your own words. **TIP** Make sure you understand the meanings of technical terms such as *wireless carrier* and *universal ring.*

3. Draw rough diagrams or illustrations to help readers' understanding or to highlight important information.

4. Create an outline showing how you will organize your explanation. For example, you may wish to include a brief opening paragraph to explain that you will offer two options for downloading ringtones: one costly, one free.

5. Refer to your outline, as well as your notes and sketches, as you begin to draft your explanation.

Comparing Narrative Poems

A **narrative poem** combines elements of fiction and poetry to tell a story.

- Like short stories, narrative poems usually include characters, setting, plot, conflict, and point of view.

- Like other poems, narrative poetry uses sound devices like rhythm and rhyme to bring out the musical qualities of language.

- Like other poetry, narrative poetry uses figurative language to create memorable images or word pictures. Figurative language includes *similes,* or comparisons of unlike things using *like* or *as*, and *metaphors,* or comparisons in which one thing is spoken of as if it were another kind of thing.

Narrative poetry is well suited to a wide range of stories. For example, narrative poems may tell about heroic deeds, amazing events, or larger-than-life characters. In contrast, the form may also be used to relate everyday stories about ordinary people.

The poems presented here blend elements of fiction and poetry in a memorable way. As you read the poems, look for ways in which they each demonstrate elements of narration and poetry. Note your ideas on a chart like the one shown.

**Common Core
State Standards**

Reading Literature

4. Determine the meaning of words and phrases as they are used in a text, including figurative and connotative meanings; analyze the impact of rhymes and other repetitions of sounds on a specific verse or stanza of a poem or section of a story or drama.

6. Analyze how an author develops and contrasts the points of view of different characters or narrators in a text.

Writing

9. Draw evidence from literary or informational texts to support analysis, reflection, and research.

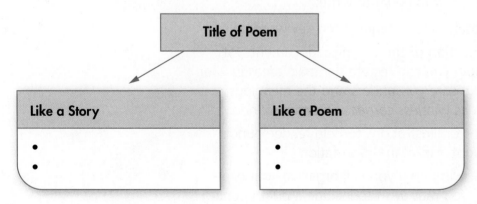

- Vocabulary flashcards
- Interactive journals
- More about the authors
- Selection audio
- Interactive graphic organizers

www.PHLitOnline.com

What is the best way to *communicate?*

Writing About the Big Question

In each of these narrative poems, the characters' actions reveal their feelings more than the words they say. Use this sentence starter to develop your ideas about the Big Question.

How you act can **communicate** more than what you say because _____.

Meet the Authors

Alfred Noyes (1880–1958)
Author of "The Highwayman"

The Englishman Alfred Noyes was a poet and a critic. Despite his great love for England's history and landscape, he moved to the United States to teach at Princeton University in New Jersey. There, he continued writing poems about legendary figures like Robin Hood.

Gregory Djanikian (b. 1949)

Author of "How I Learned English"

Born in Alexandria, Egypt, Gregory Djanikian moved to the United States at age eight with his family. Today he directs a creative writing program at the University of Pennsylvania and runs poetry workshops. Djanikian's experiences of immigrating and tackling a new language provided ideas for poems such as "How I Learned English."

The Highwayman

Alfred Noyes

Background This poem takes place centuries ago, when highways were just dirt roads, and *highwayman* meant "robber." Travelers on horseback or in carriages stopped at inns to eat, sleep, and avoid the dangers of isolated highways in the dark of night. Although travelers feared outlaws, many—like Robin Hood, Pancho Villa, and Jesse James—became legendary.

Vocabulary
torrent (tôr´ ənt) *n.* flood

Narrative Poems
Describe the setting of this poem in your own words.

Part One

The wind was a torrent of darkness among the gusty
    trees.
The moon was a ghostly galleon[1] tossed upon cloudy seas.
The road was a ribbon of moonlight over the purple
    moor,[2]
And the highwayman came riding—
        Riding—riding—
5 The highwayman came riding, up to the old inn door.

He'd a French cocked-hat on his forehead, a bunch of lace
    at his chin,
A coat of the claret velvet, and breeches of brown doeskin.
They fitted with never a wrinkle. His boots were up to the
    thigh.
10 And he rode with a jeweled twinkle,
        His pistol butts a-twinkle,
His rapier hilt[3] a-twinkle, under the jeweled sky.

---

1. galleon (gal´ ē ən) *n.* large Spanish sailing ship.
2. moor (moor) *n.* open, rolling land with swamps.
3. rapier (rā´ pē ər) **hilt** large cup-shaped handle of a rapier, which is a type of sword.

Over the cobbles he clattered and clashed in the dark
    innyard.
He tapped with his whip on the shutters, but all was
    locked and barred.
15 He whistled a tune to the window, and who should be
    waiting there
But the landlord's black-eyed daughter,
            Bess, the landlord's daughter,
Plaiting a dark red love knot into her long black hair.

And dark in the dark old innyard a stable wicket creaked
20 Where Tim the ostler[4] listened. His face was white and
    peaked.
His eyes were hollows of madness, his hair like moldy
    hay,
But he loved the landlord's daughter,
            The landlord's red-lipped daughter.
Dumb as a dog he listened, and he heard the robber
    say—
25 "One kiss, my bonny[5] sweetheart, I'm after a prize
    tonight,
But I shall be back with the yellow gold before the
    morning light;
Yet, if they press me sharply, and harry me through the
    day,
Then look for me by moonlight,
            Watch for me by moonlight,
30 I'll come to thee by moonlight, though hell should bar the
    way."

He rose upright in the stirrups. He scarce could reach her
    hand,
But she loosened her hair in the casement.[6] His face
    burnt like a brand[7]
As the black cascade of perfume came tumbling over his
    breast;
And he kissed its waves in the moonlight,
35   (O, sweet black waves in the moonlight!)
Then he tugged at his rein in the moonlight, and galloped
    away to the west.

Narrative Poems
What do you know so far about the main characters in this narrative poem?

Reading Check
What did Tim overhear?

4. **ostler** (äs´ lər) *n.* stable worker.
5. **bonny** (bän´ ē) *adj.* Scottish for "pretty."
6. **casement** (kās´ mənt) *n.* window frame that opens on hinges.
7. **brand (brand)** *n.* piece of burning wood.

Spiral Review
Figurative Language Identify the metaphor in this stanza. What effect does it have on the reader?

Vocabulary
bound (bound) *v.* tied

Narrative Poems What problem, or conflict, does Bess face?

Part Two

He did not come in the dawning. He did not come at noon;
And out of the tawny sunset, before the rise of the moon,
When the road was a gypsy's ribbon, looping the purple moor,
A redcoat troop came marching—
Marching—marching—
King George's men[8] came marching, up to the old inn door.

They said no word to the landlord. They drank his ale instead
But they gagged his daughter, and bound her, to the foot of her narrow bed.
Two of them knelt at her casement, with muskets at their side!
There was death at every window;
And hell at one dark window;
For Bess could see, through her casement, the road that he would ride.

They had tied her up to attention, with many a sniggering jest.[9]
They had bound a musket beside her, with the muzzle beneath her breast!
"Now, keep good watch!" and they kissed her. She heard the doomed man say—
Look for me by moonlight;
Watch for me by moonlight;
I'll come to thee by moonlight, though hell should bar the way!

She twisted her hands behind her; but all the knots held good!
She writhed her hands till her fingers were wet with sweat or blood!
They stretched and strained in the darkness, and the hours crawled by like years,

8. King George's men soldiers serving King George of Great Britain.
9. sniggering (snig´ ər iŋ) **jest** sly joke.

◄ **Critical Viewing**
What details of this
painting capture
the mood of the
poem? **[Connect]**

Till, now, on the stroke of midnight,
  Cold, on the stroke of midnight,
60 The tip of one finger touched it! The trigger at least was
  hers!

The tip of one finger touched it. She strove no more for
  the rest.
Up, she stood up to attention, with the muzzle beneath
  her breast.
She would not risk their hearing; she would not strive
  again;
For the road lay bare in the moonlight;
65   Blank and bare in the moonlight;
And the blood of her veins, in the moonlight, throbbed to
  her love's refrain.

Tlot-tlot; tlot-tlot! Had they heard it? The horsehoofs ringing
  clear;
Tlot-tlot, tlot-tlot, in the distance? Were they deaf that
  they did not hear?
Down the ribbon of moonlight, over the brow of the hill,

Narrative Poems
How does line 60 build
suspense in the narra-
tive?

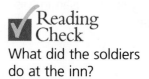
Reading
Check
What did the soldiers
do at the inn?

The Highwayman **633**

70 The highwayman came riding—
                    Riding—riding—
The redcoats looked to their priming![10] She stood up,
    straight and still.

Tlot-tlot, in the frosty silence! Tlot-tlot, in the echoing
    night!
Nearer he came and nearer. Her face was like a light.
75 Her eyes grew wide for a moment; she drew one last deep
    breath,
Then her finger moved in the moonlight,
                    Her musket shattered the moonlight,
Shattered her breast in the moonlight and warned him—
    with her death.

He turned. He spurred to the west; he did not know who
    stood
80 Bowed, with her head o'er the musket, drenched with her
    own blood!
Not till the dawn he heard it, and his face grew gray to
    hear
How Bess, the landlord's daughter,
                    The landlord's black-eyed daughter,
Had watched for her love in the moonlight, and died in
    the darkness there.

85 Back, he spurred like a madman, shouting a curse to the
    sky,
With the white road smoking behind him and his rapier
    brandished[11] high.
Blood-red were his spurs in the golden noon; wine-red
    was his velvet coat;
When they shot him down on the highway,
                    Down like a dog on the highway,
90 And he lay in his blood on the highway, with a bunch of
    lace at his throat.

And still of a winter's night, they say, when the wind is in
    the trees,
When the moon is a ghostly galleon tossed upon cloudy
    seas,

---

10. priming (prī′ miŋ) *n.* explosive used to set off the charge in a gun.
11. brandished (bran′ dishd) *adj.* waved in a threatening way.

When the road is a ribbon of moonlight over the purple
    moor,
A highwayman comes riding—
                    Riding—riding—
95 A highwayman comes riding, up to the old inn door.

Over the cobbles he clatters and clangs in the dark
    innyard.
He taps with his whip on the shutters, but all is locked
    and barred.
He whistles a tune to the window, and who should be
    waiting there
100 But the landlord's black-eyed daughter,
                    Bess, the landlord's daughter,
Plaiting a dark red love knot into her long black hair.

Critical Thinking

1. **Key Ideas and Details** **(a)** At the beginning of the narrative, how does the highwayman tell Bess he has arrived? **(b) Infer:** What does this method of communication tell you about their relationship?

2. **Key Ideas and Details** **(a)** Identify three details that make the highwayman seem like a romantic figure. **(b) Compare and Contrast:** How do these details compare with the details about Tim the ostler? **(c) Infer:** How do you think the king's men learned where to find the highwayman?

3. **Integration of Knowledge and Ideas** **Draw Conclusions:** What do the last two stanzas suggest about the love between Bess and the highwayman?

4. **Integration of Knowledge and Ideas** **(a)** In what ways do Bess and the highwayman communicate their love for each other? Explain your answer. **(b)** Based on the details in this poem, what do you think the author would say is the best way to express love? *[Connect to the Big Question: What is the best way to communicate?]*

Cite textual evidence to support your responses.

How I Learned English
Gregory Djanikian

It was in an empty lot
Ringed by elms and fir and honeysuckle.
Bill Corson was pitching in his buckskin[1] jacket,
Chuck Keller, fat even as a boy, was on first,
His t-shirt riding up over his gut,
Ron O'Neill, Jim, Dennis, were talking it up
In the field, a blue sky above them
Tipped with cirrus.[2]
          And there I was,
Just off the plane and plopped in the middle
Of Williamsport, Pa., and a neighborhood game,
Unnatural and without any moves,
My notions of baseball and America
Growing fuzzier each time I whiffed.[3]

So it was not impossible that I,
Banished to the outfield and daydreaming
Of water, or a hotel in the mountains,
Would suddenly find myself in the path
Of a ball stung[4] by Joe Barone.
I watched it closing in
Clean and untouched, transfixed
By its easy arc before it hit
My forehead with a thud.
          I fell back.
Dazed, clutching my brow,
Groaning, "Oh my shin, oh my shin,"
And everybody peeled away from me
And dropped from laughter, and there we were,
All of us writhing on the ground for one reason
Or another.

5 (line 5)
10 (line 10)
15 (line 15)
20 (line 20)
25 (line 25)
30 (line 30)

---

1. **buckskin** *adj.* yellowish-gray leather made from the hide of a deer.
2. **cirrus** (sir′ əs) *n.* high, thin clouds.
3. **whiffed** (hwift) *v.* struck out.
4. **stung** *v.* hit hard.

◀ **Critical Viewing**
Which details in this photograph reveal that this player knows how to field a baseball? Explain. **[Analyze]**

Narrative Poems
What do you know so far about the main character?

Vocabulary
transfixed (trans fikst′) *adj.* rooted to the spot

writhing (rīth′ iŋ) *adj.* squirming, often in response to pain

Reading Check
What happens to the speaker when Joe hits a ball into the outfield?

Someone said "shin" again,
There was a wild stamping of hands on the ground,
A kicking of feet, and the fit
Of laughter overtook me too,
35 And that was important, as important
As Joe Barone asking me how I was
Through his tears, picking me up
And dusting me off with hands like swatters,
And though my head felt heavy,
40 I played on till dusk
Missing flies and pop-ups and grounders
And calling out in desperation things like
"Yours" and "take it," but doing all right,
Tugging at my cap in just the right way,
45 Crouching low, my feet set,
"Hum baby" sweetly on my lips.

Spiral Review
Figurative Language
What does the simile in line 38 tell readers?

Narrative Poems
How do you know that the speaker's feelings about baseball have changed?

Cite textual evidence to support your responses.

Critical Thinking

1. **Key Ideas and Details (a)** What details in lines 1–9 tell you a baseball game is underway? **(b) Infer:** Why does the speaker have trouble with the game?

2. **Key Ideas and Details (a)** What help does Joe Barone offer the speaker in lines 35–38? **(b) Interpret:** Why does the speaker choose to continue playing?

3. **Key Ideas and Details Speculate:** How might the outcome of the day have been different for the speaker if he had not been hit in the head?

4. **Integration of Knowledge and Ideas Draw Conclusions:** Do you think playing baseball will help the speaker learn English? Why or why not?

5. **Integration of Knowledge and Ideas (a)** Name at least three nonverbal ways characters in this poem communicate. **(b)** Why are the players' actions more important to the speaker than words? *[Connect to the Big Question: What is the best way to communicate?]*

Comparing Narrative Poems

1. Craft and Structure Narrative poems have many of the same elements as short stories. Use a chart like this one to find examples of short story elements in each poem.

Short Story Element	Highwayman	How I Learned English
Setting		
Characters		
Point of View		
Conflict (Problem to be solved)		
Outcome of conflict		

2. Craft and Structure (a) In each poem, identify a musical element and explain its effect. **(b)** In each poem, identify and interpret an instance of figurative language.

Timed Writing

Explanatory Text: Essay

In an essay, explain how each poet creates contrasts between characters' points of view. Then, compare the effects the contrasts add—suspense, humor, and so on. **(40 minutes)**

5-Minute Planner

1. Read the prompt carefully and completely.

2. Gather your ideas by jotting down answers to these questions:
- Who narrates each poem? How is point of view developed?
- What different interests, motives, or perceptions do characters have?
- What important information do some characters know that others do not? What effect does this situation create?

3. Draw evidence from each poem, taking notes on similarities and differences. Use these notes as you write your essay.

4. Reread the prompt, and then draft your essay.

Writing Workshop

Common Core State Standards

Writing

1. Write arguments to support claims with clear reasons and relevant evidence.

1.a. Introduce claim(s), acknowledge alternate or opposing claims, and organize the reasons and evidence logically.

1.b. Support claim(s) with logical reasoning and relevant evidence, using accurate, credible sources and demonstrating an understanding of the topic or text.

7. Conduct short research projects to answer a question, drawing on several sources and generating additional related, focused questions for further research and investigation.

Write an Explanatory Text

Exposition: Problem-and-Solution Essay

Defining the Form A **problem-and-solution essay** identifies and explains a problem and offers one or more possible solutions to it. You might use elements of this type of writing in editorials, letters to authorities, and proposals.

Assignment Choose a problem with which you are familiar, and propose one or more solutions. Include these elements:

✔ a *thesis* that clearly states the problem

✔ an interesting *introduction*

✔ body paragraphs with *step-by-step solutions*

✔ *supporting details with facts and examples* to support each solution

✔ a strong *conclusion*

✔ error-free writing, including *correct use of participles*

To preview the criteria on which your essay may be judged, see the rubric on page 645.

 Writing Workshop: *Work in Progress*

Review the work you did on pages 599 and 619.

Prewriting/Planning Strategy

Identify a problem and possible solution. Think of problems that could inspire a strong essay. Consider problems in your town or city or in your school by reading local print or online newspapers or talking to other students. Once you decide on a problem, use a chart like this one to brainstorm for possible solutions.

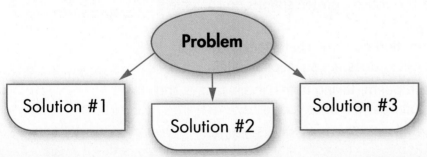

Making Your Ideas Convincing

Ideas make up the content of any piece of writing. You may have several thoughts about problems and solutions that come from your research and your own experience. To successfully persuade your readers, select the best ideas, then add convincing supporting details. Follow these tips to write a powerful essay.

Narrowing Your Focus After you choose a general problem for your essay, it is time to narrow the focus. If you write about a problem that is very broad, the solutions may be too complex. Break the problem down into smaller parts. Determine who your audience is. Then, imagine a part of the problem that your audience can help solve. To give focus to your ideas, write a thesis statement that clearly states the problem.

Explaining the Problem Your introduction should include a clear explanation of the problem. Use accurate, specific language when you explain your topic. While researching several sources, develop your ideas by answering the following questions before you write.

Who	What	When	Where	Why	How
Who is responsible for the situation?	What negative effects come from this problem?	When did the problem start?	Where is the problem most prevalent?	Why is this situation a problem now?	How did the problem develop over time?

Providing Elaboration To persuade readers that your solutions will be effective, you must provide relevant evidence and details that support each solution. Use the following techniques:

- Include accurate data, statistics, or research that supports your ideas. Quote expert opinions that favor your solutions.

- Interview people to gather anecdotes about the issue. Be sure to talk to people who know about your subject.

- Explain in detail exactly how and why your solution will be successful. Convince readers that the solution makes sense with step-by-step descriptions.

> **PH WRITING COACH**
>
> Further instruction and practice are available in *Prentice Hall Writing Coach*.

Drafting Strategies

Introduce the problem. Begin your essay by stating your thesis, or main idea. Grab your readers' attention with a bold statement or question about the problem that you will address.

Develop your ideas. In the body of your essay, build your argument by presenting information. If you are presenting one solution, move through it step-by-step. If you are suggesting several possible solutions, arrange them in an order that makes logical sense. Treat each one separately and clearly. Use your ideas from the Writer's Toolbox to fully develop your ideas. Finally, craft a concluding statement that supports your thesis and leaves a memorable thought in readers' minds.

Revising Strategies

Use the present tense. To make a convincing argument, use the present tense when you present your supporting details. For example, if you are presenting the opinion of an expert, consider using the following style:

> **Weak:** The supervisor at the city water plant *stated* that he *will support* the Clean Water Act.

> **Better:** The supervisor at the city water plant *states* that he *supports* the Clean Water Act.

Peer Review

Ask a classmate to read your essay. Then, have him or her complete a response using the following format. Request that your reviewer be as specific as possible about any areas that need improvement. Use your peer reviewer's response to revise your problem-and-solution essay. If you are unclear about any feedback, ask your reviewer for clarification.

Peer Reviewer Questions	Yes or No	How can I improve my essay?
Can you identify the problem?		
Is my solution (or solutions) reasonable?		
Do I provide enough support for each solution I propose?		
Is my essay convincing?		
Does my conclusion inspire action?		

Common Core State Standards

Writing

1. Write arguments to support claims with clear reasons and relevant evidence.

1.c. Use words, phrases, and clauses to create cohesion and clarify the relationships among claim(s), reasons, and evidence.

1.e. Provide a concluding statement or section that follows from and supports the argument presented.

Language

1.c. Place phrases and clauses within a sentence, recognizing and correcting misplaced and dangling modifiers.

Sentence Fluency	Voice	Organization	Word Choice	Ideas	Conventions

Revising Sentences Using Participles

To make your sentences flow smoothly, combine sentences using participles and participial phrases. A **participle** is a verb form that acts as an adjective, modifying a noun or pronoun. **Present participles** end in *-ing*. **Past participles** usually end in *-ed*, but may have an irregular ending, such as *-en* in *spoken*.

past participle   noun

She banged her fist against the <u>closed</u> <u>windows</u>.

A **participial phrase** consists of a participle and its modifiers. A **misplaced modifier** is placed far away from the word it describes.

Misplaced modifier: <u>I</u> heard her voice listening to the song.
Solution: Listening to the song, <u>I</u> heard her voice.

A **dangling modifier** is not logically connected to any word in the sentence.

Dangling modifier: Raising the flag, the <u>wind</u> felt strong.
Solution: Raising the flag, the <u>sailors</u> felt the strong wind.

Fixing Choppy Passages Using Participles To fix a choppy passage, identify sentences that can be combined. Then rewrite the passage using one or more of the following methods:

1. Combine sentences using a present participle.

▶ **Example:** We arranged a tour. We would walk the grounds.
We arranged a <u>walking</u> tour of the grounds.

2. Combine sentences using a past participle.

▶ **Example:** The food is cooked. It will not spoil.
The <u>cooked</u> food will not spoil.

3. Combine Sentences using a participial phrase.

▶ **Example:** Marissa ate her food quickly. She was running late. <u>Running late,</u> Marissa ate her food quickly.

Grammar in Your Writing

Choose three paragraphs in your draft. Read the paragraphs aloud, highlighting any passages that sound choppy. Using one of the methods above, fix the choppy passages by combining sentences.

PH **WRITING COACH**

Further instruction and practice are available in *Prentice Hall Writing Coach*.

Student Model: Nicole Eras, Cedarhurst, NY

Have you ever wanted to go to a concert or a big sporting event, and tried to get seats? You try to get them as soon as they go on sale and in the first two minutes, they're gone. Ticket brokers buy most of the seats right before anybody else can get to them and then they sell them at astronomical prices. This problem affects people of all ages, but especially teenagers. It is unfair and we should find a possible solution.

This problem has shown up in a popular concert I saw recently. Ticket brokers have systems that allow them to buy big blocks of tickets in a short amount of time. Then they make their money reselling tickets. Brokers bought most of the tickets and sold them to people for about $360. When teenagers got their tickets in the mail, they saw the original cost on the ticket was $60! This is all illegal. It is unfair to teenagers who have a right to buy them at the original price. The performer of the concert has filed a lawsuit against these ticket brokers.

Several states have anti-scalping laws. In New York State, for example, it is legal to buy tickets and resell them for $5 more or 10% more than the original price. This would make a $60 ticket cost $65 or $66, not $360. Brokers often sell them to people for more than three times the original cost! What makes it even worse is that the government doesn't really enforce this law. I say that the government should start enforcing it. Police should investigate the Web sites that ticket brokers use, and even arrest the people the police catch.

As part of the unfair broker system, there are also people who work for the brokers and buy the tickets in line at the concert and resell them there. These are the people you might meet at the concert who try to sell you $1000 seats. This is illegal, and I think that we should have police at these affairs to try to scout out these so-called workers.

In addition to the online broker system, which is mostly illegal, there are also licensed brokers. Licensed brokers are allowed to resell at a higher rate because they can charge a large service fee. They do this because they are allowed, and no one is stopping them. I think that this is not right. No one should rob people of their money. The only people who should be allowed to buy tickets are those who stand in line or get tickets from official vendors themselves.

So, the next time that you try to get tickets to a concert and they're either all sold out or available for a really high price, you now know why. You might think that it's unfair, unlawful, and just not right. If the police and other government officials would act, it would allow the REAL fans to enjoy seeing their favorite stars.

Nicole introduces the problem in a clearly stated thesis.

In the body, she further explains the problem by providing detailed evidence.

Nicole gives possible solutions to different parts of the problem she discusses.

She ends with a strong conclusion that reminds her readers of the seriousness of the problem and the need for a solution.

Editing and Proofreading.

Focus on Spelling: Words With Suffixes Follow these spelling rules:

- If a one-syllable word ends in a vowel and a consonant, double the consonant before adding -*ed* or -*est*. (*hot* becomes *hottest*)

- If a word has more than one syllable and ends in one vowel followed by one consonant, and *if the accent is on the last syllable*, double the consonant before adding -*ed* or -*est*. (*patrol* becomes *patrolled*)

- If a word ends in a consonant followed by a silent *e*, drop the *e* before adding -*ing*. (*describe* becomes *describing*)

- If a word ends in *y*, change *y* to *i* before adding -*es* or -*ed*. (*ability* becomes *abilities*)

Spiral Review
Earlier in the unit, you learned about **infinitives and infinitive phrases** (p. 598) and **appositives and appositive phrases** (p. 618). Make sure you have used them correctly in your essay.

Publishing and Presenting

Prepare an advice column. Turn your essay into a question and answer, as if it appeared in an advice column. As a class, publish your columns under a collective name, such as *Ask Amanda* or *Dear Dan*.

Be a talk-show guest. With a partner, take on the role of a talk-show guest who has been asked to give advice about the problem addressed in your essay. Take turns being the host and the guest.

Reflecting on Your Writing

Writer's Journal Jot down your answer to this question:

How might you approach a problematic issue in the future?

Rubric for Self-Assessment

Find evidence in your writing to address each category. Then, use the rating scale to grade your work.

Criteria	Rating Scale
	not very / very
Focus: How clearly does your thesis state the problem?	1 2 3 4 5
Ideas: How thoroughly do you explain the problem in an introduction?	1 2 3 4 5
Support/Elaboration: How developed is your support for each solution, including facts and examples?	1 2 3 4 5
Style: How persuasive is your language in the conclusion?	1 2 3 4 5
Sentence Fluency: How well do you avoid choppy sentences, especially by using participles and participle phrases?	1 2 3 4 5
Conventions: How correct is your spelling of words that contain suffixes?	1 2 3 4 5

© Leveled Texts

Build your skills and improve your comprehension of poetry with texts of increasing complexity.

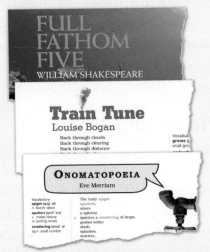

The poems in **Poetry Collection 5** explore responsibility, individuality, and the musicality of rain.

The poems in **Poetry Collection 6** present ideas of loss, rhythmic travel, and watery words.

© Common Core State Standards

Meet these standards with either **Poetry Collection 5** (p. 650) or **Poetry Collection 6** (p. 658).

Reading Literature

4. Determine the meaning of words and phrases as they are used in a text, including figurative and connotative meanings; analyze the impact of rhymes and other repetitions of sounds on a specific verse or stanza of a poem or section of a story or drama. *(Reading Skill: Paraphrase; Literary Analysis: Sound Devices; Writing: Paraphrase)*

Writing

9.a. Apply grade 7 Reading standards to literature. *(Writing: Paraphrase)*

Speaking and Listening

4. Use appropriate eye contact, adequate volume, and clear pronunciation. *(Speaking and Listening: Poetry Reading)*

6. Adapt speech to a variety of contexts and tasks, demonstrating command of formal English when

indicated or appropriate. *(Speaking and Listening: Poetry Reading)*

Language

1.a. Explain the function of phrases and clauses in general and their function in specific sentences.

1.b. Choose among simple, compound, complex, and compound-complex sentences to signal differing relationships among ideas. *(Conventions: Independent and Subordinate Clauses)*

4.c. Consult general and specialized reference materials, both print and digital, to find the pronunciation of a word or determine or clarify its precise meaning or its part of speech. *(Writing: Paraphrase)*

5.b. Use the relationship between particular words to better understand each of the words. *(Writing: Paraphrase)*

Reading Skill: Paraphrase

When you **paraphrase,** you restate something in your own words. To paraphrase a poem, you must first understand it. Just as when you read prose in paragraphs, you should look for a poem's main idea and the details that support it. **Reading aloud according to punctuation** can help you identify complete thoughts in a poem. Observe the following rules when you read poetry:

- Keep reading when a line has no end punctuation.
- Pause at commas, dashes, and semicolons.
- Stop at periods, question marks, or exclamation points.

As you read, note the punctuation to help you paraphrase.

Literary Analysis: Sound Devices

Sound devices use the sound of words to create musical effects that appeal to the ear. These sound devices are used in poetry:

- **Onomatopoeia** is the use of words with sounds that suggest their meanings.
- **Alliteration** is the repetition of sounds at the beginnings of words.
- **Repetition** is the repeated use of words, phrases, or rhythms.

Using the Strategy: Sound Device Chart

The chart below gives examples of each type of sound device. As you read, notice the author's use of these devices in poetry.

Examples	
Onomatopoeia	The *shooshing* of skis
Alliteration	*m*aggie and *m*illie and *m*olly and *m*ay Went down to the beach (to play one day)
Repetition	To the swinging and the ringing *Of the bells, bells, bells,* *Of the bells, bells, bells, bells*

What is the best way to *communicate?*

Writing About the Big Question

Each poem in Poetry Collection 5 has a musical quality that helps bring an idea to life. Use this sentence starter to develop your ideas about the Big Question.

Poets and song writers might use musical language in their work because it can **produce** _____ for readers.

While You Read Look for sounds that add to your enjoyment of the poem.

Vocabulary

Read each word and its definition. Decide whether you know the word well, know it a little bit, or do not know it at all. After you read, see how your knowledge of each word has increased.

- **withered** (wi*th*´ ərd) *adj.* dried up (p. 651) *Raisins are withered grapes.* wither *v.*

- **curdled** (kʉrd´ ʹld) *adj.* rotten (p. 651) *After a hot day, milk in the broken thermos was curdled.* curdle *v.* curdling *v.*

- **rancid** (ran´ sid) *adj.* spoiled and smelling bad (p. 651) *Frozen food turned rancid during the blackout.* rancidness *n.*

- **expectancy** (ek spek´ tən sē) *n.* a feeling that something is about to happen (p. 652) *She awoke with a sense of expectancy on her birthday.* expectant *adj.* expectantly *adv.* expect *v.* expectation *n.*

- **stutter** (stut´ ər) *v.* speak in a hesitant or faltering way (p. 652) *Some people stutter when they are nervous.* stuttering *v.* stutterer *n.* stuttered *v.*

- **slather** (sla*th*´ ər) *v.* spread on thickly (p. 654) *Sunscreen works best when you slather it on.* slathered *v.*

Word Study

The **Latin suffix -ancy** or **-ency** means "the state of being."

The narrator of "One" waits with **expectancy**, or in the state of expecting that something will happen.

Shel Silverstein

(1932–1999)

Author of "Sarah Cynthia Sylvia Stout Would Not Take the Garbage Out" (p. 650)

Shel Silverstein was a cartoonist, composer, folk singer, and writer. He began writing poetry at an early age, before he had a chance to study any of the great poets. "I was so lucky that I didn't have anyone to copy," he has said. Silverstein is best known for two books of poetry, *Where the Sidewalk Ends* and *A Light in the Attic*. His poem "The Unicorn Song" was recorded by the Irish Rovers.

James Berry

(b. 1925)

Author of "One" (p. 652)

James Berry grew up in Jamaica, in a small village by the sea. He learned to read before he was four years old and began writing stories and poems when he got to school. In 1948, Berry moved to England, and soon after that, he began writing seriously. His poems include both English and Creole, the language he spoke growing up in Jamaica.

Eve Merriam

(1916–1992)

Author of "Weather" (p. 654)

Eve Merriam was born and raised in Philadelphia, Pennsylvania. Although she also wrote fiction, nonfiction, and drama, Merriam had a lifelong love of poetry. "I do think poetry is great fun," she said. "That's what I'd like to stress more than anything else: the joy of the sounds of language."

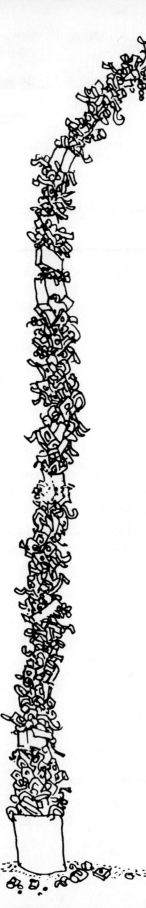

Sarah Cynthia Sylvia Stout Would Not Take the Garbage Out

Shel Silverstein

Sarah Cynthia Sylvia Stout
Would not take the garbage out!
She'd scour[1] the pots and scrape the pans,
Candy[2] the yams and spice the hams,
5 And though her daddy would scream and shout,
She simply would not take the garbage out.
And so it piled up to the ceilings:
Coffee grounds, potato peelings,
Brown bananas, rotten peas,
10 Chunks of sour cottage cheese.
It filled the can, it covered the floor,
It cracked the window and blocked the door
With bacon rinds[3] and chicken bones,
Drippy ends of ice cream cones,
15 Prune pits, peach pits, orange peel,
Gloppy glumps of cold oatmeal,
Pizza crusts and withered greens,
Soggy beans and tangerines,
Crusts of black burned buttered toast,

---

1. **scour** (skour) *v.* clean by rubbing vigorously.
2. **candy** (kan´dē) *v.* coat with sugar.
3. **rinds** (rīndz) *n.* tough outer layers or skins.

20 Gristly bits of beefy roasts . . .
   The garbage rolled on down the hall,
   It raised the roof, it broke the wall . . .
   Greasy napkins, cookie crumbs,
   Globs of gooey bubble gum,
25 Cellophane from green baloney,
   Rubbery blubbery macaroni,
   Peanut butter, caked and dry,
   Curdled milk and crusts of pie,
   Moldy melons, dried-up mustard,
30 Eggshells mixed with lemon custard,
   Cold french fries and rancid meat,
   Yellow lumps of Cream of Wheat.
   At last the garbage reached so high
   That finally it touched the sky.
35 And all the neighbors moved away,
   And none of her friends would come to play.
   And finally Sarah Cynthia Stout said,
   "OK, I'll take the garbage out!"
   But then, of course, it was too late . . .
40 The garbage reached across the state,
   From New York to the Golden Gate.
   And there, in the garbage she did hate,
   Poor Sarah met an awful fate,
   That I cannot right now relate[4]
45 Because the hour is much too late.
   But children, remember Sarah Stout
   And always take the garbage out!

---

4. **relate** (ri lāt´) *v.* tell.

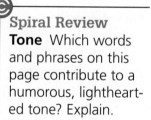

Vocabulary
withered (with´ ərd)
adj. dried up

Sound Devices
Which sound device
does the poet use in
line 24? Explain.

Vocabulary
curdled (kʉrd´
´ld) *adj.* rotten

rancid (ran´ sid)
adj. spoiled and
smelling bad

Ⓒ
Spiral Review
Tone Which words
and phrases on this
page contribute to a
humorous, lighthearted tone? Explain.

◀ **Critical Viewing**
The author drew
the cartoons that
accompany the poem.
How does the art
add to the poem's
humor? **[Assess]**

One
James Berry

Only one of me
and nobody can get a second one
from a photocopy machine.

Nobody has the fingerprints I have.
5 Nobody can cry my tears, or laugh my laugh
or have my expectancy when I wait.

But anybody can mimic my dance with my dog.
Anybody can howl how I sing out of tune.
And mirrors can show me multiplied
10 many times, say, dressed up in red
or dressed up in grey.

Nobody can get into my clothes for me
or feel my fall for me, or do my running.
Nobody hears my music for me, either.

15 I am just this one.
Nobody else makes the words
I shape with sound, when I talk.

But anybody can act how I stutter in a rage.
Anybody can copy echoes I make.
20 And mirrors can show me multiplied
many times, say, dressed up in green
or dressed up in blue.

Paraphrase
How does the punctuation help you understand the meaning of lines 9–11?

Vocabulary
expectancy (ek spek´ tən sē) *n.* a feeling that something is about to happen
stutter (stut´ ər) *v.* speak in a hesitant or faltering way

WEATHER

Eve Merriam

Dot a dot dot   dot a dot dot
Spotting the windowpane.
Spack a spack speck   flick a flack fleck
Freckling the windowpane.

5 A spatter a scatter   a wet cat a clatter
A splatter a rumble outside.
Umbrella umbrella umbrella umbrella
Bumbershoot barrel of rain.

Slosh a galosh   slosh a galosh
10 Slither and slather and glide
A puddle a jump a puddle a jump
A puddle a jump puddle splosh
A juddle a pump a luddle a dump a
Puddmuddle jump in and slide!

Vocabulary
slather (sla*th*´ ər) *v.*
spread on thickly

Sound Devices
Which sound devices does the poet use in the last stanza? Explain.

Critical Thinking

@ 1. **Key Ideas and Details (a) Infer:** What lesson might readers learn from "Sarah Cynthia . . ."? **(b) Analyze:** Do you think the poet intended to teach a lesson? Why or why not?

@ 2. **Key Ideas and Details** Identify three things that the speaker of "One" says are unique about him.

@ 3. **Craft and Structure (a)** Identify three made-up words in "Weather." **(b) Interpret:** What emotions or qualities do these words bring to the poem?

@ 4. **Craft and Structure** Which of these poems has the most musical quality? Give examples from the poem to support your answer.

@ 5. **Integration of Knowledge and Ideas** Why do you think these poets used musical sound devices to express their ideas? *[Connect to the Big Question: What is the best way to communicate?]*

Cite textual evidence to support your responses.

Reading Skill: Paraphrase

1. Write an example from each poem in which you read according to punctuation. **Paraphrase** each example.

Poem	Example From Poem	Paraphrase
Sarah Cynthia...		
Weather		
One		

Literary Analysis: Sound Devices

2. Craft and Structure (a) Find two examples of **alliteration** in "Sarah Cynthia . . ." **(b)** How does alliteration add to the humor of the poem?

3. Craft and Structure (a) Identify two examples of **repetition** in "One." **(b)** How does the repetition reinforce the poet's message?

4. Craft and Structure (a) List two examples of **onomatopoeia** in "Weather" that imitate the sound of water. **(b)** How do these words help convey the author's ideas?

Vocabulary

Acquisition and Use For each set of words, identify the word that does not belong and explain why.

1. shrunken   withered   swollen

2. rancid   fresh   stale

3. stutter   recite   swim

4. sweet   sour   curdled

5. slather   spread   uncover

6. expectancy   anticipation   boredom

Word Study Use what you know about the **Latin suffix -ancy** or **-ency** to explain your answer to each question.

1. Does an *emergency* require immediate attention?

2. Is the *relevancy* of an argument important to a judge?

Word Study

The **Latin suffix -ancy** or **-ency** means "the state of being."

Apply It Explain how the suffix -ancy or -ency contributes to the meanings of these words. Consult a dictionary if necessary.

militancy
hesitancy
consistency

What is the best way to *communicate?*

Writing About the Big Question

In Poetry Collection 6, each poet uses sound to create an image or a certain mood in the poem. Use these sentence starters to develop your ideas about the Big Question.

Sound can **entertain** us, but it can also express _____.
We can **"listen"** to words as we read by _____.

While You Read Look for the ways that the sounds of the words add to your experience of reading the poems.

Vocabulary

Read each word and its definition. Decide whether you know the word well, know it a little bit, or do not know it at all. After you read, see how your knowledge of each word has increased.

- **fathom** (fa*th*ʹ əm) *n.* unit of length used to measure the depth of water (p. 658) *We guessed that the depth of the bay was four <u>fathoms</u>.* fathom *v.*

- **groves** (grōvz) *n.* small groups of trees (p. 659) *The farmer planted apple <u>groves</u>.*

- **garlands** (gärʹ ləndz) *n.* wreaths of flowers and leaves (p. 659) *The holiday <u>garlands</u> looked real, but they were made of plastic.*

- **spigot** (spigʹ ət) *n.* faucet; spout (p. 660) *The water from the dripping <u>spigot</u> made an annoying tapping sound.*

- **sputters** (sputʹ ərz) *v.* makes hissing or spitting noises (p. 660) *On rainy days the engine <u>sputters</u>, then stops.* sputter *v.* sputtering *adj.*

- **smattering** (smatʹ ər iŋ) *n.* small number (p. 660) *The little boy had a <u>smattering</u> of freckles on his nose.* smatter *v.*

Word Study

The **Old English suffix** *-less* means "without."

In "Full Fathom Five," a king is believed to be lost in the **fathomless,** or bottomless, depths of the ocean.

William Shakespeare

(1564–1616)

Author of "Full Fathom Five" (p. 658)

Many people regard William Shakespeare as the greatest writer in the English language. He wrote thirty-seven plays, many of which are still performed frequently today. They include *Romeo and Juliet*, *Hamlet,* and other classics. "Full Fathom Five" comes from *The Tempest,* one of Shakespeare's last plays.

Louise Bogan

(1897–1970)

Author of "Train Tune" (p. 659)

Louise Bogan was born in Livermore Falls, Maine, and attended the Girls' Latin School in Boston, where she developed an interest in poetry. During her writing career, Bogan became known for her compact use of language and for the traditional form of her poems. Because she was a very private person, Bogan struggled with her celebrity as a highly respected poet, critic, and lecturer.

Eve Merriam

(1916–1992)

Author of "Onomatopoeia" (p. 660)

Eve Merriam's fascination with words began at an early age. "I remember being enthralled by the sound of words," she said. This love, which led her to write poetry, fiction, nonfiction, and drama, is reflected in the poem "Onomatopoeia."

FULL FATHOM FIVE

WILLIAM SHAKESPEARE

Background "Full Fathom Five" is from Shakespeare's *The Tempest*. In the play, a spirit named Ariel sings these lines to Prince Ferdinand, whose father, King Alonso, is thought lost in a shipwreck. Ariel describes the king's death, though later it is revealed that the king is still alive.

Vocabulary
fathom (fa*th*´ əm)
n. unit of length used to measure the depth of water

Paraphrase
After which lines do you come to a complete stop when reading?

Full fathom five thy father lies;
   Of his bones are coral made;
Those are pearls that were his eyes;
   Nothing of him that doth fade
5   But doth suffer a sea change
Into something rich and strange.
Sea nymphs hourly ring his knell;[1]
                Ding-dong.
Hark! Now I hear them—ding-dong bell.

---

1. **knell** (nel) *n.* funeral bell.

Train Tune
Louise Bogan

Back through clouds
Back through clearing
Back through distance
Back through silence

5 Back through groves
Back through garlands
Back by rivers
Back below mountains

Back through lightning
10 Back through cities
Back through stars
Back through hours

Back through plains
Back through flowers
15 Back through birds
Back through rain

Back through smoke
Back through noon
Back along love
20 Back through midnight

ONOMATOPOEIA

Eve Merriam

The rusty spigot
sputters,
utters
a splutter,
5   spatters a smattering of drops,
gashes wider;
slash,
splatters,
scatters,
10 spurts,
finally stops sputtering
and plash!
gushes rushes splashes
clear water dashes.

Critical Thinking

1. **Key Ideas and Details (a)** Name two changes that the speaker describes happening to the father in "Full Fathom Five." **(b) Interpret:** Why does the poet call these changes "rich and strange"?

2. **Craft and Structure (a)** Describe the length of the lines in the poem "Onomatopoeia." **(b) Analyze:** How do the line lengths contribute to the effect of the poem on the reader?

3. **Key Ideas and Details** Which of these poems has the most musical quality? Give examples from the poem to support your answer.

4. **Key Ideas and Details (a)** What emotion does the speaker mention in "Train Tune"? **(b) Speculate:** Why do you think the poet includes this detail? **(c) Discuss:** Share your responses with a partner. Then, discuss how talking about someone else's response did or did not change your answer.

5. **Integration of Knowledge and Ideas (a)** Which poem evokes the strongest response in you? Explain. **(b)** How do the sounds of the poem contribute to your response? *[Connect to the Big Question: What is the best way to communicate?]*

After You Read
Poetry Collection 6

Full Fathom Five •
Train Tune •
Onomatopoeia

Reading Skill: Paraphrase

1. In a chart like this one, write an example from each poem in which you read according to punctuation rather than stopping at the end of a line. Then, **paraphrase** each example.

Poem	Example From Poem	Paraphrase
Full Fathom Five		
Train Tune		
Onomatopoeia		

Literary Analysis: Sound Devices

2. Craft and Structure (a) What **sound device** is used in the title "Full Fathom Five"? **(b)** Find an example of another sound device in the poem.

3. Craft and Structure (a) Identify the **repetition** in "Train Tune." **(b)** What effect does this device have when you read the poem out loud?

4. Craft and Structure (a) Identify three words from "Onomatopoeia" that sound like falling water. **(b)** How do the sounds of the words help convey the author's meaning?

Vocabulary

Acquisition and Use For each set of words, identify the word that does not belong and explain why.

1. spigot   faucet   closet
2. sputters   creaks   opens
3. prairies   groves   orchards
4. fathom   depth   color
5. surplus   bit   smattering
6. garlands   wreaths   bushes

Word Study Use what you know about the **Old English suffix** **-less** to explain your answer to each question.

1. If a person is *friendless*, is he popular?
2. Would a *worthless* necklace be considered valuable?

Word Study

The **Old English suffix** **-less** means "without."

Apply It Explain how the suffix *-less* contributes to the meanings of these words. Consult a dictionary if necessary.

fearless
ceaseless
meaningless

Integrated Language Skills

Poetry Collections 5 and 6

Conventions: Independent and Subordinate Clauses

Poetry Collection 5

A **clause** is a group of words with its own subject and verb. The two major types of clauses are *independent clauses* and *subordinate clauses*.

An **independent clause** has a subject and a verb and can stand by itself as a complete sentence. A **subordinate clause** has a subject and a verb but is only part of a sentence. It begins with a subordinating conjunction such as *although, but, because, since, when,* and *if.*

Poetry Collection 6

Comparing Two Kinds of Clauses	
Independent	**Subordinate**
S V He arrived this morning.	S V *if* he arrived this morning
S V The mosque has a golden dome.	S V *since* the mosque has a dome

Practice A Identify the independent and subordinate clauses in each sentence.

1. Miss Stout's house was a mess because she would not take out the garbage.

2. If old food is not thrown away, it begins to smell.

3. When raindrops fall, it sounds like music.

4. Every person is unique, since no two people are exactly like.

© **Reading Application** In Collection 5, find one sentence with an independent clause and one sentence with a subordinate clause. Explain the role of these clauses in the sentences.

Practice B Identify the subordinate clause in each sentence. Then, use the subordinate clause to write a new sentence.

1. Although the king had not died, Ariel sang of his death.

2. If a spigot becomes rusty, it can be difficult to turn.

3. When you ride trains, you see scenery.

4. The chugging of a train can lull you to sleep if you allow it to.

© **Writing Application** Write two sentences about what poetry means to you. Use two subordinate clauses.

PH WRITING COACH Further instruction and practice are available in *Prentice Hall Writing Coach.*

Writing

Informative Text Write a **paraphrase** of one of the poems you read in either Poetry Collection 5 or 6.

- Read over each stanza of the original poem to identify the poet's main idea.
- Use a dictionary to define words you do not know. Replace these words with familiar synonyms, or words that have the same meaning.
- Restate the entire poem in your own words.
- Reread your paraphrase, making sure it has the same meaning as the original. Make revisions as necessary.

Grammar Application Check your writing to make sure you have correctly used main and subordinate clauses.

Writing Workshop: *Work in Progress*

Prewriting for Persuasion For a persuasive essay you might write, list three issues that affect you, your school, or your community. Next to each item, jot down why you would like this issue addressed. Put this Issues List in your writing folder.

Speaking and Listening

Presentation of Ideas Present a **poetry reading** of one of the poems from Poetry Collection 5 or 6. Follow these tips as you prepare your reading:

- Rehearse your readings alone and with a small group.
- Be sure you are pronouncing each word correctly, and read according to the punctuation.
- Practice reading slowly and with expression in your voice. You may decide to emphasize certain words or ideas by raising or lowering the volume of your voice. Do not read with a sing-song tone. Be sure that your reading sounds natural.
- Speak clearly, and prepare to make eye contract periodically with your audience.
- Ask your classmates for feedback on your reading and make changes based on their suggestions.

After you have finished rehearsing, hold a reading for the class.

Common Core State Standards

L.7.1.a, L.7.1.b, L.7.4.c, L.7.5.b; W.7.9.a; SL.7.4, SL.7.6
[For the full wording of the standards, see page 646.]

Use this prewriting activity to prepare for the **Writing Workshop** on page 698.

www.PHLitOnline.com
- Interactive graphic organizers
- Grammar tutorial
- Interactive journals

© Leveled Texts

Build your skills and improve your comprehension of poetry with
texts of increasing complexity.

The poems in **Poetry Collection 7**
honor people important to
the speaker, or focus on the
speaker's own identity.

The poems in **Poetry Collection 8**
celebrate memorable characters
or experiences.

© Common Core State Standards

Meet these standards with either **Poetry Collection 7** (p. 668) or **Poetry Collection 8** (p. 676).

Reading Literature
4. Determine the meaning of words and phrases as they are
used in a text, including figurative and connotative meanings;
analyze the impact of rhymes and other repetitions of
sounds on a specific verse or stanza of a poem or section of
a story or drama. *(Literary Analysis: Sound Devices)*

Writing
6. Use technology, including the Internet, to produce and
publish writing and link to and cite sources as well as to
interact and collaborate with others, including linking to
and citing sources. *(Writing: Poem)*

7. Conduct short research projects to answer a question,
drawing on several sources and generating additional
related, focused questions for further research and
investigation. *(Research and Technology: Survey)*

Speaking and Listening
1.c. Pose questions that elicit elaboration and respond to
others' questions and comments with relevant

observations and ideas that bring the discussion back on
topic as needed. *(Research and Technology: Survey)*

Language
1.b. Choose among simple, compound, complex, and
compound-complex sentences to signal differing relationships
among ideas. *(Conventions: Sentence Structures)*

5.b. Use the relationship between particular words to better
understand each of the words. *(Vocabulary: Analogy)*

6. Acquire and use accurately grade-appropriate general
academic and domain-specific words and phrases; gather
vocabulary knowledge when considering a word or phrase
important to comprehension or expression. *(Vocabulary:
Word Study)*

Reading Skill: Paraphrase

To **paraphrase** means to restate something in your own words to make the meaning clear to yourself. If you are unsure of a poem's meaning, **reread** it to clarify its meaning.

- First, look up definitions of unfamiliar words in the original passage and replace them with words you know.
- Identify the author's main ideas. **Restate** the passage using your own, everyday words.
- Reread the passage to make sure your version makes sense.

Using the Strategy: Paraphrasing Chart

Use a chart like the one below to help you paraphrase as you read.

Original	Unfamiliar Words	Dictionary Definitions of Unfamiliar Words	Paraphrase
Half in dreams, he saw his sire. With his great hands full of fire.	sire	sire = father	Only half awake, he saw his father. His big hands were glowing with light.

Literary Analysis: Sound Devices

Rhythm and rhyme are two techniques poets use to give poems a musical effect. **Rhythm** is a poem's pattern of stressed (´) and unstressed (˘) syllables. **Rhyme** is the repetition of sounds at the ends of words. A poem's rhythmical pattern is called **meter.** Meter is measured in feet, or units of stressed and unstressed syllables. A **rhyme scheme** is a pattern of rhymes. In this example, the words *sire* and *fire* create a rhyme. Each metrical foot is set off by slashes.

> Hálf / ĭn dreáms / hĕ sáw / hĭs síre /
>
> Wíth / hĭs greát / hănds fúll / ŏf fíre.

What is the best way to *communicate?*

Writing About the Big Question

In Poetry Collection 7, the poets convey feelings about people who are important to them. Use these sentence starters to develop your ideas about the Big Question.

Using words to **express** our feelings about others can help us reveal _____.

People sometimes **react** emotionally to words because _____.

While You Read Consider how each poet communicates ideas and emotions.

Vocabulary

Read each word and its definition. Decide whether you know the word well, know it a little bit, or do not know it at all. After you read, see how your knowledge of each word has increased.

- **coveted** (kuv´ it əd) *v.* wanted; desired (p. 668) *The hockey team coveted the trophy.* covetous *adj.* covetously *adv.* covetousness *n.*

- **kinsmen** (kinz´ mən) *n.* male relatives (p. 668) *My kinsmen were all farmers.* kin *n.* kinfolk *n.* kinswomen *n.*

- **envying** (en´ vē iŋ) *v.* wanting something that someone else has (p. 669) *I cannot help envying Karina's beautiful singing voice.* envy *n.* envious *adj.*

- **passion** (pash´ ən) *n.* strong feelings of love or hate (p. 670) *Bob's passion for cooking inspires him to try a new recipe every week.* passionate *adj.* passionately *adv.*

- **profound** (prō fo͝und´) *adj.* deeply or intensely felt (p. 670) *You have my profound sympathy for your loss.* profoundly *adv.* profundity *n.*

- **banish** (ban´ ish) *v.* send away (p. 672) *The king will banish the troublemaker to a distant village.* banishment *n.*

Word Study

The **Latin prefix im-** means "in," "into," or "toward."

"Martin Luther King" portrays King as an **impassioned** man because he conveyed the strong feelings within himself to others.

Edgar Allan Poe

(1809–1849)

Author of "Annabel Lee" (pp. 668–669)

Edgar Allan Poe won great literary success but suffered much personal loss in his life. His mother died when he was just two years old. He finished "Annabel Lee" about a year after the death of his beloved wife, Virginia. One Poe expert believes that the title character of this poem represents all the women Poe loved and lost in his life.

Raymond Richard Patterson

(1929–2001)

Author of "Martin Luther King" (p. 670)

Raymond Patterson's poetry appears in many anthologies. A native New Yorker, Patterson taught for many years at New York City College. His passion for sharing his knowledge of African American history was reflected in his newspaper column, "From Our Past," and in poems such as "Martin Luther King."

Emily Dickinson

(1830–1886)

Author of "I'm Nobody" (p. 672)

Emily Dickinson was born in Amherst, Massachusetts. In college, she grew so homesick that she returned home after just one year. After that, she rarely left her house. Quietly, however, she was writing the 1,775 poems that would make her famous after her death. In these brief works, she created a poetic self that flashes with humor and intelligence.

Annabel Lee

Edgar Allan Poe

Rhythm and Rhyme
Which syllables are stressed in the first two lines?

It was many and many a year ago,
    In a kingdom by the sea.
That a maiden there lived whom you may know
    By the name of Annabel Lee;—
And this maiden she lived with no other thought
    Than to love and be loved by me.

She was a child and I was a child,
    In this kingdom by the sea.
5   But we loved with a love that was more than love—
    I and my Annabel Lee—
With a love that wingèd seraphs[1] of Heaven
    Coveted her and me.

And this was the reason that, long ago,
    In this kingdom by the sea,
A wind blew out of a cloud by night
    Chilling my Annabel Lee;
So that her highborn kinsmen came
    And bore her away from me,
10   To shut her up in a sepulcher[2]
    In this kingdom by the sea.

Vocabulary
coveted (kuv´ it əd)
v. wanted; desired

kinsmen (kinz´ mən)
n. male relatives

---

1. **wingèd seraphs** (ser´ efs) *n.* angels.
2. **sepulcher** (sep´ əl kər) *n.* vault or chamber for burial; tomb.

The angels, not half so happy in Heaven,
    Went envying her and me:—
Yes! that was the reason (as all men know,
    In this kingdom by the sea)
That the wind came out of a cloud, chilling
    And killing my Annabel Lee.

But our love it was stronger by far than the love
    Of those who were older than we—
    Of many far wiser than we—
15 And neither the angels in Heaven above
    Nor the demons down under the sea,
Can ever dissever³ my soul from the soul
    Of the beautiful Annabel Lee:—

For the moon never beams without bringing
    me dreams
Of the beautiful Annabel Lee;
And the stars never rise but I see the bright eyes
    Of the beautiful Annabel Lee;
20 And so, all the nighttide, I lie down by the side
Of my darling, my darling, my life and my bride,
    In her sepulcher there by the sea—
    In her tomb by the side of the sea.

---

3. **dissever** (di sev ´ ər) v. separate; divide.

▲ **Critical Viewing**
Compare the emotions
this photograph conveys
with those the speaker
feels upon looking at
the sea. **[Connect]**

Paraphrase
How would you para-
phrase lines 15–18?

Vocabulary
envying (en´ vē iŋ) v.
wanting something
that someone else has

Martin Luther King

Raymond Patterson

Background Martin Luther King, Jr. (1929–1968) was a great civil rights leader. He used nonviolent methods to help end legal discrimination against African Americans in the United States. Tragically, in 1968, while fighting for justice and equality, he was assassinated at the age of thirty-nine.

Vocabulary

passion (pash´ ən)
n. strong feelings of love or hate

profound (prō foʊnd´)
adj. deeply or intensely felt

▶ **Critical Viewing**
What characteristics of Martin Luther King, Jr., does this photograph show? **[Infer]**

He came upon an age
Beset[1] by grief, by rage—

His love so deep, so wide,
He could not turn aside.

5 His passion, so profound,
He would not turn around.

He taught a suffering earth
The measure of man's worth.

For this he was slain,
10 But he will come again.

---

1. Beset (bē set´) *adj.* attacked from all sides; harassed.

Spiral Review
Connotation
What is the connotation of the word *nobody* in this poem?

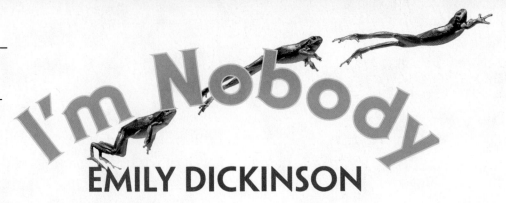

I'm Nobody

EMILY DICKINSON

Vocabulary
banish (ban′ ish)
adj. send away

I'm Nobody! Who are you?
Are you—Nobody—too?
Then there's a pair of us!
Don't tell! they'd banish us—you know!

5   How dreary—to be—Somebody!
How public—like a Frog—
To tell your name—the livelong June—
To an admiring Bog!

Critical Thinking

Cite textual evidence to support your responses.

1. **Key Ideas and Details (a)** In "Annabel Lee," how does the speaker react to Annabel Lee's death? **(b) Infer:** What will prevent the separation of the speaker's soul from Annabel Lee's soul?

2. **Key Ideas and Details (a) Interpret:** In "Martin Luther King," what does the poet mean by King's "passion, so profound"? **(b) Synthesize:** Using ideas from the poem, name two qualities that are important in a leader. Explain your answer.

3. **Integration of Knowledge and Ideas (a)** In "I'm Nobody," what does the speaker say will happen if it is revealed that she is "Nobody"? **(b) Infer:** How does the speaker feel about this consequence? **(c) Apply:** In what way does the poem suggest some of the difficulties celebrities face today?

4. **Integration of Knowledge and Ideas** Which of these poems do you think expresses the most emotion toward its subject? Explain. *[Connect to the Big Question: What is the best way to communicate?]*

Reading Skill: Paraphrase

1. Reread the following lines, and then **paraphrase** them.
   (a) "Annabel Lee": lines 9–10
   (b) "Martin Luther King": lines 1–2
   (c) "I'm Nobody": lines 5–8
2. Identify two words in these poems that you might look up in a dictionary to help you paraphrase meaning.

Literary Analysis: Sound Devices

© **3. Craft and Structure** Do these poems have **rhythmic patterns**? Explain.

© **4. Craft and Structure** Use a chart like this to analyze each poem's **rhyming patterns**.

Poem	Rhyming Words
Annabel Lee	
Martin Luther King	
I'm Nobody	

Vocabulary

© **Acquisition and Use** An **analogy** shows a relationship between a pair of words. Use a word from the list on page 666 to complete each analogy. Your choice should make a word pair whose relationship matches that of the first two words.

1. enter : exit :: _____ : welcome
2. ate : consumed :: _____ : wanted
3. excellent : great :: _____ : intense
4. cat : feline :: _____ : relative
5. enjoying : smiling :: _____ : glaring
6. disinterest : indifference :: _____ : enthusiasm

Word Study Use the context of the sentences and what you know about the **Latin prefix im-** to explain your answer.

1. Is a U.S. *immigrant* someone who came to this country?
2. If someone is *imprisoned*, is that person free?

Word Study

The **Latin prefix im-** means "in," "into," or "toward."

Apply It Explain how the **prefix im-** contributes to the meanings of these words. Consult a dictionary if necessary.

imbue
implode
imperil

What is the best way to *communicate?*

Writing About the Big Question

The poems in Poetry Collection 8 show different ways—some serious, some humorous—that poets communicate ideas about a memorable character or experience. Use this sentence starter to develop your ideas about the Big Question.

Messages that **entertain** us can also **teach** us _____.

While You Read Consider what lessons each poem may have to teach readers.

Vocabulary

Read each word and its definition. Decide whether you know the word well, know it a little bit, or do not know it at all. After you read, see how your knowledge of each word has increased.

- **incessantly** (in ses´ ənt lē) *adv.* without stopping (p. 677) *He annoyed his friends by talking incessantly during the movie.* incessant *adj.* cease *v.*

- **uncommonly** (un käm´ ən lē) *adv.* remarkably (p. 677) *She was an uncommonly talented singer.* uncommon *adj.* common *adj.*

- **sage** (sāj) *n.* very wise person (p. 677) *The sage wisely advised daily exercise and the company of friends.* sagest *adj.* sagacity *n.*

- **supple** (sup´ əl) *adj.* able to bend easily; flexible (p. 677) *Rubber is a supple material.* suppler *adj.* supplest *adj.*

- **harness** (här´ nis) *n.* equipment used to drive a horse or to attach it to a vehicle (p. 679) *He bravely grabbed the harness of the runaway horse.* harness *v.*

- **downy** (dou´ nē) *adj.* soft and fluffy (p. 679) *The fur on the rabbit was downy.* down *n.* downiest *adj.*

Word Study

The **Old English prefix** **un-** means "not."

In "Father William," a man is described as **uncommonly** large because it is not common for a person to be so big.

Lewis Carroll

(1832–1898)

Author of "Father William" (p. 676)

Lewis Carroll is the pen name of Charles Dodgson, a mathematics professor who was born in England. Under his pen name, Dodgson wrote *Alice's Adventures in Wonderland* and *Through the Looking Glass*. Like these classic novels, his poems are noted for their clever wordplay, nonsensical meanings, and delightfully zany worlds.

Robert Frost

(1874–1963)

Author of "Stopping by Woods on a Snowy Evening" (p. 678)

Robert Frost was born in San Francisco but moved across the country to New England when he was eleven. This region of the country proved to be inspirational for him as a writer. Frost's most popular poems describe New England country life and landscapes. Of these poems, "Stopping by Woods on a Snowy Evening" is considered one of his best. Frost won the Pulitzer Prize four times—more than any other poet.

Gwendolyn Brooks

(1917–2000)

Author of "Jim" (p. 680)

Gwendolyn Brooks began writing at the age of seven and published her first poem, "Eventide," at age thirteen. As an adult, Brooks wrote hundreds of poems, many of which focus on the African American experience. In 1950, she became the first African American to win a Pulitzer Prize.

Father William

Lewis Carroll

Background This poem, which comes from *Alice's Adventures in Wonderland*, is an amusing conversation between a father and son. Lewis Carroll wrote it as a humorous spoof on a serious poem by Robert Southey. In this version, Carroll pokes fun at the false ideas society often has about the way older people speak and behave.

"You are old, Father William," the young man said,
  "And your hair has become very white;
And yet you incessantly stand on your head—
  Do you think, at your age, it is right?"

5   "In my youth," Father William replied to his son,
  "I feared it might injure the brain;
But, now that I'm perfectly sure I have none,
  Why, I do it again and again."
"You are old," said the youth, "as I mentioned before.
10   And have grown most uncommonly fat;
Yet you turned a back-somersault in at the door—
  Pray, what is the reason of that?"

"In my youth," said the sage, as he shook his gray locks,
  "I kept all my limbs very supple
15 By the use of this ointment—one shilling[1] the box—
  Allow me to sell you a couple?"

"You are old," said the youth, "and your jaws are too weak
  For anything tougher than suet;[2]
Yet you finished the goose, with the bones and the beak—
20   Pray, how did you manage to do it?"
"In my youth," said his father, "I took to the law,
  And argued each case with my wife;
And the muscular strength, which it gave to my jaw
  Has lasted the rest of my life."

25 "You are old," said the youth, "one would hardly suppose
  That your eye was as steady as ever;
Yet you balanced an eel on the end of your nose—
  What made you so awfully clever?"

"I have answered three questions, and that is enough,"
30   Said his father. "Don't give yourself airs!
Do you think I can listen all day to such stuff?
  Be off, or I'll kick you downstairs!"

---

1. **shilling** (shil´iŋ) *n.* British coin.
2. **suet** (sōō´it) *n.* fat used in cooking.

Vocabulary
incessantly (in ses´ ənt lē) *adv.* without stopping
uncommonly (un käm´ ən lē) *adv.* remarkably
sage (sāj) *n.* very wise person
supple (sup´ əl) *adj.* able to bend easily; flexible

Spiral Review
Connotation What idea does the poet convey by using the word *sage*?

Paraphrase
How would you paraphrase "Don't give yourself airs!"?

Stopping by Woods on a Snowy Evening

ROBERT FROST

Background A poem may contain several levels of meaning. In "Stopping by Woods on a Snowy Evening," the speaker is a traveler passing through the winter countryside. On one level, his journey may be regarded simply as a trip through the woods. As you read the poem, however, look for a deeper meaning that relates to a journey through life.

Whose woods these are I think I know.
His house is in the village, though;
He will not see me stopping here
To watch his woods fill up with snow.

5 My little horse must think it queer
To stop without a farmhouse near
Between the woods and frozen lake
The darkest evening of the year.

He gives his harness bells a shake
10 To ask if there is some mistake.
The only other sound's the sweep
Of easy wind and downy flake.

The woods are lovely, dark, and deep,
But I have promises to keep,
15 And miles to go before I sleep,
And miles to go before I sleep.

Rhythm and Rhyme
In lines 1–8, which lines end with rhyming words?

Vocabulary
harness (här´ nis) *n.* equipment used to drive a horse or attach it to a vehicle

downy (dou´ nē) *adj.* soft and fluffy

Jim
Gwendolyn Brooks

There never was a nicer boy
Than Mrs. Jackson's Jim.
The sun should drop its greatest gold
On him.

5 Because, when Mother-dear was sick,
He brought her cocoa in.
And brought her broth, and brought her bread.
And brought her medicine.

And, tipping,[1] tidied up her room.
10 And would not let her see
He missed his game of baseball
Terribly.

Rhythm and Rhyme
Which syllables are stressed in lines 5–6?

---

1. **tipping** (tip´ in) *v.* tiptoeing.

Critical Thinking

Cite textual evidence to support your responses.

1. **Key Ideas and Details (a)** In "Father William," what details from the poem describe Father William's appearance? **(b) Analyze:** How does his appearance make his actions seem especially surprising?

2. **Key Ideas and Details (a)** In "Stopping by Woods on a Snowy Evening," why has the speaker stopped? **(b) Infer:** What about the place captures his attention?

3. **Craft and Structure (a)** What words in Frost's poem describe sights and sounds? **(b) Apply:** What is the mood, or feeling, of the poem?

4. **Key Ideas and Details (a)** In "Jim," what tasks does the boy perform for his mother? **(b) Infer:** What detail tells you that Jim is not selfish?

5. **Integration of Knowledge and Ideas** Why do you think the author of "Stopping by Woods on a Snowy Evening" uses a snowy night to communicate the idea of the journey through life? Explain. *[Connect to the Big Question: What is the best way to communicate?]*

Reading Skill: Paraphrase

1. Reread the following lines, and then **paraphrase** them.

   (a) lines 13–16 of "Father William"

   (b) lines 11–12 of "Stopping by Woods on a Snowy Evening"

   (c) lines 3–4 of "Jim"

2. Identify two words in these poems that you might look up in a dictionary to help you paraphrase meaning.

Literary Analysis: Sound Devices

ⓒ **3. Craft and Structure (a)** Do the poems have **rhythmic patterns**? Explain. **(b)** Which poem has the most interesting rhythm? Explain.

ⓒ **4. Craft and Structure** Use a chart like this to analyze **rhyme.**

Poem	Rhyming Words
Father William	
Stopping by Woods…	
Jim	

Vocabulary

ⓒ **Acquisition and Use** Answer each question by writing a complete sentence that includes the italicized vocabulary word.

1. If a car alarm wails *incessantly*, is it annoying?

2. What qualities does a person need to be considered a *sage*?

3. How can exercise help give you a *supple* body?

4. Why are you likely to remember an *uncommonly* good meal?

5. Is burlap considered a *downy* material?

6. Why would a parachutist need a *harness*?

Word Study Use the context of the sentences and what you know about the **Old English prefix un-** to explain your answer.

1. Are people persuaded by *unconvincing* arguments?

2. If you are *unfit* for service, are you likely to do a good job?

Word Study

The **Old English prefix un-** means "not."

Apply It Explain how the prefix *un-* contributes to the meanings of these words. Consult a dictionary if necessary.

unpredictable
unintended
uninformed

Integrated Language Skills

Poetry Collections 7 and 8

Poetry Collection 7

Conventions: Sentence Structures

A **simple sentence** is one *independent clause*—a group of words that has a subject and a verb and can stand by itself as a complete thought. A **compound sentence** consists of two or more independent clauses linked by a word such as *and*, *but*, or *or*. A **complex sentence** contains one independent clause and one or more subordinate clauses—a group of words that has a subject and verb but is not a complete thought. A **compound-complex sentence** consists of two or more independent clauses and one or more subordinate clauses.

Poetry Collection 8

Simple sentence:	We planned a picnic.
Compound sentence:	We planned a picnic, but it rained. ind. clause ind. clause
Complex sentence:	Because it rained, we are indoors. subord. clause ind. clause
Compound-complex sentence:	Because it rained, we are indoors, but it is still a fun time. subord. clause ind. clause ind. clause

Practice A Identify each sentence as simple, compound, or complex.

  1. The speaker loved Annabel Lee.

  2. He still loves Annabel Lee, even though she has died.

  3. Dr. King spread his powerful message far and wide.

  4. Many people think they are important, but they are not.

© **Reading Application** In Poetry Collection 7, find one simple sentence and one complex sentence.

Practice B Write a sentence for each numbered item. Then, identify its structure.

  1. Tell why a poet would use humor.

  2. Describe why a poet would use rhythm and rhyme.

  3. Explain why a poet would choose to express himself or herself through poetry.

  4. Describe a scene from one of the poems you have read.

© **Writing Application** Write a paragraph about the qualities of a good leader. Use all four types of sentence structure.

PH | **WRITING COACH** | Further instruction and practice are available in *Prentice Hall Writing Coach*.

Writing

Poetry Write a **poem** about a person you know.

- Choose someone to whom you would like to pay tribute or who evokes a strong emotion in you.

- Take notes to describe the person and include details that convey your feelings about him or her.

- Draft your lines. Then, after you have expressed your ideas and feelings, use *rhythm* to add a musical quality to your poem.

- Type your poem on a computer using a word-processing or publishing program. Use text editing features such as the thesaurus and spell-check as you revise and edit your poem. Post your poem on the classroom Web site.

Grammar Application Check your writing to be sure your sentence structures are effective.

Writing Workshop: *Work in Progress*

Prewriting for Persuasion Choose one of the items on the Issues List in your writing portfolio. Divide your paper in half lengthwise. List three points that support your view in the left column and three arguments against your view in the right. Put this Support Chart in your writing portfolio.

Research and Technology

Build and Present Knowledge Conduct a **survey,** asking class-mates to rate the poems from Poetry Collection 7 or 8 according to specific categories, such as best character description, best use of language, or best rhythm, rhyme, and meter.

- Formulate the survey questions. Evaluate your questions to be sure they are clear and answerable.

- Count the number of votes that each poem receives for each category. Then, note which poems received the most votes in each category.

- With a small group, discuss the survey results. As a group, generate questions to evaluate whether the survey was or was not effective and why.

Common Core State Standards

L.7.1.b; W.7.6, W.7.7; SL.7.1.c
[For the full wording of the standards, see page 664.]

Use this prewriting activity to prepare for the **Writing Workshop** on page 698.

PHLit Online!
www.PHLitOnline.com

- Interactive graphic organizers
- Grammar tutorial
- Interactive journals

Test Practice: Reading

Paraphrase

Poetry Selection

Directions: *Read the selection. Then, answer the questions.*

I have a little shadow that goes in and out with me,
And what can be the use of him is more than I can see.
He is very, very like me from the heels up to the head;
And I see him jump before me, when I jump into my bed.
            — *from* "My Shadow" by Robert Louis Stevenson

1. Which is the *best* paraphrase of
line 1?
 A. It is hard to watch my shadow.
 B. I have a shadow, and it is very small.
 C. My shadow goes everywhere I go.
 D. My shadow is always going some-
 where.

2. Which is the *best* paraphrase of
line 2?
 A. The more I see my shadow, the more
 useful he becomes.
 B. My shadow has more uses than I ever
 knew.
 C. I have no idea what my shadow is
 good for.
 D. My shadow is useful only when I can
 see him.

3. Which is the *best* paraphrase of
line 3?
 A. My shadow likes the way I look.
 B. My shadow and I look very much alike.
 C. My shadow is like me only in certain
 ways.
 D. My shadow has heels and a head.

4. To paraphrase a poem, you might do all
of the following *except*—
 A. look up unfamiliar words in a
 dictionary.
 B. reread parts that are difficult.
 C. ignore the punctuation.
 D. replace words you don't know with
 words you know.

5. After which line would you come to a
complete stop?
 A. after lines 1 and 4
 B. after lines 2 and 4
 C. after lines 3 and 4
 D. after lines 2 and 3

Writing for Assessment

Rewrite "My Shadow" in your own
words. Limit your paraphrase to just two
sentences, but be sure to include the
poem's main idea. Use the punctuation
to help you.

Nonfiction Selection

Directions: *Read the selection. Then, answer the questions.*

Robert Louis Stevenson may be best known for writing novels such as *Treasure Island* and *The Strange Case of Dr. Jekyll and Mr. Hyde*, but these represent only one aspect of his writing talent. Many people do not realize that Stevenson was an accomplished writer in other genres as well. Stevenson traveled extensively during his life and often described his journeys in books and essays. He also wrote a book of poetry called *A Child's Garden* in which he tried to capture memories of his childhood. In addition to these published works, Stevenson sent <u>numerous</u> letters throughout his life. In 1899, after Stevenson's death, a collection of some of these letters was published and sold. Anyone who has enjoyed page after page of Stevenson's novels may want to get a taste of his other writing as well.

1. What is the *best* way to paraphrase the first sentence of this passage?
  A. Stevenson is known for writing novels but he had other writing talents too.
  B. Adventure novels are fun to read.
  C. Stevenson wrote in a variety of genres.
  D. Authors can use their talents to write a wide variety of works.

2. Which word could replace the underlined word *numerous* without changing the meaning of the sentence?
  A. few
  B. numbered
  C. wordy
  D. many

3. What is the *best* way to restate the phrase "traveled extensively" for an audience of small children?
  A. vacationed in Europe
  B. visited many places
  C. went out
  D. saw many things

4. What is the *best* way to paraphrase the last line of this passage?
  A. Stevenson's novels as well as his other writings are enjoyable.
  B. If you enjoy reading large books, you'll enjoy reading more Stevenson.
  C. People who like Stevenson's novels may want to read his other work, too.
  D. Read Stevenson's adventure novels if you want a good story.

Writing for Assessment

Connecting Across Texts
Think about the process of paraphrasing a poem versus paraphrasing a piece of nonfiction. In a paragraph, describe things a reader must consider when paraphrasing in these two genres. Use your own experience to support your ideas.

www.PHLitOnline.com
• Online practice
• Instant feedback

Reading for Information

Analyzing Expository Texts

Magazine Article

Educational Song

Common Core State Standards

Reading Informational Text
5. Analyze the structure an author uses to organize a text, including how the major sections contribute to the whole and to the development of the ideas.

Language
6. Acquire and use accurately grade-appropriate general academic and domain-specific words and phrases; gather vocabulary knowledge when considering a word or phrase important to comprehension or expression.

Reading Skill: Determine the Main Idea

The **main idea** is the central point or message conveyed in a passage or text. **Details** are the facts and examples that develop, or support, the main idea. One way to determine the main idea of a passage or text is through **paraphrasing,** or restating in your own words. When you paraphrase sentences or paragraphs, you retell all the details, but replace, combine, or rearrange words in a way that shows your understanding. Paraphrasing passages can help you to understand how they develop main ideas.

As you read, identify words that can be replaced or combined. Use a chart like the one shown to help you paraphrase.

Sentence or Passage	Replacement Words	Paraphrase
Rap is about words, but rhythm makes them more powerful.	rhythm = beat more powerful = stronger but = although	Although words are the point of rap, its beat makes it stronger.

Content-Area Vocabulary

These words appear in the selections that follow. You may also encounter them in other content-area texts.

- **composition** (käm´ pə zish´ ən) *n.* work of music, art, or literature
- **innovative** (in´ə vā´ tiv) *adj.* original; using new ideas or methods
- **junction** (juŋk´ shən) *n.* point where two or more things are joined

Features:

- content intended for informational or leisure reading
- illustrations or photographs that accompany the text
- text that may be written for a general or specific audience

The Rhythms of Rap

Kathiann M. Kowalski

Rap is about society; some songs get notoriety. But do your feet tap, when you hear rap?

Lots of rap tracks make you move along with them. Rap is about words, but rhythm makes them more powerful.

"Rhythm is the feeling of movement in time," explains Miami University (OH) music professor Chris Tanner. "Rhythm is the term we use in music for dividing time. Music can't exist without rhythm." In other words, one sound with no break is just noise. Play a sequence of notes for a certain time each, and you get music.

As music moves forward in time, your brain notes the duration of individual sounds and groups them together into bunches that let you perceive rhythm in the music. It could be the hammering lyrics of a rap artist. Or, it could be the beginning of Beethoven's *Fifth Symphony*: "Bum, bum, bum, bummm. Bum, bum, bum, bummm."

Saying Their Songs

Rap as a popular music style started in the late 1970s.

But, notes music professor Adam Krims at the University of Alberta, "In some form or another, this kind of music has been around for about 250 years. It continues very old practices of rhyming and rhythm among African Americans."

The author provides historical details to support her main ideas.

Rap's style of rhythmic delivery sets it apart from talking or other styles of *declamatory* (words recited with music) delivery. "In rap, you're not just talking," notes Krims, "You're really foregrounding [bringing up front] the rhythmic aspects of what you're doing."

It's somewhat like the difference between reading a textbook and reading Dr. Seuss's *Green Eggs and Ham* aloud. However, stresses Krims, "Rap actually takes a lot of practice to do even slightly well." Effective rhythmic phrasing really draws listeners into the lyrics of an MC ("MC" is the same as "emcee" and stands for "master of ceremonies"—a name rap artists commonly use).

Often an MC works with words' natural

Odyssey Magazine   March, 2002

emphasis. Other times, the artist may deform words. "You purposely deliver them in a way that's a little perverse," explains Krims. So instead of "California," an MC might say "Californ-eye-ay."

In the Background

Sampling serves up yet more rhythms in rap. "Sampling is taking a little bit of music from another source," says Krims. Sampling may be the artist's own **composition**. It may be a segment from another popular song or even a classical piece.

The musician then makes a "loop" of the segment, which means that it's played over and over. Sampling adds background melody and harmony. Each bit of sampling also adds its own rhythms to a rap song.

The Beat Goes On

Underlying rap and almost all music is its pulse, or beat. "There are all kinds of rhythms going on in a *Sousa* march, but what do people march to?" says Tanner. It's not the rhythmic phrasing of the melody. Instead, he says, "They move their feet to the underlying pulse of the music."

Rap and other popular music forms often spell out the beat explicitly with drums. "Any popular music that we're used to usually has that characteristic," notes Tanner. "That's why it's fun to dance to. In fact, popular music is often designed for movement."

"Meter is simply organizing pulses into a regular cyclical pattern," adds Tanner. Instead of an endless series of beats, the musician may play cycles of "ONE, two, Three, four." This meter, known as "common time," stresses the first beat most. The third beat gets slight emphasis, too. Meter sets up a hierarchy, which the listener's brain can then remember and anticipate. That makes it possible for you to tap your foot or clap in time with the music.

Tempo is how fast a piece of music delivers its meter. Too slow, and a rap song sounds like a *dirge*, or funeral song. Too fast, and the brain can't perceive individual sounds. The music becomes one big blur. Choose a tempo that's just quick enough, and listeners want to move with the music. Speed it up slightly or slow it down in places, and listeners respond to the music's different moods.

What Makes It Cool?

Hearing rhythm patterns in a song, listeners form expectations of what comes next. If music doesn't give enough for listeners to form those expectations, it sounds chaotic and grating. If music gets too predictable, however, it becomes boring.

Sophisticated rap music provides an **innovative** mix that satisfies and sometimes surprises listeners' expectations. With lyrics, an MC might stop in the middle of a line or give some offbeat accents. Sampling or the drum track may stress different notes than those that would usually be emphasized in the meter—a technique called *syncopation*.

Revel in the rhythms of your favorite music. Innovative rhythms not only move music forward in time, but they also make rap—and many other types of music—cool.

> The final paragraph states one of the main ideas of the article.

SCHOOLHOUSE ROCK
Conjunction Junction

Music & Lyrics: Bob Dorough
Performed by: Jack Sheldon
Animation: Phil Kimmelman and Associates

Conjunction Junction, what's your function?
Hooking up words and phrases and clauses.
Conjunction Junction, how's that function?
I got three favorite cars
That get most of my job done.
Conjunction Junction, what's their function?
I got "and," "but," and "or,"
They'll get you pretty far.

"And":
That's an additive, like "this and that."
"But":
That's sort of the opposite,
"Not this but that."
And then there's "or":
O-R, when you have a choice like
"This or that."
"And," "but," and "or,"
Get you pretty far.

Conjunction Junction, what's your function?
Hooking up two boxcars and making 'em run right.
Milk and honey, bread and butter, peas and rice.
Hey that's nice!
Dirty but happy, digging and scratching,
Losing your shoe and a button or two.
He's poor but honest, sad but true,
Boo-hoo-hoo-hoo-hoo!

> The song opens with a question followed by a statement of the main idea.

> This stanza provides examples of conjunctions and supports the main idea of the song.

Conjunction Junction, what's your function?
Hooking up two cars to one
When you say something like this choice:
"Either now or later"
Or no choice:
"Neither now nor ever"
Hey that's clever!
Eat this or that, grow thin or fat,
Never mind, I wouldn't do that,
I'm fat enough now!

Conjunction Junction, what's your function?
Hooking up phrases and clauses that balance, like:
Out of the frying pan and into the fire.
He cut loose the sandbags,
But the balloon wouldn't go any higher.
Let's go up to the mountains,
Or down to the sea.
You should always say "thank you,"
Or at least say "please."

> This stanza repeats the main idea of the song, and then provides additional examples as supporting details.

Conjunction Junction, what's your function?
Hooking up words and phrases and clauses
In complex sentences like:

Conjunction Junction, what's your function?
Hooking up cars and making 'em function.
Conjunction Junction, how's that function?
I like tying up words and phrases and clauses.
Conjunction Junction, watch that function.
I'm going to get you there if you're very careful.
Conjunction Junction, what's your function?
I'm going to get you there if you're very careful.
Conjunction Junction, what's your function?
I'm going to get you there if you're very careful.

Comparing Expository Texts

1. Craft and Structure (a) Explain the differences in the way each text organizes and develops main ideas and supporting details. Give an example from each text. **(b)** Do you think either type of text is better suited for educating readers about a topic? Explain your response.

Content-Area Vocabulary

2. (a) Determine the verb forms of *composition* and *innovative*. **(b)** Use all four words in a brief paragraph about music.

⏱ Timed Writing

Explanatory Text: Paraphrase

Format
The prompt gives specific directions about the length of the assignment.

Choose either the magazine article or the educational song and paraphrase it. Use your own words to emphasize the same points as the source selection. Your paraphrase should be no longer than the original text.
(30 minutes)

Academic Vocabulary
When you *emphasize* a point in your writing, you stress its importance through word choice and details.

5-Minute Planner

Complete these steps before you begin to write:

1. Read the prompt. Look for highlighted key words.

2. Decide which text you are going to paraphrase, the magazine article or the educational song.

3. Read through the text and identify any unfamiliar words. Jot down a few synonyms, or words with similar meanings, that you can use in your paraphrase to replace those words.

4. Closely reread each section of the magazine article or song lyrics, and note the main ideas and supporting details. Jot down phrases that you can use to express the author's points in your own words.

Comparing Imagery

In poetry, an **image** is a word or phrase that appeals to one or more of the five senses. Writers use **imagery** to bring poetry to life with descriptions of how their subjects look, sound, feel, taste, and smell. Look at these examples:

- The phrase "the sweet, slippery mango slices" appeals to the senses of taste and touch.
- The phrase "glaring lights and wailing sirens" appeals to the senses of sight and hearing.

Writers also create **mood** through their use of images, words, and descriptive details. Mood is the feeling created in the reader by a literary work or passage. The mood of a work may be described with adjectives such as *joyous, gloomy, cozy,* or *frightening.*

To fully appreciate images and mood in a poem, determine the meaning of any unfamiliar words that the poet uses—including words the poet has made up. Also, pay close attention to the connotations of words—their emotional associations—as well as to their figurative, or nonliteral, meanings.

Both "Miracles" and "in Just—" contain images that appeal to the senses. On a chart like the one shown, track the images in the two poems. After you read, use your chart to help you compare the authors' use of imagery.

Common Core
State Standards

Reading Literature
4. Determine the meaning of words and phrases as they are used in a text, including figurative and connotative meanings; analyze the impact of rhymes and other repetitions of sounds on a specific verse or stanza of a poem or section of a story or drama.

Writing
1. Write arguments to support claims with clear reasons and relevant evidence.

Sense	Images	
	"Miracles"	"in Just—"
Sight		
Hearing		
Touch/Movement		
Taste		
Smell		

PHLit
Online!
www.PHLitOnline.com

- Vocabulary flashcards
- Interactive journals
- More about the authors
- Selection audio
- Interactive graphic organizers

What is the best way to *communicate?*

Writing About the Big Question

In both of these selections, the writers use imagery to paint vivid pictures in the minds of readers. Consider how descriptive language can help readers "see" exactly what the writer sees. Use these sentence starters to develop your ideas.

Descriptive words can **enrich** a piece of writing because _____.

When writing **produces** a picture in the mind of a reader, the reader can understand _____.

Meet the Authors

Walt Whitman (1819–1892)
Author of "Miracles"

Walt Whitman worked at many occupations during his life. He was a carpenter, teacher, and newspaper reporter. During the Civil War, he nursed his wounded brother and other soldiers.

The Father of American Poetry In 1855, Whitman published the first edition of *Leaves of Grass*—poems that no established publisher would touch. In this book, Whitman abandoned regular rhyme and rhythm in favor of free verse, which followed no set pattern. Now considered a masterpiece, the book led critics to regard Whitman as the father of American poetry.

E. E. Cummings (1894–1962)
Author of "in Just—"

Edward Estlin Cummings first published a collection of poetry in the early 1920s. The work stood out, among other reasons, because of Cummings's original use of language and unusual punctuation, capitalization, and word spacing. In fact, the author's name usually appears the way he wrote it, with no capitals—as e. e. cummings.

A Sense of Humor Cummings often wrote poems that were playful and humorous. These poems reflected his attitude that "the most wasted of all days is one without laughter."

Miracles
Walt Whitman

Why, who makes much of a miracle?
As to me I know of nothing else but miracles,
Whether I walk the streets of Manhattan,
Or dart my sight over the roofs of houses toward the sky,
5   Or wade with naked feet along the beach just in the edge
        of the water,
Or stand under trees in the woods,
Or talk by day with any one I love . . .
Or sit at table at dinner with the rest.
Or look at strangers opposite me riding in the car,
10 Or watch honeybees busy around the hive of a summer
        forenoon
Or animals feeding in the fields,
Or birds, or the wonderfulness of insects in the air,
Or the wonderfulness of the sundown, or of stars shining
        so quiet and bright,
Or the exquisite delicate thin curve of the new moon in
        spring;
15 These with the rest, one and all, are to me miracles,
The whole referring, yet each distinct and in its place.

To me every hour of the light and dark is a miracle,
Every cubic inch of space is a miracle,
Every square yard of the surface of the earth is spread
        with the same,
20 Every foot of the interior swarms with the same.

To me the sea is a continual miracle,
The fishes that swim—the rocks—the motion of the
        waves—
the ships with men in them,
What stranger miracles are there?

◀ La Bonne Aventure (Good Fortune) 1939, Rene Magritte Museum Boymans-van Beuningen, Rotterdam ©2000 C. Herscovici, Brussels/Artists Rights Society (ARS) New York

◀ **Critical Viewing**
Identify a line in the poem that relates to this painting. Explain your choice. **[Connect]**

Imagery
Which image in the first seven lines appeals to the sense of touch?

Vocabulary
exquisite (eks´ kwiz it) *adj.* beautiful in a delicate way

distinct (di stiŋkt´) *adj.* separate and different

Critical Thinking

1. Key Ideas and Details (a) List events that the speaker calls miracles. **(b) Infer:** Why is the sea a "continual miracle"?

2. Integration of Knowledge and Ideas Why do you think Whitman decided to use poetry to describe the beauty around him? *[Connect to the Big Question: What is the best way to communicate?]*

Cite textual evidence to support your responses.

Miracles **695**

in Just–  E. E. Cummings

in Just—
spring   when the world is mud-
luscious the little
lame balloonman

5   whistles   far   and wee

and eddieandbill come
running from marbles and
piracies and it's
spring

10   when the world is puddle-wonderful

the queer
old balloonman whistles
far   and   wee
and bettyandisbel come dancing

15   from hop-scotch and jump-rope and

it's
spring
and
    the

20   goat-footed

balloonMan   whistles
far
and
wee

Critical Thinking

1. Key Ideas and Details (a) What scene does the speaker describe? **(b) Analyze:** Why do you think he uses unusual words such as "mud-luscious"?

2. Craft and Structure Cummings breaks many language conventions. When do you think it is OK for a writer to break grammatical rules? *[Connect to the Big Question: What is the best way to communicate?]*

Cite textual evidence to support your responses.

Comparing Imagery

1. Craft and Structure Give an example from each poem of an **image** that appeals to each of the following senses: **(a)** hearing; **(b)** touch. Explain the meaning, including connotations, of key words in each image.

2. Craft and Structure (a) Using a chart like the one shown, identify and explain sight images in each poem. Explain the meaning, including connotations, of key words in each image. **(b)** Which poem has more vivid sight images?

Miracles	in Just—
Image:	Image:
Effect:	Effect:

⏱ Timed Writing

Argument: Recommendation

Write an essay that recommends one of the two poems to someone your age. Choose the poem that you believe provides more effective examples of imagery. Include details from the text to support your claim. **(40 minutes)**

5-Minute Planner

1. Read the prompt carefully and completely.

2. Gather your ideas by jotting down answers to these questions:
   • What do you find fascinating or distinctive about the imagery in the poem you are recommending?
   • Which images are most meaningful to you?
   • In what ways is the imagery in the poem you chose more effective than the imagery in the other poem?

3. Review the graphic organizer you completed as you read the poems to help you address the questions above.

4. Reread the prompt, and then draft your essay.

Writing Workshop

 **Common Core State Standards**

Writing
1. Write arguments to support claims with clear reasons and relevant evidence.
1.a. Introduce claim(s), acknowledge alternate or opposing claims, and organize the reasons and evidence logically.
1.b. Support claim(s) with logical reasoning and relevant evidence, using accurate, credible sources and demonstrating an understanding of the topic or text.

Write an Argument

Exposition: Persuasive Essay

Defining the Form A **persuasive essay** presents arguments for or against a particular position. You might use elements of this form of writing in editorials or reviews.

Assignment Write a persuasive essay that persuades readers to share your point of view on an issue about which you feel strongly. Your persuasive essay should feature the following elements:

✔ a *clear statement of your position* on an issue that has more than one side

✔ the *context* surrounding the issue

✔ *persuasive evidence* and *logical reasoning* that support your claims

✔ language that *appeals to both reason and emotion*

✔ an *appropriate organizational structure* for an argument

✔ statements that *acknowledge opposing views and offer counterarguments*

✔ error-free writing, including *proper sentence structure*

To preview the criteria on which your persuasive essay may be judged, see the rubric on page 705.

 Writing Workshop: *Work in Progress*

Review the work you did on pages 663 and 683.

WRITE GUY
Jeff Anderson, M.Ed.

What Do You Notice?

Word Choice

The following sentences are from Louis L'Amour's "The Final Frontier." Read them several times.

If we are content to live in the past, we have no future. And today is the past.

With a partner, discuss the writer's word choice and message. Then, think about ways you can convey a message effectively in your writing.

Reading-Writing Connection

To get the feel for persuasion, read "The Eternal Frontier" by Louis L'Amour, on page 500.

Prewriting/Planning Strategies

Hold a roundtable. With a group, hold a roundtable discussion of problems in your school. Raise as many different issues as possible. Jot down topics that spark strong feelings in you. Choose from these subjects for your essay topic.

Make a quick list. Fold a piece of paper in thirds lengthwise. In the first column, write issues and ideas that interest you. In the second column, write a descriptive word for each idea. In the third column, give an example that supports your description. Make sure each issue has an opposing side. Choose the issue or idea that interests you most.

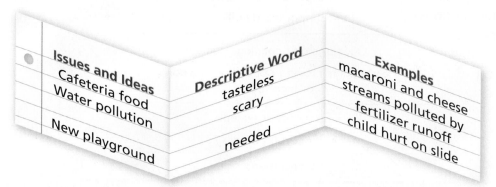

Issues and Ideas	Descriptive Word	Examples
Cafeteria food	tasteless	macaroni and cheese
Water pollution	scary	streams polluted by fertilizer runoff
New playground	needed	child hurt on slide

Narrow your focus. Evaluate your topic to be sure you can fully and effectively discuss it. For example, the topic "violence in the media" would cover violence on news reports, in movies, and on television. To write an effective persuasive essay, you should consider focusing on violence in one medium, not all three.

Gather evidence to support your position. Conduct research either in the library, on the Internet, or by interviewing experts on your topic. Gather the following types of support from accurate, credible sources:

Facts: statements that can be proved true

Statistics: facts presented in the form of numbers

Anecdotes: brief stories that illustrate a point

Quotations from Authorities: statements from leading experts

Examples: facts, ideas, or events that support a general idea

Anticipate counterarguments. Make a list of the arguments people might have against your position. For each, identify a response that you can use to address the issues in your essay.

Drafting Strategies

**Common Core
State Standards**

Writing

1.c. Use words, phrases, and clauses to create cohesion and clarify the relationships among claim(s), reasons, and evidence.

1.d. Establish and maintain a formal style.

1.e. Provide a concluding statement or section that follows from and supports the argument presented.

Develop and support your thesis statement. To keep your position clear to your readers, review your notes and develop a *thesis statement*—one strong sentence that sums up your argument. Include this statement in your introduction.

Organize to emphasize your arguments.
As you draft, present the supporting evidence you have gathered, starting with your least important points and building toward your most important ones. Use transitional words and phrases to unify your writing and show the relationships among your ideas. Address opposing concerns and counterarguments directly—do not avoid them. Delete information that does not support or add anything to your argument. Write a powerful conclusion that follows the logic of the evidence and supports your argument. Consider the method shown in the pyramid.

Introduction and thesis

• First set of arguments
• Supporting details

• Concerns and counterarguments
• Statements proving opposition is weak or incorrect

• Strongest argument
• Supporting details

Conclusions

Choose precise words. Forceful language helps convey your point and builds support for your position. Create a speaker's voice by using precise, lively words that will stir readers' emotions and appeal to their sense of reason.

> **Vague:** a *good* candidate
>
> **Precise:** a *trustworthy* candidate
> an *intelligent* candidate

Appeal to your audience. Use words that your audience will understand. If you are writing for teenagers, use informal language, but avoid slang and maintain standard English. If you are writing to a government official, use a formal style and serious language. Also, choose words that add interest and encourage readers to continue reading.

Writers on Writing

Pat Mora On Supporting a Point

Pat Mora is the author of "Maestro" (p. 578), "The Desert Is My Mother" (p. 579), and "Bailando" (p. 580).

When I was a university administrator, a friend mentioned that her daughter, Gabriela, wanted writing advice. I've always liked to write letters, so I wrote a persuasive essay as a letter to Gabi. The letter/essay became part of my collection *Nepantla: Essays from the Land in the Middle.* From the time I was in high school, I was intrigued by essays, perhaps because I like seeing how writers express their beliefs convincingly.

> *"I write because I'm a reader."*
> — Pat Mora

Professional Model:

from *"To Gabriela, A Young Writer"*

I know that the society we live in and that the movies, television programs, and commercials we see, all affect us. It's not easy to learn to judge others fairly, not because of the car they drive, the house they live in, the church they attend, the color of their skin, the language they speak at home. It takes courage to face the fact that we all have ten toes, get sleepy at night, get scared in the dark. Some families, some cities, some states, and even some countries foolishly convince themselves that they are better than others. And then they teach their children this ugly lie. It's like a weed with burrs and stickers that pricks people.

How are young women who are African American, Asian American, American Indian, Latinas, or members of all the other ethnic groups supposed to feel about themselves? Some are proud of their cultural roots. . . .

I played with different human similarities. Humans have arms and eyes. There's something so basic about the words "ten toes," though.

The right comparison, or metaphor, is like a shortcut to the reader's feelings and imagination. We all know the discomfort of stickers.

Here and throughout, I'm building my argument by using lists of examples to support my thesis. I'm building a case.

Revising Strategies

Highlight your main points. To check your organization, highlight each main point. Then, use one or more of these strategies:

- If a reader needs to know one main point in order to understand a second one, make sure the first main point comes *before* the second.

- If one main point means the same as another, combine them, or combine the paragraphs in which they appear.

- If one main point is stronger than the others, move it to the end of your essay.

Common Core State Standards

Writing
1.c. Use words, phrases, and clauses to create cohesion and clarify the relationships among claim(s), reasons, and evidence.

Language
2. Demonstrate command of the conventions of standard English capitalization, punctuation, and spelling when writing.

Model: Revising to Highlight Main Points

The best way a person can make his or her voice heard is by voting on Election Day! In the United States, the government is elected by each and every voting citizen. In some other countries, people do not have the right to vote. Their leaders are in power, and the people sometimes do not have a way to make their opinion heard. Their voices are silent, and they must listen to what their leaders tell them to do. Our system is not always perfect, but it does give us the chance to keep trying to make things better.

Combine sentences to show connections. To improve your writing, combine short, choppy sentences to stress the connections between ideas.

Similar Ideas: The town permits skating on the lake. We don't have the money to open a rink.

Combined: The town permits skating on the lake *because* we don't have the money to open a rink.

Opposing Ideas: The food is better heated. Most classrooms do not have microwave ovens.

Combined: The food is better heated, *but* most classrooms do not have microwave ovens.

Peer Review
Read your draft to a group of peers. Ask if the order of your main points is logical. Consider their responses as you revise.

Revising Fragments and Run-on Sentences

The most basic sentence contains a single **independent clause**— a group of words including a subject and a verb and expressing a complete idea.

Fixing Sentence Fragments

A **fragment** is a group of words that does not express a complete thought. It is often missing a subject, a verb, or both.

Fragments: I'll read my report. As long as you read yours, too.

To fix a fragment, first identify the incomplete sentence. Then, make a complete sentence out of it.

Corrected: I'll read my report as long as you read yours, too.

Fixing Run-on Sentences

A **run-on sentence** occurs when two or more independent clauses are joined without proper punctuation.

Run-on: We dove into the water, we swam fast.

To fix run-ons with sentence combining, use the following methods:

- Use punctuation to correctly indicate where ideas end.

  Corrected: We dove into the water. We swam fast.

- Use a comma and a coordinating conjunction such as *and, or, so*, or *but* to express ideas of equal importance.

  Corrected: We dove into the water, and we swam fast.

- Use a semicolon and a subordinating conjunctions to show the relationship between ideas.

  Corrected: We dove into the water; then, we swam fast.

> **PH** **WRITING COACH**
>
> Further instruction and practice are available in *Prentice Hall Writing Coach*.

Common Subordinating Conjunctions				
after although as	as long as because before	even though if since	so that though unless	until when where

Grammar in Your Writing

Choose a paragraph in your draft and circle any fragments or run-ons you find. Fix these sentence errors using the methods above.

Student Model: Amanda Wintenburg, Daytona Beach, FL

Decide the Future

To you, voting may seem like just a waste of time, just a mere piece of paper with boxes on it, that you have to go through to mark which person you want for that particular job. But to me, it's something more, much more. . . it's your chance to decide the future. Everyone who is eligible should take advantage of the right to vote.

I'm not the only one who thinks voting should be a top priority for people. For years, companies and organizations have supplied numerous reminders and reasons to explain when and why you vote. You've seen the commercials; they've all told us about it. Although there is no financial profit in convincing people to vote, money is being spent to make sure it happens. That should tell you something.

Eenie, meenie, miney mo, . . . maybe you don't want to vote because you feel as if you don't know enough about the candidates to make an informed decision. However, newspapers, television broadcasts, performance records—all these fact-based sources of information are available to the interested voter who wants to make a responsible choice. Find out what the candidates have been doing and what they plan to do. Make your decision based on information.

In many countries, voting is not an option. In countries with kings and queens, leaders are born into their positions. In other countries, the leaders take control rather than being voted into a leadership role. Often leaders who are not elected can be corrupt or tyrannical, because the people can't remove them from power. We are citizens of a free country in which we have the right to vote. Whether or not the system works perfectly, it is better than a system with no voting. Vote because you can. Remind yourself that not everyone is as lucky.

If you don't vote, you have less control over your own life. Voting is your chance to make your voice heard. It's your chance to decide the future.

In the opening paragraph, Amanda points out the two "sides" to the voting issue. She follows with her thesis statement.

This evidence supports the idea that voting matters.

Here, Amanda identifies and addresses readers' concerns and counterarguments.

Amanda reminds readers that not everyone has the right to vote. She uses language that appeals to both reason and emotion.

Editing and Proofreading

Review your draft to correct errors in spelling, grammar, and punctuation.

Focus on Punctuation: Be sure to use the correct end mark for each kind of sentence in your essay. Use a period at the end of a statement, a question mark at the end of a question, and an exclamation mark at the end of a statement that indicates strong feeling. In addition, use a dash for additional emphasis or to offset important information.

Publishing and Presenting

Consider one of the following ways to share your writing:

Give a speech. Use your persuasive essay as the basis for a speech that you give to your classmates.

Submit a newspaper article. Many local newspapers will publish well-written persuasive essays if they appeal to the newspaper's audience. Submit your composition and see what happens.

Reflecting on Your Writing

Writer's Journal Jot down your answer to this question:

What part of the writing process was most challenging? Explain.

Spiral Review

Earlier in the unit, you learned about **independent and subordinate clauses** (p. 662) and **sentence structures** (p. 682). Review your essay to be sure that you have used a variety of sentence structures and have formed each kind correctly.

PH WRITING COACH

Further instruction and practice are available in *Prentice Hall Writing Coach.*

Rubric for Self-Assessment

Find evidence in your writing to address each category. Then, use the rating scale to grade your work.

Criteria	Rating Scale
	not very very
Focus: How clearly is your position stated?	1 2 3 4 5
Organization: How organized is your argument or judgment?	1 2 3 4 5
Support/Elaboration: How persuasive is your evidence?	1 2 3 4 5
Style: How well do you balance language to appeal to reason and emotion?	1 2 3 4 5
Conventions: How correct is your grammar, especially your use of independent clauses?	1 2 3 4 5

Vocabulary Workshop

Connotation and Denotation

The **denotation** of a word is its dictionary meaning. A word's **connotations** are the ideas associated with that word. Those ideas and feelings might be positive or negative. Understanding connotations can help you to choose the right words in your writing. The following chart shows an example of three words with the same denotation and different connotations. Notice the various shades of meaning among the three words.

Common Core State Standards

Language

4.c. Consult general and specialized reference materials, both print and digital, to find the pronunciation of a word or determine or clarify its precise meaning or its part of speech.

5.c. Distinguish among the connotations (associations) of words with similar denotations (definitions).

Word	Denotation	Connotation	Example Sentence
postpone	to put off until a later time	to reschedule, usually due to something out of one's control	We had to *postpone* the party because the hostess became ill.
delay		to hold off on something for a short amount of time	The heavy morning traffic will *delay* the city's buses.
procrastinate		to put something off that is undesirable by doing another thing	I *procrastinate* every day by watching television before doing my homework.

Practice A Each of the following words has a positive, neutral, or negative connotation. For each word pair, identify which word has a more positive connotation. If necessary, use a dictionary to check each word's denotation.

1. noise, sound
2. screech, holler
3. grab, obtain
4. discontinue, quit
5. brainy, intelligent
6. aware, alert

Practice B Sometimes connotations of words can help you see degrees of meaning. For example, the words *large* and *enormous* have the same basic meaning, but *enormous* implies greater size than *large*. Rewrite each of the following sentences by replacing the italicized word. The new word should have the same denotation but a connotation that implies a greater degree of the original word. If necessary, use a dictionary or a thesaurus to help you.

1. The coach was *angry* after the team's poor performance.
2. My little sister loves to *bother* me when I have friends over.
3. We *eat* our lunch as soon as we sit down at the table.
4. The marching band from Southern California was *good*.
5. My mother was *happy* when I told her my grade on the test.
6. The weather in the desert is *hot*.
7. The rides at the amusement park were *fun*.
8. My cousin from Georgia is *nice*.
9. I drank a *large* glass of water after the race.
10. After playing a game of "fetch," my dog was *tired*.

Activity Each of the following words has neutral connotations. Use a thesaurus to find synonyms, or words with a similar meaning, for each word. Find at least one synonym with positive connotations and one synonym with negative connotations. Use a graphic organizer like the one shown to organize your synonyms. The first one has been completed as an example.

difficult   aged   calm   brave   humble

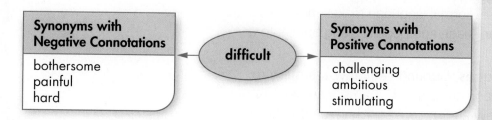

Comprehension and Collaboration

Work with a partner to write two separate paragraphs about a fictional inventor. One partner's paragraph should describe the inventor as a visionary. The other's should describe the inventor as a dreamer. When you have finished writing, exchange paragraphs and discuss how the connotations of the words *visionary* and *dreamer* influenced your descriptions of the inventor.

Communications Workshop

Evaluating Media Messages and Advertisements

Common Core State Standards

Speaking and Listening

2. Analyze the main ideas and supporting details presented in diverse media and formats and explain how the ideas clarify a topic, text, or issue under study.

3. Delineate a speaker's argument and specific claims, evaluating the soundness of the reasoning and the relevance and sufficiency of the evidence.

Media messages and advertisements appear on television, the Internet, and radio. To ensure you understand and respond appropriately to these messages, critically evaluate them, using the strategies in this workshop.

Learn the Skills

Use these strategies to complete the activity on page 709.

Determine the purpose. Identify the purpose, or goal, of the message. Some messages are meant to inform, to persuade, or to entertain. Some messages are attempts to sell you something or to convince you to do something.

Analyze images and sounds. Think critically about what you see and hear. Some images are designed to sell instead of to inform. Notice how the mood created by music and sounds influences your decisions.

Challenge the claims and evidence. Analyze the accuracy of the claims. Consider whether the reasoning is logical and whether sufficient and relevant evidence supports the claims.

Identify propaganda techniques. To effectively analyze logic, be alert to techniques involving faulty reasoning.

- **Slant and Bias:** Beware of any message that presents only one side of a many-sided issue.

- **Bandwagon Appeal:** Beware of messages that suggest you will feel left out if you do not do or buy something.

- **Spokespersons:** Ask yourself whether the spokesperson has the knowledge to back up his or her claims.

Analyze the use of language. Advertisers use language to appeal to certain groups of people. Formal language makes messages seem more accurate. Informal language and popular slang appeal to a young audience.

Interpret visual techniques. Lighting can draw attention to specific parts of an image or set a mood. Camera angles can influence the way you view an image. Special visual effects can change an existing image to increase appeal or interest.

Practice the Skills

© **Presentation of Knowledge and Ideas** Use what you have learned in this workshop to complete the following activity.

ACTIVITY: Evaluate Media Advertisements

Watch three television commercials. Then, follow the steps below.

- Identify the message and interpret the purpose of each commercial.
- Ask questions about the evidence that supports a claim.
- Explain how each commercial makes you feel.
- List memorable details from each commercial, such as special effects, camera angles, lighting, and music.
- Use the Interpretation Guide to interpret the advertisements.

Use the Interpretation Guide to analyze the content of each commercial.

Interpretation Guide

Visual Techniques
Which techniques does the advertisement include? Briefly explain each.
- ❑ camera angles   ❑ special effects
- ❑ special lighting   ❑ other visual

Sound Techniques
Which techniques does the advertisement include? Briefly explain each.
- ❑ music
- ❑ special effects
- ❑ other techniques

Messages
What is the message? How can you tell?

Claims and Evidence
Does the advertisement make claims about the product? If so, what are they? What evidence does the advertisement give? Is the evidence relevant? Is there enough reasonable evidence to support the claims? Explain.

Purpose
What is the purpose of the advertisement?

© **Comprehension and Collaboration** Compare your findings with those of your classmates. As a group, interpret how visual and sound techniques influence the message in an advertisement.

Cumulative Review

I. Reading Literature

**Common Core
State Standards**

RL.7.2, RL.7.4, RL.7.5; L.7.4.a; W.7.2
[For the full wording of the standards,
see the standards chart in the front of
your textbook.]

Directions: *Read the passage. Then, answer each
question that follows.*

I Wandered Lonely as a Cloud
by William Wordsworth

I wandered lonely as a cloud
That floats on high o'er vales[1] and hills,
When all at once I saw a crowd,
A host, of golden daffodils;
5   Beside the lake, beneath the trees,
Fluttering and dancing in the breeze.

Continuous as the stars that shine
And twinkle on the milky way,
They stretched in never-ending line
10   Along the margin of a bay:
Ten thousand saw I at a glance,
Tossing their heads in <u>sprightly</u> dance.

The waves beside them danced; but they
Outdid the sparkling waves in glee;
15   A poet could not but be gay,
In such a jocund[2] company;
I gazed—and gazed—but little thought
What wealth the show to me had brought:

For oft, when on my couch I lie
20   In vacant or in pensive[3] mood,
They flash upon that inward eye
Which is the bliss of solitude;
And then my heart with pleasure fills,
And dances with the daffodils.

---

1. o'er vales over valleys.
2. jocund *adj.* cheerful.
3. pensive *adj.* deeply or seriously thoughtful.

1. Which of the following are characteristics of a **lyric poem** such as this one?
   A. seventeen syllables; focuses on nature
   B. single image or idea; musical language
   C. letters and lines create a visual image
   D. no regular rhyme; no stanza pattern

2. Which of the following passages contains a **simile?**
   A. I wandered lonely as a cloud
   B. They stretched in never-ending line
   C. The waves beside them danced
   D. And then my heart with pleasure fills

3. What type of **figurative language** does Wordsworth use in lines 4–6?
   A. symbol
   A. personification
   A. metaphor
   A. simile

4. Which of the following lines contains the **sound device** of alliteration?
   A. I wandered lonely as a cloud
   B. Along the margin of a bay
   C. Outdid the sparkling waves in glee
   D. And dances with the daffodils.

5. Which lines **rhyme** in the second stanza?
   A. lines 7 and 8
   B. lines 8 and 9
   C. lines 8 and 10
   D. lines 10 and 11

6. Which of the following lines contains the most vivid **imagery?**
   A. lines 13 and 14
   B. lines 15 and 16
   C. lines 17 and 18
   D. lines 19 and 20

7. What **image** does Wordsworth **repeat** throughout the poem?
   A. sparkling waves
   B. shining stars
   C. dancing flowers
   D. lonely clouds

8. Which best summarizes the **main idea** of the poem?
   A. The speaker recalls the image of the daffodils, which comforts him when he is lonely or sad.
   B. The speaker compares the daffodils to his constant loneliness.
   C. The speaker thinks about the relationship between humans and nature.
   D. The speaker wanders through the fields and comments on nature's beauty.

9. **Vocabulary** Which word is closest in meaning to the underlined word sprightly in line 12?
   A. shiny
   B. energetic
   C. wilting
   D. moist

⏱ Timed Writing

10. Identify one **simile, metaphor,** or example of **personification** used in the poem. In an essay, **explain** how the **figure of speech** contributes to the overall meaning of the poem.

II. Reading Informational Text

Directions: *Read the passage below. Then, answer each question that follows.*

Common Core State Standards

RI.7.5; W.7.1; L.7.1, L.7.3
[For the full wording of the standards, see the standards chart in the front of your textbook.]

How to Set up an E-mail Filter

An e-mail filter sorts your e-mail, deletes unwanted junk mail, and helps you avoid e-mail scams. Follow these steps to make your e-mail inbox easier to navigate and to avoid opening annoying junk e-mails.
Step 1 Open your e-mail account and locate the "Tools," "Filters," or "Options" menu items. Usually, these are listed at the top of the screen.
Step 2 Once you have found the filters option, click on "New" to build a new folder. **TIP:** Name the folder "Junk Mail" so it is easy to find.
Step 3 Set up the rules, or conditions, for the filter. The rules are the conditions the e-mail must meet for it to take the action you want. **TIP:** One rule you can make is to send e-mails from unknown senders to your new folder. This means any message from a sender that is not listed in your address book will be sorted.
Step 4 Specify the action you want the filter to implement. Filters can sort e-mails in a folder, delete them, or take other actions your provider lists. **TIP:** If your filter sends unwanted e-mails to a folder, be sure to check it <u>periodically</u> to see if a wanted e-mail has been filtered out.
Step 5 Click "OK" or "Save" to save your new folder. **TIP:** Add new filters for different uses, such as organizing school, work, or family events.

1. Which of the following is a **key step** in setting up your e-mail filter?

   A. opening your junk mail first
   B. avoiding Internet scams
   C. checking your junk mail folder for wanted e-mails
   D. setting up the conditions of the filter

2. What is the *best* way to fully understand Step 4?

   A. Skip the difficult words.
   B. Look up the technical words or phrases.
   C. Put the language into your own words.
   D. Make a list of technical words.

3. What **purpose** do the tips after each step serve?

   A. They give advice.
   B. They summarize the main points.
   C. They provide illustrations.
   D. They clarify difficult concepts.

4. What is the **main purpose** of the passage?

   A. to inform you of junk e-mail
   B. to advise you how to organize your e-mails
   C. to inform you how to get rid of junk e-mail forever.
   D. to advise you how to send emails to different groups of people

III. Writing and Language Conventions

Directions: *Read the passage. Then, answer each question that follows.*

> (1) Many students, including myself, depend on our cell phones to talk with our parents. (2) Every day I hear from my mother what time she will pick me up. (3) The problem is that Mr. Galindo wants to ban cell phones from school. (4) The solution is simple. (5) We should be allowed to bring our cell phones to school, but we will only use them when school is over. (6) Yes, calls will be missed. (7) They can be returned after school. (8) This way everyone wins.

1. Which sentence could the writer add to explain Mr. Galindo's **main problem** with cell phones in school?

  A. Students do not pay attention during class because they are text messaging.

  B. Cell phone ring tones are annoying.

  C. Students will miss calls during the day.

  D. Students spend too much money on new cell phones and ring tones.

2. Which argument could the writer use to *best* strengthen the proposed **solution?**

  A. We will only check our messages or make calls in between classes.

  B. We will keep our phones on silent mode, and return only the important calls.

  C. We will keep our phones locked in our lockers until the last bell.

  D. Cell phones are useful in emergencies.

3. Which revision combines sentence 6 and sentence 7 with a **past participle?**

  A. Calls will be missed and can be returned after school.

  B. Students can return calls after school.

  C. Missed calls can be returned after school.

  D. After school, you can return your calls.

4. Which revision of sentence 2 includes an **infinitive?**

  A. Every day I hear from my mother the time she will pick me up.

  B. Every day my mother tells what time she will pick me up.

  C. Every day my mother calls to tell me what time she will pick me up.

  D. Every day my mother calls before she picks me up.

5. What is the *best* way for the writer to add more information to sentence 3 by using an **appositive?**

  A. The problem, declared today, is that Mr. Galindo wants to ban all cell phones from school.

  B. The problem is that Principal Galindo wants to ban all cell phones from school.

  C. The problem is that Mr. Galindo, our principal, wants to ban all cell phones from school.

  D. The problem is that Mr. Galindo wants to ban all cell phones from Arthur High School.

Performance Tasks

Directions: *Follow the instructions to complete the tasks below as required by your teacher.*

As you work on each task, incorporate both general academic vocabulary and literary terms you learned in this unit.

Common Core State Standards

RL.7.4, RL.7.5; W.7.9.a; SL.7.1, SL.7.4; L.7.1, L.7.2
[For the full wording of the standards, see the standards chart in the front of your textbook.]

Writing

ⓒ Task 1: Literature [RL.7.5; W.7.9.a]
Analyze a Poem's Form and Structure

Write an essay in which you analyze the form and structure of a poem in this unit.

- Plan to analyze the following elements of your chosen poem: rhyme, rhythm and meter, line length, stanza divisions, punctuation, capitalization, and spacing. Explain how these elements, both individually and together, contribute to the poem's meaning and effect.

- Revise your work to correct any run-on sentences or sentence fragments. Place phrases and clauses within sentences to clarify the relationships between ideas. Finally, correct misplaced or dangling modifiers.

- Publish your finished essay in the classroom library. Include a copy of the original text of the poem.

ⓒ Task 2: Literature [RL.7.4; W.7.9.a]
Analyze Word Choice

Write an essay in which you use the literal and implied meanings of words to help you interpret a poem in this unit.

- Choose a poem that features powerful words and images.
- Note examples of figurative language— such as similes, metaphors, and personification—and imagery that appeals

to the five senses. Analyze the impact of each example.

- Cite evidence from the poem to support your analysis.

- As you edit, make sure you have used correct punctuation, including commas to separate items in a series.

ⓒ Task 3: Literature [RL.7.5; W.7.9.a]
Compare and Contrast Forms of Poetry

Write an essay in which you compare and contrast two poetic forms.

- Plan your essay by determining the characteristics that define these poetic forms: lyric poetry, concrete poetry, and haiku. Choose two forms to compare and contrast in your essay.

- Pick one or more poems in each form.

- In your essay, compare the characteristics of each form, giving examples of each characteristic from the poems you have chosen.

- For each characteristic you discuss, explain how it contributes to the meaning of the poem.

- Include your topic sentence in the introductory paragraph. Organize the body of your compare-and-contrast essay to clearly show comparisons and contrasts. Use details from the poems to support your ideas.

Speaking and Listening

@ **Task 4: Literature** [RL.7.4; SL.7.4]

Analyze the Impact of Sound Devices

Give an oral presentation of an essay in which you analyze the impact of sound devices in a poem in this unit.

- Analyze the impact of rhyme and other sound devices, such as repetition or alliteration, in a poem in this unit. Consider how the sound devices affect mood, meaning, and tone in the poem.

- Organize your key points and support them with examples from the poem.

- Before your presentation, consult a print or online dictionary to find the pronunciations of unknown words.

- Deliver your presentation to the class. Use appropriate eye contact, adequate volume, and clear pronunciation.

@ **Task 5: Literature** [RL.7.4; SL.7.1]

Lead a Discussion About Word Choice

Lead a small-group discussion about the effects of word choice in a poem from this unit.

- Choose a poem to use as the basis for your discussion. Prepare by jotting down examples of specific words in the poem and noting their figurative or connotative meanings.

- Ask someone in your group to read the poem aloud. Then, allow group members to share their opinions and ideas about word choice in the poem. Follow general rules for discussion, taking turns speaking.

- Pose questions and respond to others' questions. Acknowledge new information and adjust your own ideas in response if necessary.

- Use formal English and academic vocabulary to discuss the poem.

@ **Task 6: Literature** [RL.7.4; SL.7.4]

Respond to Poetry

Present an oral response to one of the poems in this unit.

- Choose a poem that you feel is particularly effective. Determine the most important idea or message the poet conveys in the poem.

- Analyze the impact of word choice, imagery, figurative language, structure, and sound devices in the poem.

- Formulate your personal response to the poem. Ask yourself questions such as these: *Do the connotations of specific words make me feel a certain way? What pictures do I see in my mind when I read this line? What is the effect of rhyme or rhythm when I read the poem aloud?*

- Organize your response logically. State your opinion clearly in your introduction. Establish eye contact with your audience, and speak with adequate volume.

THE BIG ?

What is the best way to communicate?

At the beginning of Unit 4, you wrote a response to the Big Question. Now that you have completed the unit, write a new response. Discuss how your initial ideas have either been changed or reinforced. Cite specific examples from the literature in this unit, from other subject areas, and from your own life to support your ideas. Use Big Question vocabulary words (see p. 571) in your response.

Featured Titles

In this unit, you have read a wide variety of poems by many different poets. Continue to read on your own. Select works that you enjoy, but challenge yourself to explore new poets and works of increasing depth and complexity. The titles suggested below will help you get started.

Literature

It Doesn't Always Have to Rhyme

by Eve Merriam

This **poetry** collection is full of playful poems about poetry, including "How to Eat a Poem," "Metaphor," and a selection found in this unit, "Onomatopoeia."

The Poetry of Robert Frost: The Collected Poems

by Robert Frost   EXEMPLAR TEXT

Many readers admire Robert Frost's writing for how it captures a single thought or moment in a way that is personal but also universal. This **poetry** collection includes many of Frost's most popular poems.

When I Dance

by James Berry

This **poetry** collection pulses with the different rhythms of life in England and the Caribbean. In it, you will find the poem "One," which is also a selection in this unit.

My Own True Name

by Pat Mora

This **poetry** collection is divided into three sections: "Blooms" are poems about love and happiness, "Thorns" are poems about difficult times, and "Roots" are poems about family and home.

The Music of Dolphins

by Karen Hesse

After a plane crash, the main character in this **novel** is raised by dolphins until the Coast Guard finds her. Mila "the Dolphin Girl" learns to speak, but she longs to return to the sea.

Informational Texts

Discoveries: Pushing the Boundaries

In this book, you can read about many different ways to communicate. The **nonfiction articles** in this collection include "The Samurai of Feudal Japan" and "Challenging Assumptions."

This Land Was Made for You and Me: The Life and Songs of Woody Guthrie

by Elizabeth Partridge   EXEMPLAR TEXT

During the Great Depression of the 1930s, folksinger Woody Guthrie wandered the nation, meeting workers and writing songs. In addition to a **biography** of Guthrie, this book includes photographs, posters, letters, and drawings.

Preparing to Read Complex Texts

Attentive Reading As you read poetry on your own, ask yourself questions about the text. The questions below, along with others that you ask as you read, will help you understand and appreciate poetry.

Common Core State Standards

Reading Literature/Informational Text
10. By the end of the year, read and comprehend literature, including stories, dramas, and poems, and literary nonfiction in the grades 6–8 text complexity band proficiently, with scaffolding as needed at the high end of the range.

When reading poetry, ask yourself...

- Who is the speaker of the poem? What kind of person does the speaker seem to be? How do I know?
- What is the poem about?
- If the poem is telling a story, who are the characters and what happens to them?
- Does any one line or section state the poem's theme, or meaning, directly? If so, what is that line or section?
- If there is no direct statement of a theme, what details help me to see the poem's deeper meaning?

Key Ideas and Details

- How does the poem look on the page? Is it long and rambling or short and concise? Does it have long or short lines?
- Does the poem have a formal structure or is it free verse?
- How does the form affect how I read the poem?
- How many stanzas form this poem? What does each stanza tell me?
- Do I notice repetition, rhyme, or meter? Do I notice other sound devices? How do these techniques affect how I read the poem?
- Even if I do not understand every word, do I like the way the poem sounds? Why or why not?
- Do any of the poet's word choices seem especially interesting or unusual? Why?
- What images do I notice? Do they create clear word-pictures in my mind? Why or why not?
- Would I like to read this poem aloud? Why or why not?

Craft and Structure

- Has the poem helped me understand its subject in a new way? If so, how?
- Does the poem remind me of others I have read? If so, how?
- In what ways is the poem different from others I have read?
- What information, ideas, or insights have I gained from reading this poem?
- Do I find the poem moving, funny, or mysterious? How does the poem make me feel?
- Would I like to read more poems by this poet? Why or why not?

Integration of Ideas

THE BIG ?

Do others *see* us more clearly than we *see* ourselves?

Unit

5

PHLit
Online!
www.PHLitOnline.cor

Hear It!
- Selection summary audio
- Selection audio
- BQ Tunes

See It!
- Author videos
- Big Question video
- Get Connected videos
- Background videos
- More about the authors
- Illustrated vocabulary words
- Vocabulary flashcards

Do It!
- Interactive journals
- Interactive graphic organizers
- Grammar tutorials
- Interactive vocabulary games
- Test practice

Do others *see* us more clearly than we *see* ourselves?

We are constantly learning about ourselves through our experiences and our interactions with others. Sometimes we feel that another person truly knows and understands us. Other times, however, we might suspect that someone is making an assumption about us based on appearance or other factors. To see ourselves and others clearly, it helps to reflect on the unique characteristics of each person. Our individual qualities and beliefs about ourselves influence how others see us and how we react to the people around us.

Exploring the Big Question

Collaboration: Group Discussion Start thinking about the Big Question by making a list of ways you form impressions about other people and ways that other people form impressions about you. Describe one specific example of each of the following:

- A judgment based on appearance
- A judgment influenced by prejudice, or bias
- An insight about the way another person treats you or others
- A time another person seemed to understand your thoughts
- A perception based on another person's reaction to a difficult situation

Share your examples with a small group. Discuss whether or not each situation helped someone see another person clearly. Use the Big Question vocabulary in your discussion.

Connecting to the Literature Each reading in this unit will give you additional insight into the Big Question.

PHLit Online!
www.PHLitOnline.com
- Big Question video
- Illustrated vocabulary words
- Interactive vocabulary games
- BQ Tunes

Learning Big Question Vocabulary

© **Acquire and Use Academic Vocabulary** Academic vocabulary is the language you encounter in textbooks and on standardized tests. Review the definitions of these academic vocabulary words.

appreciate (ə prē´ shē āt´) v. be thankful for	**define** (dē fīn´) v. describe; explain
assumption (ə sump´ shən) n. act of accepting something as true without proof	**focus** (fō´ kəs) n. central point; topic
bias (bī´ əs) n. a slanted viewpoint	**identify** (ī den´ tə fī´) v. recognize; point out
characteristic (kar´ ək tər is´ tik) n. trait; feature	**ignore** (ig nôr´) v. pay no attention to

Use these words as you complete Big Question activities in this unit that involve reading, writing, speaking, and listening.

© **Gather Vocabulary Knowledge** Additional Big Question words are listed below. Categorize the words by deciding whether you know each one well, know it a little bit, or do not know it at all.

appearance	perception	reflect
image	perspective	reveal
	reaction	

Then, do the following:

1. Work with a partner to determine and write each word's definition.
2. Verify definitions by looking them up in a print or online dictionary and revising as needed.
3. Then, for each word, write an original sentence about how we see ourselves and others. Provide enough information so the meaning of each word is clear.
4. Exchange sentences with your partner to see if he or she agrees with your main points and your use of the vocabulary words.

The Elements of Drama

A drama is a story that is meant to be performed.

A **drama,** or **play,** is a story that is performed for an audience. Some dramas are presented live on a stage, while others are recorded on film. No matter what the form, a drama brings to life the words of its author, the **playwright.**

Drama is similar to fiction in many ways. Like fiction, drama focuses on **characters,** made-up people who interact in a particular **setting,** or environment. The characters are caught up in a struggle, or **conflict.** This drives the **plot**—a series of actions that build to a **climax.** The climax is the highest point

of tension. The action then winds down in a **resolution.**

Unlike fiction, drama is meant to be performed. Instead of *reading* a playwright's words, audiences see and hear actors speak the words.

The written text of a drama is called a **script.** A script consists of **dialogue,** the words spoken by the actors, and **stage directions,** the playwright's instructions about how the drama should be performed. **Acts** are the units of action in a drama. Acts are often divided into parts called **scenes.**

Elements of Drama	
Stage Directions	Stage directions are the playwright's instructions about how to perform the drama. They tell how actors should speak and move, and give details about lighting, sound effects, and costumes. These abbreviations are often used in stage directions: **C:** center stage **D:** downstage (nearest to audience) **U:** upstage (farthest from audience) **L:** stage left (audience's right) **R:** stage right (audience's left)
Dialogue	Dialogue is conversation between or among characters.
Set/Scenery	*Set* and *scenery* are terms used to describe the construction onstage that suggests the time and place of the action. A set may look like an actual place, or it may merely suggest a place.
Props	Props are small movable items, such as a doctor's clipboard or a student's notebook, that actors use to make their actions look realistic.
Acts and Scenes	Acts and scenes are the basic units of action in a drama. A full-length drama may consist of several acts, each of which may contain any number of scenes.

Changing Forms of Drama

Early Drama The earliest known written dramas came to us from the ancient Greeks. The Greeks divided drama into two basic categories that we still use today: **comedy** and **tragedy.**

Comedy	• features ordinary people in funny or ridiculous situations • usually has a happy ending • is meant to entertain, but also may point out human weaknesses and the faults of a society
Tragedy	• shows the downfall of the main character, known as the **tragic hero** • the tragic hero may be an admirable person with a fault that brings about his or her destruction • the hero might also be an ordinary person destroyed by an evil force in society

The biggest difference between a comedy and a tragedy is the way that the story ends. Comedies end in happy events, such as reunions or weddings. Tragedies end in sad events, such as deaths or partings.

After the great plays of the ancient Greeks, drama went into a decline that lasted more than one thousand years. It bloomed again during the time of English playwright William Shakespeare (1564–1616). Shakespeare and his fellow dramatists wrote both comedies and tragedies.

Drama Today The modern period has seen a tremendous growth in dramatic writing, and this growth has brought change—even in the meaning of the term *drama.* Contemporary plays and films that treat serious subjects tend to be called *dramas* now, rather than *tragedies*. These serious works are different from contemporary comedies, which, as expected, are lighter and more entertaining.

An even more important change is the way different media have altered people's experience with drama. For several thousand years, people saw dramas in only one way: live. Today, the world of drama is not limited to the stage. Here are some other common types of dramas:

- **Screenplays** are the scripts for films. They include camera angles and can allow for more scene changes than a stage play.
- **Teleplays** are scripts written for television. They contains elements similar to those in a screenplay.
- **Radio plays** are written to be performed as radio broadcasts. They include sound effects and do not require a set.

In This Section

The Elements of Drama

Analyzing Drama

Close Read: Understanding Elements of Drama
- Model Text
- Practice Text

After You Read

 Common Core State Standards

RL.7.3, RL.7.5
[For the full wording of the standards, see the standards chart in the front of your textbook.]

Analyzing Drama

Drama has its own unique way of telling stories about characters.

Common Core State Standards

Reading Literature 3. Analyze how particular elements of a story or drama interact (e.g., how setting shapes the characters or plot).

Reading Literature 5. Analyze how a drama's or poem's form or structure (e.g., soliloquy, sonnet) contributes to its meaning.

Structure in Drama The **structure,** or framework, of a drama affects the way the audience or reader finds meaning in the performance or script. The following is a typical structure for a three-act drama.

Act I	The characters, setting, and **conflict,** or problem, are introduced in the **exposition.**
Act II	In the **rising action,** the main character, or **protagonist,** tries to solve the conflict, but faces obstacles that prevent an easy solution.
Act III	The **climax,** or highest point of interest, represents a turning point in the drama. During the **falling action,** the plot moves toward the **resolution** of the conflict.

Of course, not all dramas follow a three-act structure. Many classic dramas, including most works by the Ancient Greeks and by Shakespeare, consist of five acts. One-act plays, on the other hand, contain a single act. Some one-act plays are divided into multiple scenes.

Conflict in Drama Dramatic action is driven by **conflict,** or struggle. There are two types of conflict in drama. **External conflict** occurs between a character and an outside force, such as another character. **Internal conflict** occurs within the mind of a character,

as when a character is torn between opposing feelings or goals.

Examples: External Conflict

- Two young people want to marry, but their parents will not allow it.
- A family must flee their war-torn country.

Examples: Internal Conflict

- A girl must decide if she should turn in her friend, who has committed a crime.
- A man struggles to overcome a violent past.

Action: Showing, Not Telling

Drama is moved forward entirely by spoken dialogue and physical action. Audiences who watch a play or film are not *told* what is happening. Rather, they are *shown* what happens. For example, the audience may recognize conflict by hearing anger in an actor's voice or seeing tension in his body. As a drama unfolds, various elements work together to bring the story to life. A dimly lit stage may create an emotional effect; one character's tone of voice may make another character respond in a certain way.

Obviously, the experience of reading a drama differs from that of seeing it performed. Readers experience a script more fully if they imagine the setting described in the stage directions and the way the actors' voices and movements bring the dialogue to life.

Character Development In drama, two elements are key to the development of character: stage directions and dialogue. These are the tools with which a playwright can create believable and interesting dramatic stories. Playwrights use **stage directions** to tell how characters speak, move, and interact with other characters. Playwrights create **dialogue** to reveal character in several ways.

- A character may directly express private thoughts, feelings, and conflicts in a speech.
- Personality traits may be revealed as a character interacts with other characters.
- A character may comment on another character.

In addition, playwrights may have characters deliver different types of speeches.

- A **monologue** is a long, uninterrupted speech spoken by one character to another.
- A **soliloquy** is a speech in which a character is alone and reveals private thoughts. Sometimes a soliloquy is spoken to the audience. Other times, the character is speaking only to himself or herself.
- An **aside** is a comment made by a character to the audience. It is not meant to be heard by the other characters.

To engage the audience and reader, playwrights create **complex characters** who resemble real people. Complex characters are involved in complicated relationships. Sometimes they are pulled in many directions because of difficult situations and problems.

Complex characters change as a play progresses.

Theme in Drama As in most other literary genres, drama conveys **themes,** or insights about life and human nature. The words and actions of the characters point to a drama's theme.

Examples of Theme in Drama

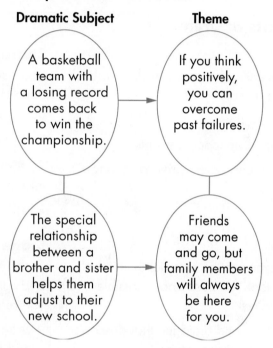

Dramatic Subject	Theme
A basketball team with a losing record comes back to win the championship.	If you think positively, you can overcome past failures.
The special relationship between a brother and sister helps them adjust to their new school.	Friends may come and go, but family members will always be there for you.

The various elements of a drama work together to convey its theme. To determine and analyze the theme of a drama, notice how the characters respond to conflicts and decide whether they change or grow as a result of their experiences. Consider how the setting—the time and place of the action—impacts characters or events. Finally, look for central ideas that are emphasized throughout the drama through the words and actions of the characters. Considering all of these elements will lead you to the central insight in a dramatic work.

Close Read: Understanding Elements of Drama

In drama, as in other genres, plot, characters, and setting propel the action forward.

The following elements are your keys to understanding a drama and its theme.

Key Elements of Drama

Plot/Action

Plot is the sequence of events in a drama. Look for details that reveal

- the passage of time;
- the importance of specific events;
- the ways that characters grow or change.

Characters

Characters in drama are described through stage directions and dialogue. As you read, look for details that reveal a character's

- appearance and background;
- personality traits;
- attitudes toward other characters;
- private thoughts and feelings.

Conflict

Conflict in drama can be external or internal. As you read, look for clues about possible conflicts, including

- stage directions and dialogue that describe a character's fears or worries;
- dialogue that expresses strong feelings;
- challenging situations.

Stage Directions

Stage directions give clues about the characters and tell how the drama should be performed. As you read, look for instructions about

- characters' movements, facial expressions, and tones of voice;
- the props and scenery;
- lighting and sound effects.

Setting

A drama usually has a specific setting that may have a strong effect on the characters and plot. As you read, consider

- the time and place of the action;
- details that describe the physical environment;
- details that make the environment challenging or dangerous.

Dialogue

Dialogue refers to the words spoken by the characters. As you read, look for dialogue that

- reveals a character's thoughts and feelings;
- moves the action forward;
- reveals the conflict.

Model

About the Text This excerpt is from the drama *Sorry, Wrong Number* by Lucille Fletcher. This popular play has been performed on stage, as a movie, and as a radio play.

---

from *Sorry, Wrong Number* by Lucille Fletcher

[SCENE: *As curtain rises, we see a divided stage, only the center part of which is lighted and furnished as* MRS. STEVENSON'S *bedroom. Expensive, rather fussy furnishings. A large bed, on which* MRS. STEVENSON, *clad in bed-jacket, is lying. A night-table close by, with phone, lighted lamp, and pill bottles. A mantle, with clock, R. A closed door, R. A window, with curtains closed, rear. The set is lit by one lamp on night-table. It is enclosed by three flats. Beyond this central set, the stage, on either side, is in darkness.*

MRS. STEVENSON *is dialing a number on the phone, as curtain rises. She listens to phone, slams down receiver in irritation.*

As she does so, we hear sound of a train roaring by in the distance. She reaches for her pill bottle, pours herself a glass of water, shakes out pill, swallows it, then reaches for the phone again, dials number nervously.]

SOUND: *Number being dialed on phone: Busy signal.*

MRS. STEVENSON (*A querulous, self-centered neurotic.*): Oh—dear! (*Slams down receiver, dials* OPERATOR.)

[SCENE: *A spotlight, L. of side flat, picks up out of peripheral darkness, figure of* 1ST OPERATOR, *sitting with headphones at a small table. If spotlight not available, use flashlight, clicked on by* 1ST OPERATOR, *illuminating her face.*]

OPERATOR: Your call, please?

MRS. STEVENSON: Operator? I've been dialing Murray Hill 4-0098 now for the last three-quarters of an hour, and the line is always busy. But I don't see how it could be that busy that long. Will you try it for me, please?

OPERATOR: Murray Hill 4-0098? One moment, please. [SCENE: *She makes gesture of plugging in call through a switchboard.*]

MRS. STEVENSON: I don't see how it could be busy all this time. It's my husband's office. He's working late tonight, and I'm all alone here in the house. My health is very poor—and I've been feeling so nervous all day....

Setting The stage directions describe a woman's "fussy" bedroom surrounded by darkness. This setting creates a somewhat unsettling feeling.

Plot/Action The action in the play will center on the character's attempts to make a phone call.

Characters Mrs. Stevenson is described in the stage directions as "querulous," or irritable, and "neurotic." We can assume that she is easily upset.

Stage Directions In the stage directions, the playwright gives specific suggestions for lighting this scene.

Dialogue Mrs. Stevenson's speech reveals her conflict. She is frightened because she is alone and unable to reach someone by phone.

© **EXEMPLAR TEXT**

Model continued

Setting Stage directions indicate and describe changes in scene and setting.

Stage Directions The playwright suggests a way to stage this scene.

Plot/Action Dialogue builds tension and suspense and moves the action forward.

OPERATOR: Ringing Murray Hill 4-0098…. *(SOUND: Phone buzz. It rings three times. Receiver is picked up at other end.)*

[SCENE: *Spotlight picks up figure of a heavyset man, seated at desk with phone on right side of dark periphery of stage. He is wearing a hat. Picks up phone, which rings three times*]

MAN: Hello.

MRS. STEVENSON: Hello…? *(A little puzzled)* Hello. Is Mr. Stevenson there?

MAN: *(into phone, as though he had not heard.)* Hello…. *(Louder)* Hello.

[SCENE: *Spotlight on left now moves from* OPERATOR *to another man,* GEORGE. *A killer type, also wearing a hat, but standing as in a phone booth. A three-sided screen may be used to suggest this.*]

2ND MAN: *(slow, heavy quality, faintly foreign accent).* Hello.

1ST MAN: Hello, George?

GEORGE: Yes, sir.

MRS. STEVENSON: *(louder and more imperious, to phone).* Hello. Who's this? What number am I calling, please?

1ST MAN: We have heard from our client. He says the coast is clear for tonight.

GEORGE: Yes, sir.

1ST MAN: Where are you now?

GEORGE: In a phone booth.

1ST MAN: OK. You should know the address. At eleven o'clock the private patrolman goes around to the bar on Second Avenue for a beer. Be sure that all the lights downstairs are out. There should be only one light visible from the street. At eleven-fifteen a subway train crosses the bridge. It makes a noise in case her window is open and she should scream.

MRS. STEVENSON: *(shocked).* Oh—HELLO! What number is this, please?

GEORGE: OK. I understand.

1ST MAN: Make it quick. As little blood as possible. Our client does not wish to make her suffer long.

GEORGE: A knife OK, sir?

1ST MAN: Yes. A knife will be OK. And remember—remove the rings and bracelets and the jewelry in the bureau drawer. Our client wishes it to look like simple robbery.

GEORGE: OK—I get— [SCENE: *Spotlight suddenly goes out on* GEORGE.] *(SOUND: A bland buzzing signal)*

Independent Practice

About the Selection Laurence Yep's novel *Dragonwings* is about Moon Shadow, a Chinese boy who becomes deeply involved in his father's quest to build an airplane. More than twenty years after writing the novel, Yep created an hour-long dramatic version of the story. Following are an excerpt from the novel, narrated by Moon Shadow, and a scene from the drama.

from the novel *Dragonwings* by Laurence Yep

I do not know when I fell asleep, but it was already way past sunrise when I woke up. The light crept through the cracks in the walls and under the shutters and seemed to delight especially in dancing on my eyes. Father lay huddled, rolled up in his blanket. He did not move when the knock came at our door. I was still in my clothes because it was cold. I crawled out of the blankets and opened the side door.

The fog lay low on the hill. Tendrils drifted in through the open doorway. At first I could not see anything but shadows, and then a sudden breeze whipped the fog away from the front of our barn. Hand Clap stood there as if he had appeared by magic. He bowed.

"There you are." He turned and called over his shoulder. "Hey, everybody, they're here."

I heard the clink of harness and the rattle of an old wagon trying to follow the ruts in the road. Toiling up the hill out of the fog was Red Rabbit, and behind him I saw Uncle on the wagon seat. The rest of the wagon was empty—I suppose to give Red Rabbit less of a load to pull. Behind the wagon came the Company, with coils of ropes over their shoulders and baskets of food. I ran down the hill, my feet pounding against the hard, damp earth. I got up on the seat and almost bowled Uncle over. For once Uncle did not worry about his dignity but caught me up and returned my hug.

Characters What does Moon Shadow's description suggest about his father's condition? What details give you this idea?

Setting Describe the setting in your own words. How could staging create this same effect?

Practice continued

"Ouch," he said, and pushed me away. He patted himself lightly on his chest. "I'm not as young as I used to be."

Then Hand Clap, Lefty, and White Deer crowded around.

"Am I ever glad you're here," I said. "Poor Father—"

Uncle held up his hands. "We know. That's why we came."

"But how? Why?" I was bursting with a dozen questions all at once.

"Why, to help you get that thing up to the top of the hill," Uncle said. "Why else would we close up our shop and take a boat and climb this abominable hill, all on the coldest, wettest day ever known since creation?"

"But you don't believe in flying machines."

Conflict What conflict does the conversation between Moon Shadow and Uncle reveal?

"I still don't," Uncle said sternly. "But I still feel as if I owe you something for what was done to you by that man who once was my son.[1] I'll be there to haul your machine up the hill, and I'll be there to haul it back down when it doesn't fly."

"We were all getting fat anyway," White Deer said, "especially Uncle."

---

1. man who once was my son Black Dog, who robbed the narrator and his father.

From the dramatization of *Dragonwings* by Laurence Yep

RED RABBIT a horse that pulls the company's laundry wagon **UNCLE BRIGHT STAR** another laundry owner **WHITE DEER** the third laundry owner	**MOON SHADOW** the narrator of the story **MISS WHITLAW** owner of a stable in San Francisco where the narrator and his father live **WINDRIDER** Moon Shadow's father

Scene 9 *Piedmont, later that day outside the stable.*

MOON SHADOW: September twenty-second, Nineteen-ought-nine.
Dear Mother. I have bad news. We are going to lose Dragonwings before father can fly it. Black Dog stole all we have, and the landlord will not give us an extension on our rent. So we'll have to move and leave Dragonwings behind. We have asked Miss Whitlaw for help, but her new house has taken up all of her money. And even if Uncle would speak to us, he has probably spent all he has on rebuilding his laundry.

*[**UNCLE BRIGHT STAR** and **MISS WHITLAW** enter from L.]*

MISS WHITLAW: I could have gotten down from the wagon by myself.

UNCLE BRIGHT STAR: Watch gopher hole.

MISS WHITLAW: I'm younger than you.

MOON SHADOW: Uncle, Miss Whitlaw!

MISS WHITLAW: How are you?

*[Shaking **MOON SHADOW's** hand. **WINDRIDER** enters from U. He now wears a cap.]*

WINDRIDER: Come to laugh, Uncle?

UNCLE BRIGHT STAR: I came to help you fly your contraption.

MOON SHADOW: But you don't believe in flying machines.

Conflict From this letter, which is performed as a monologue, what do you learn about the conflict the characters face? Is the conflict external or internal?

Stage Directions What is the meaning of "U" in the stage directions?

Practice continued

Characters Based on this speech, how does Uncle Bright Star feel about the attempt at flight?

Stage Directions What is supposed to be happening at this point in the drama? What would the audience see, as described in the stage directions?

Dialogue What effect do the call-and-response speeches of Uncle Bright Star and the others create? How does this dialogue support the illusion that is being created onstage?

UNCLE BRIGHT STAR: And I'll haul that thing back down when it doesn't fly. Red Rabbit and me were getting fat anyway. But look at how tall you've grown. And how thin. And ragged. *[Pause.]* But you haven't broken your neck which was more than I ever expected.

MISS WHITLAW: As soon as I told your uncle, we hatched the plot together. You ought to get a chance to fly your aeroplane.

UNCLE BRIGHT STAR: Flat purse, strong backs.

WINDRIDER: We need to pull Dragonwings to the very top.

UNCLE BRIGHT STAR: That hill is a very steep hill.

WINDRIDER: It has to be that one. The winds are right.

UNCLE BRIGHT STAR: Ah, well, it's the winds.

WINDRIDER: Take the ropes. *[Pantomimes taking a rope over his shoulder as he faces the audience.]* Got a good grip?

OTHERS: *[Pantomiming taking the ropes.]* Yes, right, etc.

WINDRIDER: Then pull.

[They strain. MOON SHADOW stumbles but gets right up. Stamping his feet to get better footing, he keeps tugging.]

MOON SHADOW: *[Giving up.]* It's no good.

UNCLE BRIGHT STAR: Pull in rhythm. As we did on the railroad.[1] *[In demonstration, UNCLE BRIGHT STAR stamps his feet in a slow rhythm to set the beat and the others repeat. The rhythm picks up as they move.]*
Ngúng, ngúng.
Dew gùng

OTHERS: Ngúng, ngúng.
Dew gùng

UNCLE BRIGHT STAR: *[Imitating the intonation of the Cantonese.]* Púsh, púsh.
Wòrk, wòrk.

OTHERS: Púsh, púsh.
Wòrk, wòrk.

UNCLE BRIGHT STAR: Seen gà,
Gee gá.

---

1. railroad Uncle Bright Star had helped dig tunnels through the mountains for the railroad.

[High rising tone on the last syllable.]

OTHERS: Seen gá,
Gee gá.

[High rising tone on the last syllable.]

UNCLE BRIGHT STAR: Get rìch,
Go hóme.

OTHERS: Get rìch,
Go hóme.

[MOON SHADOW, WINDRIDER, UNCLE BRIGHT STAR and MISS WHITLAW arrive D.]

MOON SHADOW: *[Panting.]* We made it. Tramp the grass down in front.

[WINDRIDER stands C as the others stamp the grass. They can't help smiling and laughing a little.]

WINDRIDER: That's enough.

MOON SHADOW: [To *MISS WHITLAW.*] Take that propeller.

[MISS WHITLAW takes her place before the right propeller with her hands resting on the blade. MOON SHADOW takes his place beside the left propeller. WINDRIDER faces U., his back to the audience.]

MISS WHITLAW: Listen to the wind on the wings.

UNCLE BRIGHT STAR: It's alive.

WINDRIDER: All right.

[MOON SHADOW and MISS WHITLAW pull down at the propellers and back away quickly. We hear a motor cough into life. Propellers begin to turn with a roar.]

UNCLE BRIGHT STAR: *[Slowly turning.]* What's wrong? Is it just going to roll down the hill?

[MISS WHITLAW crosses her fingers as they all turn to watch the aeroplane.]

MISS WHITLAW: He's up!

[WINDRIDER starts to do his flight ballet.]

MOON SHADOW: *[Pointing.]* He's turning.

UNCLE BRIGHT STAR: He's really flying.

Setting What do Moon Shadow and the others do to create the illusion of a grassy hilltop?

Stage Directions How do the actions described in the stage directions add excitement as the action builds to a climax?

Practice continued

Plot/Action How do the stage directions and dialogue help create the illusion that Windrider and Dragonwings are flying?

Dialogue What important information does this soliloquy reveal about the flight and what happened afterward? What emotions might Moon Shadow experience during this speech?

Characters What change and growth does Windrider show in this monologue?

MISS WHITLAW: I never thought I'd see the day. A human up in the sky. Off the ground.

[They turn and tilt their heads back.]

MISS WHITLAW: *[Cont'd.]* Free as an eagle.

UNCLE BRIGHT STAR: *[Correcting her.]* Like dragon.

MOON SHADOW: Father, you did it. *[Wonderingly.]* You did it.

[The aeroplane roars loudly overhead. MOON SHADOW as adult steps forward and addresses the audience.]

MOON SHADOW: I thought he'd fly forever and ever. Up, up to heaven and never come down. But then some of the guy wires[2] broke, and the right wings separated. Dragonwings came crashing to earth. Father had a few broken bones, but it was nothing serious. Only the aeroplane was wrecked. Uncle took him back to the laundry to recover. Father didn't say much, just thought a lot—I figured he was busy designing the next aeroplane. But when Father was nearly well, he made me sit down next to him.

WINDRIDER: Uncle says he'll make me a partner if I stay. So the western officials would have to change my immigration class. I'd be a merchant, and merchants can bring their wives here. Would you like to send for Mother?

MOON SHADOW: *[Going to WINDRIDER.]* But Dragonwings?

WINDRIDER: When I was up in the air, I tried to find you. You were so small. And getting smaller. Just disappearing from sight. *[Handing his cap to MOON SHADOW.]* Like you were disappearing from my life. *[He begins his ballet again.]* I knew it wasn't the time. The Dragon King[3] said there would be all sorts of lessons.

[MOON SHADOW turns to audience as an adult.]

MOON SHADOW: We always talked about flying again. Only we never did. *[Putting on cap.]* But dreams stay with you, and we never forgot.

[WINDRIDER takes his final pose. A gong sounds.]

---

2. **guy wires** wires that help to steady the plane's two sets of wings.
3. **Dragon King** In Chinese legends, most dragons are not evil creatures. Earlier in the story, Windrider relates a dream sequence in which he was given his name by the Dragon King and learned he had once been a flying dragon.

© 1. **Key Ideas and Details (a)** In the novel excerpt, how does Uncle plan to get the flying machine up the hill? **(b) Compare:** In the scene from the drama, what helps the audience grasp how Dragonwings will be moved?

© 2. **Key Ideas and Details (a) Interpret:** What does Moon Shadow mean at the end of the scene when he says, "dreams stay with you, and we never forgot"? **(b) Analyze:** What **theme** does this statement reveal?

© 3. **Key Ideas and Details Infer:** Based on the **dialogue,** how would you describe the character of Uncle Bright Star? Give specific examples.

© 4. **Key Ideas and Details Connect:** What qualities do you see in Moon Shadow that he may not see in himself?

© 5. **Key Ideas and Details Connect:** What evidence suggests that Moon Shadow does not know Uncle as well as he thinks he does?

© 6. **Craft and Structure Analyze:** If *Dragonwings* were a three-act play, in which act do you think you would find the excerpt you read? Explain.

© 7. **Integration of Knowledge and Ideas (a)** In a chart like the one shown, list examples of dialogue under the heading that reveals its use.

To Show Action	To Reveal Thoughts and Feelings	To Describe Setting
"Take that propeller"	"When I was up in the air, I tried to find you . . . Like you were disappearing from my life."	"That hill is a very steep hill."

(b) Collaborate: Compare charts with a partner. How have your ideas changed as a result of seeing other responses?

Drama Selection

Build your skills and improve your comprehension of drama with
texts of increasing complexity.

A CHRISTMAS CAROL:
SCROOGE AND MARLEY

ISRAEL HOROVITZ
from *A CHRISTMAS CAROL*
by CHARLES DICKENS

JACOB MARLEY, a specter
EBENEZER SCROOGE, not yet dead,
which is to say still alive
BOB CRATCHIT, Scrooge's clerk
FRED, Scrooge's nephew
THIN DO-GOODER
PORTLY DO-GOODER
SPECTERS (VARIOUS), carrying money-
boxes
THE GHOST OF CHRISTMAS PAST
FOUR JOCUND TRAVELERS
A BAND OF SINGERS
A BAND OF DANCERS
LITTLE BOY SCROOGE
YOUNG MAN SCROOGE
FAN, Scrooge's little sister
THE SCHOOLMASTER
SCHOOLMATES
FEZZIWIG, a fine and fair employer
DICK, young Scrooge's co-worker
YOUNG SCROOGE
A FIDDLER
MORE DANCERS
SCROOGE'S LOST LOVE

SCROOGE'S LOST LOVE'S DAUGHTER
SCROOGE'S LOST LOVE'S HUSBAND
THE GHOST OF CHRISTMAS PRESENT
SOME BAKERS
MRS. CRATCHIT, Bob Cratchit's wife
BELINDA CRATCHIT, a daughter
MARTHA CRATCHIT, another daughter
PETER CRATCHIT, a son
TINY TIM CRATCHIT, another son
SCROOGE'S NIECE, Fred's wife
THE GHOST OF CHRISTMAS FUTURE, a
mute Phantom
THREE MEN OF BUSINESS
DRUNKS, SCOUNDRELS, WOMEN OF THE
STREETS
A CHARWOMAN
MRS. DILBER
JOE, an old second-hand goods dealer
A CORPSE, very like Scrooge
AN INDEBTED FAMILY
ADAM, a young boy
A POULTERER
A GENTLEWOMAN
SOME MORE MEN OF BUSINESS

740

Read **A Christmas Carol: Scrooge and Marley, Act 1**
to find out what happens when a mean and selfish
man is forced to revisit key events from his past.

Common Core State Standards

Meet these standards with **A Christmas Carol: Scrooge and Marley, Act 1** (p. 740).

Reading Literature

3. Analyze how particular elements of a story or drama
interact. (*Literary Analysis: Dialogue*)

5. Analyze how a drama's or poem's form or structure
contributes to its meaning. (*Literary Analysis: Dialogue*)

Writing

1. Write arguments to support claims with clear reasons
and relevant evidence. **1.a.** Introduce claim(s), acknowledge
alternate or opposing claims, and organize the reasons and
evidence logically. **1.b.** Support claim(s) with logical
reasoning and relevant evidence, using accurate, credible
sources and demonstrating an understanding of the topic
or text. **1.c.** Use words, phrases, and clauses to create
cohesion and clarify the relationships among claim(s),
reasons, and evidence. (*Writing: Letter*)

7. Conduct short research projects to answer a question,
drawing on several sources and generating additional

related, focused questions for further research and
investigation. (*Research and Technology: Costume Plans*)

Language

1. Demonstrate command of the conventions of standard
English grammar and usage when writing or speaking.
(*Conventions: Interjections*)

2. Demonstrate command of the conventions of standard
English capitalization, punctuation, and spelling when
writing. (*Conventions: Interjections*)

4.b. Use common grade-appropriate Greek or Latin affixes
and roots as clues to the meaning of a word. (*Vocabulary:
Word Study*)

6. Acquire and use accurately grade-appropriate general
academic and domain-specific words and phrases; gather
vocabulary knowledge when considering a word or phrase
important to comprehension or expression. (*Vocabulary:
Word Study*)

Reading Skill: Purpose for Reading

Setting a purpose gives you a focus as you read. You may set one or more of these purposes:

- To learn about a subject
- To be entertained
- To gain understanding
- To take action or make a decision
- To be inspired
- To complete a task

To help you set a purpose, **preview a text before reading.** Look at the title, the pictures, the captions, the organization, and the beginnings of passages to help you determine your reason for reading the text.

Using the Strategy: Previewing Chart

Use a chart like the one shown to jot down details you notice as you preview. Then, use your notes to set your purpose.

Element in Work	What Is Suggested About the Work?
Title	
Pictures	
Organization, Structure, Literary Form	
Beginnings of Passages	

Literary Analysis: Dialogue

Dialogue is a conversation between characters. In a play, dialogue serves several key functions. When the play is viewed as a performance, the characters are developed entirely through dialogue. Their word choices and speech patterns give us clues to their personalities. Dialogue also advances the plot and develops the conflict.

In the script of a dramatic work, you can tell which character is speaking by the name that appears before the character's lines. Look at this example:

Mrs. Perez. Come on, kids! We're leaving.

Jen. Wait for me! *Please* wait for me!

 Do others *see* us more clearly than we *see* ourselves?

Writing About the Big Question

In Act 1 of *A Christmas Carol*, Ebenezer Scrooge is visited by a ghost who warns him to change his mean, selfish behavior toward others. Use this sentence starter to develop your ideas about the Big Question.

When we **reflect** on our actions toward others, we can learn _____.

While You Read Consider how Scrooge sees himself and how others see him.

Vocabulary

Read each word and its definition. Decide whether you know the word well, know it a little bit, or do not know it at all. After you read, see how your knowledge of each word has increased.

- **implored** (im plôrd´) *v.* begged (p. 742) *His mother implored him to be careful.* implore *v.* imploring *v.* imploringly *adv.*

- **morose** (mə rōs´) *adj.* gloomy; ill-tempered (p. 744) *The movie was so sad, the audience was morose by the end.* morosely *adv.*

- **destitute** (des´ tə to͞ot´) *n.* people living in complete poverty (p. 747) *People donated food to the destitute.* destitute *adj.* destitution *n.*

- **void** (void) *n.* emptiness (p. 752) *The hot, dry desert was a lifeless void.* void *adj.* devoid *adj.*

- **conveyed** (kən vād´) *v.* made known; expressed (p. 754) *His tightly clenched fists conveyed anger.* convey *v.* conveyable *adj.* conveyance *n.*

- **gratitude** (grat´ i to͞od´) *n.* thankful appreciation (p. 764) *The small gift filled her with gratitude.* gratuity *n.* ingratitude *n.*

Word Study

The **Latin root -grat-** means "thankful" or "pleasing."

In this play, Bob Cratchit expresses his **gratitude,** or thankfulness, for a day off from work on Christmas.

Meet
Israel Horovitz
(b. 1939)

Author of
A CHRISTMAS CAROL:
SCROOGE AND MARLEY

Israel Horovitz was born in Wakefield, Massachusetts. As a teenager, he did not like books by Charles Dickens. As he got older, however, he came to appreciate Dickens's style and stories. Now, Horovitz refers to Dickens as "a masterful storyteller." He imagines that if Dickens were alive today, the Englishman would be "our greatest television writer, or perhaps screenwriter."

Thoughts About *A Christmas Carol* As Horovitz adapted Dickens's novel into a play, he thought about which character was his favorite. The answer may surprise you: It is Scrooge, who reminds Horovitz of his own father.

BACKGROUND FOR THE PLAY
Economic and Social Change

A Christmas Carol is set in England during the nineteenth century, a time of rapid industrial growth. In this booming economy, the wealthy lived in luxury, but the poor and the working class suffered. Charles Dickens's novel, from which this drama was adapted, shows sympathy for the situation of the poor and suggests a way it might be changed.

DID YOU KNOW?
Horovitz is the author of more than fifty plays and screenplays. He is also an actor.

A CHRISTMAS CAROL:
SCROOGE AND MARLEY

ISRAEL HOROVITZ
from *A CHRISTMAS CAROL*
by CHARLES DICKENS

JACOB MARLEY, a specter
EBENEZER SCROOGE, not yet dead, which is to say still alive
BOB CRATCHIT, Scrooge's clerk
FRED, Scrooge's nephew
THIN DO-GOODER
PORTLY DO-GOODER
SPECTERS (VARIOUS), carrying money-boxes
THE GHOST OF CHRISTMAS PAST
FOUR JOCUND TRAVELERS
A BAND OF SINGERS
A BAND OF DANCERS
LITTLE BOY SCROOGE
YOUNG MAN SCROOGE
FAN, Scrooge's little sister
THE SCHOOLMASTER
SCHOOLMATES
FEZZIWIG, a fine and fair employer
DICK, young Scrooge's co-worker
YOUNG SCROOGE
A FIDDLER
MORE DANCERS
SCROOGE'S LOST LOVE

SCROOGE'S LOST LOVE'S DAUGHTER
SCROOGE'S LOST LOVE'S HUSBAND
THE GHOST OF CHRISTMAS PRESENT
SOME BAKERS
MRS. CRATCHIT, Bob Cratchit's wife
BELINDA CRATCHIT, a daughter
MARTHA CRATCHIT, another daughter
PETER CRATCHIT, a son
TINY TIM CRATCHIT, another son
SCROOGE'S NIECE, Fred's wife
THE GHOST OF CHRISTMAS FUTURE, a mute Phantom
THREE MEN OF BUSINESS
DRUNKS, SCOUNDRELS, WOMEN OF THE STREETS
A CHARWOMAN
MRS. DILBER
JOE, an old second-hand goods dealer
A CORPSE, very like Scrooge
AN INDEBTED FAMILY
ADAM, a young boy
A POULTERER
A GENTLEWOMAN
SOME MORE MEN OF BUSINESS

ACT 1

THE PLACE OF THE PLAY Various locations in and around the City of London, including Scrooge's Chambers and Offices; the Cratchit Home; Fred's Home; Scrooge's School; Fezziwig's Offices; Old Joe's Hide-a-Way.

THE TIME OF THE PLAY The entire action of the play takes place on Christmas Eve, Christmas Day, and the morning after Christmas, 1843.

SCENE 1

[*Ghostly music in auditorium. A single spotlight on* JACOB MARLEY, D.C. *He is ancient; awful, dead-eyed. He speaks straight out to auditorium.*]

MARLEY. [*Cackle-voiced*] My name is Jacob Marley and I am dead. [*He laughs.*] Oh, no, there's no doubt that I am dead. The register of my burial was signed by the clergyman, the clerk, the undertaker . . . and by my chief mourner . . . Ebenezer Scrooge . . . [*Pause; remembers*] I am dead as a doornail.
[*A spotlight fades up, Stage Right, on* SCROOGE, *in his countinghouse,*[1] *counting. Lettering on the window behind* SCROOGE *reads: "SCROOGE AND MARLEY, LTD." The spotlight is tight on* SCROOGE's *head and shoulders. We shall not yet see into the offices and setting. Ghostly music continues, under.* MARLEY *looks across at* SCROOGE; *pitifully. After a moment's pause*] I present him to you: Ebenezer Scrooge . . . England's most tightfisted hand at the grindstone, Scrooge! a squeezing, wrenching, grasping, scraping, clutching, covetous, old sinner! secret, and self-contained, and solitary as an oyster. The cold within him freezes his old features, nips his pointed nose, shrivels his cheek, stiffens his gait; makes his eyes red, his thin lips blue; and speaks out shrewdly in his grating voice. Look at him. Look at him . . .

[SCROOGE *counts and mumbles.*]

SCROOGE. They owe me money and I will collect. I will have

---

1. **countinghouse** office for keeping financial records and writing business letters.

Purpose for Reading
Based on the images, title, and other information you can quickly preview, what is your purpose for reading this play?

Reading Check
Where and when does this drama take place?

them jailed, if I have to. They owe me money and I will collect what is due me.

[MARLEY *moves towards* SCROOGE; *two steps. The spotlight stays with him.*]

MARLEY. [*Disgusted*] He and I were partners for I don't know how many years. Scrooge was my sole executor, my sole administrator, my sole assign, my sole residuary legatee,[2] my sole friend and my sole mourner. But Scrooge was not so cut up by the sad event of my death, but that he was an excellent man of business on the very day of my funeral, and solemnized[3] it with an undoubted bargain. [*Pauses again in disgust*] He never painted out my name from the window. There it stands, on the window and above the warehouse door: Scrooge and Marley. Sometimes people new to our business call him Scrooge and sometimes they call him Marley. He answers to both names. It's all the same to him. And it's cheaper than painting in a new sign, isn't it? [*Pauses; moves closer to* SCROOGE] Nobody has ever stopped him in the street to say, with gladsome looks, "My dear Scrooge, how are you? When will you come to see me?" No beggars implored him to bestow a trifle, no children ever ask him what it is o'clock, no man or woman now, or ever in his life, not once, inquire the way to such and such a place. [MARLEY *stands next to* SCROOGE *now. They share, so it seems, a spotlight.*] But what does Scrooge care of any of this? It is the very thing he likes! To edge his way along the crowded paths of life, warning all human sympathy to keep its distance.

[*A ghostly bell rings in the distance.* MARLEY *moves away from* SCROOGE, *now, heading D. again. As he does, he "takes" the light:* SCROOGE *has disappeared into the black void beyond.* MARLEY *walks D.C., talking directly to the audience. Pauses*]

The bell tolls and I must take my leave. You must stay a while with Scrooge and watch him play out his scroogey

Dialogue
What do these lines reveal about Marley's character?

Vocabulary
implored (im plôrd´) *v.* begged

---

2. **my sole executor** (eg zek´ yoo tər), **my sole administrator, my sole assign** (ə sīn´), **my sole residuary legatee** (ri zij´ oo er´ ē leg´ ə tē´) legal terms giving one person responsibility to carry out the wishes of another who has died.
3. **solemnized** (säl´ əm nīzd´) *v.* honored or remembered. Marley is being sarcastic.

life. It is now the story: the once-upon-a-time. Scrooge is busy in his counting house. Where else? Christmas eve and Scrooge is busy in his counting-house. It is cold, bleak, biting weather outside: foggy withal: and, if you listen closely, you can hear the people in the court go wheezing up and down, beating their hands upon their breasts, and stamping their feet upon the pavement stones to warm them . . .

[*The clocks outside strike three.*]

Only three! and quite dark outside already: it has not been light all day this day.

[*This ghostly bell rings in the distance again.* MARLEY *looks about him. Music in.* MARLEY *flies away.*]

SCENE 2

[*N.B.* MARLEY'*s comings and goings should, from time to time, induce the explosion of the odd flash-pot. I.H.*]

[*Christmas music in, sung by a live chorus, full. At conclusion of song, sound fades under and into the distance. Lights up in set: offices of Scrooge and Marley, Ltd.* SCROOGE *sits at his desk, at work. Near him is a tiny fire. His door is open and in his line of vision, we see* SCROOGE'S *clerk,* BOB CRATCHIT, *who sits in a dismal tank of a cubicle, copying letters. Near* CRATCHIT *is a fire so tiny as to barely cast a light: perhaps it is one pitifully glowing coal?* CRATCHIT *rubs his hands together, puts on a white comforter*[4] *and tries to heat his hands around his candle.* SCROOGE'S NEPHEW *enters, unseen.*]

SCROOGE. What are you doing, Cratchit? Acting cold, are you? Next, you'll be asking to replenish your coal from my coal-box, won't you? Well, save your breath, Cratchit! Unless you're prepared to find employ elsewhere!

NEPHEW. [*Cheerfully; surprising* SCROOGE] A merry Christmas to you, Uncle! God save you!

SCROOGE. Bah! Humbug![5]

---

4. **comforter** (kum´ fər tər) *n.* long, woolen scarf.
5. **Humbug** (hum´ bug´) *interj.* nonsense.

▼ **Critical Viewing**
How does this portrayal of Scrooge by actor George C. Scott compare with the image you picture as you read? **[Compare and Contrast]**

✓ Reading Check

What was Marley's relationship to Scrooge?

▶ **Critical Viewing**
Bob Cratchit heats his hands over a candle flame in his office. What does this action tell you about the setting? **[Infer]**

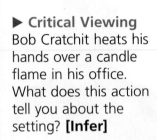

Vocabulary
morose (mə rōs´) *adj.*
gloomy; ill-tempered

NEPHEW. Christmas a "humbug," Uncle? I'm sure you don't mean that.

SCROOGE. I do! Merry Christmas? What right do you have to be merry? What reason have you to be merry? You're poor enough!

NEPHEW. Come, then. What right have you to be dismal? What reason have you to be morose? You're rich enough.

SCROOGE. Bah! Humbug!

NEPHEW. Don't be cross, Uncle.

SCROOGE. What else can I be? Eh? When I live in a world of fools such as this? Merry Christmas? What's Christmas-time to you but a time of paying bills without any money; a time for finding yourself a year older, but not an hour richer. If I could work my will, every idiot who goes about with "Merry Christmas" on his lips, should be boiled with his own pudding, and buried with a stake of holly through his heart. He should!

NEPHEW. Uncle!

SCROOGE. Nephew! You keep Christmas in your own way and let me keep it in mine.

NEPHEW. Keep it! But you don't keep it, Uncle.

SCROOGE. Let me leave it alone, then. Much good it has ever done you!

NEPHEW. There are many things from which I have derived good, by which I have not profited, I daresay. Christmas among the rest. But I am sure that I always thought of Christmas time, when it has come round—as a good time: the only time I know of, when men and women seem to open their shut-up hearts freely, and to think of people below them as if they really were fellow-passengers to the grave, and not another race of creatures bound on other journeys. And therefore, Uncle, though it has never put a scrap of gold or silver in my pocket, I believe that it has done me good, and that it will do me good; and I say, God bless it!

[*The* CLERK *in the tank applauds, looks at the furious* SCROOGE *and pokes out his tiny fire, as if in exchange for the moment of impropriety.* SCROOGE *yells at him.*]

SCROOGE. [*To the clerk*] Let me hear another sound from you and you'll keep your Christmas by losing your situation. [*To the nephew*] You're quite a powerful speaker, sir. I wonder you don't go into Parliament.[6]

NEPHEW. Don't be angry, Uncle. Come! Dine with us tomorrow.

SCROOGE. I'd rather see myself dead than see myself with your family!

NEPHEW. But, why? Why?

SCROOGE. Why did you get married?

NEPHEW. Because I fell in love.

SCROOGE. That, sir, is the only thing that you have said to me in your entire lifetime which is even more ridiculous than "Merry Christmas"! [*Turns from* NEPHEW] Good afternoon.

NEPHEW. Nay, Uncle, you never came to see me before I married either. Why give it as a reason for not coming now?

SCROOGE. Good afternoon, Nephew!

Dialogue
How does this exchange between Scrooge and his nephew show the contrast between the two characters?

Reading Check
What invitation does Scrooge's nephew offer?

---

6. **Parliament** (pär´ lə mənt) national legislative body of Great Britain, in some ways like the United States Congress.

NEPHEW. I want nothing from you; I ask nothing of you; why cannot we be friends?

SCROOGE. Good afternoon!

NEPHEW. I am sorry with all my heart, to find you so resolute. But I have made the trial in homage to Christmas, and I'll keep my Christmas humor to the last. So A Merry Christmas, Uncle!

SCROOGE. Good afternoon!

NEPHEW. And A Happy New Year!

SCROOGE. Good afternoon!

Dialogue
What can you infer about the nephew's character from his words to Cratchit?

NEPHEW. [*He stands facing* SCROOGE.] Uncle, you are the most . . . [*Pauses*] No, I shan't. My Christmas humor is intact . . . [*Pause*] God bless you, Uncle . . . [NEPHEW *turns and starts for the door; he stops at* CRATCHIT'S *cage.*] Merry Christmas, Bob Cratchit . . .

CRATCHIT. Merry Christmas to you sir, and a very, very happy New Year . . .

SCROOGE. [*Calling across to them*] Oh, fine, a perfection, just fine . . . to see the perfect pair of you: husbands, with wives and children to support . . . my clerk there earning fifteen shillings a week . . . and the perfect pair of you, talking about a Merry Christmas! [*Pauses*] I'll retire to Bedlam![7]

NEPHEW. [*To* CRATCHIT] He's impossible!

CRATCHIT. Oh, mind him not, sir. He's getting on in years, and he's alone. He's noticed your visit. I'll wager your visit has warmed him.

NEPHEW. Him? Uncle Ebenezer Scrooge? Warmed? You are a better Christian than I am, sir.

CRATCHIT. [*Opening the door for* NEPHEW; *two* DO-GOODERS *will enter, as* NEPHEW *exits*] Good day to you, sir, and God bless.

NEPHEW. God bless . . . [*One man who enters is portly, the other is thin. Both are pleasant.*]

CRATCHIT. Can I help you, gentlemen?

---

7. **Bedlam** (bed´ ləm) hospital in London for the mentally ill.

THIN MAN. [*Carrying papers and books; looks around* CRATCHIT *to* SCROOGE] Scrooge and Marley's, I believe. Have I the pleasure of addressing Mr. Scrooge, or Mr. Marley?

SCROOGE. Mr. Marley has been dead these seven years. He died seven years ago this very night.

PORTLY MAN. We have no doubt his liberality[8] is well represented by his surviving partner . . . [*Offers his calling card*]

SCROOGE. [*Handing back the card; unlooked at*] . . . Good afternoon.

THIN MAN. This will take but a moment, sir . . .

PORTLY MAN. At this festive season of the year, Mr. Scrooge, it is more than usually desirable that we should make some slight provision for the poor and destitute who suffer greatly at the present time. Many thousands are in want of common necessities; hundreds of thousands are in want of common comforts, sir.

SCROOGE. Are there no prisons?

PORTLY MAN. Plenty of prisons.

SCROOGE. And aren't the Union workhouses still in operation?

THIN MAN. They are. Still. I wish that I could say that they are not.

SCROOGE. The Treadmill[9] and the Poor Law[10] are in full vigor, then?

THIN MAN. Both very busy, sir.

SCROOGE. Ohhh, I see. I was afraid, from what you said at

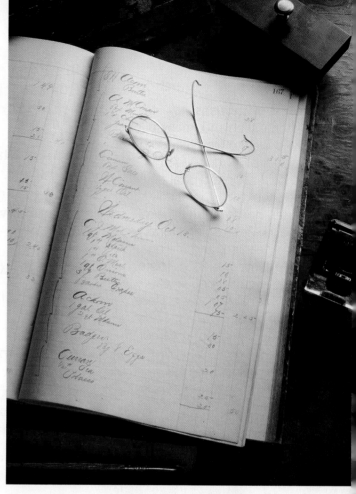

Vocabulary
destitute (des′ tə to͞ot′)
n. people living in complete poverty

Reading Check

Who do the thin man and the portly man want to help?

---

8. **liberality** (lib′ ər al′ i tē) generosity.
9. **the Treadmill** (tred′ mil′) kind of mill wheel turned by the weight of people treading steps arranged around it; this device was used to punish prisoners.
10. **the Poor Law** the original 16th-century Poor Laws called for overseers of the poor in each neighborhood to provide relief for the needy. The New Poor Law of 1834 made the workhouses in which the poor sometimes lived and worked extremely hard and unattractive.

Social Studies Connection

Union Workhouses

In Victorian England, many people who were poverty-stricken, orphaned, old, or sick lived in workhouses. On a typical day, workers woke at 5 A.M. and spent ten hours doing physical labor, such as crushing stones, sewing, cleaning, and milling corn. Bedtime was 8 P.M. There was not enough food to eat. Typically, breakfast was a piece of bread; dinner was a piece of bacon and a piece of bread or a potato; supper was a piece of bread and a piece of cheese.

Connect to the Literature

Why does Scrooge think the workhouses are adequate?

first, that something had occurred to stop them from their useful course. [*Pauses*] I'm glad to hear it.

PORTLY MAN. Under the impression that they scarcely furnish Christian cheer of mind or body to the multitude, a few of us are endeavoring to raise a fund to buy the Poor some meat and drink, and means of warmth. We choose this time, because it is a time, of all others, when Want is keenly felt, and Abundance rejoices. [*Pen in hand; as well as notepad*] What shall I put you down for, sir?

SCROOGE. Nothing!

PORTLY MAN. You wish to be left anonymous?

SCROOGE. I wish to be left alone! [*Pauses; turns away; turns back to them*] Since you ask me what I wish, gentlemen, that is my answer. I help to support the establishments that I have mentioned: they cost enough: and those who are badly off must go there.

THIN MAN. Many can't go there; and many would rather die.

SCROOGE. If they would rather die, they had better do it, and decrease the surplus population. Besides— excuse me—I don't know that.

THIN MAN. But you might know it!

SCROOGE. It's not my business. It's enough for a man to understand his own business, and not to interfere with other people's. Mine occupies me constantly. Good afternoon, gentlemen!
[SCROOGE *turns his back on the gentlemen and returns to his desk.*]

PORTLY MAN. But, sir, Mr. Scrooge . . . think of the poor.

SCROOGE. [*Turns suddenly to them. Pauses*] Take your leave of my offices, sirs, while I am still smiling.

[*The* THIN MAN *looks at the* PORTLY MAN. *They are undone. They shrug. They move to the door.* CRATCHIT *hops up to open it for them.*]

THIN MAN. Good day, sir . . . [*To* CRATCHIT] A merry Christmas to you, sir . . .

CRATCHIT. Yes. A Merry Christmas to both of you . . .

PORTLY MAN. Merry Christmas . . .

[CRATCHIT *silently squeezes something into the hand of the* THIN MAN.]

THIN MAN. What's this?

CRATCHIT. Shhhh . . .

[CRATCHIT *opens the door; wind and snow whistle into the room.*]

THIN MAN. Thank you, sir, thank you.

[CRATCHIT *closes the door and returns to his workplace.* SCROOGE *is at his own counting table. He talks to* CRATCHIT *without looking up.*]

SCROOGE. It's less of a time of year for being merry, and more a time of year for being loony . . . if you ask me.

CRATCHIT. Well, I don't know, sir . . . [*The clock's bell strikes six o'clock.*] Well, there it is, eh, six?

SCROOGE. Saved by six bells, are you?

CRATCHIT. I must be going home . . . [*He snuffs out his candle and puts on his hat.*] I hope you have a . . . very very lovely day tomorrow, sir . . .

SCROOGE. Hmmm. Oh, you'll be wanting the whole day tomorrow, I suppose?

CRATCHIT. If quite convenient, sir.

SCROOGE. It's not convenient, and it's not fair. If I was to stop half-a-crown for it, you'd think yourself ill-used, I'll be bound?

[CRATCHIT *smiles faintly.*]

CRATCHIT. I don't know, sir . . .

SCROOGE. And yet, you don't think me ill-used when I pay a day's wages for no work . . .

▼ **Critical Viewing**
Compare this actor's portrayal of Cratchit with the one on page 744. Which looks more like your idea of Cratchit? Explain. **[Compare and Contrast]**

Reading Check
How does Scrooge feel about Christmas?

A Christmas Carol: Scrooge and Marley, Act 1 **749**

▶ Critical Viewing
Describe the tone of
voice that each actor
might use to play
the scene pictured
here. **[Speculate]**

CRATCHIT. It's only but once a year . . .

SCROOGE. A poor excuse for picking a man's pocket every 25th of December! But I suppose you must have the whole day. Be here all the earlier the next morning!

CRATCHIT. Oh, I will, sir. I will. I promise you. And, sir . . .

SCROOGE. Don't say it, Cratchit.

CRATCHIT. But let me wish you a . . .

SCROOGE. Don't say it, Cratchit. I warn you . . .

CRATCHIT. Sir!

SCROOGE. Cratchit!

[CRATCHIT *opens the door.*]

CRATCHIT. All right, then, sir . . . well . . . [*Suddenly*] Merry Christmas, Mr. Scrooge!

[*And he runs out the door, shutting same behind him.* SCROOGE *moves to his desk; gathering his coat, hat, etc.* A BOY *appears at his window. . . .*]

BOY. [*Singing*] "Away in a manger . . ."

[SCROOGE *seizes his ruler and whacks at the image of the* BOY *outside. The* BOY *leaves.*]

SCROOGE. Bah! Humbug! Christmas! Bah! Humbug! [*He shuts out the light.*]

A note on the crossover, following Scene 2:

[SCROOGE *will walk alone to his rooms from his offices. As he makes a long slow cross of the stage, the scenery should change. Christmas music will be heard, various people will cross by* SCROOGE, *often smiling happily.*]

There will be occasional pleasant greetings tossed at him.

SCROOGE, *in contrast to all, will grump and mumble. He will snap at passing boys, as might a horrid old hound.*

In short, SCROOGE'S *sounds and movements will define him in contrast from all other people who cross the stage: he is the misanthrope,[11] the malcontent, the miser. He is* SCROOGE.

---

11. misanthrope (mis´ ən *thrōp*´) *n.* person who hates or distrusts everyone.

This statement of SCROOGE'S *character, by contrast to all other characters, should seem comical to the audience.*

During SCROOGE'S *crossover to his rooms, snow should begin to fall. All passers-by will hold their faces to the sky, smiling, allowing snow to shower them lightly.* SCROOGE, *by contrast, will bat at the flakes with his walking-stick, as might an insomniac swat at a sleep-stopping, middle-of-the-night swarm of mosquitoes. He will comment on the blackness of the night, and, finally, reach his rooms and his encounter with the magical specter:*[12] MARLEY, *his eternal mate.*]

---

12. **specter** (spek´ tər) *n.* ghost.

Dialogue
What do you learn about Scrooge through his words as he shuts out the light and through the description of him as he walks home?

Reading Check
Why is Cratchit taking a day off?

Vocabulary
void (void) *n.* emptiness

SCROOGE. No light at all . . . no moon . . . that is what is at the center of a Christmas Eve: dead black: void . . .

[SCROOGE *puts his key in the door's keyhole. He has reached his rooms now. The door knocker changes and is now* MARLEY'S *face. A musical sound; quickly: ghostly.* MARLEY'S *image is not at all angry, but looks at* SCROOGE *as did the old* MARLEY *look at* SCROOGE. *The hair is curiously stirred; eyes wide open, dead: absent of focus.* SCROOGE *stares wordlessly here. The face, before his very eyes, does deliquesce.*[13] *It is a knocker again.* SCROOGE *opens the door and checks the back of same, probably for* MARLEY'S *pigtail. Seeing nothing but screws and nuts,* SCROOGE *refuses the memory.*]

Purpose for Reading
Preview Scene 3. If your purpose were to find out what happens next to Scrooge, what details would you look for in the scene?

Pooh, pooh!

[*The sound of the door closing resounds throughout the house as thunder. Every room echoes the sound.* SCROOGE *fastens the door and walks across the hall to the stairs, trimming his candle as he goes; and then he goes slowly up the staircase. He checks each room: sitting room, bedrooms, slumber room. He looks under the sofa, under the table: nobody there. He fixes his evening gruel on the hob,*[14] *changes his jacket.* SCROOGE *sits near the tiny low-flamed fire, sipping his gruel. There are various pictures on the walls: all of them now show likenesses of* MARLEY. SCROOGE *blinks his eyes.*]

Bah! Humbug!

[SCROOGE *walks in a circle about the room. The pictures change back into their natural images. He sits down at the table in front of the fire. A bell hangs overhead. It begins to ring, of its own accord. Slowly, surely, begins the ringing of every bell in the house. They continue ringing for nearly half a minute.* SCROOGE *is stunned by the phenomenon. The bells cease their ringing all at once. Deep below* SCROOGE, *in the basement of the house, there is the sound of clanking, of some enormous chain being dragged across the floors; and now up the stairs. We hear doors flying open.*]

---

13. **deliquesce** (del´ i kwes´) *v.* melt away.
14. **gruel** (groo´ əl) **on the hob** (häb) thin broth warming on a ledge at the back or side of the fireplace.

Bah still! Humbug still! This is not happening! I won't believe it!

[MARLEY'S GHOST *enters the room. He is horrible to look at: pigtail, vest, suit as usual, but he drags an enormous chain now, to which is fastened cash-boxes, keys, padlocks, ledgers, deeds, and heavy purses fashioned of steel. He is transparent.* MARLEY *stands opposite the stricken* SCROOGE.]

How now! What do you want of me?

MARLEY. Much!

SCROOGE. Who are you?

MARLEY. Ask me who I was.

SCROOGE. Who were you then?

MARLEY. In life, I was your business partner: Jacob Marley.

SCROOGE. I see . . . can you sit down?

MARLEY. I can.

SCROOGE. Do it then.

MARLEY. I shall. [MARLEY *sits opposite* SCROOGE, *in the chair across the table, at the front of the fireplace.*] You don't believe in me.

SCROOGE. I don't.

MARLEY. Why do you doubt your senses?

SCROOGE. Because every little thing affects them. A slight disorder of the stomach makes them cheat. You may be an undigested bit of beef, a blot of mustard, a crumb of cheese, a fragment of an underdone potato. There's more of gravy than of grave about you, whatever you are!

[*There is a silence between them.* SCROOGE *is made nervous by it. He picks up a toothpick.*]

Humbug! I tell you: humbug!

[MARLEY *opens his mouth and screams a ghosty, fearful scream. The scream echoes about each room of the house. Bats fly, cats screech, lightning flashes.* SCROOGE *stands and walks backwards against the wall.* MARLEY *stands and screams again. This time, he takes his head and lifts it*

Dialogue
Based on this dialogue, what is Scrooge's attitude toward Marley's Ghost?

Reading Check

What does Scrooge see in the door knocker?

from his shoulders. His head continues to scream. MARLEY'S *face again appears on every picture in the room: all scream-ing.* SCROOGE, *on his knees before* MARLEY.]

Mercy! Dreadful apparition,[15] mercy! Why, O! why do you trouble me so?

MARLEY. Man of the worldly mind, do you believe in me, or not?

SCROOGE. I do. I must. But why do spirits such as you walk the earth? And why do they come to me?

MARLEY. It is required of every man that the spirit within him should walk abroad among his fellow-men, and travel far and wide; and if that spirit goes not forth in life, it is condemned to do so after death. [MARLEY *screams again; a tragic scream; from his ghosty bones.*] I wear the chain I forged in life. I made it link by link, and yard by yard. Is its pattern strange to you? Or would you know, you, Scrooge, the weight and length of the strong coil you bear yourself? It was full as heavy and long as this, seven Christmas Eves ago. You have labored on it, since. It is a ponderous chain.

[*Terrified that a chain will appear about his body,* SCROOGE *spins and waves the unwanted chain away. None, of course, appears. Sees* MARLEY *watching him dance about the room.* MARLEY *watches* SCROOGE; *silently.*]

SCROOGE. Jacob. Old Jacob Marley, tell me more. Speak com-fort to me, Jacob . . .

MARLEY. I have none to give. Comfort comes from other regions, Ebenezer Scrooge, and is conveyed by other minis-ters, to other kinds of men. A very little more, is all that is permitted to me. I cannot rest, I cannot stay, I cannot linger anywhere . . . [*He moans again.*] my spirit never walked beyond our countinghouse—mark me!—in life my spirit never roved beyond the narrow limits of our moneychang-ing hole; and weary journeys lie before me!

SCROOGE. But you were always a good man of business, Jacob.

MARLEY. [*Screams word "business"; a flash-pot explodes with him.*] BUSINESS!!! Mankind was my business. The

Purpose for Reading
What purpose for read-ing might Scrooge's question suggest to readers?

Vocabulary
conveyed (kən vād´) *v.* made known; expressed

---

15. **apparition** (ap´ ə rish´ ən) *n.* ghost.

common welfare was my business; charity, mercy, forbearance, benevolence, were, all, my business. [SCROOGE *is quaking.*] Hear me, Ebenezer Scrooge! My time is nearly gone.

SCROOGE. I will, but don't be hard upon me. And don't be flowery, Jacob! Pray!

MARLEY. How is it that I appear before you in a shape that you can see, I may not tell. I have sat invisible beside you many and many a day. That is no light part of my penance. I am here tonight to warn you that you have yet a chance and hope of escaping my fate. A chance and hope of my procuring, Ebenezer.

SCROOGE. You were always a good friend to me. Thank'ee!

MARLEY. You will be haunted by Three Spirits.

SCROOGE. Would that be the chance and hope you mentioned, Jacob?

MARLEY. It is.

SCROOGE. I think I'd rather not.

MARLEY. Without their visits, you cannot hope to shun the path I tread. Expect the first one tomorrow, when the bell tolls one.

SCROOGE. Couldn't I take 'em all at once, and get it over, Jacob?

MARLEY. Expect the second on the next night at the same hour. The third upon the next night when the last stroke of twelve has ceased to vibrate. Look to see me no more. Others may, but you may not. And look that, for your own sake, you remember what has passed between us!

▲ **Critical Viewing**
How do the actors' gestures and positions reinforce the emotion of the scene? **[Connect]**

Reading Check
Why does Marley visit Scrooge?

MARLEY *places his head back upon his shoulders. He approaches the window and beckons to* SCROOGE *to watch. Outside the window, specters fly by, carrying money-boxes and chains. They make a confused sound of lamentation.* MARLEY, *after listening a moment, joins into their mournful dirge. He leans to the window and floats out into the bleak, dark night. He is gone.*]

SCROOGE. [*Rushing to the window*] Jacob! No, Jacob! Don't leave me! I'm frightened! [*He sees that* MARLEY *has gone. He looks outside. He pulls the shutter closed, so that the scene is blocked from his view. All sound stops. After a pause, he re-opens the shutter and all is quiet, as it should be on Christmas Eve. Carolers carol out of doors, in the distance.* SCROOGE *closes the shutter and walks down the stairs. He examines the door by which* MARLEY *first entered.*] No one here at all! Did I imagine all that? Humbug! [*He looks about the room.*] I did imagine it. It only happened in my foulest dream-mind, didn't it? An undigested bit of . . . [*Thunder and lightning in the room; suddenly*] Sorry! Sorry!

[*There is silence again. The lights fade out.*]

SCENE 4

[*Christmas music, choral, "Hark the Herald Angels Sing," sung by an onstage choir of children, spotlighted, D.C. Above,* SCROOGE *in his bed, dead to the world, asleep, in his darkened room. It should appear that the choir is singing somewhere outside of the house, of course, and a use of scrim[16] is thus suggested. When the singing is ended, the choir should fade out of view and* MARLEY *should fade into view, in their place.*]

MARLEY. [*Directly to audience*] From this point forth . . . I shall be quite visible to you, but invisible to him. [*Smiles*] He will feel my presence, nevertheless, for, unless my senses fail me completely, we are—you and I—witness to the changing of a miser: that one, my partner in life, in business, and in eternity: that one: Scrooge. [*Moves to staircase, below* SCROOGE] See him now. He endeavors to pierce the

---

16. scrim (skrim) *n.* see-through fabric used to create special effects in the theater.

darkness with his ferret eyes.[17] [*To audience*] See him, now. He listens for the hour.

[*The bells toll.* SCROOGE *is awakened and quakes as the hour approaches one o'clock, but the bells stop their sound at the hour of twelve.*]

SCROOGE. [*Astonished*] Midnight! Why this isn't possible. It was past two when I went to bed. An icicle must have gotten into the clock's works! I couldn't have slept through the whole day and far into another night. It isn't possible that anything has happened to the sun, and this is twelve at noon! [*He runs to window; unshutters same; it is night.*] Night, still. Quiet, normal for the season, cold. It is certainly not noon. I cannot in any way afford to lose my days. Securities come due, promissory notes,[18] interest on investments: these are things that happen in the daylight! [*He returns to his bed.*] Was this a dream?

[MARLEY *appears in his room. He speaks to the audience.*]

MARLEY. You see? He does not, with faith, believe in me fully, even still! Whatever will it take to turn the faith of a miser from money to men?

SCROOGE. Another quarter and it'll be one and Marley's ghosty friends will come. [*Pauses; listens*] Where's the chime for one? [*Ding, dong*] A quarter past [*Repeats*] Half-past! [*Repeats*] A quarter to it! But where's the heavy bell of the hour one? This is a game in which I lose my senses! Perhaps, if I allowed myself another short doze . . .

MARLEY. . . . Doze, Ebenezer, doze.

[*A heavy bell thuds its one ring; dull and definitely one o'clock. There is a flash of light.* SCROOGE *sits up, in a sudden. A hand draws back the curtains by his bed. He sees it.*]

SCROOGE. A hand! Who owns it! Hello!
[*Ghosty music again, but of a new nature to the play. A strange figure stands before* SCROOGE—*like a child, yet at the same time like an old man: white hair, but unwrinkled skin, long, muscular arms, but delicate legs and feet. Wears*

Dialogue
What important information in Marley's opening speech will influence the rest of the play?

Spiral Review
Conflict How do details about the setting work together to increase the tension?

![Reading Check checkmark]
Reading Check
Why is Scrooge confused when he wakes up?

---

17. **ferret eyes** a ferret is a small, weasel-like animal used for hunting rabbits; this expression means to stare continuously, the way a ferret hunts.
18. **promissory** (prăm′ ĭ sôr′ ē) **notes** written promises to pay someone a certain sum of money.

white tunic; lustrous belt cinches waist. Branch of fresh green holly in its hand, but has its dress trimmed with fresh summer flowers. Clear jets of light spring from the crown of its head. Holds cap in hand. The Spirit is called PAST.]

Are you the Spirit, sir, whose coming was foretold to me?

PAST. I am.

MARLEY. Does he take this to be a vision of his green grocer?

SCROOGE. Who, and what are you?

PAST. I am the Ghost of Christmas Past.

SCROOGE. Long past?

PAST. Your past.

SCROOGE. May I ask, please, sir, what business you have here with me?

PAST. Your welfare.

SCROOGE. Not to sound ungrateful, sir, and really, please do understand that I am plenty obliged for your concern, but, really, kind spirit, it would have done all the better for my welfare to have been left alone altogether, to have slept peacefully through this night.

PAST. Your reclamation, then. Take heed!

SCROOGE. My what?

PAST. [*Motioning to* SCROOGE *and taking his arm*] Rise! Fly with me! [*He leads* SCROOGE *to the window.*]

SCROOGE. [*Panicked*] Fly, but I am a mortal and cannot fly!

PAST. [*Pointing to his heart*] Bear but a touch of my hand here and you shall be upheld in more than this!

[SCROOGE *touches the spirit's heart and the lights dissolve into sparkly flickers. Lovely crystals of music are heard. The scene dissolves into another. Christmas music again*]

Dialogue
Based on this dialogue, how has Scrooge been affected by what has happened to him so far?

SCENE 5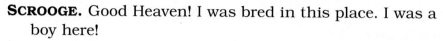

[SCROOGE *and the* GHOST OF CHRISTMAS PAST *walk together across an open stage. In the background, we see a field that is open; covered by a soft, downy snow: a country road.*]

SCROOGE. Good Heaven! I was bred in this place. I was a boy here!

[SCROOGE *freezes, staring at the field beyond.* MARLEY'S *ghost appears beside him; takes* SCROOGE'S *face in his hands, and turns his face to the audience.*]

MARLEY. You see this Scrooge: stricken by feeling. Conscious of a thousand odors floating in the air, each one connected with a thousand thoughts, and hopes, and joys, and care long, long forgotten. [*Pause*] This one—this Scrooge—before your very eyes, returns to life, among the living. [*To audience, sternly*] You'd best pay your most careful attention. I would suggest rapt.[19]

[*There is a small flash and puff of smoke and* MARLEY *is gone again.*]

PAST. Your lip is trembling, Mr. Scrooge. And what is that upon your cheek?

SCROOGE. Upon my cheek? Nothing . . . a blemish on the skin from the eating of overmuch grease . . . nothing . . . [*Suddenly*] Kind Spirit of Christmas Past, lead me where you will, but quickly! To be stagnant in this place is, for me, unbearable!

PAST. You recollect the way?

SCROOGE. Remember it! I would know it blindfolded! My bridge, my church, my winding river! [*Staggers about, trying to see it all at once. He weeps again.*]

PAST. These are but shadows of things that have been. They have no consciousness of us.

[*Four jocund travelers enter, singing a Christmas song in four-part harmony—"God Rest Ye Merry Gentlemen."*]

SCROOGE. Listen! I know these men! I know them! I remember the beauty of their song!

---

19. **rapt** (rapt) *adj.* giving complete attention; totally carried away by something.

✓ Reading Check

Who appears to Scrooge during Scene 4?

PAST. But, why do you remember it so happily? It is Merry Christmas that they say to one another! What is Merry Christmas to you, Mr. Scrooge? Out upon Merry Christmas, right? What good has Merry Christmas ever done you, Mr. Scrooge? . . .

SCROOGE. [*After a long pause*] None. No good. None . . . [*He bows his head.*]

PAST. Look, you, sir, a school ahead. The schoolroom is not quite deserted. A solitary child, neglected by his friends, is left there still.

[SCROOGE *falls to the ground; sobbing as he sees, and we see, a small boy, the young* SCROOGE, *sitting and weeping, bravely, alone at his desk: alone in a vast space, a void.*]

SCROOGE. I cannot look on him!

PAST. You must, Mr. Scrooge, you must.

SCROOGE. It's me. [*Pauses; weeps*] Poor boy. He lived inside his head . . . alone . . . [*Pauses; weeps*] poor boy. [*Pauses; stops his weeping*] I wish . . . [*Dries his eyes on his cuff*] ah! it's too late!

PAST. What is the matter?

SCROOGE. There was a boy singing a Christmas Carol outside my door last night. I should like to have given him something: that's all.

PAST. [*Smiles; waves his hand to* SCROOGE] Come. Let us see another Christmas.

[*Lights out on little boy. A flash of light. A puff of smoke. Lights up on older boy*]

SCROOGE. Look! Me, again! Older now! [*Realizes*] Oh, yes . . . still alone.

[*The boy—a slightly older* SCROOGE —*sits alone in a chair, reading. The door to the room opens and a young girl enters. She is much, much younger than this slightly older* SCROOGE. *She is, say, six, and he is, say, twelve. Elder* SCROOGE *and the* GHOST OF CHRISTMAS PAST *stand watching the scene, unseen.*]

FAN. Dear, dear brother, I have come to bring you home.

Dialogue
How do these lines reveal that a change is taking place in Scrooge?

BOY. Home, little Fan?

FAN. Yes! Home, for good and all! Father is so much kinder than he ever used to be, and home's like heaven! He spoke so gently to me one dear night when I was going to bed that I was not afraid to ask him once more if you might come home; and he said "yes" . . . you should; and sent me in a coach to bring you. And you're to be a man and are never to come back here, but first, we're to be together all the Christmas long, and have the merriest time in the world.

BOY. You are quite a woman, little Fan!

[Laughing; she drags at boy, causing him to stumble to the door with her. Suddenly we hear a mean and terrible voice in the hallway, Off. It is the SCHOOLMASTER.*]*

SCHOOLMASTER. Bring down Master Scrooge's travel box at once! He is to travel!

FAN. Who is that, Ebenezer?

BOY. O! Quiet, Fan. It is the Schoolmaster, himself!

[The door bursts open and into the room bursts with it the SCHOOLMASTER.*]*

SCHOOLMASTER. Master Scrooge?

BOY. Oh, Schoolmaster. I'd like you to meet my little sister, Fan, sir . . .

[Two boys struggle on with SCROOGE'S *trunk.]*

FAN. Pleased, sir . . . *[She curtsies.]*

SCHOOLMASTER. You are to travel, Master Scrooge.

SCROOGE. Yes, sir. I know sir . . .

[All start to exit, but FAN *grabs the coattail of the mean old* SCHOOLMASTER.*]*

BOY. Fan!

SCHOOLMASTER. What's this?

FAN. Pardon, sir, but I believe that you've forgotten to say your goodbye to my brother, Ebenezer, who stands still now

Purpose for Reading
What questions do you have about Scrooge's family? Read on to see if they are answered.

Reading Check

Where is Scrooge when his sister arrives to take him home?

awaiting it . . . [*She smiles, curtsies, lowers her eyes.*] pardon, sir.

SCHOOLMASTER. [*Amazed*] I . . . uh . . . harumph . . . uhh . . . well, then . . . [*Outstretches hand*] Goodbye, Scrooge.

BOY. Uh, well, goodbye, Schoolmaster . . .

[*Lights fade out on all but* BOY *looking at* FAN; *and* SCROOGE *and* PAST *looking at them.*]

SCROOGE. Oh, my dear, dear little sister, Fan . . . how I loved her.

PAST. Always a delicate creature, whom a breath might have withered, but she had a large heart . . .

SCROOGE. So she had.

PAST. She died a woman, and had, as I think, children.

SCROOGE. One child.

PAST. True. Your nephew.

SCROOGE. Yes.

Dialogue
What surprising aspect of Scrooge's character does this scene reveal?

PAST. Fine, then. We move on, Mr. Scrooge. That warehouse, there? Do you know it?

SCROOGE. Know it? Wasn't I apprenticed[20] there?

PAST. We'll have a look.

[*They enter the warehouse. The lights crossfade with them, coming up on an old man in Welsh wig:* FEZZIWIG.]

SCROOGE. Why, it's old Fezziwig! Bless his heart; it's Fezziwig, alive again!

[FEZZIWIG *sits behind a large, high desk, counting. He lays down his pen; looks at the clock: seven bells sound.*]

Quittin' time . . .

FEZZIWIG. Quittin' time . . . [*He takes off his waistcoat and laughs; calls off*] Yo ho, Ebenezer! Dick!

[DICK WILKINS *and* EBENEZER SCROOGE—*a young man version—enter the room.* DICK *and* EBENEZER *are* FEZZIWIG'S *apprentices.*]

---

20. apprenticed (ə pren′ tist) *v.* receiving instruction in a trade as well as food and housing or wages in return for work.

SCROOGE. Dick Wilkins, to be sure! My fellow-'prentice! Bless my soul, yes. There he is. He was very much attached to me, was Dick. Poor Dick! Dear, dear!

FEZZIWIG. Yo ho, my boys. No more work tonight. Christmas Eve, Dick. Christmas, Ebenezer!
[*They stand at attention in front of* FEZZIWIG; *laughing*]
Hilli-ho! Clear away, and let's have lots of room here! Hilli-ho, Dick! Chirrup, Ebenezer!
[*The young men clear the room, sweep the floor, straighten the pictures, trim the lamps, etc. The space is clear now. A fiddler enters, fiddling.*]
Hi-ho, Matthew! Fiddle away . . . where are my daughters?

[*The fiddler plays. Three young daughters of* FEZZIWIG *enter followed by six young male suitors. They are dancing to the music. All employees come in: workers, clerks, housemaids, cousins, the baker, etc. All dance. Full number wanted here. Throughout the dance, food is brought into the feast. It is "eaten" in dance, by the dancers.* EBENEZER *dances with all three of the daughters, as does* DICK. *They compete for the*

▲ **Critical Viewing**
Based on this photograph, what kind of a man is Fezziwig? **[Infer]**

Reading Check

Who is Fezziwig?

daughters, happily, in the dance. FEZZIWIG *dances with his daughters.* FEZZIWIG *dances with* DICK *and* EBENEZER. *The music changes:* MRS. FEZZIWIG *enters. She lovingly scolds her husband. They dance. She dances with* EBENEZER, *lifting him and throwing him about. She is enormously fat. When the dance is ended, they all dance off, floating away, as does the music.* SCROOGE *and the* GHOST OF CHRISTMAS PAST *stand alone now. The music is gone.*]

Vocabulary
gratitude (grat´ i tōōd´) *n.* thankful appreciation

PAST. It was a small matter, that Fezziwig made those silly folks so full of gratitude.

SCROOGE. Small!

PAST. Shhh!

[*Lights up on* DICK *and* EBENEZER]

DICK. We are blessed, Ebenezer, truly, to have such a master as Mr. Fezziwig!

Dialogue
What does this dialogue reveal about Scrooge's feelings for Fezziwig?

YOUNG SCROOGE. He is the best, best, the very and absolute best! If ever I own a firm of my own, I shall treat my apprentices with the same dignity and the same grace. We have learned a wonderful lesson from the master, Dick!

DICK. Ah, that's a fact, Ebenezer. That's a fact!

PAST. Was it not a small matter, really? He spent but a few pounds[21] of his mortal money on your small party. Three or four pounds, perhaps. Is that so much that he deserves such praise as you and Dick so lavish now?

SCROOGE. It isn't that! It isn't that, Spirit. Fezziwig had the power to make us happy or unhappy; to make our service light or burdensome; a pleasure or a toil. The happiness he gave is quite as great as if it cost him a fortune.

PAST. What is the matter?

SCROOGE. Nothing particular.

PAST. Something, I think.

SCROOGE. No, no. I should like to be able to say a word or two to my clerk just now! That's all!

---

21. pounds (pοundz) *n.* money used in Great Britain at the time of the story.

[EBENEZER *enters the room and shuts down all the lamps. He stretches and yawns. The* GHOST OF CHRISTMAS PAST *turns to* SCROOGE *all of a sudden.*]

PAST. My time grows short! Quick!

[*In a flash of light,* EBENEZER *is gone, and in his place stands an* OLDER SCROOGE, *this one a man in the prime of his life. Beside him stands a young woman in a mourning dress. She is crying. She speaks to the man, with hostility.*]

WOMAN. It matters little . . . to you, very little. Another idol has displaced me.

MAN. What idol has displaced you?

WOMAN. A golden one.

MAN. This is an even-handed dealing of the world. There is nothing on which it is so hard as poverty; and there is nothing it professes to condemn with such severity as the pursuit of wealth!

WOMAN. You fear the world too much. Have I not seen your nobler aspirations fall off one by one, until the master-passion, Gain, engrosses you? Have I not?

SCROOGE. No!

MAN. What then? Even if I have grown so much wiser, what then? Have I changed towards you?

WOMAN. No . . .

MAN. Am I?

WOMAN. Our contract is an old one. It was made when we were both poor and content to be so. You are changed. When it was made, you were another man.

MAN. I was not another man: I was a boy.

WOMAN. Your own feeling tells you that you were not what you are. I am. That which promised happiness when we were one in heart is fraught with misery now that we are two . . .

Dialogue
What personal change in Scrooge does this dialogue show?

Reading Check
What does the woman tell Scrooge about himself?

SCROOGE. No!

WOMAN. How often and how keenly I have thought of this, I will not say. It is enough that I have thought of it, and can release you . . .

SCROOGE. [*Quietly*] Don't release me, madame . . .

MAN. Have I ever sought release?

WOMAN. In words. No. Never.

MAN. In what then?

WOMAN. In a changed nature; in an altered spirit. In everything that made my love of any worth or value in your sight. If this has never been between us, tell me, would you seek me out and try to win me now? Ah, no!

SCROOGE. Ah, yes!

MAN. You think not?

WOMAN. I would gladly think otherwise if I could, heaven knows! But if you were free today, tomorrow, yesterday, can even I believe that you would choose a dowerless girl[22]—you who in your very confidence with her weigh everything by Gain; or, choosing her, do I not know that your repentance and regret would surely follow? I do; and I release you. With a full heart, for the love of him you once were.

SCROOGE. Please, I . . . I . . .

MAN. Please, I . . . I . . .

WOMAN. Please. You may—the memory of what is past half makes me hope you will—have pain in this. A very, very brief time, and you will dismiss the memory of it, as an unprofitable dream, from which it happened well that you awoke. May you be happy in the life that you have chosen for yourself . . .

---

22. a dowerless (dou´ er les) **girl** a girl without a dowry, the property or wealth a woman brought to her husband in marriage.

SCROOGE. No!

WOMAN. Yourself . . . alone . . .

SCROOGE. No!

WOMAN. Goodbye, Ebenezer . . .

SCROOGE. Don't let her go!

MAN. Goodbye.

SCROOGE. No!
> [*She exits.* SCROOGE *goes to younger man: himself.*]
> You fool! Mindless loon! You fool!

MAN. [*To exited woman*] Fool. Mindless loon. Fool . . .

SCROOGE. Don't say that! Spirit, remove me from this place.

PAST. I have told you these were shadows of the things that have been. They are what they are. Do not blame me, Mr. Scrooge.

SCROOGE. Remove me! I cannot bear it!
[*The faces of all who appeared in this scene are now projected for a moment around the stage: enormous, flimsy, silent.*]
> Leave me! Take me back! Haunt me no longer!

[*There is a sudden flash of light: a flare. The* GHOST OF CHRISTMAS PAST *is gone.* SCROOGE *is, for the moment, alone onstage. His bed is turned down, across the stage. A small candle burns now in* SCROOGE'S *hand. There is a child's cap in his other hand. He slowly crosses the stage to his bed, to sleep.* MARLEY *appears behind* SCROOGE, *who continues his long, elderly cross to bed.* MARLEY *speaks directly to the audience.*]

MARLEY. Scrooge must sleep now. He must surrender to the irresistible drowsiness caused by the recognition of what was. [*Pauses*] The cap he carries is from ten lives past: his boyhood cap . . . donned atop a hopeful hairy head . . . askew, perhaps, or at a rakish angle. Doffed now in honor of regret.[23] Perhaps even too heavy to carry in his present state of weak remorse . . .

---

23. **donned . . . regret** To *don* and *doff* a hat means to put it on and take it off, *askew* means "crooked," and *at a rakish angle* means "having a dashing or jaunty look."

Dialogue
What do you learn about Scrooge's past from the dialogue here?

Reading Check
Why does the woman leave Scrooge?

Purpose for Reading
How does this speech by Marley influence your purpose for reading Act 2?

[SCROOGE *drops the cap. He lies atop his bed. He sleeps. To audience*]

He sleeps. For him, there's even more trouble ahead. [*Smiles*] For you? The play house tells me there's hot cider, as should be your anticipation for the specter Christmas Present and Future, for I promise you both. [*Smiles again*] So, I pray you hurry back to your seats refreshed and ready for a miser—to turn his coat of gray into a blazen Christmas holly-red. [*A flash of lightning. A clap of thunder. Bats fly. Ghosty music.* MARLEY *is gone.*]

Critical Thinking

1. **Key Ideas and Details (a)** What scenes from his past does Scrooge visit? **(b) Draw Conclusions:** How does each event contribute to his current attitude and personality?

2. **Key Ideas and Details (a) Deduce:** What does Scrooge value in life? **(b) Draw Conclusions:** Do his values make Scrooge a happy man? Explain.

3. **Key Ideas and Details (a) Connect:** What hints suggest to you that Scrooge may change for the better? **(b) Speculate:** In the future, how might Scrooge's interactions with others differ from his interactions in the present?

4. **Integration of Knowledge and Ideas (a) Deduce:** What effects have Scrooge's past experiences had on the person he has become? **(b) Evaluate:** Based on Scrooge's past experiences, do you think he should be excused for his current attitude and behavior? Explain.

5. **Integration of Knowledge and Ideas** How do the people in Scrooge's past reveal his own behavior to him? *[Connect to the Big Question: Do others see us more clearly than we see ourselves?]*

Cite textual evidence to support your responses.

Reading Skill: Purpose for Reading

1. What clues in the title helped you to preview the content of the play?

2. **(a)** What is your **purpose for reading** this play? **(b)** How might your purpose be different if you were reading a nonfiction play about life in the workhouses of Victorian England?

Literary Analysis: Dialogue

© **3. Craft and Structure** Complete a chart like the one shown by identifying important examples of dialogue. **(a)** For each line of **dialogue** in the first column, use the second column to tell what it means. **(b)** In the third column, tell why this dialogue is important for advancing the action of the play or developing characters.

What Does It Say?	What Does It Mean?	Why Is It Important?

Vocabulary

© **Acquisition and Use** Rewrite the following sentences so that each includes a vocabulary word from the list on page 738 and retains the same basic meaning it has here.

1. Jack's gloomy expression showed that he had lost the game.

2. Her sudden inheritance meant that she would no longer live among the poor.

3. Ted's helpful gesture made me feel thankful.

4. The party helped to ease the emptiness I was feeling.

5. The grin on Dr. Jackson's face expressed his relief.

6. We begged the guard not to close the gate.

Word Study Use the context of the sentences and what you know about the **Latin root -grat-** to explain your answer.

1. If a friend helped you out of a bind, would you feel *grateful*?

2. Would *congratulations* be in order if you failed an exam?

Word Study

The **Latin root -grat-** means "thankful" or "pleasing."

Apply It Explain how the root *-grat-* contributes to the meanings of these words. Consult a dictionary if necessary.

gratuity
ingrate
gratis
gratification

Integrated Language Skills

A Christmas Carol: Scrooge and Marley, Act 1

Conventions: Interjections

An **interjection** is a part of speech that expresses a feeling, such as pain or excitement.

An interjection may be set off with a comma or an exclamation point. Interjections are used to add emphasis to your writing. When writing dialogue, use interjections to make the language sound more realistic.

Pain: Ouch! I hit my toe.
Excitement: Wow, Melissa can certainly run fast!

The chart lists some common interjections.

Wow	Whew	Well	Hey
Huh	Oh	Oops	Boy
Hmmm	Yikes	Yuck	Ugh

Practice A Identify the interjection in each sentence.

1. Hey, it is snowing outside!
2. Wow! Don't the carolers sound wonderful?
3. Yikes! It is cold in here!
4. Humph, I suppose you want to go home now!

Reading Application Find at least two different interjections in *A Christmas Carol: Scrooge and Marley*, Act 1. For each, indicate the emotion it expresses.

Practice B Add an interjection and appropriate punctuation to help express emotion in each sentence.

1. Who are you and what do you want?
2. Go away and leave me alone.
3. I do not want any more visitors.
4. Take me away from here; this is too painful to watch.

Writing Application Compare your responses with a partner, and, together, provide three interjections for each sentence above. Explain how the meaning and intensity of the sentence changes in each case.

PH WRITING COACH Further instruction and practice are available in *Prentice Hall Writing Coach.*

Writing

Argument Write a **letter** to Scrooge, telling him what he is missing in life by being cranky and negative with the people around him. Start your letter with a salutation, or greeting. Then, support the main points of your argument with clear reasons and evidence. Conclude with a closing and your signature.

- Present a balanced argument by carefully organizing the body of the letter. Fully support each claim with valid reasons and text evidence before moving on to the next one. Use transitional phrases like "another issue is . . ." or "in addition" to help unify the main argument—that there are many things Scrooge is missing.

- If you handwrite your letter, write legibly.

(For a model of a friendly-letter format, see p. R26.)

Grammar Application Check your writing to be sure your use of interjections is correct.

Writing Workshop: *Work in Progress*

Prewriting for Research For a multimedia report you may write, list four ideas in response to one of these general topics: locations around the world, nature and wildlife, or sports and athletes. Save this Ideas List in your writing portfolio.

Research and Technology

Build and Present Knowledge Prepare **costume plans** for this play. With a small group, research the clothing worn during the Victorian period in England.

- Use the Internet and library resources to gather information, photos, sketches, and descriptions.

- Determine what types of clothing different characters would have worn, based on their social positions.

- Research what kinds of clothing people wore for different seasons. Find out about the fabrics and materials that were available during the time period.

Use the information you find to plan costumes for two different characters in *A Christmas Carol*. In your plan, show or describe the types of clothing, including the colors and fabrics. Include pictures or sketches with your descriptions.

Common Core State Standards

L.7.1, L.7.2; W.7.1, W.7.1.a, W.7.1.b, W.7.1.c, W.7.7
[For the full wording of the standards, see page 736.]

Use this prewriting activity to prepare for the **Writing Workshop** on page 824.

PHLit Online!
www.PHLitOnline.com

- Interactive graphic organizers
- Grammar tutorial
- Interactive journals

Drama Selection

Build your skills and improve your comprehension of drama with texts of increasing complexity.

Read **A Christmas Carol: Scrooge and Marley, Act 2** to learn whether Scrooge changes because of visits by the ghosts of Christmas present and future.

Common Core State Standards

Meet these standards with **A Christmas Carol: Scrooge and Marley, Act 2** (p. 775).

Reading Literature
3. Analyze how particular elements of a story or drama interact. *(Literary Analysis: Spiral Review)*

5. Analyze how a drama's or poem's form or structure contributes to its meaning. *(Literary Analysis: Stage Directions)*

Writing
2. Write informative/explanatory texts to examine a topic and convey ideas, concepts, and information through the selection, organization, and analysis of relevant content. *(Writing: Tribute)*

9. Draw evidence from literary or informational texts to support analysis, reflection, and research. *(Writing: Tribute)*

Speaking and Listening
6. Adapt speech to a variety of contexts and tasks, demonstrating command of formal English when indicated or appropriate. *(Speaking and Listening: Dramatic Monologue)*

Language
1. Demonstrate command of the conventions of standard English grammar and usage when writing or speaking. *(Conventions: Double Negatives)*

2. Demonstrate command of the conventions of standard English capitalization, punctuation, and spelling when writing. *(Speaking and Listening: Dramatic Monologues)*

4.b. Use common, grade-appropriate Greek or Latin affixes and roots as clues to the meaning of a word. *(Vocabulary: Word Study)*

6. Acquire and use accurately grade-appropriate general academic and domain-specific words and phrases; gather vocabulary knowledge when considering a word or phrase important to comprehension or expression. *(Vocabulary: Word Study)*

Reading Skill: Purpose for Reading

When you **set a purpose** for reading, you decide before you read what you want to get out of a text. The purpose you set will affect the way you read and the speed of your reading. **Adjust your reading rate** to suit your purpose. For example, if you are reading directions to perform a task, you will read more slowly and carefully than if you are reading to be entertained.

- As you read drama, slow down to read stage directions carefully. They may reveal action that is not shown in the dialogue.
- Speed up to read short lines of dialogue quickly to create the feeling of conversation.
- Slow down to read longer speeches by a single character so that you can reflect on the character's words.
- If one of your purposes is to appreciate an *author's style,* or unique way of writing, slow down your pace as you read.

Using the Strategy: Reading-Rate Chart

Use this chart to help you determine your reading rate.

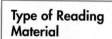 +  = **Reading Rate**

Type of Reading Material	Purpose for Reading

Literary Analysis: Stage Directions

A drama is a story told in dialogue and performed by actors in front of an audience. The script is the written text of the play. **Stage directions,** a part of the script, instruct actors how to move and speak or describe what the stage should look like. Stage directions help actors understand how to interact with the other elements of the play, such as the scenery or props. If you are reading a play instead of watching a performance, you get this information only from the stage directions. Stage directions are usually written in italic type and set off by brackets or parentheses, as in this example.

[Jen bursts through the door, stage left. There is a crack of thunder. Then, the lights go dark.]

Do others *see* us more clearly than we *see* ourselves?

Writing About the Big Question

In Act 2 of *A Christmas Carol: Scrooge and Marley*, Scrooge learns valuable lessons about himself from several ghostly visitors. Use this sentence starter to develop your ideas about the Big Question.

In order to change, we must first **identify** how our behavior affects _____ because _____.

While You Read Look for insights Scrooge gains about himself during his travels with the ghosts of Christmas present and future.

Vocabulary

Read each word and its definition. Decide whether you know the word well, know it a little bit, or do not know it at all. After you read, see how your knowledge of each word has increased.

- **astonish** (ə stän´ ish) *v.* amaze (p. 775) *The movie's sudden surprise ending will astonish you.* astonishment *n.* astonishing *v.* astonishingly *adv.*

- **compulsion** (kəm pul´ shən) *n.* driving, irresistible force (p. 777) *Jose has a compulsion to keep his room clean.* compulsive *adj.* compulsively *adv.*

- **severe** (sə vir´) *adj.* harsh (p. 778) *Winters in Alaska can be severe.* severely *adv.* severity *n.*

- **meager** (mē´ gər) *adj.* small in amount; of poor quality (p. 780) *The meager amount of food was not enough to feed the large group.* meagerly *adj.* meagerness *n.*

- **audible** (ô´ də bəl) *adj.* loud enough to be heard (p. 788) *This microphone will help to make her speech audible.* audibility *n.* audibly *adv.* audio *n.* audio *adj.*

- **intercedes** (in´ tər sēdz´) *v.* makes a request on behalf of another (p. 798) *Amelia's aunt often intercedes on her behalf.* intercede *v.* intercession *n.* intercessor *n.*

Word Study

The **Latin prefix** *inter-* means "between" or "among."

In this act, the Ghost of Christmas Future **intercedes** on behalf of Scrooge by going between him and a terrible future to protect Scrooge from what might be.

A CHRISTMAS CAROL:
SCROOGE AND MARLEY

ISRAEL HOROVITZ
from *A CHRISTMAS CAROL*
by **CHARLES DICKENS**

ACT 2

SCENE

[*Lights. Choral music is sung. Curtain.* SCROOGE, *in bed, sleeping, in spotlight. We cannot yet see the interior of his room.* MARLEY, *opposite, in spotlight equal to* SCROOGE'S. MARLEY *laughs. He tosses his hand in the air and a flame shoots from it, magically, into the air. There is a thunder clap, and then another; a lightning flash, and then another. Ghostly music plays under. Colors change.* MARLEY'S *spotlight has gone out and now reappears, with* MARLEY *in it, standing next to the bed and the sleeping* SCROOGE. MARLEY *addresses the audience directly.*]

MARLEY. Hear this snoring Scrooge! Sleeping to escape the nightmare that is his waking day. What shall I bring to him now? I'm afraid nothing would astonish old Scrooge now. Not after what he's seen. Not a baby boy, not a rhinoceros, nor anything in between would astonish Ebenezer Scrooge just now. I can think of nothing . . . [*Suddenly*] that's it! Nothing! [*He speaks confidentially.*] I'll have the

Stage Directions
What sounds establish this as a scary scene?

Vocabulary
astonish (ə stän´ ish)
v. amaze

Reading Check
What is Marley trying to figure out?

► **Critical Viewing**
Based on your knowledge of the play so far, whom do you expect this character to be? Explain. **[Hypothesize]**

clock strike one and, when he awakes expecting my second messenger, there will be no one . . . nothing. Then I'll have the bell strike twelve. And then one again . . . and then nothing. Nothing . . . [*Laughs*] nothing will . . . astonish him. I think it will work.

[*The bell tolls one.* SCROOGE *leaps awake.*]

SCROOGE. One! One! This is it: time! [*Looks about the room*] Nothing!

[*The bell tolls midnight.*]

Midnight! How can this be? I'm sleeping backwards.

[*One again*]

Good heavens! One again! I'm sleeping back and forth! [*A pause.* SCROOGE *looks about.*] Nothing! Absolutely nothing!

[*Suddenly, thunder and lightning.* MARLEY *laughs and disappears. The room shakes and glows. There is suddenly spring-like music.* SCROOGE *makes a run for the door.*]

MARLEY. Scrooge!

SCROOGE. What?

MARLEY. Stay you put!

SCROOGE. Just checking to see if anyone is in here.

Purpose for Reading
At what rate would you read these stage directions? Why?

[*Lights and thunder again: more music.* MARLEY *is of a sudden gone. In his place sits the* GHOST OF CHRISTMAS PRESENT—*to be called in the stage directions of the play,* PRESENT—*center of room. Heaped up on the floor, to form a kind of throne, are turkeys, geese, game, poultry, brawn, great joints of meat, suckling pigs, long wreaths of sausages, mince-pies, plum puddings, barrels of oysters, red hot chestnuts, cherry-cheeked apples, juicy oranges, luscious pears, immense twelfth cakes, and seething bowls of punch, that make the chamber dim with their delicious steam. Upon this throne sits* PRESENT, *glorious to see. He bears a torch, shaped as a Horn of Plenty.*[1] SCROOGE *hops out of the door, and then peeks back again into his bedroom.* PRESENT, *calls to* SCROOGE.]

---

1. **Horn of Plenty** a horn overflowing with fruits, flowers, and grain, representing wealth and abundance.

PRESENT. Ebenezer Scrooge. Come in, come in! Come in and know me better!

SCROOGE. Hello. How should I call you?

PRESENT. I am the Ghost of Christmas Present. Look upon me.

[PRESENT *is wearing a simple green robe. The walls around the room are now covered in greenery, as well. The room seems to be a perfect grove now: leaves of holly, mistletoe and ivy reflect the stage lights. Suddenly, there is a mighty roar of flame in the fireplace and now the hearth burns with a lavish, warming fire. There is an ancient scabbard girdling the* GHOST'S *middle, but without sword. The sheath is gone to rust.*]

You have never seen the like of me before?

SCROOGE. Never.

PRESENT. You have never walked forth with younger members of my family; my elder brothers born on Christmases past.

SCROOGE. I don't think I have. I'm afraid I've not. Have you had many brothers, Spirit?

PRESENT. More than eighteen hundred.

SCROOGE. A tremendous family to provide for! [PRESENT *stands*] Spirit, conduct me where you will. I went forth last night on **compulsion**, and learnt a lesson which is working now. Tonight, if you have aught to teach me, let me profit by it.

PRESENT. Touch my robe.

[SCROOGE *walks cautiously to* PRESENT *and touches his robe. When he does, lightning flashes, thunder claps, music plays. Blackout*]

Vocabulary
compulsion (kəm puĺ shən) *n.* driving, irresistible force

Reading Check
Who visits Scrooge in Scene 1?

A Christmas Carol: Scrooge and Marley, Act 2 **777**

SCENE 2

[*PROLOGUE:* MARLEY *stands spotlit,* L. *He speaks directly to the audience.*]

MARLEY. My ghostly friend now leads my living partner through the city's streets.

[*Lights up on* SCROOGE *and* PRESENT]

See them there and hear the music people make when the weather is severe, as it is now.

[*Winter music. Choral group behind scrim, sings. When the song is done and the stage is re-set, the lights will fade up on a row of shops, behind the singers. The choral group will hum the song they have just completed now and mill about the streets,*[2] *carrying their dinners to the bakers' shops and restaurants. They will, perhaps, sing about being poor at Christmastime, whatever.*]

PRESENT. These revelers, Mr. Scrooge, carry their own dinners to their jobs, where they will work to bake the meals the rich men and women of this city will eat as their Christmas dinners. Generous people these . . . to care for the others, so . . .

[PRESENT *walks among the choral group and a sparkling incense*[3] *falls from his torch on to their baskets, as he pulls the covers off of the baskets. Some of the choral group become angry with each other.*]

MAN #1. Hey, you, watch where you're going.

MAN #2. Watch it yourself, mate!

[PRESENT *sprinkles them directly, they change.*]

MAN #1. I pray go in ahead of me. It's Christmas. You be first!

MAN #2. No, no, I must insist that YOU be first!

MAN #1. All right, I shall be, and gratefully so.

MAN #2. The pleasure is equally mine, for being able to watch you pass, smiling.

MAN #1. I would find it a shame to quarrel on Christmas Day . . .

---

2. **mill about the streets** walk around aimlessly.
3. **incense** (in´ sens) *n.* any of various substances that produce a pleasant odor when burned.

Vocabulary
severe (sə vir´) *adj.* harsh

Purpose for Reading
At what rate would you read dialogue such as this? Why?

MAN #2. As would I.

MAN #1. Merry Christmas then, friend!

MAN #2. And a Merry Christmas straight back to you!

[*Church bells toll. The choral group enter the buildings: the shops and restaurants; they exit the stage, shutting their doors closed behind them. All sound stops.* SCROOGE *and* PRESENT *are alone again.*]

SCROOGE. What is it you sprinkle from your torch?

PRESENT. Kindness.

SCROOGE. Do you sprinkle your kindness on any particular people or on all people?

PRESENT. To any person kindly given. And to the very poor most of all.

SCROOGE. Why to the very poor most?

PRESENT. Because the very poor need it most. Touch my heart . . . here, Mr. Scrooge. We have another journey.

[SCROOGE *touches the* GHOST'S *heart and music plays, lights change color, lightning flashes, thunder claps. A choral group appears on the street, singing Christmas carols.*]

Stage Directions
What information in these stage directions adds to the effectiveness of the scene?

SCENE 3

[MARLEY *stands spotlit in front of a scrim on which is painted the exterior of* CRATCHIT'S *four-roomed house. There is a flash and a clap and* MARLEY *is gone. The lights shift color again, the scrim flies away, and we are in the interior of the* CRATCHIT *family home.* SCROOGE *is there, with the* spirit (PRESENT), *watching* MRS. CRATCHIT *set the table, with the help of* BELINDA CRATCHIT *and* PETER CRATCHIT, *a baby, pokes a fork into the mashed potatoes on his highchair's tray. He also chews on his shirt collar.*]

SCROOGE. What is this place, Spirit?

PRESENT. This is the home of your employee, Mr. Scrooge. Don't you know it?

SCROOGE. Do you mean Cratchit, Spirit? Do you mean this is Cratchit's home?

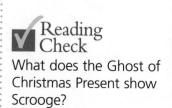
Reading Check
What does the Ghost of Christmas Present show Scrooge?

PRESENT. None other.

SCROOGE. These children are his?

PRESENT. There are more to come presently.

SCROOGE. On his meager earnings! What foolishness!

PRESENT. Foolishness, is it?

SCROOGE. Wouldn't you say so? Fifteen shillings[4] a week's what he gets!

PRESENT. I would say that he gets the pleasure of his family, fifteen times a week times the number of hours a day! Wait, Mr. Scrooge. Wait, listen and watch. You might actually learn something . . .

MRS. CRATCHIT. What has ever got your precious father then? And your brother, Tiny Tim? And Martha warn't as late last Christmas by half an hour!

[MARTHA *opens the door, speaking to her mother as she does.*]

MARTHA. Here's Martha, now, Mother! [*She laughs. The* CRATCHIT CHILDREN *squeal with delight.*]

BELINDA. It's Martha, Mother! Here's Martha!

PETER. Marthmama, Marthmama! Hullo!

BELINDA. Hurrah! Martha! Martha! There's such an enormous goose for us, Martha!

MRS. CRATCHIT. Why, bless your heart alive, my dear, how late you are!

MARTHA. We'd a great deal of work to finish up last night, and had to clear away this morning, Mother.

MRS. CRATCHIT. Well, never mind so long as you are come. Sit ye down before the fire, my dear, and have a warm, Lord bless ye!

BELINDA. No, no! There's Father coming. Hide, Martha, hide!

[MARTHA *giggles and hides herself.*]

MARTHA. Where? Here?

PETER. Hide, hide!

---

4. **Fifteen shillings** a small amount of money for a week's work.

BELINDA. Not there! THERE!

MARTHA *is hidden.* BOB CRATCHIT *enters, carrying* TINY TIM *atop his shoulder. He wears a threadbare and fringeless comforter hanging down in front of him.* TINY TIM *carries small crutches and his small legs are bound in an iron frame brace.*]

BOB AND TINY TIM. Merry Christmas.

BOB. Merry Christmas my love, Merry Christmas Peter, Merry Christmas Belinda. Why, where is Martha?

MRS. CRATCHIT. Not coming.

BOB. Not coming: Not coming upon Christmas Day?

MARTHA. [*Pokes head out*] Ohhh, poor Father. Don't be disappointed.

BOB. What's this?

MARTHA. 'Tis I!

BOB. Martha! [*They embrace.*]

TINY TIM. Martha! Martha!

MARTHA. Tiny Tim!

[TINY TIM *is placed in* MARTHA'S *arms.* BELINDA *and* PETER *rush him offstage.*]

BELINDA. Come, brother! You must come hear the pudding singing in the copper.

TINY TIM. The pudding? What flavor have we?

PETER. Plum! Plum!

TINY TIM. Oh, Mother! I love plum!

[*The children exit the stage, giggling.*]

MRS. CRATCHIT. And how did little Tim behave?

BOB. As good as gold, and even better. Somehow he gets thoughtful sitting by himself so much, and thinks the

▲ **Critical Viewing**
Based on this picture, how would you describe the relationship between Tiny Tim and his father? **[Infer]**

Reading Check

Why does Martha hide?

strangest things you ever heard. He told me, coming home, that he hoped people saw him in the church, because he was a cripple, and it might be pleasant to them to remember upon Christmas Day, who made lame beggars walk and blind men see. [*Pauses*] He has the oddest ideas sometimes, but he seems all the while to be growing stronger and more hearty . . . one would never know. [*Hears* TIM'S *crutch on floor outside door*]

PETER. The goose has arrived to be eaten!

BELINDA. Oh, mama, mama, it's beautiful.

MARTHA. It's a perfect goose, Mother!

TINY TIM. To this Christmas goose, Mother and Father I say . . . [*Yells*] Hurrah! Hurrah!

OTHER CHILDREN. [*Copying* TIM] Hurrah! Hurrah!

[*The family sits round the table.* BOB *and* MRS. CRATCHIT *serve the trimmings, quickly. All sit; all bow heads; all pray.*]

BOB. Thank you, dear Lord, for your many gifts . . . our dear children; our wonderful meal; our love for one another; and the warmth of our small fire—[*Looks up at all*] A merry Christmas to us, my dear. God bless us!

ALL. [*Except* TIM] Merry Christmas! God bless us!

TINY TIM. [*In a short silence*] God bless us every one.

All freeze. Spotlight on PRESENT *and* SCROOGE]

SCROOGE. Spirit, tell me if Tiny Tim will live.

PRESENT. I see a vacant seat . . . in the poor chimney corner, and a crutch without an owner, carefully preserved. If these shadows remain unaltered by the future, the child will die.

SCROOGE. No, no, kind Spirit! Say he will be spared!

PRESENT. If these shadows remain unaltered by the future, none other of my race will find him here. What then? If he be like to die, he had better do it, and decrease the surplus population.

[SCROOGE *bows his head. We hear* BOB'S *voice speak* SCROOGE'S *name.*]

Stage Directions
Why is the pause in Bob's speech important here?

BOB. Mr. Scrooge . . .

SCROOGE. Huh? What's that? Who calls?

BOB. [*His glass raised in a toast*] I'll give you Mr. Scrooge, the Founder of the Feast!

SCROOGE. Me, Bob? You toast me?

PRESENT. Save your breath, Mr. Scrooge. You can't be seen or heard.

MRS. CRATCHIT. The Founder of the Feast, indeed! I wish I had him here, that miser Scrooge. I'd give him a piece of my mind to feast upon, and I hope he'd have a good appetite for it!

BOB. My dear! Christmas Day!

MRS. CRATCHIT. It should be Christmas Day, I am sure, on which one drinks the health of such an odious, stingy, unfeeling man as Mr. Scrooge . . .

▲ **Critical Viewing**
Why might a director stage the scene this way, with Tiny Tim standing on the table? **[Interpret]**

Reading Check

What is wrong with Tiny Tim?

A Christmas Carol: Scrooge and Marley, Act 2 **783**

SCROOGE. Oh, Spirit, must I? . . .

MRS. CRATCHIT You know he is, Robert! Nobody knows it better than you do, poor fellow!

BOB. This is Christmas Day, and I should like to drink to the health of the man who employs me and allows me to earn my living and our support and that man is Ebenezer Scrooge . . .

MRS. CRATCHIT. I'll drink to his health for your sake and the day's, but not for his sake . . . a Merry Christmas and a Happy New Year to you, Mr. Scrooge, wherever you may be this day!

SCROOGE. Just here, kind madam . . . out of sight, out of sight . . .

BOB. Thank you, my dear. Thank you.

SCROOGE. Thank you, Bob . . . and Mrs. Cratchit, too. No one else is toasting me, . . . not now . . . not ever. Of that I am sure . . .

BOB. Children . . .

ALL. Merry Christmas to Mr. Scrooge.

BOB. I'll pay you sixpence, Tim, for my favorite song.

TINY TIM. Oh, Father, I'd so love to sing it, but not for pay. This Christmas goose—this feast—you and Mother, my brother and sisters close with me: that's my pay—

BOB. Martha, will you play the notes on the lute, for Tiny Tim's song.

BELINDA. May I sing, too, Father?

BOB. We'll all sing.

[*They sing a song about a tiny child lost in the snow—probably from Wordsworth's poem.* TIM *sings the lead vocal; all chime in for the chorus. Their song fades under, as the* GHOST OF CHRISTMAS PRESENT *speaks.*]

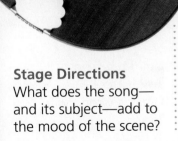

▼ **Critical Viewing**
Martha plays a lute like this one while her family sings. If this play were set in modern times, what instrument would Martha probably play? **[Apply]**

Stage Directions
What does the song—and its subject—add to the mood of the scene?

PRESENT. Mark my words, Ebenezer Scrooge. I do not present the Cratchits to you because they are a handsome, or brilliant family. They are not handsome. They are not brilliant. They are not well-dressed, or tasteful to the times. Their shoes are not even waterproofed by virtue of money or cleverness spent. So when the pavement is wet, so are the insides of their shoes and the tops of their toes. These are the Cratchits, Mr. Scrooge. They are not highly special. They are happy, grateful, pleased with one another, contented with the time and how it passes. They don't sing very well, do they? But, nonetheless, they do sing . . . [*Pauses*] think of that, Scrooge. Fifteen shillings a week and they do sing . . . hear their song until its end.

SCROOGE. I am listening. [*The chorus sings full volume now, until . . . the song ends here.*] Spirit, it must be time for us to take our leave. I feel in my heart that it is . . . that I must think on that which I have seen here . . .

PRESENT. Touch my robe again . . .

[SCROOGE *touches* PRESENT'S *robe. The lights fade out on the* CRATCHITS, *who sit, frozen, at the table.* SCROOGE *and* PRESENT *in a spotlight now. Thunder, lightning, smoke. They are gone.*]

[MARLEY *appears D.L. in single spotlight. A storm brews. Thunder and lightning.* SCROOGE *and* PRESENT *"fly" past,* U. *The storm continues, furiously, and, now and again,* SCROOGE *and* PRESENT *will zip past in their travels.* MARLEY *will speak straight out to the audience.*]

MARLEY. The Ghost of Christmas Present, my co-worker in this attempt to turn a miser, flies about now with that very miser, Scrooge, from street to street, and he points out partygoers on their way to Christmas parties. If one were to judge from the numbers of people on their way to friendly gatherings, one might think that no one was left at home to give anyone welcome . . . but that's not the case, is it? Every home is expecting company and . . . [*He laughs.*] Scrooge is amazed.

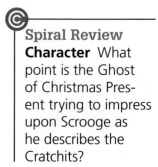

Spiral Review
Character What point is the Ghost of Christmas Present trying to impress upon Scrooge as he describes the Cratchits?

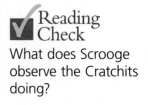

Reading Check
What does Scrooge observe the Cratchits doing?

Purpose for Reading
Why is it important
to read the change of
scene carefully?

[SCROOGE *and* PRESENT *zip past again. The lights fade up around them. We are in the* NEPHEW'S *home, in the living room.* PRESENT *and* SCROOGE *stand watching the* NEPHEW: FRED *and his wife, fixing the fire.*]

SCROOGE. What is this place? We've moved from the mines!

PRESENT. You do not recognize them?

SCROOGE. It is my nephew! . . . and the one he married . . .

[MARLEY *waves his hand and there is a lightning flash. He disappears.*]

FRED. It strikes me as sooooo funny, to think of what he said . . . that Christmas was a humbug, as I live! He believed it!

WIFE. More shame for him, Fred!

FRED. Well, he's a comical old fellow, that's the truth.

WIFE. I have no patience with him.

FRED. Oh, I have! I am sorry for him; I couldn't be angry with him if I tried. Who suffers by his ill whims? Himself, always . . .

SCROOGE. It's me they talk of, isn't it, Spirit?

FRED. Here, wife, consider this. Uncle Scrooge takes it into his head to dislike us, and he won't come and dine with us. What's the consequence?

WIFE. Oh . . . you're sweet to say what I think you're about to say, too, Fred . . .

FRED. What's the consequence? He don't lose much of a dinner by it, I can tell you that!

WIFE. Ooooooo, Fred! Indeed, I think he loses a very good dinner . . . ask my sisters, or your bachelor friend, Topper . . . ask any of them. They'll tell you what old Scrooge, your uncle, missed: a dandy meal!

FRED. Well, that's something of a relief, wife. Glad to hear it! [*He hugs his wife. They laugh. They kiss.*] The truth is, he misses much yet. I mean to give him the same chance every year, whether he likes it or not, for I pity him. Nay, he is my only uncle and I feel for the old miser . . . but, I tell you, wife: I see my dear and perfect mother's face on his own wizened cheeks and brow: brother and sister they were, and I cannot erase that from each view of him I take . . .

WIFE. I understand what you say, Fred, and I am with you in your yearly asking. But he never will accept, you know. He never will.

FRED. Well, true, wife. Uncle may rail at Christmas till he dies. I think I shook him some with my visit yesterday . . . [*Laughing*] I refused to grow angry . . . no matter how nasty he became . . . [*Whoops*] It was HE who grew angry, wife! [*They both laugh now.*]

SCROOGE. What he says is true, Spirit . . .

FRED AND WIFE. Bah, humbug!

FRED. [*Embracing his wife*] There is much laughter in our marriage, wife. It pleases me. You please me . . .

WIFE. And you please me, Fred. You are a good man . . . [*They embrace.*] Come now. We must have a look at the meal . . . our guests will soon arrive . . . my sisters, Topper . . .

FRED. A toast first . . . [*He hands her a glass.*] A toast to Uncle Scrooge . . . [*Fills their glasses*]

WIFE. A toast to him?

FRED. Uncle Scrooge has given us plenty of merriment, I am sure, and it would be ungrateful not to drink to his health. And I say . . . Uncle Scrooge!

WIFE. [*Laughing*] You're a proper loon,⁵ Fred . . . and I'm a

---

5. a proper loon a silly person.

> ✓ Reading Check
>
> What scenes does the Ghost of Christmas Present show Scrooge?

Vocabulary
audible (ô´ də bəl) *adj.*
loud enough to
be heard

proper wife to you . . . [*She raises her glass.*] Uncle Scrooge!
[*They drink. They embrace. They kiss.*]

SCROOGE. Spirit, please, make me visible! Make me **audible**! I
want to talk with my nephew and my niece!

[*Calls out to them. The lights that light the room and* FRED *and
wife fade out.* SCROOGE *and* PRESENT *are alone, spotlit.*]

PRESENT. These shadows are gone to you now, Mr. Scrooge.
You may return to them later tonight in your dreams.
[*Pauses*] My time grows short, Ebenezer Scrooge. Look you
on me! Do you see how I've aged?

SCROOGE. Your hair has gone gray! Your skin, wrinkled! Are
spirits' lives so short?

PRESENT. My stay upon this globe is very brief. It ends
tonight.

SCROOGE. Tonight?

PRESENT. At midnight. The time is drawing near!

[*Clock strikes 11:45.*]

Stage Directions
Why is the clock on
stage important to the
action?

Hear those chimes? In a quarter hour, my life will have
been spent! Look, Scrooge, man. Look you here.

[*Two gnarled baby dolls are taken from* PRESENT'S *skirts.*]

SCROOGE. Who are they?

PRESENT. They are Man's children, and they cling to me,
appealing from their fathers. The boy is Ignorance; the girl
is Want. Beware them both, and all of their degree, but
most of all beware this boy, for I see that written on his
brow which is doom, unless the writing be erased.
[*He stretches out his arm. His voice is now amplified: loudly
and oddly.*]

SCROOGE. Have they no refuge or resource?

PRESENT. Are there no prisons? Are there no workhouses?
[*Twelve chimes*] Are there no prisons? Are there no workhouses?

[*A* PHANTOM, *hooded, appears in dim light, D., opposite.*]
Are there no prisons? Are there no workhouses?

[PRESENT *begins to deliquesce.* SCROOGE *calls after him.*]

SCROOGE. Spirit, I'm frightened! Don't leave me! Spirit!

PRESENT. Prisons? Workhouses? Prisons? Workhouses . . .

[*He is gone.* SCROOGE *is alone now with the* PHANTOM, *who is, of course, the* GHOST OF CHRISTMAS FUTURE. *The* PHANTOM *is shrouded in black. Only its outstretched hand is visible from under his ghostly garment.*]

SCROOGE. Who are you, Phantom? Oh, yes, I think I know you! You are, are you not, the Spirit of Christmas Yet to Come? [*No reply*] And you are about to show me the shadows of the things that have not yet happened, but will happen in time before us. Is that not so, Spirit? [*The* PHANTOM *allows* SCROOGE *a look at his face. No other reply wanted here. A nervous giggle here.*] Oh, Ghost of the Future, I fear you more than any Specter I have seen! But, as I know that your purpose is to do me good and as I hope to live to be another man from what I was, I am prepared to bear you company. [FUTURE *does not reply, but for a stiff arm, hand and finger set, pointing forward.*] Lead on, then, lead on. The night is waning fast, and it is precious time to me. Lead on, Spirit!

[FUTURE *moves away from* SCROOGE *in the same rhythm and motion employed at its arrival.* SCROOGE *falls into the same pattern, a considerable space apart from the* SPIRIT. *In the space between them,* MARLEY *appears. He looks to* FUTURE *and then to* SCROOGE. *He claps his hands. Thunder and lightning. Three* BUSINESSMEN *appear, spotlighted singularly: One is D.L.; one is D.R.; one is U.C. Thus, six points of the stage should now be spotted in light.* MARLEY *will watch this scene from his position,* C. SCROOGE *and* FUTURE *are* R. *and* L. *of* C.]

FIRST BUSINESSMAN. Oh, no, I don't know much about it either way, I only know he's dead.

SECOND BUSINESSMAN. When did he die?

FIRST BUSINESSMAN. Last night, I believe.

SECOND BUSINESSMAN. Why, what was the matter with him? I thought he'd never die, really . . .

FIRST BUSINESSMAN. [*Yawning*] Goodness knows, goodness knows . . .

Stage Directions
The stage direction calls for Future to stretch out his hand. How does this action add to the drama of the scene?

Spiral Review
Character What valuable information does Scrooge reveal about himself?

Reading Check
What warning does the Ghost of Christmas Present give Scrooge?

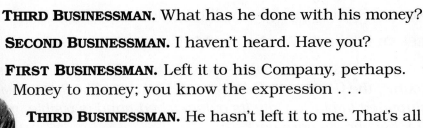

THIRD BUSINESSMAN. What has he done with his money?

SECOND BUSINESSMAN. I haven't heard. Have you?

FIRST BUSINESSMAN. Left it to his Company, perhaps. Money to money; you know the expression . . .

THIRD BUSINESSMAN. He hasn't left it to me. That's all I know . . .

FIRST BUSINESSMAN. [*Laughing*] Nor to me . . . [*Looks at* SECOND BUSINESSMAN] You, then? You got his money???

SECOND BUSINESSMAN. [*Laughing*] Me, me, his money? Nooooo!

[*They all laugh.*]

THIRD BUSINESSMAN. It's likely to be a cheap funeral, for upon my life, I don't know of a living soul who'd care to venture to it. Suppose we make up a party and volunteer?

SECOND BUSINESSMAN. I don't mind going if a lunch is provided, but I must be fed, if I make one.

FIRST BUSINESSMAN. Well, I am the most disinterested among you, for I never wear black gloves, and I never eat lunch. But I'll offer to go, if anybody else will. When I come to think of it, I'm not all sure that I wasn't his most particular friend; for we used to stop and speak whenever we met. Well, then . . . bye, bye!

SECOND BUSINESSMAN. Bye, bye . . .

THIRD BUSINESSMAN. Bye, bye . . .

[*They glide offstage in three separate directions. Their lights follow them.*]

SCROOGE. Spirit, why did you show me this? Why do you show me businessmen from my streets as they take the death of Jacob Marley. That is a thing past. You are future!

[JACOB MARLEY *laughs a long, deep laugh. There is a thunder clap and lightning flash, and he is gone.* SCROOGE *faces* FUTURE, *alone on stage now.* FUTURE *wordlessly stretches*

▲
Critical Viewing
How does the Ghost of Christmas Future differ from the other ghosts? **[Contrast]**

out his arm-hand-and-finger-set, pointing into the distance, U. There, above them. Scoundrels "fly" by, half-dressed and slovenly. When this scene has passed, a woman enters the playing area. She is almost at once followed by a second woman; and then a man in faded black; and then, suddenly, an old man, who smokes a pipe. The old man scares the other three. They laugh, anxious.]

FIRST WOMAN. Look here, old Joe, here's a chance! If we haven't all three met here without meaning it!

OLD JOE. You couldn't have met in a better place. Come into the parlor. You were made free of it long ago, you know; and the other two ain't strangers [*He stands; shuts a door. Shrieking*] We're all suitable to our calling. We're well matched. Come into the parlor. Come into the parlor . . . [*They follow him D. SCROOGE and FUTURE are now in their midst, watching; silent. A truck comes in on which is set a small wall with fireplace and a screen of rags, etc. All props for the scene.*] Let me just rake this fire over a bit . . .

[*He does. He trims his lamp with the stem of his pipe. The FIRST WOMAN throws a large bundle on to the floor. She sits beside it crosslegged, defiantly.*]

FIRST WOMAN. What odds then? What odds, Mrs. Dilber? Every person has a right to take care of themselves. HE always did!

MRS. DILBER. That's true indeed! No man more so!

FIRST WOMAN. Why, then, don't stand staring as if you was afraid, woman! Who's the wiser? We're not going to pick holes in each other's coats, I suppose?

MRS. DILBER. No, indeed! We should hope not!

FIRST WOMAN. Very well, then! That's enough. Who's the worse for the loss of a few things like these? Not a dead man, I suppose?

MRS. DILBER. [*Laughing*] No, indeed!

FIRST WOMAN. If he wanted to keep 'em after he was dead, the wicked old screw, why wasn't he natural in his lifetime? If he had been, he'd have had somebody to look after him

Stage Directions
If you were staging this play, how could you make people appear to "fly" by?

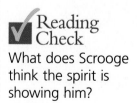

Reading Check
What does Scrooge think the spirit is showing him?

Purpose for Reading
What question about the characters directs your purpose for reading this dialogue?

when he was struck with Death, instead of lying gasping out his last there, alone by himself.

MRS. DILBER. It's the truest word that was ever spoke. It's a judgment on him.

FIRST WOMAN. I wish it were a heavier one, and it should have been, you may depend on it, if I could have laid my hands on anything else. Open that bundle, old Joe, and let me know the value of it. Speak out plain. I'm not afraid to be the first, nor afraid for them to see it. We knew pretty well that we were helping ourselves, before we met here, I believe. It's no sin. Open the bundle, Joe.

FIRST MAN. No, no, my dear! I won't think of letting you being the first to show what you've . . . earned . . . earned from this. I throw in mine.

[*He takes a bundle from his shoulder, turns it upside down, and empties its contents out on to the floor.*]

It's not very extensive, see . . . seals . . . a pencil case . . . sleeve buttons . . .

FIRST WOMAN. Nice sleeve buttons, though . . .

FIRST MAN. Not bad, not bad . . . a brooch there . . .

OLD JOE. Not really valuable, I'm afraid . . .

FIRST MAN. How much, old Joe?

OLD JOE. [*Writing on the wall with chalk*] A pitiful lot, really. Ten and six and not a sixpence more!

FIRST MAN. You're not serious!

OLD JOE. That's your account and I wouldn't give another sixpence if I was to be boiled for not doing it. Who's next?

MRS. DILBER. Me! [*Dumps out contents of her bundle*] Sheets, towels, silver spoons, silver sugar-tongs . . . some boots . . .

OLD JOE. [*Writing on wall*] I always give too much to the ladies. It's a weakness of mine and that's the way I ruin myself. Here's your total comin' up . . . two pounds-ten . . . if you asked me for another penny, and made it an open question, I'd repent of being so liberal and knock off half-a-crown.

FIRST WOMAN. And now do MY bundle, Joe.

OLD JOE. [*Kneeling to open knots on her bundle*] So many knots, madam . . . [*He drags out large curtains; dark*] What do you call this? Bed curtains!

FIRST WOMAN. [*Laughing*] Ah, yes, bed curtains!

OLD JOE. You don't mean to say you took 'em down, rings and all, with him lying there?

FIRST WOMAN. Yes, I did, why not?

OLD JOE. You were born to make your fortune and you'll certainly do it.

FIRST WOMAN. I certainly shan't hold my hand, when I can get anything in it by reaching it out, for the sake of such a man as he was, I promise you, Joe. Don't drop that lamp oil on those blankets, now!

OLD JOE. His blankets?

FIRST WOMAN. Whose else's do you think? He isn't likely to catch cold without 'em, I daresay.

OLD JOE. I hope that he didn't die of anything catching? Eh?

FIRST WOMAN. Don't you be afraid of that. I ain't so fond of his company that I'd loiter about him for such things if he did. Ah! You may look through that shirt till your eyes ache, but you won't find a hole in it, nor a threadbare place. It's the best he had, and a fine one, too. They'd have wasted it, if it hadn't been for me.

OLD JOE. What do you mean 'They'd have wasted it?'

FIRST WOMAN. Putting it on him to be buried in, to be sure. Somebody was fool enough to do it, but I took it off again . . .

[*She laughs, as do they all, nervously.*]

If calico[6] ain't good enough for such a purpose, it isn't good enough then for anything. It's quite as becoming to the body. He can't look uglier than he did in that one!

SCROOGE. [*A low-pitched moan emits from his mouth; from the bones.*] OOOOOOOooooooOOOOOooooooOOOOOOOO ooooooOOOOOOOooooooOO!

---

6. calico (kal´ i kō) *n.* coarse and cheap cloth.

Stage Directions
How do the stage directions help you picture the action in this scene?

Reading Check
Whose possessions are these people selling?

OLD JOE. One pound six for the lot. [*He produces a small flannel bag filled with money. He divvies it out. He continues to pass around the money as he speaks. All are laughing.*] That's the end of it, you see! He frightened every one away from him while he was alive, to profit us when he was dead! Hah ha ha!

ALL. HAHAHAHAhahahahahahah!

SCROOGE. OOOoooOOOoooOOOoooOOOooo OOoooOOoooOOOooo! [*He screams at them.*] Obscene demons! Why not market the corpse itself, as sell its trimming??? [*Suddenly*] Oh, Spirit, I see it, I see it! This unhappy man—this stripped-bare corpse . . . could very well be my own. My life holds parallel! My life ends that way now!

Stage Directions
What is the effect of the spirit's silence?

[SCROOGE *backs into something in the dark behind his spotlight.* SCROOGE *looks at* FUTURE, *who points to the corpse.* SCROOGE *pulls back the blanket. The corpse is, of course,* SCROOGE, *who screams. He falls aside the bed; weeping.*]

Spirit, this is a fearful place. In leaving it, I shall not leave its lesson, trust me. Let us go!

[FUTURE *points to the corpse.*]

Spirit, let me see some tenderness connected with a death, or that dark chamber, which we just left now, Spirit, will be forever present to me.

[FUTURE *spreads his robes again. Thunder and lightning. Lights up, U., in the* CRATCHIT *home setting.* MRS. CRATCHIT *and her daughters, sewing*]

TINY TIM'S VOICE. [*Off*] And He took a child and set him in the midst of them.

▶ **Critical Viewing**
Why might a director choose to place the actors playing the Cratchits this way? What do their positions reveal about the family? **[Analyze]**

SCROOGE. [*Looking about the room; to* FUTURE] Huh? Who spoke? Who said that?

MRS. CRATCHIT. [*Puts down her sewing*] The color hurts my eyes. [*Rubs her eyes*] That's better. My eyes grow weak sewing by candlelight. I shouldn't want to show your father weak eyes when he comes home . . . not for the world! It must be near his time . . .

PETER. [*In corner, reading. Looks up from book*] Past it, rather. But I think he's been walking a bit slower than usual these last few evenings, Mother.

MRS. CRATCHIT I have known him walk with . . . [*Pauses*] I have know him walk with Tiny Tim upon his shoulder and very fast indeed.

PETER. So have I, Mother! Often!

DAUGHTER. So have I.

MRS. CRATCHIT. But he was very light to carry and his father loved him so, that it was not trouble—no trouble. [BOB, *at door*] And there is your father at the door.

[BOB CRATCHIT *enters. He wears a comforter. He is cold, forlorn.*]

PETER. Father!

BOB. Hello, wife, children . . .

[*The daughter weeps; turns away from* CRATCHIT.]

Children! How good to see you all! And you, wife. And look at this sewing! I've no doubt, with all your industry,

✓ Reading Check

Whose corpse does Scrooge see?

A Christmas Carol: Scrooge and Marley, Act 2 **795**

we'll have a quilt to set down upon our knees in church on Sunday!

MRS. CRATCHIT. You made the arrangements today, then, Robert, for the . . . service . . . to be on Sunday.

BOB. The funeral. Oh, well, yes, yes, I did. I wish you could have gone. It would have done you good to see how green a place it is. But you'll see it often. I promised him that I would walk there on Sunday, after the service. [*Suddenly*] My little, little child! My little child!

ALL CHILDREN. [*Hugging him*] Oh, Father . . .

BOB. [*He stands*] Forgive me. I saw Mr. Scrooge's nephew, who you know I'd just met once before, and he was so wonderful to me, wife . . . he is the most pleasant-spoken gentleman I've ever met . . . he said "I am heartily sorry for it and heartily sorry for your good wife. If I can be of service to you in any way, here's where I live." And he gave me this card.

PETER. Let me see it!

BOB. And he looked me straight in the eye, wife, and said, meaningfully, "I pray you'll come to me, Mr. Cratchit, if you need some help. I pray you do." Now it wasn't for the sake of anything that he might be able to do for us, so much as for his kind way. It seemed as if he had known our Tiny Tim and felt with us.

MRS. CRATCHIT. I'm sure that he's a good soul.

BOB. You would be surer of it, my dear, if you saw and spoke to him. I shouldn't be at all surprised, if he got Peter a situation.

MRS. CRATCHIT. Only hear that, Peter!

MARTHA. And then, Peter will be keeping company with someone and setting up for himself!

PETER. Get along with you!

BOB. It's just as likely as not, one of these days, though there's plenty of time for that, my dear. But however and whenever we part from one another, I am sure we shall none of us forget poor Tiny Tim—shall we?—or this first parting that was among us?

Purpose for Reading
What plot information does this dialogue provide about a possible future for the Cratchits?

ALL CHILDREN. Never, Father, never!

BOB. And when we recollect how patient and mild he was, we shall not quarrel easily among ourselves, and forget poor Tiny Tim in doing it.

ALL CHILDREN. No, Father, never!

LITTLE BOB. I am very happy, I am, I am, I am very happy.

[BOB *kisses his little son, as does* MRS. CRATCHIT, *as do the other children. The family is set now in one sculptural embrace. The lighting fades to a gentle pool of light, tight on them.*]

SCROOGE. Specter, something informs me that our parting moment is at hand. I know it, but I know not how I know it.

[FUTURE *points to the other side of the stage. Lights out on* CRATCHITS. FUTURE *moves slowing, gliding.* SCROOGE *follows.* FUTURE *points opposite.* FUTURE *leads* SCROOGE *to a wall and a tombstone. He points to the stone.*]

Am I that man those ghoulish parasites[7] so gloated over? [*Pauses*] Before I draw nearer to that stone to which you point, answer me one question. Are these the shadows of things that will be, or the shadows of things that MAY be, only?

▼ **Critical Viewing**
Why do you think the sight of this tombstone terrified Scrooge? **[Connect]**

✓ Reading Check
What has happened to Tiny Tim?

---

7. **ghoulish parasites** (gōōl′ ish par′ ə sīts) man and women who stole and divided Scrooge's goods after he died.

[FUTURE *points to the gravestone.* MARLEY *appears in light well U. He points to grave as well. Gravestone turns front and grows to ten feet high. Words upon it:* EBENEZER SCROOGE: *Much smoke billows now from the grave. Choral music here.* SCROOGE *stands looking up at gravestone.* FUTURE *does not at all reply in mortals' words, but points once more to the gravestone. The stone undulates and glows. Music plays, beckoning* SCROOGE. SCROOGE *reeling in terror*]

Oh, no. Spirit! Oh, no, no!

[FUTURE'S *finger still pointing*]

Spirit! Hear me! I am not the man I was. I will not be the man I would have been but for this intercourse. Why show me this, if I am past all hope?

[FUTURE *considers* SCROOGE'S *logic. His hand wavers.*]

Oh, Good Spirit, I see by your wavering hand that your good nature intercedes for me and pities me. Assure me that I yet may change these shadows that you have shown me by an altered life!

[FUTURE'S *hand trembles; pointing has stopped.*]

I will honor Christmas in my heart and try to keep it all the year. I will live in the Past, the Present, and the Future. The Spirits of all Three shall strive within me. I will not shut out the lessons that they teach. Oh, tell me that I may sponge away the writing that is upon this stone!

[SCROOGE *makes a desperate stab at grabbing* FUTURE'S *hand. He holds firm for a moment, but* FUTURE, *stronger than* SCROOGE, *pulls away.* SCROOGE *is on his knees, praying.*]

Spirit, dear Spirit, I am praying before you. Give me a sign that all is possible. Give me a sign that all hope for me is not lost. Oh, Spirit, kind Spirit, I beseech thee: give me a sign . . .

[FUTURE *deliquesces, slowly, gently. The* PHANTOM'S *hood and robe drop gracefully to the ground in a small heap. Music in. There is nothing in them. They are mortal cloth. The* SPIRIT *is elsewhere.* SCROOGE *has his sign.* SCROOGE *is alone. Tableau. The lights fade to black.*]

SCENE 5

[*The end of it.* MARLEY, *spotlighted, opposite* SCROOGE, *in his bed, spotlighted.* MARLEY *speaks to audience, directly.*]

MARLEY. [*He smiles at* SCROOGE:] The firm of Scrooge and Marley is doubly blessed; two misers turned; one, alas, in Death, too late; but the other miser turned in Time's penultimate nick.[8] Look you on my friend, Ebenezer Scrooge . . .

SCROOGE. [*Scrambling out of bed; reeling in delight*] I will live in the Past, in the Present, and in the Future! The Spirits of all Three shall strive within me!

MARLEY. [*He points and moves closer to* SCROOGE'S *bed.*] Yes, Ebenezer, the bedpost is your own. Believe it! Yes, Ebenezer, the room is your own. Believe it!

SCROOGE. Oh, Jacob Marley! Wherever you are, Jacob, know ye that I praise you for this! I praise you . . . and heaven . . . and Christmastime! [*Kneels facing away from* MARLEY] I say it to ye on my knees, old Jacob, on my knees! [*He touches his bed curtains.*] Not torn down. My bed curtains are not at all torn down! Rings and all, here they are! They are here: I am here: the shadows of things that would have been, may now be dispelled. They will be, Jacob! I know they will be!

[*He chooses clothing for the day. He tries different pieces of clothing and settles, perhaps on a dress suit, plus a cape of the bed clothing: something of color.*]

I am light as a feather, I am happy as an angel, I am as merry as a schoolboy. [*Yells out window and then out to audience*] Merry Christmas to everybody! Merry Christmas to everybody! A Happy New Year to all the world! Hallo here! Whoop! Whoop! Hallo! Hallo! I don't know what day of the month it is! I don't care! I don't know anything! I'm quite a baby! I don't care! I don't care a fig! I'd much rather be a baby than be an old wreck like me or Marley! (Sorry, Jacob, wherever ye be!) Hallo! Hallo there!

[*Church bells chime in Christmas Day. A small boy, named* ADAM, *is seen now D.R., as a light fades up on him.*]

Purpose for Reading
Why might you read this speech by Scrooge quickly?

Reading Check
What promises does Scrooge make?

---

8. **in Time's penultimate nick** just at the last moment.

Media Connection

The Many Faces of Scrooge
The part of Ebenezer Scrooge has been played by many different actors over the years.

1983 Scrooge McDuck

1938 Reginald Owen

1951 Alistair Sim

1962 Mister Magoo

1992 Michael Caine

Connect to the Literature

Which of these actors best portrays Scrooge as you imagine him from your reading? Explain.

Hey, you boy! What's today? What day of the year is it?

ADAM. Today, sir? Why, it's Christmas Day!

SCROOGE. It's Christmas Day, is it? Whoop! Well, I haven't missed it after all, have I? The Spirits did all they did in one night. They can do anything they like, right? Of course they can! Of course they can!

ADAM. Excuse me, sir?

SCROOGE. Huh? Oh, yes, of course, what's your name, lad?

[SCROOGE *and* ADAM *will play their scene from their own spotlights.*]

ADAM. Adam, sir.

SCROOGE. Adam! What a fine, strong name! Do you know the poulterer's⁹ in the next street but one, at the corner?

ADAM. I certainly should hope I know him, sir!

SCROOGE. A remarkable boy! An intelligent boy! Do you know whether the poulterer's have sold the prize turkey that was hanging up there? I don't mean the little prize turkey, Adam. I mean the big one!

ADAM. What, do you mean the one they've got that's as big as me?

SCROOGE. I mean, the turkey the size of Adam: that's the bird!

ADAM. It's hanging there now, sir.

SCROOGE. It is? Go and buy it! No, no, I am absolutely in earnest. Go and buy it and tell 'em to bring it here, so that I may give them the directions to where I want it delivered, as a gift. Come back here with the man, Adam, and I'll give you a shilling. Come back here with him in less than five minutes, and I'll give you half-a-crown!

ADAM. Oh, my sir! Don't let my brother in on this.

[ADAM *runs offstage.* MARLEY *smiles.*]

MARLEY. An act of kindness is like the first green grape of summer: one leads to another and another and another. It would take a queer man indeed to not follow an act of kindness with an act of kindness. One simply whets the tongue for more . . . the taste of kindness is too too sweet. Gifts—goods—are lifeless. But the gift of goodness one feels in the giving is full of life. It . . . is . . . a . . . wonder.

[*Pauses; moves closer to* SCROOGE, *who is totally occupied with his dressing and arranging of his room and his day. He is making lists, etc.* MARLEY *reaches out to* SCROOGE:]

ADAM. [*Calling, off*] I'm here! I'm here!

[ADAM *runs on with a man, who carries an enormous turkey.*]

Here I am, sir. Three minutes flat! A world record! I've got the poultryman and he's got the poultry! [*He pants, out of breath.*] I have earned my prize, sir, if I live . . .

---

9. **poulterer's** (pōl′ tər ərz) *n.* British word for a store that sells poultry.

Stage Directions Why does having a spotlight of both Scrooge and Adam add drama to the scene?

Reading Check

What does Scrooge instruct Adam to do?

[*He holds his heart, playacting.* SCROOGE *goes to him and embraces him.*]

SCROOGE. You are truly a champion, Adam . . .

MAN. Here's the bird you ordered, sir . . .

SCROOGE. Oh, my, MY!!! look at the size of that turkey, will you! He never could have stood upon his legs, that bird! He would have snapped them off in a minute, like sticks of sealingwax! Why you'll never be able to carry that bird to Camden-Town. I'll give you money for a cab . . .

MAN. Camden-Town's where it's goin', sir?

SCROOGE. Oh, I didn't tell you? Yes, I've written the precise address down just here on this . . . [*Hands paper to him*] Bob Cratchit's house. Now he's not to know who sends him this. Do you understand me? Not a word . . . [*Handing out money and chuckling*]

MAN. I understand, sir, not a word.

SCROOGE. Good. There you go then . . . this is for the turkey . . . [*Chuckle*] and this is for the taxi. [*Chuckle*] . . . and this is for your world-record run, Adam . . .

ADAM. But I don't have change for that, sir.

SCROOGE. Then keep it, my lad. It's Christmas!

ADAM. [*He kisses* SCROOGE'S *cheek, quickly.*] Thank you, sir. Merry, Merry Christmas! [*He runs off.*]

MAN. And you've given me a bit overmuch here, too, sir . . .

SCROOGE. Of course I have, sir. It's Christmas!

MAN. Oh, well, thanking you, sir. I'll have this bird to Mr. Cratchit and his family in no time, sir. Don't you worry none about that. Merry Christmas to you, sir, and a very happy New Year, too . . .

[*The man exits.* SCROOGE *walks in a large circle about the stage, which is now gently lit. A chorus sings Christmas music far in the distance. Bells chime as well, far in the distance. A gentlewoman enters and passes.* SCROOGE *is on the streets now.*]

SCROOGE. Merry Christmas, madam . . .

Purpose for Reading
The positive change in Scrooge is becoming more noticeable. Will your reading rate change from here until the end of the act? Why or why not?

WOMAN. Merry Christmas, sir . . .

[*The portly businessman from the first act enters.*]

SCROOGE. Merry Christmas, sir.

PORTLY MAN. Merry Christmas, sir.

SCROOGE. Oh, you! My dear sir! How do you do? I do hope that you succeeded yesterday! It was very kind of you. A Merry Christmas.

PORTLY MAN. Mr. Scrooge?

SCROOGE. Yes, Scrooge is my name though I'm afraid you may not find it very pleasant. Allow me to ask your pardon. And will you have the goodness to—[*He whispers into the man's ear.*]

PORTLY MAN. Lord bless me! My dear Mr. Scrooge, are you serious!?!

▲ **Critical Viewing**
How do the color and movement in this photo convey Scrooge's new attitude? **[Analyze Cause and Effect]**

 Reading Check

Where does Scrooge want the turkey delivered?

SCROOGE. If you please. Not a farthing[10] less. A great many back payments are included in it, I assure you. Will you do me that favor?

PORTLY MAN. My dear sir, I don't know what to say to such munifi—

SCROOGE. [*Cutting him off*] Don't say anything, please. Come and see me. Will you?

PORTLY MAN. I will! I will! Oh I will, Mr. Scrooge! It will be my pleasure!

SCROOGE. Thank'ee, I am much obliged to you. I thank you fifty times. Bless you!

[*Portly man passes offstage, perhaps by moving backwards.* SCROOGE *now comes to the room of his* NEPHEW *and* NIECE. *He stops at the door, begins to knock on it, loses his courage, tries again, loses his courage again, tries again, fails again, and then backs off and runs at the door, causing a tremendous bump against it. The* NEPHEW *and* NIECE *are startled.* SCROOGE, *poking head into room*]

Fred!

NEPHEW. Why, bless my soul! Who's that?

NEPHEW AND NIECE. [*Together*] How now? Who goes?

SCROOGE. It's I. Your Uncle Scrooge.

NIECE. Dear heart alive!

SCROOGE. I have come to dinner. May I come in, Fred?

NEPHEW. *May you come in???!!!* With such pleasure for me you may, Uncle!!! What a treat!

NIECE. What a treat, Uncle Scrooge! Come in, come in!

[*They embrace a shocked and delighted* SCROOGE: FRED *calls into the other room.*]

NEPHEW. Come in here, everybody, and meet my Uncle Scrooge! He's come for our Christmas party!

[*Music in. Lighting here indicates that day has gone to night and gone to day again. It is early, early morning.* SCROOGE *walks alone from the party, exhausted, to his offices, opposite*

---

10. farthing (fär′ *thiŋ*) *n.* small British coin.

Stage Directions
What do Scrooge's actions tell you about his feelings at this point?

Stage Directions
How could lighting be used to show the passage of time?

side of the stage. He opens his offices. The offices are as they were at the start of the play. SCROOGE *seats himself with his door wide open so that he can see into the tank, as he awaits* CRATCHIT, *who enters, head down, full of guilt.* CRATCHIT, *starts writing almost before he sits.*]

SCROOGE. What do you mean by coming in here at this time of day, a full eighteen minutes late, Mr. Cratchit? Hallo, sir? Do you hear me?

BOB. I am very sorry, sir. I am behind my time.

SCROOGE. You are? Yes, I certainly think you are. Step this way, sir, if you please . . .

BOB. It's only but once a year, sir . . . it shall not be repeated. I was making rather merry yesterday and into the night . . .

SCROOGE. Now, I'll tell you what, Cratchit. I am not going to stand this sort of thing any longer. And therefore . . .

[*He stands and pokes his finger into* BOB'S *chest.*]

I am . . . about . . . to . . . raise . . . your salary.

BOB. Oh, no, sir, I . . . [*Realizes*] what did you say, sir?

SCROOGE. A Merry Christmas, Bob . . . [*He claps* BOB'S *back.*] A merrier Christmas, Bob, my good fellow! than I have given you for many a year. I'll raise your salary and endeavor to assist your struggling family and we will discuss your affairs this very afternoon over a bowl of smoking bishop.[11] Bob! Make up the fires and buy another coal scuttle before you dot another i, Bob. It's too cold in this place! We need warmth and cheer, Bob Cratchit! Do you hear me? DO . . . YOU . . . HEAR . . . ME?

[BOB CRATCHIT *stands, smiles at* SCROOGE: BOB CRATCHIT *faints. Blackout. As the main lights black out, a spotlight appears on* SCROOGE: C. *Another on* MARLEY: *He talks directly to the audience.*]

MARLEY. Scrooge was better than his word. He did it all and infinitely more; and to Tiny Tim, who did NOT die, he was a second father. He became as good a friend, as good a master, as good a man, as the good old city knew, or any other good old city, town, or borough in the good old world.

---

11. **smoking bishop** hot sweet orange-flavored drink.

Stage Directions
What information in the stage directions might be funny to audiences? Why?

Reading Check
What has Scrooge promised to give Bob?

And it was always said of him that he knew how to keep Christmas well, if any man alive possessed the knowledge. [*Pauses*] May that be truly said of us, and all of us. And so, as Tiny Tim observed . . .

TINY TIM. [*Atop* SCROOGE'S *shoulder*] God Bless Us, Every One . . .

[*Lights up on chorus, singing final Christmas Song.* SCROOGE *and* MARLEY *and all spirits and other characters of the play join in. When the song is over, the lights fade to black.*]

Critical Thinking

© **1. Key Ideas and Details (a)** In Scene 3, what does Scrooge learn about the Cratchit family? **(b) Analyze:** Why does Scrooge care about the fate of Tiny Tim? **(c) Draw Conclusions:** In what way is Scrooge changing?

© **2. Key Ideas and Details (a)** In Scene 4, what happens to Scrooge's belongings in Christmas future? **(b) Draw Conclusions:** What does Scrooge learn from this experience?

© **3. Key Ideas and Details (a) Analyze:** Why is Scrooge happy at the end of the play? **(b) Evaluate:** How well does he live up to his promise to learn his "lessons"?

© **4. Integration of Knowledge and Ideas Take a Position:** Do you think Cratchit and Scrooge's nephew do the right thing by forgiving Scrooge immediately? Explain, using details from the play to support your answer.

© **5. Integration of Knowledge and Ideas (a)** What does Scrooge learn from the opportunity to watch his own life? **(b)** How does he change his behavior to reflect his new insight? *[Connect to the Big Question: Do others see us more clearly than we see ourselves?]*

Cite textual evidence to support your responses.

Reading Skill: Purpose for Reading

1. Which did you read more quickly: the dialogue or the stage directions? In your answer, explain how your **purpose** affected your reading rate.

2. When you read long speeches with difficult words, what happens to your reading rate? Explain.

Literary Analysis: Stage Directions

3. **Craft and Structure** Reread the **stage directions** at the beginning of Scene 1. Then, complete a chart like the one shown to record the information the directions reveal.

Characters on Stage	Movement of Characters	Description of Lighting	Description of Sound	Other Special Effects

4. **Craft and Structure** Which stage direction in Scene 4 is especially effective in making the scene mysterious? Explain.

Vocabulary

Acquisition and Use Answer each question, then explain your answer.

1. When you speak, do you want your voice to be *audible*?

2. Would it *astonish* you if an elephant sang?

3. Would you take cover if a *severe* storm were approaching?

4. Can a family with a *meager* income build a large, fancy house?

5. Would you *intercede* if two friends were arguing?

6. Would a person with a *compulsion* to save money give away a million dollars?

Word Study Use the context of the sentences and what you know about the **Latin prefix inter-** to explain your answers.

1. Is an *international* crisis one that occurs between two states?

2. Does an *intermission* usually occur at the start of a play?

Word Study

The **Latin prefix inter-** means "between" or "among."

Apply It Explain how the prefix *inter-* contributes to the meanings of these words. Consult a dictionary if necessary.

interplanetary
interpersonal
interject

Integrated Language Skills

A Christmas Carol: Scrooge and Marley, Act 2

Conventions: Double Negatives

> **Double negatives** are two negative words used when only one is needed in Standard English.

Examples of negative words are *nothing, not, never,* and *no.* You can correct a double negative by revising the sentence.

This chart shows double negatives and ways to correct them.

Double Negative	Corrected Sentence
Coach <u>never</u> told us <u>nothing</u> about the other team.	Coach <u>never</u> told us <u>anything</u> about the other team.
Hilary does <u>not</u> have <u>no</u> cash now.	Hilary does <u>not</u> have <u>any</u> cash now.

Practice A Identify and revise the sentences that contain double negatives. Write "correct" for those sentences without double negatives.

1. Marley said that Scrooge would not be afraid of nothing now.
2. No one could show him anything surprising.
3. He was not aware the Cratchits survived on almost nothing.
4. His meanness did not have no effect on the spirit of his nephew.

© **Reading Application** In *A Christmas Carol: Scrooge and Marley,* Act 2, Scene 1, find three sentences that contain negative words.

Practice B Rewrite each sentence to correct the double negative.

1. Scrooge did not want to go nowhere with Christmas Past but knew he must.
2. The thieves believed that nobody cared nothing for Scrooge.
3. The Cratchits mourned that Tiny Tim would not be a part of their lives no more.
4. Once changed, Scrooge would not let nothing stop his acts of kindness.

© **Writing Application** Write two sentences about *A Christmas Carol: Scrooge and Marley,* Act 2, using the words *not* and *never.* Avoid using a double negative.

PH **WRITING COACH**   Further instruction and practice are available in *Prentice Hall Writing Coach.*

Writing

Argumentative Text Respond to the play by writing a **tribute,** or expression of admiration, to the changed Scrooge. Your tribute may share brief stories from the drama that show how Scrooge has transformed his life. It may also reflect on the events or experiences that caused Scrooge to change. As you draft, identify the new traits that make Scrooge worthy of a tribute, and include evidence from the play to support your analysis. Conclude by giving your opinion of the play and providing your own insights about whether there is a lesson that everyone can learn from Scrooge's story.

Grammar Application Check your writing to be sure you have corrected any double negatives.

Writing Workshop: *Work in Progress*

Prewriting for Research For each topic on your Ideas List, jot down a creative idea for using a visual or audio aid for use in a research report you may write. Save this Multimedia List in your writing portfolio.

**Common Core
State Standards**

**L.7.1, L.7.2, L.7.4.b, L.7.6;
W.7.2, W.7.9; SL.7.6**
[For the full wording of the standards, see page 772.]

Use this prewriting activity to prepare for the **Writing Workshop** on page 824.

Speaking and Listening

Presentation of Ideas Think about Scrooge's experiences with one of the ghosts. Then, write and present a **dramatic monologue** that shares Scrooge's thoughts.

- As you draft your monologue, write as Scrooge from the first-person point of view, using the word *I.*
- Include stage directions to indicate gestures and emotions.
- Punctuate your monologue correctly. Use a colon after the speaker's name and brackets to set off stage directions. Use commas and dashes in the monologue to indicate pauses and changes in thought.

As you prepare to present your monologue, consider these tips:
- Project your voice so that everyone can hear you.
- Follow stage directions that tell how to move or speak.
- As you rehearse, read the monologue several different ways. Try pausing at suitable moments, speaking at different speeds where a tempo change makes sense, and raising and lowering your voice for effect. Decide which techniques work and use these in your final presentation.

**PHLit
Online!**
www.PHLitOnline.com
- Interactive graphic organizers
- Grammar tutorial
- Interactive journals

Test Practice: Reading

Purpose for Reading

Fiction Selection

Directions: *Read the selection. Then, answer the questions.*

[*A single spotlight on* DAVID, *a young man in his early twenties. He appears stern and anxious as he hunches over his desk, hard at work. A MAN is seen leaving stage left.*]

David. [*fiercely*] No more interruptions!

[ERYKAH *enters stage right and approaches* DAVID *from behind. Her hands are behind her back. She is holding an object that we cannot see.*]

Erykah. [*cheerfully, in a Jamaican accent*] Hello, David!

David. [*annoyed*] What is it? [*He turns, smiles.*] Oh, Erykah. It's you.

Erykah. I'm sorry to interrupt. I can come back . . .

David. No, no. Come, sit down. For you, there is always time.

1. What is the most likely purpose a reader would have for reading this passage?
   A. to learn about a subject
   B. to make a decision
   C. to be informed
   D. to be entertained

2. For what purpose might you choose to read the play from which this scene comes slowly and carefully?
   A. to find out what happens next
   B. to analyze its characters
   C. to find a specific scene
   D. to discover when a character first appears

3. What question might a reader hope to answer by reading on?
   A. What is Erykah holding?
   B. How old is David?
   C. When was this play written?
   D. What is Erykah wearing?

4. At what rate should you read the stage directions, and why?
   A. Quickly, to give the impression of conversation.
   B. Slowly, in case action is revealed that is not shown in the dialogue.
   C. Quickly, in case something exciting happens next.
   D. Slowly, to figure out the author's main message.

Writing for Assessment

In a short paragraph, describe two different purposes a person might have for reading the play from which this passage comes. Discuss the reading rate that would best suit each purpose and identify key details from the text that support each idea.

Nonfiction Selection

Directions: *Read the selection. Then, answer the questions.*

The Development of Stanislavsky's Method

The Stanislavsky Method, also known as "the method," is a style of acting developed by Konstantin Stanislavsky in the early twentieth century. Stanislavsky, an actor and producer, believed that actors should not *appear* to feel a certain way but should instead recreate the emotions of their characters for themselves. His method became popular during his lifetime and is still used by some actors today.

Using Stanislavsky's Method

To use Stanislavsky's method, actors concentrate on feeling the same emotions their characters experience. For example, if an actor wants to appear happy on stage, she might recall a time when she felt happy in real life. Focusing on that feeling, according to Stanislavsky, helps an actor capture the emotions of a character more realistically.

1. What is the *best* way to preview this passage?
   A. Read the text.
   B. Read the headings.
   C. Reread and take notes.
   D. Carefully read each word.

2. What can you learn from a close reading of the passage?
   A. how actors use "the method"
   B. which plays Stanislavsky produced
   C. where and when "the method" was first used
   D. why actors might not want to use "the method"

3. What might be a purpose for reading this passage?
   A. to be entertained
   B. to find information about auditioning
   C. to understand an acting technique
   D. to be persuaded to see a play

4. You should read this passage at about the same rate as you would read—
   A. a comic book.
   B. a letter from a friend.
   C. an encyclopedia article.
   D. a folk tale.

Writing for Assessment

Connecting Across Texts

Why might the actors playing David and Erykah benefit from reading the description of Stanislavsky's method? Using details from both passages, explain your answer in a few sentences.

PHLit Online!
www.PHLitOnline.com
- Online practice
- Instant feedback

Reading for Information

Analyzing Argumentative and Expository Texts

Review	Review	Radio Interview

Common Core State Standards

Reading Informational Text
6. Determine an author's point of view or purpose in a text and analyze how the author distinguishes his or her position from that of others.

Language
6. Acquire and use accurately grade-appropriate general academic and domain-specific words and phrases; gather vocabulary knowledge when considering a word or phrase important to comprehension or expression.

Writing
1.b. Support claim(s) with logical reasoning and relevant evidence, using accurate, credible sources and demonstrating an understanding of the topic or text.
9. Draw evidence from literary or informational texts to support analysis, reflection, and research.

Reading Skill: Identify the Author's Perspective

In a review, the author makes a claim or gives his or her opinion about a work. In an interview, the guest speaks from his or her own experiences and knowledge. In each case, you are getting one person's perspective, or point of view. When you **identify an author's perspective,** you gain an understanding of the reasons behind his or her arguments, opinions, and statements. As you read, use a chart like this one to **trace the development of the author's** (or speaker's) **perspective.**

Statement	Perspective
"A new take on an old classic always offers fresh insights."	The writer approaches classic story adaptations with a positive attitude.
"A retelling of a classic story can never live up to the original."	The writer approaches classic story adaptations with a negative attitude.

Content-Area Vocabulary

These words appear in the selections that follow. You may also encounter them in other content-area texts.

- **cast** (kast) *n.* the actors in a movie, television show, or play
- **adaptation** (ad´ ap tā´ shən) *n.* something that is produced by changing the original version
- **ensemble** (än säm´ bəl) *n.* all of the actors who participate in a performance

Features:

- informational reading
- judgment or recommendation
- original summaries or excerpts from the work often included
- text written for a general or a specific audience

A Christmas Carol

TNT

(Sun., Dec. 5, 8 p.m. ET)
Picks & Pans: Television
Full text: COPYRIGHT 1999 Time, Inc.

So you muttered "humbug" when you spied yet another version of *A Christmas Carol* on the TV schedule. Don't feel guilty. It doesn't take a spiritual descendant of Ebenezer Scrooge to notice that the Charles Dickens classic has been adapted nearly to death. (Two years ago, there was even a Ms. Scrooge.)

> The tone in the opening of the review hints at the author's perspective.

But TNT's *Carol* would be worth watching if only for the lead performance of Patrick Stewart. The ex-skipper of *Star Trek: The Next Generation* has been giving staged, one-man readings of *A Christmas Carol* for 10 years, and his approach to Scrooge is consistently interesting and intelligent. Early on, Stewart seems to be speaking on the misanthropic diatribes straight from Scrooge's flinty heart, rather than reciting thoroughly familiar quotations. And when Scrooge offers a boy a one-shilling tip, Stewart has the reformed miser feel a pang of the old parsimony.

> The author reveals his feelings about the lead actor and his previous work.

People Weekly, Dec. 6, 1999

...this *Carol* feels more like Masterpiece Theatre than seasonal merchandise...

Filmed in England with a solid supporting **cast** (including Richard E. Grant as Bob Cratchit and Joel Grey as the Spirit of Christmas Past), this *Carol* feels more like Masterpiece Theatre than seasonal merchandise—except when the filmmakers embellish Scrooge's nocturnal visions with gratuitous special effects.

Bottom line: Old story well told.
—Terry Kelleher

> The review ends with a summary of the critic's opinion.

Toned-down *Christmas Carol* has more spirit

by John Sousanis

Special to *The Oakland Press*

Director Debra Wicks has tinkered with Meadow Brook's recipe for *A Christmas Carol* just enough to make the old holiday fruitcake seem fresh. To be sure, Wicks's changes are subtle. Meadow Brook is still producing the Charles Nolte **adaptation** of Charles Dickens's Christmas classic that has been a mainstay of local theater for most of the last two decades.

The audience still is serenaded by a band of merry carolers in the lobby before the show. With its giant revolving set pieces and big bag of special effects, the production's script, set and costumes are unchanged from these many Christmases past.

But ironically, Wicks has infused the show with new energy by calming everything down a bit. In prior productions, the play's singing Londoners seemed positively hopped up on Christmas cheer to the point where one feared for the life of anyone not bubbling over with the spirit of the season.

Against this unebbing Yuletide, it was easy to forgive Scrooge of all his bah-hum-bugging. If only he had seen fit to give Tiny Tim a good spanking, we might all have enjoyed Christmas a little more. But Wicks has introduced a modicum of restraint into the Happy English populace, reducing the play's saccharine content considerably and making *A Christmas Carol* a more palatable holiday treat for adults and children.

Peter Hicks's set design for the show is, as always, enormous and gorgeous: Scrooge's storefront on a busy London street revolves to reveal the interior of the businessman's office and home, then opens on itself, providing the frame for scenes from Scrooge's boyhood, young adulthood and, of course, his potential end.

Meadow Brook's technical crew executes its stage magic without a hitch: Ghosts materialize and dematerialize in thick fogs and bolts of bright light, speaking to Scrooge in electronically altered voices and freezing the action onstage with a wave of their otherworldly hands.

The cast members take on multiple roles populating busy London in one scene, then visiting poor Scrooge in his dreams of Christmas Then, Now and Soon.

Standouts in the huge **ensemble** include John Biedenbach as Scrooge's put-upon assistant Bob Cratchit, Jodie Kuhn Ellison as Cratchit's fiercely loyal wife and Mark Rademacher, who pulls double duty as the Spirit of Christmas Present (the beefiest role in the play) and as a determined charity worker.

Scott Crownover, paying only passing attention to his English accent, takes an energetic turn as Scrooge's nephew, Fred, and Tom Mahard and Geoffrey Beauchamp have fun with a handful of roles they've been performing for years. Newcomer Sara Catheryn Wolf, fresh from three seasons at the Hilberry Theatre Company, provides an ethereal Spirit of Christmas Past.

The biggest change for longtime fans of the spectacle, however, is the replacement of Booth Coleman as Scrooge. Dennis Robertson's debut as the man in need of serious Christmas redemption is in perfect keeping with Wicks's toned-down production. If he's not quite as charismatic a miser as Coleman, Robertson is a much darker, even scarier Scrooge, which makes his ultimate transformation into an unabashed philanthropist that much more affecting.

All in all, *A Christmas Carol* is what it always has been: A well-produced, grand-scale event that is as much pageant as play. And like a beautifully wrapped gift under a well-decorated tree, it suits the season to a tee.

> This title offers clues about the author's perspective on the subject.

> The critic's point of view is affected by the fact that he has seen past productions.

Charles Dickens's *A Christmas Carol:* A Radio Interview

Philip V. Allingham, Faculty of Education, Lakehead University, Thunder Bay, Ontario

Published with the kind permission of The Canadian Broadcasting Corporation, Thunder Bay (ON) Regional Station.

Lisa Laco, Host: Well we're going to talk about

Charles Dickens right now because Charles Dickens is ever foremost in our minds this week as we get ready to read Charles Dickens' *A Christmas Carol* this weekend here in Thunder Bay. When he was about ten years old poverty forced him to take a job in a factory to provide for his family. Now he was so ashamed of his time there that he never told anyone about it, but he couldn't hide the secret totally.

> Background information provides clues about the guest's point of view.

According to Philip the experience surfaces in the actions and the attitudes of many of Charles Dickens' [characters], especially in Ebenezer Scrooge from *A Christmas Carol.* Philip Allingham is a professor in the Faculty of Education at Lakehead University in Thunder Bay; he's also a Dickens scholar. CBC reporter Cathy Alex asked him what inspired Charles Dickens to write *A Christmas Carol.*

Philip V. Allingham: He was fascinated by German ghost stories; in fact, he had written himself one in the middle of *Pickwick Papers* in 1836. In the fall of 1843 he was invited to go to Manchester, where he saw a good deal of urban poor, . . . other social ills. He and a number of other Victorian reformers including Cobden and Disraeli[1] were to speak and so he heard all the tales of horror in industrial society. He saw a great deal of it; he stayed with his sister whom he loved very much—remember Scrooge's relationship with his sister. And his sister had a little boy who was lame; he probably had what we call now Pot's disease, tuberculosis of the bone, if you can imagine. So there is Tiny Tim, who was originally by the way called "Tiny Fred" after Dickens' younger brother, but "Tiny Fred" doesn't really make it does it. So in proof he corrected that to "Tiny Tim." He also put in the famous "God bless us, everyone!"—it wasn't in the original manuscript. And I think he was also interested in trying to help the ragged schools that were trying to educate poor children at night. These children worked in factories

1. **Cobden and Disraeli** Richard Cobden (1804–1865), British politician known for defense of free trade; Benjamin Disraeli (1804–1881); British novelist and politician known for defense of landowners.

Features:

- content broadcast over radio or Internet
- a discussion between a host and a guest
- a question-and-answer format
- text intended for a listening audience

during the daytime. And so all of these things were fermenting in his mind and, like a great Coleridgian[2] dream, *A Christmas Carol* was born.

Alex: How successful was *A Christmas Carol* when it first came out, with respect to the public? How did they take to this novel?

Allingham: Everybody loved it, but everybody couldn't afford it. It was five shillings: Bob Cratchit earns only about three times that each week. So this is a huge chunk of lower middle class income; the working poor would have been locked out of it entirely. But it was very popular by word of mouth. People I think borrowed it off one another. The poor people could see it in the theaters; after half-time, they could pay a very small amount and get into the theaters and at least get the essence of the dialogue and the characters. . . .

Alex: What would Charles Dickens have been like in that period? I mean, how popular would he have been in the 1840s in England and around the world?

Allingham: His popularity grew as his ability to take on larger issues, write larger books, extend his range grew. I think his readings had a great deal to do with his popularity, so that he became a physical presence to people outside the metropolis. He was the Victorian stage; he was the Victorian sage; he was the great entertainer. He was, you know, Ringo Starr and Leonardo DiCaprio and Margaret Atwood all wrapped up in one. . . .

Alex: What do you think makes *A Christmas Carol* such a classic, that it could live on for 160 years and still resonate today the same way it would have when Dickens first wrote it?

Allingham: Well, first of all from a literary perspective it's a masterpiece

> The speaker responds to the question from the point of view, or perspective, of a Dickens scholar.

of controlled tone. We have this absolute sense, this conviction of the narrator in his relationship to us; all the [characters] are just right, in that they are very Dickensian and fully realized in a short amount of space, partly because he gets, he has this wonderful ear for dialogue for the way different people sound. And there is, of course, the timeless fairy tale quality to it that everybody has remarked on. It is, it's a remarkable change of heart for the curmudgeon miser affected by a recognition of the importance of his past and instead of trying to bury it he has to come to terms with it, even if some of it was unpleasant, which is very much a Dickens autobiographical slant on things, working in the blacking factory, hiding the secret from his family. You know, they never knew about that and he was called "The Little Gentlem'n" by the boys who worked there because they initially didn't like him at all. They realised he came from a different social class. And that sensitive little boy, that little boy died during that experience really and was reborn as a man who was determined to be terribly tough and make it. And, you see, that's the other side of Ebenezer Scrooge. All these are really just extensions of Dickens himself. So it has all kinds of critical interest for scholars, but it's also just this wonderful, heart-warming story with people that we feel we know extremely well.

Laco: Dr. Philip Allingham teaches in the Faculty of Education at Lakehead University in Thunder Bay. Speaking there with our reporter, Cathy Alex.

---

2. **Coleridgian** (1772–1834) Reference to Samuel Taylor Coleridge, British poet, best known for his fantastical poem, "The Rime of the Ancient Mariner."

Comparing Argumentative and Expository Texts

©️ **1. Key Ideas and Details** **(a) Identify the author's perspective** in each of the reviews of *A Christmas Carol* and the speaker's perspective in the radio interview. **(b)** In what ways are the perspectives similar? **(c)** In what ways do the perspectives differ? **(d)** How might a particular medium, such as a radio interview, achieve a more powerful impact than a written review? Explain.

Content-Area Vocabulary

2. (a) Remove the suffix *-tion* from the word *adaptation.* Using a print or an online dictionary, explain how removing the suffix reveals a different word that is a different part of speech. **(b)** Then, use the words *adaptation* and *adapt* in sentences that show their meaning.

⏱ Timed Writing

Analytic Text: Essay

> **Format**
> The prompt gives specific directions about the type of information to include in your essay.

In an essay, trace the perspective of the author of "Toned-Down *Christmas Carol* Has More Spirit." Support your response by providing details, words, and phrases from the text that give clues to Sousanis's point of view. Be sure to explain how each clue helps reveal his perspective. (25 minutes)

> **Academic Vocabulary**
> When you *support* your response, you provide evidence that helps show that your response is true or reasonable.

5-Minute Planner

Complete these steps to write your essay:

1. Carefully read the writing prompt, noting the highlighted key words.

2. Gather information for your response. Reread the review and jot down details, words, and phrases that hint at the author's perspective on the subject.

3. Look over the evidence you've gathered and choose the strongest points. Mark these points with a checkmark, and, for each, make notes about how it helps reveal the author's perspective.

4. Refer to your notes as you write your essay.

Comparing Literary Works

Comparing Characters

A **character** is a person who takes part in a literary work. In a drama, characters are built largely through their words and actions. When a drama is presented on the stage, characters are played by actors.

- Like main characters in stories and novels, main characters in dramas have traits that make them unique. These may include qualities such as dependability, intelligence, and selfishness.

- Like other fictional characters, those in dramas have *motives*, or reasons, for acting the way they do. For example, one character may be motivated by love, but another may be motivated by fear.

In drama, one way to develop a character is through a **foil,** a character whose behavior and attitude contrast with those of the main character. With a foil, audiences can see *good* in contrast with *bad*, or *joy* in contrast with *sadness*. When you read a drama, note what each character says and does, and find the reactions these words and actions spark in others. Notice what these things reveal to you about the characters' traits and motives.

These two excerpts from *A Christmas Carol: Scrooge and Marley* show two employers reacting to the celebration of Christmas. As you read, use a character wheel like the one shown to analyze each character. Draw conclusions about whether these characters can be classified as foils. Then, make connections across the texts by comparing the characters' reactions to the celebration.

Common Core State Standards

Reading Literature

3. Analyze how particular elements of a story or drama interact.

6. Analyze how an author develops and contrasts the points of view of different characters.

Writing

9. Draw evidence from literary or informational texts to support analysis, reflection, and research.

9.a. Apply grade 7 Reading standards to literature. *(Timed Writing)*

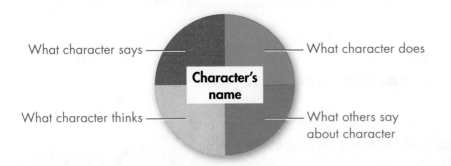

What character says — What character does

Character's name

What character thinks — What others say about character

www.PHLitOnline.com

- Vocabulary flashcards
- Interactive journals
- More about the authors
- Selection audio
- Interactive graphic organizers

818 Drama

Do others *see* us more clearly than we *see* ourselves?

Writing About the Big Question

As Bob Cratchit's boss, Ebenezer Scrooge is very different from the person he was when he worked for Fezziwig. Use this sentence starter to develop your ideas about the Big Question:

When we **reflect** on our lives, we may see differences in ourselves over time based on _____.

Meet the Authors

Charles Dickens (1812–1870)
Author of *A Christmas Carol*

English author Charles Dickens's early life was difficult. When he was a boy, his father went to prison, and young Charles had to work long hours pasting labels on bottles to earn money.

Writing As a young man, Dickens taught himself shorthand and got a job as a court reporter. In his early twenties, Dickens began to publish humorous stories. People liked his writing, and he was able to earn a living as a writer. Some of his novels are *David Copperfield, Hard Times,* and *Nicholas Nickleby.* One of his most well-known works is *A Christmas Carol*, which was published in 1843.

Israel Horovitz (b. 1939)

Author of *A Christmas Carol: Scrooge and Marley*

Israel Horovitz is a well-known playwright who lives in New York City with his wife. Horovitz is the author of more than fifty plays. His plays have introduced such actors as Al Pacino and Richard Dreyfus. *A Christmas Carol: Scrooge and Marley* was first produced in Baltimore, Maryland, in 1978.

Finding Inspiration in Tragedy Shortly after the attacks of September 11, 2001, Horovitz wrote a play about the event. The play, *3 Weeks After Paradise*, reflects his experiences during the tragedy and includes family photos and films.

from

A CHRISTMAS CAROL:
SCROOGE AND MARLEY

ISRAEL HOROVITZ
from *A CHRISTMAS CAROL* by CHARLES DICKENS

ACT 1, SCENE 2

CRATCHIT. I must be going home . . . [He snuffs out his candle and puts on his hat.] I hope you have a . . . very very lovely day tomorrow, sir . . .

SCROOGE. Hmmm. Oh, you'll be wanting the whole day tomorrow, I suppose?

CRATCHIT. If quite convenient, sir.

SCROOGE. It's not convenient, and it's not fair. If I was to stop half-a-crown for it, you'd think yourself ill-used, I'll be bound?

[CRATCHIT *smiles faintly.*]

CRATCHIT. I don't know, sir . . .

SCROOGE. And yet, you don't think me ill-used when I pay a day's wages for no work . . .

CRATCHIT. It's only but once a year . . .

SCROOGE. A poor excuse for picking a man's pocket every 25th of December! But I suppose you must have the whole day. Be here all the earlier the next morning!

CRATCHIT. Oh I will, sir. I will. I promise you. And, sir . . .

SCROOGE. Don't say it, Cratchit.

Vocabulary
snuffs (snufs) *v.* extinguishes; puts out

Character
What details here show how Scrooge feels about the holiday?

▶ **Critical Viewing**
In what ways does this actor's costume reflect Scrooge's character traits?

CRATCHIT. But let me wish you a . . .

SCROOGE. Don't say it, Cratchit. I warn you . . .

CRATCHIT. Sir!

SCROOGE. Cratchit!

[CRATCHIT *opens the door.*]

CRATCHIT. All right, then, sir . . . well . . . [*Suddenly*] Merry Christmas, Mr. Scrooge!

[*And he runs out the door, shutting same behind him.*]

ACT 1, SCENE 5

FEZZIWIG. Yo ho, my boys. No more work tonight. Christmas Eve, Dick. Christmas, Ebenezer!

[*They stand at attention in front of* FEZZIWIG; *laughing*] Hilli-ho! Clear away, and let's have lots of room here! Hilli-ho, Dick! Chirrup, Ebenezer!
[*The young men clear the room, sweep the floor, straighten the pictures, trim the lamps, etc. The space is clear now. A* fiddler *enters, fiddling.*]
    Hi-ho, Matthew! Fiddle away . . . where are my daughters?

[*The fiddler plays. Three young daughters of* FEZZIWIG *enter followed by six young male* suitors. *They are dancing to the music. All employees come in: workers, clerks, housemaids, cousins, the baker, etc. All dance. Full number wanted here. Throughout the dance, food is brought into the feast. It is "eaten" in dance, by the dancers.* EBENEZER *dances with all three of the daughters, as does* DICK. *They compete for the daughters, happily, in the dance.* FEZZIWIG *dances with the daughters.* FEZZIWIG *dances with* DICK *and* EBENEZER. *The music changes:* MRS. FEZZIWIG *enters. She lovingly scolds her husband. They dance. She dances with* EBENEZER, *lifting him and throwing him about. She is enormously fat. When the dance is ended, they all dance off, floating away, as does the music.*]

PAST. It was a small matter, that Fezziwig made those silly folks so full of gratitude.

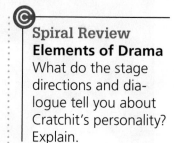

Spiral Review
Elements of Drama
What do the stage directions and dialogue tell you about Cratchit's personality? Explain.

Character
What details here show how Fezziwig feels about the holiday?

Vocabulary
fiddler (fid´ lər) *n.* person who plays a fiddle, or violin

suitors (sōōt´ ərz) *n.* men who court a woman or seek to marry her

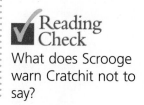

Reading Check
What does Scrooge warn Cratchit not to say?

SCROOGE. Small?

PAST. Shhh!?

[Lights up on DICK *and* EBENEZER.]

DICK. We are blessed, Ebenezer, truly, to have such a master as Mr. Fezziwig!

YOUNG EBENEZER. He is the best, best, the very and absolute best! If ever I own a firm of my own, I shall treat my apprentices with the same dignity and the same grace. We have learned a wonderful lesson from the master, Dick!

DICK. Ah, that's a fact, Ebenezer. That's a fact!

Critical Thinking

Cite textual evidence to support your responses.

@ 1. **Key Ideas and Details** **(a)** What does Cratchit say to Scrooge as Cratchit leaves? **(b) Infer:** Why do you think he says this—against Scrooge's wishes? **(c) Generalize:** What do you think this action shows about Cratchit?

@ 2. **Key Ideas and Details** **(a) Infer:** Do you think Scrooge will work on Christmas day? Why or why not? **(b) Make a Judgment:** Do you think that a boss should be required to give employees a day off for a holiday that is not celebrated by everyone? Explain.

@ 3. **Key Ideas and Details** **(a) Infer:** What kind of relationship do you think Fezziwig has with his daughters? **(b) Support:** What examples illustrate this opinion?

@ 4. **Integration of Knowledge and Ideas** **(a)** What changes in Scrooge do these scenes reveal? **(b)** What questions would you ask to learn more about the changes? **(c)** How do you think Cratchit regards the older Scrooge—with fear or pity? *[Connect to the Big Question: Do others see us more clearly than we see ourselves?]*

Comparing Characters

1. Key Ideas and Details (a) How would you describe Scrooge? **(b)** What details from the play support your ideas?

2. Key Ideas and Details (a) How would you describe Fezziwig? **(b)** What details from the play support your ideas?

3. Craft and Structure Complete a chart like the one below to compare each character's traits and motives.

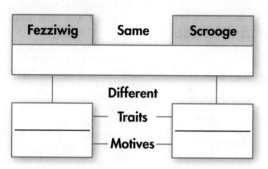

Fezziwig	Same	Scrooge

Different
Traits
Motives

4. Key Ideas and Details (a) In what ways does Fezziwig act as a foil to Scrooge? **(b)** Why is Fezziwig's character important to the play?

Timed Writing

Explanatory Text: Essay

Make connections across the texts to compare and contrast Fezziwig and Scrooge. In an essay, discuss how each character's actions and words help the playwright make a point about Scrooge and his behavior. **(40 minutes)**

5-Minute Planner

1. Read the prompt carefully and completely.

2. Gather your ideas by jotting down answers to these questions:

• Why does each character act as he does?

• What do audiences learn about Scrooge because of Fezziwig?

3. Review each scene and take notes on Fezziwig's and Scrooge's words and actions. Then, draw conclusions about the differences between the two men. Use these notes as you write your comparison-and-contrast essay.

4. Reread the prompt, and then draft your essay.

Writing Workshop

 Common Core
State Standards

Writing
2. Write informative/explanatory texts to examine a topic and convey ideas, concepts, and information through the selection, organization, and analysis of relevant content.
2.a. Introduce a topic clearly, previewing what is to follow; organize ideas, concepts, and information, using strategies such as definition, classification, comparison/contrast, and cause/effect; include formatting, graphics, and multimedia when useful to aiding comprehension.
7. Conduct short research projects to answer a question, drawing on several sources and generating additional related, focused questions for further research and investigation.
8. Gather relevant information from multiple print and digital sources, using search terms effectively; assess the credibility and accuracy of each source.

Write an Informative Text

Research: Multimedia Report

Defining the Form Presentations that include videos, slides, photographs, maps, music, or sound effects capture your attention. A presentation that uses information from both print and non-print sources is called a **multimedia report.** You might use elements of this type of writing in documentaries and research.

Assignment Create a multimedia report about a topic that interests you and that presents opportunities for audio and visual support. Your report should feature the following elements:

✔ a *focused topic* that can be covered in the time and space allotted

✔ a *clear and logical organization* that presents a main idea

✔ well-integrated *audio and visual features* from a variety of sources

✔ use of *formatting and presentation techniques* for visual appeal

✔ *effective pacing* with *smooth transitions* between elements

✔ error-free writing, including *correct usage of frequently confused words*

To preview the criteria on which your multimedia report may be judged, see the rubric on page 829.

 Writing Workshop: *Work in Progress*

Review the work you did on pages 771 and 809.

Prewriting/Planning Strategy

Flip through magazines. Scan credible magazines that explore areas you find interesting, such as travel, the arts, or sports. List possible topics and note creative ways to engage your audience. Beyond typical print sources, use multimedia sources such as reliable sites on the Internet, video documentaries, maps, photographs, music, sound, and film clips. Consider whether you will be able to find information in both print and nonprint sources, for example, by typing your topic into a search engine. Then, choose a topic.

Focus on Ideas

Your **ideas** will help you create an interesting and enjoyable multimedia report. After you have chosen your topic, look for ways to sustain your audience's interest. Make sure your ideas are original and that you have learned as much as you can about your topic.

Narrowing Your Topic If you have chosen a broad topic, like sports, narrow your topic to focus on a specific aspect. For example, focus on a favorite team, a memorable event in sports, or a specific sport you like to play. Use a chart like the one shown to help you narrow your topic.

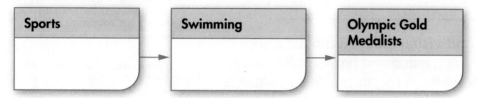

Sports		Swimming		Olympic Gold Medalists

Be sure that your topic can be covered in the allotted time and space. Once you have defined your topic and purpose, generate ideas for making that topic interesting to your audience. Ask yourself these questions:

- What do I want to say about my topic?
- Why should my audience care about my topic?
- How can I share my enthusiasm for my topic?
- Is there anything that my audience may not understand?

Connecting Your Ideas Think of past presentations you have seen. What has made them successful or unsuccessful? In other words, what makes an audience want to pay attention?

Gather as many ideas as you can regarding visual and audio aids. Research each idea and choose the ones that will work best with your topic. For example, if you are focusing on sports, you might use a video clip of a game or interview. If your topic relates to science, you might show a clip of a documentary or provide charts to support your research. Keep your content, audience, and purpose in mind as you choose your multimedia aids.

PH WRITING COACH

Further instruction and practice are available in *Prentice Hall Writing Coach*.

Drafting Strategies

Write a script. Plan every word and action in your multimedia presentation by writing a script. Use index cards to help organize your ideas. Include any words that you will speak and any stage directions that make actions and effects clear. Note when you will use each visual or audio aid.

Card 1
Visual 1: Documentary clip of a cooking show
Script: The clip I am going to show now explains how to prepare a turkey for Thanksgiving. As you will see, all of the materials are carefully laid out to make the process easier.
Actions: Press play on DVD player

Incorporate your audio and visual aids. Audio aids, such as interviews or music, can set a mood and provide information. **Visual aids,** such as spreadsheets, maps, or charts, can organize large amounts of information, making it easier to present.

Use appropriate software to design additional information, and plan to display information on posters, on computer monitors, or as handouts. Use headings, spacing, and design features to enhance the appearance of your report.

Revising Strategy

Use effective transitions. Read the final sentence of each paragraph. Then, read the opening sentence of the next paragraph. If one or both sentences clearly show the relationship between paragraphs, underline them. If you do not find a relationship, add a transitional word, phrase, or sentence to link them together. Use this tip as you revise.

To add to an idea or show sequence, use . . .	*also, and, next, equally important, furthermore, first, second, third, likewise, still, too, another, besides*
To add contrast to ideas, use . . .	*alternatively, despite, although, yet, but, conversely, instead, nor, on the other hand, however, otherwise, regardless*
To give examples or clarify ideas, use . . .	*after all, in other words, certainly, for example, such as*
To show cause and effect of ideas, use . . .	*as a result, because, for that reason, since, so that, therefore, to do this, due to*

Common Core State Standards

Writing
2.a. Introduce a topic clearly, previewing what is to follow; organize ideas, concepts, and information, using strategies such as definition, classification, comparison/contrast, and cause/effect; include formatting, graphics, and multimedia when useful to aiding comprehension.
2.c. Use appropriate transitions to create cohesion and clarify the relationships among ideas and concepts.
6. Use technology, including the Internet, to produce and publish writing.

Speaking and Listening
5. Include multimedia components and visual displays in presentations to clarify claims and findings and emphasize salient points.

Language
1. Demonstrate command of the conventions of standard English grammar and usage when writing or speaking.

Revising to Avoid Common Usage Problems

Identifying Common Usage Problems When you choose the wrong word in your writing, you can confuse readers or lead them to question the care you take with your work. The sets of words presented here are frequently confused:

- *Accept,* a verb, means "to take what is offered" or "to agree to."
- *Except,* a preposition, means "leaving out" or "other than."

  Verb: She **accepted** her award graciously.

  Preposition: Everyone **except** Anabelle went to the movie.

- *Affect,* a verb, means "to influence" or "to cause a change in."
- *Effect,* usually a noun, means "result."

  Verb: Lack of sleep can **affect** your ability to concentrate.

  Noun: What is the **effect** of getting too much sleep?

Fixing Common Usage Problems To fix a usage problem, first identify words that you often confuse. Then, correct your error using one of the following methods.

1. Identify the word's part of speech and its use in the sentence.
2. Determine the meaning you want to convey.
3. Consult a dictionary or a language handbook for clarification, then choose the correct word.

PH | WRITING COACH

Further instruction and practice are available in *Prentice Hall Writing Coach.*

Grammar in Your Writing
Choose three paragraphs in your draft. Underline each sentence that contains one of the words discussed on this page or another word you suspect you may have used incorrectly. Fix any usage problems using one of the methods described.

Other Commonly Confused Words
advice: noun, "an opinion"   **advise:** verb, "to give an opinion"
in: preposition, refers to position   **into:** preposition, suggests motion
beside: preposition, "at the side of"   **besides:** preposition, "in addition to"
farther: adjective, refers to distance   **further:** adjective, "additional" or "to a greater extent"

Student Model:
Shane Larkin and Ian Duffy, Williamston, MI

 Common Core
State Standards

Writing
6. Use technology, including the Internet, to produce and publish writing and link to and cite sources as well as to interact and collaborate with others.

Zia

Slide 1
Visual: Title and Author Slide: *Zia*, by Scott O'Dell
Script: This presentation is about the book *Zia* by Scott O'Dell. *Zia* is a sequel to the book *Island of the Blue Dolphins* and shares some of the same characters. Instead of dolphins, though, Zia and her brother see gray whales, like those heard here.

> The writers have chosen a topic that can be well covered in the time allotted to their report.

Slide 2
Visual: Whale
Sound: Whale song
Script: Reading this book got us very interested in the study of whales and how they adapt to the world around them.

Slide 3
Visual: Setting Slide
Sound: Ocean waves crashing against beach
Script: The setting of *Zia* is the southern coast of California during the Spanish colonial era. The action takes place in several locations. This is a picture of the California coast.

> The writers' choice of visual is both dramatic and appropriate to their topic, audience, and purpose.

> The writers use bold-face heads and other appropriate formatting to present the organization of their report clearly.

Video 1: Video clip of whale scanning for food
Script: From reading this book and doing a small amount of research, we discovered many ways whales can adapt to these kinds of harsh environments. Several of the toothed whales shoot a jet of water at the ocean floor. They use this jet to stir up prey hiding in the sand. These whales also have very flexible necks that help them scan the ocean floor for food.

Slide 4
Visual: Arctic shoreline
Sound: Ocean waves crashing against beach
Script: Other characteristics can help a whale live in a harsh environment. The bowhead, for instance, has several interesting physical features that allow it to live in the Arctic all the time.

> Sound effects such as this enhance the presentation.

Sound: Whale song
Script: We learned a lot about whales by reading *Zia* and doing our research, but this is only the beginning. This book has inspired us to continue our research to learn more about these amazing creatures and their adaptations to the environment.

Editing and Proofreading

Review your draft to eliminate errors in grammar, spelling, and punctuation.

Focus on presentation copies. To avoid distracting your audience with mistakes, run a spelling and grammar check on any visuals you present. Be careful, however, because spell-checkers do not catch mistakes in homophones such as *there, their,* and *they're.* You must catch these errors yourself. In addition, check the layouts of slides or handouts to be sure information is clear and error-free.

Publishing and Presenting

Consider one of the following ways to share your writing:

Present your report. Perform your multimedia report for your classmates. Ask them to evaluate what they see and hear.

Post your work. Post your report to an approved Web site. Add links to your online sources and, if possible, invite and respond to comments.

Reflecting on Your Writing

Writer's Journal Jot down your answer to these questions:

What was the most effective visual aid or audio aid you used in your presentation? Why?

Spiral Review

Earlier in the unit, you learned about **interjections** (p. 770) and **double negatives** (p. 808). Check the use of interjections in your multimedia report. Review your essay to be sure that you have corrected any sentence that contains a double negative.

Rubric for Self-Assessment

Find evidence in your writing to address each category. Then, use the rating scale to grade your work.

Criteria	Rating Scale
	not very very
Focus: How clearly focused is your topic?	1 2 3 4 5
Organization: How logical is your organization?	1 2 3 4 5
Support/Elaboration: How effective are your audio and visual features?	1 2 3 4 5
Style: How smooth are the transitions between elements?	1 2 3 4 5
Conventions: How correct is your word usage?	1 2 3 4 5
Ideas: Does your report have a specific purpose with original ideas?	1 2 3 4 5

The Monsters Are Due on Maple Street

Drama Selection

Build your skills and improve your comprehension of drama with texts of increasing complexity.

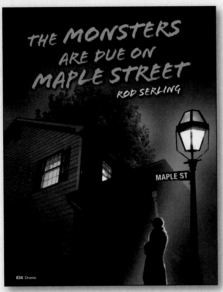

834 Drama

Read **The Monsters Are Due on Maple Street** to find out what happens when a group of frightened neighbors become suspicious of one another.

Common Core State Standards

Meet these standards with **The Monsters are Due on Maple Street** (p. 834).

Reading Literature

2. Determine a theme or central idea of a text and analyze its development over the course of the text; provide an objective summary. *(Reading Skill: Summarize)*

3. Analyze how particular elements of a story or drama interact. *(Literary Analysis: Characters' Motives)*

7. Compare and contrast a written story, drama, or poem to its audio, filmed, staged, or multimedia version, analyzing the effects of techniques unique to each medium. *(Research and Technology: Film Version)*

Spiral Review: RL.7.5

Writing

2.b. Develop the topic with relevant facts, definitions, concrete details, quotations, or other information and

examples. **2.c.** Use appropriate transitions to create cohesion and clarify the relationships among ideas and concepts. *(Writing: Summary)*

6. Use technology, including the Internet, to produce and publish writing. *(Writing: Summary)*

9.a. Apply *grade 7 Reading standards* to literature. *(Writing: Summary)*

Language

2. Demonstrate command of the conventions of standard English capitalization, punctuation, and spelling when writing. *(Conventions: Sentence Functions and Endmarks)*

4.b. Use common, grade-appropriate Greek or Latin affixes and roots as clues to the meaning of a word. *(Vocabulary: Word Study)*

Reading Skill: Summarize

A **summary** is a brief statement that presents only the central ideas and most important details of a text. Summarizing helps you review and understand what you are reading.

To summarize, you must first **distinguish between important and unimportant** details. Ask yourself questions like the following:

- Is this detail necessary for my understanding of the literary work?
- Would the literary work hold together without this information?

As you read, pause periodically to recall and restate only the key events and important details.

Literary Analysis: Characters' Motives

A **character's motives** are the reasons for his or her actions. Motives are usually related to what a character wants, needs, or feels. A character's motives may affect the way events unfold in a plot. For example, a character who wants to keep a secret may try to mislead other characters.

To identify characters' motives, examine the way they speak, think, and respond to situations and to other characters. Then, ask yourself why they behave as they do.

Using the Strategy: Character Web

As you read, use a graphic organizer like the one shown to explore each character's motives.

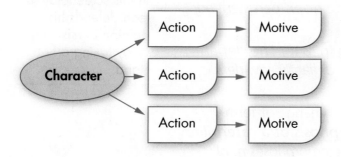

Do others *see* us more clearly than we *see* ourselves?

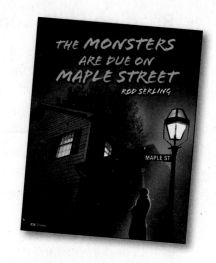

Writing About the Big Question

In *The Monsters Are Due on Maple Street*, mysterious events cause neighbors to become frightened and fearful. Use this sentence starter to develop your ideas about the Big Question:

Fear can influence our **perception** of others by _____.

While You Read Consider whether the neighbors are able to see themselves clearly.

Vocabulary

Read each word and its definition. Decide whether you know the word well, know it a little bit, or do not know it at all. After you read, see how your knowledge of each word has increased.

- **transfixed** (trans fikst´) *adj.* fascinated (p. 836) *He was transfixed by the TV show about penguins. transfix v.*

- **flustered** (flus´ tərd) *adj.* nervous; confused (p. 838) *The flustered bus driver took many wrong turns. fluster v.*

- **sluggishly** (slug´ ish lē) *adv.* as if lacking energy (p. 838) *The tired hikers walked sluggishly down the trail. sluggish adj. sluggishness n.*

- **persistently** (pər sist´ ənt lē) *adv.* firmly and steadily (p. 839) *The dog scratched persistently at the door. persistent adj. persist v. persistence n.*

- **defiant** (dē fī´ ənt) *adj.* boldly resisting (p. 840) *The defiant colonists demanded independence. defiantly adv. defy v. defying v.*

- **metamorphosis** (met´ ə môr´ fə sis) *n.* change of form (p. 843) *We witnessed the metamorphosis of a caterpillar into a butterfly. metamorphic adj. metamorphoses n. pl.*

Word Study

The **Latin root** *-sist-* means "stand."

In this screenplay, a teen defends his opinion **persistently**, or by taking a firm stand.

Meet
Rod Serling
(1924–1975)

Author of

THE MONSTERS ARE DUE ON MAPLE STREET

Rod Serling once said that he did not have much imagination. This is an odd statement from a man who wrote more than 200 television scripts.

Quick Success Serling did not become serious about writing until he was in college. Driven by a love for radio drama, he earned second place in a national script contest. Soon after, he landed his first staff job as a radio writer. Serling branched out into writing for a new medium—television—and rocketed to fame.

DID YOU KNOW?

In the 1950s and 1960s, television censors banned scripts that appeared to question American society.

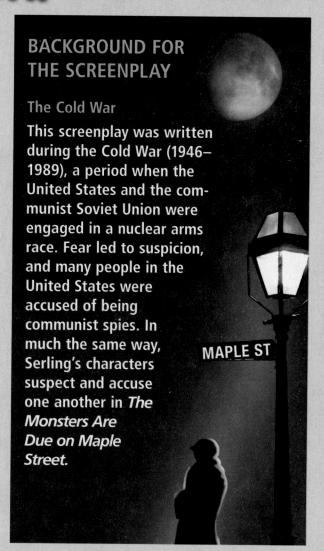

BACKGROUND FOR THE SCREENPLAY

The Cold War

This screenplay was written during the Cold War (1946–1989), a period when the United States and the communist Soviet Union were engaged in a nuclear arms race. Fear led to suspicion, and many people in the United States were accused of being communist spies. In much the same way, Serling's characters suspect and accuse one another in *The Monsters Are Due on Maple Street.*

MAPLE ST

THE MONSTERS ARE DUE ON MAPLE STREET

ROD SERLING

CHARACTERS

NARRATOR   FIGURE ONE   FIGURE TWO

RESIDENTS OF MAPLE STREET

STEVE BRAND   WOMAN   MAN TWO
CHARLIE'S WIFE   DON MARTIN   PETE VAN HORN
MRS. GOODMAN   SALLY (*TOMMY'S MOTHER*)   CHARLIE
MRS. BRAND   LES GOODMAN   TOMMY   MAN ONE

ACT 1

[*Fade in on a shot of the night sky. The various nebulae and planet bodies stand out in sharp, sparkling relief, and the camera begins a slow pan across the Heavens.*]

NARRATOR'S VOICE. There is a fifth dimension beyond that which is known to man. It is a dimension as vast as space, and as timeless as infinity. It is the middle ground between light and shadow—between science and superstition. And it lies between the pit of man's fears and the summit of his knowledge. This is the dimension of imagination. It is an area which we call The Twilight Zone.

[*The camera has begun to pan down until it passes the horizon and is on a sign which reads "Maple Street." Pan down until we are shooting down at an angle toward the street below. It's a tree-lined, quiet residential American street, very typical of the small town. The houses have front porches on which people sit and swing on gliders, conversing across from house to house. STEVE BRAND polishes his car parked in front of his house. His neighbor, DON MARTIN, leans against the fender watching him. A Good Humor man rides a bicycle and is just in the process of stopping to sell some ice cream to a couple of kids. Two women gossip on the front lawn. Another man waters his lawn.*]

✓ Reading
Check
What is the fifth dimension?

NARRATOR'S VOICE. Maple Street, U.S.A., late summer. A tree-lined little world of front porch gliders, hop scotch, the laughter of children, and the bell of an ice cream vendor.

[*There is a pause and the camera moves over to a shot of the Good Humor man and two small boys who are standing alongside, just buying ice cream.*]

NARRATOR'S VOICE. At the sound of the roar and the flash of light it will be precisely 6:43 P.M. on Maple Street.

[*At this moment one of the little boys,* TOMMY, *looks up to listen to a sound of a tremendous screeching roar from overhead. A flash of light plays on both their faces and then it moves down the street past lawns and porches and rooftops and then disappears.*

Various people leave their porches and stop what they're doing to stare up at the sky. STEVE BRAND, *the man who's been polishing his car, now stands there* transfixed, *staring upwards. He looks at* DON MARTIN, *his neighbor from across the street.*]

STEVE. What was that? A meteor?

DON. [*Nods*] That's what it looked like. I didn't hear any crash though, did you?

STEVE. [*Shakes his head*] Nope. I didn't hear anything except a roar.

MRS. BRAND. [*From her porch*] Steve? What was that?

STEVE. [*Raising his voice and looking toward porch*] Guess it was a meteor, honey. Came awful close, didn't it?

MRS. BRAND. Too close for my money! Much too close.

[*The camera pans across the various porches to people who stand there watching and talking in low tones.*]

NARRATOR'S VOICE. Maple Street. Six-forty-four P.M. on a late September evening. [*A pause*] Maple Street in the last calm and reflective moment . . . before the monsters came!

[*The camera slowly pans across the porches again. We see a man screwing a light bulb on a front porch, then getting down off the stool to flick the switch and finding that nothing happens.*

Another man is working on an electric power mower. He plugs in the plug, flicks on the switch of the power mower, off and on, with nothing happening.

Summarize
Do you think the flash of light is an important or unimportant detail? Explain.

Vocabulary
transfixed (trans fikst) *adj.* fascinated

Through the window of a front porch, we see a woman pushing her finger back and forth on the dial hook. Her voice is indistinct and distant, but intelligible and repetitive.]

WOMAN. Operator, operator, something's wrong on the phone, operator!

[MRS. BRAND *comes out on the porch and calls to* STEVE.]

MRS. BRAND. [*Calling*] Steve, the power's off. I had the soup on the stove and the stove just stopped working.

WOMAN. Same thing over here. I can't get anybody on the phone either. The phone seems to be dead.

[*We look down on the street as we hear the voices creep up from below, small, mildly disturbed voices highlighting these kinds of phrases:*]

VOICES.

Electricity's off.

Phone won't work.

Can't get a thing on the radio.

My power mower won't move, won't work at all.

Radio's gone dead!

[PETE VAN HORN, *a tall, thin man, is seen standing in front of his house.*]

VAN HORN. I'll cut through the back yard . . . See if the power's still on on Floral Street. I'll be right back!

[*He walks past the side of his house and disappears into the back yard.*

The camera pans down slowly until we're looking at ten or eleven people standing around the street and overflowing to the curb and sidewalk. In the background is STEVE BRAND'S *car.*]

STEVE. Doesn't make sense. Why should the power go off all of a sudden, and the phone line?

DON. Maybe some sort of an electrical storm or something.

CHARLIE. That don't seem likely. Sky's just as blue as anything. Not a cloud. No lightning. No thunder. No nothing. How could it be a storm?

Characters' Motives
Why do the characters come out of their homes?

Reading Check
What strange event occurs just before Maple Street loses electricity?

▲ **Critical Viewing**
What impression does this illustration convey about life on Maple Street? **[Analyze]**

Vocabulary
flustered (flus´ tərd)
adj. nervous; confused

sluggishly (slug´ ish lē)
adv. as if lacking energy

WOMAN. I can't get a thing on the radio. Not even the portable.

[*The people again murmur softly in wonderment and question.*]

CHARLIE. Well, why don't you go downtown and check with the police, though they'll probably think we're crazy or something. A little power failure and right away we get all flustered and everything.

STEVE. It isn't just the power failure, Charlie. If it was, we'd still be able to get a broadcast on the portable.

[*There's a murmur of reaction to this.* STEVE *looks from face to face and then over to his car.*]

STEVE. I'll run downtown. We'll get this all straightened out.

[*He walks over to the car, gets in it, turns the key. Looking through the open car door, we see the crowd watching him from the other side.* STEVE *starts the engine. It turns over sluggishly and then just stops dead. He tries it again and this time he can't get it to turn over. Then, very slowly and reflectively, he turns the key back to "off" and slowly gets out of the car.*

The people stare at STEVE. *He stands for a moment by the car, then walks toward the group.*]

STEVE. I don't understand it. It was working fine before . . .

DON. Out of gas?

STEVE. [*Shakes his head*] I just had it filled up.

WOMAN. What's it mean?

CHARLIE. It's just as if . . . as if everything had stopped. [*Then he turns toward* STEVE.] We'd better walk downtown.

[*Another murmur of assent at this.*]

STEVE. The two of us can go, Charlie. [*He turns to look back at the car.*] It couldn't be the meteor. A meteor couldn't do this.

[*He and* CHARLIE *exchange a look, then they start to walk away from the group.*

We see TOMMY, *a serious-faced fourteen-year-old in spectacles who stands a few feet away from the group. He is halfway between them and the two men, who start to walk down the sidewalk.*]

TOMMY. Mr. Brand . . . you better not!

STEVE. Why not?

TOMMY. They don't want you to.

[STEVE *and* CHARLIE *exchange a grin, and* STEVE *looks back toward the boy.*]

STEVE. Who doesn't want us to?

TOMMY. [*Jerks his head in the general direction of the distant horizon*] Them!

STEVE. Them?

CHARLIE. Who are them?

TOMMY. [*Very intently*] Whoever was in that thing that came by overhead.

[STEVE *knits his brows for a moment, cocking his head questioningly. His voice is intense.*]

STEVE. What?

TOMMY. Whoever was in that thing that came over. I don't think they want us to leave here.

[STEVE *leaves* CHARLIE *and walks over to the boy. He kneels down in front of him. He forces his voice to remain gentle. He reaches out and holds the boy.*]

STEVE. What do you mean? What are you talking about?

TOMMY. They don't want us to leave. That's why they shut everything off.

STEVE. What makes you say that? Whatever gave you that idea?

WOMAN. [*From the crowd*] Now isn't that the craziest thing you ever heard?

TOMMY. [*Persistently but a little intimidated by the crowd*] It's always that way, in every story I ever read about a ship landing from outer space.

Characters' Motives
Why does Tommy warn Charlie and Steve not to leave?

Vocabulary
persistently (pər sist′ ənt lē) *adv.* firmly and steadily

Reading Check
What happens when Steve tries to start his car?

WOMAN. [*To the boy's mother,* SALLY, *who stands on the fringe of the crowd*] From outer space, yet! Sally, you better get that boy of yours up to bed. He's been reading too many comic books or seeing too many movies or something.

SALLY. Tommy, come over here and stop that kind of talk.

STEVE. Go ahead, Tommy. We'll be right back. And you'll see. That wasn't any ship or anything like it. That was just a . . . a meteor or something. Likely as not—[*He turns to the group, now trying to weight his words with an optimism he obviously doesn't feel but is desperately trying to instill in himself as well as the others.*] No doubt it did have something to do with all this power failure and the rest of it. Meteors can do some crazy things. Like sunspots.

DON. [*Picking up the cue*] Sure. That's the kind of thing—like sunspots. They raise Cain[1] with radio reception all over the world. And this thing being so close—why, there's no telling the sort of stuff it can do. [*He wets his lips, smiles nervously.*] Go ahead, Charlie. You and Steve go into town and see if that isn't what's causing it all.

[STEVE *and* CHARLIE *again walk away from the group down the sidewalk. The people watch silently.*

TOMMY *stares at them, biting his lips, and finally calling out again.*]

TOMMY. *Mr. Brand!*

[*The two men stop again.* TOMMY *takes a step toward them.*]

TOMMY. Mr. Brand . . . please don't leave here.

[STEVE *and* CHARLIE *stop once again and turn toward the boy. There's a murmur in the crowd, a murmur of irritation and concern as if the boy were bringing up fears that shouldn't be brought up; words which carried with them a strange kind of validity that came without logic but nonetheless registered and had meaning and effect. Again we hear a murmur of reaction from the crowd.*

TOMMY *is partly frightened and partly defiant as well.*]

TOMMY. You might not even be able to get to town. It was that way in the story. Nobody could leave. Nobody except—

---

1. raise Cain badly disturb.

Characters' Motives
Why does Tommy's mother want him to stop talking?

Vocabulary
defiant (dē fī´ ənt)
adj. boldly resisting

STEVE. Except who?

TOMMY. Except the people they'd sent down ahead of them. They looked just like humans. And it wasn't until the ship landed that—

[*The boy suddenly stops again, conscious of the parents staring at them and of the sudden hush of the crowd.*]

SALLY. [*In a whisper, sensing the antagonism of the crowd*] Tommy, please son . . . honey, don't talk that way—

MAN ONE. That kid shouldn't talk that way . . . and we shouldn't stand here listening to him. Why this is the craziest thing I ever heard of. The kid tells us a comic book plot and here we stand listening—

[STEVE *walks toward the camera, stops by the boy.*]

STEVE. Go ahead, Tommy. What kind of story was this? What about the people that they sent out ahead?

TOMMY. That was the way they prepared things for the landing. They sent four people. A mother and a father and two kids who looked just like humans . . . but they weren't.

[*There's another silence as* STEVE *looks toward the crowd and then toward* TOMMY. *He wears a tight grin.*]

STEVE. Well, I guess what we'd better do then is to run a check on the neighborhood and see which ones of us are really human.

[*There's laughter at this, but it's a laughter that comes from a desperate attempt to lighten the atmosphere. It's a release kind of laugh. The people look at one another in the middle of their laughter.*]

CHARLIE. There must be somethin' better to do than stand around makin' bum jokes about it.

[*Rubs his jaw nervously*] I wonder if Floral Street's got the same deal we got. [*He looks past the houses.*] Where is Pete Van Horn anyway? Didn't he get back yet?

[*Suddenly there's the sound of a car's engine starting to turn over. We look across the street toward the driveway of* LES GOODMAN'S *house. He's at the wheel trying to start the car.*]

Summarize
Do you think Steve's comment will prove to be important as the story develops? Why or why not?

Reading
Check
What does Tommy say about the people who were sent from outer space?

Overview of family walking dog on the street, William Low, Courtesy of the artist

▲ **Critical Viewing**
How do the colors
in this illustration
contrast with the
mood of the drama?
Explain. **[Compare
and Contrast]**

Summarize
Why might this detail
about a car starting be
important?

SALLY. Can you get it started, Les? [*He gets out of the car, shaking his head.*]

GOODMAN. No dice.

[*He walks toward the group. He stops suddenly as behind him, inexplicably and with a noise that inserts itself into the silence, the car engine starts up all by itself.* GOODMAN *whirls around to stare toward it.*

The car idles roughly, smoke coming from the exhaust, the frame shaking gently.

GOODMAN'S *eyes go wide, and he runs over to his car.*

The people stare toward the car.]

MAN ONE. He got the car started somehow. He got his car started!

[*The camera pans along the faces of the people as they stare, somehow caught up by this revelation and somehow, illogically, wildly, frightened.*]

WOMAN. How come his car just up and started like that?

SALLY. All by itself. He wasn't anywheres near it. It started all by itself.

[DON *approaches the group, stops a few feet away to look toward* GOODMAN'S *car and then back toward the group.*]

DON. And he never did come out to look at that thing that flew overhead. He wasn't even interested. [*He turns to the faces in the group, his face taut and serious.*] Why? Why didn't he come out with the rest of us to look?

CHARLIE. He always was an oddball. Him and his whole family. Real oddball.

DON. What do you say we ask him?

[*The group suddenly starts toward the house. In this brief fraction of a moment they take the first step toward performing a* metamorphosis *that changes people from a group into a mob. They begin to head purposefully across the street toward the house at the end.* STEVE *stands in front of them. For a moment their fear almost turns their walk into a wild stampede, but* STEVE'S *voice, loud, incisive, and commanding, makes them stop.*]

STEVE. Wait a minute . . . wait a minute! Let's not be a mob!

[*The people stop as a group, seem to pause for a moment, and then much more quietly and slowly start to walk across the street.* GOODMAN *stands alone facing the people.*]

GOODMAN. I just don't understand it. I tried to start it and it wouldn't start. You saw me. All of you saw me.

[*And now, just as suddenly as the engine started, it stops and there's a long silence that is gradually intruded upon by the frightened murmuring of the people.*]

GOODMAN. I don't understand. I swear . . . I don't understand. What's happening?

DON. Maybe you better tell us. Nothing's working on this street. Nothing. No lights, no power, no radio. [*And then meaningfully*] Nothing except one car—yours!

[*The people pick this up and now their murmuring becomes a loud chant filling the air with accusations and demands for action. Two of the men pass* DON *and head toward* GOODMAN, *who backs away, backing into his car and now at bay.*]

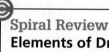

GOODMAN. Wait a minute now. You keep your distance—all of you. So I've got a car that starts by itself—well, that's a freak thing, I admit it. But does that make me some kind of a criminal or something? I don't know why the car works—it just does!

[*This stops the crowd momentarily and now* GOODMAN, *still backing away, goes toward his front porch. He goes up the steps and then stops to stand facing the mob.*
    We see a long shot of STEVE *as he comes through the crowd.*]

STEVE. [*Quietly*] We're all on a monster kick, Les. Seems that the general impression holds that maybe one family isn't what we think they are. Monsters from outer space or something. Different than us. Fifth columnists[2] from the vast beyond. [*He chuckles.*] You know anybody that might fit that description around here on Maple Street?

GOODMAN. What is this, a gag or something? This a practical joke or something?

[*We see a close-up of the porch light as it suddenly goes out. There's a murmur from the group.*]

GOODMAN. Now I suppose that's supposed to incriminate me! The light goes on and off. That really does it, doesn't it? [*He looks around the faces of the people.*] I just don't under-stand this— [*He wets his lips, looking from face to face.*] Look, you all know me. We've lived here five years. Right in this house. We're no different from any of the rest of you! We're no different at all. Really . . . this whole thing is just . . . just weird—

WOMAN. Well, if that's the case, Les Goodman, explain why—

[*She stops suddenly, clamping her mouth shut.*]

GOODMAN. [*Softly*] Explain what?

STEVE. [*Interjecting*] Look, let's forget this—

CHARLIE. [*Overlapping him*] Go ahead, let her talk. What about it? Explain what?

WOMAN. [*A little reluctantly*] Well . . . sometimes I go to bed late at night. A couple of times . . . a couple of times I'd come out on the porch and I'd see Mr. Goodman here in the wee

2. **Fifth columnists** people who help an invading enemy from within their own country.

Summarize
Briefly explain what has happened to Goodman and his car up to this point.

hours of the morning standing out in front of his house . . . looking up at the sky. [*She looks around the circle of faces.*] That's right, looking up at the sky as if . . . as if he were waiting for something. [*A pause*] As if he were looking for something.

[*There's a murmur of reaction from the crowd again.*

We cut suddenly to a group shot. As GOODMAN *starts toward them, they back away frightened.*]

GOODMAN. You know really . . . this is for laughs. You know what I'm guilty of? [*He laughs.*] I'm guilty of insomnia. Now what's the penalty for insomnia? [*At this point the laugh, the humor, leaves his voice.*] Did you hear what I said? I said it was insomnia. [*A pause as he looks around, then shouts.*] I said it was insomnia! You fools. You scared, frightened rabbits, you. You're sick people, do you know that? You're sick people—all of you! And you don't even know what you're starting because let me tell you . . . let me tell you—this thing you're starting—that should frighten you. As God is my witness . . . you're letting something begin here that's a nightmare!

ACT 2

[*We see a medium shot of the* GOODMAN *entry hall at night. On the side table rests an unlit candle.* MRS. GOODMAN *walks into the scene, a glass of milk in hand. She sets the milk down on the table, lights the candle with a match from a box on the table, picks up the glass of milk, and starts out of scene.*

MRS. GOODMAN *comes through her porch door, glass of milk in hand. The entry hall, with table and lit candle, can be seen behind her.*

Outside, the camera slowly pans down the sidewalk, taking in little knots of people who stand around talking in low voices. At the end of each conversation they look toward LES GOODMAN'S *house. From the various houses we can see candlelight but no electricity, and there's an all-pervading quiet that blankets the whole area, disturbed only by the almost whispered voices of the people as they stand around. The camera pans over to one group where* CHARLIE *stands. He stares across at* GOODMAN'S *house.*]

Summarize
In a few sentences, summarize the action of Act 1.

Characters' Motives
What emotions motivate Goodman to shout?

Reading Check
Why is the crowd following Goodman?

We see a long shot of the house. Two men stand across the street in almost sentry-like poses. Then we see a medium shot of a group of people.]

SALLY. [*A little timorously*] It just doesn't seem right, though, keeping watch on them. Why . . . he was right when he said he was one of our neighbors. Why, I've known Ethel Goodman ever since they moved in. We've been good friends—

CHARLIE. That don't prove a thing. Any guy who'd spend his time lookin' up at the sky early in the morning—well, there's something wrong with that kind of person. There's something that ain't legitimate. Maybe under normal circumstances we could let it go by, but these aren't normal circumstances. Why, look at this street! Nothin' but candles. Why, it's like goin' back into the dark ages or somethin'!

[STEVE *walks down the steps of his porch, walks down the street over to* LES GOODMAN'S *house, and then stops at the foot of the steps.* GOODMAN *stands there, his wife behind him, very frightened.*]

GOODMAN. Just stay right where you are, Steve. We don't want any trouble, but this time if anybody sets foot on my porch, that's what they're going to get—trouble!

STEVE. Look, Les—

GOODMAN. I've already explained to you people. I don't sleep very well at night sometimes. I get up and I take a walk and I look up at the sky. I look at the stars!

MRE. GOODMAN That's exactly what he does. Why this whole thing, it's . . . it's some kind of madness or something.

STEVE. [*Nods grimly*] That's exactly what it is—some kind of madness.

CHARLIE'S VOICE. [*Shrill, from across the street*] You best watch who you're seen with, Steve! Until we get this all straightened out, you ain't exactly above suspicion yourself.

STEVE. [*Whirling around toward him*] Or you, Charlie. Or any of us, it seems. From age eight on up!

WOMAN. What I'd like to know is—what are we gonna do? Just stand around here all night?

Summarize
Is Charlie's statement about candles important? Why or why not?

Spiral Review
Elements of Drama
How do the stage directions build the tension?

Streetlight, 1930, Constance Coleman Richardson, Indianapolis Musem of Art

CHARLIE. There's nothin' else we can do! [*He turns back looking toward* STEVE *and* GOODMAN *again.*] One of 'em'll tip their hand. They got to.

STEVE. [*Raising his voice*] There's something you can do, Charlie. You could go home and keep your mouth shut. You could quit strutting around like a self-appointed hanging judge and just climb into bed and forget it.

CHARLIE. You sound real anxious to have that happen, Steve. I think we better keep our eye on you too!

DON. [*As if he were taking the bit in his teeth, takes a hesitant step to the front*] I think everything might as well come out now. [*He turns toward* STEVE.] Your wife's done plenty of talking, Steve, about how odd you are!

CHARLIE. [*Picking this up, his eyes widening*] Go ahead, tell us what she's said.

Characters' Motives
Why does Steve want Charlie to be quiet?

Reading Check

Why does Goodman go out and stare at the sky early in the morning?

▲ **Critical Viewing**
Why does night's darkness, shown in this illustration, make the people of Maple Street more fearful? **[Hypothesize]**

[*We see a long shot of* STEVE *as he walks toward them from across the street.*]

STEVE. Go ahead, what's my wife said? Let's get it all out. Let's pick out every idiosyncrasy of every single man, woman, and child on the street. And then we might as well set up some kind of kangaroo court.[3] How about a firing squad at dawn, Charlie, so we can get rid of all the suspects? Narrow them down. Make it easier for you.

DON. There's no need gettin' so upset, Steve. It's just that . . . well . . . Myra's talked about how there's been plenty of nights you spent hours down in your basement workin' on some kind of radio or something. Well, none of us have ever seen that radio—

[*By this time* STEVE *has reached the group. He stands there defiantly close to them.*]

CHARLIE. Go ahead, Steve. What kind of "radio set" you workin' on? I never seen it. Neither has anyone else. Who you talk to on that radio set? And who talks to you?

---

3. **kangaroo court** unofficial court that does not follow normal rules.

STEVE. I'm surprised at you, Charlie. How come you're so dense all of a sudden? [*A pause*] Who do I talk to? I talk to monsters from outer space. I talk to three-headed green men who fly over here in what look like meteors.

[STEVE'S *wife steps down from the porch, bites her lip, calls out.*]

MRE. BRAND. Steve! Steve, please. [*Then looking around, frightened, she walks toward the group.*] It's just a ham radio set, that's all. I bought him a book on it myself. It's just a ham radio set. A lot of people have them. I can show it to you. It's right down in the basement.

STEVE. [*Whirls around toward her*] Show them nothing! If they want to look inside our house—let them get a search warrant.

CHARLIE. Look, buddy, you can't afford to—

STEVE. [*Interrupting*] Charlie, don't tell me what I can afford! And stop telling me who's dangerous and who isn't and who's safe and who's a menace. [*He turns to the group and shouts.*] And you're with him, too—all of you! You're standing here all set to crucify—all set to find a scapegoat[4]—all desperate to point some kind of a finger at a neighbor! Well now look, friends, the only thing that's gonna happen is that we'll eat each other up alive—

[*He stops abruptly as* CHARLIE *suddenly grabs his arm.*]

CHARLIE. [*In a hushed voice*] That's not the only thing that can happen to us.

[*Cut to a long shot looking down the street. A figure has suddenly materialized in the gloom and in the silence we can hear the clickety-clack of slow, measured footsteps on concrete as the figure walks slowly toward them. One of the women lets out a stifled cry. The young mother grabs her boy as do a couple of others.*]

TOMMY. [*Shouting, frightened*] It's the monster! It's the monster!

[*Another woman lets out a wail and the people fall back in a group, staring toward the darkness and the approaching figure.*]

---

4. **scapegoat** person or group blamed for the mistakes or crimes of others.

Characters' Motives
What do you think Steve is feeling at this point?

Characters' Motives
What explains the characters' fearful actions here?

Reading Check
What does Steve have in his basement?

▲ **Critical Viewing**
How does this image help communicate the ideas of the play? **[Connect]**

We see a medium group shot of the people as they stand in the shadows watching. DON MARTIN joins them, carrying a shotgun. He holds it up.]

DON. We may need this.

STEVE. A shotgun? [He pulls it out of DON'S hand.] Good Lord—will anybody think a thought around here? Will you people wise up? What good would a shotgun do against—

[Now CHARLIE pulls the gun from STEVE'S hand.]

Characters' Motives
Why does Charlie pull the shotgun from Steve's hands?

CHARLIE. No more talk, Steve. You're going to talk us into a grave! You'd let whatever's out there walk right over us, wouldn't yuh? Well, some of us won't!

[He swings the gun around to point it toward the sidewalk. The dark figure continues to walk toward them.

The group stands there, fearful, apprehensive, mothers clutching children, men standing in front of wives. CHARLIE slowly raises the gun. As the figure gets closer and closer he suddenly pulls the trigger. The sound of it explodes in the stillness. There is a long angle shot looking down at the figure, who suddenly *lets out a small cry, stumbles forward onto his knees and then falls forward on his face. DON, CHARLIE, and STEVE race forward over to him. STEVE is there first and turns the man over. Now the crowd gathers around them.*]

STEVE. [*Slowly looks up*] It's Pete Van Horn.

DON. [*In a hushed voice*] Pete Van Horn! He was just gonna go over to the next block to see if the power was on—

WOMAN. You killed him, Charlie. You shot him dead!

CHARLIE. [*Looks around at the circle of faces, his eyes frightened, his face contorted*] But . . . but I didn't know who he was. I certainly didn't know who he was. He comes walkin' out of the darkness—how am I supposed to know who he was? [*He grabs* STEVE.] Steve—you know why I shot! How was I supposed to know he wasn't a monster or something? [*He grabs* DON *now.*] We're all scared of the same thing. I was just tryin' to . . . tryin' to protect my home, that's all! Look, all of you, that's all I was tryin' to do. [*He looks down wildly at the body.*] I didn't know it was somebody we knew! I didn't know—

[*There's a sudden hush and then an intake of breath. We see a medium shot of the living room window of* CHARLIE'S *house. The window is not lit, but suddenly the house lights come on behind it.*]

WOMAN. [*In a very hushed voice*] Charlie . . . Charlie . . . the lights just went on in your house. Why did the lights just go on?

DON. What about it, Charlie? How come you're the only one with lights now?

GOODMAN. That's what I'd like to know.

[*A pause as they all stare toward* CHARLIE.]

GOODMAN. You were so quick to kill, Charlie, and you were so quick to tell us who we had to be careful of. Well, maybe you had to kill. Maybe Peter there was trying to tell us something. Maybe he'd found out something and came back to tell us who there was amongst us we should watch out for—

[CHARLIE *backs away from the group, his eyes wide with fright.*]

Summarize
How do you know that Pete Van Horn's death is an important detail?

Reading Check
Who shoots Pete Van Horn?

CHARLIE. No . . . no . . . it's nothing of the sort! I don't know why the lights are on. I swear I don't. Somebody's pulling a gag or something.

[*He bumps against* STEVE, *who grabs him and whirls him around.*]

STEVE. *A gag?* A gag? Charlie, there's a dead man on the sidewalk and you killed him! Does this thing look like a gag to you?

[CHARLIE *breaks away and screams as he runs toward his house.*]

CHARLIE. No! No! Please!

[*A man breaks away from the crowd to chase* CHARLIE.

We see a long angle shot looking down as the man tackles CHARLIE *and lands on top of him. The other people start to run toward them.* CHARLIE *is up on his feet, breaks away from the other man's grasp, lands a couple of desperate punches that push the man aside. Then he forces his way, fighting, through the crowd to once again break free, jumps up on his front porch. A rock thrown from the group smashes a window alongside of him, the broken glass flying past him. A couple of pieces cut him. He stands there perspiring, rumpled, blood running down from a cut on the cheek. His wife breaks away from the group to throw herself into his arms. He buries his face against her. We can see the crowd converging on the porch now.*]

VOICES.

It must have been him.

He's the one.

We got to get Charlie.

[*Another rock lands on the porch. Now* CHARLIE *pushes his wife behind him, facing the group.*]

CHARLIE. Look, look I swear to you . . . it isn't me . . . but I do know who it is . . . I swear to you, I do know who it is. I know who the monster is here. I know who it is that doesn't belong. I swear to you I know.

GOODMAN. [*Shouting*] What are you waiting for?

Characters' Motives
What motivates Charlie to claim that he knows who the monster is? Explain.

WOMAN. [*Shouting*] Come on, Charlie, come on.

MAN ONE. [*Shouting*] Who is it, Charlie, tell us!

DON. [*Pushing his way to the front of the crowd*] All right, Charlie, let's hear it!

[CHARLIE'S *eyes dart around wildly.*]

CHARLIE. It's . . . it's . . .

MAN TWO. [*Screaming*] Go ahead, Charlie, tell us.

CHARLIE. It's . . . it's the kid. It's Tommy. He's the one!

[*There's a gasp from the crowd as we cut to a shot of* SALLY *holding her son* TOMMY. *The boy at first doesn't understand and then, realizing the eyes are all on him, buries his face against his mother.*]

SALLY. [*Backs away*] That's crazy! That's crazy! He's a little boy.

WOMAN. But he knew! He was the only one who knew! He told us all about it. Well, how did he know? How could he have known?

[*The various people take this up and repeat the question aloud.*]

VOICES.

How could he know?

Who told him?

Make the kid answer.

DON. It was Charlie who killed old man Van Horn.

WOMAN. But it was the kid here who knew what was going to happen all the time. He was the one who knew!

[*We see a close-up of* STEVE.]

STEVE. Are you all gone crazy? [*Pause as he looks about*] Stop.

[*A fist crashes at* STEVE'S *face, staggering him back out of the frame of the picture.*
    There are several close camera shots suggesting the coming of violence. A hand fires a rifle. A fist clenches. A hand grabs the hammer from VAN HORN'S *body, etc. Meanwhile, we hear the following lines.*]

> **Summarize**
> What details show that Charlie finds it hard to say who to blame?

Reading Check

According to Charlie, who is the monster?

DON. Charlie has to be the one—Where's my rifle—

WOMAN. Les Goodman's the one. His car started! Let's wreck it.

MRS. GOODMAN. What about Steve's radio—He's the one that called them—

MRS. GOODMAN. Smash the radio. Get me a hammer. Get me something.

STEVE. Stop—Stop—

CHARLIE. Where's that kid—Let's get him.

MAN ONE. Get Steve—Get Charlie—They're working together.

[*The crowd starts to converge around the mother, who grabs the child and starts to run with him. The crowd starts to follow, at first walking fast, and then running after him.*

We see a full shot of the street as suddenly CHARLIE'S *lights go off and the lights in another house go on. They stay on for a moment, then from across the street other lights go on and then off again.*]

Summarize
Is the detail about lights going on and off in various homes important? Why or why not?

MAN ONE. [*Shouting*] It isn't the kid . . . it's Bob Weaver's house.

WOMAN. It isn't Bob Weaver's house. It's Don Martin's place.

CHARLIE. I tell you it's the kid.

DON. It's Charlie. He's the one.

[*We move into a series of close-ups of various people as they shout, accuse, scream, interspersing these shots with shots of houses as the lights go on and off, and then slowly in the middle of this nightmarish morass of sight and sound the camera starts to pull away, until once again we've reached the opening shot looking at the Maple Street sign from high above. The camera continues to move away until we dissolve to a shot looking toward the metal side of a space craft, which sits shrouded in darkness. An open door throws out a beam of light from the illuminated interior. Two figures silhouetted against the bright lights appear. We get only a vague feeling of form, but nothing more explicit than that.*]

FIGURE ONE. Understand the procedure now? Just stop a few of their machines and radios and telephones and lawn mowers . . . throw them into darkness for a few hours, and then you just sit back and watch the pattern.

FIGURE TWO. And this pattern is always the same?

FIGURE ONE. With few variations. They pick the most dangerous enemy they can find . . . and it's themselves. And all we need do is sit back . . . and watch.

FIGURE TWO. Then I take it this place . . . this Maple Street . . . is not unique.

FIGURE ONE. [*Shaking his head*] By no means. Their world is full of Maple Streets. And we'll go from one to the other and let them destroy themselves. One to the other . . . one to the other . . . one to the other—

[*Now the camera pans up for a shot of the starry sky and over this we hear the* NARRATOR'S *voice.*]

NARRATOR'S VOICE. The tools of conquest do not necessarily come with bombs and explosions and fallout. There are weapons that are simply thoughts, attitudes, prejudices—to be found only in the minds of men. For the record, prejudices can kill and suspicion can destroy and a thoughtless frightened search for a scapegoat has a fallout all its own for the children . . . and the children yet unborn. [*A pause*] And the pity of it is . . . that these things cannot be confined to . . . The Twilight Zone!

Critical Thinking

1. Key Ideas and Details (a) How do the people on Maple Street single out Les Goodman in Act I? **(b) Interpret:** What qualities of his cause the reaction? **(c) Deduce:** What does this suggest about what is really happening on Maple Street?

2. Key Ideas and Details (a) Why does Charlie shoot Pete Van Horn? **(b) Infer:** What does the crowd's response to this shooting suggest about how clearly they are thinking? Cite at least two examples to support your response.

3. Key Ideas and Details (a) Who accuses Tommy after the shooting, and why? **(b) Connect:** Why are people prepared to believe such an accusation? **(c) Support:** How do the events of the play support this statement: "The tools of conquest do not necessarily come with bombs and explosions and fallout"?

4. Integration of Knowledge and Ideas (a) Draw Conclusions: Who are the monsters on Maple Street? **(b) Discuss:** Share your responses with a partner. Then, discuss how hearing someone else's responses did or did not change your answers.

5. Integration of Knowledge and Ideas (a) How do the neighbors regard each other in the story? **(b)** How do the aliens regard the residents of Maple Street? **(c)** Whose perspective is more clear-eyed? Explain. *[Connect to the Big Question: Do others see us more clearly than we see ourselves?]*

Cite textual evidence to support your responses.

Reading Skill: Summarize

1. At the beginning of the play, the electricity goes off, and phones and radios stop working. Are these important or unimportant details? Explain your answer.

2. **Summarize** the play using a chart like the one shown.

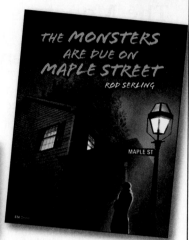

Important Details From Beginning	Important Details From Middle	Important Details From End

Summary:

Literary Analysis: Characters' Motives

© 3. **Key Ideas and Details** Explain the **character's motives** in each of these examples: **(a)** Pete Van Horn walks from his neighborhood to the next one. **(b)** Charlie shoots Pete Van Horn. **(c)** Goodman accuses Charlie of being one of the others.

© 4. **Key Ideas and Details** What is the motivation of Figure One? How does his motivation shape the plot?

Vocabulary

© **Acquisition and Use** Write a single sentence using both words.

1. transfixed; film
2. flustered; teacher
3. sluggishly; engine
4. persistently; nagged
5. defiant; teenager
6. metamorphosis; tadpole

Word Study Use the context of the sentences and what you know about the **Latin root -sist-** to explain your answer.

1. Is an *assistant* someone who will not help you?
2. If you *insist* on doing something, are you expressing yourself in a firm manner?

Word Study

The **Latin root -*sist*-** means "stand."

Apply It Explain how the root -*sist*- contributes to the meanings of these words. Consult a dictionary if necessary.

consistent
resistance
subsist

Integrated Language Skills

The Monsters Are Due on Maple Street

Conventions: Sentence Functions and Endmarks

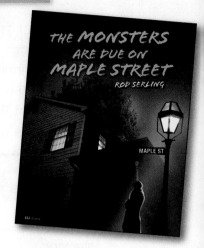

Sentences are classified into four categories based on their **function.** Each type of sentence calls for its own specific punctuation mark(s).

Catagory	Function	Endmark	Example
Declarative	to make statements	.	Our cat chased a squirrel up a tree.
Interrogative	to ask questions	?	Where did I put my jacket?
Imperative	to give commands	. *or* !	Put your books away. Don't touch that stove!
Exclamatory	to call out or exclaim	!	That's a great idea!

Practice A Identify the function of each sentence below.

1. The neighbors came out of their homes.
2. What caused them to be afraid?
3. There are monsters on the street!
4. Don't jump to conclusions about people.
5. Pete went to see if the next street had electricity.

© **Reading Application** In *The Monsters Are Due on Maple Street,* find one declarative sentence, one interrogative sentence, one imperative sentence, and one exclamatory sentence.

Practice B Follow the directions to write a sentence that performs the indicated function.

1. Make a statement about the flash of light on Maple Street.
2. Ask a question about the loss of electricity in the neighborhood.
3. Issue a command to Les Goodman about his car.
4. Call out a warning to Pete Van Horn as he approaches his neighbors in Act 2.

© **Writing Application** Write four sentences about events that take place in *The Monsters Are Due on Maple Street.* Use one declarative sentence, one interrogative sentence, one imperative sentence, and one exclamatory sentence.

PH WRITING COACH Further instruction and practice are available in *Prentice Hall Writing Coach.*

Writing

Common Core State Standards

L.7.2, L.7.4.b; W.7.2.b, W.7.2.c, W.7.6, W.7.9.a
[For the full wording of the standards, see page 830.]

Informative Text Write a **summary** of Act 1 or 2 of the screenplay.

- Include only the main ideas and most significant details.

- Use your own words, except when including quotations.

- Be sure your summary reflects the act's underlying meaning, or theme, not just the superficial details. Relay facts, not personal reactions.

- Use effective transitions between sentences to unify important ideas. For example, you might use words like *next*, *finally*, *at first*, and *however* to link events.

Type your summary using a word processing program. Use the spell-check feature to make sure that your spelling is accurate.

Grammar Application Check to be sure you have correctly punctuated your writing.

Writing Workshop: *Work in Progress*

Prewriting for Exposition For a cause-and-effect essay, make a list of three questions you have that begin with the word *Why*. The subject of each sentence is a *cause*. The answers to each question are *effects*. Keep this Question List in your writing portfolio.

Use this prewriting activity to prepare for the **Writing Workshop** on page 878.

Research and Technology

Build and Present Knowledge Plan how you would prepare a **film version** of any scene from the screenplay. Consider how you could use the medium to portray the scene in a unique way. Follow these steps to complete the assignment:

- List the events that occur in the scene.
- Plan the camera angles that will best illustrate the action.
- Consider using special sound or lighting effects.
- Think about the background and interests of your audience.
- Organize the details and sequence of your film to make it interesting and exciting to your audience.

If a camera is available and you have the time, film the scene.

Compare and contrast your filmed version of the scene with the original screenplay version.

PHLit Online!
www.PHLitOnline.com
- Interactive graphic organizers
- Grammar tutorial
- Interactive journals

Test Practice: Reading

Summarize

Fiction Selection

Directions: *Read the selection. Then, answer the questions.*

(1) A strange orange glow shone through the cracks in the toolshed walls. Carrie was troubled by the spooky light she noticed as she opened the pale blue back door to let her cat out for the night. Miss Kitty, who usually sprang for freedom as soon as the door opened, hung back hesitantly.

(2) Creeping carefully but nervously toward the shed, Carrie had the feeling her curiosity might get her into trouble. Mom and Dad were scheduled to return soon from a meeting at school, and she knew she should wait and let them explore the cause of the light. Patience had never been one of her strongest virtues, though.

1. Which detail from paragraph 1 should be included in a summary?
   A. The shed walls were cracked.
   B. An orange glow shone from the shed.
   C. Carrie let her cat out for the night.
   D. The back door was a pale blue color.

2. Which of the following is the *best* one-sentence summary of paragraph 1?
   A. A spooky light in the shed frightened Carrie and her cat.
   B. A light in the shed frightened Miss Kitty, who usually went out at night.
   C. When Carrie opened the door to let the cat out, she saw a light in the shed.
   D. Miss Kitty's behavior made it clear that something scary was in the shed.

3. What detail does *not* belong in a summary of paragraph 2?
   A. Carrie is not waiting for her parents.
   B. Carrie is often in trouble.
   C. Carrie is creeping towards the shed.
   D. Carrie is not a patient person.

4. What key detail adds suspense to paragraph 2?
   A. Carrie knew she should wait.
   B. Mom and Dad had a meeting at school.
   C. Carrie crept carefully but nervously toward the tent.
   D. Patience had never been one of her strongest virtues.

5. Which detail should come first in a summary of the entire selection?
   A. Carrie knew she should wait.
   B. Carrie opened the door of the shed.
   C. Carrie's cat hung back from the door.
   D. Carrie saw a strange orange glow.

Writing for Assessment

Write a one-sentence summary of paragraph 2. Be sure to include only the most important ideas and details.

Nonfiction Selection

Directions: *Read the selection. Then, answer the questions.*

(1) Imagine trying to find your tent in a packed campground after a long day at a nearby music festival. With thousands of campers spread out across the field, it could take hours—unless you live in Europe and have a new cellphone-activated tent.

(2) Launched recently by one of Europe's largest telecommunications companies, this tent has a special gray antenna rising from its center, and its edges are lined with luminous ribbing. When a tent owner sends a text message to a special phone number, the antenna flashes, and the entire tent glows bright orange.

(3) Although the tents are not yet available for sale in the United States, American camping retailers are interested in incorporating the technology into their equipment. Soon, campers around the world might more easily find their way "home to their domes"—so long as everyone else doesn't run out and buy one too!

1. Which of these details should *not* be included in a summary of paragraph 1?
   A. A cellphone activates the tent.
   B. The tents are available in Europe.
   C. Music festivals can be long.
   D. Locating a tent may be difficult.

2. What is the *best* one-sentence summary of paragraph 1?
   A. Campers attend crowded music festivals with thousands of other campers.
   B. Campers with cellphone-activated tents can locate their campsites easily.
   C. European campers have trouble finding their tents in crowded fields.
   D. Campers can buy cellphone-activated tents.

3. A summary of paragraph 2 should include the detail that each tent—
   A. is a popular choice for campers.
   B. has a special phone number.
   C. was manufactured in Europe.
   D. has a gray, flashing antenna.

4. Which detail should *not* be included in a summary of paragraph 3?
   A. American campers are not yet able to buy these special tents.
   B. The tents will be available to campers around the world.
   C. American retailers want to incorporate the technology into their equipment.
   D. If everyone buys a glowing tent, they will not be so useful.

Writing for Assessment

Connecting Across Texts

Imagine that the glowing light in the first passage is caused by the tent described in the second passage. Write a three-sentence summary of the first passage, incorporating this new information.

PHLit Online!
www.PHLitOnline.com
- Online practice
- Instant feedback

Reading for Information

Analyzing Argumentative Texts

Editorial	Editorial

Common Core State Standards

Reading Informational Texts
6. Determine an author's point of view or purpose in a text and analyze how the author distinguishes his or her position from that of others.

9. Analyze how two or more authors writing about the same topic shape their presentations of key information by emphasizing different evidence or advancing different interpretations of facts.

Language
6. Acquire and use accurately grade-appropriate general academic and domain-specific words and phrases; gather vocabulary knowledge when considering a word or phrase important to comprehension or expression.

Reading Skill: Identify Bias and Stereotyping

In persuasive writing, authors provide evidence to support their claims. As a good reader, you should **assess that evidence, deciding if it is adequate and accurate.** When judging a text, look for bias and stereotyping. A **bias** is a leaning toward a certain position. A **stereotype** unfairly suggests that all members of a group are exactly the same. The following chart gives examples and explanations of bias and stereotyping.

	Example	How It Works
Bias	"He *won* the election with his plans for reform." "He *stole* the election with a web of empty promises."	Two writers describe the same event differently, based on their personal feelings.
Stereotyping	"All teenagers are lazy."	The writer makes an unsupported claim about a group of people in order to sway readers' opinions.

Content-Area Vocabulary

These words appear in the selections that follow. You may also encounter them in other content-area texts.

- **derring-do** (der´ iŋ dōō´) *n.* daring deeds
- **lobbying** (läb´ ē iŋ) *v.* trying to influence the members of a lawmaking group
- **junket** (juŋ´ kit) *n.* a trip paid for with the public's money

Veteran Returns, Becomes Symbol

Editorial in the *Minneapolis Star and Tribune*, January 19, 1998

John Glenn went into orbit in 1962 and took America's hearts soaring with him. Who better to fire the nation's imagination again about the promise of space exploration?

NASA has done itself and its cause great good by announcing that Glenn, the astronaut-turned-U.S. senator, will fly into space once more. Though Glenn has represented Ohio in the Senate for five terms and run for president once, many Americans still consider his name synonymous with the nation's manned space program.

At a time when all astronauts were esteemed as America's best and brightest, Glenn stood out. Though not the first American in space, nor the one to seize the space-race prize—a moon landing—Glenn possessed an appeal that surpassed that of his peers.

Just as Glenn's orbital heroics inspired America when he was a young man, by joining the shuttle crew in October at age 77, he can inspire the nation again. He can reignite curiosity about the benefits and challenges for humankind that lie beyond Earth. He can let a watchful public share vicariously[1] his delight at leaving Earth's bounds once more.

And he can again be an exemplar for his generation—a generation already setting new standards for vigor and productivity past age 70. Glenn's flight should dramatically demonstrate that age is no limit to derring-do, nor to service to one's country.

Volunteering for a space ride isn't an option for most septuagenarians.[2] But many of Glenn's contemporaries are also volunteering, lending a hand to the young, old, sick and needy in their own communities. As America honors Glenn's past and future career in space, let the nation also take grateful note of the good works senior citizens are doing here on the ground.

---

1. **vicariously** (vī ker′ ē əs lē) *adv.* Indirectly; through the experience of another; by sympathy or imagination.
2. **septuagenarians** (sep′ too ə jə ner′ ē ənz) *n.* Persons between the ages of 70 and 80.

The Wrong Orbit: Senator Has No Legitimate Business Blasting into Space

Editorial in The *Kansas City Star*, January 20, 1998

Most Americans think of political lobbying as something done by special interest groups trying to curry favor with lawmakers to affect some legislation. Not so in the case of Sen. John Glenn and his former employer, the National Aeronautics and Space Administration.

Glenn, a Democratic senator from Ohio, has lobbied NASA for some time in hope of returning to space. Glenn, who will turn 77 in July, was the first American to orbit the Earth.

He plans to retire from the Senate, but for his next engagement he wants to strap on a space suit under the pretense of scientific merit. Glenn says his space jaunt would help the space program understand the effects of weightlessness on the aging human form. (C'mon, Senator, it's doubtful even you believe that, so don't expect anyone else to.)

There are much better uses for the taxpayers' money than Glenn's planned junket in space via the Discovery mission in October. Besides, as the senator ought to

know, workers in the space program are being laid off around the country due to downsizing at NASA. And there's something questionable, if not downright indecent, about a U.S. senator who has been a NASA ally in Congress, calling on the space agency for a favor. Whether on this planet or another, a quid pro quo[1] is the same.

John Glenn became a hero after his pioneering space flight, and he parlayed that status into what was said to be a successful political career. His political career was jeopardized by his involvement in the Keating Five scandal, and he became excessively shrill this year during committee hearings as the Senate defender of the Democratic presidential fund-raising debacle.[2]

Certainly, there are times when good science and good politics mix, as happened with the launch of the U.S. space program as part of the space race with the former Soviet Union.

But Glenn's proposed junket in space is neither good science nor good politics.

---

1. *quid pro quo* (kwid prō kwō) *n.* Latin phrase meaning "this for that"; a thing given or done in exchange for another.
2. **Keating Five . . . fund-raising debacle** (di bä´ kəl) *n.* The Keating Five were five senators, including John Glenn, who received contributions from Charles Keating, a businessman under criminal investigation. In 1997, the Senate and the Justice Department investigated White House fund-raising practices.

Comparing Argumentative Texts

© **1. Key Ideas and Details** **(a)** Identify differences between the arguments made in each editorial. **(b)** Identify instances of **bias** and **stereotyping** in each editorial.

Content-Area Vocabulary

2. (a) Remove the suffix *-ing* from the word *lobbying.* Using a print or an online dictionary, explain how removing the suffix reveals a different word that is a different part of speech. **(b)** Use the words *lobbying* and *lobby* in sentences that show their meaning.

🕐 Timed Writing

Argumentative Text: Evaluation

> **Format**
> The prompt gives directions about what to write and the type of information to include.

Choose one of the editorials about John Glenn's plans to travel in space, and write an evaluation of the piece. Tell whether the author successfully argued and supported his or her claims. Use details from the text to support your answer. (30 minutes)

> **Academic Vocabulary**
> When you *support* your answer, you provide details, examples, and facts to show that your answer is reasonable and logical.

5-Minute Planner

Complete these steps to write your evaluation:

1. Read the writing prompt carefully from start to finish. Be sure that you fully understand the assignment. **TIP** When reading a prompt, look for verbs such as "choose," "write," and "tell." These words are often important to understanding what you are being asked to do.

2. Gather information for your evaluation by rereading the editorial that you have chosen to evaluate. Jot down the author's claims and details that support each claim.

3. Determine whether the author's supporting details are based in fact or opinion, whether they are biased or unbiased, and whether they include emotional language. Use this information to decide if you are persuaded to accept the author's claims.

4. Use your notes about the author's claims to keep your thoughts focused as you write your evaluation.

Comparing Literary Works

Comparing Dramatic Speeches

Dramatic speeches are spoken by characters in a play. These speeches can move the action forward and reveal more about the characters. Dramatic speeches are an important part of the structure, or organization, of a drama. There are two main types of dramatic speeches:

- **Dialogue** is conversation between or among characters in a drama. It reveals characters' traits and helps develop conflict.

- **Monologues** are long, uninterrupted speeches that are spoken by a single character. They reveal the private thoughts and feelings of the character.

The following selections are both dramatic speeches. The excerpt from *Grandpa and the Statue* is a dialogue, and *My Head Is Full of Starshine* is a monologue. Both provide information and details about the characters. Some details are told directly through the words a character speaks. For example, a character may say, "I am happy." Other details are supplied indirectly. For example, if a character constantly disagrees with others, you can infer that he or she is angry or argumentative. As you read, use a chart like the one below to record what you learn about the main characters in these dramatic speeches.

Common Core State Standards

Reading Literature
5. Analyze how a drama's or poem's form or structure contributes to its meaning.

Writing
2. Write informative/explanatory texts to examine a topic and convey ideas, concepts, and information through the selection, organization, and analysis of relevant content.
2.b. Develop the topic with relevant facts, definitions, concrete details, quotations, or other information and examples. *(Timed Writing)*

	Grandpa and the Statue	My Head Is Full of Starshine
Main Characters		
Description of Characters		
How I Learned About Characters		

www.PHLitOnline.com

- Vocabulary flashcards
- Interactive journals
- More about the authors
- Selection audio
- Interactive graphic organizers

Do others *see* us more clearly than we *see* ourselves?

Writing About the Big Question

In each of these selections, what characters say reveals a lot about them. Use this sentence starter to develop your ideas.

The best way to **appreciate** someone is to _____.

Meet the Authors

Arthur Miller (1915–2005)
Author of *Grandpa and the Statue*

Arthur Miller is considered among the finest American playwrights. Most of his plays focus on the problems of ordinary people. Born in New York City, Miller was unable to finish high school because of the Depression. In 1934, he convinced the University of Michigan to accept him as a student anyway.

Promising Playwright In 1947, Miller saw his first play, *All My Sons,* open on Broadway. *Death of a Salesman* (1949), perhaps his most famous play, won a Pulitzer Prize and made Miller internationally famous. *Grandpa and the Statue* was originally written as a radio drama in 1944.

Peg Kehret (b. 1936)
Author of *My Head Is Full of Starshine*

Before Peg Kehret began writing books for children, she wrote radio commercials, plays, and stories for magazines.

Animal Lover Kehret is a longtime volunteer for animal welfare causes and has won an award for her work with animals. For years, she and her husband traveled around the United States so that Kehret could speak at schools and libraries. The couple traveled in a motor home so that their pets could go with them.

from Grandpa and the STATUE

ARTHUR MILLER

SHEEAN. [*Slight brogue*[1]] A good afternoon to you, Monaghan.

MONAGHAN. How're you, Sheean, how're ya?

SHEEAN. Fair, fair. And how's Mrs. Monaghan these days?

MONAGHAN. Warm. Same as everybody else in summer.

SHEEAN. I've come to talk to you about the fund, Monaghan.

MONAGHAN. What fund is that?

SHEEAN. The Statue of Liberty fund.

MONAGHAN. Oh, that.

SHEEAN. It's time we come to grips with the subject, Monaghan.

MONAGHAN. I'm not interested, Sheean.

SHEEAN. Now hold up on that a minute. Let me tell you the facts. This here Frenchman has gone and built a fine statue of Liberty. It costs who knows how many millions to build. All they're askin' us to do is contribute enough to put up a base for the statue to stand on.

MONAGHAN. I'm not . . . !

SHEEAN. Before you answer me. People all over the whole United States are puttin' in for it. Butler Street is doin' the same. We'd like to hang up a flag on the corner

1. **brogue** (brōg) *n.* Irish accent.

◀ **Critical Viewing**
What can you see in this photograph that you do not usually see in pictures of the Statue of Liberty? **[Analyze]**

ⓒ

Spiral Review
Characters How would you describe the relationship between Sheean and Monaghan? Explain.

✓ Reading Check
What does Sheean want from Monaghan?

▲ **Critical Viewing**
Why might Monaghan
be unwilling to con-
tribute after seeing
these pieces of the
statue? **[Infer]**

Dramatic Speeches
What characteristics of
Monaghan do the lines
of dialogue on this page
reveal?

saying—"Butler Street, Brooklyn, is one hundred per cent behind the Statue of Liberty." And Butler Street is a hundred per cent subscribed except for you. Now will you give us a dime, Monaghan? One dime and we can put up the flag. Now what do you say to that?

MONAGHAN. I'm not throwin' me good money away for somethin' I don't even know exists.

SHEEAN. Now what do you mean by that?

MONAGHAN. Have you seen this statue?

SHEEAN. No, but it's in a warehouse. And as soon as we get the money to build the pedestal they'll take it and put it up on that island in the river, and all the boats comin' in from the old country will see it there and it'll raise the hearts of the poor immigrants to see such a fine sight on their first look at this country.

MONAGHAN. And how do I know it's in this here warehouse at all?

SHEEAN. You read your paper, don't you? It's been in all the papers for the past year.

MONAGHAN. Ha, the papers! Last year I read in the paper that they were about to pave Butler Street and take out all the holes. Turn around and look at Butler Street, Mr. Sheean.

SHEEAN. All right. I'll do this: I'll take you to the warehouse and show you the statue. Will you give me a dime then?

MONAGHAN. Well . . . I'm not sayin' I would, and I'm not sayin' I wouldn't. But I'd be more likely if I saw the thing large as life, I would.

SHEEAN. [Peeved] All right, then. Come along.

[*Music up and down and out*]

[*Footsteps, in a warehouse . . . echo . . . they come to a halt.*]

Now then. Do you see the Statue of Liberty or don't you see it?

MONAGHAN. I see it all right, but it's all broke!

SHEEAN. *Broke!* They brought it from France on a boat. They had to take it apart, didn't they?

MONAGHAN. You got a secondhand statue, that's what you got, and I'm not payin' for new when they've shipped us something that's all smashed to pieces.

SHEEAN. Now just a minute, just a minute. Visualize what I'm about to tell you, Monaghan, get the picture of it. When this statue is put together it's going to stand ten stories high. Could they get a thing ten stories high into a four-story building such as this is? Use your good sense, now Monaghan.

MONAGHAN. What's that over there?

SHEEAN. Where?

▼ **Critical Viewing**
What tools and equipment might be needed to reassemble the statue? **[Draw Conclusions]**

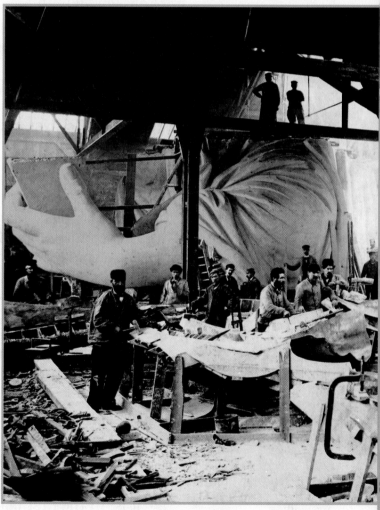

MONAGHAN. That tablet there in her hand. What's it say? July Eye Vee (IV) MDCCLXXVI . . . what . . . what's all that?

SHEEAN. That means July 4, 1776. It's in Roman numbers. Very high class.

MONAGHAN. What's the good of it? If they're going to put a sign on her they ought to put it: Welcome All. That's it. Welcome All.

SHEEAN. They decided July 4, 1776, and July 4, 1776, it's going to be!

MONAGHAN. All right, then let them get their dime from somebody else!

SHEEAN. Monaghan!

MONAGHAN. No, sir! I'll tell you something. I didn't think there was a statue but there is. She's all broke, it's true, but she's here and maybe they can get her together. But even if they do, will you tell me what sort of a welcome to immigrants it'll be, to have a gigantic thing like that in the middle of the river and in her hand is July Eye Vee MCDVC . . . whatever it is?

SHEEAN. That's the date the country was made!

MONAGHAN. The divil with the date! A man comin' in from the sea wants a place to stay, not a date. When I come from the old country I git off at the dock and there's a feller says to me, "Would you care for a room for the night?" "I would that," I sez, and he sez, "All right then, follow me." He takes me to a rooming house. I no sooner sign me name on the register—which I was able to do even at that time—when I look around and the feller is gone clear away and took my valise[2] in the bargain. A statue anyway can't move off so fast, but if she's going to welcome let her say welcome, not this MCDC. . . .

SHEEAN. All right, then, Monaghan. But all I can say is, you've laid a disgrace on the name of Butler Street. I'll put the dime in for ya.

MONAGHAN. Don't connect me with it! It's a swindle, is all it is. In the first place, it's broke; in the second place, if

---

2. **valise** (və lēs´) *n.* small suitcase.

they do put it up it'll come down with the first high wind that strikes it.

SHEEAN. The engineers say it'll last forever!

MONAGHAN. And I say it'll topple into the river in a high wind! Look at the inside of her. She's all hollow!

SHEEAN. I've heard everything now, Monaghan. Just about everything. Good-bye.

MONAGHAN. What do you mean, good-bye? How am I to get back to Butler Street from here?

SHEEAN. You've got legs to walk.

MONAGHAN. I'll remind you that I come on the trolley.

SHEEAN. And I'll remind you that I paid your fare and I'm not repeating the kindness.

MONAGHAN. Sheean? You've stranded me!

[Music up and down]

Dramatic Speeches
List three adjectives you would use to describe Monaghan based on this dialogue.

Critical Thinking

1. **Key Ideas and Details (a)** Why does Monaghan object to the Roman numbers on the tablet the statue holds? **(b) Connect:** Do you agree with him? Explain why or why not.

2. **Key Ideas and Details (a) Infer:** Judging from the dialogue, how do you think that Sheean and Monaghan know each other? **(b) Speculate:** Do you think that they are good friends? Why or why not?

3. **Key Ideas and Details (a) Summarize:** List three excuses that Monaghan gives for not giving a dime to Sheean. **(b) Predict:** Do you think Monaghan will ever give money for the pedestal? Explain.

4. **Integration of Knowledge and Ideas (a)** What does Sheean learn about Monaghan from their conversation? Use details to explain. **(b)** Do you think it is good to learn the truth about someone even if it makes you like him or her less? Explain. *[Connect to the Big Question: Do others see us more clearly than we see ourselves?]*

Cite textual evidence to support your responses.

My Head Is Full of Starshine

A Monologue
Peg Kehret

My friend, Pam, says my head is full of starshine. She laughs when she says it. What she really means is that she doesn't always understand the poems I write, but she's glad that I write them.

She means she recognizes that I'm not like her, but it's OK for me to be different.

Pam is practical. Every night before she goes to sleep, Pam makes a list of what she needs to do the next day. She puts down items like return library books and hem dress for Margo's party on Saturday. When the list is made, she numbers the items in order of importance. If it's critical, it's Number One. Pam has never had to pay an overdue fine at the library and when Saturday arrives, her dress will not only be hemmed, it will be washed, ironed, and ready to wear.

I have a long history of library fines. Twenty cents here, fifty cents there. I'm always amazed to notice that a book is overdue. It just never seems like three weeks could go by so quickly. When Saturday comes, I'll be rummaging frantically through my closet, hoping to find something decent to wear to the party. But I wrote a birthday poem for Margo that I like a lot. It took me two days; I think Margo will like it, too.

My mother often wonders aloud why I can't be more like Pam. Just once, according to my mother, it would be nice to know more than twenty-four hours in advance that your child is performing in a school concert. I always forget to bring home the notices, or else I write something on the back and stick them in my desk. Either way, Mom doesn't get them in time to make plans.

On my last report card, Mr. Evans, my science teacher, wrote that I am not working up to my potential. He said I tend to daydream, instead of paying attention in class. I have to admit that's true, especially when we were learning about insects. Pam found the unit on insects fascinating. Too fascinating, if you ask me. One day she sat beside me in the cafeteria and announced that ladybugs eat aphids, spider mites, white-flies and mealybugs.

I said, "Yuck."

Pam continued blissfully on, informing me that ladybugs eat several times their own weight in insects every day. I put down my peanut butter sandwich and told Pam that the conversation was not very appetizing, but she was so excited about ladybugs that she didn't even hear me. She just babbled

Dramatic Speeches
What clue tells you this is a monologue and not a dialogue?

Vocabulary
practical (prak´ ti kəl) *adj.* levelheaded; efficient; realistic

rummaging (rum´ ij iŋ) *v.* searching through

potential (pō ten´ shəl) *n.* possibility; capability

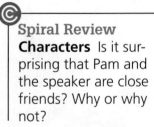

Spiral Review
Characters Is it surprising that Pam and the speaker are close friends? Why or why not?

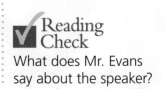
Reading Check
What does Mr. Evans say about the speaker?

on about how even the ladybug larvae eat insects and how a company in California collects the ladybugs and sells them to fruit growers, to eat the aphids off the fruit trees. I finally moved to a different table, but by then my appetite was gone.

Pam got an A in science. I only get As in English. Some kids moan and complain whenever they have to write an essay or a story, but I love assignments like that. I have a whole notebook full of ideas for stories and poems that I intend to write someday. I also have a list of good titles. My favorite title is "Magic Mud in Kansas City," but so far I haven't been able to think of a story to go with it.

I will, though. I always do. Usually it happens when I least expect it, like when I'm sitting in science class trying not to get sick as I listen to how certain animals eat their young. When Mr. Evans talks about gross things like that, I pretend my chair is a flying carpet, and I watch myself float out the window, up past the flagpole and over the trees. Sometimes I pretend that I fly beyond the moon, to a different galaxy, where I meet wonderful creatures with purple beards who ride on giant rabbits.

Maybe Pam is right. My head is full of starshine. Except for those library fines, I'm glad it is.

Dramatic Speeches
What do the details in this passage tell you about the speaker?

Critical Thinking

Cite textual evidence to support your responses.

1. **Key Ideas and Details (a) Compare and Contrast:** Which details from the text show how Pam is different from the speaker? **(b) Infer:** How does it make the speaker feel when Pam tells her that she has a head full of starshine? **(c) Draw Conclusions:** What does this detail tell you about their friendship?

2. **Key Ideas and Details (a) Analyze:** What does the last paragraph reveal about the speaker's feelings about herself? **(b) Speculate:** How do you think an actor playing the role of the speaker could use body language and vocal tone to express these feelings?

3. **Integration of Knowledge and Ideas** Even though they are quite different, Pam and the speaker are friends. What do you think they see in each other? Explain. *[Connect to the Big Question: Do others see us more clearly than we see ourselves?]*

Comparing Dramatic Speeches

© **1. Craft and Structure (a)** Rewrite these lines of dialogue as a monologue delivered by Sheean. **(b)** Rewrite these lines of the monologue as a dialogue between the speaker and Pam. **(c)** Share your chart with a partner.

from Grandpa and the Statue	As a Monologue
SHEEAN. I've come to talk to you about the fund, Monaghan. MONAGHAN. What fund is that? SHEEAN. The Statue of Liberty Fund. MONAGHAN. Oh, that.	
from My Head Is Full of Starshine	As a Dialogue
She means she recognizes that I'm not like her, but it's OK for me to be different.	

© **2. Craft and Structure (a)** Can you learn more about a character from a monologue or from a dialogue? Explain. **(b)** Can you learn more about a character in a play or in a story told by a narrator? Explain.

⏱ Timed Writing

Explanatory Text: Essay

Compare and contrast a dramatic speech given by each speaker. In an essay discuss how these dramatic speeches shape your attitude toward the characters. **(35 minutes)**

5-Minute Planner

1. Read the prompt carefully and completely.
2. Gather your ideas by answering these questions:
   - Which ideas in the speeches are familiar to you?
   - Which character do you feel you know best? Why?
3. Review each selection and take notes on the differences between the way the two speeches are presented. Use these notes as you write your essay.
4. Reread the prompt, and then draft your essay.

Writing Workshop

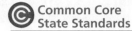 **Common Core State Standards**

Writing

2. Write informative/explanatory texts to examine a topic and convey ideas, concepts, and information through the selection, organization, and analysis of relevant content.

7. Conduct short research projects to answer a question, drawing on several sources and generating additional related, focused questions for further research and investigation.

Write an Explanatory Text

Exposition: Cause-and-Effect Essay

Defining the Form A **cause-and-effect essay** explains why something happens or what happens as a result of something else. You may use this type of writing in lab reports, historical accounts, persuasive essays, magazine articles, and speeches.

Assignment Write a cause-and-effect essay about a question or issue that interests you. Include the following elements.

✔ a *well-defined topic* that can be covered in a few pages

✔ information gathered from *reference materials and resources*

✔ *detailed, factual explanations* of events or situations and the *relationships among them*

✔ a clear organization with *transitions that indicate the relationships among details*

✔ error-free writing, including *correct subject-verb agreement*

To preview the criteria on which your cause-and-effect essay may be judged, see the rubric on page 885.

 Writing Workshop: *Work in Progress*

Review the work you did on page 859.

WRITE GUY
Jeff Anderson, M.Ed.

What Do You Notice?

Cause-and-Effect Relationships

The following sentences are from Robert Zimmerman's "Life Without Gravity." Read them several times.

Floating about in space is too easy. If astronauts don't force themselves to exercise, their muscles become so feeble that when they return to Earth they can't even walk.

Discuss these questions with a partner:

- What do you notice about these sentences?
- How are the ideas in the second sentence related to the idea presented in the first sentence?

Think about ways you might show cause-and-effect relationships in your writing.

Reading-Writing Connection

To get the feel for cause-and-effect writing, read "Life Without Gravity" by Robert Zimmerman on page 424.

Prewriting/Planning Strategies

Choose a topic. Use one of these strategies:

- **Brainstorming** Sometimes the best way to find a topic is to just start writing. Write for five minutes about whatever questions come to mind. Use phrases such as "What causes . . ." or "Why does . . ." to begin each question. Circle any questions that could make a good topic.

- **Imagining a Walk** Close your eyes and imagine yourself walking through a house, apartment, or other place you know well. Observe the objects, people, or activities that you "see" along the way. To find items that suggest cause-and-effect relationships, ask, "What caused this?" or "What effects does this have?" Jot down several ideas, then choose your topic from these items.

Narrow your topic. A topic with many causes and effects, such as the causes and effects of storms, is far too broad. Instead, narrow your topic to focus on a single cause or a single effect. For example, the effects of a tornado—a single cause—would be appropriate. Use a web like the one shown to narrow your topic. Write your topic in the center and surround it with subtopics. Then, note causes or effects connected to each subtopic. Consider whether any of the subtopics would make a good focus for your essay.

Conduct research. Do research to fill in any gaps in your knowledge about your topic. First ask yourself a series of questions about your topic to guide your research. Then, use library resources and online references, or interview an expert on the topic to find answers to the questions you posed. Continue to generate focused questions for further research. Use a two-column chart to help you gather details. In one column, list the causes involved in your event or situation. In the other column, list the effects.

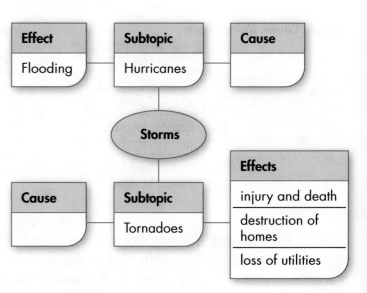

Drafting Strategies

 **Common Core State Standards**

Writing

2.a. Introduce a topic clearly, previewing what is to follow; organize ideas, concepts, and information, using strategies such as definition, classification, comparison/contrast, and cause/effect; include formatting, graphics, and multimedia when useful to aiding comprehension.

2.b. Develop the topic with relevant facts, definitions, concrete details, quotations, or other information and examples.

4. Produce clear and coherent writing in which the development, organization, and style are appropriate to task, purpose, and audience.

Write a strong introduction. Your introduction is the first thing your audience will read. Include a sentence or two explaining the importance of your topic and then identify the main points you will make in your essay.

Organize logically. Before you begin the body of your essay, decide how you want to organize your details. Use these suggestions:

- If you are writing about one effect with many causes, devote one paragraph to each cause and one paragraph to the effect.

- If you are writing about a single cause with many effects, devote a paragraph to each effect.

- If you are writing about a series of causes and effects, organize your paragraphs in chronological, or time, order.

Single Cause, Many Effects **Many Causes, Single Effect**

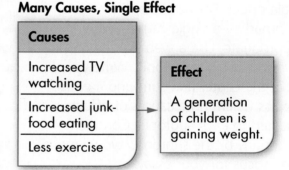

Explain causes and effects. Prove the cause-and-effect relationships you describe. As you draft, explain the logic of each cause-and-effect relationship you present. Use specific statistics, dates, names, or places whenever possible. Consider adding text features, such as headings and charts, to clarify your main ideas. Avoid plagiarism by giving credit to any ideas you use that are not your own, following a standard format for citation.

Use the SEE technique. For each main idea you identify, use the SEE technique to add depth to your essay. In a paragraph, first, write a **S**tatement. Next, write a sentence that **E**xtends the idea. Finally, write a sentence that **E**laborates on the extension.

Writers on Writing

Laurence Yep On Showing Causes and Effects

> Laurence Yep is the author of an excerpt from the novel *Dragonwings* (p. 728) and an excerpt from the dramatization *Dragonwings* (p. 730).

I often get asked what caused me to write *Dragonwings*, and the passage that follows is from an article that I wrote about it. The revisions show how much work I do on a draft. Mark Twain once said, "The difference between the almost right word and the right word is . . . the difference between the lightning bug and the lightning." As you'll see, I tried to find the "right word" to show what inspired me to write this novel.

" . . . it takes me a minimum of seven drafts . . ."
— Laurence Yep

Professional Model:

from *"A Cord to the Past"*

As a writer and as an individual, I have been drawn to the stories of those Chinese Americans who have learned to live with a kind of grace on the borderland between two cultures. . . . What first ~~attracted~~ drew me to the story of Fung Joe Guey, the Chinese American aviator, was the scope of his mind. Here was a Chinese American who ~~He~~ had built and flown his own airplane just six years after the Wright brothers had flown at Kitty Hawk. In fact, I did not incorporate all of his real mechanical achievements in the novel, Dragonwings—which included his own telephone system. When his ~~imaginary~~ fictional counterpart, Windrider, dreams that he is a dragon, it was symbolic of Fung Joe Guey's own imagination: that ability to grasp with the mind and heart what he could not grasp with the hand.

I substituted "drew" for "attracted" because I wanted to indicate the effect of Fung Joe Guey's life on me, how compelled I was to write the story.

I reversed the word order to emphasize his specialness. The normal order would only make it a statement of fact.

I changed "imaginary" to "fictional" because I used "imagination" shortly afterwards. I didn't want to sound repetitive.

Revising Strategies

State main ideas clearly. Simply by starting a new paragraph, you signal readers that a new idea is coming up. Effective writers clearly state the main idea in each paragraph. To analyze the connections among your other sentences, use color-coding.

Reread each paragraph. Use two highlighters—one color to mark phrases that present causes and another to mark those that discuss effects. Evaluate the connections between the two. Go back and add transitions such as *because of* and *as a result* to help readers see cause-and-effect connections.

Common Core State Standards

Writing
2.c. Use appropriate transitions to create cohesion and clarify the relationships among ideas and concepts.

Language
1. Demonstrate command of the conventions of standard English grammar and usage when writing or speaking.

Model: Color-Coding Causes and Effects

A generation of children is gaining weight. Instead of running and playing outside, many children sit in front of the TV, play video games or surf the Internet. While doing so, young children often eat junk food to pass the time. Because this time is so unstructured, they don't monitor how much food they are actually eating. In time, these young children are becoming very overweight.

Use the appropriate verb tense. Generally, you should use one verb tense consistently throughout your paper. However, to show the order of events, you may need to shift tenses. Review your draft to determine the tenses of most of your verbs. Circle any verbs that are in a different tense. If these verbs do not show events happening at different times or if they show a recurring event, consider changing them.

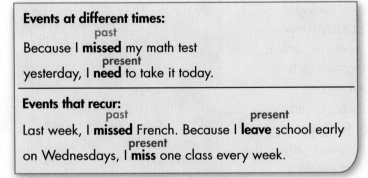

Events at different times:
                       past
Because I **missed** my math test
                present
yesterday, I **need** to take it today.

Events that recur:
              past   present
Last week, I **missed** French. Because I **leave** school early
                 present
on Wednesdays, I **miss** one class every week.

Peer Review

Ask a classmate to review your draft to help you determine whether you have logical cause-and-effect links.

Correcting Subject-Verb Agreement with Compound Subjects

Incorrect subject-verb agreement occurs whenever a subject disagrees with its verb in number.

Identifying Compound Subjects A compound subject consists of two subjects joined by a conjunction such as *and, or,* or *nor.* When the subjects joined are plural, they take a plural verb. When the subjects joined are singular, the following rules will help you make sure that a compound subject agrees with its verb.

Two or more singular subjects joined by *and* take a plural verb.

▶ **Example:** *Running **and** tennis* **are** both fun sports.

Singular subjects joined by *or* or *nor* take a singular verb.

▶ **Example:** *Running **or** playing tennis* **is** good exercise.
Neither *running **nor** playing tennis* **is** a waste of time.

When singular and plural subjects are joined by *or* or *nor*, the verb must agree with the closer subject.

▶ **Example:** Neither the *roast **nor** the *potatoes* **are** cooking.
Concert *tickets **or** a fancy *dinner* **is** a great gift.

PH | WRITING COACH

Further instruction and practice are available in *Prentice Hall Writing Coach*.

Fixing Subject-Verb Agreement To fix subject-verb agreement with compound subjects, use one of the following methods.

1. If the subjects joined are plural, use a plural verb.

2. If the subjects are singular and joined by *and*, use a plural verb. See the example above.

3. If the subjects are singular and joined by *or* or *nor*, use a singular verb. See the examples above.

4. If singular and plural subjects are joined by *or* or *nor*, the verb agrees with the closer subject. See examples above.

Grammar in Your Writing

In your draft, underline any subjects joined by *and, or,* or *nor.* Then, circle the verbs. If necessary, fix the subject-verb agreement using one of the methods above.

Student Model: Sarah Langsam, South Orange, NJ

 Common Core
State Standards

Language
2.b. Spell correctly.

The Invention of Cell Phones

Imagine our world today without cell phones. This portable way of communicating is a part of many people's everyday lives. If we did not have cell phones, moms would not be able to call from the store, more kids might have trouble staying in touch, and emergencies would be harder to report.

> Sarah defines her topic in the first paragraph.

However people did, and still do, manage without them. Cell phones weren't invented that long ago. In 1973, Dr. Martin Cooper invented the first portable handset and soon after created the first prototype of a cellular phone. Four years later, cell phones became available to the public and cell phone testing began.

> Sarah uses facts in her explanation.

What effect has the invention of cell phones had on the world? With everything in life there are pros and cons. Today, most teenagers own cell phones. This means there is no excuse for not letting a parent or guardian know where you are or for not having your cell phone charged. And of course the most important thing is never to lose your phone.

> Sarah restates her topic and begins to support it with examples.

Cell phones have caused a change in our economy. Although the cost of cell phones has gone down greatly over the years, they are still very expensive. As a result, for families that are not very wealthy, owning a cell phone might affect their income badly. However, loads of money is coming in to phone companies every month from cell phone bills.

Many people say that cell phones cause a disturbance. You cannot go on a train or shop in a mall without constantly hearing phones ring and listening to other people's conversations. The effect of this is that more people are stressed and being disturbed by cell phones. Others are disturbed by not having cell phones. A teacher in school left her cell phone at school over the weekend. She was in the office on Monday recalling her story angrily, reporting that it was an awful experience and that she could not function without her phone.

> Sarah gives examples to show how cell phones can be disturbing.

Although there are many negative aspects of cell phones, these items have also caused our world to be more secure. If you ask people why they first bought their cell phone, many will mention safety. Cell phones are very effective when people get into car accidents and can call "911" immediately. Parents can always know where their kids are.

The invention of cell phones has changed our lives immensely. There are positive and negative effects. However, despite the nuisance some cell phones present, I believe the safety issues cell phones solve can make us all feel a little more secure.

> Sarah sums up the effects of cell phones in her conclusion.

Editing and Proofreading

Focus on spelling irregular plurals.

- Change *y* to *i* and add *-es* to nouns that end in a consonant and *y (memory/memories)*.
- Do not change the *y,* but add *-s* to nouns that end in a vowel and *y* (play/plays, key/keys).
- For most nouns ending in *f* or *fe,* change the *f* or *fe* to *ve* and add *-s.* (elf/elves, wife/wives).

Some nouns' base spelling changes in the plural form *(foot/feet).* Nouns that are not countable do not have plural forms *(cash).*

Spiral Review
Earlier in the unit, you learned about **sentence functions and endmarks** (p. 858). Check your essay to be sure that you have used endmarks correctly to punctuate your sentences.

Publishing and Presenting

Consider one of the following ways to share your writing:

Present a diagram. On a posterboard or an overhead slide, create a diagram of the cause-and-effect chain in your essay. Read your essay aloud, pointing out appropriate parts of the diagram as you go.

Produce a talk show. Work with a partner, taking turns being a talk-show host and a guest expert. Answer questions about your topic. Then, ask questions about your partner's topic.

Reflecting on Your Writing

Writer's Journal Jot down your answer to this question:

Which prewriting strategy was most useful for generating a topic?

Rubric for Self-Assessment

Find evidence in your writing to address each category. Then, use the rating scale to grade your work.

Criteria	Rating Scale (not very → very)				
	1	2	3	4	5
Focus: How well is your topic defined?	1	2	3	4	5
Organization: How organized is your information from reference materials?	1	2	3	4	5
Support/Elaboration: How well do your facts explain the relationships between events?	1	2	3	4	5
Style: How smooth are the transitions between elements?	1	2	3	4	5
Conventions: How correct is your word usage?	1	2	3	4	5

Vocabulary Workshop

Borrowed and Foreign Words

English contains more **borrowed and foreign** words than any other language in the world. If you say "take the car out of the garage, because we are going to the ranch in the canyon," you have used words borrowed from both Spanish and French.

The English language is infused with words from other cultures and languages. These words enrich our language and are a road-map to our history. The chart shows words that are borrowed from other languages.

Common Core State Standards

Language
3. Use knowledge of language and its conventions when writing, speaking, reading, or listening.
4.c. Consult general and specialized reference materials, both print and digital, to find the pronunciation of a word or determine or clarify its precise meaning or its part of speech.
4.d. Verify the preliminary determination of the meaning of a word or phrase.

Word	Borrowed from	Meaning
taco	Spanish	a tortilla filled with meat and vegetables
denim	French	cotton fabric used for making jeans
sketch	Dutch	to draw quickly
piano	Italian	a large musical instrument
ski	Scandinavian	sliding on long boards over snow or water

Practice A Choose one of the borrowed words from the chart to complete each sentence. After completing the sentence, write the language it came from.

1. When it's cool in the springtime, I wear my _____ jacket.

2. Alfonso can play a simple tune on the _____.

3. Carita uses shredded lettuce when she makes a _____.

4. Most artists draw a _____ before they begin to paint.

5. I like to _____ all day when there is enough snow on the ground.

Practice B The list shows common examples of borrowed words. Choose at least three of the borrowed words and write a short paragraph using those words. If necessary, use a dictionary.

Culture of Origin	Food	Clothing	Animals
Morocco			gorilla
China	ketchup		
France		jeans	
Germany	hamburger		
Italy	spaghetti		
Native American	squash	moccasin	
Spain and Latin America		poncho	coyote

Activity Create a glossary of borrowed and foreign words. Make notecards like the one shown for words such as the following:

cous cous	futon	mirage
mukluk	mufti	timpani

Challenge yourself to create notecards for at least six more borrowed or foreign words. Verify your work by checking a dictionary.

Word:

Pronunciation:

Part of Speech:

Definition:

Origin of Culture:

Comprehension and Collaboration

Using a dictionary, identify five words commonly used in English that come from each of these languages: Spanish, Japanese, Italian, and a language of your choice.

Communications Workshop

Conducting an Interview

When you research a topic, you may sometimes find it necessary to interview someone in order to get the information you need. Follow these steps to conduct a successful interview.

Learn the Skills
Use these strategies to complete the activity on page 889.

An interview is a conversation powered by questions and answers. Before the interview, have a list of probing questions that will elicit the information you need.

Identify your purpose. It is important that you know what kind of information you would like to get from the interview. Do background research on your topic to focus your questions.

Create probing questions. Use your research to write a list of questions. You will use this list at the interview, but you can also ask other questions that come to mind as you listen. You may need to ask follow-up questions to clarify points and get examples.

Listen carefully. Listening is more than just hearing. Sometimes you think you know what someone is going to say, so you do not really hear what they *are* saying. Break this habit by rephrasing what the speaker said, or by asking for clarification before moving on. If you are listening to acquire new information or to evaluate a point of view, pay close attention to both main points and details. Here are some tips for listening effectively:

- Do not look around. Focus your eyes and ears on the speaker.
- Concentrate on what the speaker is saying. Do not be distracted by his or her manner of speaking.
- Put away anything that may distract you.
- Keep a pencil and paper handy to take notes.

Eliminate barriers to listening. Avoid distractions when listening. Sit close to the speaker and stay focused on what he or she is saying, not on other things that are going on in the room.

Take notes. Taking notes will help you remember what a speaker says. Do not write down every word. Instead, try to capture the speaker's main points and a few supporting details. Later, review your notes to be sure you understand them.

Common Core State Standards

Speaking and Listening

1.a. Come to discussions prepared, having read or researched material under study; explicitly draw on that preparation by referring to evidence on the topic, text, or issue to probe and reflect on ideas under discussion.

1.b. Follow rules for collegial discussions, track progress toward specific goals and deadlines, and define individual roles as needed.

1.c. Pose questions that elicit elaboration and respond to others' questions and comments with relevant observations and ideas that bring the discussion back on topic as needed.

Practice the Skills

Ⓒ **Presentation of Knowledge and Ideas** Use what you have learned in this workshop to complete the following activity.

> ### ACTIVITY: Conduct an Interview
>
> Interview a community member, friend, or relative on a subject about which he or she is knowledgeable. If possible, ask a partner to videotape your interview. Follow the steps below.
> - Before the interview, do background research on your topic.
> - Make a list of focused questions.
> - Listen carefully, analyze main ideas and details, rephrase what the speaker says, and ask for clarifications as needed.
> - Focus on what the speaker is saying, and block out distractions.
> - Take notes to capture the main ideas and details.

Refer to the Interview Checklist as you prepare for your interview. Then, use the checklist to give feedback on the videotapes of your classmates' interviews.

> ### Interview Checklist
>
> **Preparing for the Interview**
> Does the preparation meet all of the requirements of the activity?
> Check all that apply.
>
> ❏ The purpose of the interview is clear.
> ❏ The interviewer has performed background research on the topic.
> ❏ The list of questions is designed to draw out interesting answers.
> ❏ The questions are focused and clear.
>
> **Conducting the Interview**
> Did the interviewer follow rules for listening? Check all that apply.
>
> ❏ The interviewer concentrated on what the speaker said.
> ❏ The interviewer rephrased main ideas and details and asked for clarifications.
> ❏ The interviewer sat close to the speaker and avoided distractions.
> ❏ The interviewer took notes.

Ⓒ **Comprehension and Collaboration** With your classmates, review the completed Interview Checklists. As a group, discuss which aspects of the interview process were most challenging and which were most rewarding.

Cumulative Review

**Common Core
State Standards**

RL.7.3, RL.7.5; L.7.4.a; W.7.2
[For the full wording of the standards, see the standards chart in the front of your textbook.]

I. Reading Literature

Directions: *Read this excerpt from a play. Then, answer each question that follows.*

[*LUKE is riding in the front passenger seat of MOM'S new van. She has just picked him up from school.*]

Luke: I got an A on that English essay. Mr. Hornsby said it was "insightful."

Mom: [*distractedly*] That's nice, honey.

Luke: Yeah, I got a goal in soccer during gym today, too. Steve was in the goal. You know Steve, right? He's really huge. But I just snuck one past him. My gym teacher said she was impressed.

Mom: [*raising an eyebrow*] Do you have any other amazing <u>accomplishments</u> to report?

Luke: Well . . . I wrote that really long thank you note to Grandma. And, um—I'm really proud that I've been getting to school on time. I haven't missed homeroom once. Mia has missed it at least eight times.

Mom: Let's leave your sister out of this.

Luke: I'll probably get a perfect attendance award.

Mom: [*mildly*] I doubt it. There was that day you were sick.

Luke: Oh. . . Well, I still think I deserve some kind of reward.

Mom: [*holding back a smile*] Like what?

Luke: [*hopefully*] I saw an awesome new computer at the store.

Mom: I was thinking of something much less expensive.

Luke: [*slumps in his seat, then brightens as a new idea comes to him*] Can the guys spend the night? We want to watch the game.

Mom: Well . . .

Luke: [*warming to his topic*] The game won't be over until 11. Later if it goes into extra innings.

Mom: Well, it is Friday night. I think that sounds okay.

Luke: And you have to order pizza.

Mom: [*smiling*] I'd be happy to provide pizza to such an accomplished scholar and athlete.

Luke: And Mia has to spend the night at Grandma's.

Mom: I thought we were leaving your sister out of this.

Luke: [*looking excited*] Exactly! And that's why she needs to be left out of the house for my sleep over.

Mom: Now, that's what I call insightful.

1. What is Luke's **motive** for bragging to his mother?
   A. He wants to play soccer.
   B. He wants her to give him a reward.
   C. He wants to prove he is smarter than his sister.
   D. He wants to use his mom's computer.

2. Which sentence *best* describes Mom's reaction to her son's bragging?
   A. She is amused.
   B. She does not really care what he is saying.
   C. She is angry.
   D. She is not listening.

3. Which event in the play's **plot** happens first?
   A. The boys order pizza.
   B. Luke does well in school.
   C. Mom allows Luke's friends to stay over.
   D. Luke gets a perfect attendance reward.

4. Which sentence *best* describes the **conflict** in the play?
   A. Luke and Mia both have trouble getting to school on time.
   B. Luke and his mother disagree about the appropriate reward for his hard work at school.
   C. Luke's mom wants him to work harder in school and sports.
   D. Luke's mom wants to ignore his sister.

5. **Vocabulary** Which word or phrase is closest in meaning to the underlined word accomplishments?
   A. grades
   B. soccer goals
   C. achievements
   D. compliments

6. How do the **stage directions** contribute to the play?
   A. They tell the actors where to sit or stand.
   B. They tell the audience where to look.
   C. They give the reader more information about the character's position, expressions, and emotions.
   D. They tell you what the characters look like.

7. Which of Mom's **character traits** is evident in this passage?
   A. She has a sense of humor.
   B. She is very strict when it comes to her children's grades in school.
   C. She enjoys the company of her children's friends.
   D. She does not like to reward her children.

8. Which of the following *best* describes the **dramatic form** of this passage?
   A. dialogue
   B. monologue
   C. act
   D. set

Timed Writing

9. In a short essay, explain whether the **characters** in the play can be described as **foils. Support** your answer with **details** from the text.

GO ON

II. Reading Informational Text

Directions: *Read the passage. Then, answer each question that follows.*

**Common Core
State Standards**

RI.7.1, RI.7.5; L.7.1
[For the full wording of the standards, see the standards chart in the front of your textbook.]

Would you like an extra hour to sleep each morning? If so, you are not alone. Most American teenagers get about seven hours of sleep each night. Sleep researchers say adolescents and young teens actually need 9.2 hours. That is more than adults and young children need.

Stumbling through the day like a zombie can be dangerous. For example, the National Highway Traffic Safety Administration says young, sleepy drivers are involved in about 50,000 accidents each year. Lack of sleep can also result in poor grades.

Some adults think teenagers who sleep late are lazy. However, Professor Mary Carskadon, a sleep researcher at Brown University, says sleeping in is healthy. She thinks schools should start later. Most high schools in the United States start classes at 7 a.m. Carskadon says 8, or 8:30, would be a better time.

Not only do teenagers need more sleep, but they need it at differ-ent times. <u>Melatonin</u> is a hormone produced daily by the human brain. It tells you that you are sleepy. Research shows that teenagers produce melatonin later at night than other people do. The result is that teen-agers are often wide awake when their parents want them to go to sleep. Teenagers' melatonin levels remain high in the early morning. That means they are still sleepy, even after school has started.

1. What is the author's **main argument?**
   A. Schools should start classes later.
   B. Mary Carskadon is the expert on sleep.
   C. Teenagers should sleep more at night.
   D. Teenagers need more sleep in the morning.

2. What is one **claim** the author uses to sup-port the main argument?
   A. Teenagers produce melatonin later at night than other people.
   B. Schools should begin at 8 or 8:30.
   C. Most teenagers are lazy because they do not get enough sleep.
   D. Teenagers are forced to go to bed when they are wide awake.

3. Which piece of **evidence** supports Professor Carskadon's **assertion** that it is healthy for teenagers to sleep in?
   A. Teenagers produce more melatonin than their parents.
   B. Teenagers' melatonin levels remain high in the morning.
   C. Teenagers are often sleepy even once school has started.
   D. Sleepy drivers are involved in car accidents.

III. Writing and Language Conventions

Directions: *Read the script for the multimedia report. Then, answer each question that follows.*

Slide 1 (1) Visual: Title Slide: Stick Insects
(2) *Script:* There are 2,000 species of stick insects, including 41 in North America. (3) They are the coolest bugs in you're backyard!
Slide 2 (4) *Visual:* Walking Stick
(5) *Script:* Adults look like sticks and their eggs resemble seeds. (6) This is called camouflage. (7) Birds cannot eat bugs they cannot see.
Slide 3 (8) *Visual:* Huge walking stick on man's face
(9) *Script:* India is home to some of the world's biggest stick insects. (10) Some are over twelve inches long. (11) In the United States, we do not have none this large.

---

1. Which of these titles best indicates the **focus** of the author's topic?
  A. Insects I Love
  B. How to Find a Stick Insect in Your Backyard
  C. Learning About Stick Insects
  D. Keeping Stick Insects as Pets

2. Which of the following is an accurate summary of the report's **organization?**
  A. slide, introduction, slide
  B. slide, slide, slide
  C. introduction, script, slide
  D. slide, script, slide, script, slide, script

3. Where could the writer most effectively put the **interjection,** "Wow"?
  A. At the beginning of sentence 2
  B. Before introducing the second slide
  C. After sentence 10
  D. At the very end of the presentation

4. Which of the following revisions to sentence 3 corrects a **common usage** error?
  A. Their the coolest bugs in you're backyard!
  B. They are the coolest bugs in you backyard!
  C. There the coolest bugs in your backyard!
  D. They are the coolest bugs in your backyard!

5. How should sentence 11 be revised to fix a **double negative?**
  A. In the United States, we don't have none this large.
  B. In the United States, we do not have any this large.
  C. In the United States, we do not have any.
  D. We do not have none this large in the United States.

Performance Tasks

**Common Core
State Standards**

RL.7.2, RL.7.3, RL.7.5, RL.7.7; W.7.2,
W.7.2.a, W.7.2.b, W.7.2.c, W.7.2.f,
W.9.a; SL.7.4, SL.7.5; L.7.1, L.7.2, L.7.3
[For the full wording of the standards,
see the standards chart in the front of
your textbook.]

Directions: *Follow the instructions to complete the tasks
below as required by your teacher.*

*As you work on each task, incorporate both general academic
vocabulary and literary terms you learned in this unit.*

Writing

Task 1: Literature [RL.7.3; W.7.2]

Analyze Setting

*Write an essay in which you analyze how the
setting of* A Christmas Carol *shapes the
characters or plot.*

- Identify details from the play that reveal the
  time period as nineteenth-century England.

- Discuss how the playwright used the
  historical time to support the major points
  in the play. Point out the kind of work
  people did and the way they socialized.
  Discuss differences between the wealthy
  and the poor, and analyze why these class
  differences existed.

- Develop your ideas with relevant details,
  information, or examples from the play.

- Use appropriate transitions to show
  relationships between or among your ideas.
  Show comparisons with transitions such as
  likewise, similarly, and *in addition to.* Show
  contrasts with transitions such as *on the
  other hand* or *in contrast.*

Task 2: Literature [RL.7.5; W.7.2]

Analyze Dramatic Structure

*Write an essay in which you analyze how a
drama's structure adds to its meaning.*

- Choose a drama in this unit and analyze its
  parts, including its division into acts or
  scenes and its dialogue and stage
  directions. Explain how each part of the
  drama contributes to the characterization,
  setting, mood, and tone.

- Develop your analysis with examples from
  the drama. Use transitions to clarify the
  relationships between or among ideas.

- As you edit, make sure there is agreement
  between subjects and verbs and between
  pronouns and antecedents. Check for
  correct spelling.

Task 3: Literature [RL.7.3; W.7.2]

Analyze Characters' Motives

*Write an essay in which you analyze the
motives of various characters in "The Monsters
Are Due on Maple Street."*

- Select at least two characters from the play
  upon which to base your essay.

- Cite several examples of dialogue that tell
  what each character says, thinks, or does or
  that reveal a character's reasons for taking
  an action. Remember that information
  contained in stage directions might provide
  clues to a character's motives.

- Explain the connections between the
  characters' actions and specific events in the
  plot. Discuss why the characters behave in
  similar or different ways, and cite evidence
  from the play to support your response.

- Use a strategy, such as comparison-and-
  contrast organization, to organize your
  ideas logically. Use transitions and
  transitional phrases to connect your
  sentences and paragraphs smoothly.

- Provide a concluding statement that
  supports the information you present.

Speaking and Listening

Ⓒ Task 4: Literature [RL.7.7; SL.7.5]

Analyze Techniques in Different Media

Give a multimedia presentation in which you compare and contrast a script from this unit to its film or stage version.

- Read a drama from this unit. Consider how you visualized the presentation. Then, view a film or stage version of the same drama.

- Compare and contrast the written drama with its film or stage version. Analyze the effects of techniques that are unique to each medium. For example, consider the effects of lighting, sound, color, and camera angles in a film.

- Include multimedia components, such as film clips, tape recordings, or visual displays to clarify your claims about the different techniques used in the formats and to emphasize the major points of your presentation.

- Choose words and phrases for your intended effect and eliminate wordiness or repeated ideas.

Ⓒ Task 5: Literature [RL.7.3, RL.7.5; SL.7.4]

Analyze Dialogue

Give an oral presentation in which you analyze the dialogue in a play in this unit.

- Analyze examples of dialogue in your chosen play that provide key information about a character. Discuss the character's word choice, syntax, and possibly dialect.

- Cite specific passages of dialogue to support your analysis of the character. Explain how the dialogue, in addition to developing the character, also advances the plot and develops the conflict in the play.

- As you give your oral presentation, use appropriate eye contact, adequate volume, and clear pronunciation.

- If necessary, consult a digital dictionary to find the pronunciations of unknown words from the text.

Ⓒ Task 6: Literature [RL.7.2, SL.7.4]

Present a Summary

Give a presentation in which you identify the theme of one of the plays in the unit. Support your suggested theme's development in an objective summary of the text.

- In the introduction of your presentation, state your interpretation of the theme, or insight about life, of your chosen play.

- Use your own words to summarize the main ideas and significant details from the beginning, middle, and end of the play. Include events and ideas that support the theme you suggest. Do not include your personal opinions or reactions to the play.

- Use transitions such as *first, next,* and *then* to clarify the order of event in your summary.

- As you speak, establish eye contact with your audience. Speak with appropriate volume, and pronounce words and phrases clearly.

THE BIG ?

Do others see us more clearly than we see ourselves?

At the beginning of Unit 5, you wrote a response to the Big Question. Now that you have completed the unit, write a new response. Discuss how your initial ideas have been either changed or reinforced. Cite specific examples from the literature in this unit, from other subject areas, and from your own life to support your ideas. Use Big Question vocabulary words (see p. 721) in your response.

Featured Titles

In this unit, you have read a variety of dramatic works. Continue to read on your own. Select works that you enjoy, but challenge yourself to explore new playwrights and works of increasing depth and complexity. The titles suggested below will help you get started.

Literature

Roald Dahl's Charlie and the Chocolate Factory: A Play
Adapted by Richard R. George

In this **play,** adapted from Dahl's novel, poor Charlie Bucket wins one of five golden tickets to tour Willy Wonka's chocolate factory—a place no one has been allowed inside for a long time. As his spoiled competitors start disappearing, the question remains: Can Charlie outlast the others in Wonka's fun-house world of chocolate rivers and everlasting chewing gum?

Eight Science Fiction Plays

Included in this wide-ranging science-fiction collection are the **plays** *Only Slightly Different* by Bruce Goldstone and *A Clash of Wills* by Mary Canrobert.

Sorry, Wrong Number and The Hitchhiker
by Lucille Fletcher
Dramatists Play Service, Inc., 1998 **EXEMPLAR TEXT**

In the first of these two suspenseful **plays,** a woman overhears a plot to kill her. In the second, a man on a cross-country trip is followed by a ghostly hitchhiker.

Days of the Knights
by Christopher Maynard

Lord Henry's castle is under attack! Mixing **fiction** with **nonfiction,** Maynard re-creates a medieval siege, complete with knights and armor, battlements and drawbridges, swords and longbows. Readers learn interesting facts as they witness a thrilling battle.

Dragonwings
by Laurence Yep
Dramatists Play Service, Inc., 1998 **EXEMPLAR TEXT**

In this **play,** set in the early twentieth century, eight-year-old Moon Shadow sails from China to San Francisco to live with a father he has never met. He quickly comes to admire his fascinating father, Windrider, who dreams of building a flying machine and is willing to endure scorn, hardship, and prejudice to make his dream come true.

Short Dramas and Teleplays

This collection of **plays** features such writers as Jack London, Mark Twain, and Edgar Allan Poe. Many of these plays feature characters that gain a better understanding of themselves through their interactions with others.

Informational Texts

Creating the X-Men: How Comic Books Come to Life
by James Buckley, Jr.

In this **nonfiction** text, comic book creators take readers behind the scenes to show how they use character, dialogue, plot, and design to bring their popular superheroes to life.

Gandhi: A Photographic Story of a Life
by Amy Pastan

Gandhi proved that nonviolent, peaceful movements can succeed in creating powerful changes. His **biography** shows the impact one person can have, even when confronting a mighty empire.

Preparing to Read Complex Texts

Attentive Reading As you read on your own, ask yourself questions about the text. The questions shown below and others that you ask as you read will help you learn and enjoy literature even more.

 **Common Core State Standards**

Reading Literature/Informational Text 10. By the end of the year, read and comprehend literature, including stories, dramas, and poems, and literary nonfiction in the grades 6–8 text complexity band proficiently, with scaffolding as needed at the high end of the range.

When reading drama, ask yourself...

- Who is the main character? What struggles does this character face?
- What other characters are important? How do these characters relate to the main character?
- Where and when does the play take place? Do the time and place of the setting affect the characters? If so, how?
- Do the characters, settings, and events seem real? Why or why not?
- How does the play end? How does the ending make me feel?
- What theme or insight do I think the playwright is expressing? Do I find that theme to be important and true?

© **Key Ideas and Details**

- Does the play have a narrator? If so, what information does the narrator provide?
- Does the playwright include background information? If so, how does this help me understand what I am reading?
- How many acts are in this play? What happens in each act?
- Does the dialogue sound like real speech? Are there specific passages that seem especially real? Are there any that seem false?
- What do the stage directions tell me about the ways characters move, speak, and feel? In what other ways do I learn about the characters?
- At what point in the play do I feel the most suspense? Why?
- What speech or passage in the play do I like the most? Why?
- Does the playwright seem to have a positive or a negative point of view? How do I think the playwright's point of view affects the story?
- Do I agree with the playwright's point of view? Why or why not?

© **Craft and Structure**

- Does the play remind me of others I have read or seen? If so, how?
- In what ways is the play different from others I have read or seen?
- What new information or ideas have I gained from reading this play?
- What actors would I choose to play each role in this play?
- If I were to be in this play, what role would I want?
- Would I recommend this play to others? Why or why not?

© **Integration of Ideas**

THE BIG ?

Community or *individual*— which is more important?

898

Themes in the Oral Tradition

www.PHLitOnline.com

Hear It!
- Selection summary audio
- Selection audio
- BQ Tunes

See It!
- Author videos
- Big Question video
- Get Connected videos
- Background videos
- More about the authors
- Illustrated vocabulary words
- Vocabulary flashcards

Do It!
- Interactive journals
- Interactive graphic organizers
- Grammar tutorials
- Interactive vocabulary games
- Test practice

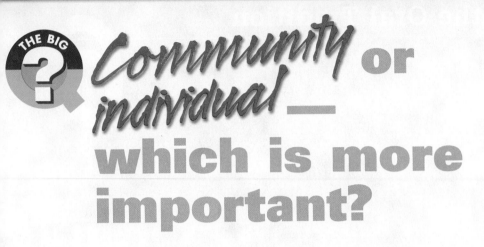

Community or individual— which is more important?

In many parts of our lives, we celebrate the individual—encouraging people to reach their personal best and to pursue their own dreams. Each individual has unique qualities and beliefs. However, an individual may also be part of a family or group that shares common cultural beliefs, traditions, or customs. Even these families and groups are part of a larger community.

Communities help individuals by providing services, support, and opportunities. Yet, sometimes the rights or desires of an individual may conflict with those of his or her community. In these cases, it can be difficult to find a fair solution.

Exploring the Big Question

Collaboration: One-on-One Discussion Start thinking about the Big Question by making a list of conflicts between individuals and their communities. Describe one specific example of each of the following situations:

- A school rule that students do not believe is fair
- A situation in which one family member does not want to do what the rest of the family is doing
- A sacrifice that one person is asked to make in order to help many others
- A decision made by someone in power that affects a large group of people

Share your examples with a partner. For each example, discuss whether the interests of the community or the individual seem more important. Use the Big Question vocabulary in your discussion.

Connecting to the Literature Each reading in this unit will give you additional insight into the Big Question.

PHLit
Online!
www.PHLitOnline.com
- Big Question video
- Illustrated vocabulary words
- Interactive vocabulary games
- BQ Tunes

Learning Big Question Vocabulary

Common Core State Standards

Speaking and Listening
1. Engage effectively in a range of collaborative discussions with diverse partners on *grade 7 topics, texts, and issues,* building on others' ideas and expressing their own clearly.

Language
6. Acquire and use accurately grade-appropriate general academic and domain-specific words and phrases; gather vocabulary knowledge when considering a word or phrase important to comprehension or expression.

Acquire and Use Academic Vocabulary Academic vocabulary is the language you encounter in textbooks and on standardized tests. Review the definitions of these academic vocabulary words.

---

common (käm´ ən) *adj.* shared; public

community (kə myoo´ nə tē) *n.* group living in a particular area

culture (kul´ chər) *n.* customs of a group or community

diversity (də vur´ sə tē) *n.* variety

duty (doot´ ē) *n.* responsibility

environment (en vī´ rən mənt) *n.* surroundings

individual (in´də vij´ oo əl) *n.* single person or thing

team (tēm) *n.* group with a common goal

tradition (trə dish´ ən) *n.* custom, as of a group or culture, handed down

unify (yoo´ nə fī´) *v.* bring together as one

unique (yoo nēk´) *adj.* one-of-a-kind

Use these words as you complete Big Question activities in this unit that involve reading, writing, speaking, and listening.

Gather Vocabulary Knowledge Additional Big Question words are listed below. Categorize the words by deciding whether you know each one well, know it a little bit, or do not know it at all.

---

custom   family   group

ethnicity

Then, do the following:

1. Discuss the meaning of each word with a partner. Then, verify each meaning using a dictionary.
2. Next, use each word in an original paragraph that gives examples of what community and individuality mean to you. Provide context clues for every vocabulary word you use.
3. Remember that context clues might be definitions, synonyms, antonyms, examples, or explanations.
4. Finally, take turns reading your paragraph with a partner. If, during the readings, the meaning of any Big Question word is still unclear, work with your partner to clarify it.

Elements of Folk Literature

Folk literature is a genre of writing that has its roots in the oral tradition.

The Oral Tradition Stories were told long before reading and writing began. These stories were handed down through the ages by word of mouth. The sharing of stories by word of mouth is called the **oral tradition.**

Folk literature is a genre of writing that originated in the oral tradition. Once writing and books were invented, the stories were collected and retold in print. Myths, legends, folk tales, and fables are all forms of folk literature.

The Importance of the Storyteller Stories in the oral tradition were created thousands of years ago. No one knows for sure who the first storytellers were. As stories were passed down, new storytellers added and changed details. These details reflected the storyteller's roots and **cultural perspective,** or view of the world. That viewpoint was shaped by the storyteller's background and experiences.

Theme is the central idea, message, or insight about life that a story conveys.

Some works of folk literature have **universal themes**—themes that are repeated across many cultures and over many time periods. They express insights into life and human nature that many people understand and find important. The struggle of good against evil is an example of a universal theme.

Other works of folk literature—especially fables—present their theme in the form of a **moral.** A moral is a lesson about life that is stated directly, usually at the very end of the work.

Purposes of Folk Literature The **purpose** of a piece of literature is the reason it was written. The purpose of some forms of folk literature may be to explain or teach. For example, a myth may explain a natural phenomenon, and a fable may teach a lesson about life. Other types of folk literature may have the simple purpose of entertaining readers.

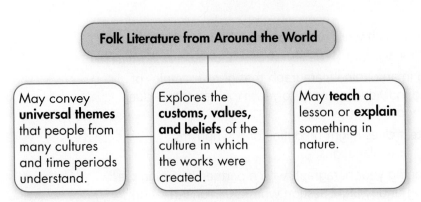

Folk Literature from Around the World

May convey **universal themes** that people from many cultures and time periods understand.

Explores the **customs, values, and beliefs** of the culture in which the works were created.

May **teach** a lesson or **explain** something in nature.

Forms of Folk Literature

Myths are tales that relate the actions of gods, goddesses, and the heroes who interact with them. Many cultures have their own collections of myths, or **mythology.**

Legends are traditional stories based on real-life events. As these stories are told and retold, fact often changes to fiction, and the characters often become larger than life.

Tall tales often focus on a central hero who performs impossible feats.

Folk tales may deal with real people or magical characters. They reflect the values and beliefs of the culture in which they were created.

Fables are brief stories or poems that often feature animal characters who act and speak like humans. They usually end with a moral that is directly stated.

Epics are long narrative poems important to the history of a nation or culture. They tell of a larger-than-life hero who goes on a dangerous journey, or **quest.**

In This Section

Elements of Folk Literature

Determining Themes in Folk Literature

Examining Structure and Theme

Close Read: Story Development and Theme
- Model Text
- Practice Text

After You Read

 Common Core State Standards

RL.2
[For the full wording of the standards, see the standards chart in the front of your textbook.]

Characteristics of Folk Literature

Here are some common characteristics you will see as you read folk literature.

Characteristic	Definition	Often Featured In...
Heroes and heroines	Larger-than-life figures who overcome obstacles or participate in exciting adventures	Myths Legends Epics
Quest	A journey filled with adventure that the hero or heroine goes on to achieve an important goal	Myths Legends Epics
Trickster	A clever character who can fool others but often gets into trouble	Folk tales Fables
Personification	A type of figurative language in which nonhuman subjects are given human qualities	Myths Fables
Hyperbole	A type of figurative language that uses exaggeration, either for comic effect or to express strong emotion	Tall tales Myths Epics
Dialect	Language spoken by people in a particular region or group	Tall tales Folk tales

Determining Themes in Folk Literature

Common Core State Standards

Reading Literature
2. Determine a theme or central idea of a text and analyze its development over the course of the text.

Folk literature expresses themes— insights about life and human nature.

Folk literature is rich with humor, adventure, romance, suspense, and drama. At the same time, it is the themes of these stories that have made them meaningful to readers of many generations and cultures.

Stated Themes Themes in folk literature take different forms. Sometimes, the theme is directly stated at the end of the story as a moral, or lesson. For example, look at the retelling of Aesop's fable, "The Lion and the Mouse."

Example: The Lion and the Mouse

A tiny mouse accidentally crossed paths with a ferocious lion. The lion was about to eat the mouse, when the mouse pleaded with the lion to let him go. "If you do, I promise to help you one day," the mouse said. The mighty lion doubted he would ever need the help of a tiny mouse, but he let the mouse go. One day, the lion became trapped in a hunter's net. The little mouse heard the lion's roars and came to his aid. In a few minutes, the mouse had gnawed his way through the net, setting the lion free.

Moral: One act of kindness often leads to another.

Implied Themes As in other literary genres, themes in folk literature are sometimes implied, or suggested, rather than stated. Clues to these themes lie in the details that describe setting, characters, and plot. Stories with implied themes require the reader to analyze the details to see what they reveal about the deeper meaning of the story.

Universal Themes A universal theme is an insight or lesson that appears in literature across cultures and throughout different periods in history. These themes are "universal" because they express ideas that are meaningful to most people. Here are a few universal themes that are commonly found in folk literature. They reflect ideas that have been understood for many generations.

- Goodness is eventually rewarded.
- Inner beauty is more important than outward appearance.
- Those who always want more are never satisfied.
- Cleverness and courage can overcome brute strength.
- Those who plan carefully now can avoid problems in the future.

Examining Structure and Theme

The structural elements of a work of folk literature contribute to its theme.

Folk literature of various types contains structural elements that contribute to the development of theme. As you read, look for these elements.

Repetition Folk literature often features the repetition of events, dialogue, descriptions, and sound patterns. Repetition adds rhythm to the text. It can also help build suspense and emphasize main ideas. For example, in the well-known tale of "The Three Little Pigs," the following lines of dialogue are repeated three times.

Example: Repetition

"Little pig, little pig, let me come in."

"Not by the hair of my chinny chin chin."

"Then I'll huff, and I'll puff, and I'll blow your house in."

Patterns Many works of folk literature share a common pattern, or repeated element. For example, many stories begin and end with such familiar phrases as "Once upon a time" and "They lived happily ever after." Another common structural element found in folk literature is the pattern of three. Many stories feature three important characters, three wishes, or three tasks.

Archetypes An archetype is an element that occurs regularly in literature from around the world and throughout history. Oral storytellers have used archetypes to convey such universal themes as the power of love or the importance of bravery. Here are some common archetypes found in folk literature:

Plot	• a dangerous journey • a struggle between a good character and an evil one • an explanation of how something came to be
Characters	• a brave hero • trickster, or wise fool • talking animals
Ideas	• magic in the normal world • hero or heroine helped by supernatural forces • evil disguised as good

Flat Characters Folk literature often features characters who seem to have only one main trait, such as kindness, cruelty, wisdom, or foolishness. Such characters are **flat,** or one-sided. They are not like real people, who usually have many different sides to their personalities. Flat characters can help storytellers express important themes. For example, in "Snow White," the evil queen remains evil throughout the tale, while Snow White herself remains kind and good. Together, these opposing characters help develop the theme that kindness is stronger than cruelty.

Close Read: Story Development and Theme

All types of folk literature share traits that contribute to story development and theme.

Folk tales, fables, legends, and myths have different elements that make them distinct. However, all folk literature shares certain qualities, or traits. As you read folk literature, notice details that help develop the story. Think about how the story's development helps express a theme.

Plot

Plot is the sequence of events in a story. In folk literature, the plot often has twists and turns. It frequently develops around one of these ideas:

- a journey, or quest, that includes a series of challenges or tests;
- the physical transformation of a character;
- a character who wears a disguise to hide his or her identity.

Repetition and Patterns

The use of repetition and patterns in folk literature helps unify a story, move it toward its end, and reveal the theme. As you read, look for

- the repetition of dialogue and descriptions;
- patterns of three;
- plot patterns, such as the breaking of a magic spell or a competition between two characters.

Characters

The characters in folk literature may have special skills or powers, or may display only one main trait. As you read, notice

- characters with exaggerated talents, magical abilities, or superhuman powers;
- animal characters with human traits;
- characters with one-sided personalities.

Setting

In folk literature, consider how certain common settings affect story development. These settings include

- challenging or threatening landscapes;
- severe or unexpected weather;
- supernatural worlds.

Theme

Theme is the central message of a story. As you read,

- look for a statement that expresses a moral;
- think about what lessons the characters learn or how a character changes or is transformed;
- notice how repetition and patterns work to keep the story moving toward its central message.

Model

About the Text Aesop's fables have been enjoyed for centuries, but the fact is that no one knows for sure who composed these stories. According to traditional belief, Aesop was a Greek slave who lived during the sixth century B.C. However, some scholars doubt his existence.

"The Travelers and the Bear"
from *Aesop's Fables*
retold by Jerry Pinkney

Two men were traveling through the forest together on a lonely trail. Soon they heard a sound up ahead as if heavy feet were trampling through the underbrush.

"It could be a bear!" one whispered with alarm, and quickly as he could, he scrambled up a tall tree. He had barely reached the first branch when a huge brown bear thrust aside the bushes and stepped out onto the path.

Hugging the trunk with both arms, the first traveler refused to lend a hand to his terrified companion, who threw himself on the ground and prepared for death.

The bear lowered its great head and sniffed at the man, ruffling his hair with its nose. Then, to the amazement of both men, the fierce beast walked away.

The first traveler slid down from his tree. "Why, it almost looked as if the bear whispered something in your ear," he marveled.

"It did," said the second traveler. "It told me to choose a better companion for my next journey."

Misfortune is the true test of friendship.

Setting The forest is a typical threatening setting in folk literature. The words *lonely* and *heavy* suggest that the travelers may encounter something dangerous.

Plot Surprising events, such as the departure of the bear, are a common element of story development in folk literature.

Theme A combination of details—the threat of the bear, the refusal of the first traveler to help his companion, and the bear's advice—develop the story and reveal the theme. As in many fables, the theme is stated directly as a moral at the end of the story.

Independent Practice

About the Selections The following stories by author Jon Scieszka are twisted versions of traditional folk literature. Even though Scieszka tells these stories in a humorous way, the stories still contain many of the common traits found in traditional folk literature.

Character What common characteristic of fables describes the characters of Grasshopper and his mom?

"Grasshopper Logic" from *Squids Will Be Squids* by Jon Scieszka and Lane Smith

One bright and sunny day, Grasshopper came home from school, dropped his backpack, and was just about to run outside to meet his friends.

"Where are you going?" asked his mom.

"Out to meet some friends," said Grasshopper.

"Do you have any homework due tomorrow?" asked his mom.

"Just one small thing for History. I did the rest in class."

"Okay" said Mom Grasshopper. "Be back at six for dinner."

Grasshopper hung out with his friends, came home promptly at six, ate his dinner, then took out his History homework.

His mom read the assignment and freaked out.

Plot How does Grasshopper's assignment compare to the challenges that are often featured in folk literature?

"Rewrite twelve Greek myths as Broadway musicals. Write music for songs. Design and build all sets. Sew original costumes for each production."

"How long have you known about this assignment?" asked Mom Grasshopper, trying not to scream.

"I don't know," said Grasshopper.

Theme How does Grasshopper's behavior in the fable contribute to the idea expressed in the moral?

Moral
There are plenty of things to say to calm a hopping mad grasshopper mom. "I don't know" is not one.

"The Other Frog Prince" from *The Stinky Cheese Man and Other Fairly Stupid Tales* by Jon Scieszka and Lane Smith

Once upon a time there was a frog. One day when he was sitting on his lily pad, he saw a beautiful princess sitting by the pond. He hopped in the water, swam over to her, and poked his head out of the weeds.

"Pardon me, O beautiful princess," he said in his most sad and pathetic voice. "I wonder if you could help me."

The princess was about to jump up and run, but she felt sorry for the frog with the sad and pathetic voice.

So she asked, "What can I do to help you, little frog?"

"Well," said the frog. "I'm not really a frog, but a handsome prince who was turned into a frog by a wicked witch's spell. And the spell can only be broken by the kiss of a beautiful princess."

The princess thought about this for a second, then lifted the frog from the pond and kissed him.

"I was just kidding," said the frog. He jumped back into the pond and the princess wiped the frog slime off her lips.

The End.

Patterns What does the familiar opening suggest about how the plot will unfold?

Plot What does the author want readers to believe will happen next in the story? What elements of folk literature does the author use to make readers believe this?

Theme This outcome puts a humorous twist on this famous fairy tale. Based on the outcome, how would you state the story's theme?

Practice continued

Character How are Duckbilled Platypus and BeefSnakStik® similar to and different from the characters that typically appear in fables?

Theme What details in the story contribute to the development of the idea expressed in the moral?

"Duckbilled Platypus vs. BeefSnakStik®" *from Squids Will Be Squids* **by Jon Scieszka and Lane Smith**

"I have a bill like a duck and a tail like a beaver," bragged Duckbilled Platypus.

"So what?" said BeefSnakStik®. "I have beef, soy protein concentrate, and dextrose."

"I also have webbed feet and fur," said Duckbilled Platypus.

"Who cares?" said BeefSnakStik®. "I also have smoke flavoring, sodium erythorbate, and sodium nitrite."

"I am one of only two mammals in the world that lay eggs," said Duckbilled Platypus.

"Big deal," said BeefSnakStik®. "I have beef lips."

Moral
Just because you have a lot of stuff, don't think you're so special.

1. **Key Ideas and Details** **(a) Summarize:** Summarize the plot of each story, making sure not to include your own opinions or judgments. **(b) Analyze:** Which of the stories has a surprise ending?

2. **Key Ideas and Details** **(a) Infer:** Why does Grasshopper call his History assignment "small." **(b) Generalize:** What makes the details of the assignment so funny?

3. **Key Ideas and Details** **(a) Describe:** What tone of voice does the frog use with the princess? **(b) Compare:** Does the frog have the same attitude or tone of voice as BeefSnakStik®? Explain. **(c) Interpret:** What makes these characters funny?

4. **Key Ideas and Details** **(a) Describe:** What is the argument between Duckbilled Platypus and BeefSnakStik® about? **(b) Draw Conclusions:** Why is neither one of these characters likely to win this argument?

5. **Key Ideas and Details** **(a) Analyze:** What makes the moral or lesson of each tale funny? Cite details in support of your answer. **(b) Evaluate:** In your opinion, which story is the funniest, and why?

6. **Craft and Structure** **(a) Interpret:** Explain the attitude toward life and literature that the fables reflect. **(b) Apply:** Is one type of reader likelier than other types to appreciate this attitude? Explain.

7. **Integration of Knowledge and Ideas** **(a) Compare:** Compare the style of Scieszka's fables with the style of a traditional fable with which you are familiar. **(b) Evaluate:** Which type of fable do you prefer? Explain.

8. **Craft and Structure** **(a)** In a chart like the one shown, list examples of hyperbole and personification in each story.

Fable/Fairy Tale	Hyperbole	Personification
Grasshopper Logic		
The Other Frog Prince		
Duckbilled Platypus vs. BeefSnakStik®		

(b) Collaborate: Discuss your chart with a classmate. Explain how your understanding of each fable has grown.

© Leveled Texts

Build your skills and improve your comprehension of myths with texts of increasing complexity.

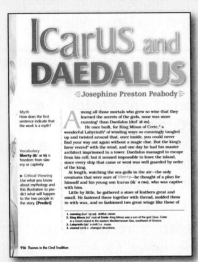

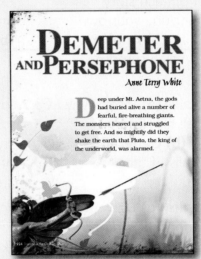

Read **"Icarus and Daedalus"** to find out what happens when a man and his son use homemade wings to make a daring escape.

Read **"Demeter and Persephone"** to find out how a mother reacts when the god of the underworld kidnaps her daughter.

© Common Core State Standards

Meet these standards with either **"Icarus and Daedalus"** (p. 916) or **"Demeter and Persephone"** (p. 924).

Reading Literature
2. Determine a theme or central idea of a text and analyze its development over the course of the text. *(Literary Analysis: Spiral Review)*

Writing
3. Write narratives to develop real or imagined experiences or events using effective technique, relevant descriptive details, and well-structured event sequences. **3.a.** Engage and orient the reader by establishing a context and point of view and introducing a narrator and/or characters; organize an event sequence that unfolds naturally and logically. **3.b.** Use narrative techniques, such as dialogue, pacing, and description, to develop experiences, events, and/or characters. *(Writing: Myth)*

Speaking and Listening
1.a. Come to discussions prepared, having read or researched material under study; explicitly draw on that preparation by referring to evidence on the topic, text, or issue to probe and reflect on ideas under discussion.
1.c. Pose questions that elicit elaboration and respond to others' questions and comments with relevant observations and ideas that bring the discussion back on topic as needed. *(Speaking and Listening: Debate)*

Language
2. Demonstrate command of the conventions of standard English capitalization, punctuation, and spelling when writing. *(Conventions: Punctuation Marks)*

4.b. Use common, grade-appropriate Greek or Latin affixes and roots as clues to the meaning of a word. *(Vocabulary: Word Study)*

Reading Skill: Cause and Effect

A **cause** is an event, action, or feeling that produces a result. That result is called an **effect.** In some literary works, multiple causes result in a single effect. In other works, a single cause results in multiple effects. Effects can also become causes for events that follow. This linking of causes and effects propels the action in a narrative forward.

As you read, **ask questions to analyze cause-and-effect relationships.** Ask yourself questions like these:

- What happened? Why?
- What will happen as a result of this?

Using the Strategy: Cause-and-Effect Web

As you read, use a chart like the one below to determine cause-and-effect relationships.

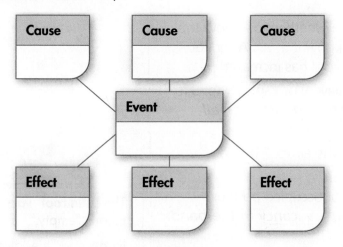

Literary Analysis: Myth

Since time began, people have tried to understand the world around them. Ancient peoples created **myths**—stories that explain natural occurrences and express beliefs about right and wrong.

Every culture has its own collection of myths, or *mythology.* In many of these myths, gods and goddesses have human traits, while human heroes possess superhuman traits. As you read, notice the ways that myths explore universal themes and explain the world in human terms.

PHLit Online!

www.PHLitOnline.com

Hear It!
- Selection summary audio
- Selection audio

See It!
- Get Connected video
- Background video
- More about the author
- Vocabulary flashcards

Do It!
- Interactive journals
- Interactive graphic organizers
- Self-test
- Internet activity
- Grammar tutorial
- Interactive vocabulary games

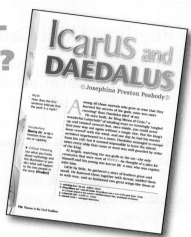

Community or *individual* — which is more important?

Writing About the Big Question

In "Icarus and Daedalus," a boy ignores important advice from his father. Use this sentence starter to develop your ideas about the Big Question.

> When **individuals** become so focused on their own desires that they do not listen to others, _____ can happen because _____.

While You Read Look for reasons why Icarus does not listen to his father, choosing instead to satisfy his own desires.

Vocabulary

Read each word and its definition. Decide whether you know the word well, know it a little bit, or do not know it at all. After you read, see how your knowledge of each word has increased.

- **liberty** (lib′ ər tē) *n.* freedom from slavery or captivity (p. 916) *The U.S. Constitution grants liberty and justice to all citizens.* liberties *n.* liberation *n.*

- **aloft** (ə loft′) *adv.* high up; flying; in the air (p. 918) *The soaring bird was aloft.* lofty *adj.*

- **vacancy** (vā′ kən sē) *n.* emptiness; unoccupied position (p. 918) *The drummer quit, leaving a vacancy in the band.* vacant *adj.* vacate *v.*

- **reel** (rēl) *v.* spin; whirl (p. 918) *Seeing her favorite movie star in person made her head reel.* reeling *v.* reeled *v.*

- **sustained** (sə stānd′) *adj.* supported (p. 918) *During the long hike, they were sustained by their hearty breakfast.* sustain *v.* sustenance *n.*

- **captivity** (kap tiv′ i tē) *n.* imprisonment; (p. 918) *The man wished to be released from captivity.* captive *adj.* captor *n.* capture *v.*

Word Study

The **Latin root -vac-** means "empty."

Icarus and Daedalus are at first frightened by the **vacancy,** or emptiness, of the sky.

Meet
Josephine Preston Peabody (1874–1922)

Author of

Icarus and DAEDALUS

Josephine Preston Peabody was born in Brooklyn, New York, and moved with her family to Massachusetts when she was ten years old. Since both of her parents loved literature and the theater, it is no surprise that Peabody learned to love reading and writing as a child. Her talent became obvious at an early age. She published a poem in *The Women's Journal* when she was fourteen and her first book—*Old Greek Folk-Stories Told Anew*—when she was twenty-three. "Icarus and Daedalus" is from this collection.

A Teacher and Writer After attending Radcliffe College in Cambridge, Massachusetts, Peabody published her first book of poems in 1898. From 1901 to 1903, she taught English literature at Wellesley College. Peabody continued to write plays and poetry throughout her life.

> ## DID YOU KNOW?
> **Peabody was a supporter of women's right to vote.**

BACKGROUND FOR THE MYTH
Greek Mythology

The ancient Greeks believed in a complex collection of gods and goddesses, ruled by Zeus. Zeus ruled with his wife, Hera, from atop Mount Olympus. Beneath Zeus in rank were many lesser gods and goddesses, each linked to ideas or qualities in nature. The ancient Greeks believed that the gods taught lessons to people who were too proud or arrogant. As you read this myth, consider the lesson that Daedalus needs to learn.

Icarus and DAEDALUS

❧ Josephine Preston Peabody ❧

Myth
How does the first sentence indicate that the work is a myth?

Among all those mortals who grew so wise that they learned the secrets of the gods, none was more cunning[1] than Daedalus (ded´ əl əs).

He once built, for King Minos of Crete,[2] a wonderful Labyrinth[3] of winding ways so cunningly tangled up and twisted around that, once inside, you could never find your way out again without a magic clue. But the king's favor veered[4] with the wind, and one day he had his master architect imprisoned in a tower. Daedalus managed to escape from his cell; but it seemed impossible to leave the island, since every ship that came or went was well guarded by order of the king.

Vocabulary
liberty (lib´ ər tē) *n.* freedom from slavery or captivity

At length, watching the sea-gulls in the air—the only creatures that were sure of liberty—he thought of a plan for himself and his young son Icarus (ik´ ə rəs), who was captive with him.

▶ **Critical Viewing**
Use what you know about mythology and this illustration to predict what will happen to the two people in the story. **[Predict]**

Little by little, he gathered a store of feathers great and small. He fastened these together with thread, molded them in with wax, and so fashioned two great wings like those of a bird. When they were done, Daedalus fitted them to his own shoulders, and after one or two efforts, he found that

---

1. **cunning** (kun´ in) *adj.* skillful; clever.
2. **King Minos** (mī´ nəs) **of Crete** King Minos was a son of the god Zeus. Crete is a Greek island in the eastern Mediterranean Sea, southeast of Greece.
3. **Labyrinth** (lab´ ə rinth´) *n.* maze.
4. **veered** (vird) *v.* changed directions.

Cause and Effect
Why does Daedalus make wings out of feathers?

Myth
What lesson does Daedalus try to teach Icarus?

Spiral Review
Theme What universal theme involving parents and their children is hinted at in the paragraph beginning, "For Icarus, these cautions…"?

Vocabulary
aloft (ə loft´) *adv.* high up; flying; in the air

vacancy (vā´ kən sē) *n.* emptiness; unoccupied position

reel (rēl) *v.* spin; whirl

sustained (sə stānd´) *adj.* supported

captivity (kap tiv´ i tē) *n.* imprisonment

by waving his arms he could winnow[5] the air and cleave it, as a swimmer does the sea. He held himself aloft, wavered this way and that with the wind, and at last, like a great fledgling,[6] he learned to fly.

Without delay, he fell to work on a pair of wings for the boy Icarus, and taught him carefully how to use them, bidding him beware of rash adventures among the stars. "Remember," said the father, "never to fly very low or very high, for the fogs about the earth would weigh you down, but the blaze of the sun will surely melt your feathers apart if you go too near."

For Icarus, these cautions went in at one ear and out by the other. Who could remember to be careful when he was to fly for the first time? Are birds careful? Not they! And not an idea remained in the boy's head but the one joy of escape.

The day came, and the fair wind that was to set them free. The father bird put on his wings, and, while the light urged them to be gone, he waited to see that all was well with Icarus, for the two could not fly hand in hand. Up they rose, the boy after his father. The hateful ground of Crete sank beneath them; and the country folk, who caught a glimpse of them when they were high above the treetops, took it for a vision of the gods—Apollo,[7] perhaps, with Cupid[8] after him.

At first there was a terror in the joy. The wide vacancy of the air dazed them—a glance downward made their brains reel.

But when a great wind filled their wings, and Icarus felt himself sustained, like a halcyon bird[9] in the hollow of a wave, like a child uplifted by his mother, he forgot everything in the world but joy. He forgot Crete and the other islands that he had passed over: he saw but vaguely that wingèd thing in the distance before him that was his father Daedalus. He longed for one draft of flight to quench the thirst of his captivity: he stretched out his arms to the sky and made towards the highest heavens.

Alas for him! Warmer and warmer grew the air. Those arms, that had seemed to uphold him, relaxed. His wings wavered, drooped. He fluttered his young hands vainly—he was falling—and in that terror he remembered. The heat of the sun

---

5. **winnow** (win´ ō) *v.* beat, as with wings.
6. **fledgling** (flej´ liŋ) *n.* young bird.
7. **Apollo** (ə päl´ ō) *n.* the Greek god of music, poetry, and medicine; identified with the sun.
8. **Cupid** (kyōō´ pid) *n.* in Roman mythology, the god of love, son of Venus.
9. **halcyon** (hal´ sē ən) **bird** *n.* legendary sea bird, which the ancient Greeks believed could calm the sea by resting on it.

He fluttered
his young
hands vainly—
he was falling...

had melted the wax from his wings; the feathers were falling, one by one, like snowflakes; and there was none to help.

He fell like a leaf tossed down the wind, down, down, with one cry that overtook Daedalus far away. When he returned, and sought high and low for his poor boy, he saw nothing but the birdlike feathers afloat on the water, and he knew that Icarus was drowned.

The nearest island he named Icaria, in memory of the child; but he, in heavy grief, went to the temple of Apollo in Sicily, and there hung up his wings as an offering. Never again did he attempt to fly.

Critical Thinking

Cite textual evidence to support your responses.

©️ 1. **Key Ideas and Details** **(a)** Where is Daedalus when the story begins? **(b) Analyze:** In what ways does Daedalus show how clever he is?

©️ 2. **Key Ideas and Details** **(a)** Who is Icarus? **(b) Infer:** What does Daedalus reveal about himself through his words to Icarus?

©️ 3. **Key Ideas and Details** **(a)** Summarize the warning Daedalus gives Icarus. **(b) Infer:** What do Icarus's actions reveal about his character?

©️ 4. **Key Ideas and Details** **(a) Compare and Contrast:** Compare and contrast Icarus's experience of flying with Daedalus's experience. **(b) Evaluate:** What does this difference reveal about their characters? Explain.

©️ 5. **Integration of Knowledge and Ideas** **(a) Take a Position:** Does Daedalus share any responsibility for Icarus's fall? Why or why not? **(b) Discuss:** Share your answer with a classmate. How has your answer grown or changed?

©️ 6. **Integration of Knowledge and Ideas** **(a)** Why does Icarus ignore his father's advice? **(b)** What is the result of Icarus's actions? **(c)** What happens when an individual puts his or her own desires before everything else? *[Connect to the Big Question: Community or individual—which is more important?]*

Reading Skill: Cause and Effect

1. Answer these questions to analyze **cause-and-effect** relationships in the myth:

(a) What happens to Icarus at the end of the myth? Why?

(b) What happens to Daedalus? Why?

2. What effect does the sun have in the myth?

Literary Analysis: Myth

3. Key Ideas and Details What superhuman qualities does Daedalus possess?

4. Craft and Structure Complete a chart like the one shown to describe the lessons the **myth** teaches through each character.

Character	Lesson	How Taught
Icarus		
Daedalus		

Vocabulary

Acquisition and Use For each item, write a single sentence using the words indicated.

1. vacancy; hole

2. sustained; noise

3. liberty; prisoner

4. aloft; eagle

5. reel; boxer

6. captivity; animals

Word Study Use context and what you know about the **Latin root -vac-** to explain your answer to each question.

1. Is it wise to *evacuate* a town if a powerful hurricane is approaching?

2. If you *vacate* your house, do you stay at home?

Word Study

The **Latin root -vac-** means "empty."

Apply It Explain how the root -vac- contributes to the meanings of these words. Consult a dictionary if necessary.

vacation

vacuous

vacuum

 **Community** *or individual —* **which is more important?**

Writing About the Big Question

In "Demeter and Persephone," the characters of Demeter and Pluto indulge their own desires at the expense of others. Use this sentence starter to develop your ideas about the Big Question.

When making a decision that will affect the greater **community,** a person is responsible for _____.

While You Read Consider how others suffer to satisfy the desires of Pluto and Demeter.

Vocabulary

Read each word and its definition. Decide whether you know the word well, know it a little bit, or do not know it at all. After you read, see how your knowledge of each word has increased.

- **defies** (dē fīz´) *v.* resists or opposes boldly or openly (p. 926) *She defies the law by driving too fast. defy v. defiant adj.*

- **monarch** (man´ ərk) *n.* ruler, like a king or queen (p. 926) *The people bowed before the monarch. monarchy n.*

- **dominions** (də min´ yəns) *n.* governed countries or territories (p. 927) *Canada and Australia were once dominions of the British empire. dominion n.*

- **intervene** (in´ tər vēn´) *v.* come between as an influence to help settle an action or argument (p. 927) *My mother will often intervene in the fights between my brothers. intervention n.*

- **realm** (relm) *n.* kingdom (p. 928) *The entire realm was saddened by the king's death.*

- **abode** (ə bōd) *n.* home; residence (p. 930) *The governor's residence was an elegant abode. abide v.*

Word Study

The **Latin root -dom-** means "master" or "building."

Pluto snatches Persephone and takes her to his underground **dominions,** the territories he rules.

▲ White's "Demeter and Persephone" appears in this treasury of myths and legends.

Author of
DEMETER AND PERSEPHONE

Anne Terry White, who was born in Ukraine (then part of Russia), was one of the leading writers of nonfiction for children. White's first two books were *Heroes of the Five Books,* a look at figures of the Old Testament, and *Three Children and Shakespeare,* a family discussion of four of Shakespeare's plays. She wrote them to introduce her own children to great works of literature.

A Life of Learning In addition to being a writer, White was an editor, a translator, and an authority on ancient Greece. She shares this knowledge in her retelling of the myth of Demeter and Persephone.

DID YOU KNOW?
White wrote books about the stars, rocks, rivers, archaeology, and mountains in her "All About" series.

BACKGROUND FOR THE MYTH
Seasonal Changes

Ancient Greeks explained the changing seasons with the story of "Demeter and Persephone." Today, scientists explain these changes differently. The Earth completes one revolution around the sun during the course of a year. As the Earth travels, its tilt causes different parts of its surface to receive more of the sun's light. In regions getting more sunlight, it is summer. In areas getting less sunlight, it is winter.

DEMETER AND PERSEPHONE

Anne Terry White

Deep under Mt. Aetna, the gods had buried alive a number of fearful, fire-breathing giants. The monsters heaved and struggled to get free. And so mightily did they shake the earth that Pluto, the king of the underworld, was alarmed.

She saw Pluto as he drove around with his coal-black horses...

"They may tear the rocks asunder and leave the realm of the dead open to the light of day," he thought. And mounting his golden chariot, he went up to see what damage had been done.

Now the goddess of love and beauty, fair Aphrodite (af´ rə dīt´ ē), was sitting on a mountainside playing with her son, Eros.[1] She saw Pluto as he drove around with his coal-black horses and she said:

"My son, there is one who defies your power and mine. Quick! Take up your darts! Send an arrow into the breast of that dark monarch. Let him, too, feel the pangs of love. Why should he alone escape them?"

At his mother's words, Eros leaped lightly to his feet. He chose from his quiver[2] his sharpest and truest arrow, fitted it to his bow, drew the string, and shot straight into Pluto's heart.

The grim King had seen fair maids enough in the gloomy underworld over which he ruled. But never had his heart been touched. Now an unaccustomed warmth stole through his veins. His stern eyes softened. Before him was a blossoming valley, and along its edge a charming girl was gathering flowers. She was Persephone (pər sef´ ə nē), daughter of Demeter (di mēt´ ər), goddess of the harvest. She had strayed from her companions, and now that her basket overflowed with blossoms, she was filling her apron with lilies and violets. The god looked at Persephone and loved her at once. With one sweep of his arm he caught her up and drove swiftly away.

"Mother!" she screamed, while the flowers fell from her apron and strewed the ground. "Mother!"

And she called on her companions by name. But already they were out of sight, so fast did Pluto urge the horses on. In

---

1. **Eros** (er´ äs) in Greek mythology, the god of love; identified by the Romans as Cupid.
2. **quiver** (kwiv´ ər) case for arrows.

a few moments they were at the River Cyane.[3] Persephone struggled, her loosened girdle[4] fell to the ground, but the god held her tight. He struck the bank with his trident.[5] The earth opened, and darkness swallowed them all—horses, chariot, Pluto, and weeping Persephone.

From end to end of the earth Demeter sought her daughter. But none could tell her where Persephone was. At last, worn out and despairing, the goddess returned to Sicily. She stood by the River Cyane, where Pluto had cleft the earth and gone down into his own dominions.

Now a river nymph[6] had seen him carry off his prize. She wanted to tell Demeter where her daughter was, but fear of Pluto kept her dumb. Yet she had picked up the girdle Persephone had dropped, and this the nymph wafted[7] on the waves to the feet of Demeter.

The goddess knew then that her daughter was gone indeed, but she did not suspect Pluto of carrying her off. She laid the blame on the innocent land.

"Ungrateful soil!" she said. "I made you fertile. I clothed you in grass and nourishing grain, and this is how you reward me. No more shall you enjoy my favors!"

That year was the most cruel mankind had ever known. Nothing prospered, nothing grew. The cattle died, the seed would not come up, men and oxen toiled in vain. There was too much sun. There was too much rain. Thistles[8] and weeds were the only things that grew. It seemed that all mankind would die of hunger.

"This cannot go on," said mighty Zeus. "I see that I must intervene." And one by one he sent the gods and goddesses to plead with Demeter.

But she had the same answer for all: "Not till I see my

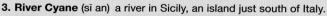

3. **River Cyane** (sī an) a river in Sicily, an island just south of Italy.
4. **girdle** (gʉrd´ əl) *n.* belt or sash for the waist.
5. **trident** (trīd´ ənt) *n.* spear with three points.
6. **river nymph** (nimf) *n.* goddess living in a river.
7. **wafted** (wäft´ əd) *n.* carried.
8. **thistles** (this´ əlz) *n.* stubborn, weedy plants with sharp leaves and usually purplish flowers.

Myths
What details in this paragraph reveal that the story is a myth?

Vocabulary
dominions (də min´ yəns) *n.* governed countries or territories
intervene (in tər vēn´) *v.* come between as an influence to help settle an action or argument

Reading Check
Who is Pluto?

daughter shall the earth bear fruit again."

Zeus, of course, knew well where Persephone was. He did not like to take from his brother the one joyful thing in his life, but he saw that he must if the race of man was to be preserved. So he called Hermes[9] to him and said:

"Descend to the underworld, my son. Bid Pluto release his bride. Provided she has not tasted food in the realm of the dead, she may return to her mother forever."

Down sped Hermes on his winged feet, and there in the dim palace of the king, he found Persephone by Pluto's side. She was pale and joyless. Not all the glittering treasures of the underworld could bring a smile to her lips.

"You have no flowers here," she would say to her husband when he pressed gems upon her. "Jewels have no fragrance. I do not want them."

When she saw Hermes and heard his message, her heart leaped within her. Her cheeks grew rosy and her eyes

Vocabulary
realm (relm)
n. kingdom

9. **Hermes** (hʉr´ mēz) a god who served as a messenger.

Mythology Connection

Gods and Goddesses

The ancient Greeks and Romans had different names for their gods and goddesses. In the diagram below, the Roman name for the god or goddess is given in parentheses. In their traditions, each god and goddess had control or power in a different area.

Poseiden (Neptune)
god of the sea

Zeus (Jupiter)
ruler of gods and men

Hera (Juno)
goddess of marriage

Demeter (Ceres)
goddess of agriculture

Hades (Pluto)
god of the underworld

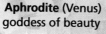

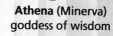

Hermes (Mercury)
messenger of the gods

Aphrodite (Venus)
goddess of beauty

Ares (Mars)
god of war

Athena (Minerva)
goddess of wisdom

Persephone (Proserpina)
goddess of springtime

Connect to the Literature **Why do you think that ancient peoples told stories about gods and goddesses such as Demeter and Persephone?**

---

sparkled, for she knew that Pluto would not dare to disobey his brother's command. She sprang up, ready to go at once. Only one thing troubled her—that she could not leave the underworld forever. For she had accepted a pomegranate[10] from Pluto and sucked the sweet pulp from four of the seeds.

With a heavy heart Pluto made ready his golden car.[11] He helped Persephone in while Hermes took up the reins.

"Dear wife," said the King, and his voice trembled as he spoke, "think kindly of me, I pray you. For indeed I love you truly. It will be lonely here these eight months you are away.

✓ **Reading Check**
What does Zeus want Pluto to do?

---

10. pomegranate (päm´ ə gran´ it) *n.* round fruit with a red leathery rind and many seeds.
11. car (kär) *n.* chariot.

And if you think mine is a gloomy palace to return to, at least remember that your husband is great among the immortals. So fare you well—and get your fill of flowers!"

Straight to the temple of Demeter at Eleusis, Hermes drove the black horses. The goddess heard the chariot wheels and, as a deer bounds over the hills, she ran out swiftly to meet her daughter. Persephone flew to her mother's arms. And the sad tale of each turned into joy in the telling.

So it is to this day. One third of the year Persephone spends in the gloomy abode of Pluto—one month for each seed that she tasted. Then Nature dies, the leaves fall, the earth stops bringing forth. In spring Persephone returns, and with her come the flowers, followed by summer's fruitfulness and the rich harvest of fall.

Vocabulary
abode (ə bōd') *n.*
home; residence

Critical Thinking

Cite textual evidence to support your responses.

1. **Key Ideas and Details** **(a)** Why did Pluto take Persephone to his kingdom? **(b) Analyze:** What does Pluto's nickname, "the grim King," suggest about his emotional outlook on the world?

2. **Key Ideas and Details** **(a)** What does Demeter do when she discovers her daughter is lost? **(b) Make a Judgment:** Do you think her actions were justifiable? Why or why not? **(c) Discuss:** Share your answer with a classmate. How has your response grown or changed?

3. **Key Ideas and Details** **(a)** How is Persephone reunited with her mother? **(b) Speculate:** How might their experiences in this myth change each of the three main characters?

4. **Key Ideas and Details** **(a)** How does nature change as Persephone moves between Earth and the underworld? **(b) Synthesize:** How do the powerful emotions of the main characters account for the changing of the seasons?

5. **Integration of Knowledge and Ideas** **(a)** What was the consequence of Demeter's actions? **(b)** How did humankind suffer as a result of one individual's impulses? *[Connect to the Big Question: Community or individual—which is more important?]*

After You Read

Demeter and Persephone

Reading Skill: Cause and Effect

1. Answer these questions to analyze **cause-and-effect** relationships in the myth:
   (a) What happens to Persephone at the end of the myth? Why? **(b)** What happens to Demeter? Why?

2. Describe the effect of the giants struggling to get free at the beginning of the myth.

Literary Analysis: Myth

© 3. **Key Ideas and Details** What human qualities does Pluto possess?

© 4. **Craft and Structure** Complete a chart like the one shown to describe the lessons the **myth** teaches through each character.

Character	Lesson	How Taught
Demeter		
Persephone		
Pluto		

Vocabulary

© **Acquisition and Use** For each item, write a single sentence using the words indicated.

1. realm; distant
2. intervene; argument
3. monarch; ancient
4. dominions; powerful
5. defies; stubborn
6. abode; family

Word Study Use the context of the sentences and what you know about the **Latin root -dom-** to explain your answer to each question.

1. If you behave in a *domineering* manner, are you being humble?
2. If a building *dominates* a city skyline, is it hard to see?

Word Study

The **Latin root -dom-** means "master" or "building."

Apply It Explain how the root -dom- contributes to the meanings of these words. Consult a dictionary if necessary.

domain
dominant
predominate

Integrated Language Skills

Icarus and Daedalus • Demeter and Persephone

Conventions: Punctuation Marks

Review the chart to learn the functions of several common **punctuation marks.**

Punctuation / Usage	Example
colon (:) A *colon* introduces information that defines, explains, or provides a list of what is referred to before.	Lily brought many toys to the beach: buckets, shovels, balls, and floats.
semicolon (;) *Semicolons* are used in compound sentences.	We spent all morning riding our bikes; then we had a picnic.
hyphen (-) A *hyphen* is used to join two or more separate words into a single word.	Billy ordered a double-scoop, bubble-gum-flavored ice cream.
dash (—) *Dashes* are used to set off information that interrupts a thought.	On our way to the cinema— it had just opened— we stopped for gas.
bracket ([ ] ( )) A commonly used type of bracket is the parenthesis. Parentheses provide information that could be left out of a sentence without changing its meaning.	My brother Raf (the shyest person in our family) declined to make a speech at the party.

Practice A Identify each punctuation mark in this paragraph, and explain its function.

Daedalus and his son Icarus—a lively young boy—were trapped on Crete. King Minos was fickle (among other character flaws) and would imprison his loyal subjects on a whim. Daedalus fastened feathers together; he molded them in with wax to make wings.

ⓒ **Reading Application** In "Icarus and Daedalus," find one sentence that contains dashes, one that contains parentheses, one that contains a colon, and one that contains a semicolon.

Practice B Rewrite the paragraph below, using punctuation, so that each sentence makes sense.

Aphrodite her beauty is legendary urged her son to pierce Pluto's heart with an arrow of love. He swooped down from the sky he snatched Persephone and descended deep into the ground.

ⓒ **Writing Application** Write a brief paragraph about the myth you read, using each of the following types of punctuation at least once: hyphen, dash, parentheses, colon, and semi-colon.

PH WRITING COACH Further instruction and practice are available in *Prentice Hall Writing Coach.*

Writing

Common Core State Standards

L.7.2, L.7.4.b; W.7.3.a, W.7.3.b; SL.7.1.a, SL.7.1.c
[For the full wording of the standards, see page 912.]

Narrative Text You may have wondered why leaves change colors in the fall or what causes an earthquake. Write a short **myth** that explains a natural phenomenon that fascinates you. The following tips will help you.

- Think of a natural phenomenon and a creative explanation for its occurrence.
- Limit the number of characters to keep the story simple.
- Develop your characters by describing their appearance and actions and by showing how they relate to other characters.
- Plan the action of your story by identifying a problem and its solution.

Grammar Application Check your writing to be sure you have used punctuation correctly.

Writing Workshop: *Work in Progress*

Prewriting for Workplace Writing For a business letter that you might write, imagine you are planning an elaborate party. Develop a Wish List of five places where you would like to hold the party. Keep the Wish List in your writing portfolio.

Use this prewriting activity to prepare for the **Writing Workshop** on page 982.

Speaking and Listening

Comprehension and Collaboration With a small group, conduct a **debate.** If you read "Icarus and Daedalus," debate whether or not Daedalus shares any responsibility for Icarus' fall. If you read "Demeter and Persephone," debate whether or not Demeter was justified in changing the weather on Earth. Each side should prepare an argument and material to support the argument.

- Appoint a leader for your debate team and choose a person to act as a moderator, or discussion leader.
- Before the debate, consider what the opposing arguments might be and prepare counterarguments to address them.
- Volunteer your own opinions and make contributions to your team. Cite evidence that is logical and supported by your reading.
- Respond directly to questions and pose your own.
- After the debate, meet with your group to provide constructive feedback about how well speakers conveyed logical ideas.

PHLit
Online!
www.PHLitOnline.com
- Interactive graphic organizers
- Grammar tutorial
- Interactive journals

© Leveled Texts

Build your skills and improve your comprehension of fiction and
literary nonfiction with texts of increasing complexity.

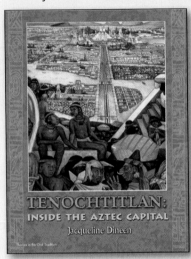

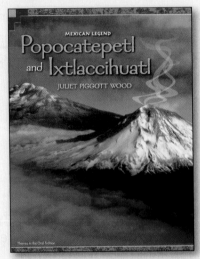

Read **"Tenochtitlan: Inside the
Aztec Capital"** to learn about
life in the ancient Aztec city of
Tenochtitlan.

Read **"Popocatepetl and
Ixtlaccihuatl"** to learn what
happens when a selfish emperor
interferes with true love.

© Common Core State Standards

Meet these standards with either **"Tenochtitlan: Inside the Aztec Capital"** (p. 938) or **"Popocatepetl
and Ixtlaccihuatl"** (p. 946).

Reading Literature
9. Compare and contrast a fictional portrayal of a time,
place, or character and a historical account of the same
period as a means of understanding how authors of fiction
use or alter history. (*Literary Analysis: Legend and Fact;
Writing: Description and Comparison*)

Spiral Review: RL.2
Writing
1.a. Introduce claim(s), acknowledge alternate or opposing
claims, and organize the reasons and evidence logically.
1.b. Support claim(s) with logical reasoning and relevant
evidence, using accurate, credible sources and
demonstrating an understanding of the topic or text.
(*Speaking and Listening: Persuasive Speech*)

2. Write informative/explanatory texts to examine a topic
and convey ideas, concepts, and information through the
selection, organization, and analysis of relevant content.

2.b. Develop the topic with relevant facts, definitions,
concrete details, quotations, or other information and
examples. (*Writing: Description*)

Speaking and Listening
4. Present claims and findings, emphasizing salient points
in a focused, coherent manner with pertinent descriptions,
facts, details, and examples; use appropriate eye contact,
adequate volume, and clear pronunciation. (*Speaking and
Listening: Persuasive Speech*)

Language
2. Demonstrate command of the conventions of standard
English capitalization, punctuation, and spelling when
writing. **2.a.** Use a comma to separate coordinate
adjectives. (*Conventions: Commas*)

4.b. Use common, grade-appropriate Greek or Latin
affixes and roots as clues to the meaning of a word.
(*Vocabulary: Word Study*)

Reading Skill: Cause and Effect

A **cause** is an event or situation that produces a result. An **effect** is the result produced. In a story or an essay, each effect may eventually become a cause for the next event. This results in a cause-and-effect chain that propels the action forward.

As you read, think about the causes and effects of events. If you do not clearly see the cause-and-effect relationships in a passage, **reread to look for connections** among the words and sentences.

Some words that identify causes and effects are *because, due to, for this reason,* and *as a result.*

Using the Strategy: Cause-and-Effect Chain

Notice the clue words in this **cause-and-effect chain**.

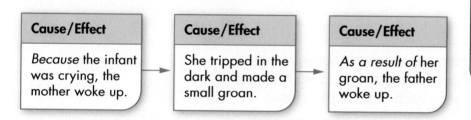

Cause/Effect	Cause/Effect	Cause/Effect
Because the infant was crying, the mother woke up.	She tripped in the dark and made a small groan.	*As a result of* her groan, the father woke up.

Literary Analysis: Legend and Fact

A **legend** is a traditional story about the past. A **fact** is something that can be proved to be true. Before legends were written down, they were passed on orally. Legends are based on facts that have grown into fiction in the many retellings over generations.

Every culture has its own legends to immortalize famous people. Most legends include these elements:

- a human who is larger than life
- fantastic elements
- roots or basis in historical facts
- events that reflect the culture that created the story

As you read, compare and contrast the historical facts about the ancient Aztec city of Tenochtitlan with a legend about that same city.

THE BIG ? *Community* or *individual —* which is more important?

Writing About the Big Question

"Tenochtitlan: Inside the Aztec Capital," describes how the Aztecs designed their city to prevent crop damage and protect against flooding. Use this sentence starter to develop your ideas about the Big Question.

When people work together for a **common** cause, they can help not only themselves but _____.

While You Read Look for details that show how the Aztecs worked to benefit the entire community.

Vocabulary

Read each word and its definition. Decide whether you know the word well, know it a little bit, or do not know it at all. After you read, see how your knowledge of each word has increased.

- **causeways** (kôz´ wāz´) *n.* roads across wet ground or shallow water (p. 939) *High waves washed away the causeways.* *causeway n.*

- **irrigation** (ir´ ə gā´ shən) *n.* the act of supplying water to land or crops (p. 940) *Irrigation makes farming possible in dry regions.* *irrigate v. irrigated v. irrigating v.*

- **nobility** (nō bil´ ə tē) *n.* people with a high rank in society (p. 940) *The nobility threw fancy parties.* *noble adj. nobleness n. nobly adv.*

- **outskirts** (out´ skɐrtz´) *n.* parts of a district far from the center of a city (p. 941) *The mall is on the outskirts of the city.*

- **reeds** (rēdz) *n.* tall, slender grasses that grow in marshy land (p. 941) *The reeds blew in the wind.* *reedy adj. reedier adj.*

- **goblets** (gäb´ lits) *n.* bowl-shaped drinking containers without handles (p. 942) *We broke two goblets during Thanksgiving dinner.* *goblet n.*

Word Study

The **Old English prefix** *out-* means "outside" or "more than."

This article describes how poor people built their homes on the **outskirts**, or areas outside the center, of an ancient Aztec city.

Author of
TENOCHTITLAN: INSIDE THE AZTEC CAPITAL

▲ "Tenochtitlan: Inside the Aztec Capital" appears in Dineen's book *The Aztecs.*

Jacqueline Dineen began her career as an editor for an educational publisher in London before she turned to writing children's books. She has written books on a variety of subjects, including science, history, and geography. Among them are *Lift the Lid on Mummies, The Early Inventions,* and *Food From the Sea.*

Text and Images In "Tenochtitlan: Inside the Aztec Capital," Dineen uses a skillful mix of description, eyewitness accounts, maps, photographs, and art to give readers a sense of what it took to build the city.

DID YOU KNOW?
Dineen has written more than eighty books.

BACKGROUND FOR THE ESSAY
The Origins of Mexico City
Mexico City, the capital of Mexico, was built on the ruins of the ancient Aztec city of Tenochtitlan. The city itself sat on an island in the center of a lake called Texcoco. Over the years, the lake was slowly drained to make room for the growing city. Because Mexico City is located on a drained lakebed, the effects of earthquakes have been severe. The city is slowly sinking several inches a year. "Tenochtitlan: Inside the Aztec Capital" presents factual information about the people and activities of the legendary city.

TENOCHTITLAN:
INSIDE THE AZTEC CAPITAL
Jacqueline Dineen

The Lake City of Tenochtitlan

The city of Tenochtitlan[1] began on an island in the middle of a swampy lake. There the Aztecs built their first temple to Huitzilopochtli.[2] The place was given the name Tenochtitlan, which means "The Place of the Fruit of the Prickly Pear Cactus." Later on the name was given to the city that grew up around the temple. The Aztecs rebuilt their temples on the same site every 52 years, so the first temple eventually became the great Temple Mayor[3] that stood at the center of the city.

The city started as a collection of huts. It began to grow after 1385, while Acamapichtli[4] was king. The Aztecs were excellent engineers. They built three causeways over the swamp to link the city with the mainland. These were raised roads made of stone supported on wooden pillars. Parts of the causeways were bridges. These bridges could be removed to leave gaps and this prevented enemies from getting to the city. Fresh water was brought from the mainland to the city along stone aqueducts.[5]

Inside the City

The Spaniards' first view of Tenochtitlan was described by one of Cortés's[6] soldiers, Bernal Diaz: "And when we saw all those towns and level causeway leading into Mexico, we were astounded. These great towns and buildings rising from the water, all made of stone, seemed like an enchanted vision."

By that time Tenochtitlan was the largest city in Mexico. About 200,000 people lived there. The houses were one story high and had flat roofs. In the center of the city was a large square. The twin temple stood on one side, and the king's palace on another. Officials' houses made of white stone also lined the square. There were few roads. People traveled in canoes along canals.

Floating Gardens

Tenochtitlan was built in a huge valley, the Valley of Mexico, which was surrounded by mountains. Rivers flowed from the

---

◄ **Critical Viewing**
What features of the city described in the text are shown on this map? **[Connect]**

Vocabulary
causeways (kôz´wāz´) *n.* roads across wet ground or shallow water

Legend and Fact
How might the Spaniards' reactions to their first sight of Tenochtitlan have sparked the beginning of a legend?

Reading Check

Who built the city of Tenochtitlan?

---

1. **Tenochtitlan** (tā nôch´ tēt län´) *n.* ancient Aztec capital located in what is now Mexico City.
2. **Huitzilopochtli** (wēt sē lō pōch´ tlē)
3. **Mayor** (mä yōr´) *adj.* (Sp.) main.
4. **Acamapichtli** (ä kä mä pēch´ tlē)
5. **aqueducts** (ak´ wə dukts´) *n.* large bridgelike structures made for bringing water from a distant source.
6. **Hernando Cortés** (er nän´ dō kōr tes´) Spanish adventurer (1485–1547) who conquered what is now central and southern Mexico.

Vocabulary
irrigation (irʹə gāʹ shən) *n.* the act of supplying water to land or crops
nobility (nō bilʹə tē) *n.* people with a high rank in society

Cause and Effect
What are two reasons the Aztecs built an embankment?

mountains into Lake Texcoco, where Tenochtitlan stood. The lake was linked to four other shallow, swampy lakes. The land around the lakes was dry because there was very little rain. The Aztecs dug ditches and piled up the earth to make islands in the shallow parts of the lake. These chinampas, or swamp gardens, could be farmed. The ditches carried water into larger canals that were used for irrigation and as waterways to the city.

Texcoco and the lake to the south contained fresh water, but the northern lakes contained salt water, which was no good for irrigation. The Aztecs built an embankment[7] 10 miles long to keep out the salt water and also to protect the city from flooding.

Feeding the People
Archaeologists think that when Tenochtitlan was at its greatest, about one million people lived in the Valley of Mexico. That included Tenochtitlan and the 50 or 60 city-states on the mainland surrounding the lakes. Food for all these people had to come from farming.

Historians are not sure how many people in Tenochtitlan were farmers, but they think it may have been between one third and one half of the population. The rest were the nobility, craftspeople, and others. Each chinampa was only big enough to grow food for one family. Most people in Tenochtitlan depended on food from outside the city.

As the city grew, more and more land was drained for farming and for building. Farmers had no tools except simple hoes and digging sticks, but the loose soil was fertile and easy to turn. The main crop was corn, but farmers also grew tomatoes, beans, chili peppers, and prickly pears. They grew maguey cactus for its fibers and to make a drink called pulque. Cacao trees were grown in the hottest areas. The seeds were used for trading and to make a chocolate drink.

Inside an Aztec Home
There were big differences between a rich Aztec home and a poor one. The nobles' houses were like palaces. They were one story high and built around

---

7. **embankment** (em bankʹ mənt) *n.* wall of earth built to keep water back.

a courtyard. Each of the four sides contained four or five large rooms. The courtyards were planted with flower and vegetable gardens. Some houses on the island in the center of the city were built of adobe—bricks made from mud and dried in the sun. Adobe is still used for building in Mexico today. These grand houses and palaces were whitewashed so that they shone in the sun. The Spanish soldier Bernal Diaz described buildings that looked like "gleaming white towers and castles: a marvelous sight."

There is very little evidence about the buildings in Tenochtitlan and hardly any about the poor people's houses. What we do know has been pieced together from scattered historical records such as documents that record the sale of building sites on the chinampa gardens. All of the poorer people's homes were built on the chinampas on the outskirts of the city. Because the chinampas would not take the weight of stone, houses had to be built of lighter materials such as wattle-and-daub. This was made by weaving reeds together and then plastering them with mud. We know that the outskirts of the city were divided into groups of houses inside walled areas, or compounds. A whole family lived in each compound. The family consisted of a couple, their married children, and their grandchildren. Every married couple in the family had a separate house of one or two rooms. All the

Spiral Review
Central Idea How does the author support the idea that the homes of rich and poor Aztecs were very different?

Vocabulary
outskirts (out skʉrtz´) *n.* parts of a district far from the center of a city

reeds (rēdz) *n.* tall, slender grasses that grow in marshy land

▼ **Critical Viewing** What details in this picture suggest the Aztecs' daily activities? **[Analyze]**

houses opened onto an outdoor patio that belonged to the whole family.

Outside the house, the families often kept turkeys in pens. The turkeys provided eggs and meat. There was also a beehive for honey. Most families had a bathhouse in the garden.

Furniture and Decoration

Aztec houses were very plain inside. Everyone slept on mats of reeds that were spread on the dirt floor at night. Families had cooking pots and utensils made of clay. There were goblets for pulque and other drinks, graters for grinding chilis, and storage pots of various designs. Reed baskets were also used for storage. Households had grinding stones for grinding corn into flour. There was also a household shrine with statues of the gods.

The houses had no windows or chimneys, so they must have been dark and smoky from the cooking fire. There were no doors, just an open doorway. Even the palaces had open doorways with cloths hanging over them.

Vocabulary
goblets (gäb´ lits) *n.* bowl-shaped drinking containers without handles

Critical Thinking

1. **Key Ideas and Details (a)** Describe one way the Aztecs shaped their environment to suit their needs. **(b) Make a Judgment:** How did this improve their lives?

2. **Key Ideas and Details (a)** Name one element of the environment that shaped the Aztecs' lives. **(b) Draw Conclusions:** How well did the Aztecs deal with that element? Explain.

3. **Craft and Structure Analyze:** How does the author use factual information to present a clear picture of ancient Aztec life?

4. **Integration of Knowledge and Ideas** How did each individual's efforts contribute to the good of the Aztec community? *[Connect to the Big Question: Community or individual—which is more important?]*

Cite textual evidence to support your responses.

Reading Skill: Cause and Effect

1. What might have **caused** the Aztecs to remove the bridges from the causeways?

2. Reread the essay to find an **effect** for each of these causes:

   (a) The city of Tenochtitlan was built on a lake.

   (b) The city grew.

   (c) Aztec houses had no windows or chimneys.

Literary Analysis: Legend and Fact

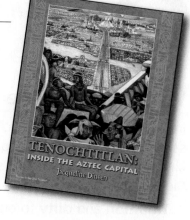

© **3. Key Ideas and Details (a)** Identify three **facts** from the essay. **(b)** Identify two predictions or assumptions made by archaeologists that are likely to be true but cannot be proved.

© **4. Integration of Knowledge and Ideas** Use the chart below to explain what facts in this essay could be used to create an interesting **legend** about Tenochtitlan.

Facts from the essay	Possible use in a legend

Vocabulary

© **Acquisition and Use** Answer each of the following questions.

   1. What type of buildings might you find on the *outskirts* of a modern city?

   2. Where do *reeds* grow?

   3. What might you do with a set of *goblets*?

   4. When might it be useful to build a *causeway*?

   5. In what way is *irrigation* useful to farmers?

   6. Why would you expect members of the *nobility* to live in fancy homes?

Word Study Use the context of the sentences and what you know about the **Old English prefix out-** to explain your answers.

   1. If you *outbid* me, did you bid more or less than I did?

   2. What do you risk by engaging in an activity that has been *outlawed*?

Word Study

The **Old English prefix out-** means "outside" or "more than."

Apply It Explain how the prefix *out-* contributes to the meanings of these words. Consult a dictionary if necessary.

outcast

outnumber

outpatient

Community or *individual —* which is more important?

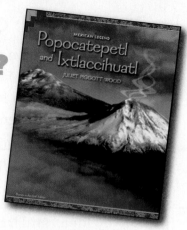

Writing About the Big Question

In "Popocatepetl and Ixtlaccihuatl," an Aztec princess is expected to sacrifice true love in order to assume her responsibilities as ruler of a kingdom. Use this sentence starter to develop your ideas about the Big Question.

Tradition and **duty** to one's community sometimes require a person to _____.

While You Read Look for details that suggest the Emperor does not consider the future results of his actions.

Vocabulary

Read each word and its definition. Decide whether you know the word well, know it a little bit, or do not know it at all. After you read, see how your knowledge of each word has increased.

- **shortsightedness** (short´ sīt´ id nəs) *n.* condition of not considering the future effects of something (p. 948) *Her shortsightedness left her unprepared for the storm.* shortsighted *adj.* shortsightedly *adv.*

- **feebleness** (fē´ bəl nəs) *n.* weakness (p. 949) *His feebleness did not stop the old man from walking his beloved dog.* feeble *adj.* feebly *adv.* feebler *adj.*

- **decreed** (di krēd´) *v.* officially ordered (p. 949) *The Queen decreed the day a holiday.* decree *v.* decreeing *v.*

- **relished** (rel´ isht) *v.* enjoyed; liked (p. 950) *Her grandmother relished time alone with a good book.* relish *v.* relish *n.*

- **unanimous** (yo͞o nan´ ə məs) *adj.* based on complete agreement (p. 951) *Beth was elected president by a unanimous vote.* unanimously *adv.* unanimity *n.*

- **routed** (rout´ əd) *v.* completely defeated (p. 952) *The king's men routed the invaders.* rout *v.*

Word Study

The **Latin prefix** *uni-* means "having or consisting of only one."

In this legend, the Aztec warriors are **unanimous,** or sharing one opinion, about who is responsible for their victory.

Author of
Popocatepetl and Ixtlaccihuatl

Juliet Piggott Wood discovered her love for learning about different cultures while living in Japan, where her grandfather was a legal advisor to Prince Ito. Wood's interest in Japan inspired her to produce several books on Japanese history and folklore. Her fascination with one culture led to research about others. She went on to co-author a book retelling famous fairy tales from around the world.

Far and Wide In World War II, Wood served in England in the Women's Royal Naval Service. Her experience in that war may have influenced her to write about other military battles, especially the legendary Aztec battle described in her book on Mexican folk tales. Clearly a person with many talents, Wood expanded her nonfiction list with a work on famous regiments in Queen Alexandra's Royal Army Nursing Corps.

DID YOU KNOW?
Wood co-authored a book retelling famous fairy tales from around the world.

BACKGROUND FOR THE LEGEND
The Oral Tradition
The oral tradition is the collection of songs, stories, and poems that are passed from generation to generation by word of mouth. People used the traditional stories to communicate shared beliefs and to explain their world. In "Popocatepetl and Ixtlaccihuatl," you will see how the storyteller shares Aztec beliefs through a tale about teenagers who fall in love.

Popocatepetl
and Ixtlaccihuatl

JULIET PIGGOTT WOOD

Before the Spaniards came to Mexico and marched on the Aztec capital of Tenochtitlan[1] there were two volcanoes to the southeast of that city. The Spaniards destroyed much of Tenochtitlan and built another city in its place and called it Mexico City. It is known by that name still, and the pass through which the Spaniards came to the ancient Tenochtitlan is still there, as are the volcanoes on each side of that pass. Their names have not been changed. The one to the north is Ixtlaccihuatl [ēs′ tlä sē′ wät′ əl] and the one on the south of the pass is Popocatepetl [pô pô kä te′ pet′ əl]. Both are snowcapped and beautiful, Popocatepetl being the taller of the two. That name means Smoking Mountain. In Aztec days it gushed forth smoke and, on occasion, it does so still. It erupted too in Aztec days and has done so again since the Spaniards came. Ixtlaccihuatl means The White Woman, for its peak was, and still is, white.

Perhaps Ixtlaccihuatl and Popocatepetl were there in the highest part of the Valley of Mexico in the days when the earth was very young, in the days when the new people were just learning to eat and grow corn. The Aztecs claimed the volcanoes as their own, for they possessed a legend about them and their creation, and they believed that legend to be true.

There was once an Aztec Emperor in Tenochtitlan. He was very powerful. Some thought he was wise as well, whilst others doubted his wisdom. He was both a ruler and a warrior and he kept at bay those tribes living in and beyond the mountains surrounding the Valley of Mexico, with its huge lake called Texcoco [tä skō′ kō] in which Tenochtitlan was built. His power was absolute and the splendor in which he lived was very great.

It is not known for how many years the Emperor ruled in Tenochtitlan, but it is known that he lived to a great age. However, it was not until he was in his middle years that his wife gave him an heir, a girl. The Emperor and Empress loved the princess very much and she was their only child. She was a dutiful daughter and learned all she could from her father about the art of ruling, for she knew that when he died she would reign in his stead in Tenochtitlan.

◀ **Critical Viewing**
Why do you think volcanoes like these inspired ancient peoples? **[Speculate]**

✔ Reading Check
Explain the meaning of each mountain's name.

---

1. **Tenochtitlan** (tä noch′ tēt län′) the Aztec capital, conquered by the Spanish in 1521.

Vocabulary
shortsightedness
(short´ sīt´ id ness)
n. condition of not
considering the future
effects of something

Cause and Effect
What causes Ixtla to
be serious?

Her name was Ixtlaccihuatl. Her parents and her friends called her Ixtla. She had a pleasant disposition and, as a result, she had many friends. The great palace where she lived with the Emperor and Empress rang with their laughter when they came to the parties her parents gave for her. As well as being a delightful companion Ixtla was also very pretty, even beautiful.

Her childhood was happy and she was content enough when she became a young woman. But by then she was fully aware of the great responsibilities which would be hers when her father died and she became serious and studious and did not enjoy parties as much as she had done when younger.

Another reason for her being so serious was that she was in love. This in itself was a joyous thing, but the Emperor forbade her to marry. He wanted her to reign and rule alone when he died, for he trusted no one, not even his wife, to rule as he did except his much loved only child, Ixtla. This was why there were some who doubted the wisdom of the Emperor for, by not allowing his heiress to marry, he showed a selfishness and shortsightedness towards his daughter and his empire which many considered was not truly wise. An emperor, they felt, who was not truly wise could not also be truly great. Or even truly powerful.

The man with whom Ixtla was in love was also in love with her. Had they been allowed to marry their state could have been doubly joyous. His name was Popocatepetl and Ixtla and his friends all called him Popo. He was a warrior in the service of the Emperor, tall and strong, with a capacity for gentleness, and very brave. He and Ixtla loved each other very much and while they were content and even happy when they were together, true joy was not theirs because the Emperor continued to insist that Ixtla should not be married when the time came for her to take on her father's responsibilities.

This unfortunate but moderately happy relationship between Ixtla and Popo continued for several years, the couple pleading with the Emperor at regular intervals and the Emperor remaining constantly adamant. Popo loved Ixtla no less for her father's stubbornness and she loved him no less while she studied, as her father demanded she should do, the art of ruling in preparation for her reign.

When the Emperor became very old he also became ill. In his feebleness he channeled all his failing energies towards instructing Ixtla in statecraft, for he was no longer able to exercise that craft himself. So it was that his enemies, the tribes who lived in the mountains and beyond, realized that the great Emperor in Tenochtitlan was great no longer, for he was only teaching his daughter to rule and not ruling himself.

The tribesmen came nearer and nearer to Tenochtitlan until the city was besieged. At last the Emperor realized himself that he was great no longer, that his power was nearly gone and that his domain was in dire peril.

Warrior though he long had been, he was now too old and too ill to lead his fighting men into battle. At last he understood that, unless his enemies were frustrated in their efforts to enter and lay waste to Tenochtitlan, not only would he no longer be Emperor but his daughter would never be Empress.

Instead of appointing one of his warriors to lead the rest into battle on his behalf, he offered a bribe to all of them. Perhaps it was that his wisdom, if wisdom he had, had forsaken him, or perhaps he acted from fear. Or perhaps he simply changed his mind. But the bribe he offered to whichever warrior succeeded in lifting the siege of Tenochtitlan and defeating the enemies in and around the Valley of Mexico was both the hand of his daughter and the equal right to reign and rule, with her, in Tenochtitlan. Furthermore, he decreed that directly he learned that his enemies had been defeated he would instantly cease to be Emperor himself. Ixtla would not have to wait until her father died to become Empress and, if her father should die of his illness or old age before his enemies were vanquished,

Cause and Effect
What was one effect of the Emperor's becoming old and ill?

Vocabulary
feebleness (fē′ bəl nəs) *n.* weakness

decreed (di krēd′) *v.* officially ordered

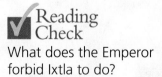

Reading Check
What does the Emperor forbid Ixtla to do?

he further decreed that he who overcame the surrounding enemies should marry the princess whether he, the Emperor, lived or not.

Ixtla was fearful when she heard of her father's bribe to his warriors, for the only one whom she had any wish to marry was Popo and she wanted to marry him, and only him, very much indeed.

The warriors, however, were glad when they heard of the decree: there was not one of them who would not have been glad to have the princess as his wife and they all **relished** the chance of becoming Emperor.

And so the warriors went to war at their ruler's behest, and each fought trebly[2] hard for each was fighting not only for the safety of Tenochtitlan and the surrounding valley, but for the delightful bride and for the right to be the Emperor himself.

Even though the warriors fought with great skill and even though each one exhibited a courage he did not know he possessed, the war was a long one. The Emperor's enemies were firmly entrenched around Lake Texcoco and Tenochtitlan by the time the warriors were sent to war, and as battle followed battle the final outcome was uncertain.

The warriors took a variety of weapons with them; wooden clubs edged with sharp blades of obsidian,[3] obsidian machetes,[4] javelins which they hurled at their enemies from troughed throwing boards, bows and arrows, slings and spears set with obsidian fragments, and lances, too. Many of them carried shields woven from wicker and covered in tough hide and most wore armor made of thick quilted cotton soaked in brine.

The war was long and fierce. Most of the warriors fought together and in unison, but some fought alone. As time went on natural leaders emerged and, of these, undoubtedly Popo was the best. Finally it was he, brandishing his club and shield,

Vocabulary
relished (rel´isht)
v. enjoyed; liked

▼ **Critical Viewing**
How does this picture relate to the details of the battle in the story? **[Connect]**

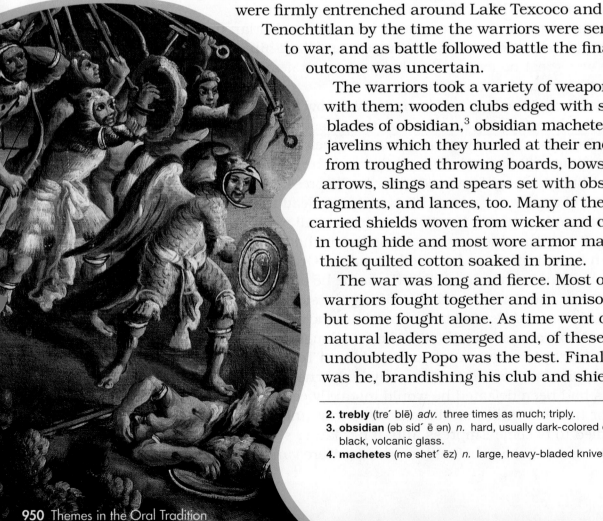

2. **trebly** (tre´ blē) *adv.* three times as much; triply.
3. **obsidian** (əb sid´ ē ən) *n.* hard, usually dark-colored or black, volcanic glass.
4. **machetes** (mə shet´ ēz) *n.* large, heavy-bladed knives.

who led the great charge of running warriors across the valley, with their enemies fleeing before them to the safety of the coastal plains and jungles beyond the mountains.

The warriors acclaimed Popo as the man most responsible for the victory and, weary though they all were, they set off for Tenochtitlan to report to the Emperor and for Popo to claim Ixtla as his wife at last.

But a few of those warriors were jealous of Popo. Since they knew none of them could rightly claim the victory for himself (the decision among the Emperor's fighting men that Popo was responsible for the victory had been unanimous), they wanted to spoil for him and for Ixtla the delights which the Emperor had promised.

These few men slipped away from the rest at night and made their way to Tenochtitlan ahead of all the others. They reached the capital two days later, having traveled without sleep all the way, and quickly let it be known that, although the Emperor's warriors had been successful against his enemies, the warrior Popo had been killed in battle.

It was a foolish and cruel lie which those warriors told their Emperor, and they told it for no reason other than that they were jealous of Popo.

When the Emperor heard this he demanded that Popo's body be brought to him so that he might arrange a fitting burial. He knew the man his daughter had loved would have died courageously. The jealous warriors looked at one another and said nothing. Then one of them told the Emperor that Popo had been killed on the edge of Lake Texcoco and that his body had fallen into the water and no man had been able to retrieve it. The Emperor was saddened to hear this.

After a little while he demanded to be told which of his warriors had been responsible for the victory but none of the fighting men before him dared claim the successful outcome of the war for himself, for each knew the others would refute him. So they were silent. This puzzled the Emperor and he decided to wait for the main body of his warriors to return and not to press the few who had brought the news of the victory and of Popo's death.

Legend and Fact
What does the account of the battle suggest about the Aztecs' attitudes toward war?

Vocabulary
unanimous (yo͞o nan′ ə məs) *adj.* based on complete agreement

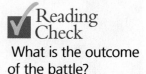
Reading Check
What is the outcome of the battle?

Social Studies Connection

Tenochtitlan

Archaeologists believe that at one time, more than 200,000 people lived in Tenochtitlan, the Aztec capital city in the middle of the giant lake Texcoco. Approximately one half of the population were farmers. Much of the farming was done on small island gardens surrounding the city. People living in Tenochtitlan depended on food the farmers grew outside the city. They also depended on water from outside the city, which was carried to the city by a system of aqueducts.

Because of its location and dependence on outside food and water, the city would have been helpless in the face of a siege. With no way to get in or out to get food, a siege would soon lead to starvation.

Connect to the Literature

Based on the situation, do you think the rewards offered by the Emperor in this story were appropriate? Explain.

Then the Emperor sent for his wife and his daughter and told them their enemies had been overcome. The Empress was thoroughly excited and relieved at the news. Ixtla was only apprehensive. The Emperor, seeing her anxious face, told her quickly that Popo was dead. He went on to say that the warrior's body had been lost in the waters of Lake Texcoco, and again it was as though his wisdom had left him, for he spoke at some length of his not being able to tell Ixtla who her husband would be and who would become Emperor when the main body of warriors returned to Tenochtitlan.

But Ixtla heard nothing of what he told her, only that her beloved Popo was dead. She went to her room and lay down. Her mother followed her and saw at once she was very ill. Witch doctors were sent for, but they could not help the princess, and neither could her parents. Her illness had no name, unless it was the illness of a broken heart. Princess Ixtlaccihuatl did not wish to live if Popocatepetl was dead, and so she died herself.

The day after her death Popo returned to Tenochtitlan with all the other surviving warriors. They went straight to the palace and, with much cheering, told the Emperor that his enemies had been routed and that Popo was the undoubted victor of the conflict.

The Emperor praised his warriors and pronounced Popo to be the new Emperor in his place. When the young man asked first to see Ixtla, begging that they should be married at once before being jointly proclaimed Emperor and Empress, the Emperor had to tell Popo of Ixtla's death, and how it had happened.

Popo spoke not a word.

He gestured the assembled warriors to follow him and together they sought out the few jealous men who had given the false news of his death to the Emperor. With the army of warriors watching, Popo killed each one of them in single combat with his obsidian studded club. No one tried to stop him.

That task accomplished Popo returned to the palace and, still without speaking and still wearing his stiff cotton armor, went to Ixtla's room. He gently lifted her body and carried it out of the palace and out of the city, and no one tried to stop him doing that either. All the warriors followed him in silence.

When he had walked some miles he gestured to them again and they built a huge pile of stones in the shape of a pyramid. They all worked together and they worked fast while Popo stood and watched, holding the body of the princess in his arms. By sunset the mighty edifice was finished. Popo climbed it alone, carrying Ixtla's corpse with him. There, at the very top, under a heap of stones, he buried the young woman he had loved so well and for so long, and who had died for the love of him.

That night Popo slept alone at the top of the pyramid by Ixtla's grave. In the morning he came down and spoke for the first time since the Emperor had told him the princess was dead. He told the warriors to build another pyramid, a little to the southeast of the one which held Ixtla's body and to build it higher than the other.

He told them too to tell the Emperor on his behalf that he, Popocatepetl, would never reign and rule in Tenochtitlan. He would keep watch over the grave of the Princess Ixtlaccihuatl for the rest of his life.

The messages to the Emperor were the last words Popo ever spoke. Well before the evening the second mighty pile of stones was built. Popo climbed it and stood at the top, taking a torch of resinous pine wood with him.

Vocabulary
routed (rout´ əd) v. completely defeated

✓ Reading Check
What does Popo ask the Emperor when he returns?

Legend and Fact
Are the volcanoes real?
How do you know?

And when he reached the top he lit the torch and the warriors below saw the white smoke rise against the blue sky, and they watched as the sun began to set and the smoke turned pink and then a deep red, the color of blood.

So Popocatepetl stood there, holding the torch in memory of Ixtlaccihuatl, for the rest of his days.

The snows came and, as the years went by, the pyramids of stone became high white-capped mountains. Even now the one called Popocatepetl emits smoke in memory of the princess whose body lies in the mountain which bears her name.

▶ **Critical Viewing**
What details in this photo are similar to the details of Popo's actions in the story? **[Analyze]**

Critical Thinking

Cite textual evidence to support your responses.

1. **Key Ideas and Details (a)** Why are Ixtla and Popo unable to marry? **(b) Analyze:** What qualities make the two well matched?

2. **Key Ideas and Details (a)** Why does Popo refuse to become emperor and rule in Tenochtitlan? **(b) Draw Conclusions:** Based on this legend, what traits do you think the Aztecs admired?

3. **Key Ideas and Details Compare and Contrast:** How do the factual account and the legend convey the size and magnificence of Tenochtitlan and the Aztec empire? **Analyze:** What elements are present in the legend that you would not find in a factual account?

4. **Integration of Knowledge and Ideas (a) Interpret:** What lesson does the legend suggest? **(b) Evaluate:** Can this lesson be applied in modern times?

5. **Integration of Knowledge and Ideas (a)** Was the Emperor's decision at the story's beginning better for the individual or the community? **(b)** Is it ever important to consider the needs of a community over the needs of an individual? Explain. *[Connect to the Big Question: Community or individual—which is more important?]*

Reading Skill: Cause and Effect

1. Reread the legend to find an **effect** for each of these **causes.**

(a) The Emperor does not allow his daughter to marry.

(b) The Emperor spends all his time teaching Ixtla statecraft.

(c) The warriors lie to the Emperor about Popo's death.

(d) Ixtla hears that Popo is dead.

2. According to the legend, what **causes** the volcano to smoke?

Literary Analysis: Legend and Fact

ⓒ 3. Key Ideas and Details Identify two **facts** in this story. How do you know that they are facts?

ⓒ 4. Integration of Knowledge and Ideas Use the chart below to help you identify which events in this **legend** might have been based on historical events.

Events from Legend	Possible Historic Connection

Vocabulary

ⓒ Acquisition and Use Answer each question and then explain your answer.

1. If something is *decreed*, is it undecided?

2. If a vote is *unanimous*, does everyone agree?

3. If one's enemies have been *routed*, have the enemies won?

4. Is *shortsightedness* useful when making decisions for the future?

5. Would *feebleness* prevent a person from exercising?

6. If you *relished* the last book you read, did you enjoy it?

Word Study Use the context of the sentences and what you know about the **Latin prefix uni-** to explain your answers.

1. How many wheels does a *unicycle* have?

2. If two people speak in *unison*, do they speak at the same time?

Word Study

The **Latin prefix uni-** means "having or consisting of only one."

Apply It Explain how the prefix *uni-* contributes to the meanings of these words. Consult a dictionary if necessary.

unity
unilateral
uniform

Integrated Language Skills

Tenochtitlan: Inside the Aztec Capital • Popocatepetl and Ixtlaccihuatl

Conventions: Commas

A **comma** signals a brief pause. A *semicolon* signals a stronger separation than a comma.

Using Commas	Example
Use a comma before a conjunction that joins independent clauses in a compound sentence.	John thought he was late, and he rushed through the parking lot.
Use a comma after an introductory word, phrase, or clause.	If you go to the play, how will you get your homework finished?
Use commas to separate three or more words, phrases, or clauses in a series.	The café offered fruit juice, iced tea, and sparkling water.
Use a comma to separate adjectives of equal rank.	We received a warm, joyful welcome from our neighbors.

Practice A Explain how the comma in each sentence is used.

1. Tenochtitlan rose from the center of a shallow, swampy lake.
2. Workers in Tenochtitlan built causeways, irrigation ditches, and stately homes.
3. In the center of the city, the homes of the nobility lined a large square.
4. Many people built swamp gardens in the lake, but they were only big enough to grow food for one family.

Ⓒ **Reading Application** In "Tenochtitlan: Inside the Aztec Capital," find three sentences that contain commas and explain how each comma is used.

Practice B Rewrite the following sentences, inserting commas as necessary.

1. In the great city of Tenochtitlan there once lived a stubborn and foolish Emperor.
2. His daughter fell in love with a great warrior but the Emperor would not allow them to marry.
3. Because of his stubbornness he lost his daughter his greatest warrior and the respect of his subjects.

Ⓒ **Writing Application** Write five sentences about two people who are in love. At least one of the sentences should be a compound sentence, one should contain items in a series, and one should include a direct quotation.

PH **WRITING COACH** Further instruction and practice are available in *Prentice Hall Writing Coach*.

Writing

Common Core State Standards

L.7.2, L.7.2.a; RL.7.9; W.7.1.a, W.7.1.b, W.7.2, W.7.2.b; SL.7.4

[For the full wording of the standards, see page 934.]

Informative Text Write a short **description** of the ancient city of Tenochtitlan based on the selections. Review "Tenochtitlan" and "Popocatepetl and Ixtlaccihuatl." Jot down details about the time, place, and overall environment of the city, as well as details about the lives of its inhabitants. Refer to your notes as you draft your description.

Next, draw on your notes to write a brief **comparison** of the selections. Identify the common historical elements that the article and the legend refer to. Finally, explain the ways in which the legend adapts or alters historical fact.

Grammar Application Check your writing to be sure you have correctly used commas, especially after introductory words, phrases, or clauses and to separate adjectives of equal rank.

Writing Workshop: *Work in Progress*

Prewriting for Workplace Writing Choose one of the locations from the Wish List in your portfolio and write a brief sentence stating your purpose for writing to that specific service provider. Save this Purpose Sentence in your writing portfolio.

Use this prewriting activity to prepare for the **Writing Workshop** on page 982.

Speaking and Listening

Presentation of Ideas Deliver a **persuasive speech** based on your reading. If you read "Tenochtitlan," your goal is to persuade authorities that building a city in the middle of a lake is a good idea. If you read "Popocatepetl and Ixtlaccihuatl," your goal is to persuade the Emperor to allow Popo and Ixtla to marry.

- On a note card, write your position and a short statement explaining the reasons for your position.
- List the main points that support your position on additional cards. Use solid evidence, including facts, statistics, and quotations from authorities, to overcome opposing views.
- Jot down phrases that will remind you of your points, rather than writing complete sentences.
- Refer to your note cards as you deliver your speech.
- As you deliver your speech, establish eye contact, adjust your volume, and pronounce each word clearly.

PHLit Online!
www.PHLitOnline.com
- Interactive graphic organizers
- Grammar tutorial
- Interactive journals

Test Practice: Reading

Cause and Effect

Fiction Selection

Directions: *Read the selection. Then, answer the questions.*

Lisa clutched her camera, afraid of missing the moment when a whale would soar out of the water. She had seen dolphins playing in the ocean when she was five years old. As a result, Lisa dreamed of one day becoming a marine biologist. Now, in honor of her thirteenth birthday, she had dragged her older brother Phil whale watching. "I'm freezing! Why do we have to whale-watch in the winter?" Phil said. Lisa glanced at Phil, who was dripping with ocean water. Over his shoulder, she noticed a massive shape rising out of the water. Phil turned and followed her gaze. "Wow!" he said in a stunned voice. "That whale is so cool! This is great." Lisa smiled at her brother's amazement as she happily snapped photos of the humpback whale.

1. Lisa has her camera ready because—
   A. she wants to photograph a whale.
   B. her brother needs to borrow it.
   C. she hopes to be a photographer.
   D. the camera might be broken.

2. What caused Phil to go whale watching?
   A. He wants a photograph of a whale, and he has convinced Lisa to come.
   B. His parents asked him to go, and he loves whales.
   C. He wants to be a marine biologist, and he has to do a science project.
   D. It is Lisa's birthday, and she wants him to go.

3. Which phrase in the story signals a cause-and-effect relationship?
   A. Now,
   B. had seen
   C. As a result
   D. Over his shoulder,

4. What effect does seeing the whale have on Phil and Lisa?
   A. Phil is glad he came, but Lisa is disappointed.
   B. Phil is annoyed that he is wet, but Lisa is thrilled to get a photograph.
   C. Both Phil and Lisa are excited to see the whale.
   D. Both Phil and Lisa are too tired to appreciate seeing the whale.

Writing for Assessment

Write a paragraph describing the cause-and-effect chain leading from Lisa's seeing dolphins when she is five years old to Phil and Lisa's whale-watching years later.

Nonfiction Selection

Directions: *Read the selection. Then, answer the questions.*

During summers off the coast of Alaska, long hours of sunshine warm the icy waters. Microscopic water plants begin to bloom, and tiny marine animals flock to the warming waters to feed on them. The tiny animals, in turn, lure giant humpback whales to the waters.

Humpbacks eat these tiny animals, but they also eat larger fish, such as sardines and mackerel. In fact, humpback whales spend most of their time eating because they need an enormous amount of food to remain active and warm. Each whale eats between 4,500 and 5,000 pounds of food each day!

As autumn nears, the days grow shorter, causing the water to cool. Food is not as plentiful in the cooler water. Because of this, the humpback whales move to warmer waters, traveling past California toward Hawaii. There they stay until summer days call them northward.

1. What is the effect of longer hours of sunshine?
  A. Microscopic plants begin to bloom.
  B. Whales create a bubble net.
  C. Humpback whales swim toward Hawaii.
  D. Sardines and mackerel are plentiful.

2. Why do humpback whales spend so much time eating?
  A. Food takes a long time to consume.
  B. Hunting takes a lot of energy.
  C. They require a lot of food to stay active and warm.
  D. They need to eat as much as they can before the waters cool.

3. The water cools because—
  A. the days grow shorter as autumn nears.
  B. the whales eat lots of fish in the water.
  C. winds blow colder air over the ocean.
  D. the days are longer in summer.

4. What is the *main* reason humpback whales leave the waters of Alaska?
  A. The sun shines for more hours per day as autumn nears.
  B. Fewer fish are in the water after the whales have been there.
  C. The whale's food supply is not as plentiful in the cooler water.
  D. The humpback whales always spend the winter near Alaska.

Writing for Assessment

Connecting Across Texts

In the first passage, Phil asks why he and Lisa can only whale-watch in the winter. Use details from both passages to explain the cause-and-effect relationship that answers his question. In your response, explain where Lisa and Phil might be.

www.PHLitOnline.com
- Online practice
- Instant feedback

Reading for Information

Analyzing Expository Texts

Textbook Article

Question and Answer

© **Common Core State Standards**

Reading Informational Text
5. Analyze the structure an author uses to organize a text, including how the major sections contribute to the whole and to the development of the ideas.

Writing
2.a. Introduce a topic clearly, previewing what is to follow; organize ideas, concepts, and information, using strategies such as definition, classification, comparison/contrast, and cause/effect.
2.c. Use appropriate transitions to create cohesion and clarify the relationships among ideas and concepts.

Language
4.c. Consult general and specialized reference materials, both print and digital, to find the pronunciation of a word or determine or clarify its precise meaning or its part of speech.
6. Acquire and use accurately grade-appropriate general academic and domain-specific words and phrases; gather vocabulary knowledge when considering a word or phrase important to comprehension or expression.

Reading Skill:
Analyze Cause-and-Effect Organization

When you **analyze cause-and-effect organization,** you look at the way relationships between events are presented in a text. Some texts show how several events or conditions (causes) produce a single effect. Others show how a single event can have several effects. To understand how causes and effects are organized in a text, begin by identifying and analyzing cause-and-effect relationships. Ask questions like the ones shown to find relationships between events.

Questions for Analyzing Cause-and-Effect Relationships	
What happened?	Winter
Why did this happen? **(cause)**	Earth's axis tilted away from the sun.
What has happened or will happen as a result? **(effect)**	Sunlight hit our hemisphere less directly; the days were colder.

Content-Area Vocabulary

These words appear in the selections that follow. You may also encounter them in other content-area texts.

- **spectrum** (spek´trəm) *n.* the band of colors formed when a beam of light is passed through a prism or is broken up by some other means

- **wavelengths** (wāv´ leŋths´) *n.* (in physics) the distances between the tops of waves of energy, such as sound or light, that follow each other

- **stratosphere** (strat´ə sfir´) *n.* the part of Earth's atmosphere that extends from about seven miles above the surface to 31 miles

Features:

- instructional reading
- headings and subheadings that organize material
- clearly identified concepts, ideas, or topics
- charts, diagrams, or other visuals
- text written for a student audience

The Seasons on Earth

from *Prentice Hall Science Explorer*

Most places outside the tropics and polar regions have four distinct seasons: winter, spring, summer, and autumn. But there are great differences in temperature from place to place. For instance, it is generally warmer near the equator than near the poles. Why is this so?

How Sunlight Hits Earth

Figure 1 shows how sunlight strikes Earth's surface. Notice that sunlight hits Earth's surface most directly near the equator. Near the poles, sunlight arrives at a steep angle. As a result, it is spread out over a greater area. That is why it is warmer near the equator than near the poles.

> Phrases such as *as a result* and *that is why* indicate cause-and-effect relationships.

Less direct sunlight

Most direct sunlight

Less direct sunlight

Axis

Equator

Figure 1 Sunlight Striking Earth's Surface Near the equator, sunlight strikes Earth's surface more directly and is less spread out than near the poles.

> This section of the article explains the cause-and-effect relationship shown in the diagrams.

Earth's Tilted Axis

If Earth's axis were straight up and down relative to its orbit, temperatures would remain fairly constant year-round. There would be no seasons. Earth has seasons because its axis is tilted as it revolves around the sun.

Notice in Figure 2 that Earth's axis is always tilted at an angle of 23.5° from the vertical. As Earth revolves around the sun, the north end of its axis is tilted away from the sun for part of the year and toward the sun for part of the year.

Summer and winter are caused by Earth's tilt as it revolves around the sun. The change in seasons is not caused by changes in Earth's distance from the sun. In fact, Earth is farthest from the sun when it is summer in the Northern Hemisphere.

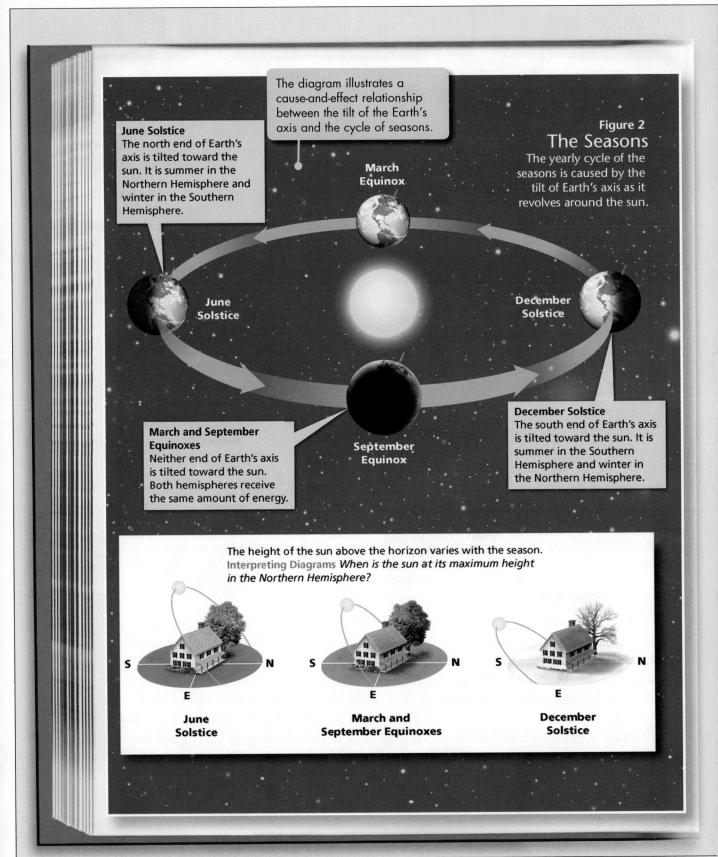

The diagram illustrates a cause-and-effect relationship between the tilt of the Earth's axis and the cycle of seasons.

Figure 2
The Seasons
The yearly cycle of the seasons is caused by the tilt of Earth's axis as it revolves around the sun.

June Solstice
The north end of Earth's axis is tilted toward the sun. It is summer in the Northern Hemisphere and winter in the Southern Hemisphere.

March Equinox

June Solstice

December Solstice

March and September Equinoxes
Neither end of Earth's axis is tilted toward the sun. Both hemispheres receive the same amount of energy.

September Equinox

December Solstice
The south end of Earth's axis is tilted toward the sun. It is summer in the Southern Hemisphere and winter in the Northern Hemisphere.

The height of the sun above the horizon varies with the season.
Interpreting Diagrams *When is the sun at its maximum height in the Northern Hemisphere?*

June Solstice

March and September Equinoxes

December Solstice

What Gives the Sunrise and Sunset its Orange Glow?

GantDaily
March 11th, 2007
Meghan Holohan, Research at Penn State

The question-and-answer format outlines causes and effects.

In Key West, Florida, tourists flock to Mallory Square at the end of the day to watch the sun set. Street performers entertain waiting crowds with magic and vendors sell souvenirs of the daily sunset celebration. Flashes click as tourists try to capture the beautiful orange sun as it disappears behind the sparkling blue ocean.

In almost every location around the globe, the sky appears orange at sunrise and sunset. What causes this colorful phenomenon?

Sunlight is composed of a multicolored **spectrum**, just like a rainbow, explains Jon Nese, senior lecturer in meteorology at Penn State. Combined together, its different **wavelengths** are perceived as white light when they enter the Earth's atmosphere.

That atmosphere is made up of a mixture of gaseous molecules, mostly nitrogen and oxygen, with some water vapor and trace gases thrown in. These molecules, clumped more densely close to Earth where the atmosphere is thickest, create tiny obstacles for traveling light waves to navigate.

The light at the longest wavelengths—red, orange, and yellow—sails more easily over these atmospheric speed bumps, while the shorter

blue and violet rays get bounced left and right as they journey towards us, in a process called "scattering."

At "solar noon," when the sun appears at its highest point in the daytime sky, light reaches us most directly, passing through less atmosphere on the way, reducing the scattering effect. When the spectrum remains together, the light we see is the familiar yellowish-white look of sunshine.

But as the Earth turns during the day and the sun drops toward the horizon, sunbeams enter the atmosphere at a slant and pass through a denser swath of air before they reach us. "When the short rays at the violet and blue end of the spectrum are deflected out in all directions, they can't get to our eyes," Nese notes, "while the orange and red wavelengths dominate our perception of the sky's color."

This paragraph begins an explanation of the cause of colorful skies.

While people in Key West almost always view orange sunsets, residents in heavily populated cities often see red. That's due to pollution in the air, says Nese. Older residents of Donora, Pennsylvania, a town on the outskirts of Pittsburgh, recall beautiful red sunsets at the height of coke production decades ago, due to the coal dust in the air.

Pollution particles are larger than the molecules of atmospheric gases, Nese explains. Even orange and yellow light waves have a hard time passing through. Red—which is composed of the longest wavelengths in the visible spectrum—is the most successful at streaming past the particles, creating a scarlet sky.

Volcanic activity can produce the same effect. In April of 1982, sunrises and sunsets were fiery red across most of the United States after the El Chichon volcano erupted in Mexico, spewing ash clear into the **stratosphere**. Red rays were the only visible light rays long enough to slice through the clouds of dense ash and sulfur dioxide.

Here, the article points out another possible cause for red skies.

While science has unlocked the secrets of the sky's many shades, "to many, the scientific explanation is secondary," Nese admits.

"There's something magical, even mysterious, about it because the colors only appear near sunrise and sunset, and few people really understand why."

GantDaily Editor's Note: This article is part of the feature, "A Probing Question." Presented through the Pennsylvania State University, researchers answer questions on things to wake up the kid in you.

Comparing Expository Texts

© 1. Craft and Structure **(a)** Compare the **cause-and-effect organization** of the textbook article and the question-and-answer text. In which text do you find cause-and-effect relationships more clearly identified? **(b)** Which text cites more effects resulting from a single cause? Explain.

Content-Area Vocabulary

2. Consulting a specialized reference, such as a dictionary of earth science, find two scientific words in addition to *stratosphere* that are formed by adding a prefix to the root *-sphere-*. Define each of the three words and their prefixes, using a dictionary as needed.

⏱ Timed Writing

Explanatory Text: Essay

> **Format**
> The prompt directs you to write a brief essay. Therefore, you will need to express your ideas in three to five paragraphs.

> Extend the chain of causes and effects in the textbook article by explaining how the cycle of seasons affects your area. Write a brief essay that explains some of the effects caused by changes in the weather and the number of daylight hours. (40 minutes)

> **Academic Vocabulary**
> When you *extend* an idea, you build on it or apply it to new situations.

5-Minute Planner

Complete these steps to write your explanation:

1. Carefully read the writing prompt. Look for key words shown in highlighted colors.

2. Reread the textbook article. As you read, find cause-and-effect relationships. **TIP** Make a list of words and phrases such as *because, as a result,* and *for this reason* that show relationships between ideas.

3. Jot down notes about how life in your area changes with the seasons. For example, wintry cold means more time indoors.

4. Organize your notes so that you can clearly see the relationships between causes and effects. Then, refer to your notes and your list of words and phrases as you draft your essay.

Comparing Literary Works

The Voyage *from*
Tales from the Odyssey •
To the Top of Everest

Comparing Universal Themes

A **universal theme** is a message about life that is expressed in many different cultures and time periods. Universal themes include concepts such as the value of courage and the danger of greed. You can identify the universal theme in a literary work by focusing on the main character, thinking about conflicts the character faces, and noticing the changes that come about as a result of those conflicts.

Universal themes are important ideas, so many cultures present these themes prominently in **epics**—stories or long poems about larger-than-life heroes. In many ways, an epic can be seen as a portrait of the culture that produced it. Ancient epics were recited as entertainment and passed down from storyteller to storyteller. Epics express a culture's values and its perspective on universal themes, such as bravery. Other **epic conventions,** or characteristics, are listed in the chart below.

Epics and their themes are an important part of the literature of different cultures. New generations often create works inspired by these epics. For example, it is not unusual to find an **allusion,** or reference, to the ancient Greek epic the *Odyssey* in a new adventure story. As you read these selections, use a chart like this to note the examples of epic conventions that help point toward a universal theme.

Common Core State Standards

Reading Literature

2. Determine a theme or central idea of a text and analyze its development over the course of the text; provide an objective summary of the text.

3. Analyze how particular elements of a story or drama interact.

Writing

2. Write informative/explanatory texts to examine a topic and convey ideas, concepts, and information through the selection, organization, and analysis of relevant content.

Epic Conventions	from *Tales from the Odyssey*	"To the Top of Everest"
dangerous journey		
characters who help	Goddesses Ino and Athena	
broad setting		
serious, formal style		

www.PHLitOnline.com

- Vocabulary flashcards
- Interactive journals
- More about the authors
- Selection audio
- Interactive graphic organizers

THE BIG ? Community or individual — which is more important?

Writing About the Big Question

Both of these selections show that travel can enrich individuals and shape their views. Use this sentence starter to develop your ideas.

When individuals travel to other places, their **communities** can also benefit because _____.

Meet the Authors

Mary Pope Osborne (b. 1949)
Author of *Tales from the Odyssey*

Mary Pope Osborne has lived an adventurous life. As a child, she never stayed in one place for long. Her father was in the military, and the family moved seven times before Mary was fifteen. As a young adult, she explored sixteen Asian countries with friends, including Iraq, Iran, Afghanistan, Pakistan, India, and Nepal.

Pope Osborne did not begin to write until she was in her thirties. Today, she is best known for her series, *The Magic Tree House.* "I'm one of those very lucky people who absolutely loves what they do for a living," Pope Osborne says. "There is no career better suited to my eccentricities, strengths, and passions than that of a children's book author."

Samantha Larson (b. 1988)
Author of "To the Top of Everest"

In 2007, American Samantha Larson became the youngest person to climb the "Seven Summits"—the highest mountains on each of the seven continents. Larson climbed her first, Mount Kilimanjaro in Africa, at the age of 12. She finished her quest on May 17, 2007, when she successfully reached the top of Mt. Everest at the age of 18.

Larson says "Everest was much harder, longer, and higher" than the other peaks she had tackled in the past. "There were a lot of difficult moments," Larson recalls. "It was one big challenge, but I never gave up hope completely. Deep down I thought I would make it."

THE VOYAGE

from **Tales from the Odyssey**

MARY POPE OSBORNE

In the early morning of time, there existed a mysterious world called Mount Olympus. Hidden behind a veil of clouds, this world was never swept by winds, nor washed by rains. Those who lived on Mount Olympus never grew old; they never died. They were not humans. They were the mighty gods and goddesses of ancient Greece.

The Olympian gods and goddesses had great power over the lives of the humans who lived on earth below. Their anger once caused a man named Odysseus to wander the seas for many long years, trying to find his way home.

Almost three thousand years ago, a Greek poet named Homer first told the story of Odysseus' journey. Since that time, storytellers have told the strange and wondrous tale again and again. We call that story the Odyssey.

◀ **Critical Viewing**
In what ways does this image reflect the description of gods and goddesses in these three paragraphs? **[Connect]**

With his hands gripping the rudder, Odysseus skillfully guided his raft over the waves. He never slept. All night, he kept his eyes fixed on the stars that Calypso had told him to watch—the Pleiades and the Bear.

Day after day and night after night, Odysseus sailed the seas. Finally, on the eighteenth day, he saw the dim outline of mountains on the horizon.

As Odysseus steered his raft toward the shore, dark clouds gathered overhead. The water began to rise. The wind began to blow, until it was roaring over the earth and sea.

Has Poseidon discovered my raft? Odysseus wondered anxiously. *Does he now seek his final revenge?*

For many years, Poseidon, mighty ruler of the sea, had been angry with Odysseus for blinding his son, the Cyclops. Now it seemed he was trying to destroy Odysseus once again. The wind roared from the north, south, east, and west. Daylight plunged into darkness. Odysseus feared he was about to come to a terrible, lonely end.

Suddenly an enormous wave crashed down on Odysseus' raft. Odysseus was swept overboard and pulled deep beneath the sea. He struggled wildly to raise his head above the water and breathe.

When his head finally broke the surface, Odysseus saw his raft swiftly moving away across the water. He swam as fast as he could toward the wooden craft. He grabbed the timbers and pulled himself aboard.

Then, as the wind swirled the raft across the water, Odysseus saw an astonishing sight. A sea goddess was floating like a gull on top of the waves.

Seemingly impervious to the great storm, she floated near his raft and climbed aboard.

"My friend," she said, "I am Ino, the White Goddess, who guides sailors in storms. I know not why Poseidon is angry with you. But I know this: for all the torture he has inflicted upon you, he will not kill you. But you must leave your raft at once and swim for the shore. Take my veil, for it is enchanted. You will come to no harm as long as you possess it. As soon as you reach land, you must throw it back into the sea."

Vocabulary
impervious (im pʉr´ vē əs) *adj.* not affected by something

inflicted (in flikt´ əd) *v.* delivered something painful

Reading Check
Who climbs aboard Odysseus' raft?

With these words, the White Goddess removed her enchanted veil and gave it to Odysseus. Then she disappeared back into the wild seas.

At that moment, a huge wave crashed down on Odysseus' raft, ripping it to pieces. Clutching Ino's veil, Odysseus pulled himself onto a wooden plank and rode it as if it were a horse. Then he dove down into the sea.

Suddenly, all the winds died down—except the north wind. Odysseus felt that Athena[1] was holding the other winds back, so he could swim safely and swiftly to some distant shore. For two days and two nights, with the north wind gently flattening the waves before him, he swam and floated on the calm sea.

On the third day, the north wind died away and the sea was completely calm. Odysseus saw land ahead. With a burst of joy, he swam toward the rocky shore.

In an instant, the wind and waves returned. With a thundering roar, sea spray rained down on him.

Odysseus struggled to keep his head above the churning water, seeking a place to go ashore.

Angry waves were pounding the reefs with great force. *I'll be dashed against the rocks if I try to swim ashore now,* he thought desperately.

But once again, Odysseus felt the presence of Athena. A giant wave picked him up and carried him over the rocks toward the beach. But before Odysseus could crawl ashore to safety, another wave dragged him back into the sea and pulled him under the water.

Odysseus swam desperately, escaping the waves pounding the shore. Soon he came to a sheltered cove. He saw a riverbank free of rough stones. As he swam toward the bank, he prayed to the gods to save him from the angry attack of Poseidon.

Suddenly the waves were still. But when Odysseus tried to haul himself ashore, his body failed him. He had been defeated by the storm. It had ripped his flesh and robbed his muscles of their strength. He was passing in and out of consciousness.

---

1. **Athena** *n.* goddess of wisdom and protector of Odysseus.

Universal Themes
Which epic convention appears in this paragraph?

Spiral Review
Theme What is Odysseus's relationship to the sea?

Gasping for breath, he pulled off Ino's veil and threw it back into the sea. Then he used his last bit of strength to drag himself out of the water and throw himself into the river reeds.

If I lie here all night, I shall die from the cold and damp, he thought. *If I go farther ashore and pass out in a thicket, wild beasts will devour me.* No matter what evils lay ahead, he knew he had to push on. On bleeding hands and knees, he crawled to a sheltered spot under an olive tree, a tree sacred to the goddess Athena.

Odysseus lay down in a pile of dead leaves. With his bloody hands, he spread leaves over his torn body. Like a farmer spreading ashes over the embers of his fire, he tried to protect the last spark of life within him.

Mercifully, the gray-eyed goddess slipped down from the heavens and appeared at his side. She closed his weary eyes and pulled him down into a sweet sleep that took away his pain and sorrow.

Universal Themes
Based on this paragraph, what trait do you think the ancient Greeks valued in heroes?

Critical Thinking

1. Key Ideas and Details (a) How does Odysseus react to the storm at sea? **(b) Generalize:** Choose three adjectives that describe Odysseus. **(c) Speculate:** Why do you think the goddesses help Odysseus?

2. Key Ideas and Details (a) Make a Judgment: Do you think Odysseus will survive his injuries? **(b) Support:** Find several passages in the text that support your answer.

3. Integration of Knowledge and Ideas Infer: How would you describe ancient Greek culture after reading this passage based on an ancient Greek myth?

4. Integration of Knowledge and Ideas Odysseus struggles mightily against beings more powerful than he is. Do you think his story can teach lessons to individuals, communities, or both? Explain your answer, using details from the text. *[Connect to the Big Question: Community or individual—which is more important?]*

Cite textual evidence to support your responses.

TO THE TOP OF EVEREST

Samantha Larson Blog

Friday, March 30, 2007

Here we go ⟶ Kathmandu!

Today is the day! Our bags are (nearly) packed and we're (just about) ready to go. I've got eleven hours to run around doing last minute errands before our plane takes off.

I arrived back in Long Beach from New York last Saturday, where I've been since our return from Cho Oyu. When I wasn't training by running, swimming at the pool, taking dance classes, or rock climbing, I was taking oboe lessons, French, and photography classes. Hopefully I'll be able to take some great pictures on this expedition!

It has been a very exciting week in all our general trip preparation mayhem, filled with lots of gear sorting and fedex package arrivals. But now my dad and I are pretty much all set to go.

See you in Kathmandu!

◄ **Critical Viewing**
Which details in this photograph suggest Larson is about to go on a dangerous journey?

Reading Check
How did Larson train for her expedition?

▼ Critical Viewing
Why would a person
have to be brave to
attempt the climb seen
here? [Deduce]

Monday, April 2, 2007
Kathmandu
After nearly 24 hours of travel we finally arrived in
Kathmandu yesterday afternoon. Doug, my dad, and I met
up with the rest of the team (Victor, James, and Wim) at our
hotel in Kathmandu. We had a group meeting where we went
over the route we are going to take to base camp, and then we
picked up some odds and ends at one of the dozens of local
climbing stores.

The team is flying to Lukla to begin the trek to base camp
early tomorrow morning.

Wednesday, April 4, 2007
Namche Bazar
Yesterday after a very scenic flight and a heart-
stopping landing on a small airstrip perched on
the side of a mountain, we arrived in Lukla to
begin the trek to base camp. Lukla was filled
with excitement as porters organized their
loads and trekkers began their journeys. From
Lukla, we hiked for about 4 hours through
the beautiful Nepalese countryside, passing
through several villages until we reached the
village of Monjo, where we stayed the night
in the Monjo Guesthouse. I think my dad
and I got the big sleep that we needed to
catch up on our jetlag; around 4 in the
afternoon, we decided to take a "nap"
that lasted until 7 the next morning!

Thursday, April 12, 2007
Base Camp
We made it to base camp yesterday
afternoon. Today we are going
to practice crossing the ladders
over the Khumbu Ice Fall. We
are well and safe.

En route here we visited
Lama Gesa and he blessed
our journey. It was an
amazing experience!

I am going to try and connect my laptop and charge it with my solar charger—we will see if that works.

More to follow.....

Monday, April 16, 2007
Rest Day

Yesterday we got an early start for our first time through the icefall. We left around 6:30 in the morning, with the idea that we would turn around 11—we did not necessarily have a destination in mind, it was more for acclimatization[1] and to get an idea of what the icefall was like. However, at 11 we were about half an hour from the top of the icefall, so we decided to just continue to the top.

It was quite fun climbing up the icefall. The ladders that we had to cross over crevasses[2] were especially exciting. I was pretty tired by the time we got back to base camp, but today was a rest day (our first), so I've had plenty of time to recover.

Tomorrow we are going up to camp one to spend the night. Camp one is about an hour further than we went yesterday. The next day we will go up to tag camp two and then come back down to base camp.

Thursday, April 19, 2007
Puja

The day before yesterday we all made it up to camp one to spend the night. This time we were able to get through the Khumbu Icefall an hour quicker than the last. We had a pretty good night at camp one; my dad and I both had a bit of a headache at first, but we were both able to eat and sleep well.

Camp one is at the start of the Western Cwm.[3] Yesterday, from camp one we continued up the Cwm to camp two. The cwm

1. **acclimatization** (ə klī′ mə tə zā′ shən) *n.* process of allowing the body to adjust to the climate, especially at high altitude.
2. **crevasses** (krə vas′ əz) *n.* deep cracks in ice or a glacier.
3. **Western Cwm** *n.* a broad valley at the base of Mount Everest

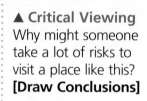

▲ **Critical Viewing**
Why might someone take a lot of risks to visit a place like this? **[Draw Conclusions]**

Universal Themes
How is Lama Gesa's role in this selection similar to Athena's role in "The Voyage"?

Reading Check
How long did it take to travel to Kathmandu?

is infamous for being very uncomfortably hot, but yesterday it was actually really nice. It was very beautiful, and we could see the summit of Everest, which we haven't been able to see since before we got to base camp. After we tagged camp two we came all the way back down to base camp. It was a long day, and we all returned pretty tired. However, it was nice to be back in base camp, and after dinner we watched Mission Impossible III on Ben's laptop (from the London Business School team). Unfortunately the power ran out about half way through, but I have been asked to charge up my laptop so we can finish tonight.

Today was the Puja, which is a ceremony that the Sherpas organize. A Lama comes up and performs many chants to ask the mountain gods for permission to climb the mountain, and to ask for protection. I had my ice ax and my crampons[4] blessed in the ceremony. As part of the ceremony, they also put out long lines of prayer flags coming out from the stupa where the ceremony was performed. Afterwards, they passed out lots of yummy treats.

While we were up at camp one, the shower tent was set up here at base camp. It's just a little bucket of water with a hose attached to it, but definitely 15 minutes of heaven.

Saturday, April 28, 2007
Base Camp

We are back at base camp! We came down from camp two yesterday, and arrived just in time for lunch. We were delayed a bit in the morning because we were radioed from base camp that there was a break in the icefall, and we didn't want to leave until we knew that the "ice doctors" had fixed up the route. As we came down, we found that the break was in a flat area known as the "football field" that we had previously designated as a "safe" area to take a little rest. And the whole shelf just collapsed!

Now that we have spent a night at camp three, we are done with the acclimatization process. We are going to take a few days for rest and recovery, and then we just wait for good weather to make a summit bid. We plan to go back down to Pengboche tomorrow so we can really get a good rest at lower altitude before our summit attempt.

Spiral Review
Central Idea Why do you think the Sherpas organize a blessing ceremony?

Universal Themes
Which details in this entry show that Larson and her team face great dangers as they continue to climb?

Vocabulary
designated (dez´ ig nāt´ əd) *v.* identified; pointed out

Here is what we have been up to these past few days:
4/23/07
Yesterday we all made it up to camp one for the night. We were joined by Tori from the London Business School team, because she wasn't feeling 100% when her team went up the day before.

Today we all came up to camp two. It was very hot coming up the Cwm this time, and we all had heavy packs because we had to bring up what we had left at camp one the last time we stayed there. It certainly made it a lot harder work!

4/24/07
Despite the fact that I caused us to get a later start than planned this morning (I had a particularly hard time getting out of my warm sleeping bag into the cold air) we accomplished our goal for the day. We went up the very first pitch of the Lhotse Face, and are now back at camp two for the evening.

4/26/07
Yesterday we went about halfway up the Lhotse face to camp three to spend the night. This was a new record for my dad and me, as our highest night ever! Camp three is at about 23,500 feet, and our previous highest night was at camp two on Cho Oyu, at 23,000 feet. We arrived at camp three around noon, and then had a lot of time to kill in our tents, as it wasn't really safe to go more than five feet outside the tent without putting on crampons and clipping into the fixed ropes. Thankfully, I had not yet reached a hypoxic[5] level where I couldn't enjoy my book.

Coming up the Lhotse Face was a bit windy, and some parts were pretty icy. It gets fairly steep, so I was glad to have my ascender, which slides up the rope, but not back down, so you can use it as a handhold to pull yourself up.

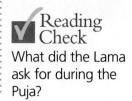

✓ Reading Check

What did the Lama ask for during the Puja?

---

5. **hypoxic** (hī päk´ sik) *adj.* having too little oxygen.

Sunday, May 6, 2007
Back from Holiday
We're back at base camp from our little holiday down the mountain.

Now that we are back in base camp, we are just waiting till we can go for our summit attempt. The ropes are not yet fixed to the summit. Once the ropes are fixed, we hope there will soon be a good weather window.

Friday, May 11, 2007
Base Camp
We're still at base camp. Hopefully we'll be able to go up soon though.

We've tried to hold on to our fitness these past few days by doing some sort of activity each day. We've been ice climbing in a really neat cave near base camp, and we've also been on hikes up Pumori to Pumori base camp, and then up to camp one. Pumori is a 7145-meter mountain near Everest.

Saturday, May 12, 2007
Still at Base Camp
It looks like we're going to be able to go up soon for our summit attempt. Fingers crossed!

We've gotten our oxygen masks and tested them out. I was able to get my oxygen saturation back up to 100% this morning! After I turned off the oxygen, I only had a few seconds of being at pseudo sea-level before it went back down, though.

We're all getting a little restless hanging around base camp.

Monday, May 14, 2007
Camp 2
We finally started our summit push yesterday, making our way from base camp to camp two. We don't have internet access up here, but we were able to relay this information to our correspondents in New York via phone. We're taking a rest day today, and plan to press on tomorrow. If all goes well, we should summit on the 17th.

Universal Themes
How do you know that Larson is willing to face challenges to meet her goal?

Vocabulary
saturation (sach´ ə rā´ shən) *n.* the state of being completely filled

Thursday, May 17, 2007

Summit!

We made it to the top! Now all we have to do is get back down...

Wednesday, May 23, 2007

Back Home!

We've been in a big rush getting back home, and I haven't been able to update for awhile, as I have not had internet access. We woke up this morning at 16,000 feet in a village called Lobuche, and this evening my dad and I arrived back at sea-level in Long Beach! The rest of the team are celebrating in Kathmandu—my dad and I skipped out on the celebration to make it back in time for my brother Ted's college graduation in New York.

The day after we summitted, we came down from the South Col (camp 4) to camp 2. I was very tired at that point, but glad that we had all made it back safely lower on the mountain. It was amazing how after being to almost 30,000 feet, 20,000-foot camp 2 felt like it was nearly at sea-level!

The day after that, we came back down to base camp, where we received lots of warm hugs and congratulations. We only had one night back at base camp, as the next day (the 20th), we packed up our bags and headed down the valley. Base camp had a strange, empty feeling—it was sad to leave my little tent that had been my home for the past 2 months! My dad, Doug, Wim, and I were hoping to get a helicopter out of Lobuche on the 21st to save a little time, but Victor and

✓ Reading Check

How does Larson stay fit while waiting to go to the summit?

We made it to the top! Now all we have to do is get back down...

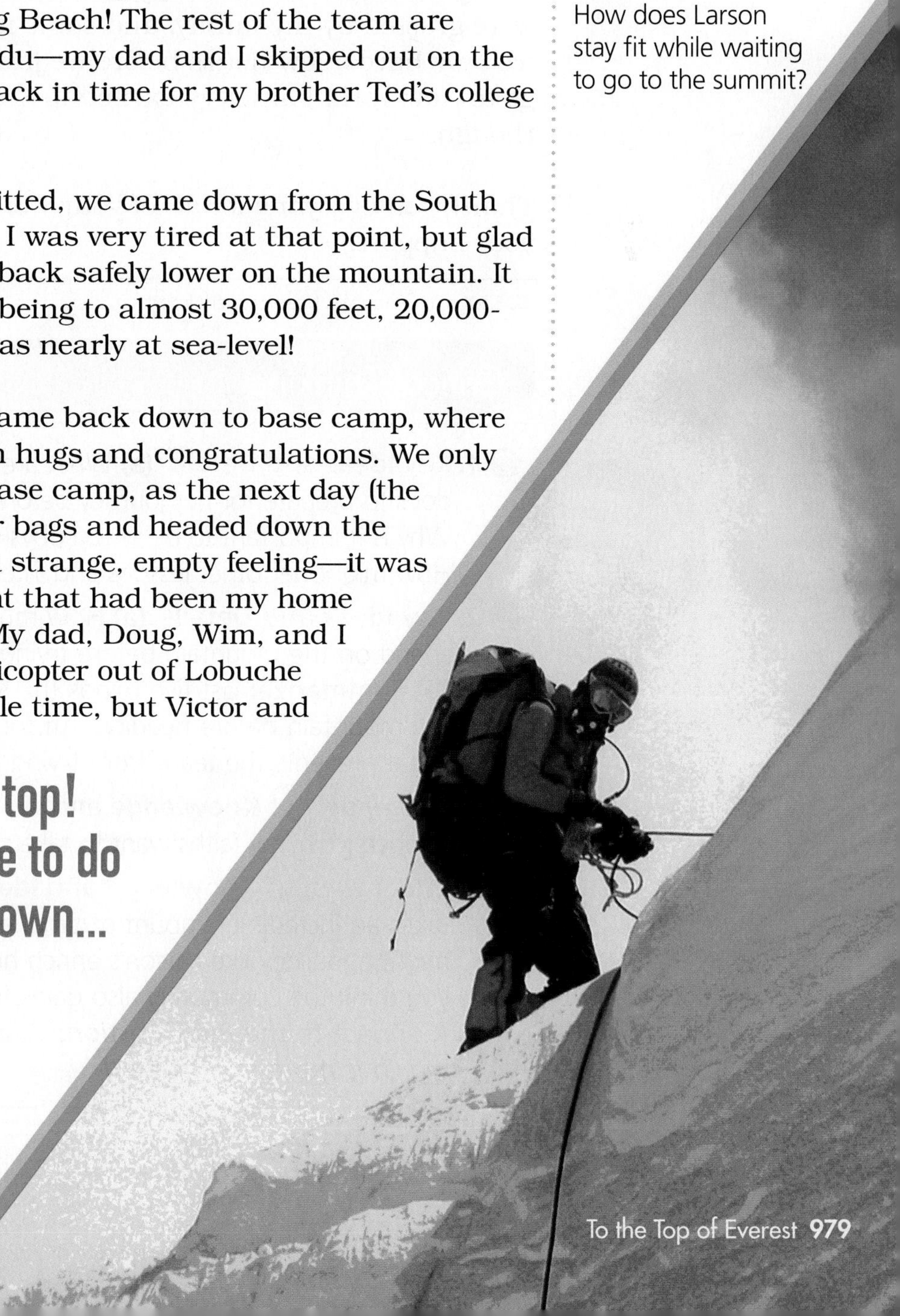

James decided to walk down to the Lukla airstrip to fly out to Kathmandu on the 23rd. However, even though we awoke on the 21st to a beautiful, clear day in Lobuche, apparently there were clouds lower down the valley, so the helicopter couldn't fly in until the 23rd either. It was kind of hard waiting those two days in Lobuche. We were just an hour away from a hot shower and a big meal, if only those clouds would clear!

Once the helicopter landed in Kathmandu, I was greeted by a mob of journalists and cameramen. I was so surprised! After nearly 20 hours of travel, my dad and I landed at LAX[6] and were greeted by my family, and some more news people. Now we only have a few hours before we jump back on a plane to go to New York! I am very excited to see my mom and brother though.

Thank you everyone for all of your wonderful comments and your support!!!

Universal Themes
What details here suggest some people consider Larson and her team heroes?

---

6. **LAX** *n.* Los Angeles International Airport.

Critical Thinking

Cite textual evidence to support your responses.

1. **Key Ideas and Details (a)** What are some of the things Larson does to prepare for her journey before leaving home? **(b) Infer:** Why is it important to be in top physical shape? **(c) Deduce:** How might her other lessons and interests affect her trip?

2. **Key Ideas and Details (a)** How much time does Larson spend on the mountain before trying to reach the summit? **(b) Summarize:** List five things the team does with its time on the mountain before heading out for the summit. **(c) Deduce:** What prevents the team from trying to summit earlier?

3. **Integration of Knowledge and Ideas Speculate:** Why might climbers of many faiths want to take part in the Puja ceremony?

4. **Integration of Knowledge and Ideas** Climbing Mt. Everest takes an incredible amount of time, effort, and money. **(a)** How might a journey like Larson's enrich her as an individual? **(b)** Do you think the community also gains from her success? Explain. *[Connect to the Big Question: Community or individual— which is more important?]*

After You Read

The Voyage *from* Tales
from the Odyssey •
To the Top of Everest

Comparing Universal Themes

© 1. Key Ideas and Details Compare and contrast Larson's voyage with Odysseus's.

	Odysseus	Samantha Larson
Journey undertaken		
Attitude of character		
Obstacles character must overcome		
Outcome		

© 2. Craft and Structure (a) Why might you include an allusion to the *Odyssey* if you were writing about Larson for your school paper? **(b)** Would you describe her as a "hero"? Explain.

© 3. Integration of Knowledge and Ideas One theme of the *Odyssey* is the triumph of bravery over power. Do you think "To the Top of Everest" expresses the same message? Why or why not? If not, how would you state its central idea?

⏱ Timed Writing

Explanatory Text: Essay

In an essay, compare and contrast the themes of the classic epic tale "The Voyage" with the modern account "To the Top of Everest." Explain how time and place influence the theme of each selection. (40 minutes)

5-Minute Planner

1. Read the prompt carefully and completely.
2. Jot down answers to these questions:
   - What is the universal theme of each selection?
   - How do the heroes overcome obstacles?
   - How does each form—epic tale or nonfiction blog—affect your response?
3. Take notes on which epic conventions are used in each selection. Record how the place and time influence the events. Then, jot down differences between the two selections.
4. Reread the prompt, and then draft your essay.

Writing Workshop

 **Common Core State Standards**

Writing

2. Write informative/explanatory texts to examine a topic and convey ideas, concepts, and information through the selection, organization, and analysis of relevant content.

2.a. Introduce a topic clearly, previewing what is to follow; organize ideas, concepts, and information, using strategies such as definition, classification, comparison/contrast, and cause/effect; include formatting, graphics, and multimedia when useful to aiding comprehension.

4. Produce clear and coherent writing in which the development, organization, and style are appropriate to task, purpose, and audience.

Write an Informative Text

Workplace Writing: Business Letter

Defining the Form A **business letter** is a brief but formal written communication with a specific purpose. People write business letters to provide or request information, to express an opinion, or to issue a complaint. You might use elements of this form in memos, proposals, or letters to an author or newspaper.

Assignment Write a business letter requesting information from a company or an organization. Include these elements:

- ✔ standard *business letter format*
- ✔ a *clear statement* of your request
- ✔ *transitions* that unify your ideas
- ✔ *formal* and polite *language*
- ✔ an appropriate and logical *organizational structure*
- ✔ error-free writing, including the *correct use of commas*

To preview the criteria on which your business letter may be judged, see the rubric on page 987.

 Writing Workshop: *Work in Progress*

Review the work you did on pages 933 and 957.

Prewriting/Planning Strategy

Organize the facts. Briefly, state your purpose for writing. Then, jot down your contact information to ensure that the recipient can respond to your letter. Use the library, Internet, or customer service department to locate the recipient's name, title, and business address. Use an organizer like this to keep track of your information.

Company or Organization	Purpose for Writing	Contact Information	Details
Greenhaus Dance Company	To get information about the faculty	Name: Rita Moore Title: Director Address: 2 Main St., Chicago, IL 80808	I want to know the dance background of the various faculty members.

Organizing a Letter

Organization is essential when writing a letter. The correct organization will give your letter credibility. Remember, you are writing to a business or organization that receives letters every day, so it is important to show that you have taken the time to use the correct format. Follow the tips below to organize your letter.

Choosing an Appropriate Format Follow this standard business letter format so the recipient can easily locate information.

- **Heading:** your address and the date of the letter
- **Inside Address:** the name and address that shows where the letter will be sent
- **Greeting:** the recipient's name, *Dear Sir, Dear Madam,* or *To Whom It May Concern*, followed by a colon
- **Body:** your purpose for writing
- **Closing:** *Sincerely*, or *Respectfully*, followed by a comma
- **Signature:** your full name and your signature above it

In **block format,** each part of the letter begins at the left margin. In **modified block format,** the heading, the closing, and the signature are indented to the center of the page. See a sample on page R27.

Getting to the Point Begin your letter by telling your reader why you are writing. You might begin with a phrase such as, *I am writing to you concerning*, or, *The reason for my letter is to request. . .* Once you have stated your purpose, give reasons why the business or organization should grant your request. Use a web to organize your thoughts.

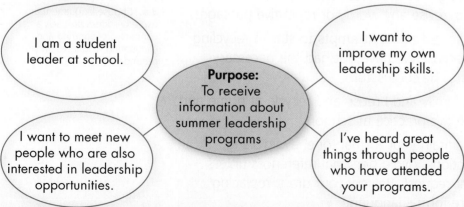

I am a student leader at school.

I want to improve my own leadership skills.

Purpose: To receive information about summer leadership programs

I want to meet new people who are also interested in leadership opportunities.

I've heard great things through people who have attended your programs.

Drafting Strategies

Use formal language. The tone of your letter should be friendly, yet serious and respectful. Remember, you are writing to a specific audience and for an intended purpose. You will not be using the same tone or language as you would in an e-mail to a friend or close relative. Use conventional English and avoid slang or a chatty, conversational style. You want your audience to take you seriously, especially if you expect your reader to grant your request.

Informal Language	Formal Language
I love your cooking show! It would be awesome if you could send me your tasty recipes!	I have always enjoyed cooking. I watch your show to learn new recipes and to learn about new foods and cooking techniques. I would appreciate it if you would share some of your recipes with me.

Develop the body. Use the web you made in your prewriting to develop the body of your letter. The body should elaborate and specify your request and should include supporting details. The business or organization must understand what you are requesting or why you are requesting it. Always end by thanking the recipient.

Link your ideas. An effective letter has unity—its details relate to a main idea. As you draft, use transitions between sentences to show how your ideas are related.

Revising Strategies

Eliminate irrelevant details. The details you include in your business letter should support your main points. Delete unnecessary information, including extra—but not key—details from your personal life. You are contacting a busy professional, so include only essential information. Also, revise any wordy or repetitive passages.

> **Relevant Detail:** Our school's past attempts to start a recycling program have failed, because we have not had the necessary information or supplies to be successful.

> **Irrelevant Detail:** My family and I reuse and recycle at home and I would like to continue this practice at school.

Check your tone. To maintain your formal tone, avoid slang, colloquialism, and contractions. Avoid personal references unless they are necessary to your request. Review your draft, replacing casual passages with more formal language.

Common Core State Standards

Writing

2.b. Develop the topic with relevant facts, definitions, concrete details, quotations, or other information and examples.

2.c. Use appropriate transitions to create cohesion and clarify the relationships among ideas and concepts.

2.e. Establish and maintain a formal style.

2.f. Provide a concluding statement.

Language

2.a. Use a comma to separate coordinate adjectives.

3.a. Choose language that expresses ideas precisely and concisely, recognizing and eliminating wordiness and redundancy.

Revising Incorrect Use of Commas

A **comma** is a punctuation mark used to indicate a brief pause. The following examples illustrate some common misuses of commas.

Rule: Commas separate two adjectives in a series, but not the adjective from the noun.

    Misused: My favorite drink is a cool, refreshing, lemonade.

    Correct: My favorite drink is a cool, refreshing lemonade.

Rule: Commas do not separate parts of a compound subject.

    Misused: After dinner, my friend Annie, and her sister Emma, left.

    Correct: After dinner, my friend Annie and her sister Emma left.

Rule: Commas separate clauses that include both a subject and its verb, not parts of a compound verb.

    Misused: The candidate looked out at the audience, and laughed.

    Correct: The candidate looked out at the audience and laughed.

Rule: Commas do not separate parts of a compound object.

    Misused: He made a sundae with whipped cream, and sprinkles.

    Correct: He made a sundae with whipped cream and sprinkles.

PH WRITING COACH

Further instruction and practice are available in *Prentice Hall Writing Coach*.

Fixing Incorrect Use of Commas Follow these rules:

1. Add a comma or commas:

- before a conjunction that separates two independent clauses in a compound sentence.
- to separate three or more words, phrases, or clauses.
- to separate adjectives of equal rank.
- to set off an introductory adverb clause.

2. Eliminate the comma:

- if it comes directly between the subject and the verb of a sentence.
- if it separates an adjective from the noun that follows it.
- if it separates a compound subject, verb, or object.

Grammar in Your Writing

Reread your letter, noting compound subjects, verbs, and objects. If necessary, revise the sentences using one of the methods above.

Student Model: Melissa Gornto, Durham, NC

© Common Core
State Standards

Writing
6. Use technology, including the Internet, to produce and publish writing.
Language
2.b. Spell correctly.

Melissa Gornto
1436 Any Street
Durham, NC 27713

September 23, 2010

14th District Judicial Bar Board
Government Office Building, Office #33
67 Sherman Street
Durham, NC 27713

Dear Sir or Madam:

I am writing to you concerning financing for the trip that my classmates and I are taking to London. I see it as a great educational opportunity to learn about a different culture, history, and way of life. We do not know much about the British society, and this is a chance for us to find out the real information.

If you were to help us with the monetary grant, a weight would be lifted off our shoulders concerning the money issue. Using the money, we would be able to go to London, where we could see many things. We would be able to go to Buckingham Palace, Stonehenge, and Big Ben. This is also a great educational opportunity because it allows us to see the English way of life, including the different monetary system and the difference in speech. They may speak English, but that doesn't mean the words have the same sound or definition. So, if you will, look at this as a once-in-a-lifetime opportunity to learn many different things that aren't taught in schools.

Thank you for your time regarding this matter. Please take this trip into consideration and help us out. If you do, you won't have to worry about us not being grateful. This is an adventure my fellow classmates and I would love to go on. Once again, thank you for your time.

Sincerely,

Melissa Gornto
Melissa Gornto

Melissa uses block format in her business letter, setting all elements at the left margin.

Melissa clearly states her purpose.

Melissa uses friendly, yet formal language.

Editing and Proofreading

A letter with mistakes makes a poor impression and may signal that the writer is not serious in his or her request. Review your draft to eliminate errors in grammar, spelling, and punctuation.

Focus on spelling. Use the Internet or phone directories to verify that the name, title, and address of the recipient are spelled correctly. Carefully reread your letter to check for any other spelling errors.

Publishing and Presenting

Consider one of the following ways to share your writing:

Swap letters. Trade letters with a classmate. Read the letter carefully. Then, write a realistic response to the request for information.

Send your letter. Use e-mail or standard mail to send your request for information to the company or organization you have selected. Maintain the correspondence as needed. If you send your letter by standard mail, sign it and neatly write the address on the envelope before mailing.

Reflecting on Your Writing

Writer's Journal Jot down your answer to this question:

In the process of writing, what did you learn about the business or organization you chose?

Rubric for Self-Assessment

Find evidence in your writing to address each category. Then, use the rating scale to grade your work.

Spiral Review
Earlier in the unit, you learned about **punctuation marks** (p. 932) and **commas** (p. 956). Check your letter to be sure that you have correctly used commas and other punctuation marks.

Criteria	Rating Scale not very / very
Focus: How clearly have you stated your request?	1 2 3 4 5
Organization: How well have you organized your letter according to standard business format?	1 2 3 4 5
Support/Elaboration: How well do the details support your request?	1 2 3 4 5
Style: How formal and polite is your language?	1 2 3 4 5
Conventions: How correct is your grammar, especially your use of commas?	1 2 3 4 5
Organization: Does your letter follow the correct organizational pattern, and is the body written in a logical pattern?	1 2 3 4 5

© Leveled Texts

Build your skills and improve your comprehension of folk tales with texts of increasing complexity.

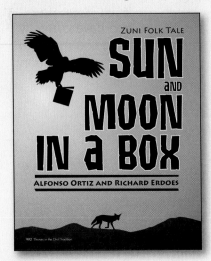

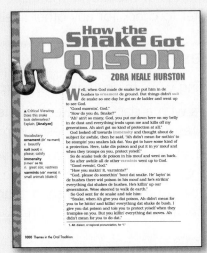

Read **"Sun and Moon in a Box"** to learn what happens when Eagle and Coyote borrow a sacred Native American box.

Read **"How the Snake Got Poison"** to find out how the snake learns to protect himself.

© Common Core State Standards

Meet these standards with either **"Sun and Moon in a Box"** (p. 992) or **"How the Snake Got Poison"** (p. 1000).

Reading Literature
2. Determine a theme or central idea of a text and analyze its development over the course of the text; provide an objective summary of the text. *(Literary Analysis: Spiral Review; Writing: Oral Summary)*

Writing
2. Write informative/explanatory texts to examine a topic and convey ideas, concepts, and information through the selection, organization, and analysis of relevant content. **2.b.** Develop the topic with relevant facts, definitions, concrete details, quotations, or other information and examples. **2.f.** Provide a concluding statement or section that follows from and supports the information or explanation presented. *(Writing: Plot Summary)*

3. Write narratives to develop real or imagined experiences or events using effective technique, relevant descriptive details, and well-structured event sequences. **3.a.** Organize an event sequence that unfolds naturally and logically.

3.b. Use narrative techniques, such as dialogue, pacing, and description, to develop experiences, events, and /or characters. *(Speaking and Listening: Story)*

Speaking and Listening
4. Use appropriate eye contact, adequate volume, and clear pronunciation. *(Speaking and Listening: Story)*

Language
2. Demonstrate command of the conventions of standard English capitalization, punctuation, and spelling when writing. *(Conventions: Capitalization)*

5.b. Use the relationship between particular words to better understand each of the words. *(Vocabulary: Analogy)*

6. Acquire and use accurately grade-appropriate general academic and domain-specific words and phrases; gather vocabulary knowledge when considering a word or phrase important to comprehension or expression. *(Vocabulary: Word Study)*

Reading Skill: Compare and Contrast

- A **comparison** tells how two or more things are alike.
- A **contrast** tells how two or more things are different.

Often, you can understand an unfamiliar concept by using your prior knowledge to compare and contrast. For example, you may understand an ancient culture better if you look for ways it is similar to and different from your own culture. You might also find similarities and differences between a story told long ago and one that is popular today. To help you compare and contrast stories, ask questions such as the following:

- Does this character make me think of someone I know or someone I have encountered in books, television shows, or movies?
- Is this plot similar to one I have seen elsewhere?
- What traditions does this story emphasize that are similar to or different from my own?

Literary Analysis: Cultural Context

Stories such as fables, folk tales, and myths are influenced by the **cultural context,** or background, customs, and beliefs, of the people who originally told them. Recognizing the cultural context will help you understand and appreciate what you read.

Using the Strategy: Cultural Context Chart

Use a chart like the one shown to identify the cultural context of a literary work. Consider the impact that cultural context might have on the author's intended theme, or message about life.

Story Title	
Time	Customs
Place	Beliefs

PHLit Online!
www.PHLitOnline.com

Hear It!
- Selection summary audio
- Selection audio

See It!
- Get Connected video
- Background video
- More about the author
- Vocabulary flashcards

Do It!
- Interactive journals
- Interactive graphic organizers
- Self-test
- Internet activity
- Grammar tutorial
- Interactive vocabulary games

Community or *individual* — **which is more important?**

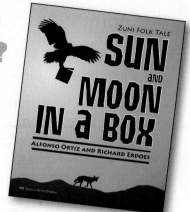

ZUNI FOLK TALE

SUN and MOON IN a BOX

ALFONSO ORTIZ AND RICHARD ERDOES

Writing About the Big Question

In "Sun and Moon in a Box," the foolish actions of Coyote and Eagle bring winter to the world. Use this sentence starter to develop your ideas about the Big Question.

When an **individual** puts his or her own needs ahead of the community, the results can be _____.

While You Read Consider whether Coyote or Eagle bears greater responsibility for causing problems for the community.

Vocabulary

Read each word and its definition. Decide whether you know the word well, know it a little bit, or do not know it at all. After you read, see how your knowledge of each word has increased.

- **regretted** (ri gret´ əd) *v.* felt sorry about (p. 993) *Antonia* *regretted her decision to stay up so late.* regret *n.* regretful *adj.* regrettable *adj.*

- **reliable** (ri lī´ ə bəl) *adj.* dependable (p. 994) *I did not ask* *Lisa for help because she is not reliable.* reliably *adv.* rely *v.* relying *v.*

- **curiosity** (kyoor´ ē äs´ ə tē) *n.* desire to learn or know (p. 994) *Unable to control her curiosity, she peeked inside* *the package.* curious *adj.* curiously *adv.*

- **pestering** (pes´ tər iŋ) *v.* annoying; bothering (p. 995) *Cal kept* *pestering his father for a car.* pester *v.* pest *n.*

- **relented** (ri lent´ əd) *v.* gave in (p. 995) *Larry finally relented* *and agreed to come with me.* relentless *adj.* relentlessly *adv.* relent *v.*

- **cunning** (kun´ iŋ) *adj.* sly; crafty (p. 996) *Her cunning plan* *took everyone by surprise.* cunningly *adv.*

Word Study

The **Latin suffix** *-ity* means "state," "quality," or "condition of."

This folk tale shows how too much **curiosity**, the state of feeling a strong desire to know, can lead one to make unwise choices.

SUN AND MOON IN A BOX

Richard Erdoes (b. 1912)

Richard Erdoes was born in Frankfurt, Germany. He studied art and later worked as a caricaturist sketching humorous portraits for several German daily newspapers.

On the Move In 1939, when the Nazis occupied Austria, Erdoes fled to France. He moved to New York in 1940. There, he worked as an illustrator for newspapers and magazines. While working at *Life* magazine, Erdoes took pictures for an article on a Sioux reservation, and his eyes were opened to the conditions there. Since then, he has written more than twenty books on the American West.

Alfonso Ortiz (1939–1997)

Alfonso Ortiz was born in San Juan, a Tewa pueblo in northern New Mexico. He earned degrees in both sociology and anthropology, and spent many years of his life as a university professor.

An Advocate for Native Americans During his teaching career, Ortiz brought scholars from the community to the university to share their knowledge with students and teachers. He also worked with the Association on American Indian Affairs and served as president of the organization for fifteen years.

DID YOU KNOW?

- Erdoes has lectured at many universities, including Yale, Princeton, and Dartmouth.
- Ortiz taught at Rutgers, UCLA, Princeton, and the University of Mexico.

BACKGROUND FOR THE FOLK TALE
Folk Tales

Many cultures have folk tales that are similar to the folk tales of other cultures. Stories about creation, the discovery of fire, and the origin of the seasons come from many different lands and peoples. As you read folk tales from different cultures, you can see how each culture changes the story to suit its own values and customs.

SUN AND MOON IN A BOX

Alfonso Ortiz and Richard Erdoes

oyote and Eagle were hunting. Eagle caught rabbits. Coyote caught nothing but grasshoppers. Coyote said: "Friend Eagle, my chief, we make a great hunting pair."

"Good, let us stay together," said Eagle.

They went toward the west. They came to a deep canyon. "Let us fly over it," said Eagle.

"My chief, I cannot fly," said Coyote. "You must carry me across."

"Yes, I see that I have to," said Eagle. He took Coyote on his back and flew across the canyon. They came to a river. "Well," said Eagle, "you cannot fly, but you certainly can swim. This time I do not have to carry you."

Eagle flew over the stream, and Coyote swam across. He was a bad swimmer. He almost drowned. He coughed up a lot of water. "My chief," he said, "when we come to another river, you must carry me." Eagle <u>regretted</u> to have Coyote for a companion.

© **Spiral Review**
Theme In some cultures, coyotes are trickster characters. How might Eagle's willingness to listen to Coyote contribute to this folk tale's theme?

Vocabulary
regretted (ri gret´ əd) *v.* felt sorry about

✓ Reading Check
Why do Eagle and Coyote stay together?

They came to Kachina Pueblo.[1] The Kachinas were dancing. Now, at this time, the earth was still soft and new. There was as yet no sun and no moon. Eagle and Coyote sat down and watched the dance. They saw that the Kachinas had a square box. In it they kept the sun and the moon. Whenever they wanted light they opened the lid and let the sun peek out. Then it was day. When they wanted less light, they opened the box just a little for the moon to look out.

"This is something wonderful," Coyote whispered to Eagle.

"This must be the sun and the moon they are keeping in that box," said Eagle. "I have heard about these two wonderful beings."

"Let us steal the box," said Coyote.

"No, that would be wrong," said Eagle. "Let us just borrow it."

When the Kachinas were not looking, Eagle grabbed the box and flew off. Coyote ran after him on the ground. After a while Coyote called Eagle: "My chief, let me have the box. I am ashamed to let you do all the carrying."

"No," said Eagle, "you are not reliable. You might be curious and open the box and then we could lose the wonderful things we borrowed."

For some time they went on as before—Eagle flying above with the box, Coyote running below, trying to keep up. Then once again Coyote called Eagle: "My chief, I am ashamed to let you carry the box. I should do this for you. People will talk badly about me, letting you carry this burden."

"No, I don't trust you," Eagle repeated. "You won't be able to refrain from opening the box. Curiosity will get the better of you."

"No," cried Coyote, "do not fear, my chief, I won't even think of opening the box." Still, Eagle would not give it to

---

1. **Kachina Pueblo** (kə chē´ nə pweb´ lō) Native American village.

Vocabulary
reliable (ri lī´ ə bəl) *adj.* dependable
curiosity (kyoor´ ē äs´ ə tē) *n.* desire to learn or know

Cultural Context
What details show that this is a Native American story set in the Southwest?

him, continuing to fly above, holding the box in his talons. But Coyote went on pestering Eagle: "My chief, I am really embarrassed. People will say: 'That lazy, disrespectful Coyote lets his chief do all the carrying.'"

"No, I won't give this box to you," Eagle objected. "It is too precious to entrust to somebody like you."

They continued as before, Eagle flying, Coyote running. Then Coyote begged for the fourth time: "My chief, let me carry the box for a while. My wife will scold me, and my children will no longer respect me, when they find out that I did not help you carry this load."

Then Eagle relented, saying: "Will you promise not to drop the box and under no circumstances to open it?"

"I promise, my chief, I promise," cried Coyote. "You can rely upon me. I shall not betray your trust."

Then Eagle allowed Coyote to carry the box. They went on as before, Eagle flying, Coyote running, carrying the box in his mouth. They came to a wooded area, full of trees and bushes. Coyote pretended to lag behind, hiding himself behind some bushes where Eagle could not see him. He could not curb his curiosity. Quickly he sat down and opened the box. In a flash, Sun came out of the box and flew away, to

Compare and Contrast
How do Coyote's and Eagle's feelings about responsibility differ?

Vocabulary
pestering (pes´ tər iŋ) *v.* annoying; bothering
relented (ri lent´ əd) *v.* gave in

the very edge of the sky, and at once the world grew cold, the leaves fell from the tree branches, the grass turned brown, and icy winds made all living things shiver.

Then, before Coyote could put the lid back on the box, Moon jumped out and flew away to the outer rim of the sky, and at once snow fell down from heaven and covered the plains and the mountains.

Eagle said: "I should have known better. I should not have let you persuade me. I knew what kind of low, cunning, stupid creature you are. I should have remembered that you never keep a promise. Now we have winter. If you had not opened the box, then we could have kept Sun and Moon always close to us. Then there would be no winter. Then we would have summer all the time."

Vocabulary
cunning (kun´ in)
adj. sly; crafty

Critical Thinking

Cite textual evidence to support your responses.

1. **Key Ideas and Details (a) Support:** Make a two-column chart. In the first column, write sentences or comments from other characters that give details about what Coyote is like. In the second column, explain what you think each detail reveals about Coyote. **(b) Discuss:** In a small group, discuss your lists. Then, choose the best details from each list to share with the class.

2. **Key Ideas and Details (a)** What does Coyote say to Eagle when Eagle is carrying the box? **(b) Infer:** Why do you think he says this? **(c) Infer:** Why do you think Eagle finally agrees to give the box to Coyote?

3. **Integration of Knowledge and Ideas Make a Judgment:** In your opinion, does Eagle share any responsibility for the appearance of the first winter? Why or why not?

4. **Integration of Knowledge and Ideas (a)** How do Coyote's ignorance and selfishness cause harm to others? **(b)** Which character bears more blame for losing the sun and moon? Why? *[Connect to the Big Question: Community or individual—which is more important?]*

Reading Skill: Compare and Contrast

1. Use a Venn diagram like the one shown to **compare and contrast** Eagle and Coyote. Think about how they look, their abilities, and how they react to responsibility.

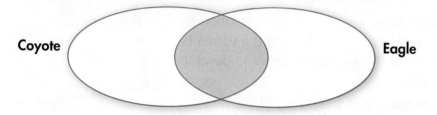

Coyote   Eagle

Literary Analysis: Cultural Context

© **2. Key Ideas and Details** Describe where Coyote and Eagle are when they first see the box. How do these details help you understand the **cultural context** of the story?

© **3. Integration of Knowledge and Ideas** What Zuni beliefs and values are revealed in this folk tale?

Vocabulary

© **Acquisition and Use** An **analogy** shows the relationship between a pair of words. Use a word from the vocabulary list on page 990 to complete each analogy. Your choice should make a word pair that matches the relationship between the first two words.

1. came in : went out :: _____ : stood firm

2. insult : anger :: _____ : annoyance

3. famous : unknown :: _____ : undependable

4. felt pride : accomplishment :: _____ : mistake

5. amiable : friendly :: _____ : sly

6. kindness : cruelty :: _____ : disinterest

Word Study Use the context of the sentences and what you know about the **Latin suffix -ity** to explain your answer.

1. Would a supervisor appreciate a worker's *productivity*?

2. If I show *sensitivity,* am I being thoughtful?

Word Study

The **Latin suffix -ity** means "state," "quality," or "condition of."

Apply It Explain how the suffix -ity contributes to the meanings of these words. Consult a dictionary if necessary.

density
integrity
reliability

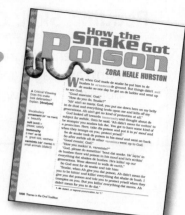

Community or *individual* — which is more important?

Writing About the Big Question

In "How the Snake Got Poison," God must figure out a solution to keep the snake from being killed by the varmints, and the varmints from being killed by the snake. Use this sentence starter to develop your ideas about the Big Question.

When the needs of the **individual** and the needs of the larger **group** are in conflict, it is helpful to _____ because _____.

While You Read Look for details that suggest both the snake's needs and the varmints' needs are important.

Vocabulary

Read each word and its definition. Decide whether you know the word well, know it a little bit, or do not know it at all. After you read, see how your knowledge of each word has increased.

- **ornament** (or´ nə ment´) *v.* beautify (p. 1000) *I put lights in the tree to ornament the patio.* ornament *n.* ornamental *adj.* ornamentation *n.*

- **suit** (soot) *v.* please; satisfy (p. 1000) *As nice as they were, the flowers did not suit her.* suitable *adj.* suitability *n.* suitably *adv.*

- **immensity** (i men´ sə tē) *n.* great size; vastness (p. 1000) *The search team had to spread out because of the canyon's immensity.* immense *adj.* immensely *adv.*

- **varmints** (vär´ mənts) *n.* small animals (dialect) (p. 1000) *Varmints got into the grain silo to eat.* varmint *n.*

Word Study

The **Latin suffix -ity** means "state," "quality," or "condition of."

In this folk tale, God looks toward **immensity.** The author uses this word to describe the enormous size of the universe.

Author of

How the Snake Got Poison

Zora Neale Hurston, the daughter of a preacher and a schoolteacher, grew up in the small town of Eatonville, Florida. In 1925, Hurston headed to New York and became part of the Harlem Renaissance, a creative movement among African Americans.

Hurston's Career Hurston collected folklore in the southern United States and in Jamaica, Haiti, Bermuda, and Honduras. Her first book, *Jonah's Gourd Vine*, was published in 1934. Although Hurston's writing was popular, she was not able to make a living from it and died penniless. In 1973, author Alice Walker found Hurston's grave and placed a gravestone on the site.

BACKGROUND FOR THE FOLK TALE

Dialect

Dialect is the form of a language that is spoken by people in a particular region or social group. It differs from standard English in pronunciation, grammar, word choice, and sentence structure. Dialect used in the retelling of a folk tale honors the oral tradition by helping the reader "hear" how the story was first told. The dialect in "How the Snake Got Poison" reflects its roots in African American folklore.

DID YOU KNOW?
Hurston studied anthropology at Barnard College and Columbia University, in New York.

How the Snake Got Poison

ZORA NEALE HURSTON

Well, when God made de snake he put him in de bushes to ornament de ground. But things didn't suit de snake so one day he got on de ladder and went up to see God.

"Good mawnin', God."

"How do you do, Snake?"

"Ah[1] ain't so many, God, you put me down here on my belly in de dust and everything trods upon me and kills off my generations. Ah ain't got no kind of protection at all."

God looked off towards immensity and thought about de subject for awhile, then he said, "Ah didn't mean for nothin' to be stompin' you snakes lak dat. You got to have some kind of a protection. Here, take dis poison and put it in yo' mouf and when they tromps on you, protect yo'self."

So de snake took de poison in his mouf and went on back.

So after awhile all de other varmints went up to God.

"Good evenin', God."

"How you makin' it, varmints?"

"God, please do somethin' 'bout dat snake. He' layin' in de bushes there wid poison in his mouf and he's strikin' everything dat shakes de bushes. He's killin' up our generations. Wese skeered to walk de earth."

So God sent for de snake and tole him:

"Snake, when Ah give you dat poison, Ah didn't mean for you to be hittin' and killin' everything dat shake de bush. I give you dat poison and tole you to protect yo'self when they tromples on you. But you killin' everything dat moves. Ah didn't mean for you to do dat."

---

1. **Ah** dialect, or regional pronunciation, for "I."

Vocabulary
ornament (ōr´ nə ment´) v. beautify
suit (so̅o̅t) v. please; satisfy
immensity (i men´ sə tē) n. great size; vastness
varmints (vär´ mənts) n. small animals (dialect)

Social Studies Connection

DUKE
ELLINGTON
AND HIS COTTON CLUB ORCHESTRA
BLACK AND TAN
with FREDI WASHINGTON

Music

The Harlem Renaissance

During the 1920s and '30s in New York City, a talented group of African American writers, artists, and musicians took part in a cultural movement that became known as the Harlem Renaissance.

Blues great Bessie ▶ Smith and musicians such as jazz legend Duke Ellington performed at the famous Cotton Club nightclub.

Zora Neale Hurston, Countee Cullen, and Langston Hughes brought the African American experience to life through their writing.
▼

Arts

Literature

Into Bondage, 1936 by Aaron Douglas, Corcoran Gallery of Art.

▲
The photographs of James Van Der Zee and the paintings of Aaron Douglas captured the look and feel of the times.

Connect to the Literature   How did works like Hurston's folk tale, "How the Snake Got Poison," contribute to the Harlem Renaissance?

Compare and Contrast
How does the varmints' problem compare with the snake's problem at the beginning of the story?

De snake say, "Lawd, you know Ah'm down here in de dust. Ah ain't got no claws to fight wid, and Ah ain't got no feets to git me out de way. All Ah kin see is feets comin' to tromple me. Ah can't tell who my enemy is and who is my friend. You gimme dis protection in my mouf and Ah uses it."

God thought it over for a while then he says:

"Well, snake, I don't want yo' generations all stomped out and I don't want you killin' everything else dat moves. Here take dis bell and tie it to yo' tail. When you hear feets comin' you ring yo' bell and if it's yo' friend, he'll be keerful. If it's yo' enemy, it's you and him."

So dat's how de snake got his poison and dat's how come he got rattles.

Critical Thinking

Cite textual evidence to support your responses.

1. **Key Ideas and Details** Which arguments from two conflicting sides does the folk tale present?

2. **Key Ideas and Details** **(a)** Find three examples of dialect in the story. **(b) Speculate:** Why do you think Hurston chose to tell the story in dialect?

3. **Key Ideas and Details** **(a)** In your notebook, describe the two arguments that the snake makes in the story. **(b) Analyze:** Tell whether you think each argument was effective and explain why you think so. **(c) Discuss:** Share your responses with a partner. Then discuss how looking at someone else's responses did or did not change your opinion.

4. **Key Ideas and Details** **(a)** What is God's final decision? **(b)** How does this decision affect both the snake and the varmints?

5. **Integration of Knowledge and Ideas** **(a) Analyze:** Explain why the varmints and the snake did not work out their problems together. **(b) Apply:** What might this situation reveal about people and their ways of interacting? **(c) Apply:** How does this story illustrate the concept of "balance of nature"?

6. **Integration of Knowledge and Ideas** **(a)** Why do the snake and varmints need protection from each other? **(b)** Why must a compromise be made to help settle this conflict between an individual and a group? *[Connect to the Big Question: Community or individual—which is more important?]*

Reading Skill: Compare and Contrast

1. Use a Venn diagram like the one shown to **compare and contrast** the snake and the varmints at the beginning of the story. Think about how they look and their abilities.

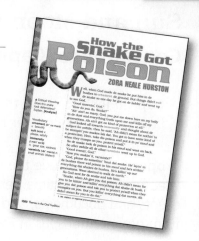

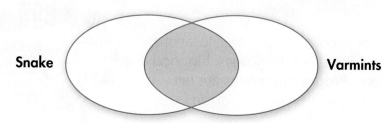

Snake   Varmints

Literary Analysis: Cultural Context

© 2. Craft and Structure How does the author's use of **dialect** help you understand the **cultural context** of the story?

© 3. Integration of Knowledge and Ideas In the story, God says to the snake, "You got to have some kind of protection." What does this statement show about beliefs within the culture where the story originated?

Vocabulary

© Acquisition and Use An **analogy** shows the relationship between a pair of words. Use a word from the vocabulary list on page 998 to complete each analogy. Your choice should make a word pair that matches the relationship between the first two words. Explain the relationship.

1. cold : hot :: _____ : smallness

2. ignore : neglect :: _____ : satisfy

3. critters : creatures :: _____ : vermin

4. hiking : trekking :: _____ : decorate

Word Study Use the context of the sentences and what you know about the **Latin suffix -ity** to explain your answer.

1. Can gentle stretching increase your *flexibility*?

2. Would your *mobility* be affected by a broken leg?

Word Study

The **Latin suffix -ity** means "state," "quality," or "condition of."

Apply It Explain how the suffix *-ity* contributes to the meanings of these words. Consult a dictionary if necessary.
probability
vanity
sincerity

Integrated Language Skills

Sun and Moon in a Box • How the Snake Got Poison

Conventions: Capitalization

Capital letters signal the beginning of a sentence or quotation and identify proper nouns and adjectives.

Proper nouns include the names of people, geographical locations, specific events and time periods, organizations, languages, historical events and documents, and religions. **Proper adjectives** are derived from proper nouns, as in *France/French* and *Canada/Canadian*.

Sentence beginning: My dog ran away.

Quotation: I yelled, "Come back!"

Proper nouns: Michael, Queen Elizabeth, U.S. Constitution, Friday

Proper adjectives: Mexican, Jeffersonian, Irish

Practice A Identify the proper nouns and adjectives in each sentence, and tell what each names (geographic location, historical event, etc.) or describes.

1. Richard Erdoes is a German artist who became interested in Native American culture after moving to America.

2. As president of the Association on American Indian Affairs, Alfonso Ortiz did much to help his people.

3. Their story "Sun and Moon in a Box" retells a Zuni folk tale.

4. The Zunis are an ancient American Indian people who live in the Southwest.

Ⓒ **Reading Application** In "Sun and Moon in a Box," find two sentences that contain quotations and two additional sentences that each contain a different type of proper noun.

Practice B Rewrite the following sentences, correcting the capitalization.

1. in this folk tale, african american writer zora neale hurston retells a story she first heard as a child in florida.

2. the story explains how god helped snake protect himself against other creatures.

3. to get god's attention, snake climbed a ladder and called, "good mawnin', god."

4. in the end, god settles on a compromise that meets the needs of both snake and the varmints.

Ⓒ **Writing Application** Write three sentences about a folk tale you have read. In your sentences, use at least one quotation, one proper adjective, and two proper nouns.

PH WRITING COACH Further instruction and practice are available in *Prentice Hall Writing Coach*.

Writing

Common Core State Standards

L.7.2, L.7.5.b, L.7.6; RL.7.2; W.7.2, W.7.2.b, W.7.2.f, W.7.3, W.7.3.a, W.7.3.b; SL.4
[For the full wording of the standards, see page 988.]

Informative Text Write a **plot summary** of either "Sun and Moon in a Box" or "How the Snake Got Poison."

- Take notes to describe each element of the folk tale: setting, major characters, main events, and final outcome.

- Use your notes to write your summary. Include one major event from the beginning, middle, and end of the story.

- Conclude your summary by stating a possible theme that logically supports the ideas you present.

Remember to remain objective, avoiding your personal reactions and including only the most important ideas and details.

Grammar Application Check your writing to be sure you have used correct conventions of capitalization.

Writing Workshop: *Work in Progress*

Prewriting for Research For a research report that you may write, list six ideas in response to one or more of the following topics: science, technology, society, or the environment. Save this Ideas List in your writing portfolio.

Use this prewriting activity to prepare for the **Writing Workshop** on page 1040.

Speaking and Listening

Comprehension and Collaboration With a partner, find five unusual facts about an animal. Include these facts in a **story** about the animal that does not reveal the animal's name. Present the story to your classmates, and ask them to guess the animal. Make your presentation entertaining and effective by using these ideas:

- Organize the plot of your story so that it unfolds naturally and is engaging and interesting to your readers.

- Include narrative techniques such as dialogue and description that help to develop your story characters and events.

- Create suspense by withholding certain details until later in the story.

- As you read, use facial expressions and body movements that enhance and support the story.

- Adjust your speaking rate, volume, and tone to suit the action of your story. Pronounce words clearly, and use appropriate expression.

- Make eye contact with your audience from time to time.

PHLit Online!
www.PHLitOnline.com
- Interactive graphic organizers
- Grammar tutorial
- Interactive journals

ⒸLeveled Texts

Build your skills and improve your comprehension of folk tales in the oral tradition with texts of increasing complexity.

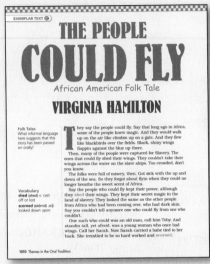

Read **"The People Could Fly"** to learn the story of enslaved Africans who find freedom in a unique way.

Read **"All Stories Are Anansi's"** to find out how Anansi earns the right to own all the stories in the world.

ⒸCommon Core State Standards

Meet these standards with either **"The People Could Fly"** (p. 1010) or **"All Stories Are Anansi's"** (p. 1018).

Reading Literature
3. Analyze how particular elements of a story or drama interact. *(Literary Analysis: Folk Tale)*

Writing
1. Write arguments to support claims with clear reasons and relevant evidence. **1.a.** Introduce claim(s), acknowledge alternate or opposing claims, and organize the reasons and evidence logically. **1.b.** Support claim(s) with logical reasoning and relevant evidence, using accurate, credible sources and demonstrating an understanding of the topic or text. *(Writing: Review)*

2.a. Introduce a topic clearly, previewing what is to follow; organize ideas, concepts, and information, using strategies such as definition, classification, comparison/contrast, and cause/effect. **2.b.** Develop the topic with relevant facts, definitions, concrete details, quotations, or other information and examples. **2.f.** Provide a concluding statement or section that follows from and supports the

information or explanation presented. *(Speaking and Listening: Television News Report)*

Speaking and Listening
4. Present claims and findings, emphasizing salient points in a focused, coherent manner with pertinent descriptions, facts, details, and examples; use appropriate eye contact, adequate volume, and clear pronunciation. *(Speaking and Listening: Television News Report)*

Language
2. Demonstrate command of the conventions of standard English capitalization, punctuation, and spelling when writing. *(Conventions: Abbreviations)*

3.a. Choose language that expresses ideas precisely and concisely, recognizing and eliminating wordiness and redundancy. *(Writing: Review)*

4.b. Use common, grade-appropriate Greek or Latin affixes and roots as clues to the meaning of a word. *(Vocabulary: Word Study)*

Reading Skill: Compare and Contrast

When you **compare and contrast**, you recognize similarities and differences. You can compare and contrast elements in a literary work by **using a Venn diagram** to examine character traits, situations, and ideas.

- First, reread the text to locate the details you will compare.
- Then, write the details on a diagram like the one below.

Recording these details will help you understand the similarities and differences in a literary work.

Using the Strategy: Character Diagram

As you read, use a Venn diagram to compare and contrast the characters of the folk tales that follow.

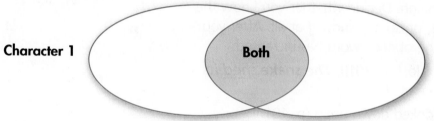

Character 1   Both   Character 2

Literary Analysis: Folk Tales

A form of fiction, a **folk tale** is a story that is composed orally and then passed from person to person by word of mouth. Though they originate in this **oral tradition,** most folk tales are eventually collected and written down. Similar folk tales are told by different cultures throughout the world, using common character types, plot elements, and themes. Folk tales often teach a lesson about life and clearly differentiate between good and evil. Folk tales are part of the oral tradition that also includes fairy tales, legends, myths, fables, tall tales, and ghost stories. As you read, notice how common elements of folk tales work together to give meaning to the story.

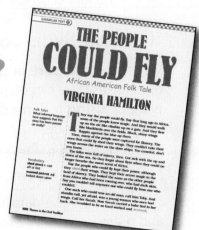

Writing About the Big Question

In "The People Could Fly," a character uses ancient African magic to free his people. Use this sentence starter to develop your ideas about the Big Question.

> Stories can sometimes **unify** people who share a common struggle because _____.

While You Read Consider how the idea of enslaved people flying to freedom may have inspired a community of people.

Vocabulary

Read each word and its definition. Decide whether you know the word well, know it a little bit, or do not know it at all. After you read, see how your knowledge of each word has increased.

- **shed** (shed) *v.* cast off or lost (p. 1010) *The snake <u>shed</u> its skin several times last year.* shedding *v.*

- **scorned** (skôrnd) *adj.* looked down upon (p. 1010) *Lisa was <u>scorned</u> by her teammates because of her refusal to come to practice.* scorn *v.* scornful *adj.* scornfully *adv.*

- **hoed** (hōd) *v.* weeded or loosened soil with a metal hand tool (p. 1011) *Lisa <u>hoed</u> the garden until she developed blisters.* hoe *v.* hoe *n.*

- **croon** (krōōn) *v.* sing or hum quietly and soothingly (p. 1011) *When you <u>croon</u> that lullaby, I get sleepy.* crooned *v.* crooning *v.* crooner *n.*

- **mystery** (mis´ tə rē) *n.* something unexplained, unknown, or kept secret (p. 1012) *Peter wanted to solve the <u>mystery</u> before he read the last chapter.* mysterious *adj.* mysteries *n.*

- **shuffle** (shuf´ əl) *v.* walk with dragging feet (p. 1013) *We heard the tired man <u>shuffle</u> down the hallway.* shuffling *v.* shuffled *v.* shuffler *n.*

Word Study

The **Greek root -myst-** means "secret."

This folk tale tells a story about the African **mystery**, or secret, of people who could fly.

Author of

THE PEOPLE
COULD FLY

"I started writing as a kid," Virginia Hamilton once said. "It was always something I was going to do." The author of countless novels, stories, and collections of African American folk tales, Hamilton has been called "America's most honored writer of books for children."

Stories of the Past Hamilton was raised in a house of gifted storytellers. She described her childhood as ideal, saying "I heard 'tells' every day of my life from parents and relatives." Some of those stories were about slavery, and most were about the past. As a result, the past came to play an important role in Hamilton's writing. She developed a unique style, combining elements of history, myth, legend, and dream to bring her stories to life.

DID YOU KNOW?
As a child, Hamilton was a cheerleader and captain of the girls' basketball team. She also ran track and sang in her school choir.

BACKGROUND FOR THE FOLK TALE
African American Folk Tales

"The People Could Fly" is a freedom tale, a kind of folk tale that enslaved Africans told to keep their hopes alive, despite the hardships they faced. Like many freedom tales, "The People Could Fly" contains images of freedom and escape as well as many references to the original storyteller's native Africa.

THE PEOPLE COULD FLY

African American Folk Tale

VIRGINIA HAMILTON

Folk Tales
What informal language here suggests that this story has been passed on orally?

They say the people could fly. Say that long ago in Africa, some of the people knew magic. And they would walk up on the air like climbin up on a gate. And they flew like blackbirds over the fields. Black, shiny wings flappin against the blue up there.

Then, many of the people were captured for Slavery. The ones that could fly shed their wings. They couldn't take their wings across the water on the slave ships. Too crowded, don't you know.

The folks were full of misery, then. Got sick with the up and down of the sea. So they forgot about flyin when they could no longer breathe the sweet scent of Africa.

Vocabulary
shed (shed) *v.* cast off or lost
scorned (skôrnd) *adj.* looked down upon

Say the people who could fly kept their power, although they shed their wings. They kept their secret magic in the land of slavery. They looked the same as the other people from Africa who had been coming over, who had dark skin. Say you couldn't tell anymore one who could fly from one who couldn't.

One such who could was an old man, call him Toby. And standin tall, yet afraid, was a young woman who once had wings. Call her Sarah. Now Sarah carried a babe tied to her back. She trembled to be so hard worked and scorned.

From **The People Could Fly** by Virginia Hamilton, illustrated by Leo and Diane Dillon.

The slaves labored in the fields from sunup to sundown. The owner of the slaves callin himself their Master. Say he was a hard lump of clay. A hard, glinty[1] coal. A hard rock pile, wouldn't be moved. His Overseer[2] on horseback pointed out the slaves who were slowin down. So the one called Driver[3] cracked his whip over the slow ones to make them move faster. That whip was a slice-open cut of pain. So they did move faster. Had to.

Sarah hoed and chopped the row as the babe on her back slept.

Say the child grew hungry. That babe started up bawling too loud. Sarah couldn't stop to feed it. Couldn't stop to soothe and quiet it down. She let it cry. She didn't want to. She had no heart to croon to it.

"Keep that thing quiet," called the Overseer. He pointed his finger at the babe. The woman scrunched low. The Driver

Vocabulary
hoed (hōd) *v.* weeded or loosened soil with a metal hand tool
croon (krōōn) *v.* sing or hum quietly and soothingly

 Reading Check
What special gift do some of the people in this tale have?

---

1. **glinty** (glint´ ē) *adj.* shiny; reflecting light.
2. **Overseer** (ō´ vər sē´ ər) *n.* someone who watches over and directs the work of others.
3. **Driver** *n.* someone who forced (drove) the slaves to work harder.

The People Could Fly **1011**

cracked his whip across the babe anyhow. The babe hollered like any hurt child, and the woman fell to the earth.

The old man that was there, Toby, came and helped her to her feet.

"I must go soon," she told him.

"Soon," he said.

Sarah couldn't stand up straight any longer. She was too weak. The sun burned her face. The babe cried and cried, "Pity me, oh, pity me," say it sounded like. Sarah was so sad and starvin, she sat down in the row.

"Get up, you black cow," called the Overseer. He pointed his hand, and the Driver's whip snarled around Sarah's legs. Her sack dress tore into rags. Her legs bled onto the earth. She couldn't get up.

Toby was there where there was no one to help her and the babe.

"Now, before it's too late," panted Sarah. "Now, Father!"

"Yes, Daughter, the time is come," Toby answered. "Go, as you know how to go!"

He raised his arms, holding them out to her. "*Kum . . . yali, kum buba tambe,*" and more magic words, said so quickly, they sounded like whispers and sighs.

The young woman lifted one foot on the air. Then the other. She flew clumsily at first, with the child now held tightly in her arms. Then she felt the magic, the African mystery. Say she rose just as free as a bird. As light as a feather.

The Overseer rode after her, hollerin. Sarah flew over the fences. She flew over the woods. Tall trees could not snag her. Nor could the Overseer. She flew like an eagle now, until she was gone from sight. No one dared speak about it. Couldn't believe it. But it was, because they that was there saw that it was.

Say the next day was dead hot in the fields. A young man slave fell from the heat. The Driver come and whipped him. Toby come over and spoke words to the fallen one. The words of ancient Africa once heard are never remembered completely. The young man forgot them as soon as he heard them. They went way inside him. He got up and rolled over on the air. He

> ### The young woman lifted one foot on the air. Then the other. She flew clumsily at first…

Vocabulary
mystery (mis´ tə rē) *n.* something unexplained, unknown, or kept secret

rode it awhile. And he flew away.

Another and another fell from the heat. Toby was there. He cried out to the fallen and reached his arms out to them. *"Kum kunka yali, kum . . . tambe!"* Whispers and sighs. And they too rose on the air. They rode the hot breezes. The ones flyin were black and shinin sticks, wheelin above the head of the Overseer. They crossed the rows, the fields, the fences, the streams, and were away.

"Seize the old man!" cried the Overseer. "I heard him say the magic *words.* Seize him!"

The one callin himself Master come runnin. The Driver got his whip ready to curl around old Toby and tie him up. The slaveowner took his hip gun from its place. He meant to kill old, black Toby.

But Toby just laughed. Say he threw back his head and said, "Hee, hee! Don't you know who I am? Don't you know some of us in this field?" He said it to their faces. "We are ones who fly!"

And he sighed the ancient words that were a dark promise. He said them all around to the others in the field under the whip,

". . . buba yali . . . buba tambe. . . ."

There was a great outcryin. The bent backs straightened up. Old and young who were called slaves and could fly joined hands. Say like they would ring-sing.[4] But they didn't shuffle in a circle. They didn't sing. They rose on the air. They flew in a flock that was black against the heavenly blue. Black crows or black shadows. It didn't matter, they went so high. Way above the plantation, way over the slavery land. Say they flew away to *Free-dom.*

And the old man, old Toby, flew behind them, takin care of them. He wasn't cryin. He wasn't laughin. He was the seer.[5] His gaze fell on the plantation where the slaves who could not fly waited.

---

4. **ring-sing** joining hands in a circle to sing and dance.
5. **seer** (sē´ ər) *n.* one who has supposed power to see the future; prophet.

▲ **Critical Viewing**
What are some reasons why a person might wish to fly? **[Speculate]**

Vocabulary
shuffle (shuf´ əl) *v.* walk with dragging feet

Reading Check

What did Sarah do to escape the Overseer?

Compare and Contrast
How is Toby's position now different from his position at the beginning of the story?

"*Take us with you!*" Their looks spoke it but they were afraid to shout it. Toby couldn't take them with him. Hadn't the time to teach them to fly. They must wait for a chance to run.

"Goodie-bye!" The old man called Toby spoke to them, poor souls! And he was flyin gone.

So they say. The Overseer told it. The one called Master said it was a lie, a trick of the light. The Driver kept his mouth shut.

The slaves who could not fly told about the people who could fly to their children. When they were free. When they sat close before the fire in the free land, they told it. They did so love firelight and *Free-dom,* and tellin.

They say that the children of the ones who could not fly told their children. And now, me, I have told it to you.

Critical Thinking

Cite textual evidence to support your responses.

1. Key Ideas and Details (a) Describe: What words would you use to describe the living conditions of many African Americans during the time this story originated? **(b) Support:** Describe three details that help you understand these living conditions.

2. Craft and Structure (a) Infer: What are the "magic words" Toby says? **(b) Interpret:** Why do you think the author includes these words in the story?

3. Key Ideas and Details (a) What happens when Toby says the "magic words"? **(b) Draw Conclusions:** What do you think "flying" really means?

4. Key Ideas and Details (a) Who is called Master? **(b) Contrast:** Who is the real "master" in the story? **(c) Evaluate:** Do you think this folk tale inspires hope? Explain.

5. Integration of Knowledge and Ideas What effect might freedom tales, like this folk tale, have had on enslaved or otherwise oppressed people? *[Connect to the Big Question: Community or individual—which is more important?]*

Reading Skill: Compare and Contrast

1. **Compare and contrast** the personalities of Toby and the Overseer. How are they similar? How are they different?

2. Use a Venn diagram to compare and contrast "The People Could Fly" with another story you have read in this book. In your diagram, include details about setting, plot, and characters.

Literary Analysis: Folk Tales

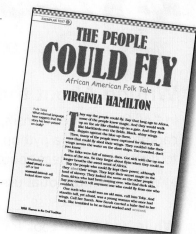

3. **Craft and Structure** Use a chart like the one shown to identify examples of the elements of **folk tales** that you find in this story and explain how they contribute to the meaning of the story.

Elements:	Characters	Plot Events	Lesson	Theme
Examples:				

Vocabulary

Acquisition and Use For each item, write a single sentence correctly using the words indicated.

1. shuffle; dance
2. scorned; opinion
3. croon; lullaby
4. shed; leaves
5. hoed; planting
6. mystery; movie

Word Study Use the context of the sentences and what you know about the **Greek root -myst-** to explain your answer to each question.

1. Would a *mysterious* disappearance be easy to solve?
2. If I am *mystified* by your answer to my question, how might I respond?

Word Study

The **Greek root -myst-** means "a secret rite."

Apply It Explain how the root *-myst-* contributes to the meanings of these words. Consult a dictionary if necessary.

mystique
mystical
mysticism

Writing About the Big Question

In "All Stories Are Anansi's," Anansi the spider uses trickery to capture a hornet, a python, and a leopard. Use this sentence starter to develop your ideas about the Big Question.

When an **individual** uses others for personal gain, he risks _____ _____ because _____.

While You Read Look for details that show how Anansi gained the trust of those around him.

Vocabulary

Read each word and its definition. Decide whether you know the word well, know it a little bit, or do not know it at all. After you read, see how your knowledge of each word has increased.

- **yearned** (yʉrnd) *v.* wanted very much (p. 1019) *I yearned for some hot chocolate on that cold winter night.* *yearn* v. *yearning* n.

- **gourd** (gôrd) *n.* hard-shelled fruit (p. 1020) *We drank water from a gourd.* *gourds* n.

- **python** (pī´ than´) *n.* large snake (p. 1020) *The python kills its prey by squeezing it.*

- **dispute** (di spyoot´) *n.* disagreement (p. 1020) *They had not spoken in several days because of a dispute.* *dispute* v. *disputant* n. *disputable* adj.

- **opinion** (ə pin´ yən) *n.* belief based on what seems true or probable (p. 1021) *His opinion was based on a book he read.* *opinionated* adj.

- **acknowledge** (ak näl´ ij) *v.* recognize and admit (p. 1022) *I acknowledge that you were right and I was wrong.* *acknowledgement* n. *acknowledged* v.

Word Study

The **Old English root -know-** means "understand."

In this folk tale, the Sky God decrees that all storytellers must **acknowledge**, or understand and admit, that the tales they tell belong to Anansi.

Meet
Harold Courlander
(1908–1996)

Author of
ALL STORIES
ARE ANANSI'S

Harold Courlander is best known for his collections of folk tales from around the world. He once told an interviewer that his interest in folk tales arose from the rich multicultural environment in his hometown of Detroit, Michigan.

World Traveler During Courlander's career, he published more than thirty-five books. As he traveled around the world, he made sound recordings of the music and stories of African, African American, and Native American cultures. About his work, Courlander has said, "I think of myself primarily as a narrator. I have always had a special interest in using fiction and nonfiction narration to bridge communication between other cultures and our own."

DID YOU KNOW?
For five years, Courlander worked as a farmer. He was also a historian and a United Nations press officer.

BACKGROUND FOR THE FOLK TALE

The Trickster in Folk Tales

"All Stories Are Anansi's" is a trickster tale. Typically, the trickster is an animal character, such as a spider, a fox, or a coyote, that tries to fool others. In some tales, he succeeds. In others, he himself is fooled. In American, African, and West Indian folklore, tricksters take advantage of larger and stronger animals through cunning or magic.

ALL STORIES ARE ANANSI'S

AFRICAN FOLK TALE • HAROLD COURLANDER

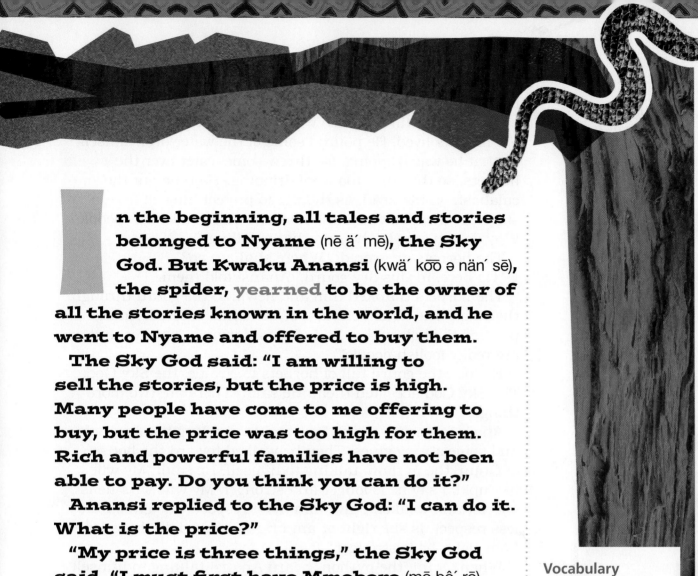

In the beginning, all tales and stories belonged to Nyame (nē ä´ mē), **the Sky God. But Kwaku Anansi** (kwä´ kōō ə nän´ sē), **the spider,** yearned **to be the owner of** all the stories known in the world, and he went to Nyame and offered to buy them.

The Sky God said: "I am willing to sell the stories, but the price is high. Many people have come to me offering to buy, but the price was too high for them. Rich and powerful families have not been able to pay. Do you think you can do it?"

Anansi replied to the Sky God: "I can do it. What is the price?"

"My price is three things," the Sky God said. "I must first have Mmoboro (mō bô´ rō), the hornets. I must then have Onini (ō nē´ nē), the great python. I must then have Osebo (ō sä´ bō), **the leopard. For these things I will** sell you the right to tell all stories."

Anansi said: "I will bring them."

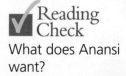

Vocabulary
yearned (yʉrnd) *v.* wanted very much

Reading Check
What does Anansi want?

Vocabulary
gourd (gôrd) *n.*
hard-shelled fruit

python (pī´ thən´) *n.*
large snake

dispute (di spyo͞ot´)
n. disagreement

Folk Tale
What lesson does the
hornets' experience
teach?

He went home and made his plans. He first cut a gourd from a vine and made a small hole in it. He took a large calabash[1] and filled it with water. He went to the tree where the hornets lived. He poured some of the water over himself, so that he was dripping. He threw some water over the hornets, so that they too were dripping. Then he put the calabash on his head, as though to protect himself from a storm, and called out to the hornets: "Are you foolish people? Why do you stay in the rain that is falling?"

The hornets answered: "Where shall we go?"

"Go here, in this dry gourd," Anansi told them.

The hornets thanked him and flew into the gourd through the small hole. When the last of them had entered, Anansi plugged the hole with a ball of grass, saying: "Oh, yes, but you are really foolish people!"

He took the gourd full of hornets to Nyame, the Sky God. The Sky God accepted them. He said: "There are two more things."

Anansi returned to the forest and cut a long bamboo pole and some strong vines. Then he walked toward the house of Onini, the python, talking to himself. He said: "My wife is stupid. I say he is longer and stronger. My wife says he is shorter and weaker. I give him more respect. She gives him less respect. Is she right or am I right? I am right, he is longer. I am right, he is stronger."

When Onini, the python, heard Anansi talking to himself, he said: "Why are you arguing this way with yourself?"

The spider replied: "Ah, I have had a dispute with my wife. She says you are shorter and weaker than this bamboo pole. I say you are longer and stronger."

Onini said: "It's useless and silly to argue when you can find out the truth. Bring the pole and we will measure."

So Anansi laid the pole on the ground, and the python came and stretched himself out beside it.

"You seem a little short," Anansi said.

The python stretched further.

"A little more," Anansi said.

"I can stretch no more," Onini said.

"When you stretch at one end, you get shorter at the

---

1. **calabash** (kal´ ə bash´) *n.* large fruit that is dried and made into a bowl or cup.

other end," Anansi said. "Let me tie you at the front so you don't slip."

He tied Onini's head to the pole. Then he went to the other end and tied the tail to the pole. He wrapped the vine all around Onini, until the python couldn't move.

"Onini," Anansi said, "it turns out that my wife was right and I was wrong. You are shorter than the pole and weaker. My opinion wasn't as good as my wife's. But you were even more foolish than I, and you are now my prisoner."

Anansi carried the python to Nyame, the Sky God, who said: "There is one thing more." Osebo, the leopard, was next. Anansi went into the forest and dug a deep pit where the leopard was accustomed to walk. He covered it with small branches and leaves and put dust on it, so that it was impossible to tell where the pit was. Anansi went away and hid. When Osebo came prowling in the black of night, he stepped into the trap Anansi had prepared and fell to the bottom. Anansi heard the sound of the leopard falling, and he said: "Ah, Osebo, you are half-foolish!"

When morning came, Anansi went to the pit and saw the leopard there.

"Osebo," he asked, "what are you doing in this hole?"

"I have fallen into a trap," Osebo said. "Help me out."

"I would gladly help you," Anansi said. "But I'm sure that if I bring you out, I will have no thanks for it. You will get hungry, and later on you will be wanting to eat me and my children."

"I swear it won't happen!" Osebo said.

"Very well. Since you swear it, I will take you out," Anansi said.

He bent a tall green tree toward the ground, so that its top was over the pit, and he tied it that way. Then he tied a rope to the top of the tree and dropped the other end of it into the pit.

"Tie this to your tail," he said.

Osebo tied the rope to his tail.

"Is it well tied?" Anansi asked.

"Yes, it is well tied," the leopard said.

"In that case," Anansi said, "you are not merely half-foolish, you are all-foolish." And he took his knife and cut the other

Vocabulary
opinion (ə pin´ yən) *n.* belief based on what seems true or probable

Compare and Contrast
What word does Anansi use to describe both the hornets and the python after he catches them?

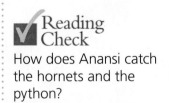
Reading Check
How does Anansi catch the hornets and the python?

Spiral Review
Theme How does Anansi's story show that sometimes cleverness beats strength?

Vocabulary
acknowledge
(ak näl´ ij) *v.* recognize and admit

rope, the one that held the tree bowed to the ground. The tree straightened up with a snap, pulling Osebo out of the hole. He hung in the air head downward, twisting and turning. And while he hung this way, Anansi killed him with his weapons.

Then he took the body of the leopard and carried it to Nyame, the Sky God, saying: "Here is the third thing. Now I have paid the price."

Nyame said to him: "Kwaku Anansi, great warriors and chiefs have tried, but they have been unable to do it. You have done it. Therefore, I will give you the stories. From this day onward, all stories belong to you. Whenever a man tells a story, he must acknowledge that it is Anansi's tale."

In this way Anansi, the spider, became the owner of all stories that are told. To Anansi all these tales belong.

Critical Thinking

Cite textual evidence to support your responses.

1. **Key Ideas and Details** **(a) Infer:** What can you infer about the hornets, the python, and the leopard from the fact that they listen to Anansi? **(b) Interpret:** In what way do these animals resemble humans in their behavior?

2. **Key Ideas and Details** **(a) Infer:** What is Anansi's attitude toward the other animals? **(b) Support:** What details reveal this attitude?

3. **Key Ideas and Details** **(a)** What does the Sky God ask Anansi to do? **(b) Draw Conclusions:** Why is Anansi able to do what warriors and chiefs have failed to do? **(c) Apply:** What qualities or characteristics are revealed by his success?

4. **Integration of Knowledge and Ideas** **(a) Interpret:** How would you describe Anansi's personal code of behavior? **(b) Evaluate:** Do you approve or disapprove of Anansi's behavior? Explain.

5. **Integration of Knowledge and Ideas** **(a)** How did Anansi gain the trust of those around him? **(b) Analyze:** Are his accomplishments admirable? Explain. **(c) Evaluate:** Was Anansi justified in using the creatures for personal gain? Why or why not? *[Connect to the Big Question: Community or individual—which is more important?]*

Reading Skill: Compare and Contrast

1. Compare and contrast the hornets, the python, and the leopard. How are they similar? How are they different?

2. Use a Venn diagram to compare and contrast "All Stories Are Anansi's" with another story you have read in this book. In your diagram, include details about setting, plot, and characters.

Literary Analysis: Folk Tales

© 3. Craft and Structure Use a chart like the one shown to identify examples of the elements of **folk tales** that you find in this story and explain how they contribute to the meaning of the story.

Elements:	Characters	Plot Events	Lesson	Theme
Examples:				

Vocabulary

© Acquisition and Use For each item, write a single sentence correctly using the words indicated.

1. yearned; warmth

2. gourd; dip

3. python; grass

4. dispute; movie

5. opinion; chocolate

6. acknowledge; right

Word Study Use the context of the sentences and what you know about the **Old English root -know-** to explain your answer to each question.

1. If an actor is *unknown*, have many people heard of him?

2. If you are having computer problems, would it be useful to call someone with technical *know-how*?

Word Study

The **Old English root -know-** means "understand."

Apply It Explain how the root **-know-** contributes to the meanings of these words. Consult a dictionary if necessary

knowledge
unbeknownst

Integrated Language Skills

The People Could Fly • All Stories Are Anansi's

Conventions: Abbreviations

An **abbreviation** is a shortened form of a word or phrase, such as *Dr.* for *Doctor* or *Rd.* for *Road.*

Most abbreviations end with a period. Abbreviations are useful when taking notes or writing lists.

Instance	Example	Abbreviation
Common Titles	Captain	Capt.
Academic Degrees	Master of Business Administration	M.B.A.
States	Maryland	MD
Addresses	Street	St.
Traditional Measurements	foot	ft.
Metric Measurements	centimeter	cm

Most abbreviations should not be used in formal writing.

Practice A Correct these items by substituting the words that are represented by the abbreviations.

1. The overseer did not have one oz. of compassion for the hungry infant.
2. When Toby uttered the magic words, Sarah rose up 50 ft. in the air.
3. The overseer chased her down Hilltop Rd.
4. She was on her way to a new home in a free place, like Boston, MA.

ⓒ Reading Application In "The People Could Fly" find a sentence containing a word that could be abbreviated in a list.

Practice B Identify the words that these abbreviations represent.

1. Mr.
2. Indianapolis, IN
3. U.N. press officer
4. WW II
5. M.D.

ⓒ Writing Application Locate the meanings for these commonly used abbreviations: *rpm; govt.; mgr.; e.g.; km; Sen.* Then, write four sentences that each use one of the abbreviations correctly.

PH WRITING COACH   Further instruction and practice are available in *Prentice Hall Writing Coach.*

Writing

 Argument Write a **review** of "The People Could Fly" or "All Stories Are Anansi's" to argue whether others will enjoy the tale.

- First, review story elements, such as characters, description, dialogue, and plot, in order to choose your position.
- State your opinion, acknowledging that some readers may not agree with you. Then, support your ideas with details from the story. Organize an effective argument by giving your strongest reasons or evidence at the beginning.

Revise your word choice to use words that are precise and descriptive. For example, replace "good" with "entertaining" or "comical," or change "boring" to "simplistic" or "predictable."

Grammar Application Check your writing to be sure you have used abbreviations correctly.

Writing Workshop: *Work in Progress*

Prewriting for Research Choose two ideas from the Ideas List in your portfolio. For each topic, jot down three different types of resources that are likely to provide you with enough information for an in-depth report. Save this Resource List in your writing portfolio.

Use this prewriting activity to prepare for the **Writing Workshop** on page 1040.

 **Common Core State Standards**

L.7.2, L.7.3.a; W.7.1, W.7.1.a, W.7.1.b, W.7.2.a, W.7.2.b, W.7.2.f; SL.7.4
[For the full wording of the standards, see page 1006.]

Speaking and Listening

 Presentation of Ideas Prepare a **television news report** that provides a clear interpretation of story events.

- Get ready by summarizing the main points of the story.
- Organize your main points by beginning with the most important point or event. Follow these points with supporting ideas.
- Describe events in your own words. Include facts about when and where the incidents took place, using details from the story.
- Include an interview with an eyewitness—someone who saw events and can provide an on-the-scene reaction. In your report, use quotations to add credibility and bring the action to life.
- Conclude your report with an insight about the meaning of the events and the characters' actions.
- Present your news report to a small group. Speak clearly and vary your voice to emphasize key points.

PHLit Online!
www.PHLitOnline.com
- Interactive graphic organizers
- Grammar tutorial
- Interactive journals

Test Practice: Reading

Compare and Contrast

Fiction Selection

Directions: *Read the selection. Then, answer the questions.*

As Jamal, Doug, and I left our cabin on the first day of camp, Jamal begged Doug and me to join the basketball tournament with him. "No way," said Doug. "I can't stand team sports! Let's go swimming instead."

"Come on," Jamal said to me, "You played basketball last year. We're not tall, but we're both fast. We'll be great together!"

"Okay," I said. "Basketball is fun. But I really hope we all work on the play together again this summer." Both Doug and Jamal nodded enthusiastically. We all met while acting in the camp play last summer, and I knew none of us would want to miss it this year.

1. What is one similarity between Jamal, Doug, and the narrator?
  A. They share a love of team sports.
  B. They have been friends for many years.
  C. They share an interest in acting.
  D. They hope to become actors.

2. One difference between Jamal and Doug is
  A. Jamal loves team sports; Doug does not.
  B. Doug is the narrator's friend, but Jamal is not.
  C. Doug is a talented actor, while Jamal gives weak performances.
  D. Jamal wants to go swimming, but Doug does not.

3. What is one similarity between the narrator and Jamal that Doug does not share?
  A. They both want to swim.
  B. They are both slow.
  C. They both go to camp.
  D. They both enjoy basketball.

4. Based on details in this passage, you can conclude that
  A. the narrator does not have much in common with Jamal.
  B. the narrator has qualities in common with both boys.
  C. the narrator has more in common with Jamal.
  D. the narrator has more in common with Doug.

Writing for Assessment

In a few sentences, summarize the similarities and differences between Doug and Jamal.

Nonfiction Selection

Directions: *Read the selection. Then, answer the questions.*

Equipment required for playing football includes helmets, mouthpieces, and a lot of thick padding. Because players often make physical contact, they must be well protected. They can wear up to ten pounds of gear during a game. The action in football is stop-and-go. A player holds the ball and runs, while others try to tackle him. Many football players are large and muscular. Their size makes it hard for opposing players to move them out of the way.

In soccer, players wear shorts, shirts, and stiff pads to protect their shins. Players mostly use their feet to move the ball, but they are allowed to use any body part other than their arms. They sometimes bounce the ball off their heads. The action in soccer is nonstop. Most soccer players are lean and muscular so that they can move quickly back and forth across the field.

1. According to the passage, in what way are football and soccer alike?
  A. Both require helmets.
  B. Both have non-stop action.
  C. Both are played by muscular athletes.
  D. Both require a lot of padding.

2. In contrast to soccer, football players—
  A. can hold the ball in their hands.
  B. never make contact with other players.
  C. wear pads to protect their shins.
  D. need very little gear.

3. Which statement is *most* accurate?
  A. Football requires players to be strong; soccer requires them to be aggressive.
  B. Football requires players to be strong; soccer requires them to be quick.
  C. Football is a team sport; soccer is an individual sport.
  D. Football is difficult to learn; soccer is easy.

4. What is the *best* title for this selection?
  A. Football and Soccer: What's the Difference?
  B. Stories From the School's Playing Fields
  C. How to Play Soccer and Football
  D. Why Football Is a Better Game than Soccer

Writing for Assessment

Connecting Across Texts
Which sport described in the second passage is Jamal more suited to play? Write a paragraph, using details from both selections to support your response.

www.PHLitOnline.com
• Online practice
• Instant feedback

Reading for Information

Analyzing Argumentative Texts

Editorial

Editorial

Common Core State Standards

Reading Skill: Analyze Point of View

Editorials reflect a writer's **point of view,** or opinion, on an issue. An editorial writer develops his or her point of view using various techniques, such as including persuasive language or providing specific evidence. When writers with differing points of view write about the same subject, they may focus only on evidence that supports their argument. Use the chart to help you **analyze the authors' point of view** in the editorials that follow.

Reading Informational Text
6. Determine an author's point of view or purpose in a text and analyze how the author distinguishes his or her position from that of others.

9. Analyze how two or more authors writing about the same topic shape their presentations of key information by emphasizing different evidence or advancing different interpretations of facts.

Writing
1.a. Introduce claims, and organize the reasons and evidence logically. **1.b.** Support claim(s) with logical reasoning and relevant evidence, demonstrating an understanding of the topic or text. **1.e.** Provide a concluding statement or section that follows from and supports the argument presented. *(Timed Writing)*

Techniques for Developing Point of View	Example
A clearly stated position	"School dress codes promote a sense of unity."
Supporting statistics, facts, and examples	"Students are more focused when distractions such as fashion choices are eliminated."
Persuasive techniques and language	"The self-confident manner of uniformed students makes a positive impression on visitors."
Arguments that address opposing views	"Some people believe that dress codes discourage individuality, yet there are many other creative outlets."
A concluding statement that reinforces the author's point of view	"Schools with dress codes shift the focus from fashion to education, which is exactly where it should be."

Content-Area Vocabulary

These words appear in the selections that follow. You may also encounter them in other content-area texts.

- **habitats** (hab´ ə tats) *n.* places where specific animals or plants naturally live or grow

- **vulnerable** (vul´ nər ə bəl) *adj.* open to attack

- **resources** (ri sôrs´ iz) *n.* any supplies that will meet a need

Zoos: Joys or Jails?

Rachel F., San Diego, CA

Imagine your family lives in a luxurious mansion where all your needs are provided for. There are gardens and daily walks and all your favorite foods.

Suddenly, you're taken from your home and shipped to a place where people come from far and wide to ogle at you, thinking they are learning about your lifestyle. Sometimes, your captors force you to perform for thousands of people.

Your life has changed drastically. Welcome to the zoo!

Although the circumstances and reasons for animals being in zoos vary, its concept has faults many don't notice during their visit with the animals. Animals in many zoos are kept in areas that are much smaller than their natural **habitats**. As a result, animals behave differently than they would in their natural surroundings. Animals like big cats are accustomed to roaming territories of up to 10 square miles.

One of the best aspects of the zoo is its emphasis on education. Signs tell visitors about the animals and their behavior in the wild, but notice how the majority say the animals were born in the zoo. Unfortunately, the adaptive behavior due to small cages gives visitors a skewed perception of how the animals actually behave in the wild.

The title of the editorial briefly presents two sides of the issue.

The most important point is presented first and is supported with statistics.

Although the idea of education to protect and preserve animals is excellent, is the zoo really setting a good example of treatment or representing the natural actions of these creatures?

Some advocates say that zoos protect and save endangered species. Despite today's advanced breeding techniques, animals raised in the zoo or other places of captivity are not learning the survival techniques they would in the wild. These animals would be very **vulnerable** if released and would encounter difficulties coping. Would it not be more beneficial to raise them in their natural habitat?

In this way scientists wouldn't face as many risks in reintroducing captive animals raised into the wild.

Helping endangered species in the wild gives them a better chance for survival and reproduction. Scientists should only revert to the zoo if the necessary funding or habitat for breeding is not available.

Animals are not just brought to the zoo to protect their species, but also to provide entertainment. Many animals' lives will include performing for visitors. Four shows are performed every day at the San Diego Zoo. The zoo should be reserved for education and protecting endangered species, not an amusement park where animals are trained to perform.

Although the zoo is trying to be helpful in providing shows about the animals, it is harming those it intends to protect. The zoo has good intentions in its educational purposes, and in breeding endangered species, but animals shouldn't perform or be treated in a manner that could change their behaviors from how they act in the wild.

Though zoos are meant to be a joy to viewers and teach lessons about our earth, the zoo jails its inhabitants and passes on faulty knowledge. The wild animals in our world are a wonder, and they must be preserved. At the zoo they are treated with care, but they should be treated with reverence.

Next time you visit a zoo, look at the enclosure of the tigers and watch the seals balance a ball on their noses, and then think about what you are really learning from your day at the zoo.

The editorial concludes with a strong, direct statement.

KID TERRITORY:
Why Do We Need Zoos?

San Diego Zoo Staff

It's an interesting question that many people wonder about. Why have people created zoos, and why are they important now?

The idea of a zoo actually started a long time ago, in the ancient cultures of China, the Middle East, and then the Roman Empire. As people started to travel more, for longer distances to explore the unknown, they began to discover animals and plants that they had never seen or heard of before. They were fascinated by these amazing creatures. Travelers reported back to their communities and their leaders what they had seen. Rulers like emperors, sultans, and kings often wanted to prove how wealthy and powerful they were, to each other and to their subjects. One way to do that was to "collect" some of these animals, and allow people to come and see them. These collections were called menageries, and usually only the rich and powerful had them.

But that changed as time went on, and eventually it was countries and then individual cities that had collections of exotic animals for people to come and see, and they were no longer reserved only for wealthy rulers. Zoology is the study of animals, so these became zoological collections. You guessed it—that was then shortened to the word we use now: zoos.

Zoos open to the public

At first most zoos only had a limited number of animals, usually the ones people had heard about but never seen in person, like lions, bears, giraffes, hippos, and other big and impressive species. Then as zoos became more popular, and traveling to get animals became more possible, zoos started to represent animals from particular countries and parts of the world. Zoologists studied these animals to find out more about them: what they ate, how they grew, how they had young, and how they behaved, among other things. But zoos were open to the general public, too, so everyone could find out about animals.

Connecting with critters

Zoos today still serve that important purpose: they allow us to study and find out more about animals that we would not understand otherwise.

Editorial

Features:
- text written for newspapers, magazines, and online publications
- a particular point of view expressed by a writer
- strong arguments
- persuasive techniques

The title of the editorial clearly identifies the issue.

The author provides historical context for the issue.

People are curious and want to know about the world around them, and that especially includes the animals and plants with which we share the Earth. In addition to studying animals in zoos, scientists are also able to go out to the countries where animals live and study them in the field, or their habitat. But most people cannot do that, so zoos allow them to see and connect with what would otherwise be unavailable to them.

Helping wildlife

These days we also have cable TV, though, and there are lots of wild animal shows that we can watch. So why still have zoos? One of the most important reasons is conservation. Humans are destroying the Earth's habitats at a very fast pace, in order to make space, food, and products for ourselves. But that leaves less and less room for animals and plants. Zoos and wildlife parks are places where we can protect species that are in trouble, so they don't disappear from the Earth completely.

People do have different opinions about that, though. Some people think that animals should not be kept by humans for any reason, and that if they go extinct, then that's the way it should be. Other people think that animals are precious resources, an important part of the Earth, and that we should do everything we can to protect them, especially since we are the ones putting them in danger in the first place. Some people feel that there is lots of wild space and that animals should only live there. Other people feel that there is very little wild space left, that animals are contained by humans in some way no matter where they are, and it is up to us to take care of them the best we can. It's a discussion that will probably go on for a long time, especially as more and more species become endangered.

The author acknowledges opposing arguments.

There is another thing that zoos accomplish, which could be one of the most important of all. Zoos give people the opportunity to see animals in person, often up close, to watch them, realize how alike we are in many ways, to understand them, and to appreciate them. It's amazing to come almost face to face with an elephant or tiger, for example, to see how big it is, to feel its power, to look in its eyes; or to see an orangutan or gorilla amble right by you, holding its baby or playing chase with its brother or sister. It is said that people only love what they understand, and they only protect what they love. Zoos may be the last stand for wild species, the place where humans can grow to love them, and then work to protect them.

The editorial concludes with a reinforcement of the author's point of view.

Comparing Argumentative Texts

1. Key Ideas and Details (a) Compare the **point of view** of each author on zoos. **(b)** Are the different points of view on the problem of extinction caused by disagreement over facts or by different interpretations of the same set of facts? Explain.

Content-Area Vocabulary

2. Use the words *habitats, vulnerable,* and *resources* in a paragraph in which you explain your opinion of zoos.

⏱ Timed Writing

Argument: Editorial

Format and Audience
The prompt gives specific directions about what to write and information about your audience. Therefore, write an essay that is four or five paragraphs long and uses clear, formal language.

Write a brief editorial for a school newspaper about an issue that affects your community or the nation. For example: building affordable housing versus protecting animal habitats. Use supporting details to develop your argument. (35 minutes)

Academic Vocabulary
When you write and *develop* an argument, you introduce your ideas, provide supporting evidence, and conclude with a restatement of your most important ideas.

5-Minute Planner

Complete these steps to write your editorial:

1. Choose an issue that affects your community or the nation.

2. Write a sentence that clearly states your point of view.

3. Make notes that give reasons, facts, descriptions, and examples in support of your claims. **TIP** Including language that evokes positive or negative emotions can sway readers.

4. Scan the two editorials to get ideas about how to structure and develop your argument. Finalize your organizational plan.

5. Consult your notes as you write your editorial. Conclude with a final paragraph that summarizes your argument in memorable phrases.

Comparing Tone and Theme

The **tone** of a literary work is the writer's attitude toward a subject. The tone can often be described in one word, such as *playful* or *serious.* Tone is produced by factors such as these.

- Word choice: The words a writer chooses may be formal or informal, fancy or simple, energetic or mournful. The connotations, or emotional associations, of words help to create tone.

- Sentence structure: Simple, direct sentences can add a conversational tone. Long, complex ones can create a dignified tone.

Because a writer's tone expresses an attitude towards the writer's subject, it can help convey a theme. The **theme** is the main message in a literary work—an insight about people or life. One example is "Love conquers all." Sometimes the author states the theme explicitly, or directly. More often, however, the theme is implied. To understand a text's theme, pay attention to the author's tone, as well as to the lessons that characters learn.

The poem "The Fox Outwits the Crow" and the fable "The Fox and the Crow" have similar characters, settings, and plots. However, the authors have different attitudes toward their subjects. As you read, use a chart like the one shown to analyze the tone and theme of each selection.

	Details I Notice	What Details Show About Tone/Theme
Title: "The Fox and the Crow"	"Good day, Mistress Crow," he cried.	formal
Title:		

Common Core
State Standards

Reading Literature

2. Determine a theme or central idea of a text and analyze its development over the course of the text.

3. Analyze how particular elements of a story or drama interact.

5. Analyze how a drama's or poem's form or structure contributes to its meaning.

Writing

2.b. Develop the topic with relevant facts, definitions, concrete details, quotations, or other information and examples. *(Timed Writing)*

www.PHLitOnline.com

- Vocabulary flashcards
- Interactive journals
- More about the authors
- Selection audio
- Interactive graphic organizers

Community or *individual* — which is more important?

Writing About the Big Question

Each of these selections ends with a moral, or life lesson, about how to get along with others. Use this sentence starter to develop your ideas about the Big Question.

A **common** difficulty in getting along with others is _____ because _____.

Meet the Authors

William Cleary (b. 1926)
Author of "The Fox Outwits the Crow"

William Cleary is a writer, composer, filmmaker, and poet who lives in Burlington, Vermont. He has written twelve books on spirituality, published five collections of religious music, and composed a musical comedy that was performed at the 1988 Olympics. He has retold eighty of Aesop's fables in verse.

Aesop (about 620–560 B.C.)

Author of "The Fox and the Crow"

People have enjoyed Aesop's fables for centuries. However, very little is known about the origin of these well-known tales—including who actually wrote them.

Many Theories Aesop may have been an enslaved person who lived on the Greek island of Samos, a spokesman who defended criminals in court, or an advisor for one of the Greek kings. The most widely held theory, however, is that Aesop was not an actual person at all. Rather, the theory holds, as the stories were told over and over in ancient Greece, people invented an imaginary author for them.

▲ Aesop as imagined by the Spanish painter Diego Velazquez, b. 1599

One day a young crow snatched a fat piece of cheese
From the porch of a house made of stone,
Then she flew to the top of a Juniper Tree
To enjoy her good fortune alone.

But a fox passing by got a whiff of the cheese,
The best of his favorite hors d'oeuvres,
So he called to the crow, *Hey, you glamorous thing,*
Does your voice match your beautiful curves?

The crow was so pleased by the flattering words
She quickly took out a libretto,[1]
How fondly that fox will listen, she thought,
To hear how I caw in falsetto.[2]

She opened her mouth—and the cheese tumbled out,
Which the fox gobbled up full of malice
While he chuckled to think how that dim-witted crow
Could believe she was MARIA CALLAS.[3]

MORAL: Attending to flattery comes at a high price.

---

1. **libretto** (li bret′ ō) *n.* the text of an opera.
2. **falsetto** (fôl set′ ō) *n.* an artificially high voice.
3. **Maria Callas** (kal′ əs) (1923–1977) U.S. opera singer.

Critical Thinking

1. **Key Ideas and Details (a)** What does the crow think after the fox flatters her? **(b) Analyze:** What do her thoughts reveal about the crow?
2. **Key Ideas and Details (a)** To what does the poet compare the crow's voice? **(b) Support:** Why is this amusing?
3. **Key Ideas and Details (a) Connect:** How do the characters' actions support the moral? Explain. **(b) Evaluate:** Is this an easy or difficult lesson to learn? Explain.
4. **Integration of Knowledge and Ideas (a)** Who was more to blame—the crow or the fox? Explain. **(b)** Would you rather have someone like the crow or the fox in your community? Explain. *[Connect to the Big Question: Community or individual—which is more important?]*

Cite textual evidence to support your responses.

THE FOX AND THE CROW
AESOP

A Fox once saw a Crow fly off with a piece of cheese in its beak and settle on a branch of a tree. "That's for me, as I am a Fox," said Master Reynard,[1] and he walked up to the foot of the tree.

"Good day, Mistress Crow," he cried. "How well you are looking today: how glossy your feathers; how bright your eye. I feel sure your voice must surpass that of other birds, just as your figure does; let me hear but one song from you that I may greet you as the Queen of Birds."

The Crow lifted up her head and began to caw her best, but the moment she opened her mouth the piece of cheese fell to the ground, only to be snapped up by Master Fox. "That will do," said he. "That was all I wanted. In exchange for your cheese I will give you a piece of advice for the future—

MORAL: Do not trust flatterers."

Vocabulary
glossy (glôs´ ē) *adj.* smooth and shiny

surpass (sər pas´) *v.* be superior to

flatterers (flat´ ər ərz) *n.* those who praise a person insincerely

---

1. **Master Reynard** (ren´ ərd) the fox in the medieval beast epic *Reynard the Fox*; therefore, a proper name for the fox in other stories.

Critical Thinking

1. Key Ideas and Details (a) How does the Fox persuade the Crow to drop the piece of cheese? **(b) Infer:** How does the Fox's attitude change when he gets the cheese?

2. Craft and Structure (a) Draw Conclusions: What human character traits do the animal characters in the fable represent? **(b) Support:** What details in the fable support your answer?

3. Integration of Knowledge and Ideas How could learning the moral of this story help people in communities get along better? *[Connect to the Big Question: Community or individual—which is more important?]*

Cite textual evidence to support your responses.

Comparing Tone and Theme

1. Key Ideas and Details Compare the tone of the fable "The Fox and the Crow" with that of the poem "The Fox Outwits the Crow" by completing a diagram like this one.

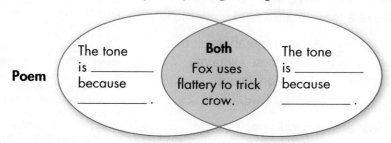

Poem

The tone is _____ because _____ .

Both
Fox uses flattery to trick crow.

The tone is _____ because _____ .

Fable

2. Key Ideas and Details Explain the theme of each selection in your own words.

3. Craft and Structure (a) Explain how the structure of the poem—its division into stanzas and use of rhyme—adds to its effect. **(b)** Are poems or fables better for teaching lessons? Why?

Timed Writing

Explanatory Text: Essay

In an essay, compare the relationship between tone and theme in each selection. **(40 minutes)**

5-Minute Planner

1. Read the prompt carefully and completely.

2. Reread and take notes on the tone of each selection. Support your ideas with concrete details and examples from the selections. Then, jot down whether the genre affected the tone. Finally, analyze the effect of tone on the theme. Gather your ideas by jotting down answers to these questions:
   - What is each writer's tone, or attitude, toward the characters?
   - In what ways did the genre affect the presentation of story events?
   - What is the theme of each selection?
   - Which selection illustrates its theme more effectively?

3. Reread the prompt, and then draft your essay.

Writing Workshop

 Common Core State Standards

Writing
2. Write informative/explanatory texts to examine a topic and convey ideas, concepts, and information through the selection, organization, and analysis of relevant content.

7. Conduct short research projects to answer a question, drawing on several sources and generating additional related, focused questions for further research and investigation.

8. Gather relevant information from multiple print and digital sources, using search terms effectively; assess the credibility and accuracy of each source; and quote or paraphrase the data and conclusions of others while avoiding plagiarism and following a standard format for citation.

Write an Informative Text

Research: Research Report

Defining the Form A **research report** analyzes information gathered from reference materials, observations, interviews, or other sources to present a clear and accurate picture of a topic or answer to a question.

Assignment Write a research report about a contemporary issue that interests or affects you. Your report should feature these elements:

✔ an overall *focused topic* or main idea to be analyzed

✔ *relevant and tightly drawn questions* on the topic

✔ a thesis statement with a *clear and accurate perspective*

✔ a *clear organization* and *smooth transitions*

✔ *appropriate facts* and *relevant details* to support main point

✔ visuals or media to support key ideas

✔ accurate, *complete citations* identifying research materials by means of *footnotes* or *bibliography*

✔ a strong *concluding statement*

To preview the criteria on which your research report may be judged, see the rubric on page 1049.

 Writing Workshop: *Work in Progress*

Review the work you did on pages 1005 and 1025.

WRITE GUY
Jeff Anderson, M.Ed.

What Do You Notice?

Facts and Details

The following passage is from Barbara Jordan's "All Together Now."

President Lyndon B. Johnson pushed through the Civil Rights Act of 1964, which remains the fundamental piece of civil rights legislation in this century. The Voting Rights Act of 1965 ensured that everyone in our country could vote.

Discuss these questions with a partner:

• What do you notice about the passage?
• What factual evidence does the writer provide?

Think about ways you can support your writing with research.

Prewriting/Planning Strategies

Watch and browse. Look through print, multimedia, and digital sources, such as recent magazines or newspapers, newscasts, and the Internet. List current events, issues, or subjects of interest and the questions they spark in you. Choose your topic from among these ideas.

After you choose your topic, make sure it is narrow enough to cover in a short report. For example, "illiteracy" is too broad a topic for a research paper. Narrow the topic by asking focused questions such as "How serious a problem is illiteracy in the United States?"

Use a variety of primary and secondary sources. Use both **primary sources** (firsthand or original accounts, such as interview transcripts and newspaper articles) and **secondary sources** (accounts that are not original, such as encyclopedia entries or an online library catalog) in your research.

Determine topics or key terms and check for them in indexes or type them into search engines. Prioritize information essential to your report. Collect relevant and objective, or neutral, information. Ensure the credibility and accuracy of each source. Crosscheck information from the Internet or an interview whenever possible by consulting printed sources.

Take notes. Use different strategies to take notes:

- Use index cards to create note cards and source cards. Write one note per card and note the source and page number.

- Photocopy articles and copyright pages; then highlight relevant information.

- Print articles from the Internet or copy them directly into a "notes" folder.

You will use these notes to help you write original text.

Record your research. Copying from sources without citing them is **plagiarism,** an act that has serious academic and legal consequences. Without giving credit to a source, you are stealing another person's words. It is important to use ethical practices when conducting research.

Whether you are paraphrasing, summarizing, or using a direct quotation, you must credit the source. You can give credit by writing a *bibliography*, a list of the print and nonprint sources you have used. Review pages R34–R35 to see the appropriate format for citing sources in a bibliography.

Note Card

> **Education**
> Papp, p.5
>
> Only the upper classes could read.
>
> Most of the common people in Shakespeare's time could not read.

Source Card

> Papp, Joseph
> and Kirkland, Elizabeth
>
> **Shakespeare Alive!**
>
> New York: Bantam Books, 1988

Drafting Strategies

Common Core State Standards

Writing

2.a. Include formatting, graphics, and multimedia when useful to aiding comprehension.

2.b. Develop the topic with relevant facts, definitions, concrete details, quotations, or other information and examples.

2.f. Provide a concluding statement or section that follows from and supports the information or explanation presented.

7. Conduct short research projects to answer a question, drawing on several sources and generating additional related, focused questions for further research and investigation.

9. Draw evidence from literary or informational texts to support analysis, reflection, and research.

Develop a main idea or thesis. Review your prewriting notes to determine the overall focus of your report. Then, write a sentence that expresses your main idea. This sentence is called a **thesis statement.** As you draft, add facts, details, statistics, and examples that support and develop your thesis statement.

Thesis: *Whales are among the most intelligent mammals on Earth.*

Supporting detail: *Whales have developed an elaborate series of sounds that serves as a language that allows them to communicate across vast stretches of water.*

Pose relevant questions. When you research, you may come up with more questions about your topic. The questions you ask yourself should be relevant to your thesis and tightly drawn. This means you should not stray too far from the perspective you convey in your report.

Make an outline. Group your prewriting notes by category. Use Roman numerals (I, II, III) to number your most important points. Under each Roman numeral, use capital letters (A, B, C) for the supporting details. Use your outline as a guide for developing your draft by turning your draft, notes into complete sentences. As you draft, review the data you have collected.

- Refer to the notes you made on index cards in the prewriting and researching stage.

- Confirm that the supporting details you include directly relate to the thesis statement.

- Delete any irrelevant information you have gathered.

Outline format

Thesis Statement
  I. First main point
    A. First supporting detail
    B. Second supporting detail
  II. Second main point
    A. First supporting detail
    B. Second supporting detail

Include visuals to support key ideas. Using charts or other visual aids allows you to present detailed information that might otherwise interrupt the flow of your report. In your writing, introduce the visual and explain its purpose. Direct readers to reference these aids as needed. To create visual aids, carry out these steps:

- Use databases and spreadsheets to organize, manage, and prepare information for your report.

- Clarify your charts, graphs, and tables by using headings and adding appropriate spacing.

- Vary the color and design of your visual aids as you display different types of information.

Provide a satisfying conclusion. Your conclusion should bring together your main ideas logically in a way that *proves* your thesis statement for the reader. For example, if your thesis is about the causes of the Civil War and the body of your report analyzes these causes in detail, your conclusion would show how these related causes combined to produce a war.

Writers on Writing

Jon Scieszka On Using Research in Fiction

> Jon Scieszka is the author of "Grasshopper Logic" (p. 908) and "Duckbilled Platypus vs. BeefSnakStik®" (p. 910) from *Squids Will Be Squids* and "The Other Frog Prince" from *The Stinky Cheese Man and Other Fairly Stupid Tales* (p. 909).

"I do research . . . to learn about the history of stories."
— Jon Scieszka

Here's an early draft of the beginning of a *Time Warp Trio* novel. The Time Warp guys can travel anywhere in time. So to make their adventures come alive, I have to know every detail I can about the place and time they travel to—in this case, Italy hundreds of years ago.

I read everything I can find for at least a month before I start writing. I want to know what kind of food people of that time and place ate, how they brushed their teeth, what they wore for underwear.

Professional Model:

from *"Da Wild, Da Crazy, Da Vinci"*

"Ready! . . . Aim! . . ."

> All of the *Time Warp* books start in the middle of some action. I figured these would be two great action words that everyone knows.

"Wait," yelled Sam. He fixed his glasses to ~~get~~ take a better look ~~around~~. "~~I think~~ We're supposed to be in Italy."

Fred, Sam, and I were standing with our backs to a steep, sandy hill. ~~In front of us sat~~ It looked like it could be Italy. But there was a ~~scary~~ strange-looking invention ~~sitting in front of us~~—a wooden, flying-saucer-shaped thing, about as big as an ice cream truck.

> The challenge in writing history-based fiction is to introduce the real history in a natural way. This tank really was one of Italian artist Leonardo da Vinci's inventions.

~~But that~~ The size wasn't the scary part. The scary part was the guns sticking out of it. The even scarier part was knowing the word that usually comes after "Ready! Aim!"

"You're ~~both~~ lucky we didn't end up in a giant toilet," said Fred. "But now you better figure out what to do about those guns pointed our way."

> My characters set up the history for me. Here Fred mentions an invention we find out about later—the flush toilet.

Revising Strategies

Analyze your organization. Look over your draft and analyze your organization to see if it matches your outline. Stop at the end of each paragraph and refer to your outline. Follow these steps:

1. Mark each paragraph with the Roman numeral and capital letter from your outline and write a key word or phrase to identify the subject of the paragraph.

2. If all the paragraphs with the same Roman numeral are not next to each other, decide whether the change is an improvement. If it is not, correct it.

Check your facts. Read through your draft to verify that the facts, statistics, and quotations you cite are accurate. Don't rely on your memory—refer to the original source material as you work. With the exception of direct quotations, be sure you have written the information in your own words.

Vary sentence length. To add interest to your writing, vary the length of your sentences. Underline or highlight sentences in your draft in alternating colors so you can easily see differences in length. Then, review your color coding. Combine short, choppy sentences or break up longer sentences if there are too many of either.

Writing

2.c. Use appropriate transitions to create cohesion and clarify the relationships among ideas and concepts.

5. With some guidance and support from peers and adults, develop and strengthen writing as needed by revising, focusing on how well purpose and audience have been addressed.

8. Assess the credibility and accuracy of each source; and quote or paraphrase the data and conclusions of others while avoiding plagiarism and following a standard format for citation.

Language

1. Demonstrate command of the conventions of standard English grammar and usage when writing.

Model: Revising to Vary Sentence Length

Basketball has been played in various forms for hundreds of years. The modern sport was introduced in 1891. An instructor at a YMCA was looking to keep his students active during the long New England winters.

The basketball hoop was made from a peach basket **with** ~~. The basket had~~ a closed bottom. Soon, the players realized that if they removed the bottom, the game could be played quicker.

Review

Ask a classmate, your teacher, or another adult to read your report to determine if the organization of your draft is clear. If your reader finds areas that require transitions, consider revising your draft by adding a word, phrase, or sentence that shows the connection between your paragraphs. Use transitions such as *at first, finally,* or *as a result* to show relationships between ideas.

Ask the reader for feedback as to whether or not you have supported your thesis statement adequately. Revise your report as needed based on your reviewer's comments.

Revising to Correct Use of Pronoun Case

Many pronouns change form according to usage. *Case* is the relationship between a pronoun's form and its use.

Personal Pronouns	
Nominative Case	**Objective Case**
I, we	me, us
you	you
he, she, it, they	him, her, it, them

Using Personal Pronouns Personal pronouns in the **nominative case** may be the subject of a verb or a predicate nominative—a noun or pronoun that renames the subject.

> **Subject:** <u>She</u> plays soccer. Cassie and <u>I</u> play soccer, too.

> **Predicate Nominative:** Beckham's biggest fans are Jenna and <u>I</u>.

Personal pronouns in the **objective case** have three uses: as a direct object, as an indirect object, and as the object of a preposition.

> **Direct Object:** Jason invited Raf and <u>me</u> to the game.

> **Indirect Object:** Paul had given <u>him</u> two extra tickets.

> **Object of a Preposition:** All three of <u>us</u> were grateful to <u>him</u>.

Fixing Incorrect Use of Personal Pronouns Mistakes with pronouns usually occur when the subject or object is compound.

1. **To test a pronoun in a compound subject, use just the pronoun with the verb in the sentence.** For example, in the sentence, "Cassie and me play soccer," "me play" clearly sounds wrong. The nominative case *I* is needed.

2. **To test a pronoun in a compound object, use the pronoun by itself after the verb or preposition.** For example, in the sentence, "Jason invited Raf and I to the game," "Jason invited I" sounds wrong. The objective case *me* is needed.

Grammar in Your Writing
Choose two paragraphs in your draft. Underline every sentence that contains a pronoun as part of a compound subject or a compound object. Use the methods above to fix any pronouns used incorrectly.

PH WRITING COACH

Further instruction and practice are available in *Prentice Hall Writing Coach*.

Hatching Chirpers

A hen's egg is an amazing thing. Sitting in the nest, it seems as if it is an inanimate, or lifeless, object, but it contains everything that is needed to make a chick. In order for the chick to grow inside the egg, however, the right external conditions are needed. Under normal circumstances, these conditions are provided by the hen. They can also be reproduced and regulated in an incubator. My investigation was to discover whether the hen or the incubator would more efficiently and effectively provide the right external conditions. My hypothesis is that an incubator can provide the right external conditions more effectively and efficiently. Let's find out.

A chicken egg should take about twenty-one days to incubate, or take form. During that time, the eggs must be kept warm. The ideal temperature is between 99 and 100 degrees Fahrenheit. In addition, the eggs must be rotated, or turned, every eight to twelve hours. If they remain in one position for longer than that, the chick can become stuck to one side of the egg and may not form properly (Johnson 14–16).

Usually, the temperature and the turning are handled by the hen that sits on the nest. She regulates the temperature of the eggs by getting off the nest or standing above the eggs if the eggs begin to get too warm. When they have had some time to cool, she gets back on the nest. The hen turns the eggs by poking at them with her beak until each egg rolls a little to one side, eventually turning from its original position (Scott).

An incubator performs these same functions. The temperature inside the incubator is measured and regulated by a thermostat that tells the heater when to turn on and when to turn off. In this way, the temperature of the eggs is kept at a constant 99 degrees. The eggs sit on a device that rolls them every eight hours. This device is controlled by an electronic timer. It is dependable because it is automatic and does not require a person to push a button for the eggs to turn. It is more efficient than a hen, because all the eggs get turned equally and consistently (Little Giant 2–6).

In the first paragraph, Laura identifies her main topic, the question she is investigating. In this science report, she provides a hypothesis—a proposition that the research will prove or disprove. This statement gives her perspective or viewpoint on the topic.

Accurate facts and details gathered through the formal research process are presented. Since these are specific statistics that a reader might want to check, the writer gives the source.

The report is organized to give balanced information about both methods being investigated—natural hatching and incubation.

Based on the fact that conditions in the incubator are more consistent and controlled, I concluded that an incubator sets the ideal conditions more efficiently, and I hypothesized that it would hatch eggs more effectively. To test my hypothesis, I observed four hens sitting on a total of twenty-four eggs and placed twenty-four eggs in an incubator. Each egg was marked with a small *x* so that I could observe how frequently and completely each egg was turned. Chart A shows specific observations over a twenty-five-day period.

Chart A

Day	Incubator Observations	Nest Observations
Day 1	**6:45 AM:** After placing the turner in the incubator, I put the 24 eggs on the turner. The temperature leveled off at 100 degrees. The eggs have warmed up quickly. **5:33 PM:** The turner is working efficiently—eggs are tilted appropriately.	**7:10 AM:** After placing the 24 eggs on the nests in the cage, I put food and water in the cage. Then, I placed the hens in the cage. **6:01 PM:** All hens are on the eggs.
Day 5	X marks on the eggs show that eggs have made a complete turn.	X marks on the eggs show that the eggs were not turned completely since I last checked.
Day 10	The turner seems to be tilting the eggs efficiently—X marks show a complete turn.	X marks show that 18 eggs were turned, but 6 were not.
Day 15	The temperature of the eggs is at a steady 100 degrees.	Two hens have moved off the nest for a brief time. Temperature of the eggs right now is 97 degrees.
Day 25	The incubator has hatched thirteen out of the twenty-four eggs.	The hens have hatched ten out of the twenty-four eggs.

Detailed information that would interrupt the flow of the report is presented in a separate chart for readers to reference as needed.

In general, the incubator eggs received much more consistent attention to their condition. The machine did not need to stop to eat or exercise, as the hens did. The marks on the eggs showed that the eggs under the hens did not always get completely turned. Sometimes, some of the eggs were turned and some were not. In addition, the hens sometimes left the nest for as long as an hour. When the temperature of the eggs was measured after a hen had been gone a long time, the egg temperature was sometimes as low as 97 degrees.

After twenty-five days, the hens had hatched ten out of the twenty-four eggs, and the incubator had hatched thirteen. The difference between the two numbers is not great enough to say that one way of incubating is more effective than the other. The incubator is definitely more efficient at delivering ideal conditions than the hens were. However, since the increased efficiency does not result in a higher number of hatches, maybe "ideal" conditions are not required for a successful hatch.

Writing
8. Follow a standard format for citation.

Laura concludes by explaining whether the research did or did not support her original hypothesis.

Bibliography

Johnson, Sylvia A. *Inside an Egg*. Minneapolis: Lerner Publications Company, 1982.

Kruse Poultry Feed. *Care and Feeding of Baby Chicks*.

Little Giant Instruction Manual for Still Air Incubator and Automatic Egg Turner. Miller Mfg. Co., So. St. Paul, MN, 1998.

Scott, Wyatt. Personal Interview. 1 Dec. 2000.

Selsam, Millicent E. *Animals as Parents*. Canada: George J. McLeod Limited, 1965.

In the bibliography, the writer lists all the works from which she gathered information used in her report. Some teachers prefer a "Works Cited" list, which lists only the sources that are actually cited, or noted, in a research report.

Editing and Proofreading

Focus on citations. Cite the sources for quotations, factual information, and ideas that are not your own. Some word-processing programs have features that allow you to create footnotes and endnotes. If you are using MLA style, citations should appear in parentheses directly after the information cited. Include the author's last name and the relevant page number.

Example: *The Atlantic Ocean has a total area of 41.1 million square miles (Smith 676).*

Publishing and Presenting

Create a reference list. Following the format your teacher prefers, create a bibliography or Works Cited list of the information you used to write your research report. (For more information, see Citing Sources, pp. R34–R35.)

Give an oral presentation. Use your research report as the basis for an oral presentation on your topic. Keep your audience in mind and revise accordingly as you prepare your presentation.

Reflecting on Your Writing

Writer's Journal Jot down your answer to this question:
What research strategy did you find most useful?

Rubric for Self-Assessment

Find evidence in your writing to address each category. Then, use the rating scale to grade your work.

Criteria	Rating Scale
	not very .... very
Focus: How clearly stated is your thesis?	1 2 3 4 5
Organization: How effective is your organization of information?	1 2 3 4 5
Support/Elaboration: How accurate and thorough are your supporting facts and details?	1 2 3 4 5
Style: How smooth are your transitions?	1 2 3 4 5
Conventions: How complete and accurate are your citations?	1 2 3 4 5

Spiral Review
Earlier in the unit, you learned about **capitalization** (p. 1004) and **abbreviations** (p. 1024). Check your research report to be sure that you have used both capitalization and abbreviations correctly.

PH **WRITING COACH**
Further instruction and practice are available in *Prentice Hall Writing Coach*.

Vocabulary Workshop

Figurative Language

Figurative language is language that is not meant to be taken literally. Most types of figurative language are based on imaginative comparisons, lending ordinary things extraordinary qualities. The use of figurative language makes writing vivid and expressive. Refer to this chart to see common types of figurative language and examples of each.

**Common Core
State Standards**

Language
5. Demonstrate understanding of figurative language, word relationships, and nuances in word meanings.
5.a. Interpret figures of speech in context.
5.b. Use the relationship between particular words to better understand each of the words.

Type of Figurative Language	Example
Simile: a comparison of two apparently unlike things using *like, as, than,* or *resembles.*	The sky is <u>like</u> a patchwork quilt.
Metaphor: a description of one thing as if it were another.	The sky <u>is</u> a patchwork quilt.
Analogy: an extended comparison of relationships. An analogy shows how the relationship between one pair of things is like the relationship between another pair.	Walter lives like a sheet of paper blown along a windy street. He is carried this way and that way with no control of his direction.
Personification: a figure of speech giving human characteristics to a nonhuman subject.	The <u>sea</u> was <u>angry</u> that day, my friends.
Paradox: a statement, an idea, or a situation that seems contradictory but actually expresses a truth.	The more things change, the more they stay the same.
Idiom: an expression whose meaning differs from the meanings of its individual words.	It was raining cats and dogs last night.

Practice A Identify each instance of figurative language in these sentences as a *simile* or *metaphor.*

1. Because I studied for several nights, the quiz was a breeze.

2. The winter night was so quiet that every sound was as clear as a bell.

3. Ivan's dog is the sunshine of his life.

4. After shoveling snow for several hours, I slept like a log last night.

5. A ghost of a moon shone over the fields.

Practice B Identify the *simile, metaphor, idiom,* or *analogy* in each sentence. Then, use context clues to explain the meaning of each.

1. Tyrone understands people very well; he reads them like a book.
2. I tried to get my friend to change his mind, but he was a mule.
3. Two peas in a pod, Simon and Jack liked exactly the same music.
4. Seeing the fascinating art in the museum sparked my interest in sculpture.
5. After she won the diving competition, Elana was as happy as a lark.
6. Learning the times tables is like riding a bike; once you learn it, you never forget it.
7. After losing the concert tickets, Kevin was as mad as a hornet.
8. Her hair was a cloud of snowy white.

www.PHLitOnline.com
- Illustrated vocabulary words
- Interactive vocabulary games
- Vocabulary flashcards

Activity With a partner, browse through a current magazine. Search through the articles to find at least two examples of each type of figurative language. Use a note card like the one shown to list the examples you have found. Then, explain the meaning of each simile, metaphor, analogy, and idiom. Use the context clues in the article to help your understanding.

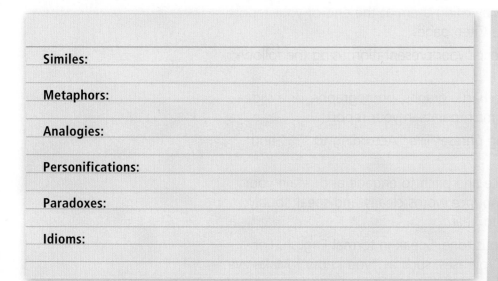

Similes:

Metaphors:

Analogies:

Personifications:

Paradoxes:

Idioms:

Comprehension and Collaboration

With a partner, write a scene with dialogue between two characters, taking care to use no figurative language. Then, rewrite the dialogue, adding idioms, analogies, similes, and metaphor. Compare your scenes. Which one sounds more realistic? Why?

Communications Workshop

Research Presentation

These guidelines will help you through the processes of conducting research, writing a report, and presenting it to an audience.

Learn the Skills

Use these strategies to complete the activity on page 1053.

Generate questions. Consider what you would like to discover about your topic. Pose relevant and concise questions to guide your research and help you to stay on topic.

Evaluate your sources. Prepare to use both print and electronic sources, such as databases, the Internet, and magazines. Evaluate the credibility, scope, and objectivity of each source.

- Is the source known for its correct facts?
- Does a Web site have *.edu* or *.org* at the end of the Web address?
- Does the publication date fall within the last three years?

Organize your information. Take notes from each source to answer your research questions. Include only the information that is meaningful to your topic. Use your notes to develop an outline.

Write the report. Organize the report to include an introduction, several body paragraphs, and a conclusion. Avoid **plagiarism** by paraphrasing instead of copying information directly from each source. Credit your sources by citing them at the end of your report on a Bibliography or Works Cited page.

Present your report. Practice your presentation using the following techniques.

- Use graphics, such as charts, graphs, photographs, or a slide-show to enhance the main points in your report.
- Credit sources by using phrases like "According to . . ." and "In the book by . . . ."
- Vary your speaking rate and pitch to engage and retain your listeners' interest. Pronounce words clearly and speak loudly enough for everyone to hear.
- Use a natural but serious tone. Speak in formal English. For example, avoid "filler" phrases, such as "you know." Make eye contact and use hand gestures to emphasize certain points.

Common Core State Standards

Speaking and Listening
4. Present claims and findings, emphasizing salient points in a focused, coherent manner with pertinent descriptions, facts, details, and examples; use appropriate eye contact, adequate volume, and clear pronunciation.

5. Include multimedia components and visual displays in presentations to clarify claims and findings and emphasize salient points.

6. Adapt speech to a variety of contexts and tasks, demonstrating command of formal English when indicated or appropriate.

Practice the Skills

© **Presentation of Knowledge and Ideas** Use the skills you learned in this Workshop to complete the following activity.

ACTIVITY: Delivering a Research Report

Prepare a research presentation by following the steps below. Then, deliver the report to your class.

- Develop your major research question.
- Gather research and organize your report.
- Present your research report to your classmates.
- Use the Research Guide to plan your report.

Use a Research Guide like the one below to develop your presentation.

Research Guide

Major Research Question:

Brainstorm to list ideas that address the research topic:

Open-ended research questions:

1.   3.

2.   4.

Research plan: Jot down notes explaining your plan for researching each question.

Assessment of sources: Briefly demonstrate the reliability and credibility of each source. Then, explain why one source is more useful than another.

Synthesize the research: Draw conclusions about and summarize or paraphrase each source to synthesize the research.
Conclusions: _____ Summary: _____

Organize your research: Think about your purpose and audience when you organize your presentation.
Purpose of the research: _____ Audience: _____

© **Comprehension and Collaboration** At the end of your presentation, invite your audience to discuss, respond to, or ask questions about your presentation. Then, listen to your classmates present their reports. Interpret the purpose of each report by explaining the content, evaluating the delivery of the presentation, and asking questions or making comments about the evidence that supports the claims.

Cumulative Review

Common Core
State Standards

RL.7.2; W.7.1.b; L.7.4.a
[For the full wording of the standards, see the standards chart in the front of your textbook.]

I. Reading Literature

Directions: *Read the story. Then, answer each question that follows.*

Jack and the Beanstalk

Once upon a time, a boy named Jack lived with his widowed mother. There came a hard winter, and the two had little to eat. The woman said, "Jack, take the cow to market, and sell her. We need the money to buy food."

On his way to the market, Jack met a butcher who showed him some magical beans. Jack traded the cow for the beans, and proudly returned home. His mother was angered by Jack's foolishness and threw the beans out the window.

By the next morning, the beans had grown into an incredibly tall plant. Curious, Jack climbed the beanstalk and found a fine castle at the top. There, an old woman appeared and told him this story:

"Once, a knight lived in this castle with his lady and infant son. A monstrous giant grew jealous of their happiness. He killed the knight, but the lady and her son fled to the village where they remained hidden for many years. Jack, that lady is your mother. This castle is rightfully yours. To win it back, you must get the hen that lays golden eggs. Are you ready?"

"Yes, for my father's honor, it is my <u>duty</u>," Jack said.

Jack crept into the castle, and hid in a closet. He peered out of the huge keyhole. Soon he heard heavy steps and a voice like thunder crying out for his supper. It was the giant! The giant's head scraped the ceiling as he walked through the kitchen.

After he ate an enormous meal of meats and potatoes, the giant picked up an ordinary-looking brown hen and said to her, "Lay!" She instantly laid a golden egg. "Lay!" said the giant again. She laid another. This went on until the giant grew bored and fell fast asleep.

Jack crept out and tiptoed across the room. He grabbed the hen and ran like lightning. With a tremendous roar, the giant woke up and sprang after Jack. Quickly, Jack scrambled down the beanstalk. With the giant right behind him, Jack took his axe and chopped down the beanstalk. The giant fell with a crash and lay dead.

The old woman reappeared. "Jack, you have shown courage. Your inheritance is restored to you." So, Jack and his mother lived happily ever after in the castle with the hen that lays golden eggs.

1. What type of story is "Jack and the Beanstalk"?
   A. a myth
   B. a folk tale
   C. a novel
   D. a play

2. What event in the **plot** happens first?
   A. Jack sells the cow.
   B. The beanstalk grows.
   C. The giant kills Jack's father.
   D. Jack snatches the hen that lays the golden eggs.

3. What **values** do Jack's actions reveal?
   A. He is not afraid of giants.
   B. He feels a sense of responsibility toward his family.
   C. He does not believe that beans can have magical powers.
   D. He thinks it is important to be quick and clever.

4. Stories such as this one often feature a character who helps the main character. Who helps Jack?
   A. nobody
   B. his mother
   C. the butcher
   D. the old woman

5. What **character trait** is most important, according to this story?
   A. intelligence
   B. kindness
   C. bravery
   D. gardening skills

6. What is the **theme** of the story?
   A. Butchers are not trustworthy.
   B. Good things come to those who wait.
   C. Giants are greedy.
   D. Courage will be rewarded.

7. What characteristic of the **oral tradition** is *not* shown in this story?
   A. wondrous events
   B. a message that is repeated across many cultures
   C. animal characters that behave like humans
   D. a brave hero

8. **Vocabulary** Which word or phrase is closest in meaning to the underlined word <u>duty</u>?
   A. expectation
   B. responsibility
   C. castle
   D. chore

 Timed Writing

9. Write a **review** of "Jack and the Beanstalk." In your review, tell whether or not it makes a good bedtime story. **Support** your opinions and ideas with **concrete details** and **examples** from the story.

 GO ON

II. Reading Informational Text

Directions: *Read the passage. Then, answer each question that follows.*

**Common Core
State Standards**

RI.7.5, RI.7.6; L.7.2
[For the full wording of the standards, see the standards chart in the front of your textbook.]

Pet ownership is a wonderful way for children to learn responsibility. I didn't always think so, but then my daughter changed my mind.

Anna was four when she began asking for a dog. I always said no. Anna was the kind of child who "forgot" her homework and never made her bed. Whenever Anna asked for a dog, I'd tell her that she needed to be more responsible before I would feel comfortable putting her in charge of a living creature.

Then, one day a little dog followed Anna home. We put up signs, but nobody claimed the dog. It seemed like she was meant to be ours.

Anna was twelve when the lost dog we named Coco joined the family. I didn't expect her to take care of the dog without help, but I was pleasantly surprised. Anna used to <u>dawdle</u> on her way home from school, always taking the long way. Suddenly, she was running home to feed Coco and take her for a walk. Anna used to tease me for picking up garbage at the park. Now she carries a bag and a glove with her so she can pick up broken glass. She doesn't want Coco to cut her paws. More surprisingly, Anna has become more responsible about things that have nothing to do with Coco—things like getting dressed in the morning and remembering her homework. Anna isn't the only one who is happy that Coco followed her home. I'm happy too!

1. What is the **author's argument** at the beginning of the passage?
  A. Children should demonstrate responsibility before getting a pet.
  B. Owning a pet can teach responsibility.
  C. Twelve is too young to own a dog.
  D. Children should help around the house.

2. According to the passage, what is one **effect** of Anna getting a dog?
  A. She comes home more quickly.
  B. She gets more exercise.
  C. She makes new friends.
  D. She stops arguing with her mother.

3. What does the author say is one **effect** of allowing a child to own a pet?
  A. Your house will need frequent vacuuming.
  B. You will need to put signs up around the neighborhood.
  C. The child will make his or her own bed.
  D. The child will become more responsible.

4. What **point of view** does the author express at the end of the passage?
  A. Children should demonstrate responsibility before getting a pet.
  B. Owning a pet can teach responsibility.
  C. Children should help around the house.
  D. Coco is a sweet dog.

III. Writing and Language Conventions

Directions: *Read the passage. Then, answer each question that follows.*

(1) October 3, 2010

(2) Dear Johnson Construction

   (3) Our baseball team has not replaced its uniforms in five years. (4) A $200 donation would allow us to purchase new shirts for each team member. (5) To show our thanks and gratitude we will put the name of your business on each shirt. (6) Spectators will see that you support an organization that gives kids something positive to do after school. (7) Please help support this talented Pleasantville team.

   (8) Thank you,

   (9) Joe Green

1. Which additional sentence would *best* state the author's **request**?
   A. The Pleasantville baseball team is in need of your financial support.
   B. We would appreciate it if you could donate team uniforms.
   C. Please, give us money.
   D. If you could donate your time and expertise, it would be greatly appreciated.

2. Which of the following revisions correctly uses a **colon**?
   A. October 3, 2010:
   B. Dear Johnson Construction:
   C. Please: help support this important Pleasantville tradition.
   D. Thank you:

3. Which elements of a **standard business letter** are missing from Joe's letter?
   A. inside address and sender's address
   B. inside address and closing
   C. closing and sender's address
   D. sender's address and postscript

4. Which of the following revisions correctly uses a **comma**?
   A. To show our thanks, and gratitude, we will put the name of your business on each shirt.
   B. To show our thanks and gratitude, we will put the name of your business on each shirt.
   C. To show, our thanks and gratitude, we will put the name of your business on each shirt.
   D. To show our thanks and gratitude we will put the name of your business, on each shirt.

STOP

Performance Tasks

Common Core
State Standards

RL.7.2, RL.7.3, RL.7.9; W.7.9.a; SL.7.1, SL.7.4
[For the full wording of the standards, see the standards chart in the front of your textbook.]

Directions: *Follow the instructions to complete the tasks below as required by your teacher.*

As you work on each task, incorporate both general academic vocabulary and literary terms you learned in this unit.

Writing

Task 1: Literature [RL.7.9; W.7.9.a]
Analyze the Use of Historical Fact in Fiction and Nonfiction

Write an essay that compares and contrasts the use of facts in a work of fiction and a work of nonfiction.

- Explain that you will discuss similarities and differences in the use of facts in "Tenochtitlan: Inside the Aztec Capital" and "Popocatepetl and Ixtlaccihuatl."

- Identify at least three facts in the article and three facts in the legend. Explain at least two similarities and differences in the ways each author uses these facts. Consider the purpose each fact serves.

- Explain whether the author of the work of fiction has changed any facts. If so, identify how the fact was changed and the purpose for the change.

- Write a thesis statement summarizing your ideas.

- Support your thesis statement by citing specific details from the texts.

- Summarize your ideas in a conclusion.

Task 2: Literature [RL.7.2; W.7.9.a]
Analyze the Development of a Theme or Main Idea

Analyze a theme or main idea from one work of fiction in this unit and write an objective summary of that story.

- Choose one story from this unit to analyze. Identify a theme or main idea of that story.

- Write down how this theme or main idea is developed through characters' actions and story events.

- To make sure you understand the development of the idea, write an objective summary of the story.

- In your summary, use your own words to retell main ideas and story details.

- Include events from each part of the story to ensure completeness.

- Leave out minor ideas and details and avoid including personal opinions.

- Add transitions, such as *first, next,* and *finally,* to show the order of events.

Task 3: Literature [RL.7.2; W.7.9.a]
Analyze a Universal Theme

Identify a theme in a story and show how it is universal by identifying the same theme in other stories.

- Identify a universal theme of a story in this unit. Be sure that the theme contains a message about life that is found in other cultures and eras.

- Connect your universal theme to specific details from the story, including character traits, settings, conflicts, and the changes or results of these conflicts.

- Explain how the same theme can be found in other works you have read.

Speaking and Listening

© Task 4: Literature [RL.7.3; SL.7.4]

Analyze the Characters in a Folk Tale

Plan a presentation in which you analyze the characters and character development in a folk tale in this unit.

- Choose a folk tale from the unit and identify specific details about the characters, their personality traits, the conflicts they face, how the setting influences their choices, and what they learn as a result of their conflicts.
- Present your ideas, facts, details, and quotations in a clear, logical order.
- Extend the ideas in your presentation by discussing the ways in which the characters' behavior reflects the beliefs of the culture that produced the tale.
- Practice delivering your presentation, focusing on expression, pacing, volume, enunciation, and eye contact.

© Task 5: Literature [RL.7.3; SL.7.4]

Analyze the Plot in a Folk Tale

Plan a presentation in which you analyze the plot elements of a folk tale in this unit.

- Choose a folk tale from the unit and identify the main events in the plot.
- Identify the rising action, conflict, climax, falling action, and resolution.
- Discuss how events in the plot are influenced by other story elements, such as setting and characters.
- Present your ideas in a logical order.
- Include visual displays, such as plot diagrams, to clarify claims and emphasize important points.

© Task 6: Literature [RL.7.2; SL.7.1]

Analyze and Discuss Theme

Analyze a theme from a story in this unit and determine which customs and beliefs it reflects. Then, organize a discussion with a small group of classmates about the value of the story's message.

- Determine the theme of a story in this unit. Analyze how it is developed over the course of the story through plot events and characters' actions.
- List questions about customs and beliefs that arise as you analyze theme. Explore one question in your analysis. Conduct research as needed.
- Evaluate whether the story still contains a meaningful message for today's readers. Support your arguments with clear and relevant reasons.
- Discuss your findings with a small group. Be sure to come to the discussion having read the story and evaluated its message.
- Use vocabulary that accurately expresses your ideas.

THE BIG ?

Community or individual—which is more important?

At the beginning of Unit 6, you wrote a response to the Big Question. Now that you have completed the unit, write a new response. Discuss how your initial ideas have either changed or been reinforced. Cite specific examples from the literature in this unit, from other subject areas, and from your own life to support your ideas. Use Big Question vocabulary words (see p. 901) in your response.

Featured Titles

In this unit, you have read a variety of literary works that originated in the oral tradition. Continue to read on your own. Select works that you enjoy, but challenge yourself to explore new writers and works of increasing depth and complexity. The titles suggested below will help you get started.

Literature

The People Could Fly: American Black Folktales
by Virginia Hamilton   EXEMPLAR TEXT

These twenty-four **folktales** celebrate the strength and resourcefulness of the people who survived slavery. The collection includes the selection "The People Could Fly," which is included in this unit.

Myths and Folktales Around the World
by Robert Potter

This collection includes traditional **myths and folktales** about famous figures, such as King Arthur, as well as new tales based on historical events, such as the sinking of the *Titanic*.

Trojan Horse
by David Clement-Davies

This modern retelling of the classic **myth** describes the clever use of a huge wooden horse in a bitterly fought battle to rescue the beautiful Helen of Troy.

The Adventures of Ulysses
by Bernard Evslin
Scholastic, 1969

In this modern interpretation of the classic **myth,** Ulysses and his men begin the journey home to Greece after conquering Troy—only to find they have angered the gods and must face many dangers along the way.

The Time Warp Trio: It's All Greek to Me
by Jon Scieszka

In this funny **novel,** Joe and his friends accidentally find themselves trapped in ancient Greece. With only a cardboard thunderbolt and painted apple as weapons, they must outwit the gods to survive the dangers of Hades and Mount Olympus.

Thirteen Moons on Turtle's Back
by Joseph Bruchac

The thirteen **poems** in this collection of myths and legends represent the thirteen moon cycles that make up the year in traditional Native American folklore.

Informational Texts

Around the World in a Hundred Years
by Jean Fritz

Jean Fritz uses a playful tone to explore the topic of explorers, like Columbus and Magellan, who ventured into unmapped territory from 1421 to 1522. This **nonfiction** book describes what happened when the explorers met the inhabitants of the lands they called "the Unknown."

The Great Fire
by Jim Murphy   EXEMPLAR TEXT

Using many personal accounts, Jim Murphy's **nonfiction** book tells the tale of Chicago's tragic Great Fire in 1871. This fascinating history tells how the fire began, how people responded, and how it was finally contained. Find out the true story behind one of the greatest disasters ever to be blamed on a cow.

Preparing to Read Complex Texts

Attentive Reading As you read on your own, ask yourself questions about the text. The questions shown below and others that you ask as you read will help you learn and enjoy literature even more.

 **Common Core State Standards**

Reading Literature/Informational Text 10. By the end of the year, read and comprehend literature, including stories, dramas, and poems, and literary nonfiction in the grades 6–8 text complexity band proficiently, with scaffolding as needed at the high end of the range.

When reading texts from the oral tradition, ask yourself …

- From what culture does this text come? What do I know about that culture?
- What type of text am I reading? For example, is it a myth, a legend, or a tall tale? What characters and events do I expect to find in this type of text?
- Does the text include the elements I expected? If not, how does it differ from what I expected?
- What elements of the culture do I see in the text? For example, do I notice beliefs, foods, or settings that have meaning for the people of this culture?
- Does the text teach a lesson or a moral? If so, is this a valuable lesson?

Key Ideas and Details

- Who is retelling or presenting this text? Do I think the author has changed the text from the original? If so, how?
- Does the text include characters and tell a story? If so, are the characters and plot interesting?
- What do I notice about the language used in the text? Which aspects seem similar to or different from the language used in modern texts?
- Does the text include symbols? If so, do they have a special meaning in the original culture of the text? Do they also have meaning in modern life?

Craft and Structure

- What does this text teach me about the culture from which it comes?
- What, if anything, does this text teach me about people in general?
- Does this text seem like others I have read or heard? Why or why not?
- Do I know of any modern versions of this text? How are they similar to or different from this one?
- If I were researching this culture for a report, would I include passages from this text? If so, what would those passages show?
- Do I enjoy reading this text and others like it? Why or why not?

Integration of Ideas

Resources

Glossary

Big Question vocabulary appears in **blue type**. High-utility Academic vocabulary is <u>underlined</u>.

A

abode (uh BOHD) *n.* home; residence

acknowledge (ak NOL ihj) *v.* recognize and admit

acquainted (uh KWAYNT uhd) *adj.* familiar

adequate (AD ih kwiht) *adj.* enough; sufficient

adolescence (ad uh LEHS uhns) *n.* time when a young person is developing into an adult

aloft (uh LAWFT) *adj.* high up; flying; in the air

<u>**analyze**</u> (AN uh lyz) *v.* break down into parts and examine carefully

antidote (AN tih doht) *n.* remedy; cure

apparent (uh PAR uhnt) *adj.* seeming

appearance (uh PIHR uhns) *n.* how a person or thing looks or seems

<u>**appreciate**</u> (uh PREE shee ayt) *v.* be thankful for

approvingly (uh PROOV ihng lee) *adv.* consentingly

aptitude (AP tuh tood) *n.* talent; ability

arid (AR ihd) *adj.* dry and barren

<u>**assumption**</u> (uh SUHMP shuhn) *n.* belief or acceptance that something is true

astonish (uh STON ihsh) *v.* amaze

atmospheric (at muh SFEHR ihk) *adj.* having to do with the air surrounding Earth

<u>**attitude**</u> (AT uh tood) *n.* mental state involving beliefs, feelings, and values

audible (AW duh buhl) *adj.* loud enough to be heard

avid (AV ihd) *adj.* eager and enthusiastic

<u>**awareness**</u> (uh WAIR nehs) *n.* knowledge gained from one's own perceptions or from information

awe (aw) *n.* mixed feelings of fear and wonder

B

babbled (BAB uhld) *v.* murmured; talked foolishly or too much

ban (ban) *n.* an order forbidding something

banish (BAN ihsh) *v.* send away; exile

believable (bih LEE vuh buhl) *adj.* having the ability to draw out belief or trust

bellow (BEHL oh) *v.* roar deeply

<u>**bias**</u> (BY uhs) *n.* tendency to see things from a slanted or prejudiced viewpoint

bigots (BIHG uhts) *n.* narrow-minded, prejudiced people

blander (BLAND uhr) *adj.* more tasteless

bound (bownd) *v.* tied

brawny (BRAW nee) *adj.* strong and muscular

burrow (BUR oh) *v.* dig a hole for shelter

C

canyon (KAN yuhn) *n.* long narrow valley between high cliffs

captivity (kap TIHV uh tee) *n.* imprisonment; caught and held prisoner

cattails (KAT taylz) *n.* tall reeds with furry, brown spikes, found in marshes and swamps

causeways (KAWZ wayz) *n.* roads across wet ground or shallow water

<u>**challenge**</u> (CHAL uhnj) *v.* dare; a calling into question

<u>**characteristic**</u> (kar ihk tuh RIHS tihk) *n.* trait; feature

clusters (KLUHS tuhrz) *n.* numbers of things of the same sort that are grouped together; bunch

coax (kohks) *v.* use gentle persuasion

<u>**common**</u> (KOM uhn) *adj.* ordinary; expected

communal (kuh MYOON uhl) *adj.* shared by all

<u>**communicate**</u> (kuh MYOO nuh kayt) *v.* share thoughts or feelings, usually in words

<u>**communication**</u> (kuh myoo nuh KAY shuhn) *n.* activity of sharing information or speaking

<u>**community**</u> (kuh MYOO nuh tee) *n.* group of people who share an interest or who live near each other

compelled (kuhm PEHLD) *v.* forced

competition (kom puh TIHSH uhn) *n.* event or game in which people or sides attempt to win

compromise (KOM pruh myz) *n.* the settling of differences in a way that allows both sides to feel satisfied

compulsion (kuhm PUHL shuhn) *n.* driving, irresistible force

<u>**conclude**</u> (kuhn KLOOD) *v.* bring to a close; end

conflict (KON flihkt) *n.* clash or fight between opposing groups or people

consolation (KON suh LAY shuhn) *n.* something that comforts a disappointed person

conspired (kuhn SPYRD) *v.* planned together secretly

contradiction (KON truh DIHK shuhn) *n.* difference between two conflicting things that reveals only one is true

contraption (kuhn TRAP shuhn) *n.* strange device or machine

<u>**contribute**</u> (kuhn TRIHB yoot) *v.* add to; enrich

conveyed (kuhn VAYD) *v.* made known; expressed

conviction (kuhn VIHK shuhn) *n.* belief

<u>**convince**</u> (kuhn VIHNS) *v.* persuade; cause to accept a point of view

coveted (KUHV iht uhd) *v.* wanted; desired

croon (kroon) *v.* sing or hum quietly and soothingly

crouches (KROWCH uhz) *v.* stoops or bends low

crucial (KROO shuhl) *adj.* important; critical

crystal (KRIHS tuhl) *adj.* made of clear, brilliant glass

culminated (KUHL muh nayt uhd) *v.* reached its highest point or climax

culprit (KUHL priht) *n.* guilty person

culture (KUHL chuhr) *n.* collected customs of a group or community

cunning (KUHN ihng) *adj.* sly; crafty

cunningly (KUHN ihng lee) *adv.* cleverly

cupboard (KUHB uhrd) *n.* cabinet with shelves for cups, plates, and food

curdled (KUR duhld) *adj.* rotten

curiosity (kyur ee OS uh tee) *n.* desire to learn or know

custom (KUHS tuhm) *n.* accepted practice

D

dabbling (DAB lihng) *v.* wetting by dipping, splashing, or paddling in the water

danger (DAYN juhr) *n.* exposure to possible harm, injury, or loss

debate (dih BAYT) *v.* argue in an attempt to convince

deceive (dih SEEV) *v.* to make someone believe something that's not true

decreed (dih KREED) *v.* officially ordered

defiant (dih FY uhnt) *adj.* boldly resisting

defies (dih FYZ) *v.* resists or opposes boldly or openly

define (dih FYN) *v.* determine the nature of or give the meaning of

deserts (dih ZURTS) *v.* leaves, especially a military post

designated (DEHZ ihg nayt uhd) *v.* pointed out; marked

desire (dih ZYR) *n.* wish or want

desolate (DEHS uh liht) *adj.* lonely; solitary

desperate (DEHS puhr iht) *adj.* hopeless; very great desire or need

destiny (DEHS tuh nee) *n.* the seemingly inevitable succession of events; one's fate

destitute (DEHS tuh toot) *n.* people living in complete poverty

devastated (DEHV uh stayt uhd) *v.* destroyed; completely upset

devastating (DEHV uh stayt ihng) *adj.* destructive; overwhelming

dignitaries (DIHG nuh tehr eez) *n.* people holding high positions or offices

diplomats (DIHP luh mats) *n.* government employees who work with other nations

disagreement (DIHS uh GREE muhnt) *n.* difference or conflict between people or groups

discipline (DIHS uh plihn) *n.* training; self-control

discover (dihs KUHV uhr) *v.* find or explore

dislodge (dihs LOJ) *v.* force from a position or place

dismal (DIHZ muhl) *adj.* dark and gloomy

dispelled (dihs PEHLD) *v.* driven away; made to disappear

dispute (dihs PYOOT) *n.* disagreement

distinct (dihs TIHNGKT) *adj.* separate and different

distract (dih STRAKT) *v.* draw attention away

diversions (duh VUR zhuhnz) *n.* amusements

diversity (duh VUR suh tee) *n.* variety, as of groups or cultures

dominions (duh MIHN yuhnz) *n.* governed countries or territories

downy (DOW nee) *adj.* soft and fluffy

duty (DOO tee) *n.* responsibility; obligation

E

elaboration (ih lab uh RAY shuhn) *n.* adding of more details

elective (ih LEHK tihv) *n.* optional course

emerged (ih MURJD) *v.* came into view; became visible

emphatic (ehm FAT ihk) *adj.* felt or done with strong feeling

enrich (ehn RIHCH) *v.* make better; improve in quality

entertain (ehn tuhr TAYN) *v.* amuse; put on a performance

environment (ehn VY ruhn muhnt) *n.* surroundings; the natural world

envying (EHN vee ihng) *v.* wanting something that someone else has

epidemic (ehp uh DEHM ihk) *n.* outbreak of a contagious disease

equality (ih KWOL uh tee) *n.* social state in which all people are treated the same

ethnicity (ehth NIHS uh tee) *n.* racial or cultural background

evading (ih VAYD ihng) *v.* avoiding

evaluate (ih VAL yoo ayt) *v.* judge; determine the significance of

evaporated (ih VAP uh rayt uhd) *v.* changed from a liquid to a gas

evidence (EHV uh duhns) *n.* proof in support of a claim or statement

evidently (ehv uh DEHNT lee) *adv.* clearly; obviously

examine (ehg ZAM uhn) *v.* study in depth; look at closely

exertion (ehg ZUR shuhn) *n.* physical work

expectancy (ehk SPEHK tuhn see) *n.* that which is expected

expectations (ehks pehk TAY shuhnz) *n.* things looked forward to

expense (ehk SPEHNS) *n.* financial cost

experiment (ehk SPEHR uh mehnt) *n.* test to determine a result

explain (ehk SPLAYN) *v.* make plain or clear

explore (ehk SPLAWR) *v.* investigate; look into

express (ehk SPREHS) *v.* say or communicate a feeling

exquisite (EHKS kwih ziht) *adj.* beautiful in a delicate way

extenuating (ehk STEHN yoo ayt ihng) *adj.* giving a reason for; excusing

exultant (ehg ZUHL tuhnt) *adj.* expressing great joy or triumph

F

facts (fakts) *n.* accepted truths or reality

factual (FAK choo uhl) *adj.* based on or limited to what is real or true

falsely (FAWLS lee) *adv.* incorrectly; untruthfully

family (FAM uh lee) *n.* people related by blood or having a common ancestor

fascinated (FAS uh nayt uhd) *adj.* captivated

fathom (FATH uhm) *n.* unit of length used to measure the depth of water

feeble (FEE buhl) *adj.* weak; infirm

feebleness (FEE buhl nuhs) *n.* weakness

fiction (FIHK shuhn) *n.* something invented or imagined

fiddler (FIHD luhr) *n.* person who plays a fiddle, or violin

flatterers (FLAT uhr uhrz) *n.* those who praise a person insincerely

fluent (FLOO uhnt) *adj.* able to write with ease

flushed (fluhsht) *v.* drove from hiding

flustered (FLUHS tuhrd) *adj.* nervous; confused

focus (FOH kuhs) *n.* central point or topic of investigation

forage (FAWR ihj) *n.* food for domestic animals

formidable (FAWR muh duh buhl) *adj.* impressive

forsythia (fawr SIHTH ee uh) *n.* shrub with yellow flowers that blooms in early spring

fragrant (FRAY gruhnt) *adj.* sweet smelling

frontier (fruhn TIHR) *n.* the developing, often uncivilized, region of a country; any new field of learning

fundamental (FUHN duh MEHNT uhl) *adj.* basic; forming a foundation

furrowed (FUR ohd) *v.* wrinkled

G

garlands (GAHR luhndz) *n.* wreaths of flowers and leaves

garments (GAHR muhnts) *n.* clothes

gauge (gayj) *v.* estimate or judge

generate (JEN uhr ayt) *v.* create

globules (GLOB yoolz) *n.* drops of liquid

glossy (GLAWS ee) *adj.* smooth and shiny

goblets (GOB lihts) *n.* bowl-shaped drinking containers without handles

gourd (gawrd) *n.* a fruit; the dried shell is used as a cup

granite (GRAN iht) *n.* hard gray rock

gratitude (GRAT uh tood) *n.* thankful appreciation

group (groop) *n.* collection or set, as of people

groves (grohvz) *n.* small groups of trees

guidance (GY duhns) *n.* advice or assistance

gumption (GUHMP shuhn) *n.* courage; enterprise

guzzle (GUHZ uhl) *v.* drank greedily

H

harness (HAHR nihs) *n.* equipment used to drive a horse or attach it to a vehicle

haunches (HAWN chuhz) *n.* upper legs and hips of an animal

hexagons (HEHK suh gonz) *n.* six-sided figures

hind (hynd) *adj.* rear

hoarding (HAWR dihng) *v.* accumulating and storing a supply as a reserve

hoed (hohd) *v.* weeded or loosened soil with a metal hand tool

hors d'oeuvres (awr DUHRVZ) *n.* savory foods served as appetizers

huddled (HUHD uhld) *v.* crowded or nestled close together

I

identify (y DEHN tuh fy) *v.* recognize as being

ignorant (IHG nuhr uhnt) *adj.* not knowing facts or information

ignore (ihg NAWR) *v.* refuse to notice; disregard

ignored (ihg NAWRD) *v.* paid no attention to

image (IHM ihj) *n.* picture; representation

immensely (ih MEHNS lee) *adv.* a great deal; very much

immensity (ih MEHN suh tee) *n.* immeasurable largeness or vastness

impervious (ihm PUR vee uhs) *adj.* not affected by something

impetus (IHM puh tuhs) *n.* driving force

implored (ihm PLAWRD) *v.* begged

improvised (IHM pruh vyzd) *v.* composed or performed on the spur of the moment

improvising (IHM pruh vy zihng) *v.* making up or inventing on the spur of the moment

incessantly (ihn SEHS uhnt lee) *adv.* without stopping

indispensable (ihn dihs PEHN suh buhl) *adj.* absolutely necessary

individual (ihn duh VIHJ oo uhl) *n.* single person or thing

inflicted (ihn FLIHKT uhd) *v.* made someone suffer something painful or bad

inform (ihn FORM) *v.* tell; give information about

information (ihn fuhr MAY shuhn) *n.* knowledge gained through study or experience

initiation (ih nihsh ee AY shuhn) *n.* process by which one becomes a member of a group

inquire (ihn KWYR) *v.* ask in order to learn about

insight (ihn syt) *n.* ability to see the truth; an understanding

integration (ihn tuh GRAY shuhn) *n.* the end of separation of cultural or racial groups

intercedes (ihn tuhr SEEDZ) *v.* makes a request on behalf of another

intermixed (ihn tuhr MIHKST) *adj.* mixed together

interplanetary (ihn tuhr PLAN uh tehr ee) *adj.* between planets

interrupted (ihn tuh RUHPT uhd) *v.* broken into or upon a thought, discussion, etc.; not continuous

intervene (ihn tuhr VEEN) *v.* come between as an influence to modify, settle, or hinder some action or argument

interview (IHN tuhr vyoo) *v.* ask a series of questions of a person in order to gain information

intricate (IHN trih kiht) *adj.* complex; detailed

investigate (ihn VEHS tuh gayt) *v.* examine thoroughly

irrigation (ihr uh GAY shuhn) *n.* supplying water with ditches, canals, or sprinklers

J

justifies (JUHS tuh fyz) *v.* excuses; explains

K

kinsmen (KIHNZ muhn) *n.* male relatives

knowledge (NOL ihj) *n.* result of learning; awareness

L

laborious (luh BAWR ee uhs) *adj.* taking much work or effort

learn (lurn) *v.* gain knowledge or skills

legislation (lehj ihs LAY shuhn) *n.* law

liberty (LIHB uhr tee) *n.* freedom from slavery or captivity

listen (LIHS uhn) *v.* pay attention to; heed

loathed (lohthd) *v.* hated

longhorns (LAWNG hawrnz) *n.* breed of cattle with long horns

luminous (LOO muh nuhs) *adj.* giving off light

M

malice (MAL ihs) *n.* ill will

malicious (muh LIHSH uhs) *adj.* spiteful; hateful

manned (mand) *adj.* having human operators on board

meager (MEE guhr) *adj.* of poor quality; small in amount

media (MEE dee uh) *n.* collected sources of information, including newspapers, television, and the Internet

meek (meek) *adj.* timid; not showing anger

merely (MIHR lee) *adv.* no more than; and nothing else; simply

metamorphosis (meht uh MAWR fuh sihs) *n.* change of form

minnow (MIHN oh) *n.* small schooling fish

miracle (MIHR uh kuhl) *n.* a remarkable event or thing; marvel

misunderstanding (mihs uhn duhr STAN dihng) *n.* state where words or a point of view fail to be communicated

monarch (MON uhrk) *n.* hereditary rule, like a king or queen

morose (muh ROHS) *adj.* gloomy

mortality (mawr TAL uh tee) *n.* condition of being mortal, or having to die eventually

mourning (MAWR nihng) *n.* expression of grief, especially after someone dies

murmuring (MUR muhr ihng) *v.* making low, indistinct sounds

mystery (MIHS tuhr ee) *n.* something unexplained, unknown, or kept secret

N

neglected (nih GLEHKT uhd) *v.* failed to take care of

nobility (noh BIHL uh tee) *n.* people with a high rank in society

nonchalantly (NON shuh lahnt lee) *adv.* casually indifferent

O

obsession (uhb SEHSH uhn) *n.* extreme interest in something, which prevents you from thinking about anything else

obstacle (OB stuh kuhl) *n.* something in the way

ominous (OM uh nuhs) *adj.* threatening

opinion (uh PIHN yuhn) *n.* belief based on what seems true or probable

opposition (op uh ZIHSH uhn) *n.* state of being against

optimist (OP tuh mihst) *n.* someone who takes the most hopeful view of matters

ornament (AWR nuh muhnt) *v.* beautify

outcome (OWT kuhm) *n.* way something turns out

outskirts (OWT skurts) *n.* a district far from the center of a city

P

parallel (PAR uh lehl) *adv.* extending in the same direction and at the same distance apart

parson (PAHR suhn) *n.* minister

passion (PASH uhn) *n.* strong feelings of love, hate or fear

patriotic (pay tree OT ihk) *adj.* love and support for one's own country

paupers (PAW puhrz) *n.* people who are very poor

peasants (PEHZ uhnts) *n.* owners of small farms; farm laborers

peeved (peevd) *adj.* irritated; annoyed

penned (pehnd) *v.* locked up in a small enclosure

perceive (puhr SEEV) *v.* adopt a point of view; see

perception (puhr SEHP shuhn) *n.* the act of becoming aware of through one or more of the senses

perch (purch) *n.* roost for a bird; seat

perfunctorily (puhr FUHNGK tuh ruh lee) *adv.* done without care merely as a routine; superficially

perilous (PEHR uh luhs) *adj.* dangerous

permanent (PUR muh nuhnt) *adj.* lasting or intended to last forever

perpetual (puhr PEHCH yoo uhl) *adj.* constant; unending

persistently (puhr SIHS tuhnt lee) *adv.* firmly and steadily

perspective (puhr SPEHK tihv) *n.* point of view

pestering (PEHS tuhr ihng) *v.* annoying; bugging

plaited (PLAYT uhd) *adj.* braided

plausible (PLAW zuh buhl) *adj.* believable

porridge (PAWR ihj) *n.* soft food made of cereal boiled in water or milk

potential (puh TEHN shuhl) *n.* possibility; capability

practical (PRAK tih kuhl) *adj.* level-headed; efficient; realistic

precaution (prih KAW shuhn) *n.* something you do to prevent something bad or dangerous from happening

preliminary (prih LIHM uh nehr ee) *adj.* coming before or leading up to the main action

presumptuous (prih ZUHMP choo uhs) *adj.* overconfident; arrogant

prickly (PRIHK lee) *adv.* sharply pointed; thorny

produce (pruh DOOS) *v.* make; create

profound (pruh FOWND) *adj.* deeply or intensely felt

promote (pruh MOHT) *v.* encourage; contribute to the growth of

proposal (pruh POH zuhl) *n.* plan; offer

python (PY thon) *n.* large snake

Q

quest (kwehst) *n.* a long search for something

question (KWEHS chuhn) *v.* challenge the accuracy of; place in doubt

R

rancid (RAN sihd) *adj.* spoiled and smelling bad

rash (rash) *adj.* too hasty

react (ree AKT) *v.* respond to; act with respect to

reaction (ree AK shuhn) *n.* response to an influence, action, or statement

readapted (ree uh DAPT uhd) *v.* gradually adjusted again

reality (ree AL uh tee) *n.* state or quality of being real or true

realm (rehlm) *n.* kingdom

reassuring (ree uh SHUR ihng) *adj.* having the effect of restoring confidence

reeds (reedz) *n.* tall, slender grasses that grow in marshy land

reel (reel) *v.* spin; whirl

reflect (rih FLEHKT) *v.* think about; consider

refugee (REHF yoo JEE) *n.* person who flees home or country to seek shelter from war or cruelty

refuse (REHF yooz) *n.* trash; waste

regretted (rih GREHT uhd) *v.* felt sorry about

relation (rih LAY shuhn) *n.* connection between two or more things

relented (rih LEHNT uhd) *v.* gave in

reliable (rih LY uh buhl) *adj.* dependable

relished (REHL ihsht) *v.* enjoyed; liked

remote (rih MOHT) *adj.* far away from anything else

repressive (rih PREHS ihv) *adj.* overly strict

reproach (rih PROHCH) *n.* disapproval; criticism

resilient (rih ZIHL yuhnt) *adj.* able to spring back into shape

resolution (rehz uh LOO shuhn) *n.* end of a conflict in which one or both parties is satisfied

resumed (rih ZOOMD) *v.* began again; continued

reveal (rih VEEL) *v.* make known; show

revived (rih VYVD) *v.* came back to life or consciousness

righteous (RY chuhs) *adj.* morally good and fair

routed (ROWT uhd) *v.* soundly defeated

rummaging (RUHM ihj ihng) *v.* searching through something

S

sage (sayj) *n.* very wise person

saluting (suh LOOT ihng) *v.* honor by performing an act or gesture

saturation (sach uh RAY shuhn) *n.* state of being completely filled

savored (SAY vuhrd) *v.* tasted or experienced with delight

scorned (skawrnd) *adj.* looked down upon

scowl (skowl) *v.* look at someone or something in an angry or disapproving way

sensitive (SEHN suh tihv) *adj.* easily hurt

sentimental (sehn tuh MEHNT uhl) *adj.* emotional; showing tender feeling

severe (suh VIHR) *adj.* harsh

shed (shehd) *v.* cast off or lose

shipments (SHIHP muhntz) *n.* the delivery or the act of sending goods

shortsightedness (shawrt SY tihd nuhs) *n.* lack of foresight

shuffle (SHUHF uhl) *v.* walk with dragging feet

simultaneously (sy muhl TAY nee uhs lee) *adv.* at the same time

sinewy (SIHN yoo ee) *adj.* tough and strong

slackening (SLAK uhn ihng) *adj.* easing; becoming less active

slather (SLATH uhr) *v.* spread on thickly

sluggishly (SLUHG ihsh lee) *adv.* as if lacking energy

smattering (SMAT uhr ihng) *n.* a small number

snuffs (snuhfs) *v.* extinguishes; puts out

solemn (SOL uhm) *adj.* serious; somber

speak (speek) *v.* use language; express in words

spectators (SPEHK tay tuhrz) *n.* people who watch

spied (spyd) *v.* watched secretly

spigot (SPIHG uht) *n.* faucet; spout

spines (spynz) *n.* backbones

sputters (SPUHT uhrz) *v.* makes hissing or spitting noises

strategy (STRAT uh jee) *n.* set of plans used to gain success or achieve an aim

strive (stryv) *v.* struggle

struggle (STRUHG uhl) *n.* fight

stutter (STUHT uhr) *v.* speak in a hesitant or faltering way

suit (soot) *v.* please; satisfy

suitable (SOO tuh buhl) *adj.* appropriate

suitors (SOO tuhrz) *n.* men who court a woman or seek to marry her

summoned (SUHM uhnd) *v.* called together

supple (SUHP uhl) *adj.* able to bend easily; flexible

surpass (suhr PAS) *v.* be superior to

sustained (suh STAYND) *adj.* supported; maintained

swerve (swurv) *n.* curving motion

T

teach (teech) *v.* share information or knowledge

team (teem) *n.* group united in a common goal

technology (tehk NOL uh jee) *n.* practical application of science to business or industry

telegram (TEHL uh gram) *n.* message transmitted by telegraph

timid (TIHM ihd) *adj.* shy; fearful

tolerant (TOL uhr uhnt) *adj.* accepting; free from bigotry or prejudice

torrent (TAWR uhnt) *n.* flood

tradition (truh DIHSH uhn) *n.* custom, as of a social group or culture

transfixed (trans FIHKT) *adj.* fascinated

transformation (trans fuhr MAY shuhn) *n.* change

translates (trans LAYTS) *v.* expresses the same thing in another form

translucent (trans LOO suhnt) *adj.* allowing light through

transmit (trans MIHT) *v.* send or give out

truth (trooth) *n.* something supported by fact or reality

tumultuously (too MUHL choo uhs lee) *adv.* noisily and violently

twine (twyn) *n.* strong string or cord of strands twisted together

U

ultimate (UHL tuh miht) *adj.* final

unanimous (yoo NAN uh muhs) *adj.* based on complete agreement

uncommonly (uhn KOM uhn lee) *adv.* remarkably

unconsciously (uhn KON shuhs lee) *adv.* thoughtlessly

understand (uhn duhr STAND) *v.* grasp or reach knowledge with respect to something

understanding (uhn duhr STAN dihng) *n.* agreement; end of conflict

unify (YOO nuh fy) *v.* bring together as one

unique (yoo NEEK) *adj.* one of a kind

unravel (uhn RAV uhl) *v.* become untangled or separated

utter (UHT uhr) *v.* speak

V

vacancy (VAY kuhn see) *n.* emptiness; unoccupied position

varmints (VAHR muhnts) *n.* vermin

veranda (vuh RAN duh) *n.* open porch, usually with a roof

verge (vurj) *n.* edge; brink

vital (VY tuhl) *adj.* extremely important or necessary

void (voyd) *n.* emptiness

vowed (vowd) *v.* promised solemnly

W

weasel (WEE zuhl) *n.* small mammal that eats rats, mice, birds, and eggs

whiff (hwihf) *n.* smell; scent

whimper (HWIHM puhr) *v.* make low, crying sounds

withered (WIHTH uhr) *adj.* dried up

wonderment (WUHN duhr muhnt) *n.* feeling of surprise or astonishment

wonders (WUHN duhrz) *n.* things that cause astonishment; marvels

writhing (RYTH ihng) *adj.* squirming, often in response to pain

wrought (rawt) *v.* shaped; made; shaped by hammering

Y

yearned (yurnd) *v.* wanted very much

Spanish Glossary

El vocabulario de Gran Pregunta aparece en **azul**. El vocabulario académico de alta utilidad está <u>subrayado</u>.

A

abode / domicilio *s.* hogar; residencia

acknowledge / aceptar *v.* reconocer; admitir

acquainted / conocido *adj.* familiar

adequate / adecuado *adj.* bastante; suficiente

adolescence / adolescencia *s.* época de desarrollo en la que una persona joven se convierte en adulto

aloft / en vuelo *adj.* en lo alto; volando; en el aire

<u>**analyze / analizar**</u> *v.* separar las partes de un todo y examinar detenidamente

antidote / antídoto *s.* remedio; cura

apparent / aparente *adj.* simulado

appearance / apariencia *s.* aspecto o parecer de una persona o cosa

<u>**appreciate / apreciar**</u> *v.* estar agradecido

approvingly / con aprobación *adv.* con consentimiento

aptitude / aptitud *s.* talento; habilidad

arid / árido *adj.* seco; baldío

<u>**assumption / suposición**</u> *s.* creencia o aceptación de la existencia de algo

astonish / pasmar *v.* asombrar

atmospheric / atmosférico *adj.* relativo al aire que rodea la Tierra

<u>**attitude / actitud**</u> *s.* estado mental determinado por creencias, sentimientos y valores

audible / audible *adj.* lo suficientemente alto para que se pueda oír

avid / ávido *adj.* ansioso y entusiasmado

<u>**awareness / conciencia**</u> *s.* conocimiento adquirido por medio de la percepción o de información

awe / sobrecogimiento *s.* sentimientos encontrados de temor y asombro

B

babbled / balbuceó *v.* murmuró; habló sin saber o demasiado

ban / prohibición *s.* orden que impide algo

banish / desterrar *v.* expulsar; exiliar

believable / creíble *adj.* tener la habilidad de inculcar credibilidad o confianza

bellow / bramar *v.* rugir profundamente

bias / parcial *s.* tendencia a interpretar las cosas de manera sesgada o prejuiciosa

bigots / intolerantes *s.* personas de mentalidad cerrada, prejuiciosas

blander / insípido *adj.* sin sabor

bound/ sujeto *v.* atado

brawny / fornido *adj.* fuerte y musculoso

burrow / excavar *v.* cavar un hollo como refugio

C

canyon / cañón *s.* paso estrecho entre dos montañas

captivity / cautiverio *s.* encarcelamiento; detenido como prisionero

cattails / espadañas *s.* plantas herbáceas de tallo alto con hojas en forma de espada que se encuentran en lugares húmedos

causeways / calzada elevada *s.* camino sobre terreno húmedo o agua poco profunda

<u>**challenge / desafiar**</u> *v.* retar; cuestionar

<u>**characteristic / característica**</u> *s.* rasgo; facción

clusters / grupos *s.* conjunto de cosas similares; montón

coax / convencer *v.* persuadir de manera sutil

<u>**common / común**</u> *adj.* ordinario; frecuente y muy sabido

communal / comunal *adj.* compartido por todos

<u>**communicate / comunicar**</u> *v.* compartir pensamientos o sentimientos, usualmente con palabras

<u>**communication / comunicación**</u> *s.* acto de compartir información o de hablar

<u>**community / comunidad**</u> *s.* grupo de personas que tienen un interés en común o que viven cerca el uno del otro

compelled / obligado *v.* forzado

competition / competencia *s.* evento o juego en que las personas o bandos pretenden ganar

compromise / solución *s.* convenio satisfactorio entre dos partes

compulsion / compulsión *s.* impulso irresistible

<u>**conclude / concluir**</u> *v.* terminar; finalizar

<u>**conflict / conflicto**</u> *s.* choque o lucha entre grupos opuestos

consolation / consolación *s.* algo que alivia la pena de una persona decepcionada

conspired / conspiró *v.* planeó de manera secreta

contradiction / contradicción *s.* diferencia entre dos cosas conflictivas que demuestra que sólo una es cierta

contraption / artilugio *s.* aparato o mecanismo extraño

<u>**contribute / contribuir**</u> *v.* agregar; enriquecer

conveyed / comunicó *v.* hizo saber; expresó

conviction / convicción *s.* creencia

<u>**convince / convencer**</u> *v.* persuadir; incitar a aceptar un punto de vista

coveted / codició *v.* quiso; deseó

croon / canturrear v. cantar o tararear silenciosa y dulcemente

crouches / acuclillar v. agacharse o doblarse a un nivel bajo

crucial / crucial adj. importante; crítico

crystal / cristal adj. hecho de vidrio claro y brillante

culminated / culminó v. alcanzó su punto más alto o clímax

culprit / inculpado s. persona culpable

culture / cultura s. conjunto de modos de vida y costumbres de un grupo o una comunidad

cunning / astuto adj. hábil; taimado

cunningly / astutamente adv. ingeniosamente

cupboard / gabinete s. mueble con repizas para tazas, platos y comida

curdled / cortado adj. podrido

curiosity / curiosidad s. deseo de aprender o saber

curiosity / curiosidad s. estado en el que se quiere aprender más sobre un tema

custom / costumbre s. lo que se hace comúnmente

D

dabbling / chapuzar v. zambullirse, sumergirse o patalear en el agua

danger / peligro s. exposición a posible daño, lesión o pérdida

debate / debate v. argumento que pretende convencer

deceive / engañar v. hacer a alguien creer lo que no es cierto

decreed / decretó v. creó un mandato oficial

defiant / desafiante adj. que resiste valientemente

defies / desafía v. que se resiste o se opone valientemente o de manera abierta

define / definir v. determinar la naturaleza o establecer el significado de algo

deserts / desertar v. dejar, abandonar, especialmente un puesto militar

designated / designó v. señaló; maró

desire / deseo s. acción de desear o querer

desolate / desolado adj. solo; solitario

desperate / desesperado adj. sin esperanzas; con gran deseo o necesidad

destiny / destino s. aparente secuencia de sucesos inevitables

destitute / indigentes adj. personas que viven en pobreza absoluta

devastated / devastado adj. destruido; completamente disgustado

devastating / devastador adj. destructivo; arrollador

dignitaries / dignatarios s. personas investidas de un cargo elevado

diplomats / diplomáticos s. empleados del gobierno que trabajan con otras naciones

disagreement / desacuerdo s. diferencia o conflicto entre dos grupos o personas

discipline / disciplina s. entrenamiento; autocontrol

discover / descubrir v. encontrar o explorar

dislodge / desplazar v. mover a la fuerza de una posición o lugar

dismal / lúgubre adj. oscuro y sombrío

dispelled / disipó v. alejó; hizo desvanecer

dispute / disputa s. desacuerdo

distinct / distinto adj. separado y diferente

distract / distraer v. apartar la atención

diversions / diversiones s. formas de entretenimiento

diversity / diversidad s. variedad de grupos o culturas

dominions / dominios s. países o territorios gobernados

downy / suave adj. blando y esponjoso

duty / deber s. responsabilidad; obligación

E

elaboration / elaboración s. unión de más detalles

elective / opción s. curso o decisión que se puede tomar

emerged / sobresalió v. apareció a la vista; se volvió visible

emphatic / enfático adj. que se siente o se hace con fuerza

enrich / enriquecer v. mejorar

entertain / entretener v. divertir; hacer una presentación

environment / medio ambiente s. lo que nos rodea; el mundo natural

envying / envidiando v. queriendo lo que otro posee

epidemic / epidemia s. proliferación de una enfermedad contagiosa

equality / igualdad s. estado de la sociedad en el que todas las personas se tratan de la misma manera

ethnicity / etnicidad s. origen cultural o racial

evading / evadiendo v. evitando

evaluate / evaluar v. juzgar; determinar el significado de algo

evaporated / evaporó v. cambió de líquido a gas

evidence / evidencia s. prueba que apoya un reclamo o argumento

evidently / evidentemente adv. claramente; obviamente

examine / examinar v. estudiar a fondo; observar detenidamente

exertion / esfuerzo s. trabajo físico

expectancy / expectativa s. lo que se espera

expectations / expectativas s. esperanzas de lo que viene

expense / gasto s. costo financiero

experiment / experimento s. prueba que determina un resultado

explain / explicar v. esclarecer o aclarar

explore / explorar v. investigar; examinar

express / expresar v. hablar de o comunicar un sentimiento

exquisite / refinado adj. hermoso y delicado

extenuating / atenuar v. aliviar la gravedad de una situación

exultant / jubiloso adj. que expresa gran alegría o triunfo

F

facts / hechos s. la verdad o la realidad

factual / basado en hechos adj. basado en o limitado a lo que es real o verdadero

falsely / falsamente adv. de manera incorrecta o incierta

family / familia s. personas de relación consanguínea o que tienen un ancestro en común

fascinated / fascinado adj. encantado

fathom / braza s. unidad de longitud para medir la profundidad del agua

feeble / débil adj. flojo; enclenque

feebleness / debilidad s. falta de fuerza

fiction / ficción s. lo inventado o imaginado

fiddler / violinista s. persona que toca el violín

flatterers / alabadores s. personas que halagan a otra persona con poca sinceridad

fluent / fluido adj. que escribe con facilidad y soltura

flushed / expulsó v. obligó a salir de un lugar

flustered / nervioso adj. agitado; confuso

focus / enfoque n. punto central o tema de investigación

forage / forraje s. comida para animales domésticos

formidable / formidable adj. imponente; impresionante

forsythia / forsitia s. arbusto de flores amarillas que florece a principios de laprimavera

fragrant / fragante adj. que emana un aroma dulce

frontier / frontera s. región bajo desarrollo de un país; cualquier campo nuevo de aprendizaje

fundamental / fundamental adj. básico; que forma una base

furrowed / arrugar v. hacer pliegues

G

garlands / guirnalda s. corona de flores y hojas

garments / prendas s. ropa

gauge / medir v. estimar o juzgar

generate / spanish copy to come

globules / glóbulos s. gotas

glossy / lustroso adj. liso y brillante

goblets / copa s. envase para tomar que no tiene asas

gourd / mate s. fruta; la coraza seca se usa como taza

granite / granito s. piedra de color gris

gratitude / gratitud s. agradecimiento

group / grupo s. conjunto o agrupación, como de personas

groves / arboleda s. grupo pequeño de árboles

guidance / orientación s. consejo o asistencia

gumption / arrojo s. coraje; empuje

guzzle / engullir v. tragar atropelladamente

H

harness / arnés s. equipo que se usa para maniobrar un caballo o ajustarlo a un vehículo

haunches / ancas s. las patas posteriores de un animal

hexagons / hexágonos s. figuras de seis lados

hind / trasero adj. que está en la parte de atrás

hoarding / acaparando v. acumulando y almacenando provisiones como reservas

hoed / limpió con la azada v. cavó y removió tierra con una herramienta de metal

hors d'oeuvres / entremeses s. platillos sabrosos para picar antes de la comida

huddled / agrupado v. atestado o arrimado

I

identify / identificar v. reconocer como existente

ignorant / ignorante adj. que no sabe los hechos o que no tiene la información apropiada

ignore / ignorar v. hacer caso omiso; desconocer

ignored / ignoró v. no le prestó atención

image / imagen n. retrato; representación

immensely / inmensamente adv. de gran extremo; mucho

immensity / inmensidad s. cantidad inconmesurable o enorme

impervious / insensible adj. que no es afectado por algo

impetus / ímpetu s. fuerza motriz

implored / implorado v. suplicado

improvised / improvisó v. hizo o presentó de manera espontánea

improvising / improvisando v. creando o inventando espontáneamente

incessantly / incesante adv. sin parar

indispensable / indispensable adj. absolutamente necesario

individual / individuo s. una sola persona o cosa

inflicted / inflijió v. que ha causado sufrimiento o daño

inform / informar v. decir; dar información de algo

information / información s. conocimiento adquirido por medio de estudio o de la experiencia

initiation / iniciación s. proceso por el cual uno se convierte en miembro de un grupo

inquire / preguntar v. cuestionar con el fin de aprender

insight / perspicacia *s.* habilidad de ver la verdad; entendimiento

integration / integración *s.* fin de la separación cultural o de grupos raciales

intercedes / intercede *v.* actúa por otra persona

intermixed / mixto *adj.* compuesto de elementos diferentes

interplanetary / interplanetario *adj.* entre planetas

interrupted / interrumpido *v.* se refiere a un pensamiento o discusión que se ha detenido; sin continuidad

intervene / interviene *v.* que toma parte en una situación como influencia para modificar, resolver o estropear una acción o argumento

interview / entrevistar *v.* hacer una serie de preguntas a una persona con el fin de obtener información

intricate / intricado *adj.* complejo; detallado

investigate / investigar *v.* examinar a fondo

irrigation / irrigación *s.* suministro de agua a acequias, canales o regaderas

J

justifies / justifica *v.* que da escusas; explica

K

kinsmen / parientes *s.* familiares; en inglés se usan dos palabras diferentes para referirse a los hombres o a las mujeres que son miembros de la familia

knowledge / conocimiento *s.* el resultado de conocer; acción de tener presente

L

laborious / laborioso *adj.* que cuesta bastante trabajo o esfuerzo

learn / aprender *v.* obtener conocimiento o destrezas

legislation / legislación *s.* ley

liberty / libertad *s.* autonomía de la esclavitud o cautiverio

listen / escuchar *v.* prestar atención; atender

loathed / abominado *v.* odiado

longhorns / ganado longhorn *s.* tipo de ganado que se caracteriza por sus cuernos largos

luminous / luminoso *adj.* que despide luz

M

malice / malicia *s.* mala intención

malicious / malicioso *adj.* que tiene mala intención; odioso

manned / tripulado *adj.* que tiene un operador humano abordo

meager / exiguo *adj.* precario; escaso

media / medios de comunicación *s.* conjunto de fuentes de información incluyendo periódicos, televisión y la Internet

meek / manso *adj.* tímido; que no demuestra enfado

merely / meramente *adv.* no más de; y nada más; sencillamente

metamorphosis / metamorfosis *s.* en estado de cambio

minnow / pececillo *s.* pez pequeño

miracle / milagro *s.* suceso o cosa extraordinaria; maravilla

misunderstanding / malentendido *s.* estado en el que palabras o un punto de vista no logra ser comunicado

monarch / monarca *s.* dominio por carácter hereditario, como el de un rey o una reina

morose / lúgubre *adj.* sombrío

mortality / mortalidad *s.* condición de ser mortal, o de tener que morir en algún momento

mourning / luto *s.* expresión de pena, especialmente después de que alguien muere

murmuring / murmurando *v.* haciendo ruidos bajos e indescifrables

mystery / misterio *s.* algo inexplicable, desconocido o que se mantiene bajo secreto

N

neglected / descuidó *v.* no logró cuidar

nobility / nobleza *s.* personas de alto nivel en la sociedad

nonchalantly / con toda tranquilidad *adv.* despreocupado, con indiferencia

O

obsession / obsesión *s.* interés extremo en algo que previene pensar en cualquier otra cosa

obstacle / obstáculo *s.* algo que se interviene en el camino

ominous / siniestro *adj.* amenazante

opinion / opinión *s.* creencia basada en lo que parece ser cierto o probable

opposition / oposición *s.* estar en contra

optimist / optimista *s.* alguien que tiende a ver las cosas de la manera más favorable

ornament / adornar *v.* embellecer

outcome / resultado *s.* la manera en que algo se resuelve

outskirts / alrededores *s.* distritos lejos del centro de una ciudad

P

parallel / paralelo *adj.* que se extiende en la misma dirección y está separado siempre a la misma distancia

parson / pastor *s.* ministro

passion / pasión *s.* sentimientos fuertes de amor, odio o temor

patriotic / patriótico *adj.* sentir gran amor y apoyo por su país de origen

paupers / pobres *s.* gente necesitada

peasants / campesinos *s.* dueños de pequeñas fincas; trabajadores de fincas

peeved / molesto *adj.* irritado; fastidiado

penned / acorralado *adj.* encerrado en un área pequeña

perceive / percibir *v.* aceptar un punto de vista; ver

perception / percepción *s.* estar conciente por medio de uno o más sentidos

perch / percha *s.* palo para que los pájaros y aves se posen; asiento

perfunctorily / superficialmente *adv.* hecho sin mucho cuidado, como parte de una rutina

perilous / arriesgado *adj.* peligroso

permanent / permanente *adj.* duradero o que debe durar para siempre

perpetual / perpetuo *adj.* constante; sin fin

persistently / persistentemente *adv.* de manera firme y constante

perspective / perspectiva *s.* punto de vista

pestering / molestando *v.* fastidiando; irritando

plaited / entretejido *adj.* trenzado

plausible / plausible *adj.* creíble

porridge / gacha *s.* comida blanda compuesta de cereal hervido en agua o leche

potential / potencial *s.* posibilidad; capacidad

practical / práctico *adj.* sensato; eficiente; realista

precaution / precaución *s.* lo que se hace para prevenir que ocurra algo malo o peligroso

preliminary / preliminar *adj.* que viene antes o anticipando el acto principal

presumptuous / presumido *adj.* con exceso de confianza en sí mismo; arrogante

prickly / espinoso *adj.* puntiagudo; con espinas

produce / producir *v.* hacer; crear

profound / profundo *adj.* que se siente grave o intensamente

promote / promover *v.* animar; contribuir al crecimiento de algo

proposal / propuesta *s.* plan; oferta

python / pitón *s.* culebra de gran tamaño

Q

quest / búsqueda *s.* seguimiento extenso

question / cuestionar *v.* desafiar la precisión de algo; poner en duda

R

rancid / rancio *adj.* dañado y maloliente

rash / imprudente *adj.* muy precipitado

react / reaccionar *v.* responder; hacer algo al respecto

reaction / reacción *s.* respuesta a una influencia, acción o afirmación

readapted / se adaptó de nuevo *v.* se ajustó gradualmente otra vez

reality / realidad *s.* estado o calidad de ser real o verdadero

realm / dominio *s.* reino

reassuring / tranquilizante *adj.* que alivia o da confianza

reeds / cañas *s.* hierbas de tallo alto que crecen en pantanos

reel / girar *v.* dar vueltas; enrollar

reflect / refleccionar *v.* pensar en algo; considerar

refugee / refugiado *s.* persona que huye de su hogar o país en busca de asilo debido a la guerra o crueldad

refuse / basura *s.* desperdicios; desechos

regretted / arrepentirse *v.* sentir pesar por algo

relation / relación *s.* referencia, respeto

relented / cedió *v.* se dejó convencer

reliable / confiable *adj.* del que se puede depender

relished / deleitar *v.* causar placer; gozar; disfrutar

remote / remoto *adj.* muy lejos de cualquier cosa

repressive / represivo *adj.* altamente estricto

reproach / reproche *s.* desgracia, culpa

resilient / resistente *adj.* fuerte; que puede recobrar su estado original

resolution / resolución *s.* fin satisfactorio de un conflicto

resumed / recobrar *v.* volver al estado original

reveal / revelar *v.* hacer saber; demostrar

revived / revivió *v.* volvió a la vida o recobró consciencia

righteous / recto *adj.* que actúa de manera justa

routed / derrotó *v.* venció

rummaging / hurgando *v.* buscando entre cosas

S

sage / erudito *s.* sabio

saluting / homenajear *v.* honrar con un acto o gesto

saturation / saturación *s.* condición en la que se está completamente lleno

savored / saboreó *v.* degustó o apreció con placer

scorned / desdeñar *v.* menospreciar

scowl / fruncir el ceño *v.* mirar a alguien o algo con ira o desaprobación

sensitive / sensible *adj.* que se hiere con facilidad

sentimental / sentimental *adj.* que demuestra sentimientos compasivos

severe / severo *adj.* duro

shed / mudar *v.* perder o cambiar

shipments / remesa *s.* envío o acto de trasportar objetos

shortsightedness / falta de visión *s.* carencia de proyección en el futuro

shuffle / arrastrar *v.* caminar sin levantar los pies

simultaneously / simultáneo *adv.* al mismo tiempo

sinewy / vigoroso *adj.* recio y fuerte

slackening / aminorando *v.* relajando; volviéndose menos activo

slather / untar *v.* extender de manera generosa

sluggishly / perezosamente *adv.* sin energía

smattering / poquito *s.* cantidad pequeña

snuffs / extinguir *v.* apagar

solemn / solemne *adj.* serio; sombrío

speak / hablar *v.* usar lenguaje; expresar con palabras

spectators / espectadores *s.* personas que ven con atención

spied / espiar *v.* observar a escondidas

spigot / grifo *s.* llave; espita

spines / espinazo *s.* vértebras

sputters / chisporrotear *v.* hacer ruidos explosivos o sibilante

strategy / estrategia *s.* planes para alcanzar el éxito o lograr un objetivo

strive / esforzarse *v.* luchar

struggle / lucha *s.* pelea

stutter / tartamudear *v.* hablar sin fluidez o de manera entrecortada

suit / convenir *v.* ser placentero; satisfacer

suitable / adecuado *adj.* apropiado

suitors / pretendientes *s.* hombres que cortejan o buscan el matrimonio

summoned / convocar *v.* citar o llamar a una reunión

supple / ágil *adj.* que usa su cuerpo con facilidad y soltura

surpass / superar *v.* ser superior

sustained / sostenido *adj.* apoyado; mantenido

swerve / viraje *s.* movimiento en curva

T

teach / enseñar *v.* compartir información o conocimiento

team / equipo *s.* grupo unido por una meta en común

technology / tecnología *s.* aplicación práctica de las ciencias en negocios o en la industria

telegram / telegrama *s.* mensaje transmitido por telégrafo

timid / tímido *adj.* reservado, temeroso

tolerant / tolerante *adj.* que acepta; libre de resistencia o prejuicios

torrent / torrente *s.* inundación

tradition / tradición *s.* costumbre, de un grupo social o cultura

transfixed / embelesado *adj.* fascinado

transformation / transformación *s.* cambio

translates / trasladar *v.* mover de un lado al otro

translucent / translúcido *adj.* que permite pasar la luz

transmit / transmitir *v.* enviar o repartir

truth / verdad *s.* lo que se corrobora con hechos o la realidad

tumultuously / tumultuoso *adv.* de manera ruidosa y violenta

twine / bramante *s.* cordón delgado o grueso, con las hebras entretejidas

U

ultimate / último *adj.* final

unanimous / unánime *adj.* basado en un acuerdo total

uncommonly / extraordinariamente *adv.* fuera de lo común

unconsciously / inconscientemente *adv.* con poca consideración; sin pensarlo

understand / entender *v.* llegar a conocer y comprender algo

understanding / entendimiento *s.* acuerdo; fin de un conflicto

unify / unificar *v.* juntar para formar uno solo

unique / único *adj.* sin otro de su especie

unravel / desenmarañar *v.* desenredar o separar

utter / pronunciar *v.* articular

V

vacancy / vacante *s.* desocupado, vacío; cargo disponible

varmints / alimañas *s.* insectos

veranda / veranda *s.* porche descubierto, usualmente con techo

verge / borde *s.* orilla; límite

vital / vital *adj.* de extrema importancia o necesario

void / vacío *s.* desocupado

vowed / juró *v.* prometió solemnemente

W

weasel / comadreja *s.* mamífero pequeño que se alimenta de ratas, ratones, aves y huevos

whiff / olorcillo *s.* olor; aroma

whimper / quejido *v.* llanto, lamento

withered / marchitado *adj.* que se ha secado

wonderment / maravilla *s.* asombro

wonders / maravillas *s.* cosas que causan asombro

writhing / retorcido *adj.* contorcionado, usualmente a causa de dolor

wrought / forjó *v.* dio forma; fabricó; dio forma al martillar

Y

yearned / anhelar *v.* desear vehemente

Literary Terms

ALLITERATION *Alliteration* is the repetition of initial consonant sounds. Writers use alliteration to draw attention to certain words or ideas, to imitate sounds, and to create musical effects.

ALLUSION An *allusion* is a reference to a well-known person, event, place, literary work, or work of art. Allusions allow the writer to express complex ideas without spelling them out. Understanding what a literary work is saying often depends on recognizing its allusions and the meanings they suggest.

ANALOGY An *analogy* makes a comparison between two or more things that are similar in some ways but otherwise unalike.

ANECDOTE An *anecdote* is a brief story about an interesting, amusing, or strange event. Writers tell anecdotes to entertain or to make a point.

ANTAGONIST An *antagonist* is a character or a force in conflict with a main character, or protagonist.

See *Conflict* and *Protagonist.*

ARGUMENT See *Persuasion.*

ATMOSPHERE *Atmosphere,* or *mood,* is the feeling created in the reader by a literary work or passage.

AUTHOR'S ARGUMENT An *author's argument* is the position he or she puts forward, supported by reasons.

AUTHOR'S PURPOSE An *author's purpose* is his or her main reason for writing. For example, an author may want to entertain, inform, or persuade the reader. Sometimes an author is trying to teach a moral lesson or reflect on an experience. An author may have more than one purpose for writing.

AUTOBIOGRAPHY An *autobiography* is the story of the writer's own life, told by the writer. Autobiographical writing may tell about the person's whole life or only a part of it.

Because autobiographies are about real people and events, they are a form of nonfiction. Most autobiographies are written in the first person.

See *Biography, Nonfiction,* and *Point of View.*

BIOGRAPHY A *biography* is a form of nonfiction in which a writer tells the life story of another person. Most biographies are written about famous or admirable people.

Although biographies are nonfiction, the most effective ones share the qualities of good narrative writing.

See *Autobiography* and *Nonfiction.*

CHARACTER A *character* is a person or an animal that takes part in the action of a literary work. The main, or *major,* character is the most important character in a story, poem, or play. A *minor* character is one who takes part in the action but is not the focus of attention.

Characters are sometimes classified as flat or round. A *flat character* is one-sided and often stereotypical. A *round character,* on the other hand, is fully developed and exhibits many traits—often both faults and virtues. Characters can also be classified as dynamic or static. A *dynamic character* is one who changes or grows during the course of the work. A *static character* is one who does not change.

See *Characterization, Hero/Heroine,* and *Motive.*

CHARACTERIZATION *Characterization* is the act of creating and developing a character. Authors use two major methods of characterization—*direct* and *indirect.* When using direct characterization, a writer states the *characters' traits,* or characteristics.

When describing a character indirectly, a writer depends on the reader to draw conclusions about the character's traits. Sometimes the writer tells what other participants in the story say and think about the character.

See *Character* and *Motive.*

CLIMAX The *climax,* also called the turning point, is the high point in the action of the plot. It is the moment of greatest tension, when the outcome of the plot hangs in the balance.

See *Plot.*

COMEDY A *comedy* is a literary work, especially a play, which is light, often humorous or satirical, and ends happily. Comedies frequently depict ordinary characters faced with temporary difficulties and conflicts. Types of comedy include *romantic comedy,* which involves problems between lovers, and the *comedy of manners,* which satirically challenges social customs of a society.

CONCRETE POEM A *concrete poem* is one with a shape that suggests its subject. The poet arranges the letters, punctuation, and lines to create an image, or picture, on the page.

CONFLICT A *conflict* is a struggle between opposing forces. Conflict is one of the most important elements of stories, novels, and plays because it causes the action. There are two kinds of conflict: external and internal. An *external conflict* is one in which a character struggles against some outside force, such as another person. Another kind of external conflict may occur between a character and some force in nature.

An *internal conflict* takes place within the mind of a character. The character struggles to make a decision, take an action, or overcome a feeling.

See *Plot.*

CONNOTATIONS The *connotation* of a word is the set of ideas associated with it in addition to its explicit meaning. The connotation of a word can be personal, based on individual experiences. More often, cultural connotations—those recognizable by most people in a group—determine a writer's word choices.

See also *Denotation.*

COUPLET A *couplet* is two consecutive lines of verse with end rhymes. Often, a couplet functions as a stanza.

CULTURAL CONTEXT The *cultural context* of a literary work is the economic, social, and historical environment of the characters. This includes the attitudes and customs of that culture and historical period.

DENOTATION The *denotation* of a word is its dictionary meaning, independent of other associations that the word may have. The denotation of the word *lake,* for example, is "an inland body of water." "Vacation spot" and "place where the fishing is good" are connotations of the word *lake.*

See also *Connotation.*

DESCRIPTION A *description* is a portrait, in words, of a person, place, or object. Descriptive writing uses images that appeal to the five senses —sight, hearing, touch, taste, and smell.

See *Images.*

DEVELOPMENT See *Plot.*

DIALECT *Dialect* is the form of a language spoken by people in a particular region or group. Dialects differ in pronunciation, grammar, and word choice. The English language is divided into many dialects. British English differs from American English.

DIALOGUE A *dialogue* is a conversation between characters. In poems, novels, and short stories, dialogue is usually set off by quotation marks to indicate a speaker's exact words.

In a play, dialogue follows the names of the characters, and no quotation marks are used.

DICTION *Diction* is a writer's word choice and the way the writer puts those words together. Diction is part of a writer's style and may be described as formal or informal, plain or fancy, ordinary or technical, sophisticated or down-to-earth, old-fashioned or modern.

DRAMA A *drama* is a story written to be performed by actors. Although a drama is meant to be performed, one can also read the script, or written version, and imagine the action. The *script* of a drama is made up of dialogue and stage directions. The *dialogue* is the words spoken by the actors. The *stage directions,* usually printed in italics, tell how the actors should look, move, and speak. They also describe the setting, sound effects, and lighting.

Dramas are often divided into parts called *acts.* The acts are often divided into smaller parts called *scenes.*

DYNAMIC CHARACTER See *Character.*

ESSAY An *essay* is a short nonfiction work about a particular subject. Most essays have a single major focus and a clear introduction, body, and conclusion.

There are many types of essays. An *informal essay* uses casual, conversational language. A *historical essay* gives facts, explanations, and insights about historical events. An *expository essay* explains an idea by breaking it down. A *narrative essay* tells a story about a real-life experience. An *informational essay* explains a process. A *persuasive essay* offers an opinion and supports it. A *humorous essay* uses humor to achieve the author's purpose. A *reflective essay* addresses an event or experience and includes the writer's personal insights about the event's importance.

See *Exposition, Narration,* and *Persuasion.*

EXPOSITION In the plot of a story or a drama, the *exposition,* or introduction, is the part of the work that introduces the characters, setting, and basic situation.

See *Plot.*

EXPOSITORY WRITING *Expository writing* is writing that explains or informs.

EXTENDED METAPHOR In an *extended metaphor,* as in a regular metaphor, a subject is spoken or written of as though it were something else. However, extended metaphor differs from regular metaphor in that several connected comparisons are made.

See *Metaphor.*

EXTERNAL CONFLICT See *Conflict.*

FABLE A *fable* is a brief story or poem, usually with animal characters, that teaches a lesson, or moral. The moral is usually stated at the end of the fable.

See *Irony* and *Moral.*

FANTASY A *fantasy* is highly imaginative writing that contains elements not found in real life. Examples of fantasy include stories that involve supernatural elements, stories that resemble fairy tales, stories that deal with imaginary places and creatures, and science-fiction stories.

See *Science Fiction.*

FICTION *Fiction* is prose writing that tells about imaginary characters and events. Short stories and novels are works of fiction. Some writers base their fiction on actual events and people, adding invented characters, dialogue, settings, and plots. Other writers rely on imagination alone.

See *Narration, Nonfiction,* and *Prose.*

FIGURATIVE LANGUAGE *Figurative language* is writing or speech that is not meant to be taken literally. The many types of figurative language are known as *figures of speech.* Common figures of speech include metaphor, personification, and simile. Writers use figurative language to state ideas in vivid and imaginative ways.

See *Metaphor, Personification, Simile,* and *Symbol.*

FIGURE OF SPEECH See *Figurative Language.*

FLASHBACK A *flashback* is a scene within a story that interrupts the sequence of events to relate events that occurred in the past.

FLAT CHARACTER See *Character.*

FOIL A *foil* is a character whose behavior and attitude contrast with those of the main character.

FOLK TALE A *folk tale* is a story composed orally and then passed from person to person by word of mouth. Folk tales originated among people who could neither read nor write. These people entertained one another by telling stories aloud—often dealing with heroes, adventure, magic, or romance. Eventually, modern scholars collected these stories and wrote them down.

Folk tales reflect the cultural beliefs and environments from which they come.

See *Fable, Legend, Myth,* and *Oral Tradition.*

FOOT See *Meter.*

FORESHADOWING *Foreshadowing* is the author's use of clues to hint at what might happen later in the story. Writers use foreshadowing to build their readers' expectations and to create suspense.

FREE VERSE *Free verse* is poetry not written in a regular, rhythmical pattern, or meter. The poet is free to write lines of any length or with any number of stresses, or beats. Free verse is therefore less constraining than *metrical verse,* in which every line must have a certain length and a certain number of stresses.

See *Meter.*

GENRE A *genre* is a division or type of literature. Literature is commonly divided into three major genres: poetry, prose, and drama. Each major genre is, in turn, divided into lesser genres, as follows:

1. *Poetry:* lyric poetry, concrete poetry, dramatic poetry, narrative poetry, epic poetry

2. *Prose:* fiction (novels and short stories) and nonfiction (biography, autobiography, letters, essays, and reports)

3. *Drama:* serious drama and tragedy, comic drama, melodrama, and farce

See *Drama, Poetry,* and *Prose.*

HAIKU The *haiku* is a three-line Japanese verse form. The first and third lines of a haiku each have five syllables. The second line has seven syllables. A writer of haiku uses images to create a single, vivid picture, generally of a scene from nature.

HERO/HEROINE A *hero* or *heroine* is a character whose actions are inspiring or noble. Often heroes and heroines struggle to overcome the obstacles and problems that stand in their way. Note that the term *hero* was originally used only for male characters, while heroic female characters were always called *heroines.* However, it is now acceptable to use *hero* to refer to females as well as to males.

HISTORICAL CONTEXT The *historical context* of a literary work includes the actual political and social events and trends of the time. When a work takes place in the past, knowledge about that historical time period can help the reader understand its setting, background, culture, and message, as well as the attitudes and actions of its characters. A reader must also take into account the historical context in which the writer was creating the work, which may be different from the time period of the work's setting.

HUMOR *Humor* is writing intended to evoke laughter. While most humorists try to entertain, humor can also be used to convey a serious theme.

IDIOM An *idiom* is an expression that has a meaning particular to a language or region. For example, in "Seventh Grade," Gary Soto uses the idiom "making a face," which means to contort one's face in an unusual, usually unattractive way.

IMAGERY See *Images.*

IMAGES *Images* are words or phrases that appeal to one or more of the five senses. Writers use images to describe how their subjects look, sound, feel, taste, and smell. Poets often paint images, or word pictures, that appeal to the senses. These pictures help you to experience the poem fully.

INTERNAL CONFLICT See *Conflict.*

IRONY *Irony* is a contradiction between what happens and what is expected. There are three main types of irony. *Situational irony* occurs when something happens that directly contradicts the expectations of the characters or the audience. *Verbal irony* is something contradictory that is said. In *dramatic irony,* the audience is aware of something that the character or speaker is not.

JOURNAL A *journal* is a daily, or periodic, account of events and the writer's thoughts and feelings about those events. Personal journals are not normally written for publication, but sometimes they do get published later with permission from the author or the author's family.

LEGEND A *legend* is a widely told story about the past—one that may or may not have a foundation in fact. Every culture has its own legends—its familiar, traditional stories.

See *Folk Tale, Myth,* and *Oral Tradition.*

LETTERS A *letter* is a written communication from one person to another. In personal letters, the writer shares information and his or her thoughts and feelings with one other person or group. Although letters are not normally written for publication, they sometimes do get published later with the permission of the author or the author's family.

LIMERICK A *limerick* is a humorous, rhyming, five-line poem with a specific meter and rhyme scheme. Most limericks have three strong stresses in lines 1, 2, and 5 and two strong stresses in lines 3 and 4. Most follow the rhyme scheme *aabba.*

LYRIC POEM A *lyric poem* is a highly musical verse that expresses the observations and feelings of a single speaker. It creates a single, unified impression.

MAIN CHARACTER See *Character.*

MEDIA ACCOUNTS *Media accounts* are reports, explanations, opinions, or descriptions written for television, radio, newspapers, and magazines. While some media accounts report only facts, others include the writer's thoughts and reflections.

METAPHOR A *metaphor* is a figure of speech in which something is described as though it were something else. A metaphor, like a simile, works by pointing out a similarity between two unlike things.

See *Extended Metaphor* and *Simile.*

METER The *meter* of a poem is its rhythmical pattern. This pattern is determined by the number of *stresses,* or beats, in each line. To describe the meter of a poem, read it emphasizing the beats in each line. Then, mark the stressed and unstressed syllables, as follows:

Mў fáth | ĕr wás | thĕ fírst | tŏ héar |

As you can see, each strong stress is marked with a slanted line (´) and each unstressed syllable with a horseshoe symbol (˘). The weak and strong stresses are then divided by vertical lines (|) into groups called feet.

MINOR CHARACTER See *Character.*

MOOD See *Atmosphere.*

MORAL A *moral* is a lesson taught by a literary work. A fable usually ends with a moral that is directly stated. A poem, novel, short story, or essay often suggests a moral that is not directly stated. The moral must be drawn by the reader, based on other elements in the work.

See *Fable.*

MOTIVATION See *Motive.*

MOTIVE A *motive* is a reason that explains or partially explains a character's thoughts, feelings, actions, or speech. Writers try to make their characters' motives, or motivations, as clear as possible. If the motives of a main character are not clear, then the character will not be believable.

Characters are often motivated by needs, such as food and shelter. They are also motivated by feelings, such as fear, love, and pride. Motives may be obvious or hidden.

MYTH A *myth* is a fictional tale that explains the actions of gods or heroes or the origins of elements of nature. Myths are part of the oral tradition. They are composed orally and then passed from generation to generation by word of mouth. Every ancient culture has its own mythology, or collection of myths. Greek and Roman myths are known collectively as *classical mythology.*

See *Oral Tradition.*

NARRATION *Narration* is writing that tells a story. The act of telling a story is also called narration. Each piece is a *narrative.* A story told in fiction, nonfiction, poetry, or even drama is called a narrative.

See *Narrative, Narrative Poem,* and *Narrator.*

NARRATIVE A *narrative* is a story. A narrative can be either fiction or nonfiction. Novels and short stories are types of fictional narratives. Biographies and autobiographies are nonfiction narratives. Poems that tell stories are also narratives.

See *Narration* and *Narrative Poem.*

NARRATIVE POEM A *narrative poem* is a story told in verse. Narrative poems often have all the elements of short stories, including characters, conflict, and plot.

NARRATOR A *narrator* is a speaker or a character who tells a story. The narrator's perspective is the way he or she sees things. A *third-person narrator* is one who stands outside the action and speaks about it. A *first-person narrator* is one who tells a story and participates in its action.

See *Point of View.*

NONFICTION *Nonfiction* is prose writing that presents and explains ideas or that tells about real people, places, objects, or events. Autobiographies, biographies, essays, reports, letters, memos, and newspaper articles are all types of nonfiction.

See *Fiction.*

NOVEL A *novel* is a long work of fiction. Novels contain such elements as characters, plot, conflict, and setting. The writer of novels, or novelist, develops these elements. In addition to its main plot, a novel may contain one or more subplots, or independent, related stories. A novel may also have several themes.

See *Fiction* and *Short Story.*

NOVELLA A fiction work that is longer than a short story but shorter than a novel.

ONOMATOPOEIA *Onomatopoeia* is the use of words that imitate sounds. *Crash, buzz, screech, hiss, neigh, jingle,* and *cluck* are examples of onomatopoeia. *Chickadee, towhee,* and *whippoorwill* are onomatopoeic names of birds.

Onomatopoeia can help put the reader in the activity of a poem.

ORAL TRADITION *Oral tradition* is the passing of songs, stories, and poems from generation to generation by word of mouth. Folk songs, folk tales, legends, and myths all come from the oral tradition. No one knows who first created these stories and poems.

See *Folk Tale, Legend,* and *Myth.*

OXYMORON An *oxymoron* (pl. *oxymora*) is a figure of speech that links two opposite or contradictory words in order to point out an idea or situation that seems contradictory or inconsistent but on closer inspection turns out to be somehow true.

PERSONIFICATION *Personification* is a type of figurative language in which a nonhuman subject is given human characteristics.

PERSPECTIVE See *Narrator* and *Point of View.*

PERSUASION *Persuasion* is used in writing or speech that attempts to convince the reader or listener to adopt a particular opinion or course of action. Newspaper editorials and letters to the editor use persuasion. So do advertisements and campaign speeches given by political candidates. An *argument* is a logical way of presenting a belief, conclusion, or stance. A good argument is supported with reasoning and evidence.

See *Essay.*

PLAYWRIGHT A *playwright* is a person who writes plays. William Shakespeare is regarded as the greatest playwright in English literature.

PLOT *Plot* is the sequence of events in which each event results from a previous one and causes the next. In most novels, dramas, short stories, and narrative poems, the plot involves both characters and a central conflict. The plot usually begins with an *exposition* that introduces the setting, the characters, and the basic situation. This is followed by the *inciting incident,* which introduces the central conflict. The conflict then increases during the *development* until it reaches a high point of interest or suspense, the *climax.* The climax is followed by the *falling action,* or end, of the central conflict. Any events that occur during the *falling action* make up the *resolution* or *denouement.*

Some plots do not have all of these parts. Some stories begin with the inciting incident and end with the resolution.

See *Conflict.*

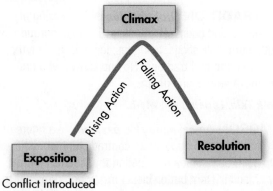

Conflict introduced

POETRY *Poetry* is one of the three major types of literature, the others being prose and drama. Most poems make use of highly concise, musical, and emotionally charged language. Many also make use of imagery, figurative language, and special devices of sound such as rhyme. Major types of poetry include *lyric poetry, narrative poetry,* and *concrete poetry.*

See *Concrete Poem, Genre, Lyric Poem,* and *Narrative Poem.*

POINT OF VIEW *Point of view* is the perspective, or vantage point, from which a story is told. It is either a narrator outside the story or a character in the story. *First-person point of view* is told by a character who uses the first-person pronoun "I."

The two kinds of *third-person point of view,* limited and omniscient, are called "third person" because the narrator uses third-person pronouns such as he and she to refer to the characters. There is no "I" telling the story.

In stories told from the *omniscient third-person point of view,* the narrator knows and tells about what each character feels and thinks.

In stories told from the *limited third-person point of view,* the narrator relates the inner thoughts and feelings of only one character, and everything is viewed from this character's perspective.

See *Narrator.*

PROBLEM See *Conflict.*

PROSE *Prose* is the ordinary form of written language. Most writing that is not poetry, drama, or song is considered prose. Prose is one of the major genres of literature and occurs in fiction and nonfiction.

See *Fiction, Genre,* and *Nonfiction.*

PROTAGONIST The *protagonist* is the main character in a literary work. Often, the protagonist is a person, but sometimes it can be an animal.

See *Antagonist* and *Character.*

REFRAIN A *refrain* is a regularly repeated line or group of lines in a poem or a song.

REPETITION *Repetition* is the use, more than once, of any element of language—a sound, word, phrase, clause, or sentence. Repetition is used in both prose and poetry.

See *Alliteration, Meter, Plot, Rhyme,* and *Rhyme Scheme.*

RESOLUTION The *resolution* is the outcome of the conflict in a plot.

See *Plot.*

RHYME *Rhyme* is the repetition of sounds at the ends of words. Poets use rhyme to lend a songlike quality to their verses and to emphasize certain words and ideas. Many traditional poems contain *end rhymes,* or rhyming words at the ends of lines.

Another common device is the use of *internal rhymes,* or rhyming words within lines. Internal rhyme also emphasizes the flowing nature of a poem.

See *Rhyme Scheme.*

RHYME SCHEME A *rhyme scheme* is a regular pattern of rhyming words in a poem. To indicate the rhyme scheme of a poem, one uses lowercase letters. Each rhyme is assigned a different letter, as follows in the first stanza of "Dust of Snow" by Robert Frost:

The way a crow	*a*
Shook down on me	*b*
The dust of snow	*a*
From a hemlock tree	*b*

Thus, the stanza has the rhyme scheme *abab*.

RHYTHM *Rhythm* is the pattern of stressed and unstressed syllables in spoken or written language.

See *Meter*.

ROUND CHARACTER See *Character*.

SCENE A *scene* is a section of uninterrupted action in the act of a drama.

See *Drama*.

SCIENCE FICTION *Science fiction* combines elements of fiction and fantasy with scientific fact. Many science-fiction stories are set in the future.

SENSORY LANGUAGE *Sensory language* is writing or speech that appeals to one or more of the five senses.

See *Images*.

SETTING The *setting* of a literary work is the time and place of the action. The setting includes all the details of a place and time—the year, the time of day, even the weather. The place may be a specific country, state, region, community, neighborhood, building, institution, or home. Details such as dialects, clothing, customs, and modes of transportation are often used to establish setting. In most stories, the setting serves as a backdrop—a context in which the characters interact. Setting can also help to create a feeling, or atmosphere.

See *Atmosphere*.

SHORT STORY A *short story* is a brief work of fiction. Like a novel, a short story presents a sequence of events, or plot. The plot usually deals with a central conflict faced by a main character, or protagonist. The events in a short story usually communicate a message about life or human nature. This message, or central idea, is the story's theme.

See *Conflict, Plot,* and *Theme*.

SIMILE A *simile* is a figure of speech that uses *like* or *as* to make a direct comparison between two unlike ideas. Everyday speech often contains similes, such as "pale as a ghost," "good as gold," "spread like wildfire," and "clever as a fox."

SOUND DEVICES *Sound devices* are techniques used by writers to give musical effects to their writing. Some of these include *onomatopoeia, alliteration, rhyme, meter,* and *repetition*.

SPEAKER The *speaker* is the imaginary voice a poet uses when writing a poem. The speaker is the character who tells the poem. This character, or voice, often is not identified by name. There can be important differences between the poet and the poem's speaker.

See *Narrator*.

SPEECH A *speech* is a work that is delivered orally to an audience. There are many kinds of speeches suiting almost every kind of public gathering. Types of speeches include *dramatic, persuasive,* and *informative*.

STAGE DIRECTIONS *Stage directions* are notes included in a drama to describe how the work is to be performed or staged. Stage directions are usually printed in italics and enclosed within parentheses or brackets. Some stage directions describe the movements, costumes, emotional states, and ways of speaking of the characters.

STAGING *Staging* includes the setting, lighting, costumes, special effects, and music that go into a stage performance of a drama.

See *Drama*.

STANZA A *stanza* is a group of lines of poetry that are usually similar in length and pattern and are separated by spaces. A stanza is like a paragraph of poetry—it states and develops a single main idea.

STATIC CHARACTER See *Character*.

SURPRISE ENDING A *surprise ending* is a conclusion that is unexpected. The reader has certain expectations about the ending based on details in the story. Often, a surprise ending is *foreshadowed,* or subtly hinted at, in the course of the work.

See *Foreshadowing* and *Plot*.

SUSPENSE *Suspense* is a feeling of anxious uncertainty about the outcome of events in a literary work. Writers create suspense by raising questions in the minds of their readers.

SYMBOL A *symbol* is anything that stands for or represents something else. Symbols are common in everyday life. A dove with an olive branch in its beak is a symbol of peace. A blindfolded woman holding a balanced scale is a symbol of justice. A crown is a symbol of a king's status and authority.

SYMBOLISM *Symbolism* is the use of symbols. Symbolism plays an important role in many different types of literature. It can highlight certain elements the author wishes to emphasize and also add levels of meaning.

THEME The *theme* is a central message in a literary work. A theme can usually be expressed as a generalization, or a general statement, about human beings or about life. The theme of a work is not a summary of its plot. The theme is the writer's central idea.

Although a theme may be stated directly in the text, it is more often presented indirectly. When the theme is stated indirectly, or implied, the reader must figure out what the theme is by looking at what the work reveals about people or life.

TONE The *tone* of a literary work is the writer's attitude toward his or her audience and subject. The tone can often be described by a single adjective, such as *formal* or *informal, serious* or *playful, bitter* or *ironic.* Factors that contribute to the tone are word choice, sentence structure, line length, rhyme, rhythm, and repetition.

TRAGEDY A *tragedy* is a work of literature, especially a play, that results in a catastrophe for the main character. In ancient Greek drama, the main character is always a significant person—a king or a hero—and the cause of the tragedy is a tragic flaw, or weakness, in his or her character. In modern drama, the main character can be an ordinary person, and the cause of the tragedy can be some evil in society itself. The purpose of tragedy is not only to arouse fear and pity in the audience, but also, in some cases, to convey a sense of the grandeur and nobility of the human spirit.

TURNING POINT See *Climax.*

UNIVERSAL THEME A *universal theme* is a message about life that is expressed regularly in many different cultures and time periods. Folk tales, epics, and romances often address universal themes like the importance of courage, the power of love, or the danger of greed.

WORD CHOICE See *Diction.*

Tips for Literature Circles

As you read and study literature, discussions with other readers can help you understand and enjoy what you have read. Use the following tips.

- ## Understand the purpose of your discussion

  Your purpose when you discuss literature is to broaden your understanding of a work by testing your own ideas and hearing the ideas of others. Keep your comments focused on the literature you are discussing. Starting with one focus question will help to keep your discussion on track.

- ## Communicate effectively

  Effective communication requires thinking before speaking. Plan the points that you want to make and decide how you will express them. Organize these points in logical order and use details from the work to support your ideas. Jot down informal notes to help keep your ideas focused.

  Remember to speak clearly, pronouncing words slowly and carefully. Also, listen attentively when others are speaking, and avoid interrupting.

- ## Consider other ideas and interpretations

  A work of literature can generate a wide variety of responses in different readers. Be open to the idea that many interpretations can be valid. To support your own ideas, point to the events, descriptions, characters, or other literary elements in the work that led to your interpretation. To consider someone else's ideas, decide whether details in the work support the interpretation he or she presents. Be sure to convey your criticism of the ideas of others in a respectful and supportive manner.

- ## Ask questions

  Ask questions to clarify your understanding of another reader's ideas. You can also use questions to call attention to possible areas of confusion, to points that are open to debate, or to errors in the speaker's points. To move a discussion forward, summarize and evaluate conclusions reached by the group members.

  When you meet with a group to discuss literature, use a chart like the one shown to analyze the discussion.

Work Being Discussed:	
Focus Question:	
Your Response:	Another Student's Response:
Supporting Evidence:	Supporting Evidence:

Tips for Improving Reading Fluency

When you were younger, you learned to read. Then, you read to expand your experiences or for pure enjoyment. Now, you are expected to read to learn. As you progress in school, you are given more and more material to read. The tips on these pages will help you improve your reading fluency, or your ability to read easily, smoothly, and expressively.

Keeping Your Concentration

One common problem that readers face is the loss of concentration. When you are reading an assignment, you might find yourself rereading the same sentence several times without really understanding it. The first step in changing this behavior is to notice that you do it. Becoming an active, aware reader will help you get the most from your assignments. Practice using these strategies:

- Cover what you have already read with a note card as you go along. Then, you will not be able to reread without noticing that you are doing it.

- Set a purpose for reading beyond just completing the assignment. Then, read actively by pausing to ask yourself questions about the material as you read.

- Use the Reading Strategy instruction and notes that appear with each selection in this textbook.

- Stop reading after a specified period of time (for example, 5 minutes) and summarize what you have read. To help you with this strategy, use the Reading Check questions that appear with each selection in this textbook. Reread to find any answers you do not know.

Reading Phrases

Fluent readers read phrases rather than individual words. Reading this way will speed up your reading and improve your comprehension. Here are some useful ideas:

- Experts recommend rereading as a strategy to increase fluency. Choose a passage of text that is neither too hard nor too easy. Read the same passage aloud several times until you can read it smoothly. When you can read the passage fluently, pick another passage and keep practicing.

- Read aloud into a tape recorder. Then, listen to the recording, noting your accuracy, pacing, and expression. You can also read aloud and share feedback with a partner.

- Use *Hear It!* Prentice Hall Literature Audio program CDs to hear the selections read aloud. Read along silently in your textbook, noticing how the reader uses his or her voice and emphasizes certain words and phrases.

Understanding Key Vocabulary

If you do not understand some of the words in an assignment, you may miss out on important concepts. Therefore, it is helpful to keep a dictionary nearby when you are reading. Follow these steps:

- Before you begin reading, scan the text for unfamiliar words or terms. Find out what those words mean before you begin reading.

- Use context—the surrounding words, phrases, and sentences—to help you determine the meanings of unfamiliar words.

- If you are unable to understand the meaning through context, refer to the dictionary.

Paying Attention to Punctuation

When you read, pay attention to punctuation. Commas, periods, exclamation points, semicolons, and colons tell you when to pause or stop. They also indicate relationships between groups of words. When you recognize these relationships you will read with greater understanding and expression. Look at the chart below.

Punctuation Mark	Meaning
comma	brief pause
period	pause at the end of a thought
exclamation point	pause that indicates emphasis
semicolon	pause between related but distinct thoughts
colon	pause before giving explanation or examples

Using the Reading Fluency Checklist

Use the checklist below each time you read a selection in this textbook. In your Language Arts journal or notebook, note which skills you need to work on and chart your progress each week.

Reading Fluency Checklist
☐ Preview the text to check for difficult or unfamiliar words.
☐ Practice reading aloud.
☐ Read according to punctuation.
☐ Break down long sentences into the subject and its meaning.
☐ Read groups of words for meaning rather than reading single words.
☐ Read with expression (change your tone of voice to add meaning to the word).

Reading is a skill that can be improved with practice. The key to improving your fluency is to read. The more you read, the better your reading will become.

Types of Writing

Good writing can be a powerful tool used for many purposes. Writing can allow you to defend something you believe in or to show how much you know about a subject. Writing can also help you share what you have experienced, imagined, thought, and felt. The three main types of writing are argument, informative/explanatory, and narrative.

Argument

When you think of the word *argument*, you might think of a disagreement between two people, but an argument is more than that. An argument is a logical way of presenting a belief, conclusion, or stance. A good argument is supported with reasoning and evidence.

Argument writing can be used for many purposes, such as to change a reader's point of view or opinion or to bring about an action or a response from a reader.

There are three main purposes for writing a formal argument:

- to change the reader's mind

- to convince the reader to accept what is written

- to motivate the reader to take action, based on what is written

The following are some types of argument writing:

Advertisements An advertisement is a planned message meant to be seen, heard, or read. It attempts to persuade an audience to buy a product or service, accept an idea, or support a cause. Advertisements may appear in print, online, or in broadcast form.

Several common types of advertisements are public-service announcements, billboards, merchandise ads, service ads, and political campaign literature.

Persuasive Essay A persuasive essay presents a position on an issue, urges readers to accept that position, and may encourage a specific action. An effective persuasive essay

- Explores an issue of importance to the writer

- Addresses an issue that is arguable

- Uses facts, examples, statistics, or personal experiences to support a position

- Tries to influence the audience through appeals to the readers' knowledge, experiences, or emotions

- Uses clear organization to present a logical argument

Forms of persuasion include editorials, position papers, persuasive speeches, grant proposals, advertisements, and debates.

Informative/Explanatory

Informative/explanatory writing should rely on facts to inform or explain. Informative/explanatory writing serves some closely related purposes: to increase readers' knowledge of a subject, to help readers better understand a procedure or process, or to provide readers with an enhanced comprehension of a concept. It should also feature a clear introduction, body, and conclusion. The following are some examples of informative/explanatory writing:

Cause-and-Effect Essay A cause-and-effect essay examines the relationship between events, explaining how one event or situation causes another. A successful cause-and-effect essay includes

- A discussion of a cause, event, or condition that produces a specific result

- An explanation of an effect, outcome, or result

- Evidence and examples to support the relationship between cause and effect

- A logical organization that makes the explanation clear

Comparison-and-Contrast Essay A comparison-and-contrast essay analyzes the similarities and differences between or among two or more things. An effective comparison-and-contrast essay

- Identifies a purpose for comparison and contrast

- Identifies similarities and differences between or among two or more things, people, places, or ideas

- Gives factual details about the subjects

- Uses an organizational plan suited to the topic and purpose

Descriptive Writing Descriptive writing creates a vivid picture of a person, place, thing, or event. Most descriptive writing includes

- Sensory details—sights, sounds, smells, tastes, and physical sensations

- Vivid, precise language

- Figurative language or comparisons

- Adjectives and adverbs that paint a word picture

- An organization suited to the subject

Types of descriptive writing include descriptions of ideas, observations, remembrances, travel brochures, physical descriptions, functional descriptions, and character sketches.

Problem-and-Solution Essay A problem-and-solution essay describes a problem and offers one or more solutions to it. It describes a clear set of steps to achieve a result. An effective problem-and-solution essay includes

- A clear statement of the problem, with its causes and effects summarized for the reader

- The most important aspects of the problem

- A proposal of at least one realistic solution

- Facts, statistics, data, or expert testimony to support the solution

- A clear organization that makes the relationship between problem and solution obvious

Research Writing Research writing is based on information gathered from outside sources. A research paper—a focused study of a topic—helps writers explore and connect ideas, make discoveries, and share their findings with an audience. An effective research paper

- Focuses on a specific, narrow topic, which is usually summarized in a thesis statement

- Presents relevant information from a wide variety of sources

- Uses a clear organization that includes an introduction, body, and conclusion

- Includes a bibliography or works-cited list that identifies the sources from which the information was drawn

Other types of writing that depend on accurate and insightful research include multimedia presentations, statistical reports, annotated bibliographies, and experiment journals.

Workplace Writing Workplace writing is probably the format you will use most after you finish school. In general, workplace writing is fact-based and meant to communicate specific information in a structured format. Effective workplace writing

- Communicates information concisely

- Includes details that provide necessary information and anticipate potential questions

- Is error-free and neatly presented

Common types of workplace writing include business letters, memorandums, résumés, forms, and applications.

Narrative

Narrative writing conveys experience, either real or imaginary, and uses time to provide structure. It can be used to inform, instruct, persuade, or entertain. Whenever writers tell a of story, they are using narrative writing. Most narrative-writing types share certain elements, such as characters, a setting, a sequence of events, and, often, a theme. The following are some types of narration:

Autobiographical Writing Autobiographical writing tells a true story about an important period, experience, or relationship in the writer's life. Effective autobiographical writing includes

- A series of events that involve the writer as the main character

- Details, thoughts, feelings, and insights from the writer's perspective

- A conflict or an event that affects the writer

- A logical organization that tells the story clearly

- Insights that the writer gained from the experience

Types of autobiographical writing include personal narratives, autobiographical sketches, reflective essays, eyewitness accounts, and memoirs.

Short Story A short story is a brief, creative narrative. Most short stories include

- Details that establish the setting in time and place

- A main character who undergoes a change or learns something during the course of the story

- A conflict or a problem to be introduced, developed, and resolved

- A plot, the series of events that make up the action of the story

- A theme or message about life

Types of short stories include realistic stories, fantasies, historical narratives, mysteries, thrillers, science-fiction stories, and adventure stories.

Writing Friendly Letters

Writing Friendly Letters

A friendly letter is much less formal than a business letter. It is a letter to a friend, a family member, or anyone with whom the writer wants to communicate in a personal, friendly way. Most friendly letters are made up of five parts:

- ✔ the heading
- ✔ the salutation, or greeting
- ✔ the body
- ✔ the closing
- ✔ the signature

The purpose of a friendly letter is often one of the following:

- ✔ to share personal news and feelings
- ✔ to send or to answer an invitation
- ✔ to express thanks

Model Friendly Letter

In this friendly letter, Betsy thanks her grandparents for a birthday present and gives them some news about her life.

11 Old Farm Road
Topsham, Maine 04011

April 14, 20—

Dear Grandma and Grandpa,

    Thank you for the sweater you sent me for my birthday. It fits perfectly, and I love the color. I wore my new sweater to the carnival at school last weekend and got lots of compliments.

    The weather here has been cool but sunny. Mom thinks that "real" spring will never come. I can't wait until it's warm enough to go swimming.

    School is going fairly well. I really like my Social Studies class. We are learning about the U.S. Constitution, and I think it's very interesting. Maybe I will be a lawyer when I grow up.

    When are you coming out to visit us? We haven't seen you since Thanksgiving. You can stay in my room when you come. I'll be happy to sleep on the couch. (The TV is in that room!!)

    Well, thanks again and hope all is well with you.

Love,

Betsy

> The **heading** includes the writer's address and the date on which he or she wrote the letter.

> The **body** is the main part of the letter and contains the basic message.

> Some common **closings** for personal letters include "Best wishes," "Love "Sincerely," and "Yours truly."

Writing Business Letters

Formatting Business Letters

Business letters follow one of several acceptable formats. In **block format,** each part of the letter begins at the left margin. A double space is used between paragraphs. In **modified block format,** some parts of the letter are indented to the center of the page. No matter which format is used, all letters in business format have a heading, an inside address, a salutation or greeting, a body, a closing, and a signature. These parts are shown and annotated on the model business letter below, formatted in modified block style.

Model Business Letter

In this letter, Yolanda Dodson uses modified block format to request information.

Students for a Cleaner Planet
c/o Memorial High School
333 Veteran's Drive
Denver, CO 80211

January 25, 20—

Steven Wilson, Director
Resource Recovery Really Works
300 Oak Street
Denver, CO 80216

Dear Mr. Wilson:

Memorial High School would like to start a branch of your successful recycling program. We share your commitment to reclaiming as much reusable material as we can. Because your program has been successful in other neighborhoods, we're sure that it can work in our community. Our school includes grades 9–12 and has about 800 students.

Would you send us some information about your community recycling program? For example, we need to know what materials can be recycled and how we can implement the program.

At least fifty students have already expressed an interest in getting involved, so I know we'll have the people power to make the program work. Please help us get started.

Thank you in advance for your time and consideration.

Sincerely,

Yolanda Dodson

Yolanda Dodson

The **heading** shows the writer's address and organization (if any) and the date.

The **inside address** indicates where the letter will be sent.

A **salutation** is punctuated by a colon. When the specific addressee is not known, use a general greeting such as "To whom it may concern:"

The **body** of the letter states the writer's purpose. In this case, the writer requests information.

The **closing** "Sincerely" is common, but "Yours truly" or "Respectfully yours" are also acceptable. To end the letter, the writer types her name and provides a **signature.**

21st-Century Skills

New technology has created many new ways to communicate. Today, it is easy to contribute information to the Internet and send a variety of messages to friends far and near. You can also share your ideas through photos, illustrations, video, and sound recordings. *21st Century Skills* gives you an overview of some ways you can use today's technology to create, share, and find information. Here are the topics you will find in this section.

- ✔ Blogs
- ✔ Multimedia Elements
- ✔ Social Networking
- ✔ Podcasts
- ✔ Widgets and Feeds
- ✔ Wikis

BLOGS

A **blog** is a common form of online writing. The word *blog* is a contraction of *Web log*. Most blogs include a series of entries known as *posts*. The posts appear in a single column and are displayed in reverse chronological order. That means that the most recent post is at the top of the page. As you scroll down, you will find earlier posts.

Blogs have become increasingly popular. Researchers estimate that 75,000 new blogs are launched every day. Blog authors are often called *bloggers*. They can use their personal sites to share ideas, songs, videos, photos, and other media. People who read blogs can often post their responses with a comments feature found in each new post.

Because blogs are designed so that they are easy to update, bloggers can post new messages as often as they like, often daily. For some people blogs become a public journal or diary, in which they share their thoughts about daily events.

Types of Blogs

Not all blogs are the same. Many blogs have a single author, but others are group projects. These are some common types of blog:

- ✔ Personal blogs often have a general focus. Bloggers post their thoughts on any topic they find interesting in their daily lives.

- ✔ Topical blogs focus on a specific theme, such as movie reviews, political news, class assignments, or health-care opportunities.

Web Safety

Always be aware that information you post on the Internet can be read by everyone with access to that page. Once you post a picture or text, it can be saved on someone else's computer, even if you later remove it.

Using the Internet safely means keeping personal information personal. Never include your address (e-mail or real), last name, or telephone numbers. Avoid mentioning places you can be frequently found. Never give out passwords you use to access other Web sites and do not respond to e-mails from people you do not know.

Anatomy of a Blog

Here are some of the features you can include in a blog.

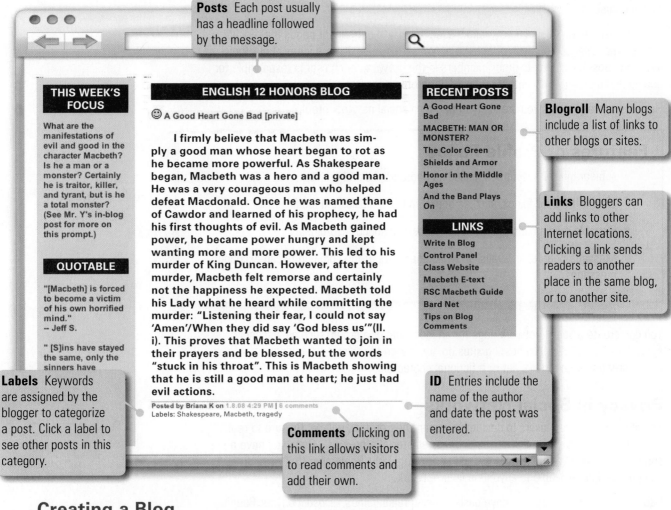

Posts Each post usually has a headline followed by the message.

Blogroll Many blogs include a list of links to other blogs or sites.

Links Bloggers can add links to other Internet locations. Clicking a link sends readers to another place in the same blog, or to another site.

Labels Keywords are assigned by the blogger to categorize a post. Click a label to see other posts in this category.

Comments Clicking on this link allows visitors to read comments and add their own.

ID Entries include the name of the author and date the post was entered.

THIS WEEK'S FOCUS

What are the manifestations of evil and good in the character Macbeth? Is he a man or a monster? Certainly he is traitor, killer, and tyrant, but is he a total monster? (See Mr. Y's in-blog post for more on this prompt.)

QUOTABLE

"[Macbeth] is forced to become a victim of his own horrified mind."
— Jeff S.

" [S]ins have stayed the same, only the sinners have

ENGLISH 12 HONORS BLOG

☺ A Good Heart Gone Bad [private]

    I firmly believe that Macbeth was simply a good man whose heart began to rot as he became more powerful. As Shakespeare began, Macbeth was a hero and a good man. He was a very courageous man who helped defeat Macdonald. Once he was named thane of Cawdor and learned of his prophecy, he had his first thoughts of evil. As Macbeth gained power, he became power hungry and kept wanting more and more power. This led to his murder of King Duncan. However, after the murder, Macbeth felt remorse and certainly not the happiness he expected. Macbeth told his Lady what he heard while committing the murder: "Listening their fear, I could not say 'Amen'/When they did say 'God bless us'"(II. i). This proves that Macbeth wanted to join in their prayers and be blessed, but the words "stuck in his throat". This is Macbeth showing that he is still a good man at heart; he just had evil actions.

Posted by Briana K on 1.8.08 4:29 PM | 6 comments
Labels: Shakespeare, Macbeth, tragedy

RECENT POSTS

A Good Heart Gone Bad
MACBETH: MAN OR MONSTER?
The Color Green
Shields and Armor
Honor in the Middle Ages
And the Band Plays On

LINKS

Write In Blog
Control Panel
Class Website
Macbeth E-text
RSC Macbeth Guide
Bard Net
Tips on Blog Comments

Creating a Blog

Keep these hints and strategies in mind to help you create an interesting and fair blog:

- ✔ Focus each blog entry on a single topic.

- ✔ Vary the length of your posts. Sometimes, all you need is a line or two to share a quick thought. Other posts will be much longer.

- ✔ Choose font colors and styles that can be read easily.

- ✔ Many people scan blogs rather than read them closely. You can make your main ideas pop out by using clear or clever headlines and boldfacing key terms.

- ✔ Give credit to other people's work and ideas. State the names of people whose ideas you are quoting or add a link to take readers to that person's blog or site.

- ✔ If you post comments, try to make them brief and polite.

SOCIAL NETWORKING

Social networking means any interaction between members of an online community. People can exchange many different kinds of information, from text and voice messages to video images.

Many social network communities allow users to create permanent pages that describe themselves. Users create home pages to express themselves, share ideas about their lives, and post messages to other members in the network. Each user is responsible for adding and updating the content on his or her profile page.

Here are some features you are likely to find on a social network profile:

Features of Profile Pages

- A biographical description, including photographs and artwork.

- Lists of favorite things, such as books, movies, music, and fashions.

- Playable media elements such as videos and sound recordings.

- Message boards, or "walls" in which members of the community can exchange messages.

You can create a social network page for an individual or a group, such as a school or special interest club. Many hosting sites do not charge to register, so you can also have fun by creating a page for a pet or a fictional character.

Privacy in Social Networks

Social networks allow users to decide how open their profiles will be. Be sure to read introductory information carefully before you register at a new site. Once you have a personal profile page, monitor your privacy settings regularly. Remember that any information you post will be available to anyone in your network.

Users often post messages anonymously or using false names, or *pseudonyms*. People can also post using someone else's name. Judge all information on the net critically. Do not assume that you know who posted some information simply because you recognize the name of the post author. The rapid speed of communication on the Internet can make it easy to jump to conclusions—be careful to avoid this trap.

Tips for Sending Effective Messages

Technology makes it easy to share ideas quickly, but writing for the Internet poses some special challenges, as well. The writing style for blogs and social networks is often very conversational. In blog posts and comments, instant messages, and e-mails, writers often express themselves very quickly, using relaxed language, short sentences, and abbreviations. However, in a conversation, we get a lot of information from a speaker's tone of voice and body language. On the Internet, those clues are missing. As a result, Internet writers often use italics or bracketed labels to indicate emotions. Another alternative is using *emoticons*—strings of characters that give visual clues to indicate emotion:

:-) smile (happy)	:-(frown (unhappy)	;-) wink (light sarcasm)

Use these strategies to communicate effectively when using technology:

✔ Reread your messages. Before you click *Send,* read your message through and make sure that your tone will be clear to the reader.

✔ Do not jump to conclusions—ask for clarification first. Make sure you really understand what someone is saying before you respond.

✔ Use abbreviations your reader will understand.

WIDGETS AND FEEDS

A **widget** is a small application that performs a specific task. You might find widgets that give weather predictions, offer dictionary definitions or translations, provide entertainment such as games, or present a daily word, photograph, or quotation.

A **feed** is a special kind of widget. It displays headlines taken from the latest content on a specific media source. Clicking on the headline will take you to the full article.

Many social network communities and other Web sites allow you to personalize your home page by adding widgets and feeds.

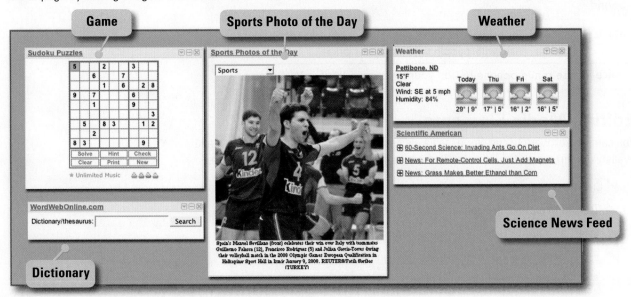

MULTIMEDIA ELEMENTS

One of the great advantages of communicating on the Internet is that you are not limited to using text only. When you create a Web profile or blog, you can share your ideas using a wide variety of media. In addition to widgets and feeds (see page R31), these media elements can make your Internet communication more entertaining and useful.

Graphics

Graphics	
Photographs	You can post photos taken by digital cameras.
Illustrations	Artwork can be created using computer software. You can also use a scanner to post a digital image of a drawing or sketch.
Charts, Graphs, and Maps	Charts and graphs can make statistical information clear. Use spreadsheet software to create these elements. Use Internet sites to find maps of specific places.

Video

Video	
Live Action	Digital video can be recorded by a camera or recorded from another media source.
Animation	Animated videos can also be created using software.

Sound

Sound	
Music	Many social network communities make it easy to share your favorite music with people who visit your page.
Voice	Use a microphone to add your own voice to your Web page.

Editing Media Elements

You can use software to customize media elements. Open source software is free and available to anyone on the Internet. Here are some things you can do with software:

✔ Crop a photograph to focus on the subject or brighten an image that is too dark.

✔ Transform a drawing's appearance from flat to three-dimensional.

✔ Insert a "You Are Here" arrow on a map.

✔ Edit a video or sound file to shorten its running time.

✔ Add background music or sound effects to a video.

PODCASTS

A **podcast** is a digital audio or video recording of a program that is made available on the Internet. Users can replay the podcast on a computer, or download it and replay it on a personal audio player. You might think of podcasts as radio or television programs that you create yourself. They can be embedded on a Web site or fed to a Web page through a podcast widget.

Creating an Effective Podcast

To make a podcast, you will need a recording device, such as a microphone or digital video camera, as well as editing software. Open source editing software is widely available and free of charge. Most audio podcasts are converted into the MP3 format. Here are some tips for creating a podcast that is clear and entertaining:

- ✔ Listen to several podcasts by different authors to get a feeling for the medium. Make a list of features and styles you like and also those you want to avoid.

- ✔ Test your microphone to find the best recording distance. Stand close enough to the microphone so that your voice sounds full, but not so close that you create an echo.

- ✔ Create an outline that shows your estimated timing for each element.

- ✔ Be prepared before you record. Rehearse, but do not create a script. Podcasts are best when they have a natural, easy flow.

- ✔ Talk directly to your listeners. Slow down enough so they can understand you.

- ✔ Use software to edit your podcast before publishing it. You can edit out mistakes or add additional elements.

WIKIS

A **wiki** is a collaborative Web site that lets visitors create, add, remove, and edit content. The term comes from the Hawaiian phrase *wiki wiki,* which means "quick." Web users at a wiki are both the readers and the writers of the site. Some wikis are open to contributions from anyone. Others require visitors to register before they can edit the content.

All of the text in these collaborative Web sites was written by people who use the site. Articles are constantly changing, as visitors find and correct errors and improve texts.

Wikis have both advantages and disadvantages as sources of information. They are valuable open forums for the exchange of ideas. The unique collaborative writing process allows entries to change over time. However, entries can also be modified incorrectly. Careless or malicious users can delete good content and add inappropriate or inaccurate information.

You can change the information on a wiki, but be sure your information is correct and clear before you add it. Wikis keep track of all changes, so your work will be recorded and can be evaluated by other users.

Citing Sources and Preparing Manuscript

Proofreading and Preparing Manuscript

Before preparing a final copy, proofread your manuscript. The chart shows the standard symbols for marking corrections to be made.

Proofreading Symbols	
Insert	$\wedge$
delete	✐
close space	$\bigcirc$
new paragraph	¶
add comma	⌃
add period	⊙
transpose (switch)	∩
change to cap	a̲
change to lowercase	ⱥ

- Choose a standard, easy-to-read font.
- Type or print on one side of unlined 8 1/2" x 11" paper.
- Set the margins for the side, top, and bottom of your paper at approximately one inch. Most word-processing programs have a default setting that is appropriate.
- Double-space the document.
- Indent the first line of each paragraph.
- Number the pages in the upper right corner.

Follow your teacher's directions for formatting formal research papers. Most papers will have the following features:

- Title page
- Table of Contents or Outline
- Works-Cited List

Avoiding Plagiarism

Whether you are presenting a formal research paper or an opinion paper on a current event, you must be careful to give credit for any ideas or opinions that are not your own. Presenting someone else's ideas, research, or opinion as your own—even if you have phrased it in different words—is *plagiarism,* the equivalent of academic stealing, or fraud.

Do not use the ideas or research of others in place of your own. Read from several sources to draw your own conclusions and form your own opinions. Incorporate the ideas and research of others to support your points. Credit the source of the following types of support:

- Statistics
- Direct quotations
- Indirectly quoted statements of opinions
- Conclusions presented by an expert
- Facts available in only one or two sources

Crediting Sources

When you credit a source, you acknowledge where you found your information and you give your readers the details necessary for locating the source themselves. Within the body of the paper, you provide a short citation, a footnote number linked to a footnote, or an endnote number linked to an endnote reference. These brief references show the page numbers on which you found the information. Prepare a reference list at the end of the paper to provide full bibliographic information on your sources. These are two common types of reference lists:

- A bibliography provides a listing of all the resources you consulted during your research.
- A works-cited list indicates the works you have referenced in your paper.

The chart on the next page shows the Modern Language Association format for crediting sources. This is the most common format for papers written in the content areas in middle school and high school. Unless instructed otherwise by your teacher, use this format for crediting sources.

MLA Style for Listing Sources

Book with one author	Pyles, Thomas. *The Origins and Development of the English Language.* 2nd ed. New York: Harcourt, 1971. Print.
Book with two or three authors	McCrum, Robert, William Cran, and Robert MacNeil. *The Story of English.* New York: Penguin, 1987. Print.
Book with an editor	Truth, Sojourner. *Narrative of Sojourner Truth.* Ed. Margaret Washington. New York: Vintage, 1993. Print.
Book with more than three authors or editors	Donald, Robert B., et al. *Writing Clear Essays.* Upper Saddle River: Prentice, 1996. Print.
Single work in an anthology	Hawthorne, Nathaniel. "Young Goodman Brown." *Literature: An Introduction to Reading and Writing.* Ed. Edgar V. Roberts and H. E. Jacobs. Upper Saddle River: Prentice, 1998. 376–385. Print. [Indicate pages for the entire selection.]
Introduction to a work in a published edition	Washington, Margaret. Introduction. *Narrative of Sojourner Truth.* By Sojourner Truth. Ed. Washington. New York: Vintage, 1993. v–xi. Print.
Signed article from an encyclopedia	Askeland, Donald R. "Welding." *World Book Encyclopedia.* 1991 ed. Print.
Signed article in a weekly magazine	Wallace, Charles. "A Vodacious Deal." *Time* 14 Feb. 2000: 63. Print.
Signed article in a monthly magazine	Gustaitis, Joseph. "The Sticky History of Chewing Gum." *American History* Oct. 1998: 30–38. Print.
Newspaper	Thurow, Roger. "South Africans Who Fought for Sanctions Now Scrap for Investors." *Wall Street Journal* 11 Feb. 2000: A1+. Print. [For a multipage article that does not appear on consecutive pages, write only the first page number on which it appears, followed by the plus sign.]
Unsigned editorial or story	"Selective Silence." Editorial. *Wall Street Journal* 11 Feb. 2000: A14. Print. [If the editorial or story is signed, begin with the author's name.]
Signed pamphlet or brochure	[Treat the pamphlet as though it were a book.]
Work from a library subscription service	Ertman, Earl L. "Nefertiti's Eyes." *Archaeology* Mar.–Apr. 2008: 28–32. *Kids Search.* EBSCO. New York Public Library. Web. 18 June 2008 [Indicate the date you accessed the information.]
Filmstrips, slide programs, videocassettes, DVDs, and other audiovisual media	*The Diary of Anne Frank.* Dir. George Stevens. Perf. Millie Perkins, Shelley Winters, Joseph Schildkraut, Lou Jacobi, and Richard Beymer. 1959. Twentieth Century Fox, 2004. DVD.
CD-ROM (with multiple publishers)	Simms, James, ed. *Romeo and Juliet.* By William Shakespeare. Oxford: Attica Cybernetics; London: BBC Education; London: Harper, 1995. CD-ROM.
Radio or television program transcript	"Washington's Crossing of the Delaware." *Weekend Edition Sunday.* Natl. Public Radio. WNYC, New York. 23 Dec. 2003. Television transcript.
Internet Web page	"Fun Facts About Gum." NACGM site. 1999. National Association of Chewing Gum Manufacturers. Web. 19 Dec. 1999 [Indicate the date you accessed the information.]
Personal interview	Smith, Jane. Personal interview. 10 Feb. 2000.

All examples follow the style given in the *MLA Handbook for Writers of Research Papers,* seventh edition, by Joseph Gibaldi.

Guide to Rubrics

What is a rubric?

A rubric is a tool, often in the form of a chart or a grid, that helps you assess your work. Rubrics are particularly helpful for writing and speaking assignments.

To help you or others assess, or evaluate, your work, a rubric offers several specific criteria to be applied to your work. Then the rubric helps you or an evaluator indicate your range of success or failure according to those specific criteria. Rubrics are often used to evaluate writing for standardized tests.

Using a rubric will save you time, focus your learning, and improve the work you do. When you know what the rubric will be before you begin writing a persuasive essay, for example, as you write you will be aware of specific criteria that are important in that kind of an essay. As you evaluate the essay before giving it to your teacher, you will focus on the specific areas that your teacher wants you to master—or on areas that you know present challenges for you. Instead of searching through your work randomly for any way to improve it or correct its errors, you will have a clear and helpful focus on specific criteria.

How are rubrics constructed?

Rubrics can be constructed in several different ways.

- Your teacher may assign a rubric for a specific assignment.

- Your teacher may direct you to a rubric in your text-book.

- Your teacher and your class may construct a rubric for a particular assignment together.

- You and your classmates may construct a rubric together.

- You may create your own rubric with criteria you want to evaluate in your work.

How will a rubric help me?

A rubric will help you assess your work on a scale. Scales vary from rubric to rubric but usually range from 6 to 1, 5 to 1, or 4 to 1, with 6, 5, or 4 being the highest score and 1 being the lowest. If someone else is using the rubric to assess your work, the rubric will give your evaluator a clear range within which to place your work. If you are using the rubric yourself, it will help you make improvements to your work.

What are the types of rubrics?

- A **holistic rubric** has general criteria that can apply to a variety of assignments. See p. R38 for an example of a holistic rubric.

- An **analytic rubric** is specific to a particular assignment. The criteria for evaluation address the specific issues important in that assignment. See p. R37 for examples of analytic rubrics.

Sample Analytic Rubrics

Rubric With a 4-point Scale

*The following analytic rubric is an example of a rubric to assess a persuasive essay.
It will help you evaluate focus, organization, support/elaboration, and style/convention.*

	Focus	Organization	Support/Elaboration	Style/Convention
4	Demonstrates highly effective word choice; clearly focused on task.	Uses clear, consistent organizational strategy.	Provides convincing, well-elaborated reasons to support the position.	Incorporates transitions; includes very few mechanical errors.
3	Demonstrates good word choice; stays focused on persuasive task.	Uses clear organizational strategy with occasional inconsistencies.	Provides two or more moderately elaborated reasons to support the position.	Incorporates some transitions; includes few mechanical errors.
2	Shows some good word choices; minimally stays focused on persuasive task.	Uses inconsistent organizational strategy; presentation is not logical.	Provides several reasons, but few are elaborated; only one elaborated reason.	Incorporates few transitions; includes many mechanical errors.
1	Shows lack of attention to persuasive task.	Demonstrates lack of organizational strategy.	Provides no specific reasons or does not elaborate.	Does not connect ideas; includes many mechanical errors.

Rubric With a 6-point Scale

*The following analytic rubric is an example of a rubric to assess a persuasive essay.
It will help you evaluate presentation, position, evidence, and arguments.*

	Presentation	Position	Evidence	Arguments
6	Essay clearly and effectively addresses an issue with more than one side.	Essay clearly states a supportable position on the issue.	All evidence is logically organized, well presented, and supports the position.	All reader concerns and counterarguments are effectively addressed.
5	Most of essay addresses an issue that has more than one side.	Essay clearly states a position on the issue.	Most evidence is logically organized, well presented, and supports the position.	Most reader concerns and counterarguments are effectively addressed.
4	Essay adequately addresses issue that has more than one side.	Essay adequately states a position on the issue.	Many parts of evidence support the position; some evidence is out of order.	Many reader concerns and counterarguments are adequately addressed.
3	Essay addresses issue with two sides but does not present second side clearly.	Essay states a position on the issue, but the position is difficult to support.	Some evidence supports the position, but some evidence is out of order.	Some reader concerns and counterarguments are addressed.
2	Essay addresses issue with two sides but does not present second side.	Essay states a position on the issue, but the position is not supportable.	Not much evidence supports the position, and what is included is out of order.	A few reader concerns and counterarguments are addressed.
1	Essay does not address issue with more than one side.	Essay does not state a position on the issue.	No evidence supports the position.	No reader concerns or counterarguments are addressed.

Sample Holistic Rubric

Holistic rubrics such as this one are sometimes used to assess writing assignments on standardized tests. Notice that the criteria for evaluation are focus, organization, support, and use of conventions.

Points	Criteria
6 Points	• The writing is strongly focused and shows fresh insight into the writing task. • The writing is marked by a sense of completeness and coherence and is organized with a logical progression of ideas. • A main idea is fully developed, and support is specific and substantial. • A mature command of the language is evident, and the writing may employ characteristic creative writing strategies. • Sentence structure is varied, and writing is free of all but purposefully used fragments. • Virtually no errors in writing conventions appear.
5 Points	• The writing is clearly focused on the task. • The writing is well organized and has a logical progression of ideas, though there may be occasional lapses. • A main idea is well developed and supported with relevant detail. • Sentence structure is varied, and the writing is free of fragments, except when used purposefully. • Writing conventions are followed correctly.
4 Points	• The writing is clearly focused on the task, but extraneous material may intrude at times. • Clear organizational pattern is present, though lapses may occur. • A main idea is adequately supported, but development may be uneven. • Sentence structure is generally fragment free but shows little variation. • Writing conventions are generally followed correctly.
3 Points	• Writing is generally focused on the task, but extraneous material may intrude at times. • An organizational pattern is evident, but writing may lack a logical progression of ideas. • Support for the main idea is generally present but is sometimes illogical. • Sentence structure is generally free of fragments, but there is almost no variation. • The work generally demonstrates a knowledge of writing conventions, with occasional misspellings.
2 Points	• The writing is related to the task but generally lacks focus. • There is little evidence of organizational pattern, and there is little sense of cohesion. • Support for the main idea is generally inadequate, illogical, or absent. • Sentence structure is unvaried, and serious errors may occur. • Errors in writing conventions and spellings are frequent.
1 Point	• The writing may have little connection to the task and is generally unfocused. • There has been little attempt at organization or development. • The paper seems fragmented, with no clear main idea. • Sentence structure is unvaried, and serious errors appear. • Poor word choice and poor command of the language obscure meaning. • Errors in writing conventions and spelling are frequent.
Unscorable	The paper is considered unscorable if: • The response is unrelated to the task or is simply a rewording of the prompt. • The response has been copied from a published work. • The student did not write a response. • The response is illegible. • The words in the response are arranged with no meaning. • There is an insufficient amount of writing to score.

Student Model

Persuasive Writing

This persuasive essay, which would receive a top score according to a persuasive rubric, is a response to the following writing prompt, or assignment:

Most young people today spend more than 5 hours a day watching television. Many adults worry about the effects on youth of seeing too much television violence. Write a persuasive piece in which you argue against or defend the effects of television watching on young people. Be sure to include examples to support your views.

Until the television was invented, families spent their time doing different activities. Now most families stay home and watch TV. Watching TV risks the family's health, reduces the children's study time, and is a bad influence on young minds. Watching television can be harmful.

> The writer clearly states a position in the first paragraph.

The most important reason why watching TV is bad is that the viewers get less exercise. For example, instead of watching their favorite show, people could get exercise for 30 minutes. If people spent less time watching TV and more time exercising, then they could have healthier bodies. My mother told me a story about a man who died of a heart attack because he was out of shape from watching television all the time. Obviously, watching TV put a person's health in danger.

> Each paragraph provides details that support the writer's main point.

Furthermore, watching television reduces children's study time. For example, children would spend more time studying if they didn't watch television. If students spent more time studying at home, then they would make better grades at school. Last week I had a major test in science, but I didn't study because I started watching a movie. I was not prepared for the test and my grade reflected my lack of studying. Indeed, watching television is bad because it can hurt a student's grades.

Finally, watching TV can be a bad influence on children. For example, some TV shows have inappropriate language and too much violence. If children watch programs that use bad language and show violence, then they may start repeating these actions because they think the behavior is "cool." In fact, it has been proven that children copy what they see on TV. Clearly, watching TV is bad for children and it affects children's behavior.

In conclusion, watching television is a bad influence for these reasons: It reduces people's exercise time and students' study time and it shows children inappropriate behavior. Therefore, people should take control of their lives and stop allowing television to harm them.

> The conclusion restates the writer's position.

Grammar, Usage, and Mechanics Handbook

Parts of Speech

Nouns A **noun** is the name of a person, place, or thing. A **common noun** names any one of a class of people, places, or things. A **proper noun** names a specific person, place, or thing.

Common Nouns	**Proper Nouns**
writer	Francisco Jiménez

Use *apostrophes* with nouns to show ownership. Add an apostrophe and *s* to show the **possessive case** of most singular nouns. Add just an apostrophe to show the possessive case of plural nouns ending in *s* or *es*. Add an apostrophe and *s* to show the possessive case of plural nouns that do not end in *s* or *es*.

Pronouns A **pronoun** is a word that stands for a noun or for a word that takes the place of a noun. A **personal pronoun** refers to (1) the person speaking, (2) the person spoken to, or (3) the person, place, or thing spoken about.

	Singular	**Plural**
First Person	I, me, my, mine	we, us, our, ours
Second Person	you, your, yours	you, your, yours
Third Person	he, him, his, she, her, hers, it, its	they, them, their, theirs

A **demonstrative pronoun** directs attention to a specific person, place, or thing.

These are the juiciest pears I have ever tasted.

An **interrogative pronoun** is used to begin a question.

Who is the author of "Jeremiah's Song"?

An **indefinite pronoun** refers to a person, place, or thing, often without specifying which one.

Many of the players were tired.

Everyone bought something.

Verbs A **verb** is a word that expresses time while showing an action, a condition, or the fact that something exists. An **action verb** indicates the action of someone or something. A **linking verb** connects the subject of a sentence with a noun or a pronoun that renames or describes the subject. A **helping verb** can be added to another verb to make a single verb phrase.

Adjectives An **adjective** describes a noun or a pronoun or gives a noun or a pronoun a more specific meaning. Adjectives answer the questions *what kind, which one, how many,* or *how much.*

The articles *the, a,* and *an* are adjectives. *An* is used before a word beginning with a vowel sound.

A noun may sometimes be used as an adjective.

family home   *science* fiction

Adverbs An **adverb** modifies a verb, an adjective, or another adverb. Adverbs answer the questions *where, when, in what way,* or *to what extent.*

Prepositions A **preposition** relates a noun or a pronoun following it to another word in the sentence.

The ball rolled <u>under</u> the table.

Conjunctions A **conjunction** connects other words or groups of words. A **coordinating conjunction** connects similar kinds or groups of words. **Correlative conjunctions** are used in pairs to connect similar words or groups of words.

both Grandpa *and* Dad   *neither* they *nor* I

Interjections An **interjection** is a word that expresses feeling or emotion and functions independently of a sentence.

"Ah!" says he—

Phrases, Clauses, and Sentences

Sentences A **sentence** is a group of words with two main parts: a complete subject and a complete predicate. Together, these parts express a complete thought.

We read that story last year.

A **fragment** is a group of words that does not express a complete thought.

"Not right away."

Subject The **subject** of a sentence is the word or group of words that tells whom or what the sentence is about. The simple subject is the essential noun, pronoun, or group of words acting as a noun that cannot be left out of the complete subject. A **complete subject** is the **simple subject** plus any modifiers. In the following example, the complete subject is underlined. The simple subject is italicized.

<u>Pony express *riders*</u> carried packages for miles.

A **compound subject** is two or more subjects that have the same verb and are joined by a conjunction.

Neither the horse nor the driver looked tired.

Predicate The **predicate** of a sentence is the verb or verb phrase that tells what the complete subject of the sentence does or is. The **simple predicate** is the essential verb or verb phrase that cannot be left out of the complete predicate. A **complete predicate** is the simple predicate plus any modifiers or complements. In the following example, the complete predicate is underlined. The simple predicate is italicized.

Pony express riders <u>*carried* packages for miles.</u>

A **compound predicate** is two or more verbs that have the same subject and are joined by a conjunction.

She *sneezed and coughed* throughout the trip.

Complement A **complement** is a word or group of words that completes the meaning of the predicate of a sentence. Five different kinds of complements can be found in English sentences: *direct objects, indirect objects, objective complements, predicate nominatives,* and *predicate adjectives.*

A **direct object** is a noun, pronoun, or group of words acting as a noun that receives the action of a transitive verb.

> We watched the *liftoff.*

An **indirect object** is a noun, pronoun, or group of words that appears with a direct object and names the person or thing that something is given to or done for.

> He sold the *family* a mirror.

An **objective complement** is an adjective or noun that appears with a direct object and describes or renames it.

> I called Meg my *friend.*

A **subject complement** is a noun, pronoun, or adjective that appears with a linking verb and tells something about the subject. A subject complement may be a *predicate nominative* or a *predicate adjective.*

A **predicate nominative** is a noun or pronoun that appears with a linking verb and renames, or explains the subject.

> Kiglo was the *leader.*

A **predicate adjective** is an adjective that appears with a linking verb and describes the subject of a sentence.

> Roko became *tired.*

Sentence Types There are four types of sentences:

1. A **simple sentence** consists of a single independent clause.
2. A **compound sentence** consists of two or more independent clauses joined by a comma and a coordinating conjunction or by a semicolon.
3. A **complex sentence** consists of one independent clause and one or more subordinate clauses.
4. A **compound-complex sentence** consists of two or more independent clauses and one or more subordinate clauses.

There are four functions of sentences:

1. A **declarative sentence** states an idea and ends with a period.
2. An **interrogative sentence** asks a question and ends with a question mark.
3. An **imperative sentence** gives an order or a direction and ends with either a period or an exclamation mark.
4. An **exclamatory sentence** conveys a strong emotion and ends with an exclamation mark.

Phrases A phrase is a group of words, without a subject and a verb, that functions in a sentence as one part of speech.

A **prepositional phrase** is a group of words that includes a preposition and a noun or a pronoun that is the object of the preposition.

> near the town   with them

An **adjective phrase** is a prepositional phrase that modifies a noun or a pronoun by telling what kind or which one.

> The house *on the corner* is new.

An **adverb phrase** is a prepositional phrase that modifies a verb, an adjective, or an adverb by pointing out where, when, in what manner, or to what extent.

> Bring your saddle *to the barn.*

An **appositive phrase** is a noun or a pronoun with modifiers, placed next to a noun or a pronoun to add information and details.

> The story, *a tale of adventure*, takes place in the Yukon.

A **participial phrase** is a participle modified by an adjective or an adverb phrase or accompanied by a complement. The entire phrase acts as an adjective.

> *Running at top speed*, he soon caught up.

An **infinitive phrase** is an infinitive with modifiers, complements, or a subject, all acting together as a single part of speech. An infinitive is the verb form that starts with *to.*

> I was happy *to sit down.*

Clauses A clause is a group of words with its own subject and verb. An **independent clause** can stand by itself as a complete sentence.

> "I think it belongs to Rachel."

A **subordinate clause** has a subject and a verb but cannot stand as a complete sentence; it can only be part of a sentence.

> "Although it was late"

Using Verbs, Pronouns, and Modifiers

Principal Parts A **verb** has four principal parts: the present, the present participle, the past, and the past participle.

Regular verbs form the past and past participle by adding *-ed* to the present form.

Present: walk	*Past:* walked
Present Participle: (am) walking	*Past Participle:* (have) walked

Irregular verbs form the past and past participle by changing form rather than by adding *-ed.*

Present: go	*Past:* went
Present Participle: (am) going	*Past Participle:* (have) gone

Verb Tense A **verb tense** tells whether the time of an action or condition is in the past, the present, or the future. Every verb has six tenses: *present, past, future, present perfect, past perfect,* and *future perfect.* The **present tense** shows actions that happen in the present. The **past tense** shows actions that have already happened. The **future tense** shows actions that will happen. The **present perfect tense** shows actions that begin in the past and continue to the present. The **past perfect tense** shows a past action or condition that ended before another past action. The **future perfect tense** shows a future action or condition that will have ended before another begins.

Pronoun Case The **case** of a pronoun is the form it takes to show its use in a sentence. There are three pronoun cases: *nominative, objective,* and *possessive.* The **nominative case** is used to name or rename the subject of the sentence. The nominative case pronouns are *I, you, he, she, it, we, you, they.*

As the subject: She is brave.
Renaming the subject: The leader is *she.*

The **objective case** is used as the direct object, indirect object, or object of a preposition. The objective case pronouns are *me, you, him, her, it, us, you, them.*

As a direct object: Tom called *me.*
As an indirect object: My friend gave *me* advice.
As an object of a preposition: She went without *me.*

The **possessive case** is used to show ownership. The possessive pronouns are *my, your, his, her, its, our, their, mine, yours, his, hers, its, ours, theirs.*

Subject-Verb Agreement To make a subject and a verb agree, make sure that both are singular or both are plural. Two or more singular subjects joined by *or* or *nor* must have a singular verb. When singular and plural subjects are joined by *or* or *nor,* the verb must agree with the closest subject.

He *is* at the door.   They *drive* home.
Either *Joe* or *you are* going.   Both *pets are* hungry.

Pronoun-Antecedent Agreement **Pronouns** must agree with their antecedents in number and gender. Use singular pronouns with singular antecedents and plural pronouns with plural antecedents. Many errors in pronoun-antecedent agreement occur when a plural pronoun is used to refer to a singular antecedent for which the gender is not specified.

Incorrect: Everyone did their best.
Correct: Everyone did his or her best.

The following indefinite pronouns are singular: *anybody, anyone, each, either, everybody, everyone, neither, nobody, no one, one, somebody, someone.* The following indefinite pronouns are plural: *both, few, many, several.* The following indefinite pronouns may be either singular or plural: *all, any, most, none, some.*

Modifiers The *comparative* and *superlative* degrees of most adjectives and adverbs of one or two syllables can be formed in either of two ways: Use *-er* or *more* to form a comparative degree and *-est* or *most* to form the superlative degree of most one- and two-syllable modifiers.

More and *most* can also be used to form the comparative and superlative degrees of most one- and two-syllable modifiers.

These words should not be used when the result sounds awkward, as in "A greyhound is *more* fast than a beagle."

Glossary of Common Usage

accept, except: *Accept* is a verb that means "to receive" or "to agree to." *Except* is a preposition that means "other than" or "leaving out." Do not confuse these two words.

Aaron sadly *accepted* his father's decision to sell Zlata.
Everyone *except* the fisherman had children.

affect, effect: *Affect* is normally a verb meaning "to influence" or "to bring about a change in." *Effect* is usually a noun, meaning "result."

among, between: *Among* is usually used with three or more items. *Between* is generally used with only two items.

bad, badly: Use the predicate adjective *bad* after linking verbs such as *feel, look,* and *seem.* Use *badly* whenever an adverb is required.

Mouse does not feel *bad* about tricking Coyote.
In the myth, Athene treats Arachne *badly.*

beside, besides: *Beside* means "at the side of" or "close to." *Besides* means "in addition to."

can, may: The verb *can* generally refers to the ability to act. The verb *may* generally refers to permission to act.

different from, different than: *Different from* is generally preferred over *different than.*

farther, further: Use *farther* when you refer to distance. Use *further* when you mean "to a greater degree or extent" or "additional."

fewer, less: Use *fewer* for things that can be counted. Use *less* for amounts or quantities that cannot be counted.

good, well: Use the predicate adjective *good* after linking verbs such as *feel, look, smell, taste,* and *seem.* Use *well* whenever you need an adverb.

its, it's: The word *its* with no apostrophe is a possessive pronoun. The word *it's* is a contraction for *it is.* Do not confuse the possessive pronoun *its* with the contraction *it's,* standing for "it is" or "it has."

lay, lie: Do not confuse these verbs. *Lay* is a transitive verb meaning "to set or put something down." Its principal parts are *lay, laying, laid, laid. Lie* is an intransitive verb meaning "to recline." Its principal parts are *lie, lying, lay, lain.*

like, as: *Like* is a preposition that usually means "similar to" or "in the same way as." *Like* should always be followed by an object. Do not use *like* before a subject and a verb. Use *as* or *that* instead.

of, have: Do not use *of* in place of *have* after auxiliary verbs like *would, could, should, may, might,* or *must.*

raise, rise: *Raise* is a transitive verb that usually takes a direct object. *Rise* is intransitive and never takes a direct object.

set, sit: *Set* is a transitive verb meaning "to put (something) in a certain place." Its principal parts are *set, setting, set, set. Sit* is an intransitive verb meaning "to be seated." Its principal parts are *sit, sitting, sat, sat.*

than, then: The conjunction *than* is used to connect the two parts of a comparison. Do not confuse *than* with the adverb *then,* which usually refers to time.

that, which, who: Use the relative pronoun *that* to refer to things or people. Use *which* only for things and *who* for people.

when, where, why: Do not use *when, where,* or *why* directly after a linking verb such as *is.* Reword the sentence.

   Faulty: Suspense is *when* an author increases tension.

   Revised: An author uses suspense to increase tension.

who, whom: Use *who* only as a subject in clauses and sentences and *whom* only as an object.

Mechanics

Capitalization

1. Capitalize the first word of a sentence.

   Young Roko glances down the valley.

2. Capitalize all proper nouns and adjectives.

   Mark Twain   Amazon River   Thanksgiving Day

3. Capitalize a person's title when it is followed by the person's name or when it is used in direct address.

   Doctor   General Khokhotov   Mrs. Price

4. Capitalize titles showing family relationships when they refer to a specific person, unless they are preceded by a possessive noun or pronoun.

   Granny-Liz   Margie's mother

5. Capitalize the first word and all other key words in the titles of books, periodicals, poems, stories, plays, paintings, and other works of art.

   from *Tom Sawyer*   "Grandpa and the Statue"

6. Capitalize the first word and all nouns in letter salutations and the first word in letter closings.

   Dear Willis,   Yours truly,

Punctuation

End Marks

1. Use a **period** to end a declarative sentence, an imperative sentence, and most abbreviations.

2. Use a **question mark** to end a direct question or an incomplete question in which the rest of the question is understood.

3. Use an **exclamation mark** after a statement showing strong emotion, an urgent imperative sentence, or an interjection expressing strong emotion.

Commas   Use commas:

1. before the conjunction to separate two independent clauses in a compound sentence.

2. to separate three or more words, phrases, or clauses in a series.

3. to separate adjectives of equal rank. Do not use commas to separate adjectives that must stay in a specific order.

4. after an introductory word, phrase, or clause.

5. to set off parenthetical and nonessential expressions.

6. with places and dates made up of two or more parts.

7. after items in addresses, after the salutation in a personal letter, after the closing in all letters, and in numbers of more than three digits.

Semicolons   Use semicolons:

1. to join independent clauses that are not already joined by a conjunction.

2. to join independent clauses or items in a series that already contain commas.

Colons   Use colons:

1. before a list of items following an independent clause.

2. in numbers giving the time, in salutations in business letters, and in labels used to signal important ideas.

Quotation Marks

1. A **direct quotation** represents a person's exact speech or thoughts and is enclosed in quotation marks.

2. An **indirect quotation** reports only the general meaning of what a person said or thought and does not require quotation marks.

3. Always place a comma or a period inside the final quotation mark of a direct quotation.

4. Place a question mark or an exclamation mark inside the final quotation mark if the end mark is part of the quotation; if it is not part of the quotation, place it outside the final quotation mark.

Titles

1. Underline or italicize the titles of long written works, movies, television and radio shows, lengthy works of music, paintings, and sculptures.

2. Use quotation marks around the titles of short written works, episodes in a series, songs, and titles of works mentioned as parts of collections.

Hyphens   Use a **hyphen** with certain numbers, after certain prefixes, with two or more words used as one word, and with a compound modifier that comes before a noun.

Apostrophes   Use apostrophes:

1. to show the possessive case of most singular nouns.

2. to show the possessive case of plural nouns ending in *s* and *es.*

3. to show the possessive case of plural nouns that do not end in *s* or *es.*

4. in a contraction to indicate the position of the missing letter or letters.

Index of Skills

Boldface numbers indicate pages where terms are defined.

Reading for Information

Reading Skills

Writing Strategies

Prewriting:

Critical Viewing

Listening and Speaking

Media Literacy

Research and Technology

Test Practice

Reading for Information

Writing for Assessment:

Index of Features

Independent Reading

Reading for Information

Literary Analysis Workshops

Literature in Context

Test Practice

Vocabulary Workshop

Index of Authors and Titles

Notes: Page numbers in italics refer to biographical information. Nonfiction appears in red.

Acknowledgments

Grateful acknowledgment is made to the following for copyrighted material: *English—Language Arts Content Standards for California Public Schools* reproduced by permission, California Department of Education, CD Press, 1430 N Street, Suite 3207, Sacramento, CA 95814.

All Children's Hospital c/o Florida Suncoast Safe Kids Coalition "2006 Safe Kids "Walk This Way" Program" from *http://www.allkids.org/body.cfm?xyzpdqabc=0&id=396&action=detail&ref=28*. Copyrgiht © 2007 All Children's Hospital. All rights reserved. Used by permission.

Miriam Altshuler Literary Agency "Treasure of Lemon Brown" by Walter Dean Myers from *Boy's Life Magazine, March 1983.* Copyright © 1983, by Walter Dean Myers. Used by permission of Miriam Altshuler Literary Agency, on behalf of Walter Dean Myers.

American Broadcasting Music, Inc. "Conjunction Junction" composed by Jack Sheldon and Bob Dorough. Copyright © 1973 American Broadcasting Music, Inc. Used by permission.

American National Red Cross "How to Recognize Venomous Snakes in North America" Copyright © 1992 by The American National Red Cross. Courtesy of the American National Red Cross. All rights reserved in all countries. Used by permission.

Americas Magazine "Mongoose on the Loose" reprinted from *Americas,* a bimonthly magazine published by the General Secretariat of the Organization of American States in English and Spanish. Content may not be copied without written permission. Used by permission.

Arte Publico Press, Inc. "Maestro" is used with permission from the publisher of *Borders* by Pat Mora. (Houston: Arte Publico Press - | University of Houston © 1986). "Bailando" from Chants by Pat Mora. Used with permission from the publisher of *Chants* (Houston: Arte Publico Press - University of Houston copyright © 1985).

Atheneum Books for Young Readers, an imprint of Simon & Schuster "Papa's Parrot" from *Every Living Thing* by Cynthia Rylant. Text copyright © 1985 Cynthia Rylant. Used by permission of Atheneum Books for Young Readers, an imprint of Simon & Schuster Children's Publishing Division.

Bantam Books, a division of Random House, Inc. "The Eternal Frontier" from *Frontier* by Louis L'Amour, Photographs by David Muench, copyright © 1984 by Louis L'Amour Enterprises, Inc. Used by permission of Bantam Books, a division of Random House, Inc.

Susan Bergholz Literary Services "My First Free Summer" by Julia Alvarez, copyright © 2003 by Julia Alvarez. First published in *Better Homes and Gardens, August 2003.* Used by permission of Susan Bergholz Literary Services, New York, NY and Lamy, NM. All rights reserved.

Brandt & Hochman Literary Agents, Inc. "The Third Wish" from *Not What You Expected: A Collection of Short Stories* by Joan Aiken. Copyright © 1974 by Joan Aiken. Any electronic copying or redistribution of the text is expressly forbidden. Used by permission of Brandt & Hochman Literary Agents, Inc.

Brooks Permissions "Jim" Copyright © 1956 from *Bronzeville Boys and Girls* by Gwendolyn Brooks. Copyright © 1956 by Gwendolyn Brooks. Used by consent of Brooks Permissions.

Curtis Brown Ltd. "Two Haiku" ("O foolish ducklings..." and "After the moon sets...") first appeared in *Cricket Songs: Japanese Haiku,* published by Harcourt. Copyright © 1964 by Harry Behn. "Suzy and Leah" first published in *American Girl Magazine.* Copyright © 1993 by Jane Yolen. *Dragonwings by Laurence Yep from Theatre For Young Audiences: Around The World In 21 Plays.* Copyright © 1992 by Laurence Yep. First appeared in *American Theatre Magazine.* Now appears in *Norton Anthology of Children's Literature.* Used by permission of Curtis Brown, Ltd. CAUTION: Professionals and amateurs are hereby warned that *Dragonwings,* being fully protected under the copyright Laws of the United States of America, the British Empire, including the Dominion of Canada, and all other countries of the Universal Copyright and Berne Conventions, are subject to royalty. All rights, including professional, amateur, motion picture, recitation, lecturing, public reading, radio and television broadcasting, and the rights of translation into foreign languages, are strictly reserved. All inquiries for *Dragonwings* should be addressed to Curtis Brown Ltd.

CA Walk to School Headquarters "Walk to School" from *www.cawalktoschool.com.* Copyright © 2006 California Center for Physical Activity.

Canadian Broadcasting Corporation "Charles Dickens's A Christmas Carol: A Radio Interview" from *http://www.victorianweb.org/authors/dickens/xmas/pva303.html.* Originally broadcast on the Canadian Broadcasting Corporation (The Great Northwest, Dec. 4, 2000). Copyright © Canadian Broadcasting Corporation. Used by courtesy of Canadian Broadcasting Corporation.

Carus Publishing Company "The Rhythms of Rap" by Kathiann M. Kowalski from *Odyssey's March 2002 issue: Music: Why Do We Love It?* Copyright © 2002, Cobblestone Publishing, 30 Grove Street, Suite C, Peterborough, NH 03458. All rights reserved. Used by permission of Carus Publishing Company.

Chronicle Books "The Travelers and the Bear" by Jerry Pinkney from *Aesop's Fables.* Copyright © 2000 by Jerry Pinkney.

City of Melbourne Stormwater Management Web Page from *http://www.melbourneflorida.org/stormwater/howyoucanhelp.htm.* Copyright City of Melbourne.

City of Oceanside City of Oceanside Clean Water Program from *www.oceansidecleanwaterprogram.org/kids.asp.* Copyright © City of Oceanside. Used by permission.

ClearyWorks "The Fox Outwits the Crow" by William Cleary from *www.clearyworks.com.* Used by permission of William Cleary, Burlington, Vermont.

Code Entertainment "The Monsters are Due on Maple Street" by Rod Serling from *The Monsters Are Due On Maple Street.* Copyright © 1960 by Rod Serling; Copyright © 1988 by Carolyn Serling, Jodi Serling, and Anne Serling. Used by permission. CAUTION: Professionals and amateurs are hereby warned that "The Monsters are Due on Maple Street," being fully protected under

Don Congdon Associates, Inc. "All Summer In A Day" by Ray Bradbury, published in *The Magazine of Fantasy and Science Fiction, March 1954*. Copyright © 1954, copyright © renewed 1982 by Ray Bradbury. From *No Gumption* by Russell Baker. Copyright © 1982 by Russell Baker. Used by permission of Don Congdon Associates, Inc.

The Emma Courlander Trust "All Stories Are Anansi's" from *The Hat-Shaking Dance And Other Ashanti Tales From Ghana* by Harold Courlander with Albert Kofi Prempeh Copyright © 1957, 1985 by Harold Courlander. Used by permission of The Emma Courlander Trust.

Crystal Springs Uplands School Crystal Springs Uplands School Theatre Contract from *http://www.csus.com/pageprint.cfm?p=1212*. Copyright © Crystal Springs Uplands School. Used by permission of the Crystal Springs Uplands School and John Hauer, Theater Manager and Production & Design Teacher.

Dell Publishing, a division of Random House, Inc. "The Luckiest Time of All" from *The Lucky Stone* by Lucille Clifton. Copyright © 1979 by Lucille Clifton. Used by permission of Dell Publishing, a division of Random House, Inc.

Demand Media, Inc. "How to Download Ringtones for a Cell Phone" from *www.ehow.com*. Copyright © 1999-2007 eHow, Inc. Article used with the permission of eHow, Inc., www.ehow.com.

Dial Books for Young Readers, a division of Penguin Young Readers Group "The Three=Century Woman" copyright © 1999 by Richard Peck, from *Past Present, Perfect Tense* by Richard Peck. Used by permission of Dial Books for Young Readers, a division of Penguin Young Readers Group, a member of Penguin Group (USA) Inc., 345 Hudson Street, New York, NY 10014. All rights reserved.

Gregory Djanikian "How I Learned English" by Gregory Djanikian from *Falling Deeply Into America*, Carnegie Mellon University, Copyright © 1989. Used by permission of the author.

Dramatists Play Service Inc. "Sorry, Wrong Number" by Lucille Fletcher. Copyright © renewed 1976, Lucille Fletcher. All rights reserved.

Dutton Children's Books From "The Tale of Mandarin Ducks" by Katherine Paterson, copyright © 1990 by Katherine Paterson, text. Used by permission of Dutton Children's Books, A Division of Penguin Young Readers Group, A Member of Penguin Group (USA) Inc. All rights reserved.

Gulf Publishing Look for the Differences (park sign) from *A Field Guide To Snakes Of California* by Philip R. Brown. Copyright © 1997.

Farrar, Straus & Giroux, LLC "Seal" from *Laughing Time: Collected Nonsense* by William Jay Smith. Copyright © 1990 by William Jay Smith. "Train Tune" from *The Blue Estuaries* by Louise Bogan. Copyright © 1968 by Louise Bogan. Copyright renewed © 1996 by Ruth Limmer. Used by permission of Farrar, Straus & Giroux, Inc.

Joanna Farrell for the Estate of Juliet Piggott Wood "Popocatepetl and Ixtlaccihuatl" by Juliet Piggott from *Mexican Folktales*. Used by permission of Mrs. J.S.E. Farrell.

Food Security Learning Center Food Security Learning Center from *www.worldhungeryear.org*. Copyright © 2007. All rights reserved. Used by permission.

Estate of Mona Gardner "The Dinner Party" by Mona Gardner from *McDougal, Littell*. Copyright © 1942, 1970. Reprinted by permission.

Georgia Department of Transportation "Safe Routes to School: It's Happening in Metro Atlanta" from *http://www.atlantabike.org/srtsfrontpage.html*. Copyright © 2007. Used by permission of Georgia Department of Transportation, Atlanta Bicycle Campaign, and the Federal Highway Administration.

Golden Books, an imprint of Random House Children's Book "The Bride of Pluto"(retitled "Demeter and Persephone") from *The Golden Treasury of Myths and Legends* by Anne Terry White, illustrated by Alice and Martin Provensen, copyright © 1959, renewed copyright © 1987 by Random House, Inc. Used by permission of Golden Books, an imprint of Random House Children's Books, a division of Random House, Inc.

June Hall Literary Agency c/o PFD "One" from *When I Dance* by James Berry (Copyright © James Berry 1990) is reproduced by permission of PFD (www.pfd.co.uk) on behalf of James Berry.

Harcourt, Inc. Excerpt from "Seventh Grade" in *Baseball in April and Other Stories*, copyright © 1990 by Gary Soto. "Fog" from Chicago Poems by Carl Sandburg, copyright © 1916 by Holt, Rinehart and Winston and renewed copyright © 1944 by Carl Sandburg. This material may not be reproduced in any form or by any means without the prior written permission of the publisher. Used by permission of Harcourt, Inc.

Harcourt Education Limited "Tenochtitlan: Inside the Aztec Capital" from *The Aztecs: Worlds Of The Past* by Jacqueline Dineen. Used by permission of Harcourt Education.

HarperCollins Publishers, Inc. "Sarah Cynthia Sylvia Stout Would Not Take the Garbage Out" from *Where the Sidewalk Ends* by Shel Silverstein. Copyright © 2004 by Evil Eye Music, Inc. Used with permission from the Estate of Shel Silverstein and HarperCollins Children's Books. From *An American Childhood*. Copyright © 1987 by Annie Dillard. "How the Snake Got Poison" from *Mules and Men* by Zora Neale Hurston. Copyright © 1935 by Zora Neale Hurston. Copyright renewed © 1963 by John C. Hurston and Joel Hurston. Used by permission of HarperCollins Publishers.

HarperTrophy, an Imprint of HarperCollins Publishers Inc. From *Dragonwings* by Laurence Yep. Copyright © 1975 by Laurence Yep. Used by permission of HarperCollins Publishers.

Harvard University Press "I'm Nobody (#288)" by Emily Dickinson. Used by permission of the publishers and the Trustees of Amherst College from *The Poems Of Emily Dickinson*, Thomas H. Johnson, ed., Cambridge, Mass.: The Belknap Press of Harvard University Press, Copyright © 1951, 1955, 1979, 1983 by the President and Fellows of Harvard College.

Helmut Hirnschall "I am a Native of North America" by Chief Dan George from *My Heart Soars*. Copyright © 1974 by Clarke Irwin. Used by permission.

Edward D. Hoch "Zoo" by Edward D. Hoch, copyright © 1958 by King Size Publications, Inc.; © renewed 1991 by Edward D. Hoch. Used by permission of the author.

The Barbara Hogenson Agency, Inc. "The Night the Bed Fell" from *My Life and Hard Times* by James Thurber. Copyright © 1933, 1961 by James Thurber. Used by arrangement with Rosemary Thurber and The Barbara Hogensen Agency, Inc. All rights reserved.

Holiday House, Inc. Copyright © 2006 by Russell Freedman from "Freedom Walkers: The Story of the Montgomery Bus Boycott." All rights reserved. Used by permission of Holiday House, Inc.

Meghan Holohan "What Gives the Sunrise and Sunset Its Orange Glow" by Meghan Holohan from *www.gantdaily.com*. Used by permission of the author.

Henry Holt and Company, Inc. Excerpt from "My Dear Cousin Tovah" from *Letters From Rifka* by Karen Hesse. Copyright © 1992 by Karen Hesse. "Stopping by Woods on a Snowy Evening" from *The Poetry Of Robert Frost* edited by Edward Connery Lathem. Copyright © 1923, 1969 by Henry Holt and Company, copyright 1951 by Robert Frost. Used by permission of Henry Holt and Company, LLC. All rights reserved.

Houghton Mifflin Harcourt "Prayers of Steel" from The Complete Poems of Carl Sandburg, Revised and Expanded Edition, copyright © 1970, 1969 by Lilian Steichen Sandburg, Trustee, reprinted by permission of Houghton Mifflin Harcourt Publishing Company. The material may not be reproduced in any form or by any means without the prior written permission of the publisher.

Hyperion Books for Children "The Voyage" (including the Prologue) from *Tales From The Odyssey - Book Four: The Gray-Eyed Goddess* by Mary Pope Osborne. Copyright © 2003 by Mary Pope Osborne. Used by permission of Hyperion Books for Children. All rights reserved.

Information Please® "Fall of the Hindenburg" *www.infoplease. com*. Information Please® Database, Copyright © Pearson Education, Inc. All rights reserved. Used by permission.

Jacksonville Zoo and Gardens "Jacksonville Zoo & Gardens Leading the Charge in Northeast Florida to Save the Frogs!" from *http://www.jaxzoo.org/about/amphibianconservationpr.asp*. All content copyright © 2008 Jacksonville Zoo and Gardens. Special appreciation to Jacksonville Zoo & Gardens, Jacksonville, FL, for information on the frog crisis.

Japan Publications, Inc. "On sweet plum blossoms," "Has spring come indeed?" and "Temple bells die out" by Bashō from *One Hundred Famous Haiku* by Daniel C. Buchanan. Copyright © 1973. Used by permission of Japan Publications, Inc.

Stanleigh Jones "He-y, Come on O-ut!" by Shinichi Hoshi translated by Stanleigh Jones from *The Best Japanese Science Fiction Stories*. Reprinted with the permission of Stanleigh Jones.

The Estate of Barbara Jordan "All Together Now" by Barbara Jordan from *Sesame Street Parents*. Used by permission of Hilgers Bell & Richards Attorneys at Law for the Estate of Barbara Jordan.

The Kansas City Star "The Wrong Orbit: Senator Has No Legitimate Business Blasting Into Space" Kansas City Star Editorial from *The Kansas City Star, 1/20/98*. Used with permission of The Kansas City Star © Copyright 2007 The Kansas City Star. All rights reserved. Format differs from original publication. Not an endorsement.

Kinseido Publishing Co., Ltd. "Conversational Ballgames" by Nancy M. Sakamoto from *Polite Fictions: Why Japanese And Americans Seem Rude To Each Other*. Used by permission.

Alfred A. Knopf, Inc. "Mother to Son" from *The Collected Poems of Langston Hughes* by Langston Hughes, edited by Arnold Rampersad with David Roessel, Associate Editor. Copyright © 1994 by The Estate of Langston Hughes. Used by permission of Alfred A. Knopf, a division of Random House, Inc.

Alfred A. Knopf Children's Books "The People Could Fly" from *The People Could Fly: American Black Folktales* by Virginia Hamilton, copyright © 1985 by Virginia Hamilton, illustrations copyright © 1985 by Leo and Diane Dillon. Used by permission of Alfred A. Knopf, an imprint of Random House Children's Books, a division of Random House, Inc.

Barbara S. Kouts Literary Agency "The Bear Boy" by Joseph Bruchac from *Flying with the Eagle, Racing the Great Bear*. Copyright © 1993 by Joseph Bruchac. Used with permission.

Samantha Larson "Everest 2007" by Samantha Larson from *www.samanthalarson.blogspot.com*. Copyright © 2006 SamanthaLarson.com. Used by permission.

Little, Brown and Company, Inc. "The Real Story of a Cowboy's Life" (The Grandest Enterprise Under God 1865–1874) from *The West: An Illustrated History* by Geoffrey Ward. Little Brown and Company. Copyright © 1996 by The West Book Project, Inc. Used by permission.

Gina Maccoby Literary Agency "MK" from *Open Your Eyes* by Jean Fritz. Copyright © 2003 by Jean Fritz. Used by permission of The Gina Maccoby Literary Agency.

Naomi Long Madgett "Life" by Naomi Long Madgett from *One and the Many*, copyright © 1956; *Remembrances of Spring: Collected Early Poems*, copyright © 1993. Used by permission of the author.

Meriwether Publishing Ltd. "My Head is Full of Starshine" from Acting Natural by Peg Kehret, copyright © 1991 Meriwether Publishing Ltd. Used by permission.

Eve Merriam c/o Marian Reiner "Onomatopoeia" from *It Doesn't Always Have To Rhyme* by Eve Merriam. Copyright © 1964, 1992 Eve Merriam. Used by permission of Marian Reiner Literary Agency.

Edna St. Vincent Millay Society "The Courage That My Mother Had" by Edna St. Vincent Millay, from *Collected Poems*, HarperCollins. Copyright © 1954, 1982 by Norma Millay Ellis. All rights reserved. Used by permission of Elizabeth Barnett, literary executor.

William Morris Agency *A Christmas Carol: Scrooge and Marley* by Israel Horovitz. Copyright © 1994 by Fountain Pen, LLC. Used by permission of William Morris Agency, LLC on behalf of the Author. All rights reserved. CAUTION: Professionals and amateurs are hereby warned that "A Christmas Carol: Scrooge and Marley" is subject to a royalty. It is fully protected under the copyright laws of the United States of America and of all countries covered by the

International Copyright Union (including the Dominion of Canada and the rest of the British Commonwealth), the Berne Convention, the Pan-American Copyright Convention and the Universal Copyright Convention as well as all countries with which the United States has reciprocal copyright relations. All rights, including professional/amateur stage rights, motion picture, recitation, lecturing, public reading, radio broadcasting, television, video or sound recording, all other forms of mechanical or electronic reproduction, such as CD-ROM, CD-I, information storage and retrieval systems and photocopying, and the rights of translation into foreign languages, are strictly reserved. Particular emphasis is laid upon the matter of readings, permission for which must be secured from the Author's agent in writing. Inquiries concerning rights should be addressed to: William Morris Agency, LLC, 1325 Avenue of the Americas, New York, NY 10019, Attn: Eric Lupfer

William Morrow & Company, Inc., a division of HarperCollins "Winter" from *Cotton Candy On A Rainy Day* by Nikki Giovanni. Copyright © 1978 by Nikki Giovanni. Used by permission of William Morrow & Company, Inc., a division of HarperCollins Publishers, Inc.

Naomi Shihab Nye "The Rider" by Naomi Shihab Nye from *Invisible*. Used by permission.

Harold Ober Associates, Inc. "Stolen Day" by Sherwood Anderson from *This Week Magazine*. Copyright © 1941 by Sherwood Anderson. Copyright renewed © 1968 by Eleanor Copenhaver Anderson. Used by permission of Harold Ober Associates Incorporated.

ODYSSEY Magazine (Cobblestone Publishing) "A Special Gift—The Legacy of 'Snowflake' Bentley" by Barbara Eaglesham from *Odyssey's December 2002 Issue: Chilly Science: Ice and Snow,* Copyright © 2002, Carus Publishing Company. Published by Cobblestone Publishing, 30 Grove Street, Suite C, Peterborough, NH 03458. All rights reserved. Used by permission of the publisher.

Ama B. Patterson "Martin Luther King" by Raymond Richard Patterson. Used by permission of the Estate of Raymond R. Patterson.

Pearson Prentice Hall "Keeping It Quiet" from *Prentice Hall Science Explorer Sound and Light*. Copyright © 2005 by Pearson Education, Inc., or its affiliates. "The Seasons on Earth" from *Prentice Hall Science Explorer Astronomy*. Copyright © 2005 by Pearson Education, Inc., or its affiliates. Used by permission.

People Weekly "Picks & Pans: A Christmas Carol (TNT)" by Terry Kelleher from *People Weekly, December 6th, 1999, Vol.52*. People Weekly Copyright © 1999 All Rights Reserved Time Inc. Used by permission.

Perseus Books "Alligator" by Bailey White from *Mama Makes Up Her Mind And Other Dangers Of Southern Living*. Copyright © 1993 by Bailey White. Used by permission of Da Capo Press, a member of Perseus Books Group. All rights reserved.

Piñata Books, an imprint of Arte Publico Press "The Desert Is My Mother/El desierto es mi madre" is used with permission from the publisher of *My Own True Name* by Pat Mora. (Houston: Arte Publico Press - University of Houston copyright © 1985).

G. P. Putnam's Sons, a division of Penguin Group (USA) Inc. "Two Kinds" from *The Joy Luck Club* by Amy Tan, copyright © 1989 by Amy Tan. Used by permission of G.P. Putnam's Sons, a division of Penguin Group (USA) Inc.

Random House, Inc. "Melting Pot" from *Living Out Loud* by Anna Quindlen, copyright © 1987 by Anna Quindlen. Used by permission of Random House, Inc.

Marian Reiner, Literary Agent "Weather" from *Catch a Little Rhyme* by Eve Merriam. Copyright © 1966 by Eve Merriam. Copyright renewed © 1994 by Dee Michel and Guy Michel. Used by permission of Marian Reiner.

Wendy Rose "Loo-Wit" by Wendy Rose from *The Halfbreed Chronicles and Other Poems*. Copyright © 1985 by Wendy Rose. Used by permission.

Santa Rosa Plateau Ecological Reserve Rattlesnakes (park sign) from *http://www.californiaherps.com/images/signs/knowyoursnakessignmt306.jpg*.

Scholastic Inc. "The Great Fire" by Jim Murphy from *Scholastic Hardcover*. Copyright © 1995 by Jim Murphy. All rights reserved. Published by Scholastic Inc.

Scribner, a division of Simon & Schuster "Rattlesnake" from *Cross Creek* by Marjorie Kinnan Rawlings. Copyright © 1942 by Marjorie Kinnan Rawlings: copyright renewed © 1970 by Norton Baskin and Charles Scribner's Sons. From *Angela's Ashes* by Frank McCourt. Copyright © 1996 by Frank McCourt. Used by permission of Scribner, an imprint of Simon & Schuster Adult Publishing Group. All rights reserved.

Seaside Music Theater "Costume Rental Policy" from *www.seasidemusictheater.org*. Copyright © 2006 Seaside Music Theater. All rights reserved. Used by Permission.

Simon & Schuster, Inc. "A Day's Wait" from *Winner Take Nothing* by Ernest Hemingway. Copyright © 1933 Charles Scribner's Sons. Copyright renewed © 1961 by Mary Hemingway.

Simon & Schuster Books for Young Readers "The Fox and the Crow" from *The Fables of Aesop Selected, Told Anew and Their History Traced* by Joseph Jacobs. Copyright © 1964 Macmillan Publishing Company. Used by the permission of Simon & Schuster Books for Young Readers, an imprint of Simon & Schuster Children's Publishing Division.

Susan Solt "Forsythia" by Mary Ellen Solt from *Concrete Poetry: A World View*. Copyright © 1968 by Mary Ellen Solt. Copyright © 1970 by Mary Ellen Solt. All rights reserved. Used by permission.

John Sousanis "Toned-down 'Christmas Carol' has more spirit" by John Sousanis, from *The Oakland Press, November 29, 2000, Vol. 156, No. 280*. Copyright © 2000 The Oakland Press. Used by permission of John Sousanis.

Star Tribune "Veteran Returns, Becomes Symbol" (Original title "Astronaut Glenn: He Can Inspire America Again") from *Minneapolis Star Tribune, January 19, 1998*. Copyright © 1998 Star Tribune, Minneapolis, MN. Used by Permission.

The Statue of Liberty-Ellis Island Foundation, Inc. "Byron Yee: Discovering a Paper Son" from *http://www.ellisisland.org/immexp/wseix_3_3.asp?* Copyright © 2000 by The Statue of Liberty-Ellis Island Foundation, Inc. www.ellisisland.org. Used by permission.

Piri Thomas "Amigo Brothers" by Piri Thomas from *Stories from El Barrio*. Used by permission of the author.

Tribute Entertainment Media Group "Indian Grey Mongoose (Herpestes edwardsi)" from *www.wildinfo.com*. Used by permission of Tribute Entertainment Media Group.

The University of Georgia "On the Boardwalk" by Amanda E. Swennes from Outreach, Winter 2007. Copyright © 2007 by the University of Georgia. Used by permission. All rights reserved.

The University of Georgia Press "Volar: To Fly" from *The Latin Deli: Prose and Poetry*. Copyright by Judith Ortiz Cofer. Used by permission of the author and The University of Georgia Press.

University of Notre Dame Press From *Barrio Boy* by Ernesto Galarza. Copyright © 1971 by University of Notre Dame Press. Used by permission of the University of Notre Dame Press. All rights reserved.

The Vagabond School of the Drama "The Flat Rock Playhouse Apprentice Showcase ad Apprentice Application Form" from *www. flatrockplayhouse.org*. Used by permission.

Viking Penguin, Inc. From *What Makes a Rembrandt a Rembrandt?* by Richard Mühlberger. Copyright © 1993 by The Metropolitan Museum of Art. "The Other Frog Prince" by Jon Scieszka and Lane Smith from *The Stinky Cheese Man & Other Fairly Stupid Tales*. Text Copyright © Jon Scieszka, 1992. Illustration © Lane Smith, 1992. "Grasshopper Logic" from *Squids Will Be Squids: Fresh Morals, Beastly Fables by Jon Scieszka,* copyright © 1998 Jon Scieszka, text. Illustrations by Lane Smith © 1998. "Duckbilled Platypus vs. BeefSnakStik®" from *Squids Will Be Squids: Fresh Morals, Beastly Fables* by Jon Scieszka, copyright © 1998 Jon Scieszka, text. Illustrations by Lane Smith © 1998. "Sun and Moon in a Box (Zuni)" from *American Indian Trickster Tales* by Richard Erdoes and Alphonso Ortiz, copyright © 1998 by Richard Erdoes & The Estate of Alphonso Ortiz. Used by permission of Viking Penguin, a division of Penguin Young Readers Group, A member of Penguin Group (USA) Inc., 345 Hudson Street, New York, NY 10014. All rights reserved.

The Wylie Agency, Inc. "Grandpa and the Statue" by Arthur Miller. Copyright © 1945 by Arthur Miller. Used with permission of The Wylie Agency. CAUTION: Professionals and amateurs are hereby warned that *Grandpa and the Statue*, being fully protected under the copyright Laws of the United States of America, the British Empire, including the Dominion of Canada, and all other countries of the Universal Copyright and Berne Conventions, are subject to royalty. All rights, including professional, amateur, motion picture, recitation, lecturing, public readin g, radio and television broadcasting, and the rights of translation into foreign languages, are strictly reserved. All inquiries for *Grandpa and the Statue* should be addressed to The Wylie Agency, Inc.

Laurence Yep "Ribbons" by Laurence Yep from *American Girl magazine, Jan/Feb 1992*. Used by permission of the author.

The Young Authors Foundation, Inc. "Zoos: Joys or Jails?" by Rachel F. from *www.teenink.com*. Copyright © 2003 by Teen Ink, The 21st Century and The Young Authors Foundation, Inc. All rights reserved. Used by permission.

Robert Zimmerman "Life Without Gravity" by Robert Zimmerman from *Muse Magazine, April 2002.* © 2002 Carus Publishing Company. All rights reserved. Used by permission, author Zimmerman owns the rights.

Zoological Society of San Diego "Kid Territory: Why Do We Need Zoos?" from *http://www.sandiegozoo.org/kids/readaboutit_ why_zoos.html*. Copyright © Zoological Society of San Diego. Used by permission of the Zoological Society of San Diego.

Note: Every effort has been made to locate the copyright owner of material reproduced on this component. Omissions brought to our attention will be corrected in subsequent editions.

Credits

Photo Credits

Kobal Collection; **800:** l. Photofest; **800:** bl. Photofest; **800:** tl. Photofest; **803:** Ebenezer Scrooge celebrating in the Guthrie Theatre's 1994 production of *A Christmas Carol* adapted by Barbara Field. Photo credit: Michal Daniel.; **813:** Photofest; **819:** t. Bettmann/CORBIS; **819:** t. ©Michal Daniel, 2003; **820:** CBS/The Kobal Collection; **822:** ©Michal Daniel, 2003; **833:** b. Bettmann/CORBIS; **834:** l. istockphoto.com; **834:** l. istockphoto.com; **834:** Bkgrnd. istockphoto.com; **834:** m. CNAC/MNAM/Dist. RÈunion des MusÈes Nationaux / Art Resource, NY; **835:** tr. istockphoto.com; **838:** *Woman on telephone as seen through window,* William Low, Courtesy of the artist.; **839:** © Paul Loven/Getty Images; **842:** *Over view of family walking dog on the street,* William Low, Courtesy of the artist; **842:** *Over view of family walking dog on the street,* (detail) William Low, Courtesy of the artist; **847:** *Streetlight,* 1930, Constance Coleman Richardson, © Indianapolis Museum of Art, Gift of Mrs. James W. Fesler.; **848:** Hans Wolf/Getty Images; **850:** William Whitehurst/CORBIS; **855:** tl. Getty Images; **855:** tr. John Springer Collection/CORBIS; **855:** bm. Photofest; **855:** br. Photofest; **855:** bl. Photofest; **867:** b. Courtesy of Peg Kehret; **867:** t. Sophie Bassouls/ CORBIS Sygma; **868:** David Nieves/Hudson Valley Aerial Photography; **870:** Courtesy of the Library of Congress; **871:** MusÈe Bartholdi, Colmar, reprod. C. Kempf"; **872:** istockphoto.com/ Joshua Haviv; **874:** Inset. Jose Luis Pelaez Inc /Getty Images; **874:** Bkgrnd. istockphoto.com; **876:** istockphoto.com; **878:** b. Charles Gupton/CORBIS; **999:** b. ©The Stock Market/Paul Loven; **1000:** ©The Stock Market/Paul Loven;

Grade 7 Unit 6 898: © Hyacinth Manning /SuperStock; **903:** t. Courtesy of the Springville Museum of Art, Springville, Utah; **904:** PEANUTS reprinted by permission of United Feature Syndicate, Inc.; **907:** Rights and Permissions will add to their acknowledgement section; **907:** b. istockphoto.com; **908-909:** Rights and Permissions will add to their acknowledgement section; **915:** t. Courtesy of the Library of Congress; **917:** Private Collection/ The Bridgeman Art Library; **919:** Mary Evans Picture Library; **924:** bl. istockphoto.com/Nicholas Monu; **924:** m. istockphoto.com/Stefan Klein; **924:** bl. istockphoto.com/Christopher Steer; **924:** b. istockphoto.com/James Warren; **924:** istockphoto.com; **925:** bl. istockphoto.com/Lise Gagne; **925:** br. istockphoto.com/Nicholas Monu; **925:** t4. istockphoto.com; **925:** tr. istockphoto.com/Clint Spencer; **926:** bl. istockphoto.com/Mike Modine; **926-927:** istockphoto.com/Ryan Burke; **927:** rb. istockphoto.com/Nicholas Monu; **928:** t. istockphoto.com/Marcin Pa-ko; **928:** t. © Leeds Museums and Galleries (City Art Gallery) U.K.; **929:** 2. The Granger Collection, New York; **929:** 1. The Granger Collection, New York; **929:** 5. The Granger Collection, New York; **929:** 3. The Granger Collection, New York; **929:** 9. The Granger Collection, New York; **929:** 7. The Granger Collection, New York; **929:** 10. Massimo Listri/CORBIS; **929:** 6. Andrea Jemolo/CORBIS; **929:** 4. Andrea Jemolo/CORBIS; **929:** 8. Mimmo Jodice/CORBIS; **929:** Bkgrnd. Paul A. Souders/CORBIS; **930:** tl. ack-figure amphora depicting Demeter, Persephone and Apollo,/Museum of Fine Arts, Budapest, Hungary, / The Bridgeman Art Library International; **937:** t. Educational and Professional Publishing.; **938:** Charles & Josette Lenars/CORBIS; **940:** The Art Archive / National Anthropological Museum Mexico/Gianni Dagli Orti; **941- 942:** The Art Archive / National Anthropological Museum Mexico / Gianni Dagli Orti; **945:** t. By permission of Mrs. J.S.E. Farrell; **945:** Ullses Ruiz/epa/CORBIS; **946:** Daniel Aguiler/Reuters/CORBIS; **947:** Werner Forman/CORBIS; **948:** Private Collection/Bridgeman Art Library; **950:** The Art Archive//Museo Franz Mayer Mexico/Gianni Dagli Orti/The Picture Desk, Inc.; **951:** Museum fur Volkerkunde, Vienna, Austria/The Bridgeman Art Library; Nationality/copyright status: out of copyright; **952:** ©Charles & Josette Lenara/CORBIS; **953:** Biblioteca Nacional de Mexico, Mexico/Giraudon/The Bridgeman Art Library; **954:** Ullses Ruiz/epa/CORBIS; **962:** David Young-Wolff/PhotoEdit; **967:** t. **968:** From Mary Pope Osborne THE GRAY-EYED GODDESS copyright (c) 2003 by Mary Pope Osborne, cover illustration by Troy Howell. Reprinted by permission of Disney/Hyperion, an imprint of Disney Book Group LLC. All rights reserved; **991:** b. AP/Wide World Photos; **991:** t. ©Bassouls Sophie/CORBIS Sygma; **992:** Darren Bennett/Animals Animals; **994:** Ron Sanford/CORBIS;

995: bl. istockphoto.com; **999:** t. The Granger Collection, New York; **999:** b. © Paul Loven/Getty Images; **1000:** © Paul Loven/Getty Images; **1001:** tm. The Granger Collection, New York; **1001:** tl. Hulton Archive/Getty Images Inc.; **1001:** m. Aaron Douglas, Into Bondage, 1936, 60 3/8 x 60 1/2, oil on canvas. In the collection of the Corcoran Gallery of Art, Washington, DC. Museum Purchase and Partial Gift of Thurlow Tibbs Jr., The Evans-Tibbs Collection. 1996.9; **1001:** tr. The Granger Collection, New York; **1001:** bmr. Bettmann/CORBIS; **1001:** tmr. Bettmann/CORBIS; **1001:** bml. Portrait of Langston Hughes (1902-1967) c. 1925, Winold Reiss, National Portrait Gallery, Washington, DC,USA/Art Resource, NY; **1001:** m. Aaron Douglas (1899-1979). Artist., 1953, Betsy Graves Reyneau, National Portrait Gallery, Smithsonian Institution/Art Resource, NY; **1001:** bl. The Granger Collection, New York; © Paul Loven/Getty Images; **1009:** t.Prentice Hall; **1009:** tr. istockphoto.com; **1011:** Book cover illustrated by Leo and Diane Dillon, © 1985 by Knopf Children, from THE PEOPLE COULD FLY (ILLUSTRATIONS ONLY) by Leo and Diane Dillon. Used by permission of Alfred A. Knopf, an imprint of Random House Children's Books, a division of Random House, Inc.; **1013:** tr. istockphoto.com/Sergey Surkov; **1017:** © 1966 by Michael Courlander; **1018:** Hans Christoph Kappel/Nature Picture Library; **1019:** t. istockphoto.com; **1019:** b. istockphoto.com; **1028:** t. Buddy Mays/CORBIS; **1029:** t. Ralph A. Clevenger/CORBIS; **1035:** t. Copyright 2004 The Burlington Free Press/Peter Huoppi; **1035:** b. Aesop, c. 1639-1640. Oil on canvas, Diego Rodriguez Velazquez, Scala/Art Resource, NY; **1040:** b. Image Source/SuperStock; **1043:** Prentice Hall

Staff Credits

The people who made up the Pearson Prentice Hall Literature team—representing design, editorial, editorial services, education technology, manufacturing and inventory planning, market research, marketing services, planning and budgeting, product planning, production services, project office, publishing processes, and rights and permissions—are listed below. Boldface type denotes the core team members.

Tobey Antao, **Margaret Antonini**, Rosalyn Arcilla, Penny Baker, James Ryan Bannon, Stephan Barth, **Tricia Battipede**, Krista Baudo, Rachel Beckman, Julie Berger, Lawrence Berkowitz, Melissa Biezin, **Suzanne Biron**, Rick Blount, **Marcela Boos**, **Betsy Bostwick**, Kay Bosworth, Jeff Bradley, Andrea Brescia, Susan Brorein, Lois Brown, **Pam Carey**, Lisa Carrillo, **Geoffrey Cassar**, Patty Cavuoto, Doria Ceraso, Jennifer Ciccone, Jaime Cohen, Rebecca Cottingham, Joe Cucchiara, Jason Cuoco, **Alan Dalgleish**, **Karen Edmonds**, **Irene Ehrmann**, Stephen Eldridge, Amy Fleming, Dorothea Fox, Steve Frankel, Cindy Frederick, Philip Fried, Diane Fristachi, Phillip Gagler, **Pamela Gallo,** Husain Gatlin, **Elaine Goldman**, Elizabeth Good, John Guild, Phil Hadad, Patricia Hade, Monduane Harris, Brian Hawkes, Jennifer B. Heart, Martha Heller, John Hill, Beth Hyslip, Mary Jean Jones, Grace Kang, Nathan Kinney, Roxanne Knoll, **Kate Krimsky**, Monisha Kumar, Jill Kushner, Sue Langan, Melisa Leong, Susan Levine, Dave Liston, **Mary Luthi**, **George Lychock**, **Gregory Lynch**, **Joan Mazzeo**, **Sandra McGloster**, Salita Mehta, Eve Melnechuk, Kathleen Mercandetti, Artur Mkrtchyan, Karyn Mueller, Alison Muff, Christine Mulcahy, Kenneth Myett, Elizabeth Nemeth, Stefano Nese, Carrie O'Connor, April Okano, Kim Ortell, Sonia Pap, Raymond Parenteau, Dominique Pickens, Linda Punskovsky, **Sheila Ramsay**, Maureen Raymond, Mairead Reddin, **Erin Rehill-Seker**, **Renee Roberts**, **Laura Ross**, Bryan Salacki, Sharon Schultz, Jennifer Serra, **Melissa Shustyk**, Rose Sievers, Christy Singer, Yvonne Stecky, **Cynthia Summers**, Steve Thomas, Merle Uuesoo, Roberta Warshaw, Patricia Williams, Daniela Velez.

Additional Credits

Lydie Bemba, Victoria Blades, Denise Data, Rachel Drice, Eleanor Kostyk, Jill Little, Loraine Machlin, Evan Marx, Marilyn McCarthy, Patrick O'Keefe, Shelia M. Smith, Lucia Tirondola, Laura Vivenzio, Linda Waldman, Angel Weyant